Law and the Behavioral Sciences

Lawrence M. Friedman

School of Law
Stanford University

and

Stewart Macaulay

Law School
University of Wisconsin

THE BOBBS-MERRILL COMPANY, INC.
A SUBSIDIARY OF HOWARD W. SAMS & CO., INC.
PUBLISHERS • INDIANAPOLIS • KANSAS CITY • NEW YORK

To my Mother and Father
From S.M.

To Leah, Mother, Jane and Amy
From L.M.F.

Preface

This is a book for use by students both in the social sciences and in law schools. The course deals, primarily, with the ways in which the legal system affects society and in which society affects the legal system. The organization of the book and the materials selected reflect the view that it is important to see the legal system as an integral part of the larger social system rather than as a set of rules, procedures and activities of officials sealed off and isolated from the rest of society.

Law is assumed to make a difference to the people and groups who are subject to it. Obviously, law as a whole does make a difference, and so, too, do particular laws and particular activities of legal officials. But the effect is not necessarily one which is deducible from a reading of the *words* of statutes and case-law. There are stringent laws in the states against sale and possession of marijuana, but more people seem to smoke marijuana all the time. Prohibition is another example of a classic problem often referred to as the "limits of legal action." The problem is classic, but so far there are no classic answers or even serious attempts at one. This book tries to gather together some of the viewpoints on the matter, and to help the student assess what is known and unknown about the impact (and lack of impact) of law.

That legal systems, on the other hand, reflect the larger society is undeniable. But this statement by itself is far too general to be very meaningful. Here too, the problem is classic and the solutions imperfect. What people or groups influence what kinds of legal action and by what means? The reflection of society in the legal system is not easy to trace. Influences travel devious and myriad routes.

There are respects, too, in which it is useful to look at the legal system in isolation—not in the dogmatic, rule-bound isolation of conceptual jurisprudence—but as a little world in itself, a social system with demands, responses, role-players and moving parts. All systems are alike in some general characteristics. Their structures, if comparable, generate comparable internal pressures which drive them to behavior of this or that kind. People working within a system, for example, will tend to try to make their tasks manageable and personally rewarding. What can one meaningfully say about the legal system as a system?

This does not mean that there are not properties unique to a legal system, compared to other social systems. Legal tasks are different from those undertaken by business corporations, the family or a university. Some of the properties and values of the legal system are of crucial importance to society as a whole. For example, the American legal system is, in part, organized around a set of values for which the phrase "due process" is a shorthand expression. Due process, in turn, has an important impact on American society, both in terms of actual results and as a value that percolates into other parts of the social order. What these consequences are is an important empirical question.

But these materials are not organized around key legal concepts such as due process. Nor are they organized about fields of law—social science and criminal law, social science and business law, and so on. A word or two may therefore be in order about the underlying theory of this book.

First, we are convinced for a variety of reasons that an integration of the study of law with social science methods and concepts is both inevitable and desirable. Classical legal research and education thought of itself as "scientific," but it took law to be a deductive science. It did not have much propensity to go out and look at the world. When this idea died (slowly), it was replaced by a new justification: the old materials were preserved, but now they were defended on the grounds that they were just the thing for the inculcation of legal method, that is, skills and habits of thought which a lawyer ought to have. Many law teachers (and even some students) still think so, but there is general agreement that beyond the first year the study of law ought to be more outward-looking. It ought to be (if one dares use the word) more *relevant* to social problems. It ought to be more empirical. There is now a good deal of emphasis on social science and empirical methods, and the trend is clearly in this direction. But elementary teaching materials for an introductory course in law and social science are badly needed.

Second, we are equally convinced that the social sciences need to study law more closely. It is a social phenomenon of great importance, and it has been unduly neglected, partly because of the insularity of legal scholarship, partly because of the insularity of the social sciences. Here too, the trend is clear: sociology of law, behavioral political science, anthropology of law, psychology and psychiatry and law, and legal economics have all received new infusions of persons and enthusiasm in the last generation. But how does the social science student enter into the legal thickets? It is possible for him to go to law school, or to take particular law school courses, but this is a wasteful method for those who do not intend to practice law and who are interested only in certain aspects of the law. Again, the solution is elementary teaching materials and an introductory course in law and social science.

There are a number of ways of organizing such materials. All are valid. One can emphasize methodology. One can present materials which accurately reflect the current state of knowledge in the various sub-fields of law and social science. This method is the classic method of organizing a "reader." It is a useful method. Many will prefer it. But we have chosen to organize our materials around themes, problems and questions about the relationship of law and society. These are the questions discussed in the beginning of this preface—the effect of law on society, and society on law, for example. Thus, a certain logic of inquiry dictates the organization which therefore does not follow current trends of emphasis in teaching and research. Sometimes the book is thin where the work is thick, or thick where the work is thin. We have also taken some trouble within sections to show how the questions have been attacked by a variety of techniques, viewpoints and methods. On some questions, then, a historian's essay will jostle against a sociologist's careful statistical study. Our law school background, perhaps, has made us value questions more than answers, at least where we doubt that the answers are eternal truths. Hopefully, however, the student *will* emerge from the class with a sense of where social science and law have arrived so far. The materials do convey some sense of the current state of the art.

Methodology is a major subtheme. We do not purport to teach students how to do social science research. Our goal is to start the student on the road toward becoming an intelligent consumer of social science. He must learn to read critically, understand the assumptions inherent in certain approaches, and be ready to challenge the inferences drawn from the evidence offered. Social science cannot be taken as a kind of magic practiced by experts. It is apparent that our law student audience needs this introduction. However, we have found that our social science students benefit too. The nature of the questions we pose in this course calls for research tactics from many areas. A graduate student in sociology, for example, tends to know the methodology in vogue in his field but has little familiarity with the procedures of social psychology, history or economics. Also, because of the nature of the subject, students of the interrelations between the legal system and society must accept research strategies which often are far less than textbook models of scientific proof. An important lesson to be drawn from the materials in this book is how to deal with "soft" methodology.

Obviously, the way this book is organized means that we have not tried to include only the major literature in the field. Some articles are omitted because they do not fit into our organization of the subject. While we think highly of the articles used, either because they are sound or because they are provocative, some have serious flaws and are here for purposes of instruction. Law school casebooks frequently present badly reasoned appellate opinions. The hope is that students will learn a critical skill by tearing them apart; there are some advantages in presenting, from time to time, a flawed social science article. Also, it is necessary to examine widely-held theories very critically. Sometimes they prove to be indefensible. Some of these theories may have value if pruned back and qualified to fit the evidence; others need to be pulled up by the roots.

An active role for both students and instructor is assumed here. These materials do not present the student with a set of propositions to memorize. Rather, the student and the instructor begin with readings and use the classes to work toward generalizations, and, if these are unobtainable, at least an appreciation of the problems which must be faced in an area. The instructor can play a greater or lesser role. At one extreme, he can lecture and assume that his class will be ready to question him on the basis of their reading. At the other extreme, he can chair a discussion where the burden of going forward with the material is left to the members of the class. In our own teaching of this course, we have attempted to relate each reading to the outline presented in the Table of Contents and to past readings, and to force the class to deal with the questions presented after the readings. In some classes we have done most of the talking while in others the students have taken over and debated the problems raised both heatedly and intelligently. It is our hope that this book can be used by teachers and students who have little or no background in law or in social science or in both fields. Obviously, background is useful, but we do not think it is essential. The problems dealt with here often are the stuff of popular journalism and most people know something about them. One need not know either how to distinguish a case from past precedent or how to run a field survey in order to study these materials. We have attempted to define terms which might be unfamiliar and to explain social science procedures in terms understandable to one with little background in the fields involved. This is a field where few people could claim to be experts. Amateurs are not only welcome but needed, if the field is to develop properly.

At various places in the book we use examples which were current when we first taught the course. (The manuscript became final in early 1969.) Undoubtedly, these will become somewhat dated. Nonetheless, they have been used to tap student interest during the first years of the life of this book. After these examples have faded, we plan to introduce newer and more current ones to our students, and any instructor who reads the newspapers will be able to do this too. The underlying problems being exemplified, unfortunately, tend to be long-lived. Vietnam protests may fade from memory, but official response to those vigorously advocating unpopular ideas is likely to remain a live issue in the United States.

Our readings and our examples are almost entirely American. The final unit poses some questions about law in a cross-cultural context. But our approach in the main body of the book—and that of the authors whose works we reprint—is greatly influenced by the problems of our society in the 1960's. We hope, however, that the materials will have relevance to students in other societies in all stages of development during the 1970's. If a particular question seems meaningless in another social system or at another time, it may be profitable to ask why it has or had meaning in the United States during the 1960's but not elsewhere.

In many instances, the materials reprinted here have been cut to emphasize themes, problems and questions about the relationship of law and social science. Only selected footnotes have been reprinted. To aid anyone referring to the original source of an article, the original footnote numbers are used and the footnotes are reproduced with citations in the same form as in the original.

Many people and organizations have helped us produce this book, and we owe them thanks. Many helpful suggestions were offered by Professor Jack Ladinsky of the Department of Sociology of the University of Wisconsin, Professor Marc Galanter of the University of Chicago and Dr. Jacqueline R. Macaulay. Both of us participated in the Russell Sage Foundation's Law and Sociology Program at the University of Wisconsin for a number of years with great profit. Professor Macaulay must acknowledge the contribution to his efforts on this book of his year at the Center for Advanced Study in the Behavioral Sciences. We are grateful for the devoted and indispensable editorial work performed by Mrs. Ruth Wright and the secretarial assistance of Mrs. Violette Moore. Finally, we owe a great debt to our students, in various disciplines, who have had so much to say about the prior mimeographed versions of this book. Their questions and criticisms have been stimulating and provocative, and we hope we have been able to meet their challenge.

Lawrence M. Friedman
Stewart Macaulay
June, 1969

Summary Table of Contents

Table of Contents

Table of Readings

Principal readings are those with page references in italics; their reading numbers in this text are given in brackets.

C

D

G

H

N

Y

Z

Chapter 1

INTRODUCTION: DEFINITIONS AND PERSPECTIVES

These materials begin with readings concerned with definitions. They ask what is the province of the study of law and social science. The first readings ask what is the sociology of law, a question likely to prompt us to turn to other behavioral sciences besides sociology. The readings also ask what is law, a problem implied by the first question as well. What are the areas of law that have been illuminated by social science theory and research? Is one to be interested in the validity of psychological assumptions inherent in rules of the law of evidence? in the relationship between the formal legal system and the knowledge and judgment of experts? in the role conflicts inherent in the task of being an appellate judge? The second question—what is law—forces us to recognize that the behavior of people dealing with each other is influenced by many forces— rewards, penalties, customary patterns of dealing and the like. Is it profitable to label some of these forces "law" and focus attention on them? What criteria are to be used, and for what purpose?

A. LAW AND SOCIAL SCIENCE: WHAT ARE THE RELATIONSHIPS?

The first three readings involve a debate between two sociologists who have been associated with the Center for the Study of Law and Society at the University of California at Berkeley and a law professor who has played a leading role in studying legal problems from a social science perspective. The debate concerns the proper questions to be asked by sociology of law and it stresses the relationship of social science to issues of legitimacy and good and bad law. To some extent, the authors are representative of the habits of thought of sociologists as compared to academic lawyers. The sociologists are more eager to mark out boundaries, to seek models for testing; the law professor far more willing to look at all the data he can find and see what he can make of it.

1. The Sociology of Law

PHILIP SELZNICK*

SOCIOLOGY TODAY (R. Merton, L. Broom & L. Cottrell eds. 1959)

The idea of dealing with legal concepts and doctrine from a sociological point of view has been vaguely familiar to at least two generations of sociologists and legal scholars. In this country, the premises of sociological jurisprudence achieved a rather quick and general victory, helped along by a pragmatic temper, an impatience with abstractions, and a setting of rapid social change. This victory, such as it is, has had but little to do with the actual researches of sociologists; nor does it reflect the particular concepts and funded knowledge of the field. It is a point of view, an approach, a sensitivity that has been accepted.

Of course, the autonomy of legal scholarship still finds considerable support. It could not be otherwise, given the technical character and intricate development of many legal notions, the peculiarities of legal history, the depth of professional pride, and the relative isolation of the law schools. But the overriding fact, it seems to me, is that legal science in America is open to new ideas and influences. Certainly the intellectual foundations for a sociological approach have been laid. There is no need today to argue the general interdependence of law and society or to insist that legal rules be tested by their practical effects. Little will be gained from further demonstrations that law serves social interests and that these interests, in turn, reflect the changing structure of society. It may even be that legal realism, legal positivism, and sociological jurisprudence have been accepted altogether too easily and that problems of great moment have received less than their due appreciation and concern. I shall return to that issue presently.

The sociology of law may be regarded as an attempt to marshal what we know about the natural elements of social life and to bring that knowledge to bear on a consciously sustained enter-

* Professor of Sociology and Director, Center for the Study of Law and Society, University of California, Berkeley. Chapter 4 of Sociology Today, pp. 115-27, edited by Robert K. Merton, Leonard Broom, and Leonard S. Cottrell, Jr. Copyright © 1959 by Basic Books, Inc., Publishers, New York. Reprinted by permission.

prise, governed by special objectives and ideals. Thus understood, legal sociology follows a pattern similar to that of industrial sociology, political sociology, and educational sociology. With some prophetic license, we can detect in all these efforts three basic stages of development.

The primitive, or missionary, stage is that of communicating a perspective, bringing to a hitherto isolated area an appreciation of basic and quite general sociological truths, such as the significance of group membership for individual behavior. This early phase characteristically includes much theoretical discussion and analysis of everyday experience. There may also be some organized research, but what there is is mostly demonstrative in function, more valuable for its educational effect than for anything else. In law, such demonstrative research has not been particularly important, in part because of the role played by fact-guided judicial decisions and by the writings of men with rich experience in legal affairs. Although most of the theoretical work in this field has been done by European social scientists, the task of communicating an elementary, not-very-sophisticated sociological perspective has been accomplished largely by American legal scholars who were influenced by European thought, and by some of the more articulate appellate judges.

The second stage belongs to the sociological craftsman. It is a muscle-flexing period marked by intellectual self-confidence, a zeal for detail, and an earnest desire to be of service. At this stage the sociologist seeks more than the communication of a general perspective. He wants to explore the area in depth, to help to solve its problems, and to bring to bear quite specific sociological techniques and ideas. There are a number of signs that the sociology of law is about to enter this stage of development.

The third stage, as I envision it, is one of true intellectual autonomy and maturity. This stage is entered when the sociologist goes beyond (without repudiating) the role of technician or engineer and addresses himself to the larger objectives and guiding principles of the particular human enterprise he has elected to study. He reasserts the moral impulse that marked the first stage of sociological interest and influence. But the third stage is of a higher, more sophisticated level than the first because the second stage has provided a sounder basis for critical analysis.

I shall limit myself here to a few remarks concerning the imminent second stage and an even briefer discussion of the ultimate third stage of development in legal sociology. Before going on to these matters, I should like to emphasize one general point. In a broad sense, there is no real problem of articulating sociological inquiry to the needs of legal development. *Sociology can contribute most to law by tending its own garden.* Truly sound knowledge regarding basic human relations and institutions will inevitably find its way into legal doctrine. Truths so well founded that no reasonable, educated man can deny them need no special means of communication beyond the ordinary channels of education. It is well to remember that, although the law is abstract, its decision-making institutions deal with a concrete and practical world. Recognition of basic truths about that world cannot be long denied. Moreover, the legal order is becoming increasingly broad in scope, touching more and more elements of society. This means that sociological research addressed to the important characteristics of society, and to the basic changes in it, will automatically have legal relevance. This relevance, of course, goes beyond bare description. It includes making the law sensitive to the values that are at stake as new circumstances alter our institutions.

If this be true, if sociologists have only to mind their own business, why a special concern for sociology of law? Perhaps the most obvious answer is that two-way communication can bring to legal analysis more rapid and direct benefits from sociological research. But as soon as this communication begins, we see that the real problem and the real opportunity stem from the incomplete and tentative character of our knowledge. There are very few incontrovertible sociological truths. Most of what we know is tentative, not only in the sense that all scientific conclusions are tentative, but also in the sense that our research in many vital areas is still primitive and pioneering. Yet legal scholars are interested in this work, and properly so, because the very least it does is to challenge older images of man and society and offer new guides for the assessment of experience. This kind of knowledge, however, cannot be absorbed directly; it must be tested within the specific areas of legal interest; it must withstand the common-sense critiques of the practical lawyer. Such communication cannot take place effectively unless sociological inquiry is made directly relevant to legal problems.

But the sociology of law has an additional, and more profound, rationale than the communication of specific sociological knowledge regarding nonlegal phenomena. The law is itself a social phenomenon, an important agency of social control. The study of the law for itself, as a part of the natural order, is very much the sociologist's business. From this standpoint the sociology of law can contribute both to the science of society itself and to the self-knowledge of legal practitioners. Since self-knowledge and moral development are so intimately related, it is plain that here lies sociology's most important special contribution. This is the distinctive office of the third, most advanced stage of legal sociology.

Stage II and Its Problems

In the second stage of development of legal sociology, as I have suggested, the main effort is to apply sociological analysis to particular problems of legal doctrine and legal institutions.

The present outcropping of interest in law on the part of sociologists has been stimulated by a number of related developments. Probably most important is the rising self-confidence among sociologists—confidence in the ability of the field to cast new light on particular areas and to help in the solution of practical problems. Another stimulus has been the development and refinement of research methods, involving not merely statistical sophistication but the identification of characteristic social factors of proven researchability. This means that at least one brand of empiricism has been available for active service, ready to form the basis of large and quickly organized research operations.

Interest in law has also been encouraged by new work in the sociology of administration. These studies have restated some older problems regarding the interplay of formal systems of social control and the spontaneous behavior of men and groups. Some of us who have worked in that field have discovered that in studying formal organizations we were also studying legal systems. It is clear that what we were learning about the functions of formal rules, the interdependence of authority and consent, and similar matters was not really new from the larger perspective of legal sociology. It is also painfully evident that some sociologists are prone to repeat mistakes of the past by overemphasizing the informal and spontaneous and deprecating the significance and the peculiar problems of a legal order.

Finally, recent years have seen a fresh approach to the relation between custom and law; today we regard the law as a more creative agency than earlier sociologists believed it to be. This new perspective has been largely stimulated and sustained by recent history in the field of race relations, especially by the Supreme Court's extension of the constitutional concept of equal protection of the laws.

These developments promise a new and fruitful period of research and analysis. But we should take a close look at the characteristic avenues by which sociologists will enter the field. Perhaps we should speak of these as temptations, the better to mark out the probable risks and pitfalls.

An obvious temptation (although also an opportunity) is to offer research technique as the peculiar contribution of the sociologist. By technique, of course, I mean the apparatus of survey and experimental research, not the more common-sense historical and reportorial data-gathering that has been the main standby of sociological classics. It seems obvious to me that quantitative research can and must play an important role in legal sociology. Any continuing program of study in that field could easily keep a staff of survey technicians busy on fruitful projects. The subjective meaning of specific rules, such as the lawyer-client privilege, for clients as well as members of the bar; the social composition of the bench and of juror panels; the self-images of lawyers, their career lines, and other matters affecting professional integrity; the quasi-legal claims and expectations of various classes of citizens—these and a host of other specific studies depend for their execution on sophisticated survey technique.

But a serious risk is entailed and should not be overlooked. If we emphasize technique, we inevitably design projects that are congenial to the skills at hand. To be sure, such projects often have a market value in that they promise information that seems to be of immediate practical use to a client. Yet we know from experience that technique-stimulated research is seldom effectively guided by significant theoretical concerns or even by matters of the greatest long-run importance to the client himself. Attempts to apply small-group theory to the study of juries may seem an exception, but in fact they are not. The study of small groups, beyond certain first principles, is one of the more weakly developed areas in sociology; if this work is pushed to the forefront in legal sociology, it will be less for the sound knowledge it can offer than for the opportunity it presents to apply sophisticated research technique.

Another approach involves a similar risk, although it also begins from a posture of strength. Here one emphasizes the fund of sociological ideas, rather than the availability of research methods. The plan is to draw upon this sociological armory in order to illuminate particular problems in the legal field, whether of doctrine or of institutional functioning. This is the approach that Leonard Broom and I would take if we were to add a chapter on the sociology of law to the second part of our introductory textbook.* The effect upon legal doctrines and institutions of a number of sociological phenomena, including

* Such a chapter has been written and is included in L. BROOM & P. SELZNICK, SOCIOLOGY: A TEXT WITH ADAPTED READINGS (4th ed. 1968) (Harper & Row). [Eds. note]

socialization, value systems, stratification, collective behavior, and demographic trends, would be studied. But the main objective of this pedagogical device is to impress upon the student the force of sociological concepts and principles; it is not offered as a substitute for the autonomous, research-oriented organization of a field of inquiry. We cannot indiscriminately apply all our sociological ideas to legal studies; we must have a theoretical ground for supposing that some notions will be more important than others.

An indifferent appreciation of the entire sociological armory encourages intellectually low-level research, for two reasons. On the one hand, there is a natural tendency to choose those socio-logical concepts or factors that are easiest to handle; since it is all sociology anyway, if no theoretical ground exists for choosing the more difficult problems this solution will seem quite respect-able. Yet the net result may be fact-gathering of a quite trivial nature. On the other hand, this same indifference may result in choosing problems of immediate interest to a client, whether or not the studies entail any advance in our general knowledge.

The alternative to these approaches is more painful. It in-volves a double intellectual commitment, to problems of greatest theoretical concern in sociology and to problems that are truly important to the legal order itself. In sociology, the roughly defined area we call "social organization" remains a challenging frontier. In this field we attempt to identify the essential char-acteristics of different types of society, to locate the key human relationships that give a social order its distinctive qualities, to discover how major groups interact and what stable arrangements result. Most of the truly great names in sociology have been identified with broad studies of this sort. At the same time, these problems are the hardest to handle and are most frequently shunned.

From the legal side, the important problems also suggest an emphasis on studies of social organization. For example, what are the limits of law as an instrument of social control? What are the capabilities of courts, as we know them and as they could be? How much does society require of these agencies? How much can legitimately be demanded? Roscoe Pound stated this problem more than a generation ago, and offered some answers.[1] But research has been wanting. This is the kind of problem that can be approached in many ways, but it surely demands both a broad theoretical perspective and an emphasis on societal

---

[1] Roscoe Pound, "The Limits of Effective Legal Action," *Int. J. Ethics*, 27 (1917), 150-67.

needs and institutional potentialities. Thus an assessment of demands upon the legal system depends on what is going on within major groups and in the relations among them. Whether modern economic institutions can autonomously safeguard their members against arbitrary treatment and undue loss of liberty depends on the nature of participation and the dynamics of internal control. The sociological answer to this question inevitably affects the role of the courts. The potential achievements and vulnerabilities of both legal and nonlegal institutions are a proper and even urgent subject for sociological inquiry.

It is an interesting paradox that theories of social organization include both the best-founded and the most questionable of sociological writings. But this is not really strange. Obviously, any effort to delineate a broad pattern of social change runs the risk of speculative overgeneralization. On the other hand, if a broad theory becomes well established, this is because it finds confirmation on many levels and in a wide variety of contexts. Thus sociology has identified some of the main characteristics of modern industrial society, including the rise and dominance of bureaucratic forms of organization. The outlines of this theory have been well developed, and many specific inferences have been drawn and tested. I am sure that any effort to ground legal doctrine on social-science knowledge must look to these theories of the origins of our social order and the direction in which it is moving. Moreover, such developmental models are most likely to have something significant to say about the probable evolution of the law itself.

There is an unfortunate tendency to think of social-science knowledge as equivalent to the conclusions of specific pieces of research. I do not doubt that every generalization must be grounded in specific empirical studies, and there is always the possibility of a logically crucial experiment. But sound general knowledge is a complex result of many diverse pieces of work, analytical and empirical, each indirectly supporting the general theory. This means that we should avoid the temptation to present social-science knowledge as based on the specific results of a limited survey or experiment, for any one of the latter may be vulnerable while the basic generalization remains firm. The general agreement among social scientists regarding the damaging effects of segregation is actually based, not on specific studies of Negroes and whites, but on a theory of personality and on quite diverse, though logically related, empirical work. The very need to defend our own conclusions should recall us to basic theory.

In calling for an emphasis on broader theoretical problems, such as arise in the interpretation of trends in social organization and in the study of cultural systems, I do not mean to say that only the broad-gauged speculative and historical writings of the sociological classics is in order. On the contrary, it is characteristic of this middle stage of development that research must be sharply focused, exploring limited problems in depth. I wish only to emphasize that this work should take its departure from our funded knowledge and carry forward the theoretical concerns that have stimulated the most fruitful and lasting contributions.

Perhaps I can best indicate the research perspective I have in mind by briefly describing a current project of my own.* This is a study of due process and job rights in modern industry. Let me say a word first about the intellectual orientation and background of the study, then something about procedure. I began with a general interest in the social sources and the dynamics of legal change. I knew from the theory of bureaucracy that significant changes should be expected in the employment relation with the shift from earlier entrepreneurial forms to the modern managerial enterprise. The same theory suggested the hypothesis that the conditions of order within the enterprise would lead management itself to sponsor a rule of law; and it also suggested that the balance of power brought about by trade unionism would not persist as a mere power arrangement but would become part of a rationalized juridical system, based on a consensus regarding the rights and duties of employees. These hypotheses regarding what Ehrlich would have called the inner order of private institutions also raised the question of whether, in the formal legal order itself, there would not be a breakdown of traditional doctrine regarding master-servant relations and the employment contract. In other words, we see a quasi-legal development in private government and we ask what significance this has for "official" legal doctrine. Here again the problem of the competence of the law, and of legitimate demands upon it, comes up in acute form.

Bearing in mind the meaning of social organization, the reader will note that this setting focuses attention on the essential characteristics of a particular relationship, the meaning of employment in the large industrial firm. At the same time, it sees this relationship against the background of changes in the social structure of the enterprise. Also, the pattern of major group relations—organized labor and management—is explored in the

---

* See P. SELZNICK, P. NONET & H. VOLLMER, LAW, SOCIETY, AND INDUSTRIAL JUSTICE (1969) (New York: Russell Sage Foundation). [Eds. note]

light of a particular hypothesis regarding the outcome of their interaction. I see this outcome as a creative movement from power to justice, from self-help through intimidation to a system of justice and legality.

These ideas are being explored and tested in a variety of ways. The outlook for managerial self-restraint is being examined through intensive study of the doctrine and practice of modern personnel management, based on interviews as well as a review of the management literature. A detailed study of labor-arbitration decisions promises to show the emergence of a code for the protection of workers against arbitrary action. In the development of this code, the collective-bargaining contract is seen not as a terminal point but as a vehicle of legal evolution, establishing the conditions for the emergence of a sense of justice as well as the machinery for specifying its meaning. We are also undertaking a survey of employees' expectations and beliefs regarding rights in a job and protection against arbitrary treatment. The correlative studies of management policy and of subjective expectations will help to determine, given the nature of the enterprise, what expectations are legitimate and provide the basis for legally recognizable rights.

My aim in these studies is, as far as possible, to bring our broad hypotheses about law and social organization down to the level of specific behaviors, specific choices, and specific attitudes. Thus, the project described above might well lead to a study of the participants in grievance machinery, both labor and management representatives, to test the hypothesis that there are discernible and ultimately compelling pressures to substitute universalist for particularist criteria of choice. This, too, would tell us something about how legal change is mediated and sustained by problem-solving on the job.

My primary concern is that this middle stage of legal sociology should fulfill its highest potentialities. It will do so, I suggest, only if it truly makes sociological theory the source of hypotheses about the law. If it does, I am confident that the problems dealt with will be significant from the standpoint of jurisprudence.

This second stage properly emphasizes the contribution of sociology. But we shall also gain as we see the legal problems press the limits of our understanding. It will not be long before we find that new basic research is needed—for example, on the meaning of the integrity of the person—if the assumptions of legal doctrine are to be tested. But I would rather have our basic understanding challenged than limit our horizons by becoming mere fact-finders. No doubt there are many matters of fact that lawyers and law professors would like to ascertain, but such fact-finding, useful as it is, should not be confused with the scholarly objectives of a sociology of law.

Whatever the difficulties of this stage, they do not include the need to wrestle with ultimate problems of definition and of philosophical perspective. A great deal of work can be carried on, even work of high theoretical content, without worrying too much about the nature of law itself, or of justice. At this stage, we can accept working notions of positive law and we can see most of our work as dealing with the social sources of legal change. By taking this practical view, we can facilitate the release of intellectual energies; it does not follow, however, that we must remain forever content with that intellectual accommodation.

Stage III and Its Problems

As we approach a more advanced stage of development, all the classic problems of legal philosophy emerge again. For at this point we should be ready to explore the meaning of legality itself, to assess its moral authority, and to clarify the role of social science in creating a society based on justice.

In a consideration of these matters, the central fact is the role of reason in the legal order. Legality as we know it is based on a combination of sovereign will and objective reason. The word *reason* has an old-fashioned ring to it, but its long life is not yet over. Reason is an authoritative ideal, and the bearers of reason have, inevitably, a creative legal role. We see this, not only in the idea and practice of grounded judicial decision-making, but in the vast body of critical literature produced by legal scholars. Whatever the lawyer's commitment to legal positivism, to the belief that law is what the legislatures and the courts enunciate and enforce, there is at least an implicit recognition that not all law is on the same level. Some law is inferior because it contains the wrong mixture of arbitrary sovereign will, including majority will, and right reason. This is especially true of judge-made law, but legislatures can also make inferior laws. An inferior legality is manifested in the disposition of judges to give a narrow construction to statutes that depart from common-law principles, and in the ease with which judicial conclusions are modified or reversed. An inherent legality is doubtless much influenced by the derivation of a rule—whether from immediate political pressures or from a larger evolution consonant with underlying principles of legal order. I think that the quality of legality, and gradations in it, will be a primary preoccupation of the sociology of law in the future, as it has been in the past. In this work, moreover, we shall have to study the relation between reason and social consensus, for we shall not be satisfied with the assumption that community sentiment, as it bears on law, is basically nonrational.

Because reason is legally authoritative, scholarship has a direct significance for law that it does not have for other fields. This is indicated by the special role of law-review articles and legal treatises cited as authority by the courts. This work usually involves a critical restatement of common-law doctrine, but it also can and does locate new rights. The restatement aspect does give this work a special status, but there is no fundamental difference between sociological learning made legally relevant and the kind of analytical writing found in the law reviews. In any case, like any other inquiry, legal reasoning cannot but accept the authority of scientifically validated conclusions regarding the nature of man and his institutions. Therefore, inevitably, sociology and every other social science have a part in the legal order.

The underlying role of reason explains why legal scholarship and the sociology of law are mainly preoccupied with common law, and therefore with judicial behavior, rather than with legislation. It is true that somewhat more emphasis in legal training is now placed on legislation, reflecting the great growth of the legislative process. It is also true that the interpretation of statutes plays a large role in the judicial process. But it is and will undoubtedly remain true that the main access to the law by legal analysts is through the judiciary. More important for legal sociology, legal doctrine is a vital part of common law but of much less importance in legislation.

A concern for the role of reason must bring with it a certain disaffection with what has come to be known as legal realism. The hard-headed effort to base our notion of law on actual behavior is certainly congenial to a sociological orientation. But human behavior is a very subtle mixture of self-restraint and impulse, idealism and self-interest, behavior guided by a long-range end-in-view and behavior compelled by day-to-day pressures. We cannot accept as more than a passing polemical formula the aphorism that the law is what the judges say it is. Taken literally, this settles nothing, for if a consistency is found in judicial behavior, searching out the underlying premises of a normative system and upholding the essential ingredients of legality, then all nonpositivist interpretations of law are still available and the problems they raise are with us still.

The ideal of reason presumes that there are principles of criticism of positive law. It also presumes, as Lon Fuller has pointed out,[3] that there are principles of criticism of "living" law. Little

---

[3] Lon L. Fuller, "American Legal Realism," *Univ. of Pa. Law Rev.*, 82 (1934), 453ff.

is gained in any ultimate sense by looking beyond positive law to actual normative behavior. We must go on to seek out the foundations in reason for choosing among human norms those that are to be given the sanction of law. This will bring us, I cannot doubt, to an acceptance of some version of a doctrine of natural law, although it may not, and perhaps should not, be called that, given its historical associations. A modern naturalist perspective may be preferable, despite the still-unsettled question of whether an objective basis of normative order can be discovered, and despite the large differences between positivism and pragmatism, affecting the ideal of reason in law, regarding the subjective component of valuation and the role of will in judgment. But whatever the philosophical auspices, the search for principles of criticism based on social naturalism must go on. Law based on reason and nature summons man to his potentialities but sees those potentialities as something that science can identify; law based on reason and nature locates the weaknesses of the human spirit, such as pride, apathy, and self-abasement, and works to offset them. The natural order, as it concerns man, is compact of potentiality and vulnerability, and it is our long-run task to see how these characteristics of man work themselves out in the structure and dynamics of social institutions.

NOTES AND QUESTIONS

1. Selznick refers briefly to the history of efforts to relate law and the social sciences. On the legal side, the picture is one of a long history of calls for action but relatively few responses until the 1950's and 1960's. In the United States, one can go back at least to the writings of Oliver Wendell Holmes, Jr. in the late 19th and early 20th centuries. He saw the solution of legal problems as resting on more than legal logic alone and advocated collaboration with what we would now call social science. "No one will ever have a truly philosophic mastery over the law who does not habitually consider the forces outside of it which have made it what it is." During the period of the first World War, Roscoe Pound called for the study of "the limits of effective legal action."

Beginning in the 1920's and 1930's, there were a number of attempts to study law empirically, or institutionally, and to bring various bodies of social science knowledge and theory to bear on legal concerns. Noteworthy was the "institutional" method of Underhill Moore at Yale; *see* "An Institutional Approach to the Law of Commercial Banking," 38 *Yale Law Journal* 703 (1929), written by Moore and Theodore S. Hope, Jr. An effort was also made to apply the accepted theories of psychology of the day to the assumptions about human behavior in the law of evidence. Efforts were made to explain law in Freudian terms. (One notable product of legal Freudianism was Jerome Frank's *Law and the Modern Mind*, published in 1930.) Those concerned with economic regulation of business turned to various schools of economic theory. A legal research center, the Institute of Law, was created at Johns Hopkins University to study legal problems through field research guided by the then current theories of behaviorism in psychology. The institute produced a number of quantitative studies of courts at work, for example, Paul F. Douglass, *The Mayors' Courts of Hamilton County, Ohio* (1933). Some attempts were made, particularly at the Columbia Law School, to restructure law school courses so that they rested on the discoveries of various social sciences. Field studies of the actual operation of law in particular settings were undertaken at a number of schools, including Wisconsin. Several law schools added social scientists (most often economists) to their faculties. However, during this period those in law schools who looked outside their own traditions were relatively few and were more likely to look to philosophy and semantics than to psychology or sociology. Considering the state of psychology and sociology at this time, this may not have been unreasonable.

After World War II, there were a number of important developments within law schools. At the University of Nebraska Law School, studies were undertaken using far more advanced social science survey techniques than existed in the 1930's. Sociologists were added to the Yale law faculty. The American Bar Foundation began a long-term study of the administration of criminal justice based on field research. The University of Chicago, backed by a large grant from the Ford Foundation, embarked on the arbitration and jury study projects in which law professors and social scientists collaborated. The results of some of these efforts will be found reflected in the readings in this volume. As Selznick indicates, most of this history involves attempts to apply social science techniques or findings to answer questions posed by legal scholars who needed facts.

On the social science side, one finds sporadic interest in law. European social theorists such as Karl Marx and Max Weber had a great concern with the role of the legal system in society, but later theory builders have devoted little if any attention to law. Anthropologists have long engaged in a continuing debate about whether or not primitive societies have legal systems or only custom, and anthropology has focused on means of dispute settlement in primitive groups as one of its interests. John R.

Commons and other institutional economists in the first part of the 20th century sought to bring about reform through legislation which would pass the judicial tests of constitutionality; this naturally concerned them with areas of law. Economists have always been concerned with the regulation of the economy; hence, at least indirectly with the law. Political science, clearly, has dealt with some aspects of the legal system, and in recent years the concerns of political scientists have become increasingly more behavioral and empirical in contrast to earlier more philosophical approaches.

Most of the interest in law and sociology came after the second World War. Of course, criminology has long been a recognized subfield of sociology, but, with a few exceptions, the emphasis there was on the criminal himself rather than on the legal system. To some extent, sociologists long labored under the burden of the dictum of the early American sociologist, William Graham Sumner (1840-1910), that "law-ways cannot change folkways." (Sumner's statement itself probably was misunderstood. *See* Ball, Simpson & Ikeda, "A Re-examination of William Graham Sumner on Law and Social Change," 14 *Journal of Legal Education* 299 (1962)). At least, they often acted as if the formal structure of the law was of minimal relevance to a description of society, social interaction and social change. After the second World War, a number of sociologists became interested in law almost by accident; they were studying particular problems and found law relevant. In the late 1940's and 1950's, those who were concerned with racial relations became interested in doing studies which might affect the legality of segregation. Their efforts were rewarded by recognition in Brown v. Board of Educ., 347 U.S. 483 (1954), the school desegregation case. Many continued their interest in law through the attempts to enforce that decision and because of the civil rights struggles of the early 1960's.

More recently collaboration between legal scholars and social scientists has been structured more formally. The Russell Sage Foundation has funded programs, centers and institutes at a number of universities including the University of California at Berkeley, Wisconsin, Northwestern, Denver and Yale. There is now a Law and Society Association, and two journals exist to encourage efforts in this direction—the *Law & Society Review* and the Law and Society section of the *Wisconsin Law Review*. Despite all these developments, however, it is only fair to note that a social science interest in law is outside the mainstream of scholarship in both law and in sociology. On the other hand, it is very common in political science.

2. In Stage II, Selznick advocates commitment to problems of "greatest theoretical concern in sociology and to problems that are truly important to the legal order itself." He offers the area of "social organization" and gives reasons why it is sociologically important. He then suggests that social organization is an important area from the legal side, and advocates studies of "the limits of effective legal action." Why are these "limits" an important legal problem? There are very few law review articles about this problem, and it is not overtly studied to any great extent in American law schools. Does this indicate that Selznick's assessment of its importance is wrong? Assuming that it is an important problem from the legal side, how does a study of social organization help one discover the limitations of law?

3. Selznick can be taken to say that social science can clarify the classic problems of legal philosophy. For example, he says "Some law is inferior because it contains the wrong mixture of arbitrary sovereign will, including majority will and right reason. . . . An inferior legality is manifested in the disposition of judges to give a narrow construction to statutes that depart from common-law principles, and in the ease with which judicial conclusions are modified or reversed." How does the arrival of collaboration between law and social science at his Stage III help us to evaluate some law as "inferior" for these reasons? Consider the following passage:

Recently the moralistic view has been widely replaced by . . . [a] . . . second fallacy . . . which is equally indefensible. That is "scientificism," the notion that social problems can be solved by applying the methods by which man has achieved increasing mastery over nature. But obviously, the basic problems are value problems, to which natural science has little relevance. To begin with, scientific knowledge confers power, but has little to say about the ends for which power is used, even by an individual. It shows *how* to do things, how to achieve a concretely defined objective, not what objectives to pursue. Further and more important, in a society dedicated to freedom, power of men over men is inherently evil, even if exercised with "good intentions," which is not very likely to be the case. Such power is to be minimized, as well as restricted in use, though it is not wholly avoidable and is often a necessary expedient, to avoid evils worse than limiting personal liberty.

Frank Knight, *Intelligence and Democratic Action* 11-12 (Harvard U. Press 1960).* Would Knight indict Selznick on a charge of "scientificism"? If so, how would you argue in Selznick's defense? Could you begin your argument usefully with the assertion that the United States is a constitutional representative government based on values and the implications of those values which are expressed in its fundamental law? For further explanations of Selznick's position, *see* Selznick, Book Review of Fuller, *The Morality of Law*, 30 *American Sociological Review* 947 (1965); Selznick, "Sociology and Natural Law," 6 *Natural Law Forum* 84 (1961); Parker, "On Values and Value Judgments in Sociology," 32 *American Sociological Review* 463, 465-66 (1967).

4. There have been a number of general treatments of the sociology of law, or, more broadly, law and society, in recent years, and a few collections of essays or readings have been published. *See, e.g.,* F. James Davis, Henry H. Foster, Jr., C. Ray Jeffery & E. Eugene Davis, *Society and the Law: New Meanings for an Old Profession* (Free Press 1962); Geoffrey Sawer, *Law in Society* (Oxford 1965); Edwin M. Schur, *Law and Society, a Sociological View* (Random House 1967); William M. Evan, *Law and Sociology, Exploratory Essays* (Free Press 1962); and Rita James Simon, *The Sociology of Law, Interdisciplinary Readings* (Chandler Publishing Co. 1968).

---

2. Legal Tasks for the Sociologist

CARL A. AUERBACH*

1 LAW & SOCIETY REVIEW 91 (1966)

I shall comment here on the theoretical framework Professor J. H. Skolnick suggests for studies in the sociology of law and the adequacy of the bibliography in his *Social Problems* article "The Sociology of Law in America: Overview and Trends."[1] While I welcome Skolnick's emphasis on theory and the "larger philosophical issues," I think his theoretical orientation would unnecessarily constrict social studies of law.

We are all indebted to Professor Skolnick for undertaking the difficult task of charting our course. Understandably, any map drawn by a single individual will most clearly reveal the particular road taken by him. But it is our purpose here to share perspectives, and I trust that my comments on Professor Skolnick's paper will contribute to this objective.

Professor Skolnick tells us that "the most important work for the sociologist of law is the development of theory growing out of empirical, especially institutional, studies" and that the "most general contribution that the sociology of law may make to social theory is that of understanding the relation between law and social organization." With these broad generalizations I agree. But at the same time, Skolnick insists that "an utterly basic question" for the sociologist of law is "how does one perceive the existence of a legal system," or, "what is there about a system of norms and rules—which exists whenever one is following any sort of model, even a blueprint—which makes it distinctively legal."

It is apparent, however, that Skolnick thinks that Professor Philip Selznick has answered this question. He quotes Selznick's statement that to "understand the distinctively legal we must

---

* Professor of Law, School of Law, University of Minnesota. Reprinted from Law and Society Review. Copyright © 1966 by the Law and Society Association. Reprinted by permission.
[1] J. H. Skolnick, *The Sociology of Law in America: Overview and Trends,* Law and Society: Supplement to Summer, 1965 Issue of SOCIAL PROBLEMS 4 (1965).

look to a special kind of obligation, an obligation to act in accordance with authoritatively determined norms." And he hazards certain generalizations which are traceable to Selznick's work—that "not all rules are lawful rules, even though these have been created by a 'legitimate' polity" and that a "rule of law . . . not only suggests controls upon arbitrary use of authority, but also implies the construction of institutions prizing and supporting man's ability to use reason to rise above subjective desire." Accordingly, Skolnick concludes, the primary task of the sociologist of law is to explore "the nature of legality and . . . the conditions under which it is most likely to emerge."

I can think of no more fruitless task. For example, I do not see how empirical studies undertaken by sociologists of law can dispose of the question whether the Nazi genocidal laws should be regarded as "lawful" rules for all scholarly and practical purposes. Skolnick sees these laws as the "most dramatic example" of the "fact" that "not all rules are lawful rules." . . . I do not understand in what sense Skolnick uses the term "fact" when he refers to the "fact" that "not all rules are lawful rules." Obviously, he has chosen to define "lawful" and the "rule of law" in a particular way that suits his purposes but which others may regard as inadequate for their purposes.

It is sometimes argued that to define "law" to include unjust laws will, in fact, encourage obedience to unjust laws. But it is also argued that to define only just laws as "law" will have the same effect because it will habituate the people to assume that the existing legal order is always just. Whether popular disobedience is more likely if people refuse to regard an unjust law as "law" is, of course, a proper question for empirical investigation. I merely wish to emphasize that recognition as "lawful" of all "positive law" (which, in Selznick's words, includes all "those public obligations *that have been* defined by duly constituted authorities"), even if it lacks "legality" in Selznick's sense, does not logically or otherwise imply a moral obligation to obey any particular legal rule or norm.

We may, for example, define and recognize the Nazi genocidal laws as "lawful" *under the Nazi legal system* and for this very reason condemn the Nazi "rule of law." We may even decide, once we acquire the power to do so, to punish the Nazi officials who executed these barbaric laws for violating the moral obligation to disobey them. Similarly, we may, if we wish, refuse to recognize a particular norm or rule as "lawful," because it is unjust, and yet be morally obligated to obey it. I am aware that at one point in his article on "Sociology and Natural Law" Selznick seeks to distinguish between his concept of "legality" and the concept of justice. But soon he acknowledges that "at least some principles of justice are ingredients of the ideal of legality." And yet he offers cogent reasons why the "positive law" should be obeyed even when it conflicts with the ideal of legality as he defines it.

It is important, of course, to make our definitions explicit so that we understand each other. I might even be persuaded to make popular use of Selznick's definition if it were shown that this would have desirable consequences for society. But I think that the sociologist of law who seeks to demonstrate the superiority of a single definition of law for all scholarly and practical purposes is wasting his time. Certainly no such demonstration is required to enable the sociologist to study law as a "normative order," or to ascertain the "universal characteristics of man and concomitant principles of justice." In short, it is not necessary to conduct a prior investigation into the nature of "legality" in order to join Selznick in the effort to establish "principles of criticism to be applied to existing positive law," based on "scientific generalizations, *grounded* in warranted assertions about men, about groups, about the effects of law itself." I accept this excellent statement by Selznick of the objective of the sociology of law. . . .

The absence of an agreed formal definition of "law" does not mean that lawyers do not know what they are talking about when they speak of the "legal" order or the "legal" system. They generally have in mind what Max Weber described as "state law" and Selznick defines as "positive law"—the rules regulating, or establishing the framework for, the behavior of the members of the society which are promulgated and enforced by the agencies of the state. Here too, I should make it clear that I do not object to Selznick's use of the term "law" to include what Max Weber called "non-state" law. Skolnick also adopts this latter use, quoting with approval Professor Lon Fuller's definition of "law" as "the [purposive] enterprise of subjecting human conduct to the governance of rules" and adding that this conception "includes the rules of a variety of institutions—corporations, clubs, churches, universities—as well as the polity itself."

But I would argue that it is important to maintain Weber's distinction between "state" and "non-state" law, not only in the interest of clarity of thought but also because of the consequences that may attend the abandonment of the distinction. To illustrate my point, I shall refer to Skolnick's discussion of the significance of "private government" for the sociologist of law. For Skolnick, the emergence of the doctrine that private government "should be subject to the same restraints under the Constitution that apply to any agency of the federal or state government" constitutes "the core subject of sociological interest in private government." While I agree with his estimate of the importance of the subject matter, it is confusing to state the problem in this manner.

As I have tried to show elsewhere, to equate the action of "private governments" with "state action" would have the consequence, among others, of making the Supreme Court of the United States, rather than the Congress of the United States, the supreme arbiter of national economic policy. Those who would welcome such an outcome—which in my opinion would impair the role of the national legislature in our democracy—should argue for it on its merits. They should not obscure the issue by contending that this consequence must be accepted because it *logically* follows from their definition of "law" and their concept of "legality."

The insistence upon a particular conception of "law" also introduces a note of confusion into Skolnick's proposals for the study of the legal profession. Skolnick maintains that the "essential interest in the legal profession, for the sociologist of law, must be in the lawyer's distinctive capacities for developing a legal order, and in the conditions under which such capacities are advanced or impeded." He then quotes with approval the following statement from Nonet and Carlin:

> As long as law remains a mere expedient for the settlement of disputes or the accommodation of conflicting interests, the lawyer's trade need hardly distinguish itself from any other occupation. . . . A fuller professional development occurs when law is viewed as an *embodiment of values.*

I am not certain that I understand these passages from Skolnick or Nonet and Carlin. I take it for granted that every lawyer participates in developing our legal order—for better or for worse—as he goes about his day-to-day tasks and that individual lawyers differ in their capacities to do their jobs. I do not see the distinction between "law" as a "mere expedient for the settlement of disputes or the accommodation of conflicting interests" and "law" as "an embodiment of values." Inevitably, in my view, values are embodied in any settlement of a dispute or accommodation of conflicting interests. We need studies that will reveal the lawyer's role in such settlements and accommodation—the sociologist's "essential interest in the legal profession" should thus be in what the profession *does.* Skolnick, Nonet and Carlin may share a particular vision of the values an ideal legal order should realize. But I do not see why it is necessary for all sociologists to share their vision in order to make significant empirical studies of the legal profession. Nor do I see why the legal "profession" is not worthy of the name if it fails to act as they think it should.

Reluctantly I have concluded that Skolnick's images of the practicing lawyer and law-teacher are not mine. Yet it is crucial for the future success of our common endeavors that we do not cling to mistaken notions of each other. Possibly, I readily acknowledge, empirical study is needed to decide who is mistaken. But permit me to point out where I differ with Skolnick.

Unlike Holmes, says Skolnick, "most practicing lawyers and law professors" do not cultivate "scholarly curiosity about the law as a social institution." "Most practicing lawyers," he explains, "are interested in knowing better how to ply their trade." "And similarly, most law professors care primarily about their stock in trade, which is in America the analysis of case law. . . . The lawyer is a practitioner and legal training stresses the logical analysis of judicial norms, a position associated with the philosophy of analytical jurisprudence." While Skolnick wisely hedges his statements by speaking of "most" practitioners and "most" law professors, he has nevertheless, in my opinion, presented to our colleagues abroad an erroneous overall impression of the concerns of the practicing lawyer and law professor and of the state of legal education in America.

After all, the legal realists did triumph and their teachings, more than any other influence, are reflected in the curricula and methods of our law schools. Even the new analytical jurisprudence inspired by linguistic philosophy is finding it difficult to make its way in America. The bibliography which Skolnick has assembled for us is studded with the works of law professors and practicing lawyers. The pioneer study of the right to privacy by Brandeis and Warren, which Skolnick thinks is still significant for sociologists, was written when both were practicing lawyers. Indeed, every practicing lawyer must be a sociologist of law in order better to ply his trade. Unfortunately, almost always, he is an untrained one.

I object to Skolnick's characterizations only because their acceptance would result in underestimating the opportunities for fruitful collaboration with practicing lawyers (including judges) and law professors in sociological studies of law. Every practicing lawyer knows that the art of advocacy—before a court, a legislative committee, an executive or administrative agency—is founded, in large measure, upon the ability to describe and evaluate the factual consequences of the alternatives open to the tribunal. He is also aware that his own—and the tribunal's—

knowledge of the social facts is inadequate. So Professor Stone
has suggested as the province of sociological jurisprudence

> the broad area of the interaction between law and legal insti-
> tutions on the one hand, and the attitudes and activities of
> men governed by these rules on the other—in brief, of the
> effect of law on men and of men on law.

In this sense, I maintain, every practicing lawyer is interested in
sociological jurisprudence. And every branch of law—private
and public—is a potential subject for sociological study on behalf
of which the energies of the law professor, the practitioner and
the judge can be enlisted. Our problem, in truth, is to devise
priorities and determine strategies for investigation.

My complaint, therefore, is that Skolnick's horizon is too limited—as is his bibliography. The empirical studies cited are concentrated in the fields of the criminal law and criminology, the
legal profession, the Chicago Jury Project* and racial desegregation. Not a single work cited deals with the legislative or executive process and the administrative process is represented only by
a few studies in criminal law administration. The focus of attention is the judicial process. Indeed, at times, Skolnick seems to
exclude all other areas from the sociologist's province. For example, he thinks that only those "policy studies" are "most central"
in the sociology of law which "reflect back upon the working of
the legal order." To illustrate his point he states: "Studies in
delinquency rehabilitation are of interest to sociology of law to
the extent that they lead to an understanding of adjudicative
behavior. If the main contribution relates to the efficiency of
correctional officials, the interest of such studies—no matter their
quality—would be mainly criminological." But why so? Why
could not studies of the efficiency of correctional officials "reflect
back upon the working of" a particular criminal code? Or form
the basis for generalizations about the administration of the
criminal law?

It has taken the law schools a long time to discover that legislative, administrative and executive processes are also part of the
"legal order." Are sociologists now to retrace our steps by taking
"adjudicative behavior" as their exclusive concern? Studies of the
legislative, executive and administrative processes merit the highest priority in any list of tasks to be done in the sociology of
law. For if one agrees with Skolnick, as I do, that the "one
broad topic" that can be said "to characterize the future of the

_____

* See Reading 44, at 427, _infra_. [Eds. note]

sociology of law . . . is legal development and change," then the study of such change requires knowledge of its principal instrument in the modern world—the legislative, executive and administrative processes. . . .

Skolnick points out that sociologists of law in America "seem increasingly interested in making jurisprudential generalizations within the context of historical trends." Such generalizations should be sought in any study of the impact of law upon social change and of social change upon the legal order. But if this is to be the case, we must not ignore the rich source of empirical data which consists of the legal records developed for purposes of law-making and law-application by state and federal judges, executives and legislators—cases, statutes and administrative and executive regulations and decisions. Professor Willard Hurst has shown us to what imaginative use these records may be put. His volumes are storehouses of "jurisprudential generalizations within the context of historical trends" which should be of great interest to all sociologists of law.

Recently, Arnold Rose called for research in the "social process by which a legislative statute is formulated and passed." We have a few such studies—by political scientists and practicing lawyers—which should not for that reason alone be excluded from a bibliography on the sociology of law. . . . Should the studies of voting behavior be excluded?

Should we also exclude the studies of the administrative process . . . ? Skolnick does not mention any of the vast number of books and articles dealing with organizational or decision-making theory. True, few of these works are concerned with administrative or executive agencies of government. But some work has been done on the process of decision-making within the administrative agencies of the federal government which should be of interest to sociologists of law.

As I indicated above, the practicing lawyer, the judge and the law professor are most interested in investigations of the social impact of particular legislative, administrative and executive rules, decisions and practices. A number of such studies have been made and should be noted. For example, should not the Kinsey studies be included?

I am certain that I have not exhausted the additional studies that ought to be listed in a bibliography on the sociology of law. . . . At any rate, what I would include reflects what I regard as proper grist for the sociology-of-law mill. And I would be disturbed if Skolnick excluded the studies I have cited solely because he thought none of them had any value for the kind of theory he thinks the sociologist of law should try to elaborate.

Yet, in spite of the numerous works I have cited, I agree with Skolnick that we should not assume that there already exists "a large body of social science findings directly relevant to lawyer-like concerns." But I would counsel my colleagues not to approach the behavioral scientist . . . with the assumption that he has nothing to contribute and a belligerent "show me" attitude. The problem, once again, is to devise priorities and strategies for investigation. Julius Stone urges that the "contributions to understanding the law" offered by the social sciences "must be marshalled and organized around the problems which confront the lawyer." I agree; but the sociologist similarly will be interested only in problems that have theoretical significance for him. Arnold Rose tells us sensibly to "get together and hammer out researchable questions of interest to both" lawyers and social scientists. Apparently, this is easier said than done.

For example, Skolnick concludes that "there is little that is exciting . . . either theoretically or philosophically" about the findings of the Chicago Jury Project—our most ambitious joint undertaking to date. Certainly, the Chicago Jury Project was marshalled and organized around a problem of significance for the lawyer. I am not competent to say whether the Project could have been organized so as to yield findings that are theoretically exciting to the sociologist. If it could have been it is a pity that it was not so organized. But even if it could not have been so organized the Chicago Jury Project yielded information of great value for any intelligent decision about the future of the jury system—a subject of lively current debate. From the point of view of a reform-minded law professor it was worth undertaking. And sociologists contributed much to make it worthwhile. If Skolnick is right projects of this sort in the future may have to rely upon the services of reform-minded sociologists or, if worse comes to worse, purchase the services of sociologists.

I know of no easy way to reach agreement that a particular research subject and research design will be significant for our society, will center on a problem of importance to the lawyer and will promise findings that are theoretically exciting to the sociologist. Skolnick and I do not even seem to agree about the merits of Dean Pound's theory of interests, which I think is of enduring theoretical importance for the sociologist of law. It enables us systematically to view the legal order of any particular society as a source of data about the values authoritatively chosen by that society. Thus it offers a significant framework for a comparative analysis of the legal orders of different societies. . . .

In my opinion these theoretical objectives [of sociologists of law] will themselves have to be formulated, tested and refined

in the light of past, present and future work of the kind that I
regard as falling within the province of the sociology of law.
Thus to me, at this juncture, the most heartening aspect of the
work going forward at Berkeley, Wisconsin and Northwestern is
not its present theoretical underpinnings but the very fact that
some sociology departments and law schools have close working
relationships.

3. Social Research on Legality
A Reply to Auerbach

JEROME H. SKOLNICK*

1 LAW & SOCIETY REVIEW 105 (1966)

Professor Auerbach makes fundamental criticisms. He can "think of no more fruitless task" than my conclusion that sociologists of law ought to explore "the nature of legality . . . and the conditions under which it is likely to emerge." "I do not," he continues, "see how empirical studies undertaken by sociologists of law can dispose of the question whether the Nazi genocidal laws should be regarded as 'lawful' rules for all scholarly purposes . . . I do not understand in what sense Skolnick uses the term 'fact' when he refers to the 'fact' that not all rules are lawful rules."

There seem to be two separable criticisms here, one having to do with legality as a theoretical model, the other with its normative aspects. I shall try to respond to each of these criticisms. I do not believe I ever suggested that sociologists of law can "dispose of" the question of whether Nazi genocidal laws should be regarded as lawful. Rather, my statement that sociologists ought to explore the nature of legality means that sociologists ought to study the conditions under which men consider certain rules to be lawful rules, and how men create, interpret and transform principles and associated rules within institutions. It also suggests that sociologists consider the meaning of governance by rules from the standpoint of the citizen. For example, what does it mean to the individual to "participate" in a "legal" order? What is universal in the adversary system and what is relative?

For such purposes the sociologist must have a point of reference as to the meaning of governance by law, or the rule of law. Although it may be true that "others" may regard the notion of the rule of law in the article as "inadequate for their purposes," I would suggest that research cannot be done without some con-

---

* Professor of Sociology, University of California, San Diego. Reprinted from Law and Society Review. Copyright © 1966 by the Law and Society Association. Reprinted by permission.

ception of the rule of law. Selznick's emphasis upon "the progressive reduction of arbitrariness" seems to be consistent with
legal writings on the meaning of the rule of law. I doubt that
Selznick "seeks to demonstrate the superiority of a single definition of law for all scholarly and practical purposes." Rather, he
is suggesting that sociological analysis of law requires a working
conception of legality even if only for research purposes. In fact,
a considerable amount of research in legal sociology has been
influenced by the problem of legality, e.g., on police, on juvenile
justice, on administrative agencies, on the jury.

Auerbach suggests (through Stone) that "excessive concentration on [the specific *differentia* of law] may indeed be a diversion." He asserts that lawyers pretty much know what they're
talking about when they speak of the legal order or the legal
system: "They generally have in mind what Max Weber described as 'state law' and Selznick defines as 'positive law'—the
rules regulating, or establishing the framework for, the behavior
of members of the society which are promulgated and enforced
by agencies of the state." It is possible, however, to entertain a
conception of a legal order that distinguishes between rules of
order—positive law, Weber's legal order—and rules directed toward constraining the arbitrary behavior of officials, e.g., search
and seizure restrictions. The conception of a legal system that
Auerbach says lawyers "generally have in mind" directs attention
to certain kinds of questions—e.g., why people violate positive
law—rather than to a concern for the behavior of authorities.
Thus Auerbach's conception of law may prove too "restrictive,"
a charge which he levels at ours. Law involves both procedure
and substance, and the relation between the two is a central issue
for empirical inquiry, as I suggested in my discussion of the relation between substantive law and its administration, including the
administration of automobile accident law. . . . By asserting that
lawyers generally know what a legal order is, Auerbach may inadvertently be seeking "to demonstrate the superiority of a single
definition of law for all scholarly and practical purposes."

Auerbach finds that my writings puzzle him. . . . As sociologists of law, we should merely be interested, he says, "in what
the profession *does*." But lawyers "do" all sorts of things—eat,
sleep, go to the theater, read, write, talk, make love. If Auerbach
is suggesting that we simply record the "behavior day" of lawyers, as Gesell tried to do with children, that is a tenable, albeit
naive, methodological stance to take. Once he begins to suggest
that some behaviors are more important to observe than others,
we want to know why. In the telling, I suspect that he will begin
to sound suspiciously like those whom he criticizes. We all are

interested in "the effect of law on men and men on law." But
this requires empirical study with guiding concepts and orienting hypotheses. *One* of these is the role of lawyers vis-à-vis the
integrity of the legal system. As Selznick recently wrote, "Certainly a continuing preoccupation of the lawyer *qua* jurist is to
enhance the integrity of the system and its procedures; but legal
craftsmanship must also be concerned with bending a received
tradition to emergent social needs, exploiting the resources of law
for practical ends. When the tension between these commitments
is faced, jurisprudence comes alive." The identification of such
central issues is required for the development of a sociology of
law.

It was for such a purpose—suggesting research issues—that the
analysis of private government was emphasized in my paper.
Auerbach misses the point when he says that the identification
of "government" in non-state groups means that the action of
such groups is "state action." This was an analytical point, and
it is a serious error to impose the special imagery of "state action," as it arises in constitutional interpretation in this country,
upon a theoretical approach to the governance in private groups.
As sociologists we are concerned with making generalizations regarding certain kinds of processes, and not at all in deciding
which branch of government should be "the supreme arbiter of
national economic policy." Generalizations might call for examination of systems of governance that do not have the official
stamp of government. We are interested in punishment systems,
not in prisons alone. We are interested in compliance with types
of authority. We are interested in the development and promulgation of rules through sanction, whether through a system of
criminal courts or faculty-student committees. We recognize that
"adjudication" is a process that takes place in many contexts—
arbitration provides a ready example—and is not only carried on
by men who are called judges. Our concern with the idea of
legality is in effect the introduction of a model in order to understand how the model develops and operates under different institutional conditions.

When I wrote that not all rules are lawful rules I was, to be
sure, using a conception of fact based upon a normatively derived model of legality. Much valuable social science has this
character. For example, political sociology considers the nature
of "democracy" and the conditions for its development; social
psychology studies the "primary group," and its determinative conditions; urban sociology investigates the nature of "community"
and the features of urban life that undermine or enhance its
maturation. Social science is replete with studies of normatively

derived models which in themselves are perhaps problematic, but not as problematic as Auerbach suggests.

Thus in the sense that I used the word "fact," it is a "fact" that there cannot be "democracy" without elections, there cannot be a "primary group" without interaction, nor a "community" without commonly held values. Similarly, as Fuller has suggested, there cannot be "legality" when authorities (1) fail to achieve rules; (2) fail to publicize or make rules available; (3) legislate retroactively; (4) make vague rules; (5) make contradictory rules; (6) require conduct beyond the powers of the affected party; (7) introduce such frequent changes in rules that subjects cannot orient their actions to them; (8) administer a set of rules different from those announced.[6] A critic may disagree with Fuller that "a total failure in any one of these eight directions does not simply result in a bad system of law; it results in something that is not properly called a legal system at all, except perhaps in the Pickwickian sense in which a void contract can still be said to be one kind of contract." Perhaps another "route to disaster" can be found, or one or two of these may be less significant than the others, just as failure to meet criteria of suffrage or frequency of elections may result in a political structure that is not properly called "democratic." But Fuller provides us with an acceptable model for pursuing empirical investigation, as good as or better than most models we experience in social science.

The heart of the controversy seems to arise from a linguistic ambiguity. The analogy to the study of "democracy" is instructive here. We ordinarily speak of a "democratic" or an "oligarchic" form of government, recognizing that political structures vary. Then we attempt to account for the development of these different political structures. The question is, are all systems of social control through rules and enforcement "legal" systems? It is possible to answer affirmatively by considering "legal structures" as being on the same conceptual level as "political structures." There *is* that ambiguity about the term "legal." For the reasons stated above—that "legality" is distinctive, that it is potentially an important research model, that a distinction between order and law is useful—I believe we will make greater advances in sociology of law research if we consider "legality" as conceptually parallel to "democracy," not to "political structure." Thus, I would again suggest that sociologists consider the nature and functioning of legality as a central concern.

Auerbach, however, may be making two other points. He may be arguing from a strictly behaviorist position that we should not

---

6 L. FULLER, THE MORALITY OF LAW 39 (1964).

study normative concepts, a position that would exclude numerous theoretical conceptions in social science. I doubt that he is saying that, though he sometimes seems to be. If so, I would simply disagree. On the contrary, I would argue that if we are to have a science of society we must study normative phenomena. Or he might be suggesting that if we study normative phenomena we should take care not to become merely spokesmen for a normative position. I agree that there is a danger here, but I am worried that the concern for a value-free social science will produce a valueless social science. The ideal of "health" is also normative, but a concern for having a healthful community does not preclude scientific inquiry into physiology or microbiology.

Like Auerbach, I would prefer to see greater collaboration between lawyers and sociologists, but I do not believe that "every practicing lawyer must be a sociologist of law in order to better ply his trade." If all Auerbach is saying is that every lawyer must be familiar with the legal order in practice as well as with "book law," he is right, of course. But the sociology of law is not merely a description of the law in action, which *some* legal realists took it to be in response to the "black letter" emphasis of many law teachers. It is also an analysis of the meaning and function of law in societies of different kinds. Unfortunately, unlike the early Holmes, most lawyers and law teachers have not concerned themselves with such questions, and I used the word "most" advisedly, to suggest a majority. Perhaps I am wrong. I hope so. I fear, however, that a review of legal writing and teaching will bear me out.

Thus, the issue is not whether there ought to be a collaboration, but, as Auerbach recognizes, what collaboration means. Auerbach agrees with Stone that the "contributions to understanding the law" offered by the social sciences "must be marshalled and organized around the problems which confront the lawyer." If they mean by this "problems which confront the legal order," I could not agree more. Such an emphasis would suggest *basic* research into the functioning of the legal order. I fear, however, that Stone means what he seems to say, i.e., that the sociologist should confine himself to *applied* research that lawyers consider useful. To use the medical analogy the lawyer, like the medical doctor, is concerned with developing vaccines. The research scientist, however, may be equally interested in understanding the nature and functioning of viruses. The two concerns are not unrelated, but there is usually a tension between those who want only to cure, and those who want also to understand.

In closing, I should like briefly to return to what Auerbach says in his chief complaint, that my "horizon is too limited." A scanning of Auerbach's horizon reveals no principle or perspectives for orienting research. A mere listing of topics and studies will not pass muster as a theoretical guideline. Certainly research into the "social process by which a legislative statute is formulated and passed" is important since it may go to the issue of the meaning of law, of how a society develops its norms for governance. Of course, studies of administrative agencies may be important, depending upon the issues they raise. Nothing in my paper suggests otherwise.

The real issue, however, is not what is studied, but how and why it is studied. Most studies of voting behavior, for example, have been concerned with explaining voting without seriously attempting to demonstrate how the variables that affect voting influence the legal order. And it is the legal order that is the central concern of the sociologist of law, not voting, not organizational dynamics, not decision-making behavior, not sexual behavior. Studies in these areas may shed light upon, or provide analytical tools for, examination of the legal order, and to the extent that they do they are relevant. In any social science field there are countless "relevant" studies. Relevance and centrality, however, are not the same thing. The concern of my paper was to suggest criteria of centrality, to respond to the question "What are distinctive theoretical issues guiding the sociology of law?" I hope that, as a result of Professor Auerbach's critique, the response to that question has been somewhat clarified.

NOTES AND QUESTIONS

1. One can distinguish between social science *in* law and a social science *of* law. That is, a study such as the Kinsey Report tells us that many people engage in sexual practices which the law declares illegal. From this discovery, a legal policymaker might conclude that (a) the law ought to be changed to make these practices legal, (b) the law ought to remain unchanged but additional resources ought to be appropriated to enforcement agencies so that the practices could be deterred and those who were not deterred could be punished, or (c) the present law and its nonenforcement represent the best compromise between groups of people with drastically different views about what sexual practices are good and bad. Thus the Kinsey data might raise a policy issue and be relevant to its resolution if not decisive. But the Kinsey Report is in one sense not a study of the legal system in operation nor of the relationship between legal and social norms. After reading the Kinsey data, one might study why the laws concerning sexual behavior do not accord with

practice, and this might be a study of the legal system or the relationship between legal and social norms.

Does the distinction between providing data for the solution of legal problems and studying the role of the legal system in society explain all the differences between Auerbach (the law professor) and Skolnick (the sociologist)? In other words, are they just talking past one another?

2. Auerbach criticizes Skolnick for having too narrow a focus. Does Auerbach set any limits on "Legal Tasks for the Sociologist"? Does it make sense to define the boundaries of a sociology of law?

3. Skolnick says at one point in his article that he is using Professor Lon Fuller's eight criteria of "legality" as a model for research purposes:

(a) Suppose one studied the operations of the Civil Aeronautics Board. One asked to what extent the CAB's operations matched and deviated from Professor Fuller's eight criteria and then reported his findings. How would these findings be valuable—that is, what kinds of conclusions could one draw from the use of this model?

(b) Fuller's model is not empirically derived. He did not study successful and unsuccessful, democratic and totalitarian, or advanced and primitive legal systems and conclude that all societies with certain characteristics had these eight features. These features appear to be closely related to current doctrines of "due process" in American constitutional law. How does this affect the usefulness of the Fuller model and the consequences that flow from its use?

4. To what extent, if at all, does Skolnick use Fuller's eight criteria as something other than a model? Suppose one concluded that the Uniform Commercial Code, an elaborate statute designed to reform commercial law and recently passed by almost all of the states in this country, had many vague rules and many contradictory rules. Would Skolnick assert that, in those states which had enacted it, the UCC was not "legal" but merely "order" imposed through extra-legal means? What would such an assertion mean?

Much of Skolnick's own work concerns the police, an institution affected by constitutional standards. *See* Reading 106, at 900, *infra*. Will the Fuller criteria work better as a model in such an area than in areas not so closely related to constitutional standards?

5. Skolnick and Auerbach debate how much the sociology of law should be concerned with the conduct of lawyers. A member of a prominent law firm has said that much of his work amounts to the lay practice of psychiatry. Businessmen often ask for what appears to be legal advice. However, a memorandum about legal rules would not do much to solve the real problem faced by executives. The businessman, because of the stress produced by a challenge to his competence and status, has been unable to define his problem and see the probable consequences of alternative courses of action. He will not see a psychiatrist or a business counselor because of the impact on his own view of his competence and status necessarily involved in seeking those kinds of help. Thus he seizes on a legal facet of his problem and turns to the lawyer who pushes the executive to think through his problem by a series of questions, ostensibly designed to obtain facts needed for the legal opinion which has been requested.

Assume that many lawyers engage in this process of "lay psychiatry." Is this process and its implications worth study? If so, is it properly the sociology of law? Can Auerbach assert that it is without being open to Skolnick's challenge that if this is true, then a lawyer's love-making is also relevant?

6. Is Skolnick's sociology of law consistent with Professor Selznick's Stage II and with Stage III?

B. THE FOCUS OF STUDY: WHAT IS LAW?

Whether one speaks of law and social or behavioral science, or of social or behavioral science used in law, one may ask what is meant by "law." The semanticists have taught us not to be satisfied with an answer from a dictionary; the word "law" refers to an idea, not to a thing, and it has many possible meanings. Hopefully, the right approach would be to ask how the term should be defined to aid in the study of law from a sociological approach. That requires a definition or specification of what the aim or approach of the student of sociology of law *is*. Professor Skolnick has given us one answer, based partly on Fuller's eight criteria. Others are possible.

We may benefit from reviewing the struggles of anthropologists over the meaning of the term law. Some primitive societies have institutions that perform the same functions as our courts, legislatures, ideals of legality and the other components we may include in our concept of law. However, these institutions may be dissimilar to ours in many ways; and other primitive societies lack such institutions altogether, yet carry out social control through other means. The anthropologist must decide what are the essential legal functions, if he is to write about the legal side of a society he is studying and compare it with the legal side of others. This is not precisely our problem, but the anthropological literature does force us to ask how much of our own implicit definition of law is institutional and how much functional. Is *law* the courts and judges? Or is it any system of rules or control?

After the ideas of Hoebel, Ehrlich, Beuscher, Malinowski and Bohannan are stated, seven examples are presented at 51-53. As to each, the question is whether or not each authority would consider the case an example of law. Hopefully, this exercise will prompt reflection on the variables which one might include or exclude—legitimacy, governmental action and so on. It might be profitable first to read the seven examples and then to consider Hoebel and company.

4. The Law of Primitive Man

E. ADAMSON HOEBEL*

What is Law?

The difficulties in achievement of a generally acceptable definition of law—a true consensus as to its essential attributes—arise from excessive parochialism, on the one hand, and, more importantly from the fact that law is but part of the social web. Its strands flow without break into the total fabric of culture and it has no clear-cut edges. Law is not sharply separable from all other forms of human action.

One may ask, "Why be concerned with definitions? Facts are the thing and quarreling over words is sterile." The answer is that although definitions are of secondary importance, they do have their functional uses.

Facts are never without their meanings, for meaningless phenomena are nonexistent. Yet, however much an overzealous empiricist may cry, "Let the facts speak for themselves!" or the rhetorician praise the persuasiveness of "eloquent facts," most phenomena are dumb and tongueless, quite incapable of speech and eloquence. If their meaning is to be put into words, man alone can do it. And to find the meaning in complex phenomena and complexes of phenomena he must abstract them, categorize them, and find realistic ways to compare one with another.

A researcher in any field must begin with the language tools and concepts that are available in his own heritage. . . . But as the researcher widens the scope of knowledge or sharpens down a point, he finds inevitably that old words must have their meanings altered or that new words must be hammered out to encompass new phenomena that are too different to be embraced in old words or concepts. . . . However, to the scientist who is also a teacher, it will always seem preferable to couch his discourse in familiar terms, if that is at all possible without effecting distortion of the facts and their meaning. . . .

* Professor of Social Anthropology, University of Minnesota. Reprinted by permission of the publishers from E. Adamson Hoebel, The Law of Primitive Man, Cambridge, Mass.: Harvard University Press, pp. 18-28. Copyright © 1954, by the President and Fellows of Harvard College.

It will soon be seen in the study of primitive law, however, that we cannot take all traditional meanings straight. When we push out from the universe of experience based on Continental and Anglo-American law into the legal world of primitive man, we find some things that are wholly new and some that are familiar but in different form. Thus it is perfectly true, as Julius Lips warned us, "Even a simple description of *facts* pertaining to law in a primitive tribe may, if we use our legal terminology, cause a distortion of the legal content of primitive institutions." This does not at all mean, however, that we must wholly reject our traditional legal terminology when we undertake an anthropology of law. It merely means that we must neither blindly nor willfully force upon primitive data that are only relatively comparable the specific content of meaning associated with our terminology. . . .

We recognize full well that in any approach to other peoples' law, thinking at all in traditional legal concepts tends to limit our perception of unfamiliar legal forms. Historians of law and analytical jurisprudes have told us, for instance, that nothing so refined and sophisticated, so well organized and logically perfected, nothing so authoritarian, so purposeful as law, could exist on the primitive level. Most anthropologists, until recently, have responded with a solemn nod. The legal life of primitive man was looked upon as being nonexistent rather than as simply unexplored.

To rationalize their blindness and to justify their neglect, they turned to the exaltation of custom. "Custom is King," became the cry. An English work [by E. S. Hartland] bearing the title of *Primitive Law*, published as late as 1924, offered the flat introductory assertion that, "Primitive law is in truth the totality of the customs of the tribe."

This, if taken literally, would mean that the patterns of pottery making, flint flaking, tooth filing, toilet training, and all the other social habits of a people, are law. Naturally enough, Sidney Hartland, the author of this assertion, did not take his proposition seriously in his subsequent discussion of what he considered to be legal topics. Yet nowhere did he indicate the basis on which he selected from the mass of customs those which he saw fit to treat as legal. Nor can the basis of selection be discerned from his treatment of the subject matter, either. . . . Yet he had perforce to utilize a hidden concept of law, if he was to write any kind of book at all on his chosen subject.

A more recent and somewhat more discriminating approach, but still custom-enchanted, may be seen in the study of East African law by J. Driberg, who proceeds on the proposition that "law comprises all those rules of conduct which regulate the behavior of individuals and communities." This, at least, rules out pottery making but still leaves us with the etiquette of handshaking as being "legal." This not uncommon fusing of law and custom by anthropologists led Clark Wissler to bless the Lynds' famous Middletown study as the first application of the methods of social anthropology to the study of an American community, embracing "the whole round of its activities," in spite of the fact, as Karl Llewellyn has observed with wry cogency, that "the legal aspects of behavior there did not seem worth canvass—or capable thereof." From this truly impressive anthropology of an American community a reader could carry away the impression that, like the reputed communities of primitive man, it lives under an automatic sway of custom without benefit of law. Such are the consequences of a lawless anthropology.

With such cues as these [William] Seagle, in his recent [1941] stimulating and provocative treatise on *The Quest for Law*, labels the first of his four chapters on primitive law, "Custom is King." That statement being so, he must have it that primitive societies are lawless and live under an "automatic *sway* of custom," which, because it is automatic, seems to suffice. Therefore, "there is no law until there are courts," and "really primitive peoples have no courts and no conception of the state." And if a people who are ordinarily recognized as primitive have courts, then *ipso facto* they are not primitive, for "to speak of the law of some African peoples as 'primitive' although they have courts and have invented many complex forms of legal transaction which compare not unfavorably with those of the ancient Babylonians is to abuse the natural [*sic*] meaning of the term."

Seagle at least is cognizant of the fact that law and custom are not one, and he truly insists that, "Only confusion can result from treating law and custom as interchangeable phenomena." He avoids doing a Hartland by arbitrarily denying in effect that there is any such thing as primitive law at all.

Thus, although the approach typified by Seagle makes it possible to separate law and custom, avoiding the fusion of the two, its logic forces the conclusion attacked by Malinowski some time ago when he wrote, "By defining the forces of law in terms of central authority, codes, courts, and constables, we must come to the conclusion that law needs no enforcement in a primitive community and is followed spontaneously." Such a conclusion, as Malinowski effectively demonstrated, is unreal and arbitrary.

A new approach and a more realistic conception as to the nature of law is clearly necessary. To make this fresh start we may properly address the question: What is law?

It is not the fiat of a sovereign—either legal or imagined. Nor is it exclusively legislative enactment. Our taking-off point will be certain modern conceptions of contemporary jurisprudence. [Benjamin N.] Cardozo has given us our best lead in his now classic declaration that a law is "a principle or rule of conduct so established as to justify a prediction with reasonable certainty that it will be enforced by the courts if its authority is challenged." This formula expands a little more elaborately and somewhat less bluntly the famous . . . dictum of [Oliver Wendell Holmes, Jr. of] 1897, "The prophecies of what the courts will do in fact, and nothing more pretentious, are what I mean by the law." From Holmes' classic statement springs the stream of legal realism of today.

In the Cardozian formulation we find four essential components: 1) the normative element; 2) regularity; 3) courts; 4) enforcement. In England a somewhat similar idea of law also took root and was given expression by [Sir John William] Salmond, who wrote in his *Jurisprudence* that law consists of "the rules in accordance with which justice is administered by the judicial tribunals of the state," and, more explicitly, "the principles enforced by the state through judicial authorities by physical force in the pursuit of justice whether attained or not."

Salmond with forthright vigor took his stand on the critical significance of the courts, as has many another legal thinker of more recent decades: "But all law, however made, is recognized and administered by the Courts, and no rules are recognized and administered by the Courts which are not rules of law. It is therefore to the Courts and not the legislature that we must go to ascertain the true nature of law." And more succinctly: "English law is nothing but the body of rules recognized and applied by English Courts in the administration of justice." In this he did not espouse the extreme position that *all* law is judge-made. He would have it that what the judges find and accept for execution or enforcement is law; what they reject is not—be it even a legislative statute. What the courts will do . . .

From the anthropological point of view such legal behaviorism makes sense and provides a handle wherewith to grasp the law. But when we consider legal matters in many primitive societies, if we must rely on courts and their predicted actions as the test of law, we are still left at sea. This is what bothered Max Radin (who well understood the anthropologist's problem) and, perhaps, led him to assert: "But there is an infallible test for recognizing whether an imagined course of conduct is lawful or unlawful. This infallible test, in our system, is to submit the question to the judgment of a court. In other systems exactly the same test will be used, but it is often difficult to recognize the court. None the less, although difficult, it can be done in almost every system at any time." Max Radin was right. But what sorts of courts did he have in mind? Some courts are difficult to identify. Among primitives they may be regularly constituted tribal courts such as the tribal council of an American Indian pueblo sitting in judicial capacity, or a court of the West African Ashanti, constituted of the chief, his council of elders, and henchmen. And even as Seagle notes, "The court of the bush is none the less a court because it does not sit every day, because it may not always employ compulsory process, because it is not housed in a permanent structure upon whose lintel is inscribed *Fiat justitia ruat caelum.*"* That type of primitive court is not too hard to recognize. Any member of the American Bar Association should readily see it for what it is. But a more obscure type of "court" may be found in the Cheyenne Indian military society.

Consider the case of Wolf Lies Down, whose horse was "borrowed" by a friend in the absence of the owner. When the friend did not return from the warpath with the horse, Wolf Lies Down put the matter before his society—the Elk Soldiers. "Now I want to know what to do," he said. "I want you to tell me the right thing." The society chiefs sent a messenger to bring the friend in from the camp of a remote band. The friend gave an adequate and acceptable explanation of his conduct and offered handsome restitution to the complainant in addition to making him his blood brother. Then said the chiefs: "Now we have settled this thing." But they went on, half as a legislature: "Now we shall make a new rule. There shall be no more borrowing of horses without asking. If any man takes another's goods without asking, we will go over and get them back for him. More than that, if the taker tries to keep them, we will give him a whipping." Can anyone deny that the Elk Soldiers were in effect sitting as a court for the entire tribe? The test is first, one of responsibility. That they knew. It is, second, one of authority. That they achieved. It is, third, one of method. Unhampered by a system of formal precedent which "required" them to judge according to the past, they recognized that the rule according to which they were settling this case was new, and they so announced it. . . .

On an even more primitive level, if an aggrieved party or his kinsmen must institute and carry through the prosecution without the intervention of a third party, there will still be a "court" if the proceedings follow the lines of recognized and established order—there will be then at least the compulsion of recognized

---

* "Let right be done, though the heavens should fall." [Eds. note]

"legal" procedure, though the ultimate court may be no more than the "bar of public opinion." When vigorous public opinion recognizes and accepts the procedure of the plaintiff as correct and the settlement or punishment meted out as sound, and the wrongdoer in consequence accedes to the settlement because he feels he must yield, then the plaintiff and his supporting public opinion constitute a rudimentary sort of "court," and the procedure is inescapably "legal."

Consider the Eskimo way of handling recidivist homicide. Killing on a single occasion merely leads to feud. (A feud, of course, marks an absence of law inasmuch as the counterkilling is not recognized as privileged by the opposite kin group. The so-called law of blood revenge is a sociological law but not a legal one.) But, among the Eskimos, to kill someone on a second occasion makes the culprit a dangerous public enemy.

Now arises the opportunity for some public-spirited man of initiative to perform a community service. He may undertake to interview, one after the other, all the adult males of the community to see if they agree that the killer had best be executed. If unanimous consent is given, he personally dispatches the murderer at the first opportunity, and no revenge may be taken on him by the murderer's relatives. Cases show that no revenge *is* taken.

A community "court" has spoken and its judgment executed. . . .

Although courts in this sense exist in primitive societies, it is not necessary to submit the concept of courts to such a strain in order to give primitive law the recognition that is its due.

The really fundamental *sine qua non* of law in any society— primitive or civilized—is the legitimate use of physical coercion by a socially authorized agent. The law has teeth, teeth that can bite if need be, although they need not necessarily be bared. . . . No matter that often the force need not be unleashed; for as Salmond notes, "Against subjects its [the law of an organized state] force is so overwhelming that its decision is usually enough to secure compliance, but force is still present though latent." . . .

However, force in law has a special meaning. Force, unqualified, means coercion—the condition that exists whenever men act, or refrain from acting, in a manner different from that which they themselves would have chosen in a given situation, because others deliberately limit the range of their choice either directly, through present control over it, or indirectly, through the threat of consequences. There are, of course, as many forms of coercion as there are forms of power. Of these, only certain methods and forms are legal. Coercion by gangsters is not legal. Even physical coercion by a parent is not legal if it is too extreme. The essentials of legal coercion are general social acceptance of the application of physical power, in threat or in fact, by a privileged party, for a legitimate cause, in a legitimate way, and at a legitimate time. This distinguishes the sanction of law from that of other social rules.

The privilege of applying force constitutes the "official" element in law. He who is generally or specifically recognized as rightly exerting the element of physical coercion is a splinter of social authority. It is not necessary that he be an official with legal office or a constable's badge. In any primitive society the so-called "private prosecutor" of a private injury is implicitly a public official pro tempore, *pro eo solo delicto*. He is not and cannot be acting solely on his own, his family's, or his clan's behalf and yet enjoy the approval or tacit support of the "disinterested" remainder of his society. If the rest of the tribal population supports him in opinion, even though not in overt action, it can only mean that the society feels that the behavior of the defendant was wrong in its broadest implications, that is, against the standards of the society as a whole. Thus it is in itself an injury to the society, although the group feeling may not be strong enough to generate overt and specific action by the group as a group and on its own initiative. Yet the private prosecutor remains the representative of the general social interest as well as that which is specifically his own. This fundamental fact is ordinarily ignored in discussions of primitive law, and it is in this sense that we may say that the difference between criminal law and private law is a difference in degree rather than in kind, although there can be no doubt that some matters touch the general interest much more vigorously than others in primitive law, as for example, sorcery, homicidal tendencies, and, frequently, treason.

These observations are not intended to deny the usefulness of our modern concept of "public" as against "private" law. Those concepts are of the greatest value in reaching an understanding of a difference in emphasis that tends to pervade the law of primitive societies as compared to the more highly organized legal systems of civilizations. Private law predominates on the primitive scene.

A third explicit feature of law is regularity. Regularity is what law in the legal sense has in common with law in the scientific sense. Regularity, it must be warned, does not mean absolute certainty. There can be no true certainty where human beings enter. Yet there is much regularity, for all society is based on it and regularity is a quality law shares with all other cultural norms. In law, the doctrine of precedent is not the unique possession of the Anglo-American common-law jurist. As we shall see, primitive law also builds on precedents, for there, too, new decisions rest on old rules of law or norms of custom, and new decisions which are sound tend to supply the foundations of future action.

Hence we may say that privileged force, official authority, and regularity are the elements that modern jurisprudence teaches us we must seek when we wish to identify law.

On this basis, for working purposes law may be defined in these terms: *A social norm is legal if its neglect or infraction is regularly met, in threat or in fact, by the application of physical force by an individual or group possessing the socially recognized privilege of so acting.*

NOTE: Eugen Ehrlich, Jacob Beuscher and Bronislaw Malinowski

Eugen Ehrlich (1862-1922), the author of *Fundamental Principles of the Sociology of Law* (Walter Moll translation, Harvard U. Press 1936), advocated a study of the "living law" in contrast to the law found in statutes and other official records. The "living law" is composed of the norms that actually govern the inner order of human associations. Not all norms are part of the living law. Legal norms govern matters of great significance to human association. They can be stated in clearer and more definite terms, and society devotes more resources to creating and stating legal norms than to other norms. Ehrlich's concept of living law focused on rules that actually guided conduct rather than on rules concerning what was to happen in case of a failure to follow the appropriate course.

It is easier to offer examples of the living law than to define it; Ehrlich was not overly concerned with precise definition or with distinguishing the legal from the nonlegal. Ehrlich lived in the Duchy of Bukovina which was then part of the Austro-Hungarian Empire and is now part of Rumania. In this Duchy lived at least nine distinct ethnic and religious groups, including Armenians, Germans, Rumanians, Russians, Jews and Gypsies. Bukovina, as part of the Empire, was formally governed by a written Civil Code, which, to a great extent, was based on Roman Law. However, such relationships as marriage, parent and child, and landlord and tenant were governed among members of these nine groups by norms very different from those in the code of the Empire. These norms were Ehrlich's living law. When formal law purports to regulate some area of conduct but other norms actually govern the behavior of a significant number of

people in this area, we have an example of living law. Ehrlich
went further and talked of the living law governing associations
in situations where the formal law was silent, but this idea introduced some ambiguity since, as we have said, not all norms were
thought of as "legal" by Ehrlich. Morals and customs could be
distinct from the living law. *See* Littlefield, "Eugen Ehrlich's
Fundamental Principles of the Sociology of Law," 19 *Maine Law
Review* 1 (1967); O'Day, "Ehrlich's Living Law Revisited—Further Vindication for a Prophet Without Honor," 18 *Western
Reserve Law Review* 210 (1966).

Ehrlich's general approach had some influence on American
pioneers in what would now be called the sociology of law. For
example, Professor William Herbert Page read a paper on Ehrlich before the Association of American Law Schools in 1914. *See*
Page, "Professor Ehrlich's Czernowitz Seminar of Living Law,"
in *Proceedings of the Fourteenth Annual Meeting of the Association of American Law Schools* 46 (1914). Page himself did little with Ehrlich's ideas during the rest of his career, but his
student and later colleague at the University of Wisconsin Law
School, the late Jacob H. Beuscher (1907-1967), carried on a great
deal of what he called "law in action" research. Beuscher, who
frequently stated his admiration for Ehrlich, did research primarily in the area of the allocation of natural resources. He took as a
starting point what traditionally has been deemed legal in American society—institutions such as courts, legislatures and the bar,
and values typically associated with the law such as due process—
and then moved out to look at other things. Sometimes the focus
was patterns of continuity in behavior and values that seemed
to be caused by a reaction to legal institutions; sometimes where
patterns of behavior seemed relatively unresponsive to an attempt by the legal system to affect them, the focus was on the
legal system itself as he attempted to explain why the law was
ineffective. Essentially his frame of reference was effective use of
the total legal system to solve social problems. If a pattern of
conduct—which another might have called law, custom, morals
or manners—was relevant to fashioning effective and acceptable
legal solutions to social problems, it was appropriate for consideration by a student of "law in action."

Bronislaw Malinowski (1884-1942) studied the people of the
Trobriand Archipelago, northeast of New Guinea; his books
about these people achieved great popularity in the 1930's and
1940's. In *Crime and Custom in Savage Society* (Routledge &
Kegan Paul, Ltd., London 1926), Malinowski traced the many
mutual rights and duties found in this society and sanctioned by

reciprocity. For example, if those who lived near the sea failed to bring fish to their trading partners who grew yams inland, the fishermen would not receive yams. Moreover, both the fishermen and the yam growers were tied together by many other mutual rights and obligations. Malinowski saw the cluster of influences that made for order and predictability in Trobriand society as primitive law. Reciprocity provided a sanction, but Malinowski stressed that the Trobriand carried out his obligations not because of his fear of sanctions but primarily because of the rewards of reciprocity, both in terms of tangible benefits to be gained and increased status.

Malinowski did not insist that everyone accept his use of the word "law" to describe these influences for order and predictability. He said he was willing to talk of "custom" rather than "law"; the key questions were whether or not a rule was obeyed, when and why. Malinowski, *Introduction to Hogbin, Law and Order in Polynesia* xxv (1934). Later he distinguished a number of meanings of the term "law."

Law (1) is the rule of determinism. It is used here in the same sense in which "law" appears in the phrase "law of science" or "law of nature". In this context we are primarily concerned with the laws of cultural determinism.

Law (2) is the rule of conduct standardized in behavior or verbally formulated. The rules of knowledge, of technology, of co-operation, of common life, and of convention, enter into this class. The rules of primitive knowledge usually occur as imperative or, at least, normative statements, since they are formulated invariably so as to fit pragmatic contexts. They bear a strong surface resemblance to other imperatives of tradition.

Law (3) applies to rules of conduct which refer to relations between individuals and groups, delimit divergent interests, and curtail disruptive physiological and sociological tendencies. Here enter most rules of property, contract, status and authority, as well as the rules protecting human life and limb, and limiting sexual rights to well-defined social relations.

Law (4) is the specific mechanism which is brought into existence when a conflict of claims arises or a rule of social conduct is broken.

Let me first state that this is not meant to be a full classification of all rules and norms of behavior, knowledge, or belief.

Malinowski, "A New Instrument for the Interpretation of Law—
Especially Primitive," 51 *Yale Law Journal* 1237 (1942).* To
what extent do Ehrlich and Malinowski differ? To what extent
are they saying the same thing in different words? Is there any
utility in attempting to distinguish "law" from "custom" and the
other forces that might press for order and predictability in
human associations?

* Reprinted by permission of the Yale Law Journal Company and Fred
B. Rothman & Company from The Yale Law Journal, Vol. 51, p. 1237 (1942).

5. The Differing Realms of the Law

PAUL BOHANNAN*

THE ETHNOLOGY OF LAW (L. Nader ed. 1965)

Law must be distinguished from traditions and fashions and more specifically, it must be differentiated from norm and from custom. A norm is a rule, more or less overt, which expresses "ought" aspects of relationships between human beings. Custom is a body of such norms—including regular deviations and compromises with norms—that is actually followed in practice much of the time.

All social institutions are marked by "customs" and these "customs" exhibit most of the stigmata cited by any definition of law. But there is one salient difference. Whereas custom continues to inhere in, and only in, these institutions which it governs (and which in turn govern it), law is specifically recreated, by agents of society, in a narrower and recognizable context—that is, in the context of the institutions that are legal in character and, to some degree at least, discrete from all others.

Just as custom includes norms, but is both greater and more precise than norms, so law includes custom, but is both greater and more precise. Law has the additional characteristic that it must be what Kantorowicz calls "justiciable," by which he means that the rules must be capable of reinterpretation, and actually must be reinterpreted, by one of the legal institutions of society so that the conflicts within nonlegal institutions can be adjusted by an "authority" outside themselves.

It is widely recognized that many peoples of the world can state more or less precise "rules" which are, in fact, the norms in accordance with which they think they ought to judge their conduct. In all societies there are allowable lapses from such rules, and in most there are more or less precise rules (sometimes legal ones) for breaking rules.

In order to make the distinction between law and other

* Professor of Social Anthropology, Northwestern University. Excerpt from American Anthropologist, Special Publication, The Ethnology of Law 33-37. Reproduced by permission of the American Anthropological Association from the American Anthropologist: Vol. 67, No. 6, Part 2 (1965).

rules, it has been necessary to introduce furtively the word "institution." . . .

A legal institution is one by means of which the people of a society settle disputes that arise between one another and counteract any gross and flagrant abuses of the rules (as we have considered them above) of at least some of the other institutions of society. Every ongoing society has legal institutions in this sense, as well as a wide variety of nonlegal institutions.

In carrying out the task of settling difficulties in the nonlegal institutions, legal institutions face three kinds of tasks: (1) There must be specific ways in which difficulties can be disengaged from the institutions in which they arose and which they now threaten and then be engaged within the processes of the legal institution. (2) There must be ways in which the trouble can now be handled within the framework of the legal institution, and (3) There must be ways in which the new solutions which thus emerge can be re-engaged within the processes of the nonlegal institutions from which they emerged. It is seldom that any framework save a political one can supply these requirements.

There are, thus, at least some aspects of legal institutions that are not shared with other institutions of society. Legal institutions—and often they alone—must have some regularized way to interfere in the malfunctioning (and, perhaps, the functioning as well) of the nonlegal institutions in order to disengage the trouble-case. There must, secondly, be two kinds of rules in the legal institutions—those that govern the activities of the legal institution itself (called . . . "procedure" by most modern lawyers), and those that are substitutes or modifications or restatements of the rules of the nonlegal institution that has been invaded (called "substantive law").

Listed above are only the minimal aspects that are all shared by all known legal institutions. There may be other aspects, as for example the commonly recognized fact that legal institutions on both the procedural and the substantive sides can be in the fullest sense innovatory.

Seen in this light, a fairly simple distinction can be made between law and custom. Customs are norms or rules (more or less strict, and with greater or less support of moral, ethical, or even physical coercion) about the ways in which people must behave if social institutions are to perform their tasks and society is to endure. All institutions (including legal institutions) develop customs. Some customs, in some societies, are reinstitutionalized at another level: they are restated for the more precise purposes of legal institutions. When this happens, therefore, law may be regarded as a custom that has been restated in order to make it amenable to the activities of the legal institutions. In this sense, it is one of the most characteristic attributes of legal institutions that some of these "laws" are about the legal institutions themselves, although most are about the other institutions of society—the familial, economic, political, ritual, or whatever.

One of the reddest herrings ever dragged into the working of orderly jurisprudence was Malinowski's little book called *Crime and Custom in Savage Society.* It is unfortunately almost the only anthropological book that appears on the standard reading list used in many law schools, "The Dean's List," and it has had an undue and all but disastrous influence on the rapprochement between anthropology and jurisprudence. Malinowski's idea was a good one; he claimed that law is "a body of binding obligations regarded as right by one party and acknowledged as the duty by the other, kept in force by the specific mechanism of reciprocity and publicity inherent in the structure of . . . society." His error was in equating what he had defined with the law. It is not law that is "kept in force by . . . reciprocity and publicity." It is custom, as we have defined it here. Law is, rather, "a body of binding obligations regarded as right by one party and acknowledged as the duty by the other" *which has been reinstitutionalized within the legal institution so that society can continue to function in an orderly manner on the basis of rules so maintained.* In short, reciprocity is the basis of custom; but the law rests on the basis of this double institutionalization. Central in it is that some of the customs of some of the institutions of society are restated in such a way that they can be "applied" by an institution designed (or, at very least, utilized) specifically for that purpose.

One of the best ways to perceive the doubly institutionalized norms, or "laws," is to break up the law into smaller components, capable of attaching to persons (either human individuals or corporate groups) and so to work in terms of "rights" and their reciprocal duties or "obligations." In terms of rights and duties, the relationships between law and custom, law and morals, law and anything else, can be seen in a new light. Whether in the realm of kinship or contract, citizenship or property rights, the relationships between people can be reduced to a series of prescriptions with the obligations and the correlative rights that emanate from these presumptions. In fact, if it is not carried too far and unduly formalized, thinking in terms of rights and obligations of persons (or role players) is a convenient and fruitful way of investigating much of the custom of many institutions. . . . Legal rights are only those rights that attach to norms that have been doubly institutionalized; they provide a means for seeing the legal institutions from the standpoint of the persons engaged in them.

The phenomenon of double institutionalization of norms and therefore of legal rights has been recognized for a long time, but analysis of it has been only partially successful. Kantorowicz, for example, has had to create the concept of "justiciability" of the law. It would be better to say that legal rights have their material origins (either overtly or covertly) in the customs of nonlegal institutions but must be *overtly restated* for the specific purpose of enabling the legal institutions to perform their task.

A legal right (and, with it, a law) is the restatement, for the purpose of maintaining peaceful and just operation of the institutions of society, of some, but never all, of the recognized claims of the persons within those institutions; the restatement must be made in such a way that these claims can be more or less assured by the total community or its representatives. Only so can the moral, religious, political, and economic implications of law be fully explored.

Law is never a mere reflection of custom, however. Rather, law is always out of phase with society, specifically because of the duality of the statement and restatement of rights. Indeed, the more highly developed the legal institutions, the greater the lack of phase, which not only results from the constant reorientation of the primary institutions, but also is magnified by the very dynamic of the legal institutions themselves. . . .

Thus, it is the very nature of law, and its capacity to "do something about" the primary social institutions, that creates the lack of phase. Moreover, even if one could assume perfect legal institutionalization, change within the primary institutions would soon jar the system out of phase again. What is less obvious is that if there were ever to be perfect phase between law and society, then society could never repair itself, grow and change, flourish or wane. It is the fertile dilemma of law that it must always be out of step with society, but that people must always (because they work better with fewer contradictions, if for no other reason) attempt to reduce the lack of phase. Custom must either grow to fit the law or it must actively reject it; law must either grow to fit the custom, or it must ignore or suppress it. It is in these very interstices that social growth and social decay take place.

Social catastrophe and social indignation are sources of much law and resultant changes in custom. With technical and moral change, new situations appear that must be "legalized." This truth has particular and somewhat different applications to developed and to less highly developed legal systems. On the one hand, in developed municipal systems of law in which means for institutionalizing behavior on a legal level are already traditionally concentrated in political decision-making groups such as legislatures, nonlegal social institutions sometimes take a very long time to catch up with the law. On the other hand, in less developed legal systems, it may be that little or no popular demand is made on the legal institutions, and therefore little real contact exists or can be made to exist between them and the primary institutions. . . . Law can, as we have seen in another context, become one of the major innovators of society, the more effective the greater a people's dependence on it.

NOTES AND QUESTIONS

1. There is a rich, long history of anthropological study of law, conveniently summarized in Laura Nader, "The Anthropological Study of Law," 67 *American Anthropologist* 3-32 (1965). In modern times, Hoebel, Malinowski, and Bohannan, who are represented in the foregoing section of this volume, have been among the more important figures in the field. Among the studies of legal anthropology, special mention should be made of *The Cheyenne Way: Conflict and Case Law in Primitive Jurisprudence,* which Hoebel wrote in collaboration with Karl N. Llewellyn, a professor of law, in 1941, in what remains a rare example of interdisciplinary enterprise in this field. A highly influential study has been Max Gluckman's *The Judicial Process Among the Barotse of Northern Rhodesia* (Manchester U. Press 1955).

2. In order to understand the definitions of law offered by these social scientists consider the following examples and decide whether or not each would view the example as law:

(a) Assume that in American middle-class society if a husband and wife send you a birth announcement, you are deemed obligated to send them a baby present.

(b) Assume that during the first World War, X, an American citizen whose parents came to this country from Germany, voiced repeated and loud opposition to President Wilson's policies concerning a war with Germany. A group called the Council of National Defense of the City of Jonesville, an organization with no connection with the government, held a meeting and discussed X's statements briefly. X was not invited and his side was not represented by anyone at the meeting. By acclamation the Council decided that X's statements were treasonous and that X should be ostracized—no one should speak to him, employ him or have any dealings with him. Members of the Council voluntarily complied with the decision. Assume that such ostracism was not illegal under the applicable state laws.

(c) The General Motors Corporation created an impartial umpire to resolve disputes between its franchised dealers and the automobile divisions of the corporation. The rights and duties of the manufacturer and the dealer are specified in detail in the selling agreement signed to create and to renew the relationship. A retired federal judge is the umpire. He operates by following procedures very similar to those used in federal courts. Assume that records of the umpire's decisions are available to representatives of both the automobile divisions and the dealers. You should recognize that a decision by the umpire against the dealer may be a far greater burden on him than the ostracism involved in case (b).

(d) Assume all the facts of case (b) with the following differences. Instead of ostracism, the Council decided to wrap X in an American flag, soak it and him with gasoline and light it. It carried out this decision before a cheering crowd of the majority of the citizens of Jonesville. (This example is not too unrealistic. On April 4, 1918, "five hundred . . . citizens in Collinsville, Illinois, who had decided that a fellow townsman, Robert Prager, was a German spy, dragged him into the street, wrapped him in the flag, and then murdered him." Scheiber, *The Wilson Administration and Civil Liberties* 50-51 (1960).*)

(e) Many patrons of bars dislike the presence of police officers in uniform and will leave bars if officers are present. A bar owner presented a "go-go girl" dancing in a revealing costume. Two uniformed police officers then came to the bar and looked carefully at each patron. They left but reappeared each hour. As a result, business suffered. The dancer then appeared in a much more modest costume.

(f) In the Employment Act of 1946, Congress declared that the ensuring of full employment was the policy and goal of the federal government. The Act set up a Council

---

of Economic Advisors to the President, and provided for an annual economic report, to be delivered by the President to the Congress. No further provisions appeared in the Act.

(g) Prior to the enactment of the Uniform Commercial Code, the Wisconsin courts enunciated a rule that, with some exceptions not relevant here, one could not sell or transfer a right he did not then have but expected to get in the future. Dairy farmers frequently were members of milk marketing cooperatives which collect and sell their milk and pay them periodically by check. A dairyman had no present right to the milk checks he expected to receive four and six months later, and under the Wisconsin rule he could not transfer a right to receive these checks. However, field research disclosed that, in Northern Wisconsin, banks regularly loaned money to dairy farmers, taking as security an assignment or transfer of the "right" to receive future milk checks. They were willing to rely on the probability that such rights would come into existence in the future.

3. Which, if any, of these examples are most significant as suggestions for further theory-building and research on the intersection of law and social science? Why?

Chapter 2

THE DESCRIPTIVE ASPECT OF LAW-IN-SOCIETY

Introductory note. One of the major tasks of the sociology of law, of related movements in other social sciences, and within the law itself, has been to bring up to date the *picture* of the legal system in operation. We often talk as if we think the legal system operated entirely in harmony with the way in which it is described or prescribed in federal and state constitutions, or in the way in which an apologist, glossing over all departures from idealized expressions, would speak of the workings of the system. Many tend to assume, in other words, a quite naive unity between the formal model of law and the way it works in the field.

Asked to describe our law (or any other system), such a naive reporter might speak in terms which fit not reality, but the ideals of formal law. Legislators debate public questions, then vote on issues in the public interest. People obey the law because of the threat of punishment or because one ought to obey it, except for some deviants who are caught by the police, arrested, tried and convicted if guilty. Defendants are freed, punished, enjoined, or ordered to pay damages as the law and the facts of the case dictate; the orders of courts and administrative agencies are carried out as prescribed; if not, the law's prescribed responses occur.

Nobody believes entirely in such a picture. On the other hand, it cannot be totally false. How does the legal system really operate? Sociology of law is a young field. It has barely begun the long hard job of excavating reality from myth. The readings that follow are examples of attempts to revise the formal model in terms of social reality. Some use the empirical tools of social science to measure reality; others construct it from one sort or another of social theory. If they have anything in common, it is their stress on the pervasiveness of what we might call a *bargaining* process in the law.

A. HOW THE UNITS OF THE FORMAL LEGAL SYSTEM WORK

1. Legislative Function

6. The Calculus of Consent

JAMES BUCHANAN AND GORDON TULLOCK*

. . . [W]e propose to examine the operation of a single collective decision-making rule, that of simple majority, under certain highly restricted assumptions. Theorists of the democratic process have, traditionally, paid little attention to the actual operation of voting rules, and they seem, by and large, to have been uninterested in making generalized predictions regarding the results of actual political decision-making. This relative neglect is explained, at least in part, by the implicit assumption that participants in collective choice seek to further the "public interest," although, . . . this concept is never defined. . . .

[O]ur purpose . . . is that of analyzing the operation of voting rules as one stage in the individual's constitutional-choice problem, that of choosing the voting rules themselves. The working of a voting rule can be analyzed only as it produces results over a series of issues.

MAJORITY VOTING WITHOUT LOGROLLING

Once it is recognized that the political process embodies a continuing stream of separate decisions, the most general model must include the possibility of vote-trading, or, to use the commonly employed American term, *logrolling*. The existence of a logrolling process is central to our general analysis of simple majority voting, but it will be helpful, by way of comparison, to consider briefly a model in which logrolling is not permitted to take place, either by legal institutions or by certain widely acknowledged moral precepts. There are certain relatively rare institutional situations in which logrolling will not be likely to occur, and in such situations the contrasting analytical model may be explana-

* Professors Buchanan and Tullock are both associated with Virginia Polytechnic Institute. The Calculus of Consent, pp. 131-45, © 1962 by University of Michigan Press, Ann Arbor, reprinted by permission.

tory. The best example is the standard referendum on a simple issue. Here the individual voter cannot easily trade his own vote on the one issue for reciprocal favors on other issues because, first, he is uncertain as to when other issues will be voted on in this way, and, second, he and his immediate acquaintances represent such a small part of the total electorate that such trading effort may not be worth while. Furthermore, the secret ballot, normally employed in such cases, makes it impossible for any external observer to tell whether voting commitments are honored or not. Under circumstances such as these, the individual voter will make his voting decision in accordance with his own preferences on the single question posed.

In this model each voter indicates his preference, and the preference of the majority of the whole group is decisive. The defect in this procedure, a serious one, . . . is that it ignores the varying intensities of preference among the separate voters. A man who is passionately opposed to a given measure and a man who is slightly favorable but does not care greatly about it are given equal weight in the process of making final decisions. It seems obvious that both of these individuals could be made better off, in terms of their own expressed preferences, if the man strongly opposed should be permitted in some way to "trade" or exchange something with the relatively indifferent supporter of the proposed measure. Applying the strict Pareto rules* for determining whether one social situation represents an improvement over another, almost any system of voting that allows some such exchange to take place would be superior to that system which weights all preferences equally on *each issue.* By way of illustration, it is conceivable that a proposal to prohibit Southern Democrats from having access to free radio time might be passed by simple majority vote in a national referendum should the issue be raised in this way. Such a measure, by contrast, would not have the slightest chance of being adopted by the decision-making process actually prevailing in the United States. The measure would never pass the Congress because the supporters of the minority threatened with damage would, if the issue arose, be willing to promise support on other measures in return for votes against such discriminatory legislation. In the complete absence of vote-trading, support for specific legislation may reach 51 per cent without much of this

---

* The reference is to concepts developed by the Italian economist and social thinker, Vilfredo Pareto. A situation represents an improvement if every individual affected by it is, in his view, better off; or if one or more individuals are better off, and none are (in their view) worse off. A situation is "optimal" when it is no longer possible to make a change which satisfies these conditions. *See* BUCHANAN & TULLOCK ch. 13. [Eds. note]

support being intense. In such cases a minimal introduction of vote-trading will insure defeat.

Without some form of vote-trading, even those voters who are completely indifferent on a given issue will find their preferences given as much weight as those of the most concerned individuals. The fact of voting demonstrates that an individual is not wholly indifferent, but many voters may, on referendum issues, be led to the polls more by a sense of duty or obligation than by any real interest in the issue to be determined. Interestingly enough, this "duty of a citizen to vote" is much emphasized as an essential feature of effective democratic process. Even the smallest preference for one side or the other may actually determine the final choice. Permitting those citizens who feel strongly about an issue to compensate in some way those whose opinion is only feebly held can result in a great increase in the well-being of both groups, and the prohibition of such transactions will serve to prevent movement toward the conceptual "social optimality" surface, under almost any definition of this term.

Note that the results under logrolling and under nonlogrolling differ only if the minority feels more intensely about an issue than the majority. If the majority is equal or more intense in its preferences, its will must prevail in either model. It is only when the intensity of preferences of the minority is sufficiently greater than that of the majority to make the minority willing to sacrifice enough votes on other issues to detach marginal voters from the majority (intense members of the majority group may, of course, make counteroffers) that the logrolling process will change the outcome. As we have suggested, the assumption of possible differences in intensity of preferences seems more acceptable than any assumption of equal intensities, and it seems clear that on many issues specific minorities may be much more interested in the outcome of political decisions.

The above discussion suggests that a reasonably strong ethical case can be made for a certain amount of vote-trading under majority-rule institutions. We emphasize, however, that our model, which incorporates the logrolling model as the general case, is not chosen because of the ethical desirability of the institutions analyzed. Positive theory must always analyze those institutions that are, in fact, general (the test of generality being the validity of the predictions made), quite independently of ethical or moral considerations. Therefore, even if vote-trading should be viewed as morally reprehensible behavior, it might still be necessary to analyze the phenomenon carefully if it were observed in the operation of real-world political processes.

Two Types of Logrolling

Logrolling seems to occur in many of the institutions of political choice-making in Western democracies. It may occur in two separate and distinct ways. In all of those cases where a reasonably small number of individuals vote openly on each measure in a continuing sequence of measures, the phenomenon seems pervasive. This is normally characteristic of representative assemblies, and it may also be present in very small governmental units employing "direct democracy." The applicability of our models to representative assemblies has already been mentioned. Under the rules within which such assemblies operate, exchanges of votes are easy to arrange and to observe. Such exchanges significantly affect the results of the political process. It seems probable that this fact provides one of the major reasons for the widespread use of representative democracy.

Logrolling may occur in a second way, which we shall call *implicit logrolling*. Large bodies of voters may be called on to decide on complex issues, such as which party will rule or which set of issues will be approved in a referendum vote. Here there is *no* formal trading of votes, but an analogous process takes place. The political "entrepreneurs" who offer candidates or programs to the voters make up a complex mixture of policies designed to attract support. In so doing, they keep firmly in mind the fact that the single voter may be so interested in the outcome of a particular issue that he will vote for the one party that supports this issue, although he may be opposed to the party stand on all other issues. Institutions described by this implicit logrolling are characteristic of much of the modern democratic procedure. Since the analysis is somewhat more incisive in the first type of logrolling, we shall not discuss the second type at this point.

A Simple Logrolling Model

Let us consider a simple model. A township inhabited by one hundred farmers who own similar farms is cut by a number of main highways maintained by the state. However, these are limited-access highways, and the farmers are permitted to enter this primary network only at the appropriate intersections with local roads. All local roads are built and maintained by the township. Maintenance is simple. Any farmer who desires to have a specific road repaired is allowed to present the issue to the whole group for a vote. If the repairing proposal is approved by a simple majority, the cost is assessed against all of the farmers as a part of the real property tax, the rate of which is automatically adjusted upward or downward so as to make revenues always equal to expenditures. The principal use of the local roads by the farmers is getting to and from the major state highways. Since these major highways cut through the whole district, there are four or five farmers dependent on each particular piece of local road, and each farmer requires at least one local road to provide him with access to the main network.

In this model the simple referendum system would result in no local road being repaired because an overwhelming majority of the farmers would vote against the repairing of any given road, considered separately. A logrolling system, however, permits the local roads to be kept in repair through the emergence of bargains among voters. The actual bargaining may take a number of forms, but most of the "solutions" will tend to be unstable. In any case, "equilibrium" involves some overinvestment of resources.

One form that an implicit bargain might take is the following: Each individual might determine, in his own mind, the general standard of maintenance that should be set for all local roads. That is to say, he would balance, according to his own scale of preferences, the costs of maintaining his own road at various levels of repair with the benefits expected, and try to reach a decision at the point where expected marginal costs equal marginal benefits. Generalizing this, he could then vote on each separate project to repair a given road in the same way that he would vote for repairs on his own road. If all voters would follow this rule of reaching decisions, we would find a schedule of voting behavior such as that shown below in Figure 12. Each mark or dot on the horizontal line represents the "idealized" standard of maintenance on all roads for a single voter. If a proposal for repairing a given road falls to the left of his own position on this scale, the individual will support it; if a proposal falls to the right of his own position, he will vote against it. If each road has at least one farmer living along it whose preference for general road repairs falls to the right of the median (A in Figure 12), then a proposal for road repair will be advanced as soon as any given road falls below this farmer's standard of maintenance. Successive further proposals would be made as the road deteriorated further. When the deterioration of any road reached the median level, a repair project would secure approval by simple majority vote. Hence, all local roads would, in this model, tend to be maintained up to the standard indicated by the median preference.

This result will not represent a fully "efficient" solution in any Pareto sense, but it is possible to support this procedure on ethical grounds. In fact, this solution seems to be the one that most of the proponents of majoritarian democracy have in mind when they discuss democratic process. In any event, we propose to use this solution, which we shall call the "Kantian," as a more or less "correct" solution against which we shall contrast our more realistic result.

If the farmers of the township generally follow such a policy in voting, then *any* single farmer could benefit himself simply by voting against all proposals to repair roads other than his own and by voting to repair his own road at each opportunity.

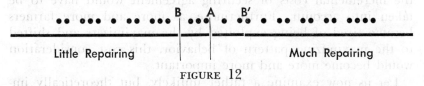

Little Repairing   Much Repairing

FIGURE 12

This single departure from the general pattern of behavior would shift the median of the schedules slightly so that the taxes on the farmer concerned would be reduced or his road kept in better-than-average repair. If the other farmers living along this road should follow the first farmer's example (we shall call such farmers "maximizers"), they would be able to shift the standards of repair so that the road on which they live would be repaired at level B' while reducing the standard on all other roads to B in Figure 12. Since the largest share of the costs of keeping their own road in repair would fall on other taxpayers, while the largest share of their own taxes would go to the repair of other roads, this change in behavior would be greatly to the advantage of the maximizers and greatly to the disadvantage of the "Kantians," although in the initial stages the disadvantages would not be concentrated to the same degree as the advantages.

If the farmers located on a second local road should also switch to a maximizing pattern of behavior, this action would have the effect of bringing the level of road-repairing on the two roads particularly affected down toward that which would prevail under the generalized Kantian system, while still further lowering the standards on the remaining "Kantian" roads. However, it seems probable that, finding themselves in this situation, the two groups of maximizers could benefit by forming a coalition designed to raise the standards of maintenance on the two roads. Let us consider the situation that would be confronted by an individual maximizer when he tries to decide whether or not to enter into such a coalition with other maximizers. Since he will pay only about 1/100 of the cost, almost any proposal to repair his own road will be supported by him. If, however, in order to obtain support for some repair project for his own road, he must also vote for the repair of another road, the individual must also count the cost to him of other repair projects. In weighing costs and benefits, he must consider not only the tax cost to himself from a proposal to repair his own road but also the tax cost to him of the other repair jobs which he must support in order to get his own proposal adopted. In the particular situation under discussion, when the farmers on all of the local roads except two are still Kantians, this added cost consideration would put few restraints on feasible projects, but some recognition of the incremental costs of securing agreement would have to be taken into account. Furthermore, as more and more farmers became tired of being exploited by the maximizers and shifted to the maximizing pattern of behavior, this cost consideration would become more and more important.

Let us now examine a rather unlikely, but theoretically important, special case. Suppose that exactly 51 of the 100 farmers follow a maximizing policy, while 49 are pure "Kantians." Let us further suppose that all of the maximizers live on some local roads, while all of the Kantians live on other roads. Under these circumstances, the Kantians clearly would never be able to get their roads repaired at all, but the level of repairs on the maximizers' roads is more difficult to determine. In order to simplify the issue somewhat, let us assume (plausibly) that these roads are maintained on such a high level that all of the Kantian farmers would vote against all further repair proposals. In this case, it would be necessary to attain the approval of all of the maximizers to carry any single repair project. A maximizing farmer, considering the repair of his own road, would necessarily be forced to take into account his share in the costs of repairing the roads of all maximizers. He would have to consider the incremental taxes that he must pay in order to repair the roads of all other parties to the bargain. His calculus requires, however, only that he compare his own marginal benefits against his own marginal costs. No knowledge of anyone else's utility function is required. The individual need only decide whether the total bargain is or is not to his advantage.

For the Kantians, note that, while no roads leading to their own farms will be repaired, they will be required to contribute toward the repair of the roads leading to the farms of the maximizers. Thus, a part of the total repair costs in the township will be paid by persons who are not parties to the decisive bargain, and, since the maximizers count only the costs to themselves when they make voting decisions, the general standard of road maintenance on the roads of the maximizers will tend to be higher than it would be if the Kantians were also included in the calculus. Under such conditions as these, where "virtue" so conspicuously would not pay, it seems likely that at least some of the Kantians would decide to switch to a maximizing policy. For simplicity, let us assume that they all do at the same time. Since these reluctant maximizers would still be in a minority, their changes of heart would not immediately redound to their private benefit. However, it might be relatively easy for this minority, acting as a coalition, to find two of the original maximizers who would, in return for a promise of very good maintenance on their own roads, desert their former colleagues. It is again obvious, however, that the new majority would now be equally susceptible to similar desertions. A permanent coalition of 51 farmers formed for the purpose of exploiting the remaining 49 could not be considered to be stable in the usual sense of this term. In the terminology of game theory, . . . any combination of 51 voters dominates any combination of less than this number, but no combination of 51 dominates all other combinations of 51.

The outcome is clearly indicated. Each farmer would enter into bilateral agreements with enough other farmers on other roads to insure that his own road is repaired. The individual farmer would then be forced to include as a part of the cost of getting his own road repaired the cost (to him) of repairing the roads of 50 other farmers. These bilateral agreements would overlap, however. Farmer A (more precisely, the group of farmers living on Road A) would bargain with Farmers B, C, . . . , M. Farmer M, on the other hand, might make up a majority bargain from an agreement with Farmer A and Farmers N, O, . . . , Z.

In counting the costs to himself involved in the repair of other roads necessary to secure the repair of his own road, each farmer would consider only the repair of those roads which he agrees to support. In this way his expenditure pattern would include as a free gift the tax payments of 49 voters. The fiscal institutions postulated insure that all 100 voters share in the costs of each repair project approved, but a minimum participation of only 51 voters in the net benefits is required by simple majority voting. The natural result would be that each road in the township would be maintained at a level considerably higher and at a greater expense than is rational from the individual standpoint of the farmers living along it. Each individual in the group would be behaving quite rationally, but the outcome would be irrational. This apparent paradox may be explained as follows: Each voter pays enough in support for the repair of other roads to attain a position of equivalence between estimated individual marginal costs and individual marginal benefits, but the payments included in his private calculus make up only a part of the costs of total road repair that he must, as a taxpayer in the community, support. There are other roads which will be repaired because of successful bargains to which he is not a party. Taken as a group, the road-repair projects for which he votes represent a good bargain for the individual; but other *ad hoc* bargains will also take place. The individual will, of course, vote against all projects included in these outside bargains, but he will be in the minority. Therefore, he will have to bear a part of the costs.

Any individual farmer who followed another course of action would be worse off, however, than the individual whose behavior is considered here. For example, a Kantian farmer would never have his own road repaired, but he would have to pay taxes for the support of other local roads. In any practical situation the whole decision-making process would tend to become one of elaborate negotiations, open and concealed, taking place at several levels of discourse. The man who is the most effective bargainer would have a considerable advantage. However, the general pattern of results may be less than optimal for all parties (optimal being defined here in terms of either the Kantian or the Paretian solution).

POSSIBLE OBJECTIONS

We may now consider certain possible objections that may be raised against the reasoning implicit in our simple logrolling model. It may be argued that those individuals whom we have called maximizers would be behaving wickedly and that ethical considerations will prevent a majority of the population in the real world from following such a course of action. Ethical and moral systems vary greatly from culture to culture, and the strength of moral restraints on private action is not readily predictable. We do not want to preclude the possible existence somewhere of a system of human behavior which could effectively restrain logrolling, but surely the American behavior pattern contains no such restraints. Under our system open logrolling is normally publicly characterized as "bad," but no real stigma attaches to those who participate in it. The press describes open logrolling arrangements without apparent disapproval, and, in fact, all of our political organizations operate on a logrolling basis. Moreover, no stigma at all attaches to implicit as opposed to open logrolling.

A second argument asserts that each farmer in our model community would soon realize that if he adopted a maximizing pattern of behavior, this would lead all other farmers to do the same thing. Since the "maximizing equilibrium" is worse for almost all farmers than the "Kantian median," each farmer would, on the basis of his own cold and selfish calculation, follow the Kantian system. This argument is familiar, and it is precisely analogous to the one which holds that no single labor union will force wage rates up for its own members because it will realize that such action will lead other unions to do the same and that the eventual outcome will simply be higher prices and wages without any increase in real incomes. There seems to be overwhelming empirical evidence that men do not act in this way. The argument overlooks the fact that there will, of course, be short-run gains to the individuals or groups who initiate action first. In addition, the argument seems to contain a logical flaw. It is based on the observation that, in any series of actions by a number of men, there must be a first step. If this can be prevented, then the whole series can be prevented. This observation is, in itself, correct; but there must also be a second, a third, and a fourth step, etc., in each series. If any one action in the series is prevented, then the whole series cannot be completed. If all of our maximizing farmers should refrain from following a maximizing course of action because each one felt that his own personal adoption of such behavior would lead to a switch to a position of "maximizing equilibrium," then, if only one of them had done so, we could construct an exactly similar argument "proving" that none of the remaining ninety-nine would follow his example. However, if the second argument is true, the first is false; hence, the chain of reasoning contains an inconsistency.

Note that our refutation of this argument does not preclude an individual's taking the attitude: "If *no one* else acts, I shall not act." However, not only must *all* members of the group assume this attitude if the argument is to be valid, but *each* member of the group must also believe that *all* other members will take this attitude. This combination of attitudes, which would amount to complete mutual trust, seems highly improbable in any real-world situation. The argument that all individuals in the group will be worse off than if they all adopted Kantian norms of behavior does have some relevance for the support of *constitutional* changes in the decision-making rules or institutions for choice. While it may never be to the interest of the individual to refrain from adopting a maximizing attitude, given the rules as laid down, it may well be to his long-range interest to support a change in these rules themselves, which, by definition, will be *generally applicable.*

ALTERNATIVES

One means through which the separate farmers in our model might enter into a bargain so as to insure results somewhat closer to the Kantian median would be the development of a specific formula that would determine when a road should be repaired. Yet another means would be the delegation of decision-making authority to a single individual or small group. These become practicable institutions, however, only within the confines of a set of closely related issues that may be expected to arise: in our model, separate proposals for road repair. In the more general and realistic case where governmental units must consider a continuing stream of radically different projects, neither an agreed-on formula nor a single expert or group of experts would seem feasible. A formula that would permit the weighing of the costs and the benefits of such diverse programs as building irrigation projects in the West to increase agricultural production, paying farmers in the Midwest to decrease agricultural production, giving increased aid to Israel, and dredging Baltimore's harbor, is inconceivable. There could not, therefore, be any real agreement on any automatic or quasi-automatic system of allocating collective resources, and the delegation of authority to make such decisions would mean the abandonment of the legislative process as such. We are reduced to the reaching of separate decisions by logrolling processes, given the constitutional rules as laid down in advance.

MAJORITY RULE AND EXTERNAL COSTS

This is by no means so much a tragedy as our simple model may have appeared to suggest. Implicit in the comparison of the logrolling solution with the Kantian solution has been the idea that the external costs imposed on the individual by the "maximizing equilibrium" exceed those resulting from the Kantian "equilibrium." This will be true if individual farmers are primarily interested in the repair of their own roads, as our model postulates. If, by contrast, some or all of the farmers should be genuinely and intensely interested in the standards of general road repair over the whole township, the Kantian solution might be worse than the maximizing one. This is because the Kantian solution under simple majority rule can take no account of varying intensities in individual standards. For example, if there should exist a minority of farmers who feel very intensely that much more should be spent on road repairs than the majority of other voters, whose standards are somewhat indifferently held, the maximizing solution, which does result in a standard of general repair above the Kantian median, may be more "desirable" on certain commonly acknowledged welfare grounds than the Kantian solution. In this case the introduction of logrolling into the Kantian model could be beneficial to all parties.

A central feature of our analysis is the demonstration that the operation of simple majority rule, quite independently of any assumption about individual motivation, will almost always impose external costs on the individual. If more than a simple majority is required for decision, fewer resources will be devoted to road-building in our model, and the individual comparison of marginal benefits and marginal costs would tend to approach more closely the calculus required by the economists' standard criteria for attaining a Pareto-optimality surface. . . . [H]owever, when any consideration of more inclusive voting rules is made, the incremental costs of negotiating bargains must also be taken into account.

GENERALIZATIONS

Some of these points will be discussed later. We shall now inquire as to what extent our simple logrolling model can be generalized. It would appear that any governmental activity which benefits specific individuals or groups in a discriminatory fashion and which is financed from general taxation would fit our model well. It is not, of course, necessary that the revenues employed in paying for the projects be collected equally from all voters, either in terms of tax rates or tax collections. The minimum necessary condition is that the benefits from public activity be significantly more concentrated or localized than the costs. This is a very weak condition, and many budgetary patterns seem to meet it. If the taxes are collected by indirect methods so that individuals cannot really tell how much they individually pay for each specific public-service project, this accentuates the distortions described by our analytical model. In the marginal case the individual may be indifferent about projects benefiting others, the costs of which seem slight to him and also difficult to measure. Under these circumstances he would be particularly likely to trade his support for such projects, which may appear costless or nearly so, for reciprocal support for his own pet proposals.

Additional types of governmental activity may also be fitted into the analysis. Other forms of taxation-expenditure problems are most easily incorporated. First, we may suppose that there is some governmental activity that provides general benefit to all voters, e.g., police protection, which is financed out of general taxation. In this case the maximizing solution and the Kantian solution will tend to be identical to the extent that the benefits and the taxes are truly general. However, as soon as general taxation is departed from, parallel reasoning to that above demonstrates that special tax exemptions and favors to individuals and groups will be introduced.

On the tax side of the fiscal account, if a given sum of money is to be raised, we should expect the revenue-raising pattern to include general taxes that are, relatively, "too heavy," but which are riddled with special exemptions for all sorts of groups. The result is that of greatly reducing the efficacy of any generally accepted norms for fiscal organization (such as progression in taxes) that are supposedly adopted. The pattern that we are able to predict as a result of our analysis thus seems to be descriptive of existing fiscal institutions, quite independently of the moral justification of the behavior that our model incorporates. General and diffuse taxes, characterized by many special exemptions, finance budgets in which public services are designed, at least to a large degree, to benefit particular groups in the society. There is clearly no apparent conflict between the predictions that emerge initially from our model and fiscal reality as it is commonly interpreted.

If our analysis is to be applied even more generally to all public activity, it must be radically generalized. For any individual voter all possible measures can be arrayed according to his intensity of interest. His welfare can be improved if he accepts a decision contrary to his desire in an area where his preferences are weak in exchange for a decision in his favor in an area where his feelings are stronger. Bargains among voters can, therefore, be mutually beneficial. Potentially, the voter should enter into such bargains until the marginal "cost" of voting for something of which he disapproves but about which his feelings are weak exactly matches the expected marginal benefits of the vote or votes secured in return support for issues in which he is more interested. Thus, he will expect to benefit from the total complex of issues which enter into his set of bargains with his fellows. In making such bargains, however, the individual must try to gain the assent of only a bare majority of other voters, not of all of them. On any given issue he can simply ignore 49 per cent of the individual decision-makers. This means that he can afford to "pay" more for other support because a part of the inconvenience caused by the measure will fall on parties who are not members of the decisive bargaining coalition.

Unfortunately, from the point of view of the individual voter, the converse also holds true. Bargains will certainly be concluded in which the single voter does not participate. Yet he will have to bear a part of the costs of action taken. As a result, the whole effect of the measures which result from his bargains and on which he votes on the winning side will be beneficial to him; but this will tend, normally, to be only slightly more than one half of all "bargained" measures passed, and the remainder will be carried out adverse to his interest. The same result would hold true for the *average* voter under a pure referendum system. The whole problem analyzed here can be eliminated by changing the rule which compels the minority to accept the decisions of the majority without compensation. So long as this rule is employed to make collective decisions, the individual voter must expect to incur external costs as a result of public or collective action.

NOTES AND QUESTIONS

1. In the second paragraph of the selection printed here, Buchanan and Tullock use the expression "constitutional choice." It should be noticed that by "constitution" they do not literally and necessarily mean a formal written document of organic law. Any agreed-upon framework of voting and procedural rules for a legislative body would be a "constitution" in their sense.

2. Buchanan and Tullock argue that, even in a democracy, the majority does not always get its way because one must take into account the intensity of minority feelings. Hence, if a vast majority weakly favors regulation of the sale of cigarettes, but a minority (of tobacco growers and sellers) very strongly opposes, it is perfectly likely that regulation will fail; the minority will "buy off" enough of the majority to get its way.

Does this explain why it has so often proved difficult to pass Civil Rights legislation in Congress? or to enact a program of medical care for the aged?

Can one argue that the picture of the legislative process given by Buchanan and Tullock is fatally defective because it does not take into account the institutional structure of legislatures—such factors as the seniority system, the use of committees, the existence of two houses? How might Buchanan and Tullock answer such an argument?

3. Buchanan and Tullock try to show that the logrolling process results in "overinvestment." In the example of the farmers (*see* pp. 59-64, *supra*) a farmer teams up with fifty other farmers to vote for road repairs on his road and those of his partners. As a rational man, he calculates his benefits and his costs. The benefits are the repairs to his roads, and the costs are the taxes he will have to pay. But these taxes will be levied on *all* 100 farmers, while they will be only needed to pay for the roads that run by the farms of fifty-one. In other words, he can count on a "gift" of taxes from forty-nine farmers, who will get no road repairs. So, our farmer will vote for a *higher* level of repair to his road and that of his coalition-partners than he would if he were going to be taxed to support repairs on all 100 roads. Unfortunately, all farmers will enter into coalitions, hence our farmer will sometimes find himself a member of the minority, taxed to support repairs of a group of roads none of which benefit him. All roads, therefore, will be kept in repair at a level greater than the farmers individually would have chosen if they calculated benefits and costs in one package. This is the "overinvestment" to which Buchanan and Tullock refer.

Some examples may clarify Buchanan and Tullock's argument in their description of "A Simple Logrolling Model." At 60-61, *supra*, they describe the "Kantian" approach. Each farmer "would balance, according to his own scale of preferences, the costs of maintaining his own road at various levels of repair with the benefits expected, and try to reach a decision at the point where expected costs equal marginal benefits." For simplicity, assume there are only ten farmers rather than the authors' 100. Assume further that each can translate his cost-benefit judgment into a decision that he will vote for a repair on any road that costs *no more* than a certain amount. That is, one farmer will vote for any repair that costs, say, $10 or less, another sets the maximum at $20 or less and so on. Finally, assume that the ten farmers' cost-benefit judgments produce the following neat pattern of maximum figures:

		4					6			
Farmer No.:	1	2	3	4		5	6	7	8	9	10
Maximum:	$10	20	30	40		50	60	70	80	90	100

Since it takes six votes to approve any project, the repair level will be $50 since farmers Nos. 10, 9, 8, 7, 6 and 5 would vote for any repair of that amount, and since farmer No. 5, whose vote is needed for a majority, would not vote for any greater amount.

At 61, *supra*, the authors first talk of a single farmer who became a "maximizer." He will vote for any repair to his own road but against all other repairs. This means that "the taxes on the farmer concerned would be reduced or his road [would be] kept in better-than-average repair." First, assume farmer No. 3, one of the original minority, adopted this position. The level of repair on all roads but his would remain at $50 since his vote is not needed for a majority at this point. However, he could increase the level of repair to his own road to $60, since farmers No. 6 to No. 10 would vote for a $60 repair and farmer No. 3's vote added to theirs would make a majority. Second, assume that farmer No. 8, one of the original majority, was the one who adopted the maximizing strategy. His road would remain repaired at the $50 level since for six votes farmer No. 8 would still have to join with farmers Nos. 10, 9, 7, 6 and 5 and since farmer No. 5 would vote for no more than a $50 repair. However, all of the other roads would not remain maintained at the $50 level, thus saving farmer No. 8 taxes. The vote then would be:

	4				6					
Farmer No.:	8	1	2	3	4	5	6	7	9	10
Maximum:	$0	10	20	30	40	50	60	70	90	100

and so all other roads would be maintained at the $40 level. (Farmer No. 8 has deserted the old majority and now farmers Nos. 10, 9, 7, 6 and 5 need farmer No. 4's vote to get any road repaired, and he will only vote for repairs that cost $40 or less.)

Buchanan and Tullock next suggest that other farmers living on farmer No. 8's road might adopt the maximizing strategy. Suppose farmer No. 9 joins farmer No. 8 in a coalition, voting to repair their road at any level but voting against any repair on any other road. Their road would still be repaired at the $50 level, the original "Kantian" outcome since farmer No. 5's vote would still be needed for a majority. (Notice that if, instead of farmer No. 9, farmer No. 8 lived on the same road as farmer No. 3, one of the old minority, then farmer No. 3's vote on their road would increase the level to $60 since farmer No. 5's vote would no longer be needed.) However, the coalition would produce a tax saving for them since the level of repair to other roads would drop to $30.

	4				6					
Farmer No.:	8	9	1	2	3	4	5	6	7	10
Maximum:	$0	0	10	20	30	40	50	60	70	100

Obviously the more who join the coalition from the ranks of farmers Nos. 3, 4, 5, 6, 7 and 10, the lower the general level of repair and the lower the taxes.

How do Buchanan and Tullock go about constructing their picture of the operation of a legislative body? To what extent can it be said to be empirical? What assumptions about human behavior do they make? Are these justified?

4. What are the political implications of the analysis presented by Buchanan and Tullock? Does it follow that the welfare state necessarily involves a higher degree of government activity and of taxation than is rational? Distinguish carefully between the power of their theoretical constructs to *explain* past events and the implications, if any, for policy, that might flow out of their view of the operation of legislative bodies.

5. Do Buchanan and Tullock provide a theoretical justification for restraints on the power of a majority? the Bill of Rights? protection for private property interests?

6. Empirical studies of the legislative process, including informal bargaining and logrolling, have been undertaken by political scientists, particularly in the last generation. One well-known case study is S. Bailey, *Congress Makes a Law: The Story Behind the Employment Act of 1946* (Columbia U. Press 1950). There is also a large general literature on Congress, how it operates, and what it does. One short, general treatment by a political scientist is Lewis A. Froman, *The Congressional Process, Strategies, Rules, and Procedures* (Little, Brown 1967). The literature on state legislatures is somewhat less rich. A convenient short collection of materials is *State Legislatures in American Politics* (A. Heard ed., Prentice-Hall 1966), one of the American Assembly series.

7. The Buchanan and Tullock study concerns itself with one aspect of the work of legislatures: passing laws. That indeed is the most notable and most important way in which legislatures "make law," in other words, seek to influence behavior of their constituents and others. In theory, legislatures investigate facts or listen to demands for action, and then pass laws to remedy situations which call for change.

There is considerable evidence that legislatures sometimes use other means to influence or change behavior. One method is the use of persuasion, propaganda, or publicity. Speeches and news releases exhort action or inaction. The investigating committee, notoriously, has been sometimes used (or abused) for the purpose of creating a climate in which action will take place quite apart from any laws that are passed or may be passed; sometimes, the committee has little or no intention of recommending laws at all.

[Reading 7]

8. An article by Ted Finman and Stewart Macaulay,* "Freedom to Dissent: The Vietnam Protests and the Words of Public Officials," 1966 *Wisconsin Law Review* 632, examines the work of the Internal Security Subcommittee of the Senate Committee on the Judiciary, and its study "The Anti-Vietnam Agitation and the Teach-In Movement, The Problem of Communist Infiltration and Exploitation." This study, compiled under the leadership of Senator Thomas Dodd of Connecticut, has this to say about the purposes for which it was conducted:

> It is . . . the purpose of the study . . . to try to establish whether the Communist Party and its various affiliates have succeeded in infiltrating and manipulating and exploiting the so-called teach-in movement and the anti-Vietnam agitation in general, and, if so, to what extent and in what manner.
>
> I hope that the facts here set forth, will, among other things, assist loyal critics of administration policy to purge their ranks of the Communists and crypto-Communists, so that the national debate on Vietnam policy can be carried forward as a discussion between honest men, unencumbered by the participation of the Communists, who have been seeking to subvert the entire process of free debate, as they seek to subvert our society.

The article by Professors Finman and Macaulay argues that the evidence compiled by the Staff Study for the allegations it contained was weak and distorted. They conclude:

> In our view, the process by which the subcommittee sought to infer that Communists or extremists controlled "the anti-Vietnam movement" made the publication of the staff study an irresponsible act. Passing this point, however, we turn to the question whether the subcommittee made its charges in a way that minimized unintended side effects. In the study's introduction Senator Dodd did indicate that the appropriate response to its conclusions would be for non-Communists to purge their ranks of Communists and crypto-Communists. Whatever the doubts about this, he did not call for a broader purge. Also he said that honest critics, as he defined them,

---

* The co-authors are Professors of Law, University of Wisconsin. Copyright © 1966 by The Wisconsin Law Review. Reprinted by permission.

had a position that "commands respect, and their voices must be heard, no matter how much any of us may disagree with them, if the processes of democracy are not to be stultified." Moreover, one of the staff study's conclusions was that the "great majority of those who have participated in anti-Vietnam demonstrations and in teach-ins are loyal Americans who differ with administration policy in Vietnam for a variety of reasons, ranging from purely strategic considerations to pacifism." Shortly after the study was released, Senator Dodd reportedly denied as "completely untrue" the charges of critics that the study tarred all anti-Vietnam demonstration participants as Communists. Nonetheless, as we have seen, one of the study's conclusions was that the "control of the anti-Vietnam movement has clearly passed from the hands of the moderate elements who may have controlled it, at one time, into the hands of Communists and extremist elements who are openly sympathetic to the Vietcong and openly hostile to the United States. . . ." One can wonder to what extent this finding undercut all the cautionary words designed to lessen side effects. Moreover, the subcommittee issued a press release describing its study. It stressed the conclusion that control had passed to the Communists and extremists, and its cautionary words were only that not "all of those who disagree with the Administration's policy on Vietnam or who participate in demonstrations against this policy are Communists or Communist dupes." Most people, of course, were likely to read not the study itself, but newspaper stories based on the press release; and while Senator Dodd is to be commended for making some attempt to blunt side effects, the staff study and press release probably did little to lessen the risks of deterring dissent and inducing punishment without due process.

Like logrolling, the manipulation of public opinion by committees of Congress and by individual congressmen is not usually thought of as part of the ideal role of a legislature except insofar as an "educational" function is conceded to the elected representatives. To what extent can and should such practices as these of the Dodd Committee be curbed? Are they defects of our particular system, or are they inevitable dangers of the fact that the central authorities are powerful and their actions newsworthy?

9. A kind of "logrolling" goes on *between* branches of government, as well as *within* Congress. In July, 1968, President Lyndon Johnson nominated Justice Abe Fortas to be Chief Justice of the United States, and Homer Thornberry to be an Associate Justice

of the United States Supreme Court. The minority leader, Senator Everett Dirksen of Illinois, announced his support for these nominations. It was widely rumored that this support was gotten for a price. The price was "a reprieve for a Dirksen pet, the moribund Subversive Activities Control Board. . . . [It] seemed clear that an extension of the life of the SACB was at least part of the price Dirksen was getting for his help. This was evident when it became known that Attorney General Ramsey Clark, on orders from the White House, had filed petitions with the SACB charging seven individuals with membership in the Communist Party, and asking the SACB to so declare them. Clark's petition was filed on June 30, just hours before the end of the fiscal-year deadline when the SACB otherwise would have ceased to exist because it had nothing to do." *Newsweek*, July 15, 1968, at 27-28.*

Interestingly enough, the nomination of Mr. Justice Fortas failed to secure senatorial assent—an example of logrolling that failed. *See* Reading 98, at 848, *infra*. And in 1969, Mr. Justice Fortas resigned from the Supreme Court because of his relationship with an individual who had sought favors from lower level officials in the Johnson administration.

* Reprinted by permission.

2. Administrative Process

8. The Politics of Property Taxation

**GLENN W. FISHER AND
ROBERT P. FAIRBANKS***

12 ADMINISTRATIVE SCIENCE QUARTERLY 48
(June 1967)

The political process is considered analogous to a game structured by the rules (the system). The game is in no sense a trivial one, or of the zero-sum type;** rather, the pay-offs to some players are real and do not necessarily cancel out with the losses of other players. The strategies adopted are the result of the self-defined goals of the players and their appraisal of the total situation. The success of a particular player depends not only upon external social and economic conditions, but also upon how well acquainted he is with both the political process and system. Players do not always know the significant elements to consider because of the complexity of the system or because of a poor understanding of the process. That the game is a serious one cannot be overemphasized. Net gains and net losses do occur, sometimes as the result of combinations that attempt to limit the game or keep others from becoming aware of it.

The model or framework for analysis used here can also be utilized to analyze decision making for the property tax in any state or, with some modifications and development, to analyze a particular aspect of the property tax process more intensively. Because important aspects of the political system vary from state to state, however, analysis here is confined to the state of Illinois. This permits the use of actual rather than hypothetical examples.

---

* Glenn W. Fisher, Professor, Institute of Government and Public Affairs, University of Illinois at Urbana; Robert P. Fairbanks, Associate Professor, Graduate School of Public Affairs, State University of New York at Albany.

** A "zero-sum game" is one in which (assuming two players) a gain to one is a loss to the other. [Eds. note]

MODEL

Basic Relationships

Some simple arithmetic relationships must be considered in the choice of a strategy by anyone wishing to influence property-tax decisions. The tax rate is determined by dividing the tax levy (expressed in dollars) by the assessed value of all taxable property within the jurisdiction of the local unit of government levying the tax. The tax to be paid by a particular taxpayer is computed by multiplying the tax rate by the assessed value of his property.

Using these relationships, one can make a preliminary analysis of possible strategies. Assume, for example, that the goal of a taxpayer is to reduce his tax. One possible strategy would be to influence the governing board of the taxing unit to reduce the tax levy. Success of this strategy would result in a lower tax rate, would reduce the tax of all taxpayers proportionally, and would reduce the level of services performed by the governmental unit. If the taxpayer values the governmental services financed by the levy or fears that an attempt to reduce the levy will encounter too much opposition, he might consider it more feasible to attempt to reduce the assessed value of his own property as a means of reducing his tax liability. This might be accomplished by influencing the assessing authorities or by removing property from the jurisdiction of the taxing district on assessment day. Since this would reduce the aggregate tax base, it would result in a slight rise in the tax rate. The net effect would be a shifting of taxes to other taxpayers. Or the taxpayer could bring about an increase in the total tax base without an increase in his own assessed value, again gaining at the expense of other taxpayers. The difficulties of successfully pursuing this strategy are obvious, but the intricacies of decision making in property taxation are such that it must not be summarily ruled out.

A rather different kind of strategy would be to attempt to get the state legislature to impose a limit on the tax rate that can be levied by the local governmental unit. Such a limit would be of value to a taxpayer if the limit is less than the rate which would have been imposed in the absence of the limitation. Success of this strategy would limit the tax levy and possibly the services provided. . . .

Tax Protests by Railroad Corporations

This case study is a description of the attempts by Illinois railroads to obtain property tax relief (the goal) at the local level by paying their taxes under protest (the strategy). It can be considered as a simple game with relatively uncomplicated interactions. The choice of strategy by railroad corporations is relatively uncomplicated for the following reasons:

1. They are large corporations with little direct interest in the welfare of particular communities and thus little interest in the size of the tax levy for a particular local governmental unit.[15] Thus their interest in smaller tax bills is not complicated by concern for the governmental units and the services they render.

2. Railroad properties being large cannot be readily moved for tax advantage and the services rendered to a particular community are strictly controlled by state and federal governments. Consequently the railroad is economically vulnerable to local political action in that local officials have little need to bargain with a railroad or to offer concessions as they would to attract and hold desirable industry.[16]

3. They exert little political power in most local communities, partly because of their economic vulnerability, but also because railroad employees are not apt to make up a significant portion of the voters in a community, and because the public image of railroads is often poor.

4. Railroad operating property is assessed by the State Department of Revenue, so that local officials have little or no control over the assessed value of a railroad.

5. The value of railroad property is large in relation to net earnings, so that property taxes affect profits more strongly than in many industries.

6. As large organizations subject to very detailed regulations, they are accustomed to operating "by the book"; therefore they may be predisposed to strategies which take advantage of legal technicalities.

These factors indicate that railroads have a strong interest in reducing their property taxes, but that the strategies open to them are seriously limited as compared with other taxpayers. Because of their lack of political influence in a community, it would be useless to attempt to reduce tax levies by leading a campaign for lower or more efficient expenditure. Because they

---

15 This is not to suggest that railroads have no interest in the welfare of the communities they serve, but that their broad general interest does not entail great concern about the effect of their actions on the tax collection of particular local governmental units.

16 This, of course, must be modified for communities that have major railroad installations, such as freight yards and shops.

are assessed by the state, they can do nothing at the local level about the level of assessment; because of economic and regulatory factors, they can rarely exert much influence upon local policies by threats or promises. Given these limitations and the very complex nature of Illinois property tax law, a natural strategy is to attack the legal validity of local tax levies. This strategy has, in fact, been pursued on a wide and continuing basis in Illinois.

In a typical case the railroad pays its taxes under protest and then, through a local attorney, files an action alleging a long list of irregularities in the levy. A sample of the objections raised against the 1961 levies of a downstate municipality follows:

1. Objection to an appropriation for employee hospitalization insurance, on the ground that municipalities were not specifically authorized to furnish such insurance to their employees.

2. Objection to an appropriation for "other capital outlays," on the ground that the wording was not specific.

3. Objection to a rate of .018 extended to pay a judgment against the city, on the ground that the city had no authority to extend this tax outside the corporate fund limit.

4. Objection to an appropriation for the street and bridge fund, on the ground that the salaries item applied to both roads and bridges. Cases were cited which held that road salaries and bridge salaries had to be shown separately. Also objection that tree removal was a corporate expense and could not be paid from the road and bridge fund.

5. Objection to park levy, on the ground that in computing the 1961 rate limit under a formula provided by statute, a rate of .20 was used as the 1945 limit instead of the correct limit of .10. This resulted in a 1961 legal limit of .029 rather than the rate of .059 extended. The purported 1945 limit of .20 was established by ordinance, although the statutes required a referendum.

6. Objection to rate of .075 for police protection, on the ground that the referendum claiming to increase the limit in 1946 was improperly worded.

Local government officials have little choice of counter strategies. To permit the objections to go to trial would tie up the protested funds for several years, would be expensive, and, perhaps most serious of all, would alert other taxpayers to the fact that some of the current taxes were of questionable legality. This might encourage a wave of tax protests and result in a serious erosion of the tax yield. In most cases, the only feasible strategy is to negotiate an out-of-court settlement. Usually this occurs at a meeting between a representative of the state's attorney, the railroad attorneys, and perhaps representatives of the local government units affected. To some extent the outcome of the bargaining depends upon the participants' knowledge of the law and to some extent upon their ability to bluff. It is expected that a considerable amount of negotiation will take place on disputed points. The objections cited were settled as follows:

1. The objection to the levy for employee hospitalization was sustained.[17]

2. The objection to appropriation for other capital outlays was overruled when it was pointed out that this appropriation was from nonproperty tax revenues.

3. The objection to the levy for the judgment fund was sustained. City officials pointed out to the authors that municipalities could, without referendum, sell judgment fund bonds to meet judgments against the city and that tax levies to service bonds were not subject to tax limits. This was not pointed out to the railroad attorneys for fear they would start objecting to this procedure.

4. The objection to the failure to separate street salaries and bridge salaries was sustained, but it was agreed to overrule the objection to tree removal expense as a street and bridge expense.

5. The objection to the park levy was sustained.

6. The objection to the police protection levy was overruled on the grounds that the referendum was held on April 9, 1946, and that the statute upon which the railroad was relying had been amended effective January 1, 1946.

In subsequent years, tax district officials try to correct the defects that led to objections. For example, salaries in the road and bridge fund would be itemized in a different way in the following year, although the railroads might object to the new method also. Some defects are not so easily corrected, however. To remove the objection to the park levy, municipal officials would have to convince the railroad attorneys that the interpretation of law accepted in the 1961 negotiations was wrong, allow the case

---

[17] The next session of the state legislature granted municipalities specific authority to pay employees hospitalization insurance. Thus a short-run strategy created demand for changes in the system, which, in turn, changed the constraints in the next period. Care must be taken not to pursue strategies that are so successful as to have long-run repercussions.

to go to trial, and win a favorable ruling on the point, or publicly admit that past levies had been above the legal limit and seek to win public approval of a higher rate in a referendum. The last two alternatives have obvious drawbacks, and local officials may prefer to continue to refund the disputed amounts to those who file protests.

The outcome of successive short-run strategies may result in long-run changes. For example, if local officials are able to eliminate enough sources of objections or feel confident enough of their position to take a firm stand on compromises, it may become unprofitable for railroads and their attorneys to continue to object. It is also possible that widespread publicity might change the situation enough to cause one or both sides to reappraise their position.

Changes may occur when "outsiders" become aware of the bargaining process and seek to achieve their own goals in similar fashion. In one downstate county, an attorney who became aware of the annual railroad objections began to file identical objections to the levies upon his own property and the property of his clients. Such action constituted a clear threat to the strategy of both railroads and local governmental officials, and both took action to discourage it. In succeeding years the railroads tried to prevent this "coattail riding" by waiting until the last day to file objections, and county officials denied the attorney the customary privilege of removing legal documents from the courthouse for copying. The attorney countered by filing a general objection and then amending it with specific charges copied from the railroad's objections at a later date. Social pressure was applied in the form of unfriendly remarks from courthouse personnel, and the attorney suspects that efforts to raise assessments on some of the property of his clients were related to his filing of objections. Later, the railroads dropped the practice of filing objections in this county. Whether this curtailment was related to the attorney's actions, to a shift of railroad personnel and interest to state-wide assessment cases, or for other reasons, is uncertain.

Protests by Other Corporations

Other industries with substantial properties in a community may have different goals and face circumstances that suggest different strategies. It is not realistic, for example, to assume that a nonrailroad corporation will always be interested primarily in reducing the size of its tax bill. The local community is often the residence of company officials and employees, and the attractiveness of the community may be a direct asset to the firm. If so, the goals of the firm may be concerned with the purposes of the tax and the efficiency with which tax funds are expended rather than with minimizing taxes. Strategies may therefore differ from the railroad strategies described. Furthermore, many firms have greater political and economic strength in the local community, yet because their property is locally assessed, they may be more vulnerable to unfavorable actions by local authorities.

These circumstances suggest that the taxpayer has a much wider range of strategies available and that the possible responses by governmental officials are more diverse; therefore, it is much more difficult to describe a case as typical. As a result, tax protests by industrial taypayers appear to be relatively infrequent in many counties. In one downstate case, a number of industries represented by a single attorney filed protests, which alleged that rates extended for several municipal funds were illegal. After the protested funds had gone into escrow for three years, city officials compromised on the case in order to get the desperately needed funds.[19] As a result of the attention focused upon the protest, the state's attorney in the county ruled that illegal rates were being extended, and the city was plunged into a financial crisis. The city council then imposed a tax upon utility services and scheduled a public referendum and obtained approval of higher property tax limits.

Negotiation of assessment is probably more common than paying taxes under protest. It is difficult, however, to know how much negotiation occurs, or how much the outcome differs from what it would have been in the absence of negotiation.[20] Even if the researcher were allowed to observe the process, it would in some cases be difficult to identify true negotiation. In the case of complex properties, it is not unusual for the assessor to request information from the owner or builder. In other cases, owners and builders often feel that it is to their advantage to provide certain information about costs, dimensions, and construction methods to the assessor before it is requested. Such exchanges of information almost inevitably take on some of the characteristics of bargaining and are strategies. In a few communities, it is known that city officials or development groups take an active part in the process—relaying information between

---

[19] The city's case rested upon legal opinion that the formula limits were unconstitutional because they were not uniform among similar cities. This view has been supported by an attorney prominent in the field of municipal law, but his opinion has not prevailed in Illinois courts.

[20] The recently revealed property tax scandals in western United States suggest that negotiation in those states has sometimes involved the bribery of assessment officials. Cf. *Newsweek*, March 7, 1966, 29-30.

the industry and the assessor and otherwise acting as intermediaries. In one such community, there is an established schedule of minimum assessment ratios for various kinds of industrial and commercial property. Negotiations occur, but no assessment may go below the minimum. In other communities, stress is placed upon the fact that all industrial and commercial properties are assessed at the same percentage of actual value. Officials in these municipalities are quick to point out that they are just as interested in keeping existing industries healthy and expanding as in attracting new industry.

Assessors' Strategies

. . . . What strategies do assessors actually choose and how do the other participants respond? The strategy depends upon the set of conditions the assessor must consider, and how he perceives these conditions and his own role. Some assessors see themselves as technical experts, whose role it is to assess all property at the required percentage of value and to make no concessions to political pressures. Such a role, of course, is the one almost always urged by tax reformers and by the assessor's own professional association. But such a strategy is difficult to pursue. In the last 20 years, property values have been increasing. This means that an assessor pursuing this policy would have had to increase property tax values on each assessment date and thus would have made every property owner aware of the role of assessment in determining his property tax bill. Furthermore the different kinds and classes of property have not increased in value at the same rate; therefore the assessor would not have been able to apply a simple percentage increase but would have had to change the assessment by different amounts for property of different types, for property in different parts of town, and for different age classes. This would certainly have caused many complaints, a large number of appeals to boards of review, and threats of political retaliation at the next election. Thus, one effect of the technical-expert strategy is to make active participants of many formerly inactive participants. Taxpayers who had become habituated to existing levels of assessment are forcefully made aware of the role that assessment plays in determining their tax and become active in an effort to reduce their assessment by negotiation, by legally challenging the assessment, or by attempting to vote the assessor out of office.

. . . . A much safer and less demanding strategy is roll copying. The point of this strategy is to make as few changes in individual assessments as possible. Unfortunately for the assessor who wants to follow it, however, it is often necessary to make changes. To maintain all assessments unchanged would mean that the total assessed value of the area would be unchanged except for addition of new construction and deletion of destroyed property. In a period of rising property values, it would mean a decline in the general assessment level.

Such a strategy almost invariably encounters opposition from the tax-levying officials, who are often very anxious to obtain additional tax revenues. Tax levy limits may prevent the raising of rates and make increases in the assessed value the only way to increase such revenues unless legislative limits are changed. Even when limits do not prevent higher rates, tax-levying officials prefer increased assessed values to increased rates, so that responsibility for higher taxes can be placed upon assessing officials. In addition, intercounty equalization serves as a source of pressure for higher assessment levels.

For these reasons, the assessor who adopts roll copying as a basic strategy must also seek a way of increasing total assessed value. One obvious source of additional value is newly constructed property. It is often possible to assess such property at a higher level than the average existing level without encountering serious opposition, unless the property belongs to a highly knowledgeable and politically powerful real estate developer.

The assessor may turn to a particular kind or class of property. The choice may be made on the basis of political and economic vulnerability, it may involve a choice of classes whose assessment is most in need of revision, or it may be a combination of the two. In Chicago, for example, property is divided into a large number of classes. The assessor has developed methods and formulas that vary with the characteristics of the property. Periodically, these formulas and methods are brought up-to-date for one or more classes. Often these revisions are badly needed and do result in improved assessment of property within the class; but they also provide an opportunity for increasing the total value of the class. This procedure is administratively defensible, since it would be expensive and wasteful of manpower to attempt to revise all classes at once, but it also has the political advantage of confining opposition in any one year to a single class of property owners. In other cases, a single or small number of industrial or commercial properties will be singled out for large assessment increases. This phenomenon is best known in New Jersey, where it has been given the name "tax lightning."

. . . . Another possible strategy is to cultivate mass political support by publicly proclaiming a policy of "soaking the rich," the rich usually being a small number of large corporations. The conditions under which such a strategy can be successfully carried out would seem to be rather rare, but it was successfully pursued for over forty years by the assessor in a major downstate Illinois City. This strategy might be considered to have some elements of the tax-lightning strategy but differs in that there, the primary motive is not to get public credit for overassessing the big taxpayer, but simply to do the maximum roll copying and so avoid increases for the more numerous average taxpayer.

NOTES AND QUESTIONS

1. In what respect does the method used by Fisher and Fairbanks differ from that used by Buchanan and Tullock? Exactly what is it that they set out to *prove*? How successful are they?

2. You will have noted that some players in the property tax game use litigation or the threat of litigation as a strategic device to gain leverage in their bargaining with an administrative agency. This type of use of litigation is by no means unique. Can you think of other examples? Is this a legitimate use of adjudication? What are your criteria for determining legitimacy? *See also*, on a related point, Clement Vose, "Litigation as a Form of Pressure Group Activity," Reading 72, at 624, *infra*.

3. Does the evidence marshalled by Fisher and Fairbanks indicate to you that the property tax system is in need of reform? If so, how would you reform it? What additional information would you need, if any, that a social scientist might be able to provide?

4. The essay by Fisher and Fairbanks utilizes techniques which have become common and widely accepted among political scientists in the analysis of the behavior of judges, administrators and private parties. These scholars have, first of all, assumed that persons operating politically are striving to maximize certain personal, political or interest-group goals, rather than merely following the idealized blueprint of their offices. Once we stop believing that the idealized blueprint is the sole guide of behavior—*e.g.*, that judges want merely to decide "according to the law," or that legislators are looking for "the public interest"—we must find out, not only how they behave, but *why* they behave as they do. This has led scholars into a search for general rules of human behavior in attaining desired ends. Some feel that one can go quite far in explaining human behavior by constructing mathematical models of behavior. For example, there has been a great deal of interest in *game theory*, the theory that describes the mathematically optimal strategies for winning certain kinds of

simple games. These scholars have been impressed with the analogy between two persons both trying to win a game, and two actors in the political arena both trying to achieve conflicting results. The possible use of game theory in analysis of judicial decision-making, along with other techniques, has been explored by Glendon Schubert in his book, *Quantitative Analysis of Judicial Behavior* (Free Press 1959). Other political scientists have examined legal behavior, using more-or-less the same behavioral assumptions as the game theorists, particularly that legal acts are usefully looked at as rational, political choices directed toward the achievement of the actor's goals and desires, but without attempting to construct mathematical models. They have tried to break down, analyze, and measure the behavior of judges, for example, into tactics ("maneuverings designed to obtain advantages in dealing with colleagues, lower court judges, other government officials, interest groups, or the public at large") and strategies ("over-all plans under which such maneuverings against specific obstacles are co-ordinated and for which scarce resources are allocated in order to further the accomplishment of the broad policy objective"). The quotations are from Walter F. Murphy's *Elements of Judicial Strategy* 9-10 (U. of Chicago Press 1964), itself a notable example of the tactical and strategic analysis of judicial decision-making in the United States Supreme Court.

Strategic analysis has been most highly developed in the study of international relations in the work of such scholars as Herman Kahn and Thomas Schelling. Much of this work has been vigorously criticized for its inappropriate use of the concept of probability and its lack of empirical support for its factual assumptions. *See, e.g.,* Rapoport, *Strategy and Conscience* (Harper & Row 1964).

5. "Bargaining" is or can be analyzed as a coldly rational process. For psychological, religious or emotional reasons, a potential bargainer may refuse to bargain, out of "principle." *See* Reading 18, at 175, *infra,* V. Aubert, distinguishing between conflicts of value and conflicts of interest.

Would one expect to find "elements of bargaining" in the negotiating process between reluctant draft boards and young men who claim the status of a conscientious objector? *See* Robert L. Rabin, "Do You Believe in a Supreme Being—The Administration of the Conscientious Objector Exemption," 1967 *Wisconsin Law Review* 642, 671-72.

9. Law and the Balance of Power

STEWART MACAULAY*

[*Law and the Balance of Power* is a study of the attempted use of formal and informal legal processes by automobile dealers to alter the balance of power between themselves and the manufacturers who franchise them.

One of the main problems, as the dealers saw it, was that the terms of their franchise agreements permitted the manufacturer to cancel them on short notice and without any particular reason. In a number of states, the dealers successfully persuaded the legislature to enact laws to deal at least partially with this problem. Wisconsin was one of these states. Its statute, first enacted in 1937, gave power to the state motor vehicle department to issue licenses to manufacturers of automobiles and their representatives, without which they could not operate in the state. The statute also empowered the department to revoke licenses under certain circumstances—for example, unfair termination of a franchise.]

The state administrative-licensing legislation also allows the licensing agency to suspend or revoke a manufacturer or its representative's license for canceling a franchise "unfairly, without due regard to the equities of said dealer and without just provocation. . . ." This requisite goes a good deal beyond the provisions of the federal Good Faith Act as it has been construed. The standard in the state statutes could have quite broad application and give a dealer real "job security." However, it is very difficult to determine how the standard has been or will be applied. Manufacturers might well fear the chance of unfair decisions under this language, and only a course of administration could set guidelines.

Textual analysis indicates some of the possibilities. The first requirement for a valid termination is that it be for "just provocation." Can a manufacturer assert that it has complied if it cancels only for a dealer's failure to perform his duties as written

---

* Professor of Law, University of Wisconsin. Law and the Balance of Power, The Automobile Manufacturers and their Dealers, pp. 148-58, published by the Russell Sage Foundation, 1966. Reprinted by permission.

in the franchise? Perhaps, but the phrase connotes more than "legal cause." At the least the franchise duty probably would have to be reasonable as written and as applied, and the violation probably would have to be material. For example, it seems unlikely that a good-faith but unreasonable determination that sales were inadequate would be enough—the manufacturer might be provoked but would its provocation be "just"?

Although there is "just provocation" under these statutes, that is not enough. The termination must also be with "due regard to the equities of said dealer. . . ." On one hand, this could mean that a manufacturer must take into account factors personal to the dealer and not related to the mutual profit of manufacturer and dealer. Why did the dealer default? What will the impact of cancellation be on him? Does the past conduct of the dealer give him a right to a greater period of default and more "second chances"? For example, suppose a dealer had a good service record and had managed to stay in business selling a manufacturer's cars when they were unpopular nationally. The dealer has a heart attack and his sales fall off drastically because he cannot supervise the business as before. Cancellation will hurt him physically and psychologically as well as financially. Are these his "equities"? Or, on the other hand, are the "equities of said dealer" who has given a manufacturer just provocation financial only? The phrase may give him no more than a right to reasonable termination benefits, such as the repurchase of cars, parts, signs, and the like and help in disposing of the premises. While today all manufacturers grant such benefits in their franchises, when the first of the state statutes was drafted much less was offered.

While one can speculate, these questions can be answered only by considering the practices of the various state agencies. However, the available information is no more than suggestive since relatively few cases have reached the formal stage under these statutes. One case in Tennessee and one in Rhode Island could be explained as involving decisions that the terminations were without "just provocation." In the Tennessee case, a Ford dealer had been terminated for failure to outsell a rival Chevrolet dealer. As we have seen, the Ford franchise as written requires the manufacturer to consider much more than this to find sales unsatisfactory. In the Rhode Island case, the licenses of four Lincoln-Mercury representatives were revoked.

When the representative from the attorney-general's department sought to determine if Ford had given consideration to a not-too-healthy economic situation in Woonsocket

as a reason for the slow sale of cars, [the New England District Sales Manager for Lincoln-Mercury] . . . contended
that *good management could overcome any economic condition.*

Under the franchises in effect at this time, there was no mention
of considering local conditions. Apparently, the Rhode Island
commission insisted that, in practice, it be added to the definition of satisfactory sales for provocation to be just. Today Ford
and all other manufacturers seem to agree as all franchises require consideration of local conditions. Obviously, the New England district sales manager's statement was nonsense. Ford's real
position was that a dealer assumed the risk of a local recession,
and it is just this objective impersonal approach that the state
statutes were designed to overturn.

My information on the "equities" language comes from a review of the transcripts of all of the formal hearings before the
Wisconsin Department of Motor Vehicles. In no case that went
this far were the "equities" of the dealer a major factor. In all
of them the commissioner viewed the provocation as "just" and
very clear. Apparently, the commissioners have assumed that as
the degree of provocation increases, the equities of the dealer
decrease and do not present a problem. For example, suppose a
dealer was canceled for intentionally defrauding the manufacturer and his customers out of large amounts of money. The
dealer's past loyal service and the impact of cancellation on his
health as well as any worry about his lost reliance expenses will
not weigh much now. The case the manufacturers have said they
fear—the nice but inefficient dealer who will be terribly hurt by
cancellation and who cannot be canceled for his lifetime—does
not appear in the Department's hearing files.

Up to this point, *formal* proceedings under the state administrative-licensing legislation have been described. However, in
many states the existence of the formal licensing system has
prompted *informal* systems to develop. And, indeed, one would
expect effective regulation to prompt compliance or pressures for
compromise and settlement rather than formal hearings and judicial review. A detailed description of the practices in Wisconsin
will be given and then there will be a report about what is known
of similar practices elsewhere.

The life history of a dispute in Wisconsin involves an elaborate
filtering process designed to screen out worthy cases and settle
them.[749] Suppose a manufacturer is dissatisfied with a Wisconsin
dealer's sales and is convinced that efforts to correct bad practices

---

[749] The discussion that follows is based on interviews.

will be unsuccessful. In some cases, the manufacturer may take one of two steps. It may call the Department of Motor Vehicles and ask to discuss how to cancel the dealer and still keep its license in Wisconsin. At this stage the Department will not discuss specific cases, but it will give general advice, stressing that it wants a detailed file on the dealer with clear evidence of poor performance.

Alternatively, the manufacturer's representatives will talk with Louis Milan, executive vice-president of the Wisconsin Automotive Trades Association (WATA) and the man most responsible for the existence of the Wisconsin administrative-licensing legislation. The factory will give him a detailed report on the dealer's shortcomings. Often Mr. Milan will know the dealer's side of the story because of his continuing contacts with the members of his association. He will tell the factory representative whether or not he thinks it has a case for cancellation that complies with the Wisconsin statute. In many instances he has agreed that the manufacturer has good reason to cancel. If the dealer's sales are not in line with the sales of other dealers selling the same car in his zone (the immediate area of the state near the dealer), Mr. Milan believes that unless the dealer can prove that there is some good explanation, the factory has a right to cancel. The comparison with zone sales has been used as a standard for so long that it is customary and generally accepted by the dealers. However, Mr. Milan qualifies his acceptance of the zone-performance standard by insisting that the manufacturer consider why the particular dealer's sales fell behind those of dealers in his area. Two cases are common and both should excuse the dealer. A local industry may close, putting a substantial number of people out of work; or a drought or crop failure in a farm area may limit the income of a dealer's customers. Not only will people in the area put off purchasing new cars; some may default on time sales and the dealer may have to pay the finance company the unpaid balance on repossessions of cars he sold during the previous two years. Second, a dealer's below-average sales should be excused where flaws in the manufacturer's distribution system are responsible for a large part of the trouble. At the beginning of the model year, metropolitan dealers tend to get many more of the best-selling models than the small town or rural dealers. Moreover, special orders can be delayed and customers may cancel. The factory should not be able to set a high quota, offer little cooperation in getting cars to a dealer when he can sell them, and then blame the dealer for poor performance. Mr. Milan is not so ready to accept comparisons of a dealer's sales with those in his district or region (usually his state and an area like the

Great Lakes States) since those ratios ignore all of the local factors.

Mr. Milan does not think the "due regard for the equities of said dealer" language of the statute gives the dealer help where his poor sales over a period of time are caused by ill health or where cancellation will have an unusually adverse effect on the dealer. If a dealer can get a fair allocation of cars and there are no circumstances that make potential customers unable to buy, a dealer must produce sales. If a dealer is sick, he must get a good manager or sell out. The equities of a dealer require consideration of the economic facts of his particular case and fair termination benefits or help in selling out to a replacement dealer. Mr. Milan strongly believes that a dealer must perform a contract if there is "mutuality." The sales requirement in a franchise is one example; performing commitments is another. If a dealer has been given a second chance on condition that he will do things over and above the franchise, he must meet these commitments or he has no remedy. He said that one must read the statutory language in light of the indefinite standards imposed by the franchises of the 1930's and 1940's, and in light of the absence of termination benefits then. At that time dealers' sales were judged by generalized formulas such as the national average requirement (if Buick sold 8 per cent of the cars in the nation, the Buick dealer in Stoughton, Wisconsin, had to sell 8 per cent of the cars sold there) which did not take into account particular factors such as local conditions or the factory's own part in a dealer's poor sales.

If Mr. Milan thinks that the factory's evidence is inadequate, the manufacturer may drop the matter, do a better job of gathering evidence, or urge the dealer to get out of business voluntarily and find a buyer for the dealership who will make a tempting offer. If Mr. Milan thinks that the factory has a case for cancellation, then it is free to proceed. At a minimum, it will not face a formal or informal amicus curiae brief from WATA before the department in a license-revocation proceeding. Also the manufacturer may benefit from the chance to make the first presentation to Mr. Milan; the one making a charge has some advantage in persuasion. Of course, a manufacturer can choose not to seek advice from the department or Mr. Milan, and begin termination proceedings within its organization as it would in any other state.

Once the manufacturer's local personnel give the dealer notice that termination has been recommended to their superiors in the company, or even earlier if the dealer discovers what is likely to happen, the dealer usually will take some action. Most frequently he will meet with Mr. Milan. If Mr. Milan has seen the manufacturer's file, if the dealer's story does not add new facts, and if Mr. Milan thinks the cancellation is justified, he will advise the dealer to accept the inevitable. He will tell the dealer he has no case and advise him how to get the best settlement on termination benefits. This advice will usually end the matter because the dealers view Mr. Milan as the authority on the statute. However, if Mr. Milan disagrees with the factory's decision to terminate, often he will telephone the appropriate factory officials and discuss the case with them. Frequently, he can obtain at least a second chance for the dealer to improve. He has known many of these officials for years, and he can avoid bureaucratic channels and talk directly to the man with authority. Undoubtedly a great deal of his power comes from such personal relationships. He is willing to listen to the manufacturer's side and the factory official may change Mr. Milan's view about the merits of the dealer's case. If Mr. Milan cannot obtain relief by personal contact and he still thinks the dealer's case is worthy, he will advise the dealer how to pursue his legal rights. One important item of information given the dealer will be the names of attorneys with experience in dealer termination cases. If the case presents an issue of significance to WATA, it will enter the case as an amicus curiae; this has been done frequently, especially where the manufacturer has pressed for a restrictive construction of the statute or challenged its constitutionality.

Dealers may talk with officials of the Wisconsin Department of Motor Vehicles. The officials will describe its procedures for a license suspension or revocation and tell the dealer about his right to file a complaint. They will also stress that the Department itself cannot give the dealer any relief but can only take licenses away or deny new ones to a dealer who has been selected to replace him. The dealer probably will know that this may be leverage enough to give him bargaining power in his negotiations with the manufacturer. While the dealer will be told of his right to file a complaint, department officials will suggest an informal approach first. The Department does not view its major function as holding formal hearings and suspending or revoking licenses. Rather it is proud of its informal mediating activities which "both bring about better solutions and save the taxpayers' money." (Under the statute the state, rather than the losing party, pays the cost of formal hearings.)[751] A Department official will write to the manufacturer stating the facts as alleged, that the case is likely to go to a formal hearing if nothing is done, but that the Department would be glad to lend its good offices

---

[751] Wis. Stat. § 218.01(5)(b) (1963).

if the manufacturer wishes to come in and talk to the dealer. The manufacturers almost always accept the invitation; the Department has a good deal of opportunity to make things difficult for an uncooperative factory, and all factories need the Department's cooperation in many different kinds of matters.

Then the Department will hold what is called a "prehearing conference," for which authority has been found in the Wisconsin Administrative Procedure Act.[752] Usually the manufacturer will send to the meeting officials from Detroit with authority to make decisions, one or more lawyers from its Detroit staff, and sometimes the local representative who made the decisions the dealer is complaining about. The dealer and his lawyer will be present. Thus the dealer will be able to break out of the factory's chain of command and be represented by a lawyer fairly early in the decision-making process. Often these informal meetings become heated. Yet frequently communication between manufacturer and dealer is reestablished because these arguments take place before representatives of the Department who can and do ask searching questions which must be answered. The combatants are forced to deal with each other's arguments; the Department officials can deflate untenable stands; and they can force both sides to make concessions. After an hour or two usually the parties will ask for a recess, leave the meeting room, and work out a settlement. The dealer may get another chance or he may be offered enough to prompt a "voluntary involuntary" termination. Usually this ends the matter. However, if the Department were to think that a violation which was against the public interest had occurred, it would continue the case through a formal hearing although the dealer might have no interest in pursuing the matter. Obviously, the Department could not do this too often without seriously impairing its mediation function.

What standards will the Department apply in this mediation process? "The key question is what did the dealer agree to do when you look at the contract."[753] Accordingly, the Department has looked primarily for "just provocation" rather than at "the equities of the dealer." While "just provocation" means cause under the terms of the franchise, the Department also insists that a manufacturer's judgments be reasonable and the dealer's default material. "A dealer must be more than barely below the passing

---

[752] WIS. STAT. §§ 227.08, .06, .07 (1963). It is clear that the draftsmen of the Wisconsin administrative-licensing act did not contemplate this development since the Wisconsin Administrative Procedure Act was passed in 1943, about six years after the manufacturer-licensing provisions were enacted in 1937. See Wis. Laws 1943, ch. 375, at 670.

[753] Interview with Department official.

mark before termination is justified—you do not take away a man's life work unless the failure is clear, if the dealer is trying hard to perform."[754] The Department accepts as evidence of inadequate sales a comparison between a dealer's percentage of his sales objective and the percentage of all dealers in his zone and between a dealer's percentage of the sales of a competing make and that of the other dealers selling his make. It is careful to see that the comparisons are meaningful. Sometimes a factory representative says, "We just can't work with that dealer." This is not enough; the manufacturer must show a specific cause.

The "equities of the dealer" concept enters in several ways. The Department presses manufacturers to work to rehabilitate dealers and give them an opportunity to succeed. Moreover, it considers long and faithful service and attempts to induce a manufacturer to give it some weight. However, this factor is persuasive only where there is a chance that a dealer can perform if given another year or two. It does not serve to protect a dealer from the requirement that he sell the percentages of his sales objective which most comparable dealers attain; it serves only to give him slightly more time to meet the standard where he has a chance of success.

If the Department's prehearing conference does not produce a settlement satisfactory to the dealer, there will be a formal hearing on revocation or suspension of the licenses of the manufacturer, its representative, or both. It is not surprising that there have been so few formal hearings so far and that no formal hearing has resulted in a suspension or revocation. One would expect the manufacturer to have a strong hand at this stage: any case that gets this far probably has failed to be settled by Mr. Milan of WATA, the Department's informal procedures, and any internal review of the manufacturer which took place.

These informal procedures, which likely exist only because of the potential exercise of the formal license revocation system, give Wisconsin dealers a great deal more bargaining power in settlement negotiations than dealers have in states where similar informal procedures do not exist. Moreover, one would expect that the existence of the informal process also acts to some degree as a deterrent; one would expect manufacturers to decide more close cases in favor of dealers in Wisconsin than elsewhere. Since the manufacturer has no clear line as to what is and is not permitted. the safe course is to do nothing that might be questionable. Unfortunately, this may be inconsistent with demanding the utmost efficiency from dealers and pushing them hard to get it.

---

[754] *Ibid.*

Apparently the elaborate informal system found in Wisconsin is the most highly developed one existing. However, most of the states with administrative-licensing statutes have some similar practices. . . .

Letters from administrative officials in several states also indicate the effect of their statutes: "While . . . it is not the intention that the Board shall be an arbitration body . . . in practice in many cases it works out that way, as many cases are resolved in the course of investigation or informal hearing." "In all of these cases the Commission informally interceded along the same line of procedure as used in Wisconsin. . . ." "The absence of formal complaints . . . may be attributed to efforts on the part of our field investigators and other parties concerned resulting in voluntary settlement and thus eliminating the possibility of a formal hearing." Of course, in some states the administrative-licensing statute is not enforced formally or informally and is a dead letter. In one such state, administration of the act was given to a state agency which is grossly understaffed and already charged with enforcing many statutes of clear importance. The legislature has never been willing to appropriate enough money to provide for enforcement.[759] The legislation thus has no more than some vague deterrent force—the statute is dormant today, but too gross a case might create the incentive to enforce the act.

In few of the states with administrative-licensing laws do the trade association managers play a role similar to Mr. Milan's in Wisconsin. Some make telephone calls to factory officials; others help a dealer get a lawyer or assist the dealer in making a presentation before a factory's internal review system. One reason for the difference is that in many states the law is administered by a group of dealers who sit as the state commission. They can handle informal negotiations very effectively since they have an official position as well as personal contacts with the manufacturers.

The manufacturers ought to have few serious complaints about the meaning of the Wisconsin statute as it has evolved through both the formal and informal procedures. Since failure to perform either the franchise commitments or promises beyond the franchise requirements is recognized as "just provocation" if those requisites are administered particularistically, one has fairly good guidelines and good evidence that no "dealer always wins" policy is being applied. In fact, one could even raise the opposite question. Have the formal and informal systems in Wisconsin fairly followed the language of the statute and fully considered all of the equities of the low-volume dealer? Perhaps he has an inter-

---

759 Interview with the dealers' trade association manager in the state.

est in "special interest" protectionist policies that is not being carried out by either the state agency or his trade association. While one who values the virtues of volume selling cannot feel too sympathetic toward him, the possibility of such an argument indicates that there have been no facts discovered in Wisconsin to indicate that manufacturers are being greatly harmed. However, the available information on practices in other states is not sufficient to rule out the possibility of protectionist policies prevailing over notions of due process, performance of commitments, and efficiency, and to assure us that the manufacturers have reasonably clear guidelines.

NOTES AND QUESTIONS

1. In what sense can it be said that the system described in operation by Professor Macaulay deviates from the formal model? What do we mean by "formal"? Is there anything in the behavior described that is inconsistent with the terms of the governing statute?

2. There are innumerable kinds of administrative proceedings. You may know of many of them, at least by name: regulation of the securities market and dealers in securities by the SEC; regulation of air transport, travel and safety by the FAA and CAB; the administration of state and local welfare programs; licensing of doctors, lawyers, nurses, accountants and many other occupations and professions; building codes and housing codes and their enforcement. The administration of the property tax was considered in the prior reading. What aspects of the processes described in the two preceding articles coincide, and which do not? What aspects might be plausibly guessed at as typical of administrative process, and which might not be? How would you go about testing your guesses?

3. Various groups have a stake in the relationship between manufacturers and dealers, including the general car-buying and car-driving public. Whose interests are protected by the informal processes described in the reading on automobile dealers? Whose interests are not?

10. Arrest: The Decision to Take a Suspect into Custody

WAYNE R. LAFAVE*

[Professor LaFave's study examines the conditions under which the police decide "to take custody of a person suspected of criminal behavior." (p. 3) Why do the police arrest some suspects and not others? When do the police choose to enforce the law with full rigor, and when do they not?

In an early chapter of the book, Professor LaFave briefly reviews the formal law of arrest. Statutes usually do *not* give the police discretion to arrest or not arrest—at least not obviously. Many statutes impose a duty on the police to arrest "all" violators of the criminal law. (p. 76) But the statutes cannot be said to provide any authoritative answer to the if, when and how of police discretion. The case-law is equally unhelpful. Some cases even imply that the exercise of discretion not to arrest, where the suspect seems clearly to have violated the law, is always improper. Other cases recognize the necessity for discretion.

The following excerpts illustrate two kinds of discretion: the decision not to arrest, and the decision to arrest for purposes other than prosecution. The materials were drawn from field studies in Kansas, Michigan and Wisconsin.]

NONINVOCATION BECAUSE OF LIMITED ENFORCEMENT RESOURCES

There are not sufficient resources available to the police for them to proceed against all the conduct which the legislature may actually desire subjected to enforcement. As a consequence, discretion must be exercised in deciding how to allocate the resources that do exist. As Thurman Arnold has said, to deny

* Wayne R. LaFave is Professor of Law at the College of Law, University of Illinois. Published by Little, Brown and Company (1965), pp. 102-12, 114-16, 119-24, 451-59, reprinted by permission.

discretion at this point would be "like directing a general to attack the enemy on all fronts at once."[1] The police and other enforcement agencies are given the general responsibility for maintaining law and order under a body of criminal law defining the various kinds of conduct against which they may properly proceed. They are then furnished with enforcement resources less than adequate to accomplish the entire task. Consequently, discretionary enforcement occurs in an attempt to obtain the best results from these limited means. In this sense, the budgetary appropriation is an establishment of policy (the general level of enforcement for which the public is willing to pay) and an indirect delegation of power by the legislative to the administrative branch.

Much of the criminal conduct coming to the attention of the police does not lead to arrest. Often a warning is given; this is the form of action least demanding on available enforcement resources.[3] Though warnings are generally issued on a haphazard basis, they are regularly used in some situations where the conduct is thought not serious enough to justify an arrest.

Even more serious offenses do not necessarily lead to arrest, however. This may occur, for example, when the police view the conduct as conforming to the normal standards of the group involved; when the victim is not seriously interested in prosecution; or when the victim's plight, considering his own misconduct, is not thought worthy of official attention. Factors such as these influence the police in their adjustment of enforcement priorities.[4]

Before discussing the particular criteria employed, one general observation can be made. Although police decisions not to arrest do lessen the burden upon the prosecutor's office, the courts, the prisons, and the correctional agencies, there is no evidence to

---

[1] Arnold, The Symbols of Government 153 (1935).

[3] In this analysis, warning is not considered a form of invocation of the process. Warning might be viewed as one kind of invocation, inasmuch as the offender learns that his violation has come to official attention and the warning, hopefully, serves to prevent future offenses. However, no established policy exists with regard to the issuance of a warning, except that some police manuals state that a warning may be given for "minor offenses." It is generally quite an arbitrary matter whether a decision not to invoke, as the phrase is used here, is accompanied by a warning. Thus any attempt to select for separate discussion decisions to invoke by warning would tend to give a distorted picture of current practice.

[4] Of course, not all police attempts to allocate law enforcement resources take the form of decisions on whether or not to arrest a particular offender. Priorities of enforcement are largely set by the manner in which a particular police agency is organized. An examination of the distribution of manpower among specialized subagencies may be particularly revealing in this respect.

indicate that they are especially prompted by this consideration.[5] Rather, the practice of not arresting is generally adopted to conserve *police* resources, either those which would be used to arrest, book, and detain the suspect or those necessarily involved later in the process, such as for police testimony at the trial.

This is not to say that the predictable action at later stages of the process has no bearing on police allocation of enforcement resources. Police may not arrest if they believe that there is no likelihood of prosecution or conviction. Also, if the predictable punishment is thought to be either too strict or too lenient, arrest is less likely unless the police have means of influencing the nature of the penalty. Finally, if the conduct is such that it is thought that the criminal process cannot provide the appropriate punishment, deterrence, or rehabilitation, the police may again devote their resources to other cases.[7] Combinations of these factors will appear in the situations which follow.

A. Trivial Offenses

Police manuals often advise the officer that warning rather than arrest is appropriate when only minor violations are concerned. This has the effect of conserving enforcement resources for more serious conduct.

1. *Traffic violations.*

Illustration No. 1: A police officer saw a motorist make an illegal left turn. The officer stopped the driver, brought the violation to his attention, but did not make an arrest and did not write a ticket.

---

[5] Criticism of police lack of consideration for these other agencies was noted only once. A judge of Recorder's Court, Detroit, was critical of the police going into a bar to arrest a drunk, and said: "If the police did this in every bar in Detroit they would have time for nothing else, and if they did the jails would not hold all the drunks."

[7] The police may consider the alternative methods available. The conduct may be best dealt with by a private agency of a civic, recreational, religious, educational, or welfare nature, or by a governmental agency not under the criminal justice system.

Where the conduct calls for penal treatment, it would appear that it could be effectively dealt with by the criminal administration process. However, the distinction between penal treatment and the administration of welfare services is often not clear, even in theory. See Allen, The Borderland of the Criminal Law: Problems of "Socializing" Criminal Justice, 32 Social Serv. Rev. 107 (1958). Even when welfare services are called for, law enforcement agencies may have to handle the situation because of a lack of appropriate public or private welfare facilities. Thus Allen notes that unmarried pregnant women were convicted when they were unable to pay for the necessary hospital expenses and the subsequent care of the child, so that the burden was shifted to the state. Id. at 109.

The use of a warning rather than making an arrest or issuing a ticket is common in cases involving minor traffic offenses. Indeed, the discretion which the officer has the power to exercise in such cases is so well known to the motoring public that an individual motorist is likely to protest if arrested or given a ticket. The practical necessity for the warning alternative in traffic cases is widely acknowledged even by those who deny the propriety of police discretion for more serious offenses. The volume of minor traffic cases is so great that it would be very costly to subject them all to the formal criminal process.[11]

Officers engaged in traffic enforcement in each of the three states studied indicated that the decision to issue a warning rather than a regular citation in a given case is left to the discretion of the individual patrolman. Specific guidance as to what kind of case deserves only a warning is rarely given, except for some written policy on the toleration levels on speeding.[12] The result is that warnings are sometimes given for illegal turns, rolling stops, and the like, but the process is invoked for the same conduct on other occasions, and it is not possible to observe any uniform enforcement pattern in this area. Invocation is the rule, however, if the violation results in a person actually being injured or put in a dangerous situation.[13] Of course, when a warning proves ineffective, then invocation of the process against the violator can be expected. But, unless warnings are made a matter of record, these repeated violations usually are not known.[14]

2. Juvenile offenses.

Illustration No. 2: Residents near a drive-in restaurant complained to the police that a disturbance of the peace was occurring in their neighborhood. A patrol car was dispatched to the scene, and the officers found a group of

---

[11] In one study it was concluded that in Berkeley, California, three million traffic violations were occurring daily, and that full enforcement would require 14,000 traffic officers. Cal. State Dept. of Education, Cal. Peace Officers Training Publication No. 71, Police Supervisory Control 26 (1957).

[12] Thus the radar unit in one Wisconsin community was instructed that when operating in a 25 m.p.h. zone, speeds up to 32 m.p.h. were to be ignored, speeds from 32 to 38 m.p.h. were to be considered cases for warning cards, and drivers going above 38 m.p.h. were to receive regular traffic citations.

[13] Therefore, whereas a speeder on a lonely road might not be arrested, another person driving at the same place, and at the same speed, would be if the traffic were heavy.

[14] Probably the best system observed was in Eau Claire, Wisconsin. There, when a warning is issued, the driver signs a warning card, a copy of which is placed on file. Should a particular driver receive three warnings within a year, the process is invoked with respect to the third violation.

teenagers singing, shouting, and racing the engines of their cars, which created a considerable disturbance. The officers administered severe warnings to the youths and then left.

Minor offenses by juveniles are not usually considered important enough to warrant expenditure of any substantial amount of police enforcement resources. The usual opinion is that such conduct, while proscribed by the penal statutes, is merely a consequence of the minor's immature judgment or youthful exuberance and poses no major threat to society if not proceeded against fully. Thus youthful offenders are often given a warning and sent on their way when the violation is not serious. This frequently occurs in small cities, but in the larger metropolitan areas, such as Detroit and Milwaukee, the warning is more likely to come after arrest. Even in large urban areas, however, it is still common for individual patrolmen to dispose of cases by some means other than arrest.

The level of toleration of juvenile offenses cannot be stated with any great degree of certainty. However, the chance of arrest is great when force or violence has been used against an innocent victim outside the juvenile's social group. Nonviolent property crimes are not thought to warrant arrest unless the amount of damage involved is great or the technique employed is professional in nature. The juvenile's past record is considered very important; it is for this reason that the decision whether to proceed against the juvenile must sometimes wait until after arrest, when it can be determined whether the youth has a record.

The most obvious reason why the police do not feel that petty juvenile offenders need to be arrested is that the offenses are not serious enough to justify official concern. In many cases a warning appears to accomplish all that is necessary. In other cases, although the police consider the juvenile's conduct serious enough to merit punishment, no arrest is made because the officer feels that the juvenile court is too lenient.

The fact that special treatment is given to the juvenile offender following arrest, during trial, and in sentencing and correction might be thought to bring nonenforcement in this area into question. Since these procedures are designed to rehabilitate, it might be argued that it is desirable to subject all youths who commit crimes to arrest and thus to rehabilitative treatment. This consideration does sometimes prompt a peace officer to make an arrest in circumstances which would not be thought to merit the expenditure of police resources were an adult involved. However, in many other cases, the police conclude either that the need for rehabilitative treatment is not great enough to justify the expenditure of their resources or that an arrest would have harmful consequences for the juvenile regardless of what the objectives of the juvenile process are in theory.

3. Drunkenness.

> *Illustration No. 3:* A patrolman came upon a man stag-
> gering down the street. The man was clearly intoxicated
> but, while his gait was unsteady, he was able to walk with-
> out any great risk of falling. Upon questioning the man,
> the patrolman learned that he was on his way home and
> that he lived about a block away. No arrest was made.

Another offense which occurs frequently but is not subject to full enforcement is drunkenness. Even though the statutes in Kansas and Michigan prohibit being intoxicated in public, a substantial number of persons observed in such condition are not arrested. If the person is not a habitual drunk, it is unusual for him to be taken into custody unless he cannot care for his own safety or is likely to cause harm to another. If the drunk is creat-ing a nuisance, this will increase the probability of arrest, but if the disturbance can be stopped and there does not appear to be a significant likelihood of further trouble, an arrest still might not be made. Drunks are often told at the time of arrest that they are being arrested for their own protection, and this fact may be incorporated into the arrest report. An arrest is not usually made when the person evinces a willingness and ability to go home, and in this respect the proximity of the offender's home is a relevant factor. In practice there is a lower level of tolerance for the "skid row" drunk, but this is because arrest is the only way in which to insure his safety.

The intoxicated person who is most likely to cause harm to others is the one who is driving or who is likely to drive if not arrested. While arrest under these circumstances is more likely, the police sometimes utilize an alternative if one is available. Persons under the influence of alcohol who are seen entering cars may be allowed to take a cab home, and even those who have been stopped for erratic driving are sometimes permitted to park their car and resume their journey home by taxi. One tactic which an officer may use when he finds a drunk sleeping in a car is to remove the keys from the ignition and either take them with him or hide them in the back seat of the car, or under the floor rug, thus insuring that the person will not drive until he is sufficiently sober to recover the keys. . . .

B. Conduct Thought to Reflect the Standards of a Community Subgroup

Illustration No. 4: A report that a stabbing had taken place came in to the station of a precinct predominantly Negro in population. An officer reported to the address and learned that a Negro woman had seriously stabbed her husband with a pair of scissors. The husband commented that there had been a little argument and requested transportation to the hospital. The officer, who had served in the precinct for some time, had reported to such calls in the past and had received similar responses. Although the conduct constituted a felonious assault, no official action was taken.

Differential treatment of racial groups may take many forms in law enforcement. One possibility is that members of minority groups may be arrested or may have even more serious action taken against them when they have not in fact engaged in criminal conduct. This quite obviously is improper. A second possibility is that laws which generally are not enforced may be enforced only when violated by members of certain minority groups. Such a practice is not so easy to evaluate, and it is harder for the individual defendant to establish, because it is almost impossible to present adequate proof of the discrimination. A third possibility, and the one of concern here, is the failure to enforce certain laws which are enforced when members of certain minority groups are not involved. This obviously is not thought disadvantageous by the offender himself, but it may be of concern to the victim or to other members of the minority group.

This kind of unequal enforcement of the law frequently occurs when Negroes are involved, particularly in large metropolitan areas such as Detroit. Such offenses as bigamy and open and notorious cohabitation are overlooked by law enforcement officials,[38] and arrests often are not made for carrying knives[39] or for robbery of other Negroes.[40] However, the practice is most strikingly illustrated by the repeated failure of the police to arrest Negroes for a felonious assault upon a spouse or acquaintance unless the victim actually insists upon prosecution.

---

[38] These offenses came to official attention principally when aid to dependent children was sought or when a domestic dispute was being dealt with.

[39] A car occupied by ten Negro youths was stopped and switch-blade knives were found on each of them. The knives were taken, but no arrests were made.

[40] Only one such case was observed, and the facts are unusual because the offender recouped his losses at gunpoint from his co-gamblers but then returned the money before the police located him.

This practice is most apparent in one predominantly Negro precinct in Detroit. The average officer, after spending several months in that precinct, becomes accustomed to the offenses which he is regularly called upon to handle; he accepts the double standard and applies it without question. He does not look upon a stabbing, for example, with the same degree of seriousness as would an officer in one of the other precincts. While settling differences with a knife cannot properly be called the established standard of behavior for Negroes, the officer repeatedly called to cases of this kind is apt to conclude that it is, particularly since his contacts with Negroes are usually confined to the law-breaking, and not the law-abiding, Negro. Thus what might appear to be an aggravated assault to an officer assigned elsewhere would, to the officer in this precinct, be looked upon merely as a family disturbance.

Usually the victim of such an assault does not wish to have the offender prosecuted. Even arrest is not usually desired; the police are called because they are able to provide the victim with ambulance service to the hospital. While the attitude of the victim is an important factor in the exercise of police discretion generally, the assault cases between Negroes are the only apparent situations in which the victim controls the arrest decision when the offense is a serious one. Although the reluctance of the victim to cooperate makes successful prosecution difficult and in many cases impossible, the willingness of the police to accept the decision of the victim indicates that they are not greatly concerned about the problem. . . .

C. Victim Does Not or Will Not Request Prosecution

Police nonenforcement is also the rule when the victim of a minor offense does not wish to expend his own time in the interests of successful prosecution. This occurs not only with minor property crimes, when the victim is concerned primarily with restitution, but also with many offenses arising out of family relationships or other associations, such as that between landlord and tenant or employer and employee.

The reluctance of the victim to prosecute makes conviction difficult or impossible and is at least some indication that the offense is not serious enough to justify the expenditure of time and effort of the police and prosecutor. In those cases arising out of a private relationship, resolution of the difficulty without prosecution may appear to be a more desirable alternative. For these reasons, the police frequently decide to apply their resources to other offenses.

1. *Victim interested only in restitution.*

> *Illustration No. 5:* A merchant called the police after having apprehended a shoplifter in his store. When the merchant was asked by the officer whether he was willing to appear in court to testify, he replied that he could not take time out from his work for this. The officer declined to arrest the shoplifter.

When small amounts of property have been taken without force of violence, the criminal process is not usually invoked unless the victim indicates that he is willing to cooperate in the prosecution of the case. In cases in which the police recover all or a substantial portion of the stolen property, it is likely that the victim will ask that the matter be dropped so that he need not take the time to appear in court. The police usually do not take further action in such cases. Cases of larceny are frequently concluded in this way, as is an occasional burglary. If force or violence has been used in obtaining the property, however, the victim's desire is seldom determinative, although action might not be taken if the act was impulsive and the victim is an acquaintance of the offender. In any of these cases, if the police have already expended considerable resources in investigating the offense, they are less likely to abide by the victim's wishes. In fact, in such a case steps will probably be taken to persuade the victim to commit himself to cooperate in the prosecution.

Probably the most significant category of conduct in which recovery of the stolen property concludes the victim's interest in prosecution is shoplifting. When shoplifters are caught, they are usually apprehended in the act, which results in immediate recovery of the stolen goods. Merchants generally are unwilling to prosecute, asserting that they cannot afford the time away from the store to testify in court or that they do not want to risk a loss of good will. The police reaction is typified by the following statement by an experienced officer to a "rookie":

> Now if that situation ever comes up with you, don't take the person to the station unless you can get somebody to agree to sign a complaint. When I first got on, I went to this store just like we did tonight. I took the shoplifter to the station, booked him through, and then one of the policewomen came up and asked me who the complainant was. Being green, I just looked at her and said, "I don't know." The policewoman informed me that the best thing to do was to turn the individual loose, and that it was a good thing we had not booked him in county jail.

For a while this store manager would not sign complaints; all he wanted the police to do was to throw a little scare into the suspect and get him out of his hair. Now, however, since we have adopted the policy of not taking them unless he will sign a complaint, things have improved, and he only calls when he intends to sign a complaint.

Thus nonenforcement in this type of situation conserves police resources in two ways: no further action need be taken in the particular case, and calls for police service from merchants are substantially diminished. . . .

2. Victim in continuing relationship with offender.

Illustration No. 7: An officer responding to a call learned that the complainant wanted his neighbor arrested for tearing down a part of his fence. The officer's investigation disclosed that this was merely the latest chapter in a continued neighborhood dispute between the complainant and offender. Although the property destruction was a criminal violation, the officer declined to take any official action.

A combination of factors may result in nonenforcement when the criminal conduct involves two persons who are in a continuing legitimate relationship with each other, such as neighbors, landlord and tenant, or parties to a contract. Generally, the police feel that such disputes are principally private in nature and that so long as the conduct is not serious, enforcement resources need not be diverted to it.

Obviously an arrest should not be made when the conduct is not criminal and would warrant only a civil action. The police are warned against acting in such cases and in fact do refuse assistance. However, they may not arrest even when the conduct is criminal if a civil remedy is available to the injured party. The availability of a civil remedy is thought adequate by the police, and their hesitation to act may be increased by a fear of giving an undue advantage to one of the parties. Also, the fact that the victim can resolve his difficulty by terminating his relationship with the offender is important. Thus a landlord was advised to evict his tenant when he wanted criminal action brought against a member of the tenant's household who caused malicious damage to the premises. Similarly, an employer was told that he could handle the situation himself when a minor burglary was found to be an "inside job" perpetrated by an employee.

In such cases, the police are not likely to take any action unless the victim asserts a strong desire for prosecution. They may even discourage the complainant if they feel that he is motivated by spite and that prosecution would only strain a necessarily continuing relationship, such as that between neighbors. The continuing relationship also makes it more likely that the victim will change his mind about prosecution.

Often the police refer these matters to another agency. Putting the burden on the victim to see the prosecutor or magistrate conserves police resources in two ways: first, no action is necessary unless the victim fails to "cool off" and continues his demand for prosecution, and, second, future complaints of this kind to the police are likely to diminish. The police feel that other agencies should take care of restitution cases. The exception is Detroit, where a specialized agency within the police department itself will aid insistent complainants in obtaining restitution.

3. Victim a member of offender's family.

> *Illustration No. 8:* A call was received at the precinct reporting a disturbance of the peace. The officer responding to the call found that the disturbance was due to a family squabble. Although the man was still hitting his wife when the officer arrived, the officer did not make an arrest but merely restored order and left.

The police are sometimes advised to avoid arrest in domestic disputes where possible. For example, the Detroit Police Manual provides:

> When a police officer is called to a disturbance in a private home having family difficulties, he should recognize the sanctity of the home and endeavor diplomatically to quell the disturbance and create peace without making an arrest.
>
> In any case where an officer suspects that a disturbance may result in the injury of any person, it is advisable for the officer to take the person causing such disturbance into custody, at least temporarily, even though it may be against the wishes of the family involved.

This is the policy generally followed in all three states.[67] The police dislike becoming involved in family disputes,[68] and calls

---

[67] For example, when a Detroit officer reported to a family dispute in which a man had struck his wife, the officer told the man that he was acquainted with the man's employer and cautioned him that any further trouble might result in his losing his job. When the husband promised not to resort to physical violence again the officer departed.

[68] Confirming this is the statement of a police official quoted in another study: "You know, if there is one thing these men hate more than anything else it is to go out on a call for a family quarrel. You ought to see

or service may be refused when it does not appear that arrest is essential to maintain order,[69] or when demands upon police services are particularly heavy.[70]

In any event, an officer is unlikely to make an arrest in cases of intrafamily disturbances involving minor offenses such as unaggravated assaults[71] if the offended spouse does not insist upon prosecution. Even if the victim-spouse asserts a desire to prosecute, the officers may still refrain from arresting if it appears likely that the victim will later change his or her mind. Because the police do not wish to expend resources on cases in which the victim will later refuse to cooperate in prosecution, steps are sometimes taken to make it difficult for the insistent victim to change his mind later. In Wichita, the victim-spouse may be taken to the station immediately to sign a complaint before arrest, or the victim may also be arrested in an attempt to insure appearance in court the following day. In Milwaukee the police determine the victim's true desires by giving him a referral memorandum which may later be used to obtain a warrant. The clerk of municipal court, who issues warrants in both ordinance and statute violation cases, will issue warrants under a charge of common drunk or assault upon complaint of the spouse only after a three-day "cooling-off" period. In Detroit the police try to discourage prosecution by the victim-spouse, but they may refer the spouse to the Misdemeanor Complaint Bureau, which does undertake to mediate more serious family disputes. The full burden is on the victim, who must go to the Misdemeanor Complaint Bureau, and no arrest is made in cases where mediation is the goal.

There are exceptions to this policy. Sometimes the circumstances are such that arrest becomes necessary regardless of the offended spouse's attitude. For example, if the police have had to respond to the same address on a number of occasions, an

---

their faces when they hear that call come over the radio." Westley, The Police: A Sociological Study of Law, Custom and Morality 115 (unpublished Ph.D. thesis No. 1197, Dept. of Sociology, Univ. of Chicago, 1951).

[69] For example, a woman called a Michigan State Police post to complain about domestic trouble. The corporal on duty suggested that the woman spend the night elsewhere and then reprimanded the husband over the phone, but declined to send an officer out to make an arrest. Both parties were informed that the state police have no right to take action in a problem such as this except to preserve the peace.

[70] Especially during the hours when police patrol cars are most busy, Detroit precinct dispatchers screen out those family disturbances in which there does not appear to be any threat of excessive violence.

[71] Occasionally officers also decide not to arrest in cases of intrafamily felonious assault, but this was rarely observed except where the parties were Negroes . . . or persons the police referred to as "hillbillies."

arrest will be made. Also, if the officer feels that the incident cannot be closed by a brief lecture, the offender will be taken into custody. Finally, a threat of subsequent serious harm will prompt a decision to arrest even when the victim does not desire prosecution.

D. Victim Involved in Misconduct

Illustration No. 9: A man entered a precinct station and complained that he had just been cheated of $20. Asked to explain, he said that he had given the money to a prostitute who had agreed to meet him at a certain time and place, but that she had failed to appear. The police, although familiar with this kind of racket, subjected the complainant to some ridicule, suggested that he had learned his lesson, and sent him on his way.

In some situations a crime is committed upon a person who is himself engaged in criminal conduct at the time. Indeed, the person's misconduct often increases the likelihood that he will become a victim of criminal action. Such is the case, for example, when a prostitute is mistreated as a direct result of her illegal activity, or when both parties to a fight are at fault. Despite the fact that the criminal activity of the victim would not be a defense in a criminal prosecution of the other party, the police are reluctant to arrest in such cases.

The most frequently observed situation of this kind is that in which a man has been tricked out of funds given to a prostitute or pimp. If the victim is insistent the police may attempt to shame him out of desiring police action, but if this is unsuccessful they may proceed to arrest the offender. Often the police will question the victim in an attempt to determine the extent of his own culpability. He will be asked how long he has lived in the vicinity, and an attempt will be made to learn whether he was sufficiently familiar with the area to know that he was exposing himself to this kind of offense by going there.

There is no established department policy to refuse to arrest under these circumstances, and informal policy has not developed to the point where all such cases are treated in the same way. An officer may detain the prostitute long enough to obtain a return of the victim's money; he may arrest and jail the prostitute; he may detain for a while both the prostitute and the man; or he may release the prostitute but detain the victim for a short time. Those officers who refuse to take action in these cases probably do so in part because they know that such a case cannot be successfully prosecuted. It is not likely that a warrant will be

issued if the complainant does not have "clean hands," and judges
are reluctant to convict in cases of this kind. . . .

ARREST TO CONTROL THE PROSTITUTE

A. The Practice of Arresting Prostitutes for Purposes Other than Prosecution

Suspected prostitutes are clearly the largest category of offenders
arrested in Detroit for purposes other than prosecution. Practically all of these arrests are made in one city precinct, in a relatively small area where streetwalking by individual prostitutes
flourishes. There are no houses of prostitution; rather, patrons
are solicited on the streets and in taverns and other public places,
and then escorted to nearby rooms.

The arrest of suspected prostitutes without intent of prosecution is almost exclusively a practice of the precinct officer. While
some of these arrests are made by regular patrol car officers, a
great majority of them are brought about by officers assigned to
the precinct "whore squads." These officers operate with unmarked cars, and although they are uniformed, they remove their
caps to prevent easy identification. Members of these squads do
not conceal their identity to the extent of plainclothes officers attempting to make accosting and soliciting cases. They are interested only in preventing the girls from seeing them approach in
time to take shelter in some nearby residence. Each night these
squads arrest from forty to fifty women believed or known to be
prostitutes. Most of these women are arrested as they are standing in doorways or on street corners, or while they are slowly
walking down the street. On occasion, they are pursued into res-
idences in the area or are arrested while sitting in a restaurant
or other public place. Occasionally the officers see and arrest a
girl as she is in the process of making a contact with a man.

A booking of D.P.I. (Disorderly Persons Investigation) is always used in this precinct for prostitutes who are not to be prosecuted. In other precincts, where prostitution is far less of a problem, the bookings are either D.P.I. or "investigation of larceny
from the person." The latter booking is based upon the fact that
many of these girls participate in the "Murphy game."* The
procedure is the same whichever entry is made. The women are
not searched at the time of booking at the precinct, but are immediately placed in a large detention area reserved for women pris-

---

* In the "Murphy game" one tells the victim that he knows how to
make contact with a prostitute. The victim gives the one playing the game
money, and he leaves to make the arrangements but never returns. [Eds.
note]

oners. When the number of D.P.I.'s reaches ten, the patrol wagon transports them to the women's detention quarters located at police headquarters. There the women are searched and finger-printed.

On the morning after arrest (except Sundays), a registered nurse reports to the women's detention quarters at 6:30. She immediately takes a smear and culture on each girl with a D.P.I. booking, and if the girl is not a "regular customer" a treatment record is prepared. By 8:00 A.M. the girls are ready for a brief examination by a doctor, also an employee of the city health department. The results are obtained from the laboratory before 11:00 A.M. At this time the girls are called out one at a time for a brief interview with a patrolman from the vice bureau. This officer observed that most of them "would not tell me the right time of day." However, he does manage to build some pandering cases on information obtained from those few, usually inexperienced, prostitutes who will identify their pimps. The infected prisoners are given medication and are asked to report back the next day, which most of them do. In fact, they are not released if they refuse to take medication or refuse to promise to return the following day. Ordinarily, most of these women are back on the street by 11:00 A.M.

The magnitude of this program is indicated by the fact that arrests of the above type often comprise nearly half of this precinct's total arrests. For example, an analysis of all of the bookings in this precinct for a typical two-day period disclosed a total of 75 arrests, 34 of which were D.P.I.'s. The "cleanup squad," charged with vice enforcement at the precinct level, reported 2942 D.P.I. arrests in a six-month period, in which time arrests for accosting and soliciting totaled only 53. There are no departmental statistics which accurately portray how many D.P.I. arrests are made in comparison with the number of prostitutes arrested for purposes of prosecution.

B. Criteria for Selection of Those Who Are Arrested

The objective of the police is to arrest women presently working as prostitutes, who have been or will be guilty of accosting and soliciting, regardless of whether the offense takes place in view of the officer or whether the girl is actually on the street for this purpose at the time of arrest. However, the officers do require some indication that the woman is in fact a prostitute before making an arrest.

For purposes of comparison, it is helpful to identify the amount of evidence of guilt that the police generally feel is necessary in order to make an arrest for accosting and soliciting which will result in prosecution and conviction. First, it is necessary to establish the word, act, or deed by the woman which constitutes the actual accosting, and which shows that the woman accosted the officer and not vice versa. Second, the officer attempts to determine the nature of the immoral act suggested by the woman. Third, the officer is expected to establish the fee requested by the prostitute. If any one of these is lacking, it is not likely that an accosting arrest will be made.

In contrast, a considerable number of the D.P.I. arrests are made upon the basis of the woman's reputation and past record. Thus, if a woman is found in an area in which prostitution is practiced and it is known or thought that she has a past record of arrests for accosting and soliciting or D.P.I., she will be taken into custody.

Often the fact that the girl is a prostitute will be substantiated by the girl herself. She may object to being taken in before she has been able to make any money, or else may object upon the ground that she "was not hustling today." But when a woman is arrested upon the basis of her past record, the officers are not concerned with whether or not she is presently soliciting. Prostitutes may be arrested even if they are in a restaurant or on the street for some other purpose at the time of their arrest. While the prostitutes seem resigned to the fact that they are going to be "D.P.I.'d" if found on the street for purposes of prostitution, they object to this when they consider themselves "off duty." One prostitute brought before the station lieutenant asked, "Is it fair to take us out of the restaurant while we are eating?"

Other women, even in the absence of any knowledge on the officer's part as to a past record, will be arrested when found late at night in areas with a high incidence of prostitution. In such an area, the mere fact that a woman is slowly walking down the street, standing on a corner, or standing in a doorway may be the basis for arrest. In the colder months the prostitutes in these areas are often recognizable by their typical dress for protection against the weather—white leather coats and high boots.

The arrest of women just because they are on the streets at night undoubtedly results in some women being unintentionally subjected to the D.P.I. process, although this does not seem to occur frequently. Often the officers will question the suspect in an attempt to determine if she is in fact a prostitute. It is not uncommon for them to detect some flaw in an elaborate story given by the woman. When confronted with the inconsistency, the woman frequently admits that she is a prostitute. Sometimes the police check the woman's story and learn that she is going to or from a legitimate job, in which case no arrest is made. The mere fact that the woman has no regular employment may result in her being D.P.I.'d even without further evidence that she is a prostitute.

If the woman is accompanied by or is talking to men, she is likely to be arrested unless the men are relatives. Usually she is questioned to determine if she knows all her male associates. Often she can name one but not the other, which leads the officers to believe that she is a prostitute and that one of the men is her pimp. A woman who stops to talk to men in a car will usually be suspect. Association of a woman with men of another race usually results in an immediate conclusion that she is a prostitute. If a Negro woman is found in the company of a white man, she is usually confronted by the police and taken to the station unless it is clear that the association is legitimate.

While officers assigned to the "whore squads" are skilled in determining who is in fact a prostitute, some arrests are made of women who are not prostitutes. Review of these arrests at the precinct station by the lieutenant in charge does not always follow as a matter of course. If the lieutenant is involved in some other task, the woman will be sent directly to the lock-up. When there is review, the lieutenant usually waves on the known prostitutes, but may question the others. Even this varies according to which lieutenant is on duty. Some lieutenants lock up all the women brought in, and if they complain, they are told that this is a mere check and that they will be released in the morning. Often questioning by the lieutenant will establish that the girl is a prostitute. Occasionally either questioning or a check of the girl's record will convince the lieutenant that the girl should be released immediately. Even with the most cautious lieutenant on duty, it is presumed that the girl brought in is a prostitute, and she is released only if it is quite definitely shown that she is not.

C. Reasons for the Practice

While part of the process involves a health examination, it is clear that the police view this as merely a side benefit, and that the practice of arresting suspected prostitutes without intent of prosecution is thought necessary by the police as the only effective means available to deal with prostitution. Said one key official in the department, "Disorderly persons investigation arrests, as practiced primarily in one of the precincts, is a harassment program. The police department has no other means of dealing with prostitution." Similarly, another department official empha-

sized that an officer makes a D.P.I. arrest to accomplish several
purposes:

> First, to get them off the street; second, as a means of harass-
> ment. It's a deterrent. They know when certain officers are
> on the job they are very likely to be picked up and they
> won't go over on that corner. These particular women I
> referred to are not only prostitutes but they are decoys for
> the so-called Murphy game. There have been persons mur-
> dered who came into contact with them. As a general rule,
> in fact almost invariably, these women are out there at two
> o'clock when the saloons close, when the prospective cus-
> tomers have a lot of liquor in them. They don't want to go
> home; they are looking for strange experiences. And we've
> had murders. We had one fellow that was found in an ash-
> can. Now what should we do under those circumstances?
> There's our problem—we have no crimes committed in the
> presence of the police officer, nothing that legally warrants
> the arrest. Shall we say, "Well, now because our hands are
> tied, we are going to let these women alone"?

Thus, the police view the program as a way of removing prostitutes from the street, and thereby also decreasing the amount of
other potential criminal activity. . . .

[The] police do not view [the existing statutes on accosting
and soliciting] . . . as an effective means of dealing with the
great number of prostitutes. In the first place, limitations upon
resources make it difficult to build cases against a significant number of the prostitutes. Secondly, the actual making of a case by
a police officer presents many difficulties. The statutory definition of the offense requires that the woman "accost, solicit or
invite another . . . by word, gesture or any other means, to
commit prostitution . . ." On the basis of their experience in
the local trial courts, the police have concluded that they must
prove the woman was the initiator, that the specific nature of the
immoral act was suggested, and that the specific price was agreed
upon. Not only is the experienced prostitute often able to identify plainclothes officers, but she may routinely avoid making any
statements encompassing all three elements.

As a consequence, the police have considerable difficulty obtaining convictions in accosting cases. Judges frequently dismiss
such prosecutions, giving as a reason the defense of entrapment,
or "enticement" in situations where it is doubtful whether the
doctrine of entrapment, as defined in appellate opinions, is applicable. According to the police, dismissals have been granted in
accosting cases where the officer used a Cadillac, because "every-

one knows that the police officers use cheap cars"; where the officer disguised himself as a taxi driver or uniformed laborer; where the officer made a telephone call to a number which he had obtained and which he was told belonged to a prostitute; where the officer stopped his car beside a prostitute on a street corner when she had not beckoned to him; and where the officer bought the girl a few drinks or otherwise spent some time with her before the accosting.

Some police attribute the difficulty to the fact that some judges do not properly understand the doctrine of entrapment. However, it seems apparent that the frequent dismissals on grounds of entrapment are merely symptoms reflecting a much deeper difference of opinion between the police and the judges. Such dismissals are often attributable to a variety of assumptions or opinions about the prostitution problem. Some judges believe that unorganized prostitution is not a serious offense, that vice in Detroit is at an irreducible minimum, and that consequently there is too great an allocation of police time and resources to vice enforcement and too little to crimes involving serious harm to persons and property. Another view is that the individual prostitute is to be "pitied" rather than "persecuted" by prosecution and conviction. Some judges feel that the methods used by police to induce women to solicit prostitution are overly aggressive, even if not technically sufficient to constitute entrapment. One judge labels this "enticement" rather than "entrapment."

The police appear to be partly responsible for the difficulty. They have not always been properly instructed in making accosting cases, and some cases have been presented in which these reactions against police methods might be expected. The difficulty is compounded because the police, knowing of the judicial hostility, sometimes feel compelled to embellish their testimony to make a better case. The judge is often able to detect this, and may conclude that the officers probably are also distorting other aspects of the case. These factors often contribute to minimum fines being imposed in cases where a conviction is obtained.

The judicial concern with the accosting and soliciting cases is not reflected in a similar attitude toward the D.P.I. program. Judges who are aware of the D.P.I. program informally approve of it. They feel that the police department is simply making an attempt to cut down the nuisance aspect of prostitution, particularly in areas of the city where law-abiding citizens are likely to be accosted. Thus, while the D.P.I. program may have been originally attributable to the refusal to convict in accosting cases, it now appears that the reluctance to convict is in part due to an attitude by the courts that the D.P.I. program is an adequate alternative. As a consequence, police rely heavily on the D.P.I. program as a method of control. One high-ranking police official said that he felt the situation could be changed only through an interchange of information at the highest level and a forthright disclosure of the views of the police, the prosecutor, and the courts.

NOTES AND QUESTIONS

1. The LaFave study was the first monograph to appear out of a major investigation of the administration of criminal justice in the United States, under the general editorship of Frank J. Remington, Professor of Law at the University of Wisconsin. The American Bar Foundation is sponsoring the study. The second volume in the series, *Conviction: The Determination of Guilt or Innocence Without Trial*, by Donald J. Newman, was published in 1966. A third volume, Lawrence P. Tiffany, Donald M. McIntyre, Jr. & Daniel L. Rotenberg, *Detection of Crime*, was published in 1967. Another product of the Bar Foundation study is Robert O. Dawson, "The Decision to Grant or Deny Parole: A Study of Parole Criteria in Law and Practice," 1966 *Washington University Law Quarterly* 243.

In recent years, scholarly interest in the police has markedly increased. *See, e.g.,* David J. Bordua ed., *The Police: Six Sociological Essays* (John Wiley 1967); David H. Bayley & Harold Mendelsohn, *Minorities and the Police, Confrontation in America* (Free Press 1969). An excerpt from Jerome Skolnick's study of a police department, *Justice Without Trial: Law Enforcement in Democratic Society*, appears at 900, *infra*.

2. In what ways does Professor LaFave go beyond conventional legal research in gathering his materials? What are the advantages and disadvantages of so doing?

3. The presentation by Professor LaFave is nonquantitative. His materials are not presented in the form of tables, graphs and charts; and there are no statistics. Professor LaFave worked with data, much of which had been gathered by others, and which was observational but not quantitative. What are the advantages and disadvantages of this approach to the gathering of data in a study of police behavior?

4. Professor LaFave gives many reasons why police practice does not conform with the rules which theoretically govern their behavior. Some of these reasons relate to the structure of police forces, that is, how police forces are organized and run; some relate to the resources available to the police; some to the values

of the public; some to the behavior of the members of the public who violate the law; some to the values held by the police themselves. Which of these are most important in LaFave's view? in yours?

5. LaFave presents evidence that the police themselves are deviants: they are not obeying the rules which are supposed to govern their own behavior. Does the deviance of the police, as described in these excerpts, constitute, in your view, a major social problem? Why? A major legal problem? Why? *See Rights in Conflict,* a report submitted by Daniel Walker, Director of the Chicago Study Team, to the National Commission on the Causes and Prevention of Violence (1968). This report deals with the response of the Chicago police to demonstrations during the Democratic National Convention in 1968. It said that the "nature of the response was unrestrained" and that there was "indiscriminate police violence on many occasions." Could one argue that this deviant conduct was, to some extent, related to the kind of deviant conduct described by LaFave?

6. Harassment is frequently used to deal with homosexuals in Los Angeles County and probably elsewhere. For example, a marked patrol car can be parked in front of a suspected "gay bar." The police may check to see whether the fire department regulations regarding the maximum number of occupants have been violated by ordering all patrons to line up for a count. They may check identification frequently during an evening. Upon leaving, the patrons may be arrested for minor crimes such as jaywalking or failing to come to a full stop before crossing the sidewalk when leaving a parking lot. *See* "Project, The Consenting Adult Homosexual and the Law: An Empirical Study of Enforcement and Administration in Los Angeles County," 13 *UCLA Law Review* 643, 719-20 (1966). Most of these methods are within the letter of the law, but they are not applied to patrons of other bars.

Compare the following judicial opinion: Lenske v. United States, 383 F.2d 20, 27-28 (9th Cir. 1967).

Lenske, a lawyer, was convicted in a trial without a jury of evading payment of his federal income tax. The government's case was based on the "net worth" method. It began with Lenske's assets and liabilities at a certain time and compared them with his net worth at a much later time. It then reconstructed his earnings and expenditures during this period, relying primarily on Lenske's tax returns. It established to the trial court's satisfaction that one could not arrive at Lenske's present net worth without additional unreported income. The United

States Court of Appeals for the Ninth Circuit ruled that the trial judge erred in denying Lenske's motion for a new trial and reversed the conviction.

Additional separate opinion of MADDEN, Judge:

As appears in the second paragraph of the opinion of the court, a Special Agent was assigned to the investigation of the defendant's tax case. The Special Agent and the Revenue Agent thereafter devoted their full time for two and one-half years to this assignment.

On June 13, 1961, the Special Agent made his report to his superior, the District Director of Internal Revenue. The report consisted of 37 closely type-written pages, followed by an appendix of 84 pages which listed 468 exhibits, and the names and addresses of 315 witnesses who would be available to testify for the prosecution if criminal proceedings were initiated. The report recommended criminal prosecution. Near the beginning of the report, under the heading, "History of Taxpayer," after stating, among other things, that Lenske had been born in Russia, reared in Minneapolis, had been a resident of Portland, Oregon, since 1925, had lived in the same house since 1936, and had no known criminal record, the report continued:

> "Representatives of the Federal Bureau of Investigation, Portland, and the Intelligence Division of the Portland Police Department stated that they have reason to believe that Mr. Lenske is a communist. In fact, they each maintain an extensive file on Mr. Lenske."

The report then stated that attached to the report were Exhibit 3A, a newspaper clipping stating that Lenske and another lawyer had called a meeting for the purpose of forming a local chapter of the Lawyers' Guild, and Exhibit 3B, which indicated "Mr. Lenske's thinking on the subject of Cuba, Laos, China, etc." I take judicial notice that the Lawyers' Guild is a national organization including many left-wing lawyers. I take judicial notice that there is in this country and in the world a great variety of "thoughts on Cuba, Laos, China, etc."

An examination of the exhibits shows that Exhibit 3A is a short news story stating that another lawyer and Lenske had called a meeting at a hotel for the purpose of organizing a local chapter of the Lawyers' Guild, and that a feature of the meeting would be the showing of a controversial film "Operation Abolition." Exhibit 3B is a rather long letter to the editor, from Lenske, in which Lenske expresses the thought that in "Cuba, Laos, China, etc." this country's actions had been in violation of our own laws and treaties, and in violation of international law.

I regard what I have recited above as a scandal of the first magnitude in the administration of the tax laws of the United States. It discloses nothing less than a witch-hunt, a crusade by the key agent of the United States in this prosecution, to rid our society of unorthodox thinkers and actors by using federal income tax laws and federal courts to put them in the penitentiary. No court should become an accessory to such a project.

When the Special Agent's report came in to his superiors, with his naive disclosure at the very beginning of his report that he placed high among the reasons why Lenske should be criminally prosecuted for income tax evasion Lenske's being a left-wing lawyer and having unorthodox political and social ideas, his superiors should have immediately removed him from the case and discarded every judgment which was contained in his recommendation. The Special Agent had given his superiors express notice that he was confused with regard to his duties and with regard to the basic ideals of his government. Discarding two and one-half years of dedicated endeavor of the Special Agent would have been a small price to pay to get the Government and its awesome taxing authority back on the path of fairness and decency.

The judgments which the Special Agent formed and embodied in his recommendation that Lenske be criminally prosecuted can only be described as grotesque. His two and one-half years of investigation had convinced him that Lenske had evaded taxes in the amount of $11,465.74 for the year 1955. The trial resulted in a finding that Lenske's taxes for 1955 would have been $414.78. The Special Agent determined Lenske's taxes to be 27 times as much as the court found them to be. On an examination testing his accuracy, the Special Agent would have scored less than 4 out of a possible 100. For the year 1957 the Special Agent's report said that Lenske had evaded $19,412.88 in taxes. The judgment of the court was that his taxes were $1006.18. The Special Agent's report thus charged Lenske with nineteen times as much tax as the court found that he owed. The Special Agent's score was less than 6 out of a possible 100. For the year 1958, the report said Lenske should have paid $7,746.85. The court found that his taxes were $4,682.99, but that he had paid $2,000 in estimated tax. That left him owing $2,682.99. The Special Agent testified that he had, in his investigation, conducted perhaps 1500 interviews. He might well have found time to look at the Government's record of Lenske's 1958 payments of $2,000 of estimated tax. The Special Agent's report thus attributed three times as much tax to Lenske as he owed for 1958. This was the Special Agent's best score, some 33 out of a possible 100. For 1956, the Special Agent's report said that Lenske should have paid a tax of $5,225.77. The court found that Lenske had no taxable income for 1956, but had a loss of $9,231.59. The Special Agent's examination score for 1956 would be, then, some almost incalculable number below zero.

The Special Agent was, so far as the record shows, technically competent and experienced. Such gross miscalculations as we have recited make it evident that some element, foreign to the functions and duties of a government tax officer, was corroding his judgment. Whether that corrosive element was that he had views differing from Lenske's about the Lawyers' Guild, or about "Cuba, Laos, China, etc." or about other political and social problems, or was something else that we cannot even imagine, the consequence is that no confidence whatever should be placed in the Special Agent's conclusions in this case. Yet he was not only the Government's investigator but the Government's principal witness in the trial. Under his supervision the complicated charts and computations were prepared. He presented and explained them to the court. He testified that he interviewed more than 500 witnesses, perhaps as many as 1500, and read "thousands, thousands" of documents.

I am authorized by Judge Hamley to say that he shares my opinion of the gross impropriety of the motivation of the Government's investigation of this case.

If the attempted conviction of Lenske offends you, do you feel the same way about using the income tax laws to put men like Al Capone in jail, that is, gangsters and members of organized crime syndicates, rather than people with unpopular political beliefs?

See also the discussion of "covert functions" of the criminal law in Herbert L. Packer, *The Limits of the Criminal Sanction* 293-95 (Stanford U. Press 1968).

7. It has been argued that the goal of law enforcement should be full application of all laws. It is recognized that there always will be a margin for judgment as to whether or not the law has

been broken. Since we now have so many obsolete laws, we could not immediately move to a policy of full enforcement but great efforts are justified to get as near this goal as possible. *See* Joseph Goldstein, "Police Discretion Not to Invoke the Criminal Process: Low-Visibility Decisions in the Administration of Justice," 69 *Yale Law Journal* 543 (1960). But one may ask, first, whether full enforcement is even possible, and second, whether it would not involve many hidden costs and disruptions, no matter how much improvement is made in the formal law. *See* Friedman, "Legal Rules and the Process of Social Change," Reading 53, at 492, *infra*.

Perhaps the difficulties of full enforcement are best alleviated by restricting the scope of criminal sanctions to especially blameworthy conduct and avoiding criminal sanctions that cannot be fully enforced. *See* Herbert L. Packer, *The Limits of the Criminal Sanction* 286-90 (Stanford U. Press 1968).

8. Another "low-visibility" decision is the decision whether to prosecute or whether to turn an offender in to the police at all. LaFave presents some data on this point. A recent and most illuminating study, Gerald D. Robin, "The Corporate and Judicial Disposition of Employee Thieves," 1967 *Wisconsin Law Review* 685, deals with the way in which department stores handle employees caught stealing from the firm. The overall prosecution rate for the three major stores which were the subject of the study was 17%; one store prosecuted a mere 2% of its 584 offenders during the period of the study.

On prosecutors' decision-making, *see* "The Prosecutorial Discretion—A Comment," by John Kaplan, 60 *Northwestern Law Review* 174 (1965); Jerome H. Skolnick, "Social Control in the Adversary System," 11 *Journal of Conflict Resolution* 52, 54-60 (1967). For an empirical study of police and prosecutor discretion, *see* "Project, Marijuana Laws: An Empirical Study of Enforcement and Administration in Los Angeles County," 15 *UCLA Law Review* 1499 (1968).

11. The Practice of Law as Confidence Game: Organizational Cooptation of a Profession

ABRAHAM S. BLUMBERG*

1 LAW & SOCIETY REVIEW 15 (1967)

Scant attention—apart from explorations of the legal profession itself—has been given to the sociological examination of legal institutions, or their supporting ideological assumptions. Thus, for example, very little sociological effort is expended to ascertain the validity and viability of important court decisions, which may rest on wholly erroneous assumptions about the contextual realities of social structure. A particular decision may rest upon a legally impeccable rationale; at the same time it may be rendered nugatory or self-defeating by contingencies imposed by aspects of social reality of which the lawmakers are themselves unaware.

Within this context, I wish to question the impact of three recent landmark decisions of the United States Supreme Court; each hailed as destined to effect profound changes in the future of criminal law administration and enforcement in America.

[The cases referred to are Gideon v. Wainwright, 372 U.S. 335 (1963), which "required states and localities henceforth to furnish counsel in the case of indigent persons charged with a felony"; Escobedo v. Illinois, 378 U.S. 478 (1964), in which the "court asserted that counsel must be permitted when the process of police investigative effort shifts from merely investigatory to that of accusatory"; and Miranda v. Arizona, 384 U.S. 436 (1966), which held that "police interrogation of any suspect in custody, without his consent, unless a defense attorney is present, is prohibited by the self-incrimination provision of the Fifth Amendment." Blumberg continues:]

---

* Abraham S. Blumberg, Ph.D., Professor of Sociology and Law, City University of New York. Reprinted from Law and Society Review. Copyright © 1967 by the Law and Society Association. Reprinted by permission.

In all three decisions, the Supreme Court reiterates the traditional legal conception of a defense lawyer based on the ideological perception of a criminal case as an *adversary, combative* proceeding, in which counsel for the defense assiduously musters all the admittedly limited resources at his command to *defend* the accused. The fundamental question remains to be answered: Does the Supreme Court's conception of the role of counsel in a criminal case square with social reality?

The task of this paper is to furnish some preliminary evidence toward the illumination of that question. Little empirical understanding of the function of defense counsel exists; only some ideologically oriented generalizations and commitments. This paper is based upon observations made by the writer during many years of legal practice in the criminal courts of a large metropolitan area. No claim is made as to its methodological rigor, although it does reflect a conscious and sustained effort for participant observation.

Court Structure Defines Role of Defense Lawyer

The overwhelming majority of convictions in criminal cases (usually over 90 per cent) are not the product of a combative, trial-by-jury process at all, but instead merely involve the sentencing of the individual after a negotiated, bargained-for plea of guilty has been entered. Although more recently the overzealous role of police and prosecutors in producing pretrial confessions and admissions has achieved a good deal of notoriety, scant attention has been paid to the organizational structure and personnel of the criminal court itself. Indeed, the extremely high conviction rate produced without the features of an adversary trial in our courts would tend to suggest that the "trial" becomes a perfunctory reiteration and validation of the pretrial interrogation and investigation.

The institutional setting of the court defines a role for the defense counsel in a criminal case radically different from the one traditionally depicted. Sociologists and others have focused their attention on the deprivations and social disabilities of such variables as race, ethnicity, and social class as being the source of an accused person's defeat in a criminal court. Largely overlooked is the variable of the court organization itself, which possesses a thrust, purpose, and direction of its own. It is grounded in pragmatic values, bureaucratic priorities, and administrative instruments. These exalt maximum production and the particularistic career designs of organizational incumbents, whose occupational and career commitments tend to generate a set of priorities. These priorities exert a higher claim than the stated ideological goals of "due process of law," and are often inconsistent with them.

Organizational goals and discipline impose a set of demands and conditions of practice on the respective professions in the criminal court, to which they respond by abandoning their ideological and professional commitments to the accused client, in the service of these higher claims of the court organization. All court personnel, including the accused's own lawyer, tend to be coopted to become agent-mediators[10] who help the accused redefine his situation and restructure his perceptions concomitant with a plea of guilty.

Of all the occupational roles in the court the only private individual who is officially recognized as having a special status and concomitant obligations is the lawyer. His legal status is that of "an officer of the court" and he is held to a standard of ethical performance and duty to his client as well as to the court. This obligation is thought to be far higher than that expected of ordinary individuals occupying the various occupational statuses in the court community. However, lawyers, whether privately retained or of the legal-aid, public defender variety, have close and continuing relations with the prosecuting office and the court itself through discreet relations with the judges via their law secretaries or "confidential" assistants. Indeed, lines of communication, influence and contact with those offices, as well as with the Office of the Clerk of the court, Probation Division, and with the press, are essential to present and prospective requirements of criminal law practice. Similarly, the subtle involvement of the press and other mass media in the court's organizational network is not readily discernible to the casual observer. Accused persons come and go in the court system schema, but the structure and its occupational incumbents remain to carry on their respective career, occupational and organizational enterprises. The individual stridencies, tensions, and conflicts a given accused person's case may present to all the participants are overcome, because the formal and informal relations of all the groups in the court setting require it. The probability of continued future relations and interaction must be preserved at all costs.

This is particularly true of the "lawyer regulars" i.e., those defense lawyers, who by virtue of their continuous appearances in behalf of defendants, tend to represent the bulk of a criminal

---

[10] I use the concept in the general sense that Erving Goffman employed it in his ASYLUMS: ESSAYS ON THE SOCIAL SITUATION OF MENTAL PATIENTS AND OTHER INMATES (1961).

court's non-indigent case workload, and those lawyers who are not "regulars," who appear almost casually in behalf of an occasional client. Some of the "lawyer regulars" are highly visible as one moves about the major urban centers of the nation, their offices line the back streets of the courthouses, at times sharing space with bondsmen. Their political "visibility" in terms of local club house ties, reaching into the judge's chambers and prosecutor's office, are also deemed essential to successful practitioners. Previous research has indicated that the "lawyer regulars" make no effort to conceal their dependence upon police, bondsmen, jail personnel. Nor do they conceal the necessity for maintaining intimate relations with all levels of personnel in the court setting as a means of obtaining, maintaining, and building their practice. These informal relations are the *sine qua non* not only of retaining a practice, but also in the negotiation of pleas and sentences.

The client, then, is a secondary figure in the court system as in certain other bureaucratic settings. He becomes a means to other ends of the organization's incumbents. He may present doubts, contingencies, and pressures which challenge existing informal arrangements or disrupt them; but these tend to be resolved in favor of the continuance of the organization and its relations as before. There is a greater community of interest among all the principal organizational structures and their incumbents than exists elsewhere in other settings. The accused's lawyer has far greater professional, economic, intellectual and other ties to the various elements of the court system than he does to his own client. In short, the court is a closed community.

This is more than just the case of the usual "secrets" of bureaucracy which are fanatically defended from an outside view. Even all elements of the press are zealously determined to report on that which will not offend the board of judges, the prosecutor, probation, legal-aid, or other officials, in return for privileges and courtesies granted in the past and to be granted in the future. Rather than any view of the matter in terms of some variation of a "conspiracy" hypothesis, the simple explanation is one of an ongoing system handling delicate tensions, managing the trauma produced by law enforcement and administration, and requiring almost pathological distrust of "outsiders" bordering on group paranoia.

The hostile attitude toward "outsiders" is in large measure engendered by a defensiveness itself produced by the inherent deficiencies of assembly line justice, so characteristic of our major criminal courts. Intolerably large caseloads of defendants which must be disposed of in an organizational context of limited resources and personnel, potentially subject the participants in the court community to harsh scrutiny from appellate courts, and other public and private sources of condemnation. As a consequence, an almost irreconcilable conflict is posed in terms of intense pressures to process large numbers of cases on the one hand, and the stringent ideological and legal requirements of "due process of law," on the other hand. A rather tenuous resolution of the dilemma has emerged in the shape of a large variety of bureaucratically ordained and controlled "work crimes," short cuts, deviations, and outright rule violations adopted as court practice in order to meet production norms. Fearfully anticipating criticism on ethical as well as legal grounds, all the significant participants in the court's social structure are bound into an organized system of complicity. This consists of a work arrangement in which the patterned, covert, informal breaches, and evasions of "due process" are institutionalized, but are, nevertheless, denied to exist.

These institutionalized evasions will be found to occur to some degree, in all criminal courts. Their nature, scope and complexity are largely determined by the size of the court, and the character of the community in which it is located, *e.g.*, whether it is a large, urban institution, or a relatively small rural county court. In addition, idiosyncratic, local conditions may contribute to a unique flavor in the character and quality of the criminal law's administration in a particular community. However, in most instances a variety of stratagems are employed—some subtle, some crude, in effectively disposing of what are often too large caseloads. A wide variety of coercive devices are employed against an accused-client, couched in a depersonalized, instrumental, bureaucratic version of due process of law, and which are in reality a perfunctory obeisance to the ideology of due process. These include some very explicit pressures which are exerted in some measure by all court personnel, including judges, to plead guilty and avoid trial. In many instances the sanction of a potentially harsh sentence is utilized as the visible alternative to pleading guilty, in the case of recalcitrants. Probation and psychiatric reports are "tailored" to organizational needs, or are at least responsive to the court organization's requirements for the refurbishment of a defendant's social biography, consonant with his new status. A resourceful judge can, through his subtle domination of the proceedings, impose his will on the final outcome of a trial. Stenographers and clerks, in their function as record keepers, are on occasion pressed into service in support of a judicial need to "rewrite" the record of a courtroom event. Bail practices are usually employed for purposes other than simply assuring a defendant's presence on the date of a hearing in connection with his case. Too often, the discretionary power as to bail is part of the arsenal of weapons available to collapse the resistance of an accused person. The foregoing is a most cursory examination of some of the more prominent "short cuts" available to any court organization. There are numerous other procedural strategies constituting due process deviations, which tend to become the work style artifacts of a court's personnel. Thus, only court "regulars" who are "bound in" are really accepted; others are treated routinely and in almost a coldly correct manner.

The defense attorneys, therefore, whether of the legal-aid, public defender variety, or privately retained, although operating in terms of pressures specific to their respective role and organizational obligations, ultimately are concerned with strategies which tend to lead to a plea. It is the rational, impersonal elements involving economies of time, labor, expense and a superior commitment of the defense counsel to these rationalistic values of maximum production of court organization that prevail, in his relationship with a client. The lawyer "regulars" are frequently former staff members of the prosecutor's office and utilize the prestige, know-how and contacts of their former affiliation as part of their stock in trade. Close and continuing relations between the lawyer "regular" and his former colleagues in the prosecutor's office generally overshadow the relationship between the regular and his client. The continuing colleagueship of supposedly adversary counsel rests on real professional and organizational needs of a *quid pro quo*, which goes beyond the limits of an accommodation or *modus vivendi* one might ordinarily expect under the circumstances of an otherwise seemingly adversary relationship. Indeed, the adversary features which are manifest are for the most part muted and exist even in their attenuated form largely for external consumption. The principals, lawyer and assistant district attorney, rely upon one another's cooperation for their continued professional existence, and so the bargaining between them tends usually to be "reasonable" rather than fierce.

FEE COLLECTION AND FIXING

The real key to understanding the role of defense counsel in a criminal case is to be found in the area of the fixing of the fee to be charged and its collection. The problem of fixing and collecting the fee tends to influence to a significant degree the criminal court process itself, and not just the relationship of the lawyer and his client. In essence, a lawyer-client "confidence game" is played. A true confidence game is unlike the case of the emperor's new clothes wherein that monarch's nakedness was a result of inordinate gullibility and credulity. In a genuine confidence game, the perpetrator manipulates the basic dishonesty of his partner, the victim or mark, toward his own (the confidence operator's) ends. Thus, "the victim of a con scheme must have some larceny in his heart."[14]

Legal service lends itself particularly well to confidence games. Usually, a plumber will be able to demonstrate empirically that he has performed a service by clearing up the stuffed drain, repairing the leaky faucet or pipe—and therefore merits his fee. He has rendered, when summoned, a visible, tangible boon for his client in return for the requested fee. A physician, who has not performed some visible surgery or otherwise engaged in some readily discernible procedure in connection with a patient, may be deemed by the patient to have "done nothing" for him. As a consequence, medical practitioners may simply prescribe or administer by injection a placebo to overcome a patient's potential reluctance or dissatisfaction in paying a requested fee, "for nothing."

In the practice of law there is a special problem in this regard, no matter what the level of the practitioner or his place in the hierarchy of prestige. Much legal work is intangible either because it is simply a few words of advice, some preventive action, a telephone call, negotiation of some kind, a form filled out and filed, a hurried conference with another attorney or an official of a government agency, a letter or opinion written, or a countless variety of seemingly innocuous, and even prosaic procedures and actions. These are the basic activities, apart from any possible court appearance, of almost all lawyers, at all levels of practice. Much of the activity is not in the nature of the exercise of the traditional, precise professional skills of the attorney such as library research and oral argument in connection with appellate briefs, court motions, trial work, drafting of opinions, memoranda, contracts, and other complex documents and agreements. Instead, much legal activity, whether it is at the lowest or highest "white shoe" law firm levels, is of the brokerage, agent, sales representative, lobbyist type of activity, in which the lawyer acts for someone else in pursuing the latter's interests and designs. The service is intangible.

The large scale law firm may not speak as openly of their "contacts," their "fixing" abilities, as does the lower level lawyer. They trade instead upon a facade of thick carpeting, walnut panelling, genteel low pressure, and superficialities of traditional

---

14 R. L. Gasser, *The Confidence Game*, 27 FED. PROB. 47 (1963).

legal professionalism. There are occasions when even the large firm is on the defensive in connection with the fees they charge because the services rendered or results obtained do not appear to merit the fee asked. Therefore, there is a recurrent problem in the legal profession in fixing the amount of fee, and in justifying the basis for the requested fee.

Although the fee at times amounts to what the traffic and the conscience of the lawyer will bear, one further observation must be made with regard to the size of the fee and its collection. The defendant in a criminal case and the material gain he may have acquired during the course of his illicit activities are soon parted. Not infrequently the ill gotten fruits of the various modes of larceny are sequestered by a defense lawyer in payment of his fee. Inexorably, the amount of the fee is a function of the dollar value of the crime committed, and is frequently set with meticulous precision at a sum which bears an uncanny relationship to that of the net proceeds of the particular offense involved. On occasion, defendants have been known to commit additional offenses while at liberty on bail, in order to secure the requisite funds with which to meet their obligations for payment of legal fees. Defense lawyers condition even the most obtuse clients to recognize that there is a firm interconnection between fee payment and the zealous exercise of professional expertise, secret knowledge, and organizational "connections" in their behalf. Lawyers, therefore, seek to keep their clients in a proper state of tension, and to arouse in them the precise edge of anxiety which is calculated to encourage prompt fee payment. Consequently, the client attitude in the relationship between defense counsel and an accused is in many instances a precarious admixture of hostility, mistrust, dependence, and sycophancy. By keeping his client's anxieties aroused to the proper pitch, and establishing a seemingly causal relationship between a requested fee and the accused's ultimate extrication from his onerous difficulties, the lawyer will have established the necessary preliminary groundwork to assure a minimum of haggling over the fee and its eventual payment.

In varying degrees, as a consequence, all law practice involves a manipulation of the client and a stage management of the lawyer-client relationship so that at least an *appearance* of help and service will be forthcoming. This is accomplished in a variety of ways, often exercised in combination with each other. At the outset, the lawyer-professional employs with suitable variation a measure of sales-puff which may range from an air of unbounding selfconfidence, adequacy, and dominion over events, to that of complete arrogance. This will be supplemented by the affectation of a studied, faultless mode of personal attire. In the larger firms, the furnishings and office trappings will serve as the backdrop to help in impression management and client intimidation. In all firms, solo or large scale, an access to secret knowledge, and to the seats of power and influence is inferred, or presumed to a varying degree as the basic vendible commodity of the practitioners.

The lack of visible end product offers a special complication in the course of the professional life of the criminal court lawyer with respect to his fee and in his relations with his client. The plain fact is that an accused in a criminal case always "loses" even when he has been exonerated by an acquittal, discharge, or dismissal of his case. The hostility of an accused which follows as a consequence of his arrest, incarceration, possible loss of job, expense and other traumas connected with his case is directed, by means of displacement, toward his lawyer. It is in this sense that it may be said that a criminal lawyer never really "wins" a case. The really satisfied client is rare, since in the very nature of the situation even an accused's vindication leaves him with some degree of dissatisfaction and hostility. It is this state of affairs that makes for a lawyer-client relationship in the criminal court which tends to be a somewhat exaggerated version of the usual lawyer-client confidence game.

At the outset, because there are great risks of nonpayment of the fee, due to the impecuniousness of his clients, and the fact that a man who is sentenced to jail may be a singularly unappreciative client, the criminal lawyer collects his fee *in advance*. Often, because the lawyer and the accused both have questionable designs of their own upon each other, the confidence game can be played. The criminal lawyer must serve three major functions, or stated another way, he must solve three problems. First, he must arrange for his fee; second, he must prepare and then, if necessary, "cool out" his client in case of defeat[17] (a highly likely contingency); third, he must satisfy the court organization that he has performed adequately in the process of negotiating the plea, so as to preclude the possibility of any sort of embarrassing incident which may serve to invite "outside" scrutiny.

_____

[17] Talcott Parsons indicates that the social role and function of the lawyer can be therapeutic, helping his client psychologically in giving him necessary emotional support at critical times. The lawyer is also said to be acting as an agent of social control in the counseling of his client and in the influencing of his course of conduct. See T. PARSONS, ESSAYS IN SOCIOLOGICAL THEORY 382 et seq. (1954); E. GOFFMAN, *On Cooling the Mark Out: Some Aspects of Adaptation to Failure*, in HUMAN BEHAVIOR AND SOCIAL PROCESSES 482-505 (A. Rose ed., 1962). Goffman's "cooling out" analysis is especially relevant in the lawyer-accused client relationship.

In assuring the attainment of one of his primary objectives, his fee, the criminal lawyer will very often enter into negotiations with the accused's kin, including collateral relatives. In many instances, the accused himself is unable to pay any sort of fee or anything more than a token fee. It then becomes important to involve as many of the accused's kin as possible in the situation. This is especially so if the attorney hopes to collect a significant part of a proposed substantial fee. It is not uncommon for several relatives to contribute toward the fee. The larger the group, the greater the possibility that the lawyer will collect a sizable fee by getting contributions from each.

A fee for a felony case which ultimately results in a plea, rather than a trial, may ordinarily range anywhere from $500 to $1,500. Should the case go to trial, the fee will be proportionately larger, depending upon the length of the trial. But the larger the fee the lawyer wishes to exact, the more impressive his performance must be, in terms of his stage managed image as a personage of great influence and power in the court organization. Court personnel are keenly aware of the extent to which a lawyer's stock in trade involves the precarious stage management of an image which goes beyond the usual professional flamboyance, and for this reason alone the lawyer is "bound in" to the authority system of the court's organizational discipline. Therefore, to some extent, court personnel will aid the lawyer in the creation and maintenance of that impression. There is a tacit commitment to the lawyer by the court organization, apart from formal etiquette, to aid him in this. Such augmentation of the lawyer's stage managed image as this affords, is the partial basis for the *quid pro quo* which exists between the lawyer and the court organization. It tends to serve as the continuing basis for the higher loyalty of the lawyer to the organization; his relationship with his client, in contrast, is transient, ephemeral and often superficial.

DEFENSE LAWYER AS DOUBLE AGENT

The lawyer has often been accused of stirring up unnecessary litigation, especially in the field of negligence. He is said to acquire a vested interest in a cause of action or claim which was initially his client's. The strong incentive of possible fee motivates the lawyer to promote litigation which would otherwise never have developed. However, the criminal lawyer develops a vested interest of an entirely different nature in his client's case: to limit its scope and duration rather than do battle. Only in this way can a case be "profitable." Thus, he enlists the aid of relatives not only to assure payment of his fee, but he will also rely on these persons to help him in his agent-mediator role of convincing the accused to plead guilty, and ultimately to help in "cooling out" the accused if necessary.

It is at this point that an accused-defendant may experience his first sense of "betrayal." While he had perhaps perceived the police and prosecutor to be adversaries, or possibly even the judge, the accused is wholly unprepared for his counsel's role performance as an agent-mediator. In the same vein, it is even less likely to occur to an accused that members of his own family or other kin may become agents, albeit at the behest and urging of other agents or mediators, acting on the principle that they are in reality helping an accused negotiate the best possible plea arrangement under the circumstances. Usually, it will be the lawyer who will activate next of kin in this role, his ostensible motive being to arrange for his fee. But soon latent and unstated motives will assert themselves, with entreaties by counsel to the accused's next of kin, to appeal to the accused to "help himself" by pleading. *Gemeinschaft* sentiments are to this extent exploited by a defense lawyer (or even at times by a district attorney) to achieve specific secular ends, that is, of concluding a particular matter with all possible dispatch. . . .

In effect, in his role as double agent, the criminal lawyer performs an extremely vital and delicate mission for the court organization and the accused. Both principals are anxious to terminate the litigation with a minimum of expense and damage to each other. There is no other personage or role incumbent in the total court structure more strategically located, who by training and in terms of his own requirements, is more ideally suited to do so than the lawyer. In recognition of this, judges will cooperate with attorneys in many important ways. For example, they will adjourn the case of an accused in jail awaiting plea or sentence if the attorney requests such action. While explicitly this may be done for some innocuous and seemingly valid reason, the tacit purpose is that pressure is being applied by the attorney for the collection of his fee, which he knows will probably not be forthcoming if the case is concluded. Judges are aware of this tactic on the part of lawyers, who, by requesting an adjournment, keep an accused incarcerated awhile longer as a not too subtle method of dunning a client for payment. However, the judges will go along with this, on the ground that important ends are being served. Often, the only end served is to protect a lawyer's fee.

The judge will help an accused's lawyer in still another way. He will lend the official aura of his office and courtroom so that

a lawyer can stage manage an impression of an "all out" performance for the accused in justification of his fee. The judge and
other court personnel will serve as a backdrop for a scene charged
with dramatic fire, in which the accused's lawyer makes a stirring
appeal in his behalf. With a show of restrained passion, the lawyer will intone the virtues of the accused and recite the social
deprivations which have reduced him to his present state. The
speech varies somewhat, depending on whether the accused has
been convicted after trial or has pleaded guilty. In the main,
however, the incongruity, superficiality, and ritualistic character
of the total performance is underscored by a visibly impassive,
almost bored reaction on the part of the judge and other members of the court retinue.

Afterward, there is a hearty exchange of pleasantries between
the lawyer and district attorney, wholly out of context in terms
of the supposed adversary nature of the preceding events. The
fiery passion in defense of his client is gone, and the lawyers for
both sides resume their offstage relations, chatting amiably and
perhaps including the judge in their restrained banter. No other
aspect of their visible conduct so effectively serves to put even
a casual observer on notice, that these individuals have claims
upon each other. These seemingly innocuous actions are indicative of continuing organizational and informal relations, which,
in their intricacy and depth, range far beyond any priorities or
claims a particular defendant may have.

Criminal law practice is a unique form of private law practice
since it really only appears to be private practice. Actually it is
bureaucratic practice, because of the legal practitioner's enmesh-
ment in the authority, discipline, and perspectives of the court
organization. Private practice, supposedly, in a professional sense,
involves the maintenance of an organized, disciplined body of
knowledge and learning; the individual practitioners are imbued
with a spirit of autonomy and service, the earning of a livelihood
being incidental. In the sense that the lawyer in the criminal
court serves as a double agent, serving higher organizational
rather than professional ends, he may be deemed to be engaged
in bureaucratic rather than private practice. To some extent the
lawyer-client "confidence game," in addition to its other functions, serves to conceal this fact.

THE CLIENT'S PERCEPTION

The "cop-out" ceremony, in which the court process culmi-
nates, is not only invaluable for redefining the accused's perspectives of himself, but also in reiterating publicly in a formally

structured ritual the accused person's guilt for the benefit of significant "others" who are observing. The accused not only is made to assert publicly his guilt of a specific crime, but also a complete recital of its details. He is further made to indicate that he is entering his plea of guilt freely, willingly, and voluntarily, and that he is not doing so because of any promises or in consideration of any commitments that may have been made to him by anyone. This last is intended as a blanket statement to shield the participants from any possible charges of "coercion" or undue influence that may have been exerted in violation of due process requirements. Its function is to preclude any later review by an appellate court on these grounds, and also to obviate any second thoughts an accused may develop in connection with his plea.

However, for the accused, the conception of self as a guilty person is in large measure a temporary role adaptation. His career socialization as an accused, if it is successful, eventuates in his acceptance and redefinition of himself as a guilty person.[21] However, the transformation is ephemeral, in that he will, in private, quickly reassert his innocence. Of importance is that he accept his defeat, publicly proclaim it, and find some measure of pacification in it.[22] Almost immediately after his plea, a defendant will generally be interviewed by a representative of the

---

[21] This does not mean that most of those who plead guilty are innocent of any crime. Indeed, in many instances those who have been able to negotiate a lesser plea, have done so willingly and even eagerly. The system of justice-by-negotiation, without trial, probably tends to better serve the interests and requirements of guilty persons, who are thereby presented with formal alternatives of "half a loaf," in terms of, at worst, possibilities of a lesser plea and a concomitant shorter sentence as compensation for their acquiescence and participation. Having observed the prescriptive etiquette in compliance with the defendant role expectancies in this setting, he is rewarded. An innocent person, on the other hand, is confronted with the same set of role prescriptions, structures and legal alternatives, and in any event, for him this mode of justice is often an ineluctable bind.

[22] "Any communicative network between persons whereby the public identity of an actor is transformed into something looked on as lower in the local scheme of social types will be called a 'status degradation ceremony.' " H. Garfinkel, *Conditions of Successful Degradation Ceremonies,* 61 Am. J. Soc. 420-24 (1956). But contrary to the conception of the "cop out" as a "status degradation ceremony," is the fact that it is in reality a charade, during the course of which an accused must project an appropriate and acceptable amount of guilt, penitence and remorse. Having adequately feigned the role of the "guilty person," his hearers will engage in the fantasy that he is contrite, and thereby merits a lesser plea. It is one of the essential functions of the criminal lawyer that he coach and direct his accused-client in that role performance. Thus, what is actually involved is not a "degradation" process at all, but is instead, a highly structured system of exchange cloaked in the rituals of legalism and public professions of guilt and repentance.

probation division in connection with a presentence report which
is to be prepared. The very first question to be asked of him
by the probation officer is: "Are you guilty of the crime to
which you pleaded?" This is by way of double affirmation of
the defendant's guilt. Should the defendant now begin to make
bold assertions of his innocence, despite his plea of guilty, he
will be asked to withdraw his plea and stand trial on the original
charges. Such a threatened possibility is, in most instances, sufficient to cause an accused to let the plea stand and to request
the probation officer to overlook his exclamations of innocence.
The table that follows is a breakdown of the categorized responses
of a random sample of male defendants in Metropolitan Court[23]
during 1962, 1963, and 1964 in connection with their statements
during presentence probation interviews following their plea of
guilty.

It would be well to observe at the outset, that of the 724
defendants who pleaded guilty before trial, only 43 (5.94 per
cent) of the total group had confessed prior to their indictment.
Thus, the ultimate judicial process was predicated upon evidence
independent of any confession of the accused.

As the data indicate, only a relatively small number (95) out
of the total number of defendants actually will even admit their
guilt, following the "cop-out" ceremony. However, even though
they have affirmed their guilt, many of these defendants felt that
they should have been able to negotiate a more favorable plea.
The largest aggregate of defendants (373) were those who reasserted their "innocence" following their public profession of
guilt during the "cop-out" ceremony. These defendants employed differential degrees of fervor, solemnity and credibility,
ranging from really mild, wavering assertions of innocence which
were embroidered with a variety of stock explanations and ration-
alizations, to those of an adamant, "framed" nature. Thus, the
"Innocent" group, for the most part, were largely concerned
with underscoring for their probation interviewer their essential
"goodness" and "worthiness," despite their formal plea of guilty.
Assertion of his innocence at the post plea stage, resurrects a
more respectable and acceptable self concept for the accused
defendant who has pleaded guilty. A recital of the structural
exigencies which precipitated his plea of guilt, serves to embellish a newly proffered claim of innocence, which many defendants

---

23 The name is of course fictitious. However, the actual court which
served as the universe from which the data were drawn, is one of the largest
criminal courts in the United States, dealing with felonies only. Female
defendants in the years 1950 through 1964 constituted from 7-10% of the
totals for each year.

TABLE 1

Defendant Responses as to Guilt or Innocence After Pleading Guilty

N* = 724   Years — 1962, 1963, 1964

NATURE OF RESPONSE		N OF DEFENDANTS
INNOCENT (Manipulated)	"The lawyer or judge, police or D.A. 'conned me' "	86
INNOCENT (Pragmatic)	"Wanted to get it over with" "You can't beat the system" "They have you over a barrel when you have a record"	147
INNOCENT (Advice of counsel)	"Followed my lawyer's advice"	92
INNOCENT (Defiant)	"Framed"— Betrayed by "Complainant," "Police," "Squealers," "Lawyer," "Friends," "Wife," "Girlfriend"	33
INNOCENT (Adverse social data)	Blames probation officer or psychiatrist for "Bad Report," in cases where there was pre-pleading investigation	15
GUILTY	"But I should have gotten a better deal" Blames lawyer, D.A., Police, Judge	74
GUILTY	Won't say anything further	21
FATALISTIC (Doesn't press his "Innocence," won't admit "Guilt")	"I did it for convenience" "My lawyer told me it was only thing I could do" "I did it because it was the best way out"	248
NO RESPONSE		8
TOTAL		724

mistakenly feel will stand them in good stead at the time of sentence, or ultimately with probation or parole authorities.

Relatively few (33) maintained their innocence in terms of having been "framed" by some person or agent-mediator, although a larger number (86) indicated that they had been manipulated or "conned" by an agent-mediator to plead guilty, but as indicated, their assertions of innocence were relatively mild.

A rather substantial group (147) preferred to stress the pragmatic aspects of their plea of guilty. They would only perfunctorily assert their innocence and would in general refer to some adverse aspect of their situation which they believed tended to negatively affect their bargaining leverage, including in some instances a prior criminal record.

One group of defendants (92), while maintaining their innocence, simply employed some variation of a theme of following

---

* N is a symbol for the number of cases being considered. [Eds. note]

"the advice of counsel" as a covering response, to explain their guilty plea in the light of their new affirmation of innocence.

The largest single group of defendants (248) were basically fatalistic. They often verbalized weak suggestions of their innocence in rather halting terms, wholly without conviction. By the same token, they would not admit guilt readily and were generally evasive as to guilt or innocence, preferring to stress aspects of their stoic submission in their decision to plead. This sizable group of defendants appeared to perceive the total court process as being caught up in a monstrous organizational apparatus, in which the defendant role expectancies were not clearly defined. Reluctant to offend anyone in authority, fearful that clear cut statements on their part as to their guilt or innocence would be negatively construed, they adopted a stance of passivity, resignation and acceptance. Interestingly, they would in most instances invoke their lawyer as being the one who crystallized the available alternatives for them, and who was therefore the critical element in their decision-making process.

In order to determine which agent-mediator was most influential in altering the accused's perspectives as to his decision to plead or go to trial (regardless of the proposed basis of the plea), the same sample of defendants were asked to indicate the person who first suggested to them that they plead guilty. They were also asked to indicate which of the persons or officials who made such suggestion, was most influential in affecting their final decision to plead.

The following table indicates the breakdown of the responses to the two questions:

TABLE 2

Role of Agent-Mediators in Defendant's Guilty Plea

PERSON OR OFFICIAL	FIRST SUGGESTED PLEA OF GUILTY	INFLUENCED THE ACCUSED MOST IN HIS FINAL DECISION TO PLEAD
JUDGE	4	26
DISTRICT ATTORNEY	67	116
DEFENSE COUNSEL	407	411
PROBATION OFFICER	14	3
PSYCHIATRIST	8	1
WIFE	34	120
FRIENDS AND KIN	21	14
POLICE	14	4
FELLOW INMATES	119	14
OTHERS	28	5
NO RESPONSE	8	10
TOTAL	724	724

It is popularly assumed that the police, through forced confessions, and the district attorney, employing still other pressures,
are most instrumental in the inducement of an accused to plead
guilty. As Table 2 indicates, it is actually the defendant's own
counsel who is most effective in this role. Further, this phenomenon tends to reinforce the extremely rational nature of criminal
law administration, for an organization could not rely upon the
sort of idiosyncratic measures employed by the police to induce
confessions and maintain its efficiency, high production and over-
all rational-legal character. The defense counsel becomes the
ideal agent-mediator since, as "officer of the court" and confidant
of the accused and his kin, he lives astride both worlds and can
serve the ends of the two as well as his own.

While an accused's wife, for example, may be influential in
making him more amenable to a plea, her agent-mediator role
has, nevertheless, usually been sparked and initiated by defense
counsel. Further, although a number of first suggestions of a
plea came from an accused's fellow jail inmates, he tended to
rely largely on his counsel as an ultimate source of influence in
his final decision. The defense counsel, being a crucial figure
in the total organizational scheme in constituting a new set of
perspectives for the accused, the same sample of defendants were
asked to indicate at which stage of their contact with the counsel
was the suggestion of a plea made. There are three basic kinds
of defense counsel available in Metropolitan Court: Legal-aid,
privately retained counsel, and counsel assigned by the court (but
may eventually be privately retained by the accused).

TABLE 3

Stage at Which Counsel Suggested Accused to Plead

N = 724

CONTACT	PRIVATELY RETAINED		LEGAL-AID		ASSIGNED		TOTAL	
	N	%	N	%	N	%	N	%
FIRST	66	35	237	49	28	60	331	46
SECOND	83	44	142	29	8	17	233	32
THIRD	29	15	63	13	4	9	96	13
FOURTH OR MORE	12	6	31	7	5	11	48	7
NO RESPONSE	0	0	14	3	2	4	16	2
TOTAL	190	100	487	101*	47	101*	724	100

* Rounded percentage.

The overwhelming majority of accused persons, regardless of
type of counsel, related a specific incident which indicated an
urging or suggestion, either during the course of the first or

second contact, that they plead guilty to a lesser charge if this could be arranged. Of all the agent-mediators, it is the lawyer who is most effective in manipulating an accused's perspectives, notwithstanding pressures that may have been previously applied by police, district attorney, judge or any of the agent-mediators that may have been activated by them. Legal-aid and assigned counsel would apparently be more likely to suggest a possible plea at the point of initial interview as response to pressures of time. In the case of the assigned counsel, the strong possibility that there is no fee involved, may be an added impetus to such a suggestion at the first contact.

In addition, there is some further evidence in Table 3 of the perfunctory, ministerial character of the system in Metropolitan Court and similar criminal courts. There is little real effort to individualize, and the lawyer's role as agent-mediator may be seen as unique in that he is in effect a double agent. Although, as "officer of the court" he mediates between the court organization and the defendant, his roles with respect to each are rent by conflicts of interest. Too often these must be resolved in favor of the organization which provides him with the means for his professional existence. Consequently, in order to reduce the strains and conflicts imposed in what is ultimately an over-demanding role obligation for him, the lawyer engages in the lawyer-client "confidence game" so as to structure more favorably an otherwise onerous role system.

CONCLUSION

Recent decisions of the Supreme Court, in the area of criminal law administration and defendant's rights, fail to take into account three crucial aspects of social structure which may tend to render the more libertarian rules as nugatory. The decisions overlook (1) the nature of courts as formal organization; (2) the relationship that the lawyer-regular *actually* has with the court organization; and (3) the character of the lawyer-client relationship in the criminal court (the routine relationships, not those unusual ones that are described in "heroic" terms in novels, movies, and TV).

Courts, like many other modern large-scale organizations possess a monstrous appetite for the cooptation of entire professional groups as well as individuals. Almost all those who come within the ambit of organizational authority, find that their definitions, perceptions and values have been refurbished, largely in terms favorable to the particular organization and its goals. As a result, recent Supreme Court decisions may have a long range effect which is radically different from that intended or anticipated. The more libertarian rules will tend to produce the rather ironic end result of augmenting the *existing* organizational arrangements, enriching court organizations with more personnel and elaborate structure, which in turn will maximize organizational goals of "efficiency" and production. Thus, many defendants will find that courts will possess an even more sophisticated apparatus for processing them toward a guilty plea!

NOTES AND QUESTIONS

1. The articles in this section are all, in some sense or another, engaged in contrasting some sort of idealized picture of the legal system with some sort of operational reality. What is Blumberg's idealized picture of the criminal process? From what sources does he derive it? How can one tell how the criminal process is "supposed" to operate?

2. Blumberg begins by describing three recent Supreme Court cases. What is the relationship between these cases and the points that Blumberg wants to make about the criminal justice system? Is he demonstrating that the Supreme Court is uninformed about the criminal justice process? Would the court have decided differently if it had been aware of the facts that Blumberg adduces? Should it have decided these cases differently?

3. Blumberg argues that the criminal lawyer is not really a man dedicated single-mindedly to the welfare of his client; rather, he is "enmeshed" in the court "bureaucracy." What does he mean by "bureaucracy"? How has Blumberg gathered data which bears on this question? Is his description valid for all criminal lawyers? for the "typical" criminal lawyer?

[Reading 12]

4. Plea bargaining, attacked by Blumberg, has not lacked defenders, academic and otherwise. The following excerpt is from Commonwealth v. Maroney, 423 Pa. 337, 223 A.2d 699 (1966), an opinion of the Pennsylvania Supreme Court. Michael Kerekes was indicted for the murder of his wife. He pleaded not guilty, then later requested permission to plead guilty to second degree murder. The court ascertained that the prosecution would not introduce evidence to prove that he was actually guilty of first degree murder; then it accepted the changed plea. The state presented its case; the defense rested. The court found Kerekes guilty and sent him to prison.

Five years later, Kerekes filed a petition for a writ of habeas corpus, attacking the validity of his plea. In the course of its opinion, the court said:

[Kerekes, the appellant] urges us to hold that any bargain made under the threat of the electric chair is necessarily coercive and invalid. We turn to a consideration of that argument.

Although the subject of considerable criticism, plea bargaining between the prosecution and the defense is a frequently resorted to technique. In exchange for a guilty plea, the prosecutor may agree to recommend a lighter sentence, to accept a plea to a lesser included offense, or to dismiss other pending charges. . . . It has been suggested, . . . that the prosecutor's obligation is to enforce, not compromise, society's determination that certain conduct be punished and that plea bargaining will undermine the deterrent effect of criminal punishment. Plea bargaining has also been denounced as being unfair to defendants on the theory that a guilty plea induced by a promise of leniency is akin to a confession so obtained. Closely related to this objection is the fear that innocent men are apt to succumb to "bargains" offered by prosecutors more interested in a high conviction rate than truth.

Realistically, however, plea bargaining, when surrounded by proper safeguards, is frequently in the best interest of both the Commonwealth and the accused. . . . From the Commonwealth's viewpoint the inability to bargain would lead to a substantial increase in required prosecutorial manpower and in the number of necessary trials, even though a satisfactory resolution of the state's interest can often be obtained with less than the potential maximum punishment available.

From the accused's viewpoint, the abolition of plea bargaining might be disastrous, for there would then be little incentive for the state to acquiesce in less than the maximum available punishment. One can readily understand why a defendant, who has no doubt about the ability of the Commonwealth to prove its case, would be willing, in exchange for some concessions by the Commonwealth, to plead guilty, thus saving the state the expense of a protracted trial. Even when the evidence, although not overwhelming, is more than sufficient to sustain a conviction, it may well be in the defendant's best interest to plead guilty rather than to gamble and lose, when losing may result in the deprivation of liberty for an extended period of time or the death sentence. . . .

In our opinion there is neither an overriding interest of society which would prohibit such prosecutorial discretion nor must such bargaining invariably infringe upon the defendant's constitutional rights. "At its best," one noted commentator suggests "this system is superior to that of trials. A good defense lawyer can present helpful information concerning his client and his problems which may lead to the working out of a more rational disposition than would be possible through trial of the case."* Of course one appreciates the agonizing choice afforded some defendants, although for others, who desire to avoid the uncertainties of trial, the choice may be obvious. In any event we prefer this to the alternative of no choice.

While we are not willing to completely proscribe plea bargaining, we do recognize that the awesome effect of a guilty plea and the sensitive nature of the bargaining process makes certain safeguards essential. . . . Also the defendant may not enter a plea without prior consultation with his counsel and he must fully comprehend the significance of the prosecutor's inability to bind the court. Finally, before accepting a guilty plea, the trial court has the responsibility of satisfying itself that the defendant understands the meaning of the charge, the consequences of pleading guilty, and that the acceptance of the plea will not result in a miscarriage of justice. . . .

We are satisfied that under the facts of this case there is no valid reason for concluding that appellant's plea of guilty was not knowingly and understandingly entered. . . .

5. Note carefully the point made at 134 n.21, *supra*. Would the plea bargaining system be fair if all criminal defendants were guilty as originally charged? if most of them were guilty?

The concept of "guilt" is not a simple one. It may refer to whether an accused actually performed certain acts which, in the abstract, constitute a crime; or it may refer to these facts *plus* whether there are available any technical or nontechnical defenses (such as an illegal arrest) to a trial for the crime. Would

---

* The quotation is from Edward L. Barrett, Jr., Dean of the University of California School of Law at Davis, in Criminal Justice: The Problem of Mass Production, reprinted from Harry W. Jones, Editor, The Courts, The Public and the Law Explosion, pp. 85, 109. Copyright © 1965 by The American Assembly, Columbia University, New York, New York. Reprinted by permission of Prentice-Hall, Inc.

you answer the questions in the first paragraph differently for different meanings of "guilty"?

6. Blumberg has gathered together evidence that many convicted persons feel they are innocent. Does this fact call into question the fairness of the process of criminal justice? Could you argue—and would you—that this evidence is inconclusive and irrelevant?

7. Sometimes, perhaps often, the defendant who is poor gets minimal legal representation; the bargained guilty plea is less demanding of lawyer time and skill than a full scale defense before a jury. Blumberg offers one explanation—the lawyers are coopted into the criminal processing system. Another has been suggested: "Although lawyers may readily acknowledge that the poor have problems, they may be reluctant to define them as legal problems. Indeed, there is a tendency to conceive of their problems as basically social or psychological, calling for therapy rather than justice. . . . The adoption of this perspective weakens the lawyer's capacity to recognize legal rights and seek legal remedies; it also provides him with a seemingly legitimate rationale for perfunctory service and for his reluctance to serve the poor as a lawyer." Jerome E. Carlin, Jan Howard & Sheldon L. Messinger, "Civil Justice and the Poor: Issues for Sociological Research," 1 *Law & Society Review* 9, 66-67 (1966).

8. Undoubtedly, there are many bargained guilty pleas. There is still another plausible explanation: such a plea is the most rational strategy open in many, if not most, cases. The criminal justice system can be viewed as an elaborate filtering process. For example, before a typical felony defendant reaches trial court in Chicago, he has been arrested, brought to court for a preliminary hearing and indicted by a grand jury. In 1964, the police reported that they arrested about 24,000 people on felony charges. However, only 16,000 were charged with felonies and got to a preliminary hearing. Of this group, only about 4,000 were bound over to the grand jury or otherwise held for prosecution on the felony charge. In another 6,500 cases the prisoner probably was prosecuted on an included or related misdemeanor. Of the 4,000 felony defendants, only 72% plead or are found guilty. (About 22% of the cases are dismissed at the trial stage for various reasons; discounting these dismissed cases one can say about 90% of those either pleading guilty or going through a complete trial are found guilty.) *See* Dallin H. Oaks & Warren Lehman, *A Criminal Justice System and the Indigent* 31-35, 40, 40-44, 45, 59, 163 (U. of Chicago Press 1968). When a felony defendant arrives

at the trial stage, the odds are that the prosecution has a strong
case. If one accepts these facts as true, would an attorney who
fails to discuss the pros and cons of a guilty plea with his client
be perfoming his job adequately? To what extent, if at all, does
this last argument undercut Blumberg's thesis?

9. For a more sympathetic view of the criminal justice system,
but one stressing its sociological rather than formal-legal aspects,
see Jerome H. Skolnick, "Social Control in the Adversary System," 11 *Journal of Conflict Resolution* 52 (1967).

13. Non-Contractual Relations in Business: A Preliminary Study

STEWART MACAULAY*

28 AMERICAN SOCIOLOGICAL REVIEW 55
(February 1963)

What good is contract law? who uses it? when and how? Complete answers would require an investigation of almost every type of transaction between individuals and organizations. In this report, research has been confined to exchanges between businesses, and primarily to manufacturers. Furthermore, this report will be limited to a presentation of the findings concerning when contract is and is not used and to a tentative explanation of these findings.

This research is only the first phase in a scientific study.[3] The primary research technique involved interviewing 68 businessmen and lawyers representing 43 companies and six law firms. The interviews ranged from a 30-minute brush-off where not all questions could be asked of a busy and uninterested sales man-

---

* Professor of Law, University of Wisconsin. Reprinted from The American Sociological Review. Copyright © 1963 American Sociological Association. Reprinted by permission.

[3] The following things have been done. The literature in law, business, economics, psychology, and sociology has been surveyed. The formal systems related to exchange transactions have been examined. Standard form contracts and the standard terms and conditions that are found on such business documents as catalogues, quotation forms, purchase orders, and acknowledgment-of-order forms from 850 firms that are based in or do business in Wisconsin have been collected. The citations of all reported court cases during a period of 15 years involving the largest 500 manufacturing corporations in the United States have been obtained and are being analyzed to determine why the use of contract legal sanctions was thought necessary and whether or not any patterns of "problem situations" can be delineated. In addition, the informal systems related to exchange transactions have been examined. Letters of inquiry concerning practices in certain situations have been answered by approximately 125 businessmen. Interviews, as described in the text, have been conducted. Moreover, six of my students have interviewed 21 other businessmen, bankers and lawyers. Their findings are consistent with those reported in the text.

ager to a six-hour discussion with the general counsel of a large corporation. Detailed notes of the interviews were taken and a complete report of each interview was dictated, usually no later than the evening after the interview. All but two of the companies had plants in Wisconsin; 17 were manufacturers of machinery but none made such items as food products, scientific instruments, textiles or petroleum products. Thus the likelihood of error because of sampling bias may be considerable.[4] However, to a great extent, existing knowledge has been inadequate to permit more rigorous procedures—as yet one cannot formulate many precise questions to be asked a systematically selected sample of "right people." Much time has been spent fishing for relevant questions or answers, or both.

Reciprocity, exchange or contract has long been of interest to sociologists, economists and lawyers. Yet each discipline has an incomplete view of this kind of conduct. This study represents the effort of a law teacher to draw on sociological ideas and empirical investigation. It stresses, among other things, the functions and dysfunctions of using contract to solve exchange problems and the influence of occupational roles on how one assesses whether the benefits of using contract outweigh the costs.

To discuss when contract is and is not used, the term "contract" must be specified. This term will be used here to refer to devices for conducting exchanges. Contract is not treated as synonymous with an exchange itself, which may or may not be characterized as contractual. Nor is contract used to refer to a writing recording an agreement. Contract, as I use the term here, involves two distinct elements: (a) Rational planning of the transaction with careful provision for as many future contingencies as can be foreseen, and (b) the existence or use of actual or potential legal sanctions to induce performance of the exchange or to compensate for non-performance.

These devices for conducting exchanges may be used or may exist in greater or lesser degree, so that transactions can be described relatively as involving a more contractual or a less contractual manner (a) of creating an exchange relationship or (b) of solving problems arising during the course of such a relationship. For example, General Motors might agree to buy all of the Buick Division's requirements of aluminum for ten years from Reynolds Aluminum. Here the two large corporations probably would plan their relationship carefully. The plan probably would include a complex pricing formula designed to meet

---

4 However, the cases have not been selected because they *did* use contract. There is as much interest in, and effort to obtain, cases of nonuse as of use of contract. Thus, one variety of bias has been minimized.

market fluctuations, an agreement on what would happen if either party suffered a strike or a fire, a definition of Reynolds' responsibility for quality control and for losses caused by defective quality, and many other provisions. As the term contract is used here, this is a more contractual method of creating an exchange relationship than is a home-owner's casual agreement with a real estate broker giving the broker the exclusive right to sell the owner's house which fails to include provisions for the consequences of many easily foreseeable (and perhaps even highly probable) contingencies. In both instances, legally enforceable contracts may or may not have been created, but it must be recognized that the existence of a legal sanction has no necessary relationship to the degree of rational planning by the parties, beyond certain minimal legal requirements of certainty of obligation. General Motors and Reynolds might never sue or even refer to the written record of their agreement to answer questions which come up during their ten-year relationship, while the real estate broker might sue, or at least threaten to sue, the owner of the house. The broker's method of *dispute settlement* then would be more contractual than that of General Motors and Reynolds, thus reversing the relationship that existed in regard to the "contractualness" of the *creation* of the exchange relationships.

TENTATIVE FINDINGS

It is difficult to generalize about the use and nonuse of contract by manufacturing industry. However, a number of observations can be made with reasonable accuracy at this time. The use and nonuse of contract in creating exchange relations and in dispute settling will be taken up in turn.

The creation of exchange relationships. In creating exchange relationships, businessmen may plan to a greater or lesser degree in relation to several types of issues. Before reporting the findings as to practices in creating such relationships, it is necessary to describe what one can plan about in a bargain and the degrees of planning which are possible.

People negotiating a contract can make plans concerning several types of issues: (1) They can plan what each is to do or refrain from doing; e.g., S might agree to deliver ten 1963 Studebaker four-door sedan automobiles to B on a certain date in exchange for a specified amount of money. (2) They can plan what effect certain contingencies are to have on their duties; e.g., what is to happen to S and B's obligations if S cannot deliver the cars because of a strike at the Studebaker factory? (3) They can plan what is to happen if either of them fails to perform; e.g.,

what is to happen if S delivers nine of the cars two weeks late?
(4) They can plan their agreement so that it is a legally enforceable contract—that is, so that a legal sanction would be available
to provide compensation for injury suffered by B as a result of
S's failure to deliver the cars on time.

As to each of these issues, there may be a different degree of
planning by the parties. (1) They may carefully and explicitly
plan; e.g., S may agree to deliver ten 1963 Studebaker four-door
sedans which have six cylinder engines, automatic transmissions
and other specified items of optional equipment and which will
perform to a specified standard for a certain time. (2) They may
have a mutual but tacit understanding about an issue; e.g., although the subject was never mentioned in their negotiations,
both S and B may assume that B may cancel his order for the
cars before they are delivered if B's taxi-cab business is so curtailed that B can no longer use ten additional cabs. (3) They
may have two inconsistent unexpressed assumptions about an
issue; e.g., S may assume that if any of the cabs fails to perform
to the specified standard for a certain time, all S must do is repair
or replace it. B may assume S must also compensate B for the
profits B would have made if the cab had been in operation. (4)
They may never have thought of the issue; e.g., neither S nor B
planned their agreement so that it would be a legally enforceable
contract. Of course, the first and fourth degrees of planning listed
are the extreme cases and the second and third are intermediate
points. Clearly, other intermediate points are possible; e.g., S and
B neglect to specify whether the cabs should have automatic or
conventional transmissions. Their planning is not as careful and
explicit as that in the example previously given.

The following diagram represents the dimensions of creating
an exchange relationship just discussed with "X's" representing
the example of S and B's contract for ten taxi-cabs.

	Defini-tion of Perform-ances	Effect of Contin-gencies	Effect of Defective Perform-ances	Legal Sanc-tions
Explicit and careful	X			
Tacit agreement		X		
Unilateral assumptions			X	
Unawareness of the issue				X

Most larger companies, and many smaller ones, attempt to plan carefully and completely. Important transactions not in the ordinary course of business are handled by a detailed contract. For example, recently the Empire State Building was sold for $65 million. More than 100 attorneys, representing 34 parties, produced a 400 page contract. Another example is found in the agreement of a major rubber company in the United States to give technical assistance to a Japanese firm. Several million dollars were involved and the contract consisted of 88 provisions on 17 pages. The 12 house counsel—lawyers who work for one corporation rather than many clients—interviewed said that all but the smallest businesses carefully planned most transactions of any significance. Corporations have procedures so that particular types of exchanges will be reviewed by their legal and financial departments.

More routine transactions commonly are handled by what can be called standardized planning. A firm will have a set of terms and conditions for purchases, sales, or both printed on the business documents used in these exchanges. Thus the things to be sold and the price may be planned particularly for each transaction, but standard provisions will further elaborate the performances and cover the other subjects of planning. Typically, these terms and conditions are lengthy and printed in small type on the back of the forms. For example, 24 paragraphs in eight point type are printed on the back of the purchase order form used by the Allis Chalmers Manufacturing Company. The provisions: (1) describe, in part, the performance required, e.g., "DO NOT WELD CASTINGS WITHOUT OUR CONSENT"; (2) plan for the effect of contingencies, e.g., ". . . in the event the Seller suffers delay in performance due to an act of God, war, act of the Government, priorities or allocations, act of the Buyer, fire, flood, strike, sabotage, or other causes beyond Seller's control, the time of completion shall be extended a period of time equal to the period of such delay if the Seller gives the Buyer notice in writing of the cause of any such delay within a reasonable time after the beginning thereof"; (3) plan for the effect of defective performances, e.g., "The buyer, without waiving any other legal rights, reserves the right to cancel without charge or to postpone deliveries of any of the articles covered by this order which are not shipped in time reasonably to meet said agreed dates"; (4) plan for a legal sanction, e.g., the clause "without waiving any other legal rights," in the example just given.

In larger firms such "boiler plate" provisions are drafted by the house counsel or the firm's outside lawyer. In smaller firms such provisions may be drafted by the industry trade association, may be copied from a competitor, or may be found on forms purchased from a printer. In any event, salesmen and purchasing agents, the operating personnel, typically are unaware of what is said in the fine print on the back of the forms they use. Yet often the normal business patterns will give effect to this standardized planning. For example, purchasing agents may have to use a purchase order form so that all transactions receive a number under the firm's accounting system. Thus, the required accounting record will carry the necessary planning of the exchange relationship printed on its reverse side. If the seller does not object to this planning and accepts the order, the buyer's "fine print" will control. If the seller does object, differences can be settled by negotiation.

This type of standardized planning is very common. Requests for copies of the business documents used in buying and selling were sent to approximately 6,000 manufacturing firms which do business in Wisconsin. Approximately 1,200 replies were received and 850 companies used some type of standardized planning. With only a few exceptions, the firms that did not reply and the 350 that indicated they did not use standardized planning were very small manufacturers such as local bakeries, soft drink bottlers and sausage makers.

While businessmen can and often do carefully and completely plan, it is clear that not all exchanges are neatly rationalized. Although most businessmen think that a clear description of both the seller's and buyer's performances is obvious common sense, they do not always live up to this ideal. The house counsel and the purchasing agent of a medium sized manufacturer of automobile parts reported that several times their engineers had committed the company to buy expensive machines without adequate specifications. The engineers had drawn careful specifications as to the type of machine and how it was to be made but had neglected to require that the machine produce specified results. An attorney and an auditor both stated that most contract disputes arise because of ambiguity in the specifications.

Businessmen often prefer to rely on "a man's word" in a brief letter, a handshake, or "common honesty and decency"—even when the transaction involves exposure to serious risks. Seven lawyers from law firms with business practices were interviewed. Five thought that businessmen often entered contracts with only a minimal degree of advance planning. They complained that businessmen desire to "keep it simple and avoid red tape" even where large amounts of money and significant risks are involved. One stated that he was "sick of being told, 'We can trust old Max,' when the problem is not one of honesty but one of reaching an agreement that both sides understand." Another said that businessmen when bargaining often talk only in pleasant generalities, think they have a contract, but fail to reach agreement on any of the hard, unpleasant questions until forced to do so by a lawyer. Two outside lawyers had different views. One thought that large firms usually planned important exchanges, although he conceded that occasionally matters might be left in a fairly vague state. The other dissenter represents a large utility that commonly buys heavy equipment and buildings. The supplier's employees come on the utility's property to install the equipment or construct the buildings, and they may be injured while there. The utility has been sued by such employees so often that it carefully plans purchases with the assistance of a lawyer so that suppliers take this burden.

Moreover, standardized planning can break down. In the example of such planning previously given, it was assumed that the purchasing agent would use his company's form with its 24 paragraphs printed on the back and that the seller would accept this or object to any provisions he did not like. However, the seller may fail to read the buyer's 24 paragraphs of fine print and may accept the buyer's order on the seller's own acknowledgment-of-order form. Typically this form will have ten to 50 paragraphs favoring the seller, and these provisions are likely to be different from or inconsistent with the buyer's provisions. The seller's acknowledgment form may be received by the buyer and checked by a clerk. She will read the *face* of the acknowledgment but not the fine print on the back of it because she has neither the time nor ability to analyze the small print on the 100 to 500 forms she must review each day. The face of the acknowledgment—where the goods and the price are specified—is likely to correspond with the face of the purchase order. If it does, the two forms are filed away. At this point, both buyer and seller are likely to assume they have planned an exchange and made a contract. Yet they have done neither, as they are in disagreement about all that appears on the back of their forms. This practice is common enough to have a name. Law teachers call it "the battle of the forms."

Ten of the 12 purchasing agents interviewed said that frequently the provisions on the back of their purchase order and those on the back of a supplier's acknowledgment would differ or be inconsistent. Yet they would assume that the purchase was complete without further action unless one of the supplier's provisions was really objectionable. Moreover, only occasionally would they bother to read the fine print on the back of suppliers' forms. On the other hand, one purchasing agent insists that agreement be reached on the fine print provisions, but he represents the utility whose lawyer reported that it exercises great care in planning. The other purchasing agent who said that his company did not face a battle of the forms problem, works for a division of one of the largest manufacturing corporations in the United States. Yet the company may have such a problem without recognizing it. The purchasing agent regularly sends a supplier both a purchase order and another form which the supplier is asked to sign and return. The second form states that the supplier accepts the buyer's terms and conditions. The company has sufficient bargaining power to force suppliers to sign and return the form, and the purchasing agent must show one of his firm's auditors such a signed form for every purchase order issued. Yet suppliers frequently return this buyer's form *plus* their own acknowledgment form which has conflicting provisions. The purchasing agent throws away the supplier's form and files his own. Of course, in such a case the supplier has not acquiesced to the buyer's provisions. There is no agreement and no contract.

Sixteen sales managers were asked about the battle of the forms. Nine said that frequently no agreement was reached on which set of fine print was to govern, while seven said that there was no problem. Four of the seven worked for companies whose major customers are the large automobile companies or the large manufacturers of paper products. These customers demand that their terms and conditions govern any purchase, are careful generally to see that suppliers acquiesce, and have the bargaining power to have their way. The other three of the seven sales managers who have no battle of the forms problem, work for manufacturers of special industrial machines. Their firms are careful to reach complete agreement with their customers. Two of these men stressed that they could take no chances because such a large part of their firm's capital is tied up in making any one machine. The other sales manager had been influenced by a law suit against one of his competitors for over a half million dollars. The suit was brought by a customer when the competitor had been unable to deliver a machine and put it in operation on time. The sales manager interviewed said his firm could not guarantee that its machines would work perfectly by a specified time because they are designed to fit the customer's requirements, which may present difficult engineering problems. As a result, contracts are carefully negotiated.

A large manufacturer of packaging materials audited its records to determine how often it had failed to agree on terms and conditions with its customers or had failed to create legally binding contracts. Such failures cause a risk of loss to this firm since the packaging is printed with the customer's design and cannot be salvaged once this is done. The orders for five days in four different years were reviewed. The percentages of orders where no agreement on terms and conditions was reached or no contract was formed were as follows:

1953	75.0%
1954	69.4%
1955	71.5%
1956	59.5%

It is likely that businessmen pay more attention to describing the performances in an exchange than to planning for contingencies or defective performances or to obtaining legal enforceability of their contracts. Even when a purchase order and acknowledgment have conflicting provisions printed on the back, almost always the buyer and seller will be in agreement on what is to be sold and how much is to be paid for it. The lawyers who said businessmen often commit their firms to significant exchanges too casually, stated that the performances would be defined in the brief letter or telephone call; the lawyers objected that nothing else would be covered. Moreover, it is likely that businessmen are least concerned about planning their transactions so that they are legally enforceable contracts. For example, in Wisconsin [at the time of this study] requirements contracts— contracts to supply a firm's requirements of an item rather than a definite quantity—probably were not legally enforceable. Seven people interviewed reported that their firms regularly used requirements contracts in dealings in Wisconsin. None thought that the lack of legal sanction made any difference. Three of these people were house counsel who knew the Wisconsin law before being interviewed. Another example of a lack of desire for legal sanctions is found in the relationship between automobile manufacturers and their suppliers of parts. The manufacturers draft a carefully planned agreement, but one which is so designed that the supplier will have only minimal, if any, legal rights against the manufacturers. The standard contract used by manufacturers of paper to sell to magazine publishers has a pricing clause which is probably sufficiently vague to make the contract legally unenforceable. The house counsel of one of the largest paper producers said that everyone in the industry is aware of this because of a leading New York case concerning the contract, but that no one cares. Finally, it seems likely that planning for contingencies and defective performances are in-between cases—more likely to occur than planning for a legal sanction, but less likely than a description of performance.

Thus one can conclude that (1) many business exchanges reflect a high degree of planning about the four categories—description, contingencies, defective performances and legal sanction—but (2) many, if not most, exchanges reflect no planning, or only a minimal amount of it, especially concerning legal sanctions and the effect of defective performances. As a result, the opportunity for good faith disputes during the life of the exchange relationship often is present.

The adjustment of exchange relationships and the settling of disputes. While a significant amount of creating business exchanges is done on a fairly noncontractual basis, the creation of exchanges usually is far more contractual than the adjustment of such relationships and the settlement of disputes. Exchanges are adjusted when the obligations of one or both parties are modified by agreement during the life of the relationship. For example, the buyer may be allowed to cancel all or part of the goods he has ordered because he no longer needs them; the seller may be paid more than the contract price by the buyer because of unusual changed circumstances. Dispute settlement involves determining whether or not a party has performed as agreed and, if he has not, doing something about it. For example, a court may have to interpret the meaning of a contract, determine what the alleged defaulting party has done and determine what, if any, remedy the aggrieved party is entitled to. Or one party may assert that the other is in default, refuse to proceed with performing the contract and refuse to deal ever again with the alleged defaulter. If the alleged defaulter, who in fact may not be in default, takes no action, the dispute is then "settled."

Business exchanges in non-speculative areas are usually adjusted without dispute. Under the law of contracts, if B orders 1,000 widgets from S at $1.00 each, B must take all 1,000 widgets or be in breach of contract and liable to pay S his expenses up to the time of the breach plus his lost anticipated profit. Yet all ten of the purchasing agents asked about cancellation of orders once placed indicated that they expected to be able to cancel orders freely subject to only an obligation to pay for the seller's major expenses such as scrapped steel. All 17 sales personnel asked reported that they often had to accept cancellations. One said, "You can't ask a man to eat paper [the firm's product] when he has no use for it." A lawyer with many large industrial clients said,

> Often businessmen do not feel they have "a contract"—rather they have "an order." They speak of "cancelling the order" rather than "breaching our contract." When I began practice

I referred to order cancellations as breaches of contract, but my clients objected since they do not think of cancellation as wrong. Most clients, in heavy industry at least, believe that there is a right to cancel as part of the buyer-seller relationship. There is a widespread attitude that one can back out of any deal within some very vague limits. Lawyers are often surprised by this attitude.

Disputes are frequently settled without reference to the contract or potential or actual legal sanctions. There is a hesitancy to speak of legal rights or to threaten to sue in these negotiations. Even where the parties have a detailed and carefully planned agreement which indicates what is to happen if, say, the seller fails to deliver on time, often they will never refer to the agreement but will negotiate a solution when the problem arises apparently as if there had never been any original contract. One purchasing agent expressed a common business attitude when he said,

> if something comes up, you get the other man on the telephone and deal with the problem. You don't read legalistic contract clauses at each other if you ever want to do business again. One doesn't run to lawyers if he wants to stay in business because one must behave decently.

Or as one businessman put it, "You can settle any dispute if you keep the lawyers and accountants out of it. They just do not understand the give-and-take needed in business." All of the house counsel interviewed indicated that they are called into the dispute settlement process only after the businessmen have failed to settle matters in their own way. Two indicated that after being called in, house counsel at first will only advise the purchasing agent, sales manager or other official involved; not even the house counsel's letterhead is used on communications with the other side until all hope for a peaceful resolution is gone.

Law suits for breach of contract appear to be rare. Only five of the 12 purchasing agents had ever been involved in even a negotiation concerning a contract dispute where both sides were represented by lawyers; only two of ten sales managers had ever gone this far. None had been involved in a case that went through trial. A law firm with more than 40 lawyers and a large commercial practice handles in a year only about six trials concerned with contract problems. Less than 10 per cent of the time of this office is devoted to any type of work related to contracts disputes. Corporations big enough to do business in more than one state tend to sue and be sued in the federal courts. Yet

only 2,779 out of 58,293 civil actions filed in the United States
District Courts in fiscal year 1961 involved private contracts.
During the same period only 3,447 of the 61,138 civil cases filed
in the principal trial courts of New York State involved private
contracts. The same picture emerges from a review of appellate
cases.[9] Mentschikoff has suggested that commercial cases are not
brought to the courts either in periods of business prosperity
(because buyers unjustifiably reject goods only when prices drop
and they can get similar goods elsewhere at less than the contract
price) or in periods of deep depression (because people are unable
to come to court or have insufficient assets to satisfy any judgment that might be obtained). Apparently, she adds, it is necessary to have "a kind of middle-sized depression" to bring large
numbers of commercial cases to the courts. However, there is
little evidence that in even "a kind of middle-sized depression"
today's businessmen would use the courts to settle disputes.

At times, relatively contractual methods are used to make adjustments in ongoing transactions and to settle disputes. Demands
of one side which are deemed unreasonable by the other occasionally are blocked by reference to the terms of the agreement
between the parties. The legal position of the parties can influence negotiations even though legal rights or litigation are never
mentioned in their discussions; it makes a difference if one is
demanding what both concede to be a right or begging for a
favor. Now and then a firm may threaten to turn matters over
to its attorneys, threaten to sue, commence a suit or even litigate
and carry an appeal to the highest court which will hear the
matter. Thus, legal sanctions, while not an everyday affair, are
not unknown in business.

One can conclude that while detailed planning and legal sanctions play a significant role in some exchanges between businesses,
in many business exchanges their role is small.

Tentative Explanations

Two questions need to be answered: (A) How can business
successfully operate exchange relationships with relatively so lit-

---

[9] My colleague Lawrence M. Friedman has studied the work of the
Supreme Court of Wisconsin in contracts cases. He has found that contracts cases reaching that court tend to involve economically-marginal-busi-
ness and family-economic disputes rather than important commercial transactions. This has been the situation since about the turn of the century.
Only during the Civil War period did the court deal with significant numbers of important contracts cases, but this happened against the background
of a much simpler and different economic system. [This study has since
been published as CONTRACT LAW IN AMERICA: A SOCIAL AND ECONOMIC
CASE STUDY (1965) (U. of Wisconsin Press). Eds.]

tle attention to detailed planning or to legal sanctions, and (B) Why does business ever use contract in light of its success without it?

Why are relatively non-contractual practices so common? In most situations contract is not needed.[11] Often its functions are served by other devices. Most problems are avoided without resort to detailed planning or legal sanctions because usually there is little room for honest misunderstandings or good faith differences of opinion about the nature and quality of a seller's performance. Although the parties fail to cover all foreseeable contingencies, they will exercise care to see that both understand the primary obligation on each side. Either products are standardized with an accepted description or specifications are written calling for production to certain tolerances or results. Those who write and read specifications are experienced professionals who will know the customs of their industry and those of the industries with which they deal. Consequently, these customs can fill gaps in the express agreements of the parties. Finally, most products can be tested to see if they are what was ordered; typically in manufacturing industry we are not dealing with questions of taste or judgment where people can differ in good faith.

When defaults occur they are not likely to be disastrous because of techniques of risk avoidance or risk spreading. One can deal with firms of good reputation or he may be able to get some form of security to guarantee performance. One can insure against many breaches of contract where the risks justify the costs. Sellers set up reserves for bad debts on their books and can sell some of their accounts receivable. Buyers can place orders with two or more suppliers of the same item so that a default by one will not stop the buyer's assembly lines.

Moreover, contract and contract law are often thought unnecessary because there are many effective non-legal sanctions. Two norms are widely accepted. (1) Commitments are to be honored in almost all situations; one does not welsh on a deal. (2) One ought to produce a good product and stand behind it. Then, too, business units are organized to perform commitments, and internal sanctions will induce performance. For example, sales personnel must face angry customers when there has been a late or defective performance. The salesmen do not enjoy this and

11 The explanation that follows emphasizes a *considered* choice not to plan in detail for all contingencies. However, at times it is clear that businessmen fail to plan because of a lack of sophistication; they simply do not appreciate the risk they are running or they merely follow patterns established in their firm years ago without reexamining these practices in light of current conditions.

will put pressure on the production personnel responsible for the default. If the production personnel default too often, they will be fired. At all levels of the two business units personal relationships across the boundaries of the two organizations exert pressures for conformity to expectations. Salesmen often know purchasing agents well. The same two individuals occupying these roles may have dealt with each other from five to 25 years. Each has something to give the other. Salesmen have gossip about competitors, shortages and price increases to give purchasing agents who treat them well. Salesmen take purchasing agents to dinner, and they give purchasing agents Christmas gifts hoping to improve the chances of making a sale. The buyer's engineering staff may work with the seller's engineering staff to solve problems jointly. The seller's engineers may render great assistance, and the buyer's engineers may desire to return the favor by drafting specifications which only the seller can meet. The top executives of the two firms may know each other. They may sit together on government or trade committees. They may know each other socially and even belong to the same country club. The interrelationships may be more formal. Sellers may hold stock in corporations which are important customers; buyers may hold stock in important suppliers. Both buyer and seller may share common directors on their boards. They may share a common financial institution which has financed both units.

The final type of non-legal sanction is the most obvious. Both business units involved in the exchange desire to continue successfully in business and will avoid conduct which might interfere with attaining this goal. One is concerned with both the reaction of the other party in the particular exchange and with his own general business reputation. Obviously, the buyer gains sanctions insofar as the seller wants the particular exchange to be completed. Buyers can withhold part or all of their payments until sellers have performed to their satisfaction. If a seller has a great deal of money tied up in his performance which he must recover quickly, he will go a long way to please the buyer in order to be paid. Moreover, buyers who are dissatisfied may cancel and cause sellers to lose the cost of what they have done up to cancellation. Furthermore, sellers hope for repeat orders, and one gets few of these from unhappy customers. Some industrial buyers go so far as to formalize this sanction by issuing "report cards" rating the performance of each supplier. The supplier rating goes to the top management of the seller organization, and these men can apply internal sanctions to salesmen, production supervisors or product designers if there are too many "D's" or "F's" on the report card.

While it is generally assumed that the customer is always right, the seller may have some counterbalancing sanctions against the buyer. The seller may have obtained a large downpayment from the buyer which he will want to protect. The seller may have an exclusive process which the buyer needs. The seller may be one of the few firms which has the skill to make the item to the tolerances set by the buyer's engineers and within the time available. There are costs and delays involved in turning from a supplier one has dealt with in the past to a new supplier. Then, too, market conditions can change so that a buyer is faced with shortages of critical items. The most extreme example is the post World War II gray market conditions when sellers were rationing goods rather than selling them. Buyers must build up some reserve of good will with suppliers if they face the risk of such shortages and desire good treatment when they occur. Finally, there is reciprocity in buying and selling. A buyer cannot push a supplier too far if that supplier also buys significant quantities of the product made by the buyer.

Not only do the particular business units in a given exchange want to deal with each other again, they also want to deal with other business units in the future. And the way one behaves in a particular transaction, or a series of transactions, will color his general business reputation. Blacklisting can be formal or informal. Buyers who fail to pay their bills on time risk a bad report in credit rating services such as Dun and Bradstreet. Sellers who do not satisfy their customers become the subject of discussion in the gossip exchanged by purchasing agents and salesmen, at meetings of purchasing agents' associations and trade associations, or even at country clubs or social gatherings where members of top management meet. The American male's habit of debating the merits of new cars carries over to industrial items. Obviously, a poor reputation does not help a firm make sales and may force it to offer great price discounts or added services to remain in business. Furthermore, the habits of unusually demanding buyers become known, and they tend to get no more than they can coerce out of suppliers who choose to deal with them. Thus often contract is not needed as there are alternatives.

Not only are contract and contract law not needed in many situations, their use may have, or may be thought to have, undesirable consequences. Detailed negotiated contracts can get in the way of creating good exchange relationships between business units. If one side insists on a detailed plan, there will be delay while letters are exchanged as the parties try to agree on what should happen if a remote and unlikely contingency occurs. In some cases they may not be able to agree at all on such matters and as a result a sale may be lost to the seller and the buyer may have to search elsewhere for an acceptable supplier. Many businessmen would react by thinking that had no one raised the series of remote and unlikely contingencies all this wasted effort could have been avoided.

Even where agreement can be reached at the negotiation stage, carefully planned arrangements may create undesirable exchange relationships between business units. Some businessmen object that in such a carefully worked out relationship one gets performance only to the letter of the contract. Such planning indicates a lack of trust and blunts the demands of friendship, turning a cooperative venture into an antagonistic horse trade. Yet the greater danger perceived by some businessmen is that one would have to perform his side of the bargain to its letter and thus lose what is called "flexibility." Businessmen may welcome a measure of vagueness in the obligations they assume so that they may negotiate matters in light of the actual circumstances.

Adjustment of exchange relationships and dispute settlement by litigation or the threat of it also has many costs. The gain anticipated from using this form of coercion often fails to outweigh these costs, which are both monetary and non-monetary. Threatening to turn matters over to an attorney may cost no more money than postage or a telephone call; yet few are so skilled in making such a threat that it will not cost some deterioration of the relationship between the firms. One businessman said that customers had better not rely on legal rights or threaten to bring a breach of contract law suit against him since he "would not be treated like a criminal" and would fight back with every means available. Clearly, actual litigation is even more costly than making threats. Lawyers demand substantial fees from larger business units. A firm's executives often will have to be transported and maintained in another city during the proceedings if, as often is the case, the trial must be held away from the home office. Top management does not travel by Greyhound and stay at the Y.M.C.A. Moreover, there will be the cost of diverting top management, engineers, and others in the organization from their normal activities. The firm may lose many days work from several key people. The non-monetary costs may be large too. A breach of contract law suit may settle a particular dispute, but such an action often results in a "divorce" ending the "marriage" between the two businesses, since a contract action is likely to carry charges with at least overtones of bad faith. Many executives, moreover, dislike the prospect of being cross-examined in public. Some executives may dislike losing control of a situation by turning the decision-making power over to lawyers. Finally, the law of contract damages may not provide an adequate remedy even if the firm wins the suit; one may get vindication but not much money.

Why do relatively contractual practices ever exist? Although contract is not needed and actually may have negative consequences, businessmen do make some carefully planned contracts, negotiate settlements influenced by their legal rights and commence and defend some breach of contract law suits or arbitration proceedings. In view of the findings and explanation presented to this point, one may ask why. Exchanges are carefully planned when it is thought that planning and a potential legal sanction will have more advantages than disadvantages. Such a judgment may be reached when contract planning serves the internal needs of an organization involved in a business exchange. For example, a fairly detailed contract can serve as a communication device within a large corporation. While the corporation's sales manager and house counsel may work out all the provisions with the customer, its production manager will have to make the product. He must be told what to do and how to handle at least the most obvious contingencies. Moreover, the sales manager may want to remove certain issues from future negotiation by his subordinates. If he puts the matter in the written contract, he may be able to keep his salesmen from making concessions to the customer without first consulting the sales manager. Then the sales manager may be aided in his battles with his firm's financial or engineering departments if the contract calls for certain practices which the sales manager advocates but which the other departments resist. Now the corporation is obligated to a customer to do what the sales manager wants to do; how can the financial or engineering departments insist on anything else?

Also one tends to find a judgment that the gains of contract outweigh the costs where there is a likelihood that significant problems will arise.[12] One factor leading to this conclusion is complexity of the agreed performance over a long period. Another factor is whether or not the degree of injury in case of default is thought to be potentially great. This factor cuts two ways. First, a buyer may want to commit a seller to a detailed and legally binding contract, where the consequences of a default by the seller would seriously injure the buyer. For example, the

---

12 Even where there is little chance that problems will arise, some businessmen insist that their lawyer review or draft an agreement as a delaying tactic. This gives the businessman time to think about making a commitment if he has doubts about the matter or to look elsewhere for a better deal while still keeping the particular negotiations alive.

airlines are subject to law suits from the survivors of passengers and to great adverse publicity as a result of crashes. One would expect the airlines to bargain for carefully defined and legally enforceable obligations on the part of the airframe manufacturers when they purchase aircraft. Second, a seller may want to limit his liability for a buyer's damages by a provision in their contract. For example, a manufacturer of air conditioning may deal with motels in the South and Southwest. If this equipment fails in the hot summer months, a motel may lose a great deal of business. The manufacturer may wish to avoid any liability for this type of injury to his customers and may want a contract with a clear disclaimer clause.

Similarly, one uses or threatens to use legal sanctions to settle disputes when other devices will not work and when the gains are thought to outweigh the costs. For example, perhaps the most common type of business contracts case fought all the way through to the appellate courts today is an action for an alleged wrongful termination of a dealer's franchise by a manufacturer. Since the franchise has been terminated, factors such as personal relationships and the desire for future business will have little effect; the cancellation of the franchise indicates they have already failed to maintain the relationship. Nor will a complaining dealer worry about creating a hostile relationship between himself and the manufacturer. Often the dealer has suffered a great financial loss both as to his investment in building and equipment and as to his anticipated future profits. A cancelled automobile dealer's lease on his showroom and shop will continue to run, and his tools for servicing, say, Plymouths cannot be used to service other makes of cars. Moreover, he will have no more new Plymouths to sell. Today there is some chance of winning a law suit for terminating a franchise in bad faith in many states and in the federal courts. Thus, often the dealer chooses to risk the cost of a lawyer's fee because of the chance that he may recover some compensation for his losses.

An "irrational" factor may exert some influence on the decision to use legal sanctions. The man who controls a firm may feel that he or his organization has been made to appear foolish or has been the victim of fraud or bad faith. The law suit may be seen as a vehicle "to get even" although the potential gains, as viewed by an objective observer, are outweighed by the potential costs.

The decision whether or not to use contract—whether the gain exceeds the costs—will be made by the person within the business unit with the power to make it, and it tends to make a difference who he is. People in a sales department oppose contract. Contractual negotiations are just one more hurdle in the way of a sale. Holding a customer to the letter of a contract is bad for "customer relations." Suing a customer who is not bankrupt and might order again is poor strategy. Purchasing agents and their buyers are less hostile to contracts but regard attention devoted to such matters as a waste of time. In contrast, the financial control department—the treasurer, controller or auditor— leans toward more contractual dealings. Contract is viewed by these people as an organizing tool to control operations in a large organization. It tends to define precisely and to minimize the risks to which the firm is exposed. Outside lawyers—those with many clients—may share this enthusiasm for a more contractual method of dealing. These lawyers are concerned with preventive law—avoiding any possible legal difficulty. They see many unstable and unsuccessful exchange transactions, and so they are aware of, and perhaps overly concerned with, all of the things which can go wrong. Moreover, their job of settling disputes with legal sanctions is much easier if their client has not been overly casual about transaction planning. The inside lawyer, or house counsel, is harder to classify. He is likely to have some sympathy with a more contractual method of dealing. He shares the outside lawyer's "craft urge" to see exchange transactions neat and tidy from a legal standpoint. Since he is more concerned with avoiding and settling disputes than selling goods, he is likely to be less willing to rely on a man's word as the sole sanction than is a salesman. Yet the house counsel is more a part of the organization and more aware of its goals and subject to its internal sanctions. If the potential risks are not too great, he may hesitate to suggest a more contractual procedure to the sales department. He must sell his services to the operating departments, and he must hoard what power he has, expending it on only what he sees as significant issues.

The power to decide that a more contractual method of creating relationships and settling disputes shall be used will be held by different people at different times in different organizations. In most firms the sales department and the purchasing department have a great deal of power to resist contractual procedures or to ignore them if they are formally adopted and to handle disputes their own way. Yet in larger organizations the treasurer and the controller have increasing power to demand both systems and compliance. Occasionally, the house counsel must arbitrate the conflicting positions of these departments; in giving "legal advice" he may make the business judgment necessary regarding the use of contract. At times he may ask for an opinion from an outside law firm to reinforce his own position with the outside firm's prestige.

Obviously, there are other significant variables which influence the degree that contract is used. One is the relative bargaining power or skill of the two business units. Even if the controller of a small supplier succeeds within the firm and creates a contractual system of dealing, there will be no contract if the firm's large customer prefers not to be bound to anything. Firms that supply General Motors deal as General Motors wants to do business, for the most part. Yet bargaining power is not size nor share of the market alone. Even a General Motors may need a particular supplier, at least temporarily. Furthermore, bargaining power may shift as an exchange relationship is first created and then continues. Even a giant firm can find itself bound to a small supplier once production of an essential item begins for there may not be time to turn to another supplier. Also, all of the factors discussed in this paper can be viewed as *components* of bargaining power—for example, the personal relationship between the presidents of the buyer and the seller firms may give a sales manager great power over a purchasing agent who has been instructed to give the seller "every consideration." Another variable relevant to the use of contract is the influence of third parties. The federal government, or a lender of money, may insist that a contract be made in a particular transaction or may influence the decision to assert one's legal rights under a contract.

Contract, then, often plays an important role in business, but other factors are significant. To understand the functions of contract the whole system of conducting exchanges must be explored fully. More types of business communities must be studied, contract litigation must be analyzed to see why the nonlegal sanctions fail to prevent the use of legal sanctions and all of the variables suggested in this paper must be classified more systematically.

NOTES AND QUESTIONS

1. Among other things, Professor Macaulay's study is a study of the nonuse of formal processes of law. But most of us in our everyday life do not use formal processes of law. In what sense, then, is a study of the nonuse of law a study of law, and how does one determine which nonuses of law are (in some sense) legally relevant, or relevant to the sociology of law? Recall the discussion of the writings of Eugen Ehrlich at 43-44, *supra*. Do Macaulay and Ehrlich agree in their definitions and views of "living law"?

2. What is the formal model of contract law and its operation from which the businessmen studied here deviate? Note that there are two sorts of "deviation" discussed in the article: non-use of available tools, and use of these tools for some purpose other than their ideal or suppositious purpose.

3. Some businessmen *do* make use of business forms which have been drafted with an eye toward standard contract law, and some cases *do* go to court. Under what conditions does this occur? What does it tell us about law in general, and contract law in particular?

4. Contract litigation is sometimes used as a last resort. There are other kinds of law which are clearly used as last resorts: divorce and bankruptcy, for example. No one would find it surprising that divorce and bankruptcy are not used *except* as last resorts. If contract law and litigation are looked upon as last resort strategies and doctrines, can it then be said that the system in fact works as it is supposed to and that the nonuse of contract law and litigation is perfectly natural? If not, why not?

5. In what respects is the use and nonuse of contract law by manufacturers determined by the way business corporations are organized, rather than by the awareness and attitudes of businessmen toward law? by aspects of the organization of the judicial and legal system? Could one increase the use of contract law by changing the content of contract doctrine? Would this be a wise or unwise thing to do?

[Reading 14]

NOTE: Automobile Accidents, Settlements and the Bargaining Process

[Bargaining and settlement, rather than litigation, are the normal means of resolving disputes arising out of automobile accidents. This has long been common knowledge; but the system of dispute-settlement in automobile accident cases has not, until recently, been the subject of a major study. A group of scholars at the University of Michigan, led by Professor Alfred Conard,* examined the extent of litigation among the approximately 10,000 persons who were seriously injured in Michigan in automobile accidents in 1958. The results were published in Chapter

---

* Professor of Law, University of Michigan. Reprinted from Chapter 6, Alfred F. Conard, et al., Automobile Accident Costs and Payments. Copyright © 1964 University of Michigan Press. Reprinted by permission.

6 of *Automobile Accident Costs and Payments* (1964). A brief excerpt follows.]

Some of these persons made no attempt to collect any damages. Others tried to collect, but were unsuccessful, and they gave up without putting their cases in the hands of a lawyer. . . . The total of the two groups who thus "dropped" their claims without settlement was about 34 percent of the seriously injured individuals. Others were more fortunate; they received tort settlements without having to hire lawyers; about 17 percent were in this group, leaving 49 percent of the cases to be handled by lawyers. Very few of these lawyer-represented cases were dropped without suing or collecting, but about a third of them (16 percent of the serious ones) got settlements without having to file suit. This left 26 percent of the serious injury cases in which suits were filed for personal injuries.

Of those who filed suits, nearly half (12 percent of the cases) obtained settlements without going to trial or a pretrial conference. Of those cases which went to pretrial conference, about half were settled without going to trial. . . .

Although the number of cases settled is less at each successive stage of litigation, the same cannot be said of the amounts. Of the settlements made without lawyers, a very small percentage are over $3000; of the settlements made by lawyers after suit filed, a majority are over $3000. However, the amount of settlement does not rise at each successive stage; there are proportionately more small settlements after pretrial than between suit and pretrial; there are proportionately more small settlements after trial than between pretrial and trial. It appears that the defense pays off most of the big winners before getting to the pretrial conference, and goes to pretrial and trial chiefly in cases where there are means of defeating or holding down the recovery. . . .

B. Gross Tort Settlements

The "gross settlement" is the amount paid out by anyone, usually a liability insurance company, to settle the insured's potential liability for negligence. Even in serious cases, most of the settlements are relatively small, and the frequency of occurrence falls off rapidly as the amount rises. . . .

This distribution gains more significance when it is reduced to a smaller number of categories; and compared with the distribution of losses among the same subjects of injury. Although all of the serious injury victims had some economic loss, 45 percent of them obtained no tort settlement at all. To put it the other way around, 100 percent had a loss, but 55 percent received a tort settlement. Twenty-six percent of the serious injury victims had losses between one and a thousand dollars, but only 16 percent of the same group had settlements in this range. The disparity mounts as the amounts rise, so that 20 percent with losses over $10,000 compare with 5 percent receiving settlements over this figure. . . .

The disparity between amount of loss and of settlements does not mean that tort law is not doing the job for which it is designed—the compensation of the innocent by the guilty. Indeed, the fact that 45 percent of the injured receive no settlement might be taken to show that the tort law is working as it should in making recovery depend on negligence and freedom from contributory negligence. Viewing the matter from this point of view, one might wish to compare the percentage distributions of losses and settlements, with uncompensated cases excluded. On this basis of comparison, one finds a striking similarity between the two distributions. The only glaring dissimilarity appears in the bracket of "$10,000 or more," in which the proportion of settlements is significantly lower than the proportion of economic losses. The comparison is made in Figure 6-6.

Perhaps the most striking aspect of these distributions is the large proportion of injured persons who receive settlements which must be far below anyone's estimate of their actual loss. Tort theory, which calls for the recovery of all or nothing, offers no justification for this phenomenon. Presumably it results partly from the desire of parties to compromise rather than to gamble for the all-or-nothing result of a jury verdict and partly from the

FIGURE 6-6—COMPARISON OF AMOUNTS OF ECONOMIC LOSS
AND OF TORT SETTLEMENTS IN SETTLED CASES
(Percentage distribution of serious injury cases)

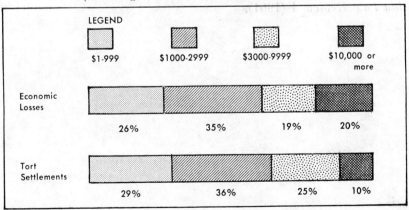

Number of interviews providing this information: 310, 183.

expectation that a jury would also compromise to reach agreement between those who want to give all and those who want to give nothing. . . .

_____

In a later part of the chapter, Conard and his associates address themselves to the question: "Why do some injury victims push their claims to ultimate judgment while others drop theirs without payment?" One might also ask "why do defendants pay some claims so generously, and others so scantily, or not at all?"

Victims who received no settlement were asked why not. Eighty percent gave reasons which involved the improbability of winning a settlement ("Nobody to collect from; nobody else at fault; the person at fault unknown or address unknown; injured person at fault, or member of family at fault," 68%; "The person at fault had no insurance, or no money," 12%). Only 1% thought collecting would be too expensive; 2% were unwilling to push the claim because the person at fault was a friend or relative. (p. 210) The reader will note how frequently the *legal* concept, fault, appears in this table. Other tables and graphs demonstrate that notions of fault, as the parties understand them, play a powerful part in determining whether the parties settle, and how much of a settlement they demand or concede. Other factors (the kind of injury, medical prognosis, disputes over the naked facts) are also important, of course.

Another empirical study of out-of-court settlements is Curtis J. Berger & Patrick J. Rohan, "The Nassau County Study: An Empirical Look into the Practices of Condemnation," 67 *Columbia Law Review* 430 (1967). *See also* Marc A. Franklin, Robert H. Chanin & Irving Mark, "Accidents, Money, and the Law: A Study of the Economies of Personal Injury Litigation," 61 *Columbia Law Review* 1 (1961).

B. THE RELATIONSHIP OF THE FORMAL LEGAL SYSTEM TO THE LESS FORMAL AND THE RELATIONSHIP OF BOTH TO THE PRIVATE SECTOR OF SOCIETY

15. Law and the Balance of Power

STEWART MACAULAY*

I. THE RELATIONSHIP BETWEEN THE LEGAL AND THE PRIVATE SYSTEMS

a. *The Nature of the Systems*

The legal system can operate in a more or less formal fashion. At one extreme, law can attempt to change or support social situations or relationships by its formal processes. Legislation can be passed. Statutes can be interpreted, and common-law doctrines can be created by courts. Disputes can be resolved in litigation or administrative proceedings. The manufacturer-dealer story involves all of this legal output; there has even been a referendum to overturn the Arkansas administrative-licensing statute. But the legal system also can operate less formally in ways not so easy to observe in a law library. For example, Senate committees can harass the president of General Motors in an effort to induce him to change corporate policies; if the information media cooperate, this can be most effective. Lawyers counseling their clients can channel conduct. In this way they can give actual or even potential formal legal action widespread effect. If, as is suspected, the manufacturers pursued a test case strategy in approaching the interpretation of the Good Faith Act,** their lawyers were giving meaning to the act in many areas by telling the sales staff to abandon many traditional practices—at least temporarily. Also administrators can advise manufacturers and dealers about their rights under state statutes and influence conduct. They can

---

* Professor of Law, University of Wisconsin. Copyright © 1966 Russell Sage Foundation, pp. 202-06. Reprinted by permission.
** A federal law of 1956, which requires manufacturers of automobiles to act in "good faith" toward their dealers in franchise matters. However, the statutory definition of "good faith" has been interpreted by the courts to cover no more than "coercion." [Eds. note]

mediate disputes in prehearing conferences without the costs of formal proceedings. For better or worse, all of this less formal legal action affects people and organizations significantly.

Private orderers, too, can operate in a more or less formal fashion. The structure of a relationship can be planned or left to evolve in response to circumstances. The manufacturer-dealer relationship has been codified in selling agreements, and procedures have been created within the manufacturers' organizations for an upward flow of communications and for review of actions taken at the local level. Other formal channels for meeting problems have been created by the manufacturers' recognition of the legitimacy of the National Automobile Dealers Association as a representative of the dealers. Of course, it is one thing to create relatively formal private procedures, and it is another thing to follow them. Often a formal contract is drafted, signed, filed away, and forgotten as businessmen prefer to work things out their own way without regard to rights and duties. We have little information about the degree to which field men insist on enforcing the provisions of franchises and when and to what extent dealers are given leeway to deviate from the formal pattern. We can expect that field men and dealers do not always "follow the book," for few superiors find it profitable to enforce all of the rules all of the time.

Disputes also can be handled more or less formally outside the legal system. At one extreme, General Motors has set up an impartial umpire to consider problems raised by dealers. The retired federal judge who was appointed adopted a procedure similar to that used in court. At the other extreme, field men and dealers settle disagreements privately and informally through negotiation. This is a bargaining process with a minimum of procedures and structure, although it takes place within a context set by the written franchise, the Good Faith Act, and, in many instances, state legislation.

b. *The Impact of the Legal on the Nonlegal Systems*

Both the more and less formal operations of the legal system have influenced the more and less formal operations of the private systems and produced the major part of whatever impact the total effort by the dealers has had. For example, the 1956 revised General Motors franchise, the elected dealer councils, and the impartial umpire were created in response to the Senate hearings. Private negotiations between field man and dealer will be affected to the extent that a manufacturer's legal department tells its sales staff that they must persuade and not order dealers to act. A field man who cannot demand action must bargain. All of these private systems have far more meaning for most dealers than lawsuits for damages under the Good Faith Act or proceedings under administrative-licensing statutes to revoke licenses of factory representatives. The major significance of these formal legal proceedings is that they support the private other-than-legal ways of dealing with the problems. This is why there is general satisfaction with the results of the dealers' use of the legal system, although one can find few reported cases under either the Good Faith Act or the state statutes which favor the dealer who brought the case. The elaborate screening systems designed to catch problem situations generally work. The law prompted most of them and keeps them safe from erosion.

2. ADVANTAGES AND DISADVANTAGES OF INFORMALITY AND PRIVATE SYSTEMS

To describe the operation of less formal legal systems and private systems for planning and solving problems is not necessarily to applaud them. Of course, each has important values. First, consider the advantages of informal legal action. For example, a publicity hearing performs an educational function, drawing attention to a problem and creating a climate for action. Unless the hearing exposes conduct which many would criticize, it fails because its findings are not news. It is one of the few techniques by which an individual legislator can initiate action rather than simply recording his vote on proposals made by the executive or the controlling group in the legislature.

Private other-than-legal dispute settlement systems also have virtues. They frequently operate at less cost and greater speed than the courts, keep problems relatively unpublicized, produce compromises instead of victories, and leave the parties happier than they would be if they had engaged in full-scale legal warfare. It seems likely that a dealer would be allowed to continue selling Fords if he won his case before the Dealer Policy Board.* One can wonder about his chances of continuing after he won a suit under the Good Faith Act.

Nonetheless, there are costs. First, informal legal systems are classified as informal because they abandon due process and procedural safeguards. It is not news that the publicity hearing can be used to sidestep these inconvenient "legal technicalities" and throw people to the mob. Individuals or organizations may be

---

* A board established within the Ford Motor Company and available to dealers for complaints about any subject, including franchise matters. [Eds. note]

forced to abandon their rights when the exercise of them is unpopular. Second, private dispute settlement has drawbacks. When two strong organizations get together to resolve differences, the resolution can be at the expense of other unrepresented interests. For example, the manufacturers and those who control dealer associations could reach decisions in private negotiations which adversely affected unrepresented dealers or the car-buying public. (This is not to say they have done so.) It is probably a little harder to do this in a public forum because of the chance of publicity and the usual attempts to give all interests a hearing.

NOTES AND QUESTIONS

1. In the preceding section, the readings demonstrated differences between actual behavior and some sort of idealized picture prescribed by the legal system. In general, not much attention was paid to the relationship between the formal and the informal realm, the public and the private.

In this unit, we examine, in a preliminary way, that relationship. It can take many forms. Law can be directed toward prohibiting conduct; or it can be supportive and permissive in nature. It can authorize people to do things they would like to do, and it can give interest groups the power and legitimacy to pursue their own ends. Can you think of examples of a supportive or permissive relationship from the excerpt from Professor Macaulay's study of auto dealers? from other readings?

The relationship between acts of private persons and formal legal rules can be quite complicated. We will take a fairly simple illustration. In Wisconsin, it is against the law to open a sealed letter addressed to another person, if done intentionally and without the consent of the sender or the addressee. WIS. STAT. ANN. § 942.05(1) (1967). Suppose a sealed letter arrives from a draft board at a young man's home. He is away. His mother is anxious to find out what is in the letter.

She may open the letter, completely unaware that a statute forbids her to. Or she may quell her curiosity and put the letter to one side, unaware of the statute, but obeying other norms. She might also accidentally open the letter, before realizing it is not addressed to her.

Let us assume the unlikely case that she *is* aware of the statute. She may nonetheless disobey and open the letter. Or she may attempt to *cope* with the legal situation—by calling up her son at work and asking his permission to open the letter. Or she may try to *evade* the statute—by holding the letter up to the light, for example. Or she may choose to *obey*, and put the letter away until her son returns. Using these various categories of response, could you classify the actions of the policemen in LaFave's study? the lawyers in Blumberg's? the businessmen in Macaulay's study of the use and nonuse of contract?

[Reading 16]

2. "Legal enforceability," wrote Karl Llewellyn, is "sometimes a factor in inducing performance by a debtor." But, he asserts, some of the debts which go to law are "bad risks"; and the possibility of enforceability may contribute to "begetting" them. "Remove the legal sanction and men will give credit with more care." "What Price Contract? An Essay in Perspective," 40 *Yale Law Journal* 704, 725 (1931).

He goes on, however, to make the following remarks in a footnote:*

. . . . Is there enough stiffening of performance-drive by the totality of legal pressures, after contract obligations have been assumed, to offset the effects (occurring before contract obligations have been assumed) which reliance on anticipated legal pressures may have in lessening credit-caution and credit-judgment? Both phases of possible legal effect are intangible, on present knowledge. The first is a step closer to tangibility than the second. My own guess is that in the main writers, both legal and other, tend to overestimate heavily the effects of law in either aspect; but that on the other hand any layman who ever gets to considering the effects of law in his own case is likely then to let the idea of it influence him for more than it really is worth. My guess is, too, that no general statement about "contract" or "credit" will in this matter be worth anything; even uninformed common sense shows huge differences to be probable between investment and commercial credit; similar differences within each field, etc., are certainly to be expected as well. And my guess is, further, that the real major effect of law will be found not so much in the cases in which law officials actually intervene, nor yet in those in which such intervention is consciously contemplated as a possibility, but rather in contributing to, strengthening, stiffening attitudes toward performance as what is to be expected and what "is done." If the contract-dodger cannot be bothered, if all he needs is a rhinoceros hide to thumb his nose at his creditor

---

* Reprinted by permission of the Yale Law Journal Company and Fred B. Rothman & Company from The Yale Law Journal, Vol. 40, p. 725 n.47 (1931).

with impunity, more and more men will become contract-dodgers. Only saps will work, in an economy of indirect, non-face-to-face contacts. And as between individual enterprises, the competition of the contract-dodger will drive the contract-keeper into lowering his own standards of performance, on pain of destruction. This work of the law-machine at the margin, in helping keep the level of social practice and expectation up to where it is, as against slow canker, is probably the most vital single aspect of contract law. For in this aspect each hospital case is a case with significance for the hundreds or thousands of normal cases. . . .

Is there any material in any of the readings thus far which sheds any light on Llewellyn's questions? How would you go about testing his hypotheses?

[Reading 17]

3. Consider the following quotation from Thomas Schelling, *Arms and Influence* 120, 140-41 (1966): *

One of the values of laws, conventions, or traditions that restrain participation in games of nerve is that they provide a graceful way out. If one's motive for declining is manifestly not lack of nerve, there are no enduring costs in refusing to compete. . . .

Typically this is the principal authority behind an arbitrator's suggestion in any dispute: the disputants having reached the point where they cannot satisfactorily negotiate an agreement themselves, and having either called in an arbitrator or had one forced upon them, there is a strong power of suggestion in whatever the arbitrator comes up with. He provides a last chance to settle on the one extant proposal; if agreement is badly desired and further negotiation out of the question, the arbitrator's suggestion may be accepted in default of any alternative.

It is worth observing that tacit negotiation of unenforceable agreements can sometimes be much more efficacious than explicit verbal negotiation of agreements that purport to carry some sanction. One difficulty with overt negotiations is that there are too many possibilities to consider, too many places to compromise, too many interests to reconcile, too many ways that the exact choice of language can dis-

---

* Professor Thomas Schelling, Center for International Affairs, Harvard University. *Arms and Influence* (1966) published by Yale University Press, reprinted by permission.

criminate between the parties involved, too much freedom of choice. In marriage and real estate it helps to have a "standard-form contract," because it restricts each side's flexibility in negotiation. Tacit bargaining is often similarly restrictive; anything that can't go without saying can't go into the understanding.

What additional relationship between formal law and informal bargaining processes, other than those already considered, is suggested here by Schelling? How important is this phenomenon?

4. Professor Macaulay stresses the virtue of "other-than-legal dispute settlement systems." They produce "compromises" instead of "victories." He thinks it likely that a dealer can stay on with Ford, even after winning his case before the Ford Dealer Policy Board—but not if he won a suit in court under the Federal Good Faith Act.

The Ford Board is deliberately informal; it not only is not a court, it does not try to behave like a court. General Motors, however, has set up a much more "judicial" procedure within its organization to handle dealer problems. Indeed, they have hired a retired federal judge to head their "court." Assuming that the General Motors "court" followed the same rules of procedure and evidence as a federal court, handed down written opinions and attempted to follow precedent (actually its operation is considerably looser), do you think it would still remain more likely that a "winner" before this court could stay on with General Motors than a winner in federal court? Why?

5. Bargaining and conciliation between affected parties, or between affected parties and government bodies may be contemplated, of course, by the formal law; it need not be extra-legal or informal. Modern labor law contemplates collective bargaining between labor and management. Government applies pressure but does not impose solutions. Civil rights statutes have often stressed "conciliation" rather than penal enforcement. An important recent study by Leon H. Mayhew, *Law and Equal Opportunity, A Study of the Massachusetts Commission Against Discrimination* (Harvard U. Press 1968) examines the way in which a state anti-discrimination agency operated.

[Reading 18]

NOTE: Vilhelm Aubert's Theory of Conflict and Conflict Resolution

Paragraph 4, above, was an inquiry into a troublesome problem. There are many kinds of institutions for settling disputes

and resolving questions of law and fact. Some are official, some
unofficial. Some are public, some private. Some are formal, some
informal. These categories overlap; the General Motors procedures are formal but private; they are unofficial from the standpoint of the government, official from the standpoint of General
Motors as a subsystem or little society in itself. The question
asked the influence on the parties and on the dispute-settlement
process of formality as against informality, publicness as against
privateness, officialness as against unofficialness.

Related problems have been explored in a fascinating essay by
Vilhelm Aubert, a well-known Scandinavian sociologist of law:
"Competition and Dissensus: Two Types of Conflict and of
Conflict Resolution."*

Aubert begins with a consideration of the concept of conflict.
Conflict is "a state existing between two (or more) individuals
characterized by some overt signs of antagonism." (p. 26) He
then goes on to distinguish between two kinds of conflict, the
conflict of interest and the *conflict of values or belief.*

A conflict of interest between two actors stems from a situation of scarcity. Both A and E want "the same thing," but there
is not enough of it available for each to have what he wants. In
this general sense the basis for a conflict is present in all trading
transactions. The seller would like to have more money than
the buyer is willing to part with, or he would like to withhold
a quantity of the product which the buyer wants to acquire. This
conflict potential is eliminated through the operation of the
market, usually so smoothly that no overt signs of conflict appear.
If a conflict comes into the open, the solution will often be a
compromise. Each party concedes to reduce his demands until
an agreement is reached, although possibly still believing that
he is contributing too much. This agreement is, therefore, not
to be interpreted as an ethical commitment to the price as an
expression of the just terms of exchange. It is merely to be interpreted as an expression of what A or E, under the given market
conditions, finds it in his own interests to do. (pp. 27-28)

Conflicts of interest are particularly prone to compromise. The
parties are not "morally involved," in the same sense as is true
of a conflict of values. It is not a matter of principle that a buyer
must buy this carload of lumber at this precise price. Moreover,
"the gain of one party is not wholly a loss to the other."

Of course, compromise is rendered less likely under certain
conditions. One party sells a car to the other. He delivers it

* Professor Vilhelm Aubert, Institute for Sociology of Law and Public
Administration, University of Oslo, Norway. The Journal of Conflict Resolution, Vol. VII (1963) pp. 26-42. Reprinted by permission.

to the curb in front of the buyer's house, but before the buyer comes home, the car is stolen. Must the buyer still pay? He can no longer achieve anything from the other party through compromise; the car is gone:

> Were there no law and no force in society, the person who wanted to terminate the interaction would have all the cards in his hand in situations where transactions had gone wrong, and there was no longer a question of sharing goods, but of sharing losses. Society, however, has been unwilling to accept that in the case of mishaps of this kind, the sheer accident of who physically possesses the undestroyed part of the exchange should always determine the solution of the conflict of interest over the sharing of a loss. (p. 28)

The legal solution, however, "in common with the solution which accident, fate, or ill will may give," tends to be an all-or-nothing solution; it "gives all to one party." Hence there is still good reason to compromise. "Although one of the parties may stand to gain by rejecting compromise, it is uncertain which party it will be." Thus, "the parties will often find it advantageous to go on with a negotiation in a spirit of compromise." Hence, there are two kinds of bargaining: one, bargaining in the market sense, which *avoids* conflict; second, bargaining in the sense of compromise that *resolves* a conflict.

Conflicts of interest do not imply any disagreement over values. It might even be said that such conflicts imply consensus, at least "on the value of the good which is sought after by both parties," for example, when two candidates seek the same office, or in cases of "sexual rivalry." Conflict of interest is thus "less fundamental" in one sense than "certain conflicts of values, in which the opponents perceive each other as the embodiment of evil."

A conflict of value is based upon a dissensus concerning the normative status of a social object. In itself there is nothing about a dissensus that should lead individuals to attack each other. Nevertheless there is no doubt that disagreements over values as well as over facts have often characterized religious and ideological wars. Such conflict behavior, however, seems almost always to be accompanied by some conflict of interest which derives from the scarcity of power and authority. (pp. 29-30)

Can conflicts of values be avoided by compromise? It is certainly possible to do so. But in such dealings the terms of exchange are quite uncertain, and a scent of the illicit pervades. A value compromise is apt to look like a sellout. Moreover, it is hard to measure compromises of values: who gives and who takes?

In real life, the two kinds of conflict are much intermingled. For example, conflicts of interest easily develop into conflicts of value, or dissensus "over facts," or both. For example, *A* and *B* compete for public office. Initially, perhaps, the dispute between them may be simply that they both want the power and prestige of the office, not to mention the salary. This would be a "pure" conflict of interest. It is highly likely, however, that they would try to persuade the voters that their conflict is one of values— *A* is a conservative, *B* a liberal—and it is likely that they and the voters would actually come to believe that the differences between *A* and *B* were differences primarily or exclusively of values. When a "strong dissensus has been expressed," the conflict becomes harder to solve, partly because bargaining and compromise become much more difficult. Note that the development of a dissensus may arise "when a pure conflict of interest is brought before a court of law. The adversaries will then be forced by the conflict-solving mechanism to formulate their opposing interests as a dissensus, over facts or law or both." (p. 32)

Dissensus (disagreement over values) does not necessarily imply conflict at all. People who disagree may simply avoid each other. For example, believers go to church, and nonbelievers do not; they need not engage in religious wars. But "when people hold strong convictions, religious, moral, political or even scientific, they often want to convert others into true believers. The reason why they want to do so may often be connected with other kinds of interests. Thus, a dissensus over religion may appear to cause crusades and religious wars, although a closer scrutiny may reveal that this had probably not happened unless there had been some clash of interests underlying the strife. . . . [Again,] if two adversaries who disagree strongly each want to propagate their faith, they will have to compete for scarce goods. Potential true believers may be numerous but are still limited. Adherents won are, at least potentially, won over from the camp of the adversary. Even more important, the contestants will compete for positions of power and authority. Each side will attempt to achieve control of resources which put them in a more advantageous position for the propagation of their beliefs. These resources are scarce, and the competition for them may be fierce. Disagreements with institutional implications seem especially to develop into hostility and conflict when they are combined with competition for power." (p. 32)

On the other hand, converting a conflict of value into one of interest does open up the possibility of a solution. The interest-dispute *can* be compromised. Power can be shared; material interests divided. In some ways, this is how democratic societies avoid struggle between competing religious and political ideologies.

Nonetheless, though the two kinds of conflict do intermingle in practice, they are distinct and have distinct characteristics. And, as Aubert's account has made clear, they at least *imply* different mechanisms for their solution. Conflicts of interest imply a bargaining or compromise solution; dissensus over facts or norm call for "law," that is, an all-or-nothing solution.

Aubert now proceeds to look at the problem from the other end, so to speak. What happens when conflicts are "handed over to the law"? The answer is clear: a conflict of interest tends to be formulated "as a dissensus, a conflict of value or belief." Possibly this has already occurred "in the heat of the conflict." But if not, "it must be effected before the parties can enter into effective litigation." In other words, an *issue* must be framed. Something else, too, happens to the conflict: the "basic interaction situation changes from a dyad to a triad," in other words, from a two-party to a three-party situation.

These two "transformations" (from interest to value or fact conflict and from diad to triad) are related. Interests are, in an important sense, subjective. When a problem is converted to one of fact or norm, it is "objectivized."

". . . [A] solution can be reached by an outsider who knows the rules of evidence and is able to perform logical manipulations within a normative structure. By comparing the available facts with the norms he can reach a verdict. As long as an interest conflict remains pure, no outsider, no third person, can, alone, arrive at any conclusion. A solution means a natural adjustment of needs.

"The preceding suggests one superiority of law to the market: it permits others, in advance and abstractly, to determine how certain conflicts are to be solved. This is what makes it possible in law to combine the function of creating predictability with the function of solving individual conflicts. Under certain conditions the 'free market' also does that, but only when the objects of the interest conflicts are replaceable or standardized. Otherwise, a solution of interest conflicts through the reciprocal adjustment of needs is ill suited to serve the need for predictability. Likewise the adjustment mechanism leaves out of consideration the notion that the solution which the parties reach may affect the rest of society." (pp. 33-34)

This situation has both advantages and disadvantages. For one thing, the conflict is not only objectivized, it is also made social and public. A bargain "leaves no mark upon the normative

order, it is not a consequence of it, nor does it become a constituent part of it." (p. 34) But when a conflict is treated at
law, there are the interests of the normative order to consider;
hence the parties are in a sense less free than they would
otherwise be.

Aubert then turns to a closer consideration of the meaning
for conflict resolution of the institutionalized third party. The
"embryo of the legal phenomenon" is to be sought, historically,
in third-party intervention to stop revenge and blood-feuding
from running rampant.

"What must always happen when a third party intervenes in
a conflict between two [parties] is that there arises a possibility
of an alliance. Instead of the stalemate 1 to 1, it can now become
2 to 1. One possibility is, of course, that the two original contestants both become antagonistic toward the third person and
decide to agree so as not to let the newcomer influence the settlement. This mechanism, bringing conflict partners together in a
common antipathy against outside interference, operates in many
situations, but mostly where a developed legal or administrative
system already exists. For the original crystallization of legal
techniques it must have been a more significant eventuality that
the newcomer might join one of the parties, thereby creating a
definitive overweight in power and making it unnecessary to
compromise with the one found to be in the wrong.

"The possibility of an alliance makes it possible, although not
necessary or even likely, that the one side will have to carry the
total loss involved in the case, that is, conform completely to the
demands of the other party. Such will rarely be the outcome
when there are only two parties, unless the power differential
between them is very great. Usually it takes the participation of
a third person to enforce a dichotomous view on the rights and
wrongs of the case. Only when one person can be defined as
guilty, liable, or responsible does the settlement take on a clear
normative meaning. It becomes something more than the settlement between E and A; it also becomes a demonstration of the
validity of a rule of behavior and a statement on past facts." (pp.
35-36)

What posture in fact does the third party take? In theory he
can ally himself with one of the parties. But should we not
rather expect him to feel that there must be "some wrong on
both sides"? "If he sides fully with one of the contestants, he
has brought his status as an outsider into some jeopardy. He has
sacrificed his unique moral standpoint in the little group." (p.
39) In terms of power and authority, he stands to gain by taking

a middle position, thus "possibly maximizing his own moral superiority." There is, then, prestige in serving as a mediator. Through the mechanism of the triad, the conflict may come to be settled "at very much the same point where the two parties would have converged if they had been able and willing to carry on with their bargaining and adjustment. To the interest of the two in reaching a compromise, is added the interest of the third person in keeping his unique role and avoiding a complete alliance." (p. 39)

But the possibility of such a "full normative alliance" cannot be ruled out. Many times the interests of society demand it. It would be a "perversion of justice" to distribute blame evenly between the criminal and his victim. Such a view, however, is specifically modern. It is fairly modern to look upon the criminal and his victim as belonging to "two different and opposing moral spheres of society, the deviants and the law-abiding citizens." In primitive societies, for example, murder took place among equals, and murder was settled by the payment of compensation.

"In the intrinsic tendency of the third party to take a middle-of-the-road view may lie one of the most primitive roots of a hierarchical moral ordering of society. If people in conflict fail to settle their differences and need a third person's intervention, they can hardly fail to bestow upon him a higher status than he had before. He performs a social service by removing stalemates and receives almost automatically a kind of moral 'tax' in addition to the actual economic rewards which he has often been given for his performance. Still, this tendency may also introduce a bias, since there is no intrinsic reason why one party to a conflict should not be predominantly right in his claims. Here lies a strong reason why the third person should be made independent, both of the need for alliance with one of the parties and of the opportunity to enhance his own social position by middle-of-the-road-ism. Hence a need for social agencies that are sufficiently strong to handle the two conflicting parties independent of alliances, and whose status is permanently secured in their professional role, independent of the outcome of individual cases.

"This is what the genuine courts attempt to establish, through organs which dispose of sufficient resources of power, thus enabling them to solve conflicts without resorting to alliances. The third party is firmly institutionalized, his social status independent of the outcome of any one case. His independence will often be demonstrated through an evening out of decisions in the long run. He may rule in favor of the insurance company in some cases, and find for the insured in some others. He may decide in favor of the wife in some divorce cases, but in favor of the husband in others." (p. 40)

In this way, a third-party mediator (deciding conflicts of interest and helping parties to reach compromises) tends to develop into a third-party judge, deciding normative questions or questions of fact.

Can a similar analysis be applied to *any* large-scale organization in which there are conflicts and disputes? In any bureaucracy, there are triadic relationships. Disputes can be referred to a superior at another administrative level for resolution. Initially, the administrative superior is interested in furthering the goals of the organization, not simply in "justice" as would be true in a law-court. Justice might even be a "great nuisance and . . . an impediment to efficient administration." (p. 41) The subordinates or clients will not feel this way, of course. They will demand justice. Hence "a strong force will operate" to tend to transform the bureaucracy into a machinery for settling disputes between subordinates or clients; efficiency "must recede into the background." This means that bureaucratic conflicts "may approach the model of private litigation and a court decision."

"The subordinates or clients consider themselves as having some minimal right of access to resources or privileges, and it is considered to be the prime duty of the superior to make decisions, and just decisions, in cases where conflicts arise over the distribution of these scarce values. A system of precedent and quasi-legal thinking may come to permeate what was originally set up as an organization devoted to effective furtherance of specified goals, and with freedom for the executive to choose the means considered most efficient to maximize the goal.

"It seems possible, then, that the mere existence of triadic relationships, which will always be a characteristic of large scale organization, tend to foster definitions of conflicts as questions of dissensus, as disagreements over rights and over operative facts. When this happens the executive is in danger of becoming a judge, and he will have strong reasons to accept some of the challenge. For how can a big organization work effectively unless the staff feel that they will be rewarded and sanctioned in accordance with the demands of justice? Justice and quasi-juridical behavior has become an element in an even more comprehensive system of means—end thinking." (p. 42)

Aubert, thus, makes an argument that is essentially different from that of Blumberg and others. They see the legal system inevitably transformed (or perverted) into a crude bargaining process; he sees, in a sense, the opposite process: the conversion of conflicts appropriate to bargaining into a cold, formal "objective" application of law. Can their viewpoints be reconciled?

Is it true that the institutionalized third party tends to transform conflicts of interest into conflicts of value? Can you think of examples which either tend to affirm or cast doubt on Aubert's thesis?

We began by suggesting that Aubert's theory had relevance to the way in which formal-informal, private-public, and official-unofficial modes of dispute-settlement interacted. Note that Aubert contains or implies, first, a *historical* or evolutionary theory of relationship; and second, a theory about the relationships between mechanisms and types of conflict, at any given time. Do the two aspects of his theory fit well with each other? Does he shed equal light on the relationship among the three pairs of opposites mentioned in the first sentence of this paragraph? And, in general, how convincing is his theory?

A number of legal scholars have advocated that courts order losses to be split equally where neither of the two parties before the court is really at fault. (Often this situation occurs where a loss has been caused by a third party who cannot be found to answer for damages, and two equally innocent litigants each seek to place the full loss on the other.) What would Aubert predict to be the likely consequence of wide use of the loss-splitting approach by the courts?

19. Bargaining and Analysis in Government

HENRY S. ROWEN*

TWO APPROACHES

The two principal approaches to the operations of Government are what have been called the Hierarchical one and the Bargaining one. The former derives from traditional administrative and economic theories, the latter from pluralist concepts of democratic government. The former has emphasized hierarchies of objectives, lines of authority, division of labor among organizational units, coordination of policies and programs, and systems efficiency. It is in this tradition that the economics of public expenditures has developed, including in recent years the technique of systems analysis. The bargaining approach is concerned mainly with the fact that individuals and groups with differing values exist, with the power they possess, and with the processes of adjustment among these groups in the workings of government. This approach is rooted in the concept of equity in a democratic society.

In recent years the bargaining view has been very much in the ascendency. For several reasons. It has deep roots in the pluralist tradition, a tradition which is widely and deeply shared in American culture. It seems to be more consistent with the actual workings of government than does the traditional hierarchically oriented administrative theory. The bargaining theorists have, of course, gone further and have not only pointed out that things don't work the way the traditional view would have it, they have adduced strong arguments as to why they shouldn't and can't.

* President, The Rand Corporation; former Assistant Director, Bureau of the Budget. Paper delivered at Annual Meeting of the American Political Science Association, September 6-10, 1966 © The APSA. Reprinted by permission. Published in Subcommittee on National Security and International Operations of the Committee on Government Operations, U.S. Senate, Selected Comment on Planning-Programming-Budgeting 44 (1967).

Third, important aspects of the theory of public expenditures have come under severe criticism. For example, the conditions to be met for Pareto optimality generally aren't met and the divergences often seem large and difficult or impossible to overcome.

So perhaps the bargaining approach is the only contender of consequence left on the field. I think it is not.

How Well Does the Present System Work?

The theory has been developed in its most interesting and recent form by C. E. Lindblom. In his latest book on this subject he asserts that independent, partisan decision makers can be coordinated in several ways in the absence of a central coordinator; that such partisan mutual adjustment is characteristic of the real world; that complex decision making is necessarily fragmented, disjointed and incremental; that having a multiplicity of interacting quasi-independent decision makers promotes rationality; that central decision making doesn't work very well; that partisan mutual adjustment facilitates agreements on values and actions; and that the process promotes consent to democratic government.

One comment on this view is that Lindblom has described the way the Government mainly works. The pulling and hauling, adversary dealings, promotion of programs, compromising, marginal adjusting, and related activities are highly visible aspects of governmental behavior from the precinct level on up. It is an important contribution to our understanding of bureaucracy to have the importance of this kind of behavior properly emphasized and to have begun to analyze it systematically.

But if this is not an inaccurate description of the workings of much of the government much of the time, how good are the results of this process, and to the extent they seem not good what can be done to improve things?

If one holds the view that means and ends of government action are indistinguishable and that all of our issues are issues of equity in a pluralistic society, it is difficult to say something meaningful about the goodness or badness of the functioning of government. Presumably the search for objective measures of governmental performance is fruitless. Any program the system produces will do as well as any other and the goodies might as well be distributed one way as another.

This is an extreme view and, I think, not tenable. (The symmetrically opposite, strict hierarchial view is even less tenable.) Not tenable for the following reasons:

Some ends are widely deemed to be better than others. Individuals and groups have preferences, not only to "Who's Right?", but also on "What's Right?". "What's Right?" often commands a high degree of agreement. There are consequences of government action that come pretty near to be objectively "good" or "bad". For example, avoidance of nuclear war, reduction of poverty at home and abroad, providing at least a minimal level of protection from crime and violence, improvement in the status of Negroes. These are widely shared objectives. Although objectives like these are abstractions, and they sometimes conflict with each other and with other objectives, and there are wider differences about ways to accomplish these ends than there is about the ends themselves, these ends do matter. And some actions do better than others at achieving these ends.

That is, efficiency matters also. This assertion might seem trivial. But if means are regarded as ends and if the purpose of the game of government is only income distribution, then why be efficient? One reason is that it has a prominent place in American culture. Another is that if one holds that there are some important objectives, it takes some minimal level of efficiency to get there. Moreover, it may take not only a strong bargaining position but even a degree of efficiency in getting income transferred to the groups deemed worthy of receiving it.

Consider technical efficiency. It seems to make a difference. Some designs of supersonic transports or space vehicles, or sewage treatment plants are better than others in the sense that payload—range or payload—thrust or plant output-input ratios—differ and some designs work better than others. In space, in defense, in transportation, in health, in crime, in flood control, in postal delivery there are many decisions made about which the question of technical efficiency is relevant.

But this is too limited a concept of efficiency. More general is an economic efficiency concept—the least cost combination of factor inputs to accomplish a given objective. Still more general is the measure of both benefits and costs in money terms.

One must be careful, however, to be sure that the same objective is being met by the various means. In the early stages of the manned lunar landing program, the two principal alternatives considered called for an earth-orbiting and a moon-orbiting stage respectively. The object in both cases was to get at least one American to the moon and back alive by 1970. There was little question about the objective being the same. (Even in examples of this kind, some members of our society might prefer one approach based not on technical or social economic criteria but on a preference among manufacturers.)

Clearly there are many cases of a type Lindblom cites where members of society have important differences both among ends and among the means for achieving given ends. The least cost solution on a highway *won't* do for many. But, the least cost solution (or at least a relatively low cost solution) is relevant and the partisan mutual adjustment process isn't all that likely to throw it up.

That is, we should not just assume that good (i.e., efficient in one of the senses described above) technical and economic decisions will be made, or even taken into account, by a system operating primarily in a partisan mutual adjustment mode. We should not assume so for several reasons:

(a) Large bureaucracies have remarkable inertia. I use the word "inertia" in the sense used in physics, as the tendency for matter (organizations) to remain at rest, if at rest or if moving, to keep moving in the same direction. The inner life of organizations and their imperviousness to changes in the external environment is often extraordinary. The celebrated case of the survival of the cavalry for decades past its useful life is a case in point, as is the continued survival of some other governmental anachronisms. The ability of a well-established organization to develop a doctrine, a theory which justifies and defends behavior against outside influences is impressive. The absence of market prices for most of the goods and services produced by government helps to maintain the inertia. So does the restricted nature of the competition that government "firms" also face.

One result is to suppress options, to conceal possibilities that don't conform. Anomalies can exist for very long periods of time with no corrective action being taken.

For example, in our Defense Department we had for many years a situation in which two services were preparing for quite different kinds of wars. Their force structure, their readiness, their logistics, and their ordnance were incompatible. These gaps persisted despite the fact that many people were aware of the problem. But doctrine was too strong. A similar gap existed between our alliance policies abroad and the forces to back up these policies.

One difficulty with leaving important issues to be thrashed out by the parties that happen to express an interest is that they can argue over the wrong issues. Some years ago there was some debate over the size of the Soviet bomber force versus our own; several years later there was a similar debate over strategic missiles. In both cases, the main issue debated was the number of

vehicles on either side; the main real issue was largely unde-
bated: the implications for the vulnerability of the forces.

(b) There are not only wide differences in the bargaining
power of the "firms," this bargaining power is not necessarily
very highly correlated with the information or the power to take
relevant action to accomplish objectives with a high degree of
efficiency.

No one can deny the power of the Bureau of Public Roads;
one might question the extent to which it has the information
to enable it to shape the structure of cities differently than it
now does through its urban highway programs or the extent to
which it would regard this as its mission in life. This power may
reflect widely shared values or the intensity with which values
are felt. But the price in technical and economic diseconomies
are often high. If all one uses as a criterion is the pragmatic test
of the firm's "sales" (the disputes it wins, the new programs introduced, the old ones sustained, the share of the budget obtained),
one hasn't much. And resources wasted often count as much as
resources well used on these criteria.

(c) Even where counteravailing power is present, one cannot
assert a high probability that the common interest will benefit.
If private firms and organized labor are capable of striking bargains which act against the common interest one shouldn't assume
that government agencies are not.

Other examples can be cited: We invest quite a lot to move
air passengers from airport to airport but have paid little attention to the increasingly significant links in the journey from
portal to and from airports. Our maritime policies which have
traditionally been worked out via the bargaining mode include
an operating subsidy which is structured so as to create a positive
incentive to overmanning of ships. Our water resources policies
favor expensive means of reducing water pollution over less expensive means. These policies have also produced flood control
projects which have generated incentives for people to overbuild
in still vulnerable flood plains. In agriculture we pay both to
take land out of agricultural production while bringing reclaimed
land in. We have a sugar subsidy program which seems to cost
three times the net incomes of the sugar producers. We spend
ten times [as much] on urban roads as on urban mass transit
without the balance between these two types of transportation
being examined.

It might be held that some of these examples simply illustrate
the principle that our political system has decided to transfer
income to specific groups, that a politically feasible way has been

found to do this, and the fact that apparently contradictory actions are taken by different parts of the government is either
evidence of income being transferred to *other* groups or is compensatory action to correct undesirable overall effects of particular
subsidies.

This is undoubtedly true—in some cases. But it is my belief,
that, on the average, instances of this type are at least as much
due to the reasons cited above: bureaucratic inertia, random
differences in bargaining power, absence of market forces, unregulated intra-governmental monopolistic practices.

WHAT CAN BE DONE?

Neither model will do. Lindblom is right about the undesir-
ability and infeasibility of a rigidly hierarchical system. But he
is, I think, too hopeful about the virtues of the largely bargaining
system we have. We need analysis as well.

What do I mean by analysis? For present purposes suffice it
to mean an attempt to define objectives, to describe alternative
means to these ends, to invent new objectives and new alternatives means, to assess benefits and costs, to take account of uncertainties, to quantify what looks useful to quantify, to isolate decisions that can be deferred from those that can't, to create options.
All this may appear ordinary. It is, but it is often difficult to
do and it hasn't been attempted much in a systematic way on
major public decisions. But it has begun to be done in a significant way with results in the Defense Department that are
impressive; I predict that results throughout other parts of government will, in time, be at least as impressive.

There are several necessary conditions for doing better: one
is that there exist a structure of adversary relationships, that over
a wide range of governmental behavior there exist mechanisms
for one group to challenge, and debate issues of common interest
with other centers. This doesn't work well if left to chance. It
requires action from a higher level. This is a familiar problem
in the operation of big corporations. It is more an important
problem in areas where market mechanisms are weak or absent.
Therefore, one subject for systematic analysis is to improve the
bargaining phenomena.

Another necessary condition is that there be a system of analysis involving many groups working from many points of view.
For no one group can assemble all of the relevant data on a
complex issue; values and facts *do* get inter-mixed; ends and
means often *do* inter-act; problems must be decomposed for analysis; analysis must be partial; all optimizations are, in some sense,

suboptimizations. One can expect, however, through more systematic analysis to narrow the vast areas in which governmental action is uninformed, arbitrary, and based on unenlightened opinion rather than data and analysis. One can create larger conceptual "islands" in which relatively good predictions can be made about the consequences of taking alternative decisions. One can even expect to connect some islands to each other through the development of broader theories. Just as economic theory was extended over time from separate theories on production and consumption and money into a unified macro-theory with major consequences for the conduct of public affairs, so we should expect to develop broader theories of health, of education, of law enforcement. And some of these might even connect. How far can this process continue? Indefinitely. (But I confess my mind boggles at the notion of the unified theory, for example, of postal service, foreign aid, and outer space.) We needn't be concerned about running out of new phenomena. New ones will be identified or become ripe at at least the rate at which old ones are mastered.

Finally, in carrying out analyses what should be done about the absence of conditions for Pareto optimality? Two things. Firstly, try in making analysis, to make corrections that move the results in what seems to be the right direction. Secondly, take some solace from the bargaining viewpoint: our system doesn't mind making interpersonal comparisons and the interactions, over time, of partisan mutual adjusters will see that rough justice gets done.

20. Civil Justice and the Poor: Issues for Sociological Research

JEROME E. CARLIN, JAN HOWARD
AND SHELDON L. MESSINGER*

1 LAW & SOCIETY REVIEW 9, 32-36, 38-42 (1966)

New Tasks. One of the characteristic features of our society is the steadily expanding scope of government. With the weakening of kinship and other traditional social units large scale formal organizations, both public and private, are called upon to perform tasks and satisfy needs that previously had been taken care of in less formal ways. The development is particularly evident in the expansion of governmental activity on behalf of the poor. This may be seen in the extension of health, education and welfare benefits through social security and welfare legislation, medicare and aid to education—and in the passage of the Economic Opportunity Act.

Along with the establishment of agencies to implement these various programs there has developed a need for insuring fairness and reasonableness, particularly in the exercise of the adjudicative or quasi-adjudicative functions of these organizations. Decisions regarding eligibility for benefits represent an important although by no means the only area of concern.

The expanded scope of the legal system is also reflected in the assumption of administrative tasks by nominally judicial agencies. Thus, to an increasing extent, courts serving the poor seem to define their principal objective as the solution of a social problem by a benevolent administrator rather than the resolution of a legal dispute by an impartial adjudicator.[93] The orientation

---

* Professor Jerome E. Carlin, Coordinator, San Francisco Neighborhood Legal Assistance Foundation; Professor Jan Howard, Center for the Study of Law and Society, University of California, Berkeley; Professor Sheldon L. Messinger, Center for the Study of Law and Society, University of California, Berkeley. Reprinted from Law and Society Review. Copyright © 1966 by the Law and Society Association. Reprinted by permission.

93 The County Court of Philadelphia, for example, in its 47th Annual Report, asserts that its domestic relations court is guided by:

the modern idea of a family court which has as its aim the coordination of the handling of all family problems in one agency, and the utilization of social skills and modern methods for the re-establish-

of such courts has been characterized as "individualized justice"; decisions are tailored to who the person is rather than to what he has done. This concern for the person, and more particularly for the rehabilitation of the disadvantaged, entails a conception of the poor as having problems rather than grievances and of needing treatment not justice. More fundamentally, however, it reflects an image of the poor as essentially incompetent, as incapable of knowing their interests or asserting them.

Not only are the poor assumed to be incompetent and treated, in effect, as wards of the court, but there is a further assumption of an essential harmony of interests between the poor citizen and the state.[96] Accordingly the task of the court is not to arrive at a determination with respect to conflicting rights, but to restore and promote social equilibrium, to heal and to cure. Indeed, the failure of parties to realize their common interests is a prime indication of their need for help. As in the therapeutic situation, stated complaints and grievances are merely the starting points for a more fundamental analysis; they are not to be taken at face value.

Given these assumptions by the court the notion of a contest between adverse interests is deplored, formal rules of evidence and procedure are avoided, and the services of counsel discouraged. The traditional model of adjudication is viewed as irrelevant to, if not preventing, a solution in the best interest of the "client."

An increasing emphasis on rehabilitation may also be noted in certain welfare agencies, with similar consequences for the legal

---

ment and strengthening of families. . . . From the outset the work of the domestic relations division in the new court was concerned with the problem of integration of family life, rather than with the strictly legal issues as to whether the family ties should be severed . . . or whether the husband had a duty to support the family members. COUNTY COURT OF PHILADELPHIA, FORTY-SEVENTH ANNUAL REPORT 195-96 (1960).

A focus on "problem solving" is also evident in the philosophy of the Juvenile Court. According to the Philadelphia report:

The welfare of the child is the guiding principle of operation in the Juvenile Division of the Municipal Court of Philadelphia. . . . The purpose of the Juvenile court law has been defined by the Supreme Court of Pennsylvania as being the "salvation of children" rather than the punishment of offenders (Commonwealth v. Fisher, 213 Pa. 48). It is the characteristics of the child and of his family more than the nature of his delinquent conduct which governs the dispositions of juvenile courts. Id. at 9, 10, 11.

96 With respect to the juvenile court it has been observed: "The delinquent . . . is not (conceived as) the enemy of society. He is society's child, and therefore the interests of the state and the child do not conflict but coincide." J. Handler, The Juvenile Court and the Adversary System: Problems of Function and Form, 1965 WIS. L. REV. 10 (1965).

rights of the poor citizen. Recipients of these agencies are seen
as reservoirs of a great many "needs," only one of which may be
the need for financial assistance. Medical care or psychiatric help
may be required; recipients may need education or job training;
instruction may be called for in managing a budget, in cleaning
up an apartment, in child training practices. The list is perhaps
endless, depending as it does on the agency officials' views of what
is required for effective family functioning. Public assistance law
is perceived by this "new style" agency as providing a mandate
for "serving" these needs. Armed with this mandate agency officials become social therapists.

If the distinctive marks of the old-style agency were suspicious-
ness and harshness, the new-style agency is characterized by a certainty that the professionals who work for the agency know what
the client "needs." And with this certainty may come a greater
intrusiveness, one that looks beyond qualifications for assistance
to the possibility of changing the moral character of recipients in
order to render them whole and competent to deal with their life
situation. To do this the new-style agent must find ways to diagnose the social and psychological defects of the poor; this obviously requires wide access to, as well as scrutiny of, the personal
and private lives of his clients.

The potential danger of the new-style agency is that it may
become a tool for total governmental control. The law would
then provide a license for regulating the detailed life activities
of those citizens "eligible" for such direction. It might well legitimize the reach of government into every circumstance that might
bear on the process of rehabilitation. Traditional guarantees of
procedural due process would be seen as unnecessary—indeed as
interfering with certain commonly desired therapeutic goals. Attorneys would become irrelevant; client dissent a sign that more
therapy was called for. Judicial review of agency decisions would
be unnecessary; judges would wonder what their role could possibly be beyond placing a ritual stamp of approval on decisions
made for reasons best understood by others. A citizen who qualified for this benign control might be stripped of his right to
mean what he said, which is perhaps the most fundamental right
of all. Although we have not yet reached such a pass, the tendency is clear enough. As sociologists we are led to explore the
forces moving the legal system toward total control and the forces
which counterbalance and counteract this movement. . . .

Reduction of Adversariness. Although court cases at all levels of
the judicial system are generally disposed of in a non-adversarial
manner, this is more likely to be the case in those tribunals that

deal with the poor. Thus, only 5 per cent of all dispositions in the Municipal Court in California in 1962 involved a formally contested trial (both sides presenting evidence in a hearing), compared with 10 per cent of all Superior Court dispositions and 12 per cent of all civil cases in the Superior Court.

The weakening of the adversary system in civil as well as in criminal cases is partly a reflection of the increasingly large volume of cases processed through inferior tribunals and the resultant pressures for more efficient procedures. This may account for the hostile reaction of many judges, particularly in traffic courts, to demands for a formal hearing.

The reduction of adversariness is also a function of the increasing emphasis on diagnosis and treatment by non-legal personnel. This is most evident in the juvenile and family courts and in commitment of the mentally ill.

The reduction of adversariness has at least three important effects on the character of the proceedings. First, it very likely hinders the accurate determination of facts. Reliance solely on the court for developing and presenting the facts may restrict information and encourage a premature labeling of the case "to try to fit it into a familiar pattern in an effort to order the mass of facts around a tentative theory." An adversary presentation, "hearing both sides of the story," tends to facilitate the exploration and sifting of facts and provides some assurance against prejudgment and partiality. Second, a non-adversary proceeding probably increases the reliance of the court on the arguments and testimony of the party having the greater resources for developing his case; this is particularly likely when one of the parties is an agency of government. An adversary proceeding on the other hand tends to place the parties on a more equal footing. Finally, the reduction of adversariness limits the opportunity of parties to challenge the bases of the court's actions and decisions and increases the burden on the court for using self-restraint in the exercise of its powers.

Abdication of Responsibility. In the many specialized tribunals it has become common practice for judges to delegate authority for decision-making to administrative personnel: probation officers, medical examiners, marriage counsellors, referees, commissioners and others. . . . This delegation of judicial authority often results, in effect, in shifting the responsibility for making decisions; the judge does little more than rubber-stamp the decisions of others.

Meaningful review of decisions made by non-judicial personnel is important because: (1) the consequences of such decisions are often punitive, (2) the "expert" determination is frequently routine and perfunctory, and (3) the affected party has little opportunity for effective participation in the "preliminary hearing" conducted by non-judicial personnel. He cannot readily present testimony or challenge the determination of the presiding or examining officer. However, given the pressures created by the large volume of cases that are finally brought to the court, the absence of clear standards for the decisions of "experts" and the lack of counsel, there is little opportunity for effective review of these precourt determinations. Thus, in these specialized tribunals delegation of responsibility for decisions seems to permit if not openly encourage unfettered official discretion.

Diffusion of Responsibility. With the increasing bureaucratization of legal institutions and the greater reliance placed on the judgments of administrative personnel, there has been a tendency to fragment responsibility for authoritative decision-making. Under these conditions it becomes difficult to determine when, on what grounds and by whom such decisions have been made. Diffusion of responsibility occurs both within and between various lower-level agencies.

Determinations regarding initial and continuing eligibility for public assistance may involve not only intake workers but case workers, supervisors and support investigators. An important consequence is that the grounds for an adverse determination, and the information upon which it is based, are often hidden from view. According to the Moreland Commission Report: "In one county, for example, 37.5 per cent of those interviewed claimed they were not told why assistance was cut off, and the case records failed to indicate that the former recipient had been given a reason." [Edward V.] Sparer observes:

> At times, a family suspended from welfare assistance because of wrongdoing or fraud cannot, even with the aid of private social workers, obtain the precise nature and ground for the suspension. Without the right to acquire this information and confront his accusers, the client is effectively precluded from disproving the charge.[122]

Diffusion of responsibility for decision-making also results from the overlapping of jurisdiction and control among various lower-level courts and agencies.

A recent study in California indicates the extent to which the functions of welfare agencies overlap those of various judicial

---

122 E. Sparer, *The Role of the Welfare Client's Lawyer*, 12 U.C.L.A. L. Rev. 361, 372 (1965).

and law enforcement agencies. In discussing the relation between welfare and the probation department of the juvenile court in handling dependent and neglected children, it was noted:

> There is no basic statewide delineation of functions. Responsibility for service varies from county to county. Frequently, both welfare departments and probation departments give service to the same family.
>
> When the child is not made a dependent child or ward of the court, casework service is usually provided by the county welfare department or by a private agency in the community. But there are exceptions. The probation departments in some counties carry a sizeable load of "informal" probation cases.[123]

Similar overlap was found in the relation between welfare and the district attorney's office in determining the whereabouts and financial status of the absent parent and in investigating alleged fraud on the part of welfare recipients.

NOTES AND QUESTIONS

1. Rowen and Carlin, Howard and Messinger raise the question whether or not the formal textbook model of the operation of the legal system has real values that are lost in an informal, case-by-case, bargaining system. Do these authors convince you that something of value has been lost when the legal system operates as described in Chapter 2, Section A, at 56-168, *supra*?

2. Do Rowen's "analysis" and Carlin, Howard and Messinger's "adversariness" have significant costs? Why has the legal system failed to give first importance to these two values and, instead, operated through bargaining and expert decision-making?

3. We will consider in more detail later the problems of experts and the legal system. *See* Chapter 4, Section D.l.c., at 630, *infra*.

4. Some might assert that Carlin, Howard and Messinger are naive in calling for adversary process for members of the "lower class." The system is designed to process them in large numbers; adversary procedure is a luxury for the middle and upper classes. *See* Golunskii & Strogovich, Reading 65, at 577, *infra*; Spartacist, Reading 67, at 587, *infra*. *See also* Friedman, Reading 53, at 492, *infra*; Leonard Zeitz, "Survey of Negro Attitudes Toward Law," 19 *Rutgers Law Review* 288 (1965).

---

[123] I. Reichert, Jr. "A Report on Relationships Between Welfare and Law Enforcement Agencies in California" 52, unpublished report, 1962.

Chapter 3

INTERCHANGES BETWEEN THE LEGAL SYSTEM AND OTHER SOCIAL SYSTEMS: ON THE IMPACT OF LAW ON SOCIETY

A. AN INTRODUCTORY NOTE

It is theoretically possible to conceive of the legal system as more or less self-contained. Some aspects of a total culture are more susceptible to influence and modification than others. In the process of modernizing, for example, a country is far more likely to discard native costumes in favor of western dress than it is to discard its native language. One way of putting this difference is to describe the linguistic system as more self-contained than fashions in dress.

It is an open question how self-contained legal systems are. The general assumption of these readings, and of *all* modern sociologists of law, is that there are at least *some* important interchanges between the legal system and other subsystems of the general society or culture. In other words, society influences law, directly and constantly. This does not mean that the legal system is not in some ways self-contained and resistant to outside influences. But all agree that it is not *totally* so. All agree, too, that law in turn influences other parts of the social system. Hence it is somewhat arbitrary to talk about one of the directions in which the influence flows, without talking about the other as well. The division of sections which follows, therefore, is for convenience and ease of analysis only. We begin in this chapter by looking at the impact of law on society.

B. CHANNELLING AND CONTROLLING BEHAVIOR: LIMITS ON
THE EFFECTIVENESS OF LAW

  1. *Individual Factors: The Response of People to Legal Action
      and the Implications for Effectiveness*

  a. *The responses*

---

21. Laws and Moral Judgments

LEONARD BERKOWITZ AND
NIGEL WALKER*

30 SOCIOMETRY 410 (1967)

There is considerable controversy as to the degree to which
criminal law should be employed in regulating private conduct.
The Wolfenden Committee in England, for example, contending that private homosexual behavior between consenting adults
should not be regarded as criminal, argued for severe restrictions
on the scope of criminal law. The Committee maintained law
should intervene as little as possible in the private lives of citizens. A number of legal scholars as well as politicians have taken
a quite different stand, however, and American history is fairly
full of attempts to control private behavior by means of criminal
law. Here we need only remember the Puritan statutes regarding
sex and the Prohibition Amendment.

Many of the points made by both sides in this controversy assume that legal control is at least partly affected by social influences. As an illustration, people advocating limitations on the
scope of criminal law frequently argue that unenforceable laws
can bring a good deal of the legal system into general disrepute.
They might be right. This type of phenomenon could well have
occurred in the Prohibition era. Those Americans who defied
the laws against the sale of alcoholic beverages might have been,
as a result, somewhat readier to break other laws as well. Even

---

* Professor Leonard Berkowitz, Chairman of the Department of Psychology,
University of Wisconsin; Nigel Walker, Oxford University. Reprinted from
Sociometry. Copyright © 1967 American Sociological Association. Reprinted
by permission.

if an individual did not himself break the Prohibition laws, seeing that many other people did so could have led him to believe law violations generally were not so bad. Social influences may also operate when a criminal law is abolished. Consider the possible consequences of new laws making, say, homosexual behavior or suicide no longer a crime. In discussing such a matter, proponents of the use of criminal laws in regulating conduct have often resorted to a contention termed by Walker[3] the "declaratory argument." This position asserts that, whether a legal prohibition acts as a deterrent or not, to repeal it would give the impression that the conduct in question is no longer regarded by society as morally wrong. Thus, removing homosexual conduct and/or suicide from the purview of criminal law supposedly places an implicit stamp of social approval on these behaviors, or at least makes them less disapproved socially, and therefore heightens the likelihood that people will engage in homosexual action and/or commit suicide. Criminal law is here regarded as providing a social definition of what is proper or improper conduct.

Walker and Argyle carried out two investigations in England as a test of this declaratory argument. One of these (by Walker) was a survey of attitudes toward attempted suicide, a form of conduct which had recently ceased to be criminal in England. No significant differences were found between those people who knew the law had been changed and those who did not have this knowledge. In the second study (by Walker and Argyle) an experiment was devised in which young men and women were informed that various actions were or were not criminal offenses. This information did not influence the subject's judgments of the moral propriety of the actions. Their judgments were successfully influenced, however, when they were given the results of a fictitious survey of peers' opinions. All in all, Walker and Argyle interpreted their findings as casting doubt on the validity of the declaratory argument.

A second test of the declaratory argument by a somewhat differently designed experiment seemed advisable, nevertheless. Walker and Argyle had found small but by no means negligible minorities among their respondents who *said* their moral attitudes toward a noncriminal activity (heavy smoking) would become more censorious if Parliament passed a law making this form of behavior a criminal offense. A different research procedure conceivably might detect shifts in moral judgments aris-

[3] Cf. N. Walker and M. Argyle, "Does the Law Affect Moral Judgments?" *British Journal of Criminology*, (1964), pp. 570-581.

ing from knowledge of the existence of a law. While we cannot trace the origins or operation of criminal law to any single set of processes, experts agree, as was noted above, that legal control is affected by social influences. Among these are social consensus and the legitimation of authority, and these influences might conceivably affect the judged propriety of actions regulated by laws.

The greater the social consensus the more likely it is, of course, that people will act in conformity with the majority view. This heightened conformity arises in part because the consensus enhances the perceived validity of the shared opinion; attitudes and beliefs that are held by all or nearly all members of the individual's reference group are frequently regarded as being probably correct. Laws may often be taken as implying a social consensus, and this implied consensus could influence attitudes toward the behavior that is the subject of the laws. Thus, unless the law is clearly violated with relatively great frequency, as happened in the case of Prohibition, the implied consensus associated with the legal definition of an action as "criminal" could result in a judgment of the action as "immoral."

But, in addition, many people also view laws as legitimate authority. Although, as [Talcott] Parsons suggested, lawyers tend to take this legitimacy for granted,[9] theory and empirical research indicate that legitimate authority can wield considerable influence over both action and attitudes. While some writers emphasize coercive processes arising from other group members in accounting for conformity to legitimate authority, most theorists stress the part played by the individual's internalized values. As an example, according to Parsons, "the well integrated personality . . . has and feels obligations to respect legitimate authority. . . ." The felt obligation, Parsons maintained, is "disinterested," and the person adheres to the prescribed code of conduct because he thinks it is "right." Something like the following may therefore happen in the case of an individual for whom a newly passed law represents legitimate authority: First, he believes the law has the right to regulate his behavior. Then, to justify his conformity to the law and lessen any cognitive dissonance*

---

[9] Legal tradition seems to favor a cost-benefit (or "decision-theory") analysis of reactions to the law, according to Professor [Stewart] Macaulay. A person weighs the benefits to him of the prohibited conduct against all the costs and the chances that he will have to pay these costs. Following this line of thought, conformity to the law could also be affected by the anticipated costs of frequent violations to the system of law and order.

* The expression "cognitive dissonance" refers to the theory worked out by Leon Festinger (A THEORY OF COGNITIVE DISSONANCE (1957)) and others,

he may feel, he may interpret the legally forbidden action as
"wrong," or morally bad. In the course of time, with several
repetitions of this process, behaviors disapproved by legitimate
authority may perhaps come to be seen as morally improper
without the intermediate behavioral compliance. Finally, as yet
another possibility, [Jerome] Frank argued that authoritative laws
are often desired because of an unresolved childish need for the
certainty of a father's commands. A person seeking the elimination of disturbing uncertainty may then attribute the father's
"rightness" to legitimate authority; it is as if he reasons, "I myself
do not know, but if the law (my father) says the action is wrong,
it must be bad."

All of these possible processes leave considerable room for individual differences. It is particularly likely that persons will differ
in their reactions to legitimate authority, and the present paper
will examine two sets of personality characteristics that may govern responses to legal controls. The first of these has to do with
social responsibility tendencies. Somewhat akin to Parson's previously cited suggestion regarding the obligations felt by "well-
integrated personalities," Berkowitz and Lutterman (unpublished
study) have described the high scorers on a Social Responsibility
Scale (SRS) as being people who have adopted many of the traditional values of their society and, consequently, often feel obligated to do the socially "right" thing. These people presumably
(a) tend to participate actively in the life of their community
rather than being alienated from their fellows, (b) have a good
deal of trust in other people and even liking for them, and (c)
possess the ego strength enabling them to postpone gratifications
and adhere to their ideals. Berkowitz and Lutterman presented
data consistent with this analysis. Also in accord with their
description, Wrightsman has reported that college students' conformity to the officially-imposed obligation to take part in psychology experiments is positively related to scores on the SRS. It
could well be, then, that high scorers on the SRS will also be
more inclined to judge legally prohibited behavior as "immoral."
Being highly traditional and feeling obligated to act in a traditionally proper manner, they may generally view deviations from
the approved code of conduct—as defined by criminal law—as
morally wrong.

which suggests that people try to bring their opinions, attitudes, values and
knowledge into consistency, and reduce any "dissonance" among them. It
would be "dissonant," the text above suggests, to feel one ought to obey the
law, and obey it, yet feel the law is wrong. Hence there is a tendency to justify one's actions, thus reducing the "dissonance." See Ball & Friedman, Reading
22, at 215, infra. [Eds. note]

The California F Scale* is conceivably also related to reactions to legitimate authority as represented by the law. While the present authors are not aware of any explicit discussion of just this point, the usual conception of the authoritarian personality might suggest that high F persons would tend to be rigidly conformistic to laws. They therefore might also be likely to state that illegal actions are immoral. Other considerations, however, lead to just the opposite prediction. [Leo] Srole has argued that the high authoritarian is actually often greatly alienated from his society, and we have just suggested that this alienation may produce only weak felt obligations to adhere to criminal laws. Then too, the original investigators of the authoritarian personality have contended that this type of individual is actually only a "pseudoconservative." He may voice the tenets of traditional conservatism but, nevertheless, supposedly possesses a violent readiness to abolish many of the institutions he says he cherishes. These violent tendencies could cause him to believe his society's criminal laws are not necessarily correct. All in all, the authoritarian may be even more ambivalent to the laws than he is said to be toward father-figures.

METHOD

SUBJECTS. The subjects in this study, carried out in England, are 41 students from Ruskin College of Oxford University and 46 students from Reading University. Only two of the Ruskin students but half of the Reading subjects are women. While there are more male than female subjects, the three experimental conditions have roughly the same ratio of men to women. The Ruskin students participated in return for a ten pound grant to their class treasury, while the Reading students came from a psychology class. A preliminary inspection of the data indicated there were no systematic differences in scores on the dependent measure between the men and women or the Ruskin and Reading subjects, and these distinctions are ignored in the following analysis.

PROCEDURE. The experiment was carried out in one session at each university. As soon as the students were all seated a two-part questionnaire was distributed. The cover page informed the subjects that the investigators were conducting "a survey of student opinions regarding different forms of conduct," and pointed out that there were no right or wrong answers since views differed on

---

* A test designed to measure the degree to which one has an "authoritarian personality." [Eds. note]

these issues. The subjects had to write down their age, sex and religious denomination, but not their names. A sample question was then provided and the subjects were given instructions as to how each question was to be answered. Each item was in the form of a statement, such as, "A person who uses public transport while he has been quarantined for scarlet fever is not doing anything morally wrong." A six-inch line having no demarcations was beneath each statement, with the ends of the line being marked either "strongly agree" or "strongly disagree." The subject was to place "a tick at the appropriate place on the rating scale" indicating how strongly he agreed or disagreed with the statement.

There were 47 such statements in Part One. Twenty were F scale items, of which 10 came from the list of "reversed" items established by Christie, Havel and Seidenberg. Three of the reversed F scale items are shown in Table 1B. There were also 16 SRS items taken from the 22 used by Berkowitz and Daniels, and 3 of these items are given in Table 1C. The remaining 11 dealt with matters of conduct. There were an equal number of positive and negative items in each personality scale.

Where Part One was the same for all students, three different conditions were established by having three different forms of Part Two: a control condition in which only repeated judgments were obtained, a condition in which peer influence was exerted, and a condition told of the existence of laws. Each of these three different forms dealt with the four statements listed in Table 1A.

The subjects receiving one form (*Test-Retest* group) read the following introduction: "You may want to alter your judgments after thinking about these issues a bit more. Here are several of the statements from Part One. Please indicate your present opinion about each statement by showing how strongly you now agree or disagree with it." The subjects getting a second version of Part Two (*Peer Opinion* condition) were told the following: "In order to stimulate you to think about some of the issues, we give you this information. A recent national survey of students similar to yourself obtained these findings. . . ." They were informed that "over 80 per cent of the students *strongly agreed*" with the statements listed as A1 and A2 of Table 1, and that "over 80 per cent of the students *strongly disagreed with*" the statements A3 and A4 from this table. Finally, in the condition of primary concern to us here (*Law* group), the introduction to Part Two read: "In order to stimulate you to think about some of the issues, we give you this information. Various recently enacted statutes are relevant to some of the previous statements." They were told that as a result of these statutes the behaviors

TABLE 1

Some of the Questionnaire Items

A. *The Four Statements Used for the Moral Judgments*
   1. A man who is drunk in a public place is acting in an immoral manner even if he is not disorderly.
   2. A person is *not* in the wrong morally if he allows someone else to borrow his car without checking this individual's license.
   3. The person who borrows money for the purpose of betting is *not* doing anything morally wrong even if he does not inform the lender why he wants the money.
   4. The individual who sees another person attempting to commit suicide and does not try to stop him is acting immorally himself.
B. *Some of the Christie-Havel-Seidenberg Modified F-Scale Items*
   4. Insults to our honour are not always important enough to bother with. (Disagree)
   25. It would be a good thing if people spent more time thinking and talking about ideas just for the fun of it. (Disagree)
   41. People should be willing to overlook failures in the manners and unpleasant habits of other people. (Disagree)
C. *Some of the Social Responsibility Scale Items*
   7. It is always important to finish anything that you have started. (Agree)
   27. It is no use worrying about current events or political matters; I can't do anything about them anyway. (Disagree)
   39. I would never let a friend down when he expected something of me. (Agree)

referred to in statements A1 and A2 were now "legally permissible," and that the actions described in statements A3 and A4 were now "illegal." Fictitious laws were cited for each.

The four statements were then again repeated in all three forms of Part Two, and the subjects were asked to indicate their *present* opinion about each statement by placing the tick at the appropriate place on the linear rating scales.

At the conclusion of the session the questionnaires were collected and the deceptions were explained. The experiment was discussed and all questions were answered.

Each item was scored by measuring the distance in quarter-inch units from one end of the linear scale. In obtaining the index of change in moral judgments for each of the four crucial statements, changes in the direction of the presumed influence were scored as positive, while changes in the opposite direction were taken as negative changes. The directions followed in the *Law* condition were employed in scoring the changes in the *Test-Retest* group.

RESULTS

Analyses of variance* were performed on the changes in moral

---

* Analysis of variance is a statistical technique which results in a ratio (F) allowing the researcher to determine the probability (p) that observed differences between two or more sets of scores could have occurred by chance. Traditionally, if the probability level is only one in twenty (".05"), the

judgments employing a 3 x 2 factorial design* composed of the three experimental conditions and the two levels of personality variable. In setting up this design the subjects within each experimental condition were first dichotomized in terms of their scores on the given personality scale (either SRS or F scale), and then cases were randomly eliminated until proportional cell frequencies had been obtained. Nine subjects were discarded in the SRS analysis, 4 from the *Test-Retest* group, 3 from the *Law* condition, and 2 from the *Peer Opinion* condition. For the F-scale analysis 15 cases were eliminated, 8 from the *Test-Retest* condition, 5 from the *Law* group, and 2 from the *Peer Opinion* condition. This procedure again resulted in roughly the same number of women in the three experimental groups.

Table 2 summarizes the findings of the analyses of variance, and shows that both designs led to the same significant effects:

TABLE 2

Results of Analyses of Variance with Subjects Classified in Terms of SRS or F-Scale Scores

		SRS		F-Scale	
	df	MS	F ratio	MS	F ratio
Conditions	2	135.30	4.36*	121.56	3.37*
Scale level	1	15.26	—	98.79	—
1 x 2	2	24.50	—	34.46	—
Ss w/in condition	72 (66)ᵃ	31.06	—	36.08	—
Items	3	191.83	7.78***	158.72	6.52**
1 x 5	6	44.94	—	49.50	—
2 x 5	3	10.33	—	2.51	—
1 x 2 x 5	6	21.29	—	16.42	—
Residual	216 (198)	24.67	—	24.35	—

ᵃ The numbers in parentheses refer to the degrees of freedom in the F-Scale analysis when these are not the same as in the SRS analysis.

* $p < .05$.
** $p < .01$.
*** $p < .001$.

researcher feels safe in assuming that similar differences will be found among other similar groups. [Eds. note]

* In an experiment involving a "3 x 2 factorial design," the combined and separate effects of two independent variables are studied. The first variable involves three categories (in the Berkowitz & Walker study, the test-retest condition, the peer opinion condition and the law condition). The second variable involves two categories (in this study, two types of subjects, "high scorers" and "low scorers" on a personality test). To say that these two variables are "independent" of each other means that both types of subjects were found in each type of situation. Since students were classified on the basis of two scores, two 3 x 2 analyses were performed here. In one analysis, the personality variable was "social responsibility"; in the other, it was "authoritarianism." [Eds. note]

(1) there were significant differences in change scores among the three experimental conditions, and (2) the judgmental changes varied across the four items. This similarity in results, whether the subjects were classified in terms of the SRS or the F scale, does not stem from a strong association between the two personality scales; disregarding the experimental conditions, there was no relationship at all between the classification of a subject as either high or low on the SRS and his high or low classification on the authoritarianism measure (chi-square=0.00).*

Looking at the top line of Tables 3 and 4, which shows the results of Duncan Range tests** of the condition means, we can see that there were reliable differences among all three groups. The subjects informed that laws existed regarding the four kinds of behavior tended to alter their judgments of the moral propriety of the actions in accord with the laws, and this change in the direction of the supposed laws was significantly greater than the change (generally in the opposite direction) occurring in the *Test-Retest* condition. The greatest shift in adjustments, however, arose in the *Peer Opinion* condition. The subject's moral opinions evidently were more strongly influenced by knowledge of the consensus among their peers as to whether the given acts were good or bad than by knowledge of the existence of laws on these matters.

TABLE 3

Mean Change in Judgments of Morality for Subjects Divided in Terms of SRS Scores

| | Experimental Conditions | | |
	Test-Retest	Law	Peer Opinion
Total Group	(24) -2.62_a	(26) $+3.19_b$	(28) $+6.46_c$
High SRS	(12) -4.42_x	(13) $+4.54_{yz}$	(14) $+4.29_{yz}$
Low SRS	(12) -0.83_{xy}	(13) $+1.85_y$	(14) $+8.64_x$

NOTE: Cells having the same subscript are not significantly different, by Duncan Multiple Range Test, at the .05 level. Separate tests were made for the Total Group and SRS-level analyses. The number of cases in each cell is given in parentheses.

---

* "Chi-square" is a statistical method used here to determine the probability that two variables are related. The finding that $x^2 = 0$ indicates that SRS scores and authoritarian scores are independent; that is, we cannot predict a subject's score on one measure from knowledge of his score on the other because they do not reflect the same underlying factors. [Eds. note]

** The "Duncan Range test" is a method of comparing each group's average score with every other group's average score which takes into account the greater probability that a relatively large difference will be observed when multiple comparisons are made than when a single comparison is made. [Eds. note]

Even though the interaction of personality scale level and experimental conditions failed to achieve the customary level of significance, we examined this interaction for heuristic purposes and also because of the conservatism of the Duncan Multiple Range Tests. As shown in Table 3, high and low scorers on the SRS tended to react somewhat differently to the experimental conditions. The high "responsibles" generally were equally affected by knowledge of the law and knowledge of their peers' opinions, and altered their judgments (in the direction of these influences) to a significantly greater extent than did the high scorers in the *Test-Retest* group. As we had expected, the low "responsibles" were somewhat less influenced by the law than were their high scoring counterparts, although this difference is not reliable, and they did not display a greater judgmental change than their similarly low scoring controls. The low "responsibles"

TABLE 4

Mean Change in Judgments of Morality for Subjects Divided in Terms of F Scale Scores

	Experimental Conditions		
	Test-Retest	Law	Peer Opinion
Total Group	(20) −3.40$_a$	(24) +1.46$_b$	(28) +5.71$_c$
High F	(10) −2.10$_{xy}$	(12) −0.25$_{xy}$	(14) +10.21$_z$
Low F	(10) −4.70$_x$	(12) +3.17$_{yz}$	(14) +1.21$_{xy}$

NOTE: Cells having the same subscript are not significantly different, at the .05 level, by Duncan Multiple Range Test. Separate tests were made for the Total Group and F-Scale-Level analyses. The number of cases in each cell is given in parentheses.

in the *Peer Opinion* group, on the other hand, exhibited a reliably greater shift in response to the information about the opinion consensus among their fellow students than did the low scorers in the other groups. The strong traditionalistic responsibility tendencies tapped by the SRS evidently produce a moderate susceptibility to both conventional influences, laws and peer opinion, while a low level of these tendencies seems to lead only to a strong susceptibility to peer consensus.

This shift in moral judgments toward the peer opinions is especially characteristic of people with relatively strong authoritarian tendencies, as is indicated in Table 4. The condition means given in this table show that the *High F* subjects altered their moral judgments toward the peer opinions to a relatively great extent, but were not influenced to any significant degree by the knowledge of the laws. The low authoritarian subjects, on the other hand, tended to be somewhat more susceptible to information regarding the existence of laws. While these people were not significantly more affected by law information than by peer opinions, it was only the *Low F Law* condition that differed reliably from the *Low F* controls. All in all, strong authoritarianism seems to produce a sensitivity to peer opinions but not necessarily to the legitimate authority represented by laws.

We might well stop at this point to discuss a matter that could be troubling the discerning reader. Having carefully studied the procedure followed in the various experimental conditions, he will have noted that the *Law* and *Peer Opinion* treatments did not attempt to influence the subjects in the same direction for Items 1 and 4. (The changes were always scored in the same direction in the *Test-Retest* and *Law* conditions, however.) Conceivably, then, differences between the Law and Peer opinion groups could be due to these differences in influence direction; it might have been easier to produce a change in one direction than in the other. What can be said about this possibility?

For one thing, the analyses of variance summarized in Table 2 did not yield any significant interaction of items by conditions, although in the case of the F scale analysis this interaction did approach significance ($F=2.03$, 6 and 222 df, $p<.10$).* The condition means involved in this interaction was subjected to a Duncan Test in order to determine where the group differences might be. The results are presented in Table 5. We note here that the *Peer Opinion* group did not differ significantly from the *Law* condition on any of the four items, and was reliably different from the control condition only on Item 2 (Borrowing money for betting purposes without informing the lender)—an item in which the influence direction was the same for all three experimental conditions.

In addition, a separate analysis of variance was conducted using only the change scores for Items 2 and 3, the items for which the change direction was the same in all three groups. The findings here paralleled the results obtained with the four-item analysis: Again, the only significant effects were for Experimental Condition ($F=3.55$, $p<.05$) and Items ($F=13.31$, $p<.001$). The

---

* *See* pp. 204-05 n.*, *supra,* discussing the "analysis of variance" used here. The statement that "$p < .10$" indicates that the probability that the observed difference would occur by chance is no more than one in ten. Berkowitz and Walker say that "this interaction did *approach* significance" since the probability that the interaction occurred by chance is greater than the conventional one-in-twenty test of significance. [Eds. note]

TABLE 5

Changes in Moral Judgments on Each Item in Each Condition—F Scale Analysis

	Items			
	1	2	3	4
Test-Retest (N=20)	+1.25 bc	−2.75 a	+0.15 ab	−2.05 ab
Law (N=24)	+0.54 ab	+0.33 ab	+1.29 bc	−0.71 ab
Peer Opinion (N=28)	+0.89 ab	−1.36 ab	+4.64 c	+1.54 bc

Cells having a subscript in common are not significantly different at the .05 level.

Condition x items interaction was again relatively large $(F=2.60)$, but this time did not even approach significance.*

All in all, inspection of Table 5 indicates the group results summarized in Tables 3 and 4 are primarily due to Items 3 and 4, and to Item 2 in the *Law* condition. These items differ considerably in content (borrowing a car, borrowing money, and preventing a person from committing suicide), and also vary in the direction of the influence attempt. They do not seem to have anything in common. What is clear is that the experimental treatments produced greater alterations in moral judgments in the case of Item 3, dealing with borrowing money for betting purposes, than on any of the other issues. All laws apparently do not produce the same modification in the judged propriety of the actions they seek to regulate, whether these laws are supported by an opinion consensus or legitimate authority.

DISCUSSION

The implications of this experiment can be summarized fairly briefly. If a number of different forms of conduct and criminal laws are sampled and if a sufficiently broad range of people are studied, relatively sensitive measures should show that knowledge of the existence of laws has modified judgments of the moral propriety of the actions regulated by these laws. There appears to be a comparatively small but nevertheless significant tendency for some people to alter their views of the morality of some actions in accord with laws specifying that these actions are legal or illegal. Knowledge of the existence of these laws, however,

---

* "$p < .05$" indicates that the probability that the observed difference would occur by chance is one in twenty; "$p < .001$" indicates that the chances are one in one-thousand. No probability level is given for the last F ratio because the probability that observed differences occurred by chance is greater than one in ten, and hence observed differences cannot safely be assumed to be other than chance differences. [Eds. note]

does not have as much effect in changing the moral judgments as knowledge of a consensus of opinions among one's peers.[22]

This distinction between laws per se and peer opinion, while conceptually important, cannot be made in many instances in the "real" world. As we indicated earlier, the extent to which criminal laws are successful in regulating conduct frequently depends upon the magnitude of the social consensus regarding the behavior with which it deals. The passage of fair housing laws may mean there is widespread agreement that racial discrimination is now more likely to be viewed as immoral. But the apparent consensus can also prove to be illusory. A person may see that a given law is frequently violated, and, as probably happened in the case of the Prohibition Amendment, the law then ceases to influence his moral judgment.[23] Sometimes only one violation is enough to break this implied consensus, particularly if it is carried out by someone high in social status.

Other considerations, nevertheless, suggest that the distinction between law effects and social consensus should be maintained. As an example, our findings indicate that the moral judgments of highly authoritarian people, as assessed by the California F scale, are quite susceptible to peer influence, but are not significantly affected by knowledge of the law. Authoritarians tend to be strongly conformistic, perhaps because of an extreme concern with social approval, but they do not necessarily accept the views of legitimate authority, at least as represented by the law. Laws

---

[22] Professor Macaulay (personal communication) has suggested that the apparent shifts in moral judgments due to knowledge of the law, or for that matter peer opinions, might be produced by . . . two somewhat different processes. On one hand, the individual might have started out by believing a certain action was morally proper or improper, and then experienced an alteration in this belief. Other persons, however, could initially have believed that the particular form of conduct was morally neutral. This suggestion essentially holds that the influence source could have placed the behavior on a dimension of moral propriety-impropriety, where initially the conduct was regarded as being irrelevant to this dimension, in addition to moving the statement's position along such a dimension. Whatever the exact process that might be involved, the present writers prefer to regard any shift in scale response as a change in moral judgment, in part for convenience and in part because this shift is presumptive evidence of some form of alteration in belief. For that matter, as Professor [Ronald] Maudsley has hypothesized, there might be very different reactions to knowledge that a certain form of conduct is now illegal and to knowledge that a given type of action no longer is illegal. The form of conduct that is regulated probably also influences the individual's response to knowledge of the law and/or peer opinion.

[23] Frequent violations of a law might also influence a person's decision-making in cost-benefit terms. Seeing that many other people transgress without apparent penalty, the individual might decide that the benefits obtained from breaking a certain law far outweigh the costs considering the low probability of being caught.

can be for them just another source of frustration. They will obey the law if they must, if deviation from the law is punished or brings disapproval, but probably not because they truly believe the law is "right." According to our results, it is primarily those persons who are deeply involved in their society, who are traditional and conventional and socially responsible, who are most likely to adopt the judgments implied by the law.

NOTES AND QUESTIONS

1. Some problems of methodology:

Berkowitz and Walker studied the reactions of eighty-seven English college students to their experiment, and then generalized from their data. The study represents laboratory social psychology as practiced by psychologists rather than the field survey more typically used by sociologists. Note that it is a follow-up study to a field survey. *See* p. 199 n.3, *supra.*

a. Does the fact that the subjects were students and English, and not even representative of all English students, indicate that one ought to question whether or not he can generalize from their findings? Can you think of reasons why a working-class American might have different views on the matters tested than the English college students? a conservative law professor? To what extent, if at all, is this difficulty avoided by Berkowitz and Walker's use of the SRS and the *F*-Scale types?

b. What advantages are inherent in the laboratory approach used by Berkowitz and Walker as compared to a field survey which uses a sample drawn to represent a given population?

2. Some substantive problems:

a. Berkowitz and Walker discuss changes in moral belief prompted by knowledge that a law has been changed. To the extent that the legal system can change one's views of right and wrong simply by informing a person that a law has been passed, it has an effective means of channelling behavior—insofar as the person's behavior is determined by his moral judgments. However, another model of individual response to law, the cost-benefit theory, is mentioned at 200 n.9, *supra.* Are these models necessarily inconsistent?

(1) In your opinion, under what kinds of circumstances would one or the other model be more useful in explaining the impact of law on the conduct of various kinds of people?

(2) Berkowitz and Walker consider situations where legal sanctions might be provided to induce compliance with a norm

or to punish violations. Some kinds of law offer rewards for conduct desired by the policymaker instead of punishments. For example, many states once offered bounties for shooting wolves or other animals thought undesirable. United States laws offer various kinds of tax incentives—to those who invest in underdeveloped or emerging nations, for example. The available evidence indicates that these incentives have had relatively little impact on the investment decisions of American businessmen and have not served to channel private capital to the nations most favored for development by American foreign policy. To what extent would you explain this result in terms of the failure of law to affect normative positions on foreign investment; to what extent in terms of an unfavorable cost-benefit judgment; to what extent in terms of any other factor?

b. One argument made by southern "moderates" on racial issues concerning acceptance of the Supreme Court's school desegregation decision was that "whether we like it or not, it is the law of the land." Does the Berkowitz and Walker study suggest the extent to which such an argument was likely to have been effective?

c. Another experiment may affect one's view of Berkowitz and Walker's findings about the impact on moral judgments of knowledge that conduct being evaluated is legally permitted or prohibited. In this later study, subjects were asked questions about hypothetical cases. In each case, the person to be judged had failed to help another in distress. In some situations, the subjects were told that the law required aid to be given; in others the law did not require aid. In some cases, the failure to give help caused serious harm or death; in others the failure to act did not result in any harm. Where the law required aid, failure to intervene was considered significantly less moral than where the law did not require one to intervene. Harmful outcomes rendered failures to give aid significantly less moral than nonharmful outcomes. *See* Harry Kaufmann, "Legality and Harmfulness of a Bystander's Failure to Intervene as Determinants of Moral Judgment," in *Altruism and Helping* 77 (Jacqueline R. Macaulay & Leonard Berkowitz eds., Academic Press 1969). To what extent, if at all, does Kaufman's study qualify Berkowitz and Walker's findings? Is help-giving behavior in some significant way different from the kinds of situations dealt with by Berkowitz and Walker? What, if anything, is the relevance of harm to the judgments made?

d. The process by which norms or moral beliefs influence behavior probably is very complex. Some psychologists stress that man cannot be viewed as a calculating machine evaluating possible actions by well-worked-out norms. More often one acts in response to situational cues and *then* may rationalize his behavior in terms of generally accepted norms. Of course, the habits that prompt the behavior may be indirectly influenced by norms or moral beliefs. For example, one may act as a norm would tell him to act because in the past he has been rewarded for such behavior by the esteem of others rather than as a response to philosophical calculation. Thus, for some people at least, a change in the law alone is unlikely to change these habits directly and quickly. *See* the articles by Darley & Latané, Aronfreed, and other contributors in J. Macaulay & L. Berkowitz eds., cited in ¶ c, *supra*. *See also* Deutscher, "Words and Deeds: Social Science and Social Policy," 13 *Social Problems* 236 (1966), which suggests that attitudes and behavior are often discrepant, and that studies of attitudes do not necessarily predict behavior.

e. What does the study tell you about the limits of effective legal action or how to make a law more effective? In answering this question, one might wish to consider the following experiment conducted by Stanley Milgram, a psychologist. He hired some forty males, between the ages of twenty and fifty, and paid them for taking part. He told the subjects that he was conducting an experiment on the effect of punishment on learning theory. They used a shock generator with switches labeled from "Slight Shock" to "Danger: Severe Shock." When the victim gave "wrong" answers to questions, the subjects were told to administer greater shock by the "scientist" conducting the "experiment." The victims were actually part of the experimental team, and the shocks administered were fake. The question was, how far would the subjects go in administering shock treatment, before they refused to go further. The general finding was a "surprising . . . strength of obedient tendencies." No subject quit before Shock Level 20, 300 volts; "at this level . . . the victim kicks on the wall and no longer provides answers." Twenty-six of the forty went on to the bitter end—more than 450 volts—administering what they thought to be extreme and dangerous shocks to the victim; despite manifestations of nervousness (including, oddly enough, laughter) and a great deal of reluctance, these subjects *did* obey. The experiment is described in Milgram, "Behavioral Study of Obedience," 67 *Journal of Abnormal and Social Psychology* 371-78 (1963).*

---

* Milgram's studies have been strongly criticized on ethical grounds. Three of the subjects underwent "full-blown, uncontrollable seizures" in the course of the experiment. Is this infliction of anxiety justifiable in the

Milgram's experiment was born out of a desire to study obedience, "the psychological mechanism that links individual action to political purpose. It is the dispositional cement that binds men to systems of authority." Many of the people accused of war crimes in Nazi Germany claimed they were merely obeying orders. Milgram's experiment indicated to him that "for many persons obedience may be a deeply ingrained behavior tendency."

In later experiments, Milgram refined his studies further by measuring the effect of group pressure on the disposition to obey. For example, if one introduces into the experiment "confederates" who defy the experimenter's authority, it reduces the propensity of the subject to follow commands blindly. *See* Milgram, "Liberating Effects of Group Pressure," 1 *Journal of Personality and Social Psychology* 127-34 (1965).

name of science? To what extent can we and should we experiment on human beings? For a critical view, *see* Kelman, *Deception in Social Research,* 3 TRANSACTION 20 (1966). [Eds. note]

22. The Use of Criminal Sanctions in the Enforcement of Economic Legislation: A Sociological View

HARRY V. BALL AND
LAWRENCE M. FRIEDMAN*

17 STANFORD LAW REVIEW 197, 220-21 (1965)

Some general features of this process of interaction are worthy of note here. The aim of regulatory law is to secure compliance by the regulated. Criminal sanctions are a technique to ensure compliance. Compliance, however, can be viewed in two lights, short- and long-run compliance. When a program of economic regulation is adopted, the attention of the legislature is usually fixed on problems of short-run compliance. The symbolic value of law as law, the fact that most people want to obey the law and will do so, has important consequences for long-run compliance. American social scientists generally agree that social sanctions can be employed deliberately to modify modes of social action—not only overt behavior, but also cognitive, affective, and conative attitudes. Less technically put, social sanctions can be used to change beliefs, attitudes, and personal values and goals; they can effectuate policy considerations by influencing what a person thinks he ought to do or what he wants to do in a particular situation.

William Graham Sumner said, "Men can always perform the prescribed act, although they cannot always think or feel prescribed thoughts or emotions." But he added that by changing conduct one induces new "experiences" that effect further changes in thoughts and emotions. The key technique is to maintain a

---

* Harry V. Ball, Professor of Sociology, University of Hawaii; Lawrence M. Friedman, Professor of Law, Stanford University. The reproduction is from an article first published in the January 1965 issue of the Stanford Law Review.

sustained demand for "strict compliance with detailed and punctilious rule." Legal institutions are therefore particularly appropriate vehicles for effecting changes in thoughts and emotions in the long run. The law may specify clear and unambiguous requirements, may provide a vigorous enforcement program, and can be equipped to maintain a long-continuing effort. Some authorities have suggested that administrative regulation is an especially useful tool for bringing about social change—it permits detailed specification of required conduct; it can modify the rules to plug loopholes as attempts at evasion appear; and it has great flexibility to adopt tactics and allocate resources toward enforcement of its regulations.

Underlying these propositions is the assumption that people tend to think that what they do is the right thing to do, even if they began to do so because they were forced to. Eventually they begin to expect similar conduct from others and, indeed, are eager to impose it upon others. As conduct becomes formalized, it lays an ideological basis for the extension of similar social norms to situations that are perceived in "analogous" terms. Ironically, some of the participants in the electrical price-fixing case reported that they first experienced price fixing when they served as industry representatives in federal price-control programs during World War II. Less dramatically, filing income tax returns and carrying drivers' licenses have become so commonplace that the public probably accepts these "customs" and, by and large, believes strongly that they are proper.

Other social scientists, however, disagree with the proposition that people learn to want to do what they have to do. Reinhard Bendix, for example, stresses how variable are the effects of coercion on personality. How a person will react to a requirement that he do something he thinks wrong and does not want to do, depends on his whole arsenal of psychological resources. Certainly people are not sheep; the countless revolutions and civil wars of human history are proof enough that law does not always convert its subjects. But surely there is some tendency for persons to provide "public justifications" for what they are actually doing. Thus the public morality must be under some pressure to correspond with required conduct. We should not be surprised to find an intergenerational "drift" toward increased moral justification of required conduct.

NOTES AND QUESTIONS

1. Is this excerpt from Ball and Friedman inconsistent with the findings and conclusions of Berkowitz and Walker?

2. Ball and Friedman assert "filing income tax returns and carrying drivers' licenses have become so commonplace that the public probably accepts these 'customs' and, by and large, believes strongly that they are proper." Since before the second World War, young men have been registering with local draft boards and accepting the classification system and its consequences. Since 1967, many young men have refused to register or to be inducted, and many prominent Americans—including several United States senators—have strongly criticized the entire system. Is this conduct and criticism inconsistent with Ball and Friedman's hypothesis about "drift" toward increased moral justification of required conduct?

3. Berkowitz and Walker did no more than tell their subjects that certain behavior had recently been declared legal or illegal by statute. Ball and Friedman suggest that, for example, the process of filling out income tax forms year after year might bring about an attitude of moral justification toward this conduct. Some programs of legal change are announced with great publicity, in all media, over an extended time (school desegregation or medicare, for example) while other kinds of legal change are introduced in a much more low-key manner. Do you think the way legal change is announced and communicated to its public affects the degree to which persons might change their views or form their views on the morality of the conduct involved in the change?

23. Social Structure and Rent-Control Violations

HARRY V. BALL*

65 AMERICAN JOURNAL OF SOCIOLOGY 598
(1960)

[Professor Ball reports on a study of "legal controls of residential rents, their differential impressions of fairness upon the landlords, and the relationships between these and violations of rent ceilings in Honolulu in 1952."

Before World War II, the ordinary law of landlord and tenant was in force in Honolulu. The market set rents, which were embodied in leases and contracts. Landlords could freely dispossess for nonpayment of rent, or simply because the lease had expired.

In 1941, rent control was introduced, under a city-county ordinance in Honolulu. It was continued under the period of martial law (1942-45), and retained by local government afterwards, through the period of Professor Ball's study, even though rent controls were abolished almost everywhere else in the country.]

As a result, the landlords of all the private rental housing units in the city were under the general legal rule not to charge more than the legally established maximum rent. Any person who wilfully violated this rule was subject, upon conviction, to penal sanctions consisting of a fine up to $1,000 or imprisonment up to a period of one year.

The inclusiveness of the Honolulu ordinance did *not* mean, however, that the legal maximum rent of every unit in 1952 had been determined by a single standard, by the application of a single criterion or set of criteria. When the ordinance was initiated in December, 1941, it specified May 27, 1941, as the "freeze" or "fair-rent" date: for all units rented on May 27, 1941, the rent and services in effect on that date were declared to constitute the "maximum-rent" and "minimum-service" standards for each unit, regardless of subsequent changes in ownership, tenancy, or

* Harry V. Ball, Professor of Sociology, University of Hawaii. Reprinted from The American Journal of Sociology. Copyright © 1960 by the University of Chicago. Published 1960, composed and printed by the University of Chicago Press, Chicago, Illinois, U.S.A. Reprinted by permission.

landlord-tenant agreements. For units which had not been rented on the fair-rent date but which had been rented sometime between May 27, 1940, and May 26, 1941, inclusive, the ordinance specified that the ceiling and service standards were to be those which had *last* existed during that specified year. Thus the statute embodied the principle that "fair rents" are those rents generally prevailing in a "normal market," and, in effect, it defined the state of the housing market of May 27, 1941, as "normal."[5]

Another provision applied to all units not rented between May 27, 1940, and May 27, 1941, but rented subsequently. The ceilings of this class of rental accommodations were to be determined by the Rent Control Commission upon the basis of the rent and services "generally prevailing for comparable housing accommodations" on the fair-rent date. The power to decide matters of "comparability" was vested entirely in the commission.

The ordinance did provide for raising the legal maximum rent of particular units under these ceilings to compensate for "substantial" increases in taxes or other operating and maintenance costs or "substantial capital improvements or alterations." But there could be no raising of the ceiling on the ground of increased market value, even if the housing accommodation had been sold to a new landlord at a cost much greater than the owner's original investment on the fair-rent date. In short, for housing rented between May 27, 1940, and May 27, 1941, or existing then but only subsequently rented there was no provision in the ordinance for explicit specific application of the concept of a "fair return upon investment" to individual accommodations.

In 1945 the Board of Supervisors intervened in a dispute between the local Rent Control Commission and the Federal Housing Administration (FHA) and amended the ordinance, directing the commission to accept the rent ceilings on new construction provided by the FHA or other authorized federal agencies. According to the rent-control administrator, these FHA ceilings provided the landlord a gross return of about 16 per cent on the cost of construction and land and were considerably higher than the ceilings then being established by the commission upon the

---

5 A short time after the adoption of Ordinance No. 941, to take account of some particularly low rentals in an otherwise "normal" market, Ordinance No. 952, April 19, 1942, was passed to amend Ordinance No. 941. Thus if, on the fair-rent date, some rent was "substantially" below that "generally prevailing for comparable housing accommodations" due to "peculiar circumstances," such as family relationships or unusually long tenancy, it could be raised to the "generally prevailing level" of the fair-rent date. The City-County Board of Supervisors eventually reduced the grounds simply to the existence of a rent substantially lower than that generally prevailing for comparable units.

basis of comparability. When, in 1947, the federal Congress exempted most new construction from federal rent control, the
board again amended this section to authorize the commission to
employ its discretion in accepting or rejecting the bases of the
ceilings set by federal agencies.

In this situation the commission did not attempt to "roll back"
the ceilings on new construction which had been established between 1945 and 1947 by the FHA. Rather, it adopted (or retained) as the major determinant of the ceilings on subsequent
new construction the federal agency's concept of 1947 of a net
return of 6.5 per cent of the total of the original cost of construction plus the asssessed value of the land.

In the light of the permanence of this special treatment for
newly constructed housing, the rent-control administrator and his
investigators tended to give comparable considerations to older
housing entering the rental market for the first time since May
27, 1940. It became a prevalent practice to establish ceilings on
these older units also upon the basis of a 6.5 per cent net return.
However, the net return in this instance was based upon an
estimate of the original cost of construction rather than the current or replacement cost. Thus it did not constitute the clear-cut
"return on investment" for the current landlord that the net-
return formula represented for landlords of newly constructed
accommodations. Rather it constituted a third class of determinations of legal maximum rent.

Thus, while the general rule that no landlord may charge a
rent in excess of the legally established maximum applied to all
landlords, a number of subclasses of landlords existed by 1952 on
the basis of the methods of determining ceilings. The ordinance,
the "law in books," had established two substatuses initially, and
then it shifted to one mandatory and one optional status. The
operations of the commission and its staff, the "law in action,"
had established three substatuses. Three classes of landlords were
created by the three ceilings, and one individual, of course, could
belong in more than one class simultaneously:

1. *Landlords with fair-rent-date ceilings.* The landlord of a
unit constructed prior to 1945 which had been given an initial
ceiling prior to 1947 according to the last rent charged between
May 27, 1940, and May 27, 1941, or the rent levels generally
prevailing for comparable housing accommodations on May 27,
1941.

2. *Landlords with fair-return ceilings.* The landlord of a unit
constructed prior to 1945 which had received its initial ceiling
in 1947 or later. The ceiling determination provided for roughly

a 6.5 per cent return on the estimated original cost of construction plus the assessed value of the land.

3. *Landlords with new-construction ceilings.* The landlord of a unit constructed in 1945 or later. For the most part, these ceilings were established to provide a 6.5 per cent return on the cost of construction plus the assessed value of the land. This approximated a net return upon investment formula.

The original expressed intent of the rent-control ordinance was to produce rents which would be fair to both landlords and tenants. But in 1952 new-construction ceilings took considerable account of the general postwar inflation, fair-return ceilings in many instances took some account of this inflation, and fair-rent-date ceilings took account of the inflation only with respect to substantial increases in direct operating costs. Thus the evidence was substantial that these differential treatments would endow the general norm not to violate ceilings with a different meaning for each subclass of landlords.

Let us turn now to a consideration of the other side of this institutional arrangement—the landlords and that part of their conduct which the legal rules regulated. The best estimates are that in Honolulu in 1952 there were about 36,000 private rental units and about 10,000 landlords. The vast majority of the landlords were small investors, described by Grebler as follows:

> He sometimes originated rental housing; more often, rental housing of certain types was built by contractors or operative builders for the purposes of immediate sale to the small investor. The structures have usually been two- to four-family dwellings, one of which is typically occupied by the owner who also frequently performs the simple management functions. The motivation of this kind of investor often is to have the net rental income carry his own housing costs. Small, non-professional investors have also entered the field of rental housing without this motivation, attracted by the social distinction of real estate ownership and expectations of above average net returns on invested capital or of capital appreciation.[9]

In Honolulu these small investors very frequently held only one or two units for rent.

The large long-term investors among landlords in Honolulu usually tended to be relatively small by Mainland standards and

---

[9] Leo Grebler, *Production of Housing* (New York: Social Science Research Council, 1950), p. 120.

to be more interested in above-average returns than some large Mainland institutions. It was very rare to find a landlord who held more than fifty units, and the large operators often controlled only one apartment building or one collection of single-family units. The large estates in Hawaii had specialized in land leases rather than in housing operations.

A few speculative sponsors had emerged in postwar Honolulu. Most of their operations centered around large apartment houses in the vicinity of Waikiki; many picked up some windfall profits, and virtually all their units had new-construction ceilings. The operative housebuilder was not yet significant in the rental market of Honolulu in 1952.

Thus, as a group, the individuals who had entered the rental housing business had usually done so for one or more of the following reasons: the social distinctions attached to landlordism, which were particularly significant in Honolulu; expectations of above-average net returns on investment or of above-average capital appreciation; or a belief that it was a safe, inflation-proof provision for retirement and a business which could be operated by relatively inexperienced survivors. Against these expectations, landlords found themselves singled out for price regulation in 1952, restricted to prices which in most instances took little or no account of inflation, and operating far more complicated businesses than anticipated.

Forty-two landlords of units with fair-rent-date ceilings and eight landlords with new-construction ceilings were interviewed to ascertain what factors they believed should be taken into account in establishing "fair rents." The landlords with the new-construction ceilings, especially the speculative sponsors, gave greatest prominence in their replies to the idea of providing a proper margin of profit, although they were consistently vague about the precise meaning of "proper."

On the other hand, the landlords with fair-rent-date ceilings, who were much more typical of Honolulu landlords, viewed the problem as a personal, complex, and relative matter. What stood out in their replies were: (1) the rents other landlords were believed to be getting for "comparable units" (with considerable variation in the criteria for "comparable"); (2) the amount by which the landlord believed, other prices and incomes had generally risen or fallen since the rent in question was established; (3) the original expectations of the landlord in terms of purchasing power—what he had specifically hoped to accomplish with his rent income; and (4) the difficulty in renting a unit at a given price. It was in terms of the last three generally, but especially

(2) and (3), that these landlords often volunteered information about the unfairness, as they saw it, of rent control.

It could be concluded that this examination of landlordism, with respect to its special motivation as an occupation and the techniques of determining "fair rent," corroborated the findings produced by the analysis of the legal structure. The multiple modes of legal maximum-rent determination did seem to constitute a gradation of restrictions upon the opportunities of landlords to establish what they considered to be "fair rents."

But were these apparent consequences actually demonstrable for individual landlords? Were individual landlords with fair-rent-date ceilings more likely to feel restricted or deprived than individual landlords with new-construction ceilings? The hypothesis was formed that the proportion of landlords who believed their legal maximum rent to be unfair would be greatest for those with fair-rent-date ceilings, intermediate for those with fair-return ceilings, and least for those with new-construction ceilings.

This hypothesis was tested against data collected from a 5 per cent sample of all rental units within the city of Honolulu which were then registered with the Rent Control Commission.[12] A questionnaire had been mailed to the landlords of each of the 1,522 rental accommodations (in the original sample) which had been established by means of a tenant interview as still in the rental market.[13] A total of 1,068 questionnaires, about 70 per cent, were available for this analysis.[14] One item in the questionnaire asked each landlord to state precisely what rent he believed would provide him a fair return. The responses to this question were classified according to (a) the kind of ceiling determination of the unit in question and (b) whether the landlord's own estimate of a fair rent was above or below the legal maximum rent, as indicated by the record for that unit in the commission's files.

The legal maximum rent was evaluated as unfair in 70.4 per cent of the responses under fair-rent-date ceilings, in 53.6 per cent of the responses under fair-return ceilings, and in 40.3 per cent of the responses under new-construction ceilings—differences statis-

---

12 The city proper was defined as Census Tracts 1 through 29 of the island of Oahu. The sample was obtained by selecting every twentieth unit in the files of the commission.

13 Of the units retained, 67.9 per cent had fair-rent-date ceilings, 17.7 per cent had fair-return ceilings, and 14.4 per cent had new-construction ceilings.

14 About 66 per cent of the questionnaires were returned by mail. A 10 per cent sample of the non-respondents was interviewed. Between respondents and non-respondents few differences were found, and those which were statistically significant were small in magnitude.

tically significant at the .01 level by the chi-square test. The null hypothesis that they had been produced by chance was rejected. The evaluations by the individual landlords of the unfairness of their ceiling rents did vary consistently with the hypothesized relative deprivations involved in the modes of determining maximum rent.

Since the differential treatments under the law did tend to provide the affected individuals with different meanings for the general norm against violating ceilings, did they also tend to produce differing rates of violation of this general norm? Inkeles has pointed out that "the need for a theory of personality is perhaps most evident in the study of those 'rates' which represent the summary or end product of thousands or millions of individual decisions and acts, yet which are of distinctive size for different societies or cultures. To illustrate . . . suicide and delinquency rates."[15] Our problem here is analogous to his, but one major qualification should be introduced. This is that different dimensions or components of personality, even different theories of personality, have varying relevance to different sets of institutional arrangements and the actions they are intended to induce or inhibit.

Now one may assume that, insofar as a landlord has a concept of a fair rent which exceeded the legal maximum for some accommodation, he is persistently motivated to seek to reduce the discrepancy. Perhaps this is not sufficient in itself to induce a landlord to violate his ceiling . But it would certainly enter the mind of any landlord who, for whatever reasons, "needs" more money, or serve as reason enough for any landlord who simply "wants" his "fair return" or whatever he originally anticipated from his rental business.

There are thus two problems: first, what the relationship was between the individual violations of ceilings and the individual evaluations of their fairness or unfairness and, second, what the final relationship was between the legal structure, as expressed in the three methods of determining ceilings and the fact of control itself, and the rates of violations of the ceilings.

To answer these questions, data on the violations among the 1,522 units in the housing sample were required. As indicated previously, the legal maximum-rent and minimum-service stand-

---

15 Alex Inkeles, "Personality and Social Structure," in R. K. Merton, L. Broom, and L. S. Cottrell, Jr. (eds.), *Sociology Today: Problems and Prospects* (New York: Basic Books, Inc., 1959), p. 251. In my paper on rents, I have taken, as a matter of strategy, the position that one should not employ a broader theory or number of ideas about personality than is required by the immediate task at hand.

ards for each of these units had been obtained from the files of the commission. At the same time, at least one adult tenant of each rental unit was interviewed to determine the rent actually paid and the services actually provided. These two sets of data were compared for each accommodation, and each was accordingly categorized as a "violation" or "non-violation."

Table 1 presents these categories of violation and non-violation cross-tabulated by the landlords' evaluations of the fairness or unfairness of their ceilings for their 1,050 responses.[16] The most striking finding was that *not one* fair response was located in the violation category. This is strong evidence for the hypothesis that having a concept of a fair rent in excess of one's legal maximum rent was a prominent component in motivating the landlord to violate his ceiling. And it was previously shown that the frequency of occurrence of this was related to the kind of determination of the ceiling involved. On the other hand, 54.6 per

TABLE 1

PERCENTAGE DISTRIBUTIONS OF CEILING VIOLATIONS AND
NON-VIOLATIONS BY LANDLORD EVALUATIONS

Evaluation of Ceiling	Violations	Non-Violations	Total
Fair	....	34.0	26.4
Don't know	....	4.2	3.3
Unfair	92.5	54.6	63.0
No response	7.5	7.2	7.3
Total	100.0	100.0	100.0
No.	232	818	1,050

cent of the non-violations also involved an evaluation of an unfair ceiling. Thus, in 67.5 per cent of the instances of declared unfairness, this, while important, was not *sufficient* to induce an act of violation.

With respect to the second question, the results of the cross-tabulation of violations by mode of ceiling determination were as expected. The proportion of violations was 29.2 per cent for fair-rent-date ceilings, 14.9 per cent for fair-return ceilings, and only 7.3 per cent for new-construction ceilings.[17] The legal structure did appear to exert more pressure on some persons than on others to engage in non-conformist rather than conformist behavior. And a substantial contribution to the understanding of the "how" was made by the intervening analyses of the differential perceptions and concomitant motivation.

It has been suggested that the real differences with regard to violations lay in opposition to rent control and that the evalua-

---

[16] The differences were statistically significant at the .01 level.
[17] The differences were statistically significant at the .01 level.

tion of unfairness by many violators may have been merely a postviolation rationalization. In other words, opposition to rent control might indicate the extent to which the violations represented an "acting-out" by individuals strongly hostile to authority in general.

Two analyses were made which tested the significance of opposition to rent control and which may be considered at least a partial test of this idea. In the questionnaire each landlord was asked, "Do you believe rent control is necessary in Honolulu at the present time?" He was asked to indicate his answer: "Yes," "Yes, but with changes in the ordinance (law)," or "No." A few respondents wrote "Don't know," or refused to answer at all.

The violation rate for those landlords who indicated rent control was not necessary was 23.2 per cent; for all others, it was 21.2 per cent. The t-test did not indicate statistical significance, and neither did a chi-square test with four degrees of freedom performed on the entire array of their responses respecting the necessity of rent control.

Finally, this hypothesis was tested: If a landlord defined his ceiling to be unfair *and* was opposed to rent control, he violated his ceiling. For reasons of sample size, this test was limited to units with fair-rent-date ceilings whose landlords had defined the ceilings to be unfair. Of the 179 violation cases in this class, 54.2 per cent of the landlord responses indicated that rent control was not necessary. Of the 321 non-violation cases, 55.1 per cent so indicated. The difference was not statistically significant, and the null hypothesis was accepted.

In short, opposition to legal rent control, as such, did not appear to play any systematic role in the act of ceiling violation by landlords in Honolulu in 1952. On the other hand, the legal restrictions placed upon previously legitimate methods for achieving still legitimate aspirations, especially that for more money, seems to have been of considerable importance. The persistent anticipation that rent control would soon be eliminated prevented any major movement from rental to other business. And the tendency to perceive one's treatment under the law to be unfair and thus to be tempted to violate the law appeared directly related to the law's severity. It only remains to stress that 77 per cent of the rental units in the city in 1952 were operated in compliance with these legal rules, in spite of widespread opposition to rent control and an overwhelming belief among landlords generally that they were being treated unfairly.

NOTES AND QUESTIONS

1. Does Professor Ball convince you that landlords who violated the rent control ordinances were not rationalizing their conduct when they later said that the legal amount of rent for their property was unfair? Isn't it possible that some landlords who believed that rent control was necessary and that their ceiling was "fair" nonetheless wanted more money and raised the rent in violation of the ordinance, hoping not to be caught, and that such landlords might finally tell Professor Ball's interviewer that the law was "unfair" in order to explain away to themselves the violation of the law? If this chain of events is possible, has Professor Ball shown that violating landlords were not merely rationalizing their behavior when they said their ceilings were unfair? Were landlords invited to characterize their ceiling rents as "fair" or "unfair" or was the judgment of fairness obtained some other way? Is the method used important?

2. Does Professor Ball say that a judgment of unfairness "caused" violations or was necessary in order to allow other causal factors to operate? During 1967 and 1968, as we have already mentioned, there was significant opposition to the Selective Service law. Some young men refused induction into the armed forces and were sent to federal prisons with sentences which, in 1967, averaged 32.1 months. Some went to Canada to avoid the draft. These face even more severe penalties if they should return to the United States. Draft resisters and evaders say that their action is prompted by opposition to the war in Vietnam; they also cite the unfair operation of the draft, which takes more poor than middle-class young men. On the other hand, many who share these views have gone into the service without overt protest. How *much* of the behavior of draft resisters is explained by their evaluation of the laws, and how much by other factors?

24. Coercion to Virtue: The Enforcement of Morals

JEROME H. SKOLNICK*

41 SOUTHERN CALIFORNIA LAW REVIEW 588, 624-26 (1968)

One way of putting oneself into the position of the potential offender is to translate the abstraction of such terms as "opiate addiction," "marihuana use," "homosexuality," into the reality of an already experienced everyday behavior. For example, the lawmaker might ask himself how he would respond to penal sanctions forbidding the smoking of cigarettes, the drinking of coffee, sexual orgasm, or any other commonly practiced activity which, if "excessively" indulged in, *might* lead to social and personal harm.

If a hypothetical lawmaker were to do this, he would first observe that penal sanctions are not necessarily the most compelling. For instance, regarding cigarette smoking, there has been an increasingly confirmed threat of cancer, severe cardio-vascular impairment and, more recently, a general tendency to shorten life. These are heavy sanctions, and if any of them were to be meted out by the State as a calculated retribution for smoking cigarettes, they would probably be regarded as cruel and unusual punishment. Yet these sanctions give every appearance of having had little effect upon the prevalence of cigarette smoking by the American population. The question is why not?

One reason is the abstract character of the sanction; the sanction is not a certainty but is instead a probability. The man who coughs heavily or turns up a suspicious looking sore in his mouth is one for whom the potential of death and disease is more likely to seem a reality. His response may be to "cut down," at least temporarily. Some stop, of course, and of those who do, even for a period of years, there are relapses. Similarly, there are people who use marihuana repeatedly, who use opium repeatedly, who

---

* Jerome H. Skolnick, Professor of Sociology, University of California, San Diego. Reprinted by permission of the Southern California Law Review.

engage in homosexual activities repeatedly, and who rarely, if ever, are caught. Marihuana users and homosexuals, especially, may continue in their use or their activity for many years without even coming into contact with law enforcement.

In addition, those who regularly use opiates, or marihuana, or who regularly engage in homosexual activities, or who regularly smoke cigarettes or drink coffee develop a set of meanings and definitions associated with the activities that make legal penalties seem especially abstract and irrelevant. The coffee drinker or smoker may plead that he cannot "get started" in the morning without nicotine or caffeine. Similarly, the illegal drug-using "outsider" develops a shared set of responses and definitions including "a special language or argot, certain artifacts, a commodity market and pricing system, a system of stratification, and ethical codes." These shared responses and definitions serve to moderate the salience of prohibitory laws. Like the exclusionary rule for the policeman, the laws take their place as another of life's obstacles to be overcome. For people who are committed to a certain activity, such as driving an automobile, associated dangers—that is, sanctions—are relevant but are not necessarily determinative in forestalling the activity. Usually, instead of changing his way of life, the individual adjusts his life so as to decrease the possibilities of the threatened sanction.

We may also inquire why the particular activity is so compelling. This is not so difficult to understand if it [is] realized that we all engage in activities which we cannot justify on rational grounds. Men who have suffered coronary attacks will continue to work at a harder pace than the doctor orders, even though the threat of death is very real. Men frequently behave in terms of a felt need which may, to those not experiencing the same situation, seem highly irrational. *The behavior of the "deviant" is not so exotic if we place ourselves in his total life situation, not merely if we ask how we would respond to his sanctions.* Narcotics laws, for example, require that the addict, who will experience serious withdrawal symptoms if he stops using narcotics, terminate his use immediately. Some addicts, in the face of these laws, have doubtless done so. In general, however, the addict does not terminate his use. Instead, he tries to find alternate means to continue his use—means which will result in a minimal possibility of legal sanction.

For these reasons—the difficulty of making rational calculations, the fact that sanctions are not necessarily invoked, that sanctions may be mitigated in the process of enforcement, that sanctions are abstract, that "deviants" develop a set of shared definitions that make sanctions even more irrelevant, that the activity being sanctioned is regarded as compelling—an increase in penalties is not likely to dissuade most "deviants" from continuing their illegal activity. Of all these reasons perhaps the most important is the "deviants' " definition of the activity. During prohibition many drinkers felt that forbidding drinking was an arbitrary assertion of State authority, based upon an unrealistic conception of alcohol and its effects. The accuracy of that assertion aside, it is important to understand that for sanctions to be meaningful they must be considered by potential violators as having a rational basis. Usually, when a sanction is invoked for a given activity, reasons are given for sanctioning the activity. If large groups in the population do not believe that the activity is wrong or harmful, especially if the "reasons" do not stand up to experience, the rule loses its authoritative character. Young people, especially, are likely to test the "reasoning" behind the rule. If drinking is forbidden, then the young will try it and measure the effects upon them as against the effects implicitly asserted by the threat of legal sanction. The same is true of marihuana. If the behavior seems not so very "harmful," or if its harmful effects seem susceptible to control, the criminal law tends to lose its authoritative character. "Because I said so" or "if you don't you'll be punished" does not usually suffice as "reasons," either in child rearing or legislation. To be effective, authority must be "legitimated" through both consent and rationality—a genuine understanding of the *total* situation. By contrast, pure *coercion* is apt to be far more limited in its capacity to enjoin behavior.

NOTES AND QUESTIONS

1. As far as one can tell from the excerpt reproduced here, what is Skolnick's methodology? How does he know that some or most people will respond to sanctions against "opiate addiction," "marihuana use" or "homosexuality" as he suggests they will? Does it matter whether those who would react as he suggests are best described as a few, many, a majority or almost all?

2. To what extent, if at all, is Skolnick's argument inconsistent with Berkowitz and Walker's findings? Undoubtedly, many high school and college students do not smoke marihuana regularly; some have tried marihuana once but have not continued to use it. Might the fact that use is illegal have exerted some influence on their judgment?

25. A Balance Theory of Coordination Between Bureaucratic Organizations and Community Primary Groups

EUGENE LITWAK AND
HENRY J. MEYER*

11 ADMINISTRATIVE SCIENCE QUARTERLY 31 (1966)

The general problem discussed here is how bureaucratic organizations and external primary groups (such as the family and neighborhood) coordinate their behavior to achieve optimal social control. It will be argued that mechanisms exist to coordinate the two forms of organizations, and that these mechanisms of coordination can be systematically interpreted by what is called a "balance theory of coordination." . . .

BALANCE THEORY

The assumption that the two forms of organization [bureaucracy and the primary group] have antithetical atmospheres can be accepted with some reservations, although much of the research of industrial sociology has sought to show that bureaucracies can be operated in a more "human relations" atmosphere than [Max] Weber would have anticipated. Nevertheless, there are basic differences between the bureaucracy and the primary group, and such differences are partly a matter of degree and partly a matter of quality. For instance, the family operates pri-

---

* Eugene Litwak, Professor at the School of Social Work, University of Michigan; Henry J. Meyer, Professor of Social Work and Sociology at the University of Michigan.

marily on the basis of nepotism and permanence of membership whereas industrial bureaucracy operates primarily on notions of merit and transitory membership. Bureaucracy and family may both permit positive affect but differ in degree, with the family permitting deep love relations.

The assumption that bureaucracies and primary groups are alternative means for the achievement of most goals must be seriously questioned. Here it is suggested that these forms of organization are complementary and that each provides necessary means for achieving a given goal. This position does not deny that the family, for example, has unique social functions, but it does assert that both primary groups and bureaucratic organizations operate in most major task areas of life and that they bring different attributes to the achievement of a given end. From a structural point of view, instead of suggesting the isolation of primary groups and bureaucracies, the position proposed here necessitates close communication between the two forms of organization.

Some of the very characteristics that have been ascribed to the formal organization and to the primary group lend plausibility to this view. One common observation notes that the bureaucratic organization is unable to deal with nonuniform or relatively unique events. This inability is usually attributed to the necessity for *a priori* rules and standardized role specifications as well as to the length of time required for the large organization to deal with an issue not previously defined. Thus, messages must move up and down long chains of communication before policy decisions can be made to meet nonuniform events. The strength of bureaucratic organizations, it is claimed, lies in the professional expertness they can provide as well as their capacity to deal with large numbers of people.

In contrast, the strength of the primary group is seen to lie in speed of adaptation and flexibility in meeting nonuniform events. The primary group is incapable of dealing with large numbers of people and is deficient in professional expertness.

Thus, the very virtues claimed for bureaucratic organizations are the defects of the primary groups; the virtues claimed for the primary group are the defects of bureaucratic organizations. For optimum achievement of many social goals—i.e., for social control—it would appear necessary to have both expert knowledge and flexibility, both breadth of coverage and speed of reaction. In short, bureaucratic and primary groups share in the achievement of functions in all areas of life. They are not necessarily competitive, nor is there a division of labor which requires each to function independently.

A Balance Theory of Coordination

The dilemma that must be faced by a theory of interorganizational relations and social control is posed by two propositions:

1. The contributions of both bureaucratic organizations and primary groups are frequently necessary to achieve maximum social control in a mature industrial society.

2. The characteristics of bureaucracies and of primary groups tend to make them incompatible, if not antithetical, as forms of social organization. A theory of coordination acknowledging both these propositions must avoid two kinds of errors. If the bureaucratic organization and external primary group are too isolated from each other, they are likely to interfere with each other and reduce the contribution of one or the other in achieving a social goal. However, if the two organizational forms are brought too close together, their antithetical atmospheres are likely to disrupt one or both organizations, again impeding the achievement of optimum social goals.

This reasoning prompts a balance theory of coordinating mechanisms that can be stated as follows: Optimum social control is most likely to occur when coordinating mechanisms develop between bureaucratic organizations and external primary groups that balance their relationships at a midpoint of social distance where they are not too intimate and not isolated from each other. This formulation requires recognition of the importance of a variety of mechanisms of coordination, ranging from those capable of bridging great social distances to those capable of increasing distance, while maintaining communication.

The idea of variable social distances bridged by varied mechanisms of coordination becomes obvious once any given large bureaucracy is examined empirically. For instance, where school systems are involved with families in which parents identify strongly with the goals of the school (e.g., middle-class families with parents in professional occupations), there is a minimum of social distance between the bureaucracy and the external primary groups. By contrast, where the schools are dealing with families who do not identify with the goals of the school (e.g., low-income migrants from the Southern Appalachian Mountains with a fundamentalist religious position), there may be a great distance between the bureaucracy and the external primary groups. Likewise industrial organizations seeking to influence the families of their employees on work conditions and worker productivity need to relate to families who identified with them as well as those families who do not. Similarly, the police seeking citizen cooperation in law enforcement must deal with persons and groups that disapprove as well as those in sympathy with the purposes of the organization.

Acknowledging variability in social distance between bureaucratic organization and external primary groups, the balance theory provides a criterion for deciding which mechanisms of coordination will provide optimum social control: mechanisms that permit communication and reduction of social distance in the case of great social distance, mechanisms that increase social distance in cases where social distance is too intimate.

Mechanisms of Coordination and Balance Theory

Theoretical consideration of issues involved in coordinating bureaucratic organizations with external primary groups is noticeably lacking in the literature on social organization. Because organizations are very much concerned with maintaining communication with external primary groups, however, it is relatively easy to find many illustrations of mechanisms of coordination. From a review of some of this literature eight reasonably distinct types have been identified, although they are often found in combination and they are not completely exclusive.

For convenience, the mechanisms are viewed as approaches by which a formal organization might seek to influence external primary groups to identify with values and norms of the organization.

1. *Detached Expert.* Professional persons (such as social workers or public health nurses) act with relative autonomy and by direct participation in external primary groups to bring group norms and values into harmony with those of the organization. They operate by becoming trusted members of the primary group the organization is seeking to influence. The use of "street gang workers" to deal with delinquent groups is an illustration.

2. *Opinion Leader.* The organization seeks to influence the members of the primary groups through "natural" leaders in neighborhoods and local communities. . . . Those utilizing mass media may unintentionally also be using an opinion leader approach. Analysis of community power suggests that in large industries management frequently uses this procedure to exercise influence.

3. *Settlement House.* A change-inducing milieu is provided through physical facilities and proximity, and through availability of professional change agents. The approach combines the traditional community center with focused educational programs. . . .

4. *Voluntary Association.* A voluntary association, bringing together members of the formal organization and the primary groups, is used as a means of communication between the two, as, for example, parent-teacher associations. The same kind of associations can be seen among other types of bureaucracies. The police have various recreational groups for children; churches have church-related clubs; hospitals have voluntary associations like the Gray Ladies; the army maintains close ties to veteran's associations; business organizations and unions often sponsor recreational associations. In all instances, the voluntary associations, whatever their explicit function, also serve as communication between the bureaucratic organizations and significant outside primary groups.

5. *Common Messenger.* Messages intended to influence are communicated through an individual who is regularly a member of both the organization and the primary groups. The school child often serves as such a messenger for communication between school and family. Communication may be very explicit as in some large industrial organizations, where employees are urged to go out and sell the idea of a better business environment to their friends and families; or it may be more subtle, such as a company's attempt to influence the wives of management by indirect socialization.

6. *Mass Media.* The formal organization tries to influence primary groups through mass communication media. The characteristics of communication through such media have been thoroughly considered in many studies. Examples of the use of this approach are common throughout the entire range of bureaucratic organizations, e.g., church, governmental, business, and other organizations.

7. *Formal Authority.* Legal or well-established norms are a basis for communicating with external primary groups. The truant officer, for example, has a legal right to link school and family. The relations of certain agencies, such as the police, to the outer community are almost solely guided by legal power. Other agencies, such as the schools, utilize some legal and some voluntary forms of communication; whereas other agencies, like business and social work agencies, depend almost solely on voluntary arrangements for communicating with outside primary groups.

8. *Delegated Function.* The organization acts through another organization, which is assumed to have better access, greater expertise, more appropriate facilities, or greater legitimacy in the

society. For instance, schools are frequently asked by organizations such as the fire department and safety councils to pass information to the homes through the school children.

Principles of Communication in Mechanisms of Coordination

These mechanisms described, their utility and limitations for narrowing or increasing social distance can be made more explicit.

For convenience, the analysis approaches the mechanisms as communications *from* the bureaucratic organization *to* the primary group. With relatively minor modifications, however, the principles can be restated so as to characterize communication *from* the primary group *to* the formal organization. The mechanisms will here be thought of as though they are purposive, that is, intended to influence.

Principle of Initiative. Where the social distance is great, it is hypothesized that those mechanisms of coordination that permit the organization to take great initiative in contacting these groups will promote communication, otherwise selective listening may prevent the message from reaching the group for which it is intended. Some of the mechanisms of coordination permit initiative by the bureaucratic organization more effectively than others. Thus, in using the detached worker approach, the bureaucratic organization sends its experts to make contact with the primary group member, in his home territory if necessary. By contrast, the voluntary association and the settlement-house approach are passive approaches requiring more initiative of the primary group. The mass-media approach, although it requires organizational initiative, leaves the decision to accept the message almost completely to the primary group members.

Principle of Intensity. To communicate across the boundaries of resistant primary groups, it is necessary to have intensive relations with primary group members in order to surmount barriers of selective interpretation and selective retention. Messages that reach a distant primary group without strong support from a trusted member are likely to be put aside or distorted. The opinion leader approach, because it depends on pre-existing influence relationships represents a mechanism of considerable intensity; so does the detached worker approach. In contrast, the mass media and common messenger approaches exert the least intensity in the coordinating process.

Principle of Focused Expertise. Much communication between bureaucratic organizations and primary groups involves simple information, such as times of meetings, announcements about speakers, descriptions of new programs, and similar details. Some communications, however, involve complex kinds of messages; for example: communicating a fundamental change in the educational policy of a school to families; communicating the employment norms of a northern, urban factory to southern rural migrants; and communicating the kind of behavior that will help a returning mental patient to his family.

The principle of focused expertise implies that the more complex the information, the more necessary the close contact between a professional expert and the group to be influenced. Furthermore, since the presentation of complex information requires the communicator to take account of unique problems any given group may have in absorbing the information and to adapt the communication accordingly, immediate feedback and response are necessary. Because of such factors, an expert in close touch with the group is required. The detached worker approach, the settlement-house approach, and the voluntary association approach are all procedures which put the expert in face-to-face contact with the external primary groups; whereas the opinion leader, the mass media, and the common messenger approaches permit only indirect access. It may be noted that great social distance usually implies that complex information must be transmitted and therefore suggests the need for focused expertise.

Principle of Maximum Coverage. It is hypothesized that better coordination will occur when a procedure can reach the largest number of external primary groups. This is not only a principle of economy, but also one of extensiveness. Procedures that reach more people without loss of effectiveness are preferred to those of limited scope. The detached expert approach is limited in the number of primary groups it can reach at a given level of resources because it requires almost a one-to-one relation between expert and group. One expert is restricted to one—maybe two groups. By contrast, the settlement house and the voluntary association can reach more people because a given expert can deal with many more groups in a given day. The common messenger approach has an even wider scope, and the mass media approach has the widest scope of all.

This enumeration of some of the major principles of communication governing the mechanisms of coordination is intended only to suggest differences in efficacy of communication procedures. Table 1 summarizes how these principles relate to the eight designated mechanisms of coordination. This table applies the principles as criteria to evaluate the suitability of a mechanism of coordination for any given state of imbalance. Obviously, there are many logical combinations of principles which have not been considered here or represented in Table 1.

APPLICATION OF BALANCE THEORY

Balance Theory of Coordination Re-examined

From the preceding presentation of mechanisms of coordination and some of the underlying communication principles in-

Table 1. Theoretical dimensions of communication, hypothesized to be operative in each mechanism of coordination.

Coordinating mechanisms	Principles of communication			
	Initiative	Intensity	Focused expertise	Coverage
Detached expert	highest	high	highest	lowest
Opinion leader	moderate	highest	low	moderate
Settlement house	moderate to low	high	high	moderate
Voluntary associations	lowest	moderate	moderate	high
Common messenger	moderate	low	lowest	high
Mass media	moderate to low	lowest	lowest	highest
Formal authority	high	moderate to low	high to low	high to low
Delegated function	high to low	high to low	high to low	high to low

volved, specific predictions can be derived from the balance theory of coordination. As illustration, the detached expert approach can be examined in terms of the principles of communication. This approach as applied to the organizations seeking to influence a primary group has the following characteristics (see Table 1):

1. It requires great initiative of the bureaucratic organization.

2. It involves intensive relations between change agent and external group.

3. It entails focused expertise, or close contact between the professional and his target group.

4. It has limited scope.

With the exception of scope, all characteristics of this mechanism are highly useful for communicating across great social distance; i.e., achieving a balance when the bureaucratic organization must deal with distant primary groups. Thus, when a school or a business seeks to communicate its goals and program to a distant family, it must take the initiative; it must use intensity of interaction to penetrate primary group boundaries, and it must make use of focused expertise to effect changes in social norms through communications of very complex messages. In northern urban communities, migrant southern white families often seem to require such an approach to achieve balance between school and family for the educational motivation of the children. Unions seeking to organize in communities unfriendly to union or management seeking to sway strong labor groups have analogous problems.

This approach is less effective for coordination when primary groups are overidentified with the bureaucratic organizations. The bureaucratic organization then does not require initiative, since the primary group will take the initiative. Intensive relations are unnecessary since there are no resistant primary group boundaries to pierce and may, indeed, evoke too much affectivity. School teachers, for example, might be tempted to evaluate children on the basis of their positive or negative feelings toward the parents, and parents might evaluate their children too exclusively on the basis of their school performance. In industry, bringing the families too close may lead to nepotism and favoritism within the organization; and among the families, it may lead to undue evaluation of family members in terms of occupational success or utility. In either case, it is likely to lead to a loss in ability to achieve occupational goals. Furthermore, the detached expert approach is extremely wasteful where families already identify with the organization, since there are other procedures (mass media and voluntary association) which can communicate to such families and reach many more of them without incurring excessive intimacy.

By similar analyses, the balance theory of coordination suggests that where great social distance exists, mechanisms such as the detached worker, opinion leader, and settlement house are more effective than mass media, common messenger, formal authority, or voluntary association approaches. These statements are intended to give only an idea of the broad applications of the theory. More precise hypotheses relating given mechanisms of coordination for different family types to optimal goal achievement depend on a more detailed analysis of the primary groups involved.

Bureaucratic Organizations and Balance Theory

Thus far, only two elements involved in balance theory have been explicitly considered in the formulation—mechanisms of coordination and external primary groups (e.g., whether they are distant or close). Little has been said about the other element of the hypothesis—the bureaucratic organization. The proposed theory of balance should be able to take account of all types of bureaucratic organizations in industrial societies.

A balance theory of coordination must be formulated to take account of two observations about bureaucratic organizations in our society: (1) that most bureaucracies must coordinate their behavior with that of outside primary groups if they are to achieve their goals successfully, and (2) that our society contains a bewildering variety of bureaucratic structures. Thus, the theory must encompass the relatively small, collegial bureaucracy of the private social work agency; the large, legalistic structure of the police force; the large industrial bureaucracy with the production and marketing goals; and the school system and the mental hospital, where requirements to conform to organizational rules may conflict with norms of professional autonomy. . . . .

Types of Bureaucratic Organization

The types of bureaucratic organizations in terms of this presentation of a balance theory of coordination can be described [as follows]. . . .

Rationalistic Model. Characterized by impersonal social relations, detailed rules governing most actions, strict hierarchy of authority, job specialization, narrow delimitation of occupational duties and privileges, evaluation on the basis of merit (knowledge, training, success on the job). . . . This type is illustrated by government bureaucracies which follow detailed legal regulations, such as those involved in administering income tax, processing applications for licenses, and so on. It is the type most familiar in industrial bureaucracies.

Human Relations Model. Exhibits personal relations, general policies rather than detailed rules, colleague rather than hierarchical structure, broad definition of the organization's goals, and evaluation on the basis of merit. Except for evaluation (employment, pay, promotion) on the basis of merit, the human relations model exhibits characteristics opposite to those of the rationalistic model. This type may be illustrated by small social work agencies, small scientific laboratories, small graduate schools, and others.

Professional Model. Incorporates both rationalistic and human relations elements, and found where both standardized, recurrent tasks and tasks requiring interpersonal skills to deal with non-standardized events are regularly required. This type of organization develops internal arrangements (such as parallel structures of authority, segregated departments) to reconcile contradictory administrative approaches. This is illustrated by hospitals, school systems, and industrial organizations with major involvements in research as well as production.

Nonmerit Model. Unlike each of the other forms, this is characterized by significant intrusion of bases other than merit for evaluation of personnel and performance; consequently criteria irrelevant to the achievement of organizational goals are introduced. Dependence on nepotism, personal friendship, discrimination on the basis of race, religion, or social class, and excessive emphasis on personal rather than organizational goals illustrate nonmerit bases of evaluation. Although these conditions may appear, intentionally or unintentionally, in the other types of organizations, when they predominate the result is distinctive enough to identify a separate organizational form. Most typical of small organizations, some large organizations as well, appear to approach this model.

Bureaucratic Organizations and Coordinating Mechanisms

At the present stage of knowledge, the relationship between bureaucratic structures and the mechanisms that link them to the outer community can be stated in a straightforward fashion if one makes the following simplifying assumption:

When administrative style and mechanisms of coordination are structurally consistent, each will operate most effectively, in achieving the given goal. Structural consistency is defined in terms of the dimensions of organization already suggested: hierarchical vs. colleague relations, impersonal vs. personalized relations, specific rules vs. policy, and so on. Each of the mechanisms may be analyzed to see which of these attributes it demands in order to operate. The detached worker approach (intended to change values or deal with distant populations, and requiring integration of the worker into the primary group) is a mechanism that promotes localized decision making, affective rather than impersonal relations, internalization of policy rather than specific rules, and diffused rather than delimited duties. In contrast, sending messages through mass media is an approach that is highly consistent with centralized authority, specific rules, impersonal work situations, delimited tasks, and so on.

The opinion leader approach requires that the good will of the leader be obtained so as to make use of his primary group attachment. This approach therefore demands affective rather than impersonal relations, localized autonomy (for the opinion leader), use of internalization of policy rather than specific rules, etc. Katz and Lazarsfeld have pointed out that this approach is often an unrecognized aspect of the more rationalistic mass media approach. Our analysis would lead to the hypothesis that it is optimally effective (e.g., the bureaucratic organization has maximal control) when it is used by a human relations administrative structure.

In contrast, agencies that use legal authority as their major means of communication must operate through rationalistic organizational structure. There are some counter trends among organizations using legal authority such as the juvenile court's stress on treatment; however, permitting localized organizational discretion often tends to subvert one of the basic tenets of the law—due process. As a consequence the use of formal authority as a means of communication puts very definite rationalistic restrictions on organizational structures.

The settlement house approach, as defined here, stresses attitude and value change. It therefore requires decentralized authority, affective and diffuse relations, and internalization of policies. It would seem most consistent with the human relations structure. In contrast, the voluntary association tends to deal with individuals who are already in sympathy with the organizational goals and who are often involved primarily in getting factual information or keeping informed. They could well operate, therefore, within the boundaries of a rationalistic administrative style. This would also hold for the common messenger approach.

When effective coordination requires the use of a range of coordinating mechanisms—where the organization is confronted by both distant and supporting primary groups—the professional organizational structure might be expected to be more effective. Thus, a school might develop a detached worker program for deviant families and at the same time promote a parent-teacher association for families who conform. The professional structure permits these mechanisms (with markedly different organizational demands) to operate within the same organization with minimal friction.

It is assumed that none of the mechanisms of coordination will be consistent with the nonmerit type of organization; that is, any other organizational structure combined with any mechanism of coordination is more likely to be effective than a nonmerit type, regardless of the mechanism of coordination employed. This assumption is based on the expectation that where the organization does not select or assign people in terms of task performance, it is less likely to achieve its task than the organization that does.

In summary, five significant combinations of coordinating mechanisms and administrative styles can be noted.[30]

1. Human relations administrative style with detached expert, opinion leader, and settlement house mechanisms.

2. Rationalistic administrative style with formal authority, voluntary association, mass media, and common messenger mechanisms.

3. Professional administrative style with combinations of mechanisms from both preceding items; e.g., detached worker and delegated function, opinion leader and mass media, etc.

4. Mismatched administrative style and mechanisms of coordination, e.g., rationalistic style and detached expert, human relations style and formal authority, and so on.

5. Nonmerit administrative style and any mechanism. . . .

CONCEPTUAL AND RESEARCH PROBLEMS

Some Conceptual Problems

. . . [S]everal questions arise sufficiently often to warrant some further comments.

Definition of Distance. Up to this point the concept of social distance has been used in an intuitive commonsensical way. In its most general sense it means that a family is socially distant from a bureaucracy where their values differ or where their capacity to implement common values differ. So a family would be most socially distant which had different values from the organization and a great capacity to implement these deviant values. By contrast, a family would be less distant which had the same values as the organization, but did not have the capacity to implement them. A family with deviant values but unable to implement them would be intermediate. This kind of general formulation will have to be elaborated and improved upon as the theory develops, but this rather general definition is no real barrier to research. Thus from the viewpoint of any given bureaucracy, whether military, school, business, or others, it is much easier to classify families as being socially close or distant from the organization empirically than to provide a general definition valid in all circumstances. More modestly put, it becomes a typical problem of measurement in the social sciences.

---

[30] The five combinations noted here do not exhaust either the theoretical or the empirical combinations. Only combinations which can easily be illustrated are cited.

Definition of a Midpoint. In addition, much greater attention has to be paid to the metric of social distance. What is the "precise midpoint" of balance? Again what is a difficult problem in the abstract becomes a typical social science problem in specific cases. It is not too difficult roughly to classify most of the families as being too involved, too distant, or intermediate, in relation to school, or military, or business organizations. The problem of measurement here is no different from that of differentiating between a middle class and a working class, a prejudiced and a nonprejudiced person, a religious or a nonreligious person. What is central about the formulation here is that it alerts the observer to three categories rather than two. . . .

Values and Social Conflict. In the discussion about social control and values, the question might well arise as to which values the proposed theory is addressed—social, individual, or which. What is crucial in these analyses of values or social goals is not who defines them, but the extent to which they require professional expertise (which bureaucracies can provide) in dealing with uniform situations as well as the nonprofessional expertise (which the primary groups can provide) when dealing with nonuniform situations. For most goals in society, both uniform and nonuniform aspects are important; therefore both bureaucracies and primary groups are necessary to maximize them. For instance, if one takes a highly personal goal, e.g., a man wants to keep the love of his wife; he could go to a professional psychiatrist; he could seek to impress her by material goods (a new car, a new house, a fur coat); or he could take her to vacation spots in far. off lands. What is characteristic of all these examples is the reliance in each case on formal organizations to provide services (e.g., cars, houses, etc.) to achieve a highly personal goal—maintaining a love relationship. It is possible to think of certain extreme situations where it would not be necessary to have both the primary group and the formal organizations, but these are not frequent. For instance, members of a classical extended family structure might consider that any help received from a bureaucracy is unnecessary. But especially in an advanced industrial society, goals that can be achieved by the primary group or the bureaucracy alone are very uncommon.

The theory formulated does not discuss potential conflicts. If the primary group has goals that are contradictory to those of the formal organizations, or if two groups in general have contradictory goals, which one is desirable? The theory gives no answer to such problems. However, it does throw some light on who might win in such a conflict. Presumably those people who have a formal organization in a balanced relationship with their primary groups are more likely to win a conflict with any other people who are missing either the formal organizations, the primary groups, or the balanced relationship between the two (all other factors held constant). This particular kind of a formulation provides an organizational basis for analyzing conflict.

Some Research Directions

To point out that there is some ideal point of social distance, as well as various linking mechanisms which increase and decrease these social distances, is still to leave many questions. This section suggests some of the initial questions and some possible research directions.

In much of the presentation, it has been assumed that the initiative for linkages comes from the formal organization. Both in principle and in fact, this is not true. There are many obvious instances where formal organizations have been the target of local primary groups, as for example the Civil Rights movements in the South. Since linkages can be initiated from either the primary group or the formal organization, the question arises—are they symmetrical? Can they be initiated from the formal organization in the same manner as the primary group? It would seem that they are not symmetrical and that this is, in part, a function of the structural characteristics of the bureaucratic organization and the primary group. It is hypothesized that the bureaucratic organization in general has more manpower and financial resources than any primary group; therefore, it can initiate community contact with almost any mechanism of coordination. By contrast, the primary group can only start with those mechanisms that require minimal financial and professional resources. For instance, the bureaucratic organizations can initiate their linkages to the community with the detached worker and the settlement house approaches, whereas the primary group might have to start with a voluntary association. The differences in group structure and the consequent asymmetry in sequencing coordinating mechanisms is an important research problem which might well be explored.

Because of their size and need for large-scale cooperation in order to exist, the bureaucratic organizations are generally more visible than the primary groups and therefore less likely to tolerate extreme forms of deviance. They can, therefore, generally be reached by much less intensive form of coordinating mechanism (e.g., the mass media) than the primary groups. Or put as a research question—are bureaucracies more susceptible to formal linkages than primary groups? It should also be noted that bureaucracies differ in the degree of their vulnerability to the public. A political machine a week before an election is more vulnerable than a week after, while wholesalers may be less vulnerable to public pressure than retailers. The entire dimension of organizational vulnerability becomes important for understanding how coordinating mechanisms affect the bureaucracy.

It is also quite clear that some bureaucracies have more of a normative base for linking to the community than others. Thus youth delinquency agencies have stronger social support than business organizations for reaching into the community. What is interesting is that business organizations have people performing many of the same functions that the social work agencies perform, but they must do so with low visibility. The differences between the public relations man in an industrial concern and the community organizer in a Community Chest program would be most interesting for highlighting the consequence of an organization needing to use their coordinating mechanisms in a latent rather than in a manifest way. More generally, the consequence of normative support for linkages becomes an interesting research question.

If an organization is not selfconscious about its coordinating mechanisms, then certain mechanisms will always be operative, such as the common messenger and the opinion leaders. What characterizes these coordinating mechanisms is their informality. When one considers that leadership in the organization is generally class related and living conditions outside the organization are generally class related, then as a consequence of these informal mechanisms, different parts of the organization become linked to different parts of the community. This, in turn, can lead to considerable tension within the organization. . . . More generally, the research question becomes: When do linkages lead to internal organizational cohesion and when to disruption? These are a few of the research issues which might profitably be pursued if one holds to the view that a bureaucracy should be neither isolated from primary groups nor brought too closely in contact with them.

NOTES AND QUESTIONS

1. Litwak and Meyer's balance theory concerns efforts by a governmental agency, charged with carrying out a program, to (a) communicate with and persuade those affected by that program to cooperate, and (b) isolate its actions from those affected by the program so it can apply its expert knowledge or the choices

of those in power unhampered by "interference" from those affected. At the outset, we must deal with objections that the second function of the theory runs contrary to democratic values or the demands of social justice. Consider two situations: first, an agency staffed by middle-class professionals is charged with retraining high school drop-outs who come from families of low socio-economic status. Second, an agency staffed by expert scientists is charged with insuring that all drugs prescribed by doctors are both safe and effective. Litwak asserts that some problems require trained experts while others are better suited to nonexpert primary group members. He notes that technological advance can shift a problem from one best suited to experts to one best left to the untrained performer. *See* Eugene Litwak, "Technological Innovation and Theoretical Functions of Primary Groups and Bureaucratic Structures," 73 *American Journal of Sociology* 468 (1968). In response to the charge that insulation of experts runs counter to democratic values, he would ask whether or not participatory democracy demanded that all decisions involved in flying a Boeing 727 jet from New York to Chicago required unanimous consent or a majority vote of the passengers. However, some problems could arise that might appropriately be left to a decision by the passengers. Suppose Chicago's airport were closed because of bad weather. The plane could land at Milwaukee or Minneapolis-St. Paul with equal safety and with about equal cost to the airline. Is this a decision best left to the experts? to the passengers? See the material on this problem at 630-98, *infra*.

2. Think of examples of all eight mechanisms of coordination identified in Litwak and Meyer's theory. In a sense, all governmental or legal acting is "formal authority"; but government can use, in addition, other mechanisms of coordination. To what extent does the police department of a large metropolitan city attempt to use the eight? Can you think of examples in the implementation of the "War on Poverty" programs of the mid-1960's? in the resolution of disputes arising out of commercial transactions? in the administration of the income tax? in the governing of a state university? In each of these areas, to what extent must one go outside the *formal* process of government to find the function being fulfilled?

Are the mechanisms of coordination and the balance theory useful only as descriptions and prescriptions for governments? Do they hence assume as a goal the implementation of decisions previously from above? Would a revolutionary group find anything of value in Litwak and Meyer? Do they tell us anything about participatory democracy?

3. Do Litwak and Meyer say that if one found all eight mechanisms of coordination operating in an agency, it necessarily would be effective in achieving its goals? or that the necessary costs would be justified by the benefits? For example, suppose the state agency charged with controlling the use of narcotics and other prohibited drugs was told by the legislature that it was particularly important to stop or significantly reduce the use of marijuana by college students. It was given an appropriation large enough so that it could make use of detached experts, opinion leaders and all the rest. Which would it be most likely to use? What would be the likely social and economic costs (including costs to the ideals of civil liberties) in using the various mechanisms. Which—if any—would be likely to succeed in reducing significantly the use of marijuana by college students?

4. Litwak and Meyer assert that the "nonmerit model" of bureaucratic organization is the most ineffective in reaching organizational goals. Graduate departments in some universities have characteristics which, in terms of the authors' criteria, might be classified as nonmerit-model bureaucracies. For example, the relationship between a major professor and his student may involve "excessive emphasis on personal rather than organizational goals." Do Litwak and Meyer mean that no doctorates will be given by departments in which there are such relationships, that the students who receive degrees necessarily will be poorly trained, or that fewer and more poorly trained students will graduate from such departments, compared to departments which reflect other models of bureaucracy?

26. On Legal Sanctions

RICHARD D. SCHWARTZ
AND SONYA ORLEANS*

34 UNIVERSITY OF CHICAGO LAW REVIEW
274, 282-300 (1967)

II

If we take seriously the task of developing a model to predict the effects of law, one of our first jobs must be to study closely the impact of sanctions on legal compliance. Accordingly, we need to examine such questions as: (1) Does the threat of punishment deter? (2) How and when does it accomplish its effects? (3) What side effects does it have? and (4) How does it compare with alternative reactions?

In order to approach these issues empirically, it was proposed some years ago that a field experiment be conducted on motivational factors affecting compliance with federal income tax laws. Recently it has become possible to carry out such a study.

Tax compliance was selected for several reasons: (1) The payment of taxes is one of the most widespread of all serious legal obligations in American society. More than a third of the total population is required by law to file federal income tax returns. Of those obligated, the overwhelming majority do so. As a result, it is possible to sample diverse groups in the population to examine the effect on compliance of various background characteristics. (2) Taxpaying is required at least annually, so that changes over time may be sequentially observed. (3) Compliance with tax law varies from full or even excessive compliance to serious evasion. It has been established that at least one-fourth of all taxpayers evade taxes to some degree. Frequency of violation has practical and methodological implications. In policy terms, it means a serious loss of revenue. According to the IRS sample audit of 1948, 1.4 billion dollars were lost in that year because of underestimations on personal returns of taxes owed to the Government. If the present study reveals legitimate and practical devices for increasing tax compliance, the government's gain could be sub-

* Richard D. Schwartz, Professor of Sociology and Law, Northwestern University; Sonya Orleans, Northwestern University Program in Law and Social Science. © University of Chicago Law Review, reprinted by permission.

stantial. Reduction in evasion may, furthermore, serve to distribute the tax burden more equitably and add to the sense of legitimacy on which the legal order presumably rests. From a methodological point of view, the pervasiveness of violations creates an opportunity for study. It means that, in principle at least, violators can be compared with those who comply, to determine the differences between them. It also opens up the possibility, exploited in this study, of examining the efficacy of different motivations through exposing taxpayers to various stimuli and observing the increases toward full compliance which result. (4) Taxpaying is behavior which can be described in detail by quantitative indices. As a result, increases in taxpaying can be rigorously described, and they can be related through powerful statistical tests to the independent variables. (5) Because income taxation is practiced in many countries and in localities within the United States, results of this study can be replicated for comparative purposes in other settings.[37]

The tax project was explicitly designed to study theoretically significant variables. The primary objective was to determine the effect of sanction threats and to compare them with appeals to conscience as determinants of legal compliance.

The technique here employed for examining tax compliance was the field experiment. This method, more widely praised than used in the social sciences, is designed to bring to natural situations some of the precision of the laboratory. In pure form, it includes the full application of the classic experimental model. This means differential application of one or more independent variables to experimental groups and the non-application of these variables to one or more control groups. The experimental and control groups are selected in such a way as to be initially comparable with each other in every way. The experimental groups are then subjected to stimuli which constitute the independent variables. The observer must be in a position to observe changes in the behavior of all groups, so as to be able to appraise the effects of each of the independent variables.

The field experiment differs from laboratory procedure, however, in that it is carried out in a situation which exists without

---

[37] Generalizations arising from studies of tax compliance cannot, of course, be freely generalized to other areas of behavior. Taxpaying differs from other forms of legal compliance in the population affected, the predominance of rational motivation, the regularity and discreteness of the act of compliance, the publicity given to its enforcement, and so forth. The findings in this sphere should therefore be examined for other kinds of legal compliance before they are used as a basis for a general theory. The need for extensive replication is increased even further if the objective is a general theory of compliance extending beyond legal to non-legal control.

instigation by the experimenter. Subjects are studied in a natural context where they would have been even if no study had been conducted. Care is taken, moreover, to avoid any awareness on the subjects' part that they are participants in an experiment. To the extent that these conditions can be maintained, it is thought that this procedure avoids a major source of distortion, and therefore permits results to be generalized with greater confidence to the "real world."

The key to this experiment lay in obtaining data on the actual taxpaying behavior of those studied. With the cooperation of the Internal Revenue Service, we obtained figures for groups of taxpayers. These groups comprise the experimental treatment groups and the controls. By giving us distributions for entire groups, the IRS complied with the statutory provision that no individual returns be disclosed.

Assignment to experimental groups followed conventional techniques. Subjects were matched individually for precision control using residential criteria from census tracts. The sample was drawn from areas where income was generally above 10,000 dollars to minimize the number of subjects whose compliance was assured by full withholding and short form filing. While this criterion prevented coverage of lower income families, it increased the chances of obtaining differential effects from the varying treatments. Subjects were then assigned to experimental or control groups on a random basis. Treatment groups consisted of 92 taxpayers in the placebo, 92 in the conscience, and 89 in the sanction group. They were interviewed during the month prior to filing their returns on their attitudes toward political and civic issues, with particular emphasis placed on tax policy.

In each of the experimental groups, questions were included which were intended to accentuate certain motives for tax payment. The "sanction-treated" group was asked questions such as the following: "A jail sentence of three years could be imposed for willful failure to pay tax on interest.[44] Under what conditions do you think the Government should impose a jail sentence?" A series of similar questions emphasized the severity of sanctions available to the government and the likelihood that tax

---

[44] Questions specified the payment of taxes on interest for two reasons. The Revenue Service had mounted a campaign during the year of the interviews to publicize the requirement of reporting interest, and this background provided a rationale for the interviewers' interest in interest. Second, we concentrated on a particular type of compliance for theoretical reasons. We predicted a relatively higher increase in compliance in the reporting of interest than in other types of compliance, especially in the group threatened with sanction. The latter effect has not occurred in findings to date, suggesting that taxpayers did not distinguish between income by source.

violators would be apprehended. The "conscience" group, on the other hand, was exposed to questions accentuating moral reasons for compliance with tax law. These included questions such as: "Would you consider a citizen's willful failure to pay tax on interest an indication that he is unwilling to do something for the country as a whole?" Similar questions posed to this group emphasized noncontroversial uses for which tax money is employed, citizen obligation to government, and the value of personal integrity.

In addition to the two treatment groups, a placebo group was selected by the same technique of precision control and random assignment. This group was given the same basic interview without any accentuation questions. A fourth group served as an untreated control. Its purpose was to determine whether the basic interview, with or without accentuation, affects taxpaying behavior.

Two kinds of data may be reported at present: interview responses and actual tax returns. The first is derived from an internal analysis of the interviews themselves. Toward the close of the interview, after the experimental treatment was given, all three groups were asked an open-ended question: "What reasons do you think taxpayers might have for reporting all the interest they earn on their tax returns?" Answers to this question were content-analyzed to determine whether normative reasons were the first given. The results of this analysis [reported in Table I] indicate that several social variables affect the manner in which taxpayers are oriented toward paying taxes and/or the manner in which they respond to different motivational appeals.

The first of these variables is social class or socio-economic status. Using the Hollingshead two-factor index of occupation and education,[51] we found no relationship between initial normative orientation, as inferred from responses in the placebo interview group, and social class (Table I, column 1). The success of conscience appeals did not vary systematically by the dimension of social class, being greater in classes II and IV than in classes I and III (Table I, column 2). There was, however, a direct relation between social class and the capacity of sanction threats

<hr>

51 The Hollingshead Index of Social Position identifies five classes, of which four are represented in our sample. These four classes range from the top executives and professionals of class I through the upper middle class II, middle and lower middle class III, to working or upper lower class IV. Only the unskilled lower class are unrepresented in this sample. For a detailed description of the characteristics of these classes as described for New Haven (where the sale was validated), see HOLLINGSHEAD & REDLICH, SOCIAL CLASS AND MENTAL ILLNESS 66-136 (1958). The techniques for generating and validating the scale are described id. at 387-407.

TABLE I

SOCIO-ECONOMIC STATUS
AND
NORMATIVE ORIENTATION TOWARD TAXPAYING
(Percentage Giving Primary Normative Response)

	Placebo		Conscience		Sanction	
Class	%	N*	%	N	%	N
I (highest)	56	13/23	71	17/24	82	22/27
II	60	15/25	87	13/15	67	16/24
III	56	15/27	71	25/35	59	16/27
IV (lowest)**	53	9/17	88	14/16	50	5/10
Total	57	52/92	[77]	69/[90]	67	59/88

* The N column shows the number giving the primary normative response over total respondents in the category. Numbers in the three groups vary slightly in each table because those who did not answer are omitted.

** Hollingshead's lowest socio-economic category was unrepresented in the sample because of a restriction to persons filing long form returns.

to elicit normative content. Column 3, Table I, shows a remarkable regularity in the relationship between normative responses after sanction threat and socio-economic status. Comparing columns 1 and 3, in Table I, we find an increase of 26% in normative orientation following the sanction threat for class I as against 7%, 3% and —3% in classes II, III, and IV respectively.

This is the first instance of a phenomenon which occurs repeatedly in the data. For class I, it appears that, while direct appeals to duty do not create a greatly increased sense of obligation, threat of sanction does. This may well indicate a major mechanism of social control. Sanctions may be most effective in preventing violations where they are converted into a sense of moral obligation. Whether this "induced morality" actually increases compliance, however, will only become apparent when it is related to behavior such as the actual taxpaying of the subjects.

Another point of interest emerges from the normative reactions of class IV as seen in Table I, row 4. Respondents in class IV show the highest gain in normative content following the conscience appeal (35%). By contrast, however, they show a slight decline following threat. In effect, they will go along with reminders of the obligation to pay taxes but will not be pushed into that position by warnings of potential punishment. The response to conscience appeals in the working class group suggests a combination of patriotism and an appreciation of the benefits provided by a welfare state. Indifference to sanctions in this stratum may relate to the reality of tax enforcement policy; i.e., the probability of tax investigation is, in fact, an increasing function of income. In addition, the working class may be somewhat more prone to view the world as dominated by luck and fate, and thus not expect a close relationship between conduct and consequence.

If such differences affect actual compliance, the practical implications for tax policy may be extremely important. Accentuation of threat, through publicized prosecutions and the like, would be called for against the rich but not against the working class. For the latter, educational campaigns emphasizing patriotic considerations appear to be more promising.

These differences by social class are consistent with reactions by educational background. Initial differences in normative content, as shown in the placebo group (Table II, column 1) are not significant, though slightly higher for college than high school

TABLE II
EDUCATION AND NORMATIVE ORIENTATION TOWARD TAXPAYING

	Placebo		Conscience		Sanction	
	%	N	%	N	%	N
College Graduate	60	28/47	78	29/37	70	35/50
College Attendance	59	10/17	75	15/20	71	12/17
High School Graduate	50	7/14	68	13/19	58	7/12
High School not completed	50	7/14	86	12/14	50	5/10

educated. Under the treatments, however, the least educated show a marked response to conscience appeals (36% increase), but no increase at all under sanction threat. College graduates, by contrast, show some evidence of threat-induced conscience (10%), even though this increase is less than the 18% produced by conscience appeals.

Taking the two variables of class and education together, what possible explanations of these findings emerge? Less educated, working class people may be more prone to respond to conscience appeals because of greater piety or naiveté, or because of a conviction that government action is needed for the solution of social problems. Alternatively, the better educated, upper class respondents may already have been exposed to such reasons for taxpaying and either accepted them—as the slightly higher proportion of normative responses for upper against lower categories in the placebo in Tables I and II suggests—or be resistant to attitude change when it is implicitly urged on them. In regard to sanction, less educated, working class individuals may be inclined to discount the prospect of prosecution being directed against them, be less worried about the experience if it should occur, and be less likely to convert the fear of sanction into normative reasons for acquiescence.

Another factor which relates to the impact of given motivation is the individual's employment status. As seen in Table III, the self-employed were slightly more normative in the placebo condition than those working for others. Subjected to conscience appeals, however, the self-employed showed a 38% increase in normative content, whereas [those employed by others] . . . were only moderately moved (12%). The effects of the conscience appeal on those working for others overshadows the limited effects of sanction threat on either group. The explanation of this finding is not immediately apparent. Perhaps those who are employed in an organization become accustomed to responding to exhortations that they comply for the good of the organization, and they extend this to the government when urged. What-

TABLE III

SELF-EMPLOYMENT AND NORMATIVE ORIENTATION TOWARD TAXPAYING

	Placebo		Conscience		Sanction	
	%	N	%	N	%	N
Self-employed	59	34/58	71	42/59	68	39/57
Employed by others	52	16/31	90	27/30	64	18/28

ever the explanation, the phenomenon is intrinsically interesting. It suggests that the increasing pervasiveness of corporations as a source of employment helps to explain tax compliance, if not the fulfillment of the general obligation of citizenship, in complex societies. Along the same lines, it may help to explain the resistance to taxation among small businessmen and farmers, as in the Poujadist movement.

Religion also emerges as a correlate of taxpaying orientation. In the placebo group, Catholics showed the most frequent normative orientation, followed by Protestants and Jews (Table IV, column 1). Subjected to the experimental interviews, however,

TABLE IV

RELIGIOUS AFFILIATION AND NORMATIVE ORIENTATION TOWARD TAXPAYING

	Placebo		Conscience		Sanction	
	%	N	%	N	%	N
Catholics	67	16/24	64	14/22	69	18/28
Protestants	52	22/42	83	34/41	67	20/30
Jews	48	10/21	76	19/25	67	20/30

Catholics showed little normative reaction to sanction threat (2%) and actually declined slightly (3%) in these responses upon being confronted with considerations of conscience. Perhaps their normative orientation is so well set by initial training or so exclusively related to an authoritative church that they do not respond to appeals or threats from other sources. By contrast, Protestants and Jews increased their normative statements to a point exceeding the Catholics under conscience appeals. Protestants showed an increase of 31% in normative content under conscience appeals, and Jews were almost equally responsive to the conscience appeal (28%). Jews showed a slightly greater normative reaction (19%) than Protestants (15%) to sanction threat, the effects of which brought Jews and Protestants virtually up to the position of the Catholics.

These diverse reactions to motivational appeals must be viewed with caution. They are based on relatively small groups which were selected from relatively well-to-do segments of the population. The correlations reported, moreover, have not, because of small numbers, been subjected to multivariate analysis to check the independence of effects. Nevertheless, the marginal analysis which has been done suggests some definite variations in initial orientation to taxpaying and in responsiveness to various motivational aspects. At a minimum, the findings suggest the following relationships:

1. Cultural and social structural factors correlate with legally relevant attitudes.
2. Conscience appeals often have a greater effect on groups with low initial normative orientations than on those who are initially high in normative orientation.
3. Sanction threat has a mixed effect on normative orientations, being capable of "inducing morality" among several categories.

It remains to be seen how these reactions relate to tax compliance. At this point, we are unable to report changes in payment in relation to social characteristics or attitudinal responses. We have received preliminary data, however, for changes in tax payments for the gross experimental and control groups. These data permit comparisons of the two experimental groups with the control group in regard to changes in tax payment on returns filed before the interview (for fiscal 1961) and after the interview (for fiscal 1962). Since the groups were randomly assigned (after matching by residence), differences in increase of taxpaying are presumably attributable to the experimental treatments.

A caveat must be entered at this point. The results obtained from the experiment are not of a magnitude which uniformly produces statistically significant differences. Some of the results reported, especially if taken separately, could well be attributed to chance. This could be the consequence of small samples, weakness of the experimental treatments, a limited amount of cheating relative to the large base of compliance, or the fluctuation of income found in all groups.

Nevertheless, the results do fall into a pattern which is highly suggestive. As indicated in Table V, column Ia, those threatened with *sanction* declared a mean increase in adjusted gross income of 181 dollars as compared with a mean decrease of 87 dollars for the placebo control (and a mean decrease of 13 dollars for the untreated control). It should also be noted, as seen in Table V, column IIIa, that income tax after credit shows a mean increase for the sanction-threatened group, compared with a decrease for the two controls.

If we look at the *number* of individuals in the sanction group who increased their adjusted gross income, this pattern is repeated. In the sanction-treated group, as shown in Table VI, 49 of 87 taxpayers, or 56%, exceeded the median dividing line set by the placebo group. The number of sanction-threatened individuals also slightly exceeded the placebo median on income tax paid.

It is equally important to note that the *conscience* appeal had a stronger effect on income reported than did the threat of sanction. Adjusted gross income reported by the conscience-appeal group showed a mean increase of 804 dollars compared with 181 dollars for those threatened with sanction (Table V, column Ia). The mean increase in AGI in the conscience group is statistically significant when compared with the placebo. Income tax payments for this group are also appreciably higher than for the sanction group or the controls. The number of conscience group members who exceeded the placebo median on adjusted gross income reported is 56 of 88 or 64% (Table VI, column I.) From this it may be inferred that more than one-fourth of the conscience group who would—in the absence of the appeal—have been below the median, were moved above it on AGI reporting. (The number of individuals who increased their taxes—Table VI, column III—also exceeded the median, although this effect is slight and statistically not significant.) These results tend to confirm the proposition that conscience appeals can be more effective than sanction threats.

Various interpretations of these results are possible. Despite efforts to avoid threats, some implication of punishment may have

TABLE V

DIFFERENCES BETWEEN 1961 AND 1962 IN REPORTED ADJUSTED GROSS INCOME DEDUCTIONS, AND INCOME TAXES AFTER CREDIT

Group	Number	I. Adjusted gross income		II. Total deductions		III. Income tax after credits	
		a. Mean of 1961-62 differences	b. Standard deviation of the observed differences	a. Mean of 1961-62 differences	b. Standard deviation of the observed differences	a. Mean of 1961-62 differences	b. Standard deviation of the observed differences
A Sanction threat	87	$181	$3,481	$278	$853	$ 11	$ 956
B Conscience appeal	88	804	4,007	177	535	243	1,189
C Placebo control	88	−87	2,858	132	571	−40	751
D Untreated control	111*	−13	3,510	320	820	−57	965

Comparison of increase, 1961-62, t Test**

	t	t	t
Sanction (A) v. Conscience (B)	1.09 (N.S.)	.88 (N.S.)	1.35 (.10) B > A
Sanction (A) v. Placebo (C)	.55 (N.S.)	1.30 (.10) A > C	.39 (N.S.)
Conscience (B) v. Placebo (C)	1.68 (.05) B > C	.53 (N.S.)	1.87 (.05) B > C
Placebo (C) v. Untreated control (D)	.14 (N.S.)	1.81 (.05) D > C	.14 (N.S.)

* Adjusted gross income tabulations are based on 110 taxpayer returns. Data for one taxpayer showing a very large decrease in adjusted gross income were excluded by the Revenue Service from the tabulations to avoid possible identification.

** BRUNK, AN INTRODUCTION TO MATHEMATICAL STATISTICS 246 (1960).

TABLE VI

NUMBERS OF TAXPAYERS IN EACH EXPERIMENTAL GROUP EXCEEDING MEDIAN INCREASE, 1961-62, OF CONTROL GROUPS IN VARIOUS ELEMENTS OF TAX REPORTING; SIGN TEST FOR SIGNIFICANCE*

Comparison	N	I. Adjusted Gross Income			II. Total Deductions			III. Income Tax after Credits		
		N > Median of C (144)	%	P	N > Median of C (97)	%	P	N > Median of C (34)	%	P
Sanction threat (A) v. Placebo (C)	87	49	56	.17	31	35	.0026	46	52	.334
Conscience appeal (B) v. Placebo (C)	88	56	64	.0073	39	44	.0838	49	56	.169
Combined experimental (A + B) v. Placebo (C)**	175	105	60	.0071	70	40	.0034	95	54	.1469

* BROWNLEE, STATISTICAL THEORY AND METHODOLOGY IN SCIENCE AND ENGINEERING 180-84 (1960). This test uses the placebo to establish a median and then computes the probability of at least the number which exceeds that median doing so by chance.

** A sign test of placebo against the medians of the untreated control shows that the two groups are very similar on AGI (P=.54, median of D=114), but very different for deductions (P=.000002, median of D=233) and somewhat so for tax (P=.084, median of D=−63). These observations reinforce the conclusion, indicated earlier, that the untreated control is not dependable in the absence of further data. In substance, this means that the bias resulting from dropouts or the interview made a difference, particularly in deductions. The similarity of AGI's of the placebo and the untreated control strongly suggests that the smaller deductions in the two experimental and the placebo groups resulted from the interview rather than from dropout bias.

been conveyed in the conscience interview. If so, the greater reporting of income by this group might have resulted from a subjective summation of threat and conscience motivations. Moreover, threats conveyed under the guise of an appeal to conscience may have led to much greater compliance because of the mechanism of threat-induced moralism noted in the interview results. On the other hand, it is possible that the subjects of these interviews were simply more responsive to appeals to conscience than to the kind of threats which apparently made at least some sanction group members dig in their heels.

There is additional evidence which suggests that some who are induced to comply by threat find ways of expressing their resentment. Deductions taken by the sanction-threatened group showed a mean increase as compared with those who were given the conscience appeal. As shown in column IIa of Table V, those threatened with sanction had a mean increase in deductions of $273, compared with $177 for the normative group. It is tempting to interpret this difference as meaning that the threatened group said: "You may beat me into admitting higher income, but I'll find a way of getting it back." One might also infer that the conscience-appeal group kept its deductions low in recognition of the importance of tax payments for the welfare of the country.[54]

These interpretations lose force, however, from the position of the two control groups on deductions. For one thing, the placebo control shows an even lower mean increase in deductions than the conscience group, a result which is not attributable to induced motivations. A second confounding fact is that the untreated control shows even higher deductions than the sanction treated group.[55] A third point to be noted is that a *minority* of members of both experimental groups increased their deductions over the median provided by the placebo (Table VI). This shows that the increase in aggregate deductions by the experimental groups is attributable to a minority of the members of each group, the minority being even smaller in the sanction than in the conscience group. If there is a heel dragging effect, then, it is found in a relatively small group. It remains to be seen

---

[54] Enrick reports some sentiment along these lines. As one subject put it: "Taxes are sure high. But of course we must be thankful for what we have, and if taxes are needed to keep the country what it is, we'll just have to pay them." Enrick, *A Pilot Study of Income Tax Consciousness*, 16 NAT'L TAX J. 169, 172 (1963).

[55] Deductions are larger in the untreated control than in the placebo by a statistically significant margin (Table V, column II). This reinforces the conclusion that the interview led to a general decrease in deductions.

whether this group can be identified as having distinctive social characteristics and attitudes.

These three findings make it prudent to interpret the suggestive differences between the two experimental groups with considerable caution. The results, nevertheless, give some evidence to support the following propositions:

1. Compliance can be increased by threat of punishment.

2. Appeals to conscience can be a more effective instrument than sanction threat for securing compliance.

Further analysis is needed to determine how these experimentally induced motives affected subgroups whose verbal reactions to the interviews varied so widely. Those results are now being prepared by the Internal Revenue Service. When completed, it is hoped that they will contribute to a fuller understanding of the motivations affecting legal compliance.

CONCLUSION

. . . . The study reported was a field experiment aimed at determining the effectiveness of sanction, as compared with an appeal to conscience and with a placebo control, in increasing normative sentiments about compliance and in heightening actual compliance in the payment of federal income taxes. The findings indicate that motivations of various kinds make a difference in taxpaying. They suggest that the two types of appeal affect normative orientation differently according to the status of those subjected to the appeals. Sanction threat increases normative orientation most markedly among the upper class, the better educated, and non-Catholics. Appeals to conscience change attitudes toward tax compliance most among the best and least well-educated, those employed by others, and Protestants and Jews. As to actual changes in tax compliance, returns currently available for the gross treatment groups suggest that conscience appeals are more effective than sanction threats, though both have some effect. The conscience appeal appears, moreover, to produce less loss through resistance, an effect implied by the increase in aggregate deductions noted in the sanction-treated group.

These results must, of course, be viewed with caution. They were obtained from a population in a given geographical area, by a novel (*i.e.*, otherwise untested) method, in an examination of a largely well-to-do population. The behavior examined, moreover, may be atypically sensitive to conscience considerations, particularly in the American urban setting. Before these results can be confidently used as a girder in the construction of a theory of legal compliance, they must be joined with studies of the same problem which use different methods, populations, and types of legal compliance. To build an adequate theory of legal compliance, much more work is needed both at the drawing board and in the field.

Nevertheless, the results of the study carry several implications for a theory of sanction. They suggest that the threat of sanction can deter people from violating the law, perhaps in important part by inducing a moralistic attitude toward compliance. This mechanism seems particularly significant when those subject to sanction threat are not trained by, and associated with, an authoritative institution other than the state. The threat of punishment appears, however, to produce some resistance to compliance. Such resistance can be minimized through alternative techniques of securing compliance, such as the utilization of appeals to conscience and to a sense of civic responsibility, motives which can be more powerful than sanction threat in increasing compliance with the law.

NOTES AND QUESTIONS

1. The article by Schwartz and Orleans is the first study reprinted in this book where it is appropriate to discuss how to read a social science article.

It is important that one without a social science background recognize that if he reads only the social scientist's conclusions and does not attempt to assess his statistics, he is placing more reliance on the social scientist's judgment and interpretative skills than he would place on the same skills of a law professor, a judge or any other scholar who works only with words. Statistics are not magic, and when an item in a table is said to be statistically significant, that significance must still somehow be explained—by logical deductions, flashes of intuition or otherwise.

2. Schwartz and Orleans commendably warn us that the "results obtained from the experiment are not of a magnitude which uniformly produces statistically significant differences. Some of the results reported, especially if taken separately, could well be attributed to chance." One without experience in social science may read past such warnings or fail to consider what they mean. Conventionally, p (the probability that a particular result was obtained by chance) must be *less* than .05 for the result to be called statistically significant. This is not a law of nature but a custom as to where a line is to be drawn; if the chances are less than one in twenty that the result was obtained by chance, one can reason *as if* it is not without offending other members of the

statistical guild. But how should one treat a result that is not statistically significant? The logic does not permit one to say that the result *was caused* by chance. Chance is only an explanation that has not been ruled out. With a different sample (a larger one, for example), a significant difference might appear. Therefore, when one fails to obtain significant results he may still theorize about relationships with the same freedom as one who does not purport to use statistics. Moreover, his "not significant" results may still serve as scraps of evidence "suggesting" certain relationships or explanations. But the conclusions so arrived at are entitled to just as much but no more weight than other theoretical or speculative work. "Science" has not "proved" anything in that case.

For example, Schwartz and Orleans, after the warning quoted at the beginning of this note, discuss a number of comparisons between the impact of the sanction, conscience and placebo treatments in their experiment (*see* pp. 257-60, *supra*). Only the difference between conscience and placebo as to the average ("the mean") adjusted gross income reported is statistically significant at the .05 level. (Of course, there are also some significant results concerning total deductions and income tax after credits.) As you will notice, many of Schwartz and Orleans' conclusions about the effectiveness of conscience appeals as compared with threat of sanction rest on these results. They do not say that they have proved these conclusions, but some readers of the *University of Chicago Law Review* might think that they asserted that they had if these readers did not read the study very carefully. Is there a real danger in presenting this kind of article to an audience unsophisticated in social science such as one composed of law professors, law students, judges, legislators and the like? How could this danger, if it exists, be minimized?

One should note that it is acceptable to make an argument based on several results which are not significant but which all point in the same direction—that is, which all indicate the same conclusion. If chance were the explanation for all the results, one would expect some results to indicate one thing and others to refute it. Schwartz and Orleans make this kind of argument at 257, *supra*.

3. A careful examination of some of the tables in the article may be profitable. What have Schwartz and Orleans proved in a statistical sense, and what conclusions may we draw from this data? The authors indicate that only when you compare the conscience appeal with the placebo (the neutral) interview do you find a statistically significant difference. Look at Tables V and

VI at 258-59, *supra.* After receiving the interview, all groups reported their adjusted gross income, took deductions and computed
an income tax due for 1962. Those who had received the conscience appeal reported an *average* adjusted gross income of $804
more than the average the members of the group had reported in
1961. All of those who had received the placebo interview reported an average of $87 *less* in 1962 than the average they re-
ported in 1961. See Table V, Column Ia. Schwartz and Orleans
can say that the conscience appeal increases the average adjusted
gross income reported as compared to the neutral interview;
this has been proved in a statistical sense.

But averages are often hard to interpret. For example, 0, 10,
20, 30 and 40 produce an average of 20; 19, 21, 19, 21 and 20
produce an average of 20; and so do 2, 1, 1, 1 and 95. For various
reasons one may want to know whether an average reflects what
most people do or the impact of an extreme case. Moreover, one
may want to know whether or not an average increase would have
occurred even if the experimental treatment had not been given.
Schwartz and Orleans report two kinds of information to help us
judge the importance of the average increases and decreases in
adjusted gross income between 1961 and 1962 in the two groups.
Clearly, we ought not be too impressed with the effectiveness of
a conscience appeal, for example, if most taxpayers change very
slightly or not at all but a high average change is produced by
one taxpayer who reports a fantastically large increase. The
authors give us, in Table V, Column Ib., the "standard deviation." This indicates that approximately two-thirds of the individual cases fall within plus or minus the average figure indicated.
For example, the average increase in adjusted gross income of
the conscience appeal group was $804, and the standard deviation
was $4,007. This means that two-thirds of the cases ranged be-
tween —3,203 and +4,811 ($804 + 4,007 = $4,811; $804 — 4,007
= $—3,203). Of course, a minus number indicates less adjusted
gross income reported in 1962 after the experiment than in 1961.
This seems a fairly wide range. Assuming that these cases are
distributed throughout this range in their "normal" statistical
pattern, this tells us that some of the conscience appeal group
actually reported much *less* adjusted gross income in 1962 after
receiving the impact of the experiment. In short, conscience
appeal does not work with everyone.

Schwartz and Orleans next offer Table VI to help further interpret the average increases from 1961 to 1962 reported in Table
V. Table VI tells us the numbers of taxpayers in each experimental group who reported more or less adjusted gross income,
deductions and tax due than the median of the placebo group

which the authors use as a control. The median is the mid-point; that is, 50% reported more than this amount and 50% less. Column I gives us more information about adjusted gross income. One hundred forty-four dollars was the median difference between what the placebo group reported in 1961 and 1962. Since there were eighty-eight people in the placebo group that means that forty-four people reported a greater increase in adjusted gross income than $144 and forty-four people reported less. Compare the conscience group in the second row. Fifty-six people, or 64%, reported more than a $144 increase between the two years, and thirty-two people, or 36%, reported less than a $144 increase. The statistical test used indicates that the probability of at least the number which exceeds the placebo median doing so by chance is less than .05, and so the difference is significant. It is possible to view the placebo results as indicating what would have happened had there been no experiment. Therefore, the increase of twelve people (14%) reporting more than this median was presumably "caused" by the conscience appeal. Again, conscience appeal has impact, but the impact only reaches some people.

Adjusted gross income is only the starting point. A taxpayer takes various deductions and credits to produce the total tax due. The experiment would have to be viewed differently if taxpayers reported more adjusted gross income after, say, a conscience appeal, but discovered or manufactured more deductions to pay the same or less tax. Schwartz and Orleans tell us about this in Table V, Column III. The conscience appeal produces an average increase of $243 in tax due in 1962 as compared to 1961. The difference between this average and the $—40 (this is, $40 less tax paid after the experiment than before) average paid by those in the placebo group is statistically significant at the .05 level. While Column II indicates that the average deductions both groups took increased, the study shows that the conscience appeal produced an average of $243 increase in taxes paid to the government. Were most taxpayers moved to make about this increase, were the taxpayers evenly distributed above and below this amount, or were there some extreme cases? The standard deviation tells us that two-thirds of the people in the conscience appeal group ranged from $—946 to $1,432, another fairly wide range.

Table VI, Column III, tells us more about the number of people who might be said to be moved by the conscience appeal to pay more tax. The median of the placebo group (the control) was an increase of $34 in tax paid from 1961 to 1962. Since there were eighty-eight people in the placebo group, that means that forty-four paid more than $34 while forty-four paid less of an increase or even a decrease. Forty-nine people (56%) in the conscience appeal group paid an increase of more than $34 while thirty-seven (44%) paid less or a decrease. Thus five more people in the conscience appeal group than in the placebo group paid more than $34, and this might be attributed to receiving the conscience appeal. However, the value of p is greater than .05, and so the experiment has not ruled out chance as an explanation of the difference. It is also quite possible too, that the increase in taxes paid is due to an extraordinarily high payment by a few people.

To what extent, then, have Schwartz and Orleans gathered data from which a theory of the degree to which a conscience appeal will be an effective sanction can be devised? Does their data tell us much about the *circumstances* under which a conscience appeal will be effective?

4. At 252-55, *supra*, Schwartz and Orleans discuss their Tables I and II. Notice the process necessarily involved in this type of research. The research design and data gathering and processing yields a table of numbers. Then one must interpret the table, and here sometimes there is room for reasonable men to differ. For example, referring to Table I, the authors say: "For class I, it appears that, while direct appeals to duty do not create a greatly increased sense of obligation, threat of sanction does." If you compare the conscience column (71%) with the placebo (56%), you will see that there is a 15% increase in the percentage giving primary normative response when the conscience appeal is used. If you compare the sanction column (82%) with the placebo (56%), you will see that there is a 26% increase. Why is a 15% increase not "a greatly increased sense of obligation" produced by a direct appeal to duty?

Then, Schwartz and Orleans say that class IV members "show a slight decline following threat" and proceed to offer suggestions why this would be the case where members of the upper lower-class are involved. The difference between the placebo and sanction case is only 3% (53% in the placebo giving primary normative response as compared to only 50% in the sanction group). Is this enough of a difference to discuss? It certainly could have been produced by chance. And what about the lengthy explanation? Would it be possible that the members of class IV typically cheat less on their income tax for many reasons and thus have little to fear from sanctions?

Finally, the authors discuss the difference in education and normative orientation toward taxpaying in Table II. They compare the difference between the least and the most educated, finding that there is no difference for "High School not completed" where the placebo interview was given and where the sanction interview was given, but that there is a 10% difference for college graduates. Notice that there is an 8% difference for high school graduates; thus it is only the high school-not-completed group that shows no increase. Does this affect the authors' argument, particularly when they combine Table I and Table II? It is possible that some of the high school graduates will fall into Class IV of Socio-Economic Status.

5. In those situations where an appeal to conscience is likely to be effective, how can a governmental agency best communicate the appeal to those most likely to respond? On the cover of the instruction booklet that accompanies tax forms, the Commissioner of Internal Revenue usually writes a short essay to taxpayers. During the administration of President John F. Kennedy, the commissioner was a former law professor, and his essay made a very explicit conscience appeal. What would Litwak and Meyer (*see* Reading 25, at 231, *supra*) suggest about the effectiveness of such essays and about other ways of making an appeal to conscience?

6. What kinds of people might be most likely to respond to a conscience appeal? Schwartz and Orleans look at socio-economic status and education. Berkowitz and Walker classified people differently, looking at high social responsibility scale people and California *F*-scale people. Which type of classification is likely to yield more useful results? Why? How could one know in advance?

7. Common sense tells us that we can sometimes control the conduct of another by threatening to punish him if he acts in a proscribed way. Schwartz and Orleans do not assert that fear of punishment is ineffective. However, the process by which a threat of punishment produces fear which produces compliance is not well understood. We know that a threat sometimes is a challenge which increases deviation—for example, "I dare you to cross this line" may force one to cross it to prove he is not a coward. Sometimes the threat produces real fear, but the target deals with his fear by distorting the message or denying that it applies to him. Sometimes the threat may prompt only better efforts to escape detection rather than compliance. One may get more compliance if he structures things so that compliance is the path of least resistance. For example, to some extent, the federal income tax Form 1040 is designed to make honest answers easier than evasions, which must be worked out in detail in order to

appear consistent with all the other information given—such as information on withholding statements and statements from banks and corporations in which the taxpayer owns stock. The psychological links between a threatening message, fear and the response to that fear which is selected is very complex and probably very loose in the sense that it depends on a host of intervening variables. *See* Howard Leventhal, "Fear—For Your Health," 1 *Psychology Today* 55 (1967).

27. Moral Suasion as an Instrument of Economic Policy

J. T. ROMANS*

56 AMERICAN ECONOMIC REVIEW 1220 (1966)

Christopher Robin goes
Hoppity, hoppity
Hoppity, hoppity, hop
Whenever I tell him politely to stop it, he
Says he can't possibly stop
——A. A. MILNE

In the fourth century, Emperor Julian the Apostate exhorted the merchants of Antioch to hold down wheat prices—with a spectacular lack of success. . . .

Long lurking in the box of little-used policy tools, moral suasion appears to be undergoing a modern-day resurrection. In recent years one can observe both a marked increase in governmental (and particularly, presidential) suasion as a policy instrument as well as (at least) a superficial increase in its effectiveness. Recent examples of moral suasion are legion: the Kennedy-U.S. Steel and Johnson-aluminum, -copper and -steel industry confrontations; implementation of wage-price guideposts; top level mediation in labor-management disputes; "voluntary" curbs on foreign investment and travel; "jawbone" exhortations to business to pass the "savings" arising from excise tax cuts on to consumers; and many, many more.

There is little evidence that moral suasion is being used wholly as a substitute for other instruments of economic policy. The increasing number and complexity of government policy objectives has led to increased use of all policy instruments, monetary, fiscal, etc. . . . [T]he instruments of policy must be at least as numerous as the number of policy objectives . . . and one way of viewing moral suasion is that government has grasped it as

---

* J. T. Romans, Associate Professor of Economics, State University of New York, at Buffalo. Reprinted from the American Economic Review.

an additional instrument to meet its increasingly numerous economic objectives. But there are many objections that can be raised concerning the use of moral suasion as a major policy instrument. Moral suasion is inequitable in that it rewards noncompliance; it constitutes extra-legal coercion by government without judicial review; it is in violation of the "rule of law"; where promises, implicit or explicit, are involved, it entails the danger of an overly familiar relationship between regulator and regulatee; its *ad hoc* character adds an additional and unnecessary element of uncertainty to business decisions; and it may frequently be used in lieu of (i.e., as an excuse for not implementing) more effective legislation.

Indicting as this list may be, it does not prove that moral suasion is inferior to other types of policy instruments. All policies have opportunity costs both in terms of their administrative and enforcement costs as well as their allocative effects on the economy. Whether moral suasion is inferior to other instruments or whether a partially effective moral suasion policy is even superior to a policy of doing nothing at all depends upon the relative costs and effectiveness of alternative policies and the value system within which the relative costs and benefits are weighed.

The purpose of this paper is not to examine the ethical or political or even all the economic implications of this increasingly popular policy instrument. Rather, the objective is to point out the necessary conditions for moral suasion to be an effective policy instrument. It will be argued that (1) the necessary conditions for a moral suasion policy to be successful in achieving any desired goal constitute a special, not a general, case in the economy; and (2) the presence of these necessary conditions may well be promoted by existing trends in the economy so that over time we may expect to see a continued increase in both the incidence and effectiveness of policies implemented through moral suasion.

Since the concern of this paper is with moral suasion only in the economic sphere, moral suasion will be defined here as the attempt to coerce private economic activity via governmental exhortation in directions not already defined or dictated by *existing* statute law. It is, in a sense, the extreme case of "rule of men" as opposed to "rule of law."

The meaning of the appellative *moral* in the term moral suasion is not at all clear. (Whoever heard of an economic policy of immoral suasion?) Possibly the purpose of the appelative is to distinguish *pure* moral suasion, an appeal for altruistic behavior, from other types of persuasion which are backed by threats of punishment and/or promises of reward. However, as a practical matter, pure moral suasion rarely has been used as serious economic policy.[1] Also, it is not at all clear how altruism enters utility functions, if in fact it ever does. Fortunately, the question of the degree to which altruistic considerations influence economic behavior is not crucial, for the basic difference between moral suasion and direct suasion via the "rule of law" is not the threat of punishment or promise of reward. Rather, it is that punishment does not *automatically and uniformly* fall upon the (apprehended) noncomplier to moral suasion as it does upon the violator of statute law. For where moral suasion is buttressed by implicit or explicit threats, even if the policy fails, the threats might not be carried out, and if only a minority does not comply the moral suasion policy is likely to be deemed a success, and no follow-up action is required or taken. (The immorality of moral suasion is quite clear here. It rewards the noncomplier and punishes the socially cooperative and conscientious.) Although, in some unworldly sense, moral suasion might carry with it no threat of punishment or promise of reward, in a real sense, if the policy constitutes anything more than innocuous pontification to the economy as a whole, it carries at a minimum the implied threat of future legislation. In addition, the threat of fully utilizing existing regulatory powers; the danger of incurring government displeasure and inspiring legal prosecution on completely unrelated grounds; the possibility of being pointed out for public ridicule and abandonment or the promise of reciprocating favors may also play a role in instances of moral suasion, both successful and unsuccessful.

Assuming intelligent government, moral suasion is exerted in the economic sphere only in instances and directions which promote the national economic welfare (as viewed from the government's objective function). Assuming rational, profit-oriented economic units, existing private economic activity is already maximizing each unit's own economic welfare. The sphere for moral suasion, or any other economic policy, is where individual profit-seeking activity does not maximize the national welfare, i.e., where the particular and the social interests diverge. Thus, moral suasion must encourage private economic units to undertake actions which are unprofitable and which they would not undertake otherwise.

It is worth noting that the strongest protagonists on the one hand and the strongest opponents of moral suasion policies on

---

[1] An exception might be appeals to patriotism in times of national emergency. The "Buy War Bonds" campaign of World War II, for example, was rather successful. To be sure, there were other incentives provided via rationing policies and in the interest paid on the bonds. But the interest rate was not *raised*.

the other, both in the abstract and on particular issues, use the lack of one or the other of the above assumptions as the main foundation of their position. Proponents of moral suasion argue that it is to the long-run benefit of private units to comply with the government persuasion ("What's good for the United States is good for General Motors . . .") implying that private units are presently acting irrationally and not maximizing (long-run) profits. On the other hand, opponents of moral suasion argue that government's position is misguided; that in fact compliance with government wishes would *not* increase national welfare (". . . and vice versa"). It is not in the national interest, they argue, to hold down aluminum or steel prices to "subsistence levels" or to take firemen off trains, etc. Neither side addresses itself to the only real dilemma: the situation where both government and private units are acting rationally in the light of their own objective functions. In what follows, intelligence and rationality are assumed on the part of all parties.[2] Eschewing from this discussion the cases where government policy is in fact not promoting the national economic welfare or where private activity is in fact not maximizing each individual unit's welfare in no way defines away the problems involved in implementing economic policy through moral suasion. On the contrary, it only disjoins those dilemmas which can be potentially resolved through intelligent and rational discourse from the dilemmas in which private and public objective functions, rationally and intelligently arrived at, are still in conflict.

Within this frame of reference, it can be somewhat tautologically asserted that moral suasion can be an effective economic policy whenever the expected cost of noncompliance is made to exceed the cost of compliance. However, there are conditions which must exist in order to so design a moral suasion policy, and these conditions severely limit the size of the set of potentially effective moral suasion policies. There are two necessary condi-

---

[2] To discuss moral suasion in any other context is in reality to discuss education, itself. Although not of direct concern here, the educational aspect should not be ignored. Education may be good even if it masquerades under the title of moral suasion, and educational benefits are frequently used to justify—or rationalize—moral suasion policies. This is the case with the wage-price guideposts, for example. The function of mediators in labor-management disputes is usually explained on educational grounds as well. Similarly the reverse case, in which government is in some sense misguided, is not an irrelevant one. The government is not tutelar nor infallible and its objective function is not necessarily equivalent to the *national welfare*. It is not *necessarily* equivalent to anything even remotely approaching it. Rather it is more equivalent to some such concept as the *majority opinion* or the *compromise of the majority power*.

tions for the success of a moral suasion policy. The first is a long-run condition only; the second is both short- and long-run.

1. *The public must support the government's position.* Strong involvement with the public interest increases both the scope for altruism as well the probability that threats will be carried out. A glare of publicity can increase the power of persuasion *ex ante* (by increasing the expected cost of noncompliance) and the degree of censure on non-compliers *ex post.* However, this is only a necessary condition for an effective moral suasion policy in the long run, for fear of public displeasure is only one of the possible threats or promises with which government might back a moral suasion policy. In the short run it may be possible to establish sufficient expectations of other costs for noncompliers. But in the long run, given that economic policies are made in a democratic framework, the public must support these policies politically. This is particularly true when moral suasion is used recurrently against the same group.

2. *The populations to be persuaded must be small.* Moral suasion appears to be completely ineffective when exerted upon a large population. Fewness makes noncompliers readily identifiable and places responsibility for the success of the policy specifically and directly upon a small number of individual units so that credit for success, or blame for failure, can be levied. The analogy with central banking practices in the United States and England is an obvious one. Moral suasion is a cornerstone of English, but not U.S. monetary policy, presumably because in England there are only five major banks which need to be persuaded. A noncooperator can be immediately identified and held up for censure. On the other hand, the Federal Reserve uses a superstructure of legalistic controls to pursue the same ends. There are too many commercial banks to identify culprits.

Furthermore, with only five banks, not only are the effects of the actions of any one bank readily visible, but any one bank itself may determine the success or failure of the policy. When there are many thousands of units, thousands may refuse to cooperate and the policy may still be deemed a success, and no retaliation is levied on noncooperators. In sum, as the size of the population to be persuaded *decreases*, the probability that punishments will actually be levied on noncompliers *increases*.

The necessity for a small population to be persuaded is particularly apparent in cases of divergent firm and industry interests, for here the opportunity cost of compliance for any one unit increases as the number of units which comply increases. In essence, the greater the number of compliers, the greater the cost of compliance. This is the composition problem familiar in agriculture where it may be to the interest of all farmers to cut production in order to raise price, but not to the interest of any one farmer to do so. If the short-run average cost curve is flat, then a small number of noncompliers can produce the market share relinquished by a large number of compliers. Contrariwise, if the average cost curve is U-shaped, then cutting output can raise costs to compliers. In either case, compliers quite likely lose absolutely and always lose relatively to noncompliers. For moral suasion to be effective here it must impose a high probability of punishment on noncompliers and for this, as I have argued, fewness is necessary.

Fewness also implies a closer and more direct correspondence between individual action and public interest. If the cost of compliance is small and the fewness condition is met, moral suasion backed by altruism alone might be effective.

The failures of modern day programs for business to voluntarily restrict investment and banks to curtail credit abroad; for vacationers to restrict their tourism abroad; or for business to pass on to consumers all "savings" from excise tax cuts can be credited directly to the fact that the population which the government was attempting to persuade was too large. (This was Emperor Julian's problem also.) On the other hand, government's relative success in imposing the wage-price guideposts in specific oligopolistic industries and in high-level mediation of labor-management disputes can be credited to the fact that the fewness condition was met.

The fewness condition imposes a severe limitation on the applicability of moral suasion as an instrument of policy, and it cannot be artificially satisfied by arbitrarily delineating a small population to be persuaded. Generally, the population to be persuaded must be as large as the population which policymakers desire to affect. One cannot, for example, successfully exert persuasion on some of the firms in a given industry to cut prices. The exception of course is where persuasion is exerted on only the price leader of an oligopolistic industry; and such industries meet the fewness condition by definition.

Fewness also implies the existence of sufficient market power to affect the public interest. Given that some level of restraint is required on economic activity, insofar as competition declines as concentration increases, substitute restraints must come from either increased governmental controls or from moral suasion. This offers a possible reason why we have observed and may continue to observe increasing use of moral suasion as an economic policy. Greater concentration in the economy increases both the effectiveness of moral suasion as well as the need for restraining policies. In addition to concentration generally, the continuing growth of firms into national vis-à-vis regional markets in response to transportation and other technological improvements encourages the use and promotes the effectiveness of moral suasion. Concentration in the national market meets the fewness condition far better than does an equal degree of concentration in regional markets. In the latter, identification with the *national* interest is not close; a moral suasion policy is more difficult to administer; the probability that implied punishments will actually be levied is much less; and insofar as intermarket competition exists on at least the regional boundaries, the need for restraining policy is less as well. The geographic organization and regional bargaining practices of many labor unions, for example, might explain why labor is (as many argue) less susceptible to moral suasion than is business whose markets are more likely to be national in scope. Increasing concentration and rise of firms into national markets along with the increasing involvement of government in the economy, a possibly more representative government in a more complex economy, and a strong desire to maintain "free institutions" even where they may conflict with other policy objectives, undoubtedly explains the rise in popularity of policies implemented through moral suasion.

NOTES AND QUESTIONS

1. What does Romans mean by moral suasion? Which, if any, of the following are examples of this phenomenon:

(a) the federal government uses the techniques of advertising in the "Smokey the Bear" campaign, designed to induce people to be more careful about lighting fires in national parks and forests;

(b) the President calls the presidents of the four largest steel companies on the telephone, asks them to roll back recently announced price rises, and says he hopes wage-price controls may not prove necessary;

(c) the President asks the public to curb the outflow of gold by restricting their travel to the western hemisphere;

(d) the President asks the heads of the three largest insurance companies to invest some of their surplus funds in the Black ghettos, as a way to avoid the possibility of social strife.

2. Does Romans introduce important qualifications to Schwartz and Orleans or are they talking about very different situations?

3. Could the use of some of Litwak and Meyer's eight mechanisms of coordination (detached expert, opinion leader, etc.) make moral suasion more effective than Romans suggests is possible? Or does Romans introduce a significant limitation on Litwak and Meyer's "balance theory"?

28. Types of Deviance and the Effectiveness of Legal Sanctions

WILLIAM J. CHAMBLISS*

1967 WISCONSIN LAW REVIEW 703

In the last analysis a legal system must be judged according to the impact it has on the social order. If that impact is largely deleterious to the lives of men, then maintaining the legal system can scarcely be justified. If, on the other hand, the law contributes in some important ways to the goals of society and its members, then there is justification for keeping it. And, of course, if the legal system is useful in certain ways but deleterious in others then this condition cries out for changes to increase its effectiveness while maintaining those aspects found to have desirable consequences.

Not all of the presumed consequences of the law are equally amenable to empirical verification. . . .

The social sciences have been concerned principally with the question of deterrence, for it is here that the impact of the legal system is most amenable to empirical and systematic evaluation.

I. THE DETERRENT INFLUENCE OF CAPITAL PUNISHMENT

The question of the deterrent influence of capital punishment has occupied the forefront in criminological research into deterrence for years. The preponderance of the evidence indicates that capital punishment does not act as a deterrent to murder. This general conclusion is based on a number of observations and researchers that have demonstrated:

(1) That murder rates have remained constant despite trends away from the use of capital punishment;

(2) that within the United States where one state has abolished capital punishment and another has not, the mur-

---

* Professor of Sociology, University of Washington, Seattle. © Wisconsin Law Review, reprinted by permission.

der rate is no higher in the abolition state than in the retention state; and

(3) that apparently the possible consequences of the act of murder are not considered by the murderer at the time of the offense.

Some of the evidence substantiating these three conclusions is presented below.

There has been a very clear tendency throughout the Western World to eliminate capital punishment. In the United States this trend away from capital punishment has taken several forms. To begin with, there has been a rapid decline in the number of states where capital punishment is mandatory if an accused is found guilty; in 1924 the death penalty was mandatory in eight states, but by 1964 it was not mandatory in any. There has also been a tendency to impose the death sentence less and less frequently. Eighty percent of those persons sentenced to death in 1933-1934 were ultimately executed; the figure was 81 percent in 1940-1945. But from 1960 to 1964 only 34 percent of the persons sentenced to death have been executed.

There has also been a steady increase in the number of states that have abolished capital punishment for various crimes. In 1920 only six states had abolished capital punishment; by 1957 the number of such states had risen to eight; and by 1965, 13 states had formally abolished capital punishment. Perhaps even more significant is the rapid decline in the number of persons actually executed. In 1951 there were 105 executions in the United States. The number of executions has steadily and precipitously declined since that time, with 15 executions in 1964, 7 in 1965, and only 1 in 1966.

Thus we see in the United States a steady and rapid alteration in the propensity to administer capital punishment. From the standpoint of deterrence, the significance of this trend is that during this same period we find *no significant change* in the murder rate (see Table 1). It would seem that if the presence of capital punishment either in principle or in fact, were a deterrent to murder, then the murder rate should have gone up as both the potential and the actual use of capital punishment declined.

A similar conclusion emerges when the murder rates of states that have retained the death penalty are compared with the murder rates of states that have abolished it. This general conclusion also holds true when one compares contiguous states—states that presumably are relatively homogeneous culturally, but where one state has retained the death penalty and the other has not (see Table 2).

TABLE 1

COMPARISON OF PRISONERS EXECUTED UNDER CIVIL AUTHORITY AND MURDER RATE, 1951-1966

Year	Number of Persons Executed	Murder Rate (per 100,000 population)
1951	105	4.8
1952	83	5.0
1953	62	4.8
1954	81	4.8
1955	76	4.8
1956	65	4.9
1957	65	4.9
1958	49	4.7
1959	49	4.8
1960	56	5.1
1961	42	4.7
1962	47	4.5
1963	21	4.5
1964	15	4.8
1965	7	5.1
1966	1	5.6

TABLE 2

ANNUAL AVERAGE MURDER RATES IN SELECTED CONTIGUOUS STATES

	Murder Rate 1959-1964
Rhode Island[a]	1.1
Connecticut[b]	1.5
Wisconsin[a]	1.3
Illinois[b]	5.1
Minnesota[a]	1.1
Iowa[b]	1.2
Wisconsin[a]	1.3
Iowa[b]	1.2
Michigan[a]	3.4
Indiana[b]	3.5

[a] abolition states
[b] death penalty states

The states that have *abolished* the death penalty do not show a substantially higher murder rate when compared with states that have retained it. In four of the five pairs of states included in the table, the abolition state has a lower murder rate. In one pair the abolition state has a higher rate. The differences are slight in every instance, and the only safe conclusion possible from this data is that there is no greater propensity to murder when capital punishment is not a possibility than when it is. The point is not that abolishing capital punishment decreases the murder rate; rather, since the murder rate does not increase, one must conclude that capital punishment is not an effective deterrent.

The same conclusion is also suggested by a study of the murder rate in Philadelphia immediately preceding and following particularly well-publicized executions. If executing someone for a capital crime is a deterrent, one would expect its influence to be at a peak when an execution was imminent or had just occurred. But Savitz found no difference in the murder rate immediately prior to and following such executions.

Some of these studies rest on the analysis of data that have serious limitations, and none of the data are as perfect as one would like. However, given the preponderance of evidence, it seems safe to conclude that capital punishment does not act as an effective deterrent to murder. This conclusion about capital punishment does not apply to punishment generally since, as is well recognized, murder and other capital offenses are usually shrouded with a great deal of emotional involvement on the part of the offender. Thus, one might well expect punishment to be less effective precisely because such offenses are less dictated by "rational" considerations of gain or loss. Therefore, one must look at what the evidence indicates about different types of offenses.

II. Drug Addiction and the Law

There is a saying among drug addicts that "once the monkey's on your back, you never shake him off." The empirical research on drug addiction strongly supports this contention. In a study of 800 addicts who were followed after treatment, it was found that 81.6 percent of them had relapsed within the first year, 93.9 percent within three years and 96.7 percent within five years. The federally run hospitals at Lexington and Fort Worth report similar recidivism rates among persons treated at these hospitals. The President's Commission on Law Enforcement and Administration of Justice has also concluded that there is a high relapse rate.

Even among persons who are presumably the most likely to be rehabilitated through treatment, the recidivism rate is exceedingly high. Synanon, an organization for the treatment of drug addicts in Los Angeles, accepts only those addicts who volunteer for treatment. In addition to volunteering, the addicts must agree to undergo rather severe "hazing" policies in order to demonstrate the sincerity of their desire to abstain from drug use. Given these conditions, it is reasonable to presume that Synanon treats only those persons whose desire to "kick the habit" is very strong. But even with these persons, the proportion who fail to complete the treatment program is in excess of 70 percent of all those who initially apply.

For the question of the deterrent influence of punishment, the significance of these statistics comes from the realization that concomitant with this propensity to recidivate has been the constantly increasing effort of the federal government to punish drug users severely. The Bureau of Narcotics has increased its efforts at control, and the formal sanctions have drastically increased in severity. Under certain federal statutes, an offender can be sentenced to prison for six years with no possibility of parole, thus making drug use one of the most severely punished crimes in the United States.

This evidence, then, suggests that drug addiction, like murder, is relatively unaffected by the threat or the imposition of punishment. But one may still raise the question of whether it is justifiable to generalize these findings to all types of offenses. Indeed, at least in one respect, drug addiction and murder share in common something that is lacking in many other types of offenses. Both of these acts are "expressive"—the act is committed because it is pleasurable in and of itself and not because it is a route to some other goal.

III. THE VIOLATION OF PARKING REGULATIONS

If murder and drug addiction anchor one extreme in a typology of criminal acts, parking law violations anchor the other. Probably no one violates parking laws simply because it is pleasurable to do so—rather, people violate these laws primarily because to do so is *instrumental* to the attainment of some other goal. Does the imposition of punishment have the same effect on parking law violators as it had on drug addicts and murderers?

A study of the violation of parking regulations by university faculty found that the propensity to violate these rules is directly related to the likelihood that offenders will be punished. In this study, a sample of faculty members was interviewed, with records being checked to establish the validity of the interview data. Information was gathered on the sample's tendency to violate the regulations during a two and one-half year period when the sanctions that could be imposed were slight and when the regulations were only sporadically enforced. Significantly, during this period over one-third of the sample reported complying with the regulations despite the mild and rarely enforced sanctions. The other members of the sample, however, reported varying degrees of rule violation, ranging from one recalcitrant who parked illegally daily (even on the lawn beside his office) and who "saved the tickets to play solitaire with," to persons who violated occasionally in order to deliver a package on campus.

There was a dramatic shift in the tendency to violate the regulations when official policies changed. In January 1956 the campus police force was greatly increased in size, thus enabling adequate coverage of all parking areas. Fines were increased from the previously established figure of 1 dollar for every offense to 1 dollar for the first offense, 3 dollars for the second offense, and 5 dollars for the third and subsequent offenses during any 12 month period. Most importantly, during this second period of more severe sanctions, illegal parking could (and did) result in the violator's car being towed away at his own expense. These changes were sufficient to alter considerably the faculty's compliant behavior. Where there had been 13 frequent violators during the light sanctioning period, there were only 2 after the change. Even these 2 violators had changed their patterns of violation considerably. One reported violating frequently, but only for a few minutes while he delivered something to a building, thus minimizing his chances of being ticketed. The other reported violating only by illegally parking in a place where he had never received a ticket, and he further commented that had he received a ticket he would have stopped parking there. Thus, in effect, all 13 frequent violators showed a reduction in the propensity to violate the laws after sanctions were imposed.

IV. White-Collar Crimes

Although the data are less systematic than one might wish, studies on the impact of enforcement on the business connected crimes show results similar to the impact of sanctions on parking violators. Where penal sanctions are imposed there is a decline in the propensity to violate the law. Clinard summarized the findings from his study of black market violations during World War II as follows:

[During the first stage of enforcement] . . . the public and business had been developing an attitude that the OPA did not mean business, that violations would be followed with only minor actions, usually simply a warning letter, and that the penalties described in the regulations were virtually meaningless. New types of violations were rapidly being devised and spreading from business concern to business concern and from consumer to consumer. . . .

As the economy was rapidly getting out of hand with this slow hit-and-miss method of price control, the government on April 28, 1942, froze the prices on nearly all uncontrolled commodities. . . . This regulation provided: "Persons violating any provision of this Regulation are subject to the criminal penalties, civil enforcement actions, and suits for treble damages provided by the Emergency Price Control Act of 1942. . . ."

. . . [T]he penalty of imprisonment, even for a short period of time, was the punishment most feared by businessmen, according to their own statements; yet it was seldom invoked as a deterrent for others. A survey of wholesale food dealers' opinions, for example, revealed that they considered imprisonment a far more effective penalty than any other government action, including fines. In fact, some 65 per cent of them made such a statement. They made remarks such as the following about jail sentences: "Jail is the only way; nobody wants to go to jail." "Everybody gets panicky at the thought of a jail sentence." "A jail sentence is dishonorable; it jeopardizes the reputation." . . . These expressions are in marked contrast to the attitudes of the same men toward the imposition of fines and other monetary penalties: "They don't hurt anybody." . . . "People are making enough money nowadays to pay a fine easily."

Clinard also reports that in districts where the OPA regulations were enforced, compliance with the rules was much more prevalent than where enforcement was lax. In one midwestern city two automobile dealers were heavily fined and one was sent to prison. Clinard reports that numerous dealers commented that they were unwilling to take the risk of being sent to prison, and the regulations were complied with. By contrast, a company that had handled over 300,000 pounds of meat in 5 months and had charged prices of 7 to 11 cents a pound in excess of the allowed ceiling was found guilty of violating the regulations. The convicted defendants were fined only 250 dollars each and given a 30 day suspended sentence. The OPA district enforcement attorney stated that attempts to enforce the regulations were simply "laughed at" after this case. . . .

V. THE SNITCH AND BOOSTER

Cameron's study of shoplifting throws still more light on the impact of punishment as a deterrent. Cameron points out that there are two types of shoplifters: the "Snitch" and the "Booster." The Booster is a professional thief whose principal form of theft is shoplifting. The Snitch (or pilferer), in contrast, is generally a respectable citizen (usually a middle-class housewife) who shoplifts in order to obtain goods she could not otherwise afford. Cameron was able to check on the recidivism of persons apprehended by careful examination of department store files. Once a person is apprehended by a store detective, a card is filed with her picture; every store in the city has access to this file. Thus it is quite likely that any previous arrest will be known. Cameron found that persons who were professional thieves invariably had prior arrest records in the stores' files but that the Snitches almost never did. For the Snitches, one arrest was almost always sufficient to insure that she would never be arrested again. It is possible, but quite unlikely, that the Snitch simply became more careful after having been arrested once. It is more likely that she was in fact deterred from further shoplifting by the experience.

> Among pilferers who are apprehended and interrogated by the store police but set free without formal charge, there is *very little or no recidivism.* . . .
>
> [O]nce arrested, interrogated, and in their own perspective, perhaps humiliated, pilferers apparently stop pilfering. The rate of recidivism is amazingly low. The reward of shoplifting, whatever it is, is not worth the cost of reputation and self-esteem. . . .
>
> One woman was observed who, thoroughly shaken as the realization of her predicament began to appear to her, interrupted her protestations of innocence from time to time, overwhelmed at the thought of how some particular person in her "in-group" would react to her arrest. Her conversation with the interrogator ran somewhat as follows: "I didn't intend to take the dress. I just wanted to see it in the daylight. [She had stuffed it into a shopping bag and carried it out of the store.] Oh, what will my husband do? I *did* intend to pay for it. It's all a mistake. Oh, my God, what will my mother say! I'll be glad to pay for it. See, I've got the

money with me. Oh, my children! They can't find out I've been *arrested*! I'd never be able to face them again!" . . .

The contrast in behavior between the pilferer and the recognized and self-admitted thief is striking. The experienced thief either already knows what to do or knows precisely where and how to find out. His emotional reactions may involve anger directed at himself or at features in the situation around him, but he is not at a loss for reactions. He follows the prescribed modes of behavior, and knows, either because of prior experience or through the vicarious experiences of acquaintances, what arrest involves by way of obligations and rights. He has some familiarity with bonding practice and either already has or knows how to find a lawyer who will act for him.

These findings suggest that the amateur shoplifter, or the Snitch, will be deterred from further criminality by the imposition of punishment, while the professional thief will be little affected by it.

The Cameron findings on professional thieves are also corroborated by other investigations. Lemert's study of the systematic check forger suggests that receiving an occasional jail sentence is merely part of the life of being a professional thief; it is accepted as one of the "hazards of the business," just as other occupational groups accept certain undesirable characteristics of their work as inevitable hazards. That arrest and jail sentence do not interrupt the ongoing interpersonal relations of professional thieves is undoubtedly an important element in rendering the punishment relatively ineffective.

But this fatalistic acceptance of imprisonment as an inevitability should not be interpreted to mean that the professional thief is wholly unresponsive to the threat of punishment. On the contrary, a much greater proportion of a thief's energy is devoted to avoiding capture and imprisonment than is devoted to stealing. Although serving an occasional sentence apparently does not deter the professional thief from crime, it must be remembered that, for a reasonably competent and skillful thief, prison sentences occur relatively infrequently.

VI. A Typology of Crime and Deterrence

The preceding summary of research findings on the deterrent influence of punishment on various types of crimes suggests some interesting contrasts. First is the contrast between acts that are "expressive" and acts that are "instrumental." Murder as an expressive act is quite resistant to punishment as a deterrent, as is

drug addiction; instrumental acts, such as violating parking regulations and shoplifting by middle-class housewives, are more likely
to be influenced by the threat or imposition of punishment.

The other major distinction suggested by the research is between persons who are highly committed to crime as a way of
life and persons whose commitment is low. Cameron talks about
this distinction in contrasting the Booster and the Snitch. She
argues that this distinction is essentially a difference in the group
support for their transgressions perceived by these different categories of offenders. More generally, one could say that persons
with a high commitment perceive group support, conceive of
themselves as criminal, and pattern their way of life around their
involvement in criminality. Persons with low commitment would,
of course, exhibit the reverse of these characteristics.

By combining these two dimensions of criminality and offender,
it is possible to construct a typology of criminal acts with clear
implications for the likelihood that a combination of offender and
offense will respond to punishment by reducing their involvement in crime. The hypothesis is that where a high commitment
to crime as a way of life is combined with involvement in an act
that is expressive, one finds the greatest resistance to deterrence
through threat of punishment. At the other extreme are acts
where commitment to crime is low and where the act is instrumental (such as the Snitch, the white-collar criminal, or the parking law violator). Here we would expect both general and specific
deterrence to be maximally effective (see Table 3).

Table 3

Types of Deviance

Degree of Commitment to Crime as a Way of Life	Type of Act	
	Instrumental	Expressive
High	Professional thief Booster Some check forgers Some murderers	Most drug addicts Some murderers Some sex offenders
Low	Snitch Parking law violator White-collar criminal Some murderers	Most murderers Some drug addicts Most sex offenders

While we can assert with some confidence that the remaining two types—high commitment-instrumental and low commitment-expressive—will fall between the two polar types, it is somewhat more difficult to know which of these types will be more responsive to punishment. It seems likely, however, that the impulsive nature of expressive acts, even when commitment to crime is low, will make such acts less amenable to punishment than instrumental acts, even though commitment is high.

We have, then, the following hierarchy of types that can be ranked according to whether or not they are likely to be deterred by punishment or the threat of it:

Most likely to be deterred: low commitment-instrumental
                               high commitment-instrumental

Least likely to be deterred: low commitment-expressive
                               high commitment-expressive

In considering this typology, it must be stressed that the sociological types represented by it do not correspond perfectly with legal types. If they did, there would be no reason for developing the typology. For example, the legal category "murder" contributes cases to at least three of the four sociological types. Probably in over 90 percent of the cases, murder is an expressive act where the commitment to crime as a way of life is low. Typically, murder occurs in an argument between two people. But there are other types of murder that would fit into the instrumental category of offenses; gangland murders, which constitute only a very small portion of the total number of murders, would, of course, be such a type. Murdering someone to collect insurance and sundry other profit-making schemes would represent instrumental types of offenses where commitment is probably low.

The above argument can now be used to throw more light on the earlier discussion of the deterrent influence of capital punishment. For if this theory is correct, then low commitment-instrumental murders should be deterred by the threat of punishment. That capital punishment does not deter now becomes dependent on the fact that most murders are expressive types of offenses.[21]

---

21 The policy question raised by this argument is a sticky one. Assuming that instrumental-type murders are deterred by capital punishment (a conclusion that is consistent with the preceding argument), then should we continue to impose capital punishment generally for murder in order to achieve that deterrent effect? The answer to this query must of course take into account the costs of such a policy. The cost of deterring instrumental murderers with capital punishment is to execute persons who would not be deterred by the threat of punishment because their acts are expressive; and in the case of murder, this represents the vast bulk of the offenders. The argument becomes even more complicated when one takes into account that

If this typology has the kind of general utility in predicting the deterrent influence of punishment that research findings suggest it should have, then a truly rational system of justice is one that will maximize its effectiveness by imposing criminal sanctions where these act as an effective deterrent, and at the same time develop alternatives to punishment where it is found to be ineffective. The implication of the foregoing analysis would be that the legal system will have little effect in reducing the frequency of such things as excessive drinking, drug use, most murders, most sex offenses, and aggravated assault. For these behaviors, alternative mechanisms of social control must be instituted.

Ironically, most of the criminal-legal effort is devoted to processing and sanctioning those persons *least* likely to be deterred by legal sanctions. Most arrests and most convictions are for relatively minor offenses, most of which are unlikely to be deterred by imposing sanctions. In 1965, for example, police reported 4,955,047 arrests to the FBI. Only 834,296 of them were for offenses that the FBI categorizes as "Type I," or "major," crimes. There is even reason to question whether this statistic is an overestimate of the proportion that are major crimes since 101,763 of these arrests were for auto theft, which in over 90 percent of the cases consists of an adolescent's borrowing an automobile for a short period of time and going for a "joy ride." In any event, well over 80 percent of the arrests made by the police are for relatively minor offenses. Although some of these offenses might be responsive to sanctions, most will not. Drunkenness accounts for a larger share of arrests made than any other single offense— in 1965, 1,535,040 arrests were for drunkenness, and this represents almost one-third of the total arrests made. Furthermore, when drunkenness-related[23] offenses are added together, they constitute *almost 50 percent* of all criminal arrests.[24] Finally, when arrests for other offenses unlikely to be deterred are considered, such as drug law violations (most of which are arrests of drug addicts),[25] aggravated assault, vandalism, and sex offenses, then the proportion of the arrests for offenses not likely to be deterred by imposing sanctions approaches 60 percent.

---

in all likelihood an instrumental murderer faces a lesser possibility of having sanctions imposed and this fact inevitably flows from the different types of offenses. One can only raise those issues here and hope that others will help pursue the answers.

23 Violation of liquor laws, driving while under the influence of alcohol, disorderly conduct, and vagrancy.

24 Total arrests in 1965 were 4,955,047; arrests for drunkenness-related offenses totaled 2,467,089.

25 *See* A. LINDESMITH, THE ADDICT AND THE LAW (1966).

That arresting persons for drunkenness is not likely to be an effective deterrent is implied by the typology. Indeed, since the bulk of such arrests are of the chronic skid row inebriate, such persons fall into the category of offenders least likely to be deterred: those with high commitment to a criminal way of life (in this case the criminal way of life consists of persistent drunkenness) and those whose acts are expressive. Studies of such offenders bear out this expectation. In their study of chronic police court inebriates, Pittman and Gordon found that the majority of these offenders were persons who had been through the "revolving door" of the police station and jail innumerable times.

> The results of our investigation negate completely the assumption that incarceration acts as a deterrent to the chronic public inebriate. . . . Of the 1,357 men committed to the Monroe County Penitentiary in 1954 on charges of public intoxication or allied offenses, only 5 were newcomers to prison life. About one-third of these men—455 to be exact— were there for their second to tenth round. Nearly 6 out of 10 (80 men) had been committed from 10 to 25 times to a penal institution, and 96 men had served 25 or more jail terms. Our study group, a random sample of their kind, includes men who have been arrested 81, 90 and 110 times for public intoxication. There is no question about it: jailing has not deterred them from further public drunkenness.[26]

Pittman and Gordon's claims are a little stronger than their data warrant. While it is true that the persons studied in the county jail show a failure of penal sanctions to deter, it may well be that many more persons who are no longer in jail but who have been arrested previously were subsequently deterred. Thus, this evidence can only be taken as suggestive, but it seems unlikely that the findings would be much different even if sampling procedures had been more reliable.

These findings contrast nicely with the common observation that systematic arrests for driving while intoxicated act as a deterrent. Many casual observers have claimed that the Scandinavian practice of arresting and severely sanctioning persons who drive while under the influence of alcohol, has the effect of greatly reducing the frequency of such events and (perhaps more importantly) of reducing the frequency with which accidents occur as a consequence of driving under the influence. Since this offense would fall logically into the category of an instrumental act (the drinking may be expressive, but driving while drunk would

---

26 D. PITTMAN & C. GORDON, REVOLVING DOOR 139-40 (1958).

clearly be instrumental by the definition given earlier), then such a finding is precisely what would be expected by the theory.

By contrast, persons likely to be deterred by imposing sanctions are, in general, the most likely to escape them. As Sutherland's analysis of white-collar crime has shown, violators of the Sherman Antitrust law are relatively free from criminal prosecution, though the imposition of punishment would be maximally effective with this type of offense. Professional thieves likewise enjoy a surprising immunity from sanctions.[30]

The incompatibility of current legal practices with the data and theoretical perspective presented here is summed up in the way the legal system typically responds to violation of antidrug laws. Relatively miniscule amounts of the legal system's energies and potentials are devoted to the development of techniques and procedures that would increase the efficiency with which persons responsible for importing, wholesaling, and distributing drugs for illegal resale are prosecuted. By contrast, great ingenuity is shown in the enforcement of antidrug laws against persons buying drugs for their own consumption. Included in these techniques are ingenious, albeit quasi-legal, methods of searching dwellings without a warrant and then, if anything is found, obtaining a warrant to make a second, "legal" search; entrapping prospective buyers; and using as informers drug addicts who are paid for informing by being given drugs for their own consumption. The likelihood that drug addicts will be deterred by sanctions, regardless of how severe or likely sanctioning may be, is exceedingly small. The wholesalers, importers, and distributors, by contrast, are generally ignored; but sanctions, if imposed, would be far more likely to be effective. As Lindesmith has pointed out, the present policy of arresting addicts and ignoring the profiteers makes about as much sense as believing that the wholesale arrest of drunks along the bowery would have curtailed the violation of prohibition laws.

VII. CONCLUSION

Before spelling out the implications of the foregoing analysis, it is essential that two general disclaimers be underlined. First, it must be reiterated that this article has assumed that deterrence is the only legitimate purpose for imposing criminal sanctions.

But there are some who would disagree with this position and who would claim other, equally important purposes for imposing

---

[30] A professional safecracker of the author's acquaintance estimated that he had been arrested for safecracking (burglary) 300 times in a career spanning some 45 years but that he had received only three prison sentences from these 300 arrests. His immunity from prosecution stemmed principally from his ability to "fix" any criminal charges brought against him.

criminal sanctions. A person may be arrested to protect him from possible harm; drunks, for example, may be put in jail to keep them from freezing to death or from having their money stolen. Or, laws may be kept "on the books" because what they express contributes something valuable to the moral climate of the society, irrespective of whether or not they are enforced. A detailed analysis of the almost infinite number of purposes claimed for the criminal law is beyond the scope of this article. No matter what such an analysis might indicate as the various legitimate purposes of the law, the fact remains that, at the very least, deterrence is a major, if not the only, purpose. Therefore, it is justifiable to consider the implications of the foregoing analysis assuming deterrence to be the sole purpose of the criminal law.

A second qualification is the tentative nature of the theory suggested here. At this point, it is of greater concern that one ask the right kind of question than that one come up with the right answer.

On the assumption, then, that the theory presented here will be confirmed by further research, what are the policy implications? One implication is quite clear. Current practices of the legal system in focusing on persons whose acts are principally expressive in character . . . [are] accomplishing very little vis à vis deterrence. Furthermore, the failure to develop techniques for imposing sanctions on instrumental type offenders omits a potentially important function for the legal order.

More specifically, what does the theory imply for lawmakers? Is it possible to write laws so that they take into account such things as the instrumental or expressive character of criminal acts? Can laws be written to take into account the person's degree of commitment to crime as a way of life? Although the task is not a simple one, the law has proven its capacity for taking into account far greater subtleties than these. Indeed, in many instances similar distinctions are made in the law. Laws imposing different penal sanctions for the "habitual offender" come close to selecting persons who are "committed to crime as a way of life." Unfortunately, such laws also pull into their net persons who are habitually expressive offenders. Indeed, one suspects that such laws are more often used to permanently incarcerate sexual offenders (who are likely to be expressive types of offenders) than to permanently incarcerate professional thieves.

Similarly, laws differentiate persons who have intent and those who do not. The notion of intent is not sufficient to differentiate expressive and instrumental acts, but the possibility of doing so through a similar legal category is certainly not farfetched.

It is conceivable that the law might prescribe, for offenders who committed an act as a means to achieving some other goal, a punishment different than the punishment prescribed for persons who committed an act because the act was satisfying in and of itself. Presumably, courts and penal institutions attempt to do this for some offenders: Arsonists, for example, are likely to receive quite different treatment if they burned a building for the pure pleasure of it than if they burned the building because it was insured for more than it was worth.

These current practices suggest that the precedent and even the mechanisms exist for making such distinctions within the legal order. The problem, then, is not that the law is unable to take such things into account; rather, the problem is that the empirical data to tell us what distinctions should be made have not been available. Then, too, there is the more basic problem of confidence in the data that is available. We are better off making social policies based on less-than-perfect data than making social policies based on no data at all. Currently, the law is based on virtually no data at all; could we really go very far wrong if we changed our policies on the basis of only tentative conclusions? It seems unlikely that things would be any worse, and there is always the chance that they would be considerably better.

NOTES AND QUESTIONS

1. Statistical inference makes use of logic and reasoning and must be subjected to rigorous analysis. In the notes following the essay by Schwartz and Orleans, we examined some assumptions underlying statistical inference in that article. Chambliss presents much less technical data. Nevertheless, one must still be careful in moving from data to conclusions. A nonstatistical article must be read as cautiously as any other.

In the first part of the article, Chambliss deals with the deterrent influence of capital punishment. He begins by arguing that capital punishment does not deter. If capital punishment were a deterrent to murder, then the murder rate should rise as the use of capital punishment declines. To prove this, he educes evidence, shown in Table 1, to the effect that the murder rate has remained constant while the number of persons executed has declined over a fifteen-year period from 105 to 1. Chambliss does not bring in any evidence to establish the implicit claim that the difference between 105 and 1 is in some way significant. The murder rate per 100,000 population in 1951 was 4.8. Assuming a population of 150 million, this means that approximately 7,500 persons were murdered in 1951. But only 105 persons were executed that year. (Presumably most of the murders for which these 105 persons were executed were committed in earlier years, but since Chambliss gives us no other data to go on, we will assume that the murder and execution rates were about the same in the preceding year or two.) Since we begin with a year, 1951, in which the execution rate is barely 1% of the murder rate, can we really assert that this is a year in which capital punishment must have deterred, if it deters at all? Was capital punishment a factor that had to be taken into account by a potential murderer? How do we know that a 1% chance of execution should deter while .1% should not, if the deterrent theory is correct?

Moreover, Table 1 does show some differences in the murder rate. Between 1964 and 1966, a rise in the number of murders parallels a sharp decline in the absolute number of persons executed. Is the difference between a rate of 4.8 and 5.6 significant in any way? To say that the figures in Table 1 are significant, or to demonstrate something real about the deterrent or non-deterrent effect of capital punishment, what is needed is some explicit theory to account for the assertion that these figures "prove" anything about capital punishment.

With regard to Table 2, the assertion is made that the pairs of contiguous states are culturally homogeneous. With regard to one pair, Wisconsin and Illinois, there appears to be a fairly large difference in the murder rate. This at least casts some doubt on whether the two are culturally homogeneous. If they are not, then one can draw no conclusions from the data. Besides, it is *possible* that Illinois would have an even higher murder rate without capital punishment; or that Wisconsin would have had an even lower murder rate had it adopted capital punishment. Table 2 does not prove to the contrary.

At 280-81, *supra*, Chambliss discusses drug addiction and the law. He attempts to show that there is no evidence that punishment deters drug addicts from the crimes associated with addiction. The first piece of evidence he adduces is a high relapse rate among addicts who have had treatment. This assumes that treatment would be a more powerful force in ending drug addiction than punishment. Hence, if treatment does not work, then punishment, a fortiori, would not work. This may be true, but it begs the question of deterrence.

At 281, *supra*, Chambliss argues against the deterrence theory by using the recidivism rate. But the only evidence he brings in deals with persons undergoing voluntary treatment. At the same time, the penalties against drug use have become more severe. Are those who undergo treatment the same people as those who are punished? If not, how can we say anything about the effect of punishment? And what about the problem of enforcement? How many persons are actually subjected to these punishments?

The discussion of drug addiction also seems to confuse two kinds of deterrence: general deterrence and special deterrence. General deterrence refers to the effect of punishment upon the general population. Special deterrence refers to the effect of deterrence upon those actually committing crimes. It is possible that punishment may deter the general population but have no effect whatsoever upon criminals and deviants themselves. That is, it is possible, at least theoretically, that severe punishments for drug addicts have no effect upon addicts who continue to violate the law, but that these punishments serve to keep out members of the general population who might otherwise be tempted to try certain drugs. When we speak of the deterrent effect of capital punishment, we are obviously not speaking of the special deterrent effect on possible repeaters; dead men commit no murders. But when we speak of the recidivism rate of drug addicts, we are obviously dealing only with special deterrence. Chambliss seems to move from a discussion of general deterrence to a discussion of special deterrence, without making the distinction very clear. Is the distinction important enough to affect his argument? Why? For a good concise discussion of the two types of deterrence, *see* Herbert L. Packer, *The Limits of the Criminal Sanction* 39-58 (Stanford U. Press 1968).

[Reading 29]

2. Does Chambliss convince you that capital punishment does not deter murder, particularly "expressive" murder, by one with low commitment to crime as a way of life? Consider further Van den Haag, "On Deterrence and the Death Penalty," 78 *Ethics* 280 (1968):*

The foregoing suggests the question posed by the death penalty: is the deterrence added (return) sufficiently above zero to warrant irrevocability (or other, less clear, disadvantages)? The question is not only whether the penalty deters but whether it deters more than alternatives and whether the difference exceeds the cost of irrevocability. (I shall assume that the alternative is actual life imprisonment so as

* Professor Ernest Van den Haag, New School of Social Research, New York City. © Ethics, published by the University of Chicago Press, reprinted by permission.

to exclude the complication produced by the release of the unrehabilitated.)

In some fairly infrequent but important circumstances, the death penalty is the only possible deterrent. Thus, in case of acute coups d'état, or of acute substantial attempts to overthrow the government, prospective rebels would altogether discount the threat of any prison sentence. They would not be deterred because they believe the swift victory of the revolution will invalidate a prison sentence and turn it into an advantage. Execution would be the only deterrent because, unlike prison sentences, it cannot be revoked by victorious rebels. The same reasoning applies to deterring spies or traitors in wartime. Finally, men who, by virtue of past acts, are already serving, or are threatened by, a life sentence, could be deterred from further offenses only by the threat of the death penalty.

What about criminals who do not fall into any of these (often ignored) classes? Professor Thorsten Sellin has made a careful study of the available statistics; he concluded that they do not yield evidence for the deterring effect of the death penalty. Somewhat surprisingly, Sellin seems to think that this lack of evidence for deterrence is evidence for the lack of deterrence. It is not. It means that deterrence has not been demonstrated statistically—not that non-deterrence has been.

It is entirely possible, indeed likely (as Sellin appears willing to concede), that the statistics used, though the best available, are nonetheless too slender a reed to rest conclusions on. They indicate that the homicide rate does not vary greatly between similar areas with or without the death penalty, and in the same area before and after abolition. However, the similar areas are not similar enough; the periods are not long enough: many social differences and changes, other than the abolition of the death penalty, may account for the variation (or lack of it) in homicide rates with and without, before and after abolition; some of these social differences and changes are likely to have affected homicide rates. I am unaware of any statistical analysis which adjusts for such changes and differences.

Homicide rates do not depend exclusively on penalties any more than other crime rates. A number of conditions which influence the propensity to crime, demographic, economic, or generally social, changes or differences—even such matters as changes in the divorce laws or in the cotton price—may influence the homicide rate. Wherefore variation or constancy cannot be attributed to variations or constancy of the penalties, unless we know that no other factor influencing the homicide rate has changed. Usually we do not. To believe the death penalty [is a] deterrent does not require one to believe that the death penalty, or any other, is the only, or the decisive, causal variable; this would be as absurd as the converse mistake that "social causes" are the only, or always the decisive, factor. To favor capital punishment, the efficacy of neither variable need be denied. It is enough to affirm that the severity of the penalty may influence some potential criminals and that the added severity of the death penalty adds to deterrence, or may do so. It is quite possible that such a deterrent effect may be offset (or intensified) by non-penal factors which affect propensity; its presence or absence, therefore, may be hard, and perhaps impossible, to demonstrate.

Contrary to what Sellin and others seem to presume, I doubt that offenders are aware of the absence or presence of the death penalty state by state or period by period. Such unawareness argues against the assumption of a calculating murderer. However, unawareness does not argue against the death penalty if by deterrence we mean a preconscious, general response to a severe but not necessarily specifically and explicitly apprehended or calculated threat. A constant homicide rate, despite abolition, may occur because of unawareness and not because of lack of deterrence: people remain deterred for a lengthy interval by the severity of the penalty in the past, or by the severity of penalties used in similar circumstances nearby.

I do not argue for a version of deterrence which would require me to believe that an individual shuns murder because of the death penalty while in North Dakota, and merrily goes to it in South Dakota, since it has been abolished there; or that he will start a murderous career, from which he had hitherto refrained, after abolition. I hold that the generalized threat of the death penalty may be a deterrent, and the more so, the more generally applied. Deterrence will not cease in the particular areas of abolition or at the particular times of abolition. Rather, general deterrence will be somewhat weakened, through local (partial) abolition. Even such weakening will be hard to detect owing to changes in many offsetting, or reinforcing, factors.

For all of these reasons, I doubt that the presence or absence of a deterrent effect of the death penalty is likely to be demonstrable by statistical means. The statistics presented by Sellin and others show only that there is no statistical proof for the deterrent effect of the death penalty. But they do not show that there is no deterrent effect. Not to demonstrate presence of the effect is not the same as to demonstrate its absence; certainly not, when there are plausible explanations for the non-demonstrability of the effect.

It is on our uncertainty that the case for deterrence must rest.

3. Does Chambliss adequately deal with the efficiency of the enforcement agency as a variable? It is almost trite to say that it is not the severity but the certainty of punishment that deters. Does Chambliss challenge this assumption?

Increases in the technology of crime detection, then, may be assumed to have an important and positive effect on the incidence of crime. The punishment rate depends initially on the detection rate; and for those criminals who operate on the cost-benefit model (and hence are deterrable), a rising detection rate should mean higher "costs" to them, hence a lower propensity to violate. (Where the cost-benefit model is inappropriate, this reasoning does not hold.)

This means, of course, that sometimes society would be well advised to put more resources into detection technology, rather than into an increase in the severity of punishment. And there are many important areas of life where this seems clearly appropriate. Indeed, the chance of avoiding nuclear war may depend on the technology of detection of violations of international agreements relating to the testing of nuclear weapons. There are other, more homely, examples. A case in point is the problem of oil pollution. Pollution of the ocean and beaches by oil from tankers has become a serious problem. Some of the pollution comes from wrecked ships, but some comes from ordinary practices of oil tankers, which often dump oily bilge at sea. Tankers do this because it is costly to carry the bilge about until it can be disposed of safely in port. There is federal legislation, but it is exceedingly difficult to enforce. Hence there have been suggestions that resources ought to be put into detection technology: chemical marking of oil, to make it possible to detect the vessel from which pollutants came; use of satellites to patrol sea lanes; and so on. The Federal Water Pollution Control Administration has awarded a contract for a computer system to "tag" oil pollution to the installation or vessel from which it originated. (This information is based upon a term paper, "The Prevention of Oil Pollution of the Sea," Dec., 1968, by Dan R. Kiely, then a third-year law student, Stanford University.)

What effect on the efficacy of sanctions do such devices as the lie detector, blood-typing and fingerprinting have?

Of course, improvement in detection does not necessarily mean a higher rate of punishment. It is possible, for example, that before the days of scientific detection more people were arrested, indicted and tried; but fewer were convicted. In other words, scientific detection and acquittal are alternative screening devices, but the rate of punishment may remain roughly the same. For what crimes would this hold true, do you think?

It goes without saying that efficiency is not the sole criterion of a detection device. Wiretapping is efficient; but many consider it inadvisable because of what they feel are harmful social byproducts.

See Rottenberg, "The Clandestine Distribution of Heroin, Its Discovery and Suppression," 76 *The Journal of Political Economy* 78 (1968).

4. How, if at all, does Chambliss' theory relate to Schwartz and Orleans' study of the impact of an appeal to conscience and of a threat of sanction? In terms of Chambliss' typology, what kind of crime is it to cheat in reporting adjusted gross income or deductions on one's income tax return?

[Reading 30]

5. As a result of the experiences many young people had in civil rights activities in the South during the early 1960's and in the later protests against the war in Vietnam, it is said that many younger middle-class Americans do not share the strong adverse emotional reaction to the idea of going to jail that is typical of their parents' generation. For some, experience in jail is a badge of honor. To the extent that this is true, does this change in attitude have relevance to a theory of deterrence? Consider the following: H. Ball & L. Friedman, "The Use of Criminal Sanctions in the Enforcement of Economic Legislation: A Sociological View," 17 *Stanford Law Review* 197, 216-17 (1965).*

It is generally accepted today that fear of criminal prosecution is an effective deterrent to businessmen, professional men, and the middle class. It follows that criminal sanctions ought to be highly effective in dealing with economic crimes.

---

* Harry V. Ball, Professor of Sociology, University of Hawaii; Lawrence M. Friedman, Professor of Law, Stanford University. © 1965 by the Board of Trustees of the Leland Stanford Junior University, first published in the January 1965 issue of the Stanford Law Review.

Also, noncriminal sanctions are presumably made more effective if the threat of criminal prosecution lurks in the background. . . .

The very effectiveness of criminal sanctions in restraining the behavior of businessmen accounts in large part for the concern over the use of criminal-penal sanctions in regulating business. Businessmen abhor the idea of being branded a criminal. Society does not particularly care whether murderers and rapists like being branded as criminals; but businessmen, after all, form a large, respectable, and influential class in our society. Therefore, effectiveness of the penal sanction in this case leads to pressure against use of the sanction. The phenomenon is a general one; middle-class persons resent being "treated like a criminal," no matter what legal rule they may violate. But rules acquire legitimacy through being adopted in the regular processes utilized in society for making rules. The legitimacy of rules derives from the use of a standardized process of adoption, as much as or more than from the subject matter with which the rules deal. Americans in general accept the proposition that it is "wrong" to violate the law, even if they feel the law acts unwisely when it prohibits certain conduct. The very fact that a criminal statute has been enacted by the legislature is a powerful factor in making the proscribed conduct illegitimate in the eyes of a potential actor, even when the actor disagrees with the purpose of the law.

Lane has suggested that there are no generic differences between the factors which produce violations of economic regulatory law and the factors which produce other criminal acts. If this is true, then economic regulation through the use of criminal sanctions poses a real dilemma for society and for the businessman. The businessman may find himself impelled toward crime; he recognizes the legitimacy of the laws which define the crime he is tempted to commit; yet he cannot concede that he is a criminal. We tend to view the criminal as a person who violates laws which we cannot see ourselves violating. In the phraseology of Harry Stack Sullivan, the criminal is that person whom we perceive from the standpoint of our own self-system as "not-me." In other cases, the criminal is the person who violates rules which we can imagine ourselves violating (or have violated in the past) but which we see as part of our "bad-me": "There but for the Grace of God go I." We are willing to condemn the conduct of the "bad-me" as "wrong," but are not likely to agree to the imposition of sanctions we feel are too severe.

6. For a different typology of sanctions, *see* Jack P. Gibbs, "Sanctions," 14 *Social Problems* 147 (1966). Another interesting treatment of sanctions, and a plea for more extensive study of this field, is Richard Arens & Harold D. Lasswell, *In Defense of Public Order, The Emerging Field of Sanction Law* (Columbia U. Press 1961).

[Reading 31]

7. Still other dimensions are suggested by the sociologist Arnold M. Rose in "Sociological Factors in the Effectiveness of Projected Legislative Remedies," 11 *Journal of Legal Education* 470, 472-73 (1959): *

When the question of the effectiveness of sanctions is raised, the *prevailing* public behavior has to be considered. Sanctions will have differing effectiveness when typical behavior, in the absence of the statute, is generally in accord with, opposed to, or completely independent of, the purpose of the statute. Under each of these three different sets of circumstances, the sanctions specified in the statute, to be effective, would have to be different. It might be hypothesized that the usual punitive sanctions of fine or imprisonment are likely to be more effective where the prevailing behavior of the majority of the population is already in accord with the goals sought by the statute. In this situation, it is only a minority that must be brought into conformity with the law, and the general population will be inclined to believe that punishment is justified for infraction. On the other hand, where the behavior sought by the statute is rarely found in the population, it seems likely that some kind of reward would be more likely to achieve the goal of the legislature. Framers of statutes have perhaps not often thought of rewards as sanctions, but this is no reason why they should not use certain rewards, such as public decorations, forgiveness on portions of the income tax, free use of public facilities for which a fee is normally charged, and so on. The principle suggested here is illustrated by a fairly recent statutory development in the field of negligent homicide by operation of a motor vehicle. The change adopted by the legislatures was not a substitution of reward for punishment, but the substitution of a lesser punishment in the place of a more severe one. In the 1920's and 1930's, many

---

* Arnold M. Rose, late Professor of Sociology, University of Minnesota. Reprinted with the permission of the Journal of Legal Education.

states passed legislation making what would otherwise be manslaughter by automobile some lesser degree of homicide, subject to a lesser penalty. These new crimes went under various names—*e.g.*, death resulting from "careless or negligent operation of a motor vehicle." Such statutes are generally regarded as legislative attempts "to get more convictions" where juries had previously balked, legislative responses to a popular feeling that manslaughter is too harsh a label and imposes too severe a penalty for a large number of cases of homicide committed through the negligent operation of automobiles.

Where there is little public knowledge of the behavior sought in the statute, it seems likely that the formation of an agency that gives publicity to violations of the statute would be an effective provision and that investigation and publicity might serve to gain conformity to the statute in lieu of sanctions. The public reprimand has been effectively used by military authorities as a means of gaining conformity, and it is reported that Soviet criminal law provides that the punishment for certain offenses may be in the form of a "public rebuke." In general, each of the possible sanctions usable in statutes should be considered in relationship to the extent of prevailing conformity to the expectations of the statute and to the degree of public knowledge concerning both the expected behavior and the statute itself.

Are the factors suggested by Rose consistent with the strategies for effectiveness that emerge from Schwartz and Orleans, Chambliss, and Ball and Friedman? Why is prevailing public behavior relevant? What assumptions about the process of compliance does Rose make?

32. The Modern Corporation and the Rule of Law

ABRAM CHAYES*

Indeed, only a little reflection is needed to make clear that generalized prescriptive commands are quantitatively and qualitatively only a small part of the body of our law.

This type of law, just because it is the most direct and brutal intervention of power into men's lives, can be employed only in a limited range of situations and for limited purposes. Even in relations which maximize the domination of one party and the subjection of another—as for example, that between officer and enlisted men—orders can be used to accomplish only quite simple things. When complex interrelations and coordinations of the kind inherent in any modern social arrangement become involved, only those purposes which are self-evidently basic and most pervasively and articulately shared can be secured by prescriptive command. "Thou shalt not kill" or the rules of the road thus ought to be seen not as the typical manifestation of law but rather as at the furthest reach of the spectrum.

Much more characteristic of the operation of the law in more complicated and indeterminate areas of social direction is the provision of facilities. To illustrate: it is possible to look at the law of contract as a command of the state not to break certain classes of promises. This is not, however, a very useful point of view if the object is to understand the role of contract law in the development of our society. For this purpose, contract must be seen as a way in which men dealing with each other can insure that their promises will outlast their transitory states of mind.

The law does not prescribe contract. It attaches no immediate normative value to the act of promising. It says only that if you wish to act, and more important, if you wish to make your action binding, in some sense, on the future, act in such and such a way. If you do not follow the approved path, the promise made to you may nevertheless be kept. But the law will lend you no aid to see that it is kept.

---

* Abram Chayes, Professor of Law, Harvard University. Reprinted by permission of the publishers from Edward S. Mason ed., The Corporation in Modern Society, pp. 31-32, Cambridge, Mass.: Harvard University Press. Copyright 1959 by the President and Fellows of Harvard College.

It will be seen that what the law of contract has provided is a device by which private persons are enabled to some extent to stabilize and make predictable—to control—the future. That is, they are enabled to make their own law to govern their own affairs. The state lends its judicial machinery to enforce this personal law, if necessary. The law appears to exhaust itself in defining the conditions on which the public force will be enlisted to effectuate the private end. And it is true that these conditions, in our system at least, are elastic enough to permit a wide range of autonomously directed private activity. The ideal of the rule of law dictates, however, that these conditions be not arbitrary, but must be rationally related to legitimate social purposes. By providing useful facilities on such condition, the legal system mobilizes powerful inducements to action in support of those purposes.

The rule of law, as here conceived, then, is concerned with regularizing and rationalizing the use of power. But it is concerned with power in both its faces—not only as an evil, to be restrained, but as a resource to be harnessed in the service of society. The creation of legal institutions which enlist the energies of men in the service of legitimate social purposes is the most important mode by which this dual end of the rule of law is approached.

NOTES AND QUESTIONS

1. Chayes suggests that contract law provides useful facilities on condition that the transaction of the one seeking to use these facilities "be rationally related to legitimate social purposes." In effect, the strategy for controlling or channelling conduct is to offer a valuable facility for a price. Did Chayes pick a good example? Recall the practices reported in Macaulay, "Non-Contractual Relations in Business," Reading 13, at 145, *supra*, and consider the likely effectiveness of controlling the power of large corporations by conditions on obtaining legal sanctions for breach of contract.

[Reading 33]

2. Law often operates as Chayes suggests, but, as one would expect, there is a price that a policymaker must pay if he would buy cooperation this way. Consider *Law and Social Process in United States History* 99-101, 190 (1960) by Willard Hurst.*

---

* Willard Hurst, Professor of Law, University of Wisconsin, reprinted by permission of Michigan Legal Publications, University of Michigan, Ann Arbor.

Professor Hurst begins by discussing some aspects of legal regulation of milk:

But [regulation] was only part of the story. We should not equate law with regulation, nor should we equate regulation with restriction. As we examine relations of law to men's efforts to direct their affairs we must note that the law's largest effects on the milk industry were promotional rather than restrictive; its Yea was more than its Nay. The promotional effects of law were felt mainly through its capacity to provide procedures for organizing action, both attracting purpose and furnishing it with facilities. The milk industry's growth proceeded by educating farmers and processors to wider ambitions for their product. In Wisconsin this was helped by the favor the law showed to associations of farmers and processors, providing them corporate status, sanctioning their initiative in sponsoring fairs, educational activities and marketing programs, and supplying public subsidies and exempting their property from taxation. This was public support by indirection. The state also offered direct encouragement to fresh venture and contrivance in the dairy industry. Two forms of direct support were especially influential. One was through the state university. The extension activities of the university were at least as effective as its on-campus instruction in persuading Wisconsin farmers and processors to adopt the quality and sanitary standards that were necessary to win wider markets. The state of dairy science and technology was the ultimate source of the industry's growth, and the university's research activity represented the state government's contribution to this source of initiative; it was at the university in 1890 that Professor S. M. Babcock devised what was to become the standard test for the butterfat content of milk. The second principal form of direct state governmental impetus toward new directions for the milk industry was road building. Roads rivaled schools in the state's budget after the turn of the century. Of special relevance to the milk industry was the fact that public money was to be had, under energetic local pressure, to develop the all-weather secondary road system which became the framework of industry operations as the motor truck took over milk transport. Finally we must note that the availability of the law to provide a regulatory framework for the industry had significance not just to police against wrongdoers but, even more important, to make possible the industry's expansion into markets of large, impersonal reach.

Many of these items of legal regulation or promotion have relevance to more than one role of law regarding social change and stability. In one view, we see law encouraging and helping men to take deliberate initiative to steer their affairs; in another aspect the same legal activity—perhaps at a later point of time—has meaning more as a factor to sustain established lines of action than to help initiate new ones. . . . The distinction may be pointed up, for example, in terms of legal regulation of quality and safety standards for milk. Once a workable pattern of regulation was established it became an indispensable sustaining influence to enable the milk industry to supply wide markets on terms that were functionally acceptable, given the needs and hazards of close-knit urban living. On the other hand, the fact that a legal order existed which made it possible to create such a framework of action was, at the outset, an influence which stimulated the imagination and will of a handful of leaders . . . to organize and obtain the kind of regulatory setting within which the industry could grow. . . .

Consider, again, the milk regulation history. Out of the growth of scientific and technical knowledge and the response of public opinion to what it learned of preventable evil, grew an expanding body of legal and practical regulation of the purity and quality of milk supply. Pasteurization, bottling, refrigeration, all required expensive additions to the investment needed for handling milk. In practice, thus, the combination of public opinion and sanitary regulation set investment requirements for entry or continuance in the business which tended to eliminate small dealers and thus to foster such economic concentration as was a prime concern of another area of public policy, embodied in the antitrust laws. The development of cooperatives might have offered a larger continuing role for smaller dealers. But such help as the law brought to this end proved too slow to affect the course of milk distribution.

3. Education is an important tactic for channelling conduct. On one hand, government officials attempt to educate the public in a wide variety of ways. Presidents address the public over television to try to gain acceptance of policies, government departments issue pamphlets justifying their program, and officials at all levels cooperate with the news media to get across their views. *See* Finman & Macaulay, Reading 7, at 73, *supra.* In a more literal sense, units of government run a system of public education, and influence what is taught in it. Local school boards and

administrators control elementary and high schools; state boards
of regents run colleges. Federal and state funds flow to various
levels of the total system, often with strings attached. Conservative or right-wing groups have long been concerned about what is
taught in the schools and its potential for affecting conduct and
attitudes towards social programs. A psychologist, Robert D.
Hess, has raised questions about the kind of education American
children are receiving, although his concern reflects a different
political view. He concluded, after studying 12,000 children in
grades two to eight in eight cities, that "elementary-school children have a highly idealized view of the Government and a very
high estimate of the power of the individual vote, combined with
an ignorance of other legitimate channels of influence." Moreover, low socio-economic status children see themselves and their
families as having much less power to influence government than
do higher status children. Hess advocates teaching the realities of
group influence and controversy and the means of social change.
Robert D. Hess, "Political Attitudes in Children: Do Our
Schoolteachers Subvert Solid Social Growth," 2 *Psychology Today*
24 (1969).

c. Defining and measuring the effectiveness of law

(1) What impact is law supposed to have?

At the outset, one can say the obvious: an effective law is one
that achieves its purpose. But the obvious often conceals a cluster
of problems. What is the purpose of a law or a program of regulation? It is not always easy to tell. Do we look to the intention or
intentions of the man who drafted the statute or the judge who
wrote the opinion creating the rule? to that of the majority of
the legislature or court who voted for it? to that of the lobbyists
who worked for the bill? to that purpose openly discussed or to
the purpose which is implicit but never mentioned? Sometimes
one can only conclude that a law had multiple and perhaps even
conflicting purposes. This is not to say that one can never be
sure of the purpose of a law, but just that one must be careful.

Moreover, there is the ends and means problem. A law may be
designed to channel behavior or control conduct to produce a
desired result. It can be ineffective, in the usual sense of the term,
when it fails to channel or control the behavior in question.
However, even when it channels or controls this behavior, it may
be ineffective if the desired result does not follow from affecting
conduct this way. Moreover, even when the desired conduct produces the desired result, there may be unanticipated and undesirable side effects. If achieving a goal at a cost a policymaker is will-

ing to pay is part of one's definition of effectiveness, such a law would be ineffective. Finally, laws can be more or less effective; few ever produce 100% compliance. Often, then, effectiveness is a normative judgment, involving one's view of the importance of channelling or controlling particular conduct and his assessment of the costs of all kinds (social as well as economic) of gaining more impact.

A detailed example may clarify all of this. Suppose the primary purpose of the law licensing lawyers is said to be to insure that those who offer legal services to the public are competent and honest. Certainly some of those who support this law seek to restrict entry into the market to minimize competition and to control the modes of competition between those who are in the market. One cannot overlook this second goal of licensing the profession. The means used to insure competency typically are a bar examination and a review by a character and fitness committee which are required of all applicants for professional status. The examination might fail to achieve the goal of insuring competent attorneys if the test were so poorly administered that applicants could cheat and not be caught or if it were so capriciously graded that some qualified candidates failed and some unqualified ones passed. However, assuming the test was not subject to this kind of distortion, it might still fail to assure that the state's attorneys would be competent if the questions asked could be answered by one who was not qualified to practice. Also the review by the character and fitness committee might involve an investigation into political belief if its members concluded that certain political positions indicated a bad character. Some might disagree with the committee's conclusion about this relationship; others might see the denial of civil liberties necessarily involved in such an investigation as an unanticipated cost they might not desire to pay. Of course, this entire process might work beautifully as a barrier to entry into the market for legal services, whatever its impact on the character and ability of the bar.

While most of those working to get a law passed or for a favorable judicial or administrative decision want to channel or control behavior, it has been suggested that frequently law has other "latent functions." Thus, one should hesitate before labelling any law as a total dead letter. Although a particular rule may not affect the conduct it purports to affect, it may serve other functions quite nicely. In summary, to talk about the effectiveness of legal action, one must specify what effect he has in mind.

34. Moral Passage: The Symbolic Process in Public Designations of Deviance

JOSEPH R. GUSFIELD*

15 SOCIAL PROBLEMS 175 (1967)

Recent perspectives on deviant behavior have focused attention away from the actor and his acts and placed it on the analysis of public reactions in labelling deviants as "outsiders." This perspective forms the background for the present paper. In it I will analyze the implications which defining behavior as deviant has for the public designators. Several forms of deviance will be distinguished, each of which has a different kind of significance for the designators. The symbolic import of each type, I argue, leads to different public responses toward the deviant and helps account for the historical changes often found in treatment of such delinquents as alcoholics, drug addicts, and other "criminals," changes which involve a passage from one moral status to another.

INSTRUMENTAL AND SYMBOLIC FUNCTIONS OF LAW

Agents of government are the only persons in modern societies who can legitimately claim to represent the total society. In support of their acts, limited and specific group interests are denied while a public and societal interest is claimed. Acts of government "commit the group to action or to perform coordinated acts for general welfare." This representational character of governmental officials and their acts makes it possible for them not only to influence the allocation of resources but also to define the public norms of morality and to designate which acts violate them. In a pluralistic society these defining and designating acts can become matters of political issue because they support or

* Joseph R. Gusfield, Professor of Sociology, University of California, San Diego. © Social Problems. Reprinted by permission of the Journal and The Society for the Study of Social Problems.

reject one or another of the competing and conflicting cultural groups in the society.

Let us begin with a distinction between *instrumental* and *symbolic* functions of legal and governmental acts. We readily perceive that acts of officials, legislative enactments, and court decisions often affect behavior in an instrumental manner through a direct influence on the actions of people. The Wagner Labor Relations Act and the Taft-Hartley Act have had considerable impact on the conditions of collective bargaining in the United States. Tariff legislation directly affects the prices of import commodities. The instrumental function of such laws lies in their enforcement; unenforced they have little effect.

Symbolic aspects of law and government do not depend on enforcement for their effect. They are symbolic in a sense close to that used in literary analysis. The symbolic act "invites consideration rather than overt reaction." There is a dimension of meaning in symbolic behavior which is not given in its immediate and manifest significance but in what the action connotes for the audience that views it. The symbol "has acquired a meaning which is added to its immediate intrinsic significance." . . . The use of the wine and wafer in the Mass or the importance of the national flag cannot be appreciated without knowing their symbolic meaning for the users. In analyzing law as symbolic we are oriented less to behavioral consequences as a means to a fixed end; more to meaning as an act, a decision, a gesture important in itself.

An action of a governmental agent takes on symbolic import as it affects the designation of public norms. A courtroom decision or a legislative act is a gesture which often glorifies the values of one group and demeans those of another. In their representational character, governmental actions can be seen as ceremonial and ritual performances, designating the content of public morality. They are the statement of what is acceptable in the public interest. Law can thus be seen as symbolizing the public affirmation of social ideals and norms as well as a means of direct social control. This symbolic dimension is given in the statement, promulgation, or announcement of law unrelated to its function in influencing behavior through enforcement.

It has long been evident to students of government and law that these two functions, instrumental and symbolic, may often be separated in more than an analytical sense. Many laws are honored as much in the breach as in performance. Robin Williams has labelled such institutionalized yet illegal and deviant behavior the "patterned evasion of norms." Such evasion occurs when law proscribes behavior which nevertheless occurs in a recurrent socially organized manner and is seldom punished. The kinds of crimes we are concerned with here quite clearly fall into this category. Gambling, prostitution, abortion, and public drunkenness are all common modes of behavior although laws exist designating them as prohibited. It is possible to see such systematic evasion as functioning to minimize conflicts between cultures by utilizing law to proclaim one set of norms as public morality and to use another set of norms in actually controlling that behavior.

While patterned evasion may perform such harmonizing functions, the passage of legislation, the acts of officials, and decisions of judges nevertheless have a significance as gestures of public affirmation. First, the act of public affirmation of a norm often persuades listeners that behavior and norm are consistent. The existence of law quiets and comforts those whose interests and sentiments are embodied in it. Second, public affirmation of a moral norm directs the major institutions of the society to its support. Despite patterned practices of abortion in the United States, obtaining abortions does require access to a subterranean social structure and is much more difficult than obtaining an appendectomy. There are instrumental functions to law even where there is patterned evasion.

A third impact of public affirmation is the one that most interests us here. The fact of affirmation through acts of law and government expresses the public worth of one set of norms, of one sub-culture vis-à-vis those of others. It demonstrates which cultures have legitimacy and public domination, and which do not. Accordingly it enhances the social status of groups carrying the affirmed culture and degrades groups carrying that which is condemned as deviant. We have argued elsewhere that the significance of Prohibition in the United States lay less in its enforcement than in the fact that it occurred. Analysis of the enforcement of Prohibition law indicates that it was often limited by the unwillingness of Dry forces to utilize all their political strength for fear of stirring intensive opposition. Great satisfaction was gained from the passage and maintenance of the legislation itself.

Irrespective of its instrumental effects, public designation of morality is itself an issue generative of deep conflict. The designating gestures are dramatistic events, "since it invites one to consider the matter of motives in a perspective that, being developed in the analysis of drama, treats language and thought primarily as modes of action." For this reason the designation of a way of behavior as violating public norms confers status and honor on those groups whose cultures are followed as the standard of conventionality, and derogates those whose cultures are considered deviant. My analysis of the American Temperance movement has shown how the issue of drinking and abstinence became a politically significant focus for the conflicts between Protestant and Catholic, rural and urban, native and immigrant, middle class and lower class in American society. The political conflict lay in the efforts of an abstinent Protestant middle class to control the public affirmation of morality in drinking. Victory or defeat were consequently symbolic of the status and power of the cultures opposing each other. Legal affirmation or rejection is thus important in what it symbolizes as well or instead of what it controls. Even if the law was broken, it was clear whose law it was.

DEVIANT NONCONFORMITY AND DESIGNATOR REACTION

In [Emile] Durkheim's analysis of the indignant and hostile response to norm-violation, all proscribed actions are threats to the existence of the norm. Once we separate the instrumental from the symbolic functions of legal and governmental designation of deviants, however, we can question this assumption. We can look at norm-violation from the standpoint of its effects on the symbolic rather than the instrumental character of the norm. Our analysis of patterned evasion of norms has suggested that a law weak in its instrumental functions may nevertheless perform significant symbolic functions. Unlike human limbs, norms do not necessarily atrophy through disuse. Standards of charity, mercy, and justice may be dishonored every day yet remain important statements of what is publicly approved as virtue. The sexual behavior of the human male and the human female need not be a copy of the socially sanctioned rules. Those rules remain as important affirmations of an acceptable code, even though they are regularly breached. Their roles as ideals are not threatened by daily behavior. In analyzing the violation of norms we will look at the implications of different forms of deviance on the symbolic character of the norm itself. *The point here is that the designators of deviant behavior react differently to different norm-sustaining implications of an act.* We can classify deviant behavior from this standpoint.

The Repentant Deviant

The reckless motorist often admits the legitimacy of traffic laws, even though he has broken them. The chronic alcoholic may well agree that both he and his society would be better if he could stay sober. In both cases the norm they have violated is itself unquestioned. Their deviation is a moral lapse, a fall from a grace to which they aspire. The homosexual who seeks a psychiatrist to rid himself of his habit has defined his actions similarly to those who have designated him as a deviant. There is a consensus between the designator and the deviant; his repentance confirms the norm.

Repentance and redemption seem to go hand-in-hand in court and church. [Gresham] Sykes and [David] Matza have described techniques of neutralization which juvenile delinquents often use with enforcement agencies.

> The juvenile delinquent would appear to be at least partially committed to the dominant social order in that he frequently exhibits guilt or shame when he violates its proscriptions, accords approval to certain conforming figures and distinguishes between appropriate and inappropriate targets for his deviance.

A show of repentance is also used, say Sykes and Matza, to soften the indignation of law enforcement agents. A recent study of police behavior lends support to this. Juveniles apprehended by the police received more lenient treatment, including dismissal, if they appeared contrite and remorseful about their violations than if they did not. This difference in the posture of the deviant accounted for much of the differential treatment favoring middle-class "youngsters" as against lower-class "delinquents."

The Sick Deviant

Acts which represent an attack upon a norm are neutralized by repentance. The open admission of repentance confirms the sinner's belief in the sin. His threat to the norm is removed and his violation has left the norm intact. Acts which we can perceive as those of sick and diseased people are irrelevant to the norm; they neither attack nor defend it. The use of morphine by hospital patients in severe pain is not designated as deviant behavior. Sentiments of public hostility and the apparatus of enforcement agencies are not mobilized toward the morphine-user. His use is not perceived as a violation of the norm against drug use, but as an uncontrolled act, not likely to be recurrent.

While designations of action resulting from sickness do not threaten the norm, significant consequences flow from such definitions. Talcott Parsons has pointed out that the designation of a person as ill changes the obligations which others have toward the person and his obligations toward them. Parsons' description sensitizes us to the way in which the sick person is a different social object than the healthy one. He has now become an object of welfare, a person to be helped rather than punished. Hostile sentiments toward sick people are not legitimate. The sick person is not responsible for his acts. He is excused from the consequences which attend the healthy who act the same way.

Deviance designations, as we shall show below, are not fixed. They may shift from one form to another over time. Defining a behavior pattern as one caused by illness makes a hostile response toward the actor illegitimate and inappropriate. "Illness" is a social designation, by no means given in the nature of medical fact. Even left-handedness is still seen as morally deviant in many countries. Hence the effort to define a practice as a consequence of illness is itself a matter of conflict and a political issue.

The Enemy Deviant

Writing about a Boston slum in the 1930's, William F. Whyte remarks:

> The policeman is subject to sharply conflicting pressures. On one side are the "good people" of Eastern City, who have written their moral judgments into law and demand through their newspapers that the law be enforced. On the other side are the people of Cornerville, who have different standards and have built up an organization whose perpetuation depends upon the freedom to violate the law.

Whyte's is one of several studies that have pointed out the discrepancies between middle-class moralities embodied in law and lower-class moralities which differ sharply from them. In Cornerville, gambling was seen as a "respectable" crime, just as antitrust behavior may be in other levels of the social structure. In American society, conflicts between social classes are often also cultural conflicts reflecting moral differences. Coincidence of ethnic and religious distinctions with class differences accentuates such conflicts between group values.

In these cases, the validity of the public designation is itself at issue. The publicly-defined deviant is neither repentant nor sick, but is instead an upholder of an opposite norm. He accepts his behavior as proper and derogates the public norm as illegitimate. He refuses to internalize the public norm into his self-definition. This is especially likely to occur in instances of "business crimes." The buyer sees his action as legitimate economic behavior and resists a definition of it as immoral and thus prohibitable. The issue of "off-track" betting illustrates one area in which clashes of culture have been salient.

The designation of culturally legitimate behavior as deviant depends upon the superior power and organization of the desig-

nators. The concept of convention in this area, as Thrasymachus
defined Justice for Socrates, is the will of the stronger. If the
deviant is the politically weaker group, then the designation is
open to the changes and contingencies of political fortunes. It
becomes an issue of political conflict, ranging group against group
and culture against culture, in the effort to determine whose
morals are to be designated as deserving of public affirmation.

It is when the deviant is also an enemy and his deviance is an
aspect of group culture that the conventional norm is most explicitly and energetically attacked. When those once designated
as deviant have achieved enough political power they may shift
from disobedience to an effort to change the designation itself.
This has certainly happened in the civil rights movement. Behavior viewed as deviant in the segregationist society has in many
instances been moved into the realm of the problematic, now
subject to political processes of conflict and compromise.

When the deviant and the designator perceive each other as
enemies, and the designator's power is superior to that of the
deviant, we have domination without a corresponding legitimacy.
Anything which increases the power of the deviant to organize
and attack the norm is thus a threat to the social dominance
symbolized in the affirmation of the norm. Under such conditions the need of the designators to strengthen and enforce the
norms is great. The struggle over the symbol of social power and
status is focused on the question of the maintenance or change
of the legal norm. The threat to the middle class in the increased
political power of Cornerville is not that the Cornerville resident
will gamble more; he already does gamble with great frequency.
The threat is that the law will come to accept the morality of
gambling and treat it as a legitimate business. If this happens,
Boston is no longer a city dominated by middle-class Yankees
but becomes one dominated by lower-class immigrants, as many
think has actually happened in Boston. The maintenance of a
norm which defines gambling as deviant behavior thus symbolizes
the maintenance of Yankee social and political superiority. Its
disappearance as a public commitment would symbolize the loss
of that superiority.

The Cynical Deviant

The professional criminal commits acts whose designation as
deviant is supported by wide social consensus. The burglar, the
hired murderer, the arsonist, the kidnapper all prey on victims.
While they may use repentance or illness as strategies to manage
the impressions of enforcers, their basic orientation is self-seek-

ing, to get around the rules. It is for this reason that their
behavior is not a great threat to the norms although it calls for
social management and repression. It does not threaten the legitimacy of the normative order.

Drinking as a Changing Form of Deviance

Analysis of efforts to define drinking as deviant in the United
States will illustrate the process by which designations shift. The
legal embodiment of attitudes toward drinking shows how cultural conflicts find their expression in the symbolic functions of
law. In the 160 years since 1800, we see all our suggested types
of non-conforming behavior and all the forms of reaction among
the conventional segments of the society. . . .

The Repentant Drinker

The definition of the drinker as an object of social shame
begins in the early nineteenth century and reaches full development in the late 1820's and early 1830's. A wave of growth in
Temperance organizations in this period was sparked by the conversion of drinking men to abstinence under the stimulus of
evangelical revivalism. Through drinking men joining together
to take the pledge, a norm of abstinence and sobriety emerged
as a definition of conventional respectability. They sought to
control themselves and their neighbors.

The norm of abstinence and sobriety replaced the accepted
patterns of heavy drinking countenanced in the late eighteenth
and early nineteenth century. By the 1870's rural and small-town
America had defined middle-class morals to include the Dry attitude. This definition had little need for legal embodiment. It
could be enunciated in attacks on the drunkard which assumed
that he shared the normative pattern of those who exhorted him
to be better and to do better. He was a repentant deviant, someone to be brought back into the fold by moral persuasion and
the techniques of religious revivalism. His error was the sin of
lapse from a shared standard of virtue. "The Holy Spirit will
not visit, much less will He dwell within he who is under the
polluting, debasing effects of intoxicating drink. The state of
heart and mind which this occasions to him is loathsome and an
abomination."

Moral persuasion thus rests on the conviction of a consensus
between the deviant and the designators. As long as the object
of attack and conversion is isolated in individual terms, rather
than perceived as a group, there is no sense of his deviant act
as part of a shared culture. What is shared is the norm of con-

ventionality; the appeal to the drinker and the chronic alcoholic is to repent. When the Woman's Anti-Whiskey Crusade of 1873-1874 broke out in Ohio, church women placed their attention on the taverns. In many Ohio towns these respectable ladies set up vigils in front of the tavern and attempted to prevent men from entering just by the fear that they would be observed. In keeping with the evangelical motif in the Temperance movement, the Washingtonians, founded in 1848, appealed to drinkers and chronic alcoholics with the emotional trappings and oratory of religious meetings, even though devoid of pastors.

Moral persuasion, rather than legislation, has been one persistent theme in the designation of the drinker as deviant and the alcoholic as depraved. Even in the depictions of the miseries and poverty of the chronic alcoholic, there is a decided moral condemnation which has been the hallmark of the American Temperance movement. Moral persuasion was ineffective as a device to wipe out drinking and drunkenness. Heavy drinking persisted through the nineteenth century and the organized attempts to convert the drunkard experienced much backsliding. Nevertheless, defections from the standard did not threaten the standard. The public definition of respectability matched the ideals of the sober and abstaining people who dominated those parts of the society where moral suasion was effective. In the late nineteenth century those areas in which temperance sentiment was strongest were also those in which legislation was most easily enforceable.

The Enemy Drinker

The demand for laws to limit alcoholic consumption appears to arise from situations in which the drinkers possess power as a definitive social and political group and, in their customary habits and beliefs, deny the validity of abstinence norms. The persistence of areas in which Temperance norms were least controlling led to the emergence of attempts to embody control in legal measures. The drinker as enemy seems to be the greatest stimulus to efforts to designate his act as publicly defined deviance.

In its early phase the American Temperance movement was committed chiefly to moral persuasion. Efforts to achieve legislation governing the sale and use of alcohol do not appear until the 1840's. This legislative movement has a close relationship to the immigration of Irish Catholics and German Lutherans into the United States in this period. These non-evangelical and/or non-Protestant peoples made up a large proportion of the urban poor in the 1840's and 1850's. They brought with them a far more accepting evaluation of drinking than had yet existed in the United States. The tavern and the beer parlor had a distinct place in the leisure of the Germans and the Irish. The prominence of this place was intensified by the stark character of the developing American slum. These immigrant cultures did not contain a strong tradition of Temperance norms which might have made an effective appeal to a sense of sin. To be sure, excessive drunkenness was scorned, but neither abstinence nor constant sobriety were supported by the cultural codes.

Between these two groups—the native American, middle-class evangelical Protestant and the immigrant European Catholic or Lutheran occupying the urban lower class—there was little room for repentance. By the 1850's the issue of drinking reflected a general clash over cultural values. The Temperance movement found allies in its political efforts among the nativist movements. The force and power of the anti-alcohol movements, however, were limited greatly by the political composition of the urban electorate, with its high proportion of immigrants. Thus the movement to develop legislation emerged in reaction to the appearance of cultural groups least responsive to the norms of abstinence and sobriety. The very effort to turn such informal norms into legal standards polarized the opposing forces and accentuated the symbolic import of the movement. Now that the issue had been joined, defeat or victory was a clear-cut statement of public dominance.

It is a paradox that the most successful move to eradicate alcohol emerged in a period when America was shifting from a heavy-drinking society, in which whiskey was the leading form of alcohol, to a moderate one, in which beer was replacing whiskey. Prohibition came as the culmination of the movement to reform the immigrant cultures and at the height of the immigrant influx into the United States.

Following the Civil War, moral persuasion and legislative goals were both parts of the movement against alcohol. By the 1880's an appeal was made to the urban, immigrant lower classes to repent and to imitate the habits of the American middle class as a route to economic and social mobility. Norms of abstinence were presented to the non-abstainer both as virtue and as expedience. This effort failed. The new, and larger, immigration of 1890-1915 increased still further the threat of the urban lower class to the native American.

The symbolic effect of Prohibition legislation must be kept analytically separate from its instrumental, enforcement side. While the urban middle class did provide much of the organizational leadership to the Temperance and Prohibition movements, the political strength of the movement in its legislative drives was in the rural areas of the United States. Here, where the problems of drinking were most under control, where the norm was relatively intact, the appeal to a struggle against foreign invasion was the most potent. In these areas, passage of legislation was likely to make small difference in behavior. The continuing polarization of political forces into those of cultural opposition and cultural acceptance during the Prohibition campaigns (1906-1919), and during the drive for Repeal (1926-1933), greatly intensified the symbolic significance of victory and defeat. Even if the Prohibition measures were limited in their enforceability in the metropolis there was no doubt about whose law was public and what way of life was being labelled as opprobrious.

After Repeal, as Dry power in American politics subsided, the designation of the drinker as deviant also receded. Public affirmation of the temperance norm had changed and with it the definition of the deviant had changed. Abstinence was itself less acceptable. In the 1950's the Temperance movement, faced with this change in public norms, even introduced a series of placards with the slogan, "It's Smart *Not* to Drink."

Despite this normative change in the public designation of drinking deviance, there has not been much change in American drinking patterns. Following the Prohibition period the consumption of alcohol has not returned to its pre-1915 high. Beer has continued to occupy a more important place as a source of alcohol consumption. "Hard drinkers" are not as common in America today as they were in the nineteenth century. While there has been some increase in moderate drinking, the percentage of adults who are abstainers has remained approximately the same (one-third) for the past 30 years. Similarly, Dry sentiment has remained stable, as measured by local opinion results. In short, the argument over deviance designation has been largely one of normative dominance, not of instrumental social control. The process of deviance designation in drinking needs to be understood in terms of symbols of cultural dominance rather than in the activities of social control.

The Sick Drinker

For most of the nineteenth century, the chronic alcoholic as well as the less compulsive drinker was viewed as a sinner. It was not until after Repeal (1933) that chronic alcoholism became defined as illness in the United States. Earlier actions taken toward promotion of the welfare of drinkers and alcoholics through Temperance measures rested on the moral supremacy of abstinence and the demand for repentance. The user of alcohol could be an object of sympathy, but his social salvation depended on a willingness to embrace the norm of his exhorters. The designation of alcoholism as sickness has a different bearing on the question of normative superiority. It renders the behavior of the deviant indifferent to the status of norms enforcing abstinence.

This realization appears to have made supporters of Temperance and Prohibition hostile to efforts to redefine the deviant character of alcoholism. They deeply opposed the reports of the Committee of Fifty in the late nineteenth century. These volumes of reports by scholars and prominent men took a less moralistic and a more sociological and functional view of the saloon and drinking than did the Temperance movement.

The soundness of these fears is shown by what did happen to the Temperance movement with the rise of the view that alcoholism is illness. It led to new agencies concerned with drinking problems. These excluded Temperance people from the circle of those who now define what is deviant in drinking habits. The National Commission on Alcoholism was formed in 1941 and the Yale School of Alcoholic Studies formed in 1940. They were manned by medical personnel, social workers, and social scientists, people now alien to the spirit of the abstainer. Problems of drinking were removed from the church and placed in the hands of the universities and the medical clinics. The tendency to handle drinkers through protective and welfare agencies rather than through police or clergy has become more frequent.

"The bare statement that 'alcoholism is a disease' is most misleading since . . . it conceals what is essential—that a step in public policy is being recommended, not a scientific discovery announced." John Seeley's remark is an apt one. Replacement of the norm of sin and repentance by that of illness and therapy removes the onus of guilt and immorality from the act of drinking and the state of chronic alcoholism. It replaces the image of the sinner with that of a patient, a person to be helped rather than to be exhorted. No wonder that the Temperance movement has found the work of the Yale School, and often even the work of Alcoholics Anonymous, a threat to its own movement. It has been most limited in its cooperation with these organizations and has attempted to set up other organizations which might provide the face of Science in league with the tone of the movement.

The redefinition of the alcoholic as sick thus brought into power both ideas and organizations antithetical to the Temperance movement. The norm protected by law and government was no longer the one held by the people who had supported Temperance and Prohibition. The hostility of Temperance people is readily understandable; their relative political unimportance is crucial to their present inability to make that hostility effective.

MOVEMENTS OF MORAL PASSAGE

In this paper we have called attention to the fact that deviance designations have histories; the public definition of behavior as deviant is itself changeable. It is open to reversals of political power, twists of public opinion, and the development of social movements and moral crusades. What is attacked as criminal today may be seen as sick next year and fought over as possibly legitimate by the next generation.

Movements to redefine behavior may eventuate in a moral passage, a transition of the behavior from one moral status to another. In analyzing movements toward the redefinition of alcohol use, we have dealt with moral crusades which were restrictive and others which were permissive toward drinking and toward "drunkards." (We might have also used the word "alcoholics," suggesting a less disapproving and more medical perspective.) In both cases, however, the movements sought to change the public designation. While we are familiar with the restrictive or enforcing movements, the permissive or legitimizing movement must also be seen as a prevalent way in which deviants throw off the onus of their actions and avoid the sanctions associated with immoral activities.

Even where the deviants are a small and politically powerless group they may nevertheless attempt to protect themselves by influence over the process of designation. The effort to define themselves as ill is one plausible means to this end. Drug addiction as well as drunkenness is partially undergoing a change toward such redefinition.[39] This occurs in league with powerful groups in society, such as social workers, medical professionals, or university professors. The moral passage achieved here reduces the sanctions imposed by criminal law and the public acceptance of the deviant designation.

The "lifting" of a deviant activity to the level of a political, public issue is thus a sign that its moral status is at stake, that legitimacy is a possibility. Today the moral acceptance of drinking, marijuana and LSD use, homosexuality, abortion, and other "vices" is being publicly discussed, and movements championing

---

[39] Many of the writings of sociologists interested in drug addiction have contained explicit demands for such redefinitions.

. . . The recent movement to redefine marijuana and LSD as legitimate is partially supported by such writings but is more saliently a movement of enemy deviants. The activities of Timothy Leary, Allen Ginsberg, and the "hipsters" is the most vocal expression of this movement.

them have emerged. Such movements draw into them far more than the deviants themselves. Because they become symbols of general cultural attitudes they call out partisans for both repression and permission. The present debate over drug addiction laws in the United States, for example, is carried out between defenders and opposers of the norm rather than between users and non-users of the drugs involved.

As the movement for redefinition of the addict as sick has grown, the movement to strengthen the definition of addiction as criminal has responded with increased legal severity. To classify drug users as sick and the victims or clients as suffering from "disease" would mean a change in the agencies responsible for reaction from police enforcement to medical authorities. Further, it might diminish the moral diaspproval with which drug use, and the reputed euphoric effects connected with it, are viewed by supporters of present legislation. Commenting on the clinic plan to permit medical dispensing of narcotics to licensed addicts, U.S. Commissioner of Narcotics Ansligner wrote:

> This plan would elevate a most despicable trade to the avowed status of an honorable business, nay, to the status of practice of a time-honored profession; and drug addicts would multiply unrestrained, to the irrevocable impairment of the moral fiber and physical welfare of the American people.

In this paper we have seen that redefining moral crusades tends to generate strong counter-movements. The deviant as a cultural opponent is a more potent threat to the norm than is the repentant, or even the sick deviant. The threat to the legitimacy of the norm is a spur to the need for symbolic restatement in legal terms. In these instances of "crimes without victims" the legal norm is *not* the enunciator of a consensus within the community. On the contrary, it is when consensus is least attainable that the pressure to establish the legal norms appears to be greatest.

NOTES AND QUESTIONS

1. Does Gusfield convince you that an unenforced law may still be highly significant because of its symbolic functions? "Legal affirmation or rejection is thus important in what it symbolizes as well or instead of what it controls. Even if the law was broken, it was clear whose law it was." *See also* Murray Edelman, *The Symbolic Uses of Politics* (U. of Illinois Press 1964); Kai T. Erikson, *Wayward Puritans: A Study in the Sociology of Deviance* (John Wiley 1966). Gusfield has treated the temperance

movement in more detail in his book, *Symbolic Crusade: Status Politics and the American Temperance Movement* (U. of Illinois Press 1963).

[Reading 35]

a. Does Gusfield assert, and do you think, that those seeking to change the law are ever satisfied with a law they know will not be enforced? Consider Stewart Macaulay, *Law and the Balance of Politics and the American Temperance Movement* (U. of Illinois Press 1963).

In the process of changing the nature of a relationship through the use of the legal system there is a pattern which involves a typical sequence of stages. In the first stage, individuals seek relief by taking their case to an agency of government. While usually individuals go to court, at times they will turn to an attorney general's office or a regulatory agency. However, usually the individual will fail if the problem requires significant changes in the law. Even if he wins, he may do so in a way that promises little to others in similar situations or his victory may come at unacceptably high costs so that others cannot use his precedent to their advantage. The second stage involves organization of a group of those aggrieved by the problem or the mobilization of a group that already exists. This group usually will attempt to "collectively bargain" with those who are creating the problem (the opponents). Collective private action succeeds sometimes. If it fails, the group reaches the third stage: collective action to induce the legal system—typically the legislature—to make changes that bring solutions. Success in lobbying usually brings about the fourth and fifth stages. The fourth stage involves attempts by the opponents to deal with the situation and responses of the proponents. The opponents may view the law in its most narrow construction and comply only that far, or, at the other extreme, they may seek to make major changes in policies or in organizational structure to modify the circumstances that caused the problem in the first place. The fifth stage involves further legal battles when someone thinks that the new legislation has not been complied with. The failure of an individual at this stage may prompt a repetition of at least part of the process—an organization may begin lobbying for repairs to its statute. These stages are like battles in a war. Victory or defeat at any point does not necessarily mean that the war has been won

---

* Professor of Law, University of Wisconsin Law School. Published by the Russell Sage Foundation, reprinted by permission.

or lost. Only when we have surveyed all of the stages and determined that it is unlikely that the cycle will begin again can we ask who won the war.

This "model" reflects what has happened in many instances. However it is clear that things are not always that neat. For example, the probability that any later stage may occur may influence any earlier stage. When one comes to court to enforce rights created by a statute (the fifth stage), often the statute is challenged on constitutional grounds. The possibility of such a challenge probably influenced the drafting of the statute (the third stage). Moreover, action in several states may influence action on a federal level which, in turn, influences action in several other states which, in turn, influences voluntary compliance elsewhere. Also those seeking legal help may skip any stage if it is obvious that they will be unsuccessful at that point.

It is likely that this pattern of stages would have to be refined to be a true model which covered all social movements that sought to control other individuals or organizations with superior market power.

The pattern described suggests that as a matter of strategy there are times when a symbolic victory will have to be accepted, simply for want of a better solution—since "better" solutions are too controversial. Might a symbolic victory be instrumental for some purposes when at a particular time a group can obtain no other type of victory? How? Is a strategic acceptance of a mere symbolic victory the kind of conduct Gusfield is describing? Is the passage of a fair housing law condemning racial discrimination in housing and employment likely to satisfy or frustrate its backers if enforcement is left to an agency which has no power except to negotiate with offending landlords and employers and attempt to persuade them to mend their ways? See the concluding chapters of Leon H. Mayhew, *Law and Equal Opportunity, A Study of the Massachusetts Commission Against Discrimination* (Harvard U. Press 1968), reviewing the effectiveness of the commission.

b. How symbolic are the victories of the groups Gusfield describes? Can one argue that symbols always have a tremendous instrumental value? To the extent this is true, what is the significance of a symbolic victory for an appraisal of the effectiveness of legal action? For example, consider the Supreme Court's decision in Brown v. Board of Educ., 347 U.S. 483 (1954). Instrumentally, it has been less than completely effective; American schools are still segregated in many areas. The decision was an important symbolic victory; is it possible that as a symbol its effect on conduct within the United States has been more significant than its actual impact on school desegregation?

c. Suppose a state legislature appeared likely to repeal its statutes making the sale and possession of marijuana illegal. Since a federal statute, buttressed by treaties with other countries, would still outlaw marijuana, the repeal would be largely symbolic in nature. Would you expect repeal to be a more simple or more difficult matter than otherwise in the light of this fact? Is the state law against sale or possession of marijuana in some sense, "effective," even if state officials spend little time trying to enforce it against anyone? Is repeal different from enactment in terms of its symbolism?

2. Gusfield presents an analysis of deviant nonconformity and designator reaction. Is this relevant to an appraisal of the effectiveness of a law?

a. To demonstrate opposition to the war in Vietnam and to the Selective Service System, several men burned their draft cards. Congress responded quickly by passing a statute making draft card burning criminal. Congressman William G. Bray of Indiana was one of the only two speakers who discussed the bill on the floor of the House. He talked of draftcard burners as a "filthy, sleazy beatnik gang," "Judas-goats," and "Communist stooges." He said, "tolerance ceases to be a virtue when it condones evil," and that if these "revolutionaries are permitted to deface and destroy their draft cards, our entire Selective Service System is dealt a serious blow."

In July of 1968, the United States Attorney in Madison, Wisconsin, announced that he would not prosecute a university student who burned his draft card during a national anti-war demonstration. The student wrote, "Now I profoundly regret what I did. Burning my draft card was an impulsive, ineffective, and irresponsible act. I wish I had not done it." The U.S. Attorney said that the student still opposed the war but realized that he should use legal means of protest.

Could Congressman Bray reasonably think that his statute had been effective in this case? would Gusfield? What does Gusfield mean by the "designators" of deviant behavior; who are they? Is the student a repentant deviant or has he accepted the norm simply to avoid going to jail?

b. Gusfield talks of different responses which are appropriate to a classification of a particular individual by a designator of deviance. As a matter of legal technique, how could the law

apply one sanction to an enemy or cynical deviant and another
to a sick or repentant deviant? The incident in Madison, Wisconsin (¶ a, *supra*) indicates that one technique would be the use
of a prosecutor's discretion. Can you think of others?

3. Can Gusfield's analysis be applied to the struggle for gun-
control legislation during the 1960's? Was this a struggle for the
designation of certain norms as the preferred norms of the society,
or was it an instrumental struggle?

4. Gusfield describes a pattern in the designation of deviants,
from repentant to enemy to sick. The pattern, he argues, fits the
history of narcotics laws and laws against consumption of alcohol.
Can you think of other cases which the pattern fits? Can you
think of any cases in which the designation of deviants has gone
the other way—from sick to enemy or to repentant?

5. One finds many statutes and ordinances in state and city
codes that are not regularly enforced. One can explain the failure to repeal such "dead-letters" in terms of symbolism. One can
explain it in terms of drift and inattention. One can never be
sure, however, that a "dead-letter" will stay dead. For example,
in Minneapolis an ordinance, passed during World War I, required the display of a large American flag at all public meetings. The ordinance rested unused, and while an American flag
was displayed at many public meetings because of custom or
because the owners of meeting places had one in the room,
meetings were held where no one thought to display a flag. On
July 16, 1966, the Chairman of the Minnesota Committee to End
the War in Vietnam was arrested during a downtown meeting in
Minneapolis called to protest American policy in Vietnam. One
of the charges was failure to display a flag. The arrest ended the
meeting which had offended at least some of those watching it. A
lower court judge later dismissed the flag display charge on the
ground that the ordinance was unconstitutional but upheld a
breach of the peace conviction.

6. The symbolic meaning of penal laws was expounded by the
great French sociologist, Emile Durkheim, in his famous book,
The Division of Labor in Society (1893). Durkheim argued that
deviance and crime are dangerous to a society not merely because
of the damage to law and order or to particular interests, but
because deviance and crime are attacks on the basic values and
norms of society; it is for this reason that they must be punished.
Criminal law and law enforcement, then, are (among other
things) ceremonies that reinforce and restate existing norms as
valid.

(2) How can the effectiveness of an existing or proposed law be measured?

Once one sees the many meanings of effectiveness of law, he next confronts the problem of measuring the particular impact he has in mind. The following selections offer several ways of making such measurements. One should consider each in terms of its accuracy and its costs, both social and economic.

36. Law and Economic Growth: The Legal History of the Lumber Industry in Wisconsin, 1836-1915

WILLARD HURST*

[Professor Hurst's book treats in detail the legal history of the Wisconsin lumber industry. The law touched on the economic concerns of this industry in many ways. One way was by granting to lumbermen franchises to use streams in the transport of lumber.]

Policy in Practice

Did law materially affect men's behavior in using the streams? If it did, in what respects, and to what extent? We can answer with some assurance so long as we ask only the more general questions.

The law did materially affect stream use. Even within the law's formal records there is ample—if mainly circumstantial—evidence of this fact, in the volume and diversity of matters brought to law concerning the streams. In the activist, opportunistic, improvising temper of nineteenth-century Wisconsin, men did not exert themselves to press and oppose, enact, amend, and repeal hundreds of statutes, and fight hundreds of lawsuits, only to celebrate a ritual. . . .

There is no way to tell how many dollars men invested in building dams or booms or altering channels which they would not have invested had the law not set the terms it did on stream improvement. We find statutes which validate dams built without prior legal license; we have no means to calculate the percentage these instances are of the whole number of unrecorded,

* Vilas Professor of Law, University of Wisconsin Law School. Reprinted by permission of the publishers from Willard Hurst, Law and Economic Growth: The Legal History of the Lumber Industry in Wisconsin, 1836-1915, pp. 225-39, Cambridge, Mass.: The Belknap Press of Harvard University Press. Copyright, 1964 by the President and Fellows of Harvard College.

unlicensed construction. On the other hand, substantial legal attention to given behavior argues that the point was probably important in the total flow of action. Thus we find not only a high original prevalence of stipulations on height and slides and exit facilities in dam and boom franchises, but also considerable activity in amending such specifications. We may infer that these franchise stipulations were not empty forms but involved matters of lively practical concern, and that there were interests active on both sides of the relation of works builder and navigator in attending to what was done or not done under such terms set by law. We cannot, however, make more finely drawn estimates than these. We should not exaggerate the representative significance of particular controversies which left uncommonly full legal records. At a few river locations there was recurrent but relatively low-key conflict. . . . Disputes which put law under unusual pressure can be especially revealing of structural or functional strength or weakness in legal process. But we must not overlook the uncommon features of such contentious histories, especially the unusual strength, intensity, and stubbornness of the competing interests, and hence the unusually sharp focus upon issues. Most stream-use practice proceeded by a succession of commonplaces. Usually issues were much less in focus, or there was less competition of interests, or competition was episodic. Usually, thus, greater play was given to custom, improvisation, and the simple cumulation of events. Because we have unusually full records of a few hard-pressed contentions, we must not take combat—let alone melodrama—as the norm. Within the common objective of promoting economic growth, the norm was, rather, a matter-of-fact concentration upon operations. Men were "practical." They concentrated on bringing things to pass.

Law made its basic claim upon stream-use behavior where it undertook to define the most elementary terms on which private will might be exercised over use of the streams. Federal and state constitutional guaranties protected such navigation as the natural condition of waters permitted. However, large-scale transport, and any development of water power, required altering natural conditions. Primarily by statute—and, with less emphasis, by common law—Wisconsin public policy required that men have or obtain a statutory franchise before they changed the natural condition of waters in any manner which might materially affect the interests of navigators or riparian landowners. Some eight hundred special statutory franchises, and scores of lawsuits before the Wisconsin Supreme Court presenting claims under general franchise legislation, attest that men established their navigation and power use of forest-area streams under such legislative li-

censes. The indication is that where the law clearly said that
men must act under the law's license they generally undertook
to regularize their conduct accordingly. . . .

As we might expect of this energetic, self-willed community,
there is evidence that men built some dams and booms without
permission of law. In twenty-seven statutes the legislature "hereby legalized" dams "heretofore built," or "now kept up," or
authorized a dam at the same location "as the unauthorized dam
built and maintained at the said point." Eight statutes apparently
legalized booms built without authority. In eight cases which
reached the Wisconsin Supreme Court the record showed erection
of dams or related works without prior legislative sanction. Several dam statutes legalized structures which had stood without
authorization for more than a generation. Thus—authorizing a
dam at a specified location on the Big Plover River in Portage
County—Laws, 1901, Chapter 261, declared: "The dam heretofore built and maintained at the place mentioned . . . built in
or about the year 1853, and the building of said dam and the
maintenance of the same to the present time is hereby validated
and legalized."

Despite such evidence, the whole record shows a striking concern by private enterprisers to legitimize their use of the streams.
The franchises which validate unauthorized works represent between 5 and 6 per cent of the whole number of special franchises;
measured by what they say, the rest authorize fresh construction.
Except [in one instance], the record shows no case in which men
undertook to improve a large collecting area or an extensive
stretch of a major stream without positive permission of law. . . .
There is little evidence of unauthorized local works construction
on the major transport rivers such as the Wisconsin, the Chip-
pewa, or the Wolf. Most of the statutes validating particular
unauthorized structures concerned secondary streams (which,
nevertheless, moved substantial log traffic). Enterprisers gave
themselves the benefit of the doubt in not waiting upon clear
legal sanction to dam streams which obviously had a very limited
navigation potential. But they did not care to commit themselves
to extensive dependence upon using improved waters on which
they did not know they had an assured right. Of the thirty-five
statutes validating originally unauthorized works, all but one
were enacted after 1865, and twenty-one were enacted after 1879;
as it moved into the full tide of growth, the industry showed
more care for the legal basis of its stream improvements. As titles
and as grants of prerogative, the law's franchises apparently taught
even a rough and tumble industry a substantial respect for the
practical values of legitimacy.

To discuss license requirements tends to emphasize the regulatory relation of law to stream-use behavior. It fits reality to begin here: licensing provided the base line both for formal policy and for industry practice in stream improvement. But it would violate reality not to turn attention promptly to the promotional impact of law upon transport and power uses of water. Men had to give some initial attention to regulation because there was at least a minimum of legally sanctioned order that was necessary for market operations. But their hearts were in promotion, not regulation. In any case, there was not a sharp division of function between these two aspects of law. Regulatory order in stream-use policy was not primarily restrictive. It served to facilitate a more effective release of productive energies than would have been possible out of random collision of wills. Formal policy was clear on this point. Hence, for example, Revised Statutes, section 1777, tendered a river improvement franchise only to that corporation "which shall have taken prior possession of such stream." . . . Entrepreneurs in effect acknowledged that the regulatory features of water law fostered productivity. The legislation which constituted the bulk of public policy on forest stream use was shaped almost wholly by the play of interests within the lumber industry; the record shows little counterpart to the wider play of interests (farmer compared with timberland investor, farmers and local businessmen relative to big city promoters, for example) which marked the growth of policy regarding public lands or railroads. Yet, with the forces in play typically drawn from within the single industry, we find a volume of legal regulation which matches that concerning public lands or railroads. There would not have been such recourse to legislation had not millmen and transporters found productive utility in so employing law. We are unlikely to draw wrong inferences when our interpretation of legal affairs is consistent with the operations-minded devotion of these men to enlarging output for market.

The promotional demand upon law was that it foster investment of money, labor, and management skills in realizing the power and transport potentials of streams. The most direct ways to this end were the furnishing of capital (out of public borrowings, or from taxes, or from public lands) and the furnishing of management (through public enterprises). Only limited recourse was made to these direct methods, and their use was of secondary importance in exploiting the waters. Federal lands and money, and at different periods some state and federal management, went into efforts to create a continuous channel between Lake Michigan and the Mississippi River via the Fox and Wisconsin rivers. The Fox-Wisconsin project aborted, particularly because of the inadequate flow and shifting sands of the Wisconsin. In any event, neither in plan nor in effect was the project of substantial importance to log or lumber transport, though as a by-product it fostered development of water power in the Fox River valley. The United States made a substantial land grant to aid construction of a canal (important to lumber shipping) from Green Bay to Lake Michigan. The federal government also invested about $200,000 in surveys and limited improvements of the Chippewa River. This activity was pressed particularly by lumber interests, but the scale of public investment was too small to be rated a major contribution to the navigation uses of the Chippewa. The United States invested more heavily and continuously to improve Mississippi navigation, but with the prime objective of aiding general steamboat traffic. The Wisconsin constitution plainly and strictly forbade investment of state general funds or management in works of internal improvement. This legal barrier may help explain why the lumber industry made no attempt to obtain such help. However, the state constitution did not forbid local government units to subsidize transport improvements. Municipalities went into considerable debt to assist railroad construction. But municipal aids to navigation were few and small; municipalities could expect little if any direct benefit from facilitating shipment of logs out of their boundaries, and apparently there were few physical situations in which local mills felt need of public help to organize common sorting or storage works.

The minor role of direct public subsidy in aid of log and lumber water transport (especially in contrast to large public aids to railroads) reflected factors of industrial and legal organization and practice, compared with which a doctrinal element like the internal improvements clause of the state constitution was of secondary account. Though it included a few sizable firms, the lumber industry of the nineteenth century developed no giants; more fragmented and commanding fewer dollars or men than did the principal railroad promoters, the lumber industry could not muster like political force to extract large favors from Congress. Lumbermen had practical power to get a great deal of what they wanted from the state legislature or local governments. However, these agencies operated on a very limited tax base, and otherwise—should legal barriers be removed—could help only out of borrowed money or out of lands given by Congress; had lumber interests seriously pressed for such aids, they would have met the overwhelming competition of the railroads. Moreover, not only the dispersed state of the lumber industry, but also the peculiarly local character of stream improvement problems, would have required that effective public subsidies be made with close attention to particular situations. Between 1840 and 1890 there was no federal or state executive establishment competent for such tasks. The time-costly and clumsy processes of contemporary legislative investigation demonstrated the practical incapacity of the legislative branch to meet such a problem; the legislature managed to grind out eight hundred special franchises for stream use only because it could—implicitly, if not explicitly—generalize most of the policy choices presented. Through public lands disposition, the federal government and the state subsidized great numbers and diversity of private operators in timber speculation and logging. They accomplished these subsidies despite the ineptness of the federal and state land offices. But here the problem was seen as a simple one (merely to hand over full initiative of decision upon the use of given resources), and in the familiar form of the fee simple title the governments had a single, well-established device by which to operate. The complete breakdown of the experiment in leasing rather than selling mineral lands attested that contemporary executive apparatus was too simple and crude to carry out any program that called for detailed operations in the field. There is no evidence that scruples of principle restrained those interested in log or lumber water transport from seeking direct public aids. What seemed practically desirable and obtainable, they sought to get. But the pattern of contemporary legal and economic institutions and practice was unfavorable to a substantial direct subsidy effort in this field.

Thus, it was mainly by indirection that law promoted investment of money, labor, and management in exploiting the power and transport potential of streams. Again, we encounter a principal theme of nineteenth-century policy—the pursuit of objectives of public concern by legitimating and supporting the exercise of private will.

As grants of title and prerogative, stream-use franchises fostered investment by creating frameworks of reasonable expectation within which men could act, knowing in what respects law allowed them to impose their will on others and in what respects law protected them against detrimental claims or actions by others. The contract clause of the federal Constitution and the policies of self-restraint which the legislature and the governors observed in applying reserved powers to amend or repeal franchises under the state constitution and statutes offered additional assurance to encourage capital commitments.

Speaking from experience of their community and its ways, contemporary lawmakers time and again asserted their conviction that the grant of franchises in fact promoted investment of private resources in stream improvements. . . . The hundreds of special stream-use franchises granted in the years that followed, as well as the general river improvement statutes, were stated almost invariably as bargains—certain privileges given, for certain performance stipulated. The bargain form attested that these practical men saw franchises as inducements to investment in stream improvements. The persistence of this style of grant, and the care taken in quite a few instances to amend details of the required consideration, attest that men found that the franchise inducement in fact operated and was taken seriously. Referring to the transport needs of the lumber industry after a generation of growth, the Wisconsin Supreme Court in 1877 thought that common experience showed that the state could obtain river improvements by granting toll right franchises, and, indeed, could get the work done on no other terms. "The state itself cannot remove such [natural] obstructions [to navigation], because it cannot be a party to carrying on any work of internal improvement, and, if such obstructions are removed, it must be done by other agencies. It is certain that no corporation or individual would [go] to the expense of making such improvements in these streams without some reward. The [Wisconsin River Improvement Company, operating under Private & Local Laws, 1853, Chapter 30] . . . alleges that it has expended over $30,000 in erecting dams for slack water, and in removing rocks from the channel of the Wisconsin river at the rapids; and how is it to be remunerated for its outlay, except by tolls upon lumber and timber which pass through the improvement?" When there was unusual controversy, and issues hence were more sharply drawn than in the ordinary course—as in repeated battles over improvement franchises on the Black River and at Eau Claire on the Chippewa—contestants and legislators alike made plain that the stakes were high, precisely because to grant or withhold, or to revoke, a franchise meant the practical difference between action or no action by particular enterprises.

That men regarded the grant of franchises as stimulating the will to act appears also from the amount of amendment of the detailed terms of franchises. It was exceptional for a stream-use franchise to be adopted just as it was introduced. By a conservative appraisal, 70 per cent of all franchise bills enacted suffered some amendment in course of passage. There was much less amendment of franchises after their enactment, but the amount of such amending activity was nonetheless substantial; about 16 per cent of all forest-area special franchises were so amended. . . .

The most numerous types of amendments dealt with matters inherently important to the title or the prerogative aspects of franchises, especially the definition of locations of franchised action and of toll rights. This activity in amendment—especially the more pervasive attention to amendments preceding original enactment—offers impressive testimony on men's attitudes. As evidence which is implicit in overt action directed to focused details of projected behavior, it can properly be taken more at face value than can the explicit rationalization men make of their decisions. By its extent, it is evidence generated from commonplace more often than from peculiarly controversial stream-use franchise situations; therefore, it is evidence likely to be the more representative of regular patterns of behavior. What this evidence suggests is that men did not regard the obtaining of a franchise as an empty form, or as of little account in affecting future behavior. Those who sought franchises—and if not they, then those who saw themselves affected by others' franchises—spent an impressive amount of energy attending to details of franchise terms. Men do not so invest energy without cause—least of all these operations-minded nineteenth-century movers and doers. The inference is that they regarded franchises as material influences upon action.

In water transport of logs or rafts there was likely to be crowding, since the bulk of product moved during short driving seasons. Whether as among competing navigators or as between navigator and millman, navigation more commonly posed factually inconsistent use claims upon a common resource than arose among different millsites. Moreover, overhead cost pressed harder on transport than on power uses of water; good business thus enforced pooling or at least co-ordination of log driving and booming activities earlier and more pervasively than it fostered concentration in woods or mill operations. As the industry developed, the statute books reflected increasing demand for law to support frameworks of organization for disciplining water traffic. The demand was natural. Traffic management meant that some men would impose their will on others, regardless of agreement; this was a relation which invited resort to law, the most distinctive function of which is to superintend the total distribution of power in a community. Too, the situation called for specially contrived legal arrangements of power—that is, for franchises. Traditional forms of private property might accommodate relations among those whose claims rested on titles to riparian lands derived from common grantors. But stream flow was a commonwealth resource; the familiar law of private property would not serve to adjust flow uses as such.

Such economic and organizational pressures help explain why there was demand for franchises to support stream management. These factors have further significance. They were pressures generated by the functional needs of efficient business and power relationships. Because of their functional origins, the growth and persistence of demand for management franchises are facts which in themselves evidence that such franchises were material elements in enlarging the scale of log and lumber transport. In 1867 a legislative committee recognized the force of such pressures of function in explaining why lumbermen on the Black River sought and obtained a franchise for the Black River Improvement Company, and continued to rely on it to legitimize the traffic management which joint use of the river required: "It had been fully demonstrated by the experience of ten years, that individual effort would do but little for the improvement of the navigation of the river, and hence the necessity of some organized corporate effort became apparent, both to the loggers and manufacturers of lumber on the river." . . .

The behavior of those who used the streams implicitly testified that the availability of a franchise was a material attraction to investment in more effective traffic organization. As their scale of operations grew, the lumbermen attached increasing value to efficient driving and booming organization as such. In the sixties and seventies men organized important joint driving arrangements on a cooperative basis; there was in these agreements no provision for tolls or dividends, but only for sharing expenses; on their face the arrangements indicated that the parties looked for no direct profit from the joint transport effort, but valued it simply as an organizational asset useful to increase eventual output. Later enterprisers commonly stipulated for tolls for their traffic management. Yet this development appears to have been of secondary significance. Most water traffic managers were involved mainly in moving their own logs or rafts; none made a great amount of money from carriage tolls; some who had the formal right to charge tolls did not exercise it. What really counted was better coordination of movement of goods. Compared with the attention given to devising better procedures of driving and booming, the absence of significant direct profit from this activity, or even of much effort to make a profit, points up the importance which lumbermen attached to achieving more effective stream-use organization as such. Men who thus estimated their interest were bound to put great store in obtaining franchises. They wanted organization to facilitate enlarged operations, but they could not safely organize as they wished without law's validation. The capital stakes were always high—not so much the investment required for stream improvements and management as the commitment of a winter's woods output which must reach market. Enterprisers needed assured definition of the

terms on which they might have access to public waters, and of
the terms on which they might expect to deal with those whose
activities would impinge on their own in the rush and hazard
of the drive. Discipline would be necessary, but even the large
operator hesitated to discipline others without knowing he had
support of law. In a showdown those who would manage traffic
wanted law's help to enforce tolls and liens and to set bounds
to liability for alleged faulty performance or civil wrong. Even
when large operators flexed their muscles, they sought color of
law for the traffic controls they would impose on others. Though
dealings were typically within a small group of operators sharing
a watershed, the pressure for organizational regularity showed
itself in increasing resort to incorporation; it was not coincidence
that the greatest relative use of the corporate form was for toll
booms and toll improvement ventures. Of course, stream traffic
organization developed as it did for business reasons, but in this
instance it was inherent in the nature of the business objectives
that the availability of a franchise should be a material inducement to action.

Having paid our respects to the promotional aspects of stream-
use franchises, we must return to the fact that they also bore
restrictive features—both the burdens they allowed the franchise
holders to impose on other persons, and the burdens they laid on
the holders for the benefit of other persons. Here especially,
when we ask what were the practical effects of franchise terms,
we must be content with inferences from scattered evidence. For
the practical meaning of these franchise features lay wholly in
the cumulative impact of operating incidents which left no regular
record.

Grantees enforced their rights to toll for use of the waters they
improved, though—as we might expect—sometimes the users contested the legitimacy of the claim or were poor risks for the
money they owed. We have noted that toll returns were not a
major item of income for improvers, and that some grantees did
not assert their right. Nonetheless, there were enough occasions
of explicit conflict in the legislature and in the courts, and sufficient activity in amending the toll terms of franchises before and
after enactment, to show that men treated these claims with respect for their practical effect. . . . Of sharper significance were
the rights of traffic management implicitly or explicitly conferred
by improvement franchises. It was over the physical control of
the passage of logs or rafts that men fought the most bitter battles in legislature and in court. The episodes of forcible self-help
which dot the record concern command of physical movement.
Most log and lumber transport flowed without acute controversy.

As the volume of traffic grew, more and more of it moved by coordinated effort under single management, and the want of conflict was the most striking evidence that men in fact used their traffic control rights, and used them with at least tolerable restraint and effect. Such an outcome matched the logic of the total situation. Workable traffic management rested on franchise rights which reflected imperatives of fact. . . .

Franchises to develop water power carried their own restrictive features. The inclusion of navigation guaranties in a dam franchise acknowledged that the grant in itself allowed the dam builder to impose on passing traffic such control of flow as was otherwise reasonable to accomplish the power use. Most licensed power dams were built, along with other works, under general statutes. Each constructed work, by its very existence, constituted an exercise of privileges to affect traffic or power uses of the waters. Beyond this feature, many works licenses (for developing power, or for navigation improvement) delegated the right of eminent domain. The delegation had two aspects. Employed at the initiative of a works builder, the eminent domain power enabled him to restrict the ordinary right of a landowner to bargain in market for the value of his property. Employed at the initiative of a flowed landowner, the eminent domain power was a limitation upon the works builder, requiring that he pay fair compensation for benefits which he obtained at the cost of inflicting certain kinds of detriment on another. We have no practical means to inventory the total use of these delegations of eminent domain authority. Two things are clear. Draftsmen of franchises put high value on including the eminent domain power; whether grantees used it or not, they wanted it in reserve. On the other hand, prevailing community values were equally clear that only through eminent domain might men be deprived of the use opportunities that went with standard titles to land surface. There was substantial legislative attention in the lumber era to drawing and redrawing the terms and procedures by which eminent domain power was made available for building dams and improving navigation. Both from its timing in the state's economic history and from the face of the statutes, it is clear that this activity had reference primarily to forest-area developments. On the other hand, there is evidence that dams were built in the north country which flowed lands that did not belong to the dam builders, and that no proceedings were taken to pay compensation and validate flowage rights. A good deal of dam building and stream improvement went on in the forest region in wild and unsettled areas. Land titles would often be in owners who held only for the value of the standing timber, or in local governments which had succeeded by tax titles to land then regarded as of little or no market value. In the circumstances, it is reasonable to infer that the operative significance of the eminent domain provisions for much of the forest country was as a reservation against exceptional difficulty or complaint.

Over-all, and despite the limitations of the evidence, we can believe that the practical impact of the stream franchises was substantial. In some aspects the emphasis was on law-fostered values of legitimacy and order. In others it was on the industry's business needs and on still broader functional requirements of the economy. The lines of influence tended to weave together, and through them the stream-use franchises became integral to the whole pattern of the industry.

NOTES AND QUESTIONS

1. Hurst sees the law performing at least three functions in dealing with conflicting interests and the use and development of the streams in nineteenth century Wisconsin. Law provided a framework of reasonable expectation within which men could act; it provided organization and discipline in using the stream; it superintended the total distribution of power in the community. How did law perform these functions? It did not perform them primarily by imposing penal sanctions or by offering tangible economic rewards. Rather the "inference is that the practical function of franchise navigation guaranties was mainly to provide legitimated criteria by which private parties stood warned and could bargain and argue out their differences." To a great extent, the process is similar to the effect of a stop sign even when it is highly unlikely that there is a traffic policeman within miles. One driver has the right of way (legitimacy) and the other does not. This is likely to affect their conduct because it affects their expectations and evaluations of the likely reactions of the other. *See* Schelling, Reading 17, at 174, *supra*.

2. What is Hurst's evidence that the law operates effectively in this manner? Why is Hurst impressed with the patterns he finds in legal records rather than with the statements of the actors? How persuasive is his evidence? Did he have any alternatives open in working with nineteenth century data?

3. Can one argue that law, in the sense Hurst uses the term, is most effective at one stage of a newly developing economy before stable systems are created which are accepted and which are supported by patterns of reciprocity?

37. Is Regulation Necessary?
California Air Transportation and National Regulatory Policy

MICHAEL E. LEVINE*

74 YALE LAW JOURNAL 1416 (1965)

Air transportation in the United States, as elsewhere in the world, is a regulated and protected industry. The present system of economic regulation was established in the Civil Aeronautics Act of 1938 and has survived virtually unchanged despite vast changes in the character of the industry and a review and reorganization of government control which resulted in the present statute, the Federal Aviation Act of 1958. Government restriction of entry into the industry and regulation of fares has fostered unnecessarily high fares, encouraged uneconomic practices, and limited the variety of service available to the public. The performance of the largest air transportation market in the world provides convincing evidence that fares are much lower and service more responsive to public needs where restrictions on entry are absent and control over fares is rarely exercised. It is time for the CAB to reconsider national regulatory policy, benefiting from twenty-seven years of accumulated experience and the remarkable example of the Los Angeles-San Francisco market.

I. THE HISTORY OF AIRLINE REGULATION

The present regulatory scheme had its beginnings in earlier government efforts, which were inspired by the desire of Congress and the Post Office to develop an airmail system. . . .

The comprehensive Airmail Act of 1934 attempted . . . to ensure competition, to make vertical integration arrangements il-

* Assistant Professor of Law, University of Southern California Law Center. Reprinted by permission of the Yale Law Journal Company and Fred B. Rothman and Company from The Yale Law Journal, Vol. 74, pp. 1416-47.

legal, and to bring rates and contracts under the jurisdiction of the Interstate Commerce Commission, although the route awards were still to be made by the Postmaster General. The Act called for the establishment of four transcontinental routes and routes on each coast. Subsidy was to be granted through a "mail pay" formula which was related to the capacity and type of equipment offered, rather than the amount of mail actually carried. Since the only organizations competent to handle the important routes were the discredited airlines, a face-saving formula was devised which enabled them to bid for the contracts. These firms and the predecessor of Eastern Airlines received the major awards, and the "big four" pattern of trunk carrier service[13] was established.

This history greatly influenced the regulatory pattern created in the 1938 Act, and has had a psychological impact upon both the carriers and their regulators. The new air transportation system was dominated by four carriers identified in the public mind with the "spoils meetings" of 1930, and hence with collusion and division of markets. Fear of "big four" domination and ultimate air transport monopoly was one of the most important sources of public pressure for the passage of the 1938 Act, and has continued to concern the Board and the public.

During the period when the attention of the public was focused upon the monopoly problems of the industry, the industry itself was becoming increasingly concerned about excessive competition. None of the legislation prior to 1938 contained any restrictions on entry. It might have been expected that in this period when mail carriage was the crucial source of revenue for air carriers, the exclusive nature of mail contracts would have acted as a barrier to entry. But entry was relatively inexpensive and, even during the depression, some individuals were willing to take a chance in aviation without a mail contract. Carriers with airmail contracts were not permitted to compete in any market for which a mail contract had been awarded to another carrier. Since mail contracts covered virtually all potentially profitable routes, the result was a government-sponsored division of markets, in which the contract carriers gave up the right to compete in other markets for monopoly rights in their own. Non-contract carriers were subject to no such restrictions and established themselves on the most profitable routes. This competition cut into the non-mail revenues of the contract carriers at the same time as the

<hr>

13 The "big four" are American Airlines, Eastern Airlines, Trans World Airlines and United Air Lines, the four largest domestic trunk (main-line) carriers. Their share of total traffic has been reduced somewhat since 1938 as a result of continuing efforts by the Board to strengthen smaller carriers.

Depression was affecting them adversely. The result was to threaten capital investments made by the established carriers during the boom years of the late 1920's and during the early 1930's while they were under the protection of a cartelized industrial structure. In addition, developing aircraft technology promised future profits, and passenger business was steadily, if slowly, growing. Thus, the industry was likely to attract still more new capital in the future. In the face of this competitive threat to past investment and future security, the airlines formed a trade association (the Air Transport Association) and pressed for protective legislation.

The new association put before Congress dire predictions of commercial chaos and impaired safety. It demanded protective legislation. The resulting Civil Aeronautics Act of 1938 provided the industry with protection so efficacious that not one carrier has been certificated to perform domestic trunk service which was not operating on May 14, 1938 and thus qualified for a certificate under the automatic-certification (grandfather) clause.

The Federal Aviation Act of 1958, successor to the 1938 Act, gives to the Federal Aviation Agency jurisdiction over the "technical" or "operational" aspects of air transportation (safety regulation, airport development, and control of the airspace). These activities are largely outside the scope of this Comment. The "economic" aspects of air transportation (*e.g.*, rates, routes, and market structure) are within the jurisdiction of the Civil Aeronautics Board, which was established by the 1938 Act and which continued virtually unchanged, but as a separate agency, under the 1958 Act. The Board is empowered under Subchapter IV of the 1958 Act to exercise supervision and control over entry into the industry, cities to be served, rates, direct subsidies, and terms of mail carriage. The Board also has the power to approve or prevent mergers, acquisitions, and transfers of control of air carriers, and actions so approved are immune from the operation of the antitrust laws.

Congress made clear the government's objectives in regulating air commerce:

> In the exercise and performance of its powers and duties under this chapter, the Board shall consider the following, among other things, as being in the public interest, and in accordance with the public convenience and necessity. . . .
>
> (c) The promotion of adequate, economical and efficient service by air carriers at reasonable charges, without unjust discriminations, undue preferences or advantages, or unfair or destructive competitive practices;

(d) Competition to the extent necessary to assure the sound development of an air-transportation system properly adapted to the needs of the foreign and domestic commerce of the United States, of the Postal Service, and the national defense; . . .

The Board is empowered to regulate entry by issuing certificates of public convenience and necessity. No carrier can engage in air transportation without such a certificate. Some carriers were certificated under the "grandfather clause" of the 1938 Act. For other carriers, the Act provides that:

> The Board shall issue a certificate authorizing the whole or any part of the transportation ordered by the application, if it finds that the applicant is fit, willing and able to perform the transportation properly, and to conform to the provisions of this chapter and the rules, regulations, and requirements of the Board hereunder, and that such transportation is required by the public convenience and necessity; otherwise such application shall be denied.

A permanent route certificate is a grant of monopoly or oligopoly power to exploit the traffic over a named group of cities arranged sequentially. Although the Board may limit the operating rights granted by a certificate, with or without limitations, a route award is potentially a valuable property. The value of a certificate is enhanced because the CAB attempts to protect the revenue of certificate holders from the effects of competition, and the certificates are transferable. Carriers pay a price, though, since government supervision is potentially so pervasive as to interfere with virtually all management prerogatives. However, even observers inclined to defend the interests of the airlines have acknowledged the munificence of the 1938 Act. . . .

In 1938, regulation seemed a small price to pay, especially since the industry appeared likely to face an annual deficit for many years to come. By 1952, however, the major airlines no longer required direct subsidy, and since then they have been less reluctant to complain about government interference. But the other protection afforded by the 1938 legislation, the freedom from new competition, has been jealously guarded. Indeed, the airlines have demonstrated an almost pathological fear of open competition, especially price competition.

This fear, dignified by twenty-five years of regulatory enforcement, has been transmogrified into a sacred truth—namely, that airlines, if allowed to compete without restrictions would engage in a frenzy of below-cost selling to the ultimate ruin of all. Such "cut-throat" destructive competition involves carriers in an over-capitalized market (*i.e.*, too many sellers) cutting fares to the point where the increase in market demand created by lower fares will not compensate for reduced unit revenues (*i.e.*, "dilution of revenues").

II.   The Economic Theory of Airline Regulation

The CAB, in regulating the industry, has shared the carriers' fear that price competition would be destructive. In addition, the Board concurs in the general belief that, unregulated, the industry would become monopolistic. The monopoly spectre has haunted the Board in two inconsistent and equally amorphous forms.

First, it is feared that without regulation the industry would be "excessively competitive." The resulting "cut-throat" competition, in addition to causing economic waste, would lead ultimately to monopoly. It is feared that such destructive competition, in which no carrier could operate profitably, would drive all but the strongest out of business. The survivor could then exercise market power and provide inferior service at monopoly fares. This fear probably had its origins in the carriers' Depression experience, where competition from unregulated lines combined with generally poor business conditions to affect adversely their investment.

Second, the CAB fears that without regulation the industry would not be competitive enough. The Board believes that monopoly would result through internal growth, merger, or collusion. This fear may have its origins in memories of the "spoils conference" and the collusion revealed by the 1934 investigation, and it is probably reinforced by recent attempted mergers.

Assuming that air transport firms behave rationally (that is, that they act to maximize gains and minimize losses), fears either of destructive competition or of monopoly must be justifiable by economic analysis to be credible. It may be that airlines are economically similar to public utilities. Or, it may be that the industry is characterized by barriers to new entry sufficiently high to allow monopolistic practices to survive unchecked by competitive forces. If neither of these is the case, it is difficult to see how the Board's economic fears are justified. Since the natural play of market forces in a public utility industry works to the public detriment, government regulation of public utilities in effect *removes* them from the competitive sector of the economy. In an industry characterized by the erection of high barriers to entry, market forces which would otherwise operate to the public benefit are stifled. The anti-trust laws seek to *preserve* the free operation of the market by preventing the erection of such barriers.

Public utilities such as telephone and power companies are described as "natural monopolies." In these industries the largest firm always has the lowest unit costs; therefore, only one firm can survive. Since the required capital investment is high and cannot be easily transferred or liquidated, new entry is costly and unlikely to occur. The established firm can use its natural cost advantages to drive out the new entrant, and since the new entrant's capital investment is immobile, it will suffer substantial losses. Such industries are regulated to prevent the output restrictions and monopoly prices which the free play of market forces would permit. There is general agreement upon the economic necessity of regulating natural monopoly industries. But Caves has demonstrated that air transportation is not a natural monopoly industry. He finds that, once minimum efficient size has been attained, scale of operations plays an insignificant role in determining costs and very large size may even be slightly disadvantageous.[42]

Public utilities such as pipelines and railroads are regulated for a different reason. These industries are characterized by high unavoidable (fixed) costs and low avoidable (variable) costs. Consequently, the average cost of each unit of output carries a high capital burden and is far greater than the marginal cost of production. The invested capital is immobile and cannot readily be liquidated or moved to a more profitable location. To recover and profit from this capital investment, such a firm must sell at average cost or above. But, faced with competition, a utility of this kind will price below average cost. The heavy burden of unavoidable costs (a product of inability to liquidate, curtail output, or move) creates pressure to reduce prices in order to use existing capacity. Any price above marginal cost will contribute *something* toward meeting fixed costs and the firm will resort to such pricing as a short-run measure. Since each reduction in price will produce a corresponding price reduction by his competitor, the market price will move inexorably toward marginal cost. At marginal cost, however, none of the firm's capital is recovered.

Regulation of such industries proceeds upon the premise that pricing practises of this kind injure the public. The theory is that industries pricing far below average cost will be unattractive

---

[42] CAVES, AIR TRANSPORT AND ITS REGULATORS 56-60 (1962), esp. Table 18, at 58 and Fig. 1, at 59.

to capital. This is said to be undesirable because "needed" services will not be provided, and technological improvement will be slowed or halted. It is further claimed that the excess capacity resulting from competitive duplication represents economic waste since immobility prevents reemployment of redundant capital. The theory holds that the strongest firm will acquire a monopoly position as the capital reserves of its competitors are depleted. Typically, such "utilities" are removed from the competitive sector by government licensing (to eliminate or restrict competition) and rate regulation (to prevent destructive or monopoly pricing).

This theory is widely, but not universally, accepted. Regardless of its economic validity, the theory provides no justification for regulating the air transport industry, for it is generally acknowledged that the air transport industry is characterized by high variable (and thus avoidable) costs, rather than high fixed costs.[43] Since aircraft can be operated over any route offering the possibility of a profit, and since there is a thriving used aircraft market,[44] capital not profitably employed can be easily reemployed or liquidated.

If it is true that the air transport industry is characterized neither by continually declining costs over feasible ranges of output, nor by a high ratio of fixed to variable costs and immobility of capital, then regulating airlines as public utilities is unjustifiable and works to the detriment of the public. For in situations other than those described, the market operates to lower prices, increase output and tailor production to suit consumer preferences.

If airlines have high avoidable and low unavoidable costs, they will not compete at prices which fail to provide adequate return, since curtailing operations will significantly reduce costs. If airline capital is mobile, then it will not remain employed in markets where the marginal rate of return is insufficient to justify its commitment. There will be no economic waste. If the airline industry is not a natural monopoly industry, then size alone will not confer market power and a small but efficient line will be able to survive competition even with a giant.

The airlines, long accustomed to uniform rates high enough to support all but the most inefficient, have come to regard price competition as almost always "cut-throat." This view depends upon the implicit assumption that all airlines operate at approximately the same level of efficiency, and that such competition

43 *Id.* at 79-82.
44 Caves, *op. cit. supra* note 42, at 106.

merely "dilutes" revenues to the disadvantage of all. But if airlines vary markedly in efficiency, technological or marketing efficiencies can confer cost advantages on the efficient carrier. Competitive pricing will then shift market shares in favor of the more
efficient carrier and, in addition, expand the market without
"diluting" revenues. Such price competition will not be destructive because the higher cost carrier will not be forced by high,
unrecoverable fixed costs to maintain capacity. If this analysis
is borne out in practice, unregulated airlines behave like competitive manufacturing and marketing firms and should not be
regulated as public utilities.

However, if the hoped-for competitive benefits to the public
would not materialize due to market imperfections, little will be
gained by removing airline regulation, unless the market imperfections are corrected. Freedom of entry is vital to the operation
of a competitive market with few sellers because it provides the
control that keeps output high and price low. On one hand, if
the price rises and makes possible a higher-than-competitive return, more capital will flow into the market and new firms will
enter, thus bringing prices down to the competitive level. Also,
freedom of entry prevents any firm from using destructive pricing
as a means to gain a monopoly. If competitors realize that selling
below cost can never be the prelude to establishing a monopoly
(due to the ever-present possibility of new entrants selling at a
competitive price), then they will regard "cut-throat" competition as suicidal. Prices will be lowered when true efficiencies give
market advantages. Since it has been demonstrated that barriers
to entry other than those artificially imposed by regulation are
relatively insubstantial in the air transport industry,[48] from an
economic standpoint, an unregulated market should operate to
the benefit of the consuming public.

But regulation of air transportation is claimed to achieve political and social as well as economic objectives. It is claimed that
regulation provides air transport to areas which would otherwise
not be served and that regulation guarantees safety. The first
may be an appropriate national policy. And no one would question the importance of the second. But neither justifies the present system of regulation.

According to one estimate, fully half of United States airline
cities do not generate enough traffic to cover the additional cost
of providing them with service.[49] Some of these cities are subsidized directly, through government payments made to the

---

[48] CAVES, *op. cit. supra* note 42, at 92, 95.
[49] *Id.* at 414.

local service carriers, but service to many is supported privately through internal subsidy. The CAB requires all carriers to serve cities and route segments that do not cover costs and to pay for such service out of profits extracted from long-haul or high-density segments served at higher-than-competitive fares. For example, United serves cities such as Elko, Nevada in return for being permitted to operate its transcontinental routes. The Board encourages even local service carriers, all of whom are subsidized directly by the government, to reduce the amount of direct subsidy by serving profitable high-density markets and using the profits to pay for service to unproductive points.

Normally, in a market economy, services which cannot be sold at a profit are not sold at all. To provide a service which does not generate enough demand to cover costs is wasteful. Resources consumed in producing this service could have been used to provide other, more desired, services elsewhere in the economy. Of course, social benefits may outweigh economic costs. But proponents of subsidy frequently purport to justify subsidized service on economic grounds, arguing that national or regional economic benefits flow from providing such transportation at low cost. Benefits are said to accrue to persons other than those purchasing the service, and hence market performance is claimed to be an inadequate measure of value. This argument cannot be tested in the abstract, but only through analysis of each claim for subsidy. Subsidy is economically justifiable so long as it does not exceed the total value of the economic benefits conferred by the service. When economic benefits are insufficient to offset costs, subsidy may be provided for purely social or political reasons or withheld, leaving the route to the free market. Withholding subsidy does not mean that small cities are denied air transportation. Smaller carriers (air taxis), private aircrafts, and charters are available at higher rates to the user but lower cost to the economy as a whole.

Non-economic justifications of subsidy are, *ex hypothesis*, beyond economic argument. But a subsidy provided on non-economic grounds ought to be designed to do as little economic harm as possible. By this standard public subsidy from general revenues is preferable to private transfer payments. It makes little economic sense to charge one group of consumers a higher-than-competitive price in order to provide similar but economically unrelated services to another group of consumers. Artificially high prices for main-line transportation decrease demand for such services, injuring those who could have profitably used the service at its true cost. Subsidizing in this way creates an allocation of resources which does not maximize output of goods and services in the economy as a whole. An efficient allocation is achieved only by employing resources where they can be most profitably used.

Defenders of internal subsidy claim that private transfer payments save taxpayers' money. Since the deficit incurred by the operation to be subsidized is independent of the source of the subsidy payments, it cannot be argued that the total cost of internal subsidy is less than the total cost of public subsidy on any given route. Moreover, it certainly cannot be argued that dollars for internal subsidy come into existence gratuitously. The citizen deprived of the opportunity to profitably use air transportation due to artificially high costs is "taxed" just as surely as if the Government collected the amount of lost profits from him. And those who travel on profitable routes, paying higher than competitive fares are "taxed" privately for the use of the service.

Finally, if output were increased by the more efficient allocations of resources which would result from the elimination of internal subsidy, the increase in total economic wealth would result in a decrease in the percentage of total revenues contributed to subsidy. Naturally, the total tax would be the same, but the taxpayer would find the bill easier to pay. Because public subsidy makes tax costs visible, benefits may be weighed against the cost of providing them. Internal subsidy makes possible disguised inefficiency.

The burden of subsidizing should fall where the benefits, economic or other, accrue. If the service is regarded as beneficial to the nation or economy as a whole, the nation should pay. If a certain geographical or economic sector is benefited, the burden of the subsidy ought to be placed there. Users of profitable routes do not benefit specially from the availability of service to unprofitable points. It is neither fair nor efficient to place the burden of subsidy on them.

The final argument advanced is that economic regulation is necessary to insure safety. This argument is based on the prediction that an unregulated market would be characterized by the proliferation of financially unstable carriers, and the assumption that financial stability contributes to safe operation. The first claim is simply untrue. The second, while true, does not justify pervasive economic regulation of the CAB variety. Expenditures to preserve high maintenance standards and permit flight cancellations when safety requires do impose short-run financial burdens. But financial stability sufficient to ensure safe operation already is a prerequisite to entry. Additional economic regulation is superfluous. The FAA is empowered to withhold air car-

rier operating certificates from carriers lacking the financial stability necessary for safe operation. No carrier can operate without
such a certificate. The FAA is determined to enforce these requirements strictly, particularly after the Paradise Airlines accident of March, 1964. The accident was caused by the combination of the airline's failure to replace a defective instrument and
the pilot's unwise decision to land under instrument conditions
and both are thought attributable to financial instability.

Profitable airlines operating in regulated markets have experienced accidents caused by negligent maintenance. No supervisory
system is perfect. But the FAA can ensure that new entrants meet
standards at least as stringent as those applied to presently-cer-
tificated carriers. Further, if public sentiment demanded, the
FAA could expand its enforcement of safety standards to include
preventative inspection. The added cost of such inspections
could be financed by a tax on air travel, so that the beneficiaries
of the inspection system—the traveling public—would pay it.
This system would provide improved safety at a relatively slight
cost and would make possible a public judgment as to whether
the safety benefits were worth the cost. Such a tax would surely
burden the consumer less than the hidden costs imposed by the
present system of economic regulation.

The present structure of air transport economic regulation was
created in response to fears and assumptions founded in the experiences of an infant industry operating in the Depression. Its
perpetuation is in part attributable to the failure of regulators
and observers to distinguish clearly the "system" from the objectives it was designed to achieve. The objectives of regulation—
economic stability, adequate and economical service to the public, and safety—could today be better achieved through a different regulatory scheme. The performance and experience of the
Los Angeles-San Francisco market demonstrates that alternative
systems may function better in fact as well as in theory.

III. CALIFORNIA, A TEST CASE

A. *Evidence*

In view of the comprehensive character of the Civil Aeronautics Act and the present worldwide agreement that entry and fare
restrictions are necessary, it is not surprising that only one major
unregulated market exists in the entire world. What is surprising is that this market—air transportation between Los Angeles
and the San Francisco-Oakland area—is the largest in the world.
Although this market is within the extensive operational jurisdiction of the FAA, it is not within the more limited economic

jurisdiction of the CAB. The economic provisions of the Act do not apply to carriers supplying purely local transportation between these two cities because they are within the same state, and transportation can be conducted without overflying another state or international waters.[59] Certificated domestic trunk carriers flying this route are subject to both Board and California Public Utilities Commission regulation, but carriers operating purely intrastate are subject only to the jurisdiction of the Commission. Although the Commission has power to regulate airline rates, it does so very flexibly. The Commission is required by statute to hold inquiries into fare increases and decreases so marked that there is reason to believe that the fare is non-compensatory, but it makes a practice of approving virtually all changes. It cannot regulate entry. Nor can it require service to any point, grant subsidy, or limit the route pattern of any enterprise. As a result, the California intrastate markets are relatively unregulated and, by world standards, are virtually free markets.[63]

Although the Los Angeles-San Francisco market has always been an important one, it was the fifth largest in the United States in 1948 (in terms of passenger miles), and became the largest only in 1961. Today, more revenue passengers travel between Los Angeles and San Francisco than between any other pair of cities in the world. More than 60 round trip non-stop

---

[59] Hence such transportation is not "interstate air transportation" within the meaning of the Act (49 U.S.C. § 1301(21)) and not subject to the jurisdiction of the Board. Because the safety jurisdiction of the Federal Aviation Agency applies to "civil aircraft in air commerce" (49 U.S.C. § 1421 (a)) and the definition of "air commerce" (49 U.S.C. § 1301(4)) is more inclusive than that of "interstate air transportation," carriage of passengers by air between the cities is subject to federal safety regulation.

[63] The CAB, in 1954, attempted to subject the intrastate carriers to the Act, but the result was inconclusive and the matter was apparently dropped. CAB v. Friedkin Aeronautics, Inc., 246 F.2d 173 (9th Cir. 1957). . . .

In California, state groups urged from time to time that the Public Utilities Commission be given broader regulatory powers. These suggestions were refined into a bill which periodically was introduced in the California Legislature, most recently as Assembly Bill No. 413, 1965 Session. To the author's great regret, the bill was passed and signed into law on June 17, 1965. The text of this Comment was prepared prior to the passage of the act and does not reflect this development.

The new act as passed amends Part 2 of Division 1 of the Public Utilities Code by adding a chapter (Chapter 4) regulating intrastate passenger air carriers. It gives the Public Utilities Commission full powers to regulate entry, rates, and such matters as ticketing, reservations, baggage handling and advertising. It does not provide for subsidy or compulsory service to unprofitable points. The Act contains a grandfather clause so worded that PSA is the only carrier likely to be eligible for a certificate of public convenience and necessity, without which no intrastate carrier is permitted to operate. . . .

flights are operated each weekday and more than 75 each Friday, Saturday, and Sunday. In March, 1965, more than 9,000 persons per day traveled between the two cities by air. The market has grown rapidly (it was only 3,500 persons per day in 1959) and has been characterized by intense competition, a wide variety of marketing strategies, and the lowest overland air fares in the world.

There are striking contrasts between the performance of this market and the performance of similar markets in the United States regulated by the CAB. For example, although the number of passengers traveling by air in the United States as a whole has increased between the years 1959 and 1964 by approximately 50 per cent, the number of travelers passing between Los Angeles and San Francisco by air has increased almost 300 per cent. Although the average jet coach fare level in the United States is approximately 5.5 cents per mile over stages considerably longer, and hence cheaper to operate, jet coach fare for the 350-mile trip from San Francisco to Los Angeles is approximately 3.9 cents per mile. Although the lowest fare between Boston and Washington, served only by CAB-certificated trunk carriers, is $24.65, Pacific Southwest Airlines, using the same modern turbo-prop equipment, carries passengers between Los Angeles and San Francisco, only 59 miles closer together, for $11.43. The jet fare is only $13.50. In other markets, obsolescent though economically viable aircraft have been rapidly retired as new aircraft have been introduced prematurely, because the fare structure has emphasized premium service and has not allowed the owner of obsolescent equipment to operate at a fare reflecting his lower capital costs. In Los Angeles-San Francisco, however, it has been common to see obsolescent equipment operated at fares reflecting the lower capital cost until replaced by new equipment so much more efficient that the capital cost charges could be amortized at fares which reflected customer demand for the new equipment.

This market is also characterized by relatively even traffic levels, without important daily or seasonal peaks. The market generates both business and "discretionary" travelers, hence the weekend traffic is slightly greater than the weekday traffic. But this discretionary travel is not seasonal, as it is in most vacation markets. This lack of pronounced peaks and dips enables a smaller carrier without other routes to employ equipment profitably on a consistent basis. The consistency makes planning more accurate for both large and small lines and contributes to the high level of efficiency which is both the cause and effect of lower fares.

Unlike most air transport markets, California is not today primarily a business and luxury market. Over 75 per cent of the travel between Los Angeles and San Francisco takes place by air. In the United States as a whole, only about 10 per cent of inter-city passengers use common carriers at all, and the airlines carry only about half of this traffic.

Four carriers are currently important factors in this market. Two of them, United Air Lines and Trans World Airlines, are among the "big four" trunklines. One of them, Western Air Lines, is one of the smallest, though one of the most profitable, domestic trunk carriers. The other, Pacific Southwest Airlines (PSA), is an intrastate carrier operating without a CAB certificate between San Francisco, Los Angeles, and San Diego. PSA is equipped with the most modern equipment and currently it and United share almost evenly over 70 per cent of the market.

The market shares of these airlines have reflected changing circumstances. General trends have emerged and then been reversed by changing competitive conditions. For example, United Air Lines' share of the market declined from a dominating 62 per cent to a barely participating 15 per cent from 1948 to the Spring of 1964, due to its unwillingness to adapt to changing competitive conditions. With United's decision to compete in earnest by offering jet service at low fares, its share rose rapidly, favored by its image as a "quality" airline, and it has regained its lost lead. PSA's share rose from insignificant in 1949 to a high of just over 50 per cent in Spring, 1962 (just before the first competitive response by the trunklines), and is presently about 35 per cent. PSA suffered from an equipment disadvantage when United entered its Boeing 727 jets in the market, but since April 9, 1965, PSA has had 727's of its own and is regaining lost ground. Western, traditionally a poor second to United among CAB-certificated carriers (1961 share: about 18 per cent), experienced spectacular growth starting in June, 1962, when it initiated low-fare services. Its market penetration reached a high of around 35 per cent, but it failed to respond quickly enough to United's jet bid and its market share is now approximately 19 per cent. Western has introduced jet service and is trying to regain some of its lost share. TWA was traditionally a follower in the market, with a historic market share of about 5 per cent. Recently it has promoted an aggressive pricing policy on its jet services and has increased its share to about 10.5 per cent.

At the beginning of 1949 United, Western, and TWA, certificated by the CAB, were the only carriers operating in the market. The generally high fare levels, the absence of restrictions on entry, the prevailing optimism about the future of air transportation, and the availability of used war-surplus transports stimulated the development of a group of small intrastate carriers in California. Low capital costs, minimum services, and high density seating kept unit costs low. By the end of the first year of operation only three of these lines—California Central, Pacific Southwest and Western Airlines of California—remained as significant factors in the market. (WAL of California, which leased equipment from and allegedly was financed by Western Airlines, Inc. is generally acknowledged to have been a "fighting ship" set up by Western for the purpose of driving the other operators out of business.) These "coach-class" carriers operated at rates which were less than half those charged by the certificated airlines (then $21.05 on United Airlines and TWA; $20.00 on Western Airlines), and were more or less ignored by United, TWA, and by Western's certificated operations. The new lines were an immediate public success and experienced load factors as high as 85 per cent. However, most of them were thinly financed and poorly managed. The largest, California Central Airlines, had considerable labor and management difficulties and finally went out of business in 1955. The smallest was PSA.

PSA was in insecure financial condition from 1952 to 1956 but by 1957 it was operating profitably, earning $196,606 in that year on revenues of $2,786,658. In 1958, its last full year of piston operation, PSA's earnings rose to $322,000 on revenues of $3,516,-000 and it carried 296,000 revenue passengers. In November of 1959, the carrier received its first three Lockheed Electras, modern turbo-prop aircraft designed for short-to-medium haul transportation. In 1960, its first full year operating this equipment, the carrier transported 621,000 passengers for revenues of $7,545,-309. According to the figures of a competitor, PSA carried 28 per cent of the total traffic between Los Angeles and San Francisco that year, as compared with 13 per cent the year before. By 1962 (its competitors still had failed to respond), PSA had increased its market penetration to 43 per cent and was now operating five Electras. The market had grown from an average of 3,500 passengers per day in 1959 to 4,200 in 1962.

On June 1, 1962, a trunk carrier for the first time responded to the competitive threat posed by PSA. Western Airlines initiated a $12.95 "Thriftair" fare between the two cities, operating obsolescent and fully depreciated DC-6B aircraft in a high-density 92-seat configuration. PSA's fare was $13.50 at the time. Western, traditionally opposed to unusually low fares, was able to operate at this low fare because it had no capital costs on the aircraft involved. The new service was an instant success, attracting either passengers who were interested in the lowest rate possible, or who were too timid to fly PSA because of its somewhat "unofficial" image (resulting from its lack of federal certification).

Thriftair became even more successful when Western abandoned the inconvenient "air bus" feature and began accepting reservations. Western's share of the market went from 15 per cent in 1961 to 32 per cent by the end of 1963, mostly at United's expense. The market continued to grow very rapidly reaching 6,800 passengers per day by the end of 1963. On February 25, 1963, Western reduced its Thriftair fare to $11.43 to increase the differential between its own and PSA's fares and thus minimize the diversionary effect of PSA's more modern Electra equipment. United's introduction of Jet Commuter service in the autumn of 1964 damaged Western's competitive position. Its now-obsolete piston equipment was inadequate competition for PSA's Electra turboprops and United's Boeing 727 jets. Western ordered four Boeing 720B's (the type it operates on long-haul routes) with special high-density seating (146 seats) for use on its California routes. It reduced but did not eliminate its DC-6B Thriftair schedules in an attempt to maintain market identity pending the introduction of the jets on April 1, 1965.

In September of 1964, after its share of the market had shrunk from 62 per cent in 1949 to 15 per cent in June of 1964, United became a serious competitor. It introduced two of its brand-new Boeing 727 jets, aircraft designed specifically for high frequency operation over short routes and offering very low aircraft-mile costs and correspondingly low seat-mile costs. These aircraft were operated exclusively between the two cities, creating an airline-within-an-airline. They were set up in a high-density configuration (114 seats) and were offered at $14.50 one way, only one dollar higher than PSA's Electra fare. Although the Boeing 727 as operated by United over this route does not offer a significant time advantage over PSA's turboprop aircraft,[99] the demonstrated consumer preference for new aircraft and jet service permitted this fare differential.

United's new service was immediately successful, and ultimately regained for it the leadership position which it had abdicated. Its well-tried marketing image, the new equipment, and the low fare attracted passengers, especially businessmen (who have traditionally favored United). Load factors were about 80 per cent, the maximum tolerable without passenger inconvenience in an operation of this kind. Initially, United operated four round trips per day using two aircraft. Within six months, it had increased the frequency to twenty round trips per day using four aircraft. Ad-

---

[99] This is because of the relatively short distance between the two cities and the elaborate air traffic procedures which United's method of operation requires. . . . PSA flies the route in its Electra in 60 minutes, while United's 727 flies it in 55 minutes.

vertising stimulated traffic. Market growth was spectacular. Even with United's quintupled scheduling, load factors remained at a comfortable and profitable two-thirds.

Despite the new competition, PSA's traffic continued to grow, although at a slower rate. To compete with United, it ordered six Boeing 727 jets for service which started April 9, 1965. It is operating these jets at $13.50 (the former Electra fare between San Francisco and Los Angeles), and United has lowered its $14.50 fare to match PSA. Western's Boeing 720B jets are offered at the $13.50 fare.

Competition has in the past prevented the market from becoming static, and the participants are now preparing for an uncertain but promising future. Because of the great productivity of PSA's and Western's jets, the capacity on this route will soon be at least tripled compared with September, 1964. Any over-capacity problem might be even more acute if PSA does not change its decision to retain its Electras. They could still be sold at a favorable price in view of the Electra's high resale value. PSA will have to find or make a market for capacity $3\frac{1}{2}$ times its March output.

Western's four-engine, 250,000 pound Boeing 720B is hardly the ideal aircraft for short haul operation. Although its aircraft-mile cost is quite low for a plane of its size and its seat-mile cost perhaps even lower than the 727's, it is a very large economic unit. Since its full capacity will be used only at peak periods, the high capital costs, the high aircraft-mile cost, the complicated ground servicing requirements and longer turn-around time may make it difficult to compete effectively on the route. Western's allocation of 720B's to this route may signify a return to the "fighting-ship" philosophy that occasioned the establishment of Western Airlines of California in 1949. Now, as then, their capital commitment is such that the aircraft could be returned to regular services, were Western to decide either that the experiment had succeeded in eliminating the "upstart" competition or that, as in 1949, such tactics were doomed to failure. It could then convert the 720B's into its normal configuration for use on more appropriate routes. Western might offer San Francisco to Los Angeles seats on its interstate flights south, and Los Angeles to San Francisco seats on its interstate flights north. This would enable them to maintain some market identity, much in the same way as TWA does.

United has considerable resources, including over sixty Boeing 727 jets in service or on order, so that if necessary more aircraft could be committed to the market. The use of this equipment would not be costless. Aside from the opportunity cost of not using it elsewhere, United must convert this equipment, since it operates the 727 on the Los Angeles-San Francisco route in a seating configuration not used elsewhere.

B. *Conclusions*

The economic evils which the air transport industry and its regulators fear will occur without regulation have not materialized in the Los Angeles-San Francisco market. Competition has not been "ruinous." Despite low fare levels, efficient firms have been able to operate profitably. PSA, with no other important source of income, has operated at a profit since 1957, and continues to do so in the face of competition from United. United's Jet Commuter service has been profitable. During the 1962-1964 period, Thriftair returned a profit for Western, but market developments since United's low-fare entry have turned this profit into a loss. Western's active promotion of its "Fanjet Commuter" suggests that it believes it can make a profit with the new service, but the overcapacity situation which the new equipment has created makes it almost certain that one of the competitors will be badly burned. Past history suggests that the burned party will be the least efficient or least adaptable firm. This market has, from the introduction of intrastate coach-class service in 1949, rewarded handsomely effective marketing and operation and penalized ruthlessly poor judgment and inefficiency.

PSA's success refutes the contention that air transport is a natural-monopoly industry. Once minimum efficient size has been reached, larger scale does not confer cost advantages. There is evidence that PSA's operating costs are lower than either United's or Western's.[109] PSA's operation is notable for its efficiency, fresh thinking, and high level of customer acceptance. It is clear that no other carrier, including United with its enormous resources (1964 revenues more than thirty times PSA's), is a more effective competitor in this market. PSA has an operation well-suited to the particular needs of its route. It preserves both an underdog

---

[109] PSA achieves a higher utilization of its equipment than its competitors, thus achieving lower capital costs per unit output. Its fuel costs are lower, because its captains spend less time on approach and climb-out due to PSA's flight procedure. . . . Since the days when its DC-3's had 31 seats, compared to the 28 of its competitors, PSA has always managed somehow to squeeze a few extra seats into the aircraft it operates. Its 727's have 122 seats, compared to United's 114, because PSA ordered its equipment without full galleys, since meals are not served on this route. United, having ordered its 727's with its system needs in mind, carries the weight and space of the idle equipment. At most times the extra seats make no difference, but at peak hours, when the load factor approaches 100%, the extra seats mean extra revenue.

appeal to the public, and an identification as a California product. It has had no difficulty financing the purchase of the most modern equipment and in this respect can only be equalled and not surpassed by its larger competitors. PSA may even have an advantage over Western, whose commitments to other routes influence it in such a way as to prevent its competing with maximum efficiency in the Los Angeles-San Francisco market. For example, rather than purchase 727's for the route, Western chose to standardize its equipment and purchased less appropriate 720B's which were already in service on its longer routes. PSA, with a fleet geared specifically to the California commuter market, and United, with its vast, diversified fleet, are in better technological positions than Western, which is neither small enough to specialize nor large enough to diversify.

PSA may even have advantages over United. Geared as it is to service in markets which emphasize premium passenger comfort and which have protected entry and fare structures, United is not experienced in the kind of marketing, passenger-handling and aircraft-handling techniques demanded by an unprotected market with an experienced and sophisticated clientele. PSA's small size makes it a less tempting target for unionization. This advantage makes possible more flexible use of personnel. PSA's flight operations are more informal than either United's or Western's, and captains have more discretion in flight planning and execution. For example, in the favorable flying weather which is usual in California, PSA's captains by VFR (Visual Flight Rules). This permits them to omit lengthy instrument approaches and departures, and results in a consistent 15 per cent reduction in flight time, which saves money for PSA. United and Western operate their California routes IFR (Instrument Flight Rules) in uniformity with their other routes, most of which are operated under less favorable flying conditions.

Lack of regulation has not caused chaos in California. Unregulated entry and price competition have not resulted in a multitude of tiny firms scrambling for passengers to the confusion of the general public. As the California market developed, advanced technology and effective marketing became essential to profitable operation; and it became increasingly difficult for a thinly-capitalized fringe operator to survive. Ultimately, no more than three important competitors remained, along with TWA's holding operation and, periodically, a fringe operator trying to find a niche in the market.

The history of Trans California Airlines illustrates the difficulties faced by a fringe operator in a mature competitive market. Trans California commenced operations in the summer of 1962.

The line operated four obsolete piston-engined Constellations and charged a fare of $10.99 one way and $21.00 round trip. It ceased operations in the fall of 1964, apparently unable to make a profit, although it was carrying more than 10,000 passengers per month at the time of its demise. The fare structure is so competitive in this market that it was unable to continue operating at fares low enough to attract passengers to its obsolete equipment.

Caves, in a discussion of capital barriers to entry and market structures,[114] cites a study by United Research, Inc., in concluding that four or five carriers are the most a well-developed short to medium-haul market can support at any one time.[115] Both marketing and technological costs account for this limitation.[116] This analysis is borne out by the California experience, and indicates that the public has little to fear from unregulated entry. Participants in a market will be naturally limited to a number which ensures both competition and technical efficiency without chaos. The free-entry California market has and will have for the immediate future approximately the same structure—two to three major carriers—as most regulated routes. The important question is whether these carriers ought to be chosen administratively or by the competitive forces of the market. And the important difference is that transportation by air in the California unregulated market can be purchased for half to seven-tenths as much as it costs elsewhere.

Structural stability should not be confused with stagnation. Although the number of firms servicing a market will remain (and have remained in California) more or less constant over time, no particular firm is guaranteed continued participation. There are no barriers to entry in the California market sufficient to protect an entrenched firm from its own inefficiency or uncompetitive pricing. PSA's successful entry in 1949 at the expense of then entrenched United attests to the ease of entry at that time. Now, PSA is strongly in favor of the licensing bill currently before the legislature. Certain of a certificate if the bill were to be enacted, PSA insists that some official distinction should protect it from the inroads of new competition. This attitude is a recognition that there is an ever-present possibility of new competition in this market. Absolute capital requirements are now considerably greater than in 1949 and the war-surplus aircraft market no longer provides obsolescent equipment at greatly reduced cost, but bar-

---

114 Caves, *op. cit. supra* note 42, at 84-97.
115 *Id.* at 96.
116 *Ibid.* This is in part because substantial scheduling and therefore substantial investment is required to create and maintain even a minimum market "identity."

riers to entry have not prevented new competition from material-
izing in the recent past. Although Trans California was unable
to survive and a prospective entrant, California Airlines, has been
unable to create a sufficiently stable capital structure to satisfy the
FAA's safety requirements, neither line's difficulties stem from
entry barriers. Rather, fares are so low and service so good that
there is little unsatisfied consumer demand. Hence, capital is not
attracted to the market. If the fares were to rise or the service
to deteriorate, new opportunities for profit might well attract new
capital.

Low fares, intensive advertising and constant innovation in
service account for the spectacular growth of the Los Angeles-San
Francisco market. This growth indicates that at least here there
is elasticity of demand for air transportation. In 1949, a Public
Utilities Commission survey disclosed that only 34 per cent of all
passengers using the newly created and inexpensive uncertificated
airlines had been diverted from regular certificated carriers. The
remaining 65 per cent either had been diverted from surface
transportation, or but for the inexpensive air transportation
would have taken no trip at all. Thus the intrastate carriers
themselves were the first impact on the market. PSA acquired
Electra equipment in 1959 and almost doubled its passenger traffic
that year. Two years later, its traffic had almost doubled again.
Even more important, during this three year period, while passengers carried in air transportation had increased for the United
States as a whole by only 10 per cent, the California market had
grown by 30 per cent. When Western introduced Thriftair in
1962, the market expanded significantly; and Western's fare reduction on Thriftair in 1963 resulted in spectacular market
growth. United's well-advertised introduction of low fare jet service almost doubled its patronage in the first nine months of operation. Between 1959 and 1964 while the United States market
grew by only 50 per cent, the California market grew by 300 per
cent.

Both the 1949 survey and the continuing attraction of great
[numbers] of travelers to air transportation suggest that the high
level of discretionary traffic over this route is an effect of low
fares. The coincidence of innovation in service plus fare reduc-
tions and spectacular market growth suggests that innovation and
low fares have in large part *caused* the market growth.

Despite the impressive and continuing "coincidence" of innovation, fare reduction and market growth, some observers trace
the growth to causes other than lack of regulation. Western Airlines, for instance, takes the position that:

[Los Angeles-San Francisco] . . . has become the world's busiest air route because of certain distinctive peculiarities which
pertain to no other route.

Most important is that the route links two large metropolitan
areas within the same state. This enables intrastate carriers to
operate without regulations by the CAB.

The two cities are 340 air miles apart. Nowhere are there
two such large cities that far apart in the same state. Furthermore, the distance is just a bit too far for comfortable ground
travel.

Los Angeles and San Francisco are located in the fastest growing part of the country. Historically, however, this development has been recent. These cities have grown to maturity
essentially in the Air Age. Ground transportation between the
two cities is not as well developed as in the East. There are,
for example, only two main highways and one railroad.

Another unique feature of this market is that the two cities—
though in the same state—are quite different. Each has its own
tourist attractions, its own charm, and a different climate.

There is far greater difference between these two cities than
between New York and Boston, which comprise the second
busiest air route in the world.

These assertions are incorrect, or at least very misleading.

That the two cities are 340 air miles apart is not unusual, unless
their location within the same state has been crucial to market
development. There are other city-pairs 340 air miles apart or
more which exchange large amounts of air traffic which have not
experienced the same growth. Location of the two cities within
the same state may create certain commercial and social ties. But
there is a similar if not quite as extensive community of interest
among the cities of the Northeast corridor (Boston, New York,
Philadelphia, and Washington) and between Chicago, Detroit,
Cleveland and New York.

Whatever "distinctive peculiarities" may account for the heavy
traffic between Los Angeles and San Francisco, that traffic need
not move by air. Ground transportation, according to the article
limited to two main highways and one railroad, is as adequate
here as elsewhere. Between Chicago and Cleveland there is one
main highway and one railroad, between Chicago and Pittsburgh
one main highway and one railroad, between Chicago and New
York one main highway and two passenger railroads, between
New York and Washington one main highway and one railroad,
and between New York and Boston one main highway and one
railroad.

On the other hand, Western takes note of the fact that the intrastate carriers can operate this route without CAB regulation. This is an implicit admission that the stimulus of competition has been an important factor in market development. The spurts in development in 1949, 1959, and 1962 have coincided too closely with competitive innovation to be discounted as accidental.

IV. A Proposal

Regulation of United States air transportation is predicated upon erroneous economic assumptions and results in unnecessarily high fares, disguised inefficiencies (such as premature replacement of equipment) and a lack of genuinely diversified service. The CAB should draw a lesson for national regulation from the Los Angeles-San Francisco market and amend the present regulatory scheme so that all markets are freed from restrictive economic regulation. The result of such deregulation would be to introduce competitive pricing on much of the national air transportation system.

Competitive pricing is unlikely to appeal to those who benefit from the protection built into the present system. The trunklines, currently protected against any real risk of demise, would undoubtedly object that the result of their twenty-five years of hard work was being taken from them. The knowledge that at least $400,000,000 has been given them in direct subsidy as a reward for their efforts or that the opportunities for unfettered competition would be almost unlimited probably would not pacify them. Despite Western's doubling of its market share between 1961 and 1963—a period during which its only important service change was the introduction of low-fare services— Western has been one of the most vociferous opponents of experimental fare reductions. And PSA, having benefited by the opportunity to enter the market free of artificial restraints, now supports legislation which would end that freedom. The free market affords opportunities to entrepreneurs from which already established firms seek to protect themselves.

Present beneficiaries of internal subsidy would probably oppose deregulation. Of course, subsidized service could be continued, but in a deregulated system the burden would fall on the beneficiaries, national or local, rather than on economically unrelated consumers. Localities accustomed to having others pay for local benefits are unlikely to welcome the opportunity to carry the burden themselves.

Any attempted deregulation would no doubt be accompanied by the usual industry warnings of impaired safety. California shows that an unregulated market is not inherently unsafe. PSA has never experienced a fatal accident. The most recent intra-state entrant, Trans California, experienced no safety problems during the two years it was in operation. The FAA will continue to enforce safety standards as prerequisites to entry and continued operation. It can always raise the standards or expand its enforcement activities.

Competitive pricing could be introduced on present-day routes either simply by abandoning route restrictions on existing trunklines, or by allowing entry to any qualified applicant. In either case carriers would still be required to file tariffs and adhere to them. Changes would be made simply by notice. Adherence to tariffs would prevent chaos and ensure sufficient certainty to enable consumers to calculate costs conveniently. However, abandoning route restrictions by allowing existing trunklines to compete would be unnecessarily restrictive. One of the reasons for PSA's success is that it "specializes" in accommodating itself to the needs of a particular market. Such specialists might well establish themselves elsewhere if given the chance. Furthermore, in California many innovations and efficiencies have been generated by carriers trying to establish themselves in a market where other carriers already have competitive "identities." Low-fare service, better operational and passenger-handling techniques, and new marketing approaches have all been pioneered in California by the intrastate carriers. Similarly, in the national market, the non-scheduled airlines provided the impetus for the trunk carriers to initiate coach service. The established trunk lines resisted this innovation.

Moreover, the airspace is public property, restrictions on the use of which were initially imposed in response to fears of economic evils. Since examination of the Los Angeles-San Francisco market shows that these fears are unjustified, there is no reason why we need continue to deny the opportunity to serve the public to those prepared to risk capital to do so. It is neither wise political nor economic policy to mark out an area of activity as the preserve of a few corporations who have the good fortune to have been operating on May 14, 1938. If these corporations, with their vast experience and talent resources, are able to adapt to competition, they should find themselves better off for it—more flexible, free of government interference, and expanding rapidly as previously untapped markets are developed. If not, it is to the public's advantage that the operation of the air transportation system be placed in more capable hands.

Allowing *any* qualified applicant to operate on competitive routes would provide a maximum competitive impetus to the market. This approach would decentralize investment decisions, eliminate the possibility of collusive agreements between grandfather carriers, and reward entrepreneurial talent. Market composition would no longer be selected arbitrarily, and public air space would become a public resource.

However, the political opposition from established carriers and subsidized communities which is certain to attend any attempted deregulation will most likely require a cautious CAB to adopt a more limited approach. But discretion is the better part of caution. If the CAB were to experiment by selecting one market to be deregulated provisionally, the established carriers might ensure the experiment's failure. They could price below cost, regarding the resulting loss as an investment, since the "failure" of the experiment would mean a return to protection and an opportunity to recoup.

Opening several markets at one time would make destructive tactics by the trunk carriers less likely, since the investment required would be greater and any attempt to compensate by requesting fare increases on their protected routes could be frustrated by an alert CAB. The difficulty with this approach is that the likelihood of the experiment proceeding without artificial distortion will increase as more traffic is affected, but so will the political opposition. The higher the rate of deregulation the greater the expected outcry from established carriers and "desubsidized" communities.

Perhaps the most politically viable alternative would be for the Board to select a limited number of new carriers to compete in high-density markets. Although this is not the most satisfactory alternative from an economic standpoint, the certification and subsequent performance of Trans Caribbean Airways in the New York-San Juan market demonstrates that such carriers, if properly selected, could dramatically [affect] existing fare levels and service patterns.[129] This approach would not produce the flexibility and

---

[129] Trans Caribbean, formerly an irregular carrier, was certificated by the Board in 1957. 26 C.A.B. 72. A temporary certificate was granted on the condition that the carrier develop a low fare service. Even before Trans Caribbean received its certificate, Pan American and Eastern (the then existing carriers on the route), lowered fares to the level of Trans Caribbean's proposed tariff. The market has grown rapidly, and Trans Caribbean has been a consistent force for low fare levels. Service at the "thrift," or lowest, fare, constituted much less than half the New York-San Juan traffic in the two years before Trans Caribbean was certificated. Trans Caribbean's aggressive promotion of even lower fares, and the competitive responses forced on American and Eastern as a result, almost doubled traffic in six years. Over 90% of the traffic at the new level travelled at the lowest fare. Trans Caribbean Airways, Direct Exhibit before the Civil Aeronautics Board, United States-Caribbean-South America Investigation, Docket No. 12895, 1965, Exhibits TC-151, p. 1; TC-156, p. 1; TC-155, p. 1.

self-regulation characteristic of a free market. Nor would it cure the present system's defect of requiring administrative determinations on matters which would be better left to the market.

Despite difficulties, deregulation, whether complete, partial, or even experimental, is worth trying. It would cost the public nothing and could point the way to a new era of mass travel. Even completely free entry would not lead to monopoly or cut-throat competition, but to a stable market configuration in which individual competitors would change relative market shares or even go out of business, but in which no more than a few carriers would operate at any one time. Free entry would not lead to oligopoly because entry costs are not too high to discourage potential competitors and the established firms would therefore be forced to keep fares low enough to avoid attracting new entrants. Subsidized service could be retained, eliminated, or modified.

Nothing prevents the Board from liberally construing the licensing provisions of the Act. Nothing would "preserve the inherent advantages of air transportation" so well as permitting its active development on the widest scale. Nothing could as effectively accomplish the "promotion, encouragement and development of civil aeronautics," as regulation which promoted high output and the prosperity of the most efficient. And nothing would as dramatically accomplish "the encouragement and development of an air transportation system properly adapted to the . . . needs of . . . the United States" as a market operating to bring transportation within the reach of consumers who are today excluded. If the success of the Los Angeles-San Francisco market were duplicated nationally, the result would be a transportation system unique in the world. A nation in which everyone could aspire to a breadth of experience hitherto reserved for tramps and retired physicians would be a remarkable place, indeed.

NOTES AND QUESTIONS

1. Levine uses at least three distinct methods to determine and evaluate the impact of airline regulation. First, he uses an *economic model* of what the airline industry would be like in the absence of regulation that restricted entry and controlled price competition. Without regulation, the opportunities for profit and the need to make an appropriate return on investment would determine the number of carriers, if any, flying between city-pairs and the type of service they would offer. Competition or the threat of competition would exert a pressure to keep fares down and the quality of service up. Next, Levine looks at the argu-

ments for regulation in situations where economic factors distort the market model so that it does not work to produce the benefits normally expected. Here he relies on *data* collected by others about the characteristics of the airline industry. For example, one assumption in the market model is ease of entry, either into a particular city-pair or into the industry itself. A railroad that found the Milwaukee to Minneapolis route unprofitable could not easily withdraw and turn to the Chicago to San Francisco route since it would have enormous costs in buying right-of-way and laying track. Thus, those railroads presently on the Chicago to San Francisco route need fear little new competition. Levine argues that this is not true in the case of airlines since the planes and ground support used to fly from Milwaukee to Minneapolis could be diverted or they could be sold on the used plane market and new equipment more suited for the longer trip purchased. Finally, Levine conducts a *case-study* of the unregulated Los Angeles to San Francisco route. He argues that, as the economic model would predict, PSA has innovated both in terms of price and type of service, and forced the larger carriers to benefit the public by meeting PSA's competition. He then is willing to generalize that, absent regulation by the CAB, essentially the California result would be found on all routes between cities approximately 400 miles apart. Since he likes the California result, he is willing to advocate ending regulation.

2. In measuring the impact of law, one problem is the absence of a *control*; that is, one rarely is able to say with confidence what behavior *would* have been like had a law *not* been passed or had a different law been passed. Schwartz and Orleans (Reading 26, at 249, *supra*) tried to solve the problem experimentally. Outside of the laboratory, it is often difficult to apply an experimental treatment to a group which one has matched in all significant respects to another group which does not receive that treatment.

In the absence of a control group or a true experiment, the effectiveness of particular rules of law may be extremely hard to measure. One can, with some difficulty, discover behavior that *seems* to be related to the existence of a rule of law, but how can one be sure whether the behavior would have been different if the law had not been passed? Take the antitrust laws, for example. Since 1890, there has been some federal legislation outlawing monopoly. One can measure the activity of the government: how many antitrust suits brought; how many companies prosecuted. It is much harder to determine the degree of concentration of industry that would have obtained in the absence of regulation.

Without a control group, the social scientist may make use of theory: theory, in other words, acts as an imaginary control group. The social scientist tries to match reality against some theoretical model. In measuring the effect of government regulation, an economist can use, instead of a control group, what economic theory tells him would have been the results of non-regulation. Since economic theory is more rigorous, exact and highly developed than theory in other social sciences, there have been more and more varied uses of economic theory as an imaginary control group to measure the effectiveness of law than is true of theory in other social sciences. *See, e.g.,* Henry G. Manne, *Insider Trading and the Stock Market* 77-110 (Free Press 1966), on the effects of different legal rules on insider trading, on the stock market and on noninside traders.

There has also developed a fairly rich literature of evaluation of actual and proposed programs of law using criteria derived from economics as the standard. This literature has a strong normative flavor to it; that is, it takes certain economic goals or axioms as its basic values, and assesses legal programs and doctrines as good or bad, depending upon whether they most efficiently or rationally achieve the economic goals or make use of theoretically correct economic means. In this regard, the literature is somewhat comparable to classical American legal writing, which is highly normative, and is constantly testing and measuring doctrines, case-results and legal theories in accordance with whether or not they are good or bad, liberal or narrow, modern or archaic. The difference—and it is a crucial one—is that the criteria for normative judgments are not "legal" but economic or strongly tinged with economic criteria, and that these criteria are open, examined, and explicit rather than implicit. The literature includes such works as Walter J. Blum & Harry Kalven, Jr., *The Uneasy Case for Progressive Taxation* (U. of Chicago Press 1953), and their study of the automobile accident problem, *Public Law Perspectives on a Private Law Problem* (U. of Chicago Press 1965). Risk allocation in the law of torts has been imaginatively treated by Guido Calabresi, beginning with "Some Thoughts on Risk Distribution and the Law of Torts," 70 *Yale Law Journal* 499 (1961). *See also* Frank J. Michelman, "Property, Utility, and Fairness: Comments on the Ethical Foundations of 'Just Compensation' Law," 80 *Harvard Law Review* 1165 (1967); William F. Baxter, "Legal Restrictions on Exploitation of the Patent Monopoly: An Economic Analysis," 76 *Yale Law Journal* 267 (1966).

The works cited have been written by law professors. Some economists, too, have tried to describe, analyze or evaluate the legal system (or parts of it) in terms of economic theory. *See, e.g.,* E. J. Mishan, "Pareto Optimality and the Law," *Oxford Economic Papers,* Nov. 1967, at 255; Gary S. Becker, "Crime and Punishment; an Economic Approach," 76 *Journal of Political Economy* 169 (1968); Simon Rottenberg, "The Clandestine Distribution of Heroin, Its Discovery and Suppression," 76 *Journal of Political Economy* 78 (1968).

3. The economist's model, generally speaking, is the theoretical picture of how a competitive market would operate. The theory was developed by the classical economists, but it has been generally acquiesced in as to *some* of its basic features by virtually all modern economists. Is there any comparable model in the other social sciences? in legal scholarship?

4. How important is the existence of an economic model of unregulated competition in Levine's study of the impact of CAB regulation? Would Levine's methods help one determine the likely impact of a change in the grounds for divorce in a particular state?

5. How important are the data collected by others to Levine's argument? For example, Levine relies on material in Richard E. Caves, *Air Transport and Its Regulators* (Harvard U. Press 1962) to establish a number of facts: that ease of entry into particular city-pairs is not difficult; that ease of entry into the airline business itself is not significantly difficult; and that there is an effective market for used aircraft. However, most of Caves' data refer to the industry before jet aircraft were introduced or before the many different types of jet aircraft that can be purchased today became available. Jet aircraft are much more expensive than the propeller aircraft they replaced. Suppose Caves' data no longer apply to conditions in the industry because of these technological changes. Does Levine still have an argument?

6. To what extent does the economic model increase the respect due generalizations drawn from Levine's case-study of the Los Angeles-San Francisco route? Without it, would you question applying the lessons drawn by Levine to the New Orleans-Memphis route? the Boston-Washington, D.C. route? the Atlanta-Pittsburgh route? Even with it, do you have any qualms about such generalizations?

38. The New York Expert Testimony Project: Some Reflections on Legal Experiments

HANS ZEISEL*

8 STANFORD LAW REVIEW 730 (1956)

IMPARTIAL MEDICAL TESTIMONY. By The Association of the Bar of the City of New York. New York: The Macmillan Company. 1956. ix + 188 pages. $3.95.

A legal innovation tentatively introduced on a limited scale is usually called an experiment. Yet even when such an experiment, in the colloquial sense of the word, is accompanied by systematic and skillful fact gathering, it will fail to reveal all the relevant effects. Only a scientifically designed, controlled experiment will do this. But the essence of a scientific experiment is to apply the experimental procedure to one group, and to withhold it from another one, called the control group. It would seem that the law, with its supreme notion of equality, cannot easily tolerate such discrimination.

It is the burden of this commentary that as we advance our notion of the law as a rational means of social control, we might reconsider this position.

These thoughts were stimulated by the recently published Report on the Medical Expert Testimony Project in the New York courts, an important milestone in the development of our civil procedures. . . .

On December 1, 1952, by a special rule from the reform-conscious first department of the appellate division, and with the help of some outside funds, the Supreme Court for the County of New York became the testing ground for an innovation in personal injury trials. Judges in this court, if in their opinion

---

* Professor of Law and Sociology, Law School, University of Chicago. The reproduction is from a book review-article first published in the July 1956 issue of the Stanford Law Review. Copyright 1956 by the Board of Trustees of the Leland Stanford Junior University.

such a procedure "would be of material aid to the just determination of the case," were empowered, after consultation with
counsel, to have the plaintiff examined by a court appointed
physician without cost to the parties. The physician is selected
from a panel, jointly prepared for this purpose by the New York
Academy of Medicine and the New York County Medical Society.
The physician is then supplied with all the medical reports in
the case, examines the patient and reports to the court, which in
turn makes the report available to the parties. Either party or
the judge may call the court expert as a witness and the parties
retain their right to call their own physician.

The Report consists of three parts: the committee report itself,
giving history and description of the plan, the experiences with it
and the results of two years of its operation; an evaluation of
the plan by the medical consultant, and miscellaneous exhibits of
forms, statistics and thumbnail summaries by the judges of the
cases disposed of after referral.

Three major accomplishments are claimed:

1. A marked increase in the number of settlements and thereby a reduction of the formidable case load of the court.

2. An improvement in the standards of justice through provision of a better process for finding the medical facts, which in
turn leads to fairer settlements and verdicts.

3. Improvement of the standards of medical diagnosis in the
field of traumatic legal medicine.

With the help of many persuasive data and inferences therefrom, the Report makes all these claims quite plausible. In fact,
the appellate division was so well satisfied with the new procedure that it decided to incorporate it as a permanent feature into
trials of personal injury cases.

To one who, as this writer, grew up in a legal tradition which
knew only impartial experts, this innovation recommends itself
naturally. But common-law lawyers may react less favorably and
may hold some or all of the views ascribed by the Report to "a
few judges and lawyers [who] have been disturbed by the special
status occupied by an impartial expert. They feel that . . . he
may usurp the functions of judge and jury. Medicine . . . is not
an exact science. . . . The opinion of a famous doctor is not
necessarily better than that of an obscure one."

And yet, with somewhat more rigor in the design of this experiment, data could have been provided which would prove (or disprove) these claims to the satisfaction of the most critical observer.

It may be instructive to put together both the evidence cited for each of the major claims and the outline of a procedure which would provide more rigorous proof.

I

The first claim concerns the increase in the number of settlements. The evidence for it is derived from one statistic and one assumption. The statistic is summarized from the descriptive text of the Report in the following table:

TABLE I

Aftermath of the 238 Cases Referred to Impartial Experts

Settled	120
in pre trial	66
before trial	36
during trial	18*
Removed to Municipal Court (claim reduced	
below the Supreme Court minimum)	9
Tried	18*
Neither settled nor yet tried	84
Examination pending	7
	238

----

* Of the 36 (18 + 18) cases that reached trial, not less than 17 were bench trials. This is, compared with the normal run of cases, a high percentage and suggests (no more) that the appointment of a court expert might also be conducive to jury waiver.

The assumption is "that most of the cases disposed of through the assistance of the Medical Expert Testimony Project . . . would have had to be tried. . . ." By relating the number of settled cases (120) to the annual number of personal injury trials in these courts (600), the Report concludes that the new procedure "would account for eliminating one-fifth of the number of trials which took place . . . while the Project was in operation." While this may indeed be true, these data hardly prove it because we cannot yet for any group of cases predict with certainty which will reach trial and which will be settled, if only at the last minute. Yet, a different method of selecting the cases for referral to the medical expert would provide data from which the accelerated elimination of cases could be estimated with great accuracy.

All personal injury claims filed would have to be randomly divided into three groups of equal size:

Group (*a*): The parties in this group would be notified that the court would under *all* circumstances appoint a neutral medical expert if a divergence between the adversary experts should appear, and the case should not be settled within a reasonable time.

Group (*b*): The parties in this group would be notified that under *no* circumstances would the court appoint a neutral expert.

Group (*c*): The parties in this group would be notified that the court *might* appoint such an expert if it thought thereby to further the cause of justice.

By comparing the progress of the settlement and jury waiver ratios in groups (*a*) and (*b*), the *direct* effect of the referral to impartial experts could be estimated.

By comparing these ratios in groups (*c*) and (*b*), the *indirect* effect of the referral procedure could be estimated, since the parties in group (*c*) might be expected to act under threat of such potential referral. This second comparison would either prove or disprove what now to the Report merely "seems highly probable," namely, "that the very existence of the Project . . . tends to deter doctors and lawyers from making . . . grossly exaggerated medical claims."

Yet even the figures given in the Report raise and half answer a puzzling question: Why was no impartial expert appointed in the 600 personal injury cases which were not settled and did reach trial? I am informed it was because the divergence of medical testimony was not sufficiently important as compared with the question of liability. But whatever the reason for the limited use of this new institution, one must expect from it at best limited court relief.

NOTES AND QUESTIONS

1. Zeisel in a later part of his review, discusses the constitutional problems of the controlled experiment technique he advocates. "The law cannot permit experiments that involve elimination of a right which the due process clause guarantees under all circumstances." Suppose a community legal services program created by the Office of Economic Opportunity decided to run an experiment. They carefully matched pending cases into pairs. In those instances where both matched defendants represented by them were found guilty by a jury, in one case they would prepare a brief supplementing and challenging the conclusions of the social worker who writes a presentence report for the judge, but in the other case the program would do nothing. After enough

cases had occurred, the Legal Services Program would have some idea about the importance of this practice if the sentences given by various judges showed a significant difference between cases where the practice was followed and cases where it was not. Do you see any due process, equal protection or ethical problems with this experiment?

2. How do you set up a true controlled experiment to test the impact of legal rules or practices? Can you ever control matters sufficiently so that you are sure that your results reflect only the variable you think you are testing? Could Levine have designed a true controlled experiment to test the impact of CAB regulation on the airlines? Do you see any political problems in putting such an experiment into practice if it could be designed? Maurice Rosenberg, *The Pretrial Conference and Effective Justice: A Controlled Test in Personal Injury Litigation* (Columbia U. Press 1964), reports on a true controlled experiment, to test the efficacy of pretrial conferences in New Jersey as a mode of solving certain problems of judicial administration. Practically, is the controlled experiment limited to this kind of nonpolitical question?

3. How do we typically test the impact of a law? For example, how do we know that Prohibition was a failure?

4. With funding from OEO, and under the supervision of the Institute for Research in Poverty of the University of Wisconsin, an experiment was mounted in New Jersey, beginning in 1968, to test the impact of proposed plans for a "negative income tax." Poor families will be given cash payments over a three-year period, and carefully tested to see how these payments affect their work and spending habits. Control groups of nonpoor families, and poor families who will not receive the payments, will also be studied.

5. There are many examples of what Zeisel calls a "legal innovation tentatively introduced on a limited scale"; but these, he says, are not scientific. Among these experiments are all sorts of "pilot" and "demonstration" projects run by government agencies. Why are they not "scientific"? Is it inherently impossible for them to achieve true "science"?

39. The Connecticut Crackdown on Speeding: Time-Series Data in Quasi-Experimental Analysis

DONALD T. CAMPBELL AND
H. LAURENCE ROSS*

3 LAW & SOCIETY REVIEW 33 (1968)

Social research frequently encounters the task of evaluating change produced in nonrandomly selected groups by events which are beyond the researcher's control. The social scientist must verify that there has in fact been a change, and that the indicated event is its cause. Illustrations are manifold: a state terminates capital punishment, and proponents of this type of punishment predict an increase in the murder rate; a school is integrated, and supporters of the reform expect to find an increase in the positive self-evaluation of Negro pupils; a natural disaster occurs in a community, and altruistic behavior is expected to increase. Because in these situations the investigator has no control over the assignment of individuals or groups to "experimental" and "control" situations, the logic of the classical experiment must be reexamined in a search for optimal interpretative procedures.

This paper introduces, in the context of a problem in applied sociology and the sociology of law, a mode of analysis designed to deal with a common class of situations in which research must proceed without the benefit of experimental control. The general methodology expounded here is termed "quasi-experimental analysis." The specific mode of analysis is the "interrupted time-series design." Perhaps its fundamental credo is that lack of control and lack of randomization are damaging to inferences of cause and effect only to the extent that a systematic consideration

* Donald T. Campbell, Professor of Sociology, Northwestern University; H. Laurence Ross, Professor of Law and Sociology, University of Denver College of Law. Reprinted from Law and Society Review. Copyright © 1968 by the Law and Society Association. Reprinted by permission.

of alternative explanations reveals some that are plausible. More complete explications of quasi-experimental analysis have appeared elsewhere;[1] this paper will merely illustrate its use in a situation where a series of observations has been recorded for periods of time both prior and subsequent to the experience of the specific event to be studied. Such data are quite commonly available, yet they are seldom fully utilized and investigators often confine themselves unnecessarily to much less satisfactory methodologies. The 1955 crackdown on speeding in the State of Connecticut furnishes an apt example of the potentialities of such quasi-experimental analysis.

In 1955, 324 people were killed in automobile accidents on the highways of Connecticut. Deaths by motor vehicle accidents had reached a record high for the decade of the fifties as the usually hazardous Christmas holidays approached. Two days before Christmas, Governor Abraham Ribicoff of Connecticut initiated an unparalleled attempt to control traffic deaths by law enforcement, and announced his crackdown on speeders in that state.

Ribicoff believed, along with many safety specialists, that excess speed was the most common contributing factor in traffic deaths, and that control of speed would result in diminished fatalities. He believed that previous efforts to control speeding under the usual court procedures and by the existing "point system" had been inadequate. In a study of three months' records of the police court in Hartford, it was noted that no more than half the persons originally charged with speeding were so prosecuted, the charge often being diminished to a less serious one. Ribicoff wanted to initiate a program with reliable procedures and strong sanctions as a means to control speeding and thus to reduce traffic deaths.

On December 23, 1955, Governor Ribicoff announced that in the future all persons convicted of speeding would have their licenses suspended for thirty days on the first offense. A second violation was to mean a sixty-day suspension, and a third convic-

---

[1] *E.g.,* D. T. Campbell & J. S. Stanley, *Experimental and Quasi-Experimental Designs for Research on Teaching,* in HANDBOOK OF RESEARCH ON TEACHING 171-246 (N. L. Gage ed. 1963) reprinted as EXPERIMENTAL AND QUASI-EXPERIMENTAL DESIGNS FOR RESEARCH (1963); D. T. Campbell, *From Description to Experimentation: Interpreting Trends as Quasi-Experiments,* in PROBLEMS IN MEASURING CHANGE (C. W. Harris ed. 1963); D. T. Campbell & K. N. Clayton, *Avoiding Regression Effects in Panel Studies of Communication Impact,* in STUDIES IN PUBLIC COMMUNICATION 99-118 (Dept. of Sociology, University of Chicago, No. 3, 1961) reprinted in Bobbs-Merrill Reprints in Sociology as S-353. For an application of this type of analysis to legal impact, *see* R. Lempert, *Strategies of Research Design in the Legal Impact Study,* 1 L. & SOC'Y REV. 111 (1966).

tion for speeding would result in indefinite suspension of the driver's license, subject to a hearing after ninety days.

The decree was put into force through the Governor's power of appointment over local judges. Under Connecticut practice, the Motor Vehicle Department was suspending licenses on the recommendation of police court judges. The judges were appointed by the Governor, who threatened loss of reappointment in 1957 to judges who appeared lax in the conviction of speeders, or who did not recommend suspension of licenses to the Motor Vehicle Department.

In the first three months of 1956, license suspensions for speeding numbered 2,855, an increase of almost 2,700 over the corresponding period in 1955. There were ten fewer fatalities, and 765 fewer arrests for speeding. The Governor was reported "encouraged" by the drop in violations and in fatalities. The press quoted him as saying, "This is positive proof that operators are not only driving slower, but are driving better."

By late May, deaths had declined from 122 in 1955 to 107 in 1956. Suspensions for speeding numbered 4,559, as against 209 in 1955. Speeding arrests had dropped 53 per cent. The Governor received a telegram of commendation for the program from the National Safety Council.

At the end of June there were twenty-two fewer fatalities than in the first six months of 1955, representing a 15 per cent reduction. Suspensions for speeding in the first six months of the year had risen from 231 to 5,398, and arrests had declined from 4,377 to 2,735. Ribicoff announced:

> Connecticut has succeeded in stopping the upward surge in highway deaths, and in the first six months of this year, contrary to the national trend, we have saved lives. Fewer people died on the highways this year than in the same period last year, in Connecticut. We did it by enforcing the law, something the safety experts said couldn't be done because the people wouldn't be behind it.

In July, a new State Police program, using unmarked police cars and making extensive use of radar, was inaugurated. The police issued a report stating that 2 per cent of the cars observed by radar on July 4 were found to be speeding; at a later date, it was claimed that no speeders were found among 53,000 cars similarly observed.

In the late summer, however, Connecticut experienced a very high number of traffic fatalities. By the beginning of September, 194 people had been killed, a number almost equal to the 195 of the comparable period in the previous year. The accident "epidemic" was embarrassing to the authorities, who retreated to defending the speeding crackdown on the grounds (a) that the fatality rate remained low in comparison with the national trend, which showed a 7 per cent increase; (b) that exposure to accidents in the State had increased by 100 million vehicle miles without an increase in deaths; and (c) that the total accident rate had risen, thereby lowering the proportion of fatal accidents to total accidents.

Fatalities were fewer in the fall of 1956, and by the end of the year Connecticut could count 284 deaths in traffic as against 324 in 1955. The Governor stated, "With the saving of forty lives in 1955, a reduction of 12.3 per cent from the 1955 motor vehicle death toll, we can say the program is definitely worthwhile."

The crackdown on speeding is still in effect in Connecticut, although it is no longer the subject of newsworthy comment. It was not entirely a political asset for the Democratic Governor. From the start, there were problems with neighboring states, which originate a substantial share of Connecticut traffic, and which at first refused to suspend licenses of drivers convicted of speeding in Connecticut. More important, many powerful individuals and groups within Connecticut resented the direct effects of the crackdown. Members of the Republican Party wanted the program "tempered with justice." The Teamsters sponsored a bill to eliminate compulsory license suspension on a first offense, and other legislation granting restricted driving permits for "hardship" cases was introduced. These efforts were not successful in officially moderating the crackdown policy.

The people of Connecticut and their officials are paying what in many instances appears to be a high price for the continuation of the crackdown on speeding. Few will feel the price is too high if it can be shown that as many as forty lives per year are being saved. However, the question must be raised as to whether the results claimed for the program in 1956 are valid in the light of both formerly and more recently available statistics on highway fatalities.

QUASI-EXPERIMENTAL ANALYSIS

Before-and-After Measures

Traffic fatalities in Connecticut for 1956, compared with 1955, are presented in Figure 1. These are the data upon which Governor Ribicoff relied in claiming success for the crackdown on speeding. Skillfully presented, such results can look impressive, but can also be fundamentally misleading.

We can speak of the evidence presented in Figure 1 as a quasi-experiment: there is a "pretest" (the 1955 figures), an "experimental treatment" (the crackdown), and a "posttest" (the 1956 figures). A substantial change is noted which one would like to ascribe to the "experimental treatment." In quasi-experimental analysis this interpretation is held to be legitimate, provided consideration is given to plausible rival explanations of the differences, with supplementary analyses being added to eliminate these where possible. In the language of quasi-experimental analysis, the data of Figure 1 constitute a One-Group Pretest-Posttest Design. This design fails to control for the six common threats to the validity of experiments specified below:

1. *History.* This term denotes specific events, other than the experimental treatment, occurring between the pretest and post-

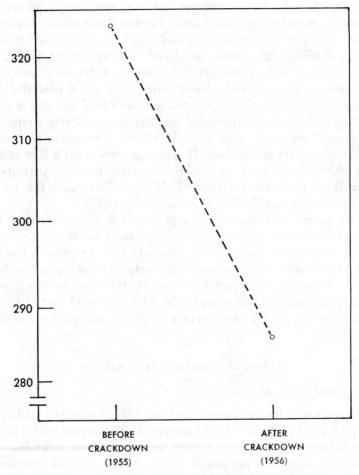

Figure 1. Connecticut Traffic Fatalities, 1955-1956

test, which might account for the change. It furnishes a "rival hypothesis" to the experimental hypothesis, a competing explanation of the before-to-after change that must be eliminated as implausible, by one means or another, before full credence can be given to the experimental hypothesis. For instance, 1956 might have been a particularly dry year, with fewer accidents due to rain and snow, or there might have been a dramatic improvement of the safety features on the 1956-model cars. In fact, neither of these is a particularly plausible rival hypothesis in this instance, and we have not encountered more likely ones, so this potential weakness may not be crucial here.

2. *Maturation.* This term originates in studies of individuals, where it refers to regular changes correlated with the passage of time, such as growing older, more tired, more sophisticated, etc. It is distinguished from history in referring to processes, rather than to discrete events. Thus, one could classify here the general long-term trend toward a reduction in automobile mileage death rates, presumably due to better roads, increased efficacy of medical care, etc. The better designs discussed below provide evidence concerning this trend in Connecticut in previous years, and in other states for the same year.

3. *Testing.* A change may occur as a result of the pretest, even without the experimental treatment. In the present instance, the assessment of the traffic death rate for 1955 constitutes the pretest. In this case it is conceivable that the measurement and publicizing of the traffic death rate for 1955 could change driver caution in 1956.

4. *Instrumentation.* This term refers to a shifting of the measuring instrument independent of any change in the phenomenon measured. In the use of public records for time-series data, a shift in the government agency recording the fatality statistics could account for such a shift. For example, suicide statistics increased a dramatic 20 per cent in Prussia between 1882 and 1883, when record keeping was transferred from the local police to the national civil service. Similarly, Orlando Wilson's reforms of the police system in Chicago led to dramatic increases in rates for most crimes, due presumably to more complete reporting. In earlier versions of the present study, the death rate per hundred million vehicle miles is computed by using the number of gallons of gasoline sold in the state to estimate the number of miles driven. The latter figure is obtained by multiplying the former by an empirically-derived constant. A decrease in the actual miles obtained per gallon, as through engines of larger horsepower or

driving at higher speeds could masquerade as a lower mileage death rate through inflating the estimate of miles driven. Conversely, if the crackdown actually reduced driving speeds, this would increase the miles-per-gallon actually obtained, leading to an underestimate of mileage driven in the post crackdown period, and consequently an overestimate of the fatality rate.

5. *Instability.* A ubiquitous plausible rival hypothesis is that the change observed is due to the instability of the measures involved. Were Figure 1 to show fatality rates for a single township, with the same 12.3 per cent drop, we would be totally unimpressed, so unstable would we expect such rates to be. In general, as is made explicit in the models for tests of significance, the smaller the population base, the greater the instability. In the uncontrolled field situation sample size is only one of many sources of instability. Much instability may be due to large numbers of change-producing events of the type which, taken individually, we have called history.

6. *Regression.* Where a group has been selected for treatment just because of its extreme performance on the pretest, and if the pretest and posttest are imperfectly correlated, as they almost always are, it follows that on the average the posttest will be less extreme than the pretest. This regression is a tautological restatement of the imperfect correlation between pretest and posttest, as it relates to pretest scores selected for their extremity. . . .

Selection for extremity (and resultant retest regression) can be seen as plausibly operating here in two ways: (a) of all states in 1955, this treatment was most likely to be applied to one with an exceptionally high traffic casualty rate; (b) for Connecticut, the most likely time in which a crackdown would be applied would be following a year in which traffic fatalities were exceptionally high.

In the true experiment, the treatment is applied randomly, without relation to the prior state of the dependent variable:* the correlation between pretest scores and exposure to treatment is zero.** Likewise, in the most interpretable of quasi-experiments, the treatment is applied without systematic relationship

---

* The dependent variable is the thing being measured which one expects will change as the result of the "treatment." Here the dependent variable is traffic deaths; the treatment is the crackdown on speeding. [Eds. note]

** A zero correlation here means that the application of treatment to any group in no way is related to or depends on what the group's pretest scores are. If the decision to apply treatment to a group depended entirely on its pretest score, the correlation between exposure to treatment and pretest scores would be perfect, which is expressed as a correlation of 1.00. [Eds. note]

to the prior status of the group. Thus, an analysis of the effects of a tornado or an earthquake can be made with confidence that the pretreatment values did not cause the tornado or the earthquake. Not so here: the high 1955 rates can plausibly be argued to have caused the treatment. That 1956 was less extreme would then be expected because of regression.[5]

Interrupted Times-Series Analysis

Figure 2 plots traffic fatalities for five years before and four years after the crackdown. This mode of quasi-experimental analysis has been labeled "Interrupted Time-Series" to distinguish it from the time-series analysis of economics. In the latter, the exogenous variable* to which cause is imputed is a continuously present variable, occurring in different degrees. In the Interrupted Time-Series, the "causal" variable is examined as an event or change occurring at a single time, specified independently of inspection of the data.

The Interrupted Time-Series design represents a use of the more extensive data which are often available even when only before-and-after measures are reported. Some potential outcomes of such a time-series analysis greatly reduce the plausibility of certain threats to validity. If the preexposure series shows but minor point-to-point fluctuations and no trend anticipating a big transtreatment shift, then maturation may not be plausible, for in most instances the plausible maturation hypothesis would have predicted shifts of the same order as the transtreatment shift in each of the pretreatment stages. Reasonable models of the testing effect would have the same implications. (In our instance, this would be on condition that the annual fatality rates had been given equal publicity.) The outcome in Figure 2 is not of this readily interpretable sort, although the trend is perhaps generally upward prior to the treatment, and steadily downward subsequently.

Judgments of the plausibility of instrumentation effects must be based upon other than time-series data. However, notice

_____

5 This issue is extremely complex. In ordinary correlation, the regression is technically toward the mean of the second variable, not to the mean of the selection variable, if these means differ. In time-series, the regression is toward the general trend-line, which may of course be upward or downward or unchanging. A more expanded analysis of the regression problem in correlation across persons is contained in Campbell & Clayton (1961) and in Campbell & Stanley (1963), both *supra* note 1.

* "Exogenous" means originating externally or developing from without. Roughly, the exogenous variable is the outside force which one says "causes" something to happen. [Eds. note]

should be taken here of a frequent unfortunate confounding: the administrative reform which is meant to produce a social change very frequently is accompanied by a coincident reform of the

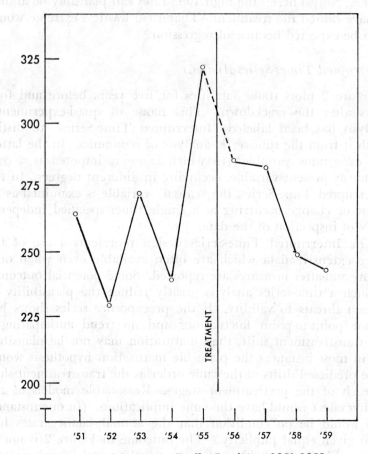

Figure 2. Connecticut Traffic Fatalities, 1951-1959

record keeping, ruling out valid inferences as to effects. The Chicago police reform cited above is a case in point. In the present instance, we have found no evidence of a change in record keeping or index computing of the type that would produce a pseudo-effect.

The likelihood of regression, or of selection for "treatment" on a basis tending to introduce regression, is supported by inspection of the time-series data. The largest change of any year is not the one after the crackdown, but is instead the upswing in the series occurring in 1954-55, just prior to the crackdown. In terms of crude fatality rates, 1955 is strikingly the highest point reached. It thus seems plausible that the high figure of 1955 caused the crackdown, and hence it seems much less likely that the crackdown caused the low figure of 1956, for such a drop would have been predicted on regression grounds in any case.

The graphic presentation of the precrackdown years provides evidence of the general instability of the accidental death rate measure, against which the 1955-56 shift can be compared. This instability makes the "treatment effect" of Figure 1 now look more trivial. Had the drop following the treatment been the largest shift in the time series, the hypothesis of effect would have been much more plausible. Instead, shifts that large are relatively frequent. The 1955-56 drop is less than half the magnitude of the 1954-55 gain, and the 1953 gain also exceeds it. It is the largest drop of the series, but it exceeds the drops of 1952, 1954, and 1958 by trivial amounts. Thus the unexplained instabilities of the series are of such a magnitude as to make the 1955-56 drop understandable as more of the same. On the other hand, it is noteworthy that after the crackdown, there are no year-to-year gains, and in this respect, the character of the time-series has changed. The plausibility of the hypothesis that instability accounts for the effect can be judged by visual inspection of the graphed figures, or by qualitative discussion, but in addition it is this one threat to validity which can be evaluated by tests of significance. These will be discussed later, and they do find some evidence of change exceeding that which the pretreatment instability would lead one to expect.

Multiple Time-Series

In many situations, time-series involving but a single experimental unit will be all that are available. In these situations, analyses on the above model are a great improvement over the usual before-and-after study. However, it is in the spirit of quasi-experimental analysis to make use of *all* available data that could help to rule out or confirm any plausible rival hypothesis. In a setting such as this, no randomly assigned control group is available. But in quasi-experimentation, even a nonequivalent control group is helpful. It provides the only control for history (for those extraneous change agents that would be expected to affect both the experimental and control group), and assists in controlling maturation, testing, and instrumentation. For Connecticut, it was judged that a pool of adjacent and similar states—New York, New Jersey, Rhode Island and Massachusetts—provided a meaningful comparison. Figure 3 plots the death rates for the control states alongside Connecticut, all data being expressed on a per 100,000 population base to bring the figures into proximity.

The control data are much smoother, due to the much larger base, *i.e.*, the canceling out of chance deviations in the annual figures for particular states.

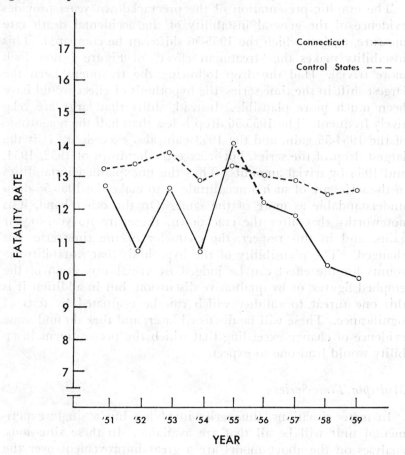

Figure 3.   Connecticut and Control States Traffic Fatalities, 1951-1959
(per 100,000 population)

While in general these data confirm the single time-series analysis, the differences between Connecticut and the control states show a pattern supporting the hypothesis that the crackdown made a difference. In the pretest years, Connecticut's rate is parallel or rising relative to the control, exceeding it in 1955. In the posttest years, Connecticut's rate drops faster than does the control, steadily increasing the gap. While the regression argument applies to the high point of 1955 and to the subsequent departure in 1956, it does not plausibly explain the steadily increasing gap in 1957, 1958, and 1959.

Figure 4 shows the comparison states individually. Note that four of the five show an upward swing in 1955, Connecticut having the largest. Note that all five show a downward trend in 1956. Rhode Island is most similar to Connecticut in both the 1955 upswing and 1956 downswing, actually exceeding Connecti-

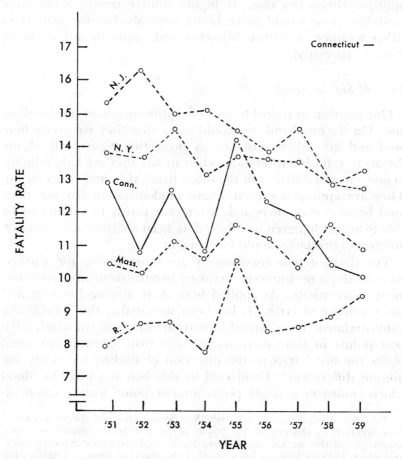

Figure 4. Traffic Fatalities for Connecticut, New York, New Jersey, Rhode Island, and Massachusetts (per 100,000 persons)

cut in the latter—in a striking argument against the hypothesis of a crackdown effect. However, the trend in 1957, 1958, and 1959 is steadily upward in Rhode Island, steadily downward in Connecticut, supporting the concept of effect.

The list of plausible rival hypotheses should include factors disguising experimental effects as well as factors producing pseudo-effects. Thus, to the list should be added *diffusion*, the tendency for the experimental effect to modify not only the experimental group, but also the control group. Thus the crackdown on speeding in Connecticut might well have reduced traffic speed and fatalities in neighboring states. . . . The comparison of posttreatment levels of Connecticut and the neighboring states might thus be invalid, or at least underestimate the effects. Conceivably one might for this reason prefer the single time-series analysis to the multiple time-series one. If highly similar remote states were available, these would make better controls, but for matters of either weather or culture adjacency and similarity are apt to be strongly associated.

Tests of Significance*

Our position in regard to tests of significance is an intermediate one. On the one hand, we would agree that they are overly honored and are [often mistaken as protecting against all of the threats to valid interpretation, when in fact they are only relevant to one—to instability. On the other hand, they are] often useful. They are appropriate even where randomization has not been used because even there it is a relevant threat to validity to be able to argue that even had these data been assigned at random,** differences this large would be frequent.

The simplest tests conceptually are those testing for a difference in slope or intercept between pretreatment and posttreatment observations. As applied here these assume linearity and independence of error. It has been shown that the "proximally autocorrelated" error typical of natural situations (in which adjacent points in time share more error than non-adjacent ones) biases the usual tests in the direction of finding too many significant differences.[8] Unaffected by this bias is a t-test by Mood which compares a single posttreatment point with a value ex-

---

* A "test of significance" tests whether or not observed differences could have occurred by chance. *See* pp. 204-05 n.*, *supra*. In the second and third paragraphs of this section, the authors discuss sophisticated statistical procedures which indicate that the odds are that the observed drop in fatalities fall just short of those conventionally accepted as statistically significant. The important conclusion in the last paragraph should be stressed: The reduction in fatalities could be due to the speeding crackdown or it could be the result of the tendency for the group with the most extreme scores at one time (Connecticut drivers in 1955) to have less extreme scores at other times. [Eds. note]

** If the various states considered in Figures 3 and 4 had been selected for treatment or no treatment (a crackdown on speeding or no crackdown) randomly, tests of significance clearly would be applicable. There is controversy among sociologists as to whether significance tests are appropriate when groups are selected other than randomly. [Eds. note]

[8] J. Sween & D. T. Campbell, *supra* note 3. The tests thus biased include tests of slope and intercept provided by H. M. WALKER & J. LEV, STATISTICAL INFERENCE 390-95, 399-400 (1953). Note that this invalidates the discussion of tests of significance in Campbell, *From Description to Experimentation*, *supra* note 1, at 220-30. The "Clayton test" presented there was found in the Monte Carlo simulation by Sween & Campbell to have additional errors leading it to be too optimistic.

trapolated from the pretreatment series.[9] None of these approached any interesting level of significance.

Glass[10] has introduced into the social sciences a more sophisticated statistical approach, based upon the work of Box and Tiao.[11] This has the advantages of realistically assuming the interdependence of adjacent points and estimating a weighting parameter thereof, of avoiding the assumption of linearity (at least in a simple or direct manner), and of weighting more heavily the observations closer to the point of treatment. A number of assumptions about the nature of the data must be made, such as the absence of cycles, but these can be examined from the data. Applying this test to monthly data, he finds a drop in fatalities not quite reaching the $P<.10$ level of significance. Using a monthly difference between Connecticut's rate and that of the pool of the four control states, still less of a significant effect is found. In what he regards as the most powerful analysis available, he computes an effect parameter for each of the four comparison states and compares the effect parameter of Connecticut with this. Connecticut shows more effect, with a significance level somewhere between $P<.05$ and $P<.07$, with a one-tailed test. A more detailed description of the method and analysis of these data is given in Glass' article. . . .

Thus on the graphic evidence of steadily dropping fatality rates, and on these marginal statistical grounds, there may be an effect. This effect, it must be restated, could be due to the crackdown, or could be due to the regression effect. (Regression effects can of course produce "statistically significant" results.)

Supplementary Analyses

In this section, we will present data that will further illustrate time-series analysis and, substantively, both indicate that the crackdown was put into effect and that it had some unanticipated and, to the policymakers, probably undesired consequences.

Figure 5 presents evidence that the crackdown was put into effect, as indicated by a great increase in suspensions of licenses

---

9 A. M. MOOD, INTRODUCTION TO THE THEORY OF STATISTICS 297-98 (1950).

10 G. V. Glass, *Analysis of Data on the Connecticut Speeding Crackdown as a Time-Series Quasi-Experiment*, 3 L. & SOC'Y REV. 55-76 (1968); T. O. Maguire & G. V. Glass, *A Program for the Analysis of Certain Time-Series Quasi-Experiments*, 27 EDUCATIONAL AND PSYCHOLOGICAL MEASUREMENT 743-50 (1967); G. V. Glass, G. C. Tiao, & T. O. Maguire, *Analysis of Data on the 1900 Revision of German Divorce Laws as a Time-Series Quasi-Experiment*, 3 L. & SOC'Y REV. (1969) (in press).

11 G. E. P. Box & G. C. Tiao, *A Change in Level of a Non-stationary Time Series*, 52 BIOMETRIKA 181-92 (1965); G. E. P. Box, *Bayesian Approaches to Some Bothersome Problems in Data Analysis* in IMPROVING EXPERIMENTAL DESIGN AND STATISTICAL ANALYSIS (J. C. Stanley ed. 1967).

for speeding. Unfortunately, we have not been able to get control state data for this and the following variables, but the single state time-series is quite convincing in itself. We regard it as confirming the appropriateness of the statistical tests that they indicate significant differences. The single-point-extrapolation t is 4.33

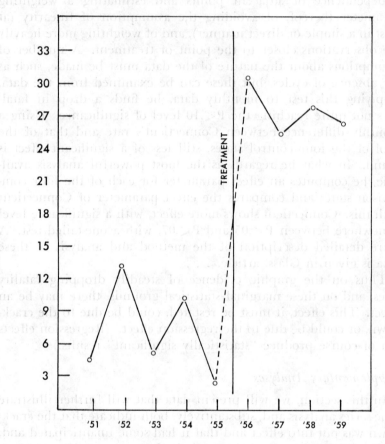

Figure 5. Suspensions of Licenses for Speeding, as a Per Cent of All Suspensions

with 4 degrees of freedom, where 3.75 is significant at the $P < .02$ level.

Figure 6 plots the percentage which speeding violations constitute of all traffic violations. This shows a decline, due presumably to greater conformity to speed limits, although it is possible that policemen and prosecutors were more willing, in the light of severe sanctions for speeding, to overlook minor infractions or to charge them as something else. While the graphic portrayal of declining speeding violations is convincing of a genuine effect, the statistical tests are not so emphatic. The single-point-extrapolation t is 2.66 with 4 degrees of freedom, not reaching the $P<.05$ level of 2.78.

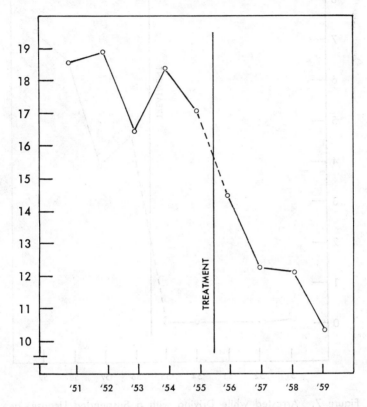

Figure 6.   Speeding Violations, as Per Cent of All Traffic Violations

From Figure 5 and the reports cited in the first section of this paper it is clear that a real change in enforcement behavior resulted. It seems likely that the proportion of drivers exceeding the speed limits on Connecticut highways actually decreased. However, over and above these desired effects there are signs of unforeseen and unwanted reactions. Figure 7 concerns persons whose licenses were further suspended because they were convicted of driving with a suspended license, expressed as a percentage of all suspensions. This jumps from an almost consistent zero to some 4 to 6 per cent. Tests of significance confirm the effect. . . . Our interpretation of this phenomenon is that automobile transportation has become a virtual necessity for many residents of the diffusely settled megalopolitan region that includes Connecticut, and these people are willing to risk very severe sanctions in order to continue daily routines that involve driving.

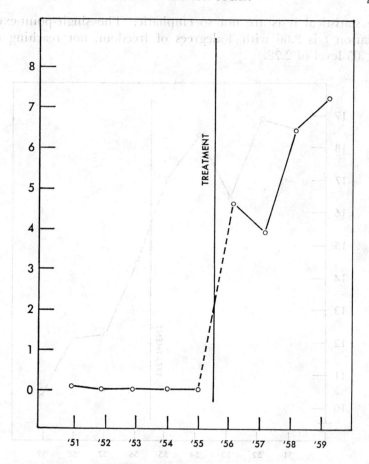

Figure 7. Arrested while Driving with a Suspended License, as Per Cent of Suspensions

Since they are willing to drive with a suspended license, suspension does not have the desired restrictive effect on this group of drivers, which is probably much larger than the number apprehended and appearing in these statistics would indicate. Alternatively, of course, the increase could result, in whole or part, from more vigorous efforts at enforcement both in the crackdown itself and in special efforts at inspection comprising a followup of the crackdown effort.

Figure 8 shows a reaction on the part of the legal system. Even with fewer speeding violations reaching the courts (Figure 6), the courts were more lenient in their handling of these cases as expressed by the proportion of not guilty decisions. Tests of significance are borderline. The single-point-extrapolation t is 2.42, which with but 4 degrees of freedom fails to reach significance at the P<.05 level, for which 2.78 would be required. Larger

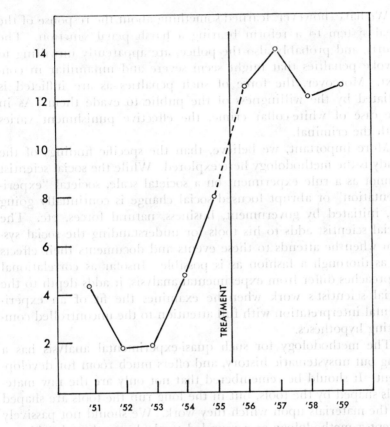

Figure 8. Per Cent of Speeding Violations Judged Not Guilty

proportions of not guilty judgments could be the result of more cases getting to court because of tightening of precourt standards, more generous handling by judges and prosecutors, or more vigorous defenses by the accused because more is at stake. The two effects shown in Figures 7 and 8 indicate a vitiation of the punitive effects of the crackdown in operation in a society where dependence on automobile transportation is acknowledged.

CONCLUSION

On the substantive side, the analysis has demonstrated that the Connecticut crackdown on speeding was a substantial enforcement effort, although some of its most punitive aspects were mitigated in practice. As to fatalities, we find a sustained trend toward reduction, but no unequivocal proof that they were due to the crackdown. The likelihood that the very high prior rate instigated the crackdown seriously complicates the inference.

We have, however, learned something about the response of the legal system to a reform bearing a harsh penal sanction. The courts, and probably also the police, are apparently unwilling to invoke penalties that might seem severe and unfamiliar in context. Moreover, the force of such penalties as are inflicted is vitiated by the willingness of the public to evade them. As in the case of white-collar crime, the effective punishment varies with the criminal.

More important, we believe, than the specific findings of the study is the methodology here explored. While the social scientist cannot as a rule experiment on a societal scale, societal "experimentation" or abrupt focused social change is continually going on, initiated by government, business, natural forces, etc. The social scientist adds to his tools for understanding the social system when he attends to these events and documents their effects in as thorough a fashion as is possible. Insofar as correlational approaches differ from experimental analysis, it adds depth to the social scientist's work when he examines the fit of an experimental interpretation with full attention to the uncontrolled competing hypotheses.

The methodology for such quasi-experimental analysis has a long but unsystematic history, and offers much room for development. It should be remembered that not only are the raw materials shaped by the tools, but in the long run the tools are shaped by the materials upon which they work. We should not passively accept a methodology as a revealed truth, but rather should test it in use with our materials. Methodology has in fact an empirical history and its constituents have the status of empirical discoveries. The classical control group experiment is not typical of the physical sciences, but instead emerged from psychological laboratory research, and is peculiar to the social sciences and their problems. Medical research has the placebo control group, and neurophysiology the sham operation control, as achievements of specific research traditions, not as logical dispensations from the philosophy of science or mathematical statistics. So too the methods for quasi-experimentation in settings like the present will emerge from an iteration of effort and criticism, in which many approaches will be rejected.

A final note on the treatment of uncontrolled variables is in order. On the one extreme there is that attitude often unwittingly inculcated in courses on experimental design, which looks askance at all efforts to make inferences where some variables have been left uncontrolled or where randomization has not taken place. In contrast, the quasi-experimental approach takes a radically different posture: any experiment is valid until proven invalid. The only invalidation comes from plausible rival explanations of the specific outcome. Regression effects and test-retest effects are such in many settings. An absence of randomization may in some specific way plausibly explain the obtained results. But unless one can specify such a hypothesis and the direction of its effects, it should not be regarded as invalidating. Subsequent consideration may uncover plausible rival hypotheses which have been overlooked, but such transitory validity is often the fate of laboratory experiments too.

At the other extreme is the naive attribution of cause which blithely fails to consider any explanations other than the author's favorite candidate. Such an orientation is likewise opposed. The quasi-experimentalist is obliged to search out and consider the available plausible rival hypotheses with all the vigilance at his command. While our coverage in this regard has been incomplete, we hope that we have at least illustrated such an approach.

NOTES AND QUESTIONS

1. Richard Lempert,* in his article, "Strategies of Research Design in the Legal Impact Study: The Control of Plausible Rival Hypotheses," 1 *Law & Society Review* 111 (1966), applies the approach of Campbell and Stanley (as cited in footnote 1 of the Campbell and Ross article) to the consequences of legal action. He raises some considerations not mentioned or developed fully by Campbell and Ross.

[Reading 40]

Campbell and Stanley . . . present eight factors which are potential threats to the internal validity of an experimental design because they provide possible sources of plausible rival hypotheses. They are: history, maturation, testing, instrumentation, regression, selection, mortality, and the interaction of certain of these factors such as selection and maturation, etc. Because of the quasi-experimental nature of legal impact studies and because of the particular nature of the law, many of these threats may be disregarded by the experimenter in this area, while others pose special problems which would not be present in the normal social-psychological quasi-experimental situation. In discussing the possible influences of these sources of plausible rival hypotheses, and for the

* Assistant Professor of Law, University of Michigan. Reprinted from Law and Society Review. Copyright © 1966 by the Law and Society Association. Reprinted by permission.

purposes of general discussion throughout this paper, we shall assume a standard experimental situation in which the experimenter is interested in assessing the effects of a certain law on the behavior of people living in states of the United States which have that law. In all cases the experimenter has available to him a sizable group of states which have different laws applying to the same subject and/or a group which is without any formal regulation of the subject.

Since administrative agencies often keep statistical records concerning the incidence of the behavior which they are supposed to regulate (*e.g.,* crime rates, types of cases reaching court) the effects of a particular law often may be measured by commonly available statistical data. Testing effects should therefore be non-existent and instrumentation effects will often be minimal, though there are some threats to validity in this area. (1) First, an investigator may be attempting to compare two states which use different methods of computing their statistical reports on the same subject. This can be controlled by utilizing data collected by national organizations which prescribe uniform methods of data collection in all states. (2) The second problem is that a state or subdivision thereof may change its methods of reporting data. . . .

Maturation, mortality and regression should also present minimal threats to the types of experimental designs which apply in this area, though there are situations when each of these features will have to be examined in detail before they can be disregarded as possible explanations of any perceived changes. For example, if a time series study were to be made of tort damage awards in two states having different legal norms, a more rapid increase in award size in one of them than in the other might be due to a difference in certain long range secular trends (maturation effects), such as inflation, rather than to the differences in the laws of the two states.

The major threats to the validity of legal impact designs are three: history, history-selection interaction; and, one peculiar to the sociology of law, the problem of distinguishing the law as it appears on the books from the "law in fact."

Of these, the determination of what the law is in fact should be preliminary to most studies. The law as it appears on the statute books may be only a partial and sometimes misleading guide as to the administered situation which in fact exists. If the law is within the province of a particular administrative agency, the agency's interpretation of the law and its activities in reference to the law must be traced. In many cases court decisions must be examined to see what "glosses" the judges have placed on the law. In still other cases there may be differential enforcement by the police in which case the system must be examined in detail at this level. In each of these cases, there are ways of getting at the character of the law as administered.

History is another potential threat to the internal validity of sociolegal experimental designs, but ordinarily it should not be too difficult to control for. It is an especially plausible rival hypothesis in the "before-and-after" type designs. . . . A coincidental historical happening can often explain a per- ceived behavior change just as well as the experimental var- iable can. This is why it is always wise to use "before-and- after" type designs in connection with a group of control states which does not have the particular law in question and which has been subject to the same historical influences as the group of affected states. If a geographically well-distrib- uted group of states with a given law can be compared with a similar group of states without the law, history may usually be ruled out as an explanatory cause for the differences in per- ceived behavior which the experimental hypothesis would suggest is caused by the law under study.

In comparing laws among states one may often want to focus on the situation in the three or four years before their passage and the situation in the years immediately after their passage. Unless the date of the passage of the laws is the same, this procedure is almost always to be avoided. Any per- ceived differences may actually be due to history, but the design itself will have failed to correct for it, and one reading the write-up of the intervention will likewise be unable to correct for it.

The legal impact theorist should also guard against the possibility that the enactment of a particular law may be only one of several similarly directed governmental inter- ventions in the same historical period.

Selection is the most severe threat which operates in a man- ner specific to sociolegal research. This is because a law represents two things, a regulatory device and (especially, but not exclusively, in a democratic political system) an ex- pression of the people's feelings about a particular issue. This variable is especially likely to be a factor where a legal system is being studied in isolation or where a whole nation is being studied. For example, to the best of my knowledge, every state in this nation has a law against incest, and there

is very little incest in this country. The mere concurrence
of these two facts does not prove that the fact that incest
is made criminal is responsible for its lack of prevalence.
Indeed the opposite is probably true. The American people
feel incest is such a bad thing that they have made a crime
of it. However, America would not be an incestuous nation
even if such laws did not exist. . . .

The types of validity threats which affect legal impact experiments are all such as to make the study of only one state
with a particular law represent a relatively poor experiment
design. Studying one state with a particular law and one
state without it is much better and can be quite impressive
if a time-linked comparison shows a sharp effect. However,
this design grows less effective the more dissimilar the states
are in other explanatory variables.

The best design will always involve a time-linked comparison of a group of states having a particular law with a
similar group of states not having that law. This design is
more valid the more heterogeneous each set of states is within
itself and the more similar the two sets of states when each
set is viewed as a whole.

Strictly speaking no experimental design is valid outside
the particular groups which were measured in the course of
the experiment, and even for those groups the internal validity would be limited to the extent to which the experimental
results are reproducible. But if experimental results could
not be generalized, there would be little sense in doing any
but the most widely encompassing experiments.

Fortunately the results of almost all experiments can be
generalized to some extent to units not involved in the
experimental situation. This generalizability is what Campbell and Stanley refer to as the external validity of the design.
By and large we can say that the greater the external validity
of a particular experimental design, the more potential applications it will have and the more it will tell one about "real
world" situations. It is in this area of external validity that
legal impact designs have a great potential strength. When
we study the impact of a law in several states we are examining what are essentially highly heterogeneous groupings
involving millions of individuals. Thus we have a strong
basis for generalizing the results of such a study to people
in all states across the United States; far stronger, for instance, than we might have for generalizing a study of racial
attitudes among students in a sociology course to students in
the same university taking an advanced biology course.

2. Campbell and Ross, and Lempert appear to be optimistic about the utility of quasi-experimental analysis in measuring the impact of law. However, note how cautious Campbell and Ross are in reaching conclusions about the impact of the Connecticut crackdown on speeding. Even if you do not think that Campbell and Ross proved much about the impact of the Connecticut crackdown, is their approach better than the one used by the Connecticut officials?

3. Chambliss, Reading 28, at 277, *supra*, discussed the deterrent influence of capital punishment using several statistical measures. To what extent, if at all, was he using Campbell and Stanley's quasi-experimental analysis? Which of the "threats to validity" does Chambliss avoid in presenting his data? Which does he disregard?

4. Could Campbell and Ross have told Governor Ribicoff anything useful before he started his crackdown on speeding? Does their method offer any help in making predictions about the potential impact of legal change?

(3) Note: Effectiveness of legal systems

The materials discussed thus far have dealt with the effectiveness of particular laws, or particular parts of a legal system. They have, of course, raised points of general applicability. But even in the aggregate, they do not provide data for testing whether this or that type of *whole legal system* is more "effective" than some other type. Is it at all meaningful to ask whether the American legal system is more "effective" than that of India, France or ancient Rome? So put, the answer is *no*. But one can ask whether one legal system is more effective than competing types in reaching a particular goal.

There has been much speculation, but little systematic research, on questions of effectiveness in this sense. The reasons are obvious. It is exceedingly difficult to define and compare legal systems. The notion of an experiment, controlled or otherwise, is impossible.

For all its difficulties, the question is well worth considering. It is particularly poignant today, when many of the legal systems of the world are undergoing rapid change, more or less directed from the top. These systems, particularly in the third world, have a vague commitment to a goal which we might call modernization, and which includes, if nothing else, a commitment to increase productivity and raise the national standard of living. There is a growing literature worth consulting that bears on the

type of legal system which can best attain these goals. *See, e.g.*,
Robert Seidman, "Law and Economic Development in Independ-
ent, English-Speaking, Sub-Saharan Africa," 1966 *Wisconsin Law
Review* 999.

[Reading 41]

Closely related is the historical question whether the industrial
revolution, which admittedly flowered in England at an early date
relative to other European countries, was sparked in any way by
the peculiar characteristics of English law. We cannot go into
the matter here in any detail. Opinions differ sharply. The modern American sociologist, Talcott Parsons,* feels that the specific
development of English law was decisive in producing the industrial revolution. In his article, "Evolutionary Universals in Society," 29 *American Sociological Review* 339, 353 (1964), he writes:

> [In England] the crucial period was the early 17th century,
> when Justice Coke asserted the independence of the Com-
> mon Law from control by royal prerogative.
>
> With this, the establishment of the organizational inde-
> pendence of the Judiciary was the crucial symbolic develop-
> ment. Substantially, the Common Law came to emphasize
> the protection of personal rights, the institution of property
> in private hands, and both freedom of contract and protec-
> tion of contractual interests far more strongly than did the
> Continental law. Common Law also emphasized both the
> adversary system, in which parties are highly independent of
> the Court, and procedural protections.
>
> Significantly, these Common Law developments were in-
> tegral parts of the more general development of British in-
> stitutions associated with the Puritan movement, excluding
> the later establishment of the independence of Parliament
> and the development of physical science.
>
> This development of English Common Law, with its adop-
> tion and further development in the overseas English-speak-
> ing world, not only constituted the most advanced case of
> universalistic normative order, but was probably decisive for
> the modern world. This general type of legal order is, in
> my opinion, the most important single hallmark of modern
> society. So much is it no accident that the Industrial Rev-

---

* Talcott Parsons, Professor in the Department of Social Relations, Harvard University. Reprinted by permission of the American Sociological Review. The article was reprinted in Parsons, Sociological Theory and Modern
Society (Free Press 1967).

olution occurred first in England, that I think it legitimate to regard the English type of legal system as a fundamental prerequisite of the first occurrence of the Industrial
Revolution. . . .

[Reading 42]

A contrasting point of view was expressed by the great German
sociologist, Max Weber,* in *Max Weber on Law in Economy and
Society* 315, 353 (Max Rheinstein ed., Harvard U. Press 1954).
Weber was trained as a lawyer and had an immense knowledge
of comparative systems of law. He felt that "modern capitalism
prospers equally and manifests essentially identical economic
traits under legal systems containing rules and institutions which
considerably differ from each other at least from a juridical point
of view." English law was in a sense *less* suitable than Continental law for the development of capitalism, since it was less
systematic, bureaucratic and logical. That capitalism "could
nevertheless make its way so well in England was largely because
the court system and trial procedure amounted until well in the
modern age to a denial of justice to the economically weaker
groups. This fact and the cost in time and money of transfers
of landed property, which was also influenced by the economic
interests of the lawyers, influenced the structure of agrarian England in the direction of the accumulation and immobilization of
landed property."

See also Chapter 4, at 507-733, *infra.*

---

2. Institutional Factors—Countervailing Pressures Limiting the Achievement of Effective Legal Control

a. A general survey

43. Prohibition: The Era of Excess

ANDREW SINCLAIR*

The drys were misled by their wide backing at the beginning of the century by the middle-class progressives of America. They were also deluded into thinking that those who helped them in the attack on the saloon would also help them in the attack on all liquor. In their eyes, the aroused millions of the American *bourgeoisie*, particularly the female of the species, would inform on any transgressor of the prohibition laws. Thus the work of enforcement officers would be a mere matter of arresting the guilty few with the approval of the righteous many. The passing of the Volstead Act** was to prove the opposite, that the many were guilty and that the arrested few were judged by the many to be righteous. It was a formidable miscalculation on the part of the drys, who were more conscious of the desirability of their reform than its possibility.

Moreover, the success of the drys went to their heads. If they had succeeded in prohibiting liquor, why should they not succeed in banning other pernicious habits? More and more, the drys forgot the practical limits of the law and remembered only their view of the good of society. And in seeking beyond the practical and the possible they made themselves ridiculous. The history of the reform crusades against the cigarette and jazz are examples of the lengths to which the moral reformers would go in courting failure and jeers. Even when they were successful, as in the

---

** Volstead Act: the popular title of the National Prohibition Act, 41 Stat. 305 (1919), passed by Congress to enforce and implement the Prohibition amendment. Andrew J. Volstead was a Congressman from Minnesota. [Eds. note]

passage of the Mann Act,* which used the federal power in interstate commerce to attack the white-slave trade and fornication across state borders, they were open to the sneers of their enemies that, while they pretended to regulate the commerce between the states, in fact they sought "to regulate commerce between the sexes."

The anticigarette crusade went hand in hand with the fight against the saloon. As the *Century* said, "The relation of tobacco, especially in the form of cigarettes, and alcohol and opium is a very close one. . . . Morphine is the legitimate consequence of alcohol, and alcohol is the legitimate consequence of tobacco. Cigarettes, drink, opium, is the logical and regular series." . . . Medical fears, similar to those exploited by the drys, were used as deterrents to possible smokers. As late as November, 1930, the *National Advocate* printed the opinion of a doctor that "sixty per cent of all babies born of mothers who are habitual cigarette smokers die before they are two years old." The opponents of the cigarette used a strategy parallel to that of the drys—they were often the same people—to secure by 1913 the passage of anticigarette laws in nine states, all in the South or in the West. The tide in favor of the prohibition of cigarettes, however, receded even faster than the dry tide. By 1929, no state forbade the smoking of cigarettes by adults.

The crusade against the new styles of dancing and jazz was another exercise in futility. In 1914, the General Federation of Women's Clubs put under a ban the tango and hesitation waltz. A clergyman added to the proscribed list the bunny hug, turkey trot, Texas Tommy, hug-me-tight, fox trot, shimmy dance, seagull swoop, camel walk, and skunk waltz. The Methodist Church would not even approve of a decorous dance step which was hopefully called the Wesleyan waltz. But worse was to come with the black bottom and the Charleston. The sexual desires of the young seemed to reign on the dance floor. And as for the growing influence of jazz on dance music, the superintendent of schools in Kansas City, Missouri, warned a thousand teachers, "This nation has been fighting booze for a long time. I am just wondering whether jazz isn't going to have to be legislated against as well." For the intoxicating influence of jazz music was held to be as dangerous as that of alcohol. "Does Jazz Put the Sin in Syncopation?" asked Anne Shaw Faulkner in the *Ladies' Home*

---

* Mann Act: a federal act of 1910, 36 Stat. 825 (1910), to control the "white slave traffic," which made it a crime to transport across state lines "any woman or girl for the purpose of prostitution or debauchery, or for any other immoral purpose." [Eds. note]

Journal in 1921; she thought it did, and she quoted a musical supervisor of a large urban high school that only forty out of two thousand best-selling songs were fit for boys and girls to sing together. Jazz was held to cause a mental drunkenness or, as Dr. Henry Van Dyke complained, "a sensual teasing of the strings of physical passion." It loosed all those moral restraints which the drys held desirable, and therefore, like alcohol, it should be prohibited. But the advent of the radio and talking picture spread the influence of jazz all over the United States and gave the Negro his first victory in America.

The excesses of the moral reformers in these losing causes did harm to the drys. For moderates were alienated from all moral reformers. Moreover, the campaign for the prohibition of liquor seemed to many to be the thin end of the wedge, the prelude to a reign of terror by moral zealots over the habits of America. When the Anti-Saloon League had presented its first petition for national prohibition as far back as 1913, the New York *World* had voiced this fear: "Tomorrow it is likely to be the Anti-Cigarette League that is clamoring for a constitutional amendment to prohibit smoking, or the Anti-Profanity League that insists on a constitutional amendment to prevent swearing, or a Eugenics Society that advocates a constitutional amendment to stop the birth of imperfect babies." The progress of the reform crusades against the cigarette and the jazzy dance merely seemed to confirm this suspicion. The field of moral reform seemed to have been taken over by fanatics. Thus all moral reform suffered. Few people tried to press for a limited good any more, a temperate betterment of a bad situation. It had to be all or nothing, either an excess or a nullification of moral legislation.

During the dominance of these concepts of law and morality, which dated from the views of the Puritans and of the pioneers, moderation and reason and respect for all law suffered. Those who were terrified by the selected laws of their chosen God tried to impose their own holy terror on their fellow citizens through the law of men. It was a hopeless task and led to scoffing at government and churches. . . .

THE UNWANTED ENFORCERS

"The willingness to exclude the saloon is largely conditioned by the opportunity to secure liquor for private use." This was the basic principle of the popular support of prohibition. Indeed, the leaders of the drys knew that they could never get a majority of the American people to give up drinking immediately. They hoped that a new generation of teetotalers would grow up from the ranks of the young, and that the protected drys would win converts among the shamed wets.

The supporters of the Eighteenth Amendment wanted primarily to outlaw the liquor trade, not to prevent dedicated wets from drinking. National prohibition was meant to stop the wet cities from swamping the dry country; only then could there be a counterattack by the rural moralists on the cities. In fact, even these limited hopes of the drys were doomed to disappointment. There was never any serious effort to enforce national prohibition until the early thirties, and by that time it was too late. After less than four years under the Volstead Act, it was clear that "three tremendous popular passions" were being satisfied, "the passion of the prohibitionists for law, the passion of the drinking classes for drink, and the passion of the largest and best-organized smuggling trade that has ever existed for money." Once legalism had turned the possession of alcohol into a popular obsession and the sale of alcohol into a new Gold Rush, enforcement of the liquor laws had no chance.

The failure of the enforcement of the Volstead Act was due to administrative stupidity, political graft, the federal structure of the United States, an antiquated legal system, and the flaws in the act itself. These interlocking and corrigible causes for failure were overshadowed by one overriding consideration, that the prohibition law could not be adequately enforced in the America of that time. Indeed, it is doubtful that national prohibition can ever be enforced, even under a dictatorship. Alcoholic drinks have been made in every civilized society in history. The Wickersham Commission itself sadly conceded, "Few things are more easily made than alcohol." The job of the Prohibition Bureau was to enforce the impossible. But it could have made a better job of this impossible task. . . .

The Prohibition Bureau was always the tool of national and state politics. . . . Political organizations had tried to accelerate or retard enforcement in given areas in accord with the dictates of political expediency. . . .

The Prohibition Bureau itself was continually kept short of men, money, and supplies by a cheeseparing Congress.

While the Volstead Act was pending in Congress, the Commissioner of Internal Revenue protested against being given the responsibility for enforcing such a thankless measure. He said that there could be no sort of adequate enforcement unless the Prohibition Bureau had the fullest co-operation from state policemen, churches, civic organizations, educational societies, charitable and philanthropic societies, and all the law-abiding citizens of the United States. The Commissioner stressed hopefully that it was "the right of the Government officers charged with the enforcement of this law to expect the assistance and moral support of every citizen, in upholding the law, regardless of personal conviction." Unfortunately, the majority of American citizens conceived of other rights—the right to patronize the bootlegger or speak-easy of their choice, and the right to keep mum about the drinking habits of their neighbors. Where the duty to inform on bootleggers was widely considered to be a wrong, prohibition agents could expect little support.

The very organization and methods of the Prohibition Bureau were hopelessly inadequate. The Bureau was not under Civil Service rules. The salaries of prohibition agents compared unfavorably with those of garbage collectors. This low pay made the agents easy victims to corruption. The total number of agents and investigators employed in prohibition enforcement varied between 1500 and 2300 men for the whole of the United States, and the entire staff of the Bureau never exceeded 4500 men. The normal rate of pay for agents was between $1200 and $2000 a year in 1920, and $2300 a year in 1930. For this inadequate wage, they were expected to work long hours and put their lives in danger from the attacks of armed bootleggers. When the bribes offered for a month's co-operation in winking at the actions of large bootlegging rings might total over one million dollars, prohibition agents were sorely tempted not to clip the wings of the goose which laid the golden eggs. In the first eleven years of the Prohibition Bureau, there were 17,972 appointments to the service, 11,982 separations from the service without prejudice, and 1604 dismissals for cause. The grounds of these dismissals included "bribery, extortion, theft, violation of the National Prohibition Act, falsification of records, conspiracy, forgery, perjury and other causes." . . .

The rapid turnover in the prohibition service, and the notoriety of some of its agents, gave it a bad name. One disgruntled prohibition administrator called the Bureau "a training school for bootleggers," because of the frequency with which agents left the service to sell their expert knowledge to their old enemies. The reasons for having such poorly qualified agents in the Bureau are hardly surprising, since the Bureau was run for eight years on the spoils system, and since there was no effort to give even the key men in the Bureau special training for their jobs until 1927. The bootleggers had more than a hundred times the appropriation of the Bureau at their disposal, and were far better organized. The inadequate were forced by their country to pursue the prepared. When drastic attempts were made to reform the Bureau by President Hoover after 1929, it was already too late.

Too many urban Americans had become disgusted with the petty thieveries of the whole service. They shared the opinion of Stanley Walker, the city editor of the New York *Herald Tribune*, that, although there were always some good prohibition agents such as Izzy Einstein and Moe Smith, "as a class, however, they made themselves offensive beyond words, and their multifarious doings made them the pariahs of New York."

An efficient enforcement agency demands three things: continuity of personnel, large enough salaries to make graft unnecessary, and public and federal co-operation. The Prohibition Bureau had none of these three essentials. The first Prohibition Commissioner, an Ohio lawyer, John F. Kramer, served for a year and a half. His promise that he would see that liquor was not manufactured, "nor sold, nor given away, nor hauled in anything on the surface of the earth nor under the sea nor in the air" was not put to the test in his short term. His successor, Roy A. Haynes, was endorsed by dry Congressman Upshaw as a man of "amazing genius and energy in organization." His four years' tenure of office did not demonstrate these qualities. His personal press releases preached the imminent collapse of bootlegging, while his political appointees made the Prohibition Bureau a center of graft and corruption. . . .

The failure of Haynes to achieve anything more than a confident manner and a few spectacular raids on New York hotels made Coolidge appoint a new head of the Prohibition Bureau, a retired General, Lincoln C. Andrews. Although Haynes kept his official position, Andrews was given all real authority. He immediately attempted to reorganize the Prohibition Bureau on military lines and to drive all political influence from the service. Senator "Sunny Jim" Watson commented cynically, "It can't be done," and he was right. General Andrews could not drive the political spoilsmen out of the Bureau. . . . The General's reorganization was largely a paper job; America was divided up into twenty-four districts, and some retired officers from the Army and Navy joined the prohibition service. General Andrews resigned in March, 1927, after offending the politicians and the drys by his forthright statements, including one admission before a Senate subcommittee in 1926 that his task would be greatly simplified by the modification of the Volstead Act to permit the sale of light wines and beer. Major Chester P. Mills, one of General Andrew's officers in New York, estimated that three-quarters of the Prohibition Bureau at the time were "ward heelers and sycophants named by the politicians."

The successors of General Andrews were the Assistant Secretary of the Treasury, Seymour Lowman, and the chief chemist of the

Prohibition Bureau, James M. Doran. The whole service was made to take the Civil Service examination, for "there were scores of prohibition agents no more fit to be trusted with a commission to enforce the laws of the United States and to carry a gun than the notorious bandit Jesse James." The result of the examination, which was the standard test, was shocking. Only two-fifths of those in the Prohibition Bureau could pass the test after two attempts. Most of the remainder were dismissed and replaced. Not until 1930 was a beginning made in setting up a stable body of men prepared to enforce prohibition. When the average length of tenure in the most difficult of the top administrative posts of the service was six months, and the prohibition commissioners themselves were not continued long in office, there was no hope of enforcing the unpopular dry laws. . . .

But if there were replacements and conflicts within the Prohibition Bureau, there were still more conflicts with other law enforcement agencies of the federal government. The Customs Service and the Coast Guard had a long and proud tradition of policing the American borders, and they were unwilling to share their knowledge with the upstart Prohibition Bureau. The border patrols of the Bureau of Immigration, formed in 1925, were also unco-operative, except when bootleggers also happened to be aliens. Rivalry between the services and the "wholesome disgust" of the other services for the despised Prohibition Bureau added to the difficulties of the enforcers of the dry laws.

Certain methods of the Prohibition Bureau gave it still more disrepute. The disguises of Izzy and Moe as undertakers or baseball players were treated as good fun; but when dry agents escorting young women posed as legitimate diners in search of a drink, they were accused of corrupting the very sex which prohibition was meant to save. Other methods of collecting information such as bribery and wire tapping did not make the American people think better of the Bureau. The fact that the chemists of the Bureau approved of putting poisonous denaturants in industrial alcohol, which might easily be diverted into the bootleg market, made them seem accomplices in murder. And the final folly of the prohibition service was to run a speak-easy of its own at the taxpayers' expense, the Bridge Whist Club at 14 East Forty-fourth Street, New York; the club sold liquor to all comers for six months and trapped a few bootleggers. But the spectacle of the Prohibition Bureau spreading the bad habits which it was charged to prevent was too much for the country. The Bridge Whist Club was closed down, and the expense accounts for the undercover agents' drinking were lopped.

But worst of all was the direct murder of innocent citizens by prohibition agents. In the opening days of the Volstead Act, there were shooting affrays between agents and bootleggers. By 1923, thirty prohibition agents had already been killed; Roy Haynes called them "our little band of martyrs." Yet the gunplay was confined, more or less, to the agents and violators of the liquor law. Unfortunately, mistakes of prohibition agents resulted in the killing of women and children, and the serious wounding of Senator Greene, of Vermont, in Washington itself. The innocent deaths of Mrs. Lillian DeKing, whose small son retaliated by shooting the responsible dry agent in the leg, of Henry Virkula, shot down while driving his family in Minnesota, and of Mildred Lee and Sheridan Bradshaw, a girl of eleven years and a boy of eight, made dry agents loathed everywhere. In a popular pamphlet, the Association Against the Prohibition Amendment claimed that more than a thousand people in ten years had been killed outright in the prohibition war between the law enforcers and the violators. Official records admitted the deaths of 286 federal officers and private citizens during this period; the officers had killed the civilians at a ratio of one officer to every three citizens.

The government showed its feelings by sending federal attorneys to defend prohibition agents accused of murder. The officers of the law were rarely convicted, even in the most flagrant cases of slaughter. The Association Against the Prohibition Amendment investigated 184 killings of citizens by prohibition agents; only six of the agents were convicted of any crime, and only one of murder in the second degree. The government seemed to be sanctioning indiscriminate killing by its officers. Although various directives were sent out ordering agents to be careful before shooting, the whole service seemed to be too quick on the draw. "What the prohibition situation needs," wrote Jane Addams, "first of all, is disarmament." Only after the Prohibition Bureau had been transferred to the Department of Justice, and the reasonable rule of Dr. A. W. W. Woodcock, was there any cessation in the shooting. . . .

The drys always maintained that national prohibition had never had a fair trial, because there was no real attempt at enforcement until ten years of bungled efforts had exhausted the tolerance of the public. . . . With the wets powerful in every Republican Cabinet, what hope was there of a zealous prosecution of the dry law? [But] . . . the political triumph of the drys was not, and could not be, translated into a social victory. In fact, if an army of federal agents had been raised to insist on the observance of the Volstead Act in the wet cities, it is probable that repeal would have come about even sooner. When Hoover began to enforce prohibition with some efficiency, he dried up its support as well as supplies of bootleg liquor.

The statistics of prohibition enforcement show the increasing efficiency of the Prohibition Bureau and the increasing volume of the bootleg trade. In 1921, a total of 95,933 illicit distilleries, stills, still worms, and fermenters were seized; this total rose to 172,537 by 1925 and to 282,122 by 1930. In the latter year, some forty million gallons of distilled spirits, malt liquor, wine, cider, mash, and pomace were also seized. The number of convictions for liquor offenses in federal courts, which had averaged about 35,000 a year after 1922, showed a startling jump under the Hoover administration to a maximum of 61,383 in 1932. Jail sentences, which reached a total of only 11,818 by 1927, rocketed to 44,678 in 1932, finally demonstrating, as President Hoover himself wrote, "the futility of the whole business."

President Hoover reckoned later that the federal government could not have come anywhere near enforcing prohibition with a police force of less than a quarter of a million men. Yet even his small efforts at enforcement were enough to write the death warrant of the Eighteenth Amendment. Prohibition had developed from a joke into a threat to all and sundry. While the situation in large cities was "not enforcement but a sort of safe regulation of the liquor-selling traffic" through the co-operation of criminals and policemen against interlopers and price cutters, the drinkers were not worried. But the moment that efficient federal agents began to put respectable citizens in jail, the situation became intolerable. Although bad enforcement disgusted America with prohibition, it was good enforcement which helped to cause the revolt of repeal.

THE DEFECTIVE ACT

The flaws in the Volstead Act were quickly revealed by the methods used by bootleggers to circumvent it. The clause relating to industrial alcohol allowed fake denaturing plants to divert the alcohol into bootleg channels by permitting the establishment of denaturing plants anywhere in the United States, once a bond had been filed and a permit issued. . . . And the home-brewing of wine and beer was itself legal under the Volstead Act, although the regulations of the prohibition unit proscribed the making of "non-intoxicating cider and fruit-juices" from dried fruits, dandelions, and rhubarb. Moreover, the legal manufacture of real beer, before its alcohol was removed and it was turned into near-beer, allowed the makers to divert large quantities of genuine ale into the ever-thirsty market.

The clauses dealing with medicinal and sacramental alcohol in the act provided more illicit liquor in America. In the House debate, Congressmen had voiced their fears of scalawag and jack-leg physicians, although no one foresaw the possibility of bootlegging ministers. The testimony of Dr. Bevan that doctors made roughly $40,000,000 in 1928 by writing medical prescriptions for whisky, the opposition of the National Association of Retail Druggists to the vast profits of the speak-easy drugstores, and proof that even sacramental wine often reached the dinner table rather than the communion cup provided damning evidence against these loopholes in the Volstead Act. . . .

Other deficiencies in the Volstead Act were evident in the prosecution of offenders. There was bad liaison between the Prohibition Bureau and the United States attorneys, and between the United States attorneys and the federal judges. . . . Many cases were dismissed because the Prohibition Bureau was held to have exceeded its legal powers while collecting evidence. Other cases were voided on technicalities. Some federal judges were obviously out of sympathy with the Volstead Act and used its complex and verbose phrasing to acquit offenders. The penalties for breaking the law were not sufficient to deter large-scale bootleggers and first offenders. Not until the passage of the Jones Act in 1929, which supplemented the Volstead Act by providing for a maximum penalty of five years in jail and a fine of $10,000 for first offenders, did the law acquire teeth enough to deter those in search of easy money from bootlegging. . . .

THE UNWILLING STATES

The problem of law enforcement in the United States also lay in the divisions between and within the states. The states had many more police officers than the federal government had—a total of some 175,000 officers of the law in 1930. But these officers were badly paid and overworked, in the interest of low taxes. The states also had different opinions, laws, and judicial practices from those of the federal government. In these discrepancies, evasion of the consequences of the law, particularly of the prohibition law, flourished. National prohibition needed central control if there was to be any efficient enforcement. This central control was impossible when a major part of enforcement was left to the individual states.

Most of the states passed laws to supplement the Volstead Act, by making evasion of the dry law a state crime as well as a federal crime. Sixteen states defined the word "intoxicating" even more stringently than did the Volstead Act. Other states forbade the possession of liquor. Some gave the state police greater powers of search and seizure. In Indiana, jewelers were forbidden to display cocktail shakers or pocket flasks in their windows. In Michigan, the savage Baumes Law made violation of the liquor laws for the fourth time punishable by life imprisonment; a mother of ten children was so sentenced for possessing one quart of gin. But, in general, there was an unmistakable hiatus in the states between the law and its enforcement. A drastic law was all very well; but the fact that the states never appropriated more than a pittance for enforcement or for policemen or for additional courts of judgment drew the teeth from these drastic laws.

The Mullan-Gage Law is a good example. The New York legislature passed this law to supplement the Volstead Act in 1921, and failed to appropriate any money to enforce its provisions. Within a week, the courts of the state were clogged up with liquor cases. Nearly 90 per cent of the accused were dismissed by the courts; 7 per cent pleaded guilty; only 20 cases out of nearly 7000 resulted in a trial by jury, conviction, and jail sentence. When Alfred E. Smith signed the repeal of the law in 1923, making New York the first state to confess to the utter failure of state prohibition enforcement, the impossibility of the job had already been demonstrated. Prohibition could not be enforced in large urban areas unless vast sums were set aside by the legislatures for the purpose, and no legislature in the United States would do this.

Not only did the states fail to enforce their own prohibition laws, but often they prevented the federal prohibition agents from doing their duty. Over and over again, zealous prohibition officers found themselves transferred or removed from their jobs because state politicians were annoyed by their efficiency. In Massachusetts, the chief prohibition officer raided a Republican party banquet where liquor was being served; his own superior officer in the Prohibition Bureau was there, and the zealous subordinate was removed for his pains. . . . In Philadelphia, the formidable General Smedley D. Butler made a valiant attempt to dry up the city. But he left his post before his two years were ended, since he found that the job was impossible. He had arrested more than 6000 people, but only 212 had been convicted in the courts. In his opinion, enforcement had not "amounted to a row of pins after the arrests were made." . . .

The Volstead Act was enforced in the United States wherever the population sympathized with it. In the rural areas of the South and West, there was effective prohibition, as there still is in certain counties. In the large cities, however, there was little

or no attempt at enforcement. The police merely aimed at regulating the worst excesses of the speak-easies. In the ports of
America, as the president of the International Seamen's Union
said, there was no such thing as enforcement or prohibition for
the seaman. "He can get all the drink that he can possibly swill
or buy, and it is strong drink." Along the main highways of the
land, roadhouses offered hard liquor to passing travelers. In addition, no tourist resort would ever dry up its means of attracting
patrons. Wherever urban conglomerations or modern communications spread, liquor spread too. . . . Enforcement was only
effective where it relied on political and religious sanctions.
Where political and religious tradition sanctioned liquor, enforcement was a farce. . . .

The states themselves showed increasing opposition to the Volstead Act. After New York had repealed its prohibition law, it
was followed in the twenties by Nevada, Montana, and Wisconsin.
In 1930, Massachusetts, Illinois, and Rhode Island all voted by
referendum to repeal their state prohibition laws. Although the
drys had won six out of ten popular referendums before 1928 on
the question of keeping the state enforcement codes in operation,
they lost ground steadily after the election of Herbert Hoover to
the White House. Their margin of victory in referendums had
always been narrow, and the growing unpopularity of prohibition during the depression turned their slight majorities into
minorities. The drys ended by opposing state referendums as a
means of expressing popular opinion, and tried to rally the legislatures alone behind the dry law. But as state after state gave
up its enforcement law, until even California with its dry strong-
hold of Los Angeles went wet in 1932, the drys could no longer
hold back the tide of popular discontent. . . .

THE BOOTLEG SPRINGS

There were five main sources of illegal liquor: imported liquor, diverted industrial alcohol, moonshine, illicit beer, and illicit
wine. The first two sources supplied most of the decent liquor
available in the early twenties. If this condition had continued
into the late twenties, there might have been some hope of adequate enforcement of the prohibition laws. But the production
of moonshine and beer and wine in the home decentralized the
making of bootleg liquor to such an extent that enforcement became impossible. Where the springs of bootleg liquor rose in
half the homes of America, there was no stopping of the flood.
. . . .

Roy Haynes referred sadly to the remark that it was impossible to keep liquor from dripping through a dotted line. The Canadian-American border was some thousands of miles long, and hardly patrolled. The Mexican border was similarly easy to cross, although it was never a major source of bootleg supply. Through these undefended frontiers, a deluge of liquor descended. Between 1918 and 1922, imports of British liquor into Canada increased six times and into Mexico eight times. Although it is impossible to calculate how much liquor was actually smuggled into America, the liquor revenues of the Canadian government increased four times during prohibition, while the consumption of spirits by the Canadian population almost halved. In the busiest smuggling area, Detroit, graft averaging two million dollars a week bought immunity for liquor traders. General Andrews calculated that the law enforcement agencies caught only one-twentieth of the liquor smuggled into America. If his estimate was accurate, the flow of liquor into America can be calculated at between five and ten million gallons a year. The Department of Commerce gave the worth of smuggled liquor at the "low estimate" of $40,000,000 a year.

Smuggled liquor was brought into the United States by sea as well as by land. Prohibition saved the economy of many poor islands off Canada and in the West Indies. Imports of liquor into St. Pierre and Miquelon, the Bahamas, and other islands would have been sufficient to keep the local population dead-drunk for hundreds of years. The liquor was exported again, however, to the fleets of rumrunners which lurked outside American territorial waters and sold their cargo to the owners of fast speedboats to run in past the Coast Guard cutters. . . .

The second spring of bootleg liquor flowed from the business of industrial alcohol. Little industrial alcohol was used in America until the beginning of this century. By 1906, however, the demand had become sufficient to secure its exemption from the excise tax on distilled liquors, once special denaturants had been added to the alcohol to render it unfit for human consumption. Between 1920 and 1930, legitimate production of industrial alcohol increased nearly four times to just over 180,000,000 proof gallons a year, although beverage alcohol was prohibited at this time. The Volstead Act carefully exempted industrial alcohol from its provisions, and set up complex rules for its supervision by the Prohibition Bureau.

The huge increase in the business of industrial alcohol was partly due to the boom in industry and partly due to bootlegging. In 1926, General Andrews referred sourly to the special denaturing plants which manufactured industrial alcohol as "nothing more or less than bootlegging organizations." He estimated that some 15,000,000 gallons of alcohol a year were diverted into boot-leg channels; the United States Attorney for the Southern District of New York lifted this figure to between 50,000,000 and 60,000,-000 gallons. Since each gallon of industrial alcohol, when doc-tored and watered and colored by bootleggers, produced three gallons of so-called whisky or gin, the amount of booze available from this source was large. But the heyday of the diversion of industrial alcohol passed in the middle twenties, and, through bet-ter regulation, the total quantity of bootlegged alcohol from this loophole had sunk to less than 15,000,000 gallons a year by 1930.

The Prohibition Bureau tried to make industrial alcohol un-drinkable by insisting on the addition of one of seventy-six de-naturants, made up from different formulas. Some of these dena-turants were harmless, such as lavender and soft soap; others were poisonous, such as iodine, sulphuric acid, and wood alcohol. The bootleggers, once they had laid their hands on the denatured al-cohol, tried to recover it for drinking purposes. . . . But the trouble was that too many bootleggers in search of quick profits did not bother to set up and pay for the expensive processes of recovery. With little more than a token effort at removing the denaturants, the bootleggers mixed industrial alcohol with glyc-erine and oil of juniper and called the product gin. Scotch whisky was made by adding caramel and prune juice and creosote to the industrial alcohol. . . .

The number of deaths due to poisonous drink in the United States gives a fair picture of the height of the influence of doc-tored industrial alcohol. The peak of these deaths was during the period 1925-1929, when some forty people in every million were dying from bad liquor each year. Most of the slaughter was caused in the New York area by the sale of bootleg containing wood alcohol, a denaturing substance which could blind and kill. . . .

The third spring of the bootleg liquor, and its chief source by the close of the twenties, was moonshine—illegal spirits distilled in America for local consumption. Moonshine had been distilled in the Appalachian Mountains since the eighteenth century, and, even before prohibition, up to two thousand illicit stills a year were seized by revenue officers. But national prohibition devel-oped the moonshining industry from small business into big busi-ness. In 1929, twelve times as many illicit stills were seized as had been seized in 1913. Methods of making high-quality liquor by speedy aging processes had made obsolete the means of both the legitimate and the illegitimate distillers of the days before the Volstead Act. By the early thirties, the huge circulation and low price of moonshine of moderate quality was a tribute to the scientific ingenuity and legal immunity of its makers. . . .

In the early days of prohibition, too many small operators with too little knowledge went into the business of operating stills. Poisonous salts of copper and lead and zinc found their way into the moonshine from defective worms and coils used in the process of distillation. The greed of amateur moonshiners made them include the "heads" of the distillation, high in aldehydes, and the "tails," shot through with fusel oil, in the final mixture. These should have been thrown away, and only the "middle run" taken. Moreover, the addition of dead rats and pieces of rotten meat to the mixture to give it a kick did not make the drink better for the health of the drinkers. . . . Only when the production of moonshine became based on the growing corn-sugar industry did its basic elements become clean enough to avoid too much contamination of the drinker's stomach. The corn-sugar industry expanded from a production of 152,000,000 pounds in 1921 to 960,000,000 pounds in 1929, making the Prohibition Bureau calculate sadly that there were at least seven or eight gallons of high-proof moonshine alcohol in circulation for every gallon of diverted industrial alcohol. This estimate put the production of moonshine made from corn sugar alone at a minimum of 70,000,-000 gallons a year, with an absolute alcohol content of some 23,000,000 gallons.

The small moonshiners were gradually taken over or pushed out by the large criminal distributors of moonshine. These distributors either ran large distilleries of their own (more than three thousand distilleries costing up to $50,000 each were captured in 1929) or else farmed out their corn sugar to hordes of home "alky cookers" in the tenements of the large cities. Corn sugar and yeast would be supplied to the alky cooker in Chicago at a cost of fifty cents a gallon. He would sell his distilled moonshine to the distributor at two dollars a gallon. The distributor would bottle it, and retail it to the speak-easy owner at six dollars a gallon. The speak-easy owner would then charge twenty-five cents for each drink, making some forty dollars on the original gallon. Local brands of moonshine had names that testified to their kick—Panther and Goat Whisky, Jackass Brandy, White Mule, White and Jersey Lightning, Yack Yack Bourbon, Soda Pop Moon, Straightsville Stuff. . . . Ten years of prohibition were calculated to have increased the consumption of spirits from all sources in America by one-tenth, when compared to the legal drinking days before the Great War.

Not all drinkers of moonshine bought the final product directly from the bootleggers. A sophisticated and economical group of

Americans preferred to "mix their own poison." They bought raw alcohol directly from the alky cookers or bootleggers or druggists. They then mixed the alcohol in their own bathtubs with quantities of glycerine and oil of juniper, according to individual taste. It was this mixture, which was known as "bathtub gin," that did much to ruin the digestion of the American middle classes. The mixture was served with quantities of ginger ale to hide the flavor, although nothing could disguise the crawling horrors of the aftereffects. . . . Moonshine was the source with which the Prohibition Bureau was least equipped to deal. Indeed, the Bureau did not attempt to deal with it. When a hundred pounds of corn sugar cost five dollars and a portable one-gallon still cost seven dollars, when the libraries of America kept a special shelf of dog-eared books on how to make liquor in the home, when the government itself issued *Farmers' Bulletins* on the methods of making alcohol, when Senator Reed could circulate in print his own recipes for making pumpkin gin and applejack, when constitutional amendments prevented the search of private homes, the attempt to stop people from making their own liquor and selling it on a small scale was impossible. . . .

The fourth major spring of booze was beer. The manufacture of legal near-beer involved the manufacture of real beer, which was then deprived of most of its alcoholic content. Many breweries were bought up by gangsters and run openly in defiance of the law. Other breweries fulfilled the letter of the law in making near-beer, and then sent supplies of the alcohol removed in the manufacturing process along with the product, so that the seller could "spike" the liquid back to its previous condition. . . .

As the increased production of corn sugar was evidence of the amount of moonshining in America, so the increased production of wort and malt syrup showed up the popular practice of illicit brewing. Wort is cooled, boiled mash from which beer is made. With the mere addition of yeast, beer can be manufactured from wort. The process of making beer from malt syrup is a little more complicated, and involves boiling. Nevertheless, the legal production of both of these non-alcoholic substances, whose chief use was in the manufacture of beer, sprang up to unrivaled heights during prohibition, increasing over six times during the space of seven years. The production of hops in the United States also continued to flourish; 15,000,000 pounds of hops were sold in 1928, enough to produce some 20,000,000 barrels of beer, according to the estimate of the Association Against the Prohibition Amendment. The suggested figures for the manufacture of home-brew in 1929, given by the Prohibition Bureau, are just under

700,000,000 gallons of beer, or about a third of the quantity consumed in 1914. These estimates are confirmed by other reliable figures.

The final major spring of bootleg was the making of wine and cider in the home. In 1920, many owners of vineyards in California had pulled up their vines, expecting financial ruin; one of them had even committed suicide. But the first six years of national prohibition brought unparalleled prosperity to the California grape growers. Shipments of grapes, wine and table and raisin, to all parts of America more than doubled. The salvation of the California grape industry was in the notorious Section 29 of the Volstead Act, which permitted the making in the home of fermented fruit juices. The section was inserted, originally, to save the vinegar industry and the hard cider of the American farmers; it was now used to save the wine of the immigrants. The California grape growers, who had often supported the drys against the local brewers and distillers and saloons in a vain effort to enlist dry support for their native industry, now found themselves saved by the dry law. They even produced a processed "grape jelly" called Vine-Glo for those who were too lazy to make their own wine. When water was added to Vine-Glo, it would make a potent wine within sixty days. . . .

A typical case of the small bootlegger was Jennie Justo, the "queen of bootleggers" in Madison, Wisconsin. She paid her way through the university there by bootlegging wine from the local Italian quarter. She drifted into the profession casually, after two journalists had asked her if she could sell them a gallon of wine each week end from her uncle's drugstore. In the end, she set up a speak-easy herself for the university students; she now claims that it was as safe and easy to run as her present tavern in Madison. She did spend six months in the Milwaukee House of Correction for bootlegging, but it was a "nice rest anyways." To her, the whole episode was a respectable way of making a living and of fulfilling a community need. The only villains in the piece were the federal officials, who trapped her by claiming to be friends of her brother.

There were many such cases among the small peddlers of bootleg and small makers of wine. And there were few means of proceeding against them. "We never would get anywhere by arresting distributors," General Andrews conceded, "because the brother or uncle of the man that is arrested takes it up and goes right on." Although the spectacle of immigrants making and selling and drinking their wine drove the drys to paroxysms of fury, so that they recommended the deportation of alien violators of the Volstead Act, nothing much could be done to stop the prac-

tice. Too many people were making too much liquor at home in
a society which resented police invasion of privacy. . . . Once a
wide knowledge of how to make passable hard liquor and beer
and wine was widely disseminated across America, and once a
depression had made all sources of income desirable, nothing
could stop the flood of homemade alcohol from swamping the
nation. . . .

THE LEGAL GAP

Between the arrest of the suspected bootlegger and his conviction, there were many ways of escape. The first loophole was the
United States Commissioner. He issued search warrants and dismissed evidence obtained through improper search and seizure.
Arrested bootleggers were brought before him for a preliminary
hearing, and it was up to him to decide whether the case warranted
a grand jury trial or not. He could put off trial of a particular
case for month after month, while the bootlegger continued with
his operations. He could refuse to believe the testimony of the
prohibition agents, and dismiss the case. One United States Attorney in New York testified that the Commissioner there dismissed nine liquor cases out of ten, or fifty thousand cases a year,
to keep the courts moderately free. Many commissioners were
appointees of state political machines and treated their cases in
the interests of their local machine. In the most flagrant instances,
the commissioners would warn a small clique of attorneys when
search warrants were issued; these attorneys would, in turn, warn
the bootleggers, so that the prohibition agents would find on their
raids "only soft drinks and church music." . . .

The second weak link in the chain of prosecution was the
United States District Attorney. His role was all-important in
securing a conviction. . . . Even where the district attorneys
were on the side of the dry law, the flood of prohibition cases
in the federal courts forced them to allow many bad practices
just to clear away the congestion. Often the offenders were persuaded to plead guilty and forego a jury trial in return for the
promise of a small fine or sentence from the judge. Sometimes
cases were dismissed outright for this purpose, or because of political pressure. During the preparation of cases, corrupt attorneys
might make slips, which would result in the quashing of the case
by the judge. Moreover, they could usually find legal grounds for
securing the continuance of a case. . . .

The third weak link was the jury. Complaints of the wet sym-
pathies of juries in liquor cases were legion. Where a prohibition
case was of such importance that it did reach trial by jury, the

jury often returned a verdict of "not guilty," despite overwhelming proofs of guilt. J. J. Britt, on the legal staff of the Prohibition Bureau, said that it was very difficult in New York or Pennsylvania "to get a verdict of any great consequence in either civil or criminal cases relating to prohibition matters." In one trial in Virginia, a member of the jury dropped a half pint of liquor in court; no action was taken, and the jury as a whole found the defendant, a bootlegging [Negro], guilty. On another occasion, a jury in San Francisco was itself put on trial for drinking up the evidence in a liquor case. Indeed, the notorious difficulty of getting dry verdicts from urban juries gave wet defendants a strong bargaining position with the district attorney; their pleas of "guilty" in return for the promise of a small fine were as much a favor to him as to them. The jury trial, instituted to protect justice, ended by becoming a method of bypassing justice.

The fourth door of escape was the judge himself. There were certain famed judges in America whose sentences on bootleggers were so light that they approached invisibility. The leniency of some judges to violators of the dry law provoked a famous outburst from Clarence True Wilson. According to him, the worst anarchists in America were not bootleggers—they were judges. He even claimed that he could call a roll of judges, "whose names would look like a criminals' list." Although he exaggerated, it is true that the American bench beneath the Supreme Court showed a surprising leniency to offenders against the Volstead Act, until the Hoover regime. . . . Only then was a determined and hopeless attempt made to enforce the dry laws. . . .

Since the beginning of the century, the number of cases tried in federal courts had been rapidly increasing. With the passage of the Mann and the National Motor Vehicle Theft and the Narcotics Acts, bringing increased legal responsibilities to the federal authorities, the number of cases terminated in the federal courts increased from 15,371 in 1910 to 34,230 in 1920, of which 5095 were prohibition cases. But then the prohibition cases increased phenomenally, and with them increased the load on the already burdened courts. By 1928, there were 58,429 prohibition cases concluded in the federal courts; two cases out of every three were terminated there. By 1932, the number of prohibition cases had risen to a maximum of 70,252. The machinery of justice was inadequate to cope with this volume of business, especially as insufficient new judgeships were created to share the load.

Faced with an impossible situation, the federal courts fell back on the expedient of "bargain days." On these days, a vast proportion of the backlog of prohibition cases was cleared off the records by quick pleas of "guilty" from the defendants, in return for low

fines or short jail sentences. Nine out of ten convictions under
the Volstead Act were obtained in "bargain days." Until 1930,
not more than one out of three convictions in federal courts
resulted in any form of jail sentence, and the average fine was
low, between $100 and $150. This method of dispensing justice
destroyed the high reputation which the federal courts had enjoyed before prohibition. . . .

But if the Volstead Act placed a severe strain on the courts of
America, it nearly burst the federal prisons. In 1916, there were
five federal prisons and penitentiaries; there were still five in
1929, although President Hoover began to build more jails to
accommodate the convicted. In 1920, those prisoners who were
serving long-term sentences in federal prisons numbered just over
five thousand; by 1930, they numbered more than twelve thousand, of whom more than four thousand had been sentenced for
violating the liquor laws. The five prisons and penitentiaries
were desperately overcrowded, since they had been built to accommodate a maximum of seven thousand prisoners. Indeed, the
federal authorities were forced to board out most of their prisoners in state and county jails, for they could not accommodate
them in their institutions.

In his Inaugural address, President Herbert Hoover promised
the reform, the reorganization, and the strengthening of the whole
judicial and enforcement system in the United States. For, in
his opinion, "rigid and expeditious justice is the first safeguard
of freedom, the basis of all ordered liberty, the vital force of
progress." And Hoover did what he said he would do. He reformed judicial procedure, the bankruptcy laws, the Federal Bureau of Investigation, and the kidnaping laws, and started to
build Alcatraz and five other prisons. He reorganized, consolidated, and increased the efficiency of the Prohibition Bureau. He
appointed the Wickersham Commission, which, despite its sloth
and evasiveness, produced a mass of absorbing information about
law enforcement in America and dealt the deathblow to prohibition.

The drys insisted on a prohibition law which could not be
enforced by their policemen and prosecutors and judges. The
failure of this enforcement was, to the wets, a proof of the failure
of the law. In fact, such a revolutionary theory as national prohibition could never have been enforced without a revolution in
criminal procedure. Yet this second revolution was not supported
by the drys, for they saw themselves as the defenders of the
ancient customs and liberties of America. Their revolution was
to restore the myth of the good old days, with its emphasis on
the American virtues of law and order.

But a law can only be enforced in a democracy when the majority of the people support that law. And the majority of the people did not support the Volstead Act. When an attempt at enforcement was made by Hoover, it was already too late. No general legal reform could satisfy a people angered by a particular law. James J. Forrester, who investigated the coal-mining regions of Pennsylvania for the Wickersham Commission, found everywhere a "strong and bitter resentment" against national prohibition among workingmen and their leaders. . . . The price that the drys paid for the partial prohibition of liquor was the cheapening of all the laws of the land, and of all the procedures of justice.

NOTES AND QUESTIONS

1. When we say that a law is unenforceable, we really mean that it cannot be enforced without an enormous expenditure of effort, time and money. We may even mean that an attempt to enforce it would be so costly in political terms that the law would be bound to be overthrown. Some laws are costly to enforce because of the nature of the laws themselves—it would be harder, for example, to enforce a law against "cheating" (which is difficult to detect and to measure) than a law against flying the flag of Communist China, since it is cheap and simple to detect violations in the latter. Perhaps a more important factor is the propensity of the relevant public to obey, evade or disobey.

How would you classify the unenforceability of the Prohibition laws, as described by Sinclair? What, in Sinclair's view, were the *causes* of the failure of Prohibition? List as many as you can. Notice that some of these causes relate to the way the laws were drafted, and purely administrative decisions about how to enforce and who would enforce. Do you think Sinclair feels that Prohibition could have succeeded if the law had been more cleverly devised and handled? Was the law "unenforceable" or simply not enforced?

2. Sinclair also lists a number of evil consequences that, in his view, flowed from the failure of Prohibition. For example, some people died or were injured by drinking adulterated liquor. Prohibition, he argues, also bred a general disrespect for law and order. How does Sinclair gather evidence for the various kinds of consequences he lists? How convincing is his evidence?

3. It is often said that the failure of Prohibition illustrates that it is impossible to "legislate morality." Or, to put the matter more intelligibly, that "in the United States . . . no piece of

legislation, or judicial decision, which does not have its roots in community beliefs, has a chance of being effectively carried out. To this extent, it is undeniable that morality cannot be legislated."

The quotation is from John P. Roche & Milton M. Gordon, "Can Morality Be Legislated," *New York Times Magazine*, May 22, 1955, at 10.* Roche and Gordon go on to say that "it would be impossible, for example, to make canasta playing a capital offense *in fact*. . . . This is a fanciful example, but in our view the Volstead Act and the Eighteenth Amendment were no less unrealistic in objective." Do you agree?

Roche and Gordon's piece was written, however, not about canasta or Prohibition, but about the Supreme Court's decision in 1954 desegregating public schools. They attempted to show that desegregation was *not* a "noble experiment" doomed to failure like Prohibition. They felt that school desegregation would work, even though Prohibition did not.

How similar to the experiment with Prohibition do you consider the following:

(a) the decision of the Supreme Court, desegregating schools;

(b) open-housing ordinances;

(c) fair employment laws;

(d) laws prohibiting the sale, possession or use of marijuana;

(e) laws forbidding public employees, including teachers and policemen, from striking;

(f) laws making adultery and fornication a crime;

(g) laws setting up minimum housing standards, and forbidding insanitary, unsafe and overcrowded conditions in the slums.

Which of these are laws "legislating morality"? Which of them are "effective" and which are not? What information would you want to know about the state of public opinion, the resources allocated to enforcement, and the administrative provisions of the laws in question, before you could answer the question fully? How far do you think the experience of Prohibition can be generalized?

On the problem of the meaning of "effective," *see* pp. 306-07, *supra*.

4. To say that one cannot legislate "morality" implies that the thrust of, and the problem with, Prohibition was that it attempted to tamper with areas of human behavior and feeling that are ex-

---

tremely difficult to reach by ordinary legislation. This is one interpretation of the failure of Prohibition. Another is that the law was not correctly structured or designed (*see* ¶ 1).

There are other possible explanations, of course. Enforcement problems may arise because of deep divisions in the population over whether a particular law is right or wrong. Before the Civil War, the federal government had enormous difficulties enforcing laws *against* the slave trade; *see* Warren S. Howard, *American Slavers and the Federal Law 1837-1862* (U. of California Press 1963), containing many interesting parallels to the Prohibition problem; but the Fugitive Slave Law ran into similar enforcement problems. Divisions in the country on the slavery question ran so deep, it was hard to enforce any major piece of legislation, either on the pro-slavery or the anti-slavery side.

Does Sinclair pay adequate attention to the fact that many people love to drink and crave liquor? If law outlaws a commodity that people consider very desirable, the effect of the law will be to increase the price of the commodity, and divert large profits from legal to illegal dealers. This phenomenon has been called the "crime tariff." Herbert L. Packer, *The Limits of the Criminal Sanction* 277-82 (Stanford U. Press 1968). An article in the *Wall Street Journal*, Dec. 18, 1968, at 1, col. 4, describes the "black market" in household help brought in from overseas:

> All the classic requirements for a thriving black market are present. . . . There is a constant demand for live-in domestics and a shortage of natives to fill it. Women from abroad, particularly the Carribean, jump at the chance to get into the U.S. And the law governing domestics from abroad is considered unreasonable and unrealistic by many, including some of those whose duty it is to enforce it.
>
> Immigration experts say many abuses arise in the illegal traffic. Some of the maids are exploited and underpaid by their employers in this country. Unscrupulous attorneys profiteer both from the domestics and the women who hire them. "Legal fees" paid by the maids range from $350 to $1,000. . . .
>
> Under law, no housewife can import a maid unless the U.S. Labor Department certifies that no American worker is available. Working conditions offered must not undermine American standards. The Labor Department also is empowered to prescribe various job particulars, including minimum pay.
>
> The latter point sends many housewives into the black market. Only the rich can afford legal maids, they complain. . . .

Here too the "crime tariff" seems to be at work. Is the black
market in household help comparable to the traffic in bootleg
liquor? *Compare* Lawrence M. Friedman, *Government and Slum
Housing: A Century of Frustration* 39-44 (Rand McNally 1968).
Professor Friedman discusses the effect of a dense network of
housing regulation on the character of the low-income housing
market, and the nature of the persons who enter the business of
supplying low-income housing.

5. Suppose you are convinced that cigarette smoking is so dangerous to health that it simply must be outlawed. Assume that
there is power in a federal agency at present to outlaw cigarettes, without fresh legislation. Would the simple prohibition
of cigarette smoking be utterly ineffective? Could you give the
agency some advice that might maximize the effectiveness of the
prohibition, and help them avoid some of the mistakes of the
Volstead Act?

6. According to Sinclair, one of the costs of the Prohibition
experiment was the "cheapening of all the laws of the land." The
notion is that unenforced or unenforceable laws lead to a general
disrespect for law; hence, unwanted deviance will be fostered or
encouraged elsewhere in the system. A person who sees no reason
why drinking should be a crime, and who sees that the law is only
fitfully enforced, will assume that the law is, in general, unjust;
and his propensity to act as a deviant in some other regard will
be increased. Or, he may become cynically tolerant of other
deviants and fail to support the society's laws in other areas.
Herbert Packer, in *The Limits of the Criminal Sanction* 305
(Stanford U. Press 1968), makes this argument about the criminality of private consensual sex offenses. The laws are, in general,
unenforced. Violators become "contemptuous" of a law they
"perceive to be both unjust and ineffectual." They react by
"strengthening their own identification as an outlaw group."
Within this group (and elsewhere), the "social stigma apart from
the criminal law" relaxes. "Otherwise law-abiding citizens" look
upon themselves as "rebels against society," not "because of
society's deeds or even society's thoughts, but simply because of
some words in a book."

Is the point well taken? What proof is there? How would one
go about showing that the statements made by Sinclair and Packer
are true or false? Do you think that the *kind* of unenforced or
misenforced law makes a difference? If so, what are the relevant
factors? *See* Berkowitz & Walker, Reading 21, at 198, *supra.*

A related point can be made about oversevere (hence under-
enforced) laws. The following letter, which appeared in the *San*

Francisco Chronicle, Jan. 28, 1969, at 32, col. 3, from H. L. Hunt, represents an extreme version of this point:

> Editor—Some "STOP" signs are often treated as a nuisance and constitute a traffic hazard by encouraging bad driving habits. On seldom-traveled streets observance can unduly slow traffic or engender disrespect for law and order. Such "STOP" signs require a delicate choice between disregarding and obeying the law. If the public becomes accustomed to disregarding unneeded signs, they may sometime fail to observe the "STOP" signs which serve a vital purpose. The results may be damage to vehicles, bloodshed, or loss of life. Signs which serve a doubtful purpose and impede traffic should be replaced with wordings the public will approve.
>
> Driving habits can be improved by diligent police chiefs selecting for their cities better words than an invariably emphatic "STOP." The public has thankfully accepted the warning "YIELD" where two or more lines of traffic must merge carefully.
>
> The International Chiefs of Police, 1319 18th Street N.W., Washington, D.C. 20036 could agree upon a title for the best warning from such words as "CHECK," "ALERT," "APPRAISE," "DANGER," "CAUTION," "PAUSE," "WARNING," "JUDGE," "DEFER," "SLOWER," "WATCH OUT," and "COURTESY."
>
> Constructively,
>
>   H. L. HUNT.
> Dallas.

7. Sinclair talks about resistance by the general public to attempts to regulate conduct. Resistance may also come, not from the general public, but from an interest group which stands to lose from the change. See the material on interest groups at 590, *infra*. One case may be singled out here for special mention. Sometimes a social problem tends to become the "property" of a particular group of experts or reformers. Recall Gusfield's discussion of temperance groups and the struggle against alcohol. Established professions are prone to develop these "property rights," and they have many ways of defending their interests, even when part of the public loses confidence in old experts and wants to turn to new ones. *See* Anthony M. Graziano, "Clinical Innovation and the Mental Health Power Structure: A Social Case History," 24 *American Psychologist* 10 (1969).

b. Some particular institutional forces

(1) Goal conflict and the decision not to enforce

When some laws cannot be enforced except at enormous cost, the decision-makers may decide not to enforce, or to adopt alternative means to pursue their goals. Some institutional means of enforcement are "high-cost"; others are "low-cost."

There are many examples of choices made by decision-makers in which the institutional frictions of particular institutions are an important consideration. Recall Macaulay's discussion of why businessmen prefer not to use litigation as a means of settling disputes. Litigation is a fairly rigid, high-cost institutional means of achieving results; it is, of course, in some instances unusually effective. See Reading 13, at 145, supra.

Some types of litigation or sanction are particularly fraught with dangers. The government often has the choice of using criminal process, or sidestepping it. Criminal law is open, notorious, and makes for headlines; sometimes government wants this, sometimes it does not. The government may indict a well-known man for income tax evasion just before the tax deadline in April; this puts the "fear of the Lord" into taxpayers. The indictment of Dr. Spock for conspiring to counsel draft evasion may have been chosen for just such a reason.

Conversely, the government may wish to avoid publicity and the martyr effect. Some opponents of the Vietnam War have refused to pay taxes; as of October 2, 1967, there were about 1,500 people who had protested against the war by attempting to withhold some of their tax payments. None had been prosecuted as of that date, although Neil Haworth, a Quaker pacifist, was later sentenced to sixty days in prison for contempt of court for failure to comply with a court order to turn over a list of his assets to the Internal Revenue Service (Peace News, Apr. 12, 1968, at 11).

The IRS has, in general, not appeared troubled by the tax dissenters. It has generally refused to make use of criminal process. Rather, the agency has levied on bank accounts, or garnisheed the incomes of tax dissenters (U.S. News & World Report, Oct. 2, 1967, at 105).

Ball and Friedman, Reading 30, at 298, supra, make a similar point about the use of criminal sanctions in enforcing child neglect laws: "The criminal law is more than a . . . catalog of rights and wrongs. [It] . . . is also a technique, a mechanism; and it is administered through highly organized institutions. Criminal justice does not consist only of penal statutes; it is also judges, bailiffs, sheriffs, policemen, district attorneys, jails, workhouses, courtrooms, files, fingerprints. Violation of the criminal law may bring the violator into contact with at least a part of this complex apparatus. Any realistic discussion of . . . criminal sanctions must take into account the impact on the accused of . . . the bringing of the accused into contact with the enforcement institutions of the criminal law. The difficulty with the use of criminal sanctions in child support cases is the impeding effect of exposing the violator to the apparatus of the criminal law; its repressive and cumbersome techniques may interfere with the goals of persuasion, negotiations, and voluntary compliance on the part of the erring father."

(2) Countervailing power

(a) Countervailing power built into the system: the jury

44. The American Jury

HARRY KALVEN, JR. AND HANS ZEISEL*

[An outstanding example of collaboration between lawyers and social scientists has been the study of the American jury system, undertaken in the 1950's at the University of Chicago Law School and financed by the Ford Foundation. Some of the results of this massive study have appeared in a number of books and scholarly articles. Other reports have yet to appear.

The American Jury is the most ambitious of the volumes to appear so far. The materials of the study were drawn exclusively from *criminal* trials. It asks the central question: what difference does the jury system make? Since the major alternative in this country to decisions by juries is decisions by judges, the study tries to find out how differently criminal trials would come out if judges decided them rather than juries.

It is, of course, extremely difficult to find out whether a judge would decide a case differently from a jury. A particular trial is a unique event, and it is either tried by judge or jury, not by both. One might simulate data by constructing mock trials; one might interview judges and juries; one might try to find out somehow what really does go on in the jury room. All these methods have limitations (though the Chicago researchers have tried them all). To get at the data for *The American Jury*, the authors chose a somewhat indirect route. They drew a sample of criminal trials in the United States, and sent out a questionnaire to the judges who presided at these trials. The judges were asked to record general information about the case; the verdict of the jury; what *they* would have decided in the absence of a

* Harry Kalven, Jr., Professor of Law, University of Chicago; Hans Zeisel, Professor of Law and Sociology, University of Chicago. Reprinted from The American Jury, pp. 242-54, 286-97, by permission of Little, Brown and Company, Boston, Mass.

jury; and, if they disagreed with the jury, their assessment of *why* the jury decided as it did. Excerpts from the study follow:]

It took several centuries of Anglo-American legal evolution for the rather sophisticated idea to emerge that the state is the other party in interest in a criminal case. For some purposes, however, it is characteristic of the jury to continue to see the criminal case as essentially a private affair.

In both tort and crime the role of the victim may, of course, become relevant. The victim may consent to the conduct or he may generate a privilege of self-defense. In tort, however, there are additional rules which tend to disqualify the plaintiff because of some participation on his side, such as contributory negligence or assumption of risk. But in theory there is no comparable concern with the victim in criminal law.

The topic then is the tendency of the jury, in crimes with victims to weigh the conduct of the victim in judging the guilt of the defendant. The cases show a bootlegging of the tort concepts of contributory negligence and assumption of risk into the criminal law. . . .

In one case the defendant and the victims apparently had been playing "chicken," that is testing each other's nerves by competitively reckless driving. The jury acquits, and the judge offers in explanation:

> Because the jury did not follow the charge of the court, they saw some evidence of contributory negligence on part of person assaulted. Contributory negligence is no defense in the laws of this state to criminal actions.

In a parallel case it appears that the victim has suggested a game of Russian roulette, and the defendant obligingly puts the gun to the victim's head. The defense to the resulting homicide charge is that the victim actually was attempting to commit suicide: some evidence of threats of suicide was introduced at the trial. The jury convicts only of manslaughter. The judge, disagreeing, states that it was the victim's suggesting Russian roulette which caused the jury's verdict.

Finally, in a negligent homicide case, a woman is charged with killing a close friend. The parties had been drinking and playing with a .22 caliber revolver, each taking turns firing it at random and playfully snapping it at each other. On one of these rounds when defendant happened to be holding the gun, it went off, killing the victim. The jury disagrees with the judge and acquits.

The contributory fault theme is found in a more familiar form in a series of negligent automobile homicide cases in which the party killed appears to the jury to also have been negligent, and accordingly the jury acquits the defendant.

> Reluctance of jurors to be severe concerning driving conduct of others, especially with possibility that deceased driver may also have been negligent.

> Victim, who drank to excess, walked or staggered across the road.

> Defendant travelled too fast, but woman (deceased) may have darted into path. . . .

In a radically different context the jury response is similar. Where the defendant is charged with molestation of an eleven-year-old girl and the jury hangs, the judge offers the following explanation of the jury's inability to reach a verdict:

> I believe the jury considered matters other than issues involved, to wit: why had the mother permitted the defendant to come to the house and why had not the mother complained earlier?

Where the defendant drives onto the scene of a previous accident which was inadequately marked off with warnings and negligently kills an ambulance driver, the jury finds the defendant guilty only of drunken driving. As the judge notes, the negligent third party on this occasion is an agent of the state.

> Jury refused to send defendant to penitentiary, apparently deciding that greater warning should have been given by officers in charge at the scene or they should have kept the lane of traffic open for use by others who desired to pass the scene.

Thus far the jury has been dealing with what in tort would be readily recognizable as contributory negligence. The idea is still evident in a series of fraud cases where the jury seems to be endorsing W. C. Field's bon mot: "You can't cheat an honest man." In one case the defendant, through a series of misrepresentations, sells poor quality goods. The judge notes:

> The victims actually received a poor grade of roof paint for their money; they were looking for a bargain and got beat at it.

In a second case the defendant is charged with misrepresenting to the victim the threat of prosecution for a liquor violation and thereby obtaining money from him for "fixing" the non-existent violation. The jury acquits. Similarly, the jury hangs in a case where the defense is that the prosecutrix, an elderly woman intent on separating from her husband, drew their life's savings from a joint bank account and gave the money to the defendant to hold until after the divorce proceedings were terminated. The defendant claims he returned the money; the prosecutrix denies this. The jury does not ignore the fact that the victim appears to have been trying to take advantage of her husband in the divorce proceedings. . . .

In the next group of cases the victim is, at most, stained by some general immorality which has left him vulnerable to the crime. As will be seen, the jury extends its analogy to cover this group of victims.

Perhaps the most vivid instance of this type of jury moralizing is a case where the defendant is charged with rolling a drunk. The judge finds grand larceny; the jury, petty larceny, and the judge explains:

> The prosecuting witness intoxicated at the time of the theft had been around to the taverns and solicited sexual intercourse and the jury did not see fit to impose a heavier crime on the defendant. This is what I think motivated the jury.

Other examples are less clearly pointed. Where the jury acquits in a case of petty theft, the victim has charged the defendants with the theft of articles from his person while he was asleep after a drinking party. The defendants, admitted prostitutes, claim that the articles were given to them in payment for services. The jury may, of course, simply have believed the defendants rather than the complainant, although the judge did not. It seems likely, however, that the jury was not too fussy about resolving the precise issue of fact and was rather taking the view that a victim who consorts with prostitutes should not be heard to complain about a petty theft.

Similarly, in a homicide case where the judge finds second degree murder, the jury, manslaughter, the decisive circumstance is that the quarrel took place in a brothel. The judge states:

> The jury would only convict of manslaughter because witnesses for both the state and the defense were all prostitutes, dope peddlers, pimps, or a combination thereof. The deceased went to a house of prostitution operated by defendants and got into a fight over the price charged. . . .

A number of disagreements arise in cases of forcible rape. Because of the distinctive legal problem here, the jury's response might have been treated as a sentiment in its own right. But these cases show so strong and interesting a resemblance to the assumption of risk theme that it seems congenial to discuss them here.

The law recognizes only one issue in rape cases other than the fact of intercourse: whether there was consent at the moment of intercourse. The jury, as we come to see it, does not limit itself to this one issue; it goes on to weigh the woman's conduct in the prior history of the affair. It closely, and often harshly, scrutinizes the female complainant and is moved to be lenient with the defendant whenever there are suggestions of contributory behavior on her part.

The rape cases are numerous enough to permit the analysis to proceed by cross-tabulation as well as by reason assessment. We begin with reason assessment.

In cases of this nature the judge will often make explicit the assumption of risk sentiment in his comments. Where a young defendant is charged with raping a seventeen-year-old girl and the jury acquits, the judge explains bluntly:

> A group of young people on a beer drinking party. The jury probably figured the girl asked for what she got. . . .

There is a series of other cases in which the point is not quite so explicit but in which the judge notes circumstances suggesting something akin to assumption of risk on the part of the victim.

> The complaining witness alleged after several beers she entered car with defendant and three other men and was driven to cemetery where act took place.

> Woman involved went to public dance and was picked up by defendant. Then went to night club and permitted defendant to take her home over unfrequented road . . . woman involved twice married and divorced, age 33.

> Prosecutrix and defendant strangers to each other; met each other at dance hall. He undertook to take her home . . . rape occurred in lonely wooded area, she drinking but not drunk. He much more under influence.

In these rape cases the jury acquits. But often it expresses disagreement by finding the defendant guilty of a lesser charge, suggesting a refinement of its policy. The jury's stance is not so much that involuntary intercourse under these circumstances is no crime at all, but rather that it does not have the gravity of rape. If given the option of finding a lesser offense, the jury will avail itself of it. However, if this option is not available, the jury appears to prefer to acquit the defendant rather than to find him guilty of rape. . . .

We turn now to the possibilities of cross-tabulation. There are in all 106 cases of forcible rape of an adult woman. Table 71* sets forth the verdict pattern. Of a total of 75 cases where the judge convicts, there are 20 normal disagreements** and 3 hung juries.

TABLE 71

Verdict Pattern for Forcible Rape Cases†

			Jury	
		Acquits	Convicts	Hangs
Judge	Acquits	24	6	1
	Convicts	20	52	3

$N = 106$

† The figures in this table and the ones that follow it do not represent percentages but the actual Number of Cases.

Table 72 then divides these cases into two categories suggested by the reason assessment: *aggravated rape*, a generic term of art, includes all cases in which there is evidence of extrinsic violence or in which there are several assailants involved, or in which the defendant and the victim are complete strangers at the time of the event; *simple rape*, another term of art, includes all other cases, that is, the cases in which none of the aggravating circumstances is present. This classification, at best a somewhat crude restatement of the hypothesis furnished by the reason assessment, serves to discriminate the jury's responses very sharply.

While in the aggravated rape cases the percentage of jury disagreement is 12 per cent, in the simple rape cases it shoots up to 60 per cent.

The analysis can be taken an important step further if we consider the disagreements on charge and examine more closely the

---

* Table 71 indicates that judge and jury agree to acquit 24 times, agree to convict 52 times. Six times the jury would convict, the judge would not, 20 times there is disagreement the other way. There were four cases of hung juries (that is, the jury could not agree). The judge would have convicted three of these defendants and acquitted one. [Eds. note]

** Kalven and Zeisel refer to a disagreement between judge and jury as "normal" if the jury acquitted where the judge would have convicted. [Eds. note]

TABLE 72
Verdict Pattern for Aggravated and Simple Rape

	Aggravated Jury			Simple Jury		
	Acquits	Convicts	Hangs	Acquits	Convicts	Hangs
Judge Acquits	11	4	—	13	2	1
Judge Convicts	5	42	2	15	10	1
			$N = 64$			$N = 42$

Per cent jury
acquittal when
judge convicts: 12% (5 + 1* out of 49) 60% (15 + ½* out of 26)

* Hung juries are here counted as ½ acquittal.

10 cases of simple rape in Table 72 where judge and jury agree to convict. It happens that in all these cases the jury was given the option of finding a lesser charge, and in all but one case the jury exercised this option. In 4 of these cases the judge agrees with the jury on the lesser charge. In 5 the jury convicts of the lesser charge, but the judge convicts of rape, leaving only one agreement on guilt where the jury convicts on the major charge. The statistical consequences of this are summarized in Table 73, which shows the verdicts in simple rape cases in terms of the response to the major charge of rape.

The result is startling. The jury convicts of rape in just 3 of 42 cases of simple rape: further, the percentage of disagreement with the judge on the major charge is virtually 100 per cent (20½ out of 22). The figures could not be more emphatic. Read

TABLE 73
Verdict Pattern for Simple Rape Cases: Rape Charge Only

	Jury Acquits*	Convicts	Hangs
Judge Acquits*	(13 + 4) 17	2	1
Judge Convicts	(15 + 5) 20	(10 − 9) 1	1
			$N = 42$

* Acquittal here means acquittal from the major charge of rape, even if convicted of a lesser charge.

in conjunction with the reason assessment, Table 73 permits the conclusion that the jury chooses to redefine the crime of rape in terms of its notions of assumption of risk. Where it perceives an assumption of risk the jury, if given the option of finding the defendant guilty of a lesser crime, will frequently do so. It is thus saying not that the defendant has done nothing, but rather that what he has done does not deserve the distinctive opprobrium of rape. If forced to choose in these cases between total acquittal and finding the defendant guilty of rape, the jury will usually choose acquittal as the lesser evil. . . .

It will be recalled that . . . we could not readily find any law against which the jury could be said to be in revolt, as it was a generation ago against Prohibition and a century and a half ago against seditious libel. Today the jury's war with the law is modest, and its sentiments cut across crimes to respond to distinctions the law does not make.

Nevertheless, there are a few crimes in which the disagreement arises largely out of the jury's antipathy to the crime itself, although the rate of disagreement is not far out of line. These crimes have two factors in common. First, they are by and large sumptuary, and we thus appear to be picking up some of the traditional hostility to sumptuary legislation. More explicitly, the jury's response is keyed to its perception that in these crimes widespread violation is tolerated. And since almost everybody is doing it, it seems a violation of the principle of evenhanded justice to single out this particular defendant for prosecution. . . .

We begin with game law violations. There is a long history of enmity toward prosecutions for such violations, reaching back to the controversies in eighteenth century England between poachers and gentry. In America the crime appears largely in the form of hunting protected animals or hunting out of season or after hours. And, as might be expected, in regions in which hunting is a popular pastime, prosecutions are not likely to sit well with the jury. Where two defendants are charged with the special crime of killing a doe and the jury hangs, the judge notes simply:

People generally do not like the game law. . . .

In another case the judge observes:

To the best of my recollection, there has never been a game law violation verdict of guilty in this county. . . .

The second category involves *gambling*. Although distinctions are suggested by some variety in the fact situations, the jury's response is general. Thus, where the charge is operating a numbers racket and the jury acquits, the judge states:

Many of our jurors play the numbers. Not illegal. It is only a violation to sell numbers—and in small doubtful cases such are our verdicts.

In another case the judge observes:

Playing numbers is not an offense. Many jurors play them and will not convict in 50 per cent of the cases.

In still another gambling case where the jury acquits, the defendant had been able to operate his numbers game with great circumspection, and hence with a minimum of records. The judge provides the reason.

I think there was ample testimony before the jury upon which it should have returned a verdict of guilty. However, juries in this area have a great reluctance to return a verdict where they find no tangible evidence of a lottery ticket. . . .

The jury in these gambling cases is moved by two considerations. . . . By legalizing all gambling in one state, by allowing track betting in half the states, and by even having the state run lotteries in some states, the law has narrowed the possible area of criminal activity here so much, that the jury has difficulty in treating any segment of gambling as a crime. We have seen the jury's sense of equity triggered by the law's failure to draw a distinction which the jury thinks the law should draw. With respect to gambling, the situation is exactly reversed. The jury is moved to leniency because in its eyes the law draws one distinction too many, thus creating an artificial boundary between what is permissible and what is criminal.

As the [judge's] comments indicate, gambling is so widespread an activity in our society that many of the very jurors who sit on these cases engage in it themselves or have acquaintances who do. There is, then, a special embarrassment in trying to persuade jurors to convict a defendant for doing something that they themselves or their friends do in their daily lives. The moral seems to be that, unless the state wants to be more serious and stringent in the regulation of gambling, the jury will not cooperate in efforts to regulate part of it through the criminal law.

. . . [T]he Prohibition era provided the most intense example of jury revolt in recent history. Our *liquor violation* cases pick up some notes, albeit faint, of these Prohibition era sentiments.

In a Kentucky case where moonshining in violation of federal law is involved and the jury acquits, the judge comments:

Routine whiskey case where violations of federal tax law pertaining to moonshining are prevalent.

Again, where the defendant is charged with selling beer in a dry
county and the jury acquits, the judge notes simply:

> Difficult generally to convict bootleggers.

And again, where the defendant is charged with selling liquor in
a dry territory and the jury acquits, the judge notes:

> This particular county adjoins the Mississippi River and al-
> coholic drink is sold just across the bridge. A very great
> number of persons maintain the belief that the law against
> selling such alcoholic drink should not be enforced, and it is
> extremely difficult to get a conviction no matter how strong
> the evidence may be. . . .

Although the gambling, game law, and liquor law violations
do not bulk large in number, the judge's comments on them suggest a persistent theme of jury hostility to particular types of
criminal regulation. Further, in many of them the sentiment is
fed by what the jury regards as an inconsistent line between legal
and illegal conduct, be it between betting at the race track and
betting in town, or between selling liquor on one side of the
Mississippi or the other. The theme that violation of the law
has become widespread and open recurs and brings with it the
embarrassment that it is difficult to find a jury whose members
are not close to the conduct they will be asked to judge. On the
other hand, it is perhaps a sign of the strength of the society and
of the democratic congruence between the people's sense of justice and the law that this best evidence of jury sentiment against
special crime categories is so modest.

One final unpopular law which illustrates the general theme
is driving under the influence of intoxicating beverages, or more
simply, *drunken driving*. The jury's response to drunken driving turns out to be interesting and complex, and in part determined by factors having little to do with sentiments on drinking.
In many cases the issue seems to be entirely evidentiary, with the
jury showing hostility to the use of drunkometers and alcometers,
so frequently relied upon in these cases. Then too, the penalty
for drunken driving is often the mandatory loss of the driver's
license for a year, a penalty which the jury regards as overly
severe. In an occasional case it is the stringency of the law's definition of the crime that offends the jury; the crime is driving
under the influence of liquor and does not require that the defendant in fact drive badly, or even that he be drunk in the
popular sense, if there is the necessary proof of alcohol in his
blood.

For the purposes of this chapter, however, we are concerned
with cases in which the judge notes an underlying community
sentiment against the crime. In a substantial number of drunken
driving cases the judge detects such a community feeling and
offers it as an explanation for disagreements. . . .

Most jurors are drinking men themselves, and, therefore,
biased. . . .

I understand that jurors in this county hesitate to convict
persons for drunk driving. In my opinion the verdict was
shocking. . . .

Few convictions in this type of case.

Hesitance to convict on part of jurors who drive and drink.

Some members of jury were favorable to drinking.

Many of the cases, of course, illustrate the difficulty already
noted in the gambling, game law, and other liquor violation
cases, namely, selecting a jury not tainted with the crime it is
asked to condemn. One comment gives homiletic expression to
the moral dilemma the jury is faced with in cases of this kind.

Perhaps some members of jury thought "There but for the
Grace of God go I."

The difficulties in jury selection are often commented on. The
vulnerable composition of the jury is at times credited directly
to the skill of defense counsel.

The defense was careful to get jury of people who drink; a
strategy that is used in cases of this kind. It is my opinion
that jurors who drink are inclined to be sympathetic to defendant when he makes a good appearance and expect more
proof of alcoholic influence than the law requires for conviction.

The historic role of the jury as a bulwark against grave official
tyranny is at best only dimly evident in its contemporary role as
a moderate corrective against undue prosecutions for gambling,
game, and liquor violations and, to some extent, drunken driving. As we review these instances of disagreement, it is apparent
that jury reaction against unpopular laws is complex: to some
extent the jurors see themselves as on trial but for the grace of
God, to some extent the jury resents the sumptuary interventions, and to some extent the jury objects to the penalty. Beyond
these points there is the recurring theme that the prosecution of

the particular defendant seems to be selective and to violate the
ideal of evenhanded administration of justice.

NOTES AND QUESTIONS

1. Review the description of the method used by Kalven and
Zeisel in gathering their data. Bear in mind that the *reasons* for
jury disagreement are distilled, not from any information provided by the jury, but from the guesses of the judges. Do you
think this fact casts some doubt on the validity of their results?

2. A number of other questions can be raised about the methodology of Kalven and Zeisel. How do we know the judge really
would have decided the case the way he says he would have? The
judges were requested to record the "verdict" before the jury
brought in *its* verdict; and the authors believe that most judges
played the game fairly. But there remains a serious objection.
In the authors' own words:

> One of the judges reported to us in conversation that he
> had wondered if he would have decided a given case as he
> did, had he been exposed to the responsibilities and full
> pressures of the actual decision. The implication was that
> he might be more legalistic on paper than he would have
> been in a real trial.

Kalven and Zeisel feel that this is a "valid point"; but they think
that there are "sufficient reasons" for taking the hypothetical
judge verdicts as "reliable." One such reason is "the vividness
with which the judge reports them." (pp. 53-54) Are you convinced?

3. A basic finding is that judge and jury agree in 75.4% of
the cases. Judge and jury both agreed that 13.4% of the defendants should be acquitted, and that 62% of the defendants should
be convicted. Adding these two figures together we obtain a figure of 75.4%, which is the total agreement rate.

Kalven and Zeisel remark that "To some . . . the fact that
judge and jury agree some 75 per cent of the time will be read
as a reassuring sign of the competence and stability of the jury
system; to others the fact that they disagree 25 per cent of the
time will be viewed as a disturbing sign of the anarchy and eccen-
tricity of the jury." (p. 57) Or, they might have added, of the
stiffness and conservatism of judges.

The disagreements tend to run in one direction. Sixty-four and
two-tenths percent of the defendants were convicted; in only
2.2% of the cases did the judge feel the jury ought to have

acquitted instead of convicted. But the judge agreed with the jury *less than half of the time* on the acquitted defendants. Of the 30.3% of defendants who were acquitted, the judge would have disagreed and convicted 16.9%; in only 13.4% of the cases did judge and jury agree. Hence the jury is considerably more "lenient" than the judge.

What is your own view of the significance of the general findings, assuming them to be correct? Whether the area of agreement and disagreement is too much or too little will depend, of course, on your view of what it is that the jury is supposed to do and how well it does it; and similarly, as to the function of the judge.

Do the general findings discussed above, and the excerpts which you have read, add up to a coherent pattern from which you can say, with more or less confidence, that the jury is performing some *general function*—for example, tempering justice with mercy for criminal defendants—different from the hypothetical or ideal function assumed by the law, or by Kalven and Zeisel, or by yourself?

4. A jury can temper justice with mercy, but, also, it can reflect community sentiment and convict the unpopular where a less representative finder-of-fact might resist the popular will. In Sheppard v. Maxwell, 384 U.S. 333 (1966), the Supreme Court ruled that newspaper publicity concerning a murder case denied the defendant a fair trial because of the high chance that the jury was prejudiced by the pretrial news coverage. Professor Rita James Simon conducted a pilot study to test how jurors react to such publicity. A sample of registered voters was drawn since this is the source of jurors in most cities. Eight hundred twenty-five people were asked to cooperate; ninety-seven were willing. These people were shown fictional newspaper stories about a murder. One group read a sensational story stressing the gory details and the criminal record of the accused. The other read a sober account of the murder. Both groups were asked their opinion of the accused's guilt. Sixteen percent more of those who read the sensational story thought that the accused was guilty than those who read the conservative story. Moreover, 10% more of the conservative story readers suspended judgment and indicated that they had no opinion than the readers of the sensational story.

Next, all subjects listened to a tape recording of a "trial" of the accused. The judge instructed the jury to disregard opinions formed by reading newspapers. After listening to the tape about 75% of the subjects thought the accused was not guilty regardless of which version of the newspaper story they had read before the trial. Before the trial only 33% who read the sensational story thought that the accused was not guilty; only 39% of those who read the conservative story thought this. Apparently, most jurors were able to put aside their preconceptions and respond to the evidence. Simon, "Murder, Juries, and the Press," 3 *Transaction* 40-42 (1966).

To what extent, if at all, does this study indicate that concern over the impact of pretrial publicity is exaggerated?

5. Notice the use of the term "legalistic" in the quotation from the judge in ¶ 2. By this the judge seems to mean a tendency to follow rules of law strictly, and to decide without reference to criteria that the law does not openly tolerate. The assumption, of course, is that juries are much less prone to be legalistic than judges—even than judges sitting without juries, and acting as it were as both judge and jury. Do you think this is so? If it is, why should it be so? And if the jury in fact uses illegitimate criteria, why do we tolerate and even treasure the jury (constitutional requirements aside)?

6. It is widely believed that juries do show biases which do not have official support in the law; and that these biases are not random, but are systematic. So, for example, southern juries are believed to be biased against Negro defendants in cases where the complaining witness is white; and juries in personal injury cases are believed to be biased against corporate defendants. How would one go about showing that such biases existed? If they were demonstrated, how would one go about eliminating them? Are they both equally harmful?

7. Recall that Auerbach and Skolnick differed about the value of the jury project. *See* Readings 2 & 3, at 18, 27, *supra.* Now that you have read a sample of the jury project findings, do you side with Auerbach, Skolnick, or neither one?

45. The Society of Captives: A Study of a Maximum Security Prison

GRESHAM SYKES*

"For the needs of mass administration today," said Max Weber, "bureaucratic administration is completely indispensable. The choice is between bureaucracy and dilettantism in the field of administration." To the officials of the New Jersey State Prison the choice is clear, as it is clear to the custodians of all maximum security prisons in the United States today. They are organized into a bureaucratic administrative staff—characterized by limited and specific rules, well-defined areas of competence and responsibility, impersonal standards of performance and promotion, and so on—which is similar in many respects to that of any modern, large-scale enterprise; and it is this staff which must see to the effective execution of the prison's routine procedures.

Of the approximately 300 employees of the New Jersey State Prison, more than two-thirds are directly concerned with the supervision and control of the inmate population. These form the custodian force which is broken into three eight-hour shifts, each shift being arranged in a typical pyramid of authority. The day shift, however—on duty from 6:20 A.M. to 2:20 P.M.—is by far the largest. As in many organizations, the rhythm of life in the prison quickens with daybreak and trails off in the afternoon, and the period of greatest activity requires the largest number of administrative personnel.

In the bottom ranks are the Wing guards, the Tower guards, the guards assigned to the shops, and those with a miscellany of duties such as the guardianship of the receiving gate or the garage.

* Gresham Sykes, Professor of Law and Sociology, University of Denver College of Law. From The Society of Captives: A Study of A Maximum Security Prison, by Gresham Sykes, pp. 40-58 (Copyright © 1958, by Princeton University Press). Reprinted by permission of Princeton University Press. Some footnotes omitted. Discussion concerning corruption of guard's authority is from Crime and Society by Gresham Sykes, © Random House, Inc., reprinted by permission.

Immediately above these men are a number of sergeants and lieutenants and these in turn are responsible to the Warden and his assistants.

The most striking fact about this bureaucracy of custodians is its unparalleled position of power—in formal terms, at least—vis-à-vis the body of men which it rules and from which it is supposed to extract compliance. The officials, after all, possess a monopoly on the legitimate means of coercion (or, as one prisoner has phrased it succinctly, "They have the guns and we don't"); and the officials can call on the armed might of the police and the National Guard in case of an overwhelming emergency. The 24-hour surveillance of the custodians represents the ultimate watchfulness and, presumably, noncompliance on the part of the inmates need not go long unchecked. The rulers of this society of captives nominally hold in their hands the sole right of granting rewards and inflicting punishments and it would seem that no prisoner could afford to ignore their demands for conformity. Centers of opposition in the inmate population—in the form of men recognized as leaders by fellow prisoners—can be neutralized through the use of solitary confinement or exile to other State institutions. The custodians have the right not only to issue and administer the orders and regulations which are to guide the life of the prisoner, but also the right to detain, try, and punish any individual accused of disobedience—a merging of legislative, executive, and judicial functions which has long been regarded as the earmark of complete domination. The officials of the prison, in short, appear to be the possessors of almost infinite power within their realm; and, at least on the surface, the bureaucratic staff should experience no great difficulty in converting their rules and regulations—their blueprint for behavior—into a reality.

It is true, of course, that the power position of the custodial bureaucracy is not truly infinite. The objectives which the officials pursue are not completely of their own choosing and the means which they can use to achieve their objectives are far from limitless. The custodians are not total despots, able to exercise power at whim, and thus they lack the essential mark of infinite power, the unchallenged right of being capricious in their rule. It is this last which distinguishes terror from government, infinite power from almost infinite power, and the distinction is an important one. Neither by right nor by intention are the officials of the New Jersey State Prison free from a system of norms and laws which curb their actions. But within these limitations the bureaucracy of the prison is organized around a grant of power which is without an equal in American society; and if the rulers of any social system could secure compliance with their rules and regulations—however sullen or unwilling—it might be expected that the officials of the maximum security prison would be able to do so.

When we examine the New Jersey State Prison, however, we find that this expectation is not borne out in actuality. Indeed, the glaring conclusion is that despite the guns and the surveillance, the searches and the precautions of the custodians, the actual behavior of the inmate population differs markedly from that which is called for by official commands and decrees. Violence, fraud, theft, aberrant sexual behavior—all are commonplace occurrences in the daily round of institutional existence in spite of the fact that the maximum security prison is conceived of by society as the ultimate weapon for the control of the criminal and his deviant actions. Far from being omnipotent rulers who have crushed all signs of rebellion against their regime, the custodians are engaged in a continuous struggle to maintain order—and it is a struggle in which the custodians frequently fail. Offenses committed by one inmate against another occur often, as do offenses committed by inmates against the officials and their rules. And the number of undetected offenses is, by universal agreement of both officials and inmates, far larger than the number of offenses which are discovered.

Some hint of the custodial bureaucracy's skirmishes with the population of prisoners is provided by the records of the disciplinary court which has the task of adjudicating charges brought by guards against their captives for offenses taking place within the walls. The following is a typical listing for a one-week period:

CHARGE	DISPOSITION
1) Insolence and swearing while being interrogated	1) Continue in segregation
2) Threatening an inmate	2) Drop from job
3) Attempting to smuggle roll of tape into institution	3) 1 day in segregation with restricted diet
4) Possession of contraband	4) 30 days loss of privileges
5) Possession of pair of dice	5) 2 days in segregation with restricted diet
6) Insolence	6) Reprimand
7) Out of place	7) Drop from job. Refer to classification committee for reclassification
8) Possession of home-made knife, metal, and emery paper	8) 5 days in segregation with restricted diet

9)	Suspicion of gambling or receiving bets	9)	Drop from job and change Wing assignment
10)	Out of place	10)	15 days loss of privileges
11)	Possession of contraband	11)	Reprimand
12)	Creating disturbance in Wing	12)	Continue in segregation
13)	Swearing at an officer	13)	Reprimand
14)	Out of place	14)	15 days loss of privileges
15)	Out of place	15)	15 days loss of privileges

Even more revealing, however, . . . are the so-called charge slips in which the guard is supposed to write out the derelictions of the prisoner in some detail. In the New Jersey State Prison, Charge Slips form an administrative residue of past conflicts between captors and captives and the following accounts are a fair sample:

This inmate threatened an officer's life. When I informed this inmate he was to stay in to see the Chief Deputy on his charge he told me if he did not go to the yard I would get a shiv in my back.   Signed: Officer A_____

Inmate X cursing an officer. In mess hall inmate refused to put excess bread back on tray. Then he threw the tray on the floor. In the Center, inmate cursed both Officer Y and myself.   Signed: Officer B_____

This inmate has been condemning everyone about him for going to work. The Center gave orders for him to go to work this A.M. which he refused to do. While searching his cell I found drawings of picks and locks.
                Signed: Officer C_____

Fighting. As this inmate came to 1 Wing entrance to go to yard this A.M. he struck inmate G in the face.
                Signed: Officer D_____

Having fermented beverage in his cell. Found while inmate was in yard.   Signed: Officer E_____

Attempting to instigate wing disturbance. When I asked him why he discarded [sic] my order to quiet down he said he was going to talk any time he wanted to and_____me and do whatever I wanted in regards to it.
                Signed: Officer F_____

Possession of home-made shiv sharpened to razor edge on his person and possession of 2 more shivs in cell. When inmate was sent to 4 Wing officer H found 3" steel blade in pocket.

I ordered Officer M to search his cell and he found 2 more
shivs in process of being sharpened.

Signed: Officer G_____

It is hardly surprising that when the guards at the New Jersey
State Prison were asked what topics should be of first importance
in a proposed in-service training program, 98 percent picked
"what to do in event of trouble." The critical issue for the
moment, however, is that the dominant position of the custodial
staff is more fiction than reality, if we think of domination as
something more than the outward forms and symbols of power.
If power is viewed as the probability that orders and regulations
will be obeyed by a given group of individuals, as Max Weber has
suggested, the New Jersey State Prison is perhaps more notable for
the doubtfulness of obedience than its certainty. The weekly records of the disciplinary court and Charge Slips provide an admittedly poor index of offenses or acts of noncompliance committed
within the walls, for these form only a small, visible segment of an
iceberg whose greatest bulk lies beneath the surface of official recognition. The public is periodically made aware of the officials'
battle to enforce their regime within the prison, commonly in the
form of allegations in the newspapers concerning homosexuality,
illegal use of drugs, assaults, and so on. But the ebb and flow of
public attention given to these matters does not match the constancy of these problems for the prison officials who are all too well
aware that "Incidents"—the very thing they try to minimize—are
not isolated or rare events but are instead a commonplace. The
number of "incidents" in the New Jersey State Prison is probably no greater than that to be found in most maximum security
institutions in the United States and may, indeed, be smaller,
although it is difficult to make comparisons. In any event, it
seems clear that the custodians are bound to their captives in a
relationship of conflict rather than compelled acquiescence, despite the custodians' theoretical supremacy, and we now need to
see why this should be so.

II

In our examination of the forces which undermine the power
position of the New Jersey State Prison's custodial bureaucracy,
the most important fact is, perhaps, that the power of the custodians is not based on authority.

Now power based on authority is actually a complex social
relationship in which an individual or a group of individuals
is recognized as possessing a right to issue commands or regula-

tions and those who receive these commands or regulations feel compelled to obey by a sense of duty. In its pure form, then, or as an ideal type, power based on authority has two essential elements: a rightful or legitimate effort to exercise control on the one hand and an inner, moral compulsion to obey, by those who are to be controlled, on the other. In reality, of course, the recognition of the legitimacy of efforts to exercise control may be qualified or partial and the sense of duty, as a motive for compliance, may be mixed with motives of fear or self-interest. But it is possible for theoretical purposes to think of power based on authority in its pure form and to use this as a baseline in describing the empirical case.

It is the second element of authority—the sense of duty as a motive for compliance—which supplies the secret strength of most social organizations. Orders and rules can be issued with the expectation that they will be obeyed without the necessity of demonstrating in each case that compliance will advance the subordinate's interests. Obedience or conformity springs from an internalized morality which transcends the personal feelings of the individual; the fact that an order or a rule is an order or a rule becomes the basis for modifying one's behavior, rather than a rational calculation of the advantages which might be gained.

In the prison, however, it is precisely this sense of duty which is lacking in the general inmate population. The regime of the custodians is expressed as a mass of commands and regulations passing down a hierarchy of power. In general, these efforts at control are regarded as legitimate by individuals in the hierarchy, and individuals tend to respond because they feel they "should," down to the level of the guard in the cellblock, the industrial shop, or the recreation yard. But now these commands and regulations must jump a gap which separates the captors from the captives. And it is at this point that a sense of duty tends to disappear and with it goes that easily-won obedience which many organizations take for granted in the naïveté of their unrecognized strength. In the prison power must be based on something other than internalized morality and the custodians find themselves confronting men who must be forced, bribed, or cajoled into compliance. This is not to say that inmates feel that the efforts of prison officials to exercise control are wrongful or illegitimate; in general, prisoners do not feel that the prison officials have usurped positions of power which are not rightfully theirs, nor do prisoners feel that the orders and regulations which descend upon them from above represent an illegal extension of their rulers' grant of government. Rather, the noteworthy fact

about the social system of the New Jersey State Prison is that
the bond between recognition of the legitimacy of control and
the sense of duty has been torn apart. . . .

Like a province which has been conquered by force of arms,
the community of prisoners has come to accept the validity of
the regime constructed by their rulers but the subjugation is not
complete. Whether he sees himself as caught by his own stupidity, the workings of chance, his inability to "fix" the case, or the
superior skill of the police, the criminal in prison seldom denies
the legitimacy of confinement.[7] At the same time, the recognition of the legitimacy of society's surrogates and their body of
rules is not accompanied by an internalized obligation to obey and
the prisoner thus accepts the fact of his captivity at one level and
rejects it at another. If for no other reason, then, the custodial
institution is valuable for a theory of human behavior because it
makes us realize that men need not be motivated to conform to a
regime which they define as rightful. It is in this apparent contradiction that we can see the first flaw in the custodial bureaucracy's assumed supremacy.

III

Since the Officials of prison possess a monopoly on the means
of coercion, as we have pointed out earlier, it might be thought
that the inmate population could simply be forced into conformity and that the lack of an inner moral compulsion to obey on
the part of the inmates could be ignored. Yet the combination
of a bureaucratic staff—that most modern, rational form of mobilizing effort to exercise control—and the use of physical violence—that most ancient device to channel man's conduct—must
strike us as an anomaly and with good reason. The use of force
is actually grossly inefficient as a means for securing obedience,
particularly when those who are to be controlled are called on
to perform a task of any complexity. A blow with a club may
check an immediate revolt, it is true, but it cannot assure effective performance on a punch-press. A "come-along," a strait-
jacket or a pair of handcuffs may serve to curb one rebellious
prisoner in a crisis, but they will be of little aid in moving more

---

7 This statement requires two qualifications. First, a number of inmates
steadfastly maintain that they are innocent of the crime with which they
are charged. It is the illegitimacy of their particular case, however, rather
than the illegitimacy of confinement in general, which moves them to protest. Second, some of the more sophisticated prisoners argue that the conditions of imprisonment are wrong, although perhaps not illegitimate or
illegal, on the grounds that reformation should be the major aim of imprisonment and the officials are not working hard enough in this direction.

than 1200 inmates through the messhall in a routine and orderly fashion. Furthermore, the custodians are well aware that violence once unleashed is not easily brought to heel and it is this awareness that lies behind the standing order that no guard should ever strike an inmate with his hand—he should always use a night stick. This rule is not an open invitation to brutality but an attempt to set a high threshold on the use of force in order to eliminate the casual cuffing which might explode into extensive and violent retaliation. Similarly, guards are under orders to throw their night sticks over the wall if they are on duty in the recreation yard when a riot develops. A guard without weapons, it is argued, is safer than a guard who tries to hold on to his symbol of office, for a mass of rebellious inmates may find a single night stick a goad rather than a restraint and the guard may find himself beaten to death with his own means of compelling order.

In short, the ability of the officials to physically coerce their captives into the paths of compliance is something of an illusion as far as the day-to-day activities of the prison are concerned and may be of doubtful value in moments of crisis. Intrinsically inefficient as a method of making men carry out a complex task, diminished in effectiveness by the realities of the guard-inmate ratio,[8] and always accompanied by the danger of touching off further violence, the use of physical force by the custodians has many limitations as a basis on which to found the routine operation of the prison. Coercive tactics may have some utility in checking blatant disobedience—if only a few men disobey. But if the great mass of criminals in prison are to be brought into the habit of conformity, it must be on other grounds. Unable to count on a sense of duty to motivate their captives to obey and unable to depend on the direct and immediate use of violence to insure a step-by-step submission to the rules, the custodians must fall back on a system of rewards and punishments.

Now if men are to be controlled by the use of rewards and punishments—by promises and threats—at least one point is patent: The rewards and punishments dangled in front of the individual must indeed be rewards and punishments from the point of view of the individual who is to be controlled. It is precisely on this point, however, that the custodians' system of rewards and punishments founders. . . .

---

8 Since each shift is reduced in size by vacations, regular days off, sickness, etc., even the day shift—the largest of the three—can usually muster no more than 90 guards to confront the population of more than 1200 prisoners. The fact that they are so heavily out-numbered is not lost on the officials.

In the first place, the punishments which the officials can inflict—for theft, assaults, escape attempts, gambling, insolence, homosexuality, and all the other deviations from the pattern of behavior called for by the regime of the custodians—do not represent a profound difference from the prisoner's usual status. It may be that when men are chronically deprived of liberty, material goods and services, recreational opportunities and so on, the few pleasures that are granted take on a new importance and the threat of their withdrawal is a more powerful motive for conformity than those of us in the free community can realize. To be locked up in the solitary confinement wing, that prison within a prison; to move from the monotonous, often badly prepared meals in the messhall to a diet of bread and water; to be dropped from a dull, unsatisfying job and forced to remain in idleness—all, perhaps, may mean the difference between an existence which can be borne, painful though it may be, and one which cannot. But the officials of the New Jersey State Prison are dangerously close to the point where the stock of legitimate punishments has been exhausted and it would appear that for many prisoners the few punishments which are left have lost their potency. To this we must couple the important fact that such punishments as the custodians can inflict may lead to an increased prestige for the punished inmate in the eyes of his fellow prisoners. He may become a hero, a martyr, a man who has confronted his captors and dared them to do their worst. In the dialectics of the inmate population, punishments and rewards have, then, been reversed and the control measures of the officials may support disobedience rather than decrease it.

In the second place, the system of rewards and punishments in the prison is defective because the reward side of the picture has been largely stripped away. Mail and visiting privileges, recreational privileges, the supply of personal possessions—all are given to the inmate at the time of his arrival in one fixed sum. Even the so-called Good Time—the portion of the prisoner's sentence deducted for good behavior—is automatically subtracted from the prisoner's sentence when he begins his period of imprisonment. Thus the officials have placed themselves in the peculiar position of granting the prisoner all available benefits or rewards at the time of his entrance into the system. The prisoner, then, finds himself unable to win any significant gains by means of compliance, for there are no gains left to be won.

From the viewpoint of the officials, of course, the privileges of the prison social system are regarded as rewards, as something to be achieved. That is to say, the custodians hold that recreation, access to the inmate store, Good Time, or visits from individuals in the free community are conditional upon conformity or good behavior. But the evidence suggests that from the viewpoint of the inmates the variety of benefits granted by the custodians is not defined as something to be earned but as an inalienable right—as the just due of the inmate which should not turn on the question of obedience or disobedience within the walls. After all, the inmate population claims, these benefits have belonged to the prisoner from the time when he first came to the institution.

In short, the New Jersey State Prison makes an initial grant of all its rewards and then threatens to withdraw them if the prisoner does not conform. It does not start the prisoner from scratch and promise to grant its available rewards one by one as the prisoner proves himself through continued submission to the institutional regulations. As a result a subtle alchemy is set in motion whereby the inmates cease to see the rewards of the system as rewards, that is, as benefits contingent upon performance; instead, rewards are apt to be defined as obligations. Whatever justification might be offered for such a policy, it would appear to have a number of drawbacks as a method of motivating prisoners to fall into the posture of obedience. In effect, rewards and punishments of the officials have been collapsed into one and the prisoner moves in a world where there is no hope of progress but only the possibility of further punishments. Since the prisoner is already suffering from most of the punishments permitted by society, the threat of imposing those few remaining is all too likely to be a gesture of futility.

IV

Unable to depend on that inner moral compulsion or sense of duty which eases the problem of control in most social organizations, acutely aware that brute force is inadequate, and lacking an effective system of legitimate rewards and punishments which might induce prisoners to conform to institutional regulations on the grounds of self interest, the custodians of the New Jersey State Prison are considerably weakened in their attempts to impose their regime on their captive population. The result, in fact, is, . . . a good deal of deviant behavior or noncompliance in a social system where the rulers at first glance seem to possess almost infinite power.

Yet systems of power may be defective for reasons other than the fact that those who are ruled do not feel the need to obey the orders and regulations descending on them from above. Systems of power may also fail because those who are supposed to rule are unwilling to do so. The unissued order, the deliberately ignored disobedience, the duty left unperformed—these are cracks in the monolith just as surely as are acts of defiance in the subject population. The "corruption" of the rulers may be far less dramatic than the insurrection of the ruled, for power unexercised is seldom as visible as power which is challenged, but the system of power still falters.

Now the official in the lowest ranks of the custodial bureaucracy—the guard in the cellblock, the industrial shop, or the recreation yard—is the pivotal figure on which the custodial bureaucracy turns. It is he who must supervise and control the inmate population in concrete and detailed terms. It is he who must see to the translation of the custodial regime from blueprint to reality and engage in the specific battles for conformity. Counting prisoners, periodically reporting to the center of communications, signing passes, checking groups of inmates as they come and go, searching for contraband or signs of attempts to escape—these make up the minutiae of his eight-hour shift. In addition, he is supposed to be alert for violations of the prison rules which fall outside his routine sphere of surveillance. Not only must he detect and report deviant behavior after it occurs; he must curb deviant behavior before it arises as well as when he is called on to prevent a minor quarrel among prisoners from flaring into a more dangerous situation. And he must make sure that the inmates in his charge perform their assigned tasks with a reasonable degree of efficiency.

The expected role of the guard, then, is a complicated compound of policeman and foreman, of cadi, counsellor, and boss all rolled into one. But as the guard goes about his duties, piling one day on top of another (and the guard too, in a certain sense, is serving time in confinement), we find that the system of power in the prison is defective not only because the means of motivating the inmates to conform are largely lacking but also because the guard is frequently reluctant to enforce the full range of the institution's regulations. The guard frequently fails to report infractions of the rules which have occurred before his eyes. The guard often transmits forbidden information to inmates, such as plans for searching particular cells in a surprise raid for contraband. The guard often neglects elementary security requirements and on numerous occasions he will be found joining his prisoners in outspoken criticisms of the Warden and his assistants. In short, the guard frequently shows evidence of having been "corrupted" by the captive criminals over whom he stands in theoretical dominance. This failure within the ranks of the rulers is seldom to be attributed to outright bribery—bribery, indeed, is usually unnecessary, for far more effective influences are at work to bridge the gap supposedly separating captors and captives.

In the first place, the guard is in close and intimate association with his prisoners throughout the course of the working day. He can remain aloof only with great difficulty, for he possesses few of those devices which normally serve to maintain social distance between the rulers and the ruled. He cannot withdraw physically in symbolic affirmation of his superior position; he has no inter-mediaries to bear the brunt of resentment springing from orders which are disliked; and he cannot fall back on a dignity adhering to his office—he is a *hack* or a *screw* in the eyes of those he con-trols and an unwelcome display of officiousness evokes that great destroyer of unquestioned power, the ribald humor of the dis-possessed.

There are many pressures in American culture to "be nice," to be a "good Joe," and the guard in the maximum security prison is not immune. The guard is constantly exposed to a sort of moral blackmail in which the first signs of condemnation, estrangement, or rigid adherence to the rules is countered by the inmates with the threat of ridicule or hostility. And in this complex interplay, the guard does not always start from a position of determined opposition to "being friendly." He holds an intermediate post in a bureaucratic structure between top prison officials—his captains, lieutenants, and sergeants—and the prisoners in his charge. Like many such figures, the guard is caught in a conflict of loyalties. He often has reason to resent the actions of his superior officers— the reprimands, the lack of ready appreciation, the incomprehen-sible order—and in the inmates he finds willing sympathizers: They too claim to suffer from the unreasonable irritants of power. Furthermore, the guard in many cases is marked by a basic am-bivalence toward the criminals under his supervision and control. It is true that the inmates of the prison have been condemned by society through the agency of the courts, but some of these prisoners must be viewed as a success in terms of a worldly system of the values which accords high prestige to wealth and influence even though they may have been won by devious means; and the poorly paid guard may be gratified to associate with a famous racketeer. Moreover, this ambivalence in the guard's attitudes toward the criminals nominally under his thumb may be based on something more than a *sub rosa* respect for the notorious. There may also be a discrepancy between the judgments of society and the guard's own opinions as far as the "criminality" of the prisoner is concerned. It is difficult to define the man convicted of deserting his wife, gambling, or embezzlement as a desperate criminal to be suppressed at all costs and the crimes of even the most serious offenders lose their significance with the passage of time. In the eyes of the custodian, the inmate tends to become a man in prison rather than a criminal in prison and the relationship between captor and captive is subtly transformed in the process.

In the second place, the guard's position as a strict enforcer of the rules is undermined by the fact that he finds it almost impossible to avoid the claims of reciprocity. To a large extent the guard is dependent on inmates for the satisfactory performance of his duties; and like many individuals in positions of power, the guard is evaluated in terms of the conduct of the men he controls. A troublesome, noisy, dirty cellblock reflects on the guard's ability to "handle" prisoners and this ability forms an important component of the merit rating which is used as the basis for pay raises and promotions. As we have pointed out above, a guard cannot rely on the direct application of force to achieve compliance nor can he easily depend on threats of punishment. And if the guard does insist on constantly using the last few negative sanctions available to the institution—if the guard turns in Charge Slip after Charge Slip for every violation of the rules which he encounters—he becomes burdensome to the top officials of the prison bureaucratic staff who realize only too well that their apparent dominance rests on some degree of co-operation. A system of power which can enforce its rules only by bringing its formal machinery of accusation, trial, and punishment into play at every turn will soon be lost in a haze of pettifogging detail.

The guard, then, is under pressure to achieve a smoothly running tour of duty not with the stick but with the carrot, but here again his legitimate stock is limited. Facing demands from above that he achieve compliance and stalemated from below, he finds that one of the most meaningful rewards he can offer is to ignore certain offenses or make sure that he never places himself in a position where he will discover them. Thus the guard— backed by all the power of the State, close to armed men who will run to his aid, and aware that any prisoner who disobeys him can be punished if he presses charges against him—often discovers that his best path of action is to make "deals" or "trades" with the captives in his power. In effect, the guard buys compliance or obedience in certain areas at the cost of tolerating disobedience elsewhere.

Aside from winning compliance "where it counts" in the course of the normal day, the guard has another favor to be secured from the inmates which makes him willing to forego strict enforcement of all prison regulations. Many custodial institutions have experienced a riot in which the tables are turned momentarily and the captives hold sway over their quondam captors; and the rebellions of 1952 loom large in the memories of the officials of the New Jersey State Prison. The guard knows that he may some day be a hostage and that his life may turn on a settling of old accounts. A fund of good will becomes a valuable form of insurance and this fund is almost sure to be lacking if he has continually played the part of a martinet. In the folklore of the prison there are enough tales about strict guards who have had the misfortune of being captured and savagely beaten during a riot to raise doubts about the wisdom of demanding complete conformity.

In the third place, the theoretical dominance of the guard is undermined in actuality by the innocuous encroachment of the prisoner on the guard's duties. Making out reports, checking cells at the periodic count, locking and unlocking doors—in short, all the minor chores which the guard is called on to perform—may gradually be transferred into the hands of inmates whom the guard has come to trust. The cellblock runner, formally assigned the tasks of delivering mail, housekeeping duties, and so on, is of particular importance in this respect. Inmates in this position function in a manner analogous to that of the company clerk in the Armed Forces and like such figures they may wield power and influence far beyond the nominal definition of their role. For reasons of indifference, laziness, or naïveté, the guard may find that much of the power which he is supposed to exercise has slipped from his grasp.

Now power, like a woman's virtue, once lost is hard to regain. The measures to rectify an established pattern of abdication need to be much more severe than those required to stop the first steps in the transfer of control from the guard to his prisoner. A guard assigned to a cellblock in which a large portion of power has been shifted in the past from the officials to the inmates is faced with the weight of precedent; it requires a good deal of moral courage on his part to withstand the aggressive tactics of prisoners who fiercely defend the patterns of corruption established by custom. And if the guard himself has allowed his control to be subverted, he may find that any attempts to undo his error are checked by a threat from the inmate to send a *snitch-kite*—an anonymous note—to the guard's superior officers explaining his past derelictions in detail. This simple form of blackmail may be quite sufficient to maintain the relationships established by friendship, reciprocity, or encroachment.

It is apparent, then, that the power of the custodians is defective, not simply in the sense that the ruled are rebellious, but also in the sense that the rulers are reluctant. We must attach a new meaning to Lord Acton's aphorism that power tends to corrupt and absolute power corrupts absolutely. The custodians of the New Jersey State Prison, far from being converted into brutal tyrants, are under strong pressure to compromise with their captives, for it is a paradox that they can insure their dominance only by allowing it to be corrupted. Only by tolerating violations of "minor" rules and regulations can the guard secure compliance in the "major" areas of the custodial regime. Ill-equipped to maintain the social distance which in theory separates the world of the officials and the world of the inmates, their suspicions eroded by long familiarity, the custodians are led into a modus vivendi with their captives which bears little resemblance to the stereotypical picture of guards and their prisoners.

NOTES AND QUESTIONS

1. Reread the description of the Experiments of Stanley Milgram at 213, *supra*. Milgram's studies have an obvious bearing on the theory of sanctions. *See* pp. 231-306, *supra*. What bearing do they have on the behavior of (a) the guard or (b) the prisoners in Sykes' study? Are the Milgram and Sykes studies inconsistent?

2. It is central to Sykes' argument that life in the New Jersey State Prison "is perhaps more notable for the doubtfulness of obedience than its certainty." On what does he base this judgment? How much obedience or compliance can one reasonably expect under the circumstances of life in the prison, and how would one decide whether there is "more" or "less" obedience? Surely most prisoners complied with most rules most of the time. Does this mean that Sykes' point is not well taken?

3. Sykes mentions many factors which, in his view, lead to the "capture" of the prison bureaucracy by the prisoners. What are these factors? To what extent are the difficulties caused by prisoners' resentment of their arrest, conviction and incarceration (so that *any* rules would be resented), and to what extent are the difficulties caused by the *content* of the rules or their modes of enforcement, such that *any group* subjected to such rules or modes of enforcement would tend not to comply? As to the latter category, could one obtain more compliance by changing the form or content of the rules? How?

[Reading 46]

NOTE: "Regulation by the Regulated" in Administrative Law

The "capture" of administrative apparatus by those ostensibly the *subjects* of regulation has been widely discussed by American political scientists, historians and specialists in administrative law.

In *Regulating Business by Independent Commission*, Marver Bernstein* went so far as to suggest that there is a definite regulatory "life cycle" that can be ascertained in the life of the independent regulatory commissions—the great federal agencies such as the Interstate Commerce Commission, the Federal Power Commission and the Civil Aeronautics Board. After a long period of "gestation," the agency is born—perhaps already "out of date" because of the "long struggle" to achieve a regulatory statute. During its youth, "its real and potential capacities contrast sharply with those of the regulated groups. It lacks administrative experience, its policy and objectives are vague and unformed, its legal powers are unclear and untested, and its relations with Congress are uncertain. On the other hand, the regulated groups are well organized, with vital interests to protect against the onslaught of the regulators." Public support reaches its climax when the statute is passed; once the statute is in effect, the public loses interest. Gradually, the commission "adjusts to conflict among the parties in interest." In the phase of "maturity," the commission becomes an accepted part of the industrial system; it takes on the functions of a "manager" rather than "a policeman." It becomes "more concerned with the general health of the industry and tries to prevent changes which adversely affect it. It is unlikely that the commission in this period, will be able to extend regulation beyond the limits acceptable to the regulated groups."

At the end of this period comes the "surrender to the regulated." "Politically isolated, lacking a firm basis of public support, lethargic in attitude and approach, bowed down by precedent and backlogs, unsupported in its demands for more staff and money, the commission finally becomes a captive of the regulated groups." What follows is "old age," in which the "primary mission is the maintenance of the *status quo* in the regulated industry and its own position as recognized protector of the industry."

The ICC has been frequently held up as the prime example of this process. The case has been elaborately documented by Samuel P. Huntington,** in "The Marasmus*** of the ICC: The Commission, the Railroads and the Public Interest," 61 *Yale Law Journal* 467 (1952). Huntington argues, for example, that

---

* Marver H. Bernstein, Professor of Politics, Princeton University. From Regulating Business by Independent Commission, by Marver H. Bernstein (Copyright © 1955, by Princeton University Press). Reprinted by permission of Princeton University Press.

** Samuel P. Huntington, School of Government, Harvard University.

*** Marasmus: a progressive wasting-away. [Eds. note]

the Commission has been more and more supine in the matter of rate regulation. The power to prescribe future maximum rates was given to the ICC in 1906. In 1911, the railroads asked for a general rate rise. The Commission refused, and laid down "rigorous criteria for the justification of rate advances." In the 1920's, the Commission began to weaken; by the 1930's, it was "exercising a benevolent paternalism"; and "since 1940 the Commission has a perfect record of giving the roads exactly what they have asked for in important passenger fare cases." It also has been extremely pliant with regard to other rates.

The cyclical theory has by no means been generally accepted. Some have denied that the commissions have departed from their original mandate. Others feel that the commissions have merely done what they set out to do: that they were designed to be "captured" from the outset. Others have argued that the commissions have, to be sure, grave defects; but that the sources of their problems are far too complex to be summed up in a single formula, and one which seems rather pat and moralistic. Some of these points of view are expressed in the following materials.

47. Railroads and Regulation 1877-1916

GABRIEL KOLKO*

The conventional interpretation of federal railroad regulation warrants a radical reappraisal, for the motives and consequences of regulation have been misunderstood. . . .

The railroads realized that they needed the protection of the federal government, and they became the leading advocates of federal regulation on their own terms. The principle of federal railroad regulation per se was accepted by an important segment of the railroad community by 1880, and the relative importance of this group increased gradually over the period until, by 1916, it included the vast majority of railroad men interested enough to leave some record of their views. The first major incident stimulating railroad support for federal regulation of railroads was the Great Strike of 1877, which came on the heels of the failure of the first efforts to create a voluntary pool structure. The strike of 1877 pointed to the danger of attacks on the railroads, not merely from the workers—whose threats were greatly exaggerated by the railroads at the time—but from the states and the Granger movement. The hostility of workers and farmers, many of whom controlled state politics, pointed to the possibility of local attacks which threatened to dislocate railroad systems that were regional, if not national, in their scope. Federal railroad regulation appeared to many railroad leaders as a safe shield behind which to hide from the consequences of local democracy, as well as a means of solving their own internal problems. In the spectrum of viewpoints on regulation, the railroads, especially after 1900, took their stand with the extreme nationalists, and were the leading advocates of this position. If the public could be led in a direction compatible with their interests, many railroad men realized, much more serious attacks could be avoided in the future.

The federal regulation of railroads from 1887 until 1916 did not disappoint the American railroad industry. If railroad leaders

---

* Gabriel Kolko, Professor of History, State University of New York, Buffalo. From Railroads and Regulation by Gabriel Kolko, pp. 231-39 (Copyright © 1965 by Princeton University Press). Reprinted by permission of Princeton University Press. Footnotes omitted.

often disagreed on the details—disagreements that extended into
their own ranks on any specific issue—the railroads nevertheless
supported the basic principle and institution of federal regulation. And, as we have seen, they enthusiastically worked for its
extension and for the supremacy of federal regulation over the
states. Rate regulation was guided by the premise that the railroads were to receive a reasonable profit and, in effect, were to
be protected from the risks and misfortunes inherent in the official ideology and economic value system of the status quo. Under
the benevolent supervision of the Interstate Commerce Commission, the conditions of the industry improved sharply, as inter-
necine competition was replaced by rate maintenance and the
elimination of rebates, and as the railroad system received protection from the attacks of both the states and powerful shippers.
The percentage of railroad stock paying dividends increased from
39 per cent in 1888 to 67 per cent in 1910, and the average rate
of dividends on all stock rose from 2.1 per cent to 5 per cent
over the same period. If the federal regulation of railroads was
only partially responsible for this improved performance, the Five
Percent decision of 1914 formalized the federal government's responsibility to maintain private profit, and the Transportation
Act of 1920 determined a level of profit which had been the
cherished and usually unattained goal of the railroads since the
1870's.

From its inception, the Interstate Commerce Commission entered into a condition of dependency on the railroads, and the
railroads quickly began relying on the Commission as a means
of attaining their own ends. Given the shortcomings of the existing law until 1903, this mutual reliance was both natural and
inevitable. . . .

Well before the end of the century the I.C.C. had reached that
stage, described in the writings of political scientists dealing with
regulatory commissions in later periods, in which its primary
function was to minister to the needs of the industry which it
was ostensibly to regulate on behalf of an amorphous, implicitly
classless, public interest.

That the Commission regarded the voluntary projects of the
railroads with solicitude . . . was the logical outcome of the key
personnel running the Commission during its early years. Indeed,
it is not unreasonable to assert that the primary commitment of
the major directors of Commission policy was essentially pro-rail-
road. Certainly Thomas Cooley can be said to qualify fully for
this appellation, and Martin Knapp* was only slightly more re-

---

* Cooley was chairman of the ICC from 1887; Knapp from 1898. [Eds.
note]

strained in his advocacy of positions identical to those of the majority of the railroads. The free interpretation of the law, the creation of informal procedures which prejudiced the rights of shippers or were administered in favor of the railroads, the outspoken public defense of pooling and legislative measures identical or nearly identical to those called for by the railroads, all suggest that the Interstate Commerce Commission was a failure from the shipper's viewpoint, and that much of the seemingly ineffective role of the Commission until 1903 was a matter of self-choice. The development after 1900 of a minority of articulate spokesmen who did not always advocate the railroad position within the Commission, was a relatively short-lived phenomenon. Wilson, in any event, turned the tide in 1914 decisively against the possibility of a genuinely neutral Commission. Ultimately, however, the very nature of the Commission concept was not conducive to the protection of the small shipper or the general consumer. Large shippers were protected by rebates or their ability to pass increased freight costs on to the consumer in the form of higher prices. The small shipper could not afford to file a formal complaint against the railroad, and was discouraged by the Commission's mediation offices from doing so. The consumer, for the most part, was left entirely helpless by the existing structure, and the Commission was ultimately an affair of consequence only to businessmen. From this viewpoint, its major function was to determine the division of business profits, not to redress the basic distribution of income, much less correct the economic imbalance that was created by the rise of a privately controlled industrial structure. Within its assumption that its basic responsibility was to the existing economic order—no one should be surprised that there was no desire by anyone to replace the fundamental system—the I.C.C. was aligned, for the most part, with the railroads.

The direction of federal regulation was not the responsibility merely of a sympathetic Commission, however. Theodore Roosevelt, whose presidency witnessed more major railroad legislation than any other, was deeply committed to the obligation of the national government to protect the railroads, not merely from the public but from themselves. He reiterated the proposition that, if modest and reasonable railroad legislation were not forthcoming, government ownership or more extreme legislation would be called for by the public. But in assigning himself the role of protector of the railroads from radicalism, he acted not merely because he was conservative but because he also accepted a theory of the general welfare that assumed, as he stated in his 1905 message to Congress, that the health of the railroad industry in the hands of its present owners would also maximize the general prosperity of the entire nation. Again and again Roosevelt repeated the assurance that he had no desire to attack the vital interests of the honest railroad men, and he frequently attacked the strongly anti-railroad actions of the states and the muckrakers. Illustrating the concept of social justice described by Anatole France's tale of the equal right of the poor man and rich man in a democracy to sleep under a bridge at night, Roosevelt called for "as much a square deal for the rich man as for the poor man." In the final analysis, Roosevelt was not interested in redressing the balance of economic power within the existing society, but in imposing vague codes of moralistic conduct on railroad men which, in their concrete implications, hardly affected the large majority of railroads in any tangible manner. . . .

Neither Roosevelt, Taft, nor Wilson ever used regulation to attack the essential interests of the railroads, and they never failed to be solicitous of the good will of the railroads. This continuity of executive policy from 1900 to 1916 is the pervasive reality in federal railroad regulation. In this respect, there was no fundamental difference on any important particulars between the New Freedom and the New Nationalism. Both left the Commission under conservative domination, and both Roosevelt and Wilson repeatedly consulted with railroad men when considering action or legislation affecting their vital welfare. In most instances the railroad men were allowed to define the boundaries, and even many of the details of proposed legislation. . . .

The basic similarity of the New Nationalism, the New Freedom, and the program of the railroads for federal control and domination points to what this writer feels to be the major significance of railroad regulation for an understanding of progressivism. Government control, per se, is not a sufficient criterion of progressivism, if by that term we mean an effort to redress the balance of economic power existing in society and to make the dominant economic forces susceptible to the control and welfare of the large majority of the people. This definition, quite properly, is the one assumed by most historians to describe progressivism. But the phenomenon described in this study was not an effort to democratize the economy via political means, but a movement to establish stability and control within the railroad industry so that railroads could prosper without the fearful consequences of cutthroat competition. It was, in fact, an effort to use political means to solve economic problems while maintaining the essential theory of social priorities and values of a capitalist economy. . . .

If one removes the traditionally positive and democratic implications from the historians' usual definition of progressivism, progressivism in operational reality becomes a political capitalism whereby important economic interests utilize the power of the federal government to solve internal economic problems which could not otherwise be solved by voluntary or non-political means. In effect, the economy was brought to a rationalized status by achieving through political means those economic ends once thought to be attainable by automatic economic mechanisms. This, in fact, is the central implication of the federal regulation of railroads, a movement supported and given dynamism by an increasingly important sector of the railroads. In this respect, federal railroad regulation was the first of many successful efforts to create rationalization and stability in the economy by political means. The goal of these efforts was not progressivism in the traditional sense, as historians have commonly interpreted that term, but a political capitalism which solved the internal problems of an industry and protected it from the attacks of a potentially democratic society.

NOTE: Occupational Licensing

A variant on the theme of "capture" of administrative agencies is the story of occupational licensing—of doctors, lawyers and hosts of other professions and occupations. The rise of occupational licensing in this country has been explored in Lawrence M. Friedman, "Freedom of Contract and Occupational Licensing 1890-1910: A Legal and Social Study," 53 *California Law Review* 487 (1965). Professor Friedman distinguishes "hostile" from "friendly" licensing; in friendly licensing, the licensed group— or rather the elite group within it—is the moving force behind licensing. This is true of the dentists, for example; state boards are controlled by the organized dentists themselves. They govern in the public interest, in theory and perhaps in practice; but they also help to maintain their own economic position, their monopoly control of the occupation, and whatever in their judgment contributes to the health of their occupation. Here too, then, what might appear to be the "capture" of a regulated group turns out, historically, to be quite otherwise: the regulators and the regulated are and always have been much the same interest group. *See* pp. 608-21, *infra*.

48. The Politics of Industry

WALTON H. HAMILTON*

The industries of transport built upon the river barge, the motorbus, and the motor truck are different in character [from that of the railroads]. Dominant features of the railroad are the privately owned right of way and the heavy overhead involved in track maintenance. Its technology makes for a few large lines which connect at terminal points, and for a rigid pattern of transportation. In contrast, the barge runs along rivers whose upkeep falls upon the Government: the waterways are open to all who may wish to use them. The boats represent only modest investments of capital, and there is no heavy overhead which needs to be spread over a large number of units. Similarly, the motorbus and motor truck run along the public highways which, tolls aside, are open to all who care to use them. Investments in vehicles are modest, and save for business considerations, there is no reason why the degree of concentration in the industry should approach that of the railroad. With them, as with the river barge, the proportion of overhead to total expense is relatively small. In railroads the certificate of convenience and necessity seems to be imperative; with these other forms of transport it is at best a convenience and at worst a source for preference.

The development of these new forms of transportation has broken the old monopoly of the railroads and set the stage for healthy competition. The drive has been thwarted in part by entrusting the regulation of competitive forms of transportation to a single agency. It was a shrewd move on the part of the railroads to bring it about that the regulation of the river barge, the motorbus, and motor truck should be lodged with the ICC. There may have been no conscious intent on the part of this agency to favor the older instrument. But over the years a body of practice has been built up which is definitely railroad-minded. In effect—if not in purpose—these forms of transportation have been delivered into the hands of a competitor.

* The late Walton H. Hamilton was an economist who was a member of the faculty of the Yale Law School from 1928 to 1947. He was admitted to the bar on special motion and practiced law in Washington, D.C., from his retirement from Yale to his death. Copyright © 1957 by Alfred A. Knopf, Inc., New York. Reprinted from pp. 59-62, by permission.

An even clearer example of the conversion of controls into sanctions is presented by one of the newest of the administrative agencies. The Civil Aeronautics Board was established by act of Congress in 1938. The congressional mandate was that the board was to establish and maintain a system of transportation by air adequate to the present and future military and commercial needs of the United States. The act envisaged a new and developing industry which would presently bring air transportation within the reach of all who travel, and allow it to assume an expanding role in the handling of cargo.

The air carriers have no rights of way to entail expense and no tracks to keep up between airports. Various services are maintained for them by the Government, and they escape a substantial part of the cost of the maintenance of airports. Yet from the first their rates have been as high as those charged for Pullman service, and until quite recently, the certificated carriers have made little attempt to capture other than the luxury trade.

At the end of the war the Government disposed of a large surplus of airplanes, and pilots trained in the service were ready to operate them. So there came into being a number of non-scheduled carriers who pioneered with a coach service at fares substantially lower than those of the certificated lines. The CAB—instead of encouraging these ventures—did its utmost to discourage. It made use of a code of regulations to subject such irregular carriers to extra costs; to keep them grounded a considerable portion of the time; to require flights to be made at inconvenient hours and on irregular schedules. After the demonstration of low-priced fares proved successful, one of the certificated carriers put on a coach flight and some of the others belatedly followed. In the same manner the venture into air cargo was pioneered by the independents.

One of the principal functions of the CAB has been to guard against entrance of newcomers into the industry. The established carriers were fitted out with certificates of convenience and necessity when the Act of 1938 was passed. In the intervening years very few additions have been made to their number. Yet had the field been left open to competition, there was no dearth of enterprising companies fit, able, and willing to take their chances —and without benefit of the subsidies enjoyed by the certificated carriers. Here an agency of Government has proved itself a willing instrument of vested carriers seeking to maintain a closed industry.

49. The Effective Limits of the Administrative Process: A Reevaluation

LOUIS L. JAFFE*

67 HARVARD LAW REVIEW 1105 (1954)

Many of the still current attitudes about the administrative process, and certain of the doctrines of administrative law, at least in their form and intensity, have been powerfully influenced by the immediate historic role of the administrative process. That history began, let us say, with the adoption of the Interstate Commerce Act of 1887. It reached its culmination in the New Deal with the creation of the Labor Board and the Securities and Exchange Commission. The administrative process was thought to have an inherent political or social orientation. There was more or less agreement as to its significance between those who hailed it and those who hated it. It was seen with hope by the one and fear by the other as capable of working continually progressive modification of the economy and the society. Supplanting private industry, it would take over the role of leadership in the "public interest." . . .

We have come to see that both the thrill and the chill failed to take into account basic factors limiting the managing and "planning" potentialities of the administrative process. These factors are inherent in our industrial organization, in our conceptions of regulation, and in our political machinery. . . .

Let us turn then to a consideration of these factors.

I

The regulated and client groups exert an effective pressure on the administrative agency in proportion to the importance of their economic function and to their organizational cohesion.

I confess at the outset that this thesis is not demonstrable. An administrative action which "favors" an industry or some defined

---

* Byrne Professor of Administrative Law, Harvard Law School. Copyright
© 1954 by The Harvard Law Review Association, reprinted by permission.

portion of it can usually be adequately explained as expressing a "correct" application of the statute or a theory of regulation which is administratively rather than industry determined. The thesis is rather a way of pointing to a significant current phenomenon, explain it as you may. This phenomenon is present where the administrative action reflects predominantly the solution desired by the industrial group. There is widespread recognition of the so-called "industry-oriented" agency. But the criticism implied in this recognition is in my opinion inadequate and misleading. There are those who say that the ICC is "railroad-minded," as if action of the ICC favorable to the railroads were a deviation from the expectable and relevant norm. The criticisms of the ICC are tendentiously documented and ultimately evasive. There can surely be no question that it was an essential element of the philosophy of the Motor Carrier Act to protect (as the drafters saw the problem) the *regulated* railroad from the *unregulated* motor carrier by subjecting both types of carrier to the same regime of regulation. In the words of a Senate Committee at a somewhat later date (1939), this was not a "railroad philosophy" but a "transportation philosophy." Obviously the implementation of this philosophy as against the previously unregulated motor carrier would favor the railroads. It may be that the ICC is more "railroad-minded" than "motor carrier-minded," but recent criticism has failed to distinguish to what extent it goes beyond the likely consequences of the kind of regulation which presently obtains in this field. The criticism pinning the blame on the ICC, and proposing perhaps this or that reshuffling of administrative power, refuses to face the problems created by regulation as such.

There is also the fact that the ICC is an old agency, that it has rigidified. This I call the arteriosclerosis theory. It is a very valuable and important theory. When the evil which gives rise to a reform has been somewhat alleviated, the initial dynamism is dispersed. There is a newly evolved status quo. It requires an exceptional effort of concern and attention to maintain human energies at high pitch, to keep courage screwed to the sticking point. Only a limited number of urgent problems can enlist this effort at any one time; the remaining problems must be handled on a routine, stand-by basis until the status quo once more becomes intolerable.

Under normal conditions, as I shall try to show, private management is inevitably the dominant *organizing* force. When the industry, after a period of reform, has been stabilized at a new level, management direction becomes the primary influence. Paradoxically, this phenomenon may be reinforced by a vague, broad delegation of administrative power! Such a delegation is a source of administrative strength in the initial reform period. The implied objectives, the climate of opinion give directing significance to the generalities of the statute. But when these objectives are realized the statutory vagueness may no longer yield a sense of mandate. External forces rush in to fill the vacuum. The arteriosclerosis theory, however, does not explain why the CAB, only 16 years of age, is fully as "industry-minded" as the ICC—in the opinion of some, more so. Perhaps, as with the ICC in recent years, the answer lies in the genesis and concept of the regulation. The "evil" to which the legislation was directed was the "instability" of the airline business. Congress wished to promote the development of the industry. The legislation was passed to attract capital and enterprise into the industry. The aim has been brilliantly achieved though sometimes despite rather than because of the regulation.

A few examples will illustrate the general thesis of effective pressure. The Civil Aeronautics Act was passed in 1938. It was an administration bill designed to develop the airline industry by a generous policy of deficit guarantee in the form of air mail pay. It was, of course, ardently supported by the airlines. There were at that time twenty airlines operating 32,335 miles of routes. The twenty were shortly reduced by failure and merger to sixteen and are now only thirteen. The CAB, though it has enormously expanded the domestic route miles to 130,000, has never certified a new domestic trunk line carrier. From 1946 to 1948 the airlines somewhat mysteriously lost $20,000,000, but since then their earnings have been dazzling: $19,000,000 in 1949 (5.9% on book assets); $41,000,000 in 1950 (12.4%); $52,000,000 in 1951 (14.9%); $59,365,000 in 1952 (14.3%). The average for 1939-1952 is 8.3%.

The certificated airlines as a unit have until recently set their face against reduction of fares to attract a substantial volume of new business; air travel in their view was a luxury, a "first-class" commodity. In this they were seconded by the CAB, which, from time to time, put obstacles in the way of the introduction of coach fare. The situation has been radically changed by one of the most bizarre and illuminating chapters in the history of regulation. A class of air carriers sometimes known as "irregulars," sometimes as "nonscheduled" ("non-skeds") were exempted by the CAB from the certification requirements. Immediately after the war there was a great supply of discharged military aviators and obsolescent equipment. The CAB concluded that the two might be put to work doing the odd jobs of air carriage ("contract" flights of one sort or another). But the planes were too large to be thus profitably employed. The non-skeds more and more scheduled semiregular flights over the more profitable long-distance routes (New York-Miami, New York-Los Angeles). They cut rates drastically and took the velvet off the first-class service, establishing a so-called "coach service." There was no question that their conduct violated the terms of their authorization. But it has taken years to put them out of business. Many of them had numerous "letters." When one was cancelled, another "was taken out from under the desk" and the operation continued. Furthermore, the Small Business Committee has championed the non-skeds and occasionally abated or postponed the CAB doom. The certificated carriers have finally capitulated and now about 30% of their traffic is coach at coach fare. The few remaining "non-skeds" are seeking certification over the principal long-distance routes on a non-subsidy basis, but all signs point to a rejection of their applications. The CAB is completely committed to the existing certificated carriers; the non-skeds have done the job of putting air service on a greatly expanded lower price basis. Like the highest flying drone, having fertilized the queen bee, they must now die.

Last year the certificated carriers requested permission to surcharge each passenger $1.00 per flight in order to even out the overhead costs of the short flight. The CAB gave temporary permission but instituted a general passenger fare investigation. When the certificated carriers moved to dismiss, the CAB split 2-2. The Board waited for a new appointment. The new member, reputedly after some vacillation, voted to dismiss;[17] but the $1.00 surcharge survived. The dissenters pointed to the present high level of profits and to the fact that the CAB has never completed a single investigation of the general rate level and has never announced a rate principle. The majority believed that the high profit might be a temporary consequence of the traffic generated by the Korean War and that any tampering with the general rate level might discourage experimentation with low coach rates.

The reader is not here intended to judge the soundness of these actions; excellent arguments can be offered to support them. The

---

[17] General Passenger Fare Investigation, Order Ser. No. E-7376 (CAB 1953). Adams, a dissenting member, said: "I cannot bring myself to believe that the Civil Aeronautics Board was established to act only responsively; or should be dedicated to a philosophy of preserving the status quo—a philosophy implied in the responsive role which certain interests would have this Board play. . . ." *Id.* at 212.

This is probably a veiled reference to the rumors that the lobbyists for the certificated carriers were very active in the Board's corridors and chambers.

matters are intricate and the material for decision cannot now be canvassed. One clue to what may seem to some a rather baffling story is the traumatic experience of 1946-48. The CAB was then told by a chorus of scolds that this slump was a consequence of its excessive certification of new routes. It was embarrassed by the heavy subsidies required to bail out the airlines. It will now do nothing at all likely to produce a recurrence. At this point, however, our only purpose is to point out that policy tends to flow along the channels congenial to the dominant certificated carriers. We shall discuss below in a related connection other examples from the ICC experience.

This phenomenon is most prominent in the completely regulated industries such as transportation. But it is not unknown in others. It has been an oft observed characteristic of agricultural price and production control through the so-called marketing agreements that the farmers, more exactly the cooperatives and the distributors, have largely determined the character of those agreements. The consumer was no doubt recognized as setting a price limit somewhere, primarily on the theory of what the market could bear. The NLRB was "captured" by the CIO from 1935-1940. I suspect that the FTC's enforcement of the Robinson-Patman Act reflects the fact that the FTC's chief political, specifically Congressional support is from the small business interest represented by Midwestern, Southern, and Western congressmen. These last two instances are obviously marginal to the argument. The balance of forces, the alliances involved are not stable, not so fixed a segment of the general social and economic structure. The type of regulation is narrow in its impact, and spasmodically applied. It does not, therefore, give rise to such relationships as exist under the Aeronautics and Transportation Acts.

It is the "planning," the industry-regulating, all-purpose administrations which are most typical of our thesis. In these situations the phenomenon loosely and invidiously described as "industry orientation" is much less a disease of certain administrations than a condition endemic in any agency or set of agencies which seek to perform such a task. It is a product of our political philosophy with its insistence on representation and the procedure through which representation functions, of our legislatures which are organized to register all functionally and socially significant groups, of our statutes which grant powers so wide that solutions will be much more the consequence of group interaction than of legislative formulation, of our theory of regulation which divorces legal command from managerial responsibility, of our dynamic industrial and economic economy which outruns prophecy and prescription, and of our administrators whose character and psychology is perforce the type of the good American.

II

The administrator develops a presumption in favor of regulation.

The charge against the ICC and the CAB is that they are "industry-minded." I would say that they are "regulation-minded" and that industry-mindedness is as much an effect as a cause. It was, for example, very clear in 1935 to Joseph Eastman, whose office, significantly enough, was Federal Coordinator of Transportation, that motor truck competition with the railroads and within the trucking industry itself must be dealt with by extending the existing system of railroad regulation. The initial impetus in the 19th century for railroad regulation came from consumer interests which demanded a curb on the monopoly power of the railroads. But there was little or no consumer demand for truck regulation. The nub of the problem was not monopoly but a too vigorous competition. The railroads, joined by rail labor, quite understandably if regulation of railroad competitive power was to continue, demanded a limit on truck competition. And in time the large trucking corporations made common cause with the railroads. In this controversy it was clear to the ICC led by Eastman (and also, it has been said, to the state commissions) that the answer was more rather than less regulation. Commissioner Eastman had recommended that air transportation be regulated: "It is believed that regulation of the kind indicated would accomplish much toward straightening out and stabilizing the industry, making it thereby a more efficient and responsible public servant. Against these advantages are to be set a possible dampening of the initiative and a partial loss of flexibility in the conduct of the industry. Much depends, of course, on how and by whom the regulation is administered." And he proposed that the ICC administer it as well as the regulation of water and motor transportation. It made for a "logical rounding out."

NOTE: Some Afterthoughts

An overriding question: the material on regulation of the regulated appears in a section of these materials on the "limits of effective legal action." In the light of the readings, you may wish to consider whether or not these materials are misplaced. Do they not rather belong with those materials which build up a bargaining model of the legal system?

One further point: dispute focuses mainly on the cause and cure of regulation by the regulated. Most of the authors begin with the assumption that the "capture" of administrative agencies is a bad thing for society. Some hold this view more strongly than others, of course. Can we question this assumption? It can be argued that every major industry *needs* a captive agency, to help it "fight its 'battles within the administrative branch of government.' " If we consolidated the separate agencies into super-agencies, the super-agencies might not, in fact, better serve the public interest; such an agency might "reconcile diverse interest groups only by curbing all of them and making them its enemies." F. C. Thayer, Jr., Review of David Corbett, "Politics and the Airlines" (U. of Toronto Press 1965), 29 *Journal of Politics* 222, 223 (1967).

(c) Enforcement officials at the action level

"Laws" are directed toward some part of the general public, but they are also directed toward enforcement agents and agencies. A statute which makes murder a crime will also express (or imply) a norm of conduct for policemen, judges and prosecutors.

Many of the readings so far have dealt with limitations on the effectiveness of law occasioned by the unwillingness, inability or ignorance of enforcement officials—the policemen in LaFave, the guards in Sykes—either as a separate, independent factor, or as the result of interaction between enforcement officials and members of the public.

The attitude of local officials toward law enforcement or their role can make or break a law or a doctrine. An interesting question is how officials resolve conflicts between their sense of duty and their allegiance to the community. Such a conflict occurred, for example, after 1954, when federal judges and other officials in the South were called upon to enforce the desegregation decisions of the United States Supreme Court, and, later, the new Civil Rights legislation.

50. Southern Judges and Negro Voting Rights: The Judicial Approach to the Solution of Controversial Social Problems

CHARLES V. HAMILTON*

1965 WISCONSIN LAW REVIEW 72

[Hamilton studied the enforcement of Negro voting rights under the Civil Rights Acts of 1957, 71 Stat. 634 (1957), and 1960, 74 Stat. 86 (1960). These acts attempted to ensure to the Negro the right to register and vote "uninhibited by restrictions based on race." Professor Hamilton studied the transcripts of cases tried before four United States district judges sitting in three southern states, interviewed attorneys in the Department of Justice and corresponded with people who had knowledge of these cases. He remarks that judicial enforcement varied greatly among judges. He found that there were "three types or characters of performance" among the judges, which he called "judicial aggressiveness," "judicial resistance," and "judicial gradualism." Judge Frank M. Johnson, Jr., of the District Court for the middle district of Alabama, was an example of an "aggressive" federal judge. In cases arising out of Macon and Montgomery counties, Judge Johnson vigorously upheld the right of Negroes to register and vote, and acted with speed and force in issuing decrees to make sure that these rights were carried into effect. For example, in Macon County, he ordered sixty-four specific Negroes registered "without reexamination or voter referees"; in Montgomery County, he issued a decree in November 1962, "whereby he personally registered 1,076 Negroes, and set forth very definite standards for registering future Negro applicants." He retained

---

* Charles V. Hamilton, Professor of Political Science, Roosevelt University, Chicago. Copyright © 1965 Wisconsin Law Review, reprinted by permission.

jurisdiction of the cases "for purposes of enforcing, modifying or extending his orders"; and took steps to see to it that he continued to be informed about how his orders were being carried out.

The federal judges in Mississippi formed a "stark contrast" to Judge Johnson. These judges "presented innumerable obstacles to the federal government's efforts to prosecute discriminatory practices by voting registrars." They represented, in Hamilton's typology, "judicial resistance." No judge in Mississippi ever found a registrar guilty of engaging in a pattern of discrimination, despite the evidence of flagrant violations of law. Harold Cox, for example, one of the Mississippi district judges, took "judicial notice" of the high rate of illiteracy among Negroes, and refused to concede that the absence of registered Negro voters had anything to do with discrimination by registrars. Naturally, the kind of strong rulings that Johnson issued were not forthcoming from Cox.

Judge Ben C. Dawkins, Jr., of Louisiana was an example of the third type, the "judicial gradualist." Government lawyers felt that Dawkins was personally a strong segregationist, but one with "respect for the law." It was therefore possible to get favorable decrees out of Dawkins. His attitudes seemed to be consonant with Cox's; but his rulings and decrees were midway between Cox and Johnson. In one case, for example:]

Judge Dawkins was impressed by the thorough preparation of the Government's case to the extent that he found virtually no dispute as to the facts. Dawkins noted that in elections prior to October 1956, Negroes "had engaged in the reprehensible practice of 'bloc voting,' " and concluded that this undoubtedly was a major motivation behind the purge. But Dawkins stated that he could not let this "alter one whit our duty under the fifteenth amendment to see to it, wherever we are called upon to do so, that there is no discrimination in voting registration because of race or color." He added: "It is to be earnestly hoped that in the future those Negroes who are qualified to vote will achieve a degree of political maturity so as to vote according to the best interests of their State and Nation rather than for their own selfish or venal purposes." Dawkins concluded that a pattern and practice of discrimination existed, but that the appointment of a voting referee was not then necessary. The names of the illegally purged Negroes were ordered restored to the rolls, and the registrar was enjoined from future discrimination. Dawkins' decree did not go as far as Johnson's decree registering the Negroes with the stroke of the pen, nor was the registrar required to make detailed monthly reports; but the case did not result in the countless delays and the weak decrees characteristic of the cases in Mississippi.

NOTES AND QUESTIONS

1. The problem of the southern judges is a problem of the interaction between community pressures and the way in which a judge perceives his own duty and his own role. Hamilton makes the simple point that this latter factor makes an enormous difference. See the material on role theory, at 824, *infra*. Does role perception have the same effect on the performance of the police in LaFave's study, the prison guards in Sykes' study, the administrators of the ICC?

Nagel, a political scientist, studied the impact of background on judicial decisions in the criminal field. He determined the proportion of the time particular judges voted for the prosecution or for the defense above or below the average for their court and compared the backgrounds of those who were prosecution or defense-minded. Statistically significant differences were found among judges based on the following characteristics: Republican or Democrat; member or nonmember of the American Bar Association; Protestant or Catholic; former prosecutor or not. In each case the first listed characteristic was associated with above average voting for the prosecution; the second with above average voting for defendants. Stuart Nagel, "Judicial Backgrounds and Criminal Cases," 53 *Journal of Criminal Law, Criminology & Police Science* 333 (1962).

Can we draw any generalizations about the importance of the personality of the administrator of the law from these various studies? How much leeway does a judge have? a policeman? an ICC commissioner? a prison guard?

2. Judge Cox is mentioned in the Hamilton article as an example of a resister. Interestingly enough, Judge Cox may later have changed his attitude toward the enforcement of civil rights legislation. Open expressions of bigotry in his courtroom seem to have ceased; and justice department officials were pleased with his handling of the trial of the men charged with the murder of Mrs. Violet Liuzzo, a civil rights worker. *See Newsweek*, Oct. 30, 1967, at 28, 29.

3. How "scientific" is the data adduced by Hamilton? How would you describe his methodology? What are the strengths and limitations of his method?

4. Consider the following:

"The business of deciding other men's disputes has never been a comfortable one; those charged with judicial functions have in all ages sought means of minimizing their personal responsibility for the decision rendered. The modern judge is likely to depict himself as an inert conduit through which the force of statutes and precedents is communicated. During periods when a general belief in witchcraft and magic exists . . . the judge [may convert] . . . the trial into a ritualistic appeal to the supernatural, in which the judge acts as a mere umpire to see that the proper forms are observed and to announce the decision when it has been determined. . . ." Lon Fuller, in Fuller & Braucher, *Basic Contract Law* 157 (1964).* *Compare* V. Aubert, Reading 18, at 175, *supra*.

Can this analysis be applied to the behavior of the southern judges, at least in part?

_____

* Lon L. Fuller and Robert Braucher, Professors of Law, Harvard Law School. Copyright © West Publishing Company, reprinted by permission.

51. The Supreme Court and the Bible Belt: Tennessee Reaction to the "Schempp" Decision

ROBERT K. BIRKBY*

10 MIDWEST JOURNAL OF POLITICAL SCIENCE
304, 312-17 (1966)

[Birkby's study deals with the reaction of school districts in Tennessee to the 1963 United States Supreme Court case of School District of Abington Township v. Schempp, 374 U.S. 203 (1963). *Schempp* held that it was unconstitutional to require a reading of the Bible, even though without comment, and to use the Lord's Prayer in public schools.

In Tennessee, state law *required* the reading of selections from the Bible "at the opening of . . . school every day." The use of the Lord's Prayer was common practice, also.

Birkby sent out questionnaires to school superintendents and to members of local school boards. He found that, of 121 school districts, seventy still followed the state law (and read from the Bible); fifty-one districts made some changes in their policy, but only one of these "completely eliminated all Bible reading and devotional exercises. The other fifty merely made student participation voluntary and left the decision whether to have devotional exercises to the discretion of the classroom teacher."

Birkby was anxious to explain the differences between the two kinds of districts. He felt extent of urbanization would be a factor; but actually, it turned out to have no relationship to compliance. Other results were also negative: "There are no significant differences in the socio-economic characteristics of changing and non-changing board members. In the changing districts, the board members did not report any overt pressure for compliance. And, by a rough test, the extent of religious pluralism in the district had no effect." Perhaps "the population of . . . Tennessee is too

---

* Robert H. Birkby, Professor of Political Science, Vanderbilt University. Reprinted from "The Supreme Court and the Bible Belt: Tennessee Reaction to the 'Schempp' Decision," Vol. 10 Midwest Journal of Political Science, 1966 by Robert H. Birkby, by permission of the Wayne State University Press. Copyright © 1966 Wayne State University Press.

homogeneous—socially, religiously, and economically—for any of these tests to be significant." But nonetheless, Tennessee's reaction called for some explanation.]

The reported response by Tennessee school districts to *Schempp* might be explained by one other hypothesis. There is in the questionnaires some support for it but not enough to make it possible to assert that it is correct. What follows then is largely speculative. The line of reasoning starts with a distinction between procedural and substantive change in policy. Policy change in any situation may take the form of (1) altering procedure without altering the policy goal, (2) changing procedure to reach a new policy goal without, however, making the new goal explicit, or (3) changing the policy goal with or without a change in procedure. Although we cannot be sure, it seems fairly safe to say that in the fifty school districts which overtly changed their policy on Bible reading and delegated the decision to the teachers there has been little change in fact. That is, it is suspected that the classroom teachers are "voluntarily" conducting Bible reading and devotional exercises just as they did before *Schempp*.[25] One might go a step further and assert, without being able to prove it, that the school boards were aware that this would probably happen. I am suggesting that the board members acted consciously either to save the substance of the program or to avoid upsetting the community status quo by making slight procedural changes. [T]he contestants who had the prizes of the game were able to keep them by responding to a rules change with a rules change of their own. A comment by a lawyer on the board of a changing district indicates the compromise nature of the policy adopted:

My personal conviction is that the Supreme Court decisions are correct, and I so told the Board and Superintendent; but I saw no reason to create controversy. If the Board had made public a decision abolishing devotional exercises, there would have been public outcry. I believe all staff members understand that the continuance of devotional exercises in their schools and in their rooms is entirely voluntary and subject to discontinuance upon objection of any individual or minority group.

There are other reasons that a board might adopt this strategy of procedural change. It could be used to reduce disagreement

---

25 This suspicion is based on unsystematic conversations with classroom teachers from two or three districts which made this formal change and on the questionnaire responses of a few superintendents who indicated doubt that any actual change had occurred.

within the board itself. It could be suggested by an individual as a means of reducing his own tensions between a desire to comply with the Court's decision and a desire to retain perceived advantages of devotional exercises. Finally, change in procedure without change in substance might be made to forestall demands for even greater change. There is nothing in the questionnaire responses to indicate which of these alternatives is correct and it is possible that all were present to some extent. If any or all of these suppositions are correct, a desire to retain the program rather than religious pluralism and urbanization would be responsible for the formal change. To this point the hypothesis does not provide an answer to the question of why the form was changed in some districts and not in others. It does emphasize that the answer must be sought in psychological rather than in demographic or socio-economic factors.

The question being asked in any impact study is why the Court's decision is not self-executing. In a different context Richard Neustadt has concluded that a self-executing order must have five characteristics: (1) the issuer of the order must be unambiguously involved in making the decision, (2) the order must be unambiguously worded, (3) the order must receive wide publicity, (4) those receiving the order must have control of the means of implementation, and (5) there must be no doubt of the individual's authority to issue the order. Neustadt was speaking of orders issued by the President but there is no reason that the same analysis cannot be applied to Court decisions. In this instance, there was no doubt that the Court did in fact make the decision though one school board member suggested that the Court was "controlled by small pressure groups." When applied to the Tennessee statute the wording of the order, although negative in content, was clear enough. There was wide publicity. The members of the boards of education had control of the means of implementation. However, the fifth factor was not so obviously present.

There was some confusion about the Court's decision. It was clear enough that required devotional exercises were forbidden but the Court did not commit itself on the status of voluntary programs such as those adopted by the fifty changing districts in Tennessee. This ambiguity caused one superintendent to assert confidently "we believe our policy [voluntary participation] is in accordance with the ruling of the Supreme Court and in accord with the desires of the people in this community."

More important is the question of the Court's authority to issue the order. The policy maker's reaction to a judicial decision will be conditioned by his perception of the Court's role in general, his beliefs concerning the importance of the challenged activity or program, his perception of the attitudes of his reference groups and constituents on the issue, and his perception of his role. The differences in policy position may be the result of a general attitude toward the Court and its role in the American system of government. The following comments are typical in content and intensity.

Changing Districts

A Surgeon: We must conform with Federal law. If we are to teach our children to obey laws we must set an example.

A Farmer: We did not want to violate any federal law.

A Superintendent: I think the Supreme Court is correct. Very few people understand the religious issue, less seem to understand what is meant by religious freedom, and relatively few seem to understand the Supreme Court's role in our government.

A Farmer: We are commanded by the Bible to be subject to civil powers as long as their laws do not conflict with laws of God.

Non-Changing Districts

A Superintendent: Impeach Earl Warren.

A Housewife: The decision of the Supreme Court seemed senseless and I could see no advantage in making changes.

A College Professor: The Supreme Court decision didn't mean a damn.

A Banker: The general public in this county do not have the respect for the U. S. Supreme Court as they once did. They think it is packed, so to speak, and doubt very much if all are qualified and unbiased and listen to the whims of the President that gave them the appointment. The standards are on a lower level than back several years ago.

A Superintendent: I am at a loss to understand the necessity for this survey. I am of the opinion that 99% of the people in the United States feel as I do about the Supreme Court's decision—that it was an outrage and that Congress should have it amended. The remaining 1% do not belong in this free world.

A Lawyer: We felt that in the absence of some good specific objection, there was no compelling reason to change previous policy.

If one had these comments without information on the policy adopted, it would not be too difficult to predict the position taken by each of these school boards.

The Court-attitude is only one of the variables affecting the impact of a judicial decision. The other major variable is the policy maker's assessment of and commitment to the challenged program or activity. Comments on the benefits and value of Bible reading and devotional exercises came only from the school board members and superintendents from the non-changing districts. These are typical:

A Farmer: I believe that if the Bible is removed from our schools and is not read that would be the first step toward removing the Holy Bible from our free society. Then we would eventually drift into heathenism.

A Merchant: This nation was founded and has grown under the firm belief in God. For those who do not believe it, there are places where they do not believe. Let them go there if they choose.

A Locomotive Engineer: I thought the Bible should be read and prayer held on account this was the only time some of our students ever had any spiritual guidance.

A Surgeon: This is a free country. If Bible reading is offensive to a very small minority then this minority may do homework or look out the window. However, we shall not discard Bible reading in order to coddle them.

A Bookkeeper: While this is a federal law, we do not intend to stick strictly to same. We permit Bible reading and devotional exercises in our school. If it was not being done, I would insist that it be done, bearing in mind that perhaps this is the only place some children are exposed to same. I cannot bear to think of communist atmosphere being exercised through our schools and children.

A Superintendent: Political leaders should read Bible and quit playing politics.

In some of these instances the belief in the importance of the program was sufficiently intense to override any desire to comply with the decision. In other instances, respondents combined attacks on the Court with a defense of the program. It seems reasonable to assume that the relative intensities of the Court-attitude and the program-attitude determined in large part the policy position taken by the school board.[31] In changing districts the board must have felt a greater obligation to follow the Court ruling than to continue to enforce their beliefs in the value of devotional exercises. In the non-changing districts *Schempp* was repudiated either because of a pre-existing negative attitude toward the Court or because of a strong belief in the value of the program, or both.

Perceptions of the attitudes of constituents or clientele are important but seem to be secondary. They play the role of reinforcing or modifying the Court-attitude and/or the program-attitude. A dentist on the board of a changing district observed that "we thought public opinion would want us to comply with Federal Law," while a chairman of a non-changing board (who did not indicate his occupation) said that the most important factor influencing him was that "we would have had complaints if we did not have Bible reading." Both of these board members were reacting to their perception of constituent attitude. The officials' constituents or clientele are not the only reference group they have. Other official bodies, such as the State Board of Education and the Commission of Education, may constitute another while non-official groups and opinion leaders could make up a third. The Commissioner's statement that Bible reading was permissible was not mentioned by any respondent but undoubtedly played a part in the making of decisions. The state has also continued to print the statutory requirement in the handbook of regulations

---

[31] The Court-attitude and the program-attitude may be either complementary or divergent. If complementary, one attitude would be positive and the other negative; they would reinforce each other and make reaching a decision relatively easy. If the two attitudes were divergent they would carry the same sign and the policy position would be unpredictable if no more were known. The possibilities and results can be diagrammed:

Court-attitude Direction	Program-attitude Direction	Policy-Position Expected
+	−	compliance
−	+	non-compliance
+	+	variable
−	−	variable

In the last two instances shown the intensity of the basic attitudes and the effect of secondary perceptions will determine the final policy position adopted.

Of those responding to this survey from changing districts only one indicated a negative Court-attitude as compared to twenty-six who expressed a favorable attitude. In non-changing districts the ratio was two favorable to thirteen negative expressions. No respondent expressed a negative program-attitude but only two from changing districts as contrasted to twenty-one from non-changing districts made positive statements. Both groups indicated a belief that their course of action had the approval of their constituents.

for teachers. This prompted one superintendent to remark that "most teachers consider Bible reading a state law since it is still in their register." And a merchant in a non-changing district said that he was influenced by the necessity of "complying with the laws of the State." Another superintendent indicated his valuation of the Court's decision by reporting that he "suggested teachers continue practices of past until forbidden by law." While official reference groups, constituents, and perceptions of the ranking of state law and Court decisions played an admitted role in the policy making process, no board member indicated that he had been influenced by any non-official reference group. However, the possibility cannot be ruled out. One superintendent justified the lack of change in his district by pointing out that the county education association had adopted a resolution favoring continued compliance with state law.

On the basis of the information available, it is impossible to weigh the value of the perceptions that went into the making of the policies. But one might hazard a guess that in the changing districts a perception of the Court as an authoritative body exercising legitimate power was strong enough to override any commitment to devotional exercises. The reverse, of course, would hold true in non-changing districts. The weight given to reference group attitudes and the direction of those attitudes probably, though not necessarily, varied in the same direction as the final policy decision and served to reinforce attitudes toward the Court or beliefs in the value of devotionals. That is, public opinion in changing districts probably was perceived by the board as favoring or at least not opposing compliance with *Schempp* and strengthened the board's desire to comply.[32]

One warning is in order. It is not asserted that procedural change to save substance and intensity of attitude explains what took place in Tennessee. All that is claimed here is that with the failure of the initial hypotheses in this study this additional explanation is possible and is supported to some extent by the response to the questionnaires.

NOTES AND QUESTIONS

1. Another political scientist, Ellis Katz, obtained questionnaire data from the "chief educational officer" of the various states (forty-one responses were usable) relating to compliance

---

[32] One board chairman reported that he and the superintendent made the decision to leave devotional exercises to the teacher's discretion "since no one else seemed to be interested."

with the *Schempp* decision. Bible reading had been most prevalent in the East and in the South. After *Schempp*, some school
superintendents reported that Bible reading had been halted in
their states, some reported it had "all but stopped," some that it
continued as before. "Most states . . . report that the . . . decision has significantly reduced Bible reading but there are specific
areas in which it is still practiced." Compliance was highest in
the East; in the South, no state "reported that the practice had
completely stopped" and almost half the reporting states stated
that Bible reading continued as before.

In general, Katz felt that those states with strong central authority over the school districts, and where the statewide officials
agreed with the decision, were those that put a halt to the practice. Other states left the matter to local option. "In most instances, state educational officials merely notified local school
districts of the content of the Supreme Court's ruling." Ellis
Katz, "The Supreme Court in the Web of Government: The
ACLU, the Supreme Court and the Bible" 237ff (unpublished
Ph.D. thesis, Columbia U. 1966).

2. Birkby's study and the Katz thesis, are examples of impact
studies—attempts to measure the actual effect of judicial decisions upon the attitudes or behavior of some segment of the
population. Such studies are surprisingly rare, even for the decisions of the United States Supreme Court. Of course, in a broad
sense, impact studies are conducted all the time: any attempt to
measure the incidence of crime, for example, is in a way an
attempt to measure the impact of law. What is rare is to try
to measure the direct effect of a particular decision of a court
(or a newly passed statute), shortly after enunciation and with
careful tools of measurement.

Surprisingly, the school prayer decisions have garnered the
lion's share of impact studies. In addition to Birkby and Katz,
there is Richard M. Johnson, *The Dynamics of Compliance:
Supreme Court Decision Making from a New Perspective* (Northwestern U. Press 1967); and William K. Muir, Jr., *Prayer in the
Public Schools: Law and Attitude Change* (U. of Chicago Press
1968). Mention should also be made of Gordon M. Patric, "The
Impact of a Court Decision: Aftermath of the McCollum Case,"
6 *Journal of Public Law* 455 (1957); Frank J. Sorauf, "*Zorach v.
Clauson*: The Impact of a Supreme Court Decision," 53 *American Political Science Review* 777 (1959); William C. Whitford,
"Strict Products Liability and the Automobile Industry: Much
Ado About Nothing," 1968 *Wisconsin Law Review* 83. *See also*
studies cited in ¶ 6, *infra*.

On the need for impact research, *see* Ernest M. Jones, "Impact Research and Sociology of Law: Some Tentative Proposals," 1966 *Wisconsin Law Review* 331; Arthur S. Miller, "On the Need for 'Impact Analysis' of Supreme Court Decisions," 53 *Georgetown Law Journal* 365 (1965); *see also* Auerbach, Reading 75, at 635, *infra.*

3. How does Birkby explain the failure of the school officials to carry into effect the *Schempp* decision? To what extent do you think the officials were reflecting the opinion of their constituents?

4. In Hamilton's study of the southern judges, we can perhaps assume that public opinion was more or less a constant in the various districts in which these judges sat. Can we make this assumption for the Tennessee school districts? Ought Birkby to have tried to measure this factor? Assuming the school districts to be roughly equal in "community sentiment," Birkby, like Hamilton, resorts to individual ("psychological rather than . . . demographic or socio-economic") factors to explain the differences in behavior. The main factor he isolates is one of attitude toward the court's authority. Could you apply the same reasoning to explain the behavior of Hamilton's judges?

5. Birkby assumes that the Supreme Court's mandate was reasonably clear and unambiguous: that it clearly outlawed the Bible reading practices indulged in in Tennessee. Birkby also assumes that this clear mandate was communicated to local officials in such a way as to leave no doubt in their minds as to the state of the law and their duties under the law. But suppose that some school officials perceived the court's opinion as ambiguous (even if it was not), would this weaken Birkby's argument that much of the noncompliance could be traced to officials' views on the legitimacy of the court's decision? In actuality, the Tennessee state authorities left the matter to local school board discretion. Does this rule out the possibility that misunderstanding or rationalization based on imaginary ambiguity was a factor in the noncompliance of some local officials?

6. In a series of decisions made in the 1960's, the Supreme Court of the United States created important rules that limited permissible police conduct in a number of respects. In Miranda v. Arizona, 384 U.S. 436 (1966), the Court held that before a suspect in custody is questioned, he must be warned that his statement can be used against him and told that he is entitled to a lawyer. Convictions based on improperly obtained evidence were to be reversed.

In a field study of police practices, Bordua and Reiss found that compliance with the requirement of warning was very low. *See* Bordua & Reiss, "Law Enforcement" in *The Uses of Sociology* 275, 294-95 (Lazarsfeld, Sewell & Wilensky eds., Basic Books 1967). In a study of practices by the police in New Haven, Connecticut, editors of the *Yale Law Journal* discovered that the *Miranda* warnings were not always given, particularly in serious cases. Moreover, the editors point out that such a warning could be given in a manner likely to nullify its effect. "The tone of a detective's voice, a few words added or omitted, the context in which a warning is given—all are factors . . . [which] may profoundly affect the suspect's understanding of his rights." Michael Wald, et al., "Interrogations in New Haven: The Impact of *Miranda*," 76 *Yale Law Journal* 1519, 1614 (1967). *See also* Richard Medalie, Leonard Zeitz & Paul Alexander, "Custodial Police Interrogation in Our Nation's Capitol: The Attempt to Implement *Miranda*," 66 *Michigan Law Review* 1347 (1968), reporting similar findings.

To what extent does Birkby's article help explain why some police departments do not carry out both the letter and the spirit of the *Miranda* decision? *See also* Krislov, *The Supreme Court in the Political Process* 134-55 (Macmillan 1965).

7. Professor Howard Becker argues that rules are enforced only when someone takes the initiative. One who wants enforcement must bring the infraction to public attention so that the infraction cannot be ignored. People are willing to do this only when they see some advantage as compared to the costs in doing this, but one's personal interest in "blowing the whistle" varies greatly with the situation. For example, those who live in large cities often ignore violations of the law and refuse to get involved. Management and labor often have a tacit compromise about which rules will or will not be enforced. Something must happen to cause these compromises to break down before action will be taken leading to enforcement. One person may or may not be able to upset the social tolerance of deviance. He is aided if he can get publicity, and often access to the communications media is vital. There are many social structures which operate to keep things quiet. For example, newspapers hesitate to print stories about the deviant practices of advertisers; police will often try to talk people out of pressing certain kinds of charges.

Sometimes the whistle is blown by a "moral entrepreneur," one who makes it his business to warn the community of threats to its values. Those who seek or hold political office may, for example, seek to enhance their own reputation—and vote-getting ability—by "exposing" what is going on at the state university.

The rewards may be less apparent when a private citizen sets out on a moral crusade to, say, force automobile manufacturers to build safer cars, as Ralph Nader did. Yet there are personal satisfactions in leading such a crusade. And crusaders have often made an impact on the law. *See* the note on Sinclair, *The Jungle*, Reading 60, at 561, *infra*.

Law enforcement officials typically are not moral crusaders. Their motivations for enforcement are different. They seldom, if ever, have sufficient resources to enforce all the laws and thus must exercise discretion. Yet they must justify the existence of their positions and they want to win the respect of significant others, such as the city council, a congressional committee, newspaper reporters —even the high officials of organized crime. Typically, too, law enforcers are sensitive to the importance of their office; one seldom finds that it pays to insult a policeman, a member of a Senate investigating committee or a judge. Thus, law enforcers decide which rules to enforce by a complex cost-benefit process which reflects their needs for status and respect, their own private evaluation of the significance of one kind of deviance from the rules as compared to another and their perception of likely reactions from significant others. For example, when Dr. Martin Luther King, Jr., was murdered, great pressure fell on the FBI and the Memphis police to find the killer. Many significant others were outraged by the murder and as time passed without an arrest, newspapers began to question the skill and the zeal of the FBI and of the Memphis police. The price of failing to produce a suspect was a significant loss of status. Finally, one must mention the "fix." Law enforcers can be paid to ignore certain crimes. Most blatantly, a prosecutor, policeman and even a judge can be paid money to ignore a violation. Less obviously, an official can understand that there are rewards for not seeing some things and penalties for seeing them. Promotion may depend on the good will of a political boss who does not want certain laws enforced; social relations for the law enforcer and his family within his circle of friends and relatives may turn on his decisions. *See* Becker, *Outsiders: Studies in the Sociology of Deviance* 121-63 (Free Press 1963). Would you qualify, add to or challenge Becker's theory?

To what extent do Hamilton, Birkby and Becker suggest that the explanation for selective enforcement of laws is to be found in the psychology of the individual who is a policeman, commissioner, prosecutor or judge; to what extent is it found in the structure of the relationship between that individual's position and that of others?

(d) Initiation of legal action

One characteristic of judicial lawmaking is that it depends heavily upon the action of private citizens. Courts make doctrine and apply rules only at the instance of litigants. Private citizens also take the initiative in many areas of administrative law. Marriage licenses, to take a simple and obvious example, are issued only to those who ask for them.

The effectiveness of law can be limited, then, not only by community sentiments which lessen obedience to law, but also by community sentiments that punish those who would initiate litigation or seek to make use of administrative channels. Some of these punishments can be very severe. They may include boycotts, physical violence, or ostracism.

The following excerpt is from Hamilton's study of southern judges.

52. Southern Judges and Negro Voting Rights: The Judicial Approach to the Solution of Controversial Social Problems

CHARLES V. HAMILTON*

1965 WISCONSIN LAW REVIEW 72, 91-93

There have been many instances of intimidation of activist Negroes. For example, Negro sharecroppers were evicted from their land in Tennessee for participation in a voter registration drive, and a Negro in Louisiana found he could not get his cotton ginned after he testified before the Civil Rights Commission. . . . Even when court actions have been instituted in spite of the threat of reprisal, the pressure brought to bear during the usually long proceedings often has been so unbearable as to produce settlements out of court. To those complainants who have been able to withstand the threat of reprisal before an action, as well as the continuous pressure during the course of the proceedings, community reprisals after the action have often been applied. Furthermore, to make matters worse, further court action to bring to account those who have been responsible for such intimidation has usually been unsuccessful.

The significant effect that these forces of reprisal external to the judicial process have had on the efficacy of judicial enforcement of voting rights can be seen in the detailed study of one case. Mrs. Ernestine Denham Talbert was a resident of George County, Mississippi. She was a teacher of ten years' experience. In 1961, she signed a one-year contract to teach and serve as part-time librarian at the Vocational High School in neighboring

* Charles V. Hamilton, Professor of Political Science, Roosevelt University, Chicago. Copyright © 1965 Wisconsin Law Review, reprinted by permission.

Greene County. Her contract was to run until the close of school in June 1962.

On the morning of January 6, 1962, Mrs. Talbert went with her husband to the registrar's office in George County to make application for a voter certificate. There were several other Negroes in the office filling out registration forms at the time. They were told to return after lunch, which they did. The registrar, Mr. Green, gave them the application forms and the oath, and he asked Mrs. Talbert to read and interpret section 50 of the Mississippi constitution. She gave her interpretation of the provision. Mr. Green then asked the Talberts if they knew their county officials. Mr. Talbert began to name them. The registrar then asked if they knew the fifteen members of the Election Commission, the group that determined the eligibility of applicants for registration. They did not know those officials. Mr. Green then asked several questions connected with the Election Commission, the answers to which the Talberts did not have for the most part. Green then advised them that there was "a lot to voting that people don't realize." At that point, he told them that the Election Commission, after its meeting in March 1962, would inform them if they were qualified to vote.

The Talberts waited until April 2, 1962, and returned to the George County registrar's office to inquire about the status of their application. There was another Negro couple present for the same purpose. The registrar informed them that he had given their applications to the Election Commission, but that the Commission wanted to talk to them personally. Mr. Green indicated that he could register persons whom he knew personally, but otherwise the applicants had to meet with the Commission. Mrs. Talbert asked him if this was the normal procedure. The registrar replied: "If you want me to disprove [sic] of your application I guarantee you I can do that. But I thought you were interested in becoming a registered voter." He then advised them that the Commission would be in session again in August. The Talberts stated that they wanted to vote in the State primaries in June. The other Negro woman applicant then noticed a notation in a ledger on the counter that the Commission would meet again on June 4, 1962.

On April 16, 1962, the United States filed a suit against the registrar of George County and the State of Mississippi under the Civil Rights Act alleging denial of voting rights to Negroes on account of their race. The complaint charged racial discrimination in the registration process. Mrs. Talbert and five other Negroes gave affidavits in that case attesting to their inability to become registered. On April 17, 1962, wide publicity was

given to the suit in Mississippi newspapers and in the press of
Mobile, Alabama. The names, addresses and educational levels
of the six Negro complainants were published with the news
stories. One week later, the press again published the identity
of the Negroes in connection with the news of a temporary
restraining order issued by the United States District Court.

About the time that this suit was filed, the Greene County
Board of Education was making its decision with respect to
which teachers would be retained for the next school year. Mrs.
Talbert was recommended by her principal for rehiring. The
recommendation, however, was not binding upon the county
school superintendent. For an unspecified reason the superintendent recommended to the Board that Mrs. Talbert not be
rehired and the Board acted affirmatively on that recommendation. . . .

NOTES AND QUESTIONS

1. Mrs. Talbert brought an action against the school board for
failing to rehire her. Her law suit was unsuccessful. Presumably,
however, it would be possible to exercise *some* control over this
kind of economic reprisal through litigation.

2. What about ostracism or private economic pressures? Is
there any way of controlling them? How can civil rights legislation ever be effective in areas of high racial tension where ostracism and economic boycott are usable weapons against civil rights
litigants and are in fact used?

c. Resource allocation as a limiting factor in law enforcement

The effectiveness of law enforcement, these materials have suggested, is a function of the *cost* of enforcement relative to the
investment by government in the means and personnel of enforcement. The cost may be high because of a propensity to disobey,
or for other reasons. Let us assume a fixed amount of deviance,
or tendency toward violation of law; the effectiveness of law
will depend upon what resources the community is willing to
invest in fighting deviance—how many policemen, for example,
the community is willing to hire.

Enforcement devices and men are a scarce resource; there never
are enough to do the job. Hence, police departments must make
choices about what laws they will strictly enforce, and which they
will not, as we noted in LaFave, Reading 10, at 97, *supra*, and
Sinclair, Reading 43, at 400, *supra*, among others. Obviously, the
level of *appropriations* is terribly important in determining how

much enforcement an agency can bring to bear on a problem. How much money is spent by government on justice determines how much justice there will be, and the particular allocations to various agencies help determine what kind of justice and for whom.

The LaFave study is full of suggestions about how subordinate agencies make accommodations based on the amount of resources at their disposal. The following excerpt takes up this problem once again, this time in the context of judicial decision-making.

53. Legal Rules and the Process of Social Change

LAWRENCE M. FRIEDMAN*

19 STANFORD LAW REVIEW 786, 798-810 (1967)

II. JUDICIAL RULES AND THE VOLUME OF BUSINESS

Institutions have normal expectations with regard to their work load. They expect to meet with certain kinds of problems in the course of a day: they expect a certain amount of work, and no more. The number of employees, the equipment available, the organizational structure are all based on these expectations. If radically new problems arise, the institution may find it hard to adapt. Equally, if too many problems of a familiar kind arise, the institution faces a crisis.

An increase in volume is not necessarily trouble. For a department store, more business—up to a point—is a blessing. The store may hire more workers, open new branches, and add on to its buildings; however, if there were a severe labor shortage or floor space could not be added at a given location, then customers might be alienated by unpleasantness, crowds, poor service, and parking troubles.

The American judicial system is in the position of the department store that cannot hire new staff easily or expand its plant. It cannot, in other words, react to increased demand simply by giving additional service. This characteristic is generally true of *all* American courts, from the United States Supreme Court to the lowest trial court. The court system responds to new demands at a tortoise-like pace. For one thing, control over personnel is not vested in the courts themselves. The labor force is relatively fixed; a court cannot reproduce; it cannot expand out of "profits." Those who control the statute books and the purse strings have allowed court systems to grow only slowly over the

---

* Lawrence M. Friedman, Professor of Law, Stanford University. The excerpt is from an article first published in the April 1967 issue of the Stanford Law Review. Copyright © 1967 by the Board of Trustees of the Leland Stanford Junior University.

years and have not allowed them to grow at all to meet the total *potential* demand for adjudication of disputes.

In the long run it is at least theoretically possible to multiply courts to keep up with changing demand. In the short run the difficulties are immense. The process of creating a new federal judgeship is laborious and delicate; it takes formal or informal action by the President, the Senate, the Senators of the proposed judge's state, and (in recent years) a committee of the American Bar Association. Sometimes a nomination is blocked or a new seat left vacant because of political quarrels not easily resolved. Even if all goes well, pressure on the docket is only slowly translated into new jobs. State court capacity is generally as difficult to expand as federal court capacity. An increase in the number of judges may require authorization from the legislature, a good deal of political jockeying, new elections, and sometimes even a constitutional change. Moreover, judgeships are typically local in their jurisdiction, and there is no bureaucratic, rational management of the work load and the staff. If the docket in a rural county is virtually empty, what could be more logical than to shift the local judge, at least part-time, to the big city, where there is tremendous congestion in the courtroom? Yet, well into the second half of the twentieth century such responses were the exception rather than the rule; until recently no state was willing to create any central coordinating body to do this.[22]

Since the number of workers (judges and clerks) is fixed, in the short run at least, courts do not have defenses against sharply rising demands. They cannot expand and contract automatically in response to the ebb and flow of litigation. Nor has there been any significant technological improvement to help the courts handle classic kinds of cases in mass. The legal system has therefore had to evolve devices and strategies to prevent a crisis in numbers.

A. *Costs of Litigation*

It is worth dwelling on gross historical changes in the character of court dockets in order to illustrate the means of meeting excessive demands for judicial services. A century ago commercial litigation made up much of the ordinary work of both trial and appellate courts. The tremendous growth in population, wealth,

---

[22] . . . Over the last century or so American law has in general resisted taking steps to make the role of a judge more like that of a civil servant (an employee and subordinate of the state) than that of an independent, free professional whose career lines and prestige derive from his relation to the bar, rather than to the state.

and commercial-industrial activities that occurred from 1850 on created such a potential for overburdening the courts that one of the following events had to happen: (1) expansion of the court system; (2) routinization and mass handling of commercial matters in the courts; (3) routinization and mass handling of commercial matters *outside* the courtroom; (4) use or expansion of a policy in favor of settlements to control the volume of litigation; (5) development of efficient dispute-settling mechanisms external to the judicial system; (6) adoption by courts or the imposition upon courts of substantive rules whose effect would be to discourage litigants from using the courts; or (7) increases in the costs of litigation sufficient to reduce its volume.

The first alternative was never adopted. No radical expansion of the court system occurred. The second was adopted where appropriate (in garnishment and collection actions, for example). The third alternative was in some ways the dominant response of the business world—the rationalization of business practices through the development of standard forms and patterns of doing business. The permissive attitude of the courts toward these devices made good sense ideologically, economically, and institutionally.

The effective use of the fourth alternative is difficult to measure. Its existence is evidenced, however, by the constantly enunciated proposition that the law favors settlement rather than litigation and by the fact that it is an unethical—even criminal—act to stir up lawsuits. It is somewhat paradoxical for an institution to declare so emphatically that public policy favors avoiding its use. There are many reasons other than case-load reasons why noncoerced settlements are preferable to trials. Yet it is also true that if no cases were settled out of court the judicial system as presently constituted could not sustain its share of the dispute-settling business.

The fifth solution, development of extrajudicial mechanisms for settling disputes, is exemplified by the rise of commercial arbitration. The sixth solution, adoption of "hostile" substantive rules, is far more difficult to attest. The seventh, increases in the cost of litigation, is often overlooked, but its institutional impact has been very great. Yet the trend toward judicial substitutes, and the acceptance by the courts of commercial routinization and extrajudicial settlement, is not unrelated to this final factor, the rise in the cost of litigation. . . .

In the twentieth century the cost of using the judicial process, especially if an appeal is made, is so high that it acts as a significant barrier against litigation that does not measure its outcome in the thousands of dollars.

The major commercial and industrial interests can afford some recourse to litigation, but they avoid the courts as much as they can. Litigation is expensive in more than dollars spent on lawyers, witness fees, court costs, and the like. It is expensive in business good will and disruptive of on-going business relationships. These undesirable effects led to the decline of commercial litigation even for those who were not deterred by the costs of actual litigation. Thus, though the tremendous expansion of business could have led to an appetite for litigation far beyond the capacities of the courts, the rising price of going to court has prevented this from happening.

With the decline of commercial litigation, the slack in the dockets was more than taken up with tort cases. In the late nineteenth century industrial accidents became a major producer of litigation. Cases of injury, death, or permanent disability were often settled, but the absence of a continuing relationship between the parties made for a situation in which a combination of costs of litigation and various, restrictive rules (such as the fellow-servant rule) did not choke off the total volume of litigation as efficiently as had been the case for commercial litigation. Jury freedom and the contingent-fee system neutralized the costs of litigation and the severity of common-law tort rules often enough to guarantee an enormous case load. The volume and acrimony of accident litigation came to be perceived as a problem by capital and labor alike.

Industrial accident law was unsatisfactory to the courts as well. First, existing law did not ration justice efficiently enough to avoid a problem of volume. Second, that law did not attain (in the view of more and more judges) equitable substantive ends. Therefore, the system imposed upon the courts a task which they could not and did not perform well, and any such task is a threat to an institution which the institution must avoid, delegate, or remove. The eventual solution (slow to develop because of the conflict of interest between business and labor) was a workmen's compensation system—a relatively stable compromise between the needs of capital and labor and a rough solution as well to the institutional problem of the courts. . . . Workmen's compensation attempted to solve the problem of volume by delegating adjudication and fact finding to a commission of experts, fully staffed and unhampered by the conventions of court law, and by reducing liability and the amount of recovery to amounts automatically determinable, thus making routinization of the work load possible. . . .

In the twentieth century, cases arising out of automobile accidents came to dominate the civil dockets. Here too the quantity

of litigation is imperfectly routinized and imperfectly controlled
by high litigation costs, and progress toward a "solution" (institutionally speaking) is slow, perhaps because there is neither real
agreement on the proper substitute nor a strong, organized movement toward one goal. On the trial level, dockets are crowded
with accident cases, and the delay between docketing and trial
can run into years in some large cities. Although the congestion
and delay in the courts have been widely criticized, the problem
seems manageable in the short run. Of course, many pending
cases are settled before they ever come to trial. It is especially
apparent in accidental-injury cases, where the litigant rarely has
an interest in the "principles" of law involved, that the economic
man would rather settle for ten dollars than sue for fifteen dollars, bearing in mind how much it will cost him in time and
money to see the matter through the courts. The very fact of
congestion is an element of cost—sometimes cruel and unjust.
Thus congestion itself encourages settlements and prevents congestion from becoming even worse.

That certain phenomena serve a rationing function in the legal
system does not mean that they are ethically "correct," except in
the special, narrow sense that they avoid or postpone radical institutional adjustments. One major drawback of allowing the price
of litigation to reduce the volume of business is that it rations
resources along class lines as well as along lines of preference. If
everybody had equal resources at his disposal, a rise in the price
of legal remedies would merely eliminate litigation of marginal
value to the litigants. A high price for opera tickets will induce
some people who could "afford" the opera to go to ball games
and musical comedies instead, or to stay home with a book. But
in a society with inequality of resources, some people will be
unable to go to the opera, no matter how strong their desires.
In the legal system, the high price of litigation means that litigation is not a practical method of resolving disputes for the average
man.

This state of affairs is not necessarily a major problem for
every society. A society may organize its legal system in such
a way that different institutions for settling disputes are available
for different ethnic groups, occupational groups, or social classes.
The medieval common law, for example, was in essence composed of rules and institutions by, for, and of the upper class.
The lower classes, indeed, were quite outside the royal common
law; its rules did not apply to their affairs, and its institutions
were beyond their grasp and their pocketbooks. Not that life
below the top was lawless. Quite the contrary. There was an
important system of minor local courts, some of them highly

informal, which deserved the title of courts of law just as much as the royal courts which usurped the name and the attention. But these local institutions did not apply the same system of rules. Just as a single, unitary nation-state is the product of more or less recent times, so is the growth of a single, unitary legal system that is relatively classless in the sense that rules do not *explicitly* distinguish between litigants on the basis of their income and station in life.

It is true and will perhaps always remain true that most affairs of life are governed by sanctions which operate automatically or without the use of formal institutions of enforcement. But the development of a single, middle-class system of law and legal institutions (rigorously controlled by a cost-rationing device) means that some social goods that are conditioned upon use of the legal process (a divorce, for example) may be beyond the reach of many members of society. Thus the high price of litigation carries its own high price: the denial, in some areas, of justice to the poor. A middle-class democratic society may consider such a situation inherently evil. To avoid this result, many forms of subsidy have been devised—legal aid, public defenders, and small claims courts, among others. Some have successfully broadened access to the legal system; some have not.[35] The recent growth of interest in improving and widening these subsidies is a recognition that some minimum of legal care should be available to the whole population, regardless of price.

The problem of defining a minimum is not peculiar to legal services; all products considered socially important and yet rationed by price (for example, medical care) present similar problems. Free vaccinations—but usually not free psychoanalysis—are provided by the state to those who cannot afford or are unwilling to buy medical care. The movement to provide legal services for the poor man faces the difficult task of deciding what kinds of legal service must be subsidized, and to what degree. There is wide agreement that a poor man arrested for murder needs and should have a good lawyer. Whether a poor man needs or deserves a free divorce, a free civil action against his landlord, or a free claim for damages for invasion of privacy is more difficult to decide and to justify.

---

[35] The small claims court finds its heaviest use not *by* the poor, but in small claims *against* the poor. For documentation of the heavy use of small claims court by unsecured creditors such as doctors and grocers, see Rapson, The Dane County Small Claims Court, 1961 (unpublished thesis in the University of Wisconsin Library).

See also Note, *The Persecution and Intimidation of the Low-Income Litigant as Performed by the Small Claims Court in California*, 21 STAN. L. REV. 1657 (1969).

The price device has on the whole been useful, however. The price of the law is a factor which, along with the formal and technical structure of the legal system, tends to keep legal and social change relatively even-paced, orderly, and free from caprice. In addition, the cost of litigation has tended to increase the predictability of the consequences that will flow from the acts of private parties.

A legal rule, of course, does not change automatically; it must be challenged, or at least an occasion must be presented at which an authoritative agency has an opportunity to change the rule, even if the rule itself is not directly challenged. Many judge-made and statutory rules, however, are never brought before courts for interpretation or review. It is, in the main, the cost of litigation that shields these rules from change. Otherwise, the inherent uncertainties in the conduct of American trials would expose these rules to challenge. Even where the outcome of a case is quite clear in terms of legal theory, a litigant must reckon with a number of intangibles which affect his actual probabilities of success. The judge and his personality, the jury and its quirks, the possibility that the other party or his witnesses will commit perjury in a persuasive manner, the ineptness of one's own attorney, accidents and miscalculations at the trial are all risks of litigation. The same uncertainties apply to evidentiary facts which before trial appear quite certain. In a legal system where courts and lawyers were free and available to all it might be worthwhile to sue for relatively trivial sums or (what is more important here) on the basis of causes of action with slim probabilities. Of course, even in such a system, powerful informal sanctions would prevent the overwhelming majority of potential suits. Friends would not sue each other for the small damages occasioned by an accidental nudge in the ribs, even if the nudge amounted to a technical assault. Many defendants might plead guilty to avoid the shame, degradation, and risk of open trial. Businessmen in profitable relationships would not sue each other for small deviations from precise contractual duties. But, clearly, in such a system many actions would be brought that would not be brought under the present system, and hence the number of opportunities of upsetting established rules would be greater.

One may look upon a rule of law as a potential command to certain subjects, a command which may be obeyed, ignored, or disputed. But to challenge the rule is costly, especially if the challenge includes litigation. A simple rule of the road—like the rule requiring drivers to keep to the right on a highway—is formally clear-cut. One does not challenge this rule of the road because the likelihood of overturning it or of modifying its mean-

ing is simply too slight to be worth the effort. Some rules equally
clear-cut in form are unclear in operation or effect, because of a
judicial gloss added in the course of repeated litigation. This
encourages challenges to the validity and scope of the rule. Such
a fate, for example, has overtaken the Statute of Frauds.

On the other hand, if litigants, for whatever reason, feel
strongly enough about an issue to challenge the averages, then
the outcome of the suit does take on an element of uncertainty.
But the cause of this uncertainty resides not only in the inherent
uncertainty of lawsuits, but in the very *fact* that somebody bothers
to sue. If the plaintiff is an isolated eccentric, he will almost
surely lose his suit, and the rule at issue will remain unchanged.
But if enough people hammer away at a rule which (in theory)
is "well settled," they stand a good chance of unsettling the rule,
for we would then have to ask: Why are so many people ham-
mering away at this "settled" rule? Either they or their lawyers
sense a possible change in the direction of the law, or the matter
is so vital to the litigants that they cannot or will not face "reality." Pioneers in civil rights cases and reapportionment cases—
or in any case in which litigants have persistently challenged "settled" rules—show something of this intensity. And in the cases
mentioned, there were indeed powerful forces seeking legal
change. The costs of access to the legal system support the legal
status quo, but they do not shut off all avenues of evolution.
These costs act as a conservative force, or, more accurately, a
channeling force; they limit access to the courts only to recognized causes of action and to unrecognized causes of action which
have many or unusually intense adherents.

In many trial court cases, of course, only facts are at issue, not
doctrine. Here too, a litigant must assess his probability of success, in relation to the stakes. A fact, like a rule, is real and
certain to the extent it goes unchallenged. Some "facts" are more
certain than others in the sense that the evidence supporting them
is convincing. But the strength of the evidence is only one influence on the likelihood that a fact will go unchallenged. Even a
"fact" certain beyond any reasonable doubt will be challenged
if the stakes are high enough. A man charged with first-degree
murder is highly likely to plead not guilty and ask for a jury
trial. The stakes are high for him—perhaps even life itself. The
costs, pains, and uncertainties of a law suit may be outweighed
by the chance—however small—of saving his neck.

A related effect of the costliness of the American legal system
is the development of what we might call networks of *reciprocal
immunities*, which help define and stabilize many common, continuing relationships. For example, the formal legal relationships

of a landlord and his tenant are spelled out in their lease. Minor infractions of duty on either side may amount to breaches of the lease, but *both* parties are protected—and given wide freedom of action in fact if not in theory—by the costliness, in money and disruption, of claiming one's "rights." So the tenant can play his radio late at night, keep a dog, and perhaps even move out a month before his lease expires without lawsuit or threat of lawsuit. And the landlord can delay small repairs or shut down the heat while the boiler is fixed without losing a tenant or suffering a lawsuit. This network of reciprocal immunities is beneficial to both parties.

Not all such networks are necessarily mutually advantageous. For example, a relationship may be so one-sided in power or authority that adverse social consequences flow from it, or many people may feel that enforcement of law or rule must be undertaken for social reasons regardless of the wishes of the immediate parties. Thus, the law of landlord and tenant is often said to be unfair to the poor tenant. The reciprocal immunities of landlord and tenant, together with the operation of a vigorously effective real estate market, permit patterns of fairly smooth and equitable transactions for middle-class and upper-class tenants (except perhaps during periods of critical imbalance in housing production). The main reason why the law is unfair to poor tenants is because, being poor, they cannot bring leverage to bear against their landlords. The call for subsidy of tenants' rights is a call for means to break through the wall of immunities—just as the criminal law is a subsidization of sanctions so that (among other things) strangers are not free to steal slightly from each other, protected from punishment or redress by a wall of cost or social relations.[37] Although the system of reciprocal immunities may operate to the detriment of some segments of society, its virtue lies in the fact that it allows for a reservoir of potentially valuable rights. Those rights can be enforced whenever there are high stakes or high intensity of desire for enforcement among bearers of the rights. Otherwise they remain below the threshold of that enforcement rate which would seriously disturb social relations among parties.

B. *Jurisdictional and Procedural Rules*

Up to this point, we have discussed how increases in the price of litigation are related to the specific institutional problem of

---

[37] Note that some instances of petty theft, particularly by juveniles or neighbors, or the children of neighbors, will probably be forgiven; and employers ignore the fact that white-collar employees take home pencils, pads, and other inexpensive items of office equipment.

volume of business. Jurisdictional and procedural rules also control the volume of business in courts. Procedural formality adds to the cost of litigation by making lawyers necessary and by requiring time-consuming effort on the part of litigants. A trial of an issue in court results in the risk of public condemnation as well as the chance of public vindication. Procedural technicality increases the difficulty of winning a lawsuit, adds an element of chance to litigation, and in turn increases the uncertainty of outcome, which is a critical element in cost. Procedural technicality as a cost-producing device characterized English royal law in the medieval period. It is much less tolerated in modern law, which has an ideological commitment to rationality and efficiency.

Jurisdictional rules are widely used to control directly the volume of upper-court business. The United States Supreme Court keeps its work load within bounds through its power over its docket. Since 1925 the case load of the Court has been almost completely discretionary. The Court may turn down cases which it deems too trivial, as well as those it deems too controversial to handle at the moment. The Court's right to refuse to hear controversial cases is the right to prevent substantive institutional crisis; the right to refuse to hear vast numbers of trivial cases is the right to prevent a crisis in volume.

The Supreme Court's freedom to choose its cases is unusual, corresponding to the unusual demands which potentially might be made upon the Court. In some states, statutes define which types of cases appellate courts *must* hear and which are discretionary. The lower the court, the less in general its leeway. As we have mentioned, courts (high and low) have been relatively inflexible institutions; they have been unable to increase productivity or staff. Limitations on the docket, or discretionary control of the docket, have allowed upper courts to retain their classic style of weighty deliberation and reasoned opinions. Lower courts, lacking the freedom of their appellate brothers and more vulnerable to the pressures of excess business, have had to countenance more and more informal processes, which—whatever other virtues they may have—succeed in limiting the docket to manageable size.

Of course, judicial institutions are not inherently incapable of handling great quantities of "cases." Mass-handling techniques can indeed be used for some kinds of business. If the social interest in rapid, efficient processing is superior to the social interest in carefully individuated justice, it is certainly possible to devise mass-production legal methods. The traffic courts, for example, handle a tremendous flow of business. Their work is mostly quite routine. The "trial" has been reduced to a formula, a vestige.

Parking tickets can be paid by mail in many cities. Other lower courts handle garnishments, debt collections, and wage assignments in fantastic numbers. Probate judges in urban centers sign hundreds of routine orders and forms each session; simple hearings on heirships and intermediate accounts are delegated to clerks or assistants.

The procedures used by courts in "trials" of this kind resemble more the procedures of record-handling and processing offices than the procedures of a court handling a murder trial or a large antitrust suit. The traffic ticket is processed on as perfunctory a basis as the recording of a deed in a county recorder's office. That one task is handled by a "court" and the other by an "office" is not often a fact of much functional importance. If one defines a court as an institution which weighs evidence, hears disputes, and renders carefully reasoned judgments, perhaps traffic and probate courts are not courts at all, but the epigones of courts, retaining from a more vital day their titles and customs. If so, then these "courts" represent not so much an adaption of judicial institutions to mass processing of routine matters, but rather an abandonment of the judicial system. The difference depends solely upon one's definition of a court.

Abandonment of the judicial system, or at least of traditional judicial procedures, has indeed been historically one major social response to the pressures of increasing business. Some work has been transferred to private institutions of conciliation; some to different agencies of government. The boards and commissions that handle industrial accident or social security claims, for example, are dealing with matters that at one time were handled, if at all, through litigation initiated by private parties. In most cases of removal of jurisdiction to administrative bodies, the courts retain a right of review—prestigious, but relatively powerless. Of course, a shift in institutional locus is more than a matter of jurisdiction. As industrial accident law shifted from court to commission, the substantive content of the rules changed too. Indeed, that was one point of the transfer. But the new rules were such that the courts would have been hard pressed to administer them without severe distortion of their classic structure.

Courts also have the power to shut off litigation by adopting a *rule of refusal*—that is, a rule refusing to acknowledge as valid a particular cause of action. Frequently, judges defend a particular rule by arguing that to abandon it would bring on an unmanageable flood of new cases. This argument can be and no doubt often is nothing more than a rationalization disguising some judicial policy choice that remains unarticulated, but it is heard so frequently that it must be at least sometimes honestly put forth. At least *sometimes* courts must deliberately adopt a rule of refusal precisely because they fear being "overwhelmed." The unspoken premise is that society will suffer if the courts are overwhelmed. A further premise is that society will be unable to rescue the courts from suffocation. Yet society certainly has the power to create an unlimited number of bypass institutions. What the courts may mean (even if they do not say so) is that a rule of refusal will preserve the institutional integrity of the courts as they now exist.

To a limited degree, such fears are justified. Rules of refusal may be needed to keep the flow of work through courts in a manageable state. Whether society benefits is another question; perhaps it is good, in some instances, to avoid short-run dislocations and institutional imbalance. Conversely, rules of refusal are harmful if the court's perception of the volume of potential business is wrong, if the claim which has been refused is otherwise justified, and if other institutions are incapable of meeting the demand in the short run. Thus, the Supreme Court might have made a dangerous mistake had it adopted a rule of refusal in the school segregation cases, fearful of the institutional consequences of so grave a decision. The Justices probably believed in their hearts that segregation was morally wrong and constitutionally unsupportable; civil rights groups had failed to get satisfaction in the legislatures; and the Court in fact weathered the crisis. Of course, it is easy to see now that twelve years have passed that the Court survived the crisis stronger than ever. It was not so easy to predict at the time.

Brown v. Board of Educ. is an excellent example of the impact of a rule of *reception* (as opposed to *refusal*) on litigation. Since the Court in effect opened up a whole new area of law, it invited Negro organizations and individual Negro plaintiffs to use litigation for an attack on this or that aspect of segregation. Such litigation had already been frequent, but the frequency now increased. Federal dockets, particularly in the South, were materially affected by many complicated, controversial cases on segregation in schools, parks, and other public facilities. It can truthfully be said that the result of the rule of reception was to create an additional demand for court services. We must be careful, however, not to overemphasize the word "create." Demand is created, not by the courts, but by society. Certainly, a Supreme Court decision which puts in question the validity of certain kinds of criminal convictions will induce numbers of petitions for redress on the strength of the new doctrine, but the basic desire of prisoners for release was not created by the Court's decision. Nor is the Court to be praised or blamed for such important social events as the rise of Negro protest movements or the sexual frankness of the modern novel. Obviously, specific Supreme Court and state court decisions strongly influenced some strategies taken by the Negro protest movement, and others encouraged bold publishers to print increasingly erotic works. Obviously, too, specific court actions play a role in social movements by sharpening public perception of problems and solutions and by directing attention to the subjects of particular litigation. But the underlying drives come to and not from the courts.

In an important—even vital—sense, a court does not control its potential docket, simply because it does not control its society. It is a member-institution in society, but not the guiding one. To do its job a court must walk a tightrope. It must be able to cope with crises or to avoid them, but it must not evade and avoid so ruthlessly as to diminish its reason for survival and lapse into ceremonial triviality (like the English sovereign). Nor must it grapple with crises in such a way as to arouse forces powerful enough to destroy it. The United States Supreme Court is in a particularly delicate position compared to other courts. It has controlled its volume of work to the point that ordinary litigation no longer reaches it. Its normal docket consists of extraordinary cases, and the necessity for striking a balance between too much avoidance and too much boldness is all the more delicate.[43]

NOTES AND QUESTIONS

1. At 499-500, Friedman discusses "reciprocal immunities" as beneficial to all concerned. "Minor infractions of duty on either side . . . [in theory give rise to a legally enforceable cause of action], but *both* parties are protected—and given wide freedom of action in fact if not in theory—by the costliness, in money and disruption, of claiming one's rights."

(a) Why is it desirable for the law to create a cause of action but to discourage suits where a small amount of money is involved by imposing cost barriers? Think of examples where it might be desirable.

(b) Is Friedman saying that the legal system was planned to work this way or that this is an unanticipated consequence of the interplay of several factors inherent in the American legal system?

---

[43] The analysis here is in terms of the institution's own perceptions and its own desires for survival. From a societal standpoint, it might be worthwhile for a particular institution to do certain jobs which are absolutely necessary at a given time, even though this meant that in the long run the institution would decay.

(c) How does Friedman discover that cost barriers serve this function? What kind of data does he rely on; what is his methodology?

2. Friedman recognizes that cost barriers produce reciprocal immunities but that the price is a denial to the poor of a chance to assert their rights. How significant a price is this? It has been asserted that the consequence is that "government by threat and fear tends to become a substitute for governance by law, and the poor accordingly become skeptical of the possibility of holding authorities accountable—they have little confidence in the efficacy of invoking the law to secure their interests."* Jerome E. Carlin, Jan Howard & Sheldon L. Messinger, "Civil Justice and the Poor: Issues for Sociological Research," 1 *Law & Society Review* 9, 78 (1966). On the other hand, it has been suggested that giving the poor causes of action and free legal services will not solve this problem completely because the poor are frequently involved in continuing relationships with welfare officials, landlords and retailers. Litigation is likely to destroy or prejudice these relationships no matter how it is conducted. The poor man may win his case but face future retaliation. *See* Joel F. Handler, "Controlling Official Behavior in Welfare Administration," 54 *California Law Review* 479 (1966).

3. At 496, Friedman comments that the "very fact of congestion is an element of cost—sometimes cruel and unjust." There is a large literature on the problem of delay in the courts, its impact on settlements and on proposals to reduce delay. *See, e.g.,* Zeisel, Kalven & Buchholz, *Delay in the Courts* (Little, Brown 1959); Rosenberg & Sovern, "Delay and the Dynamics of Personal Injury Litigation," 59 *Columbia Law Review* 1115 (1959); A. Leo Levin & Edward A. Woolley, *Dispatch and Delay, A Field Study of Judicial Administration in Pennsylvania* (Institute of Legal Research, U. of Pennsylvania 1961).

Maurice Rosenberg, *The Pretrial Conference and Effective Justice* (Columbia U. Press 1964), reports on a controlled experiment in New Jersey to determine whether pretrial conferences in personal injury cases save time for the courts by increasing pretrial settlements or by expediting trials.

Chapter 4

INTERCHANGES BETWEEN THE LEGAL SYSTEM
AND OTHER SOCIAL SYSTEMS: ON THE
IMPACT OF SOCIETY ON LAW

A. INTRODUCTION

The prior section assumed the existence of law or a law, and asked how far law or a law could be expected to be put into effect, under what conditions, and using what combination of rewards and punishments. This section asks a quite different question: how is law generated? What forces in society influence or create particular kinds of laws?

The emphasis is on the law of the United States, since that is most within the competence of editor and student alike, and since that is the legal system of most relevance to editor and student. American law, however, differs from many other systems of law, past and present, in that, as a matter of theory, the source of law is said to lie in the will of the people. There are sacred law systems which do not recognize public opinion as a valid source of law, at least in general. There are highly authoritarian systems of law which regard law as an emanation from the chief of state or from a traditional stratum of elites. American theory is clearly otherwise. Even the Constitution, which is drenched with natural law ideology, suffused with the notion of fundamental rights beyond the power of temporary majorities to interfere with, and which is itself extremely difficult to amend, is considered ultimately to be an expression of the popular will; and originally, of course, it was adopted by means of a vote. The reference to the Constitution does remind us that the theory that law is public opinion is not a simple one, even as a matter of theory, and even in so outwardly egalitarian a society as the United States. The whole idea of the "rule of law" is both an expression of an ideal of popular sovereignty and a denial of popular sovereignty as absolute. The United States, in theory, is a democracy; but it is also, in theory, a "government of laws and not of men."

Behavioral scientists, of course, are interested in human behavior as well as professed ideals, though they recognize that professed ideals profoundly influence behavior. Hence the emphasis in this section will be on the actual sources of law: who, what and how? For example, to what extent does law reflect "custom" or "public opinion"? Both of these are difficult concepts. In some very simple societies, the distinction between "public opinion," "custom" and "law" lacks clarity and focus. In some societies, there is no written language, no legal profession as such, and breaches of expected right behavior are handled, along with disputes between individuals, by leaders in a more-or-less informal setting. In these societies, the source of law is plainly "custom" and there is nothing but "custom" in these societies. But even here one can inquire as to the source of "custom." How much of the content of the norms can be explained by the fact that the tribe is nomadic? is warlike? lives in the desert? is surrounded by fierce enemies? has a high infant mortality rate? What is the precise role of economic and social forces in forming "custom"? For more complex societies, all these questions remain. In addition, there are similar problems in defining and measuring "public opinion." Then, too, the structure of the legal system itself—the way in which "custom" or "public opinion" is translated into "law" is itself an important factor—an "intervening variable."

The first reading deals with the origin of this intervening variable. Under what conditions does an informal system of social control turn into a formal system?

B. SOCIAL CONTEXT AND THE DEGREE OF FORMALITY OF THE SYSTEM OF CONTROL: WHEN DO WE FIND A "LEGAL" SYSTEM?

54. Social Factors in the Development of Legal Control: A Case Study of Two Israeli Settlements

RICHARD D. SCHWARTZ*

63 YALE LAW JOURNAL 471 (1954)

Legal control is not exercised against all disturbing behavior. Sometimes, such behavior never reaches the courts. At other times, it is not sanctioned by the courts because, we are told, it should be left to "the *interior* forum, as the tribunal of conscience has been aptly called." The effects of non-legal or informal control, whether or not adequately described in terms of "conscience," seem to be an important factor in a court's decision to withhold sanction.

The relationship between legal and informal controls can be theoretically stated and empirically described. The cultures of two Israeli communities were compared in an effort to determine the social effects of economic collectivism. One of the differences noted was that the collective community, or *kvutza*, had no distinctly legal institution, whereas the *moshav*, a semi-private property settlement, did. . . .

In the interactive aggregates of individuals which we call *social groups*, two main forms of control may be distinguished: that which is carried out by specialized functionaries who are socially

* Richard D. Schwartz, Professor of Sociology and Law, Northwestern University. Reprinted by permission of the Yale Law Journal Company and Fred B. Rothman & Company from The Yale Law Journal, Vol. 63, p. 471.

delegated the task of intra-group control, and that which is not so delegated. These will be respectively designated *legal* and *informal* controls. When, as is often the case, these two forms of control are in competition, the likelihood of legal control arising at all in a given sphere is a decreasing function of the effectiveness of informal controls. It is the thesis of this article that the presence of legal controls in the moshav, the semi-private property settlement, but not in the kvutza, the collective settlement, is to be understood primarily in terms of the fact that informal controls did not operate as effectively in the moshav as in the kvutza.

Control Systems in the Kvutza and Moshav

In most of their superficial characteristics, the two settlements are essentially similar. Both were founded at the same time, 1921, by young settlers who had come from Eastern Europe "to build a new life." Though the kvutza was smaller at first, it has grown to a population (just under 500 persons) which is almost identical in size with that of the moshav. Both are located on a slope of the Jezreel Valley where they have to deal with the same climate and similar topography. Both have about two thousand acres of land, which supports a mixed farming economy. Both populations have rejected many of the East-European Jewish customs, including traditional religious practices. Though many other Israeli collectives are left-wing socialist, the members of the kvutza under consideration resemble those of the moshav in adhering to the social-democratic political philosophy represented by the *Mapai* party.

Despite these similarities, the two communities have differed from the outset in their members' ideas about economic organization. In the kvutza, members felt they could implement the program, "from each according to his abilities, to each according to his need," as the way to create a "just society." Moshav members, many of whom had spent a few years in collectives, decided that the family should be the unit of production and distribution, and that thus a class of small independent farmers could be developed in the moshav which would provide a strong agricultural base for the country.

As far as could be ascertained, there were no initial differences in specific ideas concerning legal control. Legal jurisdiction over crimes and civil wrongs is recognized by all to reside in the State of Israel, but very few cases involving members of these settlements have been brought before the State's courts or, earlier, before the courts of the British Mandate. The minimal role of these courts has resulted from an absence of serious crime; the shielding of fellow members from British (and now to a lesser extent even Israeli) "outsiders"; and internal controls which effectively handle existing disturbances. In both settlements, the power to exercise these internal controls stems from the General Assembly, a regularly held meeting of all members in which each one present casts a single vote. This form of government works effectively in both communities, perhaps because they are small enough for everyone to be heard and homogeneous enough so that there is basic agreement on means and ends. While the kvutza meetings are more frequent and cover a broader range of issues, moshav sessions are held at least bi-weekly and are generally well attended.

In both settlements, the General Assembly delegates responsibility for certain activities to committees whose membership it approves. Committees are, if anything, more active in the kvutza, which has separate permanent groups to deal with questions of economic coordination, work assignment, education, social affairs, ceremonies, housing, community planning, and health. The moshav also has its committees, but most of these deal with agricultural matters, particularly the dissemination to individual farmers of the kind of scientific information which is handled by managers in the kvutza.

The moshav's Judicial Committee, however, is a specialized agency for which no counterpart is found in the kvutza. This Committee consists of a panel of seven members elected annually by the General Assembly for the purpose of dealing with internal disputes. Complaints by members against members are brought before the Committee either directly or by referral from the General Assembly. A hearing of the complaint is then conducted by a panel of three drawn from the larger Committee. After investigating the circumstances and hearing the direct testimony of both sides, a panel decides whether and how the defendant should bear responsibility. Fines and damages, the major types of punishment, are usually paid upon imposition, but if not, they are enforceable by the secretary of the moshav. Though these panels follow simple procedures, there can be no doubt that they have acted as an agency of legal control in the moshav.

An example will illustrate the operation of this moshav system of legal control. A fifteen-year-old boy took a neighbor's jeep without permission, picked up some of his friends, and went for a joyride outside the village. During the ride, he crashed into a tree and damaged the fender and door of the vehicle. The owner brought a complaint against him which was heard by the panel. When the boy admitted his actions, he was charged for the full cost of repairs. The debt was subsequently discharged by the boy's parents, and the case was considered closed.

By contrast, the kvutza has not delegated sanctioning responsibility to any special unit. Even when administrative or legislative action results in gain or loss to an individual, this is not its primary purpose. In the event of a dispute between workers, for example, the Work Assignment Committee or the Economic Council may decide that the interests of production would be better served if one or both of the workers were transferred. But the objective of such action is not punitive; rather it is to ensure the smooth functioning of the economy, and the decision is made in much the same manner as any decision relating to production.

In the course of its legislative work, the General Assembly of the kvutza also makes decisions which modify the gains and losses of members. Many of these are policy decisions which apply to classes of members, but sometimes an individual's behavior provides the occasion for a policy debate in the Assembly. One young member, for example, received an electric teakettle as a gift from his sister in the city. Though small gifts could be retained as personal property, the kettle represented a substantial item, and one which would draw upon the limited supply of electricity available to the entire settlement. Moreover, the kvutza had already decided against supplying each room with a kettle on the grounds that this would be expensive and would encourage socially divisive private get-togethers. By retaining the kettle, therefore, the young man was threatening the principles of material equality and social solidarity on which the kvutza is believed to rest. This at any rate was the decision of the Assembly majority following three meetings during which the issue was debated. Confronted with this decision, the owner bowed to the general will by turning his teakettle over to the infirmary where it would be used by those presumed to be in greatest need of it. No organized enforcement of the decision was threatened, but had he disregarded the expressed will of the community, his life in the kvutza would have been made intolerable by the antagonism of public opinion.

As will become apparent, it is the powerful force of public opinion which is the major sanction of the entire kvutza control system. It may be focused, as in the case of the electric teakettle, by an Assembly decision, or it may, as occurs more commonly, be aroused directly by the behavior it sanctions. In either case, it is an instrument of control which is employed not by any specialized functionaries but by the community as a whole. Since public opinion is the sanction for the entire kvutza control system, that system must be considered informal rather than legal.

We turn now to a more detailed consideration of the factors which have made this system of control so much more effective in the kvutza than in the moshav. . . .

The kvutza is in effect a large primary group whose members engage in continuous face-to-face interaction. Each able-bodied member works eight to ten hours a day, six days a week, at a job which is usually performed wholly or partially in the presence of others. The results of his efforts become known to his associates, the work manager, and the top officials who coordinate the economy. All three meals are eaten in a collective dining hall usually in the company of five other residents who happen to have arrived at the same time. Members of each sex share common washing and shower facilities, and these are used by most members at the same time, during the limited period when hot water is available. Housing is concentrated in one area of the kvutza and consists of rows of long houses, each partitioned to make six rooms, with a married couple or two roommates occupying each room. Because most rooms are surrounded by other dwellings, it is easily possible for neighbors to observe entrances and exits and even some behavior within. Child rearing is the primary responsibility of special nurses and teachers, but parents spend about two hours with their children on work days and usually more than this on their days of rest. Much of this relationship is subject to public view as parents and children stroll around the kvutza, eat together occasionally in the dining hall, or play in front of their rooms. Other leisure activities are also subject to public observation: participating in Assembly and Committee meetings, celebrating kvutza holidays, attending lectures and films, perusing newspapers and periodicals in the kvutza reading room, or taking a vacation tour of the country. Even sexual relations, particularly if they are illicit, can become the subject of general public knowledge, although this was the one type of activity excepted by a member when he said, "amongst us, all things except one are done together."

The same conditions of continuous interaction also make it possible to circulate information throughout the entire community. Mealtime and showering are two informal occasions when large numbers of people forgather and find opportunity for conversation. The shower in particular is a forum for the transmission of information where one can hear about anything from fractured ankles to broken hearts. Though "I heard it in the shower" is a kvutza equivalent for "take this with a grain of salt," much genuine news is disseminated there. Compared with these informal techniques, the weekly news bulletin and the Assembly meetings run slow supplementary seconds.

Moshav conditions do not permit as great a degree of public observation. Work is typically conducted alone, with other members of the family, or occasionally with the voluntary aid of a friend. As long as the moshav farmer maintains a solvent establishment and discharges such community obligations as payment of taxes and correct use of cooperative facilities, he is free to manage his farm as he sees fit. Meals consisting largely of produce from the farmstead are prepared by the housewife and eaten in a family dining room which occupies a central place in the home. Houses are small bungalows ranging from three to six rooms, separated from neighboring dwellings by a hundred yards or more, and screened by hedges and fruit trees. Many activities which are publicly performed in the kvutza can be, and usually are, carried out in the privacy of the moshav home, among them economic husbandry, care of clothing, showering, washing, child rearing, and such recreation as visiting, reading, and listening to the radio. There are, to be sure, places where members come into contact, such as the produce depots, cooperative store, Assembly and committee meetings, and cinema. Though such contacts provide some opportunities for the circulation of information, they are fewer and the information circulated is less complete than in the kvutza.

At least partially as a result of these differences, kvutza members do in fact learn more about the activities of more of their members than is known in the moshav. Less than a week of residence was necessary in the kvutza before virtually everyone knew the ostensible purpose of the writer's stay, whereas similar knowledge was not diffused as widely (or accurately) during two months in the moshav. Information thus transmitted is not confined to work performance and consumption, though these are of great interest, but range over such details as mail received, visitors contacted, time spent with children, and even style of underclothes worn. As a result, it becomes possible to control types of behavior in the kvutza which never become public knowledge in the moshav. . . .

Public opinion can be manifested often, swiftly, subtly, and with varying degrees of intensity in the kvutza. In the course of a day's continual interaction, positive or negative opinion may be communicated by the ways in which members glance at an individual, speak to him, pass him a requested work implement or dish of food, assign him work, give him instructions, sit next to him, and listen to his comments. To an experienced member, these small signs serve to predict more intense reactions of public acclaim or social isolation. They therefore acquire sanctioning power in and of themselves and become able to control the behavior in question before extremes are reached. In the moshav, by contrast, there are fewer opportunities to convey public opinion quickly and accurately because there is so much less contact between members in the course of the daily regime. This is an important limitation in the use of public opinion as a means of control in the moshav. . . .

[In the kvutza,] children are raised from infancy in the constant company of other children of their own age with whom they sleep, eat, bathe, dress, play, and later attend school. Though control is at first the task of the nurses, it is increasingly taken over by the children themselves. Their community is organized politically in a manner similar to the adult kvutza, with children's public opinion playing a corresponding part. When one child was caught stealing bananas reserved for the babies, the Children's Assembly decided to punish the culprit by abrogating *their own* movie privileges. Though this was explained to the adults on the grounds that all were involved in the guilt of one, a reason of at least equal importance was the children's expectation that this reaction would provide such a loss to all the children that a potential wrongdoer would repeat the precipitating action at his peril. At any rate, the practice of stealing was greatly reduced following this reaction.

During their years of training, the kvutza children become very alert to their peers' opinions, on which they are dependent for virtually all their satisfactions. While they are growing up, this force is used to ensure conformity to the standards of the children's community. These standards may conflict with those of the adult community, resulting in behavior which seems wild and capricious to the adults. But adult members remark repeatedly on the suddenness with which, following their accession to formal membership at eighteen, children of the kvutza "mature," *i.e.*, learn to conform to adult standards. This is in contrast to the moshav where adolescence is a period of great stress extending over several years. Moshav children, brought up in the close-knit farm family under their parents' control, never seem to develop the great respect for public opinion characteristic of the kvutza.

Supplementing migration and socialization practices are the day-to-day experiences of adult kvutza members. Quick and accurate response to public opinion enables the member to align his behavior with community standards, and thus to enhance his chances of attaining the acceptance and prestige which are needed for even small advantages. In the kvutza environment, one is rewarded for responding to the unfavorable reaction of his comrades when he talks too long in the Assembly, does not volunteer for emergency work service, wears inappropriate clothes, or debunks a kvutza celebration. Failure to respond has been known to result in serious difficulties, such as that experienced by a teacher who so antagonized public opinion by declining to dig trenches during Israel's War of Independence that he was denied a requested change of job a full year later.

In the moshav, this kind of pressure is exerted less frequently and effectively, if for no other reason than that there are fewer gains for which the individual is dependent on the community. Near self-sufficiency in economic affairs makes it difficult for the moshav to exert informal control. Primary reliance is placed on sanctions such as fines or, in a few cases of economic failure, expulsion from the settlement. . . .

The effectiveness of kvutza informal controls is enhanced by a system of norms classifying all behavior with reference to desirability. This system is detailed, generally unambiguous, applicable to wide, clearly defined segments of the population, and well known to the members. As a result it provides consistent guides for the application of sanction and at the same time forewarns potential sanctionees of the consequences of their acts. Such norms, found in every sphere of kvutza life, are particularly striking in economic matters.

Work activities in the kvutza are directed toward maximizing the production of agricultural goods and the performance of domestic services. Each able-bodied adult resident is expected to work in some unit, either an agricultural branch (*e.g.*, orchard, poultry, or sheep) or a domestic service (*e.g.*, kitchen, laundry, or school). Labor allocations are made by a Work Assignment Committee on the basis of economic requirements of each unit, ability of workers to meet those requirements, and lastly the preferences of each worker. Workers learn of their assignments either orally or by notice posted on the bulletin board. This assignment is understood to mean, unless otherwise specified, that the worker will report to the manager of the given unit within a reasonable time (about fifteen minutes) after the morning bell has rung, and work there, except for breakfast, lunch, and siesta, until the evening bell signals the end of the working day. Some assignments (*e.g.*, nursery, dairy, trucking, and night watch) require special hours, but these are explicitly stated and the kvutza assigns a functionary to rouse such workers and notify them of the start of their workday. Illness constitutes the major reason for exemption from this norm, and all sick persons are expected to consult the resident community physician who decides whether and for how long the patient is to abstain from work.

Each worker is expected to cooperate with the individual recognized by all as the coordinator or manager of his unit. Usually such recognition is relatively spontaneous, based upon superior knowledge, skill, leadership ability, and seniority. When no single individual is clearly superior in these regards, the Economic Council recommends reassignments which bring about this result. As a consequence, the worker typically has someone to whom he turns for guidance whenever he is uncertain as to the correct course of action. On their part, managers, though exercising considerable discretion, are expected to turn to the Economic Council for guidance in significant decisions. Ultimately, the Council itself is responsible to the General Assembly. All kvutza members are expected to perform their various activities to the best of their individual abilities. These abilities are recognized to vary widely, but kvutza members maintain that a certain level of performance exists for each worker in a given kind of job. Though a worker's prestige varies with the height of this level, he may be well esteemed if he consistently meets even a low standard of performance. Since the level of performance is set by the worker's *better* performances, he is likely to be considered a violator of this very significant norm if he is erratic and frequently falls below his standard. In an economy which has abolished wages and private profit, these work norms are of great importance in maintaining production.

Consumption activities in the kvutza are also controlled with the aid of explicit general norms. Objectives which these are supposed to serve include distribution according to need, frugality, solidarity, and of course adequate sustenance of the population. Since differential need is very difficult to ascertain, the kvutza tendency has been to distribute scarce items equally, on the assumption that need is generally equal. Exceptions are made in instances where this is obviously not the case, for example, when youth, age, illness, or pregnancy furnishes grounds for special diet, housing, or medical care. Aside from these, however, consumption of scarce goods is supposed to be as nearly equal as possible. Adults are expected to eat together in the common dining hall at specified times. There they are served meals which are planned by the dietician with an eye toward fitting the budget adopted by the General Assembly. Crops drawn directly from the land are usually sufficiently abundant to permit unrestricted consumption, but other foods such as margarine, fish, meat, hard cheese, and eggs are distributed in limited equal quantities. Though the norms governing such consumption may be a mystery to new arrivals, members are fully aware of them. Occasionally questions arise as to the kinds of dishes for which a given serving may be exchanged, but these are authoritatively settled by the dietician. Similarly, clothes are expected to be issued equally except for differences of sex and size. Women are permitted a small degree of discretion in the selection of materials, but no one may exceed the ration and standard for a given sex, of such items as work shirts, work shoes, and sweaters. In housing, correct behavior is even less complicated: one is expected to live in the room assigned by the Housing Committee, whose discretion is limited by policies established in the General Assembly. Explicit general norms also cover such matters as participation in kvutza festivals, visiting of children by parents, and preservation of a minimal privacy in rooms. . . .

Kvutza members want their society to survive and be productive. They have set up an economic system which requires diligent and cooperative work by all if it is to succeed. Any behavior which is deemed non-diligent and which does not appear to contribute to the required coordination of effort will be viewed as threatening loss to kvutza productivity. Such behavior would include failure to work at one's top ability and to comply with one's work assignment; failure in these respects would be interpreted as causing loss to the kvutza. Similarly, anyone who receives more than an equal share in food, clothes, or housing is threatening the goal of a "just society" and subjecting the other members to "relative deprivation." While variations in the other direction—too much work or substandard consumption—are less of a cause for concern, they also seem to be a source of disturbance, perhaps because vicarious experience makes such behavior unpleasant to those who observe it. Whatever the reasons, strict compliance with these norms is generally considered desirable, while violation of them is typically viewed as a loss to the members as a whole.

One of the greatest weaknesses of kvutza controls arises from failure to specify the identity and special privileges of the high-prestige members. Managers and old-timers are distinguished in fact from the ordinary workers and "simpletons" in the deference shown them and, within narrow limits, in the preference they may receive in housing, furniture, travel, and education for their children. Deviations from the general norms by the "important" people are less disturbing than if performed by ordinary members, since kvutza public opinion recognizes their special worth and power. But difficulties sometimes arise from uncertainty as to how important a given individual is and what privileges, if any, are due him.

Such problems tend to be minimized by a denial that important people are treated differently in any way, or that there is in fact a special managerial status. That an equalitarian society should be unwilling to recognize such privileges is not surprising. Material advantages given the important people are rationalized in terms of the norms and their accepted exceptions. For example, new housing units, built by the kvutza to accommodate an increased population, were made more elaborate than earlier ones by the inclusion of shower and toilet facilities. These units were designated from the first as "old-timers' housing," and it was explained that the increased age of this group made it difficult for them to use the central facilities. On closer questioning, however, it was revealed that these rooms were not intended for other inhabitants who were also advancing in years, namely, a few recent immigrants of middle-age and several resident parents of members. Though the physical need of such persons was at least as great as that of the old-timers, no one even considered the possibility that they should be given modern accommodations as permanent quarters. Actually the reason was a feeling of injustice that so much be given to people who had done so little for the kvutza, but this was never publicly articulated and the fiction prevailed that the distribution met the requirement of "equal or according to need." Accordingly, the behavior, which was in fact a non-disturbing deviation from the general norm, was classified as acceptable behavior and was not negatively sanctioned as were other deviations from the norm.

In most areas, however, norms have been developed which clearly distinguish acceptable from disturbing behavior in a given situation for a clearly delimited category of persons. Ambiguities which arise are usually brought before the General Assembly and are conclusively resolved by its decision. Sometimes the kvutza reaches a consensus informally. The resultant norms are applied with a high degree of certainty. Though for our purposes the reasons need not be spelled out, it would appear that kvutza norms can be unambiguous and simple because behavioral alternatives and variations are sharply limited and because a homogenous population is in general agreement in distinguishing desirable from undesirable behavior among these clear and limited alternatives.

Moshav norms, by contrast, are far less explicit, uniformly applied, or generally agreed upon. While it is important that a farmer manage his own holdings effectively and be a good neighbor, the exact pattern of actions by which this can be accomplished has never been authoritatively laid down. In most areas, the individual is likely to have his own ideas about the proper behavior in a given circumstance. On particular occasions involving the duty to aid one's sick neighbor, cooperation in the use of machinery, and a member's violation of State ration controls, widespread difference of opinion was discerned among moshav members. This difference was partly attributed to the influence on each member of such factors as the effect of the particular behavior on his own economic interest; his relations with the actor in question; and his conception of the responsibility owed to the moshav by its members.

Such crucial questions as property relations in the family and between neighbors are still being deliberated and moshav members vary widely in their views on such matters. The problem of succession is just beginning to arise with regularity, and its importance and difficulty for a village with limited, indivisible and inalienable farmsteads may hardly be over-estimated. Perhaps a uniform set of norms will be evolved over a period of time to deal with such problems, or perhaps the problems, especially concerning property, defy informal concensus. At any rate, for the present, there is little agreement. It is small wonder, then, that the moshav system of informal controls has been supplemented by a specialized group of deliberators able to make norms and to ensure their sanction by legal means. . . .

Tendency toward Informal Sanction:

As far as could be ascertained, the conditions which promoted effective informal control existed from the first or arose early in the history of the kvutza. Since it started out as a small settlement with a homogeneous population, it was, if anything, even more of a primary group during its formative years than at present. There is sufficient evidence in reports of old-timers to indicate that pertinent behavior was readily perceived, that public opinion was an easily implemented and effective sanction, and that unambiguous norms defined the circumstances under which such sanctions should be employed. There were, to be sure, instances where these controls failed to work, as for example in regard to the use of spending money. An early norm permitted each member to take as much money from a common fund as he felt he needed for personal expenses. In practice this is said to have resulted in low expenditures by the "idealistic" members and disproportionately high ones by those with a weaker sense of social responsibility. When public opinion proved incapable of controlling this socially disturbing behavior, the General Assembly modified the norm to stipulate a yearly amount for each member's personal use. Clarification of the distinction between acceptable and disturbing behavior in this area permitted the effective application of negative sanction to the latter, with the result that few members exceeded their allotted amount thereafter. The desired result was achieved by changes which increased the effectiveness of informal sanction rather than substituting legal controls for them.

Because effective informal control was achieved in the kvutza, the tendency for its subsequent use was increased. That this tendency was high is indicated not only by the many successful instances of its use, but perhaps even more by the persistence with which it was employed on the rare occasions when it failed. Most striking among the illustrations of this is the case of a woman who was considered by the entire kvutza to be anti-social. Soon after her arrival she began to behave very aggressively, quarreling with all her fellow workers in the kitchen and even striking them. Though the use of violence against a fellow member was shocking to the other members, only the usual mild sanctions were at first applied. For some reason, however, social disapproval failed to deter the woman. She continued the same course of behavior through seven years, during which she was subjected to more vigorous informal controls and was at the same time denied formal membership. But she was never subjected to force, expulsion, or even to material disadvantage. Only during her eighth year in the kvutza was a different type of sanction directed against her: she was given no work assignment and was deprived of the opportunity to work for the kvutza. After a year in which her isolation was thus increased, she bowed to the pressure and left the kvutza. Whether the new sanction be designated informal or legal, it is clear that it was an alternative to the traditional informal sanctions of public opinion. That it was employed only after seven years of persistent exercise of the traditional sanctions is striking indication of the firmness with which the latter were established.

In the moshav, the tendency to exercise informal controls seems much less powerful. . . . Conditions which would minimize the effectiveness of such sanctions . . . are traceable to the economic structure of the moshav, and thus it is reasonable to assume that they also existed at the inauguration of the community. If so, they preceded the rise of legal controls which evolved gradually during the first twenty years of the settlement's history. During this period and subsequently, informal controls have regularly been tried, but have been ineffective, presumably because of inadequate information, implementation, sanction magnitude, and norms. In the course of time, members have learned that informal controls are ineffective; the resultant lowered tendency to invoke these controls, resulting in even less frequent and less vigorous attempts to use them, has further diminished their effectiveness. This attitude toward informal controls was exemplified by moshav reaction to the prank of a group of adolescents who raided a melon patch and openly ate the stolen melons. Indignation ran high because the melons had been specially cultivated for the wedding feast to be given in honor of the marriage of the farmer's daughter. Failing action by the Judiciary Committee, the feeling prevailed that there was "nothing at all to do" about it. Said one member, "If you scold those fellows, they laugh at you." So on the informal level, no serious attempt was undertaken to exert effective control.

Competing Reaction Tendencies:

Infrequent and non-vigorous exertion of informal sanctions in the moshav may result in part from the competition of legal controls as an effective alternative. It is, of course, impossible to explain the original occurrence of legal controls in these terms, but once they had become established, their success as a competing reaction could have been expected to reduce the impact of informal sanctions. Within the kvutza, there was no comparable history of legal controls which might have constituted a competing alternative to the prevailing system. Free from such competition, the impact of informal sanctions could have been expected to continue without abatement.

CONCLUSION

Several factors have been discussed with reference to their effect on social control. The kvutza was characterized by a number of conditions which, our theory suggests, engender a more effective informal control system. Presence of these factors, and the effective controls which they produced, was interpreted as a partial explanation for the failure of the kvutza to develop a legal control system. By contrast, the moshav did not possess these characteristics to the same degree as did the kvutza and accordingly failed to develop an effective informal control system. The development of legal institutions in the moshav is partially explicable in these terms. Law has thus been seen to develop where disturbing behavior occurred which was not as adequately controlled informally as it could be with the aid of legal controls. If a similar process exists in the United States, its accurate description should contribute to the prediction and evaluation of our own legislative and judicial decisions.

NOTES AND QUESTIONS

1. In order to test the impact of particular factors, a social scientist will often "hold constant" certain other factors. This is

the function of a control group. If one wants to determine whether eating too many eggs leads to heart disease, one might try to find two groups of men, similar in age and other relevant characteristics, and differing only in their consumption of eggs. Then one could measure the incidence of heart disease and more or less plausibly ascribe any differences to the eating of eggs.

What factors are "held constant" in this way in the study of the *moshav* and *kvutza*?

2. How far can the Schwartz study be generalized? Note that it is a study of two "subsystems," operating *within* an organized political state. On the other hand, like the prison in Sykes, each of the two types is more or less a "total institution," which has been defined by Erving Goffman, in *Asylums* xiii (Doubleday 1961), as "a place of residence and work where a large number of like-situated individuals, cut off from the wider society for an appreciable period of time, together lead an enclosed, formally administered round of life."

3. How much of the differences between the *moshav* and the *kvutza* can reasonably be assigned to the ideological differences between the two? how much to differences in economy and organization (granting that these in turn stem from ideological differences in large part)?

4. In light of Schwartz' description of the *moshav* and the *kvutza*, what would be the likely consequences of attempting to run the following organizations as an extended primary group (that is, more or less as a big family) with few explicit rules, without a body to decide how to react to disputes and no regularized sanction system: (a) a professional athletic team, (b) this class, (c) a law school faculty of thirty men and women, (d) a police department of 1,000 officers, (e) the Republican Party of the State of California, (f) an agency of a state charged with administering programs to aid the blind, (g) the University of California at Berkeley, and (h) the federal Internal Revenue Service? What would be the consequences of attempting to run each of these organizations as a formal legal system with a legislature, judiciary and formal sanction system?

5. To what extent are the differences between *kvutza* and *moshav* explainable as consequences of the differences between the communication networks in the two kinds of settlement? No norm or rule can be effective unless it is communicated to those who are expected to obey it or follow it. In a face-to-face group, communication problems are quite different from those groups

and societies which are larger and more diffuse. *See also* Rushing, Reading 95, at 810, *infra*.

6. Compare with Schwartz, William M. Evan & Mildred A. Schwartz, "Law and the Emergence of Formal Organization," 48 *Sociology & Social Research*, No. 3 (April 1964); Note, "A Perspective on Non-Legal Social Controls: The Sanctions of Shame and Guilt in Representative Cultural Settings," 35 *Indiana Law Journal* 196 (1960), which draws on anthropological materials.

C. THE SOCIAL CONTEXT OF LEGAL CHANGE: TOWARDS A GENERAL THEORY

55. Social Change and the Law of Industrial Accidents

LAWRENCE M. FRIEDMAN AND
JACK LADINSKY*

67 COLUMBIA LAW REVIEW 50 (1967)

Sociologists recognize, in a general way, the essential role of legal institutions in the social order. They concede, as well, the responsiveness of law to social change and have made important explorations of the interrelations involved. Nevertheless, the role law plays in initiating—or reflecting—social change has never been fully explicated, either in theory or through research. The evolution of American industrial accident law from tort principles to compensation systems is an appropriate subject for a case-study on this subject. . . .

II. DEVELOPMENT OF THE LAW OF INDUSTRIAL ACCIDENTS

A. *Background of the Fellow-Servant Rule*

At the dawn of the industrial revolution, the common law of torts afforded a remedy, as it still does, for those who had suffered injuries at the hands of others. If a man injured another by direct action—by striking him, or slandering him, or by trespassing on his property—the victim could sue for his damages. Similarly, the victim of certain kinds of negligent behavior had a remedy at law. But tort law was not highly developed. Negligence in particular did not loom large in the reports and it was not prominently discussed in books of theory or practice. Indeed, no treatise on tort law appeared in America until Francis Hilliard's in 1859; the first English treatise came out in 1860. . . .

* Lawrence M. Friedman, Professor of Law, Stanford University; Jack Ladinsky, Associate Professor of Sociology, University of Wisconsin. Copyright © 1967, Columbia Law Review. Reprinted by permission.

In theory, at least, recovery for industrial accidents might have been assimilated into the existing system of tort law. The fundamental principles were broad and simple. If a factory worker was injured through the negligence of another person—including his employer—an action for damages would lie. Although as a practical matter, servants did not usually sue their master nor workers their employers, in principle they had the right to do so.

In principle, too, a worker might have had an action against his employer for any injury caused by the negligence of any other employee. The doctrine of *respondeat superior* was familiar and fundamental law. A principal was liable for the negligent acts of his agent. As Blackstone put it:

> he who does a thing by the agency of another, does it himself. . . . If an innkeeper's servants rob his guests, the master is bound to restitution. . . . So likewise if the drawer at a tavern sells a man bad wine, whereby his health is injured, he may bring an action against the master.

Conceivably, then, one member of an industrial work force might sue his employer for injuries caused by the negligence of a fellow worker. A definitive body of doctrine was slow to develop, however. When it did, it rejected the broad principle of *respondeat superior* and took instead the form of the so-called fellow-servant rule. Under this rule, a servant (employee) could not sue his master (employer) for injuries caused by the negligence of another employee. The consequences of this doctrine were far reaching. An employee retained the right to sue the employer for injuries, provided they were caused by the employer's personal misconduct. But the factory system and corporate ownership of industry made this right virtually meaningless. The factory owner was likely to be a "soulless" legal entity; even if the owner was an individual entrepreneur, he was unlikely to concern himself physically with factory operations. In work accidents, then, legal fault would be ascribed to fellow employees, if anyone. But fellow employees were men without wealth or insurance. The fellow-servant rule was an instrument capable of relieving employers from almost all the legal consequences of industrial injuries. Moreover, the doctrine left an injured worker without any effective recourse but an empty action against his co-worker.

When labor developed a collective voice, it was bound to decry the rule as infamous, as a deliberate instrument of oppression—a sign that law served the interests of the rich and propertied, and denied the legitimate claims of the poor and the weak. . . . Conventionally, then, the fellow-servant rule is explained as a deliberate or half-deliberate rejection of a well-settled principle of law in order to encourage enterprise by forcing workmen to bear the costs of industrial injury. And the overthrow of the rule is taken as a sign of a conquest by progressive forces. . . . [But] from the standpoint of social change, good and evil are social labels based on *perceptions* of conditions, not terms referring to conditions in themselves. Social change comes about when people decide that a situation is evil and must be altered, even if they were satisfied or unaware of the problem before. In order, then, to understand the legal reaction to the problem of industrial accidents, one must understand how the problem was perceived within the legal system and by that portion of society whose views influenced the law.

B. *Birth and Acceptance of the Rule*

The origin of the fellow-servant rule is usually ascribed to Lord Abinger's opinion in *Priestley v. Fowler*,[15] decided in 1837. Yet the case on its facts did not pose the question of the industrial accident, as later generations would understand it; rather, it concerned the employment relationships of tradesmen. The defendant, a butcher, instructed the plaintiff, his servant, to deliver goods which had been loaded on a van by another employee. The van, which had been overloaded, broke down, and plaintiff fractured his thigh in the accident. Lord Abinger, in his rather diffuse and unperceptive opinion, reached his holding that the servant had no cause of action by arguing from analogies drawn neither from industry nor from trade:

If the master be liable to the servant in this action, the principle of that liability will . . . carry us to an alarming extent. . . . The footman . . . may have an action against his master for a defect in the carriage owing to the negligence of the coachmaker. . . . The master . . . would be liable to the servant for the negligence of the chambermaid, for putting him into a damp bed; . . . for the negligence of the cook in not properly cleaning the copper vessels used in the kitchen. . . .

These and similar passages in the opinion suggest that Abinger was worried about the disruptive effects of a master's liability upon his household staff. These considerations were perhaps irrelevant to the case at hand, the facts of which did not deal with the household of a nobleman, great landowner, or rich merchant; *a fortiori* the decision itself did not concern relationships within

---

[15] 150 Eng. R. 1030 (Ex. 1837).

an industrial establishment. Certainly the opinion made extension of the rule to the factory setting somewhat easier to enunciate and formulate technically. But it did not justify the existence of an industrial fellow-servant rule. The case might have been totally forgotten—or overruled—had not the onrush of the industrial revolution put the question again and again to courts, each time more forcefully. *Priestley v. Fowler* and the doctrine of *respondeat superior* each stood for a broad principle. Whether the one or the other (or neither) would find a place in the law relative to industrial accidents depended upon needs felt and expressed by legal institutions in response to societal demands. Had there been no *Priestley v. Fowler*, it would have been necessary—and hardly difficult—to invent one.

In the United States, the leading case on the fellow-servant situation was *Farwell v. Boston & Worcester Railroad Corp.*,[17] decided by Massachusetts' highest court in 1842. The case arose out of a true industrial accident in a rapidly developing industrial state. Farwell was an engineer who lost a hand when his train ran off the track due to a switchman's negligence. As Chief Justice Shaw, writing for the court, saw it, the problem of *Farwell* was how best to apportion the risks of railroad accidents. In his view, it was superficial to analyze the problem according to the tort concepts of fault and negligence. His opinion spoke the language of contract, and employed the stern logic of nineteenth century economic thought. Some occupations are more dangerous than others. Other things being equal, a worker will choose the least dangerous occupation available. Hence, to get workers an employer will have to pay an additional wage for dangerous work. The market, therefore, has already made an adjustment in the wage rate to compensate for the possibility of accident, and a cost somewhat similar to an insurance cost has been allocated to the company. As Shaw put it, "he who engages in the employment of another for the performance of specified duties and services, for compensation, takes upon himself the natural and ordinary risks and perils incident to the performance of such services, and *in legal presumption, the compensation is adjusted accordingly.*" The worker, therefore, has assumed the risk of injury—for a price. The "implied contract of employment" between the worker and employer did not require the employer to bear any additional costs of injury (except for those caused by the employer's personal negligence). . . . Shaw and his generation placed their hopes of salvation on rapid economic growth. Perhaps they were anxious to see that the tort system of accident compensation did not add

---

[17] 45 Mass. (4 Met.) 49 (1842).

to the problems of new industry. Few people imagined that accidents would become so numerous as to create severe economic and social dislocations. On the contrary, rash extension of certain principles of tort law to industrial accidents might upset social progress by imposing extreme costs on business in its economic infancy. The 1840's and 1850's were a period of massive economic development in New England and the Midwest. . . . Textiles, and then iron, spearheaded the industrial revolution; westward expansion and the railroads created new markets. Communities and states made a social contribution to the construction of railroads through cash subsidies, stock subscriptions, and tax exemptions. The courts, using the fellow-servant doctrine and the concepts of assumption of risk and contributory negligence, socialized the accident costs of building the roads. That these solutions represented the collective, if uneasy, consensus of those with authority and responsibility is supported by the fact that every court of the country, with but one transient exception, reached the same conclusion in the years immediately following *Farwell.* Moreover, the fellow-servant rule was not abolished by any legislature in these early years. Although legislative inaction is not a necessary sign of acquiescence, it at least indicates lack of a major feeling of revulsion.

C. *Weakening the Rule*

A general pattern may be discerned which is common to the judicial history of many rules of law. The courts enunciate a rule, intending to "solve" a social problem—that is, they seek to lay down a stable and clear-cut principle by which men can govern their conduct, or, alternatively, by which the legal system can govern men. If the rule comports with some kind of social consensus, it will in fact work a solution—that is, it will go unchallenged, or, if challenged, will prevail. Challenges will not usually continue, since the small chance of overturning the rule is not worth the cost of litigation. If, however, the rule is weakened— if courts engraft exceptions to it, for example—then fresh challenges probing new weaknesses will be encouraged. Even if the rule retains *some* support, it will no longer be efficient and clearcut. Ultimately, the rule may no longer serve *anybody's* purposes. At this point, a fresh (perhaps wholly new) "solution" will be attempted.

The history of the fellow-servant rule rather neatly fits this scheme. Shaw wrote his *Farwell* opinion in 1842. During the latter part of the century, judges began to reject his reasoning. The "tendency in nearly all jurisdictions," said a Connecticut court in 1885, was to "limit rather than enlarge" the range of the fellow-servant rule.[30] A Missouri judge in 1891 candidly expressed the change in attitude:

> In the progress of society, and the general substitution of ideal and invisible masters and employers for the actual and visible ones of former times, in the forms of corporations engaged in varied, detached and widespread operations . . . it has been seen and felt that the universal application of the [fellow-servant] rule often resulted in hardship and injustice. Accordingly, the tendency of the more modern authorities appears to be in the direction of such a modification and limitation of the rule as shall eventually devolve upon the employer under these circumstances a due and just share of the responsibility for the lives and limbs of the persons in its employ.[31]

The rule was strong medicine, and it depended for its efficacy upon continued, relatively certain, and unswerving legal loyalty. Ideally, if the rule were strong and commanded nearly total respect from the various agencies of law, it would eliminate much of the mass of litigation that might otherwise arise. Undoubtedly, it did prevent countless thousands of lawsuits; but it did not succeed in choking off industrial accident litigation. For example, industrial accident litigation dominated the docket of the Wisconsin Supreme Court at the beginning of the age of workmen's compensation; far more cases arose under that heading than under any other single field of law.[32] Undoubtedly, this appellate case-load was merely the visible portion of a vast iceberg of litigation. Thus, the rule did not command the respect required for efficient operation and hence, in the long run, survival.

One reason for the continued litigation may have been simply the great number of accidents that occurred. At the dawn of the industrial revolution, when Shaw wrote, the human consequences of that technological change were unforeseeable. In particular, the toll it would take of human life was unknown. But by the last quarter of the nineteenth century, the number of industrial accidents had grown enormously. After 1900, it is estimated, 35,000 deaths and 2,000,000 injuries occurred every year in the United States. One quarter of the injuries produced disabilities

---

30 Ziegler v. Danbury & N.R.R., 52 Conn. 543, 556 (1885).

31 Parker v. Hannibal & St. J.R.R., 109 Mo. 362, 397 (1891) (Thomas, J., dissenting).

32 Unpublished survey and classification of all Wisconsin Supreme Court cases 1905-1915, by Robert Friebert and Lawrence M. Friedman.

lasting more than one week. The railway injury rate doubled in the seventeen years between 1889 and 1906.

In addition to the sheer number of accidents, other reasons for the increasing number of challenges to the rule in the later nineteenth century are apparent. If the injury resulted in death or permanent disability, it broke off the employment relationship; the plaintiff or his family thereafter had nothing to lose except the costs of suit. The development of the contingent fee system provided the poor man with the means to hire a lawyer. . . .

The contingent fee system was no more than a mechanism, however. A losing plaintiff's lawyer receives no fee; that is the essence of the system. The fact is that plaintiffs won many of their lawsuits; in so doing, they not only weakened the fellow-servant rule, but they encouraged still more plaintiffs to try their hand, still more attorneys to make a living from personal injury work. In trial courts, the pressure of particular cases—the "hard" cases in which the plight of the plaintiff was pitiful or dramatic—tempted judges and juries to find for the little man and against the corporate defendant. In Shaw's generation, many leading appellate judges shared his view of the role of the judge; they took it as their duty to lay down grand legal principles to govern whole segments of the economic order. Thus, individual hardship cases had to be ignored for the sake of higher duty. But this was not the exclusive judicial style, even in the appellate courts. And in personal injury cases, lower court judges and juries were especially prone to tailor justice to the case at hand. For example, in Wisconsin, of 307 personal injury cases involving workers that appeared before the state supreme court up to 1907, nearly two-thirds had been decided in favor of the worker in the lower courts. In the state supreme court, however, only two-fifths were decided for the worker. Other states undoubtedly had similar experiences. Whether for reasons of sympathy with individual plaintiffs, or with the working class in general, courts and juries often circumvented the formal dictates of the doctrines of the common law.

Some weakening of the doctrine took place by means of the control exercised by trial court judge and jury over findings of fact. But sympathy for injured workers manifested itself also in changes in doctrine. On the appellate court level, a number of mitigations of the fellow-servant rule developed near the end of the nineteenth century. For example, it had always been conceded that the employer was liable if he was personally responsible (through his own negligence) for his worker's injury. Thus, in a Massachusetts case, a stable owner gave directions to his employee, who was driving a wagon, that caused an accident and injury to the driver (or so the jury found). The employer was held liable. Out of this simple proposition grew the so-called vice-principal rule, which allowed an employee to sue his employer where the negligent employee occupied a supervisory position such that he could more properly be said to be an alter ego of the principal than a mere fellow-servant. This was a substantial weakening of the fellow-servant doctrine. Yet some states never accepted the vice-principal rule; in those that did, it too spawned a bewildering multiplicity of decisions, sub-rules, and sub-sub-rules. "The decisions on the subject, indeed, are conflicting to a degree which, it may safely be affirmed, is without a parallel in any department of jurisprudence." This statement appeared in a treatise, written on the eve of workmen's compensation, which devoted no fewer than 524 pages to a discussion of the ramifications of the vice-principal rule.

There were scores of other "exceptions" to the fellow-servant rule, enunciated in one or more states. Some of them were of great importance. In general, an employer was said to have certain duties that were not "delegable"; these he must do or have done, and a failure to perform them laid him open to liability for personal injuries. Among these was the duty to furnish a safe place to work, safe tools, and safe appliances. . . . Had the courts been so inclined, they might have eliminated the fellow-servant rule without admitting it, simply by expanding the safe place and safe tool rules. They were never quite willing to go that far, and the safe tool doctrine was itself subject to numerous exceptions. In some jurisdictions, for example, the so-called "simple tool" rule applied:

> Tools of ordinary and everyday use, which are simple in structure and requiring no skill in handling—such as hammers and axes—not obviously defective, do not impose a liability upon employer[s] for injuries resulting from such defects.[42]

Doctrinal complexity and vacillation in the upper courts, coupled with jury freedom in the lower courts, meant that by the end of the century the fellow-servant rule had lost much of its reason for existence: it was no longer an efficient cost-allocating doctrine. Even though the exceptions did not go the length of obliterating the rule, and even though many (perhaps most) injured workers who had a possible cause of action did not or could not recover, the instability and unpredictability of operation of the common law rule was a significant fact.

---

[42] Dunn v. Southern Ry., 151 N.C. 313, 315, 66 S.E. 134-35 (1909). . . .

The numerous judge-made exceptions reflected a good deal of uncertainty about underlying social policy. The same uncertainty was reflected in another sphere of legal activity—the legislature. Though the rule was not formally abrogated, it was weakened by statute in a number of jurisdictions. . . . [By the 1850's] the railroads replaced the banks as popular bogeymen. . . . Some of the fear of excessive economic power was transferred to them. Disregard for safety was one more black mark against the railroads; farmers, small businessmen, and the emerging railroad unions might use the safety argument to enlist widespread support for general regulation of railroads, but the essential thrust of the movement was economic. The railroads were feared and hated because of their power over access to the market. They became "monopolistic" as the small local lines were gradually amalgamated into large groupings controlled by "robber barons." Interstate railroad nets were no longer subject to local political control—if anything, they controlled local politics, or so it plausibly appeared to much of the public. Farmers organized and fought back against what they identified as their economic enemy. It is not coincidental that the earliest derogations from the strictness of the fellow-servant rule applied *only* to railroads. For example, the first statutory modification, passed in Georgia in 1856, allowed railroad employees to recover for injuries caused by the acts of fellow-servants, provided they themselves were free from negligence. A similar act was passed in Iowa in 1862. Other statutes were passed in Wyoming (1869) and Kansas (1874). The chronology suggests—though direct evidence is lacking—that some of these statutes were connected with the general revolt of farmers against the power of the railroad companies, a revolt associated with the Granger movement, which achieved its maximum power in the 1870's. . . .

The Granger revolt, and similar movements, were not without lessons for the railroad companies. Despite the fall of Granger legislatures, the legal and economic position of the railroads was permanently altered. Great masses of people had come to accept the notion that the power of the railroads was a threat to farmers and a threat to the independence and stability of democratic institutions. Out of the ashes of ineffective and impermanent state regulation of railroads arose what ultimately became a stronger and more systematic program of regulation, grounded in federal power over the national economy.

The Interstate Commerce Commission was created in 1887, chiefly to outlaw discrimination in freight rates and other practices deemed harmful to railroad users. The original legislation had nothing to say about railroad accidents and safety. But this did not long remain the case. . . . In 1893, Congress required interstate railroads to equip themselves with safety appliances, and provided that any employee injured "by any locomotive, car, or train in use" without such appliances would not "be deemed . . . to have assumed the risk thereby occasioned."

The Federal Employers' Liability Act of 1908 went much further; it abolished the fellow-servant rule for railroads and greatly reduced the strength of contributory negligence and assumption of risk as defenses. Once the employers had been stripped of these potent weapons, the relative probability of recovery by injured railroad employees was high enough so that workmen's compensation never seemed as essential for the railroads as for industry generally. The highly modified FELA tort system survives (in amended form) to this day for the railroads. It is an anachronism, but one which apparently grants some modest satisfaction to both sides. Labor and management both express discontent with FELA, but neither side has been so firmly in favor of a change to workmen's compensation as to make it a major issue.

FELA shows one of many possible outcomes of the decline in efficacy of the fellow-servant rule. Under it, the rule was eliminated, and the law turned to a "pure" tort system—pure in the sense that the proclivities of juries were not interfered with by doctrines designed to limit the chances of a worker's recovery. But the railroads were a special case. Aside from the special history of regulation, the interstate character of the major railroads made them subject to national safety standards and control by a single national authority. For other industrial employers, the FELA route was not taken; instead, workmen's compensation acts were passed. In either case, however, the fellow-servant rule was abolished, or virtually so. Either course reflects, we can assume, some kind of general agreement that the costs of the rule outweighed its benefits.

D. *Rising Pressures for Change*

The common law doctrines were designed to preserve a certain economic balance in the community. When the courts and legislatures created numerous exceptions, the rules lost much of their efficiency as a limitation on the liability of businessmen. The rules prevented many plaintiffs from recovering, but not all; a few plaintiffs recovered large [awards of damages]. There were costs of settlements, costs of liability insurance, costs of administration, legal fees and the salaries of staff lawyers. These costs rose steadily, at the very time when American business, especially big business, was striving to rationalize and bureaucratize its operations. It was desirable to be able to predict costs and insure against fluctuating, unpredictable risks. The costs of industrial accident liability were not easily predictable, partly because legal consequences of accidents were not predictable. Insurance, though available, was expensive.

In addition, industry faced a serious problem of labor unrest. Workers and their unions were dissatisfied with many aspects of factory life. The lack of compensation for industrial accidents was one obvious weakness. Relatively few injured workers received compensation. Under primitive state employers' liability statutes, the issue of liability and the amount awarded still depended upon court rulings and jury verdicts. Furthermore, the employer and the insurance carrier might contest a claim or otherwise delay settlement in hopes of bringing the employee to terms. The New York Employers' Liability Commission, in 1910, reported that delay ran from six months to six years.

> The injured workman is driven to accept whatever his employer or an insurance company chooses to give him or take his chance in a lawsuit. Half of the time his lawsuit is doomed to failure because he has been hurt by some trade risk or lacks proof for his case. At best he has a right to retain a lawyer, spend two months on the pleadings, watch his case from six months to two years on a calendar and then undergo the lottery of a jury trial, with a technical system of law and rules of evidence, and beyond that appeals and perhaps reversals on questions that do not go to the merits. . . . If he wins, he wins months after his most urgent need is over.

When an employee did recover, the amount was usually small. The New York Commission found that of forty-eight fatal cases studied in Manhattan, eighteen families received no compensation; only four received over $2,000; most received less than $500. The deceased workers had averaged $15.22 a week in wages; only eight families recovered as much as three times their average yearly earnings. The same inadequacies turned up in Wisconsin in 1907. Of fifty-one fatal injuries studied, thirty-four received settlements under $500; only eight received over $1,000.

Litigation costs consumed much of whatever was recovered. It was estimated that, in 1907, "of every $100 paid out by [employers in New York] on account of work accidents but $56 reached the injured workmen and their dependents." And even this figure was unrepresentative because it included voluntary payments by employers. "A fairer test of employers' liability is afforded by the $192,538 paid by these same employers as a result of law suits or to avoid law suits, whereof only $80,888, or forty-two percent, reached the beneficiaries." A large fraction of the disbursed payments, about one-third, went to attorneys who accepted the cases on a contingent basis.

These figures on the inadequacy of recoveries are usually cited to show how little the workers received for their pains. But what did these figures mean to employers? Assuming that employers, as rational men, were anxious to pay as little compensation as was necessary to preserve industrial peace and maintain a healthy workforce, the better course might be to pay a higher *net* amount direct to employees. Employers had little or nothing to gain from their big payments to insurance companies, lawyers, and court officials. Perhaps at some unmeasurable point of time, the existing tort system crossed an invisible line and thereafter, purely in economic terms, represented on balance a net loss to the industrial establishment. From that point on, the success of a movement for change in the system was certain, provided that businessmen could be convinced that indeed their self-interest lay in the direction of reform and that a change in compensation systems did not drag with it other unknowable and harmful consequences.

As on many issues of reform, the legal profession did not speak with one voice. Certainly, many lawyers and judges were dissatisfied with the status quo. Judges complained about the burdens imposed on the court system by masses of personal injury suits; many felt frustrated by the chaotic state of the law, and others were bothered by their felt inability to do justice to injured workmen. . . .

When considerations of politics were added to those of business economics and industrial peace, it was not surprising to find that businessmen gradually withdrew their veto against workmen's compensation statutes. They began to say that a reformed system was inevitable—and even desirable. A guaranteed, insurable cost—one which could be computed in advance on the basis of accident experience—would, in the long run, cost business less than the existing system. In 1910, the president of the National Association of Manufacturers (NAM) appointed a committee to study the possibility of compensating injured workmen without time-consuming and expensive litigation, and the convention that year heard a speaker tell them that no one was satisfied with the present state of the law—that the employers' liability system was "antagonistic to harmonious relations between employers and wage workers." By 1911 the NAM appeared convinced that a compensation system was inevitable and that prudence dictated that business play a positive role in shaping the design of the law—otherwise the law would be "settled for us by the demagogue, and agitator and the socialist with a vengeance." Business would benefit economically and politically from a compensation system, but only if certain conditions were present. Business, therefore, had an interest in pressing for a specific kind of program, and turned its attention to the details of the new system. For example, it was imperative that the new system be in fact as actuarially predictable as business demanded; it was important that the costs of the program be fair and equal in their impact upon particular industries, so that no competitive advantage or disadvantage flowed from the scheme. Consequently the old tort actions had to be eliminated, along with the old defenses of the company. In exchange for certainty of recovery by the worker, the companies were prepared to demand certainty and predictability of loss—that is, limitation of recovery. The jury's caprice had to be dispensed with. In short, when workmen's compensation became law, as a solution to the industrial accident problem, it did so on terms acceptable to industry. Other pressures were there to be sure, but when workmen's compensation was enacted, businessmen had come to look on it as a positive benefit rather than as a threat to their sector of the economy.

E. *The Emergence of Workmen's Compensation Statutes*

The change of the businessmen's, the judge's, and the general public's attitudes toward industrial injuries was accelerated by the availability of fresh information on the extent of accidents and their cost to both management and workers. By 1900, industrial accidents and the shortcomings of the fellow-servant rule were widely perceived as *problems* that had to be solved. After 1900, state legislatures began to look for a "solution" by setting up commissions to gather statistics, to investigate possible new systems, and to recommend legislation. The commissions held public hearings and called upon employers, labor, insurance companies, and lawyers to express their opinions and propose changes. A number of commissions collected statistics on industrial accidents, costs of insurance, and amounts disbursed to injured workmen. By 1916, many states and the federal government had received more-or-less extensive public reports from these investigating bodies. The reports included studies of industrial accident cases in the major industries, traced the legal history of the cases, and looked into the plight of the injured workmen and their families.

From the information collected, the commissions were able to calculate the costs of workmen's compensation systems and compare them with costs under employers' liability. Most of the commissions concluded that a compensation system would be no more expensive than the existing method, and most of them recommended adoption, in one form or another, of workmen's compensation. In spite of wide variations in the systems proposed, there was agreement on one point: workmen's compensation must fix liability upon the employer regardless of fault.

Between 1910 and 1920 the method of compensating employees injured on the job was fundamentally altered in the United States. In brief, workmen's compensation statutes eliminated (or tried to eliminate) the process of fixing civil liability for industrial accidents through litigation in common law courts. Under the statutes, compensation was based on statutory schedules, and the responsibility for initial determination of employee claims was taken from the courts and given to an administrative agency. Finally, the statutes abolished the fellow-servant rule and the defenses of assumption of risk and contributory negligence. Wisconsin's law, passed in 1911, was the first general compensation act to survive a court test. Mississippi, the last state in the Union to adopt a compensation law, did so in 1948. . . .

In essence, then, workmen's compensation was designed to replace a highly unsatisfactory system with a rational, actuarial one. It should not be viewed as the replacement of a fault-oriented compensation system with one unconcerned with fault. It should not be viewed as a victory of employees over employers. In its initial stages, the fellow-servant rule was not concerned with fault, either, but with establishing a clear-cut, workable, and predictable rule, one which substantively placed much of the risk (if not all) on the worker. Industrial accidents were not seen as a social problem—at most as an economic problem. As value perceptions changed, the rule weakened; it developed exceptions and lost its efficiency. The exceptions and counter-exceptions can be looked at as a series of brief, ad hoc, and unstable compromises between the clashing interests of labor and management. When both sides became convinced that the game was mutually unprofitable, a compensation system became possible. But this system was itself a compromise: an attempt at a new, workable, and predictable mode of handling accident liability which neatly balanced the interests of labor and management.

III. The Law of Industrial Accidents and Social Theory:
Three Aspects of Social Change

This case study, devoted to the rise and fall of the fellow-servant rule, utilizes and supports a view of social change as a complex chain of group bargains—economic in the sense of a continuous exchange of perceived equivalents, though not economic in the sense of crude money bargains. It also provides a useful setting for evaluating three additional popular explanations of the origin or rate of social change. First, the apparently slow development of workmen's compensation is the classic example of what Ogburn called "cultural lag." Second, since German and English statutes were enacted prior to the American laws, the establishment of compensation schemes in America can be viewed as a case of cross-cultural influence. Third, the active role of particular participants (in Wisconsin, for example, Judge [Rouget D.] Marshall and John R. Commons) may substantiate the theory which advances the causal influence of "great men" in the process of social change. A thorough examination of these theories is not contemplated here. Students both of law and of sociology, however, may profit from a brief discussion of these theories in the context of the social change embodied in workmen's compensation statutes.

A. *The Concept of Cultural Lag*

The problem of "fair and efficient incidence of industrial accident costs," in the words of Willard Hurst, "followed a fumbling course in courts and legislature for fifty years before the first broad-scale direction [leading to workmen's compensation] was applied." In a famous book written in 1922, the sociologist William Fielding Ogburn used the example of workmen's compensation and the fifty-year period of fumbling to verify his "hypothesis of cultural lag." "Where one part of culture changes first," said Ogburn, "through some discovery or invention, and occasions changes in some part of culture dependent upon it, there frequently is a delay. . . . The extent of this lag will vary . . . but may exist for . . . years, during which time there may be said to be a maladjustment." In the case of workmen's compensation, the lag period was from the time when industrial accidents became numerous until the time when workmen's compensation laws were passed, "about a half-century, from 1850-70 to 1915." During this period, "the old adaptive culture, the common law of employers' liability, hung over after the material conditions had changed."

The concept of cultural lag is still widely used, in social science and out—particularly since its popularization by Stuart Chase in *The Proper Study of Mankind*. And the notion that law fails to adjust promptly to the call for change is commonly voiced. In popular parlance, this or that aspect of the law is often said to "lag behind the times." This idea is so pervasive that it deserves comment quite apart from its present status in sociological thought.

The lesson of industrial accident law, as here described, may be quite the opposite of the lesson that Ogburn drew. In a purely objective (nonteleological) sense, social processes—and the legal system—cannot aptly be described through use of the idea of lag. When, in the face of changed technology and new problems, a social arrangement stubbornly persists, there are *social* reasons why this is so; there are explanations why no change or slow change occurs. The legal system is a part of the total culture; it is not a self-operating machine. The rate of response to a call for change is slow or fast in the law depending upon who issues the call and who (if anybody) resists it. "Progress" or "catching up" is not inevitable or predictable. Legal change, like social change, is a change in behavior of individuals and groups in interaction. The rate of change depends upon the kind of interaction. To say that institutions lag is usually to say no more than that they are slow to make changes of a particular type. But why are they slow? Often the answer rests on the fact that these institutions are controlled by or respond to groups or individuals who are opposed to the specific change. This is lag only if we feel we can confidently state that these groups or individuals are wrong as to their own self-interest as well as that of society. Of course, people *are* often wrong about their own self-interest; they can be and are short-sighted, ignorant, maladroit. But ignorance of this kind exists among progressives as well as among conservatives—among those who want change as well as among those who oppose it. Resistance to change is "lag" only if there is only one "true" definition of a problem—and one "true" solution.

There were important reasons why fifty years elapsed before workmen's compensation became part of the law. Under the impact of industrial conditions Americans were changing their views about individual security and social welfare. Dean Pound has remarked that the twentieth century accepts the idea of insuring those unable to bear economic loss, at the expense of the nearest person at hand who can bear the loss. This conception was relatively unknown and unacceptable to judges of the nineteenth century. The fellow-servant rule could not be replaced until economic affluence, business conditions, and the state of safety technology made feasible a more social solution. Labor unions of the mid-nineteenth century did not call for a compensation plan; they were concerned with more basic (and practical) issues such as wages and hours. . . . Social insurance, as much as private insurance, requires standardization and rationalization of business, predictability of risk, and reliability and financial responsibility of economic institutions. These were present in 1909, but not in 1850.

Prior to workmen's compensation, the legal system reflected existing conflicts of value quite clearly; the manifold exceptions to the fellow-servant rule and the primitive liability statutes bear witness to this fact. These were no symptoms of "lag"; rather, they were a measure of the constant adjustments that inevitably take place within a legal system that is not insulated from the larger society but an integral part of it. To be sure, the courts frequently reflected values of the business community and so did the legislatures, but populist expressions can easily be found in the work of judges, legislatures, and juries. In the absence of a sophisticated measuring-rod of past public opinion—and sophisticated concepts of the role of public opinion in nineteenth century society—who is to say that the legal system "lagged" behind some hypothetical general will of the public or some hypothetically correct solution?

The concept of lag may also be employed in the criticism of the courts' use of judicial review to retard the efficacy of social welfare legislation. In 1911, the New York Court of Appeals declared the state's compulsory workmen's compensation act unconstitutional. As a result of this holding, the state constitution had to be amended—two years later—before workmen's compensation was legally possible in New York. Because of the New York experience, six states also amended their constitutions and others enacted voluntary plans. The issue was not finally settled until 1917, when the United States Supreme Court held both compulsory and elective plans to be constitutional. But it adds little to an understanding of social process to describe this delay in terms of the concept of cultural lag. Courts do not act on their own initiative. Each case of judicial review was instigated by a litigant who represented a group in society which was fighting for its interests as it perceived them; these were current, real interests, not interests of sentiment or inertia. This is completely apart from consideration of what social interests the courts thought they were serving in deciding these cases—interests which hindsight condemns as futile or wrong, but which were living issues and interests of the day.

Conflicts of value also arose in the legislatures when they began to consider compensation laws. The Massachusetts investigating commission of 1903 reported a workmen's compensation bill to the legislature, but the bill was killed in committee on the ground that Massachusetts could not afford to increase the production costs of commodities manufactured in the state. Once more, the emergence of compensation depended upon a perception of inevitability—which could cancel the business detriment to particular states which enacted compensation laws—and of general economic gain from the new system. It is not enough to sense that a social problem exists. Rational collective action demands relatively precise and detailed information about the problem, and clear placement of responsibility for proposing and implementing a solution. For many years legislatures simply did not consider it their responsibility to do anything about industrial injuries. Since they did not view accidents as a major social problem, and since state legislatures were weak political structures, they were content at first to leave accidents to tort law and the courts. Moreover, state agencies were not delegated the task of collecting information on the nature and extent of industrial accidents until relatively late. The Wisconsin legislature created a Bureau of Labor and Industrial Statistics in 1883, but did not provide for the collection of data on industrial accidents until 1905. When a need for accident legislation was perceived, individual legislators, under pressure of constituencies, began to introduce work accident indemnity bills. Some were inadequately drafted; most were poorly understood. In order to appraise potential legislation, investigating commissions were created to collect information, weigh the costs and report back alternative solutions.

What appears to some as an era of "lag" was actually a period in which issues were collectively defined and alternative solutions posed, and during which interest groups bargained for favorable formulations of law. It was a period of "false starts"—unstable compromise formulations by decision makers armed with few facts, lacking organizational machinery, and facing great, often contradictory, demands from many publics. There was no easy and suitable solution, in the light of the problem and the alignment of powers. Indeed, workmen's compensation—which today appears to be a stable solution—was only a compromise, an answer acceptable to enough people and interest groups to endure over a reasonably long period of time.

Part of what is later called "lag," then, is this period of false starts—the inadequate compromises by decision makers faced with contradictory interest groups pressing inconsistent solutions.

There may not *be* a "solution" in light of the alignment of interests and powers with respect to the problem at any given point in time. Perhaps only a compromise "solution" is possible. What later appears to be the final answer is in fact itself a compromise—one which is stable over some significant period of time. Sociologically, that is what a "solution" to a problem is: nothing more than a stable compromise acceptable to enough people and interest groups to maintain itself over a significant period of time. Theoretically, of course, total victory by one competing interest and total defeat of another is possible. But in a functioning democratic society, total victories and defeats are uncommon. Total defeat would mean that a losing group was so utterly powerless that it could exert no bargaining pressure whatsoever; total victory similarly would imply unlimited power. In the struggle over industrial accident legislation, none of the interests could be so described. Different perceptions of the problem, based at least in part on different economic and social stakes, led to different views of existing and potential law. When these views collided, compromises were hammered out. Workmen's compensation took form not because it was (or is) perfect, but because it represented a solution acceptable enough to enough interests to outweigh the costs of additional struggle and bargaining. If there was "lag" in the process, it consisted of acquiescence in presently acceptable solutions which turned out not to be adequate or stable in the long run. "Lag" therefore at most means present-minded pragmatism rather than long-term rational planning.

B. *Cross-Cultural Borrowing*

The adoption of workmen's compensation in America does represent an instance of what can be called conscious cross-cultural borrowing. Workmen's compensation was not an American innovation; there were numerous European antecedents. Switzerland passed a workmen's compensation act in 1881; Germany followed in 1884 with a more inclusive scheme. By 1900 compensation laws had spread to most European countries. In 1891 the United States Bureau of Labor commissioned John Graham Brooks to study and appraise the German system. His report, published in 1893, was widely distributed and successfully exposed some American opinion-leaders to the existence of the European programs. Most of the state investigating commissions also inquired into the European experience, and a number of early bills were modeled after the German and British systems.

Though workmen's compensation can therefore be viewed as an example of cross-cultural borrowing, care must be exercised in employing the concept. Successful legal solutions to social problems are often borrowed across state and national lines but this borrowing must not be confused with the actual "influence" of one legal system over another. "Influence" carries with it an implication of power or, at the least, of cultural dominance. The forces that led to a demand for workmen's compensation were entirely domestic, as this study has argued. The fact that European solutions to similar problems were studied and, to an extent, adopted here shows not dominance but an attempt to economize time, skill, and effort by borrowing an appropriate model. It would be quite wrong to detect European legal "influence" in this process. The existence of the European compensation plans was not a cause of similar American statutes. Rather, the interest shown in the foreign experiences was a response to American dissatisfaction with existing industrial accident law. Similarly, the current drive for an American *ombudsman* is not an example of the "influence" of Scandinavian law. A foreign model here sharpens discussion and provides a ready-made plan. Yet the felt need for such an officer has domestic origins.

C. *Great Men and Social Change*

Sociologists are fond of pointing out the inaccuracy of the "great-man theory of history," which holds that particular persons play irreplaceably decisive roles in determining the path of social change. The influence of single individuals, they say, is hardly as critical as historians would have us believe. The role of outstanding persons in bringing about workmen's compensation acts seems on one level quite clear. . . . Reformers and academicians served as important middlemen in mediating between interest groups and working out compromises. Their arguments legitimated the act; their zeal enlisted support of middle-class neutrals. They were willing to do the spadework of research, drafting, and propagandizing necessary for a viable law. In the passage of many other welfare and reform laws, outstanding personalities can be found who played dominant roles in creating and leading public opinion—for example, Lawrence Veiller for the New York tenement housing law of 1901, Harvey Wiley for the Federal Food and Drug Act.

The great-man hypothesis is not susceptible of proof or disproof. But the course of events underlying workmen's compensation at least suggests that social scientists are properly suspicious of placing too much reliance on a great-man view. If the view here expressed is correct, then economic, social, political and legal forces made workmen's compensation (or some alternative, such as FELA) virtually inevitable by the end of the nineteenth century. Outstanding men may be necessary in general for the implementation of social change; someone must take the lead in creating the intellectual basis for a change in perception. Nonetheless, when a certain pattern of demand exists in society, more than one person may be capable of filling that role. Particular individuals are normally not indispensable. The need is for talent—men with extraordinary ability, perseverance, and personal influence, men who can surmount barriers and accomplish significant results. Obviously, the absence of outstanding persons interested in a particular cause can delay problem solving or lead to inept, shoddy administration. The appearance of truly exceptional persons at the proper moment in history is undoubtedly not automatic. But talent, if not genius, may well be a constant in society; and the social order determines whether and in what direction existing talent will be exerted.

Thus, it would be foolish to deny that specific individuals exert great influence upon the development of social events, and equally foolish to conclude that other persons could not have done the job as well (or better) if given the opportunity. "Great men," however, must be in the right place, which means that society must have properly provided for the training and initiative of outstanding persons and for their recruitment into critical offices when needed. In difficult times, great businessmen, political leaders, musicians, or physicists will emerge. "Great men" appear "when the time is ripe"—but only insofar as society has created the conditions for a pool of creative manpower dedicated to the particular line of endeavor in which their greatness lies.

NOTES AND QUESTIONS

1. The history of the fellow-servant rule, and the development of workmen's compensation, has been used as the basis for a provocative introductory book of readings on the legal process and on the historical development of law. Carl A. Auerbach, Lloyd K. Garrison, Willard Hurst & Samuel Mermin, *The Legal Process: An Introduction to Decision-Making by Judicial, Legislative, Executive and Administrative Agencies* (Chandler Publishing Co. 1961). *See also* Philippe Nonet, *Administrative Justice* (Russell Sage Foundation 1969), which traces the history of the California Industrial Accident Commission.

2. In "The Economic Interpretation and the Law of Torts," 53 *Harvard Law Review* 365 (1940),* Roscoe Pound wrote:

> What stands out in the history of Anglo-American law is the resistance of the taught tradition in the hands of judges drawn from any class you like, . . . against all manner of economically or politically powerful interests.

He goes on to discuss *Priestley v. Fowler* and the rise of the fellow-servant rule. He argues that the rule was not the product of "a tribunal consciously expressing in legal doctrine the self interest of a dominant social or economic class." Rather, it was the result of the "conception of liability" entertained by courts and lawyers generally in the early 19th century; no court, however composed, would have decided otherwise.

> An exclusively economic interpretation of single decisions and single items of judicial action leaves out of account the tenacity of the taught tradition. It takes no account of the instinctive tendency of the lawyer to refer every case back to some general principle. It ignores the prevailing mode of thought of the time which often reflects an economic situation of the past when the taught ideal was formulated.

Do Friedman and Ladinsky ignore the "taught tradition"? Do they leave out of their reckoning the training, habits and inherited modes of thought of the legal profession? How would they respond to Pound's critique?

3. In their discussion of "lag" at 543, Friedman and Ladinsky state that:

> Theoretically . . . total victory by one competing interest and total defeat of another is possible. But in a functioning democratic society, total victories and defeats are uncommon. Total defeat would mean that a losing group was so utterly powerless that it could exert no bargaining pressure whatsoever; total victory similarly would imply unlimited power.

Doesn't this contradict Aubert's notion that some conflicts (of values) cannot be compromised? *See* Reading 18, at 175, *supra.* Do the authors imply that *all* conflicts can, in fact, be compromised—and are? What compromise was possible between those who, in 1968, opposed the war in Vietnam and the Johnson

---

* Copyright © 1940 by the Harvard Law Review Association. Reprinted by permission.

administration? between the members of the medical profession who opposed medicare and those who demanded it? between the "wets" and the "drys" during Prohibition? Was the repeal of Prohibition a "total victory" for one side and a "total defeat" for the other?

4. Is the key phrase in the passage just quoted "functioning democratic society"? Does that exclude the possibility that "lag" might be found in a totalitarian state?

5. It is notorious that in Congress a great deal of power is exercised by certain committee chairmen. Many of these chairmen are from southern states; their seats are "safe" and they accumulate seniority that is impossible to northern liberals in "swing" districts. Hence there are built-in conservative bottlenecks in the legislative process. Could not the delays to liberal legislation occasioned by these committee chairmen be fairly described as instances of "lag" between dominant public opinion and the responsiveness of law? Recall Buchanan & Tullock, "The Calculus of Consent," Reading 6, at 56, *supra*.

[Reading 56]

6. On the subject of "lag," consider also the following excerpt from Albert V. Dicey, *Lectures on the Relation Between Law and Public Opinion in England During the Nineteenth Century* (Macmillan 1914).*

Legislative opinion must be the opinion of the day, because, when laws are altered, the alteration is of necessity carried into effect by legislators who act under the belief that the change is an amendment; but this law-making opinion is also the opinion of yesterday, because the beliefs which have at last gained such hold on the legislature as to produce an alteration in the law have generally been created by thinkers or writers, who exerted their influence long before the change in the law took place. Thus it may well happen that an innovation is carried through at a time when the teachers who supplied the arguments in its favour are in their graves, or even—and this is well worth noting—when in the world of speculation a movement has already set in against ideas which are exerting their full effect in the world of action and of legislation. Bentham's Defence of Usury supplied every argument which is available against laws which

* Reprinted from pp. 33-35, by permission of Macmillan & Co., Ltd. (English rights) and the executor of the Dicey Will Trust (U.S.A. rights).

check freedom of trade in money-lending. It was published in 1787; he died in 1832. The usury laws were wholly
repealed in 1854, that is sixty-seven years after Bentham had
demonstrated their futility; but in 1854 the opponents of
Benthamism were slowly gaining the ear of the public, and
the Money-lenders' Act, 1900, has shown that the almost
irrebuttable presumption against the usury laws which was
created by the reasoning of Bentham has lost its hold over
men who have never taken the pains or shown the ability
to confute Bentham's arguments. Nor is there anything mysterious about the way in which the thought or sentiment
of yesterday governs the legislation or the politics of to-day.
Law-making in England is the work of men well advanced
in life; the politicians who guide the House of Commons,
to say nothing of the peers who lead the House of Lords,
are few of them below thirty, and most of them are above
forty years of age. They have formed or picked up their
convictions, and, what is of more consequence, their prepos-
sessions, in early manhood, which is the one period of life
when men are easily impressed with new ideas. Hence English legislators retain the prejudices or modes of thinking
which they acquired in their youth; and when, late in life,
they take a share in actual legislation, they legislate in accordance with the doctrines which were current, either generally or in the society to which the law-givers belonged, in
the days of their early manhood. The law-makers, therefore,
of 1850 may give effect to the opinions of 1830, whilst the
legislators of 1880 are likely enough to impress upon the
statute-book the beliefs of 1860, or rather the ideas which
in the one case attracted the young men of 1830, and in the
other the youth of 1860. We need not therefore be surprised
to find that a current of opinion may exert its greatest legislative influence just when its force is beginning to decline.
The tide turns when at its height; a school of thought or
feeling which still governs law-makers has begun to lose its
authority among men of a younger generation who are not
yet able to influence legislation.

1. *The Opinions of Different Kinds of Publics and Their Different Impacts*

a. *The view of the public at large*

57. Parental Authority: The Community and the Law

JULIUS COHEN, REGINALD A. ROBSON AND ALAN P. BATES*

[This important study, a rare example of close collaboration between legal scholars and social scientists, attempted to measure "the moral sense of the community," and compare this "moral sense" with "legal norms." The study was conducted in Nebraska. A trained staff of interviewers administered questions to a carefully selected sample of residents of the state. The total sample population was 860.

The questions concerned various aspects of social and legal norms relating to the authority of parents over children. A sample section of the study follows. First the question is given, as administered to the subjects, then the position of the law is stated, then the "view of the community," then a comparison of the two.]

The Issue: Parental authority to disinherit the child completely. Question 23 deals with this.

QUESTION 23A: "Suppose that either the husband or wife is dead, and the survivor willed all of his or her property to persons or groups outside the family, and left nothing at all for the children. If the parent is legally allowed to do this, it could mean

* Julius Cohen, Professor of Law, Rutgers University; Reginald A. Robson, Professor of Sociology, University of British Columbia; Alan P. Bates, Professor of Sociology, University of Nebraska. Copyright © 1958 Rutgers University Press. Reprinted from pp. 76-78, 193-95, by permission.

that the child might have to depend on some outside source for the necessities of life. On the other hand, if the parent is prevented by law from doing this, he would not be able to will his property as he sees fit. In these circumstances, do you think that the parent should legally be allowed to will all of his or her property to persons or groups outside the family and leave nothing at all for the children, or should the law prevent this?"

Position of the law: It would seem that the parent would be permitted to disinherit his offspring, except for an amount that would be required to support parentless children under 14. Beyond this exception, the privilege of testamentary disposition would not be affected by the age or economic status of the children, or by the intrinsic worth of the object of the disposition; nor would the privilege be affected if exercise of it resulted in benefit to one child and not to another.

Views of the community: In responding to the situation presented in Question 23A the members of the sample were asked to indicate whether their opinion would be affected by the fact that the child was under or over 21 years of age (23Bi and 23Bii). Following this, in Questions 23Ci and 23Cii, the factor of the economic status of the child was introduced into the picture. Next, in Questions 23Di and 23Dii, respondents were asked to take into consideration with respect to the basic issue the question of the worthiness of the recipients of the parental estate. In the final sub-question (23E), people were asked to suppose that the parent left all his assets to only one of several children, all of whom were in about the same financial circumstances. The way in which community opinion is distributed and its degree of stability in these changing contexts are recorded in Table 12.

A quick comparison of "Allow" and "Prevent" responses for all parts of this question shows that in all cases a clear majority (and in several instances a very large majority) is of the opinion that the law should not allow a parent to disinherit a child completely. We find an extremely high congruence of views where the child is under 21 years of age, where the child is poor and where the parent leaves his assets to some beneficiary unworthy to receive them.

If the child is over 21 years of age, more than a third of the population would agree that parents should be legally entitled to omit the child from the will. Likewise, where the child is well-off financially in his own right, 40.8% would support a parent's right to make no provision for the child. A much less notable, but still considerable effect is produced by the assump-

TABLE 12

SHOULD THE LAW ALLOW PARENTS TO DISINHERIT CHILDREN?
(EXPRESSED IN PERCENTAGES OF TOTAL POPULATION)

Question	Allow	Prevent	Don't Know
23A (See above.)			
23Bi and Bii			
Child is under 21 years of age.	5.5	93.4	1.2
Child is over 21 years of age.	35.5	63.4	1.2
23Ci and Cii			
Child is poor.	7.0	92.0	1.0
Child is well-off financially.	40.8	57.3	1.9
23Di and Dii			
Parents leave assets to unworthy group.	5.1	93.8	1.0
Parents leave assets to worthy group.	18.6	79.2	2.2
23E Discrimination between children exists.	19.4	78.5	2.1

tion that the parent wishes to leave all his assets to a worthy cause; 18.6% would agree that the law should support the parent with such a purpose in mind. By and large, however, there appears to be an impressively high degree of agreement in the population that parents do have an obligation to their children which extends beyond their own death.

So far as the relation between community opinion and law on this issue is concerned, it is plain that most persons in the population disagree with the law, except in the case where a parentless child under 14 would be left without support. As indicated earlier, the law in this instance would require the parent's estate to provide support for the child.

[At the end of the study, the authors summed up their findings. They found wide disharmony between social and legal norms in Nebraska. "Of the 17 issues examined, the community and the existing law would disagree as to ten, agree as to five, and perhaps evenly divide as to one. . . . The majority in the community would favor greater legal restrictions on parental authority over the child than the law presently requires." (pp. 193-94)

These findings, somewhat to the authors' surprise, reflected general community feelings and did not vary as between "social groupings." "By and large, there are no *substantial* differences between the views of the members of various social groupings within the community toward the issues we studied, based on such factors as sex, residential area, religion, age, income, parenthood, schooling and occupation." (p. 195)

Why the great variance between community and legal norms? The authors saw three major factors: the "built-in professional conservatism" of lawyers and judges, that is, Roscoe Pound's "taught tradition" (*see* p. 546, *supra*); the lack of "pressure" from the public for change; and the "inadequacy of prevailing techniques utilized by law-makers for ascertaining the moral sense of the community." (p. 195)]

58. Review of Cohen, Robson & Bates

LUKE COOPERRIDER*

57 MICHIGAN LAW REVIEW 1119 (1959)

A law professor and two sociologists report herein on a joint attempt to assess the degree of congruence between existing legal doctrine, in a defined area of application, and a factor which the authors call "the moral sense of the community." The justification for the study is provided by the law member of the team, and proceeds from the observation that legal scholars, groping for standards of criticism external to the law, seem to gravitate toward a "sense of justice," or of "injustice"—toward a view of morality, at least, which is shared, to some degree, by the people in the community wherein the law is applicable. The authors vigorously and repeatedly disclaim a position on whether or to what extent such a common moral sense should by the law be taken into account. They assert, however, that law-makers, both legislative and judicial, do in fact frequently refer to it, and the argument is that *if* the moral sense of the community is relevant at all, then it makes sense to consider how that datum may be ascertained more scientifically than by the divination or intuition of the individual judge or legislator. Their study is offered as an example of how this may be done by making use of the developed techniques of public opinion research. They do not suggest, of course, the canvassing of the community's moral sense in order to establish premises for the adjudication of individual cases. It is argued, rather, that within a given area of law it would be possible to establish community reactions to a selected battery of propositions, and that these reactions could then be used as analogical bases for prediction of community reaction to other situations in a way which, to lawyers, would be quite familiar. Their project is an experimental survey of this type in the general area of parent-child relations. . . .

It is, perhaps, unresponsive to argue the merits of the questions which were propounded to the public, for, as I have said,

* Professor of Law, University of Michigan. Copyright © 1959 Michigan Law Review. Reprinted by permission.

the authors carefully disclaim any position on the extent to which
the law should seek to effectuate the community moral sense
which they were investigating. They set out to establish a
method, not a matrix for the remaking of the law in the area
of family relations. They were, nevertheless, unable completely
to conceal their feeling that their study could be used by "law-
makers whose juristic philosophy stakes out as an objective a
high degree of harmony between the existing law and the moral
sense of the community" as a ready-made set of specifications for
law revision in the area of family law. Furthermore, as it seems
to me, their failure to consider the basic question—what bearing
should community moral attitudes have with reference to the
specific problems propounded—has led them into a fallacy which
is fundamental, and which would be very difficult to avoid in
any similar project. . . .

On . . . six issues where disagreement between law and morals
was found, the law, at the present time, occupies a position of
laissez faire. The questions relate to parental "authority" (1) to
determine whether a child may have a college education, (2) to
determine the child's religious affiliation, (3) to prevent the child
from entering a career of his own choosing, (4) to transfer
custody of a child to another person without legal supervision,
(5) to disinherit the child, and (6) to treat the child's earnings
as the parent's own property. In all six cases it is assumed that
the law bestows upon the parent the "authority" indicated,
and in all six cases the community view, according to the
survey, was that the law should "prevent" the parents from
exercising such authority. It is on these six issues that an unequivocal discrepancy is found between the law and the moral
standards of the community, and it must be principally in connection with these issues that we judge the authors' assertions
that there is a serious lag between law and public opinion, a
lag which they suggest is to be attributed to imperfections in the
political process, and to the "dissenting acquiescence" of a population too inert to resist.

Considering these six issues, it will be noted that the parental
"authority" referred to in the first three instances is nothing more
than the de facto compulsion which the parent, by the very existence of the family relation, is enabled to exert. The extent of its
legal recognition is that the state has not established procedures
for supervising it, and the probability is that if an issue between
parent and child were in some manner raised in court, the court
would refuse to interfere unless the acts by which the compulsion
was exerted were criminal, or so abusive as to place in legal
jeopardy the parent's custody of the child. In assessing the rea-

sons mentioned by the respondents for their indicated views, the authors thought that there was a noteworthy absence of feeling that the law should not intrude itself into the parent-child relationship. The percentage of those who took the "allow" position and who adverted to this point was relatively small, throughout. The authors' interpretation of this fact is exemplified by the following comment: "Although where the choice of a child's religious affiliation is concerned, there is greater expressed sentiment in the community against the role of government than when the issue relates to the availability of a college education, the predominant sentiment, nevertheless, would still recognize the need to respect the child's independent choice of religious affiliation, and, if required, to employ legal sanctions against the parent to effectuate it." (p. 171) A bit farther on the authors indicate that "Those who favored some legal control of parental authority . . . were not asked just what specific type of legal controls should be imposed: *this would have been far too involved and complicated for our undertaking.* It is fairly safe to assume that they favored *some* government-sanctioned means— the exercise of authority outside the realm of parental control for the achievement of the given ends." (p. 186. Emphasis added, in part.)

I agree that it would probably have been both impracticable and useless to have raised the "how" question with the average member of the public. But is it not of the essence? I submit that these answers cannot be taken to be, in any practical sense, a true representation of community desires, for it is apparent that the respondents had not the slightest awareness of the practical implications of their answers. Some of the questions incorporated a caveat, "if the law prevented the parents from keeping the child out of college, it would reduce parental control and increase the amount of outside authority over the family to that extent." But how much meaning does this carry to one who is not familiar with the workings of the political-legal machinery of the state? If the questions had been formulated not in the denatured "should the law allow or prevent?" form, but in the terms in which they would be faced by the legislator or the judge—"Should a statute be enacted establishing a Family Liberties Commission with power to conduct investigations into invasions by parents of certain enumerated liberties of their children, to issue subpoenas and compel testimony, and to issue cease and desist orders against parents found to have committed such invasions, and to maintain actions in court to compel obedience to such orders, etc."—or— "Should a child who feels himself aggrieved by the act of his parent refusing to him his right of free religious association be permitted to maintain in the courts an action for injunctive relief, etc."—is it likely that the citizenry would have exhibited the same enthusiasm for the Big Brother approach that this survey seems to have revealed?

The other three of the six instances of disagreement between law and morals are somewhat different, involving situations (transfer of custody, disinheritance, parental ownership of child's earnings) which can, by a lawyer, be more easily conceived of as subjects of legal regulation. As the descent of property is already regulated by law, there would be no great derangement if the applicable law excluded complete disinheritance of a child. It might be doubted that the respondents have envisioned *all* the implications, but at least the probabilities are greater here that an implementation of their views would not produce practical consequences which would shock the majority of people affected. Administrative difficulties are certainly very substantial with reference to the custody and ownership of earnings issues, however. It is easy to pass a law—"Any person who, without prior approval of the probate court, gives his child into the custody of another person (permanently? for a period in excess of ——— days? with the intent to abandon custody himself?) shall be guilty of a misdemeanor." Enforcement would be another matter, family connections being as casual as, regrettably, they sometimes are. And with reference to the child's earnings, how should the law attend to their protection? It would be possible, I suppose, to require all parents to account as fiduciaries, periodically or upon the attainment by their children of majority, but I would imagine that compliance would be secured only to the accompaniment of a considerable amount of kicking and screaming.

The subject is fascinating, and the literary qualities of the book are high. It will reward any reader, whether he is jurisprudentially oriented or simply an interested observer of the society in which he lives. As a novel experiment the study adds to the sum total of our experience whether the individual reader's conclusions with respect to the relevance and validity of the experimenters' methods are positive or negative. To me it furnishes strong evidence of the necessity for continuing close attention to the factors which make it practicable and desirable to seek some social objectives through legal standards and sanctions, while making it equally apparent that other objectives must be left to other forms of social control. I have no doubt that the moral views indicated by the survey are effective in assuring that few parents actually exercise the full extent of the "authority" over their children which the law would probably tolerate. I am equally certain that to attempt to bring the *law* into alignment with these views would be rank folly. Law does not consist solely of norms of conduct. The official sanction through which the norm is enforced is an inescapable concomitant. A personal conviction as to what, in the abstract, *ought* to be, may serve very well as a moral standard, operating through the conscience and will of the individual, but it cannot be assumed that the same conviction would survive a marriage to official compulsion.

Many of the norms which were approved by the respondents in the Nebraska survey are such that they could be brought to bear upon the community only through legal sanctions which, according to *this* reader's intuition, would be found, by the same persons who approved the norms, to be quite intolerable, and by the agents of the law to be incapable of administration. I would submit, therefore, that an inquiry into popular views of "what the law should be" can be most misleading if it does not raise, with the persons interviewed, the legislative question in all its complexity. If that question were raised, I would doubt the ability of the great majority of all citizens to respond to it in an informed and intelligent way. Query, then, whether the law-maker can expect as much help from the opinion surveyer as these authors suggest.

NOTES AND QUESTIONS

1. Did Cohen, Robson and Bates really measure the moral sense of the "community" or that of individuals in isolation? Is there a difference? Should they have separately tried to ascertain what "leaders" felt about these questions? Was it wrong to give equal weight to the opinions of educated, articulate people, and those who had never even considered the problem? *See* Herbert Marcuse, "Repressive Tolerance," in *A Critique of Pure Tolerance* 81-117 (Beacon Press 1965).

2. To what extent, if at all, should a legislator, administrator or judge consult the moral sense of the community? Consider the following:

Many things that are immoral are, nevertheless, not proper subjects for criminal punishment. And some things that unthinking public opinion has put in criminal codes ought now to be taken out. . . .

Quantification of public opinion will be useful, for example, to persuade legislators that the voters are not as benighted as some suppose. . . . But, as respects law reform, precise knowledge of prevailing public attitudes can hardly do more than indicate the limit of mass tolerance for immediate changes.

Louis B. Schwartz, "Ascertaining the Moral Sense of the Community: A Comment," 8 *Journal of Legal Education* 319, 320 (1955).* Is Schwartz's general viewpoint the same as Cooperrider's? What are the similarities and differences?

3. Cohen, Robson and Bates found that the community wanted more controls than the law afforded them. Perhaps a sophisticated survey would show that the general public is considerably less willing to allow holders of unpopular views to express themselves than are leaders and elites, and these in turn are less willing than are the courts interpreting the first amendment to the Constitution. *See, e.g.,* Samuel A. Stouffer, *Communism, Conformity and Civil Liberties* (Doubleday 1955). This would almost certainly be true on the question of tolerance for "obscene" and "pornographic" literature; and compare Birkby, Reading 51, at 476, *supra,* and the attitudes in Tennessee toward Bible reading in the schools. *Should* law reflect current community sentiments absolutely? Where should the line be drawn?

4. If the moral sense of the community should be consulted, how should it be done?

(a) What are the advantages and disadvantages of using modern survey research methods?

(b) Can one defend from a sociological point of view the use of the lawmaker's hunch or intuition about the moral sense of the community? Is the lawmaker entitled to consider himself as an adequate sample of the community's moral sense? What influences his behavior and hunches and what influences his perception of his role?

5. Contrast the argument of Friedman and Ladinsky about the validity of the concept of lag, and the findings of Cohen, Robson and Bates that law is seriously at variance with community views. Are the two notions contradictory? Recall Buchanan & Tullock, "The Calculus of Consent," Reading 6, at 56, *supra.*

6. Fowler V. Harper, reviewing Cohen, Robson & Bates in 59 *Columbia Law Review* 684, 687 (1959),** remarked:

The findings made by these scholars throw considerable doubt on the widely held sociological and juristic theory that law is the resultant of the clash of interests of different pres-

---

* Louis B. Schwartz, Professor of Law, University of Pennsylvania. Copyright © 1955. Reprinted with the permission of the Journal of Legal Education.
** Copyright © 1959 Columbia Law Review. Reprinted by permission.

sure groups in the community. The theory may be sound in some areas, but there is no substantial evidence in this study that it is relevant to the field of law under investigation.

Is the point well taken?

[Reading 59]

7. Did the authors study the right phenomenon? Should they have looked at behavior, rather than attitude? Alan Milner,* in a review of the study in 21 *University of Pittsburgh Law Review* 147 (1959), had this to say:

At the outset, the authors fail to put forward any good reason for carrying out the survey at all. It is almost as if, endowed with a grant of $11,500, they decided on an area of common interest, carried out the study and then looked around to justify its usefulness. Hence, "if the moral sense of the community is relevant to the law-making process, either as a norm for the law-maker to consider, or as a norm to follow . . . [then] modern social science techniques could be more reliably utilized for the task." But the authors expressly refuse to consider the decision-making process in any detail or to explain in what way they think the moral sense is relevant to lawmaking. It is a here-it-is-if-you-want-it attitude, with very little practical function unless many more assumptions are made or much more research is carried out. We want to know, for instance, what will happen if the law and the moral sense do not coincide and whether the moral sense should guide the law or *vice versa*? These are problems professedly outside the scope of the work but, surely, to offer any comprehensive guide to decision, the scope should have been enlarged, rather than the reader thrown back on his own imagination.

The authors are aware of these and other deficiencies. It is their constant position that the search for goals can be carried on without these extra trappings. Let us take a specific example. They (and I) know of no reliable study of *actual* parent-child *practices*. But whereas they simply lament this and proceed regardless, I would suggest that to *make* such a study should have been their first concern. A knowledge of what families do as well as what they say, is vital to an accurate study of the field. Of course, in some respects, their practices are strictly controlled. A child cannot marry below

---

* Alan Milner, Fellow of Trinity College, Oxford. Copyright © 1959 University of Pittsburgh Law Review. Reprinted by permission.

a certain age, whatever the parent may think of the rightness
or wrongness of the law. On the other hand, a parent's practice may well differ from the instruction of the law in a
matter of supervision of the child's earnings. The relevance
of "beliefs" is perhaps secondary to that of practices. . . .
The uninformed public opinion collected here showed only
too high a degree of ambiguity and circularity of reasoning.

8. Is the *legal* model of Cohen, Robson and Bates accurate?
That is, have they really measured the law with the same care
that they lavished on "public opinion"? Milner, in the book
review just cited makes this remark:

> In a study which sets out to contrast the "moral sense"
> with the "law," the latter gets an unjustifiably static treat-
> ment. "Law" to Messrs. Cohen, Robson and Bates consists
> of norms "in the more traditional sense . . . law ready to
> be applied if and when the occasion calls." This apparently
> means an application of statutes and judicial precedent with-
> out insight or imagination—a condition of immobility which
> hardly matches up to the decisions of which we know the
> courts are capable. Into all the questions of their study, for
> instance, the authors introduced "significant factual varia-
> tions" to gauge the moral sense more accurately. They nat-
> urally found the answers to their questions varying just as
> significantly. But nowhere is there the slightest suggestion
> that if a judge were faced with a similar variation, he might
> find a legal way to label it significant and so come up with
> a decision to suit his own moral sense.

9. Is the study, even on the authors' own terms, valid only for
Nebraska? valid only for the period studied? If one wished to
take community sentiments into account in another state, would
one need a fresh survey, and in what detail? How long does the
moral sense of the community last? If one decided to change the
law to conform with community sentiment (assuming that were
possible), at what point would one have to seek a fresh reading
of the public pulse? Is there a difference between immediate
public reaction to an event and a stable view held widely over a
period of time; would such a difference affect your answers to
these questions?

10. Consider the following quotation from Albert V. Dicey,
*Lectures on the Relation Between Law and Public Opinion in
England During the Nineteenth Century* (Macmillan 1914):*

---

* Reprinted from pp. 19-20, by permission of Macmillan & Co., Ltd.
(English rights) and the executor of the Dicey Will Trust (U.S.A. rights).

There exists at any given time a body of beliefs, convictions, sentiments, accepted principles, or firmly-rooted prejudices, which, taken together, make up the public opinion
of a particular era, or what we may call the reigning or
predominant current of opinion. . . .

[The] whole body of beliefs existing in any given age may
generally be traced to certain fundamental assumptions
which at the time, whether they be actually true or false,
are believed by the mass of the world to be true with such
confidence that they hardly appear to bear the character of
assumptions. . . .

In Dicey's view, did Cohen, Robson and Bates study "public
opinion" at all? What did they study? How would one ascertain
the state of "public opinion" as Dicey uses the phrase?

11. Allen Barton and Saul Mendlovitz, in "The Experience
of Injustice as a Research Problem," 13 *Journal of Legal Education* 24 (1960), propose a strategy for the use of survey methods
to aid the legal system different than that used by Cohen, Robson
and Bates. They want to take a sample of the population and
ask in what situations members of the sample have been aware of
or concerned about injustice. Then one could determine the
relationship of the legal system to this injustice—as cause or
remedy. If it turned out that the legal system itself caused injustice, one would have uncovered a serious problem which probably went undetected because it was not newsworthy. If the
injustice came from other sources and if the legal system offered
little or no remedy, this too would be a social—and legal—
problem. Suppose the sample consisted of parents or people who
had dealt with some government agency concerning their children. One might uncover a different set of problems posed by
the law of parent and child than those uncovered by Cohen,
Robson and Bates. Does this approach seem more promising
than that of Cohen, Robson and Bates? Do you see any difficulties with it? *Compare* Friedman & Macaulay, "Contract Law
and Contract Teaching: Past, Present, and Future," 1967 *Wisconsin Law Review* 805, 819-21.

[Reading 60]

NOTE: Upton Sinclair, *The Jungle*, and the Background of the First Food and Drug Act, 1906

At about the turn of the century, there was considerable agitation in the country for some form of government regulation of

the quality of food products. In particular, scandal had arisen over the quality of meat products. During the Spanish-American war, it was alleged, American soldiers were forced to eat cans of "embalmed beef." (Theodore Roosevelt testified before the Senate that he would just as soon eat his old hat as the canned food shipped to the men in Cuba.)* Some state laws were passed on quality control of food. Within the government, Dr. Harvey W. Wiley worked tirelessly to expose adulteration of food products and to achieve the enactment of legislation that would ensure the sale of safe, wholesome foods and drugs.** Wiley revealed many horrible practices of manufacturers—practices which cheated the public, and, in some cases, poisoned them. Still, a federal food and drug law had not been passed when, in 1906, Upton Sinclair published *The Jungle,* a novel about life in Chicago, centering around the stockyards.

Sinclair considered himself an ardent Socialist. He believed that capitalism was the source of the evil that he saw about him, and he became convinced, as he wrote in his autobiography, that "the heart and center of the evil lay in leaving the social treasure, which nature had created, and which every man has to have in order to live, to become the object of a scramble in the marketplace, a delirium of speculation."*** The turn of the century was a period in which socialism had considerable appeal to some American intellectuals; it was also a period in which "muckrakers" were educating the reading public about corruption, vice and degradation in American society, and about the destruction of American myths and ideals. Or so it looked to Sinclair.

Sinclair's early novels came to the attention of a radical magazine, *The Appeal to Reason.* The editor, Fred Warren, offered Sinclair $500 for serial rights to a new novel. Sinclair selected the Chicago stockyards as the scene for his book. In 1904, Sinclair went to Chicago, and for seven weeks he "lived among the wage slaves of the Beef Trust."**** Then he went home and, in furious speed, wrote a novel based on his experiences.

The Jungle tells the story of a Lithuanian immigrant named Jurgis Rudkus, who comes to the United States full of naïve

---

* Robert B. Downs, *Afterword* to THE JUNGLE (New American Library ed. 1960) at 343. Hereinafter cited as DOWNS. [Eds. note]

** Wiley's career is described in O. ANDERSON, THE HEALTH OF A NATION: HARVEY W. WILEY AND THE FIGHT FOR PURE FOOD (1968) (U. of Chicago Press). Hereinafter cited as ANDERSON. [Eds. note]

*** U. SINCLAIR, AMERICAN OUTPOST, A BOOK OF REMINISCENCES 143 (1932) (Farrar, Straus & Giroux, Inc.). Hereinafter cited as AMERICAN OUTPOST. [Eds. note]

**** *Id.* at 154. [Eds. note]

faith in America, and settles in "Packingtown," the stockyard area of Chicago. He and his family and friends find nothing tangible in the American dream. Every possible horror and tragedy is inflicted on Jurgis and his circle. He is exploited at work, in his rented home, on the streets. His wife dies in childbirth. His son drowns. Women dear to him are driven to prostitution. He is injured on the job, laid off, and eventually blacklisted. He becomes a wanderer, but ends up a convert to socialism, convinced that only through this means can the world be saved.

In the first half of the book, there are passages that vividly describe conditions in the packing plants. Tubercular pork was sold for human consumption. Old sausage, rejected in Europe and shipped back "mouldy and white," would be "dosed with borax and glycerine, and dumped into the hoppers, and made over again for home consumption." Meat was stored in rooms where "water from leaky roofs would drip over it, and thousands of rats would race about on it." The packers would put out poisoned bread to kill the rats; then the rats would die, and "rats, bread, and meat would go into the hoppers together." Most horrifying of all was the description of the men in the "cooking-rooms." They "worked in tank-rooms full of steam," in some of which there were "open vats near the level of the floor." Sometimes they fell into the vats "and when they were fished out, there was never enough of them left to be worth exhibiting—sometimes they would be overlooked for days, till all but the bones of them had gone out to the world as Durham's Pure Leaf Lard."

The book became notorious while it was still in the process of appearing, as a serial, in *The Appeal to Reason.* George P. Brett, of Macmillan & Co., gave Sinclair an advance, and offered to publish the book if he removed the "objectionable passages." But Sinclair refused. Other publishers also turned it down. Sinclair appealed to the readers of the magazine for support and they sent in enough subscription money to put out an edition of the novel. Then Doubleday, Page & Co. became interested in the book. Worried about its accuracy, they investigated the situation in Chicago. They became convinced that Sinclair was telling the truth about conditions in "Packingtown," and they published an edition of the book, early in 1906.

The Jungle created a furor when it appeared. A copy was sent to President Theodore Roosevelt, and letters from the public on the subject poured in to the President. "Mr. Dooley," the fictional creation of Finley Peter Dunne, has painted the following imaginary picture of Roosevelt's encounter with *The Jungle*:

Tiddy was toying with a light breakfast an' idly turnin' over th' pages iv th' new book with both hands. Suddenly he rose fr'm th' table, an' cryin': "I'm pizened," begun throwin' sausages out iv th' window. Th' ninth wan sthruck Sinitor Biv'ridge* on th' head an' made him a blond. It bounced off, exploded, an' blew a leg off a secret-service agent, an' th' scat-thred fragmints desthroyed a handsome row iv ol' oak-trees. Sinitor Biv'ridge rushed in, thinkin' that th' Prisidint was bein' assassynated be his devoted followers in th' Sinit, an' discovered Tiddy engaged in a hand-to-hand conflict with a potted ham. Th' Sinitor fr'm Injyanny, with a few well-directed wurruds, put out th' fuse an' rendered th' missile harmless. Since thin th' Prisidint, like th' rest iv us, has become a viggytaryan . . .

The meat-packers fought back with propaganda of their own, and they did their best to block legislation in Congress. But this time they were not successful. Roosevelt appointed two investigators, Charles P. Neill, U.S. Commissioner of Labor, and James B. Reynolds, a reformer from New York. Their report confirmed Sinclair's findings. At first, Roosevelt did not release the report of his investigators. Senator Albert Beveridge had "hammered out the draft of a meat-inspection law," which he attached as a rider to the agricultural appropriation bill. It called for post-mortem examination of meat, inspection of meat products, control of sanitation, and exclusion of "harmful chemicals and preservatives."** The packers refused to cooperate. The President then released the report.

He also applied pressure toward passage of the pure food law, which had been bottled up in Congress. In this he was greatly helped by the great public uproar over *The Jungle*. The packers and food manufacturers fought a rear-guard action. But one executive admitted that "the sale of meat and meat products has been more than cut in two."*** State food and drug officials, and Dr. Wiley, helped lobby for passage. "Public opinion" had been mobilized. In 1906, both a pure food and a meat inspection law were finally passed, and signed by the President.

What was Sinclair's reaction to all this? *The Jungle* made him famous. But to him, there was a slight element of disappointment—or irony—in the outcome. He said: "I aimed at the public's heart, and by accident I hit it in the stomach." Socialism

---

* Senator Albert Beveridge, of Indiana. [Eds. note]
** ANDERSON at 189. [Eds. note]
*** Quoted in DOWNS at 348. [Eds. note]

was not advanced by *The Jungle*, though that was Sinclair's real purpose in writing the book. He wrote in 1932 that:

> I am supposed to have helped clean up the yards and improve the country's meat supply—though this is mostly delusion. But nobody even pretends to believe that I improved the condition of the stockyard workers. They have no unions to speak of, and their wages are, in relation to the cost of living, every bit as low as they were twenty-eight years ago. Yet I don't want to be pessimistic, and say, as Jack London said to me, that by all his labors for the revolution he had perhaps brought it ten minutes nearer. I believe there are a great many Americans with a new dream in their hearts, even though they do not know how to make it effective. . . .*

NOTES AND QUESTIONS

1. What does this account of the passage of the Food and Drug Act tell us about the manner in which sharp outbursts of public opinion can be mobilized? Is there less likely to be a variance between social and legal norms in an area subject to such high public pressures as food safety, compared to the low-visibility, low-pressure areas measured by Cohen, Robson and Bates?

2. What does this account tell us about the *limits* of muck-raking, scandal and incidents as means of mobilizing public opinion and inducing legal change?

3. Think of other examples of the influence of scandal and incident on the formation of law. Compare, for instance, the role of Ralph Nader in the rise of auto safety legislation, and the blunder committed by General Motors when they attempted to "smear" his personal life.

[Reading 61]

Norman C. Miller, "GM's Snooping Boosts Prospect of Safety Law," *Wall Street Journal*, Mar. 25, 1966, at 10, col. 3:**

WASHINGTON—In the debate over the auto industry's responsibility for car safety, it would appear that General Motors Corp. is its own worst enemy.

For the admission by company officials that detectives hired by GM had harassed a vocal critic of the company's

---

* AMERICAN OUTPOST at 175-76. [Eds. note]
** Reprinted with permission of The Wall Street Journal.

car-safety program strengthens the chances that Congress will write the sort of law that GM and the other auto companies fear most—legislation that would empower Federal officials to outlaw car designs they rule unsafe.

Such legislation already has been recommended to Congress by President Johnson. The Administration's highway-safety bill would require auto makers to build cars "designed and equipped for maximum safety" and would give the Government authority to set safety standards, unless the industry devised "adequate" voluntary standards. The proposed law would be enforced by a ban on interstate shipment of cars failing to meet the standards. . . .

The auto industry believes annual styling changes are what sell cars. Thus, while prepared to accept a limited Federal involvement in the safety field, auto officials have promised an all-out campaign to persuade Congress to set tight limits on any Government power to establish design standards. The industry's first public move in this campaign will come on April 5 when auto officials are slated to testify before the Senate Commerce Committee on the Administration's proposed vehicle-safety law.

Until a few days ago Detroit was confident it could get Congress to see things its way. Industry officials believed they could cite a record of voluntary safety steps in the past several months as solid evidence that it was unnecessary for the Government to impose mandatory safety standards for car designs.

The industry's recent flurry of interest in safety, prompted by scathing criticism of GM's safety policies in Congressional hearings last July, has included: Addition of formerly optional safety equipment as standard items on 1966 cars; promises to add to all cars most, and possibly all, safety items required by the Federal Government on cars it purchases; voluntary development by GM of a collapsible steering wheel to be put on all its cars starting with 1967 models; an industry gift of $10 million to the University of Michigan for safety research, and increased safety development work by the companies' own staffs.

Moreover, the companies have greatly increased the emphasis given to safety devices in advertising. And they have mounted a high-powered public relations campaign to switch the focus of the car-safety debate away from car designs. (The $10 million safety-research grant to the University of Michigan, one high auto official has privately remarked, was a "public relations gimmick" intended to take the heat off the industry.) In countless speeches in recent months, auto executives have hammered at the theme that the companies already are doing everything they can to build safe cars, that real progress in reducing highway deaths can only come by cracking down on lawbreaking drivers and building better highways.

These efforts, auto officials believed, had gone a long way toward disarming the industry's safety critics. But now General Motors, by its own blunder, has handed them a new weapon.

The huge automobile company was caught in a clumsy attempt to have private detectives pry into the personal affairs of a young and obscure lawyer-author, Ralph Nader, whose book, "Unsafe at Any Speed," castigated the auto industry's safety policies in general and GM's in particular. Moreover, GM compounded its blunder by issuing a press release "explaining" the Nader investigation which Sen. Robert F. Kennedy (D., N.Y.) charged was "false" and which the company conceded could be "misleading." The GM statement omitted the facts, which the company was forced to admit before a Senate subcommittee, that detectives had constantly trailed Mr. Nader for a week and had sought intimate information about him from his associates.

To be sure, James M. Roche, GM president, apologized before the subcommittee for what he conceded was "harassment" of Mr. Nader by GM. Mr. Roche said no member of the company's "governing committees" had been aware of the investigation of Mr. Nader, and promised "such errors will not happen again."

The effect of Mr. Roche's candid admission of the company's mistake was largely erased, however, when top GM lawyers who had ordered the investigation testified only grudgingly about details of the spying by their detectives. A. F. Power, GM's general counsel, found himself denying that GM's agents had harassed Mr. Nader after Mr. Roche had already admitted it, then wound up conceding that if he were followed constantly himself he would consider it harassment.

Ironically, in the process of trying to put the best face on the company's probing into Mr. Nader's personal affairs, GM officials repeatedly stated that all the material their agents had uncovered indicated Mr. Nader was an eminently responsible and respectable citizen. They thus did much to undercut previous assertions by industry officials that allegations of unsafe car design were merely the mouthings of "wild-eyed critics."

In explaining that he wasn't aware of the harassment of Mr. Nader because he didn't read voluminous reports filed by the detectives, Mr. Power opened the company to charges that GM isn't concerned about what tactics are attempted to silence its critics. And by allowing a misleading public statement about the Nader investigation to stand uncorrected for almost two weeks, GM has handed critics new evidence to support their contention that the largest auto company is trying to cover up facts relating to the safety debate.

GM's inept handling of the Nader affair puts the company right back in the villain's role it has been trying to shake off, and makes a hero of one of its most determined critics. Inevitably, it has made it more difficult for Detroit to persuade Congress that the auto industry can be trusted with a safety program not enforced by law.

[Reading 62]

Arlen J. Large, "My Brother the Car, Public Irritation at Auto Defects Smooths Way for New Law," *Wall Street Journal*, Apr. 27, 1966, at 16, cols. 4 & 5:*

"For years people all over the country have been having trouble with their cars," philosophizes Sen. Dominick, the Colorado Republican. "Now this resentment is coming to the surface in the form of talk about automobile safety—and you know most people really don't care about that. It's just a way of kicking the manufacturers back."

Sen. Dominick's theory may go a long way toward explaining the astonishing ease with which Congress is preparing Federal safety fetters for one of the nation's most powerful industries. Normally, an expansion of Government controls into new territory sets off bruising Congressional battles: Witness the slugging over rules for drug labels, cigaret advertising, highway billboards, interest rate disclosure, food packaging. As a rule, proponents of new controls have to water down their original proposals in order to salvage anything.

Not so with President Johnson's plan for inducing Detroit to build safer cars. In the Senate, at least, there's enthusiastic rivalry to see who can pile more safety ideas atop the Presi-

---

* Reprinted with permission of The Wall Street Journal.

dent's initial proposal. Chairman Magnuson (D., Wash.) of the Commerce Committee, which will start assembling the safety measure in closed-door sessions in the next week or two, seems determined not to be outdone by such competitors as Sens. Ribicoff (D., Conn.), Robert Kennedy (D., N.Y.) and Minnesota's Mondale. The auto industry's main hope at this point is that the House will be a shade less zealous. . . .

As the Washington hearings progressed, Sen. Ribicoff and others began increasingly to cite specific car models sold to the public with mechanical defects. Ralph Nader, author of the book "Unsafe at Any Speed," was invited repeatedly to amplify his indictment of the early Corvair and other makes.

Politically, the result has been devastating to the industry. Confronted with examples of sticking accelerators, defective brakes and unstable steering mechanisms, few lawmakers are ready to rally to Detroit's defense. It's hard to be against legislation that people somehow hope will outlaw four-wheeled lemons. . . .

And for all its probable injustice, the sight of Detroit's powerful motor lords squirming before an indignant Senator has provided vicarious revenge for anyone who's ever felt betrayed by his beloved automobile.

4. Repeatedly, newspaper stories, books, and sensational magazine accounts have alleged corruption in municipal government, festering slum conditions, wholesale violation of housing codes, conditions of starvation in areas of the South, great gaps in airline safety, dangerous levels of air pollution, and shocking conditions in prisons and mental hospitals. Yet the response of public opinion has been, or seemed to be, much more muted than in other instances which, on the surface, seem to present less crisis and involve much less scandal. What social conditions seem likely to create a scandal that actually influences changes in law?

5. Both before and after publication of *The Jungle*, the meatpackers were rich, powerful, influential men. Yet the law was passed over their objection. Does this fact mean that the conventional interest-group theory of American government is wrong? Does it mean that the "power elite" theory is wrong? *See* pp. 575-89, *infra.*

Is the story of the passage of the Food and Drug Act consistent or inconsistent with the story of the passage of Workmen's Compensation, as viewed by Friedman and Ladinsky?

6. Related to legal change flowing from a scandal is legal change flowing from tactics of confrontation and protest. Argu-

ably, "confrontation" is a strategy designed to gain rewards by affecting public opinion in a particular way. In theory, the process involves rallying a protest group willing to take action. The action must be designed to gain attention, and usually this means conduct which the news media will find newsworthy. The protest activity is then communicated to the intended audience which, if the protest is to succeed, will demand reform. Finally, those in power meet the demands of the aroused public and the protesters achieve at least some measure of their goals.

While the theory is easy to state, execution is not always easy. It is usually difficult to mobilize a protest group, particularly if the planned activity involves some risk to the participants. Militant rhetoric often is employed to create solidarity and a willingness to act, but militancy can offend the intended audience or the holders of power. The protest activity must be newsworthy, and forms of protest tend to lose their shock value, so escalation toward more aggressive tactics is likely in order to capture or keep the attention of the media. Of course, these more aggressive tactics increase the risks to the participants and make it somewhat more difficult to recruit them. They also tend to offend a great portion of those who follow the demonstration in the news, and thus a "backlash" effect prompts counter-pressure on those who hold power to deny the protesters' demands and take repressive measures against them.

The late Dr. Martin Luther King, Jr., often was able to overcome these problems. His call to action was phrased in terms of a religion shared by many of the protesters, the national audience and the holders of power. His tactics were advertised as nonviolent, although he was willing to take the risk of provoking violence from his opponents. His successes came in situations where his followers appeared to be victims of unwarranted aggression. In Birmingham, Alabama, nonviolent demonstrators were met with police using cattle prods, police dogs and high pressure fire hoses. The scene was transmitted to the nation nightly over television. A year later the Civil Rights Act of 1964 was passed, and many credit the outrage fanned by television coverage of Birmingham with an important role in this legislative success. Finally, King was appealing to a northern white liberal audience to help change the situation in the South. In the early 1960's, this audience, at little cost to itself, could exercise a great deal of influence on the federal government with a view to procuring governmental action in another part of the country. However, other protests have been far less successful. Sometimes the price of the action demanded seems simply too high. Sometimes the public apparently views the demonstrators as having "asked for" police violence, or the police appear to be models of patience using approved nonviolent tactics to control demonstrators.

[Reading 63]

Ted Finman & Stewart Macaulay, "Freedom to Dissent: The Vietnam Protests and the Words of Public Officials," 1966 *Wisconsin Law Review* 632, 683-85:*

While provocative protests may attract attention, they are often annoying, and one may ask whether this attention getting is really necessary. Ideally a speaker whose ideas have merit should not need to resort to such tactics. In fact, however, he often must. The temptation to ignore difficult, complex problems like the war in Vietnam is great. Acceptance of the *status quo* is far simpler than trying to comprehend the mass of pertinent information and the many interrelated issues that are involved. Moreover, when it comes to foreign policy, many people feel powerless to influence the government and thus tend to ignore debate because they view it as futile. Additionally the anti-Communist character of the Vietnam struggle may give the government's policy special insulation against the charges of its critics. For these and perhaps other reasons, special measures to capture public attention may well be essential when one wants to stimulate widespread examination of a previously accepted government policy.

In this respect, it should be noted that the opponents of government policy may have no ready access to the mass media. This was true of most protesters against the war in Vietnam. Lacking the funds required for a national advertising campaign, they had to rely on the publicity that newsworthiness could buy. But at least in the early days, the people who were protesting were not newsworthy in themselves—they were neither prominent as individuals nor did they speak for prominent groups. And the message they expressed was not sufficiently shocking to command the attention of television, newspapers, and magazines. Therefore the newsworthiness of their *tactics* may have been especially important in determining how much of their position reached the public. Furthermore, the protesters needed not only to capture space in the mass media, but had also to arouse audi-

---

* Ted Finman and Stewart Macaulay, Professors of Law, University of Wisconsin. Copyright © 1966 Wisconsin Law Review. Reprinted by permission.

ence interest. Familiar devices such as a letter to the editor or a speech at a local auditorium are apt to be far less effective than a march through the center of town or a picket line around the White House. New ideas, like new products, require provocative and unusual forms of promotion to bring them to the consumer's attention. And in a market filled with competitors, a new product, especially a bitter pill, needs this vigorous promotion if it is ever to be noticed at all.

This promotional process, of course, is not a simple one; and not all forms of protest are effective in reaching all groups within the public. Indeed, something like a chain letter effect may operate. The early student protests, for example, with an initial impact confined to the academic community, may well have sparked the first teach-ins. The activities of the professors, in turn, somewhat more noteworthy, reached beyond the campus—to various nonacademic intellectuals and to some extent to the public at large. Religious leaders had also entered the discussion, and this led to a further involvement of the public. And while we cannot trace with confidence a direct causal connection, eventually open hearings were held in the Senate.

Dramatic and unusual forms of protest may have other effects conducive to heightened discussion and debate. Opposition to the war in Vietnam has been at times rather unpopular and some people, perhaps many, may in consequence have felt reluctant to express a questioning or dissident point of view. But by advertising the fact that there is a protest movement—by popularizing dissent, so to speak—the tactics of protest may have dispelled the notion that a position of dissent is necessarily a lonely or isolated one, and thus have encouraged some to speak out. Still other people may remain silent because they view the expression of dissent as radical or extreme, and hence for them, improper. But whether any given expression of dissent will be perceived as beyond the bounds of propriety often turns on the range of protest tactics currently in use; whatever lies at the far end of the spectrum has a way of being popularly equated with "radicalism." But when a new and provocative tactic appears, the range—subject to certain qualifications— may be extended; older tactics may shift toward the center and cease to be viewed as quite so shocking. If writing letters, signing petitions, and the like are the only modes of protest in use, some people inevitably will regard these acts as radical and shun them. But as different and more provocative tactics become common—picket lines, for example, or sit-ins—the over-all picture changes, and people previously unwilling to express themselves at all may now be willing to write their Congressman, or sign a petition, and so on. In brief, dramatic and unusual tactics may enhance the respectability of the more moderate forms of protest.

Those who hold government power do not lack defenses against protests. To avoid creating a televised incident in which the protesters will be viewed as innocent victims of arbitrary government action, they can respond by initiating an investigating committee which will delay action until the protest is forgotten. They can manipulate concessions, dealing with showy but marginal problems, preserving the core of their interests intact. They can attempt to discredit protest leaders or switch critical attention to the demonstrators' tactics. They can plead that money is not available to meet the demands, or that the protest is addressed to the wrong agency. *See* Michael Lipsky, "Rent Strikes: Poor Man's Weapon," 6 *Transaction* 10 (1969); Hubbard, "Five Long Summers and How They Grew," 12 *The Public Interest* (1968); Lawrence R. Velvel, "Protecting Civil Disobedience Under the First Amendment," 37 *George Washington Law Review* 464 (1969).

[Reading 64]

In light of these comments consider the following argument by Paul Salstrom in "The Need for Confrontation," 12 *Liberation* 12 (July 1967): *

> For action to be effective, it must be fresh and creative. It must be a bold and unpredictable initiative and unmask the opposition by drawing out into full view its assumptions, violence and pathology. Gandhians call this moral jiu-jitsu— the essentially friendly use of an opponent's energy to throw him—throw him *open* to examination by himself and others.
>
> In the course of six years of antidraft work . . . I've seen only one true spark struck—by four card burners at South Boston Courthouse in the spring of 1966. There the pattern of developments accidentally followed the lessons James Bevel and others had painfully learned in Birmingham and applied masterfully in Selma. The fact is that nonviolence tends to work well, only if applied (with guts) in the face of dangerous violence and witnessed by many observers. Police brutality helps, of course, and police protection hurts.

---

* Reprinted from the July 1967 issue of Liberation, 5 Beekman Street, N.Y., N.Y. 10038. Copyright 1967 by Liberation. Reprinted by permission.

South Boston is an Irish working-class ghetto. Nine pacifists were to be tried there one morning, about a year ago, for an illegal sit-down. After phoning news media for four hours the night before, four of these pacifists burned their draft cards on the Courthouse steps just before the trial. They were surrounded by several hundred tough kids who had been alerted by the cooperative media, specifically the rabble-rousing "news flashes" during the night. For twenty minutes the burners took a savage beating, both outside and inside the court-house, while a few cops and F.B.I. agents looked on. The press was on hand en masse and took a few on the chin also. (Large-scale, blow-by-blow media coverage was of the essence in the Birmingham and Selma breakthrough.) . . .

But it fizzled two weeks later. A coalition between weak-kneed clergymen and a police force more than willing to provide protection for them as they "confronted" South Boston on our pacifist behalf . . . doused the spark thoroughly. . . . We had the irony of scores of God's elect—many of them Irish Catholic priests—surrounded by hundreds of equally scared cops, swinging clubs to pretend they felt brave marching through a continuous mob of Irish men, women and children, many of whom were mad enough about the whole scene to land themselves in jail. Thus a day which could have been a national break-through—the creaming of those preachers who *would* have been brave enough to march *sans* fuzz, recorded blow-by-blow for TV newscasts across the land, and causing a furor comparable perhaps to Selma's— was instead a fizzle.

What are the limitations, if any, of confrontation tactics? Could they be used by the American Nazi Party to bar Jews from public office in a community? One lesson for "the establishment" is not to play the role of the oppressor, at least while the television cameras are present, but what are the costs if a police department does not empty buildings occupied by demonstrators sitting-in and is zealous in protecting parades by unpopular groups?

To what extent, if at all, do the successes of confrontation tactics indicate the power of public opinion and undercut "power-elite" theories of control of the legal system?

b.   Particular types of publics: the influence of interest groups on the law

(1)   Interest groups and pluralism

Introductory Note

Who makes the laws? In a democracy, theoretically, the people make the laws. But no one has ever been so naive as to believe that it is all the people who make all the laws. The very structure of American government presupposes narrower groupings representing narrower interests. The Constitution reflected the fact that small states had different interests from large states, that slaveholding states had different interests from nonslaveholding states. It was felt to be important to preserve some sort of balance between interests, at least interests defined in geographical terms. Moreover, the Bill of Rights was designed as a constitutional limitation on the power of the majority of the people to do certain things to minorities.

In modern political science, the focus of research and theory is on interest groups in the sense of more-or-less organized, nongovernmental associations whose members share some general orientation, usually an economic one. The pioneer work of Arthur Bentley, who wrote *The Process of Government* in 1908, has been rediscovered, largely since the end of the second World War, and analysis of American political life in terms of interest groups has since become part of the conventional wisdom. Modern political scientists tend to pay considerably less attention to the formal structure of government than to the groups which take advantage of the opportunities and constraints provided by governmental structure in seeking to translate their economic and social programs into law.

Once we admit that much of the law is the result of the demands and programs of "interest groups," the job of research and understanding of the lawmaking process has only begun. How the various groups meet and hammer out their differences in the political arena, how the shape, scope and enforceability of law is affected by the process—all this requires the careful observation and calculation of an enormous number of factors.

In this section, we will touch on some of the main policy and empirical questions of interest-group theory. Throughout the readings, interest groups and "lobbies" appear, in one form or another. In a highly abstract form, Buchanan and Tullock, Reading 6, at 56, *supra*, sketched out the mechanics of coalition formation, which is at the heart of interest-group politics. Among the concrete interest-group characters that have appeared so far in

our story, we have seen occupational groups—organized auto
dealers and manufacturers, meat-packers, railroads—and pressure
groups without an economic organization base, for example, the
"wets" and "drys" who struggled over Prohibition.

An earlier generation deplored the interest groups because they
represented narrow, selfish interests rather than the "public interest." Many modern political scientists, however, do not believe
in the reality of so nebulous a concept as the "public interest."
They feel that there are *only* private interests, and that the public
interest is served by a kind of marketplace competition through
the use of legitimate political means. They praise the noisy,
brawling pluralism of interest groups in the United States. They
point out that the United States has, rather successfully, prevented excessive dominance of political and economic life by
groups with overwhelming power—first, by placing certain minority rights beyond the reach of the majority; second, by fragment-
ing political power among many jurisdictions, state, federal and
local; and third, through the development of interest-group politics, so that one group balances the other, bargains and compromises must be struck, and solutions to social problems will
necessarily have to take into account the needs, desires, wants
and opinions of a great many groups. American government,
then, is "pluralistic"; its basic "axiom" is that "instead of a
single center of sovereign power there must be multiple centers
of power, none of which is or can be wholly sovereign." Robert
A. Dahl, *Pluralist Democracy in the United States: Conflict and
Consent* 24 (Rand McNally 1967). This refers not only to the
form of government, but also to the manner in which public
opinion is brought to bear on the organs of government. No
one interest group or class is sovereign; all must contend with
the others.

Not every social scientist and legal thinker agrees with the
pluralist view. Some would not be so quick to abandon the idea
of the public interest. At least some legal action can be explained
in terms of what the actor thinks is the public interest. The
next three readings provide another attack on the dominant view.
From one theoretical standpoint or another, they deny that pluralist democracy either is or can ever be pluralist.

65. Theory of the State and Law in Soviet Legal Philosophy*

S. A. GOLUNSKII AND
M. S. STROGOVICH

Sec. 1. The State and Law. The state—an organization of the authority of the dominant class . . . —is a "complex machine," with whose aid the exploiter classes in exploiter society crush and oppress the toiling masses, and the proletariat in socialist society—effectuating its dictatorship—destroys exploitation and the exploiter classes, and builds socialist society. In all its activity, the state—realizing the *will* of the dominant class to which authority belongs—defends and guarantees the interests of that class. For this, the governing class requires that the mandates of its will be binding in society—that all citizens of the state be subject to, and observe them. To this end, the exploiter class forces its will upon the exploited—dictates its will to the people, subordinates the people to itself. In a socialist state, the will of the worker class, which has abolished exploitation—thereby expressing the interests of all the toilers—is binding upon all citizens, to the end of establishing and developing socialist relationships and building a classless, communist society.

Such an expression and realization of the will of the dominant class, to the end of establishing and strengthening social arrangements advantageous and agreeable to the dominant class, are attained with the aid of *law*, binding rules of conduct (chiefly in the form of legislation) established by the dominant class, which assures observance thereof by the entire force of its apparatus of constraint: the state. "Will, if it is the state's will, must be expressed as *legislation* established by *authority*—otherwise 'will' is an empty concussion of air by an empty sound." In the *Communist Manifesto*, Marx and Engels wrote of the bourgeoisie: "Your law is merely the will of your class, erected into legislation

* Reprinted from pp. 365-66, 369-70, 372-75, by permission of the publishers from Hugh W. Babb, translator, Soviet Legal Philosophy, Cambridge, Mass.: Harvard University Press. Copyright © 1951 by the President and Fellows of Harvard College.

—a will whose content is defined by the material conditions of the existence of your class."

This proposition of the founders of Marxism revealing the class essence of bourgeois law—is the key to understanding the class essence of law of any sort, viz., the will of the dominant class elevated into legislation. This means that such will is precisely formulated and given universally binding force, becoming a rule of conduct binding upon all. The law of exploiter society always expresses the will of the class of exploiters—aided by law the exploiter classes impose their will upon the exploited popular masses. The law of socialist society likewise expresses the will of the dominant class, the worker class; and—since exploiter classes have there been destroyed, and the worker class (to which the state guidance of society belongs) expresses the interests and aspirations of all the toiling people—socialist law is the will of the soviet people elevated into legislation—the will of the people who have built socialist society under the guidance of the worker class headed by the bolshevik party.

Lenin has pointed out that "without an apparatus capable of *compelling* the observance of legal rules the law is nothing," which solves also the problem of the relationship between law and the state. This problem is still unsolved in bourgeois legal theory—as is the controversy as to which has precedence. Is the state founded on law? Or is law created by the state? The most distinct expression of the idea that the law has precedence is by those who hold the contract theory of the origin of the state: viz., that the basis of the state is a contract between citizens and the state authority, and that the conditions of this contract— as well as "natural law" established by nature independently of the state—are binding upon the latter. In another form, the idea that law has precedence was expressed in the theory of the Rechtsstaat, which holds that the state itself is a purely legal concept. Other bourgeois theorists defend the view that the state has precedence . . . and that the state creates law. From the viewpoint of the Marx-Lenin theory of the state, each of these interpretations is incorrect. Law and the state are not two distinct phenomena—one preceding the other—but are two sides of one and the same phenomenon: class dominance, which is manifested (a) in the fact that the dominant class creates its apparatus of constraint (the state), and (b) in the fact that it expresses its will in the shape of rules of conduct which it formulates (law) and which—with the aid of its state apparatus—it compels people to observe. . . . Law emerged jointly with the state, in consequence of the disintegration of the primordial-communal social order, the appearance of private property, and the division of society into classes. In class society antagonistic classes struggle *inter se* and the dominant class—aided by the instrument of constraint (the state)—holds the subordinate classes obedient, and—aided by *law*—dictates its will to them. Like the state, law is a historical phenomenon, emerging under the influence of the causes aforesaid, and—like the state—it will disappear with the disappearance of the causes which evoked it. . . .

Law, as we have seen, expresses *the will* of the dominant class, and so has a definite goal which the dominant class attains with its aid. It always regulates social relationships—systematizes and coördinates them, secures and defends them, and develops them conformably with the interests of the dominant class. It always comes as a regulation of social relationships employed by the dominant class, to strengthen its dominance, to guarantee its interests, and to resist encroachments upon that dominance and those interests. In his report at the Extraordinary VIII All-Union Congress of Soviets on the Draft of the U.S.S.R. Constitution, Stalin pointed out that in a bourgeois state "a constitution is necessary in order to make secure social arrangements agreeable and advantageous to the 'have' classes," whereas in the soviet state "a constitution is necessary in order to make secure social arrangements agreeable and advantageous to the toilers." These words, while referring directly to the Constitution—the fundamental Law, establishing the basic legal norms of supreme importance—are completely applicable as well to the entire aggregate of laws presently in force in society: to all law.

Law thus consists of norms as to which state authority guarantees their being put into operation to the end of defending, securing, and developing legal relationships and arrangements agreeable and advantageous to the dominant class. Individual legal norms, therefore—individual rules of conduct—are not a fortuitous accumulation of heterogeneous demands upon people, but are penetrated by one and the same class content and are directed at the attainment of identical goals.

Summarizing the foregoing features and indicia of law, we may define it as follows: *Law is the aggregate of the rules of conduct (norms) established or approved (sanctioned) by state authority, expressing the will of the dominant class, as to which the coercive force of the state guarantees their being put into operation to the end of safeguarding, making secure, and developing social relationships and arrangements agreeable and advantageous to the dominant class. . . .*

Sec. 3. Law and Social Relationships. Law is an aggregate of the rules of human conduct—consequently it regulates human behavior, human actions, the relationships of humans *inter se* and with organs of the state and with the state itself. Human relations in society are called social relations—it is these relations which are objects of regulation by law. At the same time, however, law itself issues out of definite social relationships which arise independently of law. Thus law—while it emanates from social relationships—regulates these social relationships as well. This dual bond between law and social relationships requires special clarification to the end that we neither dissociate law from social relationships nor ignore specific peculiarities of law which distinguish it from other sides of social life—from other social phenomena connected with it. The Marx-Lenin teaching is that social life is founded on production relationships: mutual relationships into which people enter during the production process. "The aggregate of these production relationships constitutes the economic structure of society—the true basis on which the juridic and political superstructure is raised, and with which definite forms of social consciousness correspond."[29] These production-economic relations are therefore the foundation or basis, and law is a superstructure. Law emerges out of definite economic relationships. Thus, the emergence of private property—the relationships between persons, whereby specific things are in the exclusive possession of individuals—was due to the influence of expanded production forces. It was independent of law. When the development of private property attained definite limits—when all the basic means of production had passed into private property—those who had property were bound to defend it against encroachment by those who did not have property. Then arose *the law of private property*: legal norms requiring people to refrain from encroachment on the property of another. Fulfillment of these—as of all—legal norms was guaranteed by the coercive power of the state, the class organization of property owners. *The law of private property* thus originates in factual social relationships, which arose on the basis of private property—wherefor the character of these social relationships defined as well the content of these legal norms.

Production relationships (on the basis whereof definite juridic relationships—legal relationships—arise) are formed independently of the human will, under the influence of the level to which production forces have developed. On the other hand, legal norms are always produced by conscious human activity.

Just as, in the individual, in order for him to begin to act, all the stimuli evoking his actions must inevitably pass

---

[29] MARX, Foreword to A CRITIQUE OF POLITICAL ECONOMY (Russian ed., 1938) 6.

through his head and become stimuli of his will, precisely so all the needs of human society—irrespective of what is the then dominant class—inevitably pass through the will of the state in order to attain universal significance in the form of statutes.[30]

Emanating from, and defined by, specific social relationships (production relationships in the last analysis), law is nevertheless no mere passive or mechanical reflection thereof: it actively influences social relationships—regulating them, confirming and safeguarding some, reorganizing others, etc. The Marx-Lenin teaching as to the interrelationship of foundation and superstructure establishes the point that the superstructure (and law is specifically referable to the superstructure) is defined by the foundation (production relationships—the economic structure of society), but once the superstructure has arisen, it acquires an independent existence, and exerts reflex influence upon the foundation (social relationships). In this regard, Stalin has pointed out that

> social ideas, theories, and political institutions, have arisen upon the foundation of pressing tasks of developing the material life of society—social being—and themselves thereafter react upon social being—upon the material life of society— create the conditions essential for carrying through to the end the solution of pressing problems of the material life of society, and for making the further development of that life feasible.

Thus law, also, as a part of the superstructure, reacts upon the foundation (economic relationships) out of which it emanated— being a vast organization force in society: so the law of private property, arising out of factual human relationships, wherein only some persons possessed the means of production (land, animals, slaves, etc.) in turn promoted the confirmation and further development of such factual relationships.

Safeguarded by the law of private property (the law being guaranteed by the coercive force of the state), owners were able to enjoy their property in peace and quiet—to utilize it to exploit the have-nots, and thereby still further to swell their riches. The law of private property thus subserved the still greater separation of society into "haves" and "have-nots," exploiters and exploited— although the very emergence of the law of private property was

---

[30] ENGELS, LUDWIG FEUERBACH AND THE END OF CLASSICAL GERMAN PHILOSOPHY (Russian ed., 1938) 44.

specifically associated with the factual division of society into classes. It must moreover be clearly understood that the social relations giving birth to law must not be substituted for laws—thus the law of private property must not be confused with the economic fact of private property. The part played by law in organizing social relationships can—as is true of socialist law now—be progressive, and even revolutionary (when it expresses the will of a progressive and developing class); or it may be reactionary (when it is the law of a class that is stepping out of the historical arena after outliving its historical potentialities, and becoming a reactionary force which retards social development), as is true of bourgeois law at the present time.

66. The Power Elite*

C. WRIGHT MILLS

It is very difficult to give up the old model of power as an automatic balance, with its assumptions of a plurality of independent, relatively equal, and conflicting groups of the balancing society. All these assumptions are explicit to the point of unconscious caricature in recent statements of 'who rules America.' According to Mr. David Riesman, for example, during the past half century there has been a shift from 'the power hierarchy of a ruling class to the power dispersal' of 'veto groups.' Now no one runs anything: all is undirected drift. 'In a sense,' Mr. Riesman believes, 'this is only another way of saying that America is a middle-class country . . . in which, perhaps people will soon wake up to the fact that there is no longer a "we" who run things and a "they" who don't or a "we" who don't run things and a "they" who do, but rather that all "we's" are "they's" and all "they's" are "we's." '

'The chiefs have lost the power, but the followers have not gained it,' and in the meantime, Mr. Riesman takes his psychological interpretation of power and of the powerful to quite an extreme, for example: 'if businessmen *feel* weak and dependent, they *are* weak and dependent, no matter what material resources may be ascribed to them.'

'. . . The future,' accordingly, 'seems to be in the hands of the small business and professional men who control Congress: the local realtors, lawyers, car salesmen, undertakers, and so on; of the military men who control defense and, in part, foreign policy; of the big business managers and their lawyers, finance-committee men, and other counselors who decide on plant investment and influence the rate of technological change; of the labor leaders who control worker productivity and worker votes; of the black belt whites who have the greatest stake in southern politics; of the Poles, Italians, Jews, and Irishmen who have stakes in foreign policy, city jobs, and ethnic religious and cultural organizations; of the editorializers and storytellers who help socialize the young, tease and train the adult, and amuse and annoy the aged; of the farmers—themselves warring congeries of

* From The Power Elite by C. Wright Mills, pp. 243-48. Copyright ©
1956 by Oxford University Press, Inc. Reprinted by permission.

cattlemen, corn men, dairymen, cotton men, and so on—who control key departments and committees and who, as the living representatives of our inner-directed past, control many of our memories; of the Russians and, to a lesser degree, other foreign powers who control much of our agenda of attention; and so on. The reader can complete the list.' . . .

There is some reality in such romantic pluralism, even in such a *pasticcio* of power as Mr. Riesman invents: it is a recognizable, although a confused, statement of the middle levels of power, especially as revealed in Congressional districts and in the Congress itself. But it confuses, indeed it does not even distinguish between the top, the middle, and the bottom levels of power. . . . Exactly *what*, directly or indirectly, did 'small retailers' or 'brick masons' have to do with the sequence of decision and event that led to World War II? What did 'insurance agents,' or for that matter, the Congress, have to do with the decision to make or not to make, to drop or not to drop, the early model of the new weapon? . . .

The balance of power theory . . . is a narrow-focus view of American politics. With it one can explain temporary alliances within one party or the other. It is also narrow-focus in the choice of time-span: the shorter the period of time in which you are interested, the more usable the balance of power theory appears. For when one is up-close and dealing journalistically with short periods, a given election, for example, one is frequently overwhelmed by a multiplicity of forces and causes. One continual weakness of American 'social science,' since it became ever so empirical, has been its assumption that a mere enumeration of a plurality of causes is the wise and scientific way of going about understanding modern society. Of course it is nothing of the sort: it is a paste-pot eclecticism which avoids the real task of social analysis: that task is to go beyond a mere enumeration of all the facts that might conceivably be involved and weigh each of them in such a way as to understand how they fit together, how they form a model of what it is you are trying to understand.

Undue attention to the middle levels of power obscures the structure of power as a whole, especially the top and the bottom. American politics, as discussed and voted and campaigned for, have largely to do with these middle levels, and often only with them. Most 'political' news is news and gossip about middle-level issues and conflicts. And in America, the political theorist too is often merely a more systematic student of elections, of who voted for whom. As a professor or as a free-lance intellectual, the political analyst is generally on the middle levels of power himself.

He knows the top only by gossip; the bottom, if at all, only by 'research.' But he is at home with the leaders of the middle level, and, as a talker himself, with their 'bargaining.'

Commentators and analysts, in and out of the universities, thus focus upon the middle levels and their balances because they are closer to them, being mainly middle-class themselves; because these levels provide the noisy content of 'politics' as an explicit and reported-upon fact; because such views are in accord with the folklore of the formal model of how democracy works; and because, accepting that model as good, especially in their current patrioteering, many intellectuals are thus able most readily to satisfy such political urges as they may feel.

When it is said that a 'balance of power' exists, it may be meant that no one interest can impose its will or its terms upon others; or that any one interest can create a stalemate; or that in the course of time, first one and then another interest gets itself realized, in a kind of symmetrical taking of turns; or that all policies are the results of compromises, that no one wins all they want to win, but each gets something. All these possible meanings are, in fact, attempts to describe what can happen when, permanently or temporarily, there is said to be 'equality of bargaining power.' But, . . . the goals for which interests struggle are not merely given; they reflect the current state of expectation and acceptance. Accordingly, to say that various interests are 'balanced' is generally to evaluate the *status quo* as satisfactory or even good; the hopeful ideal of balance often masquerades as a description of fact.

'Balance of power' implies equality of power, and equality of power seems wholly fair and even honorable, but in fact what is one man's honorable balance is often another's unfair imbalance. Ascendent groups of course tend readily to proclaim a just balance of power and a true harmony of interest, for they prefer their domination to be uninterrupted and peaceful. So large businessmen condemn small labor leaders as 'disturbers of the peace' and upsetters of the universal interests inherent in business-labor cooperation. So privileged nations condemn weaker ones in the name of internationalism, defending with moral notions what has been won by force against those have-nots whom, making their bid for ascendancy or equality later, can hope to change the *status quo* only by force.

The notion that social change proceeds by a tolerant give and take, by compromise and a network of vetoes of one interest balanced by another assumes that all this goes on within a more or less stable framework that does not itself change, that all issues are subject to compromise, and are thus naturally harmonious or can be made such. Those who profit by the general framework of the *status quo* can afford more easily than those who are dissatisfied under it to entertain such views as the mechanics of social change. Moreover, 'in most fields . . . only one interest is organized, none is, or some of the major ones are not.' . . .

Checks and balances may thus be understood as an alternative statement of 'divide and rule,' and as a way of hampering the more direct expression of popular aspiration. For the theory of balance often rests upon the moral idea of a natural harmony of interests, in terms of which greed and ruthlessness are reconciled with justice and progress. Once the basic structure of the American political economy was built, and for so long as it could be tacitly supposed that markets would expand indefinitely, the harmony of interest could and did serve well as the ideology of dominant groups, by making their interests appear identical with the interests of the community as a whole. So long as this doctrine prevails, any lower group that begins to struggle can be made to appear inharmonious, disturbing the common interest. 'The doctrine of the harmony of interests,' E. H. Carr has remarked, 'thus serves as an ingenious moral device invoked, in perfect sincerity, by privileged groups in order to justify and maintain their dominant position.'

67. Pluralistic Society or Class Rule?[1]

SPARTACIST*

All good political science majors know how this society functions. It is a dynamic balance of various interests and pressure groups ranging from organized labor, to downtown merchants, to the John Birch Society. Of course. To speak of class rule is to exhibit naïveté and bad taste. Worse yet, it is to "use the rhetoric of the thirties."

Now Governor [Pat] Brown [of California] (the good, gray "vector zero" product of the pluralistic society) has turned the cops loose on Berkeley students and is vowing to put down "anarchy and revolution." Does the governor's charge have any substance? The issue which first brought the students onto the scene was civil rights. In theory, racial equality is fully compatible with the present social order. Indeed, the abstract model of the society works better with racial equality than without it. Civil rights, therefore, is a reformist demand. The actual society, however, is so beset by internal contradictions and external conflicts, and racism so deeply imbedded in it, that the demand for racial equality in practice takes on a revolutionary character. Hence the crackdown on student civil liberties. The campus had to be sealed off from the community because, with the prospect of deepening struggles in the black ghettos, the students were not only a powerful force in their own right but also threatened to provide a link between the ghetto and potential anti-status-quo forces in the white community. The fight for civil rights led to a fight for civil liberties. Civil liberties, too, are theoretically a reformist issue and are even enshrined in the political constitution of the society. But the actual exercise of civil liberties by dissidents (as opposed to their theoretical expostulation by establishment intellectuals) is also a revolutionary threat and is reacted to as such by the authorities.

What have the Berkeley students uncovered? First, in pursuance of civil rights, they have taken on such bastions of private

1 Revolutionary Socialist group leaflet distributed in early December, 1964.
* Reprinted from The Berkeley Student Revolt 231-32 (Lipset & Wolin ed., Doubleday 1965), by permission of the Spartacist League of the United States.

property as the Bank of America and the Oakland *Tribune*. The response of the UC administration, which, via the Board of Regents, is responsible to these same forces, was to curtail student civil liberties. Finding themselves unable to secure their rights within the rules made and changed at will by their enemies, the FSM [Free Speech Movement*] resorted to militancy, civil disobedience, and a traditional class weapon, the strike. While the faculty sweated and equivocated, the liberal Democratic governor, who knows what power is, called out the cops.

What the Berkeley students have exposed is not merely a vast and inept bureaucracy, but a coherent ruling-class structure. It runs all the way from the agro-business, banking, mining, railroad, utility, and newspaper capitalists and their direct representatives on the Board of Regents through the Democratic governor and the university administration down to the point of application, the police club. When Brown calls the FSM revolutionary, he speaks the truth, despite the fact that FSM fights only for rights supposedly guaranteed within a democratic capitalist society. In this struggle the students, whatever their intentions may have been, have given a clear and dramatic demonstration of how bourgeois class rule works. They have shown it too moribund and fearful to grant even those rights which are supposed to be its moral justification.

These exposures are invaluable lessons for *other* actual and potential enemies of this ruling class, such as the automation victims, farm laborers, the ghetto masses, indeed, all sections of the working class. To the extent that they learn these lessons, and come to understand their stake in this Free Speech Movement, they will aid the embattled students with their numerical strength, organization, and economic power. This revelation of class power will mark a significant step in a process of increasing political and class consciousness which must lead to a movement that will have the strength to effect the final solution of the whole gamut of problems which are now the students' concern.

Pat Brown calls it "revolution."

NOTES AND QUESTIONS

1. To what extent are Golunskii and Strogovich, Mills, and "Spartacist" making the same general point about western democracies? To what extent do they differ?

---

* *See* P. JACOBS & S. LANDAU, THE NEW RADICALS 59 (1966) (Vintage Books). [Eds. note]

2. Note the definition of law given by Golunskii and Strogovich. Does this definition take into account only *formal* aspects of law, and if so, is it not possible that some aspects of the law of a bourgeois country might in fact *not* express the "will of the dominant class," but rather some ideals which are more general but which are not carried out in practice? Does "Spartacist" imply a different view of law—one which does not, on the surface, express the "will of the dominant class"?

3. Do you think C. Wright Mills would recognize the existence of a "power elite" in the Soviet Union, China or Cuba? In Mills' view, is the dominance of the United States by an interlocking clique of industrial, military and political elites due to the American economic and political system? Or is it inherent in any large modern society?

4. "Spartacist" stresses the gulf between the formal and the real, in regard to American civil rights.

(a) Is it a refutation of "Spartacist" to point out that the very concept of a basic right beyond the reach of temporary majorities recognizes that there is a tendency to oppress deviants and dissidents, and that a democracy must constantly struggle against this tendency?

(b) Does "Spartacist" ignore the symbolic and educational value of formal civil liberties? Is there a tendency for the real to approximate the ideal? Try to think of instances where the existence of ideal or paper rights has influenced the struggle toward the realization of such rights. Are your examples strong enough to refute "Spartacist"? What, in other words, is the strength of formal rights as a factor in the struggle described in "Spartacist's" pamphlet?

(2) Pressure groups and the making of law:
techniques and policy issues

68. The Washington Lawyer

CHARLES A. HORSKY*

Let us now turn to the Washington lawyer in his relation to the second major branch of the federal government—the legislative. Principally, this will have to do with lobbying—using the term in the broad sense of activity intended to influence legislative action. At the outset, however, it is worth noting that lobbying is not the only work for the Washington lawyer in the legislative field.

Washington has always had a full share of litigation challenging the powers of Congress and of congressional committees. . . . Advice to clients on when they should testify and when they may properly claim privilege has been sought and given for over a century.

Moreover, still apart from anything which can properly be called lobbying, there is what might be called the Washington lawyer's interpretation and evaluation work. A bill is introduced which, on its face, means nothing; let us say that it reads like this: "The fourth proviso of subsection (b) of Section 1 of the Act of March 2, 1937, is amended by deleting the words following the word 'assessment,' and changing the comma which follows said word to a semi-colon." The lawyer who has undertaken to advise a client on legislative developments will have a preliminary interpretation job. Likewise, in a bill which proposes new language in place of old, the lawyer will have to evaluate the potential effect of the bill in terms of how radically it breaks with the past. If the client happens to be one which does considerable business with the government, not only substantive bills but appropriation bills must be analyzed and evaluated. The process of reporting, interpreting and evaluating continues through the several legislative stages—the hearings, the committee reports, the floor debates.

At first blush, there seems to be nothing in this which calls for any particular qualifications except an access to the bills and reports. For the Washington lawyer they are conveniently at hand, but they are available in due course to lawyers everywhere. Speed, however, is often important, or at least many clients so regard it. More importantly, the evaluation of proposed legislation demands a considerable understanding of the prevailing political moods of individual Senators and Congressmen, of congressional committees, and of Congress as a whole. . . .

Recognizing, then, that the Washington lawyer has functions in connection with the legislative process which have no external impact, let us turn to the role of the Washington lawyer in lobbying—in activity intended to influence legislation. Probably that is his chief role in the legislative function. . . .

From the point of view of the Washington lawyer, there are two types of lobbying which we can promptly eliminate from discussion. First, there are activities directed at influencing legislation through the electoral process—that is, by supporting the election to the legislative body of a person with a legislative program one favors. Second, there are activities directed at influencing legislation by "educational work." If you happen to oppose the particular legislative action which is in issue, substitute for the phrase "educational work" the phrase "propaganda work." The education or propaganda may be specific, directed toward a particular bill, or it may be directed only at the establishment of a political or economic philosophy which will condition all future legislation. This latter has been called "grass roots" lobbying. The Washington lawyer, like any other citizen, may participate in both of these types of lobbying activities, but neither category has any special relation to either his location or his skills.

The other two kinds of lobbying, with which the Washington lawyer is concerned, are of a more direct sort. The first is the most direct—contacts or communications with specific legislators or legislative committees. The other is the contact with an interested government department or agency to secure its approval and cooperation in presenting and securing the passage of a bill. In each of these fields, the special competence of the lawyer is both used and useful. . . .

[Let us examine] certain concrete types of legal work designed to influence legislative action. First, let us take a sample of what is a frequent occurrence—the drafting of proposed legislation. Here there are perhaps three skills of the lawyer which are involved—the ability to write, in the sense of using words exactly and intelligibly; the appreciation, in that writing, of secondary or particular meanings of words in specific legal contexts; and finally the appreciation and wise choice of approach to a legislative solution, taking into account not only political imponderables, but also the relationship of the proposed act to other statutes, or even to the Constitution itself. . . .

In major bills, . . . private assistance in draftsmanship is usually unnecessary. In such cases, and indeed in most legislation, Congress has had since 1918, and has utilized, the drafting services of the Office of the Legislative Counsel—a title which itself recognizes the legal nature of the work. The Office frees the Congress from the necessity of relying solely upon private parties or the executive agencies of the government, but . . . does not remove either the propriety or in some cases the necessity for private parties to present their own views on problems of draftsmanship or policy.

Let us take another example, somewhat more removed from the direct contact with Congress, but nonetheless lobbying, as we have defined it—that is, activity intended to affect legislative action. This one, as it happens, has its whole background stated in the public record. The salmon canners in Alaska for many years had been engaged in a controversy with the Alaskan Indians and the Department of the Interior concerning the respective rights of the canners and the Indians to fish in certain Alaskan waters. The problem was most acute in respect to fish traps— large, fixed nets—which the canners and others had for many years maintained at strategic locations. The Indian tribes wanted fish traps too, but most of the available locations, or at least most of the best ones, were already pre-empted.

The canners proposed to resolve the controversy by legislation rather than litigation. Being politically practical, however, they recognized that without Department of Interior approval, no legislation would be likely to pass, so they sought the aid of Washington counsel in drafting a bill which would secure that approval and support when it was presented to Congress. Here, the lawyer's problem was partly legal—Indian rights in Alaska are a veritable legal nightmare—but principally the work was practical—how to balance the conflicting equities of the canners and the Indian tribes in order that they both might be more legally secure. Drafts were prepared. Many conferences were held with many Department of Interior officials—its Solicitor, representatives of its Fish and Wildlife and Indian Affairs Divisions, an Assistant Secretary and the Secretary himself. The proposed bill was drafted and redrafted and redrafted. Agreement finally was reached, and the bill was finally introduced at the request of the Department.

This once-removed-from-Congress lobbying is far more usual than might appear. Bills considered by Congress—even private bills—almost always deal with a matter which is of direct concern to some federal department or agency, and they are generally referred to that agency as a matter of course by the congressional committees. Experience teaches that seldom, if ever, does a bill slip by without the agency making its views known—by appearance in a hearing, if the bill gets that far, or by a letter to the committee which may end its legislative flight before it ever gets off the ground. Common prudence dictates, therefore, that before serious attempts are made to secure any legislative action, conferences with the interested government officials are desirable. Perhaps the lawyer's efforts are so fully successful that the bill will be proposed as a government measure. And even though there is usually not a complete agreement, by compromise or otherwise, such as in my fish-trap illustration, at least some areas of disagreement are eliminated, nonsignificant matters can be reconciled, and the later hearings focused on the critical issues. . . .

A lawyer who seeks a change in a provision of the tax law, or who, perchance, wishes to avoid a change in a particular tax provision, will usually start with the office of the Tax Legislative Counsel in the General Counsel's Office of the Treasury Department. . . . By memoranda and personal conferences on the merits of the change, or, if no change is wanted, on the merits of the present law, the lawyer will attempt to persuade the Department to accept and incorporate the lawyer's position in its tax recommendations to Congress. Memoranda and arguments are not only legal, but economic, sociological, and political; in short, in many cases they will include the same material as the departmental staff itself would prepare for the Secretary of the Treasury on the same topic. . . .

In the field of taxes, however, Congress has many ideas of its own which may be quite opposed to those of the Treasury, and for which it relies on the technical services of the staff of the Joint Committee, supplemented by information from the Treasury Department. In such an area—and again it is part of expertise to know where those areas lie—the contacts will begin with that staff, which will be consulted, argued with, and perhaps persuaded to act, or to refrain from acting. Indeed, it is one of the functions of that staff to evaluate and correlate proposals for changes in the tax law from whatever source. To the extent that the Washington lawyer can be of practical assistance to the staff, in preparing an accurate and helpful evaluation and analysis of the tax provisions in which the lawyer is interested, just to that extent may the lawyer expect that he will advantage his client's position. At this level, at least—whatever may be the determinative factors which operate at the congressional committee and floor debate stages—the decisions are almost entirely on the tax merits of the proposal, and a good brief in support of a position is as helpful as it is in a court. And let me repeat it, such activity is not confined to attempts to introduce affirmative changes; tax provisions which are helpful to your clients may equally require effort to keep them in the law.

Let us admit, however, that what we have been talking about thus far is the unusual rather than the usual type of a Washington lawyer's congressional activity. Much more common is the client who is affected by a bill with which he has had nothing to do until it is introduced. Laws being what they are and clients being what they are, more than likely the client wishes that he had never heard of it. What such a client wants is to oppose, or perhaps to favor, that bill. Why does he come to a Washington lawyer?

There are several possibilities. He may wish the lawyer to testify for him. The lawyer, being aware of the fact that on Capitol Hill one constituent is worth a platoon of lawyers, will discourage that proposal, though there are cases in which it is appropriate. . . .

A client may arrive in your office, anxious to oppose or favor a bill. Hearings may have been set, and he wants to appear, and wants you to help him to get ready. There is work for you to do.

Conversation will bring out, painfully or promptly as the case may be, why he takes the position he does, and a general flavor of the reasons he can advance. You are then in a position at once similar to but at the same time very different from that of a lawyer preparing a witness for a trial. True, you don't have to worry about the rules of evidence, but you become more keenly aware of the fact that opinion evidence and sweeping conclusions and generalizations are poor substitutes for carefully circumscribed and documented statements, charts and graphs. You also know that even though you need not fear greatly that irrelevant material will be excluded, your witness will have only a limited amount of time in which to present a position, and time spent on irrelevancies is simply time wasted. You explore the possibility of reasons other than the ones your client has thought of. You imagine all possible arguments on the other side, and determine which ones to try to meet, which ones to ignore, and which ones to try to skate over lightly. And when all of that is done, you make sure that your client understands what you have prepared, agrees with it, and can answer—you hope—such questions as the committee may put to him.

The differences from a judicial proceeding are fundamental in that the issues are always, in the large sense, political. Potential witnesses must be evaluated in terms of at least the states represented by the members of the committee. Members of Congress are not unnaturally interested in what their own constituents have to say. Perhaps such a witness is desirable even if he is not as fully qualified on the merits as you would like; you still need the tangible evidence of his interest and support. Again, the lawyer will attempt to develop, as a political device, a "polar" phrase—"retroactive laws are bad," "natural resources must be conserved," "small business," "injury to competition," "American system of free enterprise," or the like, which can be repeated and repeated. In short, the motivating factors for a member of Congress are not only the intrinsic merits of a proposal, but also its political implications, and neither can be ignored. . . .

Thus far, we would no doubt all agree that the Washington lawyer is largely exercising the normal skills and abilities of the profession—draftsmanship, marshaling of facts, distillation of issues and arguments as well as resolution of purely legal issues. Let us pursue his activities into areas where his work may be less directly legal. Either in connection with some of the activities already described, or independent of them, a Washington lawyer may be brought directly into legislative activity. Let us say that on some particular measure in which a client is interested the lines have begun to be drawn in Congress. Some of the members are known to be on the client's side. Others are doubtful. The lawyer visits, and seeks to persuade, the doubtful ones who are important, using, let us assume . . . the same sort of arguments he has made, or would have made, in a public hearing. Perhaps he may put the essential facts and arguments into a memorandum which can be distributed to many members of Congress.

With a member of Congress who is already on the client's side, the lawyer offers or suggests that he may be of additional help. Perhaps he can prepare helpful questions, or lines of questions, that may be asked during the committee hearings. Possibly he can be useful in composing the committee report. Or, assuming that the bill has reached the floor of either house, he may assist a member of Congress in preparing a speech for their common position. Members of Congress are notoriously overworked, and the lawyer may have the time and the facilities which the member lacks to analyze the record made at the hearings, or to summarize the arguments, or to suggest new ones. If the bill as it emerges from the committees is not entirely clear, and the lawyer can foresee future arguments in the Supreme Court on its proper construction, there may be substantial advantages to the client in suggestions on how the intent of the Congress might be clarified—by speeches which might be made, or by amendments which might be proposed and discussed even if they may ultimately be defeated, or by the sort of legislative cross-examination which smokes out the real purpose of the proposed law through carefully drawn questions addressed to the chairman of the committee which reported the bill, or to its principal proponent in the floor debate.

69. More About Noerr—Lobbying, Antitrust and the Right to Petition

JERROLD L. WALDEN*

14 U.C.L.A. LAW REVIEW 1211 (1967)

In *Eastern R.R. Presidents Conference v. Noerr Motors,*[14] the [United States Supreme] Court unanimously held the Sherman Act inapplicable to a combination of large railroads which had united together to conduct a widespread public relations campaign in favor of state legislation inimical to the welfare of the trucking industry. Underlying the opinion of the Court was the notion that a contrary opinion might raise problems under the right to petition guaranteed by the first amendment. Nonetheless, the plain effect of the ruling has been to turn the legislative halls of the country into a gladiator's arena where potent economic units can joust with one another (unmindful of who gets maimed in the process) under the protective sanction of the Constitution of the United States. That this opinion was written by Mr. Justice Black is particularly surprising in view of his past experience as Chairman of a Senate Committee to investigate lobbying and his onetime sponsorship of a bill to regulate lobbying. It is also contrary to his public recognition of the dangers which lobbying poses which he once expressed in the following terms:

> Contrary to tradition, against the public morals, and hostile to good government, the lobby has reached such a position of power that it threatens government itself. Its size, its power, its capacity for evil; its greed, trickery, deception and fraud condemn it to the death it deserves. . . .

II

In the latter part of 1949, the major railroads in the East launched a vehement public relations campaign against the Amer-

---

* Dean and Professor of Law, University of North Dakota. Copyright ©
UCLA Law Review. Reprinted by permission.
[14] 365 U.S. 127 (1961).

ican trucking industry. The gradual inroad by the truckers into the long-haul freight business of the roads in the post-World War II years was responsible for this action. The reaction of the railroads to this competition was in negative terms with efforts directed more toward impeding the growth of the trucking industry through legislation rather than through offsetting losses by more vigorous competitive practices, increased efficiency, and improved services. It was an acceleration of efforts that had been initiated as far back as the early 1930's to hinder the economic prosperity of the trucking industry through the use of lobbying and propaganda techniques.

In this instance, the campaign of the railroads was organized under the auspices of the Eastern Railroad Presidents Conference, an unincorporated association comprised of the presidents and trustees of some thirty-five railroads operating in the northeastern United States. The Conference had created a Committee on Competitive Transportation, replete with legal, research, and public relations subcommittees. This latter group devised, as a scheme to harass the truckers, proposals for restrictive state legislation to be sponsored by various organizations acting on behalf of the roads but without public disclosure of this relationship. In this connection, the public relations firm of Carl Byoir & Associates, Inc., was selected from a number of eager applicants to assist in effectuating the program. This firm had achieved notable success in the past in a number of similar endeavors[21] and seemed an admirable choice.[22]

Byoir went right to work. In New Jersey, New Jersey Automobile Owners, Inc., was reactivated to front for Byoir and the Presidents Conference. Falsely denying that it was in any way associated with outside interests, this organization, with the support of money contributed by the Byoir firm and charged to the Conference, conducted a forceful campaign for the revision of trucking laws to lower truck weights and increase trucking fees.

---

[21] Among Byoir's many important business clients have numbered such large firms as B. F. Goodrich, Schenley, Bendix Aviation Corporation, American Can Company, RCA, and the Great Atlantic and Pacific Tea Co. . . . Byoir boasted among its successes responsibility for a reduction of almost 50% in severance taxes in Louisiana on behalf of its client, Freeport Sulphur Co. . . . For manufacturers of floor and wall tile, Byoir had several building code changes made in some 2,000 cities. . . . For A & P, Byoir defeated a proposed chain store tax in New York which would have resulted in a $2,000,000 levy on the firm. It also conducted a winning campaign against imposition of a similar federal tax.

[22] Byoir was to be paid $75,000 a year plus all expenses incurred in the venture. It is estimated that the total cost of Byoir's services came to around $500,000 a year. *The Railroad-Trucker Brawl*, Fortune, June 1953, pp. 137, 198.

In this endeavor it was abetted by the New Jersey Citizens Tax Study Foundation, another "front" created by Byoir, which, by working closely with Dr. John S. Sly of Princeton, head of the New Jersey Tax Study Commission, was able to present the views of the railroads regarding the imposition of a weight-distance tax without disclosure of the source of these recommendations. So successful were these efforts that in 1950, certain axle weight limitations were imposed and trucking fees raised by the New Jersey Legislature.

In New York, the railroads paid for an allegedly independent survey of the highways, highway use, and revenues. Byoir operated in New York (as in New Jersey) largely through so-called "front" organizations. The Empire State Transport League was organized in order to distribute vast amounts of anti-truck propaganda throughout the state. Byoir enlisted women's organizations in the cause through the employment of Mrs. Bessie Q. Mott, a "specialist in the field of reaching women's clubs, women's interests," and Vice Chairman of the New York State Federation of Women's Clubs. Mrs. Mott freely used this title in engaging in a wide variety of activities on behalf of the railroads. Other organizations employed in New York to attain the objectives of the railroads were the Citizens Tax League of Rochester and the Citizens' Public Expenditure Survey, Inc. In the course of the New York campaign Byoir's operatives succeeded in persuading such organizations as the Rural Letter Carriers, the Grange, and the Mayors Conference to adopt resolutions demeaning the truckers. Another Byoir activity was the conducting [of] public opinion polls containing questions slanted so as to elicit responses unfavorable to the truckers. The results of the polls were widely disseminated. These efforts proved highly propitious for the railroads; the New York campaign was capped by legislation in April 1951 making New York the first state east of the Mississippi River to impose a substantial mileage tax on trucks.

In other states such as Ohio, results were "little less than phenomenal." Governor Lausche was reelected in 1952 largely on a campaign based on materials supplied by Byoir's agent to impose a ton-tax per mile on trucks. Ultimately, fees on trucks in Ohio were raised as a result of this intensive campaign.

Perhaps the crucial battleground was Pennsylvania, where for many years the railroads had been strongly entrenched in the state's economy. Here, the prevailing weight limit of 45,000 pounds for trucks made the state one of the lowest in the United States and was substantially less than that in force in any of the surrounding states. However, as a result of vigorous lobbying efforts by the truckers, the Pennsylvania Legislature had passed a bill raising the weight limit to 60,000 pounds in the 1951 session. The bill reposed on the Governor's desk for signature when Byoir entered the picture.

In an effort to obtain a gubernatorial veto, Byoir & Associates mustered the tide of public opinion against the bill. This time working through established groups such as the Pennsylvania State Grange and the Pennsylvania State Association of Township Supervisors, Byoir succeeded in stirring up grass roots opposition to the legislation. Indeed, "so insistent . . . was the opposition . . . that the Governor felt obliged to hold public hearings two days before the deadline for his decision. . . ." At this point, "The CB & A team . . . went out and organized twenty-one witnesses for twenty-one organizations against the bill. They prepared their statements and the publicity." In addition to these witnesses, the Governor had the benefit of a report of the tentative results of road tests then being conducted in Maryland to determine the effect of subjecting highways to constant wear by heavy motor vehicles. What he did not know was that the materials constituting this report were prepared in the Byoir office. As a result, the Governor vetoed the bill just six minutes before it would have become law without his signature, thus marking up another triumph for the Byoir campaign on behalf of the roads.

It can be seen from the above that the program adopted by the railroads was a collective plan of attack utilizing public relations counsel to employ so-called "capitalist front groups" to develop public opinion hostile to truckers to such a degree that the promotion of legislation inimical to the trucking interests would be feasible. These aims were facilitated by news releases containing distorted data and employing a technique which the district court characterized as "the 'Big Lie'." In addition, Byoir provided freelance writers with data from its files and secured the publication of articles in magazines with widespread circulations throughout the country.[40] In none of this activity was the true source, Byoir, or the real interests, the railroads, divulged.

The district court, characterizing the Byoir program on behalf of the railroads as a "campaign of vilification," concluded that

---

[40] Among numerous anti-truck articles based in whole or in part upon Byoir supplied data were the following: Brownell, *The Rape of Our Roads*, Readers Digest, June 1950, p. 137; Neuberger, *Who Shall Pay for Our Roads?*, Harpers, Oct. 1952, p. 86; Stearns, *Our Roads are Going to Pot*, Harpers, Sept. 1950, p. 34; Wittels, *Are Trucks Destroying Our Highways?*, Saturday Evening Post, Sept. 16, 1950, p. 19. These and other magazines in which articles based upon Byoir material against the truckers appeared "had a combined nation-wide circulation of almost 20 million in this period." . . .

the roads and Byoir had combined and conspired to restrain trade in violation of the antitrust laws by destroying the good will of the truckers and by promoting legislative restrictions on the development of the trucking industry through the tactics described above. The decision was affirmed by the court of appeals, with one judge dissenting. The Supreme Court of the United States, in a unanimous opinion written by Mr. Justice Black, reversed. The Sherman Act, concluded the Court, did not prohibit two or more persons from combining to secure the enactment of legislation or to influence executive departments, even though the *sole* purpose of undertaking such activity was to destroy competition. A contrary interpretation, said the Court, would raise grave constitutional questions in light of the right to petition guaranteed by the first amendment. While use of the "third party technique" by the employment of front organizations to achieve the desired ends constituted a practice which the Court frankly acknowledged "falls far short of the ethical standards generally approved in this country," this factor, too, was "legally irrelevant." That the truckers may have been injured economically in the process was, in the view of the Court, *damnum absque injuria.* In sum, the Court's decision not only threw the protective cordon of the Constitution around the practice of lobbying, however unethically conducted, but also opened up the legislative halls to all combinations of large interests and pressure groups which might unite to bring economic and political pressure to bear on the legislature. Viewed in this light, the decision poses a serious threat to the continued well being of the national polity.

III

An accurate history of the American legislature requires inclusion of instances of subversion of the legislative process by the lobbying tactics of the large economic interests of the nation. Interests in favor of the tariff descended upon the newly formed Congress as early as 1789, and "since then the hidden hand of the lobbyist has directed the authorship of all tariff bills that have been enacted by Congress." . . . [In 1924] Senator Mc-Kellar, writing in the *New York Times,* drew the following sorry spectacle of the National Capital:

There are lobbyists for the sugar interests, for the steel interests, for the wool interests, for the tobacco interests, for the fertilizer interests, for the cotton manufacturers' interests, for prohibition and anti-prohibition, for postal employees, for labor organizations, for railroads, for Civil Service employees, the equal rights of women, for the bonus, for those opposed to the bonus, for the Mellon plan of tax reduction, for the farmer's organizations, for the shipping interests, for Henry Ford's acquisition of Muscle Shoals, for the water power trust, for the packers, for the oil interests, for the disabled ex-servicemen, for the manufacturers, for the army, for the navy, for national aid to education, and many other special interests. Washington is honey-combed with lobbyists, the hotels are full of them.

Today, over 1,100 private individuals and organizations are officially registered in Washington as lobbyists. Another 500 persons are registered as representatives of foreign concerns or governments. These figures do not include the myriad of "Washington representatives," "five-percenters," attorneys, business associations, and others believing themselves exempt from reporting under the present laws. While these lobbyists in the nation's Capitol represent a broad range of interests, undoubtedly the most significant group from the standpoint of power and influence have been lobbyists for business interests.[60] So much money

---

60 "Business groups remained among the most powerful pressure forces affecting Congress in the 1945-65 post-war era. Taken in the aggregate, business groups were probably the single most powerful pressure force. . . ." CONGRESSIONAL QUARTERLY SERVICE, LEGISLATORS AND THE LOBBYISTS 11 (1965). The financial importance of business influence on the legislative process is shown in the following table indicating the proportionate share of all interest groups which have reported spending under the Federal Regulation of Lobbying Act.

Type of Interest	Expenditures on Lobbying (1948*—1965†)	Percent‡
Business	$36,691,196	41.5
Citizens	12,379,785	14.0
Employee and Labor	12,822,311	14.5
Farm	7,713,344	8.7
Military and Veterans	2,394,531	2.7
Professional	9,912,743	11.2
Other	6,484,257	7.3
TOTAL	$88,398,167	99.9

* 1948, first nine months only.
† 1955, omitted for lack of data.
‡ Lobby Spending, 5-11, 13-22 CONGRESSIONAL QUARTERLY ALMANAC (1944-55, 1957-66).

After the preparation of a similar tabulation of money spent to influence state legislatures, the same conclusion was reached, namely, "the summary impression has to be one of business dominance, at least so far as reported spending is concerned." LANE, LOBBYING AND THE LAW 150 (1964). Another

is spent by these large wielders of political influence that lobbying itself has developed into a "billion dollar" business.[61]

Much of today's lobbying adheres to the traditional pattern of molding legislative behavior. In the forefront, of course, are direct contacts with legislators or executive departments and agencies by interest groups or their representatives. The "social lobby" where legislators are wined and dined sumptuously by those interested in influencing legislation still fills an important role in the repertoire of today's effective lobbyists. There have been no outright instances of open bribery of Senators or Congressmen in recent years, but suspiciously large sums of money have changed hands,[67] often in the form of campaign contributions, and smaller favors have been more openly conferred.

---

study at the state level also found "A greater proportion of lobbyists are employed by business groups than by other groups, and business and professional lobbyists tend to be both better-educated and better-paid for their services than lobbyists for other groups." Patterson, *The Role of the Lobbyist: The Case of Oklahoma*, 25 J. POL. 72, 91 (1963).

[61] H.R. REP. No. 3138, 81st Cong., 2d Sess. 8 (1950). The American Medical Association, for example, is estimated to have spent between $7,000,000 and $12,000,000 in its lobbying campaign against compulsory medical insurance. DEAKIN, [THE LOBBYISTS 23 (1966)]. "Similarly, the oil industry spent at least $20,000,000 and probably $25,000,000 or more to lobby the Harris-Fullbright bill." *Ibid.* Total annual expenses for representative years reported by registered lobbying organizations to influence federal legislation appear in the following table. Again we must emphasize that because of incomplete reporting, these figures reflect only a portion of the funds that are actually spent for lobbying purposes each year.

Year	Spending*
1965	$ 5,484,413
1960	3,854,374
1955	4,365,843
1950	10,303,204
1947	5,191,856

* 22 CONGRESSIONAL QUARTERLY ALMANAC 1796 (1966).

[67] Witness the nearly $100,000 which was transferred to Bobby Baker by high executives of California savings and loan associations in the fall of 1962. Stuart Davis, Chairman of Great Western Financial Corporation, testified at the Baker trial that he handed Baker two envelopes in the Statler Hotel in Washington, D.C. on October 21, 1962. One of these envelopes contained the sum of $33,000; the other, $17,100. [Reported in the New York Times,] Jan. 13, 1967, p. 20, cols. 1-2. J. F. Marten, President of Great Western Financial Corporation, gave Baker another envelope containing $16,200 ten days later at the Carlton Hotel. *Ibid.* Mark Taper of First Charter Finance Corporation transmitted an additional $33,000 to Baker on November 9, 1962, all in $100 bills. *Id.*, Jan. 17, 1967, p. 23, col. 1. This money was

With the advent of mass communications media and the development of the art of public relations, lobbying has taken on a new twist. True, the familiar letter campaign is still employed, often with some measure of success; and personal influence continues to rank high among the salable talents of the professional lobbyist. Nonetheless, new techniques that have been adopted are much more subtle and, in the long run, more effective as well. Characteristic of the "new lobbying" is the expenditure of huge sums to underwrite massive advertising and public relations campaigns on behalf of public issues in which particular groups maintain an interest. The objective, of course, is to arouse public opinion which can then be brought to bear upon the legislature. This technique was used to good effect by the railroads in the *Noerr* case, as has already been pointed out. These more refined lobbying techniques successfully combine the effort of the skilled public relations specialist with those of the experienced lobbyist in an almost irresistible combination.

Today a broad-scale lobbying effort directed towards the enactment or defeat of major legislation brings to bear a panoply of weapons aimed at the vitals of the legislative process. In all probability, a professional lobbyist of considerable experience will be employed at a handsome fee. The person selected may be a former government employee who once ranked high in admin-

---

reputedly delivered in the form of campaign contributions "so that there would be an open door when legislation came along affecting their interests," *id.*, Jan. 20, 1967, p. 34, col. 1, although Senators for whom the money was presumably destined never received a cent. *Id.*, Jan. 13, 1967, p. 20, col. 1. Baker testified that this money was delivered to Senator Kerr. *Id.*, Jan. 21, 1967, p. 12, col. 3, and some $42,950 in cash was discovered in his safe deposit box upon the latter's untimely demise. *Id.*, Jan. 26, 1967, p. 19, col. 5. While the disposition of the proceeds still remains a controversial subject, it is certainly highly coincidental that all of these transactions were initiated at a time when Congress was considering the Revenue Act of 1962, 76 Stat. 960 (1962) (codified in scattered sections of 26 U.S.C.), which imposed substantial tax increases on savings and loan associations. As passed by the House, savings and loan associations were permitted to add 60% of their taxable income to their reserves in computing taxes. The Senate, however, had amended the bill at the behest of Senator Kerr to reduce the reserves allowed *stock* savings and loan associations to 50% of taxable income, thereby imposing an additional $10,000,000 in taxes on stock companies. S. REP. NO. 1881, 87th Cong., 2d Sess. (1962); 108 CONG. REC. 17759 (1962). Mr. Childs, former President of the Home Savings & Loan Association of Los Angeles, was introduced to Senator Kerr on September 24, 1962, by Glenn S. Troop, lobbyist for the U.S. Savings & Loan League while the bill was in conference, and it was on this date that Childs told Baker he would proceed to secure contributions from the industry. *Mirabile dictu*, on the very next day, the Senate conferees receded on the issue of a tax differential on stock savings and loan associations! N.Y. Times, Sept. 26, 1962, p. 18, col. 6; H.R. CONF. REP. NO. 2508, 87th Cong., 2d Sess. (1962).

istration echelons,[75] or perhaps an ex-Congressman or Senator. All the better if he possesses his personal key to the inner sanctums of the legislature. In any event, he will no doubt make discrete contacts with appropriate personages at the proper times. In addition, the advice of public relations departments or counsel will be sought in undertaking to stir up grass roots sentiment throughout the land by means of dissemination of a voluminous amount of propaganda on the general subject accompanied by vigorous exhortations to write or call on Congress. As a result, a stream of letters and telegrams will subsequently deluge the offices of unwitting legislators. If all goes well, the source of this spontaneous public groundswell will remain wholly concealed from both Congress and the general public. In conjunction with these efforts, campaign contributions may also be discretely seeded among selected legislators to muster support where needed.

As a result of these frenzied activities, the public interest may be the last to receive consideration in the enactment of legislation, for as a practical matter, the legislative process, because of lobbying and public relations techniques such as those described, will have aborted and been converted into a mere public ceremony fulfilling the formal requisites for legislation demanded by law but with results long since foreordained by lobbyists who have drawn the initial bills, selected committee witnesses and

---

[75] In view of the significance of personal contacts in the lobbying profession, it is not surprising to find many ex-government officials now earning a livelihood in the business of lobbying. The table below shows some former federal officials who have acted or whose law firms have acted as lobbyists in recent years as revealed by various registration laws.

Name of Official	Former Position in Government*
Dean Acheson	Secretary of State (1949-53)
Bernard L. Boutin	Administrator, GSA (1961-65)
Ralph Casey	GAO (1948-55); General Counsel House Committee on Merchant Marine & Fisheries (1955-56)
Oscar Chapman	Secretary of Interior (1949-53)
Donald S. Dawson	Adm. Ass't to President Truman (1947-53)
Michael B. Deane	Commerce, ECA, Tariff Commission Official (1936-53)
Edward F. Howry	Chairman, FTC (1953-55)
Fowler Hamilton	Administrator, AID (1961-62)
Paul Porter	Administrator, OPA (1946)
Kenneth C. Royall	Secretary of the Army (1947-49)

* 21 CONGRESSIONAL QUARTERLY ALMANAC 1460-61 (1965).

prepared their testimony, written speeches and articles for Congressmen, drafted committee reports, and seen to it that the voting tallies have been made far in advance of the sounding of the bells summoning legislators to the Chambers for the measure's consideration. Under these circumstances, Congress becomes transformed into one of Plato's shadows in the cave, confined to acting out a miracle play on behalf of the true functionaries of American Government, the lobbyists and pressure groups.

IV

Public controls over the general field of lobbying have been ill-defined and poorly drawn. The more blatant forms, such as outright bribery, have been directly prohibited. But, aside from some minor statutory restrictions contained in the Public Utility Holding Company Act of 1935 and the Merchant Marine Act of 1936, the principal statute affecting lobbying has been the Federal Regulation of Lobbying Act, a misnomer since the act contains no prohibitions or regulations governing lobbying activities.

However, the Federal Regulation of Lobbying Act does provide a scheme for registration and reporting by paid lobbyists and for the filing of statements by those who solicit and expend funds for the purpose of influencing legislation. Section 305 of the act, for example, requires that all persons receiving contributions or making expenditures to enact legislation or to influence the passage of legislation before Congress must keep detailed records of contributions and expenditures and provide quarterly summaries thereof to the Clerk of the House. Section 308 requires registration with both the Clerk of the House and the Secretary of the Senate and the filing with them of quarterly reports by lobbyists, that is, by all persons engaged for pay to influence the passage or defeat of any legislation in Congress. The United States Supreme Court held in *United States v. Harriss* [347 U.S. 612 (1954)] that these sections must be read in conjunction with section 307, thereby severely restricting the general coverage of the statute. Under the Court's interpretation, the act does not apply to persons or organizations which spend their own resources to help defeat or enact legislation no matter how heavy these expenditures may be. Nor does the law affect persons soliciting or expending money unless the *principal purpose* thereof is to influence legislation. This means that behemoth lobbying organizations such as the NAM and the Chamber of Commerce, for example, have been able to lay claim to being largely immune from the requirements of the law. A person is required to register as a lobbyist under section 308 only if he does so for pay and his principal purpose is to

influence legislation. Finally, presumably in order to assure the
constitutionality of the act, the Court has indicated that it is applicable only to "lobbying in its commonly accepted sense," that is,
to making direct contacts with Congress, and that it does not
include indirect or "grass roots" lobbying.

The Federal Regulation of Lobbying Act leaves much to be
desired. Because the act imposes no regulations, unimpeded lobbying in all forms is permitted. Further, although it is a disclosure act, many exceptions and limitations have been read into
its provisions. Thus, what remains undisclosed may be greater in
dimension than that which is revealed. In other words, however
desirable it may be to know the extent of lobbying in the legislative halls, this is not accomplished to any reliable extent by
the law as now written and construed. Nor does the act extend
to pressures exerted upon administrative agencies which are perhaps even more susceptible prey to the lobbyist than is Congress.
Another deficiency is the lack of provision for administration;
unless some complaint is made, the law is largely unenforced. . . .

Results at the state level, where regulation of lobbying has
been of longer duration, have hardly been better. While a few
states have, under certain circumstances, prohibited lobbying altogether, the majority of states regulating lobbying have done so
on the basis of full disclosure laws. The multitude of state registration laws have had a checkerboard history and yielded a minimum of results, with the unfortunate consequence that the
state legislatures today continue to fall victim to large lobbying
interests.

70. Administrative Regulation: A Study in Representation of Interests[*]

AVERY LEISERSON

[C]onflicts of organized-producer interests . . . are marked by their special vocational character as opposed to the unorganized universal interest of man as a consumer. . . .

It is true that women's organizations and consumers' leagues purport to represent the general consumer interest, but when they are effectively organized their activity is concentrated upon support of special objectives, such as lower prices, higher minimum wages for women, elimination of child labor, and so on. A further weakness of consumer organizations is their lack of effective economic strength. Economic power depends upon a collective ability to withhold or to withdraw goods or services demanded by other economic groups. Consumer organizations too often are organized around the intellectual interests of scattered individuals and are not organized so as to exert a compelling influence over particular producers in the market. For this reason consumers' general interests in low utility rates or commodity prices are often far more effectively represented by producers organizations that are not primarily consumers but whose costs are adversely affected by material and supply prices.

In view of this lack of an organized group constituency, an idealistic assumption has arisen that the government should, if it does not, represent consuming interests. It is notorious, however, that governmental bodies engaged in research to protect the consumer by letting him know what he is buying, such as the Bureau of Agricultural Economics, the Bureau of Chemistry, the Food and Drug Administration, the Bureau of Standards, are continually hampered by the opposition of producer groups not effectively counterbalanced by consumer organizations except as other producer groups may be favorably affected by the results of research. This is also true of the work of the Food and Drug

---

[*] Professor of Political Science, Vanderbilt University. Published by University of Chicago Press. Reprinted from pp. 49-51, by permission.

Administration and the Federal Trade Commission in exposing and prohibiting acts of misrepresentation and deception, although the Federal Trade Commission has self-initiating powers of a prosecuting nature which the research agencies do not possess. Unimplemented by the activities of a so-called group constituency, government agencies, to whom the task of representing or protecting a general consumer interest is delegated, are extremely handicapped.

NOTES AND QUESTIONS

1. This section deals with the influence of interest groups on the making of policy and law. Political scientists, in analyzing how law and policy are formed, have come more and more to look to the influence of interest groups, and to downgrade the influence of the general public. The concept of "the public" has not seemed meaningful. What is often referred to as "the public" is really a great number of publics; each "public" is interested in some issues but is profoundly apathetic about others. Interest groups are organized about concrete issues and interest; they originate when a group of people recognize "an identity of interests," and are "willing to organize or act in concert to promote and defend their interest . . . by attempting to shape public policy." Richard W. Gable, "Interest Groups as Policy Shapers," 319 *The Annals of the American Academy of Political and Social Science* 84 (Sept. 1958). When does an interest group succeed in shaping policy? According to Gable, it is "when it is able to identify its conception of the needs of the moment with the prevailing or predominant attitudes of a number of prominent publics and when it has access to the major centers of policy decision in government." Use of propaganda is one way interest groups attempt to mobilize other publics to support their aims. Access means opportunity, ability and skill in communicating with legislators and other persons in authority.

Gable states that there is a "fundamental paradox" in the role played by interest groups in American society. These groups are "necessary and essential elements in our policymaking process, but at the same time they can impair the effective operation of representative democracy." Also, interest groups are expected to exert influence, but officials are expected to resist that influence.

What evidence is there in Horsky and Walden confirming the existence of this "paradox"?

2. One can argue, as do many political scientists, that "pressure politics" is not only inevitable, but also desirable. Horsky is in this camp: although he recognizes some dangers, he stresses

the positive functions performed by the lawyer in his lobbyist role. The lawyer-lobbyist, for example, acts as a channel for conveying information to the legislator about the views of the group which the lobbyist represents. He helps to keep the legislator abreast of the meaning and impact of proposed, existing and pending legislation. Despite these functions, is it also possible that certain important interests will be short-changed?

Robert Paul Wolff argues that not only are some groups ignored in American pluralist politics but that pluralism is suited primarily for the solution of problems of distributive justice. Insofar as a social ill is caused by something other than the maldistribution of wealth, the system fails to offer ways of curing it. He asserts that "natural beauty, public order, the cultivation of the arts are not the special interest of any identifiable social group." As a result, one cannot solve problems here by redistributing wealth, the classic remedy of pluralism. Wolff, "Beyond Tolerance," in *A Critique of Pure Tolerance* 3, 49-50 (Beacon Press 1965).

3. There is an enormous literature on the particular type of interest-group activity called lobbying. Both Horsky and Walden, of course, deal with it. Many political scientists have written about lobbying, for example, Lester Milbrath in *Washington Lobbyists* (Rand McNally 1963). A recent article, "The Effects of Lobbying: A Comparative Assessment," by Harmon Zeigler (in Norman Luttbeg, ed., *Public Opinion and Public Policy: Models of Political Linkage,* Dorsey Press 1968, at 184) reviews the literature on the role of lobbyists in the legislative process. One group of authors argues that lobbyists are exceedingly powerful. This belief, which Zeigler calls the "mechanistic" theory, claims that lobbyists (and other interest groups) operate as powerful "transmission belts" between individual needs and government agencies. In a complex society, "secondary associations" replace "primary associations" as the "essential group referents of individuals." Individuals do not influence government as individuals. Political parties are too diffuse to act as good channels for communicating individual wants and needs to the government. Interest groups fill in the gap. They "channel communications to decision makers"; they "help structure alternative policy choices . . . help check demands made by others." They "provide functional representation." The essence of interest-group theories is that "interest groups are powerful because they monopolize access to governmental decision makers."

Some recent writers, however, have felt that there are difficulties with the mechanistic model. They find that the effects of lobbying have been much exaggerated. Lobbyists may be only a "relatively minor factor in the ultimate decision." It may even be that the lobbyists "could very easily be eliminated from the decision-making process without any appreciable change in public policy."

Zeigler's own essay is an attempt to study six states and find out which view is correct. He finds that the lobby is stronger and more effective in some states than others, and that the effect of the lobby is not easily summarized. To take one example of the variability of lobbying phenomena: Zeigler's data showed that there were many more interactions in some states between legislators and lobbyists than in others. Legislators in Oregon reported a mean of 34 interactions a week with lobbyists; legislators in Massachusetts reported a mean of 7.8. This and other differences could be accounted for in a number of ways. Structural differences between legislatures might be a factor. Some states have more legislators than others; if there are many legislators, "interaction" becomes more inefficient and costly. Cultural differences (differences in attitudes toward lobbyists and interest groups), and social and economic differences between the states in general may also play a part.

Zeigler's conclusion, after examining a number of other empirical findings in the six states studied, is that neither of the two general models can be called "universally applicable"; this suggests that "less inclusive theories are more useful."

If forced to choose between the "mechanistic" model and its opposite, which one would Horsky pick? Walden?

What revisions in Buchanan and Tullock's picture of the legislative process (Reading 6, at 56, *supra*) are rendered necessary by the material on lobbying? Is less violence done to their viewpoint if one accepts the anti-mechanistic model? Why? Which of the two models would be more congenial to Friedman and Ladinsky and their theory of the rise of the workmen's compensation statutes? Which one would be more likely to appeal to Mills, Spartacist, and Golunskii and Strogovich? Does Walden's article support the attack on the pluralist theory of American politics which these authors make?

If Zeigler is right, and neither model is "universally applicable," what factors would you guess would be most cogent in explaining differences between the various states? Also, would the effectiveness of lobbying depend upon the *subject* of the lobbying?

Note that if no one view of lobbying is correct, if lobbying differs from state to state, if it varies with the subject matter of the lobbying, if, in short, it is a highly complex phenomenon, then the problems of coping with lobbying through legislation are much greater than one might imagine if one took a more simplistic view of lobbying. What additional data, if any, would you need before you could rationally decide under what circumstances the lobbyist ought to be regulated and how regulation might be made effective? In what regards do present statutes (as described by Walden) fail to measure up? What should the aim of legislation be—to curb "abuses" such as those described by Walden, or to restructure the system so that more groups can effectively lobby, or to do some of both? Can you suggest reform measures which would be effective and at the same time politically realistic?

4. How might one go about *measuring* the impact of a lobbyist? Would it be fair to count the number of bills enacted that met with the approval of the lobby? Would one have to consider the extent to which a proposed bill was modified in the legislature? For an attempt to measure pressure group success, *see* Lawrence D. Longley, "Interest Group Interaction in a Legislative System," 29 *Journal of Politics* 637 (1967), a study of pressure groups in Tennessee. In that state, the attitude of the governor toward proposed legislation turned out to be a factor of prime importance in determining success or failure of enactment.

71. Individual Freedom and Governmental Restraints

WALTER GELLHORN*

Until the end of the nineteenth century, few occupations other than those of the lawyer and the physician were subject to state licensing. There were, of course, departures from the norm. Ohio, for example, began to license insurance solicitors in 1830, a year before attorneys were reached and 66 years before physicians came under regulation in that state. By and large, however, only three learned professions—law, medicine, and the ministry—were recognized; and only the first two of these were subject to licensing.

But with the twentieth century came a veritable deluge of licensing laws. By 1952 more than 80 separate occupations, exclusive of "owner-businesses" like restaurants and taxicab companies, had been licensed by state law; and in addition to the state laws there are municipal ordinances in abundance, not to mention the federal statutes that require the licensing of such diverse occupations as radio operators and stockyard commission agents. As long ago as 1938 a single state, North Carolina, had extended its laws to 60 occupations. One may not be surprised to learn that pharmacists, accountants, and dentists have been reached by state laws, as have sanitarians and psychologists, assayers and architects, veterinarians and librarians. But with what joy of discovery does one learn about the licensing of threshing machine operators and dealers in scrap tobacco? What of egg graders and guide-dog trainers, pest controllers and yacht salesmen, tree surgeons and well diggers, tile layers and potato growers? And what of the hypertrichologists who are licensed in Connecticut, where they remove excessive and unsightly hairs with the solemnity appropriate to their high-sounding title?

The orotundity of the hypertrichological nomenclature, while inescapably reminiscent of the ditch digger who insisted that he be called a drainage engineer, is perhaps suggestive of a more

* Betts Professor, Columbia University School of Law. Copyright © 1956 Louisiana State University Press. Reprinted from pp. 106-26, 140-44, by permission.

significant sociological development. Differentiating the professions from mere jobs is becoming increasingly difficult, if not impossible. The Church and medicine and law were early recognized as professions because, first, "their practice is based upon the theoretical study of a department of learning" and, second, "the individuals who follow them are bound to follow a certain mode of behavior and are so regarded by the public." The force of these supposedly distinguishing characteristics has much diminished through the years. Dr. Thomas Parran, former Surgeon General of the United States and now dean of the Graduate School of Public Health at the University of Pittsburgh, asserts that nurses and other "semi-professionals" must nowadays "master a body of knowledge greater in extent and usefulness for the care of the sick than all of the medical knowledge of a century ago. In addition, they have codes of ethics and possess techniques as exact as those of the brain surgeon." Moreover, the expansion of cafeteria style, tax-supported universities and colleges attended by hordes of young men and women intent solely upon vocational training as funeral directors, sales executives, hotel managers, commercial artists, playground supervisors, or the like—but all of whom are deemed to be educated in the end because they are, after all, college graduates—has made it difficult to say that this occupation is "learned" while that one is not. Greater urbanization has, in addition, made for a mounting specialization. Activities have been ever more narrowly defined. The expert or specialist has come into his own, respected for his grasp of the knowledge pertinent to his fragment of human activity. But because the specialist deals only with a fragment, he is not thought to deserve any particular deference outside that sphere. Finally, the professional man today only rarely exhibits the selflessness that once set him somewhat apart from the ordinary herd. If the professional man's dedication to the common weal was, as Harold Laski less generously believed, merely "the maintenance of the elaborate pretence of a very remote interest in the financial return for his work," then, at any rate, a skeptical generation has found the elaborate pretence less effective than perhaps it formerly was. . . .

[L]et it not be thought that occupational licensing has always, or even chiefly, been imposed rather than induced. Public recognition of scandalous conditions has occasionally led to licensing against the wishes of the licensees, as when New York and New Jersey, stirred by reports of criminality on the waterfront, forbade the employment of any dock-worker who had not first obtained the Waterfront Commission's blessing; or as when stock exchanges and brokers came under federal licensing after the financial debacle of 1929. Again, the large individual responsibility borne by physicians or lawyers, whose attentions are so important to the persons they serve but so little subject to their informed judgment, created demands from outside as well as from inside the medical and legal professions that their qualifications be tested. These, however, are the rarities. In the main, those already within the occupational group clamor for licensing, always, of course, upon the stated ground that thus the public will receive protection against the incompetent or unscrupulous—but always, also, with other less emphasized purposes. One of these is to achieve a competitive advantage or an enlarged income. The other, of an emotional rather than economic nature, though in some instances of possibly even larger importance, is to achieve a formalized recognition of the knowledge, skill, and probity required of a conscientious practitioner. Be he chiropodist or chiropractor, tile layer or horseshoer, photographer or watchmaker, dry cleaner or embalmer, the sound man may yearn for professional status and social advancement.

Successful campaigns to achieve licensure may in point of fact produce some gain for the community as a whole. Personal ambition, whether economic or social, does very often realize itself through creating some common good, as a sort of by-product. Moreover, swindlers and incompetents may in actuality be somewhat hindered by licensing laws, so that the public interest may to that extent be served just as the proponents of licensing asserted would be the case. It is hard to believe, however, that legislators are responding to any felt public need when they agree that florists and beauticians and naturopaths and shorthand reporters and all the other groupings must first be tested, sifted, and pasteurized—and then be protected against the competition of upstarts who might like to enter the occupation.

The pattern of pressure is the same all over the country. In a single session of the New Jersey legislature calls were heard for the licensing of bait fishing-boats, beauty shops, chain stores, florists, insurance adjusters, photographers, and master painters. In no instance did the calls come from citizens who had suffered at the hands of members of those groups. They came always from the affected businessmen themselves—men who probably enjoyed cursing the government for interfering with private business, but who at the same time besought their own licensing. Typically they proposed that persons already within the occupation be licensed without examination, but they prescribed extensive tests, qualifications, and delays for those who wished to share the occupational glory after passage of the law. A Wisconsin legislator, having observed the pressures at work in that state, concluded sadly that her six-year-old son could no longer reasonably aspire to become a watchmaker in Wisconsin though, fortunately, he might still hope to become President of the United States.

Who is there to resist the endeavors of the "ins" to make certain that the "outs" will remain out? Obviously those who may in future find themselves excluded from an occupation, or delayed in their entry into it, are not yet aware of the difficulties they will face; unorganized and, indeed, unknown, they remain unrepresented while licensing is debated. Who can present the public's opinion of whether it will or will not be disadvantaged by recognition of yet another profession or sub-profession? The "public" has no spokesman in these matters. Occasionally a group already on the inside will rise in might to prevent others from gaining status through licensing. The medical associations of New York, for example, managed until 1956 to thwart the ambitions of that state's psychologists, who had long been agitating for the imposition of "professional standards" upon them; and the osteopaths, having achieved New York licensure in 1907, now join with the physicians to beat off the chiropractors who actively seek a similar recognition. Unless there chances to be some such competition of ambitions, campaigns to become licensed are likely to be unopposed by anything other than inertia, a doughty foe indeed, but one that habitually yields to sustained pressure.

Some Social Consequences

Like most things of interest, occupational licensing is neither all good nor all bad. Some positive advantages do undoubtedly flow from it to the public at large as distinct from the licensees. For example, an individual who believes himself wronged by a licensee's poor service or sharp dealing may perhaps gain redress more simply and more cheaply through a licensing board than if he were remitted to a judicial remedy. Indeed, if only small sums of money are involved, the judicial remedy may be wholly illusory, while the administrative remedy may be quickly available. That much is clearly a gain. So, too, there may be gain for the public in discouraging the entrance into an occupation of unsuitable persons. Doomed from the start, they may, in their desperate efforts to survive, adopt unethical practices that debase their competitors as well. . . . [But] now, in mid-twentieth century, question arises whether the contemporary emphasis upon occupational licensing may not tend to lead us backward from a society of hopeful movement into a society of status. . . .

The philosophy of free competition has dominated the economic growth of America. Of course it has never become an obsession. At no time since the first colonists set foot on this continent has there been a policy of complete laissez faire, and one shudders to contemplate any such policy today. Nonetheless, except in the case of the so-called "natural" monopolies, governmental influence has traditionally been used to support and not to limit competition, to encourage and not to restrict personal, economic, and social mobility. That tradition, whether for good or ill, is in process of drastic revision today.

The thrust of occupational licensing, like that of the guilds, is toward decreasing competition by restricting access to the occupation; toward a definition of occupational prerogatives that will debar others from sharing in them; toward attaching legal consequences to essentially private determinations of what are ethically or economically permissible practices. . . .

State statutes sometimes allow licensed groups to govern themselves all but completely, for all the world as the guilds once did. The lawyers of California, for example, are members of an "integrated bar"—which means that they must be members of a professional association with major responsibility to examine, admit, govern, and expel them; more than half the states have similarly transformed the legal profession into an approximation of an autonomous guild. Other "professions" have been eager to enjoy the same potent independence. Thus, the chiropodists of North Carolina function under the control of a board of examiners appointed by the state pedic association and, suitably, the board reports annually to the association rather than to the governor; and in Oklahoma the dentists, flattering the lawyers by imitating them, successfully campaigned for legislative recognition of The Registered Dentists of Oklahoma, who now manage their own affairs without the intrusion of the people's representatives.

Price-fixing powers are often conferred on licensing bodies only nominally divorced from those whose prices are fixed; not unusually the powers are to be exercised in accordance with the petition or the agreement of a stated percentage of those affected. The professed reason, as a report of the Council of State Governments recently noted, is to prevent price cutting to such an extent that sanitary and health laws might be ignored in the race to show profits despite low incomes. But since only the raising of prices is allowed, and their reduction is forbidden even when the asserted occasion for their having been raised no longer exists, some question remains as to whether protection of health and sanitation is the primary objective. . . .

The field of operation having been marked out and surrounded by a high fence, those who did the marking and the fencing are loath to admit others into the fraternity. Extravagantly difficult entrance requirements are devised. In some states a high school graduate who aspires to be a master plumber must undergo a longer course of preparation than a classmate who wishes to be a physician or surgeon. When apprenticeships must be served in order to qualify for licensed status, there is no assurance that apprentices will be accepted by the masters to whom they must be articled, or that the training they will receive will in fact be related to their needs. Examination fees are set at high enough levels—sometimes as much as $100 though usually less—to discourage some who might otherwise gamble on passing an examination and being admitted. A few atypical labor unions have been roundly and no doubt rightly criticized for raising initiation fees so steeply that prospective members have been repelled rather than attracted—the glaziers in Chicago, for example, with their $1,500 fee or the truckers in Seattle with their fee of $500. As in the licensed occupations, the reason is plain. High hourly wage rates attained through collective pressure attract recruits to the trade, just as do high earnings attributable to the incomplete competition achieved through exclusionary licensing. Hence, unless something is done to frighten these hopeful newcomers away from the favored area, the number of workers may increase disproportionately to the number of jobs. Successful efforts to attain a preferred economic position may therefore unleash the most vigorous activity to prevent others from sharing it. . . .

The Intrusion of Irrelevancies

Precisely because state power is so little subject to check in this field, special care must be taken to forestall the intrusion of irrelevancies into licensing statutes. Occasionally they do creep in with a certain careless gaiety, as when Georgia enacted that each applicant for a commercial photographer's license must "submit a certificate from the board of health, showing a negative Wasserman test," or when Michigan sought to compel all barbers to be American citizens, a requirement that New York attempted also to impose upon masseurs and chauffeurs. But even the seemingly irrelevant may be sustained by a court reluctant to substitute its judgment for that of the legislature. The Supreme Court, for example, sustained a local requirement that pool hall operators be American citizens, saying merely that while the premise upon which this requirement apparently rests may not be well founded in experience, there might be local conditions unknown to the Court that would afford a rational basis for the legislative decision. And, rational or not, citizenship has come to be an unchallenged requirement for large numbers of occupations to which it has no discernible relevance. One may perhaps argue reasonably that lawyers should be citizens because their work cuts to the heart of our governmental processes and they are by definition "officers of the court," though in Britain, from which we derive so much of our professional tradition, one may be a barrister while still an alien. Not even a semblance of plausibility supports an argument that chiropodists, tree surgeons, and embalmers (among many others) must be eligible to vote before they may become eligible to seek a license.

Since 1886 race and religion have been recognized to be improper elements for consideration in connection with licensing; nevertheless they may continue to be operative though concealed factors. . . .

The Problem of Administration

Earlier pages have suggested that decisions in the licensing field may be affected by the character of the agencies that regulate an occupation—ostensibly in the public interest. A further word deserves to be said on that score.

Seventy-five per cent of the occupational licensing boards at work in this country today are composed exclusively of licensed practitioners in the respective occupations. These men and women, most of whom are only part-time officials, may have a direct economic interest in many of the decisions they make concerning admission requirements and the definition of standards to be observed by licensees. More importantly, they are as a rule directly representative of organized groups within the occupation. Ordinarily they are nominated by these groups as a step toward a gubernatorial or other appointment that is frequently a mere formality. Often the formality is dispensed with entirely, appointment being made directly by the occupational associations—as happens, for example, with the embalmers in North Carolina, the dentists in Alabama, the psychologists in Virginia, the physicians in Maryland, and the attorneys in Washington. This virtual capturing of the licensing bodies has been justified on the ground that thus political patronage and partisanship have been excluded, while expert and informed administration has been assured.

A less enthusiastic view would be that thus general consideration of the public interest has been effectively subordinated to particularized consideration of group advantage. The latter is not invariably opposed to the former, but the possibility of conflict arises frequently enough to warrant more detachment than the present system assures.

Constricting an appointing authority's choice of personnel to carry out statewide policies has been severely criticized by political scientists, as has the transfer of administrative power directly into the hands of those who are to be regulated. Experience has confirmed the theoretical objections. Minorities within an occupation tend to be ignored when the regulators are chosen by or are sympathetically associated with the dominant element. Agencies composed of public servants, according to one investigation of public administration, "are, for the most part, making an intelligent and conservative use of their Rule-Making Power— while on the other hand, those agencies which are manned, not by State employees, but by members of the vocation and occupation which they purport to regulate, are, for the most part, using the Rule-Making Power far in excess of that which could have been reasonably contemplated by the General Assembly." The investigators reported among their "most prominent discoveries" that "the rules promulgated in many instances unreasonably curtail the free exercise of competition and . . . that admission itself to some of the professions and vocations is unreasonably restricted." . . .

It is not necessary to think of occupational boards as selfish, venal, or arrogant in order to think of them as inept, inefficient, and costly. Government is surely as serious and complicated a profession (or art or trade) as, say, chiropody, manicuring, or horseshoeing. Accordingly, there is no more reason to imagine that a horseshoer can be a good bureaucrat than to imagine that a bureaucrat can be a good horseshoer. A man may be a master at paring a callus without achieving competence to conduct the formal disciplinary proceedings of a regulatory body dealing with chiropodists. The proliferation of separate boards, each staffed with experienced craftsmen who are wholly inexperienced in statecraft, gives little assurance that laws will be executed effectively. Nor does duplication of files, staffs, facilities, and offices reduce the costs of state government.

The argument is made, however, that only a board drawn from the regulated occupation can have the technical proficiency required for evaluation of license applicants. The solution of this difficulty lies not, as is supposed, in creating more and more trade-minded boards. It lies, rather, in creating a responsible administrative body that, if need be, may employ vocationally experienced staff members and that should in all instances recruit suitable advisory groups from within the affected occupation. A searching and fair chiropodist's examination cannot be drafted by a lawyer or a clergyman or a statistician; but if a licensing agency were made up of such a trio, they need not divorce themselves from the insights others can contribute. . . .

In short, expertness is needed in administering licensing programs as well as other regulatory programs. In the complex modern world, the needed expertness is that of the generalist who can weave together into a workable whole the separate expertness of the specialists.

NOTES AND QUESTIONS

1. Gellhorn concludes that occupational licensing has "gone too far. It compresses rather than liberates the economy, stratifies society instead of furthering its democratization." He makes a number of recommendations for curbing its excesses. He suggests that it "should be reserved for special cases," only when "an occupation of critical public importance has been overrun . . . by persons insensitive to their responsibilities," or when "theoretical training is a necessary step toward achieving occupational competence." Presumably most licensing laws would not survive these tests.

Gellhorn also suggests that "certification" should often be used instead of licensing. For example, some nurses are entitled to be designated as "registered nurses." In some states, anybody may "nurse the infirm for pay"; but if someone wants a *trained* nurse, "the certification of those who are registered serves to indicate the individuals of supposedly greater worth." In some states, anyone may perform "architectural planning and design," but only certified persons may call themselves "architects." Gellhorn thinks that this device informs and protects the public, without the harmful side effects that flow from the indiscriminate use of licensing.

2. For further information on occupational licensing, *see* Corrinne Lathrop Gilb, *Hidden Hierarchies: The Professions and Government* (Harper 1966); William Goode, "Community Within a Community: The Professions," 22 *American Sociological Review* 195 (1957); William Goode, "Encroachment, Charlatanism and the Emerging Professions: Psychology, Sociology, and Medicine," 25 *American Sociological Review* 905 (1960); Ronald L. Akers, "The Professional Association and the Legal Regulation of Practice," 2 *Law & Society Review* 463 (1968). On the rise of occupational licensing, with an attempt to explain some facets of the astounding growth of this form of "control," *see* Lawrence M. Friedman, "Freedom of Contract and Occupational Licensing 1890-1910: A Legal and Social Study," 53 *California Law Review*

487 (1965). See, further, the section of these materials on "Regulation by the Regulated," at 441-70, *supra*.

3. Is the manipulative use of law for "selfish" economic interests inherent in a system of representative republican government? Why have the occupations been so successful in selling a bill of goods to the legislatures—and the public? Consider the relevance of the analysis in Buchanan & Tullock, Reading 6, at 56, *supra*. Is excess occupational licensing an example of what they term "overinvestment"? Are Gellhorn's proposals for reform (¶ 1, above) hopelessly impractical? How can the excesses of occupational licensing be trimmed within the present political system?

4. Many of the readers of these materials are prospective lawyers. To what extent do you think that Gellhorn's analysis applies to the legal profession? Should lawyers be "certified" but not given an exclusive right to practice law? What about surgeons? Professor Milton Friedman, of the University of Chicago Department of Economics, argues that free entry into the practice of medicine would produce many social gains, including more and better doctors, wide varieties of insurance and prepayment plans, and forms of group practice likely to cut costs. *See* M. Friedman, *Capitalism and Freedom* 137 (U. of Chicago Press 1962). How would these benefits come about? To what extent, in practice, does the medical profession now have a "certification" system without the advantages of free entry?

5. Gellhorn's materials deal with the external relations of occupational groups. One must also consider the internal politics of occupations. Who does the "organized" bar, medical profession, or barbers' profession represent? to what degree are these occupational groups "democratic"? to what degree can they be? Should their internal workings be regulated by government? If so, why and how? Questions similar to those raised above concerning occupational groups can also be raised about interest groups in general. How "democratic" are farm groups, trade associations, unions? How closely do they "represent" their constituents? *See generally* Seymour Martin Lipset, Martin Trow & James Coleman, *Union Democracy* (Free Press 1956).

It has been argued that insulation of the leadership of a trade group from the wishes of the membership may produce results more in the public interest than a leadership that is highly responsive to its member's views. The leadership must deal with the representatives of other groups and the government who limit the freedom of action of the group's leaders. As a result, often the leaders can bargain relatively free from membership constraints. For example, the American Bar Association has a Standing Committee on the Federal Judiciary that advises the Attorney General of the United States on the qualifications of those considered for federal judgeships. The Committee is, to a great extent, insulated from the pressures of the ABA membership. "It can be argued that the Committee has been engaged in a holding action against extreme demands by lawyers for control over the selection of federal judges by the bar." Jack Ladinsky & Joel B. Grossman, "Organizational Consequences of Professional Consensus: Lawyers and Selection of Judges," 11 *Administrative Science Quarterly* 79, 105 (1966).

[Reading 72]

NOTE: Litigation and Pressure Groups

One does not, perhaps, think of the courtroom as an arena in which the conflict between interest groups is carried out. Court cases are, for the most part, struggles and disputes between individuals. Nevertheless, since courts have a great deal of power in the United States, it is natural for groups to turn to them as a forum, particularly if other avenues of political influence fail or are blocked. A group which has been unsuccessful in defeating legislation harmful to the interest of the group, may move into court to try once more to achieve group objectives. Of course, the courtroom is a rather special arena. The question will have to be framed differently than in the legislature. In the legislature, debate can focus on whether the law is in the public interest—or whether it is politically wise. Litigants will have to ask more "legal" questions. They will try to have the law declared unconstitutional, or have it "interpreted" to suit their needs, but usually without explicitly referring to their needs as a basis for argument. Pressure group activity, in court, will usually take the form of a private lawsuit between individuals, a form which masks the group interests at stake.

The editors of the *Yale Law Journal* surveyed the participation of interest groups in civil rights and civil liberties cases before the Supreme Court of the United States. They relied on experts in constitutional law at Yale and Harvard to select the significant cases from 1933 to 1963. There were 318 of these decisions. The American Civil Liberties Union had participated in 120; the National Association for the Advancement of Colored People in thirty; the American Jewish Congress in twenty-nine. Comment, "The South's Amended Barratry Laws: An Attempt to End

Group Pressure Through the Courts," 72 *Yale Law Journal* 1613, 1643-44 (1963).

Why do organizations go to court? Clement E. Vose,* in "Litigation as a Form of Pressure Group Activity," 319 *Annals of the American Academy of Political and Social Science* 20, 22 (Sept. 1958), points out that:

> Organizations support legal action because individuals lack the necessary time, money, and skill. With no delays a case takes an average of four years to pass through two lower courts to the Supreme Court of the United States. A series of cases on related questions affecting the permanent interest of a group may extend over two decades or more. The constant attention that litigation demands, especially when new arguments are being advanced, makes the employment of regular counsel economical. This may be supplemented by a legal staff of some size and by volunteer lawyers of distinction. Parties also pay court costs and meet the expense of printing the record and briefs. Organizations are better able to provide the continuity demanded in litigation than individuals. Some individuals do maintain responsibility for their own cases even at the Supreme Court level, but this is difficult under modern conditions.

Some organizations, Vose asserts, go to court to protect themselves as organizations. The Jehovah's Witnesses were involved in many constitutional cases. This religious group does a good deal of preaching and missionary work in public; it insists that its members are all "ministers" and thus draft exempt; its members refuse to salute or pledge allegiance to the flag. Hence they have frequently run afoul of the law, and have defended themselves vigorously—and with marked success.

The NAACP and other associations dedicated to racial equality have had a great deal of success as well in advancing group interests through litigation. In general, as Vose points out,

> Judicial review in the United States constitutes an invitation for groups whose lobbying fails to defeat legislation to continue opposition by litigation. The NAACP has taken advantage of this in questioning state segregation laws, and, especially before 1937, business groups of various sizes—the American Liberty League, trade associations, and corporations—contested the constitutionality of state and federal regulatory legislation. This exploitation of judicial review

---

* Professor of Government, Wesleyan University. Copyright © 1958 The American Academy of Political and Social Science. Reprinted by permission.

has been balanced by the practice of victorious groups in legislation continuing to support administrative agencies in
charge of enforcement. When statutes are challenged, organizations often support the Justice Department in Washington or a state Attorney General in defending them. This
is to say that when losers in legislation have brought test
cases in the courts, the legislative winners have aided the
official legal defense. [p. 28]

Some of these groups mentioned are economic interest groups,
others are noneconomic (the NAACP is a good example). Often
the legal question is constitutional; but sometimes it is not. Recall the use of litigation by the railroad companies in Fisher &
Fairbanks, Reading 8, at 76, *supra*. There litigation was used as
a power technique, with the actual outcome somewhat less important than, for example, in the school segregation cases.

In the instances discussed so far, the interest group has been
itself a litigant, or has promoted a "test case" in which a member
or officer of the group has acted as a plaintiff or defendant. Sometimes groups intervene as third parties, by filing a brief *amicus
curiae* (as "friend of the court"). In the last two decades, the
use of this device in the United States Supreme Court has enormously increased. The Court itself has "helped foster its development as a vehicle for broad representation of interests, particularly in disputes where political ramifications are wider than a
narrow view of common law litigation would indicate." Judges
have used the brief "to gain information from political groups,"
and to give these groups a "feeling of participation in the process of decision." Samuel Krislov, "The Amicus Curiae Brief:
From Friendship to Advocacy," 72 *Yale Law Journal* 694, 720-21
(1963).*

Krislov feels that the use of the brief, and the court's permissive attitude, is a "logical extension of realistic awareness of law
as a process of social choice and policy making." If you share
this awareness, would you advocate dropping the various restrictions on group participation in lawsuits, and allow any person
with an interest of any sort in the outcome of a lawsuit to participate? Moreover, would you consider dropping the notion that
courts in the Anglo-American system act merely on the instance
of private litigants with grievances against each other, and allow:
(a) groups to obtain declaratory judgments on the constitutionality of proposed or enacted legislation; and (b) courts to investigate

---

* Professor of Political Science, University of Minnesota. Reprinted by
permission of the Yale Law Journal Company and Fred B. Rothman & Company. From The Yale Law Journal, Vol. 72, pp. 720-21.

on their own initiative the constitutionality of proposed or enacted legislation, and to issue opinions on the subject?

Does the phenomenon described in Vose harm the adjudicative process? does it harm the legal system in general? See the essay by Lon Fuller, Reading 88, at 736, *infra*.

(3) Intellectual leadership, public opinion and the making of law

73. The Relation Between Law and Public Opinion in England[*]

A. V. DICEY

The opinion which affects the development of the law has, in modern England at least, often originated with some single thinker or school of thinkers.

No doubt it is at times allowable to talk of a prevalent belief or opinion as "being in the air," by which expression is meant that a particular way of looking at things has become the common possession of all the world. But though a belief when it prevails, may at last be adopted by the whole of a generation, it rarely happens that a widespread conviction has grown up spontaneously among the multitude. "The initiation," it has been said, "of all wise or noble things, comes and must come, from individuals; generally at first from some one individual;"[1] to which it ought surely to be added that the origination of a new folly or of a new form of baseness comes, and must in general come, at first from individuals or from some one individual. The peculiarity of individuals, as contrasted with the crowd, lies neither in virtue nor in wickedness but in originality. It is idle to credit minorities with all the good without ascribing to them most at least of the evils due to that rarest of all human qualities—inventiveness.

The course of events in England may often at least be thus described:—A new and, let us assume, a true idea presents itself to some one man of originality or genius; the discoverer of the new conception, or some follower who has embraced it with enthusiasm, preaches it to his friends or disciples, they in their

[1] Mill, *On Liberty*, p. 119.

turn become impressed with its importance and its truth, and
gradually a whole school accept the new creed. These apostles
of a new faith are either persons endowed with special ability
or, what is quite as likely, they are persons who, owing to their
peculiar position, are freed from a bias, whether moral or intellectual, in favour of prevalent errors. At last the preachers of
truth make an impression, either directly upon the general public or upon some person of eminence, say a leading statesman,
who stands in a position to impress ordinary people and thus
to win the support of the nation. Success, however, in converting
mankind to a new faith, whether religious, or economical, or
political, depends but slightly on the strength of the reasoning
by which the faith can be defended, or even on the enthusiasm
of its adherents. A change of belief arises, in the main, from the
occurrence of circumstances which incline the majority of the
world to hear with favour theories which, at one time, men of
common sense derided as absurdities, or distrusted as paradoxes.
The doctrine of free trade, for instance, has in England, for about
half a century, held the field as an unassailable dogma of economic policy, but an historian would stand convicted of ignorance
or folly who should imagine that the fallacies of protection were
discovered by the intuitive good sense of the people, even if the
existence of such a quality as the good sense of the people be
more than a political fiction. The principle of free trade may,
as far as Englishmen are concerned, be treated as the doctrine
of Adam Smith. The reasons in its favour never have been, nor
will, from the nature of things, be mastered by the majority of
any people. The apology for freedom of commerce will always
present, from one point of view, an air of paradox. Every man
feels or thinks that protection would benefit his own business,
and it is difficult to realise that what may be a benefit for any
man taken alone, may be of no benefit to a body of men looked
at collectively. The obvious objections to free trade may, as free
traders conceive, be met; but then the reasoning by which these
objections are met is often elaborate and subtle, and does not
carry conviction to the crowd. It is idle to suppose that belief in
freedom of trade,—or indeed any other creed,—ever won its way
among the majority of converts by the mere force of reasoning.
The course of events was very different. The theory of free trade
won by degrees the approval of statesmen of special insight, and
adherents to the new economic religion were one by one gained
among persons of intelligence. Cobden and Bright finally became
potent advocates of truths of which they were in no sense the
discoverers. This assertion in no way detracts from the credit
due to these eminent men. They performed to admiration the

proper function of popular leaders; by prodigies of energy, and by seizing a favourable opportunity, of which they made the very most use that was possible, they gained the acceptance by the English people of truths which have rarely, in any country but England, acquired popularity. Much was due to the opportuneness of the time. Protection wears its most offensive guise when it can be identified with a tax on bread, and therefore can, without patent injustice, be described as the parent of famine and starvation. The unpopularity, moreover, inherent in a tax on corn is all but fatal to a protective tariff when the class which protection enriches is comparatively small, whilst the class which would suffer keenly from dearness of bread and would obtain benefit from free trade is large, and having already acquired much, is certain soon to acquire more political power. Add to all this that the Irish famine made the suspension of the corn laws a patent necessity. It is easy, then, to see how great in England was the part played by external circumstances—one might almost say by accidental conditions—in determining the overthrow of protection. A student should further remark that after free trade became an established principle of English policy, the majority of the English people accepted it mainly on authority. Men, who were neither land-owners nor farmers, perceived with ease the obtrusive evils of a tax on corn, but they and their leaders were far less influenced by arguments against protection generally than by the immediate and almost visible advantage of cheapening the bread of artisans and labourers. What, however, weighed with most Englishmen, above every other consideration, was the harmony of the doctrine that commerce ought to be free, with that disbelief in the benefits of State intervention which in 1846 had been gaining ground for more than a generation.

NOTES AND QUESTIONS

1. Is Dicey expressing the "great man" theory of history, which Friedman and Ladinsky attempt to refute? Can the two points of view be reconciled?

2. Compare Adam Smith's role in laying a basis for the repeal of the corn laws with Upton Sinclair's role in laying a basis for the passage of food and drug laws, as described in the note on *The Jungle*, Reading 60, at 561, *supra.*

3. Is Dicey's account fatally defective in that he fails to take into account (a) concrete economic interests which the Adam Smith doctrines served; and (b) the "taught tradition" of the law,

which favored individualism, and hence was receptive to the principles that Smith argued for?

4. From 1964 to 1968, there was a shift in public opinion about American participation in the war in Vietnam. At least a substantial minority of the public came to view government policy as unwise if not immoral. By 1968, a number of prominent Americans were criticizing that policy. Although the point is debatable, the policy can be said to have changed to some extent during 1968; peace negotiations began and President Johnson's decision not to seek reelection both promoted policy change directly and created the opportunity for change through the political process. What was the role of protests by college students and peace groups, of the anti-war activities of college professors, of the criticism of influential journalists, and of the positions taken by those who held or sought political office in changing public opinion and in producing any change one might find in government policy? Could one say that the anti-war movement influenced several "great men" who in turn influenced policy?

c. Expert opinion: the influence of science and knowledge on law

Introductory Note

Thus far we have discussed, as a formative element in law, general public opinion and the role of interest groups, chiefly economic. The selection from Dicey has considered how, at least in Dicey's view, the bold intellectual leadership of Adam Smith spread among the English elite, and ultimately had a decisive impact on the formation of policy and law. Here we will consider the impact upon law of expert opinion—of science and what passes for science in society.

It is apparent that the law is concerned with fact, with truth, in many areas. Law generally seeks to influence behavior; it is, therefore, rational in that it concerns means appropriate to the ends in view. "Science" tells lawmakers what means pertain to what ends. Some aspects of "science" are part of common understanding but others are within the domain of "experts." Much of the lawmaking and decision-making in society is delegated to these experts. Congress, for example, may decide to outlaw the sale of food products that contain substances harmful to health. They are likely to hand over to chemists and doctors, the actual job of identifying these substances. The delegation may take place formally (by setting up an agency to decide which substances are harmful, and perhaps even by specifying that those who make the decisions must be doctors or chemists); or the lawmakers may themselves consult with experts, ascertain what the substances are, and name them in the governing statute. There is in this latter case no formal delegation of power to experts, but there has been a reliance on experts in fact.

The legal system is part of society, inescapably connected with the rest of the social system; and there is no question that advances in technology and knowledge affect the law and its institutions. At the simplest level, lawyers, courts, judges and litigants make use of the technological tools of their era, for example, courtrooms are air conditioned, clerks use typewriters, judges ride to the courtroom in cars. Lawyers may soon use computers as data retrieval devices, enabling them to locate fairly quickly cases and statutes that might have taken long hours to search for before. Nor is there much dispute that better techniques should replace lesser techniques in the gathering of evidence and the presentation of data to legislatures and courts. Courts freely admit fingerprint evidence and, not so freely, blood-test evidence and the evidence of lie-detector tests. The use of still other kinds of fact-gathering methods is under a cloud: the wiretap, for example.

Wiretapping is illegal, or questionable, not because it is not a technically valid source of information, but because (it is said) the use of wiretapping impinges upon other values. Value choices cannot be avoided by lawmakers who are called upon to decide whether or not to make use of some technically valid source of information. Torture, after all, can be said to be a rational and highly effective mode of extracting truth. But it is rejected in American society. There are, similarly, grave constitutional and ethical doubts about the use of compulsory birth control, compulsory sterilization and compulsory abortion as methods of holding down the population explosion, although there is little doubt about the efficacy of these means. (Note that there is controversy both about the *goal* of population control and about the *means* of attaining it.)

There are other problems in the use of science and expert knowledge in law. Someone has to decide, for example, who is an expert, and what areas are appropriate for expert decision. What are the boundaries of the value domain and the domain of science? The dream of those who called themselves "technocrats" was that all questions of policy would ultimately be resolved into questions amenable to rational decision by impartial experts. Few people are still dreaming that dream. But there are many unresolved problems about the proper use of experts. There are also many unresolved questions about the actual use of experts. Psychiatrists appear in court and testify that a defendant is insane. The jury finds him not guilty. Have they reached their decision *because* of the psychiatrist? Are the experts sometimes manipulated by interest groups to lend color to arguments or strategies that are valued quite apart from or despite the considerations that the experts use? In the famous school desegregation case, Brown v. Board of Educ., 347 U.S. 483 (1954), the Supreme Court mentioned with approval the finding of the lower court that school segregation "has a detrimental effect upon . . . colored children." That finding, said the Court, "is amply supported by modern authority." The Court then cited the work of a number of sociologists and social psychologists. Did this research really influence the Court, or was the Court merely using the research to buttress its decision or to convince the outside world of the "scientific" nature of its decision? Furthermore, how "scientific" were these studies? Some have openly questioned the methods used in these studies. *See, e.g.,* Herbert Garfinkel, "Social Science Evidence and the School Segregation Cases," 21 *Journal of Politics* 37 (1959). Similarly, some have questioned whether psychiatrists play a helpful role in deciding whether to send accused persons to jail, to a mental hospital, or to freedom, partly because there are doubts in the minds of many that psychiatry is truly a science. Similar doubts have been raised about the scientific nature of the recommendations of economists on which much of the country's fiscal and financial policies seem to be based.

There is no question of the value of science and expert knowledge. For example, there is general agreement that economies are better managed under the guidance of trained economists than before the days of economic science. Also, there is no doubt that if a man should not have to support an illegitimate child he did not father, it is good to have blood-test evidence to "prove" he could not be the father in order to avoid unjustly burdening him with child support. But there are many serious borderline questions about the use of science and what constitutes the domain of the expert and the domain of the man of law. The following readings center on these problems.

74. The Administrative Process*

JAMES M. LANDIS

[Landis, in the course of his book, deals with the question of judicial review over decisions and rulings of administrative agencies. It is often said that courts should have some measure of control over questions of "law" but not over mere findings of fact by the agencies. How does one determine what is "law" and what is "fact"? Professor Landis says:]

[The content of the concept law] insofar as it relates to judicial review of administrative action, reaches back to the issue of expertness. *Our desire to have courts determine questions of law is related to a belief in their possession of expertness with regard to such questions. It is from that very desire that the nature of questions of law emerges. For, in the last analysis, they seem to me to be those questions that lawyers are equipped to decide.*

To view "law" in this fashion seems to me to bring reason into our conceptions of the supremacy of law. It seems to afford some guide to molding the process of judicial review over both legislative and administrative action. It explains the variances in the scope of judicial review over administrative agencies of different compositions and charged with the disposition of different subject matters. It lends emphasis to the insistence of Mr. Justice Brandeis that differences in treatment should be accorded to findings of fact by different administrative officials, because of differences in the facts and in the qualities of the administrative to be expert in finding the facts. It removes nothing from the insistence that policy plays a commanding role in the shaping of judicial review, but in the place of a simple theory of economic determinism, or of a barren logic, it substitutes a sense of emphasis upon intellectual quality and discipline as related to a particular problem. The line of demarcation will then speak in terms of reality, in terms of an appreciation of the limitations and abilities of men, rather than in terms of political dogma or of righteous abstractions.

Of course, such a conception of law as related to spheres of judicial and administrative activity affords no definite answers. It must not do so, for the capacities of men and the nature of disciplines will vary. But it does point to the elements that should control judgment. And from the standpoint of affording conceptions of liberty real meaning, one can ask little more than to have issues decided by those best equipped for the task.

Such a conception of the nature of law does not remove the sense of battle which dominates the question of judicial review over administrative action. But it makes that contest rest upon a plane where the issues relate to the ability of men to handle subject matter. As such, the contest should partake more of that rivalry that attends the academic scene, where a passionate desire for truth makes for recognition and not resentment of achievement.

The world of today as distinguished from that of even a hundred years ago is one of many professions. We can no longer divide it, in its civil aspect, between the church, the law, and medicine. Economics, political science, sociology, social ethics, labor economics, engineering in its various branches, all are producers of disciplines relating to the arrangement of human affairs. Government today no longer dares to rely for its administration upon the casual office-seeker. Into its service it now seeks to bring men of professional attainment in various fields and to make that service such that they will envisage governance as a career. The desires of these men to share in the mediation of human claims cannot be denied; their contributions dare not casually be tossed aside.

The grandeur that is law loses nothing from such a prospect. Instead, under its banner as a commanding discipline are enlisted armies of men dedicated to the idea of justice. But to use those armies, a sense of the effectiveness of their units is essential and an instillation in those units of morale. "Courts," as Mr. Justice Stone has reminded us, "are not the only agency of government that must be assumed to have capacity to govern";[42] nor are they, one can add, the only agency moved by the desire for justice. The power of judicial review under our traditions of government lies with the courts because of a deep belief that the heritage they hold makes them experts in the synthesis of design. Such difficulties as have arisen have come because courts cast aside that role to assume to themselves expertness in matters of industrial health, utility engineering, railroad management, even bread baking. The rise of the administrative process represented the

---

[42] United States v. Butler, 297 U.S. 1, 87 (1936).

hope that policies to shape such fields could most adequately be developed by men bred to the facts. That hope is still dominant, but its possession bears no threat to our ideal of the "supremacy of law." Instead, it lifts it to new heights where the great judge, like a conductor of a many-tongued symphony, from what would otherwise be discord, makes known through the voice of many instruments the vision that has been given him of man's destiny upon this earth.

NOTES AND QUESTIONS

1. How does one determine those areas in which lawyers and judges are expert, as opposed to those areas in which others are expert? If law is merely one area of expertise among many, why should there be a "supremacy of law"? What is the basis for the claim of the law to dominance over decisions affecting other areas of life?

2. The multiplication of administrative agencies, each with a specialized mandate for regulating or controlling some aspect of economic or social life, is a striking trend of modern American government. Necessarily, these agencies make use of many experts, and they carry on their work with, on the whole, relatively little control by courts. At many points in these materials, we have noted these agencies—the CAB, occupational licensing agencies, the ICC. Clearly, they differ greatly in the degree to which they are free from interference either by courts or legislatures, in the degree to which in their day to day work they apply principles that most people would agree fall within the exclusive technical competence of some class of experts, and in the degree to which they make value choices as to which their judgment is no better or worse than the average citizen.

[Reading 75]

3. The viewpoint of the following essay should be compared with Landis' statements about the nature and scope of judicial expertness. Carl A. Auerbach, "Issues of Legal Policy in Social Science Perspective," 2 *Law & Society Review* 499 (1968):*

The call for studies of the social impact of particular judicial, legislative, administrative and executive rules, decisions and practices is sounded sporadically and acted upon but rarely. To read the recent decisions of the Supreme Court

---

* Professor of Law, University of Minnesota. Reprinted from Law and Society Review. Copyright © 1968 by the Law and Society Association. Reprinted by permission.

of the United States overruling established precedents in
many areas of our constitutional law is to catalogue a long
list of missed opportunities for social scientists. As an example of the cause for this lament, I shall present *Keyishian v.
Board of Regents*[1] which for all practical purposes overruled
Alder v. Board of Education.[2]

In *Adler*, decided in 1952, the Supreme Court, by a vote
of six to three, upheld the constitutionality of (1) the New
York Civil Service Law which barred from employment in
the civil service and the educational system anyone who (a)
advocated the overthrow of the Government by force, violence or any unlawful means, or (b) published material advocating such overthrow, or (c) organized or joined any society
advocating such doctrine; and (2) the Feinberg Law which
required the Board of Regents to adopt and enforce rules to
effectuate these provisions of the Civil Service Law and list
the organizations advocating the proscribed doctrine. Membership in such organizations was made prima facie evidence
of disqualification for employment.

Justice Minton wrote the Court's opinion, in which Chief
Justice Vinson and Justices Jackson, Burton, Reed, and Clark
joined.

Justice Black dissented, attacking the New York legislation
as another of the enactments "which make it dangerous—
this time for school teachers—to think or say anything except
what a transient majority happen to approve at the moment."

Justice Douglas also wrote a dissenting opinion in which
Justice Black joined. Justice Douglas castigated "this kind of
censorship" imposed on the public school system and the
"witch hunt" which it would produce. He also predicted
that the New York legislation "is certain to raise havoc with
academic freedom." "Any organization committed to a liberal cause, any group organized to revolt against an hysterical
trend, any committee launched to sponsor an unpopular program" will become suspect. Teachers "will tend to shrink
from any association that stirs controversy" and "freedom of
expression will be stifled." "Inevitably," Justice Douglas
claimed, the school system will be turned "into a spying
project."

> Regular loyalty reports on the teachers must be made
> out. The principals become detectives: the students, the
> parents, the community become informers. . . .

---

[1] Keyishian v. Board of Regents, 385 U.S. 589 (1967).
[2] Adler v. Board of Education, 342 U.S. 485 (1952).

What happens under this law is typical of what happens in a police state. Teachers are under constant surveillance; their pasts are combed for signs of disloyalty; their utterances are watched for clues to dangerous thoughts. . . . Fear stalks the classroom. The teacher is no longer a stimulant to adventurous thinking; she becomes instead a pipe line for safe and sound information. A deadening dogma takes the place of free inquiry. Instruction tends to become sterile; pursuit of knowledge is discouraged; discussion often leaves off where it should begin.

Justice Frankfurter also dissented, but not on the merits of the New York legislation. He pointed out that the case had been brought to the Supreme Court by eight municipal taxpayers; two were parents of children in the New York City schools and four were teachers in these schools. All the plaintiffs sought a declaratory judgment that the New York legislation was unconstitutional and an injunction against its effectuation; their motion for judgment on the pleadings was denied by the highest New York court. No steps had been taken to enforce the legislation from the time the suit began. Under these circumstances, Justice Frankfurter objected that the Court was indulging in constitutional adjudication "on merely abstract or speculative issues" instead of "on the concreteness afforded by an actual, present, defined controversy, appropriate for judicial judgment, between adversaries immediately affected by it."

. . . as the case comes to us we can have no guide other than our own notions—however uncritically extra-judicial —of the real bearing of the New York arrangement on the freedom of thought and activity, and especially on the feeling of such freedom, which are . . . part of the necessary professional equipment of teachers in a free society.

Fifteen years later, by a vote of five to four, the Supreme Court in *Keyishian* declared the New York legislation at issue in *Adler* to be unconstitutional. Justice Brennan wrote the Court's opinion, in which Chief Justice Warren and Justices Black, Douglas and Fortas joined. Justice Clark wrote the dissenting opinion, in which Justices Harlan, Stewart and White joined. Only Justices Black, Douglas and Clark had been on the Court that decided *Adler*.

Once again the Court was guided by its "own notions" of "the real bearing" of the New York arrangement on "freedom of thought and activity, and especially on the feeling of such freedom." Justice Brennan never asks whether the dire predictions made by Justice Douglas in *Adler* came true. Not once does his opinion refer to the fifteen years of experience under the New York legislation. So we are again presented with a series of assumptions and renewed predictions unsupported by any facts stated in the opinion. "The very intricacy of the plan [set up by the New York legislation] and the uncertainty as to the scope of its proscriptions make it," asserts Justice Brennan, "a highly efficient *in terrorem* mechanism."

It would be a bold teacher who would not stay as far as possible from utterances or acts which might jeopardize his living by enmeshing him in this intricate machinery. . . . The result must be to stifle that free play of the spirit which all teachers ought especially to cultivate and practice. . . . . . . the First Amendment . . . does not tolerate laws that cast a pall of orthodoxy over the classroom.

In also declaring unconstitutional a provision, added to the New York laws in 1958, that made Communist Party membership, as such, prima facie evidence of disqualification for employment, the Court states flatly that "the stifling effect on the academic mind from curtailing freedom of association in such manner is manifest, and has been documented in recent studies." But none of these studies seeks to ascertain the results of the fifteen years of experience under the New York legislation.[18] Only the Jahoda and Cook and Lazarsfeld and Thielens studies make any effort at scientific inquiry. None of these studies document or otherwise make manifest, as Justice Brennan claims, the "stifling effect on the academic mind from curtailing freedom of association" with the Communist Party.

Keyishian itself did not give the Court any opportunity to evaluate the New York legislation in action. The suit was brought by five members of the faculty of the University of Buffalo which had become part of the State University of New York in 1962. At that time, four of them—members of the teaching faculty—refused to sign certificates that they

---

[18] The studies cited are P. F. LAZARSFELD & W. THIELENS, THE ACADEMIC MIND 92-112, 192-217 (1958); F. B. BIDDLE, THE FEAR OF FREEDOM 155 *et seq.* (1951); M. Jahoda & S. Cook, *Security Measures and Freedom of Thought: An Exploratory Study of the Impact of Loyalty and Security Programs,* 61 YALE L.J. 295 (1952); R. M. MacIVER, ACADEMIC FREEDOM IN OUR TIME (1955); M. R. KONVITZ, EXPANDING LIBERTIES 86-108 (1966); C. Morris, "Academic Freedom and Loyalty Oaths," 28 LAW & CONTEMP. PROB. 487 (1963).

were not Communists, and that if they had ever been Communists, they had communicated that fact to the President of the State University. As a result, Keyishian's one-year-term contract as an instructor in English was not renewed. Two others, an Assistant Professor of English and a lecturer in Philosophy, were allowed to continue to teach because their contracts still had time to run. The fourth, an Assistant Professor of English, voluntarily resigned and the Supreme Court held he had lost his standing to maintain the suit. In June 1965, shortly before the case came to trial, the certificate requirement was rescinded.

The fifth person involved in the litigation was a library employee and part-time lecturer in English. Personnel in this classification were not required to sign the certificate but were asked to answer in writing under oath the question, "Have you ever advised or taught or were you ever a member of any society or group of persons which taught or advocated the doctrine that the Government of the United States or of any political subdivisions thereof should be overthrown or overturned by force, violence or any unlawful means?" When he refused to answer the question, he was dismissed.

Neither the plaintiffs nor the defendants in the lawsuit—nor the American Civil Liberties Union or American Association of University Professors which filed briefs as amici curiae—thought it necessary to deal with the question of the impact of the New York legislation now declared unconstitutional upon New York's educational system during the fifteen years the legislation was in effect. I do not know that anybody has written or even attempted such a study. Yet I hope that someone may be encouraged to undertake it. It would no longer affect the Supreme Court's authoritative judgment of the New York legislation in question. But it would contribute to the continuing evaluation of the work of the Supreme Court. Equally important, it would add a significant chapter to the history of the Supreme Court, for should not the most meaningful core of the Court's history be the account of the consequences of its decisions for American society?

Is a decision interpreting the First Amendment one in which lawyers and judges, as contrasted with others, are the only or exclusive experts, one in which legal expertise rests on factual assumptions which are in the domain of other experts, or one in which none of the appropriate experts are lawyers? Why do

you think that the Supreme Court failed to insist on full data on
"the fifteen years of experience under the New York legislation"
as Auerbach notes?

76. Book Review: Kinsey, Sexual Behavior in the Human Female

FOWLER V. HARPER

63 YALE LAW JOURNAL 895 (1954)*

Kinsey's findings [that many kinds of illicit sexual acts and relationships are extremely common among the public] have been viewed with surprise and alarm, with respect and disdain. No one knows the margin of error probable in his conclusions nor the extent to which they may safely be extended on a national basis. But although the margin be considerable, and due allowance made therefor, the results go far toward demolishing the assumptions of laymen as to the sex behavior of men and women in our culture. On the other hand, the results tend to confirm the guesses of most scientific persons who have made observations and speculations about sex. Few anthropologists, psychologists and still fewer psychiatrists are surprised by either book.

Of what significance are these studies for lawyers? Society frequently gets excited about sex offenders. Periodically, we are advised that sex offenses are increasing. This may only mean that the number of arrests for sex offenses has increased. Kinsey does not find confirmation for the assertion of increase in sex offenses other than that proportional to the increase in population. He also points out that most studies of sex offenses are limited to a study of sex offenders; when proper control groups are employed, the inferences drawn may be altogether different.

Kinsey obtained the histories of some thirteen hundred women who had been convicted and sentenced to penal institutions as sex offenders. Out of this study of sex offenders and of the sexual behavior of persons who have never run afoul of the law in this respect, Kinsey believes that there "should come data which may some day be used by legislators in the development of a body of sex law that may provide society with more adequate protection against the more serious types of sex offenders." He then

---

* Reprinted by permission of the Yale Law Journal Company and Fred B. Rothman & Company. From The Yale Law Journal, Vol. 63, p. 895.

goes on to say that "our present information seems to make it clear that the current sex laws are unenforced and unenforceable because they are too completely out of accord with the realities of human behavior, and because they attempt too much in the way of social control. Such a high proportion of the females and males in our population is involved in sexual activities which are prohibited by the law of most states of the union, that it is inconceivable that the present laws could be administered in any fashion that even remotely approached systematic and complete enforcement."

The impact of these studies on the law will depend on several factors, public opinion and the individual reaction of legislators included. As a sample of the latter, the results of a questionnaire sent to members of the legislature of what may be regarded as a typical New England state may be significant. A random sampling of 93 from the lower house was taken together with full coverage of the upper house.[14]

The legislators were asked whether or not, in view of Kinsey's findings that approximately 50% of the men and 25% of the women have extra-marital relations, a single act of adultery should continue to be grounds for divorce. Sixty-two and five tenths per cent said yes, 30% said no, and 7.5% did not answer the question. None thought that the criminal law relating to adultery (punishable by up to five years' confinement) should be made stricter, but only 40% thought the penalty should be reduced. As to fornication (punishable by a maximum penalty of six months), 20% thought the law should be strictly enforced, 37.5% thought it should remain the same but not strictly enforced, and 20% wanted the statute repealed. As to homosexuality and other forms of sodomy (punishable by imprisonment up to thirty years), 57.5% wanted no change in the law while only 32.5% thought it should be made less strict.

Asked whether or not they thought studies such as Kinsey's were of value to them as legislators, 45% thought so, 50% thought not, and 5% did not think. It would appear that immediate revision of the sex laws in State X is unlikely. But Alfred Kinsey is a dedicated man. He wants and will reach his goal of a hundred thousand case histories. By that time, some of our legislators may be prepared to recognize sex for what it is and what, notwithstanding the opposition of Church and State, it always has been.

---

[14] Confidential questionnaire prepared by students of Yale Law School under the supervision of the reviewer.

NOTES AND QUESTIONS

1. Why do you suppose the legislators who felt Kinsey's findings were not "of value" to them as legislators, took this position? Is it likely that the reasons were similar to those that account for the failure of the Supreme Court to seek data, as described by Auerbach?

2. The findings of Harper's survey suggest differences between public opinion and public behavior; see the questions and materials following the excerpts from Cohen, Robson & Bates, Reading 57, at 549, *supra*.

3. Has Harper's pessimism proved to be somewhat premature? Has he simply ignored the fact that impact and reform occur slowly? About fifteen years have now passed since Harper's comments, and the matter may look different now. In this period, there have been some changes in laws relating to sexual behavior. In Illinois, consensual homosexual relations between adults are no longer a crime, as a result of the latest revision of the state's penal code. The Model Penal Code of the American Law Institute, which is bound to have some influence on penal code revisions in some states, has taken the same point of view.

4. Changes in the law, as exemplified by the Illinois revision just mentioned, may come about for a variety of reasons. To what extent, would you guess, has the "liberalization" of Illinois law been influenced by "expert" opinion (such as the Kinsey report)? To what extent is Kinsey an "expert" at all on what should be the content of a criminal code?

5. The Surgeon-General of the United States issued a report which presented strong statistical evidence connecting cigarette smoking with lung cancer, as well as with emphysema, certain kinds of heart disease and other maladies. So far, no state has banned cigarette sales or cigarette smoking; there has been no "prohibition" movement afoot, and the most that can be said is that there is some possibility of curbing the advertising methods used in marketing cigarettes. Why are the experts not being followed in this case? (a) Is their expertise seriously questioned? The Tobacco Institute has, after all, questioned it. (b) Is the economic power of the Tobacco Institute the critical variable? (c) Is the public misinformed or indifferent to the question? (d) Is cigarette smoking a deep-rooted social custom, such that the attempt to legislate regarding it would be doomed to failure?

6. Laws against fornication and adultery remain on the books in the United States. Generally, these sexual offenses do not give

rise to the same sense of moral outrage, it would seem, as homosexuality. The statutes are virtually never enforced. There is no significant movement for repealing them. How can you explain the survival of these laws, though they are decried by the experts, and, apparently, have less public support than laws against homosexual behavior?

77. Prochnow v. Prochnow

274 WIS. 491, 80 N.W.2d 278 (1957)

A husband appeals from that part of a decree of divorce which adjudged him to be the father of his wife's child and ordered him to pay support money. [The husband was a plumber with a yearly income of about $5,000. The trial court ordered him to pay $50 a month child support.] The actual paternity is the only fact which is in dispute.

Joyce, plaintiff, and Robert, defendant, were married September 2, 1950 and have no children other than the one whose paternity is now in question. In February, 1953, Robert began his military service. When he came home on furloughs which he took frequently in 1953 he found his wife notably lacking in appreciation of his presence. Although he was home on furlough for eight days in October and ten in December, after August, 1953, the parties had no sexual intercourse except for one time, to be mentioned later. In Robert's absence Joyce had dates with a man known as Andy, with whom she danced in a tavern and went to a movie, behaving in a manner which the one witness who testified on the subject thought unduly affectionate. This witness also testified that Joyce told her that Robert was dull but that she and Andy had fun. She also said that a few days before Friday, March 12, 1954, Joyce told her she had to see her husband who was then stationed in Texas but must be back to her work in Milwaukee by Monday.

On March 12, 1954, Joyce flew to San Antonio and met Robert there. They spent the night of the 13th in a hotel where they had sex relations. The next day, before returning to Milwaukee, she told him that she did not love him and was going to divorce him. Her complaint, alleging cruel and inhuman treatment as her cause of action, was served on him April 8, 1954. On September 16, 1954, she amended the complaint to include an allegation that she was pregnant by Robert and demanded support money.

The child was born November 21, 1954. Robert's letters to Joyce are in evidence in which he refers to the child as his own. He returned to civilian life February 13, 1955 and on February 18, 1955, answered the amended complaint, among other things denying that he is the father of the child born to Joyce; and he counterclaimed for divorce alleging cruel and inhuman conduct on the part of the wife.

Before trial two blood grouping tests were made of Mr. and Mrs. Prochnow and of the child. The first was not made by court order but was ratified by the court and accepted in evidence as though so made. This test was conducted in Milwaukee on March 21, 1955. The second was had in Waukesha September 29, 1955, under court order. The experts by whom or under whose supervision the tests were conducted testified that each test eliminated Robert as a possible parent of the child. An obstetrician, called by Robert, testified that it was possible for the parties' conduct on March 13, 1954 to produce the full-term child which Mrs. Prochnow bore the next November 21st. Mrs. Prochnow testified that between December, 1953 and May, 1954, both inclusive, she had no sexual intercourse with any man but her husband. . . .

BROWN, Justice. The trial judge found the fact to be that Robert is the father of Joyce's child. The question is not whether, on this evidence, we would have so found: what we must determine is whether that finding constituted reversible error.

Section 328.39 (1) (a), Stats., commands:

"Whenever it is established in an action or proceeding that a child was born to a woman while she was the lawful wife of a specified man, any party asserting the illegitimacy of the child in such action or proceeding shall have the burden of proving beyond all reasonable doubt that the husband was not the father of the child. . . ."

Ignoring for the moment the evidence of the blood tests and the effect claimed for them, the record shows intercourse between married people at a time appropriate to the conception of this baby. The husband's letters after the child's birth acknowledge it is his own. The wife denies intercourse with any other man during the entire period when she could have conceived this child. Unless we accept the illegitimacy of the baby as a fact while still to be proved, there is no evidence that then, or ever, did she have intercourse with anyone else. The wife's conduct with Andy on the few occasions when the witness saw them together can justly be called indiscreet for a married woman whose husband is absent, but falls far short of indicating adultery. Indeed, appellant did not assert that Andy is the real father but left that to the imagination of the court whose imagination, as it turned out, was not sufficiently lively to draw the inference. Cynics, *among whom on this occasion we must reluctantly num-*

ber ourselves [emphasis added], might reasonably conclude that Joyce, finding herself pregnant in February or early March, made a hasty excursion to her husband's bed and an equally abrupt withdrawal when her mission was accomplished. The subsequent birth of a full-term child a month sooner than it would usually be expected if caused by this copulation does nothing to dispel uncharitable doubts. But we must acknowledge that a trial judge, less inclined to suspect the worst, might with reason recall that at least as early as the preceding August Joyce had lost her taste for her husband's embraces. Divorce offered her freedom from them, but magnanimously she might determine to try once more to save the marriage: hence her trip to Texas. But when the night spent in Robert's arms proved no more agreeable than such nights used to be she made up her mind that they could live together no more, frankly told him so and took her departure. The medical testimony concerning the early arrival of the infant does no more than to recognize eight months of gestation as unusual. It admits the possibility that Robert begat the child that night in that San Antonio hotel. Thus, the mother swears the child is Robert's and she knew, in the Biblical sense, no other man. Robert, perforce, acknowledges that it may be his. Everything else depends on such reasonable inferences as one chooses to draw from the other admitted facts and circumstances. And such inferences are for the trier of the fact. Particularly, in view of sec. 328.39 (1) (a), Stats., supra, we cannot agree with appellant that even with the blood tests left out of consideration, the record here proves beyond a reasonable doubt that Joyce's husband was not the father of her child.

Accordingly we turn to the tests. The expert witnesses agree that the tests excluded Mr. Prochnow from all possibility of this fatherhood. Appellant argues that this testimony is conclusive; that with the tests in evidence Joyce's testimony that she had no union except with her husband is insufficient to support a finding that her husband is the father. The conclusive effect of the blood test is sometimes imposed by statute, such as is found in secs. 4 and 5 of the Uniform Act on Blood Tests to Determine Paternity, presently in force in California, Michigan, New Hampshire and Oregon. But the Wisconsin statute authorizing blood tests in paternity cases pointedly refrains from directing courts to accept them as final even when they exclude the man sought to be held as father. In its material parts it reads:

"Sec. 325.23 *Blood tests in civil actions.* Whenever it shall be relevant in a civil action to determine the parentage or identity of any child, . . . the court . . . may direct any party to the action and the person involved in the controversy to submit to one or more blood tests, to be made by duly qualified physicians. . . . "Whenever such test is ordered and made the results thereof shall be receivable in evidence, but only in cases where definite exclusion is established. . . ."

This statute does no more than to admit the test and its results in evidence, there to be given such weight and credibility in competition with other evidence as the trier of the fact considers it deserves. No doubt in this enactment the legislature recognized that whatever infallibility is accorded to science, scientists and laboratory technicians by whom the tests must be conducted, interpreted and reported retain the human fallibilities of other witnesses. It has been contended before this that a report on the analysis of blood is a physical fact which controls a finding of fact in opposition to lay testimony on the subject, and the contention was rejected. . . . When the trial judge admitted the Prochnow tests in evidence and weighed them against the testimony of Mrs. Prochnow he went as far in giving effect to them as our statute required him to do. Our opinions say too often that trial courts and juries are the judges of the credibility of witnesses and the weight to be given testimony which conflicts with the testimony of others for us to say that in this case the trial court does not have that function. . . .

[I]n a bastardy action the testimony of the woman that she had timely intercourse with the man and that she had none with anyone else, if believed by the jury, is sufficient to support a verdict that he is the father of her child. . . . That is the common rule. . . . So, if Joyce and Robert were not married and the child now in question had been born to Joyce her testimony of intercourse with him, which he admits, and her denial of it with any other man would, if believed by the trier of the fact, be sufficient to establish that Robert is the child's father beyond a reasonable doubt. How much greater, then, is the sufficiency of the same testimony, when believed by the trial court, to establish such fatherhood when, the parties being married to each other, the burden of proof has been reversed by statute, *supra,* and the burden is now Robert's to prove beyond reasonable doubt that he is *not* the parent. The conclusion seems inescapable that the trial court's finding must stand when the blood-test statute does not make the result of the test conclusive but only directs its receipt in evidence there to be weighed, as other evidence is, by the court or jury. We hold, then, that the credibility of witnesses and the weight of all the evidence in this action was for the trial court and error can not be predicated upon the court's acceptance of Joyce's testimony as more convincing than that of the expert witnesses. . . .

Judgment affirmed.

WINGERT, Justice (dissenting). With all respect for the views of the majority, Mr. Chief Justice FAIRCHILD, Mr. Justice CURRIE and the writer must dissent. In our opinion the appellant, Robert Prochnow, sustained the burden placed upon him by sec. 328.39 (1) (a), Stats., of proving beyond all reasonable doubt that he was not the father of the child born to the plaintiff.

To meet that burden, appellant produced two classes of evidence, (1) testimony of facts and circumstances, other than blood tests, which create grave doubt that appellant is the father, and (2) the evidence of blood tests and their significance, hereinafter discussed. In our opinion the blood test evidence should have been treated as conclusive in the circumstances of this case.

Among the numerous scientific achievements of recent decades is the development of a method by which it can be definitely established in many cases, with complete accuracy, that one of two persons cannot possibly be the parent of the other. The nature and significance of this discovery are summarized by the National Conference of Commissioners on Uniform State Laws, a highly responsible body, in the prefatory note to the Uniform Act on Blood Tests to Determine Paternity, as follows:

"In paternity proceedings, divorce actions and other types of cases in which the legitimacy of a child is in issue, the modern developments of science have made it possible to determine with certainty in a large number of cases that one charged with being the father of a child could not be. Scientific methods may determine that one is not the father of the child by the analysis of blood samples taken from the mother, the child, and the alleged father in many cases, but it cannot be shown that a man is the father of the child. If the negative fact is established it is evident that there is a great miscarriage of justice to permit juries to hold on the basis of oral testimony, passion or sympathy, that the person charged is the father and is responsible for the support of the child and other incidents of paternity. . . . There is no need for a dispute among the experts, and true experts will not disagree. Every test will show the same results. . . .

"As to the make-up of the blood, the testing process is reasonably simple. It is practically the same thing in which the 11 million or more men were tested in determining blood types in the service. It is the same kind of test made of the blood of donors to the Red Cross and hospital blood banks. Consequently, this is one of the few classes of cases in which judgment of court may be absolutely right by use of science. In this kind of a situation it seems intolerable for a court to permit an opposite result to be reached when the judgment may scientifically be one of complete accuracy. For a court to permit the establishment of paternity in cases where it is scientifically impossible to arrive at that result would seem to be a great travesty on justice." Uniform Laws Annotated, 9 Miscellaneous Acts, 1955 Pocket Part, p. 13.

In the present case the evidence showed without dispute that the pertinent type of tests were made of the blood of the husband, the wife and the child on two separate occasions by different qualified pathologists, at separate laboratories, and that such tests yielded identical results, as follows:

	3/17/55	9/29/55
	Blood	Types
Robert Prochnow (Husband)	AB	AB
Joyce Prochnow (Wife)	O	O
David Prochnow (Child)	O	O

There is no evidence whatever that the persons who made these tests were not fully qualified experts in the field of blood testing, nor that the tests were not made properly, nor that the results were not correctly reported to the court. The tests were voluntarily submitted to by the adult parties, and with the consent of the guardian ad litem of the child.

Two qualified experts in the field also testified that it is a physical impossibility for a man with type AB blood to be the father of a child with type O blood, and that therefore appellant is not and could not be the father of the child David. Both testified that there are no exceptions to the rule. One stated "There is no difference of opinion regarding these factors amongst the authorities doing this particular work. None whatsoever." The evidence thus summarized was not discredited in any way and stands undisputed in the record. Indeed, there was no attempt to discredit it except by the wife's own self-serving statement that she had not had sexual relations with any other man during the period when the child might have been conceived. . . .

As pointed out previously, the fact that appellant has type AB blood and the child has type O blood was established by uncontradicted evidence—evidence of two tests by different experts in different laboratories at widely different times, reaching exactly the same result. The correctness of the procedures followed in making the tests and the qualifications and disinterestedness of the experts who made them and testified about them are unchallenged.

This court has frequently held that the testimony of a witness or finding of a jury which is contrary to unquestionable physical situations or common knowledge is of no weight in favor of the side it is invoked to support, and indeed may be self-destructive, being successfully impeached by its demonstrated improbability or impossibility. . . . For instance, if verified skid marks show that a car traveled on the left side of the road when and after the brakes were applied sufficiently to slide the wheels, no weight can be given to testimony of the driver and his passengers that he was at all times in the right-hand traffic lane. . . .

[T]he National Conference of Commissioners on Uniform State Laws has drafted a uniform act on blood tests to determine paternity, which has been enacted in the states of California, Michigan, New Hampshire and Oregon. The act contains the following provisions:

"§ 4. Effect of Test Results.—If the court finds that the conclusions of all the experts, as disclosed by the evidence based upon the tests, are that the alleged father is not the father of the child, the question of paternity shall be resolved accordingly. If the experts disagree in their findings or conclusions, the question shall be submitted upon all the evidence. . . .

"§ 5. Effect on Presumption of Legitimacy.—The presumption of legitimacy of a child born during wedlock is overcome if the court finds that the conclusions of all the experts, as disclosed by the evidence based upon the tests, show that the husband is not the father of the child." Uniform Laws Annotated, 9 Miscellaneous Acts, 1955 Pocket Part, pp. 20, 21.

While Wisconsin has no such legislation, the facts on which the uniform act is based are as true here as anywhere else, and should be recognized by our courts in the absence of legislation. The Constitution of the State confers the judicial power on the courts, Art. VII, sec. 2. The decision of questions of fact, and determination of the weight to be given to evidence of various types, are judicial functions exercised by the courts from time immemorial. It is the duty of the courts, as well as their power, to adopt the principles of proof best calculated to determine such questions correctly. They should not wait for the legislature to take the initiative to that end. Courts should not shut their eyes to advances in science which conclusively establish a fact, by simply repeating the age-old maxim that credibility of witnesses is for the trier of fact.

In the instant case, we are satisfied that the trial court failed to give proper weight to the unimpeached evidence with respect to blood tests, and that in so doing, and thereby holding the appellant responsible for the support of another man's child, the decision will work a grave injustice.

In coming to the conclusions above stated, we do not overlook the possibility of human error in blood testing as in other procedures. We would preserve to the party against whose contentions blood tests operate to the fullest opportunity to challenge the qualifications of the testers, the propriety of the testing procedures and the correctness of the report of their result. The plaintiff had such opportunity here, and failed to discredit the tests or the testers in the slightest degree. The tests were therefore entitled to full weight.

NOTES AND QUESTIONS

1. Notice that there were, in essence, two crucial pieces of evidence presented on the issue of paternity: first, the blood test; second, the wife's sworn testimony. What aspects of the evidence do we refer to when we say that one piece of evidence is "scientific" evidence, and the other is not? Note that almost everyone (even the judges who wrote the majority opinion) seemed to be convinced that the "scientific" evidence was, on the issue of paternity, infallible, and that Mrs. Prochnow was therefore necessarily lying on the stand. How do you explain this attitude? Was the blood test infallible?

2. If the majority felt (as seems likely) that Mrs. Prochnow was not telling the truth, on what basis could they persist in their decision? Do you think that (a) they felt certain institutional or role pressures, which outweighed their devotion to scientific truth; or (b) they felt the issue was not really one of "scientific truth," but merely took that form; or (c) they were responding to some entirely different factor?

3. In 1957, the Wisconsin legislature enacted a statute changing the law about blood tests. In a paternity proceeding, or any civil action where it is relevant "to determine the parentage or identity of any child," blood-test results "shall constitute conclusive evidence where exclusion is established." Wis. Stat. Ann. §§ 52.36, 325.23 (1957).

In the absence of any information on the legislative history of this proposal, what guesses would you make about the reasons why the legislature passed this law? Compare and contrast the process you assume to have happened with the process that resulted in passage of the first Food and Drug Act. *See* Reading 60, at 561, *supra.*

4. A defendant who is "insane" cannot be found guilty of committing most crimes. In what respects, do you think, is the issue of a person's insanity similar to the issue of paternity, that is, a question of science or fact, and in what respects do you think it is different? *See* Halleck, Reading 79, at 671, *infra.*

78. Being Mentally Ill: A Sociological Theory

THOMAS J. SCHEFF*

LEGAL AND PSYCHIATRIC SCREENING OF INCOMING PATIENTS

The data upon which this phase of the study is based were
drawn from psychiatrists' ratings of a sample of patients newly
admitted to the public mental hospitals in a Midwestern state,
official court records, interviews with court officials and psychiatrists, and our observations of psychiatric examinations in four
courts. The psychiatrists' ratings of new patients will be considered first.

In order to obtain a rough measure of the incoming patient's
qualifications for involuntary confinement, a survey of newly
admitted patients was conducted with the cooperation of the hospital psychiatrists. All psychiatrists who made admission examinations in the three large mental hospitals in the state filled out
a questionnaire for the first ten consecutive patients they examined in the month of June 1962. A total of 223 questionnaires
were returned by the 25 admission psychiatrists. Although these
returns do not constitute a probability sample of all new patients
admitted during the year, there were no obvious biases in the
drawing of the sample. For this reason, this group of patients
will be taken to be typical of the newly admitted patients in
Midwestern State.

The two principal legal grounds for involuntary confinement
in the United States are the police power of the state (the state's
right to protect itself from dangerous persons) and *parens patriae*
(the State's right to assist those persons who, because of their own
incapacity, may not be able to assist themselves). As a measure
of the first ground, the potential dangerousness of the patient,
the questionnaire contained this item: "In your opinion, if this
patient were released at the present time, is it likely he would
harm himself or others?" The psychiatrists were given six options,

---

* Professor of Sociology, University of California, Santa Barbara. Copyright © 1966 Thomas J. Scheff. Reprinted from pp. 130-53, by permission.
(Published by the Aldine Publishing Company, Chicago.)

ranging from Very Likely to Very Unlikely. Their responses were: Very Likely, 5 per cent; Likely, 4 per cent; Somewhat Likely, 14 per cent; Somewhat Unlikely, 20 per cent; Unlikely, 37 per cent; Very Unlikely, 18 per cent. (Three patients were not rated, 1 per cent.)

As a measure of the second ground, *parens patriae*, the questionnaire contained the item: "Based on your observations of the patient's behavior, his present degree of mental impairment is:

None . . . Minimal . . . Mild . . . Moderate . . . Severe . . ."

The psychiatrists' responses were: None, 2 per cent; Minimal, 12 per cent; Mild, 25 per cent; Moderate, 42 per cent; Severe, 17 per cent. (Three patients were not rated, 1 per cent.)

To be clearly qualified for involuntary confinement, a patient should be rated as likely to harm self or others (Very Likely, Likely, or Somewhat Likely), and/or as Severely Mentally Impaired. However, voluntary patients should be excluded from this analysis, since the court is not required to assess their qualifications for confinement. Excluding the 59 voluntary admissions (26 per cent of the sample) leaves a sample of 164 involuntarily confined patients. Of these patients, 10 were rated as meeting both qualifications for involuntary confinement, 21 were rated as being severely mentally impaired, but not dangerous, 28 were rated as dangerous but not severely mentally impaired, and 102 were rated as not dangerous nor as severely mentally impaired. (Three patients were not rated.)

According to these ratings, there is considerable uncertainty connected with the screening of newly admitted involuntary patients in the state, since a substantial majority (63 per cent) of the patients did not clearly meet the statutory requirements for involuntary confinement. How does the agency responsible for assessing the qualifications for confinement, the court, react in the large numbers of cases involving uncertainty?

On the one hand, the legal rulings on this point by higher courts are quite clear. They have repeatedly held that there should be a presumption of sanity. The burden of proof of insanity is to be on the petitioners, there must be a preponderance of evidence, and the evidence should be of a "clear and unexceptionable" nature.

On the other hand, existing studies suggest that there is a presumption of illness by mental health officials. [David] Mechanic describes admissions to two large mental hospitals located in an urban area in California in this way:

In the crowded state or county hospitals, which is the most typical situation, the psychiatrist does not have sufficient time to make a very complete psychiatric diagnosis, nor do his psychiatric tools provide him with the equipment for an expeditious screening of the patient. . . .

In the two mental hospitals studied over a period of three months, the investigator never observed a case where the psychiatrist advised the patient that he did not need treatment. Rather, all persons who appeared at the hospital were absorbed into the patient population regardless of their ability to function adequately outside the hospital.[7]

A comment by Brown suggests that it is a fairly general understanding among mental health workers that state mental hospitals in the United States accept all comers. In a study of 58 commitment proceedings, Miller found that some of the proceedings were "routine rituals."

Kutner, describing commitment procedures in Chicago in 1962, also reports a strong presumption of illness by the staff of the Cook County Mental Health Clinic:

Certificates are signed as a matter of course by staff physicians after little or no examination . . . The so-called examinations are made on an assembly-line basis, often being completed in two or three minutes, and never taking more then ten minutes. Although psychiatrists agree that it is practically impossible to determine a person's sanity on the basis of such a short and hurried interview, the doctors recommend confinement in 77 per cent of the cases. It appears in practice that the alleged-mentally-ill is presumed to be insane and bears the burden of proving his sanity in the few minutes allotted to him.

These citations suggest that mental health officials handle uncertainty by presuming illness. Other investigators, however, have reported conflicting findings. To ascertain if the presumption of illness occurred in Midwestern State, intensive observations of screening procedures were conducted in the four courts with the largest volume of mental cases in the state. These courts were located in the two most populous cities in the state. Before giving the results of these observations, it is necessary to describe the steps in the legal procedures for hospitalization and commitment. The process of screening persons alleged to be mentally ill can be visualized as containing five steps in Midwestern State:

---

[7] D. Mechanic, "Some Factors in Identifying and Defining Mental Illness," *Mental Hygiene*, 46 (January, 1962), pp. 66-74.

1. The application for judicial inquiry, made by three citizens. This application is heard by deputy clerks in two of the courts (C and D), by a court reporter in the third court, and by a court commissioner in the fourth court.

2. The intake examination, conducted by a hospital psychiatrist.

3. The psychiatric examination, conducted by two psychiatrists appointed by the court.

4. The interview of the patient by the guardian *ad litem*, a lawyer appointed in three of the courts to represent the patient. (Court A did not use guardians *ad litem*.)

5. The judicial hearing, conducted by a judge.

These five steps take place roughly in the order listed, although in many cases (those cases designated as emergencies) step No. 2, the intake examination, may occur before step 1. Steps 1 and 2 usually take place on the same day or the day after hospitalization. Steps 3, 4, and 5 usually take place within a week of hospitalization. (In courts C and D, however, the judicial hearing is held only once a month.)

This series of steps would seem to provide ample opportunity for the presumption of health, and a thorough assessment, therefore, of the patient's qualifications for involuntary confinement, since there are five separate points at which discharge could occur. According to our findings, however, these procedures usually do not serve the function of screening out persons who do not meet statutory requirements. At most of these decision points, in most of the courts, retention of the patient in the hospital was virtually automatic. A notable exception to this pattern was found in one of the three state hospitals; this hospital attempted to use step No. 2, the intake examination, as a screening point to discharge patients that the superintendent described as "illegitimate," i.e., patients who do not qualify for involuntary confinement. In the other two hospitals, however, this examination was perfunctory and virtually never resulted in a finding of health and a recommendation of discharge. In a similar manner, the other steps were largely ceremonial in character. For example, in court B, we observed twenty-two judicial hearings, all of which were conducted perfunctorily and with lightning rapidity. (The mean time of these hearings was 1.6 minutes.) The judge asked each patient two or three routine questions: "How do you feel?" "How are you being treated?" "Would you cooperate with the doctors if they think you should stay awhile?" *Whatever* the patient's answer, however, the judge immediately ended the hearing, managing in this way to average less than two minutes per patient. Even if the patient was extremely outspoken, no attempt was made to accommodate him. The following excerpt from an official transcript provides an example of such a case:

J. "How are you, Miss _____?"
P. "Oh, pretty good."
J. "Are they treating you all right?"
P. "Yes."
J. "Any complaints?"
P. "No. The only complaint I have is that they won't let me out."
J. "Well, do you want to get out?"
P. "Sure."
J. "What if the doctors say you should stay for a while to get well?"
P. "Well, I don't see why I was sick, come in here in the first place."
J. "Well, let's see what the doctors say. Have they examined you yet—the doctors?"
P. "Well, examine me for what? For mental condition? I'm not mental as far as that is. The ones who brought me here—I think should be examined."
J. "Who brought you here?"
P. "The Police Department. Why, they come over to my house and they just grab people just like this. They try to make me say there is two tables when there is only one. What would you expect"
J. "All right, Miss _____."
P. "Where are your laws of today? I see that the laws are not very fair, not just either, or maybe your hospital needs money. We have to come here to help pay your bills . . ." (The patient had become quite angry.)
J. "Well, we are overcrowded now."
P. "Well, then where is your justice in this world today? You have none, the way it looks to me. I think better justice should be done with your Police Department and your authority . . ."
J. "All right, Miss _____, thank you."
P. "That's all I ask you to do. There are probably many like me today are facing the same problems that I do and they are not even guilty to be put up in a mental institution . . ."
J. "All right."

It should be noted that the judge made no attempt to inform this voluble patient of her right to counsel, which might have relieved her considerably. In this court, informing the patient of her rights was supposedly done through the guardian *ad litem*. The patient, however, had no way of knowing this at the time of the hearing.

Our observations of the guardian's interviews suggested, furthermore, that the guardians were not likely to take the patient's side, since, like the examining psychiatrists, they were paid a flat fee for each case. That is, their rate of pay depended on the rapidity with which they could finish. In recommending hospitalization, they were avoiding interruption of the already-occurring process of hospitalization and treatment; hence their interview could be quite short. If, on the other hand, they wished to recommend discharge, they would have to interrupt an on-going process, take the responsibility for such interruption, and build a case for discharge. Building such a case would have required considerably more time, thus severely reducing their rate of pay.

In the twelve interviews we observed by guardians, none of the guardians informed the patient of his rights. This omission was especially striking in the three interviews of one guardian, since he was quite vocal about the rights of the patients when interviewed beforehand:

Q: "What is the function of the guardian *ad litem*?"
A: "To protect the legal rights of the ward."
Q: "What are these rights?"
A: "*One*: trial by jury.
Two: right to his own attorney.
Three: right to a hearing.
Four: right to petition for a re-examination.
I think that the right to private counsel is very important."

Noticing that in none of the three cases did he inform the patient of any of the rights he quoted above, the interviewer asked him about the third case, in which this information might have been particularly useful to the patient.

Q: "I don't remember for sure, but did you tell John _____ (the last patient interviewed) about his right to a lawyer? Was this an oversight or did you skip it purposely?"
A: "I didn't purposely skip it so that he wouldn't know about it but I was conscious of not telling him. You know lawyers don't work for nothing and I had it in the back of my mind that Mr. _____ (the patient) was not able to pay for any lawyer because, as you remember, he said he had enough to get to Minneapolis. A guy hates to refer a client when he knows that client can't pay."

What appeared to be the key role in justifying these procedures was played in step No. 3, the examination by the court-appointed psychiatrists. In our informal discussions of screening with the judges, and other court officials, these officials made it clear that although the statutes give the court the responsibility for the decision to confine or release persons alleged to be mentally ill, they would rarely if ever take the responsibility for releasing a mental patient without a medical recommendation to that effect. The question which is crucial, therefore, for the entire screening process is whether or not the court-appointed psychiatric examiners presume illness. . . .

Our observations of 116 judicial hearings raised the question of the adequacy of the psychiatric examination. Eighty-six of the hearings failed to establish that the patients were "mentally ill" (according to the criteria stated by the judges in interviews).[13] Indeed, the behavior and responses of 48 of the patients at the hearings seemed completely unexceptionable. Yet the psychiatric examiners had not recommended the release of a single one of these patients. Examining the court records of 80 additional cases, we found still not a single recommendation for release.

Although the recommendation for treatment of 196 out of 196 consecutive cases strongly suggests that the psychiatric examiners were presuming illness, particularly when we observed 48 of these patients to be responding appropriately, it is conceivable that this is not the case. The observer for this study was not a psychiatrist (he was a first year graduate student in social work) and it is possible that he could have missed evidence of disorder which a psychiatrist might have seen. It was therefore arranged for the observer to be present at a series of psychiatric examinations, in order to determine whether the examinations appeared to be merely formalities or whether, on the other hand, through careful examination and interrogation, the psychiatrists were able to establish illness even in patients whose appearance and responses were not obviously disordered. The observer was instructed to note the examiner's procedures, the criteria they appeared to use in arriving at their decision, and their reaction to uncertainty.

Each of the courts discussed here employs the services of a panel of physicians as medical examiners. The physicians are paid a flat fee of ten dollars per examination, and are usually assigned from three to five patients for each trip to the hospital.

---

[13] In interviews with the judges, the following criteria were named: appropriateness of behavior and speech, understanding of the situation, and orientation.

In court A, most of the examinations are performed by two psychiatrists, who go to the hospital once a week, seeing from five to ten patients a trip. In courts B, C, and D, a panel of local physicians is used. These courts seek to arrange the examinations so that one of the examiners is a psychiatrist, the other a general practitioner. Court B has a list of four such pairs, and appoints each pair for a month at a time. Courts C and D have a similar list, apparently with some of the same names as court B.

To obtain physicians who were representative of the panel used in these courts, we arranged to observe the examinations of the two psychiatrists employed by court A, and one of the four pairs of physicians used in court B, one a psychiatrist, the other a general practitioner. We observed 13 examinations in court A and 13 examinations in court B. The judges in courts C and D refused to give us the names of the physicians on their panels, and we were unable to observe examinations in these courts. (The judge in court D stated that he did not want these physicians harassed in their work, since it was difficult to obtain their services even under the best of circumstances.) In addition to observing the examinations by four psychiatrists, we interviewed three other psychiatrists used by these courts.

The medical examiners followed two lines of questioning. One line was to inquire about the circumstances which led to the patient's hospitalization, the other was to ask standard questions to test the patient's orientation and his capacity for abstract thinking by asking him the date, the President, Governor, proverbs, and problems requiring arithmetic calculation. These questions were often asked very rapidly, and the patient was usually allowed only a very brief time to answer.

It should be noted that the psychiatrists in these courts had access to the patient's record (which usually contained the Application for Judicial Inquiry and the hospital chart notes on the patient's behavior), and that several of the psychiatrists stated that they almost always familiarized themselves with this record before making the examination. To the extent that they were familiar with the patient's circumstances from such outside information, it is possible that the psychiatrists were basing their diagnosis of illness less on the rapid and peremptory examination than on this other information. Although this was true to some extent, the importance of the record can easily be exaggerated, both because of the deficiencies in the typical record, and because of the way it is usually utilized by the examiners.

The deficiencies of the typical record were easily discerned in the approximately one hundred applications and hospital charts which the author read. Both the applications and charts were extremely brief and sometimes garbled. Moreover, in some of the cases where the author and interviewer were familiar with the circumstances involved in the hospitalization, it was not clear that the complainant's testimony was any more accurate than the version presented by the patient. Often the original complaint was so paraphrased and condensed that the application seemed to have little meaning.

The attitude of the examiners toward the record was such that even in those cases where the record was ample, it often did not figure prominently in their decision. Disparaging remarks about the quality and usefulness of the record were made by several of the psychiatrists. One of the examiners was apologetic about his use of the record, giving us the impression that he thought that a good psychiatrist would not need to resort to any information outside his own personal examination of the patient. A casual attitude toward the record was openly displayed in 6 of the 26 examinations we observed. In these six examinations, the psychiatrist could not (or in three cases, did not bother to) locate the record and conducted the examination without it, with one psychiatrist making it a point of pride that he could easily diagnose most cases "blind."

In his observations of the examinations, the interviewer was instructed to rate how well the patient responded by noting his behavior during the interview, whether he answered the orientation and concept questions correctly, and whether he denied and explained the allegations which resulted in his hospitalization. If the patient's behavior during the interview obviously departed from conventional social standards (e.g., in one case the patient refused to speak), if he answered the orientation questions incorrectly, or if he did not deny and explain the petitioners' allegations, the case was rated as meeting the statutory requirements for hospitalization. Of the 26 examinations observed, eight were rated as "Criteria Met."

If, on the other hand, the patient's behavior was appropriate, his answers correct, and he denied and explained the petitioners' allegations, the interviewer rated the case as not meeting the statutory criteria. Of the 26 cases, seven were rated as "Criteria Not Met." Finally, if the examination was inconclusive, but the interviewer felt that more extensive investigation might have established that the criteria were met, he rated the cases as "Criteria Possibly Met." Of the 26 examined, 11 were rated in this way. The interviewer was instructed that whenever he was in doubt to avoid using the rating "Criteria Not Met."

Even giving the examiners the benefit of the doubt, the interviewer's ratings were that a substantial majority of the examinations he observed failed to establish that the statutory criteria were met. The relationship between the examiners' recommendations and the interviewer's ratings are shown in Table 2.

TABLE 2
OBSERVER'S RATINGS AND EXAMINERS' RECOMMENDATIONS

| Examiners' Recommendations | Observer's Ratings | | | |
	Criteria Met	Criteria Possibly Met	Criteria Not Met	Total
Commitment	7	9	2	18
30-day Observation	1	2	3	6
Release	0	0	2	2
Total	8	11	7	26

The interviewer's ratings suggest that the examinations established that the statutory criteria were met in only 8 cases, but the examiners recommended that the patient be retained in the hospital in 24 cases, leaving 16 cases which the interviewer rated as uncertain, and in which retention was recommended by the examiners. The observer also rated the patient's expressed desires regarding staying in the hospital, and the time taken by the examination. The ratings of the patient's desire concerning staying or leaving the hospital were: Leave, 14 cases; Indifferent, 1 case; Stay, 9 cases; and Not Ascertained, 2 cases. In only one of the 14 cases in which the patient wished to leave was the interviewer's rating Criteria Met.

Interviews ranged in length from five minutes to 17 minutes, with the mean time being 10.2 minutes. Most of the interviews were hurried, with the questions of the examiners coming so rapidly that the examiner often interrupted the patient, or one examiner interrupted the other. All of the examiners seemed quite hurried. One psychiatrist, after stating in an interview (before we observed his examinations) that he usually took about thirty minutes, stated:

> It's not remunerative. I'm taking a hell of a cut. I can't spend 45 minutes with a patient. I don't have the time, it doesn't pay.

In the eight examinations that we observed, this physician actually spent 8, 10, 5, 8, 8, 7, 17, and 11 minutes with the patients, or an average of 9.2 minutes.

In these short time periods, it is virtually impossible for the examiner to extend his investigation beyond the standard orientation questions and a short discussion of the circumstances which brought the patient to the hospital. In those cases where the patient answered the orientation questions correctly, behaved appropriately, and explained his presence at the hospital satisfactorily, the examiners did not attempt to assess the reliability of the petitioner's complaints, or to probe further into the patient's answers. Given the fact that in most of these instances the examiners were faced with borderline cases, that they took little time in the examinations, and that they usually recommended commitment, we can only conclude that their decisions were based largely on a presumption of illness. Supplementary observations reported by the interviewer support this conclusion.

After each examination, the observer asked the examiner to explain the criteria he used in arriving at his decision. The observer also had access to the examiner's official report, so that he could compare what the examiner said about the case with the record of what actually occurred during the interview. This supplementary information supports the conclusion that the examiner's decisions are based on the presumption of illness, and sheds light on the manner in which these decisions are reached:

1. The "evidence" upon which the examiners based their decision to retain often seemed arbitrary.

2. In some cases, the decision to retain was made even when no evidence could be found.

3. Some of the psychiatrists' remarks suggest prejudgment of the cases.

4. Many of the examinations were characterized by carelessness and haste.

The first question, concerning the arbitrariness of the psychiatric evidence, will now be considered. In the weighing of the patient's responses during the interview, the physician appeared not to give the patient credit for the large number of correct answers he gave. In the typical interview, the examiner might ask the patient fifteen or twenty questions: the date, time, place, who is President, Governor, etc., what is 11×10, 11×11, etc., explain "Don't put all your eggs in one basket," "A rolling stone gathers no moss," etc. The examiners appeared to feel that a wrong answer established lack of orientation, even when it was preceded by a series of correct answers. In other words, the examiners do not establish any standard score on the orientation questions, which would give an objective picture of the degree to which the patient answered the questions correctly, but seem at times to search until they find an incorrect answer.

For those questions which were answered incorrectly, it was not always clear whether the incorrect answers were due to the patient's "mental illness," or to the time pressure in the interview, the patient's lack of education, or other causes. Some of the questions used to establish orientation were sufficiently difficult that persons not mentally ill might have difficulty with them. Thus one of the examiners always asked, in a rapid-fire manner: "What year is it?" What year was it seven years ago? Seventeen years before that? etc. Only two of the five patients who were asked this series of questions were able to answer it correctly. However, it is a moot question whether a higher percentage of persons in a household survey would be able to do any better. To my knowledge, none of the orientation questions that are used have been checked in a normal population.

Finally, the interpretations of some of the evidence as showing mental illness seemed capricious. Thus one of the patients, when asked, "In what ways are a banana, an orange, and an apple alike?" answered, "They are all something to eat." This answer was used by the examiner in explaining his recommendation to commit. The observer had noted that the patient's behavior and responses seemed appropriate and asked why the recommendation to commit had been made. The doctor stated that her behavior had been bizarre (possibly referring to her alleged promiscuity), her affect inappropriate ("When she talked about being pregnant, it was without feeling,") and with regard to the question above: "She wasn't able to say a banana and an orange were fruit. She couldn't take it one step further, she had to say it was something to eat." In other words, this psychiatrist was suggesting that in her thinking the patient manifested concreteness, which is held to be a symptom of mental illness. Yet in her other answers to classification questions, and to proverb interpretations, concreteness was not apparent, suggesting that the examiner's application of this test was arbitrary. In another case, the physician stated that he thought the patient was suspicious and distrustful, because he had asked about the possibility of being represented by counsel at the judicial hearing. The observer felt that these and other similar interpretations might possibly be correct, but that further investigation of the supposedly incorrect responses would be needed to establish that they were manifestations of disorientation.

In several cases where even this type of evidence was not available, the examiners still recommended retention in the hospital. Thus, one examiner employed by court A stated that he had recommended 30-day observation for a patient whom he had thought *not* to be mentally ill, on the grounds that the patient, a young man, could not get along with his parents, and "might get into trouble." This examiner went on to say:

> We always take the conservative side (commitment or observation). Suppose a patient should commit suicide. We always make the conservative decision. I had rather play it safe. There's no harm in doing it that way.

It appeared to the observer that "playing safe" meant that even in those cases where the examination established nothing, the psychiatrists did not consider recommending release. Thus in one case the examination had established that the patient had a very good memory, was oriented, and spoke quietly and seriously. The observer recorded his discussion with the physician after the examination as follows:

> When the doctor told me he was recommending commitment for this patient too (he had also recommended commitment in the two examinations held earlier that day) he laughed because he could see what my next question was going to be. He said, "I already recommended the release of two patients this month." This sounded like it was the maximum amount the way he said it.

Apparently this examiner felt that he had a very limited quota on the number of patients he could recommend for release (less than 2 per cent of those examined).

The language used by these physicians tends to intimate that mental illness was found, even when reporting the opposite. Thus in one case the recommendation stated: "No gross evidence of delusions or hallucinations." This statement is misleading, since not only was there no gross evidence, there was not any evidence, not even the slightest suggestion of delusions or hallucinations, brought out by the interview.

These remarks suggest that the examiners prejudge the cases they examine. Several further comments indicate prejudgment. One physician stated that he thought that most crimes of violence were committed by patients released too early from mental hospitals. (This is an erroneous belief.) He went on to say that he thought that all mental patients should be kept in the hospital at least three months, indicating prejudgment concerning his examinations. Another physician, after a very short interview (8 minutes), told the observer:

> On the schizophrenics, I don't bother asking them more questions when I can see they're schizophrenic because *I*

know what they are going to say. You could talk to them
another half hour and not learn any more.

Another physician, finally, contrasted cases in which the patient's
family or others initiated hospitalization ("petition cases," the
great majority of cases) with those cases initiated by the court:

The petition cases are pretty *automatic.* If the patient's own
family wants to get rid of him you know there is something
wrong.

The lack of care which characterized the examinations is evident in the forms on which the examiners make their recommendations. On most of these forms, whole sections have been
left unanswered. Others are answered in a peremptory and uninformative way. For example, in the section entitled "Physical
Examination," the question is asked: "Have you made a physical
examination of the patient? State fully what is the present physical condition." A typical answer is "Yes. Fair.," or "Is apparently
in good health." Since in none of the examinations we observed
was the patient actually physically examined, these answers appear
to be mere guesses. One of the examiners used regularly in court
B, to the question "On what subject or in what way is derangement now manifested?" always wrote in "Is mentally ill." The
omissions, and the almost flippant brevity of these forms, together
with the arbitrariness, lack of evidence, and prejudicial character
of the examinations, discussed above, all support the observer's
conclusion that, except in very unusual cases, the psychiatric
examiner's recommendation to retain the patient is virtually
automatic.

Lest it be thought that these results are unique to a particularly backward Midwestern State, it should be pointed out that
this state is noted for its progressive psychiatric practices. It will
be recalled that a number of the psychiatrists employed by
the court as examiners had finished their psychiatric residencies,
which is not always the case in many other states. A still common practice in other states is to employ, as members of the
"Lunacy Panel," partially retired physicians with no psychiatric
training whatever. This was the case, in 1959, in Stockton, California, where I observed hundreds of hearings at which these
physicians were present. It may be indicative of some of the
larger issues underlying the question of civil commitment that,
in these hearings, the physicians played very little part; the judge
controlled the questioning of the relatives and patients, and the
hearings were often a model of impartial and thorough investigation.

Ratings of the qualifications for involuntary confinement of patients newly admitted to the public mental hospitals in a Midwestern state, together with observations of judicial hearings and psychiatric examinations by the observer connected with the present study, suggest that the decision as to the mental condition of a majority of the patients is an uncertain one. The fact that the courts seldom release patients, and the perfunctory manner in which the legal and medical procedures are carried out, suggest that the judicial decision to retain patients in the hospital for treatment is routine and largely based on the presumption of illness. Three reasons for this presumption will be discussed: financial, ideological, and political.

Our discussions with the examiners indicated that one reason that they perform biased "examinations" is that their rate of pay is determined by the length of time spent with the patient. In recommending retention, the examiners are refraining from interrupting the hospitalization and commitment procedures already in progress, and thereby allowing someone else, usually the hospital, to make the effective decision to release or commit. In order to recommend release, however, they would have to build a case showing why these procedures should be interrupted. Building such a case would take much more time than is presently expended by the examiners, thereby reducing their rate of pay.

A more fundamental reason for the presumption of illness by the examiners, and perhaps the reason why this practice is allowed by the courts, is the interpretation of current psychiatric doctrine by the examiners and court officials. These officials make a number of assumptions, which are now thought to be of doubtful validity:

1. The condition of mentally ill persons deteriorates rapidly without psychiatric assistance.

2. Effective psychiatric treatments exist for most mental illnesses.

3. Unlike surgery, there are no risks involved in involuntary psychiatric treatment: it either helps or is neutral, it can't hurt.

4. Exposing a prospective mental patient to questioning, cross-examination, and other screening procedures exposes him to the unnecessary stigma of trial-like procedures, and may do further damage to his mental condition.

5. There is an element of danger to self or others in most mental illness. It is better to risk unnecessary hospitalization than the harm the patient might do himself or others.

Many psychiatrists and others now argue that none of these assumptions are necessarily correct.

1. The assumption that psychiatric disorders usually get worse without treatment rests on very little other than evidence of an anecdotal character. There is just as much evidence that most acute psychological and emotional upsets are self-terminating.

2. It is still not clear, according to systematic studies evaluating psychotherapy, drugs, etc., that most psychiatric interventions are any more effective, on the average, than no treatment at all.

3. There is very good evidence that involuntary hospitalization and social isolation may affect the patient's life: his job, his family affairs, etc. There is some evidence that too hasty exposure to psychiatric treatment may convince the patient that he is "sick," prolonging what might have been an otherwise transitory episode.

4. This assumption is correct, as far as it goes. But it is misleading because it fails to consider what occurs when the patient who does not wish to be hospitalized is forcibly treated. Such patients often become extremely indignant and angry, particularly in the case, as often happens, when they are deceived into coming to the hospital on some pretext.

5. The element of danger is usually exaggerated both in amount and degree. In the psychiatric survey of new patients in state mental hospitals, danger to self or others was mentioned in about a fourth of the cases. Furthermore, in those cases where danger is mentioned, it is not always clear that the risks involved are greater than those encountered in ordinary social life. This issue has been discussed by Ross, an attorney:

> A truck driver with a mild neurosis who is "accident prone" is probably a greater danger to society than most psychotics; yet, he will not be committed for treatment, even if he would be benefited. The community expects a certain amount of dangerous activity. I suspect that as a class, drinking drivers are a greater danger than the mentally ill, and yet the drivers are tolerated or punished with small fines rather than indeterminate imprisonment.*

From our observations of the medical examinations and other commitment procedures, we formed a very strong impression that the doctrines of danger to self or others, early treatment, and the avoidance of stigma were invoked partly because the officials be-

---

* Ross, *Commitment of the Mentally Ill: Problems of Law and Policy*, 57 MICH. L. REV. 945, 962 (1959). [Eds. note]

lieved them to be true, and partly because they provided convenient justification for a preexisting policy of summary action, minimal investigation, avoidance of responsibility and, after the patient is in the hospital, indecisiveness and delay.

The policy of presuming illness is probably both cause and effect of political pressure on the court from the community. The judge, an elected official, runs the risk of being more heavily penalized for erroneously releasing than for erroneously retaining patients. Since the judge personally appoints the panel of psychiatrists to serve as examiners, he can easily transmit the community pressure to them, by failing to reappoint a psychiatrist whose examinations were inconveniently thorough.

NOTE

For other empirical studies of commitment procedure, *see* Note, "The Need for Reform in the California Civil Commitment Procedure," 19 *Stanford Law Review* 992 (1967); Note, "Civil Commitment of the Mentally Ill," 14 *UCLA Law Review* 822 (1967). *See also* Alan M. Dershowitz, "The Psychiatrist's Power in Civil Commitment: A Knife That Cuts Both Ways," 2 *Psychology Today* 42 (1969).

79. A Critique of Current Psychiatric Roles in the Legal Process

SEYMOUR L. HALLECK*

1966 WISCONSIN LAW REVIEW 379

It must be noted that many practical inconsistencies and injustices can arise through psychiatric involvement in the courtroom. Specifically, the writer wishes to elaborate upon the following three points. (1) For any form of criminal justice to be effective it must be consistently applied to all men regardless of race or social or economic status. The writer will note that the issue of criminal responsibility is raised with unusual selectivity. (2) Implied in any legal contest of criminality and criminal responsibility is an assumption that to find a man not guilty by reason of insanity and to send him to a state hospital is a merciful and humane act. In practice this is a highly questionable assumption. (3) Effective utilization of the plea of criminal insanity implies that psychiatrists will come to eventual agreement on a workable definition of terms such as psychosis or mental illness. The writer contends that this is unlikely.

First, the use of psychiatric testimony to determine criminal responsibility is greatest in those states which have capital punishment. Here it should be noted, however, that not every emotionally disturbed offender who is on trial for his life uses this defense. Many factors other than the degree of emotional disturbance enter into the introduction of the insanity plea. Much depends on the circumstances of the crime, the availability of forensic psychiatrists,[30] the laws of the state, the attitude of

---

* Professor of Psychiatry, University of Wisconsin; Chief Psychiatric Consultant to the Wisconsin Division of Corrections. Copyright © 1966 Wisconsin Law Review. Reprinted by permission.

[30] The guilt or innocence of an emotionally disturbed offender may become highly dependent upon the skills of the defendant's psychiatrist. The psychiatrist's manner of presentation, his personality, and his credentials may have as much influence upon the jury as his scientific data. In this sense having a good psychiatrist becomes quite similar to having a good defense attorney. Unfortunately, a good psychiatrist—like a good attorney—costs money. In many jurisdictions it is extremely difficult for a poor person to find competent psychiatric assistance.

the community, and the offender's socioeconomic class. In many jurisdictions, for example, it would be quite unlikely that an uneducated Negro offender would plead insanity or be found not guilty by reason of insanity.

Even in states which do not have a death penalty, the plea of not guilty by reason of insanity is not invoked in a consistent manner. In the State of Wisconsin there are at the present time eleven inmates confined to the state hospital for the criminally insane who have been found not guilty by reason of insanity. Of this number eight are murderers. There are probably no more than ten to twenty individuals who are currently free (some of whom have spent many years in a mental hospital) who have been acquitted by reason of insanity. This is a very small group when compared with the total number of offenders in the state, and is made up mainly of individuals who have murdered or committed other violent crimes. What is important to note here is that the plea of insanity is practically never raised unless there has been a violent crime. If some murderers are not responsible for their behavior, then it is difficult to understand why there are not forgers, burglars, car thieves, and sex offenders who are similarly nonresponsible. The explanation must be that the plea of insanity is raised only when there is a possibility of a long prison sentence.

Several years ago the author and a colleague[31] studied the records of a group of offenders who were at that time committed to the Wisconsin State Hospital for the Criminally Insane after having been transferred from the Wisconsin State Prison. The issue of not guilty by reason of insanity had *never* been raised for these offenders, but they had nevertheless been too emotionally disturbed to remain in a prison. At the time of the study there were sixty such inmates living at the state hospital. Offhand, it might be assumed that these were relatively normal men who broke down under the stress of incarceration. This, however, was not the case. Over half of the inmates studied had a history of having spent time in a mental hospital before the commission of a criminal act. An additional twenty per cent, although not having a history of previous hospitalization, had revealed such overt pecu-

---

It is only fair to note also that some jurisdictions do provide psychiatric assistance for the offender who wishes to plead insanity. In some states an impartial panel of psychiatrists may provide testimony as to the defendant's sanity. The State of Massachusetts goes even further—under the Brigg's law anyone charged with a capital offense and most felons are automatically examined to determine their sanity. See MASS. ANN. LAWS ch. 123, § 100A (1965).

[31] Dr. Richard Thurrell, Assistant Professor of Psychiatry, University of Wisconsin.

liar behavior that the issue of insanity had been raised in the probation officer's presentence report. A number of these men had to be transferred to the state hospital almost immediately after their arrival at the prison.

It must be repeated that the emotional state of these men was never raised as a legal issue. Although even the most cursory kind of examination would have revealed the presence of what most psychiatrists would call mental illness, apparently nobody even wondered if these men were responsible for their acts. Since Wisconsin is an enlightened state which has an excellent tradition of social welfare, it is difficult to rationalize the cavalier disposition of these cases. Obviously, it must be that factors other than the degree of emotional disturbance preceding the criminal act operate in the selection of those who plead insanity. Whether these factors are the economic status of the offender, the type of crime he commits, his race, the attitude of local psychiatrists, the type of negotiated plea which is made with the district attorney, or the whim of the community, psychiatrists cannot be too proud of contributing to a system which offers one kind of justice for some men and another kind for others.

If one were to argue that although these men were defined as criminals they eventually ended up in the appropriate institution anyway, it would be difficult to disagree. The point is that if only a few offenders are found nonresponsible and if other disturbed offenders must find a circuitous route to the hospital, there is reason to be skeptical as to the value of psychiatry's humanitarian contribution in the courtroom. Those who support our current system of correctional justice should be troubled by the likelihood that the majority of emotionally disturbed offenders are never given an opportunity to plead insanity. The noble victories for humanism claimed when an occasional offender is found not guilty by reason of insanity pale in comparison to the grim indifference which society accords to a much larger group of men.

Second, at the conclusion of a recent widely publicized trial in the State of Wisconsin, some of the writer's colleagues were jubilant over what they perceived to be a victory for the forces of social welfare and righteousness. In this case a man had been found not guilty of murder by reason of insanity and was returned to the state hospital for the criminally insane. In spite of the enthusiasm which so many psychiatrists show for this kind of decision, there is reason to be skeptical of its humanitarian value. This particular offender had already spent several years at the hospital for the criminally insane, having been legally confined until he had shown sufficient improvement to be psychologically competent to stand trial. He was returning to an institution where he would continue to be deprived of freedom.

It is sometimes difficult to see what advantages are offered to the man who is committed to a hospital for the criminally insane. In the State of Wisconsin (which has one of the best of such hospitals) he is still sent to a heavy security institution. His cell is located behind several formidable locked doors and he is rarely allowed to leave the hospital grounds. Opportunities for receiving help are limited because the institution is chronically understaffed. (At the time of the particular case we are referring to, the state prison had approximately three times the amount of psychiatric and psychological help available as the state hospital.) Many of the men who are sent to the state hospital are retained for as long a period or longer than they would have been if given a criminal commitment.

It is true that punitive elements are less emphatically stressed at hospitals for the criminally insane than in prisons. Both types of institutions, however, are theoretically devoted to a program of rehabilitation. It is also true that in our society there may be punitive aspects to commitment to a state hospital which are reflected in social attitudes and which may be more devastating than legally codified punishment. For many the stigma of the mental hospital is more feared than the restraints of prison. Even seriously disturbed prison inmates may be reluctant to be transferred to a hospital setting. The mental illness role is resisted on the basis that dignity, self-esteem, and chances for an earlier release would be seriously compromised. Prison inmates sense that confinement to a hospital for the criminally insane is not an evasion of punishment nor a soft touch and that continued loss of freedom by confinement to an understaffed institution is a grim prospect whether it is called punishment or treatment.

Third, terms such as insanity, mental illness, psychosis, and neurosis may be definable for purposes of professional communication but they can never be refined so that they describe concrete categories. Value judgments invariably enter into any categorization of the individual patient, and although there are criteria by which attempts can be made to separate the mentally ill from the normal or the psychotic from the neurotic, these criteria are necessarily vague and equivocal. They serve best in separating obvious disorders; they are of little value when applied to the borderline cases.

Criminal offenders tend to have personality disorders which are not readily classifiable. The psychiatrist rarely sees offenders who are either overtly disorganized or who are in good psychological health. Because of the criminal's propensity for action and because he is exposed to so many different kinds of environments, he will show unusual variation in his mental status. It is not uncommon, for example, to find an offender who is grossly disorganized while awaiting trial, who is then fully coherent during court proceedings, who later decompensates at the prison, and who still later appears to reintegrate his personality when transferred to the state hospital. In cases such as this the diagnosis of psychosis becomes almost a matter of chance. It is dependent on the training, experience, and personal philosophies of the particular psychiatrist who examines the offender and the circumstances under which the offender is examined. Attempts to use such examinations to speculate as to the offender's emotional state at the time of the crime are extremely unreliable. What too often happens is that the judge and jury are subjected to a variety of opinions all of which may disagree and all of which may have a certain relevance.

The problem can be illustrated more clearly by a hypothetical case. While the example is fictional, everything recorded here has actually happened more than once in the State of Wisconsin and certainly must have occurred in other states.

Mr. *K* was arrested for the crime of forgery. While in the county jail he was observed behaving peculiarly and the sheriff requested a psychiatric examination. A psychiatrist examined the patient and stated that he was undergoing an acute schizophrenic reaction, that he was psychotic, and that he needed immediate hospitalization. The judge then committed Mr. *K* to hospital *X* for thirty days. At that institution a thorough examination was conducted and it was concluded that Mr. *K* was suffering from a chronic schizophrenic reaction, undifferentiated type and that he was not able to stand trial. The judge then committed Mr. *K* to hospital *Y* (a hospital for the criminally insane) until he was felt to be sufficiently recovered to stand trial. After he had spent two months at hospital *Y*, the staff felt that the patient was no longer psychotic and in their report expressed the view that he would be more correctly labeled a passive-aggressive personality, aggressive type. Mr. *K* was then returned to court to stand trial for his offense. At the time of the trial, the patient's attorneys raised the plea of not guilty by reason of insanity. Two psychiatrists testified that Mr. *K* was sane at the time of his offense and two testified that he was not. During the course of a lengthy trial a great amount of psychiatric testimony was heard, and in some ways there was considerable agreement among the psychiatric witnesses. They all agreed that Mr. *K* was a seriously disturbed person. They agreed that at times his behavior was ineffective and peculiar. There was further agreement that Mr. *K* needed treatment and that it would be of benefit to him. Yet when forced to strait-jacket their testimony into issues such as responsibility and mental illness, the psychiatrists disagreed violently. The judge found that Mr. *K* was sane and sentenced him to the state prison. Within two weeks after his arrival at the prison the patient became extremely disturbed, hallucinated, and unable to function. The prison psychiatrist found him to be psychotic and he was immediately transferred to state hospital *Y*. Within a month he appeared to have recovered and hospital psychiatrists recommended his return to the prison.

There are two problems here. One is that disturbed offenders show rapid fluctuations in their emotional state. The patient's immediate environment plays a major role in whatever psychological picture predominates at a given moment. A second problem is that even though Wisconsin psychiatrists are no less homogeneous than those in other states, they do differ widely in their concepts of psychosis and mental illness, particularly as applied to so-called borderline states. As human beings who hold to a variety of ethical positions, they also differ as to the degrees to which they would hold a man responsible for his behavior. These differences characterize not only individual psychiatrists but are also true at an institutional level. Thus one hospital may regularly utilize criteria of psychosis which are quite different from those preferred by another institution which may be located just a few miles away.

It is hoped the reader has noted that in the example given psychiatrists may have disagreed as to philosophical issues and problems of categorization, but there was general agreement as to what was wrong with the patient. The writer is not arguing that psychiatry is an inconsistent discipline nor that psychiatrists must always disagree with one another. When the psychiatrist confines himself to simply trying to understand and treat the disturbed individual, he uncovers dynamic patterns and uses techniques which are relatively consistent. In the courtroom, however, it often appears that psychiatrists are a group of inconsistent, disagreeable, and even ludicrous amateur philosophers. . . .

In spite of a high level of enthusiasm and commitment, it appears that the psychiatrist has been rather ineffective in influencing the law or promoting change in social attitudes towards the criminal. If the plea of not guilty by reason of insanity is now invoked with more frequency and is more often found to be an excusing condition, it is probably because society has independently changed some of its attitudes towards the criminal, and is willing to utilize psychiatry to provide a rationale for its wish to excuse certain offenders. In most sanity trials it is extremely easy to predict the outcome if even minimal information is available as to the type of crime committed, the status of the criminal in the community, and the attitudes of that community toward the offender. The psychiatrist is used to lend scientific authenticity to a social ritual; he is much more a pawn than a knight.

ARE THERE ALTERNATIVES?

Much of what is decided in the courtroom is influenced by an awareness of what happens to the offender once he is convicted. If our correctional system were more concerned with rehabilitation than with punishment, society would not be so preoccupied with finding the mentally ill nonresponsible. If we knew that the disturbed offender would be subjected to real treatment rather than neglect or cruelty, we would have little need to wrestle with unanswerable philosophical questions. One recourse for providing a rational role for psychiatry in the legal and correctional process is, therefore, dependent upon a radical alteration of many correctional practices.

An enlightened correctional system would employ psychiatrists for only two purposes: to help diagnose, treat, and rehabilitate all classes of offenders; and to help control dangerous offenders. If punishment were not the major issue, the criminal offender believed to be emotionally disturbed would be tried in court only with regard to the question of his actual commission of the crime. Mental illness would not mitigate criminal intent. All persons found to have committed a crime (except where *mens rea* did not exist for reasons other than mental illness) would be considered fully responsible. Psychiatrists and other behavioral scientists would be able to confine their role to assisting in the determination of what is to be done with the individual offender.[34]

Many systems have been proposed which would not allow the psychiatrist to testify as to responsibility, but would use him to aid in disposition and treatment. . . .

The psychiatrist is the only expert witness who is asked to form opinions as to man's responsibility and man's punishability. The toxicologist may testify as to the amount of poison in a victim's body and give an opinion as to cause of death. The orthopedic surgeon testifies as to the degree of motor incapacitation and its possible causes. The fingerprint or ballistics expert gives opinions which are strictly limited to his field of competence. None

---

[34] An enlightened system of justice would have to do away with the death penalty. As long as we continue to execute people, psychiatrists and others will be tempted to perjure themselves for humanitarian purposes.

of these experts is ever asked to give an opinion as to the guilt or responsibility of the offender. Only the psychiatrist is asked to testify and answer questions which go beyond his own training or competence. . . .

There are undoubtedly some who would argue that lay people could not decide on the responsibility of mentally ill offenders without receiving considerable direction from psychiatrists. The writer would strongly disagree with this view. If the community wishes to punish some and excuse others, it could just as easily make such decisions itself without forcing the problem upon the psychiatrist. As things stand today, the psychiatrist is often exploited to provide a pseudoscientific rationalization for actions which the community would take anyway. Changes in the current legal code which would make the psychiatrist more of an expert witness and the judge or jury more of a decision-making body would simply put each group into its proper and traditional role.

THE PROBLEM OF PRETRIAL COMMITMENTS

One practical legal issue which society must face is what to do with the offender who does not appear to be well enough to stand trial. Irrespective of the stand it takes on the issue of criminal responsibility, a humane society cannot afford to have confused or disorganized citizens tried in its courts. It is unlikely that such persons could adequately defend themselves and receive a fair trial. In most jurisdictions an alleged offender who is unable to understand the charges against him, is unable to understand the proceedings which are to be invoked, or is unable to assist his counsel is judged incompetent. He is then committed to a unit for the criminally insane until he regains his competency. All such commitments are based upon psychiatric testimony which is heard by a judge.

On the face of it this appears to be a straightforward and humane procedure. One major problem, however, is that confinement to an institution for the criminally insane represents a loss of freedom and is experienced as a form of punishment. If the individual does not recover he can spend the rest of his life behind bars. If he recovers slowly he will still be spending time in confinement without having been convicted of a crime. Given the deplorable condition of so many of our hospitals for the criminally insane, opportunities for recovery may be sorely limited. This is complicated by the fact that some judges and district attorneys are quite reluctant to try certain individuals and therefore they subtly encourage their continued confinement in a hospital. Obviously, in such a situation the civil liberties of an emotionally disturbed offender are in great jeopardy. He may be deprived of constitutional guarantees for a speedy trial, and he is placed in a kind of double jeopardy since time spent in the hospital is not considered in terms of a future sentence. . . .

Again we find that humanistic and conscientious psychiatrists have unwittingly contributed to social injustices. Many of the psychiatrists who testify on the issue of competency to stand trial are unfamiliar with conditions in hospitals for the criminally insane. Their frequent diagnoses of incompetency are intended to help sick people, but too often they result in only an arbitrary restriction of freedom. Part of the problem lies in the vagueness of terms such as ability to understand charges, ability to understand legal proceedings, or ability to assist counsel. Obviously these terms can only be defined quantitatively. Given a group of either normal or disturbed people, there are all degrees of ability to comprehend charges and proceedings or to co-operate.

In the writer's view, psychiatrists, particularly those who are psychoanalytically oriented, expect too much of a man before they call him competent. The greater proportion of the mentally ill and mentally defective who are now judged incompetent could probably do as good a job of protecting their interests in the courtroom as most other offenders of a similar socioeconomic class. It seems that with the enormous potential threat to civil liberties involved, psychiatrists would do better to define incompetency only as the most severe case of deficiency, confusion, or disorganization. Under our current system it might be argued that this would result in a number of disturbed persons having to reach the mental hospital only after a criminal commitment. This, however, might be preferable to the frightening possibility of endless incarceration without trial.

Actually, if our hospitals for the criminally insane were upgraded to the level possible in modern psychiatry, the great majority of incompetent offenders (even if our definition of incompetency were restricted as above) would be able to recover sufficiently to return to court in a few months. The only major exceptions would be the brain-damaged and the severely defective. Unfortunately no hospital for the criminally insane approaches the adequacy of private psychiatric hospitals or even public ones. There is also great variability of policy in these hospitals. Some superintendents of hospitals for the criminally insane work diligently to return their patients to court as soon as it is humanistically possible; others do not. Some jurisdictions encourage the hospitals to return offenders as rapidly as possible; others do not. In order to improve the plight of the noncompetent offender there would not only be a need for better hospitals but also a need to exert moral pressure upon psychiatrists, judges, and attorneys to more diligently guard the right to a speedy trial.

Even if psychiatrists were more careful in defining competency and even if psychiatrists and attorneys were more diligent in returning offenders to court, there would still be serious problems. A certain number of the severely disturbed and the severely retarded would still not recover. After a year or two in a hospital for the criminally insane, some offenders simply do not change. What is to be done with this small but troublesome group?[37] One possibility would be to release these individuals from all criminal proceedings and give them a civil commitment. This would at least entitle them to the possibility of parole and release. A mentally defective person, for example, might never be legally competent but could become sufficiently well socialized so that he could live in his community. While the writer is not unaware of some of the hazards and potential injustices of civil commitment (especially when proof of deviant behavior is not established), this does seem like a more humane approach. It would allow the psychiatrist and the community to continue to restrain truly dangerous offenders in a method similar to that by which dangerous patients not faced with criminal charges are currently restrained.

NOTES AND QUESTIONS

1. To what extent would the problems described by Scheff and Halleck be alleviated by spending more money on the provision of proper psychiatric aid to the legal process?

2. Halleck refers to the "humanitarian contribution" of psychiatry to the courtroom. Consider the following quotation from Lady Barbara Wooton, *Social Science and Social Pathology* 206 (1959).*

Without question, therefore, in the contemporary attitude towards anti-social behaviour, psychiatry and humanitarianism have marched hand in hand. Just because it is so much in keeping with the mental atmosphere of a scientifically-minded age, the medical treatment of social deviants has been a most

---

[37] In the State of Wisconsin, the Department of Public Welfare can parole an incompetent offender at any time, providing the committing court does not object. This practice works well in the majority of cases. Sometimes, however, the court is reluctant to parole men who could be safely released without endangering others.

* Published by George Allen and Unwin Ltd., London. Reprinted by permission.

powerful, perhaps even the most powerful, reinforcement of humanitarian impulses; for today the prestige of human proposals is immensely enhanced if these are expressed in the idiom of medical science. Indeed we might go so far as to say that, even if the intellectual foundations of current psychiatry were to be proved to be wholly unsound, and even if psychiatric "science" was exposed as nothing more than fantasy, we might yet have cause to be grateful for the result of so beneficent a delusion.

Are there serious dangers in Lady Wooton's argument? Does it not invite or excuse acts of an elite of experts, misleading the public in the name of some assumed social good, as they define it? How much difference does it make that psychiatrists who testify in an unscientific manner may be firmly convinced of the truth of their testimony and that what they say is grounded in science?

3. In 1881, President Garfield was shot to death by Charles J. Guiteau. In the long and disorderly trial that followed, the chief defense was Guiteau's insanity. The trial turned into a battle of psychiatric experts. The defending psychiatric experts, fighting to save Guiteau's life in the face of an outraged public opinion, were engaged in the kind of humanitarian battle that Lady Wooton has described. Ironically, however, their view of "insanity" was a hodge-podge in which notions of heredity and physical symptoms of insanity played a large part, to a degree that would be totally unacceptable to modern medicine. The trial is described in Charles E. Rosenberg, *The Trial of the Assassin Guiteau: Psychiatry and Law in the Guilded Age* (U. of Chicago Press 1968).

4. The assassin Guiteau was convicted and executed despite some—to modern readers—fairly convincing evidence of insanity. Public acceptability of the leadership of experts may vary with the type of crime. Assuming roughly the same evidence—aside from the crime itself—of insanity, is there the same likelihood that a man will be found not guilty by reason of insanity if he (a) assassinates the President; (b) strangles a series of women, wholly unknown to him, over a period of years; (c) takes a gun and rides through the countryside, robbing and killing ten people; (d) rapes and murders a sixteen-year-old girl; (e) kills his wife and her lover whom he surprised in a motel room; and (f) robs graves, commits cannibalistic acts, and dissects corpses.

5. As Halleck points out, very few defendants use the insanity defense in cases of burglary or embezzlement. Why? What does

this suggest about the role of expert psychiatric opinion in the courtroom?

6. There is an enormous polemic literature on the use of psychiatry in the law. An extreme anti-psychiatric view is found in Thomas Szasz, *Law, Liberty and Psychiatry* (MacMillan 1963). Where does Halleck stand? Is Halleck saying that psychiatry is not really a science? or that its categories cannot readily be applied to the requirements of a criminal trial? or that it cannot answer the questions posed by the criminal law because these questions are not such as can be answered by the use of psychiatric procedures? What is Scheff's attitude toward the "scientific" nature of psychiatry?

7. Delegation to experts, according to Scheff, may be one way which society uses to wash its hands of a problem. Note, however, the difference between psychiatric testimony in a criminal case, and the behavior of the judges in commitment cases. In a criminal case, the psychiatrist testifies, but does not decide; that role, both formally and informally, is in the hands of judge and jury. Think of the role played by engineers in patent cases, by doctors in tort and workmen's compensation cases. What do you think explains these differences in formal and in informal roles?

Consider the following report of an experiment with jurors selected from the jury pools of Chicago, St. Louis and Minneapolis. These jurors listened to a tape recording of a trial, and were asked to decide the case and answer questions about the process.

80. Jurors' Evaluation of Expert Psychiatric Testimony

RITA M. JAMES [SIMON]*

21 OHIO STATE LAW JOURNAL 75, 94-95 (1960)

The jurors listened to a criminal trial involving a charge of incest and a plea of insanity, in which the defense had relied solely on the testimony of two psychiatrists. Both doctors had testified that the defendant was mentally ill for some period preceding the trial and the acts with which he was charged were not an unexpected result of his earlier experiences. In contrast, the prosecution relied primarily on the testimony of lay witnesses, especially the testimony of the defendant's two daughters. They did call as a final witness a psychiatrist who had not examined the defendant and who testified very briefly.

In their reactions and evaluations of the expert testimony, the jurors made several points. They distinguished the contributions made by the defense and government psychiatrists. That is, they acknowledged that a doctor's testimony not based on first hand knowledge of the subject may not be worth as much as testimony which was derived from direct contact. Generally speaking, most jurors granted to the experts the recognition appropriate to their specialized training and greater knowledge. Jurors did not, so far as can be judged at this time, indicate any differences in their evaluation of the "model" in contrast to the "typical" version of psychiatric testimony. The longer, more detailed, straightforward account was not perceived as being significantly more helpful or more influential than the shorter and more technical "typical" version. Generally, jurors indicated that they were impressed with the full scope of the experts' performance on the stand. About three quarters of the jurors indicated that the testimony was helpful, and two thirds did not believe the language they employed was too technical or that more information was needed.

---

* Professor of Sociology, Institute of Communications, University of Illinois, Urbana. Copyright © Ohio State Law Journal. Reprinted by permission.

But as to the experts influencing the jurors insofar as the verdict was concerned, this was another matter.

It was almost because the jurors recognized that these men were experts, that they were members of a profession, that it gave the jurors license to grant them a certain degree of deference which did not also oblige them to accept the witnesses' statements as directives for their own action. As experts, these witnesses had a position and a view to represent, just as a member of the Chamber of Commerce might present the businessman's view, or a union leader, the working man's perspective. These witnesses represented the views of psychiatry about criminals. It is suggested that for many of the jurors they appeared as extreme and perhaps impractical views which, in the final assessment, most jurors did not choose to accept. This interpretation, concerning the failure of the experts to influence the jurors in their ultimate decisions, that of finding the defendant guilty or insane, is strongly supported by one statistic which we have deliberately delayed reporting: of the sixty-eight juries who heard and deliberated the case, only nine, or 13 per cent, found the defendant not guilty by reason of insanity. In brief, 71 per cent of the juries in finding the defendant guilty voted against the experts, and 16 per cent were unable to arrive at a unanimous verdict.

81. The Politics of Planning for Urban Redevelopment: Strategies in the Manipulation of Public Law

SHELDON J. PLAGER AND
JOEL F. HANDLER*

1966 WISCONSIN LAW REVIEW 724

In May 1961 at the city council meeting of Center City,** the mayor announced that a multimillion dollar, nine-square-block urban redevelopment project would be built, creating a new retail shopping complex in the heart of the downtown section, one block from the main business street. Center Circle—our name for the project—will profoundly affect the people of that community. To undertake the project, for a community the size of Center City, involved a political decision of the first magnitude. It involved a major reallocation of a scarce commodity— land in the heart of the central business district; a multimillion dollar investment by the private promoters; a previously undreamed of commitment of local public resources including capital improvements in the form of parking facilities, road improvements, and utility relocations; and a program of related public controls in the form of protective zoning. It involved a major economic shift away from the existing Main Street merchants to the promoters and developers of the project and their tenants. Streets had to be vacated, traffic patterns changed, people and businesses moved. Center Circle will affect where people will shop, how they will get to and from work, where they will live, and what type of growth and development they will have in their community. . . .

---

* Both authors are Professors of Law: Plager at the University of Illinois and Handler at the University of Wisconsin. Copyright © 1966 Wisconsin Law Review. Reprinted by permission.
** This name is fictitious. [Eds. note]

The legal process attempts to structure the decision-making process so that decisions will be consistent with public goals. The people of the community decide, through their official representatives, the basic pattern of development of the community—the comprehensive plan, the zoning ordinance, the subdivision regulations, and the building codes. If change is to be made, it is submitted first to those who specialize in this aspect of public decision making: the plan commission and the planners. This unit of government hears, considers, and then recommends to the elected representatives of the people, the city council. The council, after due notice and hearing, decides what is best for the community. Other units of government which may be affected (such as agencies concerned with parking, streets and traffic, utilities, and schools) are also consulted. If these units of government are autonomous, and if their services are needed, then their consent must also be obtained.

The legally prescribed procedures for public decision making reflect a democratic value: those to be affected by the decision are to be given a meaningful opportunity to be heard—the merchants, the site residents, the taxpayers, and the other interested people and groups. This does not necessarily mean that those affected will control the shape of the redevelopment program. In decisions of this type, some will gain and some will lose. But the process does contemplate that the legally authorized decision maker (the city council) will at least consider the competing interests. This is of benefit to the decision maker, since those who are directly affected presumably know the most about their particular problems. The required use of the local planning bodies and their decision-making procedures also reflects this democratic value. And the planning bodies, in theory at least, perform the additional function of providing the council with disinterested expert help.

Public participation and the assertion and consideration of affected interests—as required by law and democratic ideals—place the promoters in something of a dilemma. The legally prescribed methods of public decision making give the various affected interests not only the opportunity to be heard, but also the opportunity to defeat the project; they can persuade the local legislature to deny the necessary support. The procedures cannot be ignored by the promoters. At some point the project has to be brought to the surface and be submitted to the formal process of governmental decision making.

The outcome of the struggle at the public level and the integrity of the decision-making process itself will depend on how well the competing interests use the relevant resources available to them. There are two resources of particular importance. The first we call political skills. The proponents of the project have to gain the explicit consent of the governmental decision makers— the council and the plan commission. Their goal is to gain official planning and legislative support without running the risks of deliberative debate. The strategy is to enter the public arena when the potential opposition is still uninformed and unorganized and then proceed through the decision-making steps before the opposition can make itself felt. Success requires secrecy during the formative stages of the plan and co-operation from those public officials who are both powerful and sympathetic. When the plan is made public, the public machinery must move promptly and swiftly, before the opposition can acquire its own political skills.

But political skills are not enough for significant land-use planning issues. Another resource has to be used. We call this planning skills. Proposals for redevelopment projects (as well as counter-proposals) appear largely in technical form: statistical tables, charts, graphs, reports, maps, and drawings. The technical paraphernalia serve several vital tactical functions. They give an air of scientific neutrality to the proposal by masking the very important value decisions. What is the "best use" of urban land? How much and what kinds of benefits can the community realize from the project? Are these benefits worth the cost? Land-use planning decisions of this scope involve judgments about values and probabilities. The decisions are political in the broadest sense. They are not susceptible of final determination by technical experts or by scientific, "objective" "facts." The technical data then tend "to conceal what is really at issue and to direct the discussion along the lines that are either irrelevant or less than fully relevant." They also help neutralize the opposition. The technical justification for the proposal is prepared and supported by experts in land use, traffic, municipal financing, and marketing. If the proposal is to be evaluated and countered successfully, then the opposition (including uncommitted governmental officials) must also use experts. Simply saying "No" or "I don't like it" is not enough. Opponents in the public arena need planning skills as well as political skills, even though basically political issues are to be decided.

Our thesis is that the success (in terms of community acceptance) of the redevelopment proposal depends primarily on whether the proponents or the opponents command the political and planning skills. The locus of the actual decision-making power (the ability to prevail in the redevelopment effort) will be determined by which of the various groups have both these skills. Neither skill without the other is sufficient. And the degree of monopoly of these skills will determine both the substantive results of the redevelopment decisions and the genuineness of the use of the legally required public decision-making apparatus. In other words, despite the goals and purposes of the legally established decision-making procedures, the integrity of that process and the rationality of planning in the public interest depend on the realities of the power relationships of the actors in the process. This is true even though the promoters are required to use the public law process and the public decision makers have veto power over the projects. . . .

The supporters of Center Circle hail the project as a great example of private capital working for the good of the community. They claim with assurance that business in Center City will increase, that there will be more jobs and more tax revenues. Given the prior condition of the land uses in the project site and the persistent economic stagnation in the community, the project, it is argued, certainly is an improvement.

There would undoubtedly be general agreement that the Center Circle complex made a significant contribution to shopping ease. The interior is handsomely appointed, and the stores are well-integrated around a central mall providing free movement from store to store without having to go outside the heated and air-conditioned structure. The project (despite its external resemblance to a penitentiary caused by its high, solid brick walls) has been awarded a citation for "excellence in environmental architecture" by a national association of architects.

Others point out, however, that these gains may be substantially offset in the long run by other, less dramatic, effects of the project. The promoters and their hired planners claimed that they were planning for the community as a whole. They did not present anything like a master plan, but they did present a plan for the redevelopment of the entire central business district and discussed its relation to the community as a whole. What they accomplished, however, was a plan for only one section of the central business district. Furthermore, the planning for their one section . . . was strictly planning for the development and protection of their commercial shopping center. The main section of the central business district, Main Street, and the section that heretofore was of most concern to those interested in improving the community as a whole, was included in the planning of the promoters if and when their shopping center expanded northward. In short, the planning for Center Circle was planning in the public interest only to the extent that the public interest is indirectly served by the bettering of private economic conditions.

At no stage in the history of the Center Circle project was systematic disinterested professional thought given to the relationship of the project to the over-all development of the community.
As noted earlier, there is no evidence that the decision makers,
public or private, paid any attention to the existing independent
studies of the area's needs.

The planning for Center Circle left unresolved four principal
problems: Main Street, traffic, land uses in the areas adjacent
to the project site . . . and the financial condition of the parking lot operation. The promoters and the public officials have
spoken optimistically about the resolution of these problems, but
the evidence to back their claims seems, so far, not convincing.
And it would seem that a failure to resolve these problems might
cost Center City in the long run more than it will gain from
the project, and could even jeopardize the success of the project
itself. Whether or not this will happen depends on the ability
of the community to prevent a further decline of Main Street
business, to come up with a successful program to handle the
impending crush of traffic, and to prevent the deterioration of
land uses surrounding the site.

The problems raised and left unresolved by Center Circle are
of considerable importance to the people of Center City. They
are the ones who will have to pay for planning errors—the inconvenience of traffic congestion, the costs of spreading blight, the
vacancies on Main Street, and the overcommitted indebtedness.
It is for this reason that the legal procedures for public decision
making concerning the allocation and use of urban land are provided. These procedures provide, on paper, full opportunity for
the assertion and consideration of the public interest in private
programs.

In substance, none of this happened in Center City. X* and
his small group of insiders, together with highly skilled outsiders—the chain [of department stores which promoted Center
Circle] and the hired planners, presented the community with
a take-it-or-leave-it package. The organs of government, instead
of serving the function of performing an independent public
scrutiny, merely implemented the private decisions and granted
the public support needed for the project. Under implicit and
explicit threats of obstructionism, not only were there no proposals for independent studies during the critical days of decision,

---

* X, a lawyer, was one of the prime movers in the Center City Project.
He was a "descendant of one of the founding families of Center City," with
a "deep civic commitment to the city. He owned, along with another, the
large hotel which was located in the project site." [Eds. note]

but the record reveals that no serious questions were ever raised by any of the responsible elected public officials. Public meetings were held, as prescribed by law, but for the most part they were used by the promoters for public relations services; with minor exceptions, no questions were raised by the citizens or the Main Street merchants. Even the two local newspapers have had only praise for the project.

NOTES AND QUESTIONS

1. Is there ever an ethical basis for misrepresenting the degree to which the experts agree on a particular point? Is there a difference between (a) stating an opinion, without qualification, when the consensus of the experts is that the matter is probable but not certain; and (b) stating an opinion, without qualification, when some experts agree with you and others do not?

For example, suppose you are a doctor called upon as an expert witness to testify in a workmen's compensation case. The question is whether a miner's lung disease was "caused" by conditions at work. You have been paid by the company. You honestly believe that this kind of disease is *never* caused by work conditions. What should your testimony be? Or, you (and almost all other doctors) honestly believe the disease is *usually* not caused by work conditions. What should you disclose?

[Reading 82]

Do you distinguish between a trial situation and a Congressional hearing? In answering this question, you might wish to consult William A. Klein, "The Incidence of the Corporation Income Tax: A Lawyer's View of a Problem in Economics," 1965 *Wisconsin Law Review* 576, 601.*

In the first part of his article, Professor Klein deals with the question whether, in the light of economic theory and economic information, one can say definitely that a corporation subject to corporate income tax can "shift" the tax to consumers or workers, or that it cannot shift it so that the burden of the tax falls on shareholders. He concludes that there is simply no way to decide.

In spite of this uncertainty, "a surprising number of experts in public finance seem to have been altogether willing, if not anxious, to offer estimates of the extent of tax shifting." Some have said the tax was completely shifted, others that it was not shifted at all. One economist went so far as to "assert, as a best

---

*Professor of Law, University of Wisconsin. Copyright 1965 Wisconsin Law Review. Reprinted by permission.

estimate, that one-third was shifted forward to consumers, one-eighth was shifted backward to workers, and the remainder was borne by shareholders." Most economists took a middle ground, asserting that some part of the tax was shifted, some part not. In their books, articles and testimony before government bodies, according to Professor Klein, many economists have not been sufficiently emphatic about the degree of uncertainty which infects the whole question of the incidence of the tax. Professor Klein goes on to remark that:

Perhaps the most distressing aspect of this phenomenon is that it is not necessary for the economist, in order to be of value in the decision-making process, to take a position specifying a probable degree of shifting. It seems to be assumed in much of the writing in economics that the way to decide the question whether the corporation tax is a good tax is to decide—on the best basis available, no matter how poor it may be—whether the tax is shifted. As some commentators have recognized, however, since the basic objective is to appraise the tax itself, it is entirely sufficient, and in fact much wiser, to insist on the position that the question of shifting is presently unanswerable. Then the issue becomes, what should be done in the face of this uncertainty? Admittedly this difference of approach is largely a matter of emphasis. The writers who offer conclusions about the degree of shifting generally do preface their remarks with an acknowledgement of the difficulty of the problem and the relatively uncertain nature of their conclusions. It strikes me that this is not enough. A book or article that offers a conclusion and gives detailed reasons to support that conclusion (or that makes an assumption) about tax shifting and then proceeds to build an elaborate policy argument from this base, while giving only passing mention to the element of uncertainty, may be seriously misleading—at least if it is intended to be read by nonexperts.

The reasons why trained economists have given misleading advice are difficult to fathom and must remain largely a matter of speculation. The possibility of intellectual laziness or incompetence seems more a conclusion than an explanation. It does not tell us why a man whose high intellectual capacity and industry have been demonstrated in one context should fail to make full use of that capacity in another context. There is of course the obvious possibility of subconscious bias, by virtue of which a particular conclusion is chosen to fit the individual's "predilections or policy program." Thus the egalitarian who wants to "soak the rich" may adopt the wish-fulfilling conclusion that the corporate tax falls on shareholders (who tend to be rich). At the same time the rich shareholder, while publicly complaining about the burden he bears, may privately be consoling himself with the assumption that the tax is in fact passed on to consumers. Another possibility is that it was originally assumed by all sides that the tax fell on the shareholders (and thus, by and large, on the rich); that a hard-fought battle ensued on this assumption; and that the initial assumption must be retained for symbolic reasons, if only to avoid public recognition of the fact that the battle may have been fought in vain. Once politicians have gotten themselves into this posture they may offer irresistable rewards (such as positions of public esteem or power) to the academician who offers the soothing opinion that their initial assumptions were not erroneous.

Whatever the reasons, the fact that economists have in fact expressed conflicting and vacillating conclusions, backed by reasoning that has proved highly vulnerable to attacks by each other, can hardly be expected to enhance the respect in which they are held by their nonexpert audience—and herein lies the pity. This kind of fallibility is, of course, not limited to economists, but no matter where it is encountered it is unfortunate. In so far as the public becomes aware of it, the role of the expert advice-giver tends to become undermined; the potency of sound, useful expert opinion, and perhaps of reason in general, tends to be impaired.

2. Compare the role of the economist in public testimony about the incidence of the corporate income tax with the testimony of psychiatrists described in Halleck, Reading 79, at 671, *supra*, and the planners in Plager & Handler, Reading 81, at 685, *supra*.

3. Did the "expert" opinion of the economists play a role in the enactment of the corporate income tax? in maintaining the system as it is? Are the economists discussed by Klein manipulating the lawmaking process for their own private interests and the interests of economists as a whole, or are they being manipulated by the process? What of the planners in Plager and Handler? the psychiatrists in Halleck?

[Reading 83]

4. In the twentieth century, government spends literally billions of dollars on science and research, partly to provide itself

with the basis for undertaking and implementing new policy and law, and partly to encourage the development of technology, strengthen national defense, and in general support what government sees as the national interest. There are enormous problems in making decisions on the direction research should take, and who should undertake it. Consider Gordon B. Baldwin, "Law in Support of Science: Legal Control of Basic Research Resources," 54 *Georgetown Law Journal* 559, 563-64, 590-91 (1966):*

Competence is best proven by prior success, by the methods the applicant proposes to use, and by the recommendations of those scientists closest to his work.

Consequently, laymen in or out of Congress are not able to make the kind of judgments required to support good science. However unwilling Congressmen may be, and however unprecedented it is to give others vast authority to expend federal funds, the selection power must be delegated to scientists competent to make these critical judgments. Such is the structure of the National Science Foundation which is merely given statutory authority to "initiate and support basic scientific research."

All these characteristics of fundamental research make colleges, universities, and private research institutes ideal centers for scientific activity. These institutions seek the most able men committed to enlarging our knowledge, support scholars in a variety of fields, and zealously promote the communication of ideas so necessary for the improvement of scientific knowledge. Yet, no individual, no industry, no university, and no private foundation can supply the equipment or hire the labor that modern science demands, and as a consequence scientists inevitably seek support from the federal government.

Legislators examining the function of science in society are similarly handicapped by their lack of scientific training. Our most creative scientists seek neither public office nor employment on congressional staffs, and consequently legislators must educate themselves or rely on information elicited during hearings. Here they are likely to be baffled by technical details, preoccupied by questions of costs, and foiled by the divided political responsibilities of scientific witnesses. The President's science advisers, for example, may be precluded from giving complete testimony if the matters in issue are within the ambit of executive privilege. These factors

---

* Professor of Law, University of Wisconsin. Copyright © 1966, Georgetown Law Journal. Reprinted by permission.

further the difficulty in communicating scientific problems, and it is hardly surprising, therefore, that legislators are often either woefully ignorant or wildly optimistic about the promises of science.

[Reading 84]

5. Much of the research that eventuates in changes in law and policy is carried on within the government itself. A relatively early example is dealt with in the following excerpt. Oscar E. Anderson, *The Health of a Nation: Harvey W. Wiley's Fight for Pure Food* (U. of Chicago Press 1958):*

[Another development] that influenced the campaign for a pure food and drug law after 1903 . . . [was] the investigations by Wiley into the effect of preservatives on human digestion and health. . . .

What Wiley had in mind when he obtained authority to study preservatives was feeding experiments that would permit an empirical conclusion as to their effect on the human organism. When he returned from his summer trip to Europe in 1902, he threw himself into the work of preparation. A kitchen and dining room were fitted out in the basement of the chemistry building, and twelve young men were recruited from the employees of the Department of Agriculture to undergo the tests. Wiley was anxious to find men of good character, for unless the subjects co-operated conscientiously, the data obtained would be of no value. All the volunteers were required to pledge themselves to follow the rules prescribed, to make the observations required, and to take no food except that provided at the experimental table. The plan was to subject the young men to a series of observations, the first of which was a "fore period," a time of careful feeding to determine the quantity of food necessary to maintain normal body weight at a constant level and to determine normal metabolism. This was followed by a "preservative period" of fifteen or twenty days to test the effects of such substances and an "after period" to restore the individual if there had been any disturbance of physical state. The conclusions were to be based on frequent physical examinations and on a comparison between the food given each man and his bodily excretions. These comparisons involved an incredible amount of detailed laboratory work, for all

---

food and waste had to be weighed and analyzed carefully. That there were difficulties Wiley was perfectly aware. No inspection of organs could be made, as would have been possible had animals instead of humans been employed. Mental anxieties might produce physical disorders, for the subjects knew they were taking preservatives. Wiley thought, however, that this would not be so serious a factor in his experiments, which were to continue several months, as in studies lasting only a few days. The self-control of each individual was an additional variable, for each had to endure the almost intolerable nuisance of carrying about containers to collect scrupulously his urine and feces. Finally, there was the bias of the investigator. This Wiley proposed to counter by trying to remove all personal prejudice and to free himself from the weight of authorities and the influence of public opinion.

In November, 1902, the tests got underway. With interruptions and many changes in personnel they were to continue for five years. Wiley had an able coadjutor in Bigelow of the Food Laboratory; nevertheless, he made it his business to give the experiments his close and detailed supervision. He tried to eat each meal with his "boys," even though it meant arriving at the bureau early in the morning and staying until six or seven in the evening. Frequently he made the physical examinations, and in emergencies he donned an apron and presided at the stove. The first preservative tested was boric acid; then in 1903 and 1904 came studies of salicylic, sulphurous, and benzoic acid, and of formaldehyde. Once the investigations were completed, a laborious job of tabulation remained, but in 1904 the boric-acid results were published as the first part of Bulletin 84, *Influence of Food Preservatives and Artificial Colors on Digestion and Health.* The evidence was produced in great detail for the benefit of serious students, but Wiley's own interpretation was affirmed concisely and positively: "It happens . . . that both boric acid and borax, when continuously administered in small doses for a long period or when given in large quantities for a short period, create disturbances of appetite, of digestion, and of health." Anticipating the argument that his study failed to show that the use of borax in butter and meat, especially when not continuous, would prove deleterious in any reasonable length of time, he argued that if the preservative were admitted in these, it would have to be admitted in every other product. He believed it might be used in a few cases in which other methods of preparation were inapplicable and decomposition would be a danger greater than the preservative, but beyond that he would not go.

In 1906 came Part II of Bulletin 84, the report on salicylic acid and its compounds. Though Wiley found it less harmful than its general condemnation would lead one to believe, he concluded that even in small quantities its influence was injurious. Not only was there no need for it, but its employment tended to induce carelessness by manufacturers in selecting, cleaning, and preserving. After 1906 additional reports, all condemnatory, were made on sulphurous and benzoic acid and their compounds and on formaldehyde. Two other reports—on copper sulphate and saltpeter—were prepared but never published. No feeding experiments were made to determine the wholesomeness of coloring materials. Bulletin 84, reporting adversely on a subject controversial in the extreme and affecting important interests, was bound to encounter dissent. Critics appeared to challenge both methods and interpretations. Wiley never wavered in his belief that his techniques and conclusions were basically valid. Since much of the criticism came from scientists in the service of firms making or using preservatives, he became more and more intolerant with his detractors. Against experts who attacked him in behalf of vested interests he was bitter. They ought not, he thought, "to be recognized as having an ethical standing with a profession whose purpose is the welfare, not the injury of mankind."

More than anything that the Bureau of Chemistry ever had done, the feeding experiments appealed to the popular imagination. This was apparent when the first newspaper announcements that Wiley was looking for volunteers to receive free board for doing nothing but eat food that at times would be poisoned brought numerous letters of application. Serious as was his intent, Wiley found himself reflecting the common attitude. When two friends from Cincinnati offered in jest to serve, he could not resist penning a letter of mock acceptance. "You will begin with a diet of borax garnished with salicylic acid—with a dish of alum on the side. You will then have a course in chromatics—beginning with the beautiful yellow of oleomargarine and including the appropriate green of the French canned peas. Rochelle salts, bicarbonate of soda, acid phosphate and basic alumina sulphate will be found delightful entrées. . . . Please report for duty about September 10th. Blanks for wills and coroners' certificates must be furnished by the guests."

Most of the publicity that the experiments received at the outset was the work of a young reporter for the *Washington Post*, George Rothwell Brown. In November, 1902, he began writing stories on the tests. Though done in a humorous vein, they were fairly straightforward accounts based on interviews with the chief chemist. Soon, however, they became so flamboyant that Wiley, worried about the impression this would create among scientists, protested to Scott C. Bone, Brown's editor. But the stories continued, some of them of a character likely to throw doubt on the accuracy of the findings. During the Christmas holidays, while Wiley was in Indianapolis, the matter was brought to a head by a series which, though written with no intent other than humor, tended to make the whole preservative study appear ridiculous. When Wiley returned, Secretary Wilson gave him strict orders against any more contact with newspapermen. The chemist was willing enough to comply, but Brown was resourceful, and when he failed to find a story, he invented one. His pieces continued to appear sporadically, not only in his own paper but in other journals throughout the country. Frequently Brown called the preservatives tested "poisons." Soon the dozen volunteers dining in the Bureau of Chemistry were referred to generally as the "poison squad," a name to which Wiley objected. Obviously, it prejudged the issue; he much preferred the more objective "hygienic table." The newspaper publicity generated a surprising amount of interest. When accounts appeared that borax produced a beautiful pink and white complexion in his boarders, several women actually wrote for more information on the wonderful discovery. Songs inspired by the poison squad soon made their debut on the minstrel stage. Wiley himself found that the experiments gave him a topic of wide appeal. From 1903 on he used the feeding studies frequently as a theme in his speeches and articles, both of which were becoming important responsibilities of his position.

The preservative investigations were a significant event in the struggle for the law. For one thing, they clarified Wiley's views on the subject. He did not think absolute prohibition warranted, but he came to a firm conclusion that preservatives should be restricted to cases of absolute necessity. The burden of proving need and harmlessness should fall on the producer, and none should be used without proper notice to the consumer. The feeding experiments were of further significance in that they helped to awaken the public to the problem of food adulteration. They were much more effective in focusing interest than mere summaries of conditions. Finally, they sharpened opposition to the food law among manufacturers. Some of those who had been working for the law, now frightened by the hardening of Wiley's position and the concern of the public, defected to the enemy. . . .

Refer back to the account of the passage of the Pure Food Act in the note on Sinclair's *The Jungle*, Reading 60, at 561, *supra*, and distinguish carefully between the role of scientific information in (a) mobilizing the public to sense the existence of a problem, and the technical possibility of attacking that problem through law; and (b) creating the body of technical knowledge that makes possible the implementation of policies set out or to be set out in law. Which of these was Dr. Wiley doing? Or was he doing both?

6. For a fascinating case study of the political problems of amassing social science data and applying it to a problem of public policy, and, incidentally, of the problems of communicating the data to the public, *see* Lee Rainwater & William L. Yancey, *The Moynihan Report and the Politics of Controversy* (M.I.T. Press 1967).

2. How Social Needs and Social Attitudes Are Fed into the Legal System

a. Introductory note

Social needs and social attitudes impinge upon and are drawn upon by the legal system in a wide variety of ways. The very term "legal system" connotes this. A system is a number of units organized to perform one or more functions, and there is an interrelationship between the units so that changes in one prompt changes in the others. In speaking of a system, one usually stresses these interrelationships and describes an on-going process rather than a static situation. Moreover, a system operates in an environment, taking in "inputs," processing them, producing "outputs" and receiving "feedback" or reactions to past or proposed outputs. David Easton, a leading political scientist, has written a description of political life in system terms. He describes how political agencies take in inputs of two kinds—demands for allocations of things valued by the society and support for the political system. (A letter to a Congressman, asking for a change in law, would be a demand; a letter praising his work or his votes would be a support.) Demands are processed and there are products (outputs) of the system—allocations of valuable goods, *e.g.*, awards of damages in law suits, legislation passed favoring one group's interest over another, or promoting a Colonel to a Brigadier General. Society, or some part of it, reacts to this output by offering new demands and by granting or withholding support. This feedback, actual or anticipated, influences output. Elected officials obviously are influenced by a potential withdrawal of support, and even dictators must be concerned not to prompt such negative feedback from their source of power that a revolution might be sparked. *See* Easton, *A Systems Analysis of Political Life* (John Wiley 1965).

The American legal system has countless points of contact with other parts of American society. We have noted many in the materials studied in the previous sections of this book. For example, presidents, senators, representatives, judges, prosecutors and even some county surveyors are elected and therefore are likely to be sensitive to potential positive and negative feedback. At times government seeks out representatives of the society or of some segment of society to participate in public operations. The jury, for instance, is used to "find facts" in law suits. Laymen serve on investigatory commissions and on school boards and housing commissions. Moreover, the media of communication serves to dramatize the action of some units in the legal system and public opinion polls supply some government officials with indications of what will and will not produce support.

Up to this point, this note has stressed social attitudes—will a program be popular, will it be ignored, will it produce a revolution? But there is another dimension: Apart from immediate popularity, what are the long run consequences of a program for society? Are they good or bad? We can think of the legal system again as having inputs and outputs; inputs are items of information about an existing situation which is viewed by someone inside government as a problem, and information about the likely consequences of possible solutions. The legal system processes the problem and produces an output in the form of a program to solve the problem (or it may produce the output of refusing any action). The program may produce feedback, in the form of information about the consequences of the program. For example, a congressional committee may hear testimony about the impact of a program, the field personnel of an administrative agency may report their experiences, a Congressman may receive many letters of protest about the operation of a program, or a court may see feedback about the consequences of its past decisions in the record of a new case brought before it. For the use of such a systems analysis approach in the study of a legal and social problem, *see* Dallin H. Oaks & Warren Lehman, *A Crim-*

inal Justice System and the Indigent: A Study of Chicago and Cook County 179-96 (U. of Chicago Press 1968).

What channels are open for both types of feedback; that is, for public reaction, and for the consequences of the program? If there are no such channels or only relatively ineffective ones, how is the operation of government affected? What are the consequences for society? We now turn to materials which bear on these questions.

85. Stability and Change in Judicial Decision-Making: Incrementalism or Stare Decisis?

MARTIN SHAPIRO*

2 LAW IN TRANSITION QUARTERLY 134 (1964)

For some time now a number of American lawyers and political scientists have been seeking to place courts and judges firmly within the matrix of politics and government rather than treating them as peculiar phenomena isolated from the rest of the governmental process. I have elsewhere called this movement "political jurisprudence." That courts are political agencies is self-evident. They are part of government, they make public policy, and they are an integral part of the law-making and enforcement process which is the central focus of political activity. If legislatures are political and executives are political, then courts must be political since all three are inextricably bound together in the process of making law, and each sometimes performs the functions that each of the others performs at other times. . . .

This article . . . seeks to show that we can describe a method of decision-making that is shared by courts and other political agencies. Such an effort is essential to political jurisprudence because it has traditionally been argued that courts are unique in that they have a peculiar, and nonpolitical, method of decision-making based on either neutral principles of law, or rational and

---

* Professor, Department of Political Science, School of Social Sciences, University of California, Irvine. Copyright © 1964 Law in Transition Quarterly. Reprinted by permission.

non-discretionary operations of legal logic, or both. If I can begin to show that judges' decisions actually exhibit the same methods as those of other policy makers in the political process, then one of the key arguments against political jurisprudence will be at least partially undermined. Let me point out again, however, that to say that the judge uses the same method of decision-making as other politicians does not necessarily mean that he is subject to the same influences, pursues the same values or has the same level of decisional power as any other given political decision-maker.

It must be added that I am concerned here only with decision-making by appellate courts and more particularly with those decisions by appellate courts that involve judicial law-making. To avoid awkward repetition, I must ask the reader to add "appellate court" to all my subsequent references to judicial decision-making.

Incrementalism

The theoretical work I propose to discuss has been done by two men who fall on the vague line between political science and economics, James March and Charles Lindblom. Both have recently presented theories of decision-making that might apply to both political and economic decisions and particularly to the peculiar mixture of politics and economics that typically occurs in what we call the "public policy" sphere. Courts are very frequently involved in just such mixed questions of politics and economics.

The theory set forth by March in his *Behavioral Theory of the Firm*[7] and Lindblom in his *Strategy of Decision*[8] (both March and Lindblom had co-authors whom I neglect simply to avoid having repeatedly to refer to the firm of Cyert, March, Braybrooke and Lindblom) will probably add another barbarism to our language—"incrementalism." For both authors are seeking to present a method of decision-making that proceeds by a series of incremental judgments as opposed to a single judgment made on the basis of rational manipulation of all the ideally relevant considerations. . . .

For a long time the ideal type for decisions in economics or politics was "rational decision-making" in which all relevant data was to be considered in the light of all relevant goals, the goals themselves to be precisely weighted according to the decision-maker's valuational priorities. The basic sticking point with rational decision-making theories is that real decision-makers just

---

[7] CYERT & MARCH, A BEHAVIORAL THEORY OF THE FIRM (1963).
[8] BRAYBROOKE & LINDBLOM, A STRATEGY OF DECISION (1963).

did not act this way. The economists found that firms did not act rationally—that is so as to maximize their profits. The political scientists found that political decision-making bodies, particularly highly bureaucratized ones, tended toward decisions that compromised the conflicting interests of various participants on an ad hoc basis without agreement on either the facts or the priority of goals. This collision of rational decision-making theories with hard facts is marked by the popularity of such notions as "satisficing" rather than maximizing and definitions of public interest in terms of legitimizing processes rather than substantive policies. At this point it might have been said that propositions about how decisions ought to be made were simply at odds with how decisions were in fact made. But then economists began to tell us that the marginal cost involved in gathering every piece of pertinent data and checking it against every available alternative policy in terms of all approved values would frequently itself be irrational in terms of input-output ratios. And students of politics began to urge that the self-preservation of a given political agency and/or the political process as a whole necessitated mediational decisions. It is not after all rational to destroy cherished institutions in the process of making "correct" public policy. Thus deviations from rational decision-making models not only did occur but ought to occur.

Incrementalism is the formal statement of this dissatisfaction with conventional models of decision-making. Let me briefly describe the tactics of incrementalism as presented by Lindblom. Lindblom begins with propositions about "margin-dependent choice." The decision-maker starts from the status quo and compares alternatives which are typically marginal variations from the status quo. Formulation and choice among alternatives is derived largely from historical and contemporary experience. It follows that only a restricted number, rather than all rationally conceivable, alternatives are considered. Moreover only a restricted number of the consequences of any given alternative are considered. And those that are chosen for consideration are not necessarily the most immediate or important but those that fall most clearly within the formal sphere of competence of the analyst and with which he feels most technically competent to deal.

In the traditional, rational model of decision-making, means are adjusted to ends, but the incrementalist often adjusts what he wants to the means available. Similarly he constantly restructures both his data and values. He uses "themes" rather than "rules." That is he does not say "if factor X is present, decision Y must follow," but "factor X is an important consideration." Lindblom's next rubric is "serial analysis and evaluation"—the notion that policy is usually made by following a long series of steps. Rather than attempting to solve the problem in one fell swoop the decision-maker whittles away at it. Indeed the analyst is likely to "identify . . . ills from which to move away rather than goals toward which to move." Finally analysis of a given policy area is likely to be carried on by several different agencies or institutions with consequently differing world views.

March in offering a "behavioral theory of the firm" presents a more analytically rigorous set of hypotheses about decision-making. . . . Let me quote March's own succinct summary.

1. Multiple, changing, acceptable-level goals. The criterion of choice is that the alternative selected meet all of the demands (goals) of the coalition.

2. An approximate sequential consideration of alternatives. The first satisfactory alternative evoked is accepted. Where an existing policy satisfies the goals, there is little search for alternatives. When failure occurs, search is intensified.

3. The organization seeks to avoid uncertainty by following regular procedures and a policy of reacting to feedback rather than forecasting the environment.

4. The organization uses standard operating procedures and rules of thumb to make and implement choices. In the short run these procedures dominate the decisions made.

. . . . March's first item, when extended from the firm to the political system, would seem to be a summary statement of the incremental politics which Lindblom says is the foundation of his strategy. For Lindblom's strategy is not an abstract model applicable to all decision-making everywhere, but is dependent on roughly the type of pluralistic politics to be found in Western constitutional democracies. No rigorous cause and effect relationship need be supposed. But a system containing multiple centers of decision-making, all or many of which have to come into agreement in order finally to arrive at and implement a decision, tends toward incremental decision-making if for no other reason than that rational decision requires a single set of rationally ordered goals, which is a condition difficult enough for one decision-maker to attain, and nearly impossible for more than one. The findings of March, and of many others who have studied large organizations, that such organizations, even though theoretically organized on a strictly hierarchical basis, in reality consist of coalitions of decision-making units each with somewhat differing goals, is what makes theories of decision derived from the organizational behavior of private firms applicable to political life.[15]

March's second and third hypotheses are obviously closely related to several of Lindblom's propositions and indeed add a certain operational precision to Lindblom's formulation. March actually reduces the boundaries of decision even further than does Lindblom. He specifies not only the consideration of a restricted number of alternatives, but of only one alternative at a time, with the first workable alternative attempted accepted as the preferred solution. Lindblom's general formulation suggests rather continuous decisional activity. March's finding that the search for alternatives begins only when the present policy fails may indicate that Lindblom's point about moving away from ills may apply not only to the direction but the initiation and timing of incremental decisions.

March's notion of feedback expresses the same thought as Lindblom's reference to historical and contemporary experience and emphasizes a point that Lindblom makes repeatedly. In the face of uncertainty about consequences the best decisional tactic is to take minor steps which will elicit new information and allow one to pull back without excessive loss if the new information indicates unexpected trouble. Finally, March notes the use of regular procedures, which also has a damping effect on change. No change at all occurs so long as the regular procedures yield acceptable results. Thus March emphasizes what is not always clear in Lindblom, that the other side of the coin of incremental *change* is a limitation and routinization of decision-making which produces a relatively slow tempo of new decisions, each of which constitutes a relatively smaller change from the status quo than even the general theory of marginal dependent choice would require.

Indeed March's emphasis on operating procedures and rules of thumb represent an important point for us. Lindblom's preoccupation with "themes" rather than rules seems to me to over-represent one political style at the expense of another. Certain political decision-makers in certain political settings may seek to avoid anything that looks like a hard and fast rule, but others, in other settings, may customarily operate through formulating and changing rules, which they take to be binding on themselves as well as others. March emphasizes that the rules are rules of

---

[15] As a concrete example, the sales division of a large firm may have quite different goals than the engineering division, and the engineering quite different goals than the safety division. Or, put somewhat differently, each division is likely to define the goals of the firm somewhat differently than the other divisions.

thumb that are modified on the basis of feedback. In short, policy makers desire several somewhat conflicting conditions for decision to operate simultaneously. They want to be free to change their minds. They want to be free to concentrate on the most important decisions and so must develop means of handling myriads of routine decisions routinely. Finally, they wish to be free of the constant pressure of those who wish them to alter decisions they have already made. Thus, in order to obtain decisional freedom, policy makers will sometimes adopt a thematic approach which, by avoiding rules, gives them maximal flexibility and may expose them to less criticism than a hard and fast rule would. Or they may adopt rules of thumb, which will relieve them of future decisions and may serve as a shield against pressure by allowing them to insist that they too are now bound by the rule and so cannot make the decision some outside group desires.

Incrementalism and Judicial Decision-Making

After this summary of the work of March and Lindblom, let me turn to the question of how notions of incrementalism may be applied to the study of courts and law. Here we are concerned with two bodies of scholars with differing interests, but two that can find a common ground in the application of incremental theory to judicial decision. First the political and social theorist is interested in constructing generalizations that will comprehend and integrate various modes of behavior. If it can be demonstrated that the theory of incrementalism adequately accounts for the decisions of judges as well as bureaucrats and business executives, then the value of the theory, qua theory, is increased since the purpose of social theory is to identify widespread regularities lying beneath superficially diverse kinds of behavior. On the other hand, from the point of view of the student of courts in particular, the successful application of incremental theory to judicial decision-making would increase our understanding of the relation of courts to other agencies that also act incrementally, and provide a new framework around which to organize what we know of the actual behavior of courts.

To the extent that incrementalism is a descriptive theory of how decisions are made, it must be tested against actual decisions. In the field of law we have a huge body of decisions relatively accurately recorded and indexed in precisely the way necessary to trace series of decisions on the same question. Moreover, legal institutions, compared to other political agencies or even large private firms, have a particularly efficient communications system which keeps all analysts relatively well informed of what the last decision was, which is, of course, essential in a strategy that uses the last decision as the base for reaching the next. Thus, at first glance, it would seem that legal materials might provide a rich and convenient body of data on which to test incremental theory. This impression is certainly bolstered by consideration of the lore of Anglo-American jurisprudence in which stare decisis and the case by case process of inclusion and exclusion play central roles. At least superficially this lore suggests series of policy decisions in which changes of policy occur incrementally, each new decision based on the previous one and differing from it on the basis of feedback from earlier results. The theory of stare decisis stands directly opposed to that of incrementalism. For the theory is that there are rational and immutable legal principles imbedded somewhere in the life of the law and that the technique of stare decisis facilitates the legal system's discovery of those principles. We are all aware of the old notion that the case is not the law but the best evidence of the legal principle. From our point of view what is interesting is that the theory behind stare decisis (which is in conflict with incrementalism) has foundered, while the technique (which is basically in harmony with incrementalism) marches bravely on. The theory has foundered on the rock of the *ratio decidendi*. First the *ratio* was thought to be what the judge said the principle involved was, then whatever principle was necessary to get from the facts to the holding, no matter what the judge said. Then it was discovered that no single case had a single *ratio*, and finally that in any given instance, not one but several lines of cases (from each of which a different *ratio* could presumably be derived) bore on any litigational situation. So the notion of solving a dispute by reference to an agreed principle disappeared and the rational theory behind stare decisis disappeared with it.

. . . [I]ncremental theories may help to orient us in the current jurisprudential disputes we encounter among legal theorists. Professor [Herbert] Wechsler's call for neutral principles[17] has been attacked basically because of the difficulty of defining "neutral"—a difficulty he himself admits. But from a slightly different point of view, his call for decisions which enunciate principles (neutral or not) that will be applicable in every future case of the same sort, is an example of a rational decision-making strategy that the incrementalists argue is not, and cannot be, employed because it makes impossible demands on the decision-maker. In-

---

[17] Wechsler, *Toward Neutral Principles of Constitutional Law*, 73 HARV. L. REV. 77 (1958). See also Wechsler, *The Courts and the Constitution*, 65 COLUM. L. REV. 1001 (1965).

deed I think the two principal and superficially contradictory criticisms of Wechsler's position are both essentially incremental arguments, and that their superficial contradiction can be resolved by translating these attacks into the language of incrementalism. Professor [Alexander] Bickel has attacked Wechsler because, if the Supreme Court were to govern its decisions by neutral principles of constitutional law, it would have to make certain major incursions on Congressional powers at inopportune moments, incursions that might create crises that would weaken the Court.[18] On the other hand, Wechsler has been criticised because so few neutral principles are available, and they are so difficult to formulate, that if the courts were to act only when they found and could articulate a neutral principle, they could hardly act at all. It is almost impossible to imagine a rule that, formulated today, would yield desirable results in every imaginable future case. In fact both these arguments boil down to the position that courts must be satisfied with incremental decisions if they are to make policy decisions at all.

. . . . Karl Llewellyn in his great retreat from judicial realism, *Deciding Appeals—The Common Law Tradition*,[20] gives us a full-blown theory of incrementalism in law, with the same mixture of descriptive and prescriptive elements we find in Lindblom, although he uses a different language than Lindblom to express fundamentally the same point of view. . . . He argues that much of the lawyer's distress at the supposed disregard by American courts of stare decisis in recent years is the result of excessive enchantment with logical deductive styles of decision-making, and that courts at their best do and should solve problems by evolving on-the-spot solutions that, given the practical limits of knowledge and prediction, seem best for the situation. He argues in effect that if lines of precedent are viewed not as fluctuations around a locus of principle, but as the record of a series of marginal adjustments designed to meet changing circumstances, then the legal system will regain for the viewer the coherence and predictability that are obscured when we attempt to view the work of the courts through the traditional theories of stare decisis. For Llewellyn finds in his own examination of the decisions of modern American courts that they typically seek to make incremental changes in policy in the light of feedback from earlier decisions. . . .

I wish now to work my way through the various propositions of incremental theory and suggest that certain aspects of judicial

---

18 Bickel, *Forward: The Passive Virtues,* 75 HARV. L. REV. 40 (1961).
20 LLEWELLYN, DECIDING APPEALS—THE COMMON LAW TRADITION (1960).

behavior at least superficially correspond to each, in the hope
that in the next few years some students of courts will examine
whether the correspondence is more than superficial. Before
doing so, however, I wish to issue a warning against a pseudo
incrementalism which has become a favorite tactic of the United
States Supreme Court. I refer to the segregation and reapportionment decisions. An uninformed observer might view the *School
Segregation Cases*[22] and the subsequent decisions outlawing segregation in one public facility after another as presenting an
incremental pattern. But it seems fairly clear that at the time
of the school decision the Justices had already made up their
minds on the desegregation of all publicly owned property. The
seeming incrementalism of the later decisions on beaches, sports
arenas, etc. is really only a product of the discrete and serial form
that litigation necessarily takes, combined with the Justices' desire to keep their cards close to the vest until each was played.
I take it that the series of decisions that has led us to one man—
one vote was of the same variety. The decisions here did formally
proceed step by small step, but with the benefit of hindsight it
now seems clear that a majority of the Justices at the time of
Baker v. Carr[24] actually jumped directly to the one man—one
vote decision which they then implemented by successive decisions. Even here, of course, some element of true incrementalism
enters since presumably the Justices could have stopped short
of full implementation in the later decisions if the adverse feedback from *Baker* had been strong enough.

On the other hand, let me suggest that the obscenity decisions
from *Roth v. United States*[26] on are incremental. Indeed since
each new decision has added a new doctrinal step, while completely preserving all the old a vertical cut through the latest
will yield a kind of geological cross section of the whole incremental history of obscenity law. All this should also indicate
that the presentation of an incremental theory of judicial decision-making does not imply that all judicial decisions are incremental. It is sufficient for a beginning to show that some of them
are and the theory is most useful in the long run if it is found
that most of them are, or that they typically are.

The heart of both March's and Lindblom's formulation is that
the analyst begins with the status quo as his base and then considers, not all possible alternatives, but those similar to the status
quo. Furthermore, March specifies that the status quo is generally

22 Brown v. Board of Educ., 347 U.S. 483 (1954).
24 369 U.S. 186 (1962).
26 354 U.S. 476 (1957). . . .

maintained until failure occurs. Failure stimulates the search for alternatives, and the first satisfactory alternative invoked is accepted. Now this seems to me a startlingly accurate description of a major variety of litigation. The typical instance in which we encounter judicial law-making is one in which one party in effect clothes himself in the existing state of the law, while the other in effect requests the court to change the law. The litigant requesting change will only succeed if he can convince the court that the existing law fails to meet the social situation, and the whole craft of the lawyer is aimed at suggesting the minimum alteration in the law necessary to help his client, for he knows it is the minimum alteration that he is most likely to get. The first satisfactory alternative, in the sense of the alternative requiring minimum change, is likely to be accepted. Indeed it might be possible on the basis of experience with judicial behavior to modify March's hypothesis from "first satisfactory alternative" to "alternative involving minimum change necessary to satisfy."

To some readers it may appear misleading to assign the legal status quo to one of the two contending parties when judicial lawmaking occurs. For in such instances the judge is often confronted with two rival interpretations of a statute which may be said to have no status quo since it is vague enough to admit the rival interpretations. Just how frequently an appellate judge chooses the interpretation that "changes" the statute because that interpretation will yield better results, rather than choosing the interpretation that he believes would maintain the status quo, is a matter for investigation. Yet while we do not know just how often this occurs, we do know that it does occur, for at least the most extreme instances, those in which a court overrules one of its previous decisions, are readily observable.

However, even in the classic instances of rival interpretations of an existing statute, each of which is equally plausible in terms of the wording of the statute and its past interpretations, the decisional situation is still basically one of marginal choice based on the status quo. The status quo is the statute's general intention, and counsel for each party argues that his specific interpretation more appropriately relates the statute to the circumstances. In a sense the judge does not face a choice between status quo and change, since, if there has been no previous authoritative interpretation of the statute on all fours with the new situation, whatever he decides will be new. Yet neither judge nor counsel are free to propose any interpretation they like. All potential interpreters are constrained by both technical canons of statutory interpretations and common sense rules of logic to stay relatively close to the statutory language. The status quo here becomes the rather vague one of the very statutory intent that is in dispute. But vague as it is, it remains an anchor around which cluster various marginal choices. While we may argue whether the value of limestone or cement ought to be used in calculating depletion allowances under a statute allowing such calculation on the basis of "the commercially marketable mineral product," no one is going to argue that the value of the bridge eventually made out of the cement should be the basis of calculation.

The very purpose of briefs is to narrow a court's range of alternatives and to present only those requiring the least movement in the law necessary to meet a new situation. I call your attention to a recurring situation in Supreme Court supervision of administrative agencies. The agency, let us say the I.R.S. [Internal Revenue Service] or the I.C.C. [Interstate Commerce Commission], finds a "loophole" in the statute. It seeks to close the loophole by administrative lawmaking. In the subsequent litigation the private party will plead the statute—that is, the status quo. The Court is likely to take the stance of defender of the Congressional act against subsequent administrative alteration unless the agency can demonstrate both the failure of the statute and that the means it has adopted to correct that failure can be harmonized with congressional intent and language. In short the whole legal context of administrative decision-making, and of judicial review of such decisions, forces both administrators and courts to operate within the narrow range of alternatives compatible with the congressional statute.

Another striking way in which the legal context of administrative decision-making enforces incrementalism can be found in the long standing practice doctrine. Courts frequently hold that the long standing practice of an administrative agency acquires the force of law. As a practical matter this does not freeze the status quo at any instant in the agency's past practice. Instead it forces the agency to put the highest priority on gradual changes, made incrementally in whatever direction the agency wants to go. If the agency can do its law-making in this way, each new decision will acquire the legal mantle of long standing practice. Any decision that deviates sharply from past practice may not only be struck down, but will damage the impression of long standing, consistent practice the agency is trying to build up to strengthen its legal position. Repeated deviation may mean the courts will fail to find any long standing practice and thus revoke the agency's license for administrative law-making, which in fact the long standing practice doctrine usually constitutes.

We have here not only the narrowing of alternatives, and a status quo basis for decision-making, but Lindblom's serial analysis and evaluation and March's reaction to feedback rather than predicting the environment. The administrative agency may in fact have made a long range forecast of the environment and formulated the great leap forward necessary to meet a new environment. But if the courts force it to meet the environment by a gradual series of shifts in its long standing practice, the agency willy nilly will pick up feedback from each shift and would have to be peculiarly bull-headed not to further modify its estimate of the environment on the basis of this feedback.

To move on, Lindblom notes that incremental decision is typically marked by the consideration of only a restricted number of consequences for any given policy. It seems to me that this proposition is identical with the old legal cliche that the great virtue of the doctrine of cases and controversies is that the judge need not decide abstract questions but is confronted with a concrete situation in which he can see the concrete consequences to the parties that will follow from one decision or another. Now to be sure, judges usually look somewhat beyond the consequences to the given litigant, but the whole context of litigation is likely to hold them closely to at least the types of claims represented by the litigants. A judge in a condemnation proceedings in which the only issue is fair value must ask himself how his decision will affect the further claims of property owners and of the city. He may consider, either consciously or unconsciously, whether the housing project to be built is one the city needs, but the rules of his game exert strong pressure on him not to do so. And he is highly unlikely to consider the consequences of urban renewal for mass transportation or the psyches of the renewed. In short he considers only those aspects of the entire problem of the most immediate concern to him even though these may not be the most important aspects of the problem as a whole in any ultimate sense. . . .

[S]ome attention to the aspect of incrementalism that Lindblom labels "adjustment of objectives to policies" may help us to view another judicial problem in the normal light of politics rather than in the shadow of the peculiar sort of debate into which students of courts often plunge. Lindblom's basic point here is that considerations of availability of means often and necessarily affect, and indeed partially define, what goals we are going to pursue. This point has, I think, always been evident in many of the more "routine" areas of law. The need to pursue certain legal goals within the context of what the real situation will bear is attested to by such concepts as "the reasonably prudent man," "innocent third party purchaser," and "last clear chance." All of these concepts represent compromises between certain ideal goals and what can actually be expected of imperfect human beings in an imperfect society. Movements toward and away from absolute warranty, for instance, have always focused on what manufacturing and marketing conditions would bear rather than notions of absolute fairness or responsibility. Somehow in these areas students of law are quite accustomed to modifying their goals and cutting their losses under the impact of the real world. Indeed such adoption of judicial behavior to reality is generally applauded and encouraged.

March's final proposition, stressing the use of standard operating procedures and rules of thumb, which in the short run dominate the decisional process, is so strikingly applicable to the legal process that little comment is necessary. The terminology is slightly different in law. But legal doctrines or rules are precisely those standard operating procedures or rules of thumb by which judicial decision-makers dispose of most of the cases that come before them. The clear and present danger rule is a familiar example, but it is hardly necessary to belabor the point that, in every field of law, doctrines which fall somewhere between the status of fixed elements in the law and random dicta by individual judges play an important part in the decision of cases. We know that in the short run most decisions are going to be routinely determined by the given state of doctrine. We also know that in the long run the doctrine is going to change. March's proposition neatly fits that strange paradox of law in which we can at one and the same time be almost absolutely sure that the case tomorrow will be decided according to doctrine X and that ten years from now doctrine X will have disappeared. The rest of incrementalism explains how and why it disappears.

We have already noted some seeming conflict between this last proposition and what Lindblom calls the "reconstructive treatment of data" under which he stresses the use of themes rather than rules. In legal materials we find a parallel situation in which courts sometimes do and sometimes do not use a fairly firm and definite rule providing that if one or more elements are present then a particular result must follow. For instance, the Supreme Court holds that if violence or the immediate threat of violence is present in a labor-management dispute, the state may intervene in matters that would otherwise be the sole concern of the National Labor Relations Board—the so-called violence exception to the primary jurisdiction of the N.L.R.B. [National Labor Relations Board]. Where courts must determine whether a given crime involves moral turpitude, they almost invariably hold that where fraud was an element in the offense, the crime does involve **turpitude.**

On the other hand courts frequently take precisely the thematic tack Lindblom describes, simply naming various factors all of which they will consider, but none of which they will bind themselves to treat as decisive. A clear example is the now largely defunct fair-trial rule under which no given lapse in criminal procedure in and of itself rendered a trial unfair, but the Supreme Court was, in each instance, to determine whether the trial was fundamentally fair as a whole. The balancing doctrine often used in conjunction with the First Amendment, where the Court weighs the interest in infringing upon speech against the interest in preserving it, is another example. Obviously under either doctrine the Court is absolutely free to decide any case any way it wants to since no single element of law or fact is allowed to dictate the legal conclusions.

This thematic approach may often be used to preserve a court's options in future decisions. Here is a quotation from a Supreme Court opinion dealing with a rather tricky problem of railway abandonment on a southern line. The Justices are quite obviously looking over their shoulders at the problem of New York commuter runs which may come before them in the future.

> In some cases . . . the question is whether abandonment may justly be permitted, in view of the fact that it would subject the communities directly affected to serious injury while continued operation would impose a relatively light burden upon a prosperous carrier. . . . In cases falling within the latter category, such as those involving vital commuter services in large metropolitan areas where the demands of public convenience and necessity are large, it is of course obvious that the Commission would err if it did not give great weight to the ability of the carrier to absorb even large deficits resulting from such services. But where, as here, the Commission's findings make clear that the demands of public convenience and necessity are slight . . . it is equally proper for the Commission, in determining the existence of the burden on interstate commerce, to give little weight to the factor of the carrier's overall prosperity.[37]

Of course it is understood that the court will do its own reweighing of the weighing it orders the Commission to do.

Perhaps the most dramatic examples of the alteration and mixture of rule of thumb and thematic techniques and the tactical advantages of each to various courts and litigants are to be found

---

[37] Southern Ry. v. North Carolina, 376 U.S. 93, 105 (1964).

in those areas, particularly labor and antitrust law, where per se rules are much in fashion. In such areas disputes about whether courts should or should not adopt per se rules are in effect disputes about whether they should use the rule or thematic approach. And, of course, courts have sometimes adopted and sometimes rejected the per se approach. Per se rules, however, offer an extreme example. Probably most common is the situation in which a court's doctrine is relatively clear and predictable, in other words, is a rule of thumb or standing operating procedure, but nevertheless is sufficiently imprecise to allow the judge some of the freedom of the thematic approach particularly through his choice of emphasis on particular portions of the relevant law and facts.

Another feature of what Lindblom calls this "reconstruction" strikes home immediately in the judicial process. "Fact-systems are reconstructed as new ones are discovered. Policy proposals are redesigned as new views of the facts are adopted." At the most elementary level, all of us have many times been struck by the way in which, in a given case, the facts look so much different in the majority opinion than in the dissent. The majority's frightened child, shivering in his cell, cut off from his loving parents, and confessing in loneliness and desperation, may become the dissenters' hardened juvenile delinquent, refusing to see his mother and confessing as a final gesture of defiance. The poor little Seventh Day Adventist, who, forbidden by her conscience to work on Saturday, is struck off the unemployment compensation rolls, moves my heart precisely because I almost instinctively think in terms of an economic system in which there are plenty of five day jobs. She moves my heart slightly less when a dissenter shows that, in the Southern town in which she lives, practically the only employment for women is in the textile mills which work a six day week. Thus the lady's religion conveniently allows her to refuse every available job and continue to live off the taxpayers indefinitely. I am not saying that judges necessarily pick and choose their facts to support their decisions, but that judges typically decide on the basis of some model or abstraction from the facts and that the way they construct this model affects their decisions. No matter what its technical relation to the doctrine of presumption of constitutionality, is not this the real story of the Brandeis brief? By the way, here attitudinal studies and incrementalism cross paths again, for judges may structure the facts of any given case to verify their pre-existing attitudes toward the parties, and the factual models on which policies are based and modified may change as new judges with different attitudes take a hand in painting the factual picture.

Finally March, within the context of the firm, and Lind-blom, dealing with the political system as a whole, emphasize that analysis is done by many participants and that the policy product of the system as a whole results from the interaction of these multiple centers of analysis. I think we can find this phenom-enon, not always but sometimes, in multi-judge courts, and in multi-court systems, for instance the circuits when interpreting federal statutes, or the highest courts of the several states in working out commercial law which must govern many interstate transactions. The basic lore of common law is, of course, one of multiple decision-making under the label of "case by case" development of the law. More concretely the typical process of federal statutory interpretation is likely to involve decisions by several circuits. Agreement among successive circuits will fix the initial interpretation. Conflict among the circuits will defer a final interpretation and, at least in theory, eventually lead to a decision by the Supreme Court. Thus the circuits form a multi-unit decision-making system in which agreement or disagreement among the units is likely to materially influence the system's final decision. To the extent that the courts of certain states find the judicial decisions of certain other states highly persuasive, legal decision-making as a mutual product of two state court systems will occur. Nearly every practicing lawyer is in possession of rough rules of thumb as to which states' reports his own state's judges are likely to treat most hospitably. Of course the chain of appeal within each of the states, and of the federal courts, particularly when there are two levels of appellate courts, con-stitutes multiple decision-making in and of itself.

Certainly, taking the role of the courts in the context of the political system as a whole, the phenomenon of multiple, inter-acting policy-making centers has been widely recognized as crucial to judicial behavior. For instance, where the federal courts make federal law by statutory interpretation, they add their decisions to those already made by Congress in passing the statute, and frequently those of the agencies responsible for administering and thus initially interpreting it. The court's decisions are likely to provoke further agency decisions and perhaps further congres-sional action, with the courts then making more decisions yet in response to new Congressional and agency action. Thus courts are part of the succession of policy decisions, none of which is decisive or final, but each of which affects all the others, that is typical of incremental decision-making. . . .

Essentially lawyers have been unable to escape from stare decisis because they continue to require some theory that will account for the fact that law changes while law stays the same. This sta-

bility cum change has often been taken to be a peculiar phenomenon of common law requiring for its explanation that peculiar
theory of the common law, stare decisis. Stability with change
is not a peculiar feature of common law but a general feature of
Anglo-American political systems. The theory of incrementalism
adequately accounts for just that respect for the status quo coupled with marginal change that stare decisis takes us down so
many tortured and basically fictional bypaths to describe. Incrementalism could thus be used as a tool for teaching and understanding judicial decision-making that would coherently organize
the actual process of decision without requiring us to drum the
ideology of stare decisis into the law student and risk his subsequent shock and alienation when he discovers that stare decisis
itself has been drummed out of the jurisprudential corps. . . .

With the decline of mechanical jurisprudence and the general
admission of the inevitability of judicial law-making, a vast unease
has fallen over legal scholarship. All the orthodox limitations on
judicial choice, which used to stabilize and confine both the
judges and the commentators, seem to have been swept away.
Deprived of these comforts, many legal scholars have fallen into
desperate fears of excessive judicial action even while approving
the actual actions of the courts. The ambivalence has not improved their scholarly disposition. Indeed in their general state
of alarm, they tend to see every hint of judicial action, either
in the courts themselves or in jurisprudential writing, as one
more step toward disaster. Anyone who is not busy in helping
to rebuild some sort of fence around judicial action and thus
in reestablishing the security and serenity that the legal profession enjoyed when the law was a grand and mysterious edifice,
but one whose structure was clear and certain to the lawyers, is
viewed as irresponsible and dangerous. Indeed there are dark
hints that they do not really love the law. . . .

This malaise can be cured, I think, when we can demonstrate
that the admission of judicial choice, that is, of the politicism of
courts, is *in and of itself* also the imposition of a set of limitations on courts. The new jurisprudence does sweep away the
traditional, mechanical limits on judicial action, but it does not
leave a vacuum that the doyens of the establishment law schools
must work desperately to fill. The new jurisprudence recognizes
the freedom of judges but also specifies the limitations on that
freedom.

Incrementalism is, it seems to me, the most effective way of
emphasizing the limiting functions of the new jurisprudence, and
hopefully comforting those who see judicial extravagance lurking
everywhere. For the core of incremental doctrine is respect for

the status quo and movement from the status quo only in short, marginal steps carefully designed to allow for further modification in the light of further developments. If you will examine all the orthodox pleas for careful and honest treatment of precedent, precise and cautious legal language, narrowly drawn holdings, respect for traditional legal concepts, and logical, case by case progress toward legal improvement, you will simply have found the message of incrementalism in the language of legal orthodoxy. Incrementalism is a theory of freedom *and* limitation. As a descriptive theory incrementalism recognizes the freedom of decision-makers, including judges, but emphasizes that in the real world decision is narrowly confined. As a prescriptive theory incrementalism requires of the judge, as political decision-maker, that he act cautiously and according to the rules of legal craftsmanship so dear to the hearts of legalists. The principal advantage of incrementalism to the legal fraternity may well be that it provides a middle and common ground for those who revel in the new found freedom of judges and those who fear the excesses of that freedom.

NOTES AND QUESTIONS

1. Professor Shapiro writes about incrementalism and the courts. To what extent does his description of the incremental process fit the actions of Congress, the presidency and administrative agencies? To what extent is he suggesting the proper behavior of courts, to what extent merely describing what courts do?

2. There are other models of decision-making. One model, of the "scientific" or "rational" process, involves identifying a problem, searching for all alternatives, predicting the likely consequences of each alternative, and evaluating all these consequences by some agreed value or values. Another model is the "irrational"; in this process, the decision-maker uses a leap of faith, or the best guess of one with experience; he reacts to events and hopes for the best.

a. Give your impressions as to how the following government decisions should be classified, based on what you know about them:

(1) The Department of Defense, over the opposition of many navy officers, decided that the aircraft carrier, "John F. Kennedy," would not be nuclear powered. The decision was based on elaborate cost-benefit studies.

(2) During a riot in the area of a large city in which most
of the residents were Black, the mayor ordered the
police removed from the area; a group of residents took
over the police function. The riot ended. The decision
was made under crisis conditions; some people were advising the mayor to call for the National Guard and the
use of massive armed force.

(3) A federal agency created a program designed to help end
poverty. Control of the program at the local level was,
in large part, in the hands of the poor and out of the
hands of political systems which run the large cities. A
mayor, whose backing was crucial in election campaigns,
objected and asked the President to give control of the
program to regular city officials. The President decided
to accede to his request.

(4) The supreme court of state X, in a case of first impression in the state, held that a novel by Henry Miller
was not obscene. Many state and federal cases were cited
in the opinion.

b. Under what circumstances are decisions likely most closely
to fit the "scientific" model? the incremental? the leap of faith?

[Reading 86]

3. Consider the following excerpt. In "The Law of the
Planned Society," 75 *Yale Law Journal* 1228, 1261-63 (1966),
Charles Reich* has written:

Congress, while it cannot fix more definite standards for
agency decisions, can insist upon broader standards: a more
sweeping definition of the agency's task and a wider list of
the values that must be considered. Is this a workable remedy for the narrowness of some agencies' vision? Perhaps it
would help to think of the delegation of power to any agency
in terms of a corporate or an institutional charter, conferring
the general government and management of a given area,
just as the Corporation of Yale University is given, not an
instruction to make rules in "the public interest," but the
"government, care, and management" of the University.
This should make clear to an agency that its responsibility
cannot be satisfied by passive balancing of competing inter-

* Professor of Law, Yale University. Reprinted by permission of the
Yale Law Journal Company and Fred B. Rothman & Company. From The
Yale Law Journal, Vol. 75, pp. 1261-63.

ests, but that it must engage in affirmative planning on its own. The charter of the Forest Service furnishes an example. It states that "[T]he Secretary of Agriculture is authorized and directed to develop and administer the renewable surface resources of national forests. . . ." Such a statutory mandate is, of course, easier to lay down where the subject matter is publicly owned. But could we not also tell the CAB that its responsibility is to administer the public air corridors of the nation and to plan, promote and regulate the national air transportation system? The FPC [Federal Power Commission] could be chartered as an agency to care for and manage the nation's hydroelectric resources. Thus the law could establish each agency as a public enterprise like the post office or the TVA [Tennessee Valley Authority] —operated in part by private enterprise but with the public agency responsible to the consumers for the ultimate product. Such a delegation would not only remind the agency of the scope of its responsibilities, it would make clear to the public where responsibility for failure lies. If television programs are objectionable, the public should be able to hold the FCC [Federal Communications Commission] accountable, and if airline service is unsatisfactory the CAB [Civil Aeronautics Board] should be an object of criticism. The public will, of course, continue to blame the private entrepreneurs as well, but the law can help the public to perceive and locate governmental responsibility.

Besides delegating power, Congress might also attempt to set down a checklist of certain basic goals or values that the agency must take into consideration. Such statements of values are no mere gesture. Experience with the Forest Service demonstrates that if a professional agency is developed and given full responsibility, it is of the nature of bureaucracy that it will take very seriously whatever guides Congress imposes. The Forest Service has its limitations of vision, but it does try to carry out its mandate faithfully. It demonstrates how well an agency can function if its basic responsibility for planning and management (with certain defined goals and values) is made clear to it and to the public.

A broader outlook can also be built into the agency itself by institutionalizing certain values which might otherwise be neglected. Why not a bureau of conservation in the highway department, a department of fisheries for the FPC, a division of educational television in the FCC? Such agencies or bureaus could be depended on to do what comes naturally to any bureau: pursue its own raison d'etre as ardently as possible. The device of bureaus to represent interests is already common in government, like the Disarmament Agency which is supposed to counteract the Pentagon. It is no longer a surprising thought that government must take measures to ensure a broad range of values and even to promote its own opposition. As government grows ever stronger, it must underwrite pluralism in ever more explicit terms.

An agency can only support a full spectrum of values if it has some way to identify all of them. This exposes a further duty of the planning agency—not merely to represent all visible values, but to seek out those which are not so readily discovered.

What problems, if any, about incrementalism and its emphasis on inputs of demands and support and feedback from past decisions are suggested by Reich? To what extent is an agency which is operating incrementally likely to have the kind of "broad outlook," and "full spectrum of values" Reich wishes them to have? *Compare* Rowen, "Bargaining and Analysis in Government," Reading 19, at 184, *supra.*

4. Many people are impatient with or deplore the slow-moving, marginal, patchwork progress of government—roughly, the incremental approach. It strikes them as a kind of drift without direction, and as incapable of solving the critical problems that face society. Incrementalism seems to favor the status quo. On the other hand, it can be defended as the way to balance the many warring interests in a pluralist society. In what areas is organized, rational central planning possible and desirable? Does it necessarily mean a more totalitarian state, either the right-wing or the left-wing version? To what extent is incrementalism an important factor in the preservation of freedom? Could one expect a "socialist" government to be created incrementally? Could one expect such a government to operate incrementally?

On incrementalism and social change, *see* Albert O. Hirschman, *Journeys Toward Progress: Studies of Economic Policy-Making in Latin America* (The Twentieth Century Fund 1963).

c. *The input and feedback process: support or a vote of no confidence*

87. Popular Democracy and Judicial Independence: Electorate and Elite Reactions to Two Wisconsin Supreme Court Elections

JACK LADINSKY AND ALLAN SILVER*

1967 WISCONSIN LAW REVIEW 128

What is most obviously interesting about judicial elections, even those to the highest of the state courts, is that they seem so very uninteresting. They are typically placid affairs of low salience, involving men usually obscure to the general public. Professional norms and codes inhibit or utterly prevent the substantive discussion of judicial decisions or legal philosophies, and incumbents are usually returned to office.

By inference, rather than observation, the judicial electorate has often been described as uninformed and apathetic. It is certainly true that the turnout for judicial elections, or the number of votes cast for judicial candidates when other offices are also at stake, is usually below the norm in Wisconsin as elsewhere. The judicial electorate is thus small; and while it may or may not be ignorant and unconcerned, it is certainly acquiescent.

The "acquiescent electorate" is not new to judicial politics. Even when the courts were ruling conservatively in hotly contested areas of economic policy, popular reaction in the form of electoral defeat was not the rule, and where it was attempted, it was typically unsuccessful.

* Jack Ladinsky, Associate Professor of Sociology, University of Wisconsin; Allan Silver, Professor of Sociology, Columbia University. Copyright © 1967 Wisconsin Law Review. Reprinted by permission.

One such episode occurred in Wisconsin in the Civil War period. When the railroads defaulted on their bonds after the Panic of 1857, many farmers who had mortgaged their farms in return for railroad certificates were faced with demands from eastern creditors. Organized into leagues, the farmers successfully obtained legislative relief. Legislation was passed favoring the farm mortgagors every year but one between 1857 and 1867. The Wisconsin Supreme Court, however, declared almost all these laws unconstitutional. During two judicial elections, in 1861 and 1863, the farmers organized challenges to incumbents who had voted with the majority in these cases, but they failed narrowly to elect their candidates. The extent to which such instances strike us today as exceptional or bizarre suggests the extent to which insulation of the elective judiciary from the normal consequences of electoral competition has become an expected and basic feature of the American polity.

An "acquiescent electorate" means that even in states that have elective judiciaries the power of governors to fill vacancies provides generously for appointive access to supreme courts. And election or reelection ordinarily implies the ratification of judges themselves, not their decisions. . . .

Whether elective or not, courts remain agencies that occasionally—even if rarely, compared to other branches of government—produce decisions with strong political and policy consequences. But they do so on a recondite basis: "the law," which in principle does not admit of popular debate, pressure, or passion. Every man and every cause may have a day in court, but they have it on the law's terms—terms that seem to rule out the familiar tests of political strength, personal influence, or moral force. If only in this procedural sense, the judiciary must remain what Tocqueville said it was, an "aristocratic element." How might "aristocracy" be legitimized in the great American democracy on those occasions that reveal and test the bases of legitimacy, when authority renders decisions of wide scope and grave consequence that displease many citizens? . . .

[T]he judiciary has unique functions that distinguish it from the executive and legislative branches. While these latter agencies of government have the legitimate as well as legal right to administer, change, or innovate, the judiciary is appropriately shielded from popular influence because it does none of these. Instead, it serves as the detached and impersonal voice of the community in applying the law. Second, the judiciary is particularly dependent upon public support for its functions because, in contrast to other branches, it lacks elective legitimation and independent means to compel conformity to its decisions.

Thus, what appears to be the most aloof of government institutions is, in another sense, the most critically dependent upon public assent to its functions. Accordingly, two themes appear in the literature that either promulgate or discuss the legitimation of the American judiciary. The first stresses majesty, the second expertise.

As majestic figures, the justices are keepers of a mystery in the pristine sense of that word: They guard the constitutional essence of the Republic, which, although embodied in words, is approached and comprehended only by special acquaintance with precedent. Their close association with the ultimate sources of sovereignty renders them men who dwell apart, uniquely garbed, esoteric, few, powerful. One joins them by means both arduous and obscure. Like priestly lawgivers, they do not make the law but find it in the Constitution and the accumulated body of precedent. Thus, they exercise no independent discretion. They are powerful and respected because the ultimate values that bind us together as a moral community speak through them.

As experts, the judges are supreme technicians. Skilled masters of their craft, they apply the principles of law to a variety of cases and changing circumstances. They are respected for learning, but learning of an essentially technical character that, like other technical skills, is open to all who succeed in acquiring it. Judges are members of the legal profession whose general conduct is governed by an honorable and responsible code, but a code of an occupation and not a priesthood.

While these images are not wholly incompatible, each stresses a different aspect of judicial authority, and the balance between them may change. Majesty is particularly appropriate to the claim that judges in a democracy exercise no independent power but are rather the detached conscience of the society. Thus, this notion does not violate democratic suppositions about the exercise of decisive power. Expertise helps justify judicial authority because it rests upon achievement that is in principle open to all. The expert makes a claim to authority not because he represents an extraordinary principle, but because he is technically qualified to exercise special functions. Furthermore, although experts are usually right, they may be wrong.

Each picture of the judiciary, together with its accompanying claim to legitimation, expresses a different view toward the judiciary as creative elite—an elite in the classic sense, superior men charged with the maintenance of standards. In the one case, however, the creative elite appears as the worthy but passive vehicle of constitutional verities. In the other, it appears quali-

fied by personal accomplishment either to uphold or to alter
an existing state of affairs by analyzing it in terms of legal
technique. . . .

[The bulk of the article deals with two judicial elections in
Wisconsin. Horace W. Wilkie was appointed to the Wisconsin
Supreme Court in May, 1962, by the governor, a Democrat, to
fill a vacancy. Wilkie was a prominent liberal Democrat.

In July, 1963, Wilkie announced he was a candidate for election to a full ten-year term. The election was slated for April,
1964. Another lawyer, Harry E. Larsen, also announced his candidacy. And on the last day for filing nominating papers, a right-
wing conservative, Howard H. Boyle, Jr., also entered the race.
"He immediately announced to the press that his campaign would
include criticism of Wilkie's record as a justice"; and, in particular, his vote with the majority of the Supreme Court in a case
that held that Henry Miller's *Tropic of Cancer* was not obscene.
In the primary, in March, 1964, Boyle surprised the experts by
coming in second, eliminating Larsen, and almost carrying Milwaukee County where liberal Democrats usually had done well.

The next month "was marked by unusually heated campaign-
ing and controversy." Boyle attacked not only Wilkie's record in
the obscenity case, but in two other cases. In one, the court
"broadly, but not totally, abrogated parental immunity from
liability for negligent torts to their children." Boyle charged
that the court here "changed the common law where the legislature had specifically refused to act." In another case, Wilkie
"upset a court-ordered obligation of a married daughter to support her aged mother when the daughter was forced by health
to retire from a government job." Boyle argued that the court
should have allowed the daughter's income to be considered.

Wilkie "countered by marshalling the financial and verbal
bipartisan support of . . . the bar, the bench, law professors,
politicians, labor, businessmen, and the press." He charged that
Boyle was attacking the court as an institution and threatening
the independence of the judiciary.

In an "unprecedented maneuver" five members of the court
publicly defended the *Tropic* decision and "assailed Boyle for the
impropriety of his attack on Wilkie." The Milwaukee Junior
Bar Association's executive body accused Boyle of violating the
"lawyers' canons of professional ethics for judicial campaigns."
Not a single major newspaper supported Boyle. Boyle did have
some support from Catholic organizations, partly because he came
out strongly for state aid to parochial schools.

Boyle lost the election, but Wilkie's plurality was a modest one. A "comparatively large electorate turned out, activated for the most part by the presidential primary."

A 1965 judicial election was in many ways similar to the Boyle-Wilkie campaign. Boyle ran again, this time against a sitting judge, Nathan S. Heffernan, who had been prominent in the Democratic Party before he became a justice. Again, Boyle eliminated a third candidate in the primary. He raised many of the same themes as before in his campaign. He attacked the "ultra-liberal" trend of the court, and he "assailed what he saw as a departure from time-honored, traditional principles." Boyle lost once more, though again by a small number of votes.

"Popular intervention had been temporarily turned back." Bench and bar were "uneasy" about the possibility of a third confrontation. Justice Thomas E. Fairchild, who wrote the *Tropic* decision, came up for reelection in 1966. "But no confrontation arose." Boyle did not enter the race; Fairchild ran unopposed. "Normality had been restored to judicial politics."

The authors studied the active workers for Wilkie and contrasted them with Boyle's troops. Wilkie's were "generally political and bar notables, men of high public office, particularly in state bar." They were older men, predominantly lawyers in medium-sized firms in metropolitan areas. Boyle workers were young and inexperienced, mostly lawyers in solo practice. More of them were Catholics, active in church and parochial school affairs. More of them were right-wing Republicans. More of them were political amateurs—for one half, this was a "first venture into judicial elections"; this was so for only one quarter of the Wilkie men. More Boyle than Wilkie men were from small-town backgrounds. In their attitude toward the court, the Boyle men espoused a "rigid, inflexible, populist, and orthodox theology." The Wilkie men constituted "an established, cosmopolitan and professional state elite."

What kinds of people, the authors ask, are "more likely to have 'populist' or 'interventionist' attitudes toward judicial authority, and what kinds 'respectful' and 'self-denying' perspectives"?

For one thing, there seem to be distinctions in the population based on age. Those over fifty-five are most likely to be "populist," preferring the elective system, partisan to nonpartisan elections, and least likely to think there is "something special" about judges compared to other public officials. Why this age phenomenon? Does it reflect "a secular trend in society," or does it reflect "changes in individuals associated with age"? Tentatively, the authors feel that "the weight of supposition is on the side of social rather than individual change."

Education, too, correlates with attitudes: the less educated are also the least "respectful." College educated voters were more likely to be for Wilkie than for Boyle.

The link between voting in these elections, and general orientations toward the judiciary was not always strong and clear. Partly, this was because of widespread "ignorance of judicial issues and the low visibility of judicial elections." Only one third of the electorate had even heard of the Court's obscenity decisions. The authors continue:]

There is another way in which the code of judicial politics operates: It is the demand for stability on the bench, which cuts across political lines and affects elites not usually associated with the courts. An important factor in Wilkie's bipartisan support was his experience as a legislator. Wilkie was known widely as a "reasonable" man, a man of strong liberal principles, but not inflexible. Thus, he was a member of the "team" and a person with whom other legislators could work, regardless of party. Moreover, as a leading lawyer Wilkie shared a profession, stance, and activity with the leadership of the state bar. Among lawyers supporting Wilkie were men who had become judicial campaign "specialists." Others, less political, were nevertheless long-respected bar activists, many of them retired judges, with sincere dedication to the idea of an independent judiciary. Wilkie was tied to all these men by common work experience and ongoing collegial relationships that had, over the years, created bonds of mutual respect, trust, and often friendship. Stability of the courts is an important matter to all these men, and their defense of stability is expressed by support of the sitting judge as long as he is widely respected as competent and honest. Wilkie enjoyed their confidence; Boyle did not.

A glance at the judicial electorate in Wisconsin confirms the impression that, even in the comparatively inflamed circumstances of the 1964-1965 period, the state judiciary has low salience. Thus only forty-six percent of the total electorate even knew that Wisconsin judges are elected, only thirty percent could tell which of two candidates was the incumbent, and only nine percent could remember anything substantive about the most recent state supreme court election (held a few months before interviewing). About eighty-five percent did not know the political parties with which the candidates had been associated.

However, the electorate's general orientations toward the judiciary are more heterogeneous. Sixty-four percent think state judges should be elected, but only forty-four percent think elected judges are typically better than those appointed by experts (with thirty-seven percent agreeing that the latter are better). One-third like the idea that judicial candidates should criticize each other's records in a campaign, and about half dislike it. Seven out of ten think it appropriate that judicial candidates should tell the people how they feel in general about issues likely to come before the court, while one-fifth think this is not a good idea. Half agree with the proposition that a majority of the people should be able to reverse a judicial decision of which they do not approve, while a third disagree. About forty percent think that the people are best qualified to assess the merits of judges, and a roughly equal proportion think that lawyers and judges are best qualified to do so. Half think of judges as distinctively "special," compared to other public officials, but a third do not. Despite these evidences of divergent orientations toward the judiciary, general satisfaction with the bench is very high—almost ninety percent think that as a group the judges are fair, just, and trying to do a good job. . . .

In Wisconsin during 1964 and 1965, the "acquiescent electorate," or part of it, stirred. Many notables in the state were aroused in response. From this distance, and at this point, one has the impression that the judicial electorate hardly knew its own strength. Mobilized only partially, both in numbers and passion, it came close to politicizing an election to the state's highest court. If for those who play the game the politics of the judiciary are really the "politics of place" rather than of issue, then for the electorate they are largely the politics of absentmindedness. But in the challenge to understandings and custom that we have been observing, this changed. For those close to the game—contestants, notables, observers—the issue became one akin to a constitutional one. The electorate appears to have gone back to acquiescence; only a few of those who voted told us that they cared about voting for a loser more than in most other elections. And Mr. Boyle did not fail to send the usual telegram of congratulations to each victorious opponent, precisely as required by American political protocol.

It is clear that at least one judicial electorate could be moved almost to the point of electing to the state supreme court a man who explicitly challenged many understandings about the functioning of an elective judiciary. At the least, judicial majesty in Wisconsin is far from sufficient to guarantee that those who render judgment cannot be challenged or replaced by the will of the people, precisely as any competitive election implies.

One cannot infer from this that "respectfulness" is declining. On the contrary, it is possible that the factors our survey suggests are associated with higher education and that the generational succession of those below late middle age, will strengthen those perspectives that made a judicial electorate hard to mobilize. But though the "ideological insulation" of the elective court from its constituency may be growing, occasions that erode acquiescence may also be multiplying as courts innovate or clarify in matters of morals and values: censorship, relationships of church and state, police practices, and the relationships of the races.

In Wisconsin, at least, the court appears to remain untouched by popular intervention. Perhaps even more striking in this respect than the court's legal philosophy is its religious composition. In a state that is two-thirds Catholic and Lutheran, four of the judges, on the seven-man supreme court in early 1966, were Congregationalists and one was Presbyterian. The sixth was a Jew, and only one was Catholic. Our survey reveals that Congregationalists number less than three percent and Presbyterians number less than four percent of the Wisconsin population. Thus, electoral pressures for religious representation appear to be weak or wholly absent. Furthermore, this religious makeup probably has long-range implications for the court's value orientation. Previous research has suggested a connection between religion and judicial decision-making. In any case, the almost total lack of representatives of the state's two major and most articulate religious groupings bespeaks a truly extraordinary degree of freedom from the need to respond in some measure to public sentiment. However, just as the power of judicial review sometimes exercises latent influence over the legislative process, so also may the potential of the judicial electorate exercise a latent influence over the mentality of the court. Such at least was the fear expressed by many of those who most actively defended the court.

On the side of the challenger, many disparities appear between activists and electorate. The activists were comparatively young; those most disposed to respond to them, late middle age or older. The activists were heavily Republican and many supported [George] Wallace [the former Governor of Alabama, who ran in the 1964 Wisconsin presidential primary on a right-wing and segregationist platform]. Those who voted for their candidate had no distinctive party background and showed little disposition to support the Wallace candidacy. Half the activists were Catholics, but religion played a smaller and less consistent role in mobilizing their following. However, activists and supporters both agreed on the matter immediately at hand: It is appropriate to vote against a judge because of disagreement with his decisions, and elected judges are preferable to appointed ones.

To what extent did the notables who defended the "independence" of the court and those who voted for the incumbent judges share congruent values? The activists were relatively better educated; so, most definitely, were their supporters in the electorate. But it is not clear that the meaning of a judicial election is the same for both groupings. Those who managed the defense of the court, in general, prefer the elective procedure, despite their harrowing experience with it. Why? Perhaps because the "politics of judicial place" can so often receive the legitimating stamp of popular confirmation. Might not this part of the electorate fit the picture of the ideal citizen in a democratic polity given us in [Gabriel] Almond and [Sidney] Verba's *The Civic Culture*— a man with a "high perception of potential influence and a lower level of actual influence," precisely an arrangement that can "help explain how a democratic political culture can act to maintain a balance between governmental elite power and governmental elite responsiveness. . . ." Perhaps one way that judicial authority is legitimated is the sense of potential control that elections bestow despite the other elements, both institutional and cultural, that militate against that control being exercised or being directly efficacious.

We found few evidences—they are qualitative in form rather than numerical—of a prevalence of judicial mystery or majesty in Wisconsin. The "ideological insulation" of the judiciary manifested in the general electorate does not appear to reflect the sophisticated rhetoric of legal and political analysts. . . . In the face of widespread disagreement with the substance of recent judicial innovations in public policy areas, public support seems more a matter of acquiescence or ignorance rather than positive endorsement, of respect for the judiciary as one kind of government official rather than as a distinctive office embodying unique functions and status. Indeed, in our interviews judges were typically respected as dignified representatives of the people and the state, as men of distinguished achievement, and rarely as aloof guardians of immutable, constitutional principles. Yet it would be unwarranted to consider this as a weakness in the cultural defense of judicial independence. Quite the contrary, the traditional view of the judiciary is so incompatible with the prevailing texture of American political culture that it is likely to erode quickly if, as some observers suggest, a new realism about judicial innovation, lawmaking, and policy intervention is taking hold.

The traditional, conservative, and elitist interpretation of judicial power, stressing its majesty, aloofness, and neutrality, developed, we suspect, as a reactive defense against a population more "populist" and interventionist in the past than it is now. Nothing has quite equaled the Progressive's proposals for court reorganization. It is also noteworthy that the formal provisions for judicial election in Wisconsin itself have gradually become more insulating since statehood. In 1889 the constitution was amended to end popular election of the chief justice in favor of elevating to that post the member with the longest continuous service; the term of office was increased from six years in 1852 to ten years in 1877; in 1913 nomination by party convention and party designation on the ballot were eliminated; the governors' appointees were originally elected for the unexpired term of their office, but since 1953 they have been elected for a full term; and in 1955 a license to practice law in Wisconsin for five years prior to election or appointment was added to the necessary qualifications for office.

Thus, as cultural populism declines . . . there is less need for the older interpretation of the judiciary's role in judicial review. . . . Nonetheless, the issue of judicial distinctiveness remains troublesome, especially as the court handles touchy issues in value fields. The court must continue to claim popular support and legitimacy as a distinctively insulated institution. . . .

But a cultural defense for judicial authority is likely to be more viable in America if it extends, rather than opposes, the primordial sense of democracy. Thus, an image of the judiciary that sees it as an instrument of popular sovereignty, albeit occupying a special place in our political arrangements, is likely to prove stronger armor than the older image. . . . Surely democracy cannot be told that a judiciary that may exercise such power is wholly untouchable. Yet at times the electorate must be induced, persuaded, or defeated if it tries vigorously to exercise its elemental power.

Perhaps the delicate and ambiguous matrix linking court and people is one of the means by which the extraordinary powers of our judiciaries receive the private sanction and acceptance of many citizens whom they disappoint and even offend on few, but great, occasions. And perhaps it is also among the means by which the courts on such occasions, for whatever reasons or motives, spoken or unrealized, take not only the law into account but [also] the people.

NOTES AND QUESTIONS

1. Note the difference between public support of the court as an institution and members of the court as individuals. Sup-

port of an institution may ultimately be based on support of its incumbents in the aggregate, but a legal system is stable when there is important public support for the institution or office, even if particular acts of the officeholders (or even particular officeholders) do not meet with the same approval. A President's popularity can sink very low, but the American public generally waits patiently or impatiently for the next election and continues, by and large, to pay respect to the office of the Presidency.

Support can be manifested in many ways—by silence or inaction, which is an extremely important way, or by positive acts. Simply acquiescing in what courts, legislatures and Presidents do is an important kind of support. Positive acts include votes at elections, letters to officeholders approving their conduct, and compliance with official requests. Nonsupport can be shown by negative votes, failures to comply, and actions ranging all the way to armed revolution.

2. From what sources do the various agencies within the legal system—courts, legislatures, administrative agencies, the police, the President—derive their *knowledge* of the level and intensity of support or nonsupport from the general public and from various segments of the public?

3. Support for the political or legal order flows from the public if and when the public believes in the *legitimacy* of the political or legal order. The great German sociologist, Max Weber, was one of the social thinkers who first developed the concept of legitimacy and attempted to classify types of legitimacy. Essentially, Weber saw three kinds of legitimacy: *traditional*, that is, the sacredness of what is customary and the adherence to customary, traditional authority; *charismatic*, "the surrender to the extraordinary . . . actual revelation or grace resting in . . . a savior, a prophet, or a hero"; and *rational*, in which legitimacy is ascribed to a "system of consciously made rational rules," and commands are valid and meet with obedience "as generally binding norms whenever such obedience is claimed by him whom the rule designates." Max Rheinstein, ed., *Max Weber on Law in Economy and Society* 336 (Harvard U. Press 1954).

What is the source, in Weber's terms, of the legitimacy of the Wisconsin Supreme Court as described by Ladinsky and Silver?

4. Ladinsky and Silver indicate one way a behavioral scientist can study legitimacy. Selznick, Reading 1, at 2, *supra,* indicates another. A psychologist has suggested still a third path:

A crucial problem which I feel warrants investigation by psychologists is the overlap between legality and morality, the possible conjoint socialization of these cognitive systems, and the effects of culture and demography. This is an obvious corollary to the psychologist's interest in the socialization of moral stages. Any understanding of the legal process should involve some attempt to understand the nature of the cognitive process in legal development. How do individuals develop a legal sense? How are senses of justice socialized? How do individuals make laws or rules? Is a sense of law, or order, or rule or orderliness inherent in the human organism and, if so, how is it manifest? What are the regularities in human behavior which indicate that legal development, like moral development, may be stimulated or retarded by culture or differentially affected by demographic factors? What are the generational differences in concepts of justice? Is it a life-cycle phenomenon? What are the personality styles, belief systems, and coping strategies of lawyers, theologians and psychologists as the justice-makers? What factors inhibit or facilitate compliance or noncompliance to law and authority?

June L. Tapp, "Psychology and the Law: The Dilemma," 2 *Psychology Today* 16, 22 (1969). Dr. Tapp is a senior research social scientist for the American Bar Foundation, the research organization sponsored by the American Bar Association. What does one gain from each approach to the study of the input of support (legitimacy)? Do the approaches differ significantly?

Chapter 5

THE LEGAL SYSTEM AS A SOCIAL SYSTEM: INTRA-SYSTEM CONSIDERATIONS

A. INTRODUCTION

A system must do a number of things to function. Two important tasks are adapting to pressures from the environment and coordinating the activities of the people who are part of the system so that they work to attain its goals. To some extent, we have already considered these matters, but in this section we will give them special emphasis. How can the legal system avoid being overburdened by too many demands? How can it control threats to its support when there is a crisis in the society and some part of the system is called upon to make allocations of values which will offend important parts of the society, whatever the allocation selected? And how is action coordinated in a system theoretically based on a separation of powers and which contains many units that can take action in a particular situation? Think of the number of federal, state and local legal agencies concerned with the problem of poverty. The task of coordination is extremely difficult, and within each agency there are problems coordinating the conduct of people both in central offices and in the field. Obviously, we have rules to solve many of these problems: rules enabling a legal agency to evade a sticky issue; rules assigning functions to the federal legislature, the state legislatures, one court and not another; and rules for the conduct of the jobs of clerk of court, legislator and investigator for an agency. But, as we shall see, rules are not the whole answer.

B. APPROPRIATENESS OF FUNCTION AND MAINTENANCE OF THE LEGAL SYSTEM

88. Adjudication and the Rule of Law

LON L. FULLER*

1960 PROCEEDINGS OF THE AMERICAN
SOCIETY OF INTERNATIONAL LAW 1-8

I

By "the limits of adjudication" I mean to indicate the very simple and familiar idea that there are certain kinds of social tasks that are not suitable raw material for the adjudicative process. We cannot solve all of our problems and disputes by referring them to judges or arbitrators. Anyone who discharges a judicial function works within a particular institutional framework. That framework is like a specialized tool; the very qualities which make it apt and efficient for one purpose make it useless for another. A sledge-hammer is a fine thing for driving stakes. It is a cumbersome device for cracking nuts, though it can be used for that purpose in a pinch. It is hopeless as a substitute for a can-opener. So it is with adjudication. Some social tasks confront it with an opportunity to display its fullest powers. For others it can be at best a *pis aller*. For still others it is completely useless.

When the question is thus stated, one is faced with the problem of clarifying the concept of adjudication itself. This is no easy task, for adjudication presents itself in many mixed forms. Sometimes, for example, it verges on mediation directed toward compromise. In this form it tends to merge with the concept of contract. At other times, when the members of a tribunal are selected in such a way as to make them representative of the various interests affected by the tribunal's decisions, adjudication verges on representative government.

---

* Professor of Law, Harvard University. Copyright © 1960 The American Society of International Law. Reprinted by permission.

One line of my thought was, then, directed toward some definition of adjudication in what might be called its unmixed manifestations; when it presents itself *simpliciter* and does not borrow its forms and methods from some other process of social decision.

The other line of thought was, as I have said, directed toward clarifying the meaning of "the rule of law." In the literature we find the rule of law identified with ideas that not only seem quite different from one another but actually opposed in meaning. It can be said—and it has been said with varying degrees of explicitness—that the rule of law exists, *first*, where there is respect for justice and human dignity; *second*, where there is constituted a law-making authority whose decrees will be obeyed even when they are unjust; *third*, where the rules established by authority are faithfully enforced by judicial processes; *fourth*, where there is an independent judiciary ready to protect the affected party against the arbitrary acts of established power, *et cetera*.

I suggest that one way of bringing coherence into this confused area is to emphasize one aspect of the process by which a state of anarchy or despotism is converted into something we can call "the rule of law." The aspect I have in mind is the process by which the party affected by a decision is granted a formally defined participation in that decision. Thus we may oppose against anarchy and naked power a society in which there are recognized voting procedures, for voting is an ancient and cherished device by which the individual is accorded a participation in decisions which affect his interests. Again, we may oppose against anarchy and untrammeled power a society organized by the principle of contract, for negotiation (directly or through representatives) is a procedure by which the affected party is granted a participation in the settlement which governs his future conduct.

Continuing along the same line of thought, we may arrive at the conclusion that the fundamental characteristic of adjudication also lies in the particular form of participation it accords to the affected party. That participation consists in the institutionally protected opportunity to present proofs and arguments for a decision in his favor. This is, in effect, nothing more than an unfamiliar formulation of a very familiar conception, that of giving the affected party "his day in court." The formulation I am offering has the advantage, I believe, of clarifying what is necessary to make the party's day in court meaningful. For one thing, he must have some conception of the issues toward which his proofs and arguments are to be directed, if his opportunity to present proofs and arguments is to be meaningful. This is a truth that has been recognized in writings as far apart as Kafka's *The Trial* and Lewis Carroll's account of the Mad Hatter's attempt to testify before the King of Hearts. It is a truth that is, however, often forgotten, I am afraid, by uncritical enthusiasts for "judicializing" every kind of social decision.

To recapitulate, the analysis presented here regards adjudication as a process of social decision characterized by the peculiar form of participation it accords to the affected party, that of presenting proofs and arguments for a decision in his favor. This conception is, I believe, capable of bringing into some kind of order notions about the proper role of adjudication that otherwise remain merely enumerative and disjunctive. I do not have time here to trace, or even to suggest, all the implications that seem to me to flow from this conception. I shall have to content myself with two.

II

The first of these has to do with the concept of the polycentric task. This is a term I have borrowed from Michael Polanyi's profound and much neglected work, *The Logic of Liberty* (1951). To anticipate my conclusion I shall assert that adjudication is a process of decision badly suited to the solution of polycentric problems.

What is a polycentric problem? Fortunately I am in a position to borrow a recent illustration from the newspapers. Some months ago a wealthy lady by the name of Timken died in New York leaving a valuable, but somewhat miscellaneous, collection of paintings to the Metropolitan Museum and the National Gallery "in equal shares," her will indicating no particular apportionment. When the will was probated the judge remarked something to the effect that the parties seemed to be confronted with a real problem. The attorney for one of the museums spoke up and said, "We are good friends. We will work it out somehow or other." What makes this problem of effecting an equal division of the paintings a polycentric task? It lies in the fact that the disposition of any single painting has implications for the proper disposition of every other painting. If it gets the Renoir, the Gallery may be less eager for the Cezanne, but all the more eager for the Bellows, *et cetera*. If the proper apportionment were set for argument, there would be no clear issue to which either side could direct its proofs and contentions. Any judge assigned to hear such an argument would be tempted to assume the rôle of mediator, or to adopt the classical solution: Let the older brother (here the Metropolitan) divide the estate into what he regards as equal shares, let the younger brother (the National Gallery) take his pick.

Let me now give a series of illustrations of polycentric problems, some of which have been assigned, with poor success, to adjudicative treatment, some of which have been proposed for adjudicative treatment, and some of which are so obviously unsuited for adjudicative decision that no one has dreamed of subjecting them to it: setting prices and wages within a managed economy to produce a proper flow of goods; redrawing the boundaries of election districts to make them correspond to shifts in population; assigning the players of a football team to their respective positions; designing a system of throughways into a metropolitan area; allocating scarce funds for projects of scientific research; allocating air routes among our various cities; drawing an international boundary across terrain that is complicated in terms of geography, natural resources, and ethnology; allocating radio and television channels to make balanced programs as accessible to the population as possible.

For problems like these it is clear that adjudication can at best be an unsatisfactory mode of decision. There is and can be no single solution or issue toward which the affected party may direct his proofs and arguments. The mode of participation in the decision accorded to him, that is, the opportunity to present proofs and arguments for a decision in his favor, therefore loses most of its meaning. If he is nevertheless "given his day in court," this concession cannot have the meaning it does for the ordinary litigant, since the deciding agency must direct its mind toward considerations much more important than those contained in the fragmentary presentation open to any single party.

To avoid misunderstanding, let me present briefly a series of clarifications and qualifications.

First, polycentricity is not merely a matter of the complexity of the issues presented to the deciding tribunal. A suit by *A* against *B* on a promissory note for $100 may present extremely complex issues, where, for example, the note was given as part of some complicated deal between the parties. It is not conplexity of issues but of patterns of decision that characterizes the polycentric problem. In the case of the promissory note the court can decide that *A* wins over *B*, without having to move *C*'s position, or to exchange *C*'s position for that of *D*. Contrast this with the football coach who, when he put A in as quarterback, has to move B from halfback to end, to retain C as a center, *et cetera.*

Second, polycentricity is not a matter merely of a multiplicity of affected parties. Indeed, as I have indicated, a polycentric problem can arise between two parties, as in the case of Mrs. Timken's will. On the other hand, if an award were offered for information leading to the capture of a particular criminal, the fact that ten claimants might appear would make for a cumbersome hearing; it would not make the problem polycentric.

Third, I am not asserting that polycentric problems are problems without rational solution. There are rational principles for building bridges of structural steel. But there is no rational principle which states, for example, that the angle between girder *A* and girder *B* must always be 45 degrees. This depends on the bridge as a whole. One cannot construct a bridge by conducting successive arguments on the angle of every pair of intersecting girders. One must deal with the whole structure at once.

Fourth, the fact that an adjudicative decision affects and enters into a polycentric relationship does not of itself mean that the adjudicative tribunal is moving out of its proper sphere. On the contrary, there is no better illustration of a polycentric relationship than an economic market, and yet the laying down of rules that will make a market function properly is one for which adjudication is generally well suited. The working out of our common law of contracts case by case has proceeded through adjudication, yet the basic principle underlying the rules thus developed is that they should promote the free exchange of goods on a polycentric market. The court gets into difficulty, not when it lays down rules about contracting, but when it attempts to write contracts.

Fifth, the polycentricity of any given problem is a matter of degree, though we need to recall Holmes' remark that a distinction may be a matter of degree and none the worse for that. For example, in the evolution of the rules of contract law, our courts often had to backtrack when they discovered that a rule that seemed proper in *Situation X* worked an injustice when applied to *Situation Y*. The problem of the unexpected side effects of a precedent is one that plagues all systems of law, including those which interpret contracts as well as those which lay down the rules for contracting. But the difficulties of this problem furnish no argument for abandoning any concern for the limits of adjudication. On the contrary, they warn us eloquently where adjudication will land if it decides it might as well quit the frying pan for the fire.

To recapitulate: When we move from a condition of anarchy to despotism toward something deserving the name of "the rule of law," one of the most important aspects of that transition lies in the fact that formal institutions are established guaranteeing to the members of the community some participation in the decisions by which their interests are affected. Adjudication is a form of social decision which is characterized by a peculiar mode of participation accorded to the affected party, this participation consisting in the opportunity to present proofs and arguments for a decision in his favor. Whatever impairs the meaning and force of that participation impairs the integrity of adjudication itself. This participation is seriously impaired where an attempt is made to deal with problems where the polycentric element, as here defined, is important and significant. Adjudication is a mode of decision badly suited for the solution of polycentric problems. When it is seriously misused in this direction the rule of law is itself impaired.

What measures, then, are open for the solution of polycentric problems? I can see only two: *contract* and *managerial author-ity*. The first is illustrated by an economic market; the second by a football coach who assigns his players to their appropriate positions.

The majority principle is itself incompetent to deal with poly-centric tasks; at least it would be incompetent if it were not so commonly supplemented by contract in the form of the political deal. Perhaps studies in voting forms . . . may yield methods of voting that will accommodate the machinery of elections to the solution of polycentric tasks.

III

The second main implication of my analysis is one that I have already mentioned, and that is that adjudication must take place within a framework of accepted or imposed standards of decision before the litigant's participation in the decision can be mean-ingful. If the litigant has no idea on what basis the tribunal will decide the case, his day in court—his opportunity to present proofs and arguments—becomes useless. Just as the judge can-not be impartial in a vacuum, so the litigant cannot join issue with his opponent in a vacuum. Communication and persuasion presuppose some shared context of principle.

Those who regard the judge's task as essentially deductive have considered that adjudication can function meaningfully only when rules have been formally laid down in advance for the decision of controversies. According to this view, in any situa-tion where the rule of law is in process of being born, we must first establish rules of decision, and then set up tribunals to administer and apply those rules in particular cases. If the estab-lished rules are insufficient to cover the area of possible controversy, then to that extent adjudication must also default as an ordering principle.

Against this view stand those who contend that rules are a kind of by-product of the adjudicative process, who indeed often seem to regard rules as an unwelcome by-product of adjudication, born of the perverse human impulse toward rationality, often manifesting itself at the cost of good sense.

With considerable simplification we can divide the opponents in this dispute into those whose slogan is: "First rules, then courts," and those who adopt the opposite slogan: "First courts, then rules." Those who take the second position—that is, those who say, "First courts, then rules"—often support their argument by references to history. It is pointed out that the two great systems of law that dominate the world today—the common law and the Roman law—took their origins in a case-by-case evolution of doctrine. Even today, when developments occur in the common law, it is often only at the end of a series of cases that the governing principle becomes clear. In the civil-law countries the codes from which courts purport to derive their principles often provide little beyond a vocabulary for stating legal results. They are filled with clauses referring to "good faith," "equity," "fair practice," and the like—standards that any court could apply without the aid of a code. One of the best of modern codes, the Swiss Code of Obligations, lays down very few rules and contents itself largely with charting the range of judicial discretion and with setting forth what might be called check-lists for the judge to consult to make certain that he has overlooked no factor properly bearing on the exercise of his discretion.

Those on the opposite side of this argument reject this historical argument. To their minds it only confirms the truth of their own slogan, "First law, then courts." In the instances mentioned there were already rules which the courts could apply. These were not, to be sure, rules of law, but they were established moral principles that were generally accepted by the litigants who came before the courts. What happens in such cases has no bearing on situations where a court attempts to project its functions into a moral and legal vacuum. Here the court will fail unless it can enter this wilderness armed with rules authoritatively laid down in advance.

It seems to me that what is needed in this dispute is some analysis of the circumstances under which rules or standards of decision can develop out of the adjudicative process without being laid down in advance; where, in other words, adjudication may reasonably be expected to produce such rules or standards as a by-product of its functioning. For we cannot assume that this will under all conditions occur. Some of our most important domestic regulative agencies were initiated in the hope that, as knowledge was gained case by case, a body of principle would emerge that would be understandable by all concerned and that would bring their decisions within the rule of law. Sometimes this has happened; sometimes our hopes that it would happen have been completely disappointed. Here is a pool of experience which ought to be tapped.

As I see it, there are two major conditions that must exist before principles of decision may be expected to emerge as a by-product of adjudication. The first is that there must be an extra-legal community, existent or in process of coming into existence, from which principles of decision may be derived. The common law of contracts developed concomitantly with the development of the economic institution of exchange. In the course of the long evolution of legal doctrine about contracts, litigants had to put up with many unpleasant manifestations of the adjudicative process—with wooden literalness, with confused analysis, with class bias, with imperfect insight and foresight. But they put up with these inconveniences because they saw that adjudication was necessary to maintain something that existed outside the courtroom that they wanted to preserve and develop. They saw also, by and large, that the principles of law laid down by the courts were themselves derived from the intrinsic demands of this extra-legal community of interest. This was just as true, I think it should be emphasized, whether the courts were laying down rules for the making of contracts, or were developing principles for the interpretation of contracts already concluded, for I believe that it is in the sphere of interpretation that the law's dependence upon extra-legal community is most direct and complete.

The first condition for the emergence of legal doctrine as a by-product of adjudication is, then, the actual or potential existence of extra-legal community. The second condition is that the adjudicative process must not, in attempting to maintain and develop extra-legal community, assume tasks for which it is radically unsuited. I hope I shall not appear to be overworking the concept of polycentricity if I say that all community is polycentric in nature, as indeed are all living relationships. Adjudication may profitably nurture extra-legal community and help it into being; it cannot create it.

It is notable that the greatest failure in American administrative law has been with respect to those agencies that were assigned, or assumed for themselves, polycentric tasks which they attempted to discharge through adjudicative forms. This has been the case with the Civil Aeronautics Board and the Federal

Communications Commission. Both of these agencies have attempted to operate as adjudicative tribunals with only the guidance of very general legislative mandates. Both have failed to build up any coherent body of doctrine that can be called a system of law. Both have failed, not because there was nothing in the way of extra-legal community they could help to develop, but because they were compelled, or thought they were compelled, to create and shape that community through adjudicative procedures. The inadequacies of the community thus built, as well as the too frequent lapses from the judicial proprieties that have characterized both agencies, are alike attributable to an attempt to use adjudicative forms for the accomplishment of tasks for which they are not suited. It is as if the courts of common law, instead of laying down rules governing the making and interpretation of contracts, had from the beginning felt compelled to write contracts for the parties, and had attempted to hold a separate hearing for each clause as the contract was being written.

My final conclusion is that, like many other precious human goals, the rule of law may best be achieved by not aiming at it directly. What is perhaps most needed is not an immediate expansion of international law, but an expansion of international community, multiplying and strengthening the bonds of reciprocity among nations. When this has occurred—or rather *as* this occurs—the law can act as a kind of midwife—or, to change the figure—the law can act as a gardener who prunes an imperfectly growing tree in order to help the tree realize its own capacity for perfection. This can occur only when all concerned genuinely want the tree to grow and to grow properly. Our task is to make them want this.

NOTES AND QUESTIONS

1. Note that Fuller does not view adjudication as a process carried on only by courts. It is a process that can be found in administrative agencies, legislatures and even universities. Nonetheless, Anglo-American courts are the model for what he means by adjudication.

2. Courts have redistricted a state so that representatives represent people and not areas, they have run school systems, managed bankrupt railroads, and they have done many other presumably polycentric tasks. Sometimes there is no other legal agency available to undertake these tasks; sometimes agencies which are available cannot act or do not want to act for political reasons. Suppose a court refused a polycentric task, solely because it was not appropriate for adjudication. Would costs to society be likely

to result from this inaction? Would there be costs to the legal system itself? under what circumstances? Was *Brown v. Board of Educ.* (the school desegregation decision) polycentric? What costs would have resulted from failure to take and decide the case? Conversely, suppose the legal system assigns what Fuller calls a polycentric task to the process of adjudication. Fuller says the results will be bad. What are these undesirable results for society? for the legal system?

3. Does Fuller prove that adjudication is an inappropriate response to a polycentric task? What method of proof does he use?

a. If the Civil Aeronautics Board has failed, as Fuller says it has, is this necessarily because it attempted to allocate airline routes by adjudication? Might it have been more successful if it had been, like most judges, relatively insulated from political pressures? CAB officials often have left the agency for well-paying jobs with airlines; airlines often hire men with political influence to lobby for their interests—this is common enough to warrant a special term for such men in industry jargon: they are called "rainmakers."

b. Aren't all major lawsuits polycentric decisions, in the sense that they have far-reaching social implications?

c. Why could a football team not allocate positions by adjudication if the process were thought worth the cost? Is this not an area where a community has developed sufficiently precise standards to which all parties could meaningfully refer in argument?

C. RULES AND MAINTENANCE OF THE SYSTEM

1. Rules and Control of the Relationship with the Environment

89. Legal Rules and the Process of Social Change

LAWRENCE M. FRIEDMAN*

19 STANFORD LAW REVIEW 786 (1967)

In recent years there has been a welcome increase in the attention paid by behavioral scientists to the legal system. A great deal of it—like much jurisprudential thought—has been process oriented. Theorists have been concerned with the way in which *decisions* are made—in whether precedent, race, education, social background, personality, or some other factor predisposes a judge toward one side or another in particular controversies. Scholars have, of course, been extremely interested in the output of legal institutions, but they have often limited their definition of output to results or decisions and have not concerned themselves with another kind of formal output—rules of law.

A decision (or result) is a unique application of preexisting rule. A rule is a general statement capable (or at least apparently capable) of application to more than one concrete situation. Rules may be as important a product of legal institutions as decisions. A great number of institutions make up the legal system (including courts, legislatures, and administrative bodies); these institutions are engaged in making and applying law, in producing both decisions and rules. Some fresh attention to rules—how they change, what institutional regularities they exhibit, what their relationship is to actual behavior of institutions, and what lifecycles they follow—may illuminate some social characteristics of legal institutions left dark in the course of research and theory devoted to the decision-making process.

* Professor of Law, Stanford University. Copyright © 1967 by the Board of Trustees of the Leland Stanford Junior University. The reproduction is from an article first published in the April, 1967 issue of the Stanford Law Review.

I. Rules of Law

A. *General Introduction*

The common word "rules" has a variety of meanings. We speak of rules of law and also of rules of the game of checkers and rules of personal behavior (as when a person says, "I go to bed at midnight as a rule" or "I make it a rule to avoid fried foods"). In general, the word "rule" is used in law to describe a proposition containing two parts: first, a statement of fact (often in conditional form) and, second, a statement of the consequences that will or may follow upon the existence of that fact, within some normative order or system of governmental control. Or, as Roscoe Pound has put it, a rule is a "legal precept attaching a definite detailed legal consequence to a definite detailed statement of fact." Pound's definition is accurate enough for present purposes. It is broad enough to include statements of common-law doctrine as well as statutory provisions, administrative regulations, ordinances, decrees of dictators, and other general propositions promulgated by legitimate authorities which are intended to govern or guide some aspect of social or individual conduct. All of these propositions may be called legal "rules" in that they all append legal consequences to given facts.

It is very clear that some of the propositions enunciated in appellate cases are (or purport to be) rules. Thus, the famous case of *Hadley v. Baxendale* asserts as a rule:

> Where two parties have made a contract which one of them has broken, the damages . . . should be such as may fairly and reasonably be considered either arising naturally . . . from such breach of contract itself, or such as may reasonably be supposed to have been in the contemplation of both parties, at the time they made the contract, as the probable result of the breach of it.[3]

To a certain set of facts (a broken contract), this rule appends certain consequences (a particular measure of damages). Statutory phrases or sentences are also rules. The heart of the federal patent law—"[w]hoever invents or discovers any new and useful process . . . may obtain a patent"—is a rule. The consequences of a rule may sometimes be omitted from the verbal formulation. But if the rule is to be operational, the consequences must be there, even if not expressed. "Thou shalt not kill" is a rule of law under the definition used here if (and only if) there is an implication that he who kills will or may be visited with conse-

---

[3] 9 Ex. 341, 354, 156 Eng. Rep. 145, 151 (Ex. 1854).

quences imposed upon him by some authority sanctioned by law. Most of the consequences mentioned so far have been punishments, but they just as easily may be rewards, as in the case of the patent rule quoted, or an outright subsidy or bounty to one who performs a given act. For example, a statute of Arizona authorizes a bounty to a person who kills a coyote and displays its skin to the proper authorities.[5]

Rules can be classified or analyzed in innumerable ways. They can be and often are examined in accordance with their subject matter—that is, from the standpoint of the kind of conduct they are directed toward: rules of criminal law, marriage and divorce, business, property, contract, and the like. All rules are directed toward conduct, and the kind of conduct they are concerned with can be called the *substantive* aspect of the rule.

In addition, however, rules have what might be called a *formal* aspect. Rules differ from each other in more than their subject matter. There are certain highly abstract categories into which rules can be sorted and classified. These correspond to the most basic and abstract categories of legal relationships. Thus, some rules grant rights, some grant privileges, some permit, some forbid, and some give positive commands. Some rules say "may" and some say "shall." Some rules of evidence set up (in legal jargon) rebuttable presumptions; others, conclusive presumptions. Differences among rules in regard to these dimensions are differences in *form*.

In addition, all rules have a *jurisdictional* aspect, or an aspect of *distribution of power*. This is an aspect of legal rules that is sometimes overlooked. A legal rule, as we use the term here, attaches consequences to facts. But consequences do not attach to conduct by themselves; someone must manipulate the strings. Each rule, to be a meaningful rule, must carry with it a ticket to some person, agency, or institution, authorizing, permitting, forbidding, or allowing some action to take place. Each rule has its institutional and distributive side as well as its formal and substantive side. It distributes, or redistributes, power within the legal system or within the social order. Without this aspect, a rule would be a mere exhortation, essentially empty or rhetorical, like the preamble to a statute.

---

[5] ARIZ. REV. STAT. ANN. § 24-821 (1956). The consequences of a legal rule are ultimately sanctions, positive or negative. But some propositions (usually referred to as rules) are merely segments of some larger rule. For example, in tax law a person who sells stock held for more than six months at a price in advance of what he initially paid realizes a long-term capital gain. This is, in common parlance, a rule, but it has meaning only insofar as it is connected with the further rule that attaches certain tax advantages to a long-term capital gain.

The distributive aspect of a rule is often implicit. An ordinary criminal statute, for example, contains no explicit jurisdictional statement; it merely defines certain conduct as criminal and assesses punishment for commission of that crime. The jurisdictional aspects of the ordinary criminal law rule are implicit and, in actuality, quite complex. They can be understood only by understanding the institutional context and the history of the common-law system. This tells us that appellate courts will have some responsibility for administration of the law—for example, by deciding its outer limits of applicability. Primarily, however, the law will be carried out by policemen, district attorneys, trial judges, and other operational arms of the criminal process. Other statutes or rules are addressed in the first instance to lawyers, or to judges, or to administrative officials. In many, but by no means all, cases the rule explicitly grants power or authority. Still other rules may be addressed to doctors, plumbers, or private citizens generally, authorizing, preferring, or forbidding certain behavior. Here too, however, there is ultimately in the background an explicit or implicit grant of jurisdiction to some governmental authority to take the steps necessary to implement the provisions of the rule.

The three aspects of a rule just discussed are interrelated. Substantive, formal, and distributive aspects of a rule cannot really be understood in isolation and cannot be sharply distinguished from each other. Nonetheless, it is useful to analyze rules according to these aspects in order to see more clearly the way aspects of rules respond to specific social and institutional conditions.[6]

---

[6] All three aspects relate to the way a rule appears on a printed page and in formal context. Rules call for or allow specific behavior on the part of the persons addressed, and on the part of those authorities charged with enforcing the rule. It is a sociological commonplace that reality does not always conform to paper norms. Some rules, to be sure, are enforced, and quite vigorously. Others are dead letters. Some are enforced selectively only, to achieve goals quite distinct from those officially contemplated by the rule books. The divergence between rule and practice is a dimension of formal authority of extraordinary importance; but it may also be a matter of moment to understand why a rule which is not enforced or is only partially enforced continues to be enunciated, or enunciated in a manner that does not reflect its true vitality. For example, let us assume two counties in a state with local-option laws. In County *A* and County *B*, liquor consumption is identical; yet County *A* is legally dry and County *B* is legally wet. County *A* does not even sporadically enforce its antiliquor laws. One cannot deduce from the texts of formal rules the actual behavior of the citizens of Counties *A* and *B* with regard to drinking and with regard to police practice toward people who drink. And there is one other critical aspect of behavior important to the operation of the legal system that cannot be deduced from the drinking and police habits of the two counties. There is a facet of the legal order in County *A* that distinguishes it from County *B* and demands sociological explanation: why is County *A* formally dry?

B. *A Note on Rule Skepticism*

One reason why more jurisprudential and sociological attention in the last generation has not been paid to rules is because
rules no longer enjoy quite the favor they once did. Indeed, it is
fashionable in the academic world to decry them. Many legal
realists described themselves as "rule skeptics," and legal education is heavily influenced by rule skepticism. Many students begin, naively, with the notion that rules of law are always precise
and that these rules can be easily and mechanically applied to
clear-cut situations. Much professorial energy is directed toward
dispelling these notions and toward demonstrating that certainty
in the law is an illusion, since life is far too complex to be
summed up in little maxims. As a result, legal scholarship is
strongly influenced by the attitudes of rule skepticism, and the
bulk of scholarly writing today is rule skeptical, in one way or
another.

Rule skepticism, reduced to the extreme, means either (1) that
some pretended rules are not the true operating rules; or (2) that
some rules are unreal in the sense that they are varied, misused,
or ignored as they are applied and that those who apply rules
actually govern in their discretion, using the rules as mere handles
or shams. The first of these two possible meanings is not an
objection to the study of rules, but only a call for more sophistication in the study. Indeed, many of the realists were rule skeptics
only in a limited sense; they recognized that their job was not to
destroy rules, but to gain more precision in understanding the
true operational rules. . . .

The second meaning of rule skepticism is a more fundamental
objection to the reality of legal rules, because it goes to the heart
of the problem of government. Laws on paper are meaningless;
they must be enforced or applied. At the cutting edge of law,
rules devolve upon human operators, not machines. In their
hands rules may become a mockery. Thus, for example, a criminal statute may say that he who commits assault suffers such-and-
such a penalty. No exceptions or mitigations are mentioned. But
the policeman who finds two men brawling in a bar may close
his eyes and ignore the fight, break up the fight and say nothing
further, or arrest the two men and throw them in jail. The district attorney may decide to let both of them go or book them
for trial. At trial the judge may dismiss the case if he wishes.
Therefore, the statutory rule is (so the argument goes) in part
or in whole unreal. The policeman, the district attorney, the
judge—these govern, not the rule.

To examine the problem more closely let us go back to a consideration of the nature of a rule. A rule is a direction; it is a tool for carrying out some task of government. Government can be effectuated either through personal surveillance or through formal directives to other persons (rules). Control exclusively through personal surveillance would be possible only for very simple societies. As society and government become more complicated, specific functions are allocated to this agency or that person, and bureaucratic organization necessarily replaces personal rule. At this point, rules enter into the structure of government. There is always, however, an operating level—a level at which laws are personally administered—by a policeman, for example. Yet, if it is true that administration at this level is never governed by rules, then government is not merely difficult, it is impossible—and no country, state, city, hospital, army, or large corporation can be run with any semblance of plan.

What is meant, then, is not that the policeman and other operating units of a system disregard formal rules altogether, but that they sometimes completely disregard them, and other times displace them a little. They may in some cases not disregard them at all. One of the major accomplishments of behavioral scientists—and of the legal realists—has been to highlight the gap between living law and book law. But this gap is not constant; it varies from region to region, from field of law to field of law, from time to time. However, the extent to which discretion is allowed and the extent to which it is actually exercised are social factors which, if we knew enough, could be explained by general laws of behavior.

Moreover, as an empirical proposition, it is probably not true that most legal rules are "unreal" in the sense that they are not or cannot be translated into behavior or enforcement. Most legal rules are in fact obeyed by those to whom they are addressed. Violations of the rules are promptly and efficiently punished. The general meaning of rules is in many—probably most—cases clear enough to form the basis of behavior. Nevertheless, there is a view among some students of the legal process that most rules are inherently uncertain and that most legal concepts are flexible and variable in meaning.[11] In the United States, habits of thought inculcated during the course of legal training may encourage this point of view. Law students learn by debating the application of doctrine to extremely difficult borderline situations derived from cases reviewed by appellate courts. One object of

---

[11] M. Gluckman, The Judicial Process Among the Barotse of Northern Rhodesia (1955).

this exercise is to train the students' minds in legal thought and develop skills of advocacy, and this object, it is believed, is best accomplished through the examination of difficult questions, rather than easy questions and well-settled law.

In fact, however, if one views impartially the whole of the legal system, it can be differentiated into three major areas. Some of the substantive content of the legal system consists of rules which are dormant—that is, there is no attempt at conscious, consistent enforcement. Other parts raise classic problems of uncertainty. These are the unsettled, but living, problems of law—such as the question of what constitutes due process of law. A third—and vital—part of the legal system consists of rules which are well settled in the special sense that they are acted upon by many persons in a particular manner and their applicability to given situations is not challenged. "Well settled" may mean, then, not that a dubious situation cannot be imagined or that the application of a rule is inherently free of doubt, but that it is *actually* free of doubt as a matter of ordinary, patterned human behavior. If most of the operating (as opposed to the dormant) rules of the legal system were not well settled in this sense, many of the normal processes and activities of life that people carry on with reference to legal rules would be profoundly altered. In a complex social and economic system, a legal system on the model of law school appellate cases would be insupportable. There are strong needs to know what is lawful and unlawful in our common, everyday actions. We need to know, for example, whether we are validly married if we go through certain forms (valid in the sense that our claim to validity will be either unchallenged or highly likely to survive any possible challenge). We need to know the permissible ranges of speed.[12] Moreover, in business affairs, we need to know that a deed in a certain form executed in a standard manner truly passes title to a piece of land. If every such transaction had to be channeled through a discretionary agency, the economic system could not survive in its present form. A market economy and a free society both impose upon the legal system a high demand for operational certainty in parts of the law which regulate important aspects of the conduct of everyday life and everyday business.[13]

The legal system must therefore limit operating rules which do not govern—that is, which do not in themselves provide a clear-

---

[12] Custom may dictate, of course, that we can exceed a posted speed limit by five or so miles per hour with impunity; but this is itself an operational certainty.

[13] *See, e.g.,* J. Hurst, Law and Economic Growth 309 (1964).

cut guide to action on the part of those persons to whom the rule is addressed. Some rules do provide the possibility of a clear-cut mandate; others do not. There is a significant difference between a rule which provides that no will is valid unless it is signed by two witnesses and a rule which provides that wills need or do not need witnesses, depending upon the circumstances and the demands of equity and good faith. Rules of the latter sort (discretionary rules)[14] are tolerable as operational realities only in those areas of law where the social order or the economy can afford the luxury of slow, individuated justice. If there is a social interest in mass handling of transactions, a clear-cut framework of nondiscretionary rules is vital.

Of course, it has to be emphasized once more that when one speaks of the needs of the social order and the economy, one is speaking of operational realities, rather than of the way rules look on paper. . . . Some rules which appear discretionary on paper may not be truly discretionary in their manner of application, and vice versa. Some formally discretionary rules do not imply discretionary practice because the discretionary feature of those rules is jurisdictional only; it is a delegation to some lower agency, which in turn may adopt nondiscretionary rules. Suppose, for example, a rule of law which purports to impose a punishment upon any person who sells "unwholesome" and "diseased" food. "Unwholesome" and "diseased" are critical items in this rule, but they obviously have no single objective meaning. Who shall decide what they mean? If the rule is statutory and if it is silent as to mode of enforcement, we may assume that the usual processes of criminal justice will provide whatever enforcement is needed or wanted. If policemen, district attorneys, and private citizens feel the law is being violated, they may invoke the criminal process. Ultimately, an appellate judge may put some additional meaning into the terms, though it is not likely that the problem will be litigated often enough for him to do so in a very precise way or that he will have the means at his command to frame intelligent regulations. He might, however, hold that some *specific* practice is a purveying of "unwholesome" food as a matter of law.

On the other hand, the task of enforcing these provisions may be handed over to an officer of the executive branch and his staff or to an administrative agency. In Wisconsin, for example, at the end of the nineteenth century it became the "duty" of the dairy and food commissioner "to enforce the laws regarding . . . the

---

[14] Friedman, *Law, Rules, and the Interpretation of Written Documents*, 59 Nw. U. L. Rev. 751 (1965).

adulteration of any article of food or drink."[15] The statutes defined "adulteration" in broad language. For example, food was adulterated if "any substance or substances have been mixed with it, so as to lower or depreciate or injuriously affect its strength, quality or purity. . . ."[16] Under these statutes the commissioner and his staff might assume the task of laying down further rules capable of clear obedience; or they might delegate rulemaking power further down the administrative hierarchy. . . .

As a general proposition, we may guess that there is a strong tendency within the legal system toward the framing of nondiscretionary rules *at some level* and that it is strongest where it is socially important to have mass, routine handling of transactions, which are channeled through some agency of the legal system, or where relative certainty of legal expectation is important. A rule *can* be nondiscretionary in operation so long as it is formally nondiscretionary at any *one* rulemaking level of the legal system (which has many, many such levels) or if it is nondiscretionary at the point of application. Consequently, the legal system may have many more discretionary rules formally speaking than operationally speaking. . . .

D. *The Function of Rules*

Legal institutions and their products serve various purposes in society; but their primary purpose is to make government possible and effective. One major function of law is social control. Within this vague, broad mandate, specialized agencies play specialized roles. A complex society must use rules as tools to govern its members. These are of various substantive types, corresponding to the components required by a system of social control. First, rules may be concerned with effectuating general policy; they will attempt to channel conduct by mapping out areas of preferred, allowed, and forbidden behavior in everyday life. Second, rules may impose sanctions on those who deviate from the norm—that is, govern the disposition of trouble cases. Third, rules may invoke or lay down some strategy for dealing with major deviations from the norm—with disorders or emergencies so great that they amount to a crisis in the system. Finally, although all rules (as we have said) have power-allocating aspects, some rules may be jurisdictional in substance; they may set up courts, grant certain kinds of business to certain agencies, and authorize officials to do certain things. Most institutions—perhaps

---

15 Wis. Stat. 1898, ch. 56(b), § 1410(a).
16 Wis. Stat. 1898, ch. 187, § 4601(2).

all—generate or operate with rules of all four types. However, there are also institutions whose overall function is to devise or to apply rules of one particular type.

Of course, the four classes of rules are not clearly differentiated from each other. They have a tendency to blend, and distinctions between types of rules are meaningful only insofar as they shed some light on the behavior of legal institutions and on the manner in which those institutions generate, adopt, and modify legal rules.

E. *Institutional Behavior*

Before proceeding, we will make explicit two simple assumptions about the behavior and nature of legal (and other) institutions. First, we assume that the people who staff legal institutions would normally like to do a good and efficient job; they prefer to satisfy legitimate demands made upon them. If they cannot satisfy the demands, they will seek some legitimate excuse for not doing so.

Second, we assume that institutions have boundaries in our society; jurisdictional limits, however vague, are placed upon the institution's authority. In some respects, institutions are subject to review, appeal, or limits of some kind on *some* area of their work; this is true of courts, administrators, policemen, and even the President. These boundaries are fixed by law, custom, public opinion, and physical necessity. Their *exact* location is in any given case likely to be unknown. Bold Presidents, bold courts, and bold incumbents of other institutions are likely to test the location of the boundary of their power. Conservative power-holders are likely to remain within the safe sphere of their traditional jurisdiction, never venturing close to the edge. It may be that the factors which influence institutional limits cannot be reduced to general rules. But it certainly is clear that all institutions have limits and that some of these limits are easier to define and to see than are others. Some institutions are less adaptable than others. They have less room either to seek new power or to satisfy new demands. . . .

Courts also have quite definite limits to their authority. The kinds of work that courts can do are prescribed by law (statutes and constitutions) and by tradition. In the light of this fact, we will proceed to examine how the courts have reacted, in their rulemaking, to certain kinds of demands made upon them. We mean to show how a legal institution reacts to pressures upon it and how it adopts rules which make an efficient response to the pressures in terms of its institutional needs. For example, when an institution in the short run has no power to expand its capacity and when the sheer volume of demands made upon it increases, it will react by framing jurisdictional rules such that the number of instances coming before it will remain more or less manageable. Or, more concretely, a court will tend to evolve rules which will limit the number of actual cases to that which it can reasonably handle.

It is important to distinguish clearly, however, between long-run and short-run responses. It is possible to show relationships between social demands and rulemaking output in the short run. It is not possible to predict, however, how institutions will evolve over the long run—to what extent they will break through their boundaries and grow in power at the expense of other institutions. Even if in 1800, let us say, one might have predicted a tremendous absolute growth in the power of central governments, one could not have said what agencies, bearing what names and descending from what other agencies, would be the major legatees of this power. It turns out that the President and his subordinate officials have gained a great deal of the power, but it might conceivably have been the Supreme Court, or Congress, or the Secretary of State (cutting down the President's role to a ceremonial kingship), or even the Vice President (by means of his power as presiding officer of the Senate), all through a chain of events quite unknowable in advance. We reject, then, at least as a long-run consideration, any notion that there is some ideal role of a "court" or a "legislature" which each of these is uniquely designed to play and which is badly served by other institutions because of their inherent qualities. One may define such a role and recognize empirically that a particular existing institution either now best performs that function or is more easily adaptable to that function than are other institutions. But this is not because of the inherent qualities of any real-life institutions. Certain important kinds of rules cannot be laid down by existing Anglo-American courts. But we should not attribute to the courts fundamental, timeless deficiencies; rather, concrete limits have been imposed upon them, partly by positive law and partly by their traditional legitimate role. As societal values change, so does the law and so do institutions; roles may be permanent, but not their institutional forms. There is no more an enduring function of a court than there is an enduring function of a king. . . .

III. JUDICIAL RULEMAKING

Courts, as we have stressed, are equipped to handle a normal flow of trouble cases (which for them are routine). They must

also be equipped to assimilate and bring about change, at least
in a gradual manner. Finally, they must be able to deal with
"crises." A "crisis" in the nonquantitative sense is a sudden demand upon the court, different from past demands, which puts
the smooth, normal functioning of the court in jeopardy. A crisis
is not simply a difficult case in the usual sense—that is, a case
which lies within a gray area of law and evokes sharply different
responses. Few judicial decisions satisfy both sides. This means
that the very nature of the work of a deciding judge is such that
some segment of society is necessarily dissatisfied with the outcome of his cases. However, it ought to be true, at least in theory,
that a judicial decision should increase net satisfactions in society—a written opinion is an attempt to demonstrate the social
utility of the actual decision to interested parties outside the
immediate circle of litigants. In a "crisis case," sharp, widespread
impact can be foreseen as the result of decision. In such a case,
demands are made on the court, which, however met, might so
alienate or disappoint one important segment of society that social
support of the court might be endangered. This kind of crisis
case is never common, and is particularly rare on the trial court
level.

The response of high courts to what they sense as a potential
source of crisis has been a frequent subject of study. Most of the
study concerns, quite naturally, the United States Supreme Court.
The arts by means of which the Supreme Court delays, equivo-
cates, and avoids some extraordinary issues are therefore well
known and have been frequently catalogued. The Court has at
its disposal an enormous arsenal of tools of defense. It can tem-
porize and compromise. It can split a case down the middle. It
can balance results against ideology by deciding a case on grounds
so narrow that those grounds evade some burning issue. The
Court also can simply refuse to hear certain cases. Others it can
accept but delay from term to term. Some matters, if delayed
long enough, will vanish or be diverted into another forum.
Finally, some issues can be decided in such a way as to limit
the notoriety of the result. The Court cannot hide the precise
outcome of its cases, but it may issue brief, unsigned, per curiam
decisions. Newspapers and trade journals are unlikely to note or
notice these low-key opinions.

Some legal scholars have bitterly attacked recent examples of
what they consider abuse of the per curiam decision. The per
curiam, in their view, is an evasion of the Court's responsibilities,
which are assumed to be such that the Court must enunciate principled decisions and lay bare its reasoning processes whenever
changes are made in the law or important matters decided. Tech-

nically there is no such requirement. The United States Supreme Court is not bound to write opinions of any particular length or degree of explicitness, but the accepted function and the role of the Court in legal and political life are such that the Court is in fact required to enunciate principled decisions in most of its major cases. Nevertheless, the Court has always felt that at times discretion is the better part of valor. The per curiam decisions may be one escape from a baffling dilemma. They can be looked upon as dangerous, but essential.

Criticism of the Court would have more force if the Court used the per curiam decision as a vehicle for dodging *most* of the issues that came before it. A consistent policy of avoiding crises, through per curiam decisions or otherwise, would bring on a crisis of its own. The Court cannot dodge all difficult issues. First of all, the Justices have taken an oath and assumed serious responsibilities. Moreover, a consistent, constant policy of maximum judicial restraint would be just as disastrous as consistent brashness and "usurpation." This is the Court's dilemma. A policy of great (and permanent) restraint robs the Court of the ultimate source of its prestige and drives away those groups which use the Court as an instrument of power. Thus, the one inescapable policy of the Court must be at all times to walk the fine line between activism, which endangers its position, and restraint, which has a similar result.

Nevertheless, any degree of activism contains potentially grave dangers for the Court. Any highly charged issue is likely to be costly. In most of its work, the Court is protected from harm by the *general* support it enjoys in the country (and as to which it does not essentially differ from other legitimate institutions—the Presidency, the Congress, officers of state). The Court's legitimacy is not likely to satisfy a man whose death sentence the Court affirms, or a white supremacist whose dearest institutions are destroyed by the "nine sociologists." Nevertheless, few people are intimately touched by the average Supreme Court decision, and the public, insofar as it can be said to have any opinion at all, holds the Court in enormous esteem. The source of this respect may be the belief that judges are not true politicians and that they decide cases honestly according to some impersonal standard of law. There may be other reasons as well. In any event, the *legitimacy* of the Court is an outstanding bulwark of protection against harmful criticism.

Some students of the Court insist that poorly written opinions, loose rhetoric, flawed logic, inconsistency of decision, and squabbling dissents damage the image of the Court and hence impair its legitimacy. This damage, if it exists, must be confined in its immediate impact to a tiny circle of law professors and scholars. Perhaps their influence spreads more widely into society over the course of time. Neither these scholars, nor the Justices of the Court, nor anyone else is sure whether this is so or not. Since the Court itself has no instruments for measuring public reaction, and certainly no mode of predicting impact other than common sense, it must rely on its own judgment as to the best course to follow, and, in appropriate cases, fall back upon a firm body of principle. Strictly as a matter of political expediency, the Court can be dangerously wrong. Most historians would call the *Dred Scott*[54] decision a serious error, and perhaps the first income tax case[55] as well. On the other hand, *Brown* now looks like a gamble that succeeded—a gamble, in the sense that the Court could not know whether society would let it keep its decision, or at what cost.

The questions posed to the Court by *Brown, Dred Scott,* and other cases of high policy and moment produce occasions of potential crisis. Crisis can be contained—or delayed—but not always or entirely, as we have noted. Once the Court has decided to meet an issue, and not evade it, is there any further strategy that can limit the risk? This depends in part on whether the crisis is *nonrecurring*—that is, can one be reasonably sure that the issue will not plague the Court in the near future in the same general form.

Two examples of highly publicized actions of the United States Supreme Court may illustrate what is meant here by "nonrecurring." In the first, *Wilson v. Girard,*[57] a serviceman was on duty in Japan, guarding a machine gun. On a nearby firing range Japanese civilians were picking up spent cartridge cases. Girard fired a cartridge case with a grenade launcher; the case struck and killed a Japanese woman. A tremendous furor arose in Japan over the incident, particularly over the question whether Japan or the United States should try Girard for the crime. The United States waived jurisdiction and Girard sought relief in the federal courts. The Supreme Court denied relief in a short per curiam opinion. The Japanese tried and convicted Girard. However, his sentence was relatively light and the issue soon receded into history.

Perhaps the furor over Girard was a symptom of deep trouble between the two nations, but if so it was only a symptom. The status-of-forces agreement had worked smoothly before the *Girard*

---

[54] Dred Scott v. Sandford, 60 U.S. (19 How.) 393 (1857).
[55] Pollock v. Farmer's Loan & Trust Co., 157 U.S. 429 (1895).
[57] 354 U.S. 524 (1957).

case; it worked smoothly afterwards. *Girard* was an "incident," as isolated as a case of murder over love. It demanded not closely reasoned articulation but clean, swift, and certain resolution by all relevant agencies. Irresolution could have turned an incident into crisis—as happened in the case of Caryl Chessman. The Court's refusal to intervene was sound statesmanship, perhaps aided by knowledge that the issue rose and fell with Girard.

The celebrated *Steel Seizure* case[60] is another example of a nonrecurring crisis, although here, in contrast to *Girard*, the Justices were sharply divided over what was to be done and filed long and contentious opinions. Here too a swift, clean-cut decision was necessary. Delay would have meant avoiding the issue completely. Here too it was understood that all parties would acquiesce in the Court's decision. Here too the precise event was not likely to recur. It is true that the Justices (and many commentators on the case) felt that a fundamental issue was at stake. The extent of the President's emergency powers, the power of the President to seize control of an industry in peacetime—there are many ways to formulate this issue. But in one sense it could be argued that the case presented no fundamental issue at all since the *Steel Seizure* case could not recur. A President might in the future seize the steel industry, and, if so, certainly the earlier case would be cited as a precedent. But in fact no two situations in which a President feels compelled to seize a major industry and which are separated by any appreciable span of time could be similar enough for the Court to feel truly bound by its prior decision. The President seizes a major industry only under extraordinary circumstances or if he is an extraordinary President. In either event his act would be uniquely time bound and of vast political importance—two factors which dilute the importance of precedent almost to the vanishing point.

Thus, paradoxically, these most crisis-like crises are not crisis producing for the Court *as an institution*. Though the underlying issues are highly controversial, they can be efficiently decided by the Court since society welcomes a once-and-for-all resolution by a legitimate, impartial tribunal. When the precise *event* or the *person* at issue is the source of the crisis, then the crisis is nonrecurring in the sense used here, and it poses (in our society) few or no long-term difficulties for the Court.

Institutionally more serious is a crisis which is made up of recurrent cases and which does not vanish with a single resolution, but which heralds a new situation for the courts. Either a new social problem emerges out of the social background (as in

---

[60] Youngstown Sheet & Tube Co. v. Sawyer, 343 U.S. 579 (1952).

the segregation cases) or a demand on the courts is met by a judicial response which in turn creates additional demand for fresh definitions of the rights and duties of the parties and the forces that they represent (as in the obscenity cases).

A rational court will attempt to reduce such a situation to institutionally manageable proportions. In the face of recurrent events, the court is therefore likely to develop a rule that can be delegated to other authorities for administration. From the standpoint of the court, this is an important element of a solution to the problem. Of course, the solution must be substantively "correct" as well; it must be in accordance with principle as the Court defines principle. But the *form* of resolution of such problems (as distinct from substance) is likely to be dictated by institutional needs. The kind of rule which emerges from a recurrent crisis of substance will be a rule which serves the formal requirements of the system and answers the substantive social demands.

What sort of solution will meet this requirement? From the formal standpoint, it is likely to be a rule which perhaps can end the constant probing by litigants for definition and the constant search for the boundaries of the rule. Such a rule will be as objective, as quantitative as possible. An objective, quantitative rule minimizes the risk of further litigation and maximizes the extent to which other private or public agencies can apply the rule, thus taking pressure for decision away from the courts. Such a rule, in form, will be either a rule of refusal or a rule expressed or expressible in quantitative form. A rule of refusal is not usually a rule which accepts and satisfies a fresh demand for social reform, but on occasion it can serve this function. For example, a court might conceivably rule that no power existed in any branch of government to censor any book on the grounds of obscenity. This would be a rule which refused to litigate the question of obscenity at all, not for jurisdictional reasons, but by obliterating the concept of obscenity as a basis for judicial exercise of discretion. Notice that such a rule is hard-and-fast and therefore expressible in quantitative terms—rules of refusal are rules whose quantitative term is zero. In essence, then, crisis situations will tend to generate in a court a movement of doctrine toward quantitative expression.

The reapportionment cases provide a neat illustration of this movement of doctrine—atypical only in the swiftness and smoothness of development. The general social background is well known. Many legislative bodies, sometimes in disregard of state constitutions, had refused to reapportion themselves in accordance with actual population distributions. Relatively speaking, cities and suburban areas were underrepresented in state legislatures. Rural areas, some of which had declined absolutely in population as well as relatively since the last reapportionment, had far more representatives than they merited on a straight population basis. In many states, apportionment in the upper house departed from a population basis even more radically than in the lower house.

In most states it was useless to ask the legislature to reform itself. Representatives were unwilling to vote themselves out of their jobs. Judicial review was a possible avenue to relief. *Colegrove v. Green*[67] brought into question the apportionment of congressional districts in Illinois. The Court, however, sidestepped the issue and adopted a rule of refusal. Mr. Justice Frankfurter thought that the question was "of a peculiarly political nature and therefore not meet for judicial determination." The doctrine he invoked (the "political question" doctrine) satisfied all the formal requirements of a rule sufficient to lay the apportionment issue at rest. It was quantitative and clear, in the sense that all rules of refusal are quantitative and clear. Moreover, the doctrine had served the Court well on other occasions when, in its judgment, tactics of evasion were necessary to preserve the structure of government from interinstitutional conflict or to safeguard the integrity of the Court.

But *Colegrove* was only a formal, not a substantive, solution to the problem of malapportionment. Some of its defects were apparent upon its face: a bare majority of the Justices deciding the case concurred in the result; two Justices did not sit; and only three Justices joined in the majority opinion. The division of the Court reflected the ultimate, social instability of *Colegrove*: it did not quiet the movement to seek judicial relief from unfair methods of apportionment. New Justices and slight variations in the facts of new cases were enough to encourage the bringing of new lawsuits. In *Gomillion v. Lightfoot*[71] the Court overturned a racially motivated gerrymander of the city boundaries of Tuskegee, Alabama. This was a further sign of the weakness in *Colegrove*, even though the racial aspect of *Gomillion* made it distinguishable and even though it was a unanimous decision whose opinion, denying the relevance of *Colegrove*, was written by Mr. Justice Frankfurter himself. The case gave fresh encouragement to potential litigants. A rule of refusal which seems to have changed from a "no" to a "maybe" is weak. A "maybe" (unlike

---

[67] 328 U.S. 549 (1946).
[71] 364 U.S. 339 (1960).

a "no") is not quantitative; hence, a weakening rule of refusal loses even its formal claim to govern.

In *Baker v. Carr*[72] a six-man majority abandoned the rule of refusal. The case concerned the apportionment of the General Assembly of Tennessee; the precise holding was that "the complaint's allegations of a denial of equal protection present a justiciable constitutional cause of action upon which appellants are entitled to a trial and a decision." Only the threshold question was decided. The Court, true to its own traditions and anxious to make only an incremental decision, held merely that the political-question doctrine no longer precluded testing legislative reapportionment against constitutional standards. But the Court deliberately refused to say anything specific about those standards.

The decision and its successors provoked much comment, scholarly and otherwise; much of it was highly critical. But from the standpoint of the Court's institutional needs, there was logic in the course of doctrinal development. To begin with, the halting, tentative reach of *Baker v. Carr* was the expression of an attitude of restraint. The political-question doctrine had been a form of jurisdictional restraint. Substantive restraint underlay the limited scope of *Baker v. Carr*. By deciding only what was absolutely necessary to the case, the Court deferred all other major decisions. The case merely asserted that the judiciary possessed a reservoir of power. It was conceivable (if unlikely) that the problem would then vanish from the judicial forum. For example, legislatures might have voluntarily apportioned themselves to please potentially interested parties and to avoid fresh litigation. Moreover, the narrowness of the decision in *Baker v. Carr* prepared the political public for further steps which, however bold, could not have been as sudden as they would have been if the Court had gone the whole way in *Baker v. Carr*. An occasion for discourse had been opened up; conceivably some sort of dim consensus might have emerged.

But, when all is said and done, a limited, discretionary, nonquantitative rule (like the rule in *Baker v. Carr*) is formally unstable; it lacks the clarity and simplicity of a rule of delegation, and its survival depends upon triviality or consensus. Yet the decision was not trivial by any stretch of the imagination; nor did it lend itself to consensus. The Court had not solved the problem of the constitutional limits of malapportionment in a *formal* sense. Quite the contrary, it had overturned a rule of refusal, enunciated a rule of acceptance, and declined (for the moment) to issue a quantitative guide. If *Baker v. Carr* was a

---

[72] 369 U.S. 186 (1962).

step toward a solution to the apportionment problem in the substantive sense, it was a step away from solution in the formal sense. It had merely opened a door. It had given encouragement and permission to others to inquire about limits, to litigate, to debate. Within a year after *Baker v. Carr* seventy-five lawsuits were filed in state and federal courts; the legality of virtually every legislature was under a cloud. Some legislatures remained deadlocked on reapportionment. Others tried to make minimal changes—changes unacceptable to groups which now sensed a powerful ally in the courts. Thus, the hoped-for stable delegation to the legislatures did not take place, and the Court was forced to meet the essential question head on. It was, in other words, asked to frame the solution itself and then to hand it on to subordinate institutions.

A crisis always looks more intense to those directly involved. The Supreme Court now faced a situation of ceaseless, fractious, and annoying litigation; of warfare between state legislatures and the federal judiciary, and between rural, urban, and suburban interests, all battling on through the years in disruptive litigation. Here, then, was a second "problem" of *Baker v. Carr.*

Substantively there was little doubt that the Court would not go back to its discarded rule of refusal. It would continue to uphold its own preferred solution, embodying an attitude toward reapportionment that would favor cities and suburbs as opposed to rural areas (or that could be so viewed) and would lean toward a theory of suffrage that would weigh as equally as possible the votes of all citizens. Formally, the Court would seek a hard-and-fast, quantitative rule that would not call for the exercise of discretion on the level of the Supreme Court and that would allow efficient and permanent delegation of the responsibility for application.

In fairly rapid order the Supreme Court proceeded to reach a solution to the reapportionment problem that met these minimum formal requirements for equilibrium. In *Gray v. Sanders*[77] the Court invalidated the "county-unit" system used in Georgia as a basis for counting votes in Democratic primary elections. Though there were hints of the coming doctrine of "one man, one vote," the opinion was still guarded and tentative. *Westberry v. Sanders,*[78] a Georgia case concerning congressional elections, broadened the hints. Finally, in June 1964 the logical end point was reached in six cases headed by *Reynolds v. Sims*[79] and all handed down on the same day.

---

[77] 372 U.S. 368 (1963).

[78] 376 U.S. 1 (1964).

[79] 377 U.S. 533 (1964).

In essence, these cases enunciated a rule that both houses of a bicameral legislature must be apportioned substantially on a population basis. Anything short of this offends the Constitution. In each of the cases Mr. Justice Harlan registered a bitter dissent. He accused the Court of ignoring history, precedent, logic, good sense, and the proper limits of judicial restraint; the rule laid down by the majority, moreover, was vague and utterly unworkable. Yet, though the majority did speak of case-by-case resolution and did disclaim the need for mathematical precision in fixing boundaries and in determining permissible deviations from absolute equality, the rule laid down by the Court was as logical, as quantitative, and hence as workable as the situation permitted. A more discretionary rule would have invited constant litigation; it would have lacked even the bare formal prerequisites of stable solution. The actual formulation—"one man, one vote"—met these formal prerequisites. It contained in itself, by virtue of its relatively clear-cut contours, at least the possibility of a stable solution—a relatively permanent and operational delegation of authority to the lower courts and, hopefully, to the state legislatures.[81]

Of course, a hard-and-fast rule is only an *attempt* to provide a solution; it was yet possible for the Court to be submerged in a storm of protest. To serve as a stable solution, the new rule must be generally accepted, or the costs of challenge, measured against the likelihood of change, must successfully deter challenges. If the new rule is unacceptable, it will be followed by more and more challenges, and the Court may either have to retreat from its rule or (even more serious) suffer losses in power or prestige. There is often, then, a period of anxious waiting. In the case of the reapportionment rule, there now seems little doubt that the rule will prevail. Despite angry cries, a proposed constitutional amendment, much fulminating in the press, and waspish carping in the law reviews, the decision seems firmly, even serenely, entrenched. . . .

---

[81] Martin Shapiro states that "with the benefit of hindsight it now seems clear that in the reapportionment cases a majority of the Justices at the time of *Baker v. Carr* actually jumped directly to the one man—one vote decision which they then implemented by successive decisions." Shapiro, *Stability and Change in Judicial Decision-Making: Incrementalism or Stare Decisis?*, 2 LAW IN TRANSITION Q. 134, 146 (1965). The speed of the trip from *Baker v. Carr* to "one man, one vote" is some evidence for this proposition. But, even if true, this would merely indicate that the consciously rational Court would deliberately choose to simulate a process which occurs without premeditation in other instances. Professor Shapiro notes that the Court "could have stopped short of full implementation in the later decisions if the adverse feed-back from *Baker* had been strong enough." *Ibid.*

When a rule can be stated in "yes-no" terms, it satisfies the conditions of quantitative certainty, and it is formally capable of stable delegation. Not all rules, however, are susceptible of statement in such terms. The political-question doctrine was a rule of refusal, capable of statement as a simple "no"; once it was abandoned, no simple "yes" rule was possible. It was necessary, then, for the Court to work its way toward a rule capable of quantitative statement in a more literal sense. As we have seen, the Court did so. But it is not always easy for appellate courts to work out quantitative rules, even when, sociologically speaking, circumstances impel the Court toward such rules and when societal patterns or the Court's great reservoir of prestige would allow any solution to be stable.

On the trial court level particular concrete decisions are often expressed in quantitative terms. Juries return verdicts in dollar amounts, figured to the penny. A verdict that the plaintiff in a tort action should recover a "reasonable" amount of damages would be insufferable; such an award could not be efficiently executed and would require one more (and unnecessary) delegation. Not all lower-court decisions are dollar decisions, but they are all extremely precise. A finding that B has title to a tract of land rather than C or that the court has no jurisdiction to hear D's claim is quantitative in the same sense as a rule of refusal, and has the same general impact—that is, it can be precisely carried out without further delegation of discretion.

Indeed, the ultimate *application* of a rule to a fact situation must be concrete or precise, or it is not an application at all. Similarly, appellate decisions take a simple "yes-no" form; they reverse or affirm. But in formulating general rules to govern whole classes of cases, courts do not find it easy to lay down obviously precise, quantitative rules. In Anglo-American law it would be completely unthinkable that a court could decree or even evolve a workmen's compensation system or a social security law. Those programs rest on statutes with elaborate quantitative tables, schedules of rates, dollars, and ages. They require a taxing system and a large administrative staff. They presuppose some means of gathering information, of evaluating it, and of devising technical instruments for carrying policy into effect. All this is beyond the *customary* power, as well as the customary role, of the courts. Laws of this form in our legal system are promulgated only by legislative bodies.

Nevertheless, courts do sometimes lay down rules which cost a great deal of public money to implement and which either invoke or imply a large administrative staff. Those rules may be embodied in decisions which, if adopted as legislative policy,

would likely have been preceded by considerable study and accompanied by careful plans for implementation. *Brown* required
complete reorganization of southern school systems. In 1964, for
example, the Court ordered a Virginia county to reopen a public
school system.

There is, nonetheless, an important distinction between these
activities and programs on the scale of workmen's compensation
and social security. Lack of staff and inability to levy taxes are
symptoms, not the underlying reality. The courts do not innovate
certain kinds of new programs because they lack power—in the
sense of legitimate authority—to do so. The legitimate authority
of the courts is defined by positive law (the federal and state constitutions and statutes on jurisdiction) and by a powerful tradition which describes the proper role of judicial agencies and the
proper mode of behavior of judges. There is nothing inherent in
a "court" to prevent it from devising new programs and, specifically, from promulgating rules in precise, quantitative terms.
There is nothing inherent in a "legislature" that prevents it from
deciding concrete cases. Historically, the institutional ancestors
of American courts and legislatures performed many tasks which,
to the modern eye, seem curious reversals of their roles. Legislatures long exercised appellate jurisdiction; the name of the highest English court (the House of Lords) preserves the memory of
this period. In the United States, too, appellate decision-making
in state legislative bodies persisted well into the nineteenth century, and county courts in the American colonies were important
administrative agencies—levying taxes and overseeing construction of roads, for example. The name of the Massachusetts General Court (a legislative body) harks back to a time when governmental functions were performed by a single authoritative body,
untroubled by notions of the separation of powers.

The legitimacy of an institution is not unchanging, and, with
respect to the courts, does not rest on a single ideal core of
meaning. Legitimacy is culturally defined; its effect on the power
and style of courts is specific to a given time and place. In the
recent history of the common-law system, it was conventionally
stated that judges could not legitimately "make law." . . .

In the main, courts still deny their power to make new law.
This denial is itself no small limitation on their power. It helps
ensure that judge-made law results in only small, incremental
changes in the existing fabric of doctrine. A great leap forward
is rare. Even constitutional law—where a major change can be
legitimated through appeal to the higher mandate of the Constitution—shuns sudden advances. The reapportionment cases, for
instance, exemplify a cautious, step-by-step movement. In gen-

eral, judge-made law inches forward in a glacial kind of creep. When a court overrules a past decision, it often claims to be redressing an error rather than changing the law. Cases make small changes in law and call them no change; big changes are called small changes. . . .

In the twentieth century, partly because of the effect of legal realism upon the style of judicial opinions, judicial creativity is somewhat less verbally restrained than it was in the late nineteenth century. . . . New theories legitimate particular kinds of bold creativity—the duty of courts to expound the Bill of Rights to protect the individual against government or the duty of courts to keep law in touch with what is deemed to be the temper of the times. Yet changes in judicial behavior, all in all, are not deep; they are style rather than substance. Change in the law, through the medium of courts, remains incremental and gradual, rather than sudden or revolutionary. There is still a commitment to the common-law approach, to evolutionary movement, and to constant recourse to grand principles of law, established precedent, or constitutional phrases as the major premises of judicial reasoning. Legal realism has not freed the courts from an obligation to society, only from an obligation to a certain style of legal logic; the pull of social responsibility, coupled with an awareness of the limits of judicial knowledge and the limits of judicial capacity to effect social change, may lead to greater, not lesser, caution in action and to greater, not lesser, accountability in principle and reasoning.

But past and present disabilities on the kind of rules that can be legitimately enunciated are an embarrassment to courts when problem situations call for rules of stable delegation, since these, as we have seen, will tend to be quantitative rules. The evolutionary, incremental character of judicial behavior in rulemaking implies (on the contrary) slow, inductive movement along a continuum, and clandestine changes in law—qualitative rules, rules expressed in terms of reasonableness, rules empty of content except as courts fill them with content, rules capable of expansion by small degrees, discretionary rules concealing the reality of change. Thus, the history of judicial systems harbors a considerable dilemma: How can the legitimate limits of judicial rulemaking be reconciled with the institutional need for quantitative rules?

One solution, frequently adopted, is to enunciate rules of a flat "yes-no" nature—rules of refusal, for example. But such rules are not always appropriate. Still another technique is to ratify or absorb into judge-made law quantitative measures whose legitimacy derives from other branches of the legal system or from elsewhere in society. One example of this technique can be seen in the course of the evolution of the Rule Against Perpetuities. The rule, in essence, puts a limit on the length of time property can be "tied up" in a family or held in a family trust. Originally phrased in terms of "reasonableness," the rule could not in the long run remain in that form, just as the rule in *Baker v. Carr* had to move in the direction of more certainty. In sharp contrast to the swiftness of *Baker v. Carr*, the evolution of the Rule Against Perpetuities from a rule of reason to a stable quantitative rule took more than a century. The process was much the same, however. A rule of "reasonableness" in perpetuities law would have precluded any stable delegation to conveyancers, lower courts, and the general public. Rational calculations in the dynastic planning of estates would have been much more difficult without a hard-and-fast rule to ensure safe predictability. Perhaps the simplest solution might have been a flat quantitative limit on the duration of trusts containing contingent interests— perhaps fifty or one hundred years; or fifty years following the duration of a life estate. A legislature might choose such a method, but it is not the style of a court. Hence the evolutionary character of the rule. The original formulation was characteristically vague; the final formulation, "lives in being plus twenty-one years," for all its irrationalities, is in theory capable of "mathematical" accuracy in application. The twenty-one-year period is not measured by anybody's minority, although the choice was not entirely accidental. It has *some* rational relationship to the period of minority, but it was powerfully influenced by the fact that twenty-one years was an available *number* with preexisting legal significance, so that it could be adopted and embodied within a rule of law without transgressing the bounds of judicial legitimacy. The history of the Rule Against Perpetuities, then, illustrates not only the tendency of courts to evolve rules that are mathematical in the broadest sense, but also one technique for solving the dilemma of how to achieve quantitative results without the legitimate means available to a legislative body.[95] . . .

---

[95] The evolution of a formally stable rule does not ensure its survival for any period. No sooner had the Rule Against Perpetuities reached its "mathematical" form than it began to decay—that is, it began to lose some of its mathematical properties. . . . A formally stable rule may indeed be all the more vulnerable to pressure in that its results are "harsh"—that is, universalistic. As we have noted, *Baker v. Carr* began a process of evolution by overturning a formally stable rule of refusal. . . . At any given time, of course, *some* changes in the law will be in the direction of bringing substantive ends into conformity with formal prerequisites, while other changes will, temporarily at least, be in the other direction by virtue of social or judicial dissatisfaction with the substantive aspect of some prior, formally stable rule.

For courts the most embarrassing area of conflict is one lacking the possibility of quantitative rulemaking, stable delegation, agreement upon policy, or any signs of a nonjudicial solution. In such areas of law the courts are continually plagued by pressure from litigation for constant redefinition and refinement. In these areas, public awareness of the problem is high, but no consensus is visible, and no solution to the substantive problem seems feasible. In such an area, the law will show a considerable degree of uncertainty and flux, prediction will be difficult, and "trends" will be ambiguous. Indeed, the very term "trend" implies a high degree of policy agreement on the part of the courts. A trend means substantive movement in one policy line toward some absolute limit. As we have seen, courts prefer making changes by degrees when they can.

Many areas of law have characteristics which rule out any current formal solution. How far the Constitution permits suppression or control of "obscene" literature and art is one such question. . . . The law is now in a period of constant testing of boundaries. The courts are the forum for dispute between those who wish to push literature further toward graphic sexuality (out of conviction or, in the case of some publishers, for gain) and those who see grave social dangers in unbridled literary sexuality. There is no obvious solution. Rules that might satisfy the *formal* requirements of stability are unacceptable—that is, either a rule allowing all censorship or all censorship of such-and-such a type, or a rule so formulated as to bar once and for all any control by the state over the limits of sexual frankness in literature and art. The Supreme Court has moved far in the direction of complete freedom of expression, but it has thus far insisted on retaining the concept of obscenity as a category of expression not protected by the first amendment. And from time to time it has gone "backwards"—for example, in the recent case of *Ginzburg v. United States*.[100] But no objective test of obscenity appeals to the Court, and perhaps such a test could never be devised. Since there is no stopping point, no consensus, and no possibility of stable delegation, the issue will remain at least temporarily where it now is: a subject of great uncertainty and backing and filling in the courts. The Supreme Court of the United States—and the high courts of the states—will continue to act as "high courts of obscenity," reading particular books, seeing particular movies, and making up their minds about them one at a time.

Ultimately, if the Court cannot solve the problem and if the problem does not vanish of its own accord (through a radical

---

[100] 383 U.S. 463 (1966).

change in popular tastes or levels of toleration), some extrajudicial solution will have to be reached. This is so because the very definition of a problem implies a social impulse toward solving it. No "issue" or "problem" lasts more than two or three generations. There are, to be sure, eternal issues or problems, but these are not problems in the sense used here; rather they are formulations of human dilemmas on so high a level of abstraction that they cannot ever really be resolved. Problems such as poverty, crime, or the ugliness of cities can exist through all time, but such specific issues as whether slavery shall exist in Missouri Territory, whether fair-housing ordinances can constitutionally be enacted, whether fetishistic literature can be sold in drug stores, and whether hospitals shall be immune from tort actions must be resolved; they cannot drag on forever. If an issue is sharply enough defined to be perceived as a "problem" by the public or some significant segment of the public, there is a strong movement toward resolution, by definition. Society has a whole battery of institutions and mechanisms for resolving current problems. Otherwise society could not survive. If the first agency to which the issue is referred cannot resolve it, those raising the issue will seek a more authoritative agency (or a more efficient one). If worst comes to worst, the issue will not find its agency, and society might even be destroyed by the ensuing struggle.

NOTES AND QUESTIONS

1. A later section of Professor Friedman's article, not reprinted here, applies his analysis to the legislative process as well. Legislatures, too, face crises of quantity and quality; and they react in ways which are somewhat similar, making use, for example, of generalization and delegation.

[Reading 90]

2. Consider the following opinion: Mitchell v. United States, 386 U.S. 972 (1967).

Petition for writ of certiorari* to the United States Court of Appeals for the Second Circuit.

March 20, 1967. Denied.

Mr. Justice DOUGLAS dissents:

---

* When the Supreme Court denies a writ of certiorari, it decides only that the case is not an appropriate one for the Court to hear. At least formally, such a denial is not a decision on the merits of the case. [Eds. note]

Petitioner did not report for induction as ordered, was indicted, convicted, and sentenced to five years imprisonment and his conviction was affirmed. 369 F.2d 323. His defense was that the "war" in Vietnam was being conducted in violation of various treaties to which we were a signatory especially the Treaty of London of August 8, 1945, 59 Stat. 1544, which in Article 6(a) declares that "waging of a war of aggression" is a "crime against peace" imposing "individual responsibility." Article 8 provides:

"The fact that the Defendant acted pursuant to order of his Government or of a superior shall not free him from responsibility, but may be considered in mitigation of punishment if the Tribunal determines that justice so requires."

Petitioner claimed that the "war" in Vietnam was a "war of aggression" within the meaning of the Treaty of London and that Article 8 makes him responsible for participating in it even though he is ordered to do so.

Mr. Justice Jackson, the United States prosecutor at Nuremberg, stated: "If certain acts in violation of treaties are crimes, they are crimes whether the United States does them or whether Germany does them, and we are not prepared to lay down a rule of criminal conduct against others which we would not be willing to have invoked against us." (International Conference on Military Trials, Dept. State Pub. No. 3880, p. 330.)

Article VI, cl. 2 of the Constitution states that "treaties" are a part of "the supreme law of the land; and the Judges in every State shall be bound thereby."

There is a considerable body of opinion that our actions in Vietnam constitute the waging of an aggressive "war."

This case presents the questions:

(1) whether the Treaty of London is a treaty within the meaning of Art. VI, cl. 2;

(2) whether the question as to the waging of an aggressive "war" is in the context of this criminal prosecution a justiciable question;

(3) whether the Vietnam episode is a "war" in the sense of the Treaty;

(4) whether petitioner has standing to raise the question;

(5) whether, if he has, it may be tendered as a defense in this criminal case or in amelioration of the punishment.

These are extremely sensitive and delicate questions. But they should, I think, be answered. Even those who think

that the Nuremberg judgments were unconstitutional by our
guarantee relating to *ex post facto laws* would have to take
a different view of the Treaty of London that purports to lay
down a standard of future conduct for all the signatories.

I intimate no opinion on the merits. But I think the petition for certiorari should be granted. We have here a recurring question in present-day Selective Service cases.

On the problem in the Mitchell case, *see also* Mora v. McNamara,
389 U.S. 934 (1967); Hughes, "Civil Disobedience and the Political Question Doctrine," 43 *New York University Law Review* 1
(1968).

a. What would be the likely consequences if the Supreme
Court of the United States had agreed to consider whether or
not the war in Vietnam was an aggressive war under the Treaty
of London, and had decided, in 1967, that it was? What impact
would such a decision have had on:

(1) those who opposed the war and were subject to the draft?
(2) the conduct of the war?
(3) the position of those who directed the war?
(4) the Supreme Court of the United States?

b. What would have been the likely consequences if the Court
had heard Mitchell's case and had decided that the war was legal?
When the Court upheld the constitutionality of a statute prohibiting the burning of draft cards, in O'Brien v. United States, 391
U.S. 367 (1968), approximately seventy women demonstrated near
the court building in Washington. They unsuccessfully demanded
to talk with the justices and eleven of the demonstrators burned
draft cards and sent the charred remains to the justices by mail.
In an era of escalating confrontation tactics, would one have
expected a decision that the war was legal to prompt large demonstrations against the Court?

[Reading 91]

c. An article by Sylvia Barnes, "The Law and the Movement,"
Guardian, Aug. 31, 1968, at 8, cols. 1-3,* states:

As we of the new left have moved from talk to action, from
theory to practice, we have collided with the brutal face of
the ruling class—the law. . . . The first understanding we
should reach is that the often-heard slogans "The courts are

* Copyright © 1968 by the Guardian, Independent Radical Newsweekly,
New York. Reprinted by permission.

a tool of the ruling class" and "The courts function as agents
of social control for the ruling class" are not merely empty
rhetoric; they're true. The law is neither impartial nor objective. It is an integral part of the regulative system of a
capitalist country, and works hand in hand with the com-
monly-accepted mores which embrace racism and hold the
sanctity of property above that of person (although it is covered with a veneer of libertarianism). . . . The courts have
never been, and are not today, objective, impartial arbitrators. Although their rulings are based on the dominant political views (which any law professor, if not a judge, will admit)
they consistently refuse even to hear the political arguments
of dissenters—even though those very arguments explain
their motives for action. Capt. Howard Levy [an army doctor who refused to give medical training to soldiers to use
in treating Vietnamese civilians because he objected to medicine being exchanged for political allegiance], Dr. Spock
[who was convicted of conspiring to induce men to evade
the draft, but whose conviction was reversed on appeal],
draft resisters, student activists and others cannot raise any
relevant political defense within the legal system.

If the refusal of the Court to decide an issue results in the
withdrawal of trust and support by the side which is seeking a
change in the law or change through the law, then cannot it be
argued that the Court should never dodge an issue for political
reasons, since a highly-charged case is dangerous whether or not
decided?

d. In Friedman's terms, is the legality of the Vietnam war a
"recurring" or a "nonrecurring" problem? What difference would
this make if the Friedman analysis is accepted?

e. In what way did President Johnson and the Congress avoid
the crisis-issue of whether or not the war in Vietnam was illegal
in their own operations, apart from challenges in the courts?

3. The penalty for refusing to be inducted in the Armed Services is a prison sentence of no more than five years, a $10,000 fine
or both. In 1965, before there was a large-scale resistance to the
draft by opponents of the war in Vietnam, the average sentence
for refusal was twenty-one months. In 1967, after such resistance
began, it was 32.1 months. A federal judge in Chicago announced
in late 1966 that he would give "draft dodgers" sentences of no
less than four years, because "willful evasion of the draft must
be stopped." The judge noted that he had twice the usual num-

ber of anti-draft cases in 1966. (In fiscal year 1966, nationally there were 642 selective service criminal cases filed; there were 1,388 in fiscal year 1967.) It was charged that militant members of minority groups were receiving the maximum five-year sentences.

Groups supporting those who refused to serve in the Armed Forces publicized the effect of a 32-month sentence. Given parole and time off for good behavior, most people with such a sentence served fourteen months. Most sentences were served in minimum security prisons in order to cut costs and to keep the draft-refusers from "contaminating" other prisoners.

Friedman speaks of a pressure toward nondiscretionary rules (p. 761), and the pressure towards making rules "as objectively quantitative" as possible. Do these facts about draft-refusal sentencing support or refute his argument?

4. Does Friedman agree or disagree with Fuller (Reading 88, at 736, *supra*) on the dangers of courts accepting the task of making "polycentric" decisions? If they disagree, what argument can be made for either position?

2. Rules and Coordination Within the Legal System
a. A system of internal control

92. The Forest Ranger: A Study in Administrative Behavior

HERBERT KAUFMAN*

PROCEDURAL DEVICES FOR PREFORMING DECISIONS

Since it is clear that the organizations for national forest administration might disintegrate if each field officer made entirely independent decisions about the handling of his district, many decisions are made for them in advance of specific situations requiring choice (once experience has indicated the kinds of situations likely to develop). . . . The field officers . . . need determine only into what category a particular circumstance falls; once this determination is made, he then simply follows the series of steps applicable to that category. Within each category, therefore, the decisions are "preformed."

Authorization, Direction, and Prohibition

The description of the course of action applicable to any category may be permissive. It may spell out several series of steps among which the employee shall choose. It may allow the option of acting or not acting, but define the steps (or alternative series of steps) to be followed if the decision is to act. A description of this kind will be called an "authorization" in this volume.

An authorization "permits" an action by guaranteeing the person who takes it that no one in the organization will impose sanctions, or cause (or seek to cause) sanctions to be imposed, on him for so doing. Indeed, in practice, it goes further; an authorization generally turns out to mean the resources of the organiza-

* Professor of Political Science at Yale University. Copyright © 1960 Johns Hopkins Press, Baltimore, published for Resources For the Future, Inc. Reprinted from pp. 91-99, 101-07, 126-40, 142-45, 149-53, by permission.

tion will be used to defend an individual attacked for acting in pursuance of the authorization. . . .

An authorization is in this sense a "grant" of power. By eliminating, or at least reducing, the risk of personal hardship, it frees the agent to do the specified thing in the specified way. Obviously, where there is no likelihood of attack from any quarter, authorizations are unnecessary; most human behavior needs no authorization. When challenge is probable, or even possible, however, authorizations are normally issued, and individuals often expend great quantities of energy in trying to get more secure guarantees from stronger guarantors.

But an authorization is a limit on behavior, too. It serves notice on those to whom it is issued that if they handle a situation in a designated category in any fashion other than those specified, they do so at their peril. . . .

Since authorizations are not normally issued, whether in writing or orally, unless the possibility of attack is believed to exist, they advise their recipients what they may *not* do as well as what they may do.

Direction is even more confining. It resembles authorization in that it describes courses of action to be taken by designated individuals should events and conditions in specified categories occur. But directions ordinarily leave no options to act or refrain from acting; they constitute notice that if cases of a given class arise, failure to take the prescribed steps will result in the imposition of penalties. They are descriptions of what must be done in particular circumstances.

Authorization and direction promote and channel action. They are supplemented by prohibitions, which are promulgated to prevent designated actions by establishing penalties for those who commit them. That is, the limits of formal powers are not left completely to inference from the terms of each permission or instruction; they are often made explicit.

Although authorizations, directions, and prohibitions (and, indeed, goals) may accurately be described in the formal sense in terms of penalties and immunities from punishment, it is quite clear that they do not depend for their effect entirely, or even mostly, on fear of organizational sanctions. Far more importantly, their effectiveness turns on the desire of organization members to observe official requirements, on the feelings of guilt—the pangs of conscience, or, in a manner of speaking, the intrapsychic sanctions—aroused in members who violate official requirements, or on the neutrality of members' sentiments with respect to particular requirements; many of these attitudes . . . are deliberately established by the leaders of the organization. In every conversation with field men in the Forest Service, it quickly becomes evident that anxieties about sanctions are by no means absent; it also becomes apparent, however, that other factors play a major part in producing adherence to requirements.

By issuing authorizations, directions, and prohibitions, it is therefore possible to influence the behavior of the members of organizations. An extensive, elaborate network of such issuances envelopes every district Ranger. The network is anchored in more than eighty Federal statutes providing explicitly for the establishment, protection, and management of the national forests; in scores of Presidential proclamations and executive orders on the same subject; in hundreds of rules, regulations, and orders of the Secretary of Agriculture; in many court decisions. It is also rooted in uncounted statutes, Presidential orders, departmental rulings, and regulations of staff agencies (the Civil Service Commission, the Bureau of the Budget, the General Services Administration, and others) governing the federal service over-all. But it is not to them directly that the Rangers look to find out what they are authorized, directed, and forbidden to do; for the Rangers, the "bible" is the *Forest Service Manual* put out by the Washington office of the Forest Service, which incorporates, explicates, and interprets the relevant legal documents applicable to the agency, and which contains also additional provisions promulgated by the Washington office under the authorizations in those documents.

The *Manual* currently in force consists of seven volumes. Three more were projected to complete the series, but, before the job could be finished, complaints about its unwieldiness led to a revision and simplification now in progress. Until this is done, however, these volumes remain in effect, serving as the agency Baedeker.

Four of the seven volumes—those dealing with General Administration, Fiscal Control, National Forest Protection and Management, and Acquisition of Lands—are issued to Rangers. (The others are concerned with activities in which Rangers have little or no part, to wit, State and Private Forestry, Forest Research, and Administrative Statistics.) They run to more than 3,000 pages, and it is difficult to think of anything likely to happen on a Ranger district that will not fall fairly unequivocally into one or another of the hundreds of categories catalogued in this *Manual*; indeed, only a fraction of the *Manual* covers most of the recurrent problems of the average district, the remaining provisions applying to events that are not ordinary occurrences anywhere, but which may conceivably come up, or may in fact have already developed here or there. . . .

The volumes of the *Manual* are looseleaf binders. Additions are inserted at appropriate points; rescinded portions are removed; amended portions are inserted after the changes in the original sections have been posted. In the course of a year, hundreds of additions, rescissions, and modifications are issued from Washington; just getting them filed and posted takes many hours every month. But, in this fashion, the categories of authorization, direction, and prohibition, are constantly defined, made more precise, and kept up to date as errors, omissions, uncertainties, and conflicts are corrected. . . .

Each region, in addition, puts out its own authorizations, directions, and prohibitions controlling field personnel. They take the form of supplements to the Service-wide *Manual*, interpreting and clarifying and rendering more specific the materials emanating from Washington so as to fit them to the needs of each Region. Printed on paper of a different color, but using the same system of classification, they are inserted in the volumes of the *Manual* beside the sections to which they refer; like the Washington office, the regional offices issue additions, changes, and rescissions, and scarcely a day goes by without at least one arriving in each Ranger's mail. Service-wide regulations form a fine mesh governing field decisions, but the mesh is tightened considerably by regional specifications. . . .

Over and above these administrative manuals are technical handbooks describing minutely the conduct of technical operations. Some are published by the Washington office, most by the regional offices. They set forth in detail the standards and procedures for timber surveys and valuation; construction and maintenance of recreation areas; location and construction and maintenance of roads; automotive and equipment maintenance; design and procurement and erection of signs; siting and building permanent improvements (warehouses, lookout towers, etc.); planting trees; fire reporting and damage appraisal. In different regions, depending on the character of their workloads, one finds different books, but none of the Ranger districts visited in the course of this study had fewer than a half dozen on hand. They add hundreds of pages of instruction for field personnel.

Some regions issue "Guides" for field personnel. These pull together the essence of existing regulations and assemble them, with explanations and additional requirements, in handbooks that are somewhat easier to read and follow and consult than the formal rules. In one region, for example, there is a "Personnel Guide," setting forth, step by step, the process of hiring people, getting them paid, keeping files on them, etc.; here, the Rangers find listed every form required for every kind of personnel action, and instructions on the execution of the forms. . . .

Finally, when most of the functions that make up resource management attain a level of activity higher than can be handled by cursory, rule-of-thumb methods, formal district plans for them are drawn up. Indeed, for two functions, the Washington office requires every Ranger district to have a plan; there is none without a fire plan and a timber plan. For the others, Regional offices establish requirements. . . .

Plans, at least as they are treated in the Forest Service, are preformed decisions. They set long-range (eighty to a hundred or more years for a function like timber management; five, ten, or twenty years for others) quantitative and qualitative goals, break these down into shorter-range objectives, and sometimes reduce these to annual targets. They spell out the steps and stages by which the goals are to be achieved, including methods of operation, and priorities by geographical area, in each district. Out of these functional plans grow the substantive targets and quotas of the Service as a whole. At the same time, once adopted, the field plans govern the actions of the field officers and their work crews; if they depart from the procedures, or fail to fulfill their quotas, and the departures are detected, they may be called to account just as if they had violated authorizations or directions or prohibitions in the *Forest Service Manual*. . . .

All functional plans of this formal kind, combined with the guides and handbooks and the *Manual* with all its supplements, constitute an impressive network of standing orders influencing Ranger behavior. They are not the whole network, though. For there is a steady flow of *ad hoc* instructions from higher headquarters to the Ranger districts—memoranda, letters, circulars. And there are inspectors (described later) and visitors from above who issue informal, oral directives in the course of their sojourns in the field. Intermittent, irregular, unpredictable, these are usually directed to very limited aspects of district management, and are of temporary duration. All the same, in the aggregate, added to the other types of preformed decisions, they provide the finishing touches to a remarkably complete means of administrative control touching every facet of official Ranger activity.

Clearance and Dispute Settlement

Yet authorization, direction, and prohibition are only *one* category of preformed decisions. Equally important in the day-to-day functioning of a district is the process of channeling decisions proposed by Rangers through higher headquarters before permitting them to take effect—that is to say, before investing them with the immunities and guarantees implicit in formal authorizations. This enables supervisors and regional foresters and their respective staffs to reshape such proposed decisions, and thereby to determine in advance what will actually take place on the Ranger districts.

The formal mechanism for ensuring review is limitation of authorization. Much of the business on a Ranger district involves transactions that can be legally completed only by higher headquarters; a sale of timber worth more than two thousand dollars, for example, can legitimately be consummated only by a forest supervisor (or by a regional forester if the volume exceeds 10 million board feet, or by the Chief if it is 50 million board feet or more), and only very small sales are below these limits. . . . While the Rangers and their subordinates do most of the physical and paper work of preparing items for higher action, the actions are not binding until the approval is obtained. Sometimes it comes almost automatically; sometimes proposals are radically modified or even rejected. The decision rests with the higher officers.

Clearance is complemented by dispute settlement as a means of bringing policy questions to the attention of higher officials for resolution. From time to time, a supervisor's staff assistant specializing in a particular function (or group of functions on the smaller forests) takes issue with the way a given Ranger manages the function that is the staff man's specialty. Staff assistants concentrating on recreation, for example, are wont to complain that this function is not given due attention, or that some activities charged to recreation management accounts would be more appropriately charged to fire control or something else. . . . In fact, each staff officer at every level, since his energies and attention are concentrated on one segment of the total spectrum of Forest Service policy, displays an inclination to feel more can be done in his function than is actually done by the men in the field. Some of them gradually, and probably inadvertently, edge over from exerting pressure to see that their work is adequately done to commanding line officers as to precisely what ought to be done. . . .

If a Ranger gives in to a staff officer, or if a staff officer does nothing about a Ranger's resistance to his actions or recommendations, such clashes subside. If a staff man attempts to pressure a Ranger into compliance, the Ranger will ordinarily protest to the forest supervisor. If a Ranger objects to staff interference or ignores staff suggestions, the staff officer may carry his case to the forest supervisor. In either event, the supervisor convenes the disputants, hears their arguments, and adjudicates the conflict. Almost without exception, this settles the matter.

The net effect of this procedure is to call to the attention of the forest supervisors (and higher line officers) policy alternatives in the management of Ranger districts that might otherwise go unnoticed. It thus gives them additional opportunities to clear the air of uncertainty, to eliminate ambiguities in standing orders, to say what will be done in particular instances. It suspends the force of decisions until they have been reviewed and approved, modified, or rejected at higher levels. It is a method of pre-forming decisions in the field that would otherwise not rise for clearance. It employs conflict for purposes of organizational integration.

That is not to say the Forest Service is constantly beset by internal wrangling. Indeed, it is a classic illustration of the process of multiple oversight of administration; although the Rangers, like all line officers below the Chief, are at the focal point of many converging lines of communication from many sources in the administrative levels above them, they find reason to object to only a fraction of the suggestions of the staff men, frequently call upon them for advice and assistance, and manage to work out many differences of opinion without resort to formal adjudicatory proceedings. But the lines of appeal are clear and available to administrative officials, and they are not unused.

The consequences of clearance and dispute settlement, however, cannot be measured by the actual frequency of their employ- ment alone. For almost every Ranger, knowing that works he undertakes and agreements he negotiates and plans he proposes (particularly if these are offensive to one of the agency's clientele) are subject to review and possible change or veto, screens out projects and requests to which the reactions of the reviewers are difficult to anticipate or likely to be negative, and concentrates instead on those more apt to win approval. If a project seems particularly desirable or necessary, or an applicant for the pur- chase of timber or the use or exchange of national forest property is especially insistent, and a Ranger therefore feels under pres- sure to proceed along a doubtful line, he normally queries his supervisor or his supervisor's staff assistants before acting. Some- times, unwilling to risk the embarrassment of having an applicant go over his head and possibly win approval for what he denied, or of commencing negotiations only to be overruled, a Ranger refers the applicants to higher headquarters in the first instance. Thus, over and above what is required by explicit regulations, there is considerable informal clearance. This avoids some clashes with staff assistants that might otherwise arise, and eliminates some rejections and vetoes and criticisms by higher headquarters. But it also gives officers at higher levels additional opportunities to preform decisions about what goes on in Ranger districts.

Of course, the absence of disputes may just as well be evidence that staff officers are failing to influence the Rangers as that the Rangers are fully compliant. So the anticipation of reactions cuts both ways—but more toward Ranger compliance with staff officers' recommendations than toward staff officers' hesitation to offer advice and suggestions. For staff officers and staff assistants are ordinarily in closer and more continual touch with supervisors than are the Rangers, and they share the supervisors' broader territorial perspectives. While the Rangers will not brook what they regard as interference in their administration of their districts, they also recognize that the shared contacts and vantage points of the line and staff officers at the higher level mean those officers are likely to see many things the same way—and for valid reasons. So the Rangers are not apt to protest vigorously unless the provocation seems to them particularly great.

Then, too, if no disputes arise a supervisor cannot be sure that excessively compliant Rangers or unduly timid staff officers are not permitting the work in the field to proceed further and further from the objectives proclaimed by Forest Service leaders. Anticipation of reactions simplifies the influence of dispute settlement as an influence on Ranger behavior because there *are* occasional reactions, they are resolved at higher levels, and more often than not are resolved in favor of the staff officers.

Clearance and dispute settlement, as a result, reach far beyond what the formal mechanisms *per se* imply. They are for this reason among the major techniques by which Ranger behavior in the field is molded by the organization.

Detecting and Discouraging Deviation

Reporting

To determine whether behavior of men in the field conforms to the requirements of preformed decisions promulgated by organization leaders, the leaders must obviously keep themselves informed about what actually goes on in the field. The easiest way for them to do so is to ask the field men what they are doing. Hence, reporting is a common characteristic of all large-scale organizations.

Reports are not the only means of finding out what happens in the field. Indeed, if reporting is not supported and supplemented by other information-gathering techniques, it may well become a relatively unreliable method. But it is convenient and effective when coupled with other devices. So it is virtually universal; the greatest part of the upward flow of administrative communications in any agency is likely to consist of reports requested by the agency leadership. . . .

Data on individual actions are primarily for financial and book-keeping purposes rather than for program and policy control; they permit administrators in the forest and regional offices to maintain surveillance of receipts and expenditures. But they also keep the higher administrative echelons informed about what their subordinates are doing. The payrolls, requisitions, and vouchers sent from the field to be charged against the functional accounts and sub-accounts established for a district constitute a running record of what goes on in the district. By consulting the record from time to time, the Rangers' superiors can keep abreast of the Rangers' activities, and they are able to assemble from such reports the statistics embodied in their own summaries.

Moreover, as noted earlier, many transactions—large timber sales, for example, and special-use permits—must be signed by supervisors and regional foresters before they take effect. As a result, these officers do not have to ask for special reports on many functions in order to compile their own reports; the information is readily at hand. . . .

Over and above regular, periodic reports of both the tabular and individual-action types, there are frequent calls for special reports on an *ad hoc* basis. In addition, the written documents are supplemented by uncounted informal reports; every time the Rangers get in touch with higher headquarters for guidance or advice or preliminary clearance of a proposed field action or to settle a dispute with a staff man, and every time a visitor from a higher level appears on a district, the Rangers' superiors get new insights into what is happening in the field.

All in all, then, the flow of information from the districts to the forests, the regions, and to Washington is steady, massive, detailed, and comprehensive. In one way or another, the Rangers themselves furnish facts revealing how closely they are adhering to the preformed decisions of the Service leaders, facts that disclose any deviations from the promulgated standards. It is doubtless true, as members of the Forest Service at every level aver, that the system of reporting has not been set up to expose deviations so much as to provide the leaders with the knowledge they need realistically to plan and guide the destinies of the agency. Distrust is not the driving force behind the system. Just the same, whatever the intentions of those who established and maintain the upward flow of reports, one result is to bring to their attention any continued departures from announced behavioral norms.

Theoretically, a field officer who does depart from announced policies, as a result of the tendencies toward fragmentation that pull at all Rangers, could falsify his reports to conceal his digression. In practice, this is seldom feasible, for misrepresentation in one report would soon produce contradictions with so many others that it would require almost all a man's time and energy as well as the most extraordinary ingenuity to tamper with all of them so as to make them consistent. What is more, many people—employees, users of national forest products and facilities—would eventually have to be drawn into the conspiracy. And even if all the reports were successfully altered, the information in the reports would then conflict with that obtained by higher levels through the other channels described in this chapter. It is almost inconceivable that manipulations of the records could long escape detection.

In any case, the incentives to falsify reports are not very strong. In the first place, the penalties for occasionally inadequate performance are far less severe than those for misrepresentation: the risks of dishonesty are infinitely greater than those of honesty. Secondly, . . . the whole ethos of the Service discourages falsification. The observer of the organization quickly gets the feeling such behavior would be regarded as not only immoral, but cowardly, unmanly, degrading to the individual and to the Service (whose members have a fierce pride in it), and that any man who practices it must end with contempt for himself for not having the courage to fight for those departures from policy that he believes right or to admit his errors when he is wrong. . . .

Official Diaries

Rangers, assistant Rangers, and their principal aides are required to keep official diaries throughout the year. The diaries show to the nearest half-hour how each workday is spent. On standard Service-wide forms, the field officers and employees record each thing they do, describing the activity in enough detail for any inspector to identify it, the functions to which the activity is chargeable, the time at which it began and was completed, and the amount of office, travel, and field time it entailed. They thus compile a full running record of the way they employ their time. . . .

Forest Service officials do not designate disclosure of deviation as the chief function of the diaries. Rather, they contend the information in the diaries is needed to enable the leaders to formulate and adjust policies and objectives to what the records show is practicable on the ground; it puts the leaders in touch with reality, and tells them as much about the shortcomings of their own programs and goals as it does about the men in the field. The diaries, they say, are designed for the guidance of the top echelons rather than to force field officers to testify against themselves. And there is no denying the diaries are used for this purpose.

But the fact remains that the diaries *also* expose deviations from decisions issued at higher levels to regulate the behavior of men in the field. The practice of keeping diaries may have been instituted for other reasons, and it may be employed in other connections. Nevertheless, exposure of deviation is one of the consequences, and few members of the organization are unaware of this.

The diaries are kept accurately for the same reasons that reports are not "doctored." In the first place, falsifying them is far too difficult. If inconsistencies between the diaries and work reports were not quickly discovered, then contradictions between what the diaries recorded and what was actually accomplished in the woods *would* soon come to light. Furthermore, discrepancies between the entries in the diary of one forest officer and those of his colleagues, subordinates, and superiors could not be long concealed. In any event, the entries are made throughout the year, so manipulating them for purposes of hiding the truth would take elaborate, long-range planning, and great investments of effort. . . .

Secondly, there is apparently a feeling of ethical, professional, and organizational obligation to keep the records straight. Members of the Service speak with obvious repugnance of tampering; it is regarded as petty and contemptible conduct, contrary to the traditions and the welfare of the agency. To be sure, few diaries are actually current, as regulations require; except for what one Ranger called "streaks of religion," during which he enters his activities faithfully at the end of each day, most men rely on their memories, aided by brief notes and consultations with co-workers, to fill out the forms for days—or even weeks—during which more urgent business was given precedence. And there is by no means unanimous enthusiasm for the diaries; some men argue that other reports supply all the information that can be gleaned from them. Still, even one Ranger who objected strongly to keeping one admitted that he is conscientious about its accuracy and completeness even though it has disclosed occasional failings for which he was reprimanded. Unquestionably, they are not precise to the minute, but they do reflect fairly closely what actually happens in the field.

The diaries are collected by higher headquarters and analyzed periodically. Current pages, kept in the field for the use of field administrators, are available to visiting inspectors. And they *are* studied by representatives of higher levels.

Along with diaries of their own activities, officers in the field are also required to maintain equipment-use records that are in effect diaries of their equipment. Each piece of apparatus and each vehicle is covered by a log in which an entry must be made every time it is employed. The ostensible objectives are to furnish cost data, and to provide information from which it can be determined whether the equipment is used enough to justify it; in the language of the Forest Service, equipment must "earn" its purchase. But discrepancies between reported use of equipment and technical and financial plans, travel allowances, travel entries in personnel diaries, and work accomplished in the woods are occasionally discovered by comparing equipment records with other documents and inspection reports. Within limits, property records and other reports must tally. They send up warning flags when what happens in the field diverges from what is enunciated as policy at the center.

District Rangers and their subordinates thus leave behind them in time a wake of paper that is a highly visible chronicle of their operations. If they stray from the designated channels, they do not ordinarily get very far before their divagations are disclosed. . . .

Inspection

In the end, however, regardless of how much of their field behavior is described in what the field men tell about their achievements, and in their inadvertent disclosures when they employ staff services, the only sure way to find out what goes on at the level where the physical work of the organization is done is to visit the field and see. This practice has been highly developed and carefully systematized in the Forest Service. . . .

TYPES OF INSPECTION

The broadest type of inspection—that is, the type that covers the broadest range of activities—is the General Integrating Inspection. . . . [A] General Integrating Inspection is designed to find out how good a job a line officer is doing when his total responsibilities are considered. Taking the whole gamut of national forest administration tasks as its subject, it reveals whether an organizational unit is administered in accord with policy, and whether everything that *could* be done *is* done.

Functional Inspections are narrower in scope but greater in depth than General Integrating Inspections. They normally concentrate on individual functions—timber management, wildlife management, recreation management, information and education, engineering, etc.—and explore in detail the way they are administered. A General Integrating Inspection takes up the balance among functions; a Functional Inspection turns to the balance among tasks within a function. A General Integrating Inspection relies on samples and general impressions; a Functional Inspection rests on minute examination and analysis of figures and methods. General Integrating Inspectors strive for "horizontal" sweep; Functional Inspectors aim at "vertical" comprehensiveness. . . .

Fiscal-Administrative Inspections—essentially, audits of fiscal operations and administrative housekeeping functions—do for office management, including accounting and record-keeping and reporting, what General Functional Inspections do for field operations. Books, files, and records are examined for maintenance according to standard. Manuals and work plans are reviewed to see if they are up-to-date and accessible. Procedures for handling paper work are studied. Diaries are checked for currency and completeness. Reporting promptness and accuracy are evaluated. Thus, not only is behavior compared with performed decisions by means of reports and records; in addition, reports and records are themselves inspected to ensure the reliability of the data they provide, and to make sure field officers are familiar with the decisions to which they are expected to conform.

Two additional types of inspection are *ad hoc* in character rather than recurrent. They are substantially hearings on major failures of one kind or another, although they are sometimes employed to see what can be learned from unusual accomplishments as well. Boards of review look into the causes and consequences of large-scale, unexpected reverses, such as huge fires; investigations are inspections of alleged misconduct on the part of forest officers. Unlike the other kinds of inspection, these occur only when something extraordinary happens; they focus on the exceedingly unusual.

Whether going along quietly and routinely or beset by catastrophe, members of the Forest Service can be as certain of inspection as they are of death and taxes. . . .

When a region is inspected by Washington, or a national forest by a regional office, the inspectors ordinarily visit randomly chosen Ranger districts, for every inspection involves study of field work.

Every Ranger interviewed has had the experience of being visited by people from Washington and region offices as well as being checked by their own respective supervisors. Since the number of inspections of one kind or another by supervisors' offices average three or more a year over and above the reviews by higher levels, every Ranger can count on at least several inspections every year; inspectors and functional specialists thus come through with high frequency, and the chances of deflections from preformed decisions going undetected are correspondingly reduced. . . .

[Yet] the more experienced Rangers are quite casual about inspection, for they know that only the most grievous mismanagement is likely to get them into serious trouble. The atmosphere of inspection is not one of a trial or even a competitive examination. In the evenings, when the work is done and the notes written up, the inspectors and the inspected gather socially to discuss personal and organizational affairs—such things as shifts of personnel, promotions, retirements, additions to staff, organization policies and strategies and problems—meeting as professional equals rather than as superiors and subordinates, or inquisitors and defendants. The practice of rotation and transfer of foresters, . . . combined with the travels of inspectors, acquaints members of the Service in each region with their co-workers; inspection is a mode of communication and of face-to-face contact that helps bind the agency into a unity. Men in the field, rather than fearing inspection, tend to welcome the opportunities it affords them to keep abreast of developments in the organization, to learn the latest rumors and gossip, and to give their own ideas to their superiors at first hand.

The fact remains, however, that the written reports following every inspection are blunt and hard-hitting; criticisms are not softened, punches are not pulled. . . .

Inspectors summarize their principal findings for the officers they investigate, and the inspected officers are thus both forewarned of what is to be reported and given a chance to answer the criticisms and thus possibly to have some of them explained or eliminated. If a report nevertheless contains material to which they object, they may submit a written protest; several of the Rangers interviewed have done so on occasion. One Ranger expressed mild annoyance at the appearance in reports of findings not actually discussed with him in advance, and another was somewhat irritated by intimations that he was unaware of deficiencies that any good forester would recognize—deficiencies, in some instances, that he himself called to the attention of the visitors. On the whole, however, the Rangers indicate they believe inspection reports are accurate and fair despite their sometimes painful candor.

But inspections are not only a mode of detection. They are also a method of communicating preformed decisions to the men in the field, of reducing the ambiguities of previously issued policy statements, and of finding out whether such policy statements require revision in the light of field experience. That is, they are an additional technique of preforming Ranger decisions, and they help determine the contents of such decisions.

For inspectors do not merely note violations of policy pronouncements and suggest in general terms that the field men look up the appropriate provisions and figure out how to conform. Rather, they indicate quite precisely what is to be done— what neglected projects should be undertaken, what activities should be reduced or halted or expanded or intensified, what procedures should be improved or corrected. They direct and prohibit action. They interpret authorizations and plans and budgets. They clarify ambiguous statements. In so doing, they claim merely to explain what policy statements and rules and regulations mean; this, in fact, is why they are said to be engaged primarily in training. Yet it is clear that they fill in whatever interstices may remain in the fabric of preformed decisions; they tighten the weave.

Not every such elaboration of the body of administrative issuances is initiated by the inspectors. To be sure, in the written documents, in the conversations during tours of the physical facilities, in the discussions of tentative findings and recommendations, and even in the informal social evenings, the visitors volunteer their ideas on a great many matters even in the course of a couple of days. But some of their advice and suggestions are requested by field men unable to interpret an instruction, or uncertain about how to resolve apparent contradictions between various provisions, or anxious to find impressive support for an interpretation on which they have been overruled by someone else. The inspectors do not simply impose themselves on the field officers; the field officers take whatever advantage they can of the presence of representatives of higher levels by inviting interpretations and elaborations of the rules. In a sense, this is a form of clearance. In any event, the Rangers elicit by their queries some of what is told them by their superiors.

At the same time that inspections increase the volume and specificity of decisions flowing *to* the field, they afford the Rangers opportunities to influence the formation of some of the decisions they will be expected to abide by. For the Rangers take advantage of the personal contacts with the inspectors to voice their complaints, their needs, their preferences, and their aspirations. If objectives are unattainable with the funds available, they point this out. If a prescribed procedure is excessively burdensome, they let the inspectors know. If they see potentialities in the management of their districts that call for amendments or additions to existing orders, they do not hesitate to urge them. . . . There is a flow of communications upwards as well as downwards within the inspection process, and it may be presumed to guide and limit to a small degree the contents of the rules and orders Rangers are called upon to observe.

Yet while inspections generate elaborations of authorizations, directions, prohibitions, and other preformed decisions, and contribute to the substance of those decisions, their *distinctive* function is to uncover deviation by field men from the behavior prescribed by the organization. Even if there were no inspectors, orders would flow out to the field, and reports and reactions would flow back to the center. But leaders would then be dependent entirely on evaluations of field accomplishments by the very men who did the physical work, men with heavy stakes in making their performance look as good as possible. Inspectors from higher levels, checking the field work, furnish more disinterested judgments as to whether or not the work conforms to policy pronouncements. In the last analysis, this is the rationale of inspection.

NOTES AND QUESTIONS

1. Kaufman mentions the strong esprit de corps of the Rangers. It is possible, of course, that this spirit—and the devotion to duty that flows from it—exists in spite of, rather than because of, the elaborate rules and regulations that hedge about the work environment of the Rangers. Is there any evidence in the piece which enables one to judge one way or the other? How would you go about testing the impact of the network of regulation on the performance of the Rangers?

2. Recall the eight mechanisms of coordination described by Litwak and Meyer (Reading 25, at 231, *supra*). How many are used in controlling the field staff of Forest Rangers as Kaufman describes it?

3. Accepting Kaufman's report as accurate, there seems to be a great difference between the behavior of Sykes' prison guards (Reading 45, at 441, *supra*) and Kaufman's forest rangers. Kaufman's rangers are said to act much more "by the book." They are much more responsive to control and coordination from above.

Why should this be the case? Do these differences suggest that there are limitations on how far one can generalize from a study of a particular agency within the legal system? In general, what is the value, if any, of a case study as Kaufman's, Sykes', or Macaulay's (Readings 13 & 15, at 145, 169, *supra*)?

b.   The problems of control

(1)   Technical problems in creating a system

93. The Regulatory Process in OPA Rationing

VICTOR A. THOMPSON*

Although not guided by conscious purpose, the development [of the legal documents related to rationing in World War II] was toward complexity, and the result was that the rationing law had to be "found" rather than read. The legal documents, as they came to be, could not have been part of a system of communication with most laymen. Various kinds of materials came to be included in the legal documents. The illustrations in this chapter will very clearly show a confusion between the idea of the legal document as a communication with the ultimate *reader* and the idea of the legal document as a communication with an intermediate *interpreter*.

AN INSTRUCTION TO THE PUBLIC

Under the terms of the Federal Register Act (Section 7), regulations of "general applicability and legal effect" are not "valid as against any person who has not had actual knowledge thereof until the duplicate originals or certified copies of the document shall have been filed with the Division" of the Federal Register. (49 Stat. 502.) Thus, legal documents which described duties which OPA [Office of Price Administration] wished to be enforceable at law had to be filed with the division of the Federal Register and were so filed. Since practically no one (other than attorneys) reads the Federal Register or has even heard of it, this method of communicating duties is obviously communication with intermediaries or interpreters rather than with ultimate readers (the persons on whom the duties were imposed—in rationing, chiefly business firms). It was also a means of communicating instructions to judges.

* Professor of Political Science, University of Illinois. Copyright © 1950. Reprinted from pp. 359-401, 406-17, by permission.

If only that material had been published in the Federal Register which was legally required to be so published (i.e., enforceable duties), the rationing regulations would have been less than half as long as they were. However, a tremendous amount of other material which either legally or practically could not become the subject of court interpretation (i.e., be enforced by law) was also included in the legal documents and thereby published in the Federal Register. Although the rationing legal documents were read by very few people other than attorneys, the legal documents were treated as though they were a principal means of communication to all people affected by rationing, in and out of OPA. A great part of the material included in rationing legal documents had no "legal effect" in theory and an even greater part had no "legal effect" in fact. Not only were the public's rights and duties described, but a tremendous number of other things were also described. Applicants were told where to pick up application forms, how to fill them out, where to mail them. They were told the form numbers of the forms they were to use, and the forms were often described as to kind of paper, number of parts, type of serialization, etc. Applicants were given instructions in the regulations which were printed in even more detail on the forms. They were told the questions they had to answer, which questions and a few more were printed on the forms. They were told what kind of pencils to use (indelibles or pen and ink) in filling out the forms (also specified on the forms). Any changes in these details, as by the revisions of a form, required an amendment to the regulations (e.g., "OPA Form R-1101" had to be changed to "OPA Form R-1101 [Rev.]" wherever the phrase was mentioned in the regulation). . . .

Much of the material included in the legal documents got there because the drafting attorneys thought the public had a "right" to be informed about it. Whether they thought this "right" was both a legal and a moral one is not completely clear. At any rate they thought it was a moral one. All the rationing attorneys thought the "right" was satisfied by the "constructive notice" of the Federal Register. Thus, the inclusion of much of the material in the legal documents was justified as "necessary" to give "notice" to the public.

Although the drafting attorneys included a tremendous amount of dull and unimportant detail in the legal documents in order to give "notice" to the public, many matters of tremendous interest to the public were excluded from the regulations (and, hence, the Federal Register) with the consent and approval of the attorneys.

One fertile source of such "hidden" material, including duties of members of the public, was the official interpretations. Most interpretations were to be found only in memoranda in the attorneys' files. Some of the more important of them came to be reproduced in mimeograph form for use of the field attorneys. These important interpretations were also printed in the OPA Service, the attorneys' looseleaf service. A very small number of them were printed in the local board looseleaf as "annotations." . . . None of them was printed in the Federal Register.
. . . .

Interpretations rarely got to the local boards, and so those which created or limited rights of applicants or conditions of eligibility had no effect on the public. However, when a district office rationing representative informed his boards in a bulletin about the existence of one of these interpretations, which sometimes happened, then all the people in the jurisdiction of those boards were vitally affected by rules about which the regulations did not inform them. . . .

Further information of great interest to the public was to be found in field instructions—not considered legal documents. These field instructions were not published in the Federal Register; they received circulation only within OPA. From the following examples the reader can judge for himself the importance to the public of some of this instructional material about which the public was never given "notice" via the Federal Register.

The fuel oil rationing program provided for the issuance of "hardship" rations to those people who simply could not get along with their fuel oil rations. Hardship rations were necessary to keep people from freezing. The regulations merely informed the applicant that he could apply for a hardship ration if his present ration was "insufficient to meet his minimum . . . requirements." Boards were instructed in the regulations to issue hardship rations only if they found the applicant's ration to be "insufficient to meet [his] minimum . . . requirements." From the provisions just quoted it is easy to see that an applicant for a hardship ration could find out very little about his "rights" by reading the regulations. How to decide what constituted insufficient fuel oil to meet minimum requirements and how much additional ration was to be issued were described in a nonlegal field instruction. This instruction informed boards that a person who still had left from his ration half or more of what he should have left (according to a table showing the percentage of the heating year which had passed) was not to be issued a hardship ration. A person who had left less than half of what he should have left was to be issued a hardship ration which would restore his total ration to what it should be (under the forementioned table). Thus, whether a person was actually able to receive a hardship ration and how much he would receive were discoverable only by reading the non-legal field instruction—not by reading the regulations. . . .

Under the annotation system of instructing boards, the legal document and the non-legal instruction became so scrambled up that both members of the public and OPA officials often failed to distinguish between them. The annotation system was a rationing field instructional technique adopted late in 1943 whereby the legal document was made the basic instructional vehicle. If a legal sentence was felt to need further elaboration, a non-legal sentence of explanation—an annotation—was interlarded into the legal text. The whole thing was printed in the local board looseleaf service. The annotations were non-legal field instructions. They are not included in any version of the legal document except the board looseleaf, and were not, therefore, printed in the Federal Register. Many of these annotations described material of more interest to the public than the legal sentences which they elaborated. Especially was this true in the field of eligibility. Eligibility rules in the regulations were usually very general. Following these general eligibility rules there were many annotations which prescribed whether or not specific groups were included within the meaning of the general rules. Sometimes official interpretations were later reprinted in the board looseleaf as annotations. More often annotations were simply a non-legal statement of a part of the plan. . . .

Another kind of material of great importance to the public which never appeared in the regulations was enforcement policy. The rule-making effect of enforcement policy is often overlooked. In legal theory, of course, a decision to take no enforcement action against a certain class of violators does not change the legal responsibility of that class to comply with the rules. In actual effect, however, an enforcement policy suspends the operation of the rules on a certain class. In this sense, rationing enforcement policy was law-making in a field where the subject matter was just as important to the individual as fines or suspension from business.

Generally speaking, enforcement policy creation was the sole responsibility of the enforcement department. Some rationing officials, however, recognizing the extreme importance of enforcement policy and its effect on their responsibility for a successful program, insisted on participating in enforcement policy creation. Thus, the fuel rationing officials, in the spring of 1943, persuaded the enforcement officials to agree not to bring any enforcement

actions for violations of the fuel oil rationing regulations which
occurred prior to February, 1943. Agreement on the type of violation for which suspension orders would be sought was also
reached. The resulting fuel oil rationing enforcement policy was
presented to the fuel oil industry advisory committee the following July and more or less grudgingly accepted by it. The enforcement policy was written up in one issue of the fuel oil industry
letter and mailed to several thousand members of the industry.
. . .

Besides the confusing profusion of legal documents already described, the legal documents were rendered poor devices of communication because of the attorneys' drafting mechanics and
attitudes toward law-making.

DRAFTING MECHANICS

Mechanical drafting devices and the writing habits of the drafting attorneys tended to make the rationing legal documents poor
communications. Drafting mechanics not only reduced the readability of the legal documents; they often rendered them completely unintelligible to anyone but a legal researcher. One of
these characteristics of legal writing with which everyone is familiar is the excessive use of cross references. There were very few
sections of the rationing regulations which a person could read
without referring to some other section or sections. Usually these
other sections referred one to still another section, etc., until one
had made some sort of complete circle in organization logic. In
the meantime, the reader had probably lost his place. Often ten
fingers were not enough to keep the pages open at all the points
involved in reading the complete rule. . . .

[One] reason for cross references was natural, human laziness.
Rather than simply refer to other sections, the drafting attorneys
could have repeated the necessary information in the new section. However, such repetition would have required more drafting time and energy. Unquestionably, one of the reasons why
cross references were used so much was because they were the
easiest way out.

[Another] reason for the excessive use of cross references was
a strong reluctance on the part of the attorneys to rephrase something already in the regulations. The attorney learns that the
best way to get a consistent reaction from a court is to use words
which the court has already interpreted. Synonyms for those
words will not do. This legally acquired attitude of the attorneys
was carried into regulation drafting, although most parts of the
regulations obviously would never be the subject of court con-

struction. The dislike of rephrasing or even repeating words and phrases was simply in the attorneys' bones. Hence, cross references to already existing legal words and phrases were resorted to.

Another drafting mechanic which made at least the amendment impossible as an instruction was the attorneys' use of the amendment as a printer's instruction. Even before OPA had acquired any looseleaf services, attorneys were drafting amendments which were simply instructions to someone to make certain changes of words and phrases on various pages of a mythical document called the regulations. Actually, what the attorneys were amending was not a document, but the "law"—"a brooding omnipresence in the skies"—something to be determined by legal (almost mathematical) research. This subconscious concept of the regulations (the "law") was completely at war with the notion of the legal document as an instruction to the field or the general public.

Shortly after fuel oil rationing began, it was discovered that the ration formula did not provide enough oil for house trailers. The rationing officials decided to allow the "maximum of the range" rather than the "mid-point of the range" for house trailer rations. These concepts were well known to boards and the change simply meant that the square foot floor area of the trailer applied to the "maximum of the range" column in a table would give the ration to be issued. The rationing officials also wanted to excuse trailer dwellers from the requirement of furnishing a dealer's certification as to the amount of oil sold for use in the trailer during the first pre-rationing year, and they also wanted to include old railroad cars used as permanent dwellings in the category of trailers. These simple plans were incorporated in the regulations by means of the following amendment—a printer's instruction of one 200-word sentence.

Subparagraph (1) of paragraph (a) of 1394.5001 is amended, a new subparagraph (16a) is added to such paragraph (a) and in subparagraph (23) of such paragraph (a), the phrase "structure, including a house trailer," is substituted for the word "structure"; in subdivision (iii) of subparagraph (1) of paragraph (a) 1394.5151, the word "or" is added after the phrase "its use"; and a new subdivision (iv) is added to subparagraph (1) of such paragraph (a); in paragraph (a) of 1394.5253 the phrase "other than a house trailer," is inserted between the phrase "in any premises," and the phrase "or for hot water"; in paragraph (a) 1394.5256 the phrase "other than a house trailer" is inserted between the words "private dwelling premises" and the words "during the heating year"; in paragraph (b) of such section, the phrase "private dwelling

premises other than a house trailer" is substituted for the
phrase "the premises"; in paragraph (c) of such section the
phrase "other than a house trailer," is inserted between the
words "private dwelling premises" and the words "and the
amount"; a new paragraph (d) is added to such section; in
1394.5259, the phrase "paragraphs (c) and (d)" is substituted
for the phrase "paragraph (c)"; in paragraph (a) of 1394.5403,
the phrase "(other than those which are house trailers)" is
inserted between the word "cars" and the word "may"; and
a new paragraph (k) is added to 1394.5902; as set forth below.

Such an amendment becomes more significant when one remembers that Federal Register reprints of amendments were obtained
and diligently mailed by some field and industry relations officers
not only to the OPA field organization but to several thousand
members of the industry for their instruction.

Another drafting practice which made the legal document useless as an instruction was the use of drafting tricks. Often the
drafting attorneys would discover that they could make some
rationing plan "legal" by changing only one or a few key words
in some strategic part of the regulations. Then, by the strenuous
application of logic to the words of the regulations, one could
discover that, sure enough, the plan was "covered." Changes
made in this way were completely uninformative to anyone but
a legal researcher. The use of these drafting tricks was, therefore, completely inconsistent with the inclusion in the regulations
of the very large amount of purely instructional and non-legal
material, described in the last chapter. However, such drafting
tricks were used a great deal. . . .

Early in 1942, the driver of an automobile which regularly
carried passengers to work was made eligible for recapped and
second grade tires. Later in the year . . . it was decided to make
all members of the car club who had cars—not just the driver—
eligible for recapped and second grade tires. In the original provision, the driver had been required to present to his local board
a certification from his plant transportation committee "that
other practicable means of transportation are not available." The
amendment extending eligibility to all members of the car club
simply changed this certification to read, "that other practicable
means of transportation, exclusive of the automobiles of other
workers, are not available." The reader can get a good idea of
the instructiveness of this amendment or of the section of the
regulations it amended by simply trying to figure out how this
change in wording could bring about the great change in the
program described above. Actually, the change in the program

was not brought about or described by the amendment but by newspapers, instructions, meetings, etc. However, the amendment satisfied the OPA attorneys, and their satisfaction was necessary in order to make the change in the program. The reaction of judges was not involved. . . .

Another device used which shows that the drafting attorneys were writing to legal researchers rather than the public was the way they often terminated provisions. Rather than remove the provision from an order or place it in an appendix, which, if writing for a looseleaf (as they usually did) they could have done, they often would insert a date before which the applicant must apply or take other action. This date was often inserted at the time of, or after, the termination of the provision. Thus, when the fuel oil hardship provision was terminated at the end of the first year of rationing, an amendment simply added between the words "may apply," the words "before September 13, 1943," making the whole phrase read "may before September 13, 1943 apply" to the board, etc. This amendment was issued September 10 and effective September 13. The newspapers would carry the story of the termination on September 10, the issuing date. The amendment or looseleaf page replacements would probably not be printed and distributed until after September 13. Thus, after September 13, a person would be informed by the legal document that he could apply for a hardship ration if he did so before September 13, a date already passed. He would be instructed fully how to apply, etc. Such a person must have thought Washington was full of practical jokers. The reason the attorneys often terminated provisions in this way was because this method did the job just as thoroughly as any other as far as the "law" was concerned. At the moment they were not thinking about the legal document as an instruction to the general public. They also may have used this device because of their desire to have the regulations describe the past as well as the present and the future. . . .

LEGAL ATTITUDES TOWARD LAW-MAKING AND THE INSTRUCTIVENESS OF THE LEGAL DOCUMENT

In addition to the mechanics of drafting a legal document, there appear to be a number of attorneys' attitudes toward law-making which also help to make the legal documents poor communications for any but legal researchers. . . .

The Drive for Accuracy

Among the rationing officials, the attorneys were the defenders of complete accuracy in all documents. Every written document was "cleared" by the attorneys for accuracy. They insisted upon completely refined and qualified statements, both in the legal documents which they drafted and in non-legal documents which they cleared. The result was often a document or statement so qualified as to be almost unreadable. The attorneys appeared not to be concerned at all with ease in reading but only with the accuracy of the statement. . . . The significance of this attitude of the attorneys was not so much that they sought accuracy as that they sacrificed readability, intelligibility, and instructiveness to accuracy, whether or not accuracy was important. Consciously or subconsciously, the drafting attorneys wrote for readers who were trained or disposed to squeeze the last drop of a conventionalized logic out of a word. . . .

Part of the drive for accuracy was the tremendous preoccupation with definitions. Every ration order had its long list of carefully defined words. Often, to solve drafting problems, a word would be given a slightly unusual definition. Thus, unless the casual reader of a ration order memorized the definitions before he started to read the order, he could very easily be misled. . . .

Where a legal statement might actually become the subject of dispute between attorneys—i.e., where duties were under discussion in courts or suspension hearings—accuracy rather than readability and instructiveness was obviously indicated. The behavior to be affected was the behavior of attorneys. Accuracy in these matters might result in fewer court cases being lost. However, where information of only general interest was involved, such as consumer eligibility and procedural provisions, the drive for complete accuracy seemed a strange waste of the powers of logic. It helped to make the legal document unintelligible to the general reader.

MAKING THE RULES KNOWN

Legal communication by the written word is not an effective means for eliciting desired reactions from persons other than attorneys. Since the great mass of people did not have legal advice, and particularly since local boards did not have it (except when they specifically requested interpretations from OPA district offices), non-legal means for communicating rationing plans to the general public and local boards were developed. Thus, despite the tremendous assumptions underlying the legal documents that they were the principal means of communicating rationing plans to all concerned, the rationing plans were actually communicated to non-attorneys chiefly by other means. Although communication with the field was verbal to an important extent, the principal non-legal communicative activity of the Washington rationing staff was the preparation of non-legal field instructions. Still other means were used to inform the general public. . . .

THE DEVELOPMENT OF INSTRUCTION TECHNIQUES

One of the earliest kinds of instruction was an instruction or guide to the exercise of discretion. Many rationing delegations were couched in very general terms. Rationing officials became conscious that boards (or district offices) might need help in interpreting these broad grants of discretionary power. The rationing attorneys became conscious of this need first and included in the regulations much material which was really only a guide to the exercise of broad discretion. . . .

Often these legal guides to a board decision simply admonished boards "to take into consideration" certain things when making decisions. Thus, the first sugar home-canning program allowed additional sugar for canning "the quantity of fruit the Board deems to be reasonable." The board was instructed by the regulations to give "due consideration to the period within which the fruit will be consumed, the past practice of the individual or family unit . . . the prevailing home canning practice in the locality. . . ."

The attorneys did not have a monopoly on the guide to decision type of instruction. When the annotation system was adopted, most annotations were guides to decision under the general rules of the regulations. They answered some of the questions which would come to a person's mind after reading the general rule in the regulations. Thus, the gasoline rationing regulations allowed unlimited amounts of gasoline "for the transportation of mail on behalf of the United States Government." One of the annotations under this rule pointed out that "persons transporting special delivery mail in privately owned automobiles are eligible for preferred mileage."

Fuel oil rationing officials consciously tried to narrow board discretion to the vanishing point. Specifically, they attempted to reduce discretion to a mathematical formula wherever possible. They realized that this approach resulted in injustice in a few unusual cases that did not fit the formula, but believed that it would actually result in less injustice than broad grants of discretion which would be interpreted in various ways by 5,500 local boards or by the same board for different applicants. An example of the tendency to narrow the board's discretion by instruction was the first year hardship ration program in fuel oil rationing. The regulations contained a tremendous grant of discretion to the boards to issue hardship rations to any person "who finds that his [ration is] insufficient to meet his minimum . . . requirements for the balance of the heating year." The board was to issue such a person an additional ration sufficient "to meet his minimum . . . needs." The field instruction reduced the adjudication and determination of hardship rations to a purely mathematical and clerical action. . . .

Even when it was impossible to reduce board discretion to a mathematical computation, the tendency among instruction conscious officials was to include in instructions as many specific applications of the general rules as they could think of in advance of board action under the general rule. In general, however, rationing officials allowed specific applications of the general rule to accumulate by the process of interpretations and appeals—by the case process—including them in the instructions one by one as specific cases were decided upon. Many of the annotations were formerly interpretations regarding specific cases. In the fuel oil regulations, boards were given power to issue rations for "any necessary purpose not otherwise specified in this Order." A great case law grew up under this provision. Finally, toward the end of rationing, this case law was reduced in the instructions (the fuel oil guide) to a list of twenty-three purposes which were "necessary" and fifteen which were not. This list covered about 99 per cent of the applications presented to boards and thus cut their discretion with regard to interpreting "necessary purpose" by about 99 per cent. . . .

In May of 1943, OPA, on contract with a private printing firm in New York, acquired a looseleaf service for local boards. Each rationing program had a section in the looseleaf. An up-to-date version of each ration order and all outstanding board letters were reproduced in the local board looseleaf service (or simply local board service), as it was called. Thus, at first, the looseleaf was chiefly a handy binder for the local board letters. For the regulations, it was a real gain. Amendments to the regulations, usually only instructions to a looseleaf printer anyway, became page replacements for the board service, and for the first time boards had accurate and up-to-date versions of the ration orders which could be kept up-to-date. The board looseleaf service was distributed at a rate of three or four per board with much larger quantities going to field offices above the boards. A few months after the board looseleaf service was acquired, the rationing de-

partment adopted the annotation system, thereby deciding to
reprint again all rationing regulations and instructions in annotated form. . . .

THE LOCAL BOARD LOOSELEAF SERVICE

The local board service was a great help to everyone in OPA.
It was becoming almost impossible to keep track of the many
board letters. The problem which the looseleaf solved as far as
the instructions were concerned was the reference problem. To
refer back to something under the letter system was almost impossible because the proper letter would not easily be found and,
even if found, had probably been changed by some other unknown letter. As for the regulations, they were meaningless without a looseleaf. The board looseleaf brought permanent organiza-
ation of material, and, once a person became familiar with that
organization, he could look up any point he wanted to. The
looseleaf service was a reference book. It was not an unmixed
blessing.

One of the chief difficulties with the looseleaf was that a person could not from it follow the changes in the program. The
changes appeared as a group of page replacements. On each of
these new pages to be inserted in place of old pages in the looseleaf was one or more new words, sentences, or paragraphs. Altogether they added up to something, but what? For practical purposes, it is impossible to reconstruct a complete story from a
group of page replacements to a looseleaf.

The device used to solve this problem was a "newsletter" which
appeared with each set of page replacements (called a "supplement"). The newsletter carried a brief reference to the change
and the new sections or sentences. As the addendum to the office
instruction on annotations stated: "The main function of the
newsletter is to point out changes on new material and should
rarely be more than 2 to 5 lines long [sic]." The instruction
writers were not allowed to describe the change in the newsletter.
A typical newsletter is the following:

Transportation of School Children.—Preferred mileage may
be allowed under some circumstances. (P. 270.10.)

All the board service newsletter did was to warn boards that a
change had been made, which they knew by virtue of receiving
the new pages, and to tell them that the change involved some
specified subject. The problem of reconstructing the change from
the page replacements was not in any way solved by the newsletter. Some changes affected dozens of sections or subsections

in the regulations. The average change affected over four sections. This was not the whole story, however. The sections affected by a change were laced to other sections through cross references, so that to determine the content of a change in the looseleaf involved a person in intricate legal research. . . .

Coupled with the board's problem of finding out what any supplement did, what changes it made, was the problem of insufficient copies of the service at the board. With some exceptions in large boards, each board received three or four copies of the looseleaf service. This number of copies did not begin to do the job of installing an important program change. Anywhere from a few to several dozen people would have to use those copies in turn. They could not take them home to study them. The distribution of the board looseleaf service, like everything else about it, emphasized the point that it was a *reference* volume. . . .

One further problem with relation to the board looseleaf deserves mention. This was the problem of keeping the looseleafs up-to-date and accurate by the prompt and correct insertion of the new pages and the discarding of the old ones. Once a looseleaf became inaccurate because of failure to insert new pages, it was almost impossible to correct it. The instructions accompanying a supplement told what pages were to be taken out and what added. If the pages to be replaced had never been inserted in the first place, a person could not be sure if the new pages were properly related to all other material in the looseleaf. Spot checks of board looseleafs taken early in 1945 indicated that most of them were not accurate or up-to-date. The only solution to this problem appears to be careful education of persons whose function it is to make the page replacements, and also careful supervision of them. Generally speaking, little work along these lines was done by the rationing department. Clerks and stenographers were not sufficiently impressed with the importance of keeping looseleafs up-to-date, or properly instructed on how to do this. The result was that probably few of the board looseleafs were accurate.

How the Public Was Instructed

The general public was not informed of its rights and duties under rationing by legal documents. Most people have never seen or even heard of any one of the many rationing legal documents. Even if everyone had received all rationing legal documents, most people would not have been instructed thereby. . . .

[T]he public was actually notified in a great variety of ways, none of them legal ways. . . . There was almost as much rationing educational activity as there was rationing planning activity.

In the first place, all rationing changes were accompanied by a news story which was released to the national wire services in Washington, and which appeared, therefore, in newspapers all over the country about three days before the change was effective. Local boards and district offices would release these stories or local versions of them over and over in the local newspapers. In addition, if any part of a program seemed to be poorly understood, information specialists in the district offices prepared further corrective stories for release in local newspapers.

Many rationing programs developed an "industry letter" or "bulletin" which was mailed out once or twice a month to all interested members of the industry, or anyone else. Any person who wished his name put on the mailing lists could have it put thereon. Trade associations received the industry letters and reproduced them for distribution to their members. The letters were reproduced quickly by a photo-offset process. Folding and addressing were by machines and took only a day or so. Most persons on the mailing lists received their copies of the industry letter within ten days of the time the letter was sent to the printer.

The industry letters contained summaries of all program changes affecting the industry, explanations of the reasons for the changes, discussions of the supply outlook, and many suggestions on how to operate effectively under the rationing rules. Occasionally, one issue of the letter would be used to summarize the industry's duties under rationing. Such an issue then became a check list of duties which many dealers posted in their offices for the information of themselves and their employees. Efforts were made to make the industry letter interesting, and it was set up with an attractive format and easy-to-read print. . . .

OPA had a separate information department charged with the duty of keeping the public informed about OPA programs. . . .

In addition to . . . various educational devices and activities . . . some rationing branches had national industry advisory committees and also local industry committees for each OPA district office. These committees were not only aids in planning but were also a channel of communication to the industry. Important program changes were carefully explained to the industry committees, and the committee members then helped to explain these changes to other members of the industry.

NOTES AND QUESTIONS

1. One of the basic requirements of effectiveness for any rule, directive, doctrine or standard enunciated within the legal system is that it be communicated to those who are expected to act on the basis of it. (Perhaps laws which are intended to be symbolic only, if there are any, are an exception.) Hence, any legal system must contain a communication network. It is instructive to analyze familiar parts of the American legal system from the standpoint of the requirements of the system for internal and external communication.

One set of rules and practices governs communications from those who wish to make use of the legal system—requirements of filing and giving notice, formal complaints in court, petitions to the legislature, and so on. Another set of rules and practices governs communications *within* the system. The American legal system is so large, and so complex, that there are real problems of information and control within it. Both Kaufman and Thompson deal directly with this problem within administrative agencies.

Particularly interesting are the problems of communicating outputs of the legal system to the public. The ways of doing so range from exceedingly direct and personal information, to highly formal published regulations. There is an enormous difference between a gigantic sign on an interstate highway, which states very simply that the speed limit is seventy m.p.h. and the involute OPA documents which Thompson discusses. What accounts for these differences? One factor is the nature of the audience and the nature of the desired response. Some of the problems that Thompson discovered in the work of the OPA stem from the fact that the legal documents were designed for a mixed audience: the actual users of OPA rulings, that is, merchants and the public, but also field offices of the OPA. There is still a third, implicit audience: the audience of lawyers who, without making actual use of the legal documents, may judge them for accuracy and craftsmanship, and if they fall short, will presumably think the worst of the draftsman. To consider this audience at all may be foolish, but Thompson feels this audience was nonetheless considered.

Compare the standard American appellate decision as a communication device. It too has multiple audiences. A Supreme Court ruling on the admissibility of confessions in criminal cases has for its audience: (a) actual and potential criminals; (b) the lawyers who serve as "brokers" of information for members of the public; (c) police officials, prosecutors and other enforcement officers; (d) lower courts expected to obey the Supreme Court ruling; (e) the general public, which is not expected to commit crimes, but which grants or withholds prestige to the Court, and which assesses the political meaning of acts of government; and (f) the legal academic community, which will judge the merits of the case from the standpoint of policy, craftsmanship and soundness as law. Can you think of still other audiences? Obviously, the appellate opinion will not reach all of these audiences with equal force and effect, and it will affect behavior in the various spheres much differently. To which audience is the Court really addressing itself? Which audience does it most try to please? Does Thompson's study suggest limitations on the effectiveness of appellate case-law and why?

In light of the nature of the regulations and the other kinds of communications coming from the OPA offices in Washington to the local rationing boards, how much discretion did the local boards have? What can we assume were the limits on that discretion?

[Reading 94]

2. OPA was an agency created during the almost unprecedented crisis of World War II. Can one argue that the chaotic system of regulations, instructions, annotations, letters and press releases actually was functional for the rationing system and that a neat system such as described by Kaufman in *The Forest Ranger* would have been dysfunctional? Compare the following from John Kenneth Galbraith, *The New Industrial State* 67 n.4 (1967):*

[For a time] during World War II . . . I was in charge of price control. Decisions on prices—to fix, raise, rearrange or, very rarely, to lower them—came to my office after an extensive exercise in group decision-making in which lawyers, economists, accountants, men knowledgeable of the product and industry, and specialists in public righteousness had all participated. Alone one was nearly helpless to alter such decisions; hours or days of investigation would be required and, in the meantime, a dozen other decisions would have been made. Given what is commonly called an "adequate" staff, one could have exercised control. But an adequate staff would be one that largely duplicated the decision-making group with adverse effect on the good nature and sense of

* Professor of Economics, Harvard University. Copyright © 1967 Houghton Mifflin Company, Boston and Hamish Hamilton Ltd., London. Reprinted by permission.

responsibility of the latter and the time required for decision. To have responsibility for all of the prices in the United States was awesome; to discover how slight was one's power in face of group decision-making was sobering. . . .

3. Thompson discusses "hidden material"—information of interest to the public about agency decision processes, criteria for making judgments and enforcement procedures—which was nonetheless not readily available to the public. One might think that the more an agency educated the public about criteria and procedures, the more compliance it would get from the public. However, some agencies like to keep much of this kind of information hidden. Should we assume that hiding information aids the agency or certain people in it, or is this situation just the product of laziness and sloppy procedure? Can you think of any functions for the use of hidden information? Recall Litwak & Meyer, Reading 25, at 231, *supra*.

4. Refer to ¶ 1 once more. How would you explain the conduct of the OPA lawyers, who were, one imagines, reasonably competent people, anxious to help OPA do its job? Why did they act in the fashion Thompson so criticizes? Why were they so neglectful of the need to communicate with the public part of their audience?

(2) The costs of a system of control

95. Organizational Rules and Surveillance: Propositions in Comparative Organizational Analysis

WILLIAM A. RUSHING*

10 ADMINISTRATIVE SCIENCE QUARTERLY
423 (1966)

Since Max Weber's writings on bureaucracy, complex organization has usually been defined by sociologists in terms of office hierarchy, specialization, formal rules, impersonality, and other familiar characteristics. It is frequently assumed that these attributes constitute a functionally interrelated whole; indeed, in Weber's ideal-type formulation this assumption is a necessary consequence of the definition of bureaucracy. The concept "bureaucracy," then, is often used to refer to an ideal or pure state in which a configuration of attributes is present. Several criticisms have been made of this formulation, two of which are particularly relevant to this paper.

First, the characteristics which are included in the definition tend not to be considered as variables. Attention is focused on the definition of an ideal or pure state, rather than on the fact that organizations may vary in terms of certain variables. And partly as a consequence of this, attention is deflected away from the fundamental questions of the degree to which the various characteristics are related and the degree to which each is separately related to nonbureaucratic variables. Since the definition assumes that the various components of bureaucracy are interrelated and, by implication, that nonbureaucratic variables exert a similar effect on each of the components, it has not encouraged the development of bureaucratic theory in the form of a series

* Professor of Sociology, Vanderbilt University, Nashville. Copyright © 1966 Administrative Science Quarterly. Reprinted by permission.

of interrelated propositions which are statements of relationship among a group of variables. In this paper, some initial efforts toward the construction of a series of propositions about bureaucratic organization are presented. Propositions deal with the relationship between two bureaucratic variables, formal rules and surveillance, and several other variables.

Rules include productivity norms and other objective means for evaluating participant performance, as well as explicit rules that prescribe specific performances. Surveillance refers to supervisory practices, that is, efforts to influence the performance of organizational participants through direct observation and face-to-face contact. Each is assumed to form a continuum, reflecting varying degrees of participant autonomy. These variables constitute two major components of what is usually considered the formal control structure of organizations and they perform similar organizational functions: each restricts, regulates, and controls participant behavior. Nevertheless, the two are not always positively associated. They are not always affected in the same way by the same variables; in fact, as will be suggested, there are circumstances in which the two may vary in opposite directions.

Since this study is concerned with organizational control, the analysis is related to the models of bureaucracy outlined by [Robert] Merton, [Philip] Selznick, and [Alvin] Gouldner, all of which revolve around the problem of organizational control. In both Merton and Gouldner the primary organizational control strategy is rule making, whereas for Selznick it is delegation. The conceptual analysis of organizational control presented here is different from these models, however.

The models of Merton, Gouldner, and Selznick are social-system models. Changes in the one component of the organization are assumed to have ramifying consequences for the whole organizational system. Each model takes as its starting point, that is, as its major independent variable, organizational control strategies, from which a number of organizational consequences, anticipated and unanticipated, are expected to stem. The effect of rule making or delegation on other components of the organization are then traced out in detail, but the effects that different structural conditions may have on the level of control and different types of control strategies is given relatively little attention. More relevant to these models are the dysfunctional consequences of rule making or delegation, and how these consequences may in turn reinforce the need for control and, therefore, the existing level of organizational control. In these social system models, then, "vicious circles" and feedback loops among organizational processes are of primary interest.

Although the analysis in this paper deals to some degree with vicious circles (e.g., the relationship between rigid organizational control and the motivation to produce), the conceptual analysis of organizational control is essentially different. There is greater concern with identifying the various structural conditions that may cause variation in organizational demands for control, and the reasons why one control strategy rather than another may be a more likely organizational response to specified structural conditions, than there is with analyzing the various consequences of these strategies. Rules and surveillance are, then, conceptualized primarily as dependent variables. The independent variables include participant performance level, organizational conflict, participant supply and demand, organizational size, and structural differentiation.

Although these variables are social-structural, the basic framework is social-psychological. The reward-cost framework of George C. Homans, and of John W. Thibaut and Harold H. Kelley provides the theoretical framework for each hypothesized relationship between social-structural conditions and organizational strategies of control. The reward-cost model is viewed as a variable which intervenes between structural variables and organizational control strategies. Rewards are generally defined as valued states of affairs, while costs refer to valued states of affairs which are forgone in the performance of a particular activity. Hence an activity, e.g., a particular control strategy, may yield high reward, but be undesirable because other values are forgone; consequently, an alternative strategy with a more desirable reward-cost balance may be chosen instead. Despite the use of this psychological model, however, the variables in most of the propositions are social-structural ones. The general orienting frame of references may be expressed as follows: Variation in conditions of social structure, acting upon the reward-cost balance of individuals in organizations, causes levels of attempted organizational control and types of control strategies to vary.

Since the analysis deals with variables like rules, surveillance, organizational conflict, and structural differentiation, which characterize all complex organizations to some degree, the propositions cut across specific types of organizations, such as hospitals, government agencies, prisons, or industrial firms. Hence, they constitute a framework for comparative research on rules and surveillance in organizations. Unfortunately, however, all propositions are not supported by research in all types of organizations. And, as is often the case in a paper such as this, all propositions are not equally supported, although no contradiction of them has been found in the literature. Some propositions have been previously stated by other authors (e.g., Proposition V), but apparently they have not been explicitly formulated within the reward-cost framework of this paper; no one has looked at the same set of variables in quite the same way. Finally, since the analysis is limited to only a selected list of variables, the reader should note that each proposition is accompanied with the qualification, "all other things being equal."

PARTICIPANT PERFORMANCE LEVEL

When the level of participant performance is high in an organization, persons who are in managerial positions are rewarded, but when performance levels are low, such persons incur costs. Bureaucratic rules may then be imposed in an effort to reduce these costs. Gouldner notes, for example, that in response to workers' low productivity, management demanded strict adherence to rules and regulations governing punch-in time, absenteeism, and use of company property. Blau finds, too, that when subordinates fail to attain adequate work quotas, formal methods for evaluating work performance are introduced. And Argyris concludes that in order "to combat reduced productivity" many managers resort to "careful definition" as well as closer inspection of employees' performance.

Proposition 1. Use of formal rules to control behavior will be greater when organizational participants fail to attain minimum performance levels than when they attain these levels.

Thus if compliance is not voluntary, formal rules may be introduced. Rules and formal regulations may, *if they are accepted by those to whom they apply*, become *functional substitutes* for participant motivation and voluntary performance. Organizations, and areas within the same organization, where performance levels are considered too low are also places where many elaborate formal rules are also likely to be found.

Such use of bureaucratic rules is not restricted to the actions of higher officials or to superior's actions against subordinates. Rushing shows that members of ancillary (i.e., subordinate) psychiatric professions try to impose formal referral procedures in response to psychiatrists' failure to send them what they consider a sufficient number of patient referrals.

Closer surveillance of recalcitrant participants may also be employed. For example, in the eighteenth century Prussian bureaucracy, where it is said that superiors believed "no official could be trusted any further than the keen eyes of his superiors could reach," an extensive and elaborate system of surveillance (including a spy system) was devised. Studies of mental hospitals show that those patients who are unable or unwilling to maintain adequate levels of functioning are closely watched, while patients who function at higher performance levels are freer to move about. Closer surveillance was management's initial reaction in Gouldner's study, as it was in Rushing's study of the psychiatric professions.

Proposition 2. Surveillance will be greater when organizational participants fail to attain minimum performance levels than when they attain these levels.

Rules and surveillance do not always achieve the results desired, however. Stringent behavior controls, because of the costs to participants, may result in reduced participant motivation and productivity, the condition that may have brought about more stringent controls. Indeed, observations indicate that both close surveillance and bureaucratic rules may intensify apathy and decrease motivation and productivity levels. Group relations may thus be caught in a "vicious circle": Group A imposes rules on Group B or engages in closer surveillance because of B's low productivity, only to find B's level of productivity decreasing even further.

Proposition 3. The greater the use of formal rules and direct surveillance, the greater the tendency for participants to lower their production.

This does not mean, however, that productivity will, in fact, always be lower; the *tendency* to restrict output and the *actual restriction* of output are not the same thing. It would seem that if the tendency is there, however, high performance levels become more dependent upon surveillance. Thus, a consequence of bureaucratic rules may be the continuation of surveillance, or even its intensification, since the tendency to perform at low productivity levels may be reinforced when stringent rules are introduced. Surveillance becomes necessary because the rule sender and rule receiver fail to agree.

Proposition 4. After rules have been introduced, surveillance will be greater when the rule receiver and rule maker are not in consensus than when they are in consensus.

Stanton Wheeler finds, for example, that prisoners who exhibit less consensus with staff on norms are those most likely to be closely watched (kept in close custody).

COSTS OF SURVEILLANCE

Surveillance may bring about compliance (i.e., higher productivity), but it may be very costly, e.g., it will require time and effort, or the expense of hiring others to do the job. In an effort to retain high production levels with fewer surveillance costs, surveillance may be replaced with rules. . . .

Proposition 5. The greater the costs of surveillance, the greater the use of formal rules.

If Proposition 5 is true, conditions that consistently increase surveillance costs should be directly related to the use of formal rules, but inversely related to surveillance. The physical distance between organizational members, particularly superiors and their subordinates, is one such condition.

Proposition 6. The greater the physical distance between superiors and subordinates, the less the use of surveillance and the greater the use of formal rules.

Herbert Kaufman's description of the organization of the United States Forest Service suggests the validity of this hypothesis. There are 792 widely scattered ranger districts, each managed by a Ranger, so that no more than three or four inspections by representatives from Washington are possible each year. Consequently, numerous formal rules, such as federal statutes, Presidential proclamations and executive orders, and a 3,000 page *Forest Service Manual* prescribe the Ranger's behavior in detail. Kaufman writes of the *Manual*: "It is difficult to think of anything likely to happen on a Ranger district that will not fall fairly unequivocally into one or another of the hundreds of categories in this *Manual*."

Difficulties in maintaining surveillance over several scattered units and the replacement of surveillance with rules are also shown in Gouldner's description of the practices employed by a safety engineer to assure that different plants engage in proper safety practices. In addition to the costs of time and effort, which increase with physical distance between superior and subordinate, the fewer and shorter personal contacts cause communication failures to increase. Rules may be employed in an effort to prevent such costs.

ORGANIZATIONAL CONFLICT

There are two general types of organizational conflict: (*1*) conflict between the organization and an outside agent and (*2*) conflict between groups within the organization.

More stringent adherence to organizational regulations is a probable internal response to outside threats. Merton's analysis of the "ritualism" of bureaucrats is consistent with this hypothesis. Because of conflict with clients, participants may defend their action and attempt to prevent further conflict by adhering rigidly to organizational rules. Clients may take their complaints to higher officials, who become concerned that clients be treated impartially, so that an even greater adherence to existing rules may be emphasized. Participants may become even more rigid in their relations with clients. Thus, increased rigidity may be an attempt to prevent the costs of the hostility of clients and the wrath of superiors. In general, therefore, as an organization undergoes threat from the outside it will become increasingly rigid. As protection from the threatening agent, new rules may be promulgated and old ones rigidly enforced.

Proposition 7. Demands for precise conformity to organizational rules will be greater during periods of conflict between the organization and an outside agent than during periods of harmony.

Internal conflict may also result in added measures of control. Although there are conflicting relationships that may be terminated by the withdrawal of one party, here only those relationships are considered in which parties are bound to the relationship, either through force or mutual dependence.

Proposition 8. To the extent that neither party withdraws, formal rules will be more extensive when internal organizational conflict exists than when harmony prevails. This proposition is based on the rationale that conflict will ordinarily produce excessive costs for both parties, and that agreed-upon rules will eliminate or reduce such costs.

Research in industrial organizations supports this proposition. Melville Dalton observes that "dysfunctional relations" between two departments in an industrial organization precipitated the process of "delimiting human behavior . . . by means of elaborate regulatory techniques." Clark Kerr's analysis of union-management relationships indicates that conflict and the threat of its eruption in strikes or lock-outs are forces which produce labor-management agreements. He further argues that important cost-reducing functions are performed by these agreements. Because the actions of each party are regulated by rules, there is a firmer basis for predicting the other's actions; so that the costs of uncertainty are removed and management and labor are able to avoid using strategies like strikes or lock-outs, which are so costly to them both. Thus, most disputes are eventually concluded and rules negotiated, because "aggressive conflict is so costly to both sides."

Internal Conflict and Organizational Rigidity in Prisons

Studies of prisons provide excellent examples of the relationship between internal conflict and organizational rigidity. Research workers indicate that the inmate-staff relationship is extremely conflictual: each party views the other with distrust and hate, the inmates want to escape but the staff must keep them in, and the inmate social code strongly opposes cooperation with prison staff. In consequence, inmate conduct is rigidly controlled by formal rules: Whom one may talk to and joke with, and when he may talk and joke, as well as whistle, sing, smoke, and urinate are organizationally defined. Since individual judgment may lead to open conflict, it is curtailed. The detailed regulation of behavior is no less true for prison employees who have close contact with inmates.

It is only with this system of enforced rules that the prison's continuous functioning in the face of mutual hostility is possible. Because the whereabouts and "movement-control" of inmates are assured, opportunities for overt expressions of hostility are limited and disruptive events such as fights, riots, and escapes are reduced. And since virtually all activities must either conform to or violate detailed and explicit rules, deviations and disturbances are relatively easy to detect. Emergency reactions, which are themselves well planned and organized, quickly arise. It is thus the potentiality of latent conflict erupting into costly overt violence, rather than compulsiveness or some other personality trait of prison officials, that makes an elaborate system of enforced rules necessary. The costs of suppressed freedom and enforcing organizational rules are less than the costs of open conflict and violence.

Relation Between Organizational Conflict and Surveillance

Surveillance will usually create higher costs than the use of rules for both the persons engaged in surveillance and the persons who are the objects of it. For the latter, rigid rules are, of course, to some degree punishing and depriving in that they curtail one's freedom of movement, even if they are the product of negotiation, for formal negotiations always involve unsought duties and obligations as well as rights and privileges. But such costs are usually less than the costs of being kept under surveillance. For then one's freedom of movement is more severely restricted, one must constantly monitor his behavior, and there is the implication that one is considered untrustworthy or incompetent. For the party who must exert control, not only is surveillance usually more costly than rules, but conditions of conflict generate additional surveillance costs. Since surveillance necessitates face-to-face contact, one is exposed to the aggressive and hostile response of supervisees. Thus, since negotiated rules are a more attractive alternative than surveillance for both parties, they are more likely to be the organizational response to conflict. And when surveillance is the initial response, there is a tendency for negotiated settlements to arise, as predicted by Proposition 5. Rules, even if supported by a system of "spot checks," are more attractive than a system of continuous checks.

Not all organizational rules are negotiated, however; and in the above discussion, parties have something to negotiate, some kind of reward to exchange; but all organizational relationships are not based on exchange. Criminals, for example, do not enter prison to seek reward from prison officials, but because they are forced to; nor are most prison rules negotiated. Under these circumstances, only constant surveillance can assure compliance. In relationships based on coercion, then, rules themselves are insufficient to elicit compliance.

Proposition 9 (a corollary to Proposition 4). In relationships based on coercion, surveillance will be greater than in relationships based on exchange.

This is not to say, however, that surveillance in these relationships is not accompanied by high costs. Surveillance will always entail the costs of time, effort, and foregoing more attractive alternative activities (including doing nothing). Consequently, the costs of assuring conformity to existing rules may be very high. This is particularly true when organizational rules become excessive in number, as is the case in prisons, where almost constant surveillance of inmates is necessary. In order to reduce surveillance costs, therefore, the staff may relax one rule, in exchange for the inmates' voluntary compliance with another rule.

PARTICIPANT SUPPLY AND DEMAND

. . . . When the organization's potential supply of participants is limited, the participants' autonomy within the organization increases and control structures are weakened. This is clear in [S. M.] Lipset's description of the Saskatchewan socialist government. Although cabinet ministers wanted to remove from office civil servants who opposed the government's policies, they were too dependent upon the technically trained subordinates to terminate their services. Because the supply of qualified persons was limited, the government had to tolerate opposition to its policies, as well as the actual deflection of them. The cost of the civil

servants' withdrawal from the government would have been greater than the cost of their opposition to government policy.

Proposition 11. The smaller the supply of potential organizational participants outside the organization, the fewer the formal
controls over participants within the organization.

This may be called the participant supply proposition. Since
participant demand increases and supply decreases when participant skill and ability rise, organizations employing highly skilled
and technically trained participants must be careful not to inhibit
participant autonomy; otherwise, they risk losing participants to
organizations with less restrictive control structures.

Proposition 12 (corollary to Propositions 10 and 11). An increase in the organizational skill structure will be accompanied by
a decrease in the use of formal rules and surveillance to control
conduct.

SIZE AND STRUCTURAL DIFFERENTIATION

In small organizations, control is rather easily achieved through
informal face-to-face relationships. Surveillance and evaluation
procedures are often by-products of contact between superiors and
subordinates which the dictates of day-to-day work make necessary. Such procedures are casual and informal, and special structures such as formal supervisory positions and formally stated
rules are unnecessary. Since little extra effort and time are required, and because supervisees are not formally confronted with
being observed and evaluated, costs to both supervisors and supervisees are minimal.

With an increase in organizational size and the "span of control," however, the frequency and intensity of contact between
superiors and subordinates in day-to-day activities decrease. If
supervisors are to continue their constant informal surveillance,
additional time and effort must be invested in organizational affairs. A less costly alternative may be available, however, if formal surveillance procedures and rules standardizing participant
conduct are instituted.

Proposition 13. With an increase in organizational size, formal
surveillance and formal rules will increase relative to informal
surveillance.

One description of the historical growth of hospitals supports
this hypothesis. When hospitals were small and many hospital
jobs relatively simple, it was through the direct supervision of
directors of nursing and hospital administrators that control and
coordination of most activities were assured. With increased size
and job complexity, however, this practice became too costly, so

that the formalization of relationships with rules and regulations took place. Formal channels of communication and procedures replaced face-to-face contact and direct supervisory control, and their importance in resolving communication and coordination increased accordingly.

As an organization grows, formal surveillance structures may take the form of full-time supervisory positions, the incumbents of which are employed with the sole purpose of supervising and evaluating participant conduct; or a formal system of periodic checks may be involved. In both cases, supervisees as well as the organization incur additional costs. Formal surveillance may suggest to supervisees that their competence is being questioned; it may also entail additional efforts toward monitoring their own behavior. Such costs may account for the observed relationships between organization size and participant dissatisfaction with supervision. In any case, adding supervisory positions entails additional costs for the organization. The anticipation of such costs may deter further organizational growth.

Note that Proposition 13 merely states that with an increase in size, both formal surveillance and formal rules will increase *relative to informal surveillance*. The relative difference between formal surveillance and formal rules with increasing organizational size is not mentioned. It is suggested, however, that since formal rules are less costly than formal surveillance, with increasing organizational growth, they will increasingly replace surveillance structures.

Proposition 14. As an organization grows, rules and regulations will increasingly replace direct surveillance as methods of organizational control.

The importance of eliciting standardized behavior in large organizations in the absence of direct surveillance has been noted by Peter Blau.

It is difficult to generalize about the effects of size unless the effects of structural differentiation and organizational complexity are also considered. Increases in size are usually accompanied by new jobs and specialties, or completely new units, such as additional plants. A greater variety of specialties and units will lead to additional problems of conflict, communication, and coordination too numerous for face-to-face contacts to resolve. Consequently, basic changes in the pattern of formal organization may be required.

Proposition 15. As an organization undergoes increasing structural differentiation, rules and regulations will increasingly replace direct surveillance as methods of organizational control.

Thus, to the extent that increases in size and structural differentiation are related, the costs of conflict and coordination are compounded, and the relationship between increased size and formal rules should be particularly strong. In cases where size and structural differentiation are not associated, results predicted in Propositions 14 and 15 might not occur. While a positive correlation between the two variables is usually assumed, the extent to which this is actually true has only begun to be investigated. . . .

In this paper an attempt has been made to formulate a series of propositions that is comparative in scope. The propositions deal with the relationship between surveillance and organizational rules, and with the relationship between these two variables and variables such as size, physical distance, participant supply and demand, and organizational conflict. Since these variables cut across specific types of organizations, the propositions should be equally valid for organizations of all types. The ultimate validity of each proposition must, of course, await comparative empirical research to test the propositions in question.

NOTES AND QUESTIONS

1. Does Rushing's article provide any basis for reconsidering whether Kaufman's description of the forest ranger rings true? Or does Kaufman's data challenge the validity of some or all of Rushing's propositions? Do Rushing's propositions shed any light on why Schwartz's two types of settlement developed different legal structures? *See* Schwartz, Reading 54, at 509, *supra*.

2. Under what conditions is it dysfunctional to increase surveillance, or to increase the number and scope of formal rules? Can one generalize? Consider the following:

(a) a camp for children uses the "buddy" system during swimming hours. Each child is assigned a partner. A lifeguard is stationed on the beach. Periodically, he calls for a show of hands. Each child must then find his "buddy" and the two clasp hands and raise them so that the guard can see them. This way the lifeguard can see immediately if any child is missing;

(b) General Motors formalizes its internal procedures for handling dealer complaints. *See* p. 170, *supra*;

(c) recall the description of the prison system in Sykes, Reading 45, at 441, *supra*, and the impact and effect of the elements of surveillance and structured rules;

(d) upper courts control lower courts, but they use *no* surveillance, review is on written records alone, and only
certain rules of conduct are formalized and made amenable to control by the higher court.

In which of these cases would *less* surveillance (or more) be
desirable? In which would *less* structured rules (or more) be
desirable?

3. Rushing uses a cost-benefit model of human behavior, an
approach identified with the social theories of George C. Homans,
a sociologist at Harvard University. (Compare the behavioral
assumptions underlying Buchanan & Tullock, Reading 6, at 56,
supra, and Fisher & Fairbanks, Reading 8, at 76, *supra.*) Do Rushing and Homans assert that individuals who hold positions in the
legal system actually make cost-benefit calculations in most instances or only that such a model reflects patterns of behavior
over time? More specifically, what would Rushing posit as a
consequence if our system were structured so that judicial inspectors checked the work of judges both as to quantity and quality, through various kinds of surveillance? Would judges, finding
their work less fulfilling, decide to slack off as to quantity and
quality? Or would they respond positively to the fear or threat
posed by inspection?

4. If rules and surveillance carry high costs in terms of the
morale of an organization's personnel, how can the main office
of an agency in Washington, D.C., or a state capital induce its
personnel in the field to carry out its policies in a uniform way?

5. Supreme Court decisions have made it clear that a city
may not prohibit one from handing out political leaflets on the
streets merely because those receiving them drop them and litter
the streets. Such an application of anti-littering ordinances is an
unconstitutional abridgment of the free speech guarantees of the
First Amendment. In 1965, members of the Queens [N.Y.] Committee to End the War in Vietnam were given summonses by a
police officer for distributing political leaflets at the exits of the
Forest Hills Stadium. The section of the Administrative Code
of New York City under which they were charged literally prohibited only distribution of "business or commercial leaflets."
The arresting officer picked up about 200 leaflets that had fallen
to the ground when people refused to accept them. The New
York District Attorney's office decided to prosecute. The trial
judge found the defendants guilty and imposed a small fine. He
said that "we cannot allow the Borough of Queens to be buried."
He explained that he would not follow the Supreme Court deci-

sions on free speech because that Court had "not considered the problem of municipal manners in large cities." The case was appealed by the New York Civil Liberties Union. The appellate court reversed the conviction in a three-sentence opinion. People v. Katz, 52 Misc. 2d 546, 275 N.Y.S.2d 996 (Sup. Ct. 1966). The case was one of at least eighteen prosecutions during 1965 and 1966, for distributing anti-war literature on the streets of New York City. *See, e.g.,* People v. Katz, 21 N.Y.2d 132, 233 N.E.2d 845 (1967); People v. Krebs, 54 Misc. 2d 576, 282 N.Y.S.2d 996 (N.Y.C. Crim. Ct. 1967); People v. Kaufman, 47 Misc. 2d 1074, 264 N.Y.S.2d 81 (N.Y.C. Crim. Ct. 1965). In three other cases in New York City, the defendants had placed anti-war bumper stickers or signs in or on their automobiles which they had driven through or parked in city parks. They were given summonses for advertising in a public park or on a parkway. The New York City traffic regulation in question bans business or advertising signs on cars in parks or on parkways; if applied to political messages, the regulation would be unconstitutional. The district attorney's office prosecuted in all three cases but trial courts dismissed the charges.

In all of these cases, the officer who issued the summons and a representative of the prosecutor's office who brought the cases to court violated relatively clear rules governing how they should have responded to political speech. Some trial judges did too. The activity of the NYCLU prompted action in court which declared the conduct of the police and prosecutors improper and of no legal effect; in cities other than New York where civil liberties organizations are not as active, the small fines imposed as compared to the costs of appeals have meant that unconstitutional convictions have remained undisturbed.

a. The Supreme Court of the United States creates rules concerning limitations on free speech activity, and appellate courts, trial courts, prosecutors and superiors on police forces are supposed to exercise surveillance over police officers who deal with the public to see that they do not violate these rules. In New York City, the rules were not honored by the police or the prosecutor. On the intervention of a private organization, the NYCLU induced the surveillance system to remove some of the consequences of noncompliance with the free speech rules. What ideas, if any, do Kaufman, Thompson and Rushing offer about how police and prosecutors could be induced to obey the law in the free speech area more often or about the likely costs of attempts to induce such compliance on their part? *See* Skolnick, Reading 106, at 900, *infra.*

b. There are many instances where control mechanisms such as appeals or private lawsuits for abuse of the powers of governmental position are ineffective as a practical matter. In some of these instances private sanctions do not exercise much control either, since the people who might be affected by noncompliance with the rules by public officials are not members of groups with much political power. Nonetheless, many, if not most, policemen, prosecutors, administrators and judges follow what they understand to be the rules announced by legislatures and courts most of the time if not always. How can we explain this?

D. ROLE THEORY, THE ACTORS IN THE LEGAL SYSTEM AND MAINTENANCE OF THE SYSTEM

1. Introduction

Sociologists typically deal with relationships between social units such as the family, the group, complex organizations with bureaucratic structures, the economy, and the total societies of nations or regions. Psychologists typically deal with individual personalities. What is the relationship between the individual, with all of his personality characteristics, and the various social units? Theorists use the concept of "role" to describe and explain the link between individuals and larger social groupings. A role is a pattern for conduct in a particular social position. There is a pattern of appropriate conduct for one who has the status of father, student, doctor of medicine, secretary, minister of a church, elder statesman in an organization and so on. These patterns are not a precise job description covering all possible contingencies, and so an individual may play his part in a fashion that reflects his personality. Even in performing a famous play by a great playwright where all of the parts are defined by tradition, an actor has wide opportunity to make the role "his."

Roles tend to be defined so that the important functions of a social organization are served; they serve to organize the division of labor. Some roles are defined more precisely and more formally than others. Formal rules, which may or may not come from the legal system, tell those who hold certain positions what they are to do or what they should not do. However, the process of role definition is typically informal. For example, suppose a young man with a law degree and two years' experience in law practice is appointed an assistant professor of law at a major university. How does he discover how to play this role? There are some very formal rules in state statutes, university regulations and his employment contract. His dean or senior colleagues may tell him of customs in the law school that are important and usually followed; implicit in such friendly advice is a warning that there are sanctions which will be imposed if he disappoints the expectations of his colleagues. He will have to discover some customs for himself. For example, at lunch his senior colleagues may criticize another law faculty member for certain conduct and praise another for different conduct. The cues may be more subtle, and he may have to discover some contours of his role by observing a disapproving expression on the faces of his important senior colleagues, assuming that he can discover who his important senior colleagues are. Of course, other contours of his role will be defined by students, secretaries or even his wife and parents. Finally, the newly-appointed assistant professor has his own concept, probably only partially defined, of his role formed by his experiences as a student, by reflection about the situation in light of the values he holds, or even by reading novels. Of course, different people will respond differently to these cues. Some young professors seek to please "the establishment." Some want to curry favor with their students. Some take a fiercely independent stance, marching to their own drum. Some seem to delight in prompting the disapproval of colleagues. We can describe these behaviors and say that each is a way of playing the role of assistant professor of law. Some personalities tend toward one style of performance, some towards another.

A person usually plays many roles at one time. For example, our newly-appointed assistant professor may find himself in the roles of professor, husband, father, son, member of a professional committee outside of the university, member of the County Executive Committee of the Republican Party and member of a city unit of the Urban League. The performance of one role may affect the performance of another. A law professor's teaching and research may be aided by insights gained in political activity, or it may be hindered if the political activity takes too much time. He may face problems of role strain. His professorial role may call for objectivity in dealing with students; his role as member of a family may call for favoritism toward his brother who is a law student. His professional role may call for a certain style of research; his membership on a Presidential task force may demand another; his political values perhaps still another.

The idea of "role" seems to reflect common sense. Yet it is not a precise concept. We talked of the role of a professor, but is there such a thing? Men of widely different background and personality get these jobs. Role theory itself recognizes that each occupant of the professorial role will be part of a different role-set. That is, the demands of family, friends and nonprofessorial associations will differ for each. Moreover, what is the appropriate way of looking at a role? Can we talk meaningfully about the role of a professor, or must we be more specific and talk of the roles of full, associate and assistant professors? of professors of law and of professors of sociology? of conservative institutionally-oriented professors? of radical nonconformist professors? In short, are the differences more important than the similarities so that there is no one role of professor, father and the like? This is a question to keep in mind in considering the materials in this section. Another overriding question is how one discovers and describes a particular role. Clearly, this is a question of fact, not something one can deduce from formal rules or a conventional definition of a particular social status.

Several distinct ideas are hidden within the concept of role. First, there are the expectations of members of the society or of significant role definers in the society about the rights and obligations of a particular position. For example, is it improper— out of role—for the president of a state university to run for the United States Senate while still holding office as university president? Are we interested in what a state assemblyman may think, what most people in the state may think, or what other university presidents may think? In brief, it may be important to specify *who* is defining the boundaries of a role, whether and why that definition is legitimate, and the importance that has been assigned to the definition. Second, there is an individual's own conception of his privileges and duties with regard to a position. A university president might think it proper to take public stands on political questions and to support candidates for political office openly; others might disagree. Third, there is a person's actual performance in a role. Finally, one can distinguish between legitimate and illegitimate role definers. A university professor might accept a vote of his department on the discretion of professors to conduct certain kinds of research; he might object vigorously if the state legislature attempted to adopt the same policy as a limit on his role as researcher. For an excellent discussion of these and other related problems, *see* Stanton Wheeler, "The Structure of Formally Organized Socialization Settings," in Brim & Wheeler, *Socialization After Childhood* (John Wiley 1966).

Role conflict is a term often used to refer to conflicting demands of two or more social statuses. A judge called upon to sentence his own son faces one set of expectations about the behavior of judges and another about the behavior of fathers. But role conflict can also come from inconsistency in expectations held by two different groups of role definers. Or, one group can hold inconsistent expectations, demanding both conduct *A* and conduct *B* even though *A* and *B* cannot both be performed.

See Derek Pugh, "Role Activation Conflict: A Study of Industrial Inspection," 31 *American Sociological Review* 835 (1966).

In this section we will consider efforts to explain the conduct of actors in the legal system in terms of role theory. Most of the materials expressly make use of role theory, but some deal with the same issues without explicitly talking in terms of "role," "role-set" and the like. One could explain the conduct of legislators, lawyers, policemen and the other actors in terms of formal rules guiding their conduct, but most would agree that this is, at best, a partial explanation. One could explain conduct in terms of personality, bias and interest of these actors, but this, too, is only a partial explanation. Does role theory, taken together with rules and personal factors, provide an adequate explanation?

2. Specific Roles of the Actors in the Legal System
a. The role of the judge

96. Dissenting Blocs on the Warren Court: A Study in Judicial Role Behavior

JOEL B. GROSSMAN*

30 JOURNAL OF POLITICS 1068 (1968)

It is impossible to understand fully the work of the Supreme Court and similar appellate bodies without focussing on the crucial role of the individual justice. Supreme Court decisions are the products of the constant and forceful interaction of judicial minds and personalities, of precedents and traditions of the past and perceptions of the future, and of the conflicts and reinforcements which develop in its relationship to other political institutions. Justices are products of their environment, past and present, and it is a large part of their task to apply the values derived from these experiences to resolving cases before them.

Contemporary students of the Court have articulated a number of techniques for studying the decision-making process. All are based on the assumption that the values and attitudes of individual justices are crucial determinants of decisional behavior, but each differs in its particular emphasis on the precise role which attitudes, values, or the backgrounds of the justices play in arriving at both individual and collegial determinations. In fact, the major disagreements among contemporary scholars seems to be over the relative importance of one or another component, rather than on the existence—or lack—of these components.

The personal values of the justices play an undeniably important role in the decision-making process, but to "explain" Su-

---

* Professor of Political Science, University of Wisconsin. Copyright © 1968, Journal of Politics. Reprinted by permission. This excerpt is based on an earlier unpublished version and differs slightly from the article as printed.

preme Court decisions exclusively in such terms vastly oversimplifies a complex process. Such a rigid view ignores both the
complex institutional framework in which the justices operate
and the process by which certain values are internalized, deemed
appropriate for judicial expression, and articulated in formal
opinions. Our concern must be not only for the dominant values
of the justices, but *how* and *why* particular values produce identifiable behavior patterns.

As a means of guiding research toward these goals, the concept
of role appears to be particularly promising. Although it has not
been widely used by judicial scholars, it has yielded excellent
results in non-judicial studies. One of its great strengths is its
flexibility and sensitivity toward the more subtle dimensions of
human behavior. Another strength (to some a deficiency) may
be that role concepts do not comprehend any particular methodology, technique, or type of empirical data in order to be effectively used. It is an ordering concept which can be serviced by
many techniques. Finally, it is particularly appropriate for use
in judicial research because it highlights the relationships between an individual justice and his environment in the *environmental* context. . . .

The concept of role is as old as man, and was probably conveyed
to social scientists through its use in drama. In its theatrical
context, the concept of role is probably common knowledge. But
its inherent ambiguity may not be widely recognized. The concept of role is used to refer to a "part" or "position" which an
actor plays. Used in this way, the actions to be taken and the
words to be spoken are the product of the dramatist. It is Shake-
speare's "Othello" or Shaw's "Major Barbara." But as most people recognize, the author is not the whole show. The actor, or
role-player, adds his own personality and interpretation to the
part; thus, Olivier's "Hamlet" or Julie Andrews' "Eliza Doolit-
tle" are not necessarily identical with the author's expectations.
The same is true in other settings; most social and political roles
are amalgams of formal rules, traditions, and the not inconsid-
erable contribution of the role-player himself. The degree to
which each of these factors contributes to the actual behavior of
the role occupant is an empirical question.

Contemporary definitions of "role" can be divided into three
categories: Those which define roles as expectations of behavior
prescribed by elements of the society (either formal or informal);
those which use the term essentially to describe the role-player's
perceptions of these expectations; and those which use the term
to describe actual behavior patterns. All of these definitions share
the concept of expectation, although they often do not define the

sources of expectation very clearly. Furthermore, they all operate on the assumption that the concept of role cannot be meaningfully applied to any individual, but to one who occupies a particular "position" in the social or political order. Role is optimally a relational concept in that it does not merely describe a set order of events, or an inflexible constellation of values. Rather it describes a relationship between an individual and the milieu in which he operates, a relationship which at various times produces different results. This is not to say that role theory does not comprehend identifiable regularities or patterns of behavior. But in exploring these patterns, the role theorist is cautioned to be unusually sensitive to the subtleties which mark all such human relationships. And it is particularly useful in evaluating the plausibility of results obtained by other methods.

The concept of "role" is here defined as the general or specific expectations of proper behavior associated with the position of Supreme Court justice, and the concept of "role behavior" is here defined as those patterns of activity which reflect a justice's perceptions of the *proper* role of a Supreme Court justice, including his adjustment of personal values and perceived role expectations. Behavior which is substantially incongruous with the role definition may be referred to as deviant role behavior.

The sources of role definers or role expectations of Supreme Court justices are many; they include the general public, the political world; the history and traditions of the Court, and perhaps most important, the articulate portions of the bench and bar, whose views are communicated to the incumbent justices in a variety of ways. As much as anyone, the latter can be said to form the Court's "constituency," from whom cues *may* be most appropriate and most heeded. Of course, not all cues come from these sources; and not all judges hold them in equal favor. The extent to which these groups actually operate as articulators of role definitions is an empirical question; here we can only posit the existence of such a relationship, and examine its accuracy.

Likewise, there is preciously little empirical data supporting the notion that there is one particular constellation of expectations which constitutes *the* Supreme Court role. There is, however, considerable qualitative and interpretive writing—by judges, lawyers, professors, and journalists—which has sought to capture the essence of the judicial role. From these we can hypothesize that the consensus judicial role, the role which seems to have acquired a sort of institutional status, consists of an amalgam of four general components: (1) expectations about the proper function of the Supreme Court in the American social, political, and legal systems; (2) expectations that the judges share in the foundation values of the society they serve; (3) expectations about the role of law in a democratic society; (4) expectations about the external and internal behavior of the justices. If these components are an accurate summary, then it is clear that the expected role of Supreme Court Justice contains prescriptions for both thought and action which are analytically separate, but closely interrelated. . . .

97. Role Theory and the Supreme Court

DOROTHY B. JAMES*

30 THE JOURNAL OF POLITICS 160 (1968)

A major problem facing those who analyze the Supreme Court involves the question of whether the decision processes are those of the Court as an institution or of individuals on it. How far does the Court form the Justice's conception of his role, and how far is that conception formed by his previous experience and opinions? To what degree are his opinions the product of the institutional setting and to what degree are they the product of prior interests? . . .

Despite an increasing degree of sophistication, the analytical techniques and conceptual tools applied to date leave unanswered questions concerning the ways in which personal attitudes influence legal interpretation and action, and what conditions their effect. Specifically, they do not provide an adequate way of describing and identifying institutional factors in judicial attitudes. Obviously a tool of analysis is needed which will set the balance between structural and behavioral factors in a manner which makes more clear how and under what conditions personal attitudes may influence judicial decisions. . . .

Robert Merton . . . described each social status as involving "an array of associated roles," which he termed "role-set."[3] More recently, Nadel has suggested that these associated roles or attributes which make up any given role are not all equivalent. He distinguished three types:[4] lowest in the hierarchy were those attributes which were peripheral to the role so that their performance might be considered optional, or permit alternatives; second were those which were sufficiently relevant to the role so that their absence or variation left it imperfect or incomplete; finally, the pivotal attributes were those on which "the role norm has zero tolerance."

---

* Professor, Lehman College, C.U.N.Y. Copyright © 1968 Journal of Politics. Reprinted by permission.

[3] Robert K. Merton, *Social Theory and Social Structure* (Glencoe, Illinois: The Free Press, 1959), p. 369.

[4] S. F. Nadel, *The Theory of Social Structure* (Glencoe, Illinois: The Free Press, 1962), pp. 31, 32.

This theoretical approach relates directly to analysis of the decision processes of the Supreme Court. If the concept of status and role is a valid analytic tool under the circumstances, we should find that the development of an individual's judicial philosophy entails three aspects: First, there will be an invarying inclusion in his philosophy of all "pivotal" role attributes. Here structural factors will be particularly important as the institutional setting itself largely determines which those pivotal attributes may be. Therefore, Justices holding widely different governmental philosophies will show little variation in their perception and recognition of these norms. On pivotal role attributes there will be little leeway for individual variation.

Second, there will be an inclusion in his philosophy of "relevant" role attributes. Here structural factors are not as controlling. Therefore, there is more leeway for individual differences. The norms are structured by the institution, and as such must be perceived as relevant for the Court. However, conflicting norms may also be structured by the institutional setting or the norm-definition may be unclear. This conflict or ambiguity permits individual choice which is likely to be based on personal factors such as a governmental philosophy or personal biases.

Finally, an individual's judicial philosophy will include "peripheral attributes" which may be optional or permit of alternatives. Here there is wide leeway for individual differences of perception and recognition as structural factors have little relevance.

The value of this particular framework for analysis of the Supreme Court is its ability to bridge the dichotomy between structural and behavioral elements. It permits one to deal with the internal ranking within a judicial philosophy to discover its structure and the types of variables which control its elements. In this way, a set of structural and behavioral elements can be organized to specific aspects of the judicial role set. In this paper it has been used in two case studies.

Research Design:

In a study of role and status of Supreme Court Justices, it is particularly appropriate to consider Justices appointed by Franklin Delano Roosevelt. Prior to their appointment, these men had been active, vocal supporters of the New Deal. They had experienced the frustration of their legislative goals by a scant majority of Justices, and had seen the crisis with the "nine old men" come to a head in President Roosevelt's 1937 court-packing plan, when the role of the Court and the individual Justice had been a mat-

ter of national concern. Their involvement thus invited the development of explicit judicial philosophies prior to their accession to the Court.

Of the eight Roosevelt appointees, two were selected for
detailed analysis, Robert H. Jackson and William O. Douglas.[6]
They stood at opposite sides of the spectrum of thought on the
Supreme Court of their day. Justice Jackson represented the
Court's conservative wing. He was a "moderate liberal" toward
civil liberty claims, and a "moderate conservative" in business
regulation and labor cases. Justice Douglas represented the liberal wing. His general position on the Court was "left-liberal"
toward civil liberty claims, business regulation, and labor cases.

The Supreme Court's Function:

The function performed by the Supreme Court in the American system of government provides the role of a Justice with
several major attributes. One such list of attributes might include: the maintaining of an orderly judicial process, acting as
an umpire of the federal system, maintaining judicial independence, exercising judicial self-restraint, and avoiding extra-judicial
activity with partisan or policy implications. Each of these major
attributes involves an array of associated aspects. Thus, maintenance of an orderly judicial process includes three aspects: the
Court's supervisory function over the federal court system, its
binding custom of giving opinions only in cases or controversies,
and its adherence to precedent. Judicial independence requires
the exercise of judicial review to protect the court system against
interference from states, military tribunals, plaintiffs, lawyers, and
the mass media of communication, especially the press. Self-restraint may be practiced by the judiciary in relation to states
and localities as well as in relation to the President, Congress and
administrative bodies.

These are relevant categories of analysis as they flow from
structural attributes of American politics. They are often con-

---

[6] The sources of information relied on for this study were primarily the
words of the Justices themselves. All of the unpublished speeches of the
two Justices were read for relevant material. They are available at the
United States Supreme Court Building in Washington, D. C. The published
works of the Justices were also consulted, as were their opinions in each
volume of the *United States Reports* during the period that they served together on the bench. This spanned volumes 314 to 347. On Monday, March
23, 1964, Justice Douglas was personally interviewed in his chambers at the
Supreme Court Building. Secondary material was also used. It included
biographies of the Justices and their colleagues and contemporaries, as well
as interpretations of their work. In the case of Justice Jackson, it included
memorial tributes as well.

sidered desirable and important norms in the Court's behavior,
yet they are not all equally relevant. Some are so essential to
the Court's role that their omission would completely negate the
concept of a Supreme Court as a judiciary and as one of the
three branches of our national government. Since these are essential to the institutional setting, they might be considered "pivotal" role attributes. Other attributes may be desirable norms
in the behavior of the Court, but they may also conflict with
other desirable norms, or have an ambiguous definition. In that
case there is more leeway for individual differences of perception, so the attribute might be considered "relevant." Finally,
some are optional or "peripheral," permitting alternative solutions which may depend heavily on personal factors of individual
perception and preference. In the following pages each role attribute will be assigned a tentative rank (pivotal, relevant, or
peripheral); then the decisions and opinions of Justices Douglas
and Jackson will be analyzed, leading to a summary on the probable rank for the particular role attribute of a Supreme Court
Justice.

Maintenance of an Orderly Judicial Process:

Maintenance of an orderly judicial process entails several aspects: supervising the federal court system, giving opinions only
in cases or controversies, and adhering to precedent. The first
aspect of this major attribute of the Justice's role is his responsibility for supervision of the federal court system. The Supreme
Court was given this responsibility by the First Judiciary Act of
1789. Further acts of Congress dealt with details of the system,
demonstrating a continuous acceptance of the need for Supreme
Court responsibility for supervision of the federal court system.
This is so essential to assure regularity of the federal law that it
would seem likely that it is a "pivotal" role attribute. Without
this function the Court can hardly fulfill its institutional responsibilities as the apex of the federal court system. We would therefore expect to find it accepted as a controlling norm by Justices
with widely divergent governmental philosophies.

Both Robert Jackson and William Douglas accepted completely
the necessity for Supreme Court supervision over the federal court
system. It was so much a constitutional "given" for Justice Jackson that he did not explicitly discuss it. He accepted it implicitly
and acted upon it, assuming it to be a necessary aspect of the
Court's function. Justice Douglas was more explicit in favoring
supervision by the Supreme Court over lower federal courts and
over federal questions rising in state courts.

The second aspect of the Court's role in maintaining an orderly judicial process is the binding custom of giving opinions only in cases or controversies in a bona fide law suit. Even where *obiter dicta* are given they must be within the context of a decision on a specific case or controversy. Advisory opinions would require an added burden on the Court's time, necessitate advice without the development of a body of evidence, and might require change once a genuine case or controversy with its individual fact structure developed. Moreover, the loss to the Court's prestige if its opinion were not followed is obvious. The case method prevents review from becoming precipitate and awaits the development of a body of evidence illuminating the actual working of the laws in question. Thus this too would seem likely as a "pivotal" role attribute, for it flows necessarily from the institutional setting.

Robert Jackson completely accepted the Supreme Court's custom of giving opinions only in cases or controversies. Justice Douglas was also forced to accept the necessity of having the Supreme Court restrict itself to deciding only cases or controversies, but he did so with greater reluctance than Justice Jackson. While he agreed that the limitation was necessary, he was unhappy with the results, and longed for a broader construction of what was entailed in the formula of case or controversy. He believed that the Court had retreated [to] the rubric of "political questions" in areas where the average person had no remedy but the judicial one.

The third aspect of maintenance of an orderly judicial process is adherence to precedent. The Supreme Court has accepted this as an important norm as it is necessary to maintain regularity of the law. However, *stare decisis* is not an absolute compulsion for the Court. Precedents are sometimes overturned, often with dramatic results as in the school integration and legislative redistricting decisions. The difficulty here is that predictability may be the essence of the law, but an unchanging law may also be a straight jacket restricting society's development. Here, therefore, is an area of conflicting norms which permit of individual variations in perception and recognition. The general practice is to adhere to precedent unless there is some compelling reason to overrule it. It might therefore be considered a "relevant" but not pivotal role attribute.

The conflicting norms of predictability and flexibility require Justices to make personal choices on the desirability of adherence to precedent. For this reason, an individual's viewpoint may alter considerably during his lifetime depending on the institution with which he is affiliated, for his institutional setting and personal experience help him to see one or the other norm as of greater significance. This conflict is mirrored in Robert Jackson's changing viewpoint on the importance of adherence to precedent.

In his earliest speech he expressed concern for stability and continuity in the law reached through adherence to previous decisions. As Solicitor General he reevaluated that preference when the Supreme Court invalidated key pieces of New Deal legislation relying primarily on post-civil war doctrines which had contradicted earlier precedents. He urged a return to the words of the Constitution rather than what had been said by succeeding generations of Justices about it. When the trend of Court decisions changed late in 1937, he was in the forefront of those who supported the reversal, and became an apologist for it. The dilemma was sharpened for him once he became a Justice and had to deal with it on a daily basis. It was clear that he did not wish to revert to his earlier position advocating strict adherence to precedent. At the same time, he could not advocate overthrowing precedent as freely as he had from the executive branch. He saw the Court's role on adherence to precedent as flexible, but felt that where an established law was overruled, it should be done "only as a matter of deliberate policy." . . .

Robert Jackson's solution for the dilemma, then, was an adherence to precedent as far as consistent with the purpose of the Constitution to create a working government for each generation. Where precedent could not be followed without harm to the system, he advocated a clear, careful explanation on the part of Justices for their reversal: "We need not be slaves to a formula but unless we can point out a rational way of reaching our conclusions they can only be accepted as resting on intuition or predilection."

Since material is not available to trace the development of William Douglas' views, we must consider solely what he said during his service on the Court.[21] His earliest speech on the subject outlined a position favoring flexibility over predictability. As time passed, he took an increasingly strong position in regard to the need for flexibility in constitutional law, on the ground that a judge must reject the "gloss" which his predecessors put on the Constitution, if he believes that it does violence to the Constitution's spirit, for the judge is sworn to uphold the document, not the opinions of his predecessors. He maintained that "the law

---

[21] His personal files contain no material from the period before he became an Associate Justice, and his numerous publications prior to that time have no reference to the judicial role. Despite an active political career prior to becoming an Associate Justice, he had developed no explicit judicial philosophy. In a personal interview on March 23, 1964, he said that he had not had time to reflect upon these points prior to his accession to the Court.

will always teem with uncertainty." As he saw it, the law but mirrored the compromises which are an essential element in the legal process of a democracy.

On the level of daily affairs he valued *stare decisis* as a means to provide uniformity and stability, and to prevent legal whim or caprice. Nevertheless, he reasserted the value of change in preference to letting the Constitution freeze into a pattern set by a past generation which might carry overtones hostile to later generations. The novel aspect of his outlook was his suggestion that courts should reexamine their own doctrines, checking to see if they were gradually overruling cases through distinguishing precedents. He claimed that: "It is this gradual process of erosion of constitutional doctrine that has the truly unsettling effect."

While flexibility was clearly preferable to the Justice, there was one area where he would restrict experimentation—the field of civil liberties. Here he maintained that adjustment to majority preferences was intolerable.

In summary, both supervision over the federal court system and the custom of giving opinions in cases or controversies are necessary aspects of the Court's function in maintaining an orderly judicial process. They are inherent in the institutional setting and might therefore be considered "pivotal" role attributes for each Justice. That they are pivotal may be seen by the cases of Justice Jackson and Douglas. Both men accepted them as necessary for the Court's function. Even though Justice Douglas preferred a broad interpretation of "case" or "controversy," he was forced to accept it as a necessary norm.

The structure of our legal system makes adherence to precedent a "relevant" but not "pivotal" attribute of the Justice's role, for it conflicts with another relevant norm, flexibility in the law. Therefore, there is room for individual differences in perception. The choice an individual makes between these two attributes will depend on his experience and his institutional and historical vantage point. Thus, as a young lawyer, Robert Jackson was firmly in favor of strict adherence to precedent; as a member of the New Deal he took a different position; and as a Justice he reached a synthesis entailing adherence to precedent as far as consistent with an effective government and careful explanation of any reversals of this doctrine. Justice Douglas entered the Court with adherence to precedent at a very low level of his scale of values. Over time he became even more firmly convinced that *stare decisis* had no place in constitutional law, and that the Court should even overrule all relevant decisions at the fall of a landmark decision.

Umpire of the Federal System:

The second major attribute of the Justice's role involves the Supreme Court's function as umpire of the federal system. The Court serves as an arbiter to prevent confrontation between the nation and the states. This aspect of the Court's function must be perceived by each Justice because of the structure of our federal legal system. However, it cannot easily be considered a "pivotal" role attribute since the meaning of "umpire of the federal system" is not clearly defined. The Court must balance the interests involved—but how; using what criteria? The fluid nature of this role attribute forces each individual Justice to make his own choice as to the criteria which the Court will apply. Therefore, this appears to be a "relevant" attribute. Although it is recognized as necessary, it allows great leeway for individual variation in perception of its meaning.

One aspect of the problem which especially touched the Court was the deference it should show decisions of state supreme courts. The Supreme Court has traditionally refused to review judgments of state courts which rest on adequate and independent grounds of state law. Since the Court refrains from entering into questions of state law, and only reviews federal questions, the Court must know whether state or federal law controlled the judgment in each case. In cases where that was not clear, Justice Jackson held that: "It seems consistent with the respect due the highest courts of the states of the Union that they be asked rather than told what they have intended." This implied an assumption on his part of the rationality of state supreme courts and their decision making process.

Justice Douglas concurred in the belief that the Supreme Court should be our referee in the federal system, but in balancing the different interests involved, the criteria he used were very different from those used by Robert Jackson. Invariably he set the balance in favor of federal rights. On the question of what degree of deference should be shown state supreme court decisions, he emphasized the need to protect federal rights against state intrusion. He therefore dissented from the majority opinion written by Justice Jackson in the case just cited. . . .

[W]hile both Justices agreed that the United States Supreme Court must function as an umpire of the federal system, they disagreed fundamentally on the criteria used. Since this particular aspect of the Justice's role is not clearly defined, each man could fall back on his own basic philosophy of government to give meaning to the role. The institutional setting made the aspect necessary, but personal factors influenced perception of its nature.

Thus it may be considered a "relevant" role attribute. Justice Jackson preferred a balance which would give adequate power to the states in dealing with purely local problems, and to the nation in dealing with questions of national scope. He would, then, permit great freedom to states in regulating those areas which the Constitution had placed squarely in their domain, such as divorce, libel or education. However, in questions relating to areas which the Constitution had given to the national government, such as interstate commerce or the contract clause, he believed that the Court should balance conflicts between state and nation in a manner which left wide leeway for national power. His basic philosophy of government has been summarized by one commentator as a desire to "concede to every element in the political system its appropriate functions—and fix upon it the responsibility for discharging them."[45] Yet the whole was meant to function too, therefore, reciprocity was essential. As the states were important elements in the political system, he was anxious to have them function well, but in a manner which would contribute to the smooth working of the entire American political system. He found the Supreme Court generally well designed to strike this balance between national and state authority.

Individual civil rights were of paramount importance in Justice Douglas' governmental philosophy. For him the Supreme Court's function as umpire of the federal system required protection of the federal system against states' rights. He viewed as the essence of democratic government the fact that individuals are protected in their rights to free speech, worship, and assembly, freedom of opportunity, the sanctity of the ballot, protection from unreasonable searches and seizures, the right of jury trial, and all the procedural rights of the first ten Amendments. Of all the rights, he held due process and freedom of speech most dear. In fact, he raised freedom of speech to almost the level of an absolute. And because individual freedom stood at the apex of his value system, he was bound to emphasize federal power over that of the states. He wrote that:

> The need has been, and is, to raise the level of law and administration in the States. There are no vocal, organized groups to do this. We deal with minorities who are usually unpopular. Their best safeguards are in constitutional guarantees that give some shelter against the passions of the day.

It was his belief that the tensions between the federal and state level would be "never ending."

---

[45] Charles Fairman, "Associate Justice of the Supreme Court," *Columbia Law Reviews*, 55 (April, 1955), 451.

Judicial Independence:

The Supreme Court must be free of undue external pressure in order adequately to act as umpire of the federal system, maintain an orderly judicial process, and protect individual rights. For this reason the Constitution provides that Justices will have life tenure during good behavior and that their salaries may not be reduced. More importantly, it is through its exercise of judicial review that the Court can protect the judicial system from undue external pressures. Thus, structural factors would seem to make this a "pivotal" norm. If judicial independence is a pivotal role attribute, we should expect to find it, and the necessary use of judicial review included in the philosophies of both Justices Jackson and Douglas.

Apparently Robert Jackson's view of a Justice's role was directly influenced by the institutions with which he was affiliated. A brief survey of his views on the exercise of judicial review suggests a curve which began at its highest point in favor of judicial review, declined markedly during his affiliation with the executive branch to a low in 1937, and rose during his service on the Court. His earliest writing enthusiastically supported judicial review as a necessary safeguard of minority rights. Within fifteen years he had switched sides and joined wholeheartedly in an attack on the Court on the ground that its conservatism was enforcing the thoughts of a past, discredited generation against the most ardent desires of the contemporary one. Shortly before his appointment as an Associate Justice he wrote: "The Constitution nowhere provides that it shall be what the judges say it is." The crux of his disagreement with the Court was that: ". . . the Constitution contemplated a really effective government," yet the government was not effectively able to deal with economic or social problems so long as a narrowly divided Court was able to read an outmoded *laissez faire* doctrine into it. However, having experienced the bitter problems involved in trying to get the Court-packing plan passed, he came to believe that the end result (leaving it to the Justices themselves to correct the Court's errors) was: "certainly easier and perhaps wiser . . . than to split our society as deeply as adoption of any formula for limiting judicial power would be likely to do." As a Justice, he continued to be concerned that the Court defer as far as possible to the will of the people expressed through their elected representatives, but he came more fully to understand and appreciate the need for judicial independence. It seemed all the more important to him after his experience with the record of the Nuremberg War Crimes Trials. He held that: "The right to fair trial is the right that stands guardian over all other rights."

Protection of individual rights was at the core of Justice Douglas' governmental philosophy. The Supreme Court, as he viewed
it, must be independent of other branches if it is to safeguard
minority rights against abridgment sanctioned by the majority.
Nevertheless, he did not overlook the possibility of judicial tyranny. Therefore, he stressed the importance of the procedural
safeguards in the Bill of Rights. The Court was to be independent of the other branches of government, but carefully restricted by Constitutional prescriptions of procedure. Regarding
the Court as a necessary safeguard for minority rights, he was
particularly anxious to keep it independent of the pressures of
public opinion. His opinion underwent a significant though not
explicit shift toward greater judicial independence of the mass
media during [his] service on the Supreme Court. Both Justices
upheld judicial independence against the states, military tribunals, and harassment by plaintiffs, prosecutors, and the press, and
both Justices upheld the Court's supervisory power over lower
courts.

In summary, judicial independence protected by the use of
judicial review is an aspect of the Justice's role which seems
clearly to be "pivotal," resulting from the institutional setting.
Without it, the Court cannot fulfill its responsibilities to umpire
the federal system, maintain an orderly judicial process, or check
and balance the power of the legislative and executive branches.
It is a norm, then, which must be accepted as controlling by all
Justices. As has [been] shown, Robert Jackson and William
Douglas both came, as Justices, to accept it in the fullest sense,
despite the fact that Justice Jackson had not valued it so highly
during his pre-Court career. . . .

Judicial Self-Restraint:

The other side of the coin of an independent judiciary is a
judiciary which leaves the other branches of government independent in the exercise of their respective powers. While it is
necessary to protect minority rights through an independent judiciary, majority rule is an essential attribute of democracy, and
that entails expression of majority will through elected representatives. This requires that the judiciary exercise restraint in
its use of judicial review. This is the fourth major attribute of
the Justice's role.

Judicial self-restraint entails a nice balance which is often easier to theorize about in general terms than to deal with on the
case by case basis of Supreme Court action. The difficulty lies

in the need for Justices to exercise restraint in the use of their function without entirely abdicating it, for the power of the Supreme Court to set aside acts of Congress, the Executive, state legislatures and state executives remains an indispensable part of our system of checks and balances. The extent to which restraint must be followed will depend upon individual perceptions of its importance. This role attribute is likely to be seen as a "relevant" one. It is structured by the institutional setting and therefore is perceived as necessary. However, self-restraint is an imprecise term subject to questions of degree. Its definition depends on the individual Justice's governmental philosophy.

Robert Jackson's opinion concerning the importance of judicial self-restraint only changed through deepening and becoming more fixed during his lifetime. . . .

What Justice Jackson conceived to be the appropriate role for a judge was one of restraint in enforcing his personal predilections, but where a choice lay between principles, he would select those which kept the law abreast of contemporary needs.

Justice Jackson believed that the Court could never be an active, first line of defense for our society for several reasons. First, unlike legislatures, courts cannot choose when to act, but must await the development of cases. This entails delays of many years, and the problems arising from individual fact structures. Often cases arise which present valuable principles in competition, requiring the Court to choose between them, or the record of an individual case may not present a solid basis for the ultimate questions involved. Further, the Court could only be a second line of defense because the "disaster potentials" in our system, such as the war power and power of inflation (money, taxing and spending), are possessed exclusively by the elected branches. . . .

Justice Douglas' viewpoint on the criteria for judicial self-restraint might be expected to differ from those of Justice Jackson as he was one of the "activists" whom Jackson deplored. Nevertheless, he viewed the Court's function in much the same terms as had Justice Jackson, recognizing judicial self-restraint as a valid norm for the Court. He felt an obligation to rely on the thoughts and acts of the community and their elected representatives. Yet, much as he admired the judge who did not write his own preferences into the law, he also admired the one who showed courage in upholding his own convictions. His awareness of the tremendous effect which Supreme Court decisions might have on a social, political, or economic situation caused him to emphasize judicial self-restraint in relation to the executive and legislative branches. Only with regard to civil liberties might self-restraint be lessened and even here he maintained that the other two branches should be given the benefit of the doubt.

A comparison of the opinions of the two Justices on judicial self-restraint with specific regard to the President, administrative bodies, and Congress shows marked similarity. Both Justices would permit a considerable margin of freedom to the President in construing his constitutional prerogatives. In the field of foreign relations they maintained that the President was supreme. Both agreed that he was solely responsible for the conduct of military affairs. Both agreed that courts should defer to the President on political questions; but that where his power was exercised in domestic matters which were not political questions, the courts had a right to require that they be exercised with due regard for the limitations placed upon them by our constitutional system.

While both Justices agreed that the judiciary should continue to exercise review over the findings of administrative bodies, they were predisposed to accept these findings as final. And both Justices gave a presumption of constitutionality to acts of Congress.

Their only area of basic disagreement arose over congressional investigations. Justice Jackson maintained that Congress alone was responsible for the behavior of its committees, whereas Justice Douglas was convinced that the Court should step in if an individual's constitutional rights were being abridged. While this is only one difference, it is crucial for the general assessment of differences between the two Justices because scholarly literature on the Court tends to stress cases involving civil liberties, rather than such areas as administrative law or foreign relations. On this basic issue of civil liberties the two Justices differed markedly, although they were in agreement on other areas involving judicial self-restraint.

In summary, the two Justices perceived judicial self-restraint as an important role attribute. However, they disagreed at least in one area on the definition of the term. Since judicial restraint is structured by the institutional setting, but not clearly defined, there is room for individual variation in perception. Therefore, it may be considered a "relevant" attribute.

Avoidance of Extra-Judicial Activity with Partisan or Policy Implications:

A concurrent norm has developed that Justices will refrain from partisan activity or political utterances for the duration of their service on the bench. Partisan speeches and activities off the bench were not unusual for Justices during the last century, but it eventually became clear that a Justice's extra curricular activities had an influence on his judicial effectiveness and on the effectiveness of the Court as a whole. Lacking its own means to enforce decisions, the Court must rely on other branches. This in turn, means that the Court is ultimately dependent upon public opinion. If the Court is generally respected by the citizenry, a President, legislator or Governor might run serious political risks in refusing to enforce its mandate, whereas he might benefit from dramatic opposition if his constituency did not support it. Thus a premium is put upon maintenance of a high degree of public respect for the Court's methods and personnel. Experience has shown that the Court's prestige has been damaged by partisan political activities on the part of members; therefore, withdrawal from the fray has developed as a norm. In the Twentieth Century, the norm of withdrawal has broadened to the point that, like a Boston dowager, only one notice of the contemporary Justice's personal life is supposed to appear in the press—his death notice. Most Justices avoid the Washington cocktail circuit, and generally engage in monastic seclusion.

Though the benefits to the Court's prestige from such seclusion are obvious, they are also irksome to most Justices. Non-partisan individuals are rarely appointed to the court. Moreover, Justices usually come to the Court in the vigorous prime of their political lives. They are also likely to have been fairly gregarious, the personality type most likely to be attracted to political life, and to climb successfully to a position from which he might be recruited for the Court. Therefore, for every Justice there is at least an initial difficult transition period. For some, that period never ends.

The norm constraining Justices from partisan or controversial political activity or utterances relies entirely on self-enforcement. Thus, it tends to depend on subjective, personal factors. It might therefore be considered a "peripheral" role attribute. If this is the case, its inclusion in an individual's judicial philosophy would be optional and might permit of variations in performance not only between Justices, but during the term in office of each individual Justice.

Robert Jackson had made many political speeches prior to his accession to the Court, but thereafter he confined himself to writing and speaking primarily on the role of courts, of lawyers and laymen in fashioning the law, of the meaning of our democratic process, and on constitutional questions. Although he recognized the norm as controlling and tried to live up to it, in two notable instances he failed. The Jackson-Black feud was one obvious instance in which both Justices seriously breached the norms of judicial conduct. A less clear-cut example was Justice Jackson's acceptance of the appointment as America's prosecutor at the Nuremberg War Crimes Trials. He viewed the Trials as legal acts, but others disagreed, considering them political. Chief Justice Stone called them a "high-grade lynching party."[83]

Justice Douglas devoted a minority of his writing and speaking to the type of legal questions which occupied Justice Jackson's mind. Except for civil liberties, his speeches, books, and articles dealt primarily with non-legal topics such as conservation, camping, travel, and literature. He also ranged frequently into politically sensitive and controversial areas of national policy formation such as our far and middle eastern foreign policy, world federalism, the United Nations, and negotiation in the Vietnamese War.

Since Justice Jackson's speeches were primarily legal, they were generally delivered before legal bodies such as bar associations and law schools. With his broader range of topics, Justice Douglas frequently addressed lay audiences. The difference is more sharply drawn in a comparison of publications. Justice Jackson's work appeared almost entirely in legal periodicals. Justice Douglas wrote for these also, but much of his writing was for mass circulation magazines.

William Douglas was regarded by many as a semi-active political figure with a desire to leave the restrictive confines of the Court with which he seemed from time to time frankly bored. He was widely considered to be President Truman's choice for Secretary of the Interior in 1946 until Chief Justice Stone wrote to the President making clear his position on "raids" on the judiciary. His name was frequently mentioned as a possible preferable Democratic presidential candidate to Harry Truman in 1948. His personal life entered the field of political debate due to three divorces and four marriages, the last two of which were highly publicized because of the youth of the brides.

The brief comparison of the two Justices suggests a temperamental and philosophical difference which influenced their recognition and acceptance of the norm in question. William Douglas had many interests, which often seemed to eclipse the law in his attention. Thus the norm's inclusion in his judicial philosophy was clearly optional. Robert Jackson's whole life was devoted to the law in its largest sense. By and large, he accepted the norm of avoidance of partisan political activity and utterances; there was notable variation, however, in his ability to

---

[83] Alpheus T. Mason, *Harlan Fiske Stone: Pillar of the Law* (New York: Viking Press, 1956), p. 716.

follow it. From these variations it would seem to be a "peripheral" role attribute.

Conclusion:

. . . . This methodology has been a useful one in giving a
greater understanding of the Court's decision processes. It has
provided a tool which sets the balance between structural and
behavioral factors in a manner which indicates the conditions
under which, and how, personal attitudes may influence judicial
decisions. Most analysis of the Supreme Court focuses on the
differences between Justices. Role theory indicates how broad is
the area of similarity in their behavior, because of the structural
factors of the role. It also indicates those areas where personal
factors may influence decisions. Yet even where personal factors
come into play, there are frequent constraints placed by the
institutional setting.

This work has the limitation of being more indicative than
exhaustive. A broader investigation covering a far wider variety
of Justices in depth is desirable to test the typology more adequately. Nevertheless, this study does suggest a fruitful means
of analyzing the Supreme Court, and the methodology could
probably be used with equal validity on other institutions.

NOTES AND QUESTIONS

1. Both Grossman and James hypothesize that certain attitudes
and values are attributes of the role of Justice of the Supreme
Court of the United States. Suppose you had at your command
all the resources you thought necessary such as unlimited funds,
the full cooperation of all government officials and the confidence
of newspaper reporters and editors. How would you establish
the content of the role or roles of Supreme Court Justice? How
would you establish which attributes of a role were "pivotal,"
"relevant," and "peripheral"? Is the task so difficult as to destroy
the value of role theory? How does James go about establishing
the content of the judicial role?

2. What does role theory tell us about the coordination and
functioning of the Supreme Court as a part of the total legal
system? Does it add to what one would find in the formal doctrines in statutes, the Constitution and past Supreme Court cases?

3. Suppose a man is nominated by the President and confirmed by the Senate as an Associate Justice of the Supreme Court,
whose judicial philosophy does not include one of what James
calls "pivotal" role attributes. Does James recognize that this

event could possibly happen? If it did, would the deviance continue? And if so, what does she indicate would be the likely consequence of such role deviance?

4. Do Grossman and James see "role" as a static or as a dynamic concept? Would the role of a Supreme Court Justice change over time? Would various attributes change from "pivotal" to "relevant" or to "peripheral"? How would this process take place?

[Reading 98]

5. How does a lawyer given a judicial appointment discover the role attributes of his new position? There is no detailed job description. *See* p. 837 n.21, *supra.* To what extent can one explain the following in terms of role theory? *Newsweek,* Sept. 23, 1968, at 30-31:*

Seventy-seven days after Lyndon Johnson nominated Abe Fortas to succeed Earl Warren as the next Chief Justice of the Supreme Court, the parliamentary paths were nearly cleared to bring the appointment to the Senate floor. But even this modest progress last week was deceptive. For at the same time, the Senate Judiciary Committee, which must first vote on the nomination, decided to hold several more last-minute hearings on Fortas's activities on and off the bench during his three years as an Associate Justice. These could only heighten the opposition—and make it more certain than ever that his nomination as Chief Justice would be the first to be blocked by the Senate since 1795.

What had gone wrong with the nomination? Just about everything, Supreme Court observers were beginning to conclude. Everything and everybody. . . .

Perhaps Lyndon Johnson's single greatest mistake was even picking an Associate Justice to elevate to the Chief Justice's chair. Historically, this has spelled trouble in the Senate because the nominee becomes a rare political target, answerable and attackable for the past performance of the Court as a whole and for his own highly visible decisions there. In Fortas's case, the focus of Senate attack has been the Court's and his own liberal rulings in obscenity cases, a viscerally sensitive, highly exploitable rallying point for those opposed to the whole activist, liberal drift of the Warren Court during the last fifteen years. . . .

Finally, Abe Fortas himself has been a major part of Abe Fortas's troubles. Probably the most damaging issue affecting the nomination, one which transcends the liberal-conservative dividing line on the bench, is the question of whether Fortas as an Associate Justice has maintained a proper, judicial distance from his old friend the President. Several senators have accused Fortas of failing to honor the separation of executive and judicial powers in his alleged dabblings in White House affairs. These backstairs chores, they say, have even extended to drafting Presidential policies and pronouncements. Abe Fortas himself admitted during the Judiciary hearings in July that he had participated in non-social contacts with the President since becoming an Associate Justice. Fortas's defenders point out that other Justices have acted as advisers to other Presidents; they point in particular to FDR's confidant and consultant Felix Frankfurter. There is indeed precedent in the Frankfurter case. But students of the High Court have argued that "It was wrong for Frankfurter."

Last week, as the Judiciary Committee reopened its hearings, it heard fresh testimony that Fortas received a whopping $15,000 fee for giving a nine-week law-school seminar during the summer. This new bit of information suggested that Fortas was at best rather careless about the sensitivities surrounding a Supreme Court Justice's off-the-court activities. Dean B.J. Tennery of American University law school testified that the money to set up the special summer course had been raised by Fortas's former law partner, Paul A. Porter, from five prominent businessmen. And Sen. Strom Thurmond, one of the major opponents of Fortas's nomination, insinuated aloud what some others no doubt may have suspected—that the seminar was a setup to supplement Fortas's Supreme Court salary with money from somewhat questionable sources.

Fortas had appeared in person at the earlier hearings and was invited to testify again before the committee. But he "respectfully" declined last week to do so. Other witnesses, however, were expected to testify early this week on the role Fortas allegedly played at the White House in drafting a law—following Robert Kennedy's assassination—to provide Secret Service protection for Presidential candidates. Then Fortas's nomination is scheduled finally to be put to a committee vote. An ample majority is expected to vote in favor, and so, no doubt, would a majority of the Senate as a whole. But an angry minority has threatened to filibuster on the

Senate floor until Congress adjourns if necessary to block confirmation—and therein lie Fortas's unhappy prospects for confirmation.

On October 2, 1968, Mr. Justice Fortas asked that his nomination as Chief Justice be withdrawn.

In light of the precedent of Mr. Justice Frankfurter's active role in advising President Roosevelt—there have been many other examples in Supreme Court history, too—how was Mr. Justice Fortas to discover that his work for President Johnson might have been deemed to be outside the role of a Supreme Court Justice by a significant group of role definers?

In May of 1969, *Life* published an article revealing that Justice Fortas had accepted a $20,000 fee from the family foundation of Louis E. Wolfson. The fee was accepted in January of 1966. In September and October of that year, Wolfson was indicted and charged with violating the federal securities laws by selling shares of a company which were not registered with the Securities and Exchange Commission and charged with participating in a conspiracy to obstruct an SEC investigation of purchases of stock in a large corporation. *Life* charged that Justice Fortas' name was used by Wolfson in his efforts to have the charges dropped. Wolfson was convicted and sentenced to eighteen months in prison. Justice Fortas returned the $20,000 to the Wolfson family foundation in December of 1966.

After the publication of the *Life* article, several Congressmen called for impeachment proceedings. On May 16, 1969, Justice Fortas resigned from the Supreme Court. He said that in December of 1965 he entered into an agreement with the Wolfson foundation to help guide its program in racial and religious cooperation. He was to be paid $20,000 a year for life and on his death his wife was to be paid $20,000 a year for her life. When he learned of the plan to indict Wolfson in June of 1966, he wrote the foundation cancelling the arrangement. In December of 1966, after the indictments, he returned the $20,000 and said that his services should be treated as a contribution to the foundation. Justice Fortas denied any wrongdoing. He conceded he had discussed Wolfson's problems with him but denied interceding in any proceeding for him. He said he was resigning to end the controversy.

The *New York Times*, May 15, 1969, at 28, cols. 1-4 (city ed.),* in an article entitled, "Guidelines on Judicial Conduct Sometimes

---

* Copyright © 1969 by The New York Times Company. Reprinted by permission.

Blurred," by E. W. Kenworthy, indicated the lack of clarity about
the standards for judges:

In the Jan. 18, 1954, issue of Time magazine, there was a
double-page advertisement by Pan American Airways with a
picture of Federal Judge Harold Medina and his wife board-
ing a Pan Am clipper bound for Bermuda.

The caption beneath the picture read in part: "Judge and
Mrs. Harold Medina both agree. It's certainly true that Pan
American knows how to run an airline."

Just a week earlier there was filed in Judge Medina's court,
the United States District Court for the Southern District of
New York, Civil Action 90-259, entitled "United States of
America versus Pan American World Airways." This was
an antitrust action against the airline.

The near juxtaposition of these events did not escape the
attention of the Justice Department, although it did nothing about it. Whether Judge Medina received payment for
what amounted to a "testimonial" for the airline was not
known. And even if he had received a payment, there was
no law prohibiting such an endorsement of a commercial
enterprise.

There was, however, Canon 25 of "The Canons of Judicial
Ethics" prepared in 1922 for the American Bar Association
by a committee headed by Chief Justice William Howard
Taft. It says in part:

An Imprecise Guideline

"A judge should avoid giving ground for any reasonable
suspicion that he is utilizing the power of prestige of his
office to persuade or coerce others to patronize or contribute,
either to the success of private business, or to charitable
enterprises."

This illustrates how imprecise is the whole area of judicial
conduct, an area in which Justice Abe Fortas is now caught
up because he accepted $20,000 from the family foundation
of Louis Wolfson, the financier, after he had taken his seat
on the Supreme Court and did not return it until 11 months
later, after Wolfson had been indicted for violating the
securities law.

The only laws governing the conduct of Federal judges
are the Constitution, which enjoins upon them "good behavior" and provides for impeachment by the House of Representatives and trial by the Senate for "treason, bribery or
other high crimes and misdemeanors," and two statutes, one

that makes it a felony for a judge to peddle influence, and another that makes it a misdemeanor for him to practice law.

Beyond these legal proscriptions, there is only "The Canons of Judicial Ethics," and as Joseph Borkin, author of "The Corrupt Judge," said today, These canons are simply a compendium of "biblical injunction, custom, common sense and 'Caesar's wife' admonitions to be above reproach."
. . .

Probably most important are those injunctions that are most vague and that leave shadowy questions up to the judge's conscience.

Thus, Canon 4 states that "a judge's official conduct should be free from impropriety and the appearance of impropriety . . . and his personal behavior, not only upon the bench and in the performance of judicial duties, but also in his everyday life, should be beyond reproach."

And Canon 24 states that "a judge should not accept inconsistent duties; nor incur obligations, pecuniary or otherwise, which will in any way interfere, or appear to interfere, with his devotion to the expeditious and proper administration of his official functions."

Supreme Court Justice Louis D. Brandeis's sense of propriety was such that he declined even to accept honorary degrees for fear that the bestowing universities might one day be a party to a suit before the court.

LACK OF CONSISTENCY

But not all Federal judges have had consistent views of "impropriety" and "inconsistent duties." For example, on the question of serving as a bank director, no canon of the A.B.A. specifically bars such service.

But in 1943 the Association's Committee on Professional Ethics stated in an opinion that "It is improper for a judge to serve as a director of a bank."

The committee based its opinion on Canon 25, which says that a judge should "not enter into such private business" as would justify suspicion that he is trying to promote that business.

But after 20 years, this opinion evidently had had no effect on several Federal judges. In 1963, The Wall Street Journal's investigative reporter Jerry Landauer disclosed exclusively that three of the six judges on the United States Court of Appeals for the Seventh Circuit, in Chicago—Elmer

J. Schackenberg, Latham Castle and Win G. Knoch—were bank directors.

As a result of this disclosure the Judicial Conference of the United States ruled that a judge could not be a bank director.

Not only is the area of judicial conduct ill-defined but also the impeachment proceeding—as Lord Bryce said in "The American Commonwealth"—is too heavy an artillery piece to bring to bear against any but constitutional violations.

Does this article persuade you that Justice Fortas had no way of knowing that members of Congress would consider his relationship with the Wolfson foundation improper? Consider the case of the man who as President accepted Justice Fortas' resignation. In 1952, it was revealed that the then Senator Richard Nixon was the beneficiary of a fund set up by wealthy California businessmen to pay campaign expenses. Nixon defended himself in a nationally televised speech and ended the criticism of the fund. Was this case significantly different from the Fortas affair? Is the definition of the role of United States Senator different in this respect from that of an Associate Justice of the Supreme Court? Consider the comments of Aubert, Reading 18, at 175, *supra*.

James mentions Jackson's acceptance of a position in prosecuting German officials at the Nuremberg trials. In more recent years, Chief Justice Earl Warren accepted the chairmanship of a commission to investigate the assassination of President John F. Kennedy. Was the Chief Justice a role deviant in so doing? What advantages and disadvantages flowed from his acceptance of the chairmanship: (a) to the commission? (b) to American society in general?

6. To what extent are the attributes discussed by James, attributes of the role of a *judge,* of an *appellate judge,* or specifically of a Justice of the United States Supreme Court? Some high court judges, for example, are authorized to give advisory opinions—in Massachusetts, for example, the highest court advises on the constitutionality of pending legislation. The United States Supreme Court, however, does not do so, and considers itself constitutionally barred from doing so.

7. Federal judges are appointed; most state and local judges are elected. However, "Unlike most countries, the United States has never possessed a group of career judges. Would-be judges must possess no special training or qualifications." Herbert Jacob,

Justice in America 89 (Little, Brown 1965). They are, however, invariably lawyers, except for the lowest local courts.

There have been some studies of the selection process, for example, Joel B. Grossman, *Lawyers and Judges: The ABA and the Politics of Judicial Selection* (John Wiley 1965); and David Danelski, *A Supreme Court Justice Is Appointed* (Random House 1964), a case study of the appointment of Pierce Butler.

What influence do you think social background and mode of appointment have on the judge's conception of his role? Do you think appointment and election would lead to different role conceptions?

99. The Judicial Role and Sentencing Behavior

DEAN JAROS AND
ROBERT I. MENDELSOHN*

11 MIDWEST JOURNAL OF POLITICAL
SCIENCE 471 (1967)

Personal Factors and Role Factors in Judicial Behavior

As recognition that the courts are political bodies thoroughly participant in the process of making and executing policies has grown, so has concern with the antecedents of judges' official acts. In the grossest sense, this concern has been manifested in two kinds of commentary. On the one hand, there are those who state that courts are not political bodies, that judges merely apply objective, certain, knowable law through fixed processes. On the other hand, "legal realists" and members of other jurisprudential schools insist that the judicial process cannot proceed in this way, that judges do and must personally affect the application of the law. We are confronted with two conceptions of the judge: an exponent of the law all of whose acts can be justified in terms of legally relevant criteria which attach to the position of judge; and a person who comes to the judgeship already encumbered with certain characteristics, which characteristics have an important bearing on how he behaves. The fact that these two conceptions are antagonistic has led to a good deal of normative discourse. To what extent should individual characteristics be allowed to displace legally relevant considerations in the decision of the court?

But which conception describes reality? In attempting to understand judicial behavior, are we to concentrate, as the legal realists would have us, on the personal characteristics of judges, or are we to examine the judicial role which transcends any par-

---

* Dean Jaros, Professor of Political Science, University of Kentucky; Robert I. Mendelsohn, Member, Department of Political Science, Wayne State University, in 1969, on leave as a Special Consultant, Committee on the Administration of Justice, Washington, D.C. Reprinted from "The Judicial Role and Sentencing Behavior," 11 Midwest Journal of Political Science (1967) by Dean Jaros and Robert I. Mendelsohn by permission of the Wayne State University Press. Copyright 1967 by Wayne State University Press.

ticular incumbent judge, and which, in the hopes of many, contains strictly legal principles? The present day clearly belongs to the realists. Systematic inquiry has shown them largely to be correct. No observer can ignore judicial attitudes and personality. But though recent scholarship has identified and assessed the causal efficacy of several personal variables, it is important in rejecting the naivete of the legalists not to discount entirely the possibility that certain kinds of judges under some circumstances are in fact primarily influenced by the expectations of their offices. It is likely that *both* personal factors and role expectations influence judicial decisions. If so, the empirical task is to specify the kinds of personal variables and role expectations that are important and to identify the conditions under which each is operative.

Through a systematic study of punishment meted out in Detroit Traffic Court, this paper examines the proposition that the sentencing behavior of judges in lower level trial courts is the consequence of the playing of a legal-professional role. It is reasonable to think that in the more structured workings of lower courts judges would be more influenced by the common expectations of how they should behave than they would in appellate courts where cases are less routine. As one moves from the "norm enforcement" end of the judicial spectrum toward the "policy making" end, expected behavior may become more difficult to identify and outlets for personal factors may become more numerous. Most previous systematic research has focussed on the appellate, "policy making" courts.

Disparities in Sentencing: A Function of Personal Factors?

Sentencing behavior and the motivation of trial court judges have attracted attention over the years. Most commentators observe that, *ceteris paribus*, the severity of sentences which judges impose on offenders varies from time to time, place to place, judge to judge, or from class of defendant to class of defendant. These disparities are regarded as evidence that trial court judges, like their appellate court counterparts, allow their personalities to influence their decisions. If the law alone governed, no such disparities would be seen. Such observations are often accompanied by condemnations of personal factors as sentencing determinants and by pleas for universal equality before the law. Indeed, such pleas are founded on a very large body of hard data citing sentencing disparities by class, race or other minority group status, sex, age, religion, and time. On the surface, at least, it appears that judges do not equally apply the law, that they have given way to social prejudices or other idiosyncrasies.

However, it is possible that normative commitment has interfered with the empirical faculties of some of these observers. A reassessment of these data casts quite a different light on the motivational processes underlying sentencing. [Edward] Green, though he does not deny the existence of disparities in gross data on sentencing, finds that they are often justifiable in legally relevant terms. For example, while the imposition of consistently heavier sentences on Negroes may suggest racial prejudice on the part of judges, in reality it is a function of differential criminal behavior patterns between Negroes and whites; Negroes commit more serious crimes and more serious crimes draw heavier penalties. Imposing controls for legally relevant criteria—primarily severity of offense and recidivism—causes the disparities to disappear. In fact, the very data upon which other authors base attacks on judges have an altogether different implication when exposed to this simple treatment. This, coupled with Green's own Philadelphia data—which show the same pattern, disparities in the gross figures which disappear with the imposition of controls— does much to weaken the impact of the studies showing disparities in sentencing.

A Professional Judicial Role

The judgeship is a position that is particularly susceptible to role analysis. Not only is it a formally specified office involving relationships with many other persons and institutions, but it has typically been held in a somewhat sacrosanct position involving much ceremony and the accoutrements of great dignity. . . .

The obligations of such a role, however, are not self-evident. Though we might intuitively feel that "society" expects judges to make decisions in accord with "norms rooted in the law," such an assumption is highly dangerous. "Society" as such holds no consensual expectations about a given position. Different role definers may have quite inconsistent expectations. Moreover, we cannot assume the primacy of the law in expectations about judicial behavior. In certain kinds of systems, relevant role definers may expect judges to behave in ways quite contrary to what can be justified in law alone.

Despite these demurrers, however, there are in fact a great many would-be role definers who expect that judges will behave in accordance with legally justifiable criteria. The judicial profession, apparently quite self-conscious, itself has much to say about appropriate behavior patterns for its members. As individuals and as members of formal councils, judges urge their colleagues to base all of their decisions in the law. Failure to do so is seen as erosive of the prestige of the legal process and ultimately injurious to the profession itself.

The organized bar formally declares very definite expectations about the behavior of judges, and these expectations prominently feature the strict legal justification of decisions. Though lawyers know that in some courts, defendants' "wealth, social position, and race do have an effect on the standard of justice," they fear this will tarnish the image of the profession; they have made quite clear their belief that this situation should be corrected by the "improvement" of the bench (i.e. increasing the conformity of decisions of legally justifiable criteria), via the mechanisms for selecting better judges.

Do these highly general statements have any role-definitional potential for members of the judicial profession in general and the judges of Detroit Traffic Court in particular? We must confess uncertainty on this matter. We have not identified the particular role definers for any judges nor have we described the specific expectations held for them. This is far short of what the ultimate in role analysis would demand. However, expectations of legal justification are ubiquitous; it would be a rare judge who was unaware of them. Moreover, despite their varied sources, these expectations are quite congruent, suggesting considerable agreement among agencies. This, coupled with the considerable prestige of these agencies, the fact that judges are socialized in them, and the at least potential sanctions which they hold over the bench, makes it quite unreasonable to assume the complete non-salience of such expectations.

Though the higher-court judge may find that they provide few guides for dealing with the relatively atypical cases that characterize appellate judicial proceedings, such norms may bulk large for the jurist of an inferior court where the relationship of the dictates of the law to unambiguous, routine cases is clear.

Rights of the Judicial Role

Roles are characterized not only by *obligations* but also by *rights*. The judge is expected to perform certain behaviors as a consequence of his position, but because of his position he may expect that others will exhibit certain kinds of behavior toward him.

Though there are great differences about how best to obtain it, there is agreement that one of the rights of the judicial role is the receipt of respect. It is expected that incumbents of other positions will accord judges deference. . . .

In a study of sentencing, we are interested in judges' expectations of respectful behavior on the part of defendants. What will a judge do if a defendant violates his expectations of being treated respectfully? We posit that the judge will impose sanctions upon him in the form of more severe sentences. Of course, blatant courtroom disrespect has always been punishable by citation for contempt. But it is possible that sanctions are imposed for less severe displays through the sentencing process.

Would this be inconsistent with the hypothesis that their role obligations require judges to sentence in accordance with legally relevant criteria? We think not because the question of respect for the bench derives from the same legal-professional role as the obligation to eschew personal factors in sentencing. Just as the efficacy of the bench might suffer if social attitudes were allowed to displace legally relevant sentencing criteria, so would it suffer if disrespect for the bench went undeterred. Judges' behavior will reflect both of these considerations.

In short, we postulate that the obligations of the judicial role require lower court judges' sentences to conform to legally relevant criteria and not to the attitudes of the judges. Second, the rights of the judicial role include the receipt of respect. Failure to receive respect, since it threatens the very sanctity of law, will be met with sanctions in the form of more severe sentences.

Method

These propositions were examined in a study of sentences imposed by the three judges of Detroit Traffic Court[22] during two one-week periods in the summer of 1966. Data were gathered on all complete cases tried during these periods. Observers, mostly secondary school teachers, were allowed, with the permission of the court, directly to observe cases being tried. The observers were trained by the authors; included in the training were three or more hours of practice observation in court. Mass training sessions were held in order to develop common decisional criteria for those observations requiring "subjective" classification.

The observers recorded the sex, race, and other similar defendant characteristics as well as the nature of the charge and the disposition of the case. The ages of defendants were estimated

22 Lest it be argued that traffic court judges are not full-fledged members of the judges' profession, it is necessary to note that these men are formally of Recorder's Court. The same status, salary and requirement for assumption of office—including a law degree—apply to all judges of such courts. Referees operating in Traffic Court are bureaucratic types not necessarily members of the legal profession. They are not included in this analysis.

and placed into one of four categories provided. No direct measurement of social class was possible under these circumstances. In the following analysis the presence or absence of an attorney is used as a surrogate variable on the ground that in this court where there is no appointed counsel, a defendant must be able to afford fees if he is to have legal advice. Recidivism was measured by observing whether previous traffic offenses were cited by the judge or admitted by the defendant.

Respectful defendant behavior was measured in two ways. First, the way in which the defendant was dressed was noted. Four categories, arranged in increasing order of court-appropriateness, were established and each defendant was classified accordingly. The category of least appropriate apparel was deemed to be work clothes, such as would be appropriate to manual labor, gardening, or other similar tasks. The second and third categories included "casual clothes," but soiled or rumpled apparel was adjudged to be less appropriate to a courtroom appearance than similar garb that was clean and neat. The fourth and most court-appropriate category was designated "business clothes;" the wearing of coat and tie or of hose and heels was sufficient to admit defendants to this group. Preliminary observation convinced us that dress was not significantly related to social class, as many defendants who appeared to be working class members donned coats and ties, while some who appeared to be professionals otherwise enjoying a day off appeared rather shabbily dressed. Admittedly, this is an impressionistic judgment, for we have no independent measure of status against which to test this proposition.

Second, six courtroom acts, seen in preliminary observation to draw negative reaction from judges, were assembled into a Demeanor Index. The number of these acts which a defendant performed constituted his demeanor score: the higher the score the less appropriate his demeanor. The behaviors are: 1) failure to use an honorific title in addressing the judge, 2) expression of disagreement with declarative statement of the judge, 3) raising of the voice, 4) use of sarcasm, 5) expression of disparagement of courts, law, or police, and 6) failure to express repentance. Testing of the instrument revealed that the modal score was two; in the rapid operation of the traffic court, only conscious effort would result in a lower score, while some belligerence was normally necessary to achieve a score of higher than two. Accordingly, in the analyses that follow, demeanor index scores are classified into three categories; appropriate (less than two), modal (two), and inappropriate (more than two).[23]

_____

[23] It should be noted that this is an index assembled for an exploratory study on limited scope. It is not a developed scale meeting requirements of

The dependent variable, sentence, was simply recorded when pronounced. In the following analyses sentences are considered as to whether they included jail confinement, and/or the amount of fine imposed.

Charges were recorded when read and subsequently trichotomized according to severity. Severity was determined on the basis of the average fine that had been imposed for convictions on given charges during the first quarter, 1966. Low severity charges were those drawing a mean fine of less than $15, moderate between $15 and $75, and high more than $75. There is substantive justification for these cut off points. The first category includes improper signal, obstructing traffic, etc., the moderate category includes most speeding cases and license violations, while the high category generally involves reckless driving or intoxication charges. Each category seems quite homogeneous.

As a reliability check, all cases were simultaneously recorded by two observers acting independently.

The imposition of jail sentences (i.e., the presence or absence of such a punishment) is analyzed through the use of Kendall's *tau* correlation,* or, where the data do not appear in categories which are ordinally scaled, through chi-square.** The imposition of fines (i.e., amount) is treated by analysis of variance and the calculation of F,*** or, if the data are on a dichotomous variable, by the difference of means test.****

As a final note on the method employed in this study, it should be observed that the judges themselves in a high-production situation such as a traffic court have only the most minimal information on which to base decisions. In fact, their position is very

---

high reliability. Findings based on its use should be regarded as suggestive only.

* *Kendall's tau* (indicated by "r" in the tables reproduced in this Reading) is a statistic which indicates the strength of the relationship (correlation) between two sets of ranks. If you have two sets of scores which can be ranked (first, second, third, etc.), each person's rank on one variable can be compared with his rank on the other variable. If everyone has the same rank on both variables (one person gets the highest score in each set, another gets the second highest in each set, etc.), *tau* equals 1.00. If ranks on one variable are unrelated to ranks on the second variable, *tau* equals zero. One can refer to a table worked out by Kendall, which gives the odds that a particular value of *tau* will be found with groups of various sizes. Conventionally, the odds must be at least one in twenty (or $p < .05$) to conclude that the particular value found is not a mere chance occurrence. [Eds. note]

** *See* p. 206 n.*, *supra.* [Eds. note]

*** *See* p. 204 n.*, *supra.* [Eds. note]

**** The difference of means test (or "*t* test") is the same as an analysis of variance applied to a case where only two groups (or sets of data) are involved. *See* p. 204 n.*, *supra.* [Eds. note]

similar to that of our observers. Thus, though there was information which was not available to the observers, such information was by and large not available to the judge either and hence probably not relevant to the decisional process.

Data: Legally Relevant Criteria

[M]any writers feel that considerations of the law play an extremely small part in motivating judges' sentencing behavior. ". . . the conclusion seems inescapable that the differences [in sentencing] are due *primarily* to diverse attitudes on the part of the individual judges toward various crimes and that the severity or lightness of the punishment depends in each instance very largely on the personality of the trial judge."[25] This view, however, is probably somewhat overstated. Most scholars, even in the light of much variance in judges' behavior, do not regard the meting out of sentences as, from a legal point of view, "totally erratic." Our hypotheses of course suggest a very large role for

TABLE 1*
SENTENCING BY LEGALLY RELEVANT CRITERIA

	Severity of Offense			Recidivism	
	Low (N = 64)	Moderate (N = 88)	High (N = 78)	First Offenders (N = 111)	Repeaters (N = 97)
Percent jailed	11	18	37	18	28
		$(r_c = .23 \ p < .001)$		$(x^2 = 4.67, 1 \ df, p < .05)$	
Mean fine	$38.09	$44.37	$79.83	$47.34	$62.88
		$(F_{2,\ 212} = 17.07, p < .001)$		(difference, $p < .05$)	

* All calculations reported in this paper were performed with computer programs that excluded missing data. Thus, total N's may not exactly correspond from table to table. The discrepancies result from inability to secure measurements on some cases or from inapplicability of certain variables.

legally relevant criteria, at least as far as the lower court judge is concerned. Conforming to expectations about his role, he must pay great heed to such factors in passing sentence on those who appear before him. It follows from this that sentencing in Detroit Traffic Court is governed by 1) the severity of the offense charged, and 2) recidivism of the defendant.

25 Matthew F. McGuire and Alexander Holtzoff, "The Problem of Sentencing in the Criminal Law," *Boston University Law Review,* Vol. 420 (1940), pp. 423, 427-28, emphasis added.

That the data reveal this to be the case is confirmation of what all but the most incautious would expect. Table 1 demonstrates the effect of severity of offense and recidivism on sentencing behavior. Both in the proportion jailed and in the mean fine imposed, there is an upward, monotonic progression across the three-category scale of severity of offense. The situation is nearly the same for recidivism. Despite the fact that our measurement of this variable was crude—merely noting whether any previous traffic offenses were mentioned in the courtroom proceedings—a very noticeable relationship is to be seen. It should be noted that these variables are quite independent of one another. Imposing controls for one will not greatly alter the relationship between the other and the judicial behavior in question.[28]

The law, then, is quite important in the sentencing behavior of these trial judges. If the bench has any aspects of legal professionalism at all, at least this much deference for legally relevant criteria should be observed.

Data: Personal Factors

It is patent, however, that even with the above data, there is still much room for judges to indulge attitudes or social preju-

---

[28] The absence of relationship between severity of charged offense and recidivism in these data can clearly be seen: $x^2 = 5.75$, 2 df, $p > .05$.
[This footnote could have been worded more precisely. Since the probability that the relationships between severity of offense and recidivism occurred by chance is greater than one in twenty ($p > .05$), conventionally one is not warranted in saying that he has proved that severity and recidivism together produce any combined effect on sentencing. The logic of this kind of analysis involves an attempt to disprove the "null hypothesis"—here, that there is no relationship between the two variables. But failing to overcome the null hypothesis of no relationship does not *prove* that there is no relationship. All one can say is that the question is still open. (Some readers may be helped by an analogy: suppose a district attorney offers evidence that a defendant killed his wife. The defendant offers no evidence. The jury finds the defendant not guilty. Since the burden of proof was on the prosecutor, we cannot say that the defendant was proven innocent but only that the prosecutor failed to carry his burden of proof.)
Here, the authors indicate that the probability that there is a relationship is greater than .05, the conventional line for statistical significance. But reference to a table of x^2 probability levels (found in most statistics textbooks) shows that the p level for $x^2 = 5.75$ with 2 degrees of freedom is about .06. In other words, the observed relationship between the two variables just misses being statistically significant. It is possible that an increase in statistical "power"—for example, increasing the number of cases in the analysis referred to—might indicate the relationship to be significant.
In light of all this, one cannot "clearly" see any "absence of relationship between severity of charged offense and recidivism." All that can be seen clearly is that the presence or absence of such a relationship is uncertain. (Eds.)]

dices. Concomitant with the expectation that judges in their legal-professional role will recognize legally relevant criteria is the expectation that they will not allow factors like defendants' age, race, and social class to color their decisions regardless of what these characteristics mean to them personally. To be sure, even judges completely unaffected by personal factors could impose differential sentences by, say, race or class. They may play other roles. For example, a southern judge, whose role as a protector of traditional social norms is more salient than that of legal-professional may well find race a very important criterion, one to which he is expected to pay great heed. Similarly, studies which have shown sentencing "discriminations" against lower-status groups may regard judges as agents of the exploiters in a class struggle.[29] Such a role would require vastly different behavior than that of a legal-professional. For cosmopolitan Detroit, we postulate the dominance of legal-professionalism and the absence of personal criteria in the sentencing process. Generally, the data support this (Table 2).

TABLE 2

SENTENCING BY PERSONAL FACTORS

	Age of Defendant		Presence of Counsel		Race of Defendant	
			With	Without		
	Juvenile	Adult	Counsel	Counsel	White	Negro
	(N = 25)	(N = 204)	(N = 81)	(N = 148)	(N = 96)	(N = 152)
Percent jailed	20	23	31	18	18	27
	($r_c = .02, p > .05$)		($x^2 = 4.75, 1\ df, p < .05$)		($x^2 = 2.45, 1\ df, p > .05$)	
Mean fine	$43.75	$56.49	$63.18	$50.41	$55.35	$55.40
	(difference, $p > .05$)		(difference, $p < .05$)		(difference, $p > .05$)	

It is conventional wisdom that young defendants receive greater leniency in the courts. This is supposedly due to the activation of judges' paternalistic attitudes by youngsters. Green finds, however, that despite appearances judges do not protect youth, but continue to act as legal-professionals when dealing with juvenile offenders. Though raw data may show lighter penalties imposed on young defendants, imposition of controls for a legally relevant variable—recidivism, which varies strongly with age—causes these relationships to disappear, thus indicating that the judges allow

29 Edwin M. Lemert and Judy Rosberg, "The Administration of Justice to Minority Groups in Los Angeles County," *University of California Publications in Culture and Society,* Vol. 2 (1948), pp. 1-28.

the legal considerations and not sentiments about youth to govern their behavior.

There is little evidence that the Detroit judges respond to the ages of defendants that appear before them. In fact, it is not even necessary to impose a control for recidivism to observe this;[31] neither jail sentences nor fines are significantly lighter for juveniles than for adults. The imposition of controls for severity of offense and for recidivism, variables known prominently to affect these judges' sentencing, has little effect. Significant relationships do not appear except for offenses of highest severity. At this level, 40% of the adults are jailed as against 20% of the juveniles; adults are fined on the average of $84.35, juveniles $47.00. Both differences are significant at .05. It appears that judges under certain circumstances do deviate from a strictly legal-professional role in dealing with young offenders. However, this deviation is neither pronounced nor widespread.

In these data there is no direct measurement of defendants' social class. The best surrogate variable, it will be remembered, is presence of legal counsel. Though crude, the index is serviceable. Moreover, it allows a direct test of the hypothesis that justice is enjoyed by those who can afford to hire lawyers. The professional on the bench should not allow considerations of this kind to color his appraisal of the legal merits of the cases he hears. As Table 2 shows, there are clearly significant relationships between presence of counsel and sentence, but they are not in the direction that the cynic would expect. The fact that defendants who hire lawyers are more likely to be punished harshly is not as surprising as it might seem when we consider legally relevant criteria which may motivate the judge. A higher proportion of defendants charged with more serious offenses have counsel; and it is precisely these more serious offenders that are more likely to go to jail or to be heavily fined. It is the nature of the offense which apparently motivates the judge—exactly what we would expect of a legal-professional. When controls are imposed for severity of offense, any relationship between counsel and extent of punishment is eliminated (for jail sentences, chi-squares between 1.3 and 2.4, none significant; for fines, differences between $1.07 and $14.28, none significant).

Thus, no advantage is conferred upon those defendants in traffic court who can afford legal counsel. This finding may seem

[31] This is due to the fact that in the Traffic Court data, recidivism and age do not co-vary ($r_c = -.07$, $p > .05$) as they do for most crime. This is not surprising, for there is no reason to expect traffic offenses to follow usual criminal behavior patterns. A traffic offense, after all, may be the result of a simple mistake.

to clash with recent declarations of the Supreme Court and other legal bodies about the importance of the right to counsel in "higher order" criminal cases. In such proceedings, it may be that counsel is critical. But in the lower court, with unambiguous cases and pressure for production, the judges' obligation to consider only legally relevant criteria may well nullify any such advantage. These data certainly suggest this to be the case.

Though assertions of racial discrimination in judicial sentencing are supported by several studies, we noted that the observed differences in penalties may be a function of racial differences in patterns of criminal behavior. Negroes reportedly commit more serious offenses than whites. Judges of course take severity of offense into account when passing sentence, and thus despite the fact that they may be playing a purely legal-professional role, gross data show stiffer penalties for Negroes. In Traffic Court, Negroes are not sentenced significantly more harshly than are whites. Moreover, this can be seen even prior to the imposition of controls for severity of offense.[33] As one would expect, the introduction of such controls in no way modifies this conclusion. A series of small and insignificant relationships (which do not all run in the same direction) is revealed. For jail sentences x^2's range between 0.00 and 2.44, none significant; for fines, differences range between \$.12 and \$12.29, none significant.

This analysis of sentencing by race does nothing to disturb our hypothesis that Traffic Court judges are engaging in behavior appropriate to a role of legal-professional. In fact, there is little in any of the analysis of judicial reaction to defendant characteristics to indicate that attitudes or other personal factors affect the imposition of sentence. Neither age, status as measured by presence of counsel, nor race of the defendant appears seriously to have deflected these judges from what would be expected of them on the basis of strict adherence to legal criteria.

Data: Rights of the Judicial Role

Although our data suggest that the judges are motivated by role expectations and not social prejudice in sentencing, this does not mean that legally relevant criteria define all of their behavior. As noted above, the judicial role may contain expectations held by judges for defendants. We have postulated that judges not only expect deferential and respectful behavior from defendants,

---

[33] This is again a function of the fact that traffic offenses do not follow patterns of other criminal behavior. That is, there is no relationship between severity of offense and race ($x^2=4.26$, $2df$, $p>.05$).

but that they react negatively to defendants who do not exhibit it. Such defendants will be more harshly sentenced.

Table 3 shows the Detroit judges' sentencing reactions to respect-related defendant behavior. That they responded negatively in sentencing the less well dressed is clearly indicated. The proportion of individuals jailed declines monotonically as mode of dress becomes increasingly appropriate. Moreover, the imposition of controls for the legally relevant variables only minimally modifies this relationship, indicating that it is not an incidental arti-

TABLE 3

SENTENCING BY RESPECT-RELATED DEFENDANT BEHAVIOR

	Court-Appropriate Dress				Demeanor		
	Least 1 (N=46)	2 (N=114)	3 (N=39)	Most 4 (N=23)	Inappropriate (N=11)	Modal (N=63)	Appropriate (N=62)
Percent jailed	43	26	23	13	18	24	21
		$(r_c=-.15, p<.01)$				$(r_c=-.01, p>.05)$	
Mean fine	$58.70	$56.49	$53.75	$58.88	$75.00	$51.31	$44.15
		$(F_{2, 181}=1.51, p>.05)$				$(F_{2, 127}=2.08, p>.05)$	

fact. Controlling for severity of offense shows that the relationship remains significant at low ($r_c = -.16$, $p<.05$) and moderate ($r_c = -.15$, $p<.05$) levels, but not at the high level ($r_c = -.12$, $p>.05$). Perhaps as the gravity of the offense increases, the obligations of the judicial role become more important than the rights.

The relationship between dress and jail sentence holds when recidivism is controlled, although again a legally relevant criterion appears to interact with dress. Among first-offenders, the effect of dress on imposition of jail sentence is mild indeed and does not attain significance ($r_c = -.08$, $p>.05$). This contrasts with a fairly strong relationship ($r_c = -.19$, $p<.01$) for defendants with records of prior traffic offenses. Perhaps judges expect repeaters, because of their past experience, to be especially knowledgeable in court-appropriate behavior.

Although we might expect dress to have similar effects upon the fines which the judges impose, this anticipation is not vindicated by the data. The gross data show no systematic relationship and none develops with the imposition of controls.

The relationship between defendants' Demeanor Index scores and sentencing behavior is less clear cut but highly suggestive.

Courtroom demeanor, it will be recalled is measured by defendant's performance or non-performance of six "inappropriate" behaviors. Higher scores indicate that more inappropriate acts were performed and that behavior was less respectful. Demeanor so measured has no bearing on whether a defendant is confined. No systematic relationships appear in these data even with the imposition of controls for severity of offense or recidivism. Our hypothesis fares little better when we consider the judges' imposition of fines. Table 3 shows that they visit harsher penalties on defendants who do not proffer the respect due incumbents of the judicial role than they do upon those who exhibit deferential behavior. However, analysis reveals that despite the fact that fines decrease monotonically as demeanor improves, the variance is not significant at the .05 level. That means of these magnitudes are not associated with significant variance is due to the fact that the distribution is skewed very heavily toward the "appropriate" end. Unhappily, there are complete observations on only eleven defendants who made "inappropriate" scores.

Controlling for severity of offense or for recidivism effects no notable changes in this relationship. Though monotonic progressions are generally retained, F values decline (to as low as .15), emphasizing the problems of the small number of observations at one end of the distribution. The data continue to contain enough hints of a relationship to maintain interest and to suggest promise for investigations conducted with better-developed instrumentation.

Thus, our hypotheses about the rights of the judicial role receive only partial confirmation. Inappropriate dress appears to draw sanctions from judges, but only in the imposition of jail sentences. Poor demeanor does not appear to affect jail sentences though there is suggestive (but not significant) evidence that it may affect the magnitude of the fines assessed the defendant.

Summary and Conclusions

Undoubtedly social attitudes, professional role considerations, and community values motivate judicial behavior. It seems likely that lower-court judges—due to their relatively structured and routinized circumstances—are more influenced by role considerations than by personal factors. The salience and role-definitional potential of general statements aimed at a wide, professional judicial audience will increase as the number of opportunities for judicial innovation declines. Such statements universally exhort judges to eschew personal predispositions and act in accordance with legally relevant criteria.

Our hypotheses that sentencing behavior in Detroit Traffic Court could be explained in terms of a legal-professional role are at least partially confirmed. Observed behavior is either directly justified in the law or otherwise a consequence of a role which emphasizes the importance of legitimate legal procedures. Legally relevant criteria in fact do show the most highly significant relationships with judges' actual behavior. Belying the fears of the most cynical observers of the judiciary, the committers of more serious offenses and the repeated offenders draw the harshest penalties. Concomitantly, legally irrelevant criteria, which could enter the judges' decisional processes as a consequence of personality or of playing an alternate role, are found to be almost totally without effect. Neither a defendant's social class nor his race affects the severity of sentence which is meted out. Though under some limited circumstances judges do appear to respond leniently to defendants' youth, evidence of judicial "irrationality" and prejudice, so prominent in other literature, are largely absent from the Detroit data.

Though the judicial role may restrict judges from using defendants' social characteristics as criteria for sentencing, it cuts two ways. The *rights* of the role include the receipt of respect by these exponents of the legal order. We posited that defendants who did not manifest this respect would be regarded as corrosive of the status of the law and that the judges would impose sanctions on them in the form of harsher punishments. The data provide us with some confirmation and with some interesting suggestive relationships. The more appropriately one dresses in court, the less likely he is to be sentenced to jail. The respect connoted by appropriate clothing does not appear to save its wearers from fines equivalent to their less well attired counterparts, however.

Courtroom demeanor does not relate to jail sentence at all. The data on fines, however, suggest stiffer penalties for those who do not exhibit deference. But since these data are troubled by a skewed distribution, the relationships do not attain statistical significance and must therefore be regarded with some qualification.

In sum, the behavior of the Detroit Traffic Court judges is generally consistent with the hypotheses we have deduced from role-theoretic considerations. Although all hypotheses were not confirmed and although demonstrated relationships were not all startlingly dramatic, the notion of a professional judicial role has demonstrated promise for the explanation of the behavior of lower-court judges.

NOTES AND QUESTIONS

1. What can we learn about judicial sentencing behavior and concepts of a legal-professional role from Jaros and Mendelsohn's study? Do their findings contradict Hamilton's conclusions about personal factors (Reading 50, at 472, *supra*)? Is it possible that Judge Cox, the segregationist, might ignore the fact that a defendant in a traffic case was Negro, yet handle a voting rights case quite differently? What is the relevance of the type of case?

Stuart S. Nagel, Professor of Political Science at the University of Illinois, studied disparities in the sentencing of defendants having different background characteristics. In selecting state cases for the year 1962, he used a procedure developed by the National Opinion Research Center for sampling; he used all of the federal criminal cases decided in 1963. He limited his attention to larceny and assault cases; there were 846 felonious assault and 1,103 grand larceny cases from the states and 196 assault and 785 interstate larceny cases from the federal system.

One who could not afford to hire his own lawyer was classified as indigent. Nagel found that the indigent were much less likely to be recommended for probation by a probation officer or to be granted probation or a suspended sentence by a judge than the nonindigent. Some of the results can be explained by the relation between race and indigence, but Nagel concluded that "indigent defendants suffer more discrimination than Negro defendants in the administration of criminal justice."

In the state larceny cases, 74% of the guilty Negroes received prison sentences while only 49% of the guilty whites did; the disparity remained when one held prior criminal record constant. In the federal larceny cases, 63% of the Negroes and 44% of the whites were recommended for prison sentences. However, the Negro was more likely to receive a shorter sentence than the white who was sentenced. There were disparities in the prison-probation data for assault cases which ran in the same direction but which were much less than in the larceny cases.

See Nagel, "Disparities in Criminal Procedure," 14 *UCLA Law Review* 1272, 1281-82, 1284-87 (1967); Nagel, "The Tipped Scales of American Justice," 3 *Transaction* 2 (1966).

To what extent, if at all, do Nagel's findings qualify or contradict those of Jaros and Mendelsohn?

2. Many judges are popularly elected. Suppose a judge were elected by an electorate biased against men who wear beards and long hair. The judge gave harsher sentences to such people. Is he departing from his legal-professional role?

3. What assumptions, if any, do Jaros and Mendelsohn make about the values implicit in the legal-professional role? Are their views consistent with a Marxist interpretation of law? How would a Marxist explain a correlation between, say, humility of demeanor and appropriateness of dress and sentencing behavior?

4. Suppose a judge has had a son killed by a driver who was speeding and lost control of his car. The judge gives all speeders the maximum sentence allowed by the law. The statute sets a range of sanctions and says nothing about how a judge is to select an appropriate sentence within that range. Is such a judge departing from his legal-professional role? Did Jaros and Mendelsohn establish that none of their Detroit traffic court judges were acting under the influence of such personal considerations?

5. What kind of judge would be more likely to be severe toward juvenile delinquents—a well-read young judge who kept up with professional literature, did not wear robes to court and was knowledgeable about delinquency, or a judge with the opposite traits? Somewhat surprisingly, a team of social scientists studying juvenile justice in the Boston area found that the more "professional" judge was the more severe; that is, he more often recommended procedures that ended up with commitment of the juvenile. Stanton Wheeler, Edna Bonacich, M. Richard Cramer & Irving K. Zola, "Agents of Delinquency Control: A Comparative Analysis," in Stanton Wheeler, Ed., *Controlling Delinquents* 31, 54ff (John Wiley 1968). These were the judges who were most concerned with delinquency as a social problem, who were most trusting of the institutions to which juveniles were sent and most open to a "social welfare ideology." Compare Scheff's findings about the behavior of judges with regard to civil commitment; and note particularly, Scheff's contrasting description of the behavior of the judge in Stockton, California. (p. 667)

Can Wheeler and Scheff's findings be plausibly explained in terms of role theory?

[Reading 100]

6. Suzanne Williams, who was seventeen years old at the time, was one of 150 people who picketed the main gate of the Electric Boat Company in Groton, Connecticut, on July 21, 1966, to protest the launching of the 41st Polaris submarine. Nine pickets, including Miss Williams, attempted to enter the shipyard and sat down at the gate blocking the path of invited spectators at the launching. They were arrested, charged with trespassing, and arraigned on the same day. In "My 67 Days in Prison," *WIN,*

Peace and Freedom Through Nonviolent Action, Vol. 2, No. 18, Oct. 20, 1966, at 2-4,* Miss Williams gave her version of what happened as follows:

> I've just gotten out of jail and I'm delighted to be free. It all happened this way. On July 21, along with others, I tried to get into the shipyard of Electric Boat in Groton, Conn. to leaflet the launching of the Polaris submarine, *Will Rogers.* As I had anticipated, I was stopped by the EB security guard and the police, told I was trespassing and asked to leave. When I refused, I was dragged across the street into a waiting bus. We asked the officers if we were under arrest, but they wouldn't tell us.
>
> We then drove to New London and parked outside the courthouse. An officer came in and began booking us. When my turn came I again asked if we were under arrest. He replied that we were and that I was charged with trespassing, resisting arrest and breach of the peace. He told us all that if we did not cooperate in court that we probably would get 30 days for contempt of court. At this point I had already decided not to cooperate, but his statement made me review the reasons for my decision.
>
> I had decided to talk to everyone in the interests of communication and courtesy, but not to cooperate physically with the court. Primarily, I noncooperated for the same reason I had gone limp when taken into custody: I felt that my actions at Electric Boat were correct, that I should not assist others in interfering with these actions. Also, while I have great respect for justice, I have a number of objections to the present court system—for instance, that the court is the tool which our government uses to punish those who oppose immoral laws such as the Selective Service Act; and that the court discriminates between rich and poor.
>
> When I declined to come forward to the bench, Judge George Kinmouth found me in contempt of court and sentenced me to 30 days. The others were continued to a later date, when most were fined $25. Throughout the 30 days I cooperated with the jail in all respects, except that I fasted from Hiroshima Day to Nagasaki Day. I can give no real reason for cooperation with the jail in view of my noncooperation with the courts, as jails are certainly bad *per se.* I merely felt that a line must be drawn somewhere in each

---

case, and was not sure I could handle noncooperation with the jail at that time. Also, I did not want to annoy the jail authorities.

On August 19 my 30 days were up and I went to Groton Circuit Court to appear before Judge Luke Stapleton on the original charges. I was again dragged into the court room, but this time was placed right in front of the bench, on the floor. The judge and I talked for several minutes. I told him why I could not, in good conscience, cooperate. He asked me questions concerning my education, employment, and various other matters. My impression was that he is a nice guy. However, when I continued to remain seated, he found me in contempt of court, and I was again sentenced, this time to 60 days. I wrote to the judge, explaining again my reasons for noncooperation, reassured him that I had nothing against him, and asked to be released. He answered immediately with a friendly telegram, but his position remained unchanged.

On Tuesday, September 27, Mr. Arnold Klau came to visit me. He is a lawyer of the American Civil Liberties Union and was interested in the facts that I had had no counsel and (most of the time) no guardian. When he understood my position in respect to the court, however, he suggested that I apply for modification of sentence, as he felt that the judge and I had the same respect for the concept of justice, and neither of us liked my imprisonment. My statement to Judge Stapleton was as follows: "I would like to apply for a reduction of my sentence to time served. My actions in court were not intended to indicate disrespect for justice. To me, the achieving of justice is one of the highest aspirations of man and those who wear the robes of justice, the symbol of such aspirations, are entitled to the decent respect of mankind. I am sorry that my actions in court were taken for disrespect. They were not so intended." The judge then drove the considerable distance from Hartford to New London, opened court, and purged me of contempt. He then asked the prosecutor to *nolle* the other charges against me, as I had already served 68 days, and the prosecutor did so. Mr. Klau had seen me at 9:00 a.m. and I was released at around 4:00 p.m. on the same day. I was surprised to find that the judge was waiting outside the jail with Mr. Klau, and actually rode in the same car with us a good deal of the way to Hartford. He was very friendly. I am convinced there are good reasons for both noncooperation and cooperation with the court. This time I was moved to the former.

I feel that my experience was, as a whole, a valuable one, although I now deplore jails and prisons more than ever.

Accepting Miss Williams' story, did Judge Kinmouth play a legal-professional judicial role? Did Judge Stapleton? Is this incident consistent with Jaros and Mendelsohn's findings? Does it indicate any difficulties with role theory?

b. The role of the lawyer

[Reading 101]

NOTE: Eulau and Sprague on Lawyers in Politics

Heinz Eulau and John D. Sprague, two political scientists, in *Lawyers in Politics: A Study in Professional Convergence,** have studied the lawyer as a legislator and compared him with non-lawyers. Their research technique was, in part, to define the lawyer's role cluster and relate it to elements of the legislator's role cluster which they discovered by coding legislator's answers to a questionnaire.

What is the lawyer's role cluster? Eulau and Sprague discuss the lawyer-client relationship in terms of the lawyer's style, focus and scope. The style is one of a trusted fiduciary who, however, is detached and not personally involved in his client's affairs. On the one hand, the attorney must not reveal communications from his client. On the other hand, he may withdraw if he does not wish to represent a client. The focus and scope involve four aspects of the lawyer's role: as advocate, as attorney, as counselor and as contact man. The *advocate* builds a case and persuades decision-makers. The *attorney* is a negotiator, mediator and arbitrator—one with power to resolve disputes but with professional distance from others; a man who can deal with third parties, particularly other lawyers, without ego involvement. The *counselor* is an adviser, but the modern counselor gives advice about the best solution for a total problem and not merely about what is and is not "legal." The counselor clarifies issues, suggests alternatives and points out the consequences of proposals. Obviously, this strategic position may give the lawyer great influence over policy choices. Finally, the *contact man* knows whom to ask, how to ask him and how to get to see him. Frequently the man with access and such knowledge has great influence.

---

* Heinz Eulau, Professor of Political Science, Stanford University; John D. Sprague, Professor of Political Science, Washington University. Published by Bobbs-Merrill Co., Inc., 1964.

Eulau and Sprague compared lawyer roles with those legislator roles which seemed similar. They wished to know whether lawyers, because of their professional role cluster, behaved differently in the legislature than non-lawyers. For example, the lawyer as an attorney who negotiates can be compared to the legislator who acts as a go-between and who bargains and compromises to reconcile divergent interests. One might expect to find lawyers easily moving from the lawyer role of attorney to the legislative role of go-between. Yet Eulau and Sprague's data show very few instances where lawyers are different from non-lawyers in taking any of the legislative roles that parallel lawyer roles. Lawyers tend to be more partisan than non-lawyers. One might see some carry-over from the role of advocate, but, as Eulau and Sprague indicate, a better explanation is that lawyers have more to gain from party loyalty than others since it is related to success in practice and the chance to gain many different kinds of government jobs. There was only one area in which there were important differences between lawyers and non-lawyers. The lawyer was viewed as an expert in his own field by non-lawyer legislators. Thus the lawyer was called on for advice on such "legal" problems as determining the constitutionality of proposals or drafting the language to be used in a bill. Moreover, he was thought to be appropriately trained to render important service on committees and to serve as committee chairman and in positions of legislative leadership.

NOTES AND QUESTIONS

1. What do Eulau and Sprague mean when they talk of the lawyer's role cluster and identify the elements within that cluster as advocate, attorney, counselor and contact man? Consider a member of the bar who specializes in representing plaintiffs in negligence cases, the General Counsel of the General Electric Corporation, a general practitioner in a city of 150,000, a lawyer who works for the Civil Aeronautics Board and the Attorney General of the United States. Will all of them be advocates, attorneys, counselors and contact men? Will some emphasize one element in the role cluster more than another? Will some or all do things not encompassed within Eulau and Sprague's categories? How do you discover what the lawyer's role is?

2. Do Eulau and Sprague convince you that lawyers have a distinct role with attributes not widely shared by others? The role of "counselor," for example, is shared with psychiatrists, ministers, deans at universities and many others. Would "middle-class professionals who counsel" be a better role description

than "lawyer"? How do you decide what are the boundaries of a role and what is its appropriate label?

3. What is the significance of the part lawyers play in the general, day to day functioning of the legal system, quite apart from their courtroom roles? Professor Willard Hurst of the University of Wisconsin Law School points out that lawyers are part of the enforcement system of the law through their work in counseling clients. Their advice often channels clients from an illegal to a legal way of achieving their goals. *See* Hurst, *The Growth of American Law: The Law Makers* 303-04, 344-45, 355-56 (Little, Brown 1950). Undoubtedly this is often the case. However, "many lawyers have difficulty in getting their clients to ask for advice before the clients have made decisions and taken action, and even in getting them to follow the advice that is given. For example, consider the embarrassment of the General Electric legal department when the price-fixing conspiracy was discovered and it was disclosed how carefully the conspirators had evaded the scrutiny of the legal staff." Macaulay, "Law Schools and the World Outside Their Doors: Notes on the Margins of 'Professional Training in the Public Interest,' " 54 *Virginia Law Review* 617 (1968). *See also* Blumberg's conception of the lawyers' performance within the system as expressed in Reading 11, at 122, *supra*.

4. What effect on the social structure can be attributed to the dominance of certain aspects of political and economic life by lawyers?

Richard A. Posner, "Natural Monopoly and Its Regulation," 21 *Stanford Law Review* 548, 623-24 (1968), analyzes government regulation of the so-called natural monopolies, and finds that government has failed to evaluate realistically the "costs and benefits of regulation"; there is far more regulation than can be justified on economic grounds. The reasons for this state of affairs lie, in part, in "the character of education in the disciplines relating to public-policy questions":

Lawyers in fact dominate the regulatory process. Commissioners and leading staff members are drawn almost wholly from their ranks. Most legislators are lawyers and so are most of the representatives of the regulated firms who appear before the agencies, and all of the judges who review regulatory action. A lawyer's training and experience are indispensable to the practical implementation of social policy. What is too readily assumed is that lawyers are also expert in the underlying policies themselves, a view that lawyers, who are among the most facile of "generalists," eagerly promote. Unhappily, the overwhelming majority of lawyers involved with regulation are largely ignorant of the principles of economics. . . . Most law schools do little to remedy this deficiency. A law student's exposure to the regulated industries is normally limited to the administrative-law class, which deals with procedural questions, not with economic policies. What law schools principally instill in their students is sensitivity to the formal processes of the law and to considerations of fairness and equity, emphases that go far to explain the continuing preoccupation of both practicing lawyers and legal scholars with the procedural and distributional questions in the regulatory field—such as how much of the pie should investors get and how much consumers. Issues as or more important to the welfare of society—issues of economic efficiency in the broadest sense of that term—are usually ignored because the province of a different discipline. . . .

In "Careers of Lawyers, Law Practice, and Legal Institutions," 28 *American Sociological Review* 47, 54 (1963), Jack Ladinsky suggested that "partly because legal talent from quality law schools has flowed heavily into the large firms for many years, there has been extensive elaboration of legal procedures to handle the problems of corporate enterprises as opposed to those to care for the problems of private citizens." Areas of law "unrelated to the operation of corporate enterprises" have not been the beneficiaries of "the same level of creativity." He mentions "public and private welfare, personal injury, divorce, home finance," where developments have been "less dramatic than developments in corporate taxation, mergers, stocks and bonds."

Is Professor Ladinsky right? Lawrence Friedman, in a review of Beryl H. Levy's *Corporation Lawyer: Saint or Sinner?* (Chilton Co. 1961), in 63 *Columbia Law Review* 1537, 1540 (1963) argues that "it is wholly erroneous to assume that, had the legal profession not mobilized itself to serve the needs of industrial incorporations, modern big business would have been strangled in infancy and the United States would have remained in the era of cottage handicrafts and subsistence agriculture."

The question—perhaps oversimplified—is whether the economic and social system molds the legal profession, or vice versa. The "right answer" is no doubt some kind of theory of interaction, not a black and white choice. But how would one go about measuring the impact of the legal profession on the social structure—and of the social structure on the legal profession?

5. Particularly in recent years, sociologists have devoted a fair amount of attention to the social background and behavior patterns of American lawyers. Mention should be made of the two studies by Jerome Carlin: *Lawyers on Their Own: A Study of Individual Practitioners in Chicago* (Rutgers U. Press 1962) (an excerpt from this study appears as Reading 102, at 880, *infra*); and *Lawyers' Ethics: A Survey of the New York City Bar* (Russell Sage Foundation 1966). Joel F. Handler did a replication study of the latter: *The Lawyer and His Community: The Practicing Bar in a Middle-Sized City* (U. of Wisconsin Press 1967). Two other recent studies are Erwin O. Smigel, *The Wall Street Lawyer: Professional Organization Man?* (Free Press 1964); and Hubert J. O'Gorman, *Lawyers and Matrimonial Cases: A Study of Informal Pressures in Private Professional Practice* (Free Press 1963). Social backgrounds of lawyers and their effect on the practice have been studied by Jack Ladinsky. *See* "Careers of Lawyers, Law Practice, and Legal Institutions," 27 *American Sociological Review* 47 (1963); and "The Impact of Social Backgrounds of Lawyers on Law Practice and the Law," 16 *Journal of Legal Education* 127 (1963).

Materials on the legal profession and on legal ethics are collected in Vern Countryman & Ted Finman, *The Lawyer in Modern Society* (Little, Brown 1966). A recent general survey is Quintin Johnstone & Dan Hopson, Jr., *Lawyers and Their Work: An Analysis of the Legal Profession in the United States and England* (Bobbs-Merrill 1967).

Two more specialized, but interesting, studies of lawyers in other countries are Walter Weyrauch, *The Personality of Lawyers: A Comparative Study of Subjective Factors in Law, Based on Interviews with German Lawyers* (Yale U. Press 1964); and Brian Abel-Smith & Robert B. Stevens, *Lawyers and the Courts: A Sociological Study of the English Legal System 1750-1965* (Harvard U. Press 1967).

6. Charles Horsky in "The Washington Lawyer," Reading 68, at 590, *supra*, makes this comment:

Certainly, I cannot vouch for the ethical standards among Washington lawyer-lobbyists. I think they are generally high, and that the principal criticism of lobbying activities is in fact directed at the non-lawyer lobbyists, who outnumber the lawyers perhaps ten to one. But neither do I challenge the assertion that there are, and will be, lawyers who recognize no limits. Vague as the ethical standards may be, there is clearly a line that no lawyer should pass. Fundamentally, there can be no more basis for a lawyer to obtain the vote of a member of Congress on the basis of friendship, or on the basis of past, present or future favors, than there is for a lawyer to obtain a vote from a judge or a juror on the same basis. The lawyer stands on a different footing from his client. John Smith, the voter, and also the man who favors H.R. 10,000, can with propriety tell his Congressman that the price of Smith's next vote or his next campaign contribution is the Congressman's own vote for H.R. 10,000. It may be poor citizenship; it may move the Congressman to vote against, rather than for, H.R. 10,000. But it is the essence of democracy, it seems to me, that voters should be able to tell a member of Congress what they want, and to tell the member that if he disagrees, he will lose that voter's support in the next campaign.

The Washington lawyer, or any other lawyer, for that matter, is not the voter. He is retained, and paid, for professional advice and services. But when he is retained, or paid, for his influence or alleged influence over a member of Congress, regardless of the merits of the issue, he is no longer acting as a lawyer. [pp. 57-58]

What does Horsky mean when he says that a lawyer who is paid for his influence over a member of Congress is no longer acting as a lawyer? What conception of a lawyer's role does Horsky express here? Does it have any empirical basis?

102. Lawyers on Their Own: A Study of Individual Practitioners in Chicago

JEROME CARLIN*

The Ethical Dilemmas of
Individual Practice

Between the official requirements of the Canons of Professional Ethics and the practical demands of individual practice there is often sharp conflict. This conflict is apparent not only in the area of getting business, but also in dealings with courts and other official agencies and in relations with clients.

The solicitation problem. . . .

The model for the present American Bar Association Canons of Ethics was the Code of Ethics adopted by the Alabama Bar Association in 1887, which was largely based upon Judge Sharswood's essay on professional ethics published in 1854. Although those responsible for drafting the early Canons were not totally unaware of the special problems created by the large metropolitan environment, the image of the profession that is unmistakably conveyed by the Canons is of the small-town bar, consisting of lawyers who are highly visible not only to one another but to their prospective clientele, and who are capable, therefore, of attracting clients by establishing a reputation in the community as competent practitioners. These conditions, of course, do not exist today in the large metropolitan centers. The individual practitioner frequently finds himself in what we have termed an invisible market for legal services, and a market, furthermore, which is controlled to a large extent by encroaching lay agencies and business brokers. The nearly universal problem of gaining visibility, or of establishing contact with someone or some agency

---

* Coordinator, San Francisco Neighborhood Legal Assistance Foundation. Copyright © 1962 Rutgers University Press. Reprinted from pp. 155-64, by permission.

that has it, leads, as we have seen, to a skeptical, if not cynical view of the passive attitude toward business-getting implicit in the Canons.* A large number of those in the sample [of Chicago lawyers engaged in solo practice], particularly in the early years although by no means confined to that stage in their careers, have assumed an aggressive attitude toward business-getting in violation of the spirit and frequently the letter of the Canons.

The problem of pay-offs and political influence. The use of personal influence and the trading or buying of favors in the courts or administrative agencies in order to obtain special treatment for a client is frowned upon by the Canons. These prohibitions, however, make certain assumptions about the operation and personnel of the courts and administrative agencies and about the law that, like the rules restricting advertising and solicitation, appear to be at odds with actual metropolitan conditions. For a variety of reasons, the use of personal influence and the trading or buying of favors become an almost indispensable part of the individual lawyer's job, especially for those lawyers with more than occasional contact with the courts and administrative agencies.

In the course of handling clients' matters, there appear to be two principal areas in which these problems are most acute. The first involves the routine processing of matters by clerks of the local courts and administrative offices. Here the lawyer is concerned with filing or checking through various documents, with having certain papers or documents certified or issued, with setting dates for hearings or appearances, or with having these dates changed. In order to secure prompt and efficient processing of these matters or to get a case or matter advanced or called ahead, to get a file in a hurry, or for minor conveniences or accommodations, the lawyer *must* take care of the clerk. Better than two out of three lawyers interviewed candidly admitted purchasing favors from clerks. In most instances, this meant giving a few dollars in the form of a tip or gratuity; almost a third also mentioned giving Christmas presents—box of cigars, carton of cigarettes, bottle of whisky—and several said they occasionally had to buy tickets of one kind or another. The lawyers with primarily a real estate or business-corporate practice, and who therefore have least contact with courts, account for most of those not mentioning the necessity for currying favor with the clerks. . . .

* Canons 27 and 28 forbid any kind of advertising or solicitation. [Eds. note]

One lawyer who has drifted out of practice, giving most of his time now to his own investments, recalled the situation as it existed when he was more active in the courts:

I don't do it any more. If it's hard to serve someone with a summons you give a few dollars to the bailiff; a few bucks to get a file to the clerk. . . . You can't get too much done without doing it. A clerk in the Municipal Court in the thirties got $1,800 a year—he has a little education, he has to be a high school graduate—$1,800 a year! Well, if you want something done in a hurry, he'll do it.

Several lawyers more actively engaged in practice made some rather strong comments about the situation:

Those officials are underpaid. Everybody's in there for what they can get.

It is essential to give money to get work done efficiently.

I maybe give them a buck to get on the docket earlier. I'm not naïve, but it doesn't sit well with me. Some lawyers carry dollar bills on them when they go into these offices.

Interviewer: Do you get favors from clerks?
Respondent: If we do, we pay.
Interviewer: At Christmastime too?
Respondent: Any time. That's one of the vicious things about the practice. Not everyone does it, but those who don't, get lost. It's a difficult situation to overcome.

A clerk will call me ahead once in a while, help me with papers.
Interviewer: Do you have to give them a couple of dollars?
Respondent: A hell of a lot more than that, five, ten dollars.
Interviewer: You give them a gift at Christmas?
Respondent: Christmas is all year round.

They all have their hands out, all the time. Jesus Christ, twenty-five, fifty dollars each time, clerks or bailiffs. Sometimes clerks can delay you for a month. . . .

The wide currency of such practices results in part from the sheer inefficiency characteristic of most of these offices, which are generally understaffed and invariably plagued with a large backlog of matters. Probably more significant, however, is the fact that almost all the personnel of these offices are political appointees grown accustomed to the favor system. And, finally, there is the tendency of a good many individual lawyers to compensate for their apparent insecurity, sense of inadequacy, and lack of confidence by acting like bigshots, passing out large tips and presents in order to ensure their being known by the clerks and other officials.

The pay-off and influence problem also arises from the application of certain local statutes and ordinances that are often grossly unrealistic, practically unenforceable, and inevitably coupled with a wide range of administrative discretion. These include most of the local tax laws (statutes dealing with tax foreclosure, personal property tax, real property tax), a large segment of municipal law (zoning ordinances, licensing statutes), and the divorce law (artificial limitations on or definition of the legal grounds for divorce). Under these conditions it is the lawyer who knows somebody in the State's Attorney's Office, in the Board of Zoning or Tax Appeals, in the Board of County Commissioners, or in a variety of other agencies and offices, or who is known by the judges, who will receive the more favorable interpretation or treatment, can expect a more advantageous adjustment or compromise, or will have his matter pushed through more expeditiously. Partly this is just a matter of paying off the right people and partly, because most of these officials are political appointees, of having the right political connections.

The fiduciary problem. A central requirement of the Canons is that the lawyer should adopt a trust or fiduciary relationship with his client, whose best interests he is supposed to promote, and that he deal directly and personally with the client without the intrusion of lay intermediaries. From what we know of the nature of individual practice, however, there appear to be strong pressures forcing the lawyer-client relationship into two deviant forms in conflict with the requirements indicated above.

1. "Clients are expendable." In the case of those lawyers specializing in personal injury, local tax, collections, criminal, and to some extent divorce work, the relationship with the client, as we have seen, is generally mediated by a broker or business supplier who may be either another lawyer or a layman. In these fields of practice the lawyer is principally concerned with pleasing the broker or of winning his approval, more so than he is with satisfying the individual client. The source of business generally counts for more than the client, especially where the client is unlikely to return or to send in other clients. The client is then expendable; he can be exploited to the full. Under these conditions, when a lawyer receives a client from a layman or a referring

lawyer, he has not so much gained a client as a piece of business, and his attitude is often that of handling a particular piece of merchandise or of developing a volume of a certain kind of merchandise. If, for example, as sometimes happens, a client who was originally referred by another lawyer returns, the question that arises is not what obligation this lawyer owes in a professional sense to the client or to the lawyer who initially referred him, but how important the referring lawyer is as a source of business. Where there is an opportunity or prospect of getting more referrals, the lawyer will follow the rule of notifying the referring lawyer (and offering him part of the fee—generally a third) as an inducement to keep sending him matters, otherwise he will not. Some lawyers even extend this policy of notifying the referring lawyer to the situation where the client refers another client, in which case both the referring client and the lawyer may get a cut:

> An ex-client referred me someone. He came [the ex-client] from a certain lawyer. Well, that lawyer still appears on the file—that's my incentive to that lawyer, otherwise he'd be afraid of the repeat. A referral fee goes to the lawyer, and maybe also some to the client who referred it.

Others won't go this far:

> If the client recommends someone else, then it's my client—I won't call the other lawyer.

One reason for the different approach of these two lawyers is that the first is a specialist in personal injury, while the second is a general practitioner and less dependent on other lawyers for business. One young lawyer refused to do any more work for an older lawyer in his suite because where the repeat business was lucrative, the older lawyer insisted on taking complete charge of the matter.

> I used to get some referrals when I came in [to the office], but I asked him to stop—I didn't like the arrangement; they were still his clients and he charged only very small fees. I'd see the client, but he'd set small fees. He used it as an accommodation to his clients to get personal injury cases, so they'd feel warm to him and send him personal injury cases. I made peanuts, but if they came back and referred another case to me, that was to be his client and his business.

In some cases the client will not even know who his lawyer is, that is to say, who is actually doing the work for him. This happens when the referring lawyer does not want the client to know that he has farmed out the matter (e.g., to a "ghost brief writer") because of the risk of losing the client to the other lawyer. As one respondent remarked:

Usually I'll let my client know I'm referring it, but it's not always wise; you can lose clients that way.

A close, trust relationship is probably rarely achieved in the type of practice to which we have just been referring, not only because of the volume-merchandising phenomenon and the importance of the broker but also because most such matters are handled on a contingency basis that gives the lawyer a direct financial stake in the matter. For this reason the client often becomes, literally, a piece of business.

2. "Clients are partners." Unlike the lawyers discussed above, the upper-level real estate and business-corporate lawyers frequently have a close, intimate relationship with their business clients, so much so in fact that many become merged with their clients on something like a business partnership basis. Well over half go in on deals with clients, principally in the area of real estate, and several are officers or on the board of directors of their clients' corporations. Under these conditions it would appear to be difficult to maintain a fiduciary relationship with the client or to adopt toward him an attitude of disinterestedness. A number of respondents recognize the dangers involved in becoming "partners" of their clients, but, nevertheless, they feel that this is the only way to "make it" financially in the law practice.

They told us in law school to stick to the law business and it will take care of you—don't go into business with your clients, no deals or arrangements, you lose your perspective, you really become a partner of your client. But this is baloney. If you're invited to go in, go in by all means; it's the only way to get any financial independence—it's the only way to make it. You can't do it practicing law, you can't get any financial security that way. Ninety per cent of the lawyers can't make it—I haven't to date.

NOTES AND QUESTIONS

1. Are Carlin's individual practitioners playing the solo lawyer role or are they failing to play the lawyer role as defined by the Canons of Ethics?

2. To what extent do personality characteristics determine role definition and role performance? Recall the socially responsible and the authoritarian personalities described by Berkowitz and

Walker (Reading 21, at 198, *supra*). Would one be more likely to follow the Canons of Ethics even where it would mean a client would lose his case than the other? Which one?

[Reading 103]

3. In a survey of lawyers in a smaller city in "down-state" Illinois, Professor Joel Handler found that lawyers generally followed the Canons of Ethics. However, in *The Lawyer and His Community: The Practicing Bar in a Middle-Sized City* 155 (U. of Wisconsin Press 1967), Professor Handler* concluded:

In Prairie City, then, we found what might be considered optimum conditions for the achievement of one of the important goals of professional ethics, that of placing service and fiduciary obligations to clients, colleagues, and the administration of justice above economic self-interest. The general prosperity, shared experiences, and professional integration of this bar could serve as supports for this goal. In both attitudes and behavior, the lawyers agreed that the rules were in general worthwhile; they agreed too on the relative importance of the rules. Yet ethical rules were sometimes rejected or ignored. [Among these lawyers] ethical behavior was related to wealth and stability of clients and to opportunities to violate ethical rules. The same factors that were related to the ethical behavior of Prairie City lawyers were also related to the ethical behavior of the New York City lawyers. In other words, when the lawyers in Prairie City were faced with pressures similar to those faced by the New York City lawyers, they tended to respond in the same way. This was true despite the fact that the Prairie City lawyers differed from the New York City lawyers in terms of social and economic backgrounds and education. The pressures, or conditions of practice, differed both qualitatively and quantitatively, and, we suggest, this accounted for most of the differences in ethical behavior between the two bars.

We interpret this to mean that the ethical commitment of Prairie City lawyers was conditioned by the characteristics of their practice. When or if the social and economic conditions of the community changed, when the bar became more

* Professor of Law, University of Wisconsin. From Joel F. Handler, The Lawyer and His Community (Madison: The University of Wisconsin Press); © 1967 by the Regents of the University of Wisconsin, p. 155. Reprinted by permission.

specialized in terms of clients and areas of practice, it would become increasingly stratified, and professional community would disintegrate. The economic conditions of practice would change and so would the commitment of lawyers to their ethical rules. Proportions of poor and unstable clients and rates of opportunities to violate would rise for certain segments of the bar, and this increase would result in higher levels of violations. As the community increased in size and economic diversity, the bar, in its social characteristics, would look more like the New York City bar; so would its commitment to professional ethics.

To what extent are roles responsive to social and economic conditions of the particular environment of the role-player? Is it meaningful to speak of the role of an individual practitioner lawyer, or are there many roles, depending on where he practices and the conditions of practice?

104. The Army Defense Counsel: Unusual Ethics for an Unusual Advocate

ARTHUR A. MURPHY*

61 COLUMBIA LAW REVIEW 233 (1961)

I. THE CHOICE

The perceptive civilian criminal lawyer often finds himself confronted with difficult ethical choices. The officer-lawyer of the Judge Advocate General's Corps appointed to defend an accused before an Army court-martial must avoid all the pitfalls which threaten the civilian trial lawyer, and a few more besides. Customs, legislatures, courts, and bar associations have provided rules and precedents in matters of ethics that the civilian lawyer may follow with some confidence. The military lawyer, however, cannot safely look to the traditions of courts-martial practice. Activities of defense counsel approved years or even months ago have been condemned by Congress or the Court of Military Appeals. Nor can military counsel anywhere find his ethical obligations "officially" defined.

If asked, most active military lawyers would probably say that the appointed defense counsel should follow the code of ethics of the civilian bar, but closer questioning and study of actual practices uncover startlingly divergent views on the ethical obligations of Army counsel and on the extent to which "professional responsibility" confines the advocate in an adversary proceeding. Thus many judge advocate officers stress the defense counsel's status as an "Army officer and a minister of justice." They see him as a member of a "team" and accordingly expect him to be mindful of the effects of his activity on discipline, to approach

* Associate Professor, Dickinson School of Law. At the time this article was written, the author was a major in The Judge Advocate General's Corps, United States Army. The views expressed in this article are those of the author and do not necessarily represent the views of The Judge Advocate General's Corps or any other governmental agency. Copyright © 1961 Columbia Law Review. Reprinted by permission.

his case with a detached attitude, to raise only plainly meritorious issues, and to cooperate with his staff judge advocate, the prosecutor, and the court. Although they would not deny the accused a "just" result, they want speed, economy, and a frictionless trial, and may even argue that defense counsel should present only such evidence as he personally believes to be true. If convinced of his client's guilt, his only duty is to "protect the rights of the accused" by objecting to improper evidence and procedure.

On the other hand, some judge advocate officers emphasize the adversary nature of court-martial proceedings and the defense counsel's primary duty of fidelity to his client. They acknowledge that the defense counsel's status as an attorney prohibits certain conduct that might help his client, but they recognize no such restraints deriving solely from his status as an Army officer. In fact, a substantial number among this group, including the author, believe that the Army defense counsel should be expected to go further in advancing the interests of his client, should be more "partisan," than his civilian counterpart. The military defense counsel must be a "partisan" in that he should follow his client's wishes more often than a civilian attorney, while defending his client's personal interests more warmly and with less regard for the countervailing interests of the court and the society in which he functions. I do not mean that defense counsel should espouse blindly the schemes and whims of corrupt or foolish clients. Professional responsibility sets limits to his partisanship, and the interests of his client will often be served best by keeping well within those limits.

So that the true relation between the conduct of military lawyers and what they profess may be better understood, this article attempts to explain the partisan philosophy of Army defense counsel, outlining its justification and illustrating its application to areas in which there is liveliest disagreement among military lawyers or in which military ethics differ most sharply from civilian ethics. Further, the ethical standards of Army lawyers in relation to the future will be discussed, with emphasis on the factors that are likely to influence those standards and the efforts that should be made to shape their development.

A. *History*

During the past 180 years the American court-martial trial has evolved from an inquisitorial into a real adversary proceeding. In the beginning there was no defense counsel—or almost none. The sixth amendment right to counsel "in all criminal prosecutions" was not intended to apply to trial by courts-martial, and the "privilege" of an accused to have even privately retained counsel in court was only grudgingly conceded. When the accused was permitted to introduce counsel, some courts-martial limited his participation to whispering advice to his client. Others allowed him to question witnesses and make arguments provided he did not become offensive or delay the course of justice. Many Army officers believed that lawyers were too addicted to legal sophistries and too ignorant of military procedure to be allowed to practice before courts-martial. . . .

Even as the right to counsel crystallized, its value to the client was limited by restrictions imposed by regulations and custom on counsel's activities. Army regulations, 1910, for example, directed the appointed counsel to "guard the interests of the prisoner by all honorable and legitimate means known to the law, *so far as they are not inconsistent with military relations.*" The then Judge Advocate General of the Army warned military lawyers against going "too far in assimilating the court-martial trial to the ordinary criminal trial" and against conducting the defense without "due regard for authority." After World War I, official publications defining the duties of defense counsel dropped the prohibition against using means that although otherwise honorable and legitimate, were "inconsistent with military relations."

From World War I to the enactment of the Uniform Code of Military Justice in 1951, the published decisions of Army Boards of Review and the Judge Advocate General indicated a growing recognition that the defense counsel should be a real adversary. At the same time, the opinions illustrated, in the evils they spotlighted, the continued vitality at the trial level of the notion that the defense counsel should be a "team player." The latter theory was also expounded in a text book widely circulated among military lawyers during World War II.

Since 1951, the new Court of Military Appeals has worked hard at eradicating this lukewarm adversary philosophy. . . .

Generally, the Court of Military Appeals analogizes the military defense counsel's duty of fidelity to client to that of an attorney in a civilian criminal case. On at least one occasion it has analogized it to the higher standards of a court-appointed counsel or public defender. However, . . . decisions . . . seem to indicate the court's awareness that the military lawyer should be more partisan than any civilian counterpart. The members of the Court of Military Appeals appear to respect a fighting defense counsel, and will find a good word for him even when they disapprove of his tactics.

II. *Conditions of Practice*

The basis of the case for partisanship lies in the peculiar conditions under which Army defense counsel practice. The Army's judicial process and the ethics of military lawyers might be explained in terms of conflict between the ideals of the military and those of the legal profession. Examples of this conflict may be seen in the long struggle to free court members and counsel from "command control" and to disabuse court members of cherished misconceptions about their functions. The military environment, the organization and operation of the typical staff judge advocate office, and the lack of contact with civilian members of the legal profession all tend to produce and perpetuate ethical misconceptions among judge advocate officers. A code different from the American Bar Association's Canons of Ethics, one that unblushingly makes a partisan of the military defense counsel, appears to be necessary if trial by court-martial is to approximate trial by civilian court in justice of proceeding and result.

The environment in which the court-martial system must operate is very different from the societal background against which civilian criminal trials are held. The Army has a defined mission, the security of the state; and the bureaucracy and clear lines of authority are an incident to that mission. Distinctive attitudes and ways of thinking, at once a cause and expression of the military environment, are characteristic of the officer corps. The mind of the representative professional officer might be described as disciplined, rigid, logical, inflexible, not intuitive, unemotional. The "military mind" emphasizes "the permanence, irrationality, weakness and evil in human nature. It stresses the supremacy of society over the individual and the importance of order, hierarchy and division of function. . . . It exalts obedience as the highest virtue of military men." In recent years the professional officer has come to expect from military personnel subjective loyalty to superiors and to the Army. He desires simple, direct solutions to problems and tends to disregard subtle factors.

The typical professional officer sees the military justice system as an adjunct of command, useful for promoting discipline and separating undesirable personnel from the service. He would like the system to reflect his own attitude of paternalism towards subordinates: fair but firm and unencumbered by legal technicalities.[35]

---

[35] These conclusions have been confirmed by the author in discussions with several hundred officers during military justice classes conducted over the last five years.

The viewpoint of the officer corps, although often modified in individuals by personal influences, is a persisting reality that shapes court-martial practice and procedure. The military mind not only affects legislation and department policy but enters the judicial process directly in the persons of the commanding generals who appoint general courts-martial, refer charges to trial, and, in case of conviction, review the findings and sentence, and in the persons of the members of courts-martial who function as a jury.

The appointed defense counsel is a member of a judge advocate section organized along bureaucratic military lines. His prospects for promotion and favorable future assignment depend upon earning the good opinion of his chief, the staff judge advocate. The latter, if he is so minded, can make life disagreeable and can, at will, relieve the defense counsel from further duty in that capacity. Since staff judge advocates are actively involved in the disposition of cases and may come under considerable pressure from the convening authority, it is not surprising to find that they often favor defense counsel who plead a substantial number of clients guilty, stipulate freely, and try their cases quickly and without complications. Although the majority of staff judge advocates do not deliberately or regularly interfere with the proper freedom of defense counsel, many do influence counsel by their attitudes and some are occasionally guilty of affirmative interference.

Conflicts of interest may also arise from the fact that the prosecutor is usually a member of the same section as the defense counsel and may be senior to him in rank or even his supervisor in unrelated work. The prosecutor who is willing to make his own job harder by urging defense counsel to contest each case to the fullest extent consistent with the interests of the client is, of course, rare.

The defense counsel may be exposed to improper influences in addition to a degree of coercion. Friendship for the staff judge advocate or prosecutor may affect his independent judgment. He may not want to embarrass "the office." Furthermore, the defense counsel is frequently young and inexperienced. He may not be immune to the notions of military expediency shared by many of the nonlawyers who sit as members of courts-martial or with whom he fraternizes. Especially if he is lazy by nature, he is likely to be attracted by a philosophy that requires great exertion only when the defense counsel "believes" in his cause. Finally, he lacks the economic incentives of civilian practice. He need not win to earn a fee or attract other clients. On the contrary, he may feel that if he is too successful his career will suffer.

Although vigorous advocacy may be inspired by a craftsman's pride, idealism, or egotism, it is nevertheless identity of interest secured by a fee that is one of the surest guarantees of effective representation in civilian practice.

These are the main reasons why the concept of the defense counsel as a "team player" is slow to die in the Army and why the Canons of Ethics of the American Bar Association are not the antidote for this pernicious concept. The Canons prescribe ideal conduct for members of a profession whose self-interest, if unbridled, would incline them to excesses in behalf of their clients. The military code, on the other hand, must be designed to counterbalance forces that tend to separate counsel from client. The Canons require lawyers to make fine distinctions and to balance carefully their duties to clients, court, and profession. The military code must relieve the defense counsel from such delicate decisions in situations in which he may be improperly influenced by factors he scarcely perceives. In short, the military code of ethics must encourage the appointed defense counsel to be more partisan than the civilian lawyer. All principles of morality, conscience, etiquette, and taste that are not strictly rules of ethics must be identified as such. The privilege of the defense counsel to act according to his own discretion absent ethical duty must be respected by his associates and superiors. He should not be censured, given a poor efficiency rating, or prematurely relieved from service as defense counsel except for incompetence or unethical behavior. . . .

B. *Pretrial Conduct Toward Other Officers*

An ethical attorney's professional conduct towards other lawyers should be characterized by candor and fairness. Judged by the standards of the civilian bar, the partisan military defense counsel may appear somewhat less than candid and fair in his relationship to the trial counsel (the military's title for a prosecutor) and the staff judge advocate. The appointed defense counsel may not properly consider himself a member of a "team," however cordial his personal relations with prosecutor and staff judge advocate. The trial counsel is his opponent in an adversary proceeding, and since the staff judge advocate usually has different aims than the defense counsel, even when the former performs his quasi-judicial functions in a truly impartial manner, the partisan defense counsel should treat his staff judge advocate more like a respected adversary than a judicial officer.

The partisan defense counsel has no general obligation to be helpful to the government. It is grossly improper for him gratuitously to volunteer advice or aid to the staff judge advocate or trial counsel when such assistance will be detrimental to the accused. The accused's attorney should keep the nature of the defense and the identity of his witnesses secret whenever he believes he can profit through surprise. He should never agree to a stipulation of fact or testimony unless he believes that the matter is of no consequence or indisputable and readily proved, or that his client will benefit either from the stipulation itself or from some concession offered in exchange by the prosecutor or staff judge advocate. He may try to win a concession even when the stipulation relates to inconsequential or uncontrovertible matter.

The staff judge advocate has no right to dictate to the defense counsel how he should prepare or try his case. The latter may disregard a request or order that he not question potential government witnesses until after the trial counsel has seen them, or that he not hamper the prosecution by telling government witnesses about their testimonial rights or their privilege to ignore an ineffective subpoena.

C. *Negotiation of Pleas*

Since 1953 it has become common practice for staff judge advocates and defense counsel to negotiate agreements under which the staff judge advocate promises, on behalf of the convening authority, to reduce the sentence adjudged by the court to an agreed punishment if the accused pleads guilty. In negotiating guilty pleas, the Army defense counsel cannot eschew the bargaining technique and consideration of extraneous circumstances. He should be concerned more with the staff judge advocate's reaction to the proposals and arguments he makes than with their inherent reasonableness or justice. When the defense counsel initiates an offer to plead guilty, he must at least urge the lightest sentence that a dispassionate lawyer would consider reasonable, and may even ask for an unreasonably light sentence. In support of his position he may argue not only such obviously relevant factors as extenuating and mitigating matters, and a particular philosophy of punishment, but also the possibilities of an acquittal, delays and difficulties he can cause, and the embarrassment the command or particular individuals may suffer if the case is contested and publicized. He may engage in some "puffing" so long as his inflated statements do not seem to be assertions that he personally knows certain facts to be true. . . .

IV. CONCLUSIONS

Partisanship . . . discourages improper police action and official practices. Those investigators, staff judge advocates, and other officials who might be willing to cut corners to avoid "troublesome" requirements of law are sometimes deterred by knowledge that a vigilant defense counsel stands ready to expose them. That the problem of "command control" has become less serious in recent years is partly due to the courage of counsel who have challenged questionable acts of their superiors.

Command control, however, is not completely dead: a convening authority may appoint as court members only those officers who share his opinions and attitudes; he may relieve from further duty a court-martial that, in his opinion, improperly acquits or shows undue leniency; members of courts-martial may be subtly intimidated by their superiors. Although the defense counsel may not be able to object successfully to such obscure forms of command influence, his partisanship may offset their prejudicial effect.

Perhaps the best argument for universal adoption of partisan ethics is that such ethical principles are already widely and successfully followed in practice, if not in name, by experienced defense counsel and judge advocates who work with them. Partisanship has been one of the factors that have improved the suspected military offender's chances of avoiding conviction or of receiving a light sentence during the last ten years. Staff judge advocates are less likely to refer a charge for trial without compelling evidence; they are readier to compromise in guilty plea negotiations; courts-martial are more prone to acquit or to impose moderate sentences. Although military lawyers differ about the quality of the resulting justice and its effect on discipline and morale, the change would seem to be for the better. There is little danger that unjustified acquittals, even if they occur, will have an adverse effect on discipline. The evidence in courts-martial cases is rarely publicized. Few men outside an accused's own unit are likely to remark on the results of a trial or have any basis for questioning the decision. Furthermore, since the American soldier's sense of justice is best satisfied by a virile adversary process, the effect of partisanship on morale is positive.[103] The threat to discipline and morale is not from a judicial

---

[103] A trial I once watched stands out in my memory. I knew from private conversation that the defense counsel had no faith in his client or case, but one would never have suspected this from the zeal and skill with which he opposed the prosecutor and presented a case for the accused. Although convicted, the soldier not only thanked his counsel but apologized to him for

system that reflects the liberal, democratic ideals of our civilian courts, but from the reluctance of some professional officers to accept such a system gracefully.[104]

Two organizational changes have been suggested for taking the defense counsel from under the real or apparent influence of the staff judge advocate and convening authority. One innovation, never seriously considered, contemplated a separate corps of civilian attorneys. The other, recently studied by the Judge Advocate General of the Army, envisions a separate corps of officers-defense counsel reporting to the Judge Advocate General, and thus less vulnerable to local control. Although either change might diminish the need for partisanship, the probable gains seem outweighed by considerations of cost, administration, efficient use of personnel and the possible disadvantage to which a defense counsel might be put as a stranger to the command, the potential witnesses, and the court members. Instead it is more feasible for the Judge Advocate General's Corps to improve the character of defense representation by pursuing two objectives: First, to educate all judge advocate personnel having any connection with courts-martial in the principles of partisan ethics; second, a long range goal, to improve military justice so that appointed defense counsel can eventually embrace the ethical ideals of the rest of the legal profession.

Promulgation of an official code, the obvious method for bringing about the change to partisan ethics, is not advisable. Drafting a code detailed enough to be helpful would be difficult, and immediate codification might inhibit desirable responsiveness to changing conditions. Although the ethical standards of a bar can by crystallized by decree, they should not be dictated in toto by court, legislature or bar association.

The change to partisanship can be accomplished best by the proper education of personnel. Whenever a staff judge advocate assigns an inexperienced defense counsel, the latter should be oriented in the ways of partisanship. More important, by his

---

not having brought him a stronger case. I talked with a master-sergeant who had also watched the trial, a hash-marked, ribboned old soldier. "It's been a long time since I saw a general court-martial," he said. "I never thought a soldier could get as fair a shake from a military court as that boy did today."

[104] It might be argued that adoption of a partisan code will brand military lawyers as a venal lot in the eyes of the profession and the public. The best answer is that there now exists suspicion among soldiers, the public, and the profession that military lawyers are not always loyal to the soldiers they represent. Since he is not selected by the accused, wears a uniform, draws Army pay, and works in the same office with those he opposes, the military defense counsel can best protect his reputation by unequivocal partisan behavior.

own impartial and fair attitude in every case, the staff judge advocate should demonstrate his sincerity in what he says. Junior officers should be given every possible opportunity to try cases in partnership with experienced lawyers; nothing will do more to improve the competency of Army trial lawyers and to dispel notions that the defense counsel should be a tepid advocate. . . .

Two larger reforms may make the need for partisanship less pressing. They require no new legislation and much has already been done to bring them about. First, each staff judge advocate should strive to eradicate any vestiges of command control within his jurisdiction. Court members should be impartially selected, and should serve out their terms subject to discharge only for incompetence on the recommendation of the law officer. Second, every judge advocate officer should do all in his power to educate lay officers in the nature of the judicial process and the adversary system. The duty of a court member to exercise independent, unbiased judgment and to accord an accused his legal rights should be impressed upon every person who may serve in that capacity. Once these ideas are universally accepted by the officers' corps, accused soldiers will be sure of fair hearings, and opposition to other court-martial reforms will dwindle.

But for the present, the military defense counsel should be the zealous and courageous partisan of his clients. There will be time enough for him to temper his outlook when partisanship is no longer an indispensable condition to justice in the Army.

NOTES AND QUESTIONS

1. Murphy's article concerns what is called role strain or role conflict. A man finds himself both in the role of defense counsel and army officer, and attributes of each of these roles pull in different directions. Civilian lawyers can be subject to similar role strain when they work for one client or are dependent on one governmental agency to supply work. *Compare* Blumberg, Reading 11, at 122, *supra.*

2. Murphy suggests ways to isolate the Army lawyer from the demands of one of his conflicting roles, and suggests changes in the attributes of the other. How effective are his proposals likely to be? Can changes in the structure of the work setting produce the kinds of role change he wants? *See* William M. Evan, "Due Process of Law in Military and Industrial Organizations," 7 *Administrative Science Quarterly* 187 (1962).

3. Consider whether and to what extent the following situations are pregnant with the possibility of role strain; how do you think any such strain is resolved:

(a) a trained lawyer acting as prosecutor in a "purge" trial in a totalitarian country;

(b) a trained Soviet lawyer acting as defense counsel for an American tourist arrested in the Soviet Union and branded as a spy;

(c) a company doctor who examines workers who are claiming compensation for injuries suffered on the job;

(d) a company doctor who has to decide whether workers have sufficiently recovered from a communicable disease to return to work;

(e) a conservative lawyer appointed to defend an accused Maoist in a trial for sedition;

(f) a devout Roman Catholic judge deciding a divorce case.

[Reading 105]

Lawyers are not necessarily or invariably apt to abandon their role as lawyers and play on the team. Wilbert E. Moore,* a sociologist with great experience studying business, comments as follows in *The Conduct of the Corporation* 184-85 (1962):

> The difficulty of integration of specialists arises from still another source. Experts tend to be dedicated as well as merely self-interested men. Self-interest alone would lead them to exaggerate their importance to the enterprise as a whole. Dedication leads them to plead their cause with deep moral fervor and to take their responsibilities so seriously that a balanced judgment, a proper consideration of other views and other functions, becomes quite unlikely.
>
> Let me illustrate this problem by comments directed at lawyers. . . . There is probably some malice in my selection, but I shall stand by my comments anyway.
>
> Because the law is ubiquitous, a pervasive feature of social life, the lawyer tends to assert the importance of legal clearance on virtually every external relationship of the corporation and some internal ones as well. This gives to lawyers, in effect, a very wide range of negative responsibilities, not of performance but of preventing unlawful or questionable performance. They hold extensive "veto powers." Now this problem would not be so serious were it not for some characteristics of the law and lawyers. The popular and relatively

---

* Formerly Professor of Sociology, Princeton University; presently on the staff of the Russell Sage Foundation. Copyright © 1962 Random House, Inc. Reprinted by permission.

desirable belief in the certainty of the law is not shared by
its experts. In many instances the legislation is unclear, the
judicial cases and precedents either ambiguous or not clearly
applicable to the questioned conduct. The lawyer commonly
does not deal in certainties but in probabilities—that is, reasoned guesses as to how judges or juries would decide if the
case went to trial.

If the probability of an adverse decision, of defeat, is
significantly above zero, the lawyer turns cautious. He is
among the most suspicious of men. Indeed, at least in corporate circles, the lawyer is a professional paranoid. His
motto is, "If in doubt, say No," and he is often in doubt.

This is a different picture of the lawyer from that of the
instrumentalist, the "slicker" who permits his client to keep
within the law while doing something ethically wrong. The
story is told of the original J. P. Morgan that his lawyer,
commenting on a proposed business deal, remonstrated, "But
you can't do that, Mr. Morgan." Mr. Morgan, the story goes,
replied, "Your job is to tell me how to do what I want to
do." Mr. Morgan's attorney may have done so, but I do
not see the modern corporation lawyer so easily subdued.
Within his own field, and it is a tremendous territory, his
word is literally law. In my opinion this has a distinctly
dampening effect on whatever spark of spirit the large corporation still permits.

Not all corporate lawyers would agree with Moore's impressions.
They argue that they are actually involved in a bargaining
process. If they obstruct the plans of a company's executives too
often, the executives will not bring problems to them. Thus
the lawyer's tactic is to object to a proposed course of action
only where it is critical to stop it. (Of course, the corporate
lawyer is the one who defines what is a critical action, and others
might disagree with his judgment.) Moreover, if a lawyer is
asked to comment, and approves of a course of action, and a
$1,000,000 lawsuit faces the company as a result, it is the lawyer
who will have to shoulder much of the blame.

3. How do institutions arrange structure and ideology to deal
with role conflict? What kinds of role conflict might a judge
face? How does the system help lessen this conflict? How does
the legal system aid the corporate lawyer in lessening his role
strain?

4. How did Murphy compile his data? What are the advantages and disadvantages of his methodology?

c. The role of the police

106. Justice Without Trial: Law Enforcement in Democratic Society

JEROME H. SKOLNICK*

The police . . . [face] the problem of managing divergent expectations of conduct. Democracy's ideological conflict between the norms governing the work of maintaining order and the principle of accountability to the rule of law provides the justification for various demands upon the policeman. He may be expected to be rule enforcer, father, friend, social servant, moralist, street-fighter, marksman, and officer of the law. The problem of organizing and defining such demands furnishes the basis for the institutional analysis of police. The problem itself suggests the situational difficulties affecting the policeman's capacity to be a responsible law enforcement official who enforces order under the rule of law.

The dilemma of the police is further complicated. It is possible in practice for applications of the rule of law as well as conceptions of order to vary. Standards for applying the rule of law are developed by the courts in the setting of specific police practices. Standards governing search and seizure practices, for example, are usually developed in narcotics cases, while standards of the legality of procedures for obtaining confessions typically arise in cases where there is an element of assault. Similarly, conceptions of order are subject to varying interpretations and tend to influence and be influenced by conditions prevailing in police work. General statements about the police conception of order and its sources can be made . . . but it is also possible to show how the generalized conception is modified by the perceived

* Professor of Sociology, University of California at San Diego. Copyright © 1966, John Wiley & Sons, Inc., Publishers. Reprinted from pp. 17-18, 20-21, 196-99, 231-42, by permission.

requirements of various police assignments. When the informer system is discussed, for example, it becomes clear that the meaning of criminal conduct is differently evaluated depending on how the perceived criminality fits in with procedures characteristically used to enforce specific categories of the law.

The division of labor within the police department (burglary, vice control, traffic control, patrol) supplies a methodological framework for observing and comparing the assumptions and outcomes of police practices in democratic society. Policing specialties generate distinctive patterns for the invocation and enforcement of the law of crimes: who first sees a criminal act, how it is reported, how apprehension takes place. In gathering participant-observational data, then, the division of police labor set the background for the working hypothesis of the study: *the characteristic pattern of enforcement, with its special arrangements for gathering information, processing offenders, and evaluating the competence of personnel, all under rule of law, determines operational law enforcement.* The idea of operational law enforcement should suggest both the attitudes and behavior of policemen responding to judicial rulings, and interpersonal relations with the accused, the prosecutor, defense attorney, judge, and whenever applicable, with the general public.

Underlying this working question is a more general and fundamental issue growing out of the concept of law enforcement. This issue is the meaning and purpose of law in democratic society. The idea of law enforcement in such a society, taken seriously, suggests that legally constituted institutions such as the police exist not only to preserve order, but to serve the rule of law as an end in itself. On the other hand, the circumstances of the occupational environment, with its associated requirements that the police maintain order, might develop a very different conception of law in police, a conception without articulation or explicit philosophical justification, but existing nevertheless. Such a conception might perceive law not primarily as an instrument for guaranteeing individual freedom, but, as in the Soviet Union, an instrument of education, as a father is a teacher of children. . . .

The meaning of law in a society is ultimately dependent upon its political and social philosophy. When law is viewed primarily as an instrument of education or as an instrument of order, rather than as a goal in itself, the society no longer conceives of punishment as a last resort, to be used only reluctantly. . . .

It is not only that the law of a total state has as its essential condition that the society conceive of itself as a single great family. Single great families where the question of values is open to discussion are imaginable. There needs to be also a conception of the inevitability of events, a sense of place in the interpretation of the grand sweep of history, a logical connection, and, ultimately, a belief in the righteousness of killing for the sake of logic. This sort of certainty as to what is right, and the willingness to adopt the most extreme punitive measures in defense of it, is the essence of the conception of law in a total state. Father knows all in such a family, and he may, if he thinks it necessary, rule by the rod. This conception of law necessarily contemplates minimal restraint on authority.

By contrast, a democratic society envisions constraint upon those who are granted the right to invoke the processes of punishment in the name of the law. They must draw their rules clearly, state them prospectively. The rules themselves must be rational, not whimsically constructed, and carried out with procedural regularity and fairness. Most important of all, rule is from below, not above. Authorities are servants of the people, not a "vanguard" of elites instructing the masses. The overriding value is consent of the governed. From it derives the principle of the accountability of authority, accountability primarily to courts of law and ultimately to a democratically constituted legislature based upon universal suffrage. . . .

ADMINISTRATIVE BIAS OF THE CRAFTSMAN

The policeman views criminal procedure with the *administrative bias of the craftsman,* a prejudice contradictory to due process of law. That is, the policeman tends to emphasize his own expertness and specialized abilities to make judgments about the measures to be applied to apprehend "criminals," as well as the ability to estimate accurately the guilt or innocence of suspects. He sees himself as a craftsman, at his best, a master of his trade. As such, he feels he ought to be free to employ the techniques of his trade, and that the *system* ought to provide regulations contributing to his freedom to improvise, rather than constricting it. . . . Like other doers, he tends to be resentful of critics who measure his value by abstract principles rather than the "reality" of the world he knows and lives and sees.

To further understand the consequence of his craftsman's bias, it must be understood that the policeman draws a moral distinction between criminal law and criminal procedure. (I have never heard a policeman actually articulate, argue, and defend the distinction, but it is implicit in his general outlook.) The distinction is drawn somewhat as follows: The substantive law of crimes is intended to control the behavior of people who willfully injure persons or property, or who engage in behaviors eventually having such a consequence, as the use of narcotics. Criminal procedure, by contrast, is intended to control authorities, not criminals. As such, it does not fall into the same *moral* class of constraints as substantive criminal law. If a policeman were himself to use narcotics, or to steal, or to assault, *outside the line of duty*, much the same standards would be applied to him by other policemen as to the ordinary citizen. When, however, the issue concerns the policeman's freedom to carry out his *duties*, another *moral* realm is entered.

Statements are often made, typically by civil libertarians, to the effect that "policemen ought not to break the law in carrying it out." From sociological vantage, the important point is the different meaning of the word "law" as used by the policeman and by his critics. Unlike the policeman, civil libertarians do not in this context draw a moral distinction between the law of crimes and criminal procedure. This is not, for the moment, to suggest that civil libertarians are wrong in the demands they make upon police. No policy judgment need be implied here. Rather, it is important to make a conceptual distinction which will help to understand the policeman's attitude toward legal constraints.

In contrast to the criminal law presumption that a man is innocent until proven guilty, the policeman tends to maintain an administrative presumption of regularity, in effect, a presumption of guilt. When he makes an arrest and decides to book a suspect, the officer feels that the suspect has committed the crime as charged. He believes that as a specialist in crime, he has the *ability to distinguish between guilt and innocence.* If pressed, and in public, most police would not advocate that criminal trials are generally unnecessary. If one talks to policemen for a period of time in private, however, the impression is gained that the policeman feels that most trials are a waste of taxpayers' money since, as one law enforcement spokesman put it, "We do not charge innocent men." Indeed, the policeman sees himself as a merciful administrator of justice as well. Vice control men feel, for example, that any "breaks" a particular defendant deserves have already been meted out according to personal discretionary standards of police, appropriate in their operational environment.

Placed in the routine context of criminal law administration, the presumption of regularity is the most obvious and commonplace assumption that can be made. That is, it *is* reasonable to assume that trained people do their jobs properly. To understand the force of this assumption, one need only observe several *voir dire* examinations of jurors in criminal cases, and notice the stress placed by the defense attorney on communicating to the jury the right of the defendant as to a presumption of innocence, and the burden of proof of the prosecution to prove its case beyond a reasonable doubt. Prosecutors, at least in Westville,* prefer to try cases before experienced jurors, and defense attorneys before a "greener" panel because each perceives that the greater the experience of a juror, the more likely is he to attribute a presumption of regularity to law enforcement, rather than a presumption of innocence to the defendant.

Among criminal lawyers, this is the fundamental distinction between those who are regarded as "prosecution-minded" and those who are termed "defense-minded." The "prosecution-minded" lawyer envisions the adjudication of criminality as a "rational" administrative task, placing much confidence in "specialists" whose job it is to deal with criminals. The "defense-minded" lawyer, on the other hand, emphasizes the peril of interfering with the liberty of a human being. He sees the sanctions as being so high that it is dangerous not to presume the innocence of the defendant. Furthermore, he is troubled that the police will behave in an arbitrary fashion, with greater concern for their own stake in the outcome than for the society's interest in justice. The consequence (and a deep and inevitable source of tension under the circumstances) is that the policeman must feel his work is being "interfered with" well beyond what a "rational" system would demand.

Accordingly, the policeman feels that criminal procedure has been unfairly weighted against him. In the policeman's administrative eyes, any "balance of advantage" lies not with the State but with the defendant. The policeman finds it difficult to fathom and to justify a system which, on the one hand, requires that he be increasingly knowledgeable and competent in general areas as well as those relating specifically to police work, and, on the other, sometimes nullifies his best efforts by interposing seemingly irrational requirements and procedural delays. . . .

OCCUPATIONAL ENVIRONMENT AND THE RULE OF LAW

Five features of the policeman's occupational environment weaken the conception of the rule of law as a primary objective of police conduct. One is the social psychology of police work, that is, the relation between occupational environment, working

---

* Skolnick's disguised name for the large western city in which he carried out his work. [Eds. note]

personality, and the rule of law. Second is the policeman's stake in maintaining his position of authority, especially his interest in bolstering accepted patterns of enforcement. Third is police socialization, especially as it influences the policeman's administrative bias. A related factor is the pressure put upon individual policemen to "produce"—to be efficient rather than legal when the two norms are in conflict. Finally, there is the policeman's opportunity to behave inconsistently with the rule of law as a result of the low visibility of much of his conduct.

Although it is difficult to weigh the relative import of these factors, they all seem analytically to be joined to the conception of policeman as *craftsman* rather than as *legal actor*, as a skilled worker rather than as a civil servant obliged to subscribe to the rule of law. The significance of the conception of the policeman as a craftsman derives from the differences in ideology of work and authority in totalitarian and nontotalitarian societies. . . .

Subordinates in totalitarian society are offered little opportunity to introduce new means of achieving the goals of the organization, since subordination implies obedience rather than initiative. . . . By contrast, in nontotalitarian society, subordinates are encouraged to introduce their own strategies and ideas into the working situation. . . . In brief, the managerial ideology of nontotalitarian society maximizes the exercise of discretion by subordinates, while totalitarian society minimizes innovation by working officials.

This dilemma of democratic theory manifests itself in every aspect of the policeman's work. . . . In explaining the development of the policeman's "working personality," the dangerous and authoritative elements of police work were emphasized. The combination of these elements undermines attachment to the rule of law in the context of a "constant" pressure to produce. Under such pressure, the variables of danger and authority tend to alienate the policeman from the general public, and at the same time to heighten his perception of symbols portending danger to him and to the community. Under the same pressure to produce, the policeman not only perceives possible criminality according to the symbolic status of the suspect; he also develops a stake in organized patterns of enforcement. To the extent that a suspect is seen as interfering with such arrangements, the policeman will respond negatively to him. On the other hand, the "cooperative" suspect, that is, one who contributes to the smooth operation of the enforcement pattern, will be rewarded. Accordingly, a detailed investigation was made of exchange relations between police and informers, in part to ascertain how informers are differentially treated according to the extent to which they support enforcement patterns, and partly to analyze how the policeman creates and uses the resources given to him.

In attempting to enrich his exchange position, the policeman necessarily involves the prosecutor in supporting his enforcement needs. The prosecutor, of course, also has a stake in the policeman's work performance, since the policeman provides him with the raw materials of prosecutorial achievement. Our observations suggested, however, that although he is ultimately the policeman's spokesman, the prosecutor performs a quasi-magisterial function by conveying a conception of legality to the policeman.

Most interesting, of course, is the basis on which the prosecutor's greater attachment to legality rests. We may point here to pertinent differences between policeman and prosecutor. One, of course, has to do with socialization. The prosecutor is a product of a law school, with larger understanding and appreciation of the judiciary and its restraints, especially constitutional ones. The policeman, on the other hand, generally has less formal education, less legal training, and a sense of belonging to a different sort of organization. Such differences in background go far to explain the development of the policeman's conception of self as a craftsman, coupled with a guildlike affirmation of worker autonomy. The policeman views himself as a specialist in criminological investigation, and does not react indifferently either to having his conclusions challenged by a distant judiciary or to having "obstacles" placed in his administrative path. He therefore views the judiciary, especially the appellate courts, as saboteurs of his capacity to satisfy what he sees as the requirements of social order. Each appellate decision limiting police initiative comes to be defined as a "handcuffing" of law enforcement, and may unintentionally sever further the policeman's attachment to the rule of law as an overriding value. In addition, the policeman is offended by judicial assumptions running contrary to a probabilistic fact—the notion of due process of law staunchly maintains a rebuttable presumption of innocence in the face of the policeman's everyday experience of an administrative presumption of regularity.

Although the prosecutor is legally accorded a wider area of discretion than the policeman, the setting of the policeman's role offers greater opportunity to behave inconsistently with the rule of law. Police discretion is "hidden" insofar as the policeman often makes decisions in direct interaction with the suspect. The prosecutor typically serves at most as advisor to these dealings. Whether it is a question of writing out a traffic citation, of arresting a spouse on a charge of "assault with a deadly weapon," or of apprehending an addict informer, the policeman has enormous power; he may halt the legal process right there. Such discretionary activity is difficult to observe. By contrast, prosecutorial discretion frequently takes place at a later stage in the system, after the initial charge has been made public. The public character of the charge may restrict the prosecutor's discretion in practice more than the policeman's, even though the scope of the prosecutor's discretion is far wider in theory.

Internal controls over policemen reinforce the importance of administrative and craft values over civil libertarian values. These controls are more likely to emphasize efficiency as a goal rather than legality, or, more precisely, legality as a means to the end of efficiency. . . .

The dilemma of democratic society requiring the police to maintain order and at the same time to be accountable to the rule of law is thus further complicated. Not only is the rule of law often incompatible with the maintenance of order but the principles by which police are governed by the rule of law in a democratic society may be antagonistic to the ideology of worker initiative associated with a nontotalitarian philosophy of work. In the same society, the ideal of legality rejects discretionary innovation by police, while the ideal of worker freedom and autonomy encourages such initiative. Bureaucratic rules are seen in a democracy as "enabling" regulations, while the regulations deriving from the rule of law are intended to constrain the conduct of officials.

The conflict between the democratic ideology of work and the legal philosophy of a democracy brings into focus the essential problem of the role of the police. The police are not simply "bad guys" or "good guys," authoritarians or heroes. Nor are they merely "men doing their jobs." They are legal officials whose tendencies to be arbitrary have roots in a conception of the freedom of the worker inhering in the nontotalitarian ideology of the relation between work and authority, a conception carried out in the context of police work. Seeing themselves as craftsmen, the police tend to conduct themselves according to the norms pertaining to a working bureaucracy in democratic society. Therefore, the more police tend to regard themselves as "workers" or "craftsmen," the more they demand a lack of constraint upon initiative. By contrast, *legal actors* are sympathetic toward the necessity for constraint and review.

PROFESSIONALISM AND POLICE CONDUCT

The idea of professionalism is often invoked as the solution to the conflict between the policeman's task of maintaining order and his accountability to the rule of law. The meaning of this idea, however, is by no means clear. In sociology, there have been two main traditions, one emphasizing professional ideals and values, the other stressing technical competence. In [Emile] Durkheim's view, what is distinctive about the idea of "professional" groups is not merely that such groups have high status, or high skill, or a politically supported monopoly over certain kinds of work, or a distinctive structure of control over work—most important is an infusion of work and collective organization with moral values, plus the use of sanctions to insure that these moral values are upheld. . . .

An alternative concept of "professionalism" is associated with a managerial view emphasizing rationality, efficiency, and universalism. This view envisages the professional as a bureaucrat, almost as a machine calculating alternative courses of action by a stated program of rules, and possessing the technical ability to carry out decisions irrespective of personal feelings. . . .

In the effort to introduce fairness, calculability, and impersonality into an American administration of criminal justice that was often riddled with corruption and political favoritism, most writers who have seriously examined police have also tended to subscribe to reforms based upon the managerial conception of "professional." . . .

There are, however, costs in developing a professional code based upon the model of administrative efficiency. Such a conception of professionalism not only fails to bridge the gap between the maintenance of order and the rule of law; in addition it comes to serve as an ideology undermining the capacity of police to be accountable to the rule of law. The idea of organization based on principles of administrative efficiency is often misunderstood by officials who are themselves responsible for administering such organizations. In practice, standardized rules and procedures are frequently molded to facilitate the tasks of acting officials. The materials of this study have clearly demonstrated that the policeman is an especially "nonmechanical" official. . . .

[A]s a system of organization, bureaucracy can hope to achieve efficiency only by allowing officials to initiate their own means for solving specific problems that interfere with their capacity to achieve productive results. Some of these procedures may arise out of personal feelings—for example, relations between police and traffic violators—while others may become a routine part of the organizational structure. Examination of a procedural code, for example, would disclose no reference to the systematic use of informants. Given the task of enforcing crimes without citizen complainants, however, it becomes necessary for police to develop alternative methods to those used to apprehend violators in "standard" or "victimizing" crimes. These techniques of apprehension may demand considerable organization and skill on the part of the individual official, skill not so much in a formal administrative sense as in the sense of knowledge and ability to work within the effective limits of formal organization. As described, for example, the informer system requires so much ability that an aesthetic of execution has come to be associated with its use; it has become such an intrinsic component of police work that the abilities of the "professional" detective have come to be defined in terms of capacity to utilize this system.

As a bureaucratic organization, however, the police and governmental institutions, increasingly and generally, have a distinctive relationship to the development of the rule of law. The rule of law develops in response to the innovations introduced by officials to achieve organizational goals. . . . Thus, for example, a body of case law has been emerging that attempts to define the conditions and limits of the use of informants. Legality, therefore, develops as the other side of the coin of official innovation. As such, it is both a variable and an achievement. To the extent that police organizations operate mainly on grounds of administrative efficiency, the development of the rule of law is frustrated. Therefore, a conception of professionalism based mainly on satisfying the demands of administrative efficiency also hampers the capacity of the rule of law to develop.

The police are increasingly articulating a conception of professionalism based on [a] narrow view of managerial efficiency and organizational interest. A sociologist is not surprised at such a development. Under the rule of law it is not up to the agency of enforcement to generate the limitations governing its actions, and bureaucrats typically and understandably try to conceal the knowledge of their operations so that they may regulate themselves unless they are forced to make disclosures. But the police in a democracy are not merely bureaucrats. They are also, or can be conceived of as, legal officials, that is, men belonging to an institution charged with strengthening the rule of law in society. If professionalism is ever to resolve some of the strains between order and legality, it must be a professionalism based upon a deeper set of values than currently prevails in police literature and the "professional" police department studied, whose operations are ordered on this literature.

The needed philosophy of professionalism must rest on a set of values conveying the idea that the police are as much an institution dedicated to the achievement of legality in society as they are an official social organization designed to control misconduct through the invocation of punitive sanctions. The problem of police in a democratic society is not merely a matter of obtaining newer police cars, a higher order technical equipment or of recruiting men who have to their credit more years of education. What must occur is a significant alteration in the ideology of police, so that police "professionalization" rests on the values of a democratic legal order, rather than on technological proficiency.

No thoughtful person can believe that such a transformation is easily achieved. In an article estimating the prospects for the rule of law in the Soviet Union, Leonard Schapiro has written, "It is perhaps difficult for dictators to get accustomed to the idea that the main purpose of law is, in fact, to make their task more difficult."[11] It is also hard for police officials in a democracy to accept this idea. . . . "Professional" police administrators in the United States often criticize those who, for example, insist that the police must act legally for their evidence against the accused to be admitted. The argument is always essentially the same: that the efficient administration of criminal law will be hampered by the adoption of procedures designed to protect individual liberties. The police administrators on the whole are correct. They have been given wide and direct responsibility for the existence of crime in the community, and it is intrinsically difficult for them to accustom themselves to the basic idea of the rule of law: "that the main purpose of law is, in fact, to make their task more difficult."

THE COMMUNITY AND POLICE CONDUCT

If the police are ever to develop a conception of *legal* as opposed to *managerial* professionalism, they will do so only if the surrounding community demands compliance with the rule of law by rewarding police for such compliance, instead of looking to the police as an institution solely responsible for controlling criminality. In practice, however, the reverse has been true. The police function in a milieu tending to support, normatively and substantively, the idea of administrative efficiency that has become the hallmark of police professionalism. Legality, as expressed by both the criminal courts community with which the police have direct contact, and the political community responsible for the working conditions and prerogatives of police, is a weak ideal. This concluding section will attempt to locate the main sources

---

[11] Leonard Schapiro, "Prospects for the Rule of Law," *Problems of Communism,* 14 (March-April, 1965), 2.

of support for the managerial concept of police professionalism.

A posthumously published article by Professor Edmond Cahn distinguishes between "the imperial or official perspective" on law and "the consumer perspective."[13] The official perspective, according to the author, is so called "because it has been largely determined by the dominant interests of rulers, governors, and other officials. In contrast, the "consumer" perspective reflects the interests and opinion of those on the receiving end of law. In the "consumer" view, therefore, constraints on the decision-making powers of officials are given more importance than the requirements of the processing system and those who carry out its administration. Cahn adds, in addition, that "A free and open society calls on its official processors to perform their functions according to the perspective of consumers." At the same time that he argues against it, however, Cahn demonstrates in his own article the empirical strength of the presumption of correctness in official conduct. So in large part do the materials in this study.

The "official perspective" is most persuasive because it operates as the "established" mode of law enforcement, in the broadest sense of that term. The administration of criminal justice has become a major industry in modern urban society. FBI data show that during 1963 there were 4,437,786 arrests reported by 3,988 police agencies covering areas totaling 127 million in population. In California alone during 1963 there were 98,535 adult felony arrests and 595,992 adult misdemeanor arrests. There were in addition 244,312 arrests of juveniles. During 1962 to 1963, the District Attorney of Los Angeles County had a staff of 546 (with 180 lawyers) and a budget of just over $4,800,000.

Under these circumstances of mass administration of criminal justice, presumptions necessarily run to regularity and administrative efficiency. The negation of the presumption of innocence permeates the entire system of justice without trial. All involved in the system, the defense attorneys and judges, as well as the prosecutors and policemen, operate according to a working presumption of the guilt of persons accused of crime. As accused after accused is processed through the system, participants are prone to develop a routinized callousness, akin to the absence of emotional involvement characterizing the physician's attitude toward illness and disease. That the accused is entitled to counsel is an accepted part of the system, but this guarantee implies no specific affirmation of "adversariness" in an interactional sense.

---

[13] "Law in the Consumer Perspective," *University of Pennsylvania Law Review,* 112 (November, 1963), 1-21.

Indeed, the most respected attorneys, prosecuting and defense alike, are those who can "reasonably" see eye-to-eye in a system where most defendants are guilty of some crime.

The overwhelming presence of the "official" system of justice without trial provides normative support for the policeman's own attachment to principles of administrative regularity in opposition to due process of law. Under such circumstances, it should not be surprising to find the policeman adopting the "official" perspective too, since his role is to make the initial decision as to whether a charge has been warranted. Having made the charge, he of all people can hardly be expected to presume the innocence of the defendant. He has, in practice, listened to the defendant's story and assured himself of the latter's culpability. In his own mind, there are numerous guilty parties whom he has not arrested because he does not feel their cases will hold up in court, even though he is personally convinced of their guilt to a moral certainty. Police may feel most strongly about the "irrationality" of due process, but in fact other role players in the system of criminal justice may also be observed to be more concerned with efficiency than legality. If the policeman is the strongest advocate of a "rational bureaucratic" system emphasizing factual over legal guilt, he may well be simply because it is the definition of his ability as a worker that is most affected by the application of the rule of law.

An "order" perspective based upon managerial efficiency also tends to be supported by the civic community. The so-called power structure of the community, for example, often stresses to the police the importance of "keeping the streets clear of crime." . . . The police, quite sensitive to press criticism, find little support for the rule of law from that quarter. Indeed, when a newspaper runs an editorial, or a political figure emphasizes the importance of "making the streets safe for decent people," the statements are rarely qualified to warn law enforcement officials that they should proceed according to the rule of law. On the contrary, such injunctions are typically phrased as calls for zealous law enforcement or strict law enforcement. . . .

The emphasis on the maintenance of order is also typically expressed by the political community controlling the significant rewards for the police—money, promotions, vacations. Mayors, city councilmen, city managers draw up police budgets, hire and fire chiefs of police, and call for "shake-ups" within the department. Even the so-called "liberal" politician is inclined to urge police to disregard the rule of law when he perceives circumstances as exceedingly threatening. . . .

In contrast to that of political authority, the power of appellate courts over the police is limited. In practice, the greatest authority of judges is to deny the merit of the prosecution. Thus, by comparison to the direct sanctions held by political authority, the judiciary has highly restricted *power* to modify police behavior. Not only do appellate courts lack direct sanctions over the police but there are also powerful political forces that, by their open opposition to the judiciary, suggest an alternative frame of reference to the police. By this time, however, the police have themselves become so much a part of this same frame of reference that it is often difficult to determine whether it is the political figure who urges "stricter law enforcement" on the policeman, or the law enforcement spokesman who urges the press and the politician to support his demands against laws "coddling criminals," by which he typically means rulings of appellate courts upholding constitutional guarantees, usually under the Fourth, Fifth, Sixth, and Fourteenth Amendments. Whether the policeman is the "man in the middle," . . . as police prefer to present themselves, or whether police have by this time come to be the tail wagging the press and the politician, is the subject for another study. Beyond doubt, however, there are enough forces within the community, perhaps by now including the police themselves, to provide the working policeman with a normative framework praising managerial efficiency and opposing due process of law.

NOTES AND QUESTIONS

1. Skolnick does not find the policemen he studied in the same kind of role conflict as Murphy's army defense counsel. Rather, the conflict is over who is to define the role and what values shall govern. Notice that many occupational groups in our society such as lawyers, professors, plumbers and barbers have wide power to define their own occupational role attributes. Can we view the police-craftsman role as part of this trend toward self-definition of roles?

2. What does Skolnick suggest about the source of definition of the attributes of a role? What part is played by ideology; what part by a system of rewards and punishments inherent in the structure of the system in which the role is found? Is Skolnick's suggestion consistent with Handler's at 886, ¶ 3, *supra*?

3. During the Democrat Party National Convention in Chicago in August, 1968, the Chicago police used riot sticks to beat some demonstrators and those watching them in downtown Chicago. Richard Daley, mayor of Chicago, defended the police;

he said that one had to understand that some of the police had
been extremely provoked by the demonstrators who screamed
obscenities at the police, carried weapons and threw rocks and
other objects. Was the mayor's statement a definition of attributes of the police-professional role; or was he saying that a man
cannot be expected to continue playing this kind of role in the
face of certain kinds of provocation? *See* Daniel Walker, *Rights
in Conflict, Report to National Commission on the Causes and
Prevention of Violence* (1968). At least 37% of the police officers
interviewed in a study thought it proper to use violence to force
a citizen to respect police authority. *See* William A. Wesley,
"Violence and the Police," 59 *American Journal of Sociology* 34,
39 (1953). On the police, *see also* LaFave, Reading 10, at 97,
supra.

4. What does Skolnick mean by "legality as an end in itself"?
See Selznick, Reading 1, at 2, *supra;* Skolnick, Reading 3, at 27,
supra.

5. For the use of role theory concepts in the analysis of an
administrative agency, *see* Joseph Lazar, "The Human Sciences
and Legal Institutional Development: Role and Reference
Group Concepts Related to the Development of the National
Railroad Adjustment Board," 31 *Notre Dame Lawyer* 414 (1956).
See also Peter M. Blau, *The Dynamics of Bureaucracy: A Study
of Interpersonal Relations in Two Governmental Agencies* (U. of
Chicago Press, rev. ed. 1963).

Chapter 6

LAW, CULTURE, AND HISTORY

A. INTRODUCTORY NOTE

These materials began, many pages back, with an exploration of the question—what is law? In Chapter 5, attention was focused not upon "law" but upon the *legal system*. There is a difference between the law of the United States and the legal system of the United States; the latter phrase, whatever else it means, implies a structure of interconnected parts, and it implies a *process* in which law is made, unmade, applied and misapplied. Judges are not part of the law, but they *are* part of the legal system. The Uniform Commercial Code is a part of the law of all but a few of the states, at least in some formal sense, but one cannot deduce its place in the *system* without knowing a good deal more about its efficacy, who invokes it, and what its relationship is to other parts of the law and other legal actors.

Just as one can speak of the structure and process of American law, in short, of the legal *system* of the United States, one can speak of the legal system of France, Japan or of any other sovereign nation; and so, too, of the legal system of any more-or-less self-contained community, tribe or culture. The Cheyenne Indians had a legal system, and, in a sense, so do racial and ethnic groups in the urban ghettos. The readings thus far have concentrated on only one legal *system,* and on the law of only one nation, the United States. Moreover, the focus has been basically contemporary, with only a little attention paid to historical, comparative and cross-cultural aspects of law. Questions of the limits of the effectiveness of law were asked primarily with regard to the United States, under present conditions. Of course, social science research and social science theory commonly face the problem of deciding how far specific findings can be generalized, how much a concept or hypothesis depends upon facts that hold true for this time and this culture only. If theory is sound, and if research takes the right variables into account, it may be possible to generalize widely. The ideal for the social sciences is the situation of the physical sciences; what is true of falling bodies in New York today is true of them in Brisbane tomorrow and Nairobi yesterday. Needless to say, the social sciences are years away from the level of "science" that physics and biochemistry have achieved.

Despite the fact that the materials in this volume so far have been rooted in a specific time and place, it would be fair to ask of each reading or essay whether its arguments or results might be extended backwards and forwards in time, and horizontally across land and water to other cultures. Sometimes the notes and questions have specifically addressed themselves to the question of the level of generality achieved or achievable by the readings. In almost every case, it would be profitable for readers to speculate—or at least to speculate on what additional knowledge one would need to make cross-cultural speculation worthwhile.

In a sense, neither the comparative nor the historical aspects of law has been neglected by scholarship. The history of law is a recognized academic specialty and has been so for quite some time. Comparative law is taught at many law schools. But research and theory on what we might call the "macroscopic" questions of the sociology of law are underdeveloped. By "macroscopic" questions we mean such questions as: what is the relationship between whole legal systems and their cultures? what general types or families of legal systems exist, and how are they related to each other historically and culturally? what are the distinctive features of legal systems in industrialized nation-states, and how do they differ from those of feudal or theocratic states, or pre-literate tribal or nomadic societies? How culturally specific is law, and how much of it can be borrowed profitably from one society to another? Is there a meaningful sense in which law can be said to be evolutionary—in other words, is there evidence that legal systems pass through "stages" or "phases" in some sort of inevitable sequence?

Obviously, questions such as these are exceedingly difficult to research. They do not lend themselves to experimentation. Survey research is possible only for contemporary times; moreover, it is expensive, and it is not feasible in some cultures. Before any of the broad questions posed can be answered, or even researched, a lot of theoretical spade work is necessary. Although some of the most illustrious names in the history of the social study of law—Sir Henry Maine, Emile Durkheim, Max Weber—have addressed themselves to some of these grand and elusive questions, their speculations do not amount to a coherent theory, or even part of one.

However, after a period of some neglect, basic historical and comparative questions are beginning to be asked again. One reason, perhaps, lies in the growth of interest in problems of underdeveloped countries. The old colonial empires are dissolving; mass communications and technology are making the societies of the world more closely connected. The new sovereign nations, in the process of "modernization," are attempting to devise new legal systems in line with their current needs and aspirations, or, at the least, attempting to reform their old ones. This raises the question of the cultural specificity of legal institutions.

This unit begins with an excerpt from the work of the famous German sociologist Max Weber. Weber was originally trained as a lawyer, and had an amazing knowledge of history of law and comparative law. His well-known typology of legal systems, and his remarks on the historical development of legal systems, are almost inevitably the jumping-off point for speculation on the relationship between culture, history and law.

B. TYPOLOGIES OF LEGAL SYSTEMS

107. Max Weber on Law in Economy and Society

MAX RHEINSTEIN ED. (1954)*

A body of law can be "rational" in several different senses, depending on which of several possible courses legal thinking takes toward rationalization. Let us begin with the apparently most elementary thought process, viz., generalization, i.e., in our case, the reduction of the reasons relevant in the decision of concrete individual cases to one or more "principles," i.e., legal propositions. This process of reduction is normally conditional upon a prior or concurrent analysis of the facts of the case as to those ultimate components which are regarded as relevant in the juristic valuation. Conversely, the elaboration of ever more comprehensive "legal propositions" reacts upon the specification and delimitation of the potentially relevant characteristics of the facts. The process both depends upon, and promotes, casuistry.** However, not every well-developed method of casuistry has resulted in, or run parallel to, the development of "legal propositions of high logical sublimation." Highly comprehensive schemes of legal casuistry have grown up upon the basis of a merely paratactic association analogy of extrinsic elements. In our legal system the analytical derivation of "legal propositions" and the decision of specific cases go hand in hand with the synthetic work of "construction" of "legal relations" and "legal institutions," i.e., the determination of which aspects of a typical

* Reprinted by permission of the publishers from Edward Shils, trans., Max Rheinstein ed. [Professor Emeritus, University of Chicago Law School], Max Weber on Law in Economy and Society, pp. 61-64, 303-09, 313-21, 351-56, Cambridge, Mass.: Harvard University Press. Copyright © 1954 by the President and Fellows of Harvard College.

** Casuistry is a method of thinking about problems involving the application of general principles to specific cases in a manner which often discloses limitations on a principle because of special circumstances or the influence of other equally valid principles. The term is also loosely and generally used to refer to excessively formal, logical, technical reasoning. [Eds. note]

kind of communal or consensual action are to be regarded as *legally* relevant, and in which logically consistent way these relevant components are to be regarded as *legally* coördinated, i.e., as being in "legal relationships." Although this latter process is closely related to the one previously described, it is nonetheless possible for a very high degree of sublimation in analysis to be correlated with a very low degree of constructional conceptualization of the legally relevant social relations. Conversely, the synthesis of a "legal relationship" may be achieved in a relatively satisfactory way despite a low degree of analysis, or occasionally just because of its limited cultivation. This contradiction is a result of the fact that analysis gives rise to a further logical task which, while it is compatible with synthetic construction, often turns out to be incompatible with it in fact. We refer to "systematization," which has never appeared but in late stages of legal modes of thought. To a youthful law, it is unknown. According to present modes of thought it represents an integration of all analytically derived legal propositions in such a way that they constitute a logically clear, internally consistent, and, at least in theory, gapless system of rules, under which, it is implied, all conceivable fact situations must be capable of being logically subsumed lest their order lack an effective guaranty. Even today not every body of law (e.g., English law) claims that it possesses the features of a system as defined above and, of course, the claim was even less frequently made by the legal systems of the past; where it was put forward at all, the degree of logical abstraction was often extremely low. In the main, the "system" has predominantly been an external scheme for the ordering of legal data and has been of only minor significance in the analytical derivation of legal propositions and in the construction of legal relationships. The specifically modern form of systematization, which developed out of Roman law, has its point of departure in the logical analysis of the meaning of the legal propositions as well as of the social actions. The "legal relationships" and casuistry, on the other hand, often resist this kind of manipulation, as they have grown out of concrete factual characteristics.

In addition to the diversities discussed so far, we must also consider the differences existing as to the technical apparatus of legal practice; these differences to some extent associate with, but to some extent also overlap, those discussed so far. The following are the possible type situations:

Both lawmaking and lawfinding may be either rational or irrational. They are "formally irrational" when one applies in lawmaking or lawfinding means which cannot be controlled by the

intellect, for instance when recourse is had to oracles or substitutes therefor. Lawmaking and lawfinding are "substantively
irrational" on the other hand to the extent that decision is influenced by concrete factors of the particular case as evaluated upon
an ethical, emotional, or political basis rather than by general
norms. "Rational" lawmaking and lawfinding may be of either
a formal or a substantive kind. All formal law is, formally at
least, relatively rational. Law, however, is "formal" to the extent
that, in both substantive and procedural matters, only unambiguous general characteristics of the facts of the case are taken into
account. This formalism can, again, be of two different kinds.
It is possible that the legally relevant characteristics are of a tangible nature, i.e., that they are perceptible as sense data. This
adherence to external characteristics of the facts, for instance, the
utterance of certain words, the execution of a signature or the
performance of a certain symbolic act with a fixed meaning, represents the most rigorous type of legal formalism. The other type
of formalistic law is found where the legally relevant characteristics of the facts are disclosed through the logical analysis of
meaning and where, accordingly, definitely fixed legal concepts
in the form of highly abstract rules are formulated and applied.
This process of "logical rationality" diminishes the significance of
extrinsic elements and thus softens the rigidity of concrete formalism. But the contrast to "substantive rationality" is sharpened, because the latter means that the decision of legal problems
is influenced by norms different from those obtained through
logical generalization of abstract interpretations of meaning. The
norms to which substantive rationality accords predominance include ethical imperatives, utilitarian and other expediential rules,
and political maxims, all of which diverge from the formalism
of the "external characteristics" variety as well as from that which
uses logical abstraction. However, the peculiarly professional,
legalistic, and abstract approach to law in the modern sense is
possible only in the measure that the law is formal in character.
In so far as the absolute formalism of classification according to
"sense-data characteristics" prevails, it exhausts itself in casuistry.
Only that abstract method which employs the logical interpretation of meaning allows the execution of the specifically systematic
task, i.e., the collection and rationalization by logical means of
all the several rules recognized as legally valid into an internally
consistent complex of abstract legal propositions. . . .

Present-day legal science, at least in those forms which have
achieved the highest measure of methodological and logical rationality, . . . proceeds from the following five postulates: viz., first,
that every concrete legal decision be the "application" of an ab-

stract legal proposition to a concrete "fact situation"; second, that it must be possible in every concrete case to derive the decision from abstract legal propositions by means of legal logic; third, that the law must actually or virtually constitute a "gapless" system of legal propositions, or must, at least, be treated as if it were such a gapless system; fourth, that whatever cannot be "construed" legally in rational terms is also legally irrelevant; and fifth, that every social action of human beings must always be visualized as either an "application" or "execution" of legal propositions, or as an "infringement" thereof. . . .

The Anti-Formalistic Tendencies of Modern Legal Development. From a theoretical point of view, the general development of law and procedure may be viewed as passing through the following stages: first, charismatic legal revelation through "law prophets"; second, empirical creation and finding of law by legal honoratiores, i.e., law creation through cautelary jurisprudence and adherence to precedent; third, imposition of law by secular or theocratic powers; fourth and finally, systematic elaboration of law and professionalized administration of justice by persons who have received their legal training in a learned and formally logical manner. From this perspective, the formal qualities of the law emerge as follows: arising in primitive legal procedure from a combination of magically conditioned formalism and irrationality conditioned by revelation, they proceed to increasingly specialized juridical and logical rationality and systematization, passing through a stage of theocratically or patrimonially conditioned substantive and informal expediency. Finally, they assume, at least from an external viewpoint, an increasingly logical sublimation and deductive rigor and develop an increasingly rational technique in procedure.

Since we are here only concerned with the most general lines of development, we shall ignore the fact that in historical reality the theoretically constructed stages of rationalization have not everywhere followed in the sequence which we have just outlined, even if we ignore the world outside the Occident. We shall not be troubled either by the multiplicity of causes of the particular type and degree of rationalization that a given law has actually assumed. As our brief sketch has already shown, we shall only recall that the great differences in the line of development have been essentially influenced, first, by the diversity of political power relationships, which . . . have resulted in very different degrees of power of the imperium vis-à-vis the powers of the kinship groups, the folk community, and the estates; second, by the relations between the theocratic and the secular powers; and,

third, by the differences in the structure of those legal honoratiores who were significant for the development of a given law
and which, too, were largely dependent upon political factors.

Only the Occident has witnessed the fully developed administration of justice of the folk-community . . . and the status group
stereotyped form of patrimonialism; and only the Occident has
witnessed the rise of the rational economic system, whose agents
first allied themselves with princely powers to overcome the
estates and then turned against them in revolution; and only
the West has known "Natural Law," and with it the complete
elimination of the system of personal laws and of the ancient
maxim that special law prevails over general law. Nowhere else,
finally, has there occurred any phenomenon resembling Roman
law and anything like its reception. All these events have to a
very large extent been caused by concrete political factors, which
have only the remotest analogies elsewhere in the world. For
this reason, the stage of decisively shaping law by trained legal
specialists has not been fully reached anywhere outside of the
Occident. Economic conditions have, as we have seen, everywhere
played an important role, but they have nowhere been decisive
alone and by themselves. To the extent that they contributed
to the formation of the specifically modern features of present-day
occidental law, the direction in which they worked has been by
and large the following: To those who had interests in the commodity market, the rationalization and systematization of the law
in general and, with certain reservations to be stated later, the
increasing calculability of the functioning of the legal process in
particular, constituted one of the most important conditions for
the existence of economic enterprise intended to function with
stability and, especially, of capitalistic enterprise, which cannot
do without legal security. Special forms of transactions and special procedures, like the bill of exchange and the special procedure for its speedy collection, serve this need for the purely
formal certainty of the guaranty of legal enforcement.

On the other hand, the modern and, to a certain extent, the
ancient Roman, legal developments have contained tendencies
favorable to the dilution of legal formalism. At a first glance,
the displacement of the formally bound law of evidence by the
"free evaluation of proof" appears to be of a merely technical
character. . . . [T]he primitive system of magically bound proof
was exploded through the rationalism of either the theocratic
or the patrimonial kind, both of which postulated procedures
for the disclosure of the real truth. Thus the new system
clearly appears as a product of substantive rationalization. Today,
however, the scope and limits of the free evaluation of proof are

determined primarily by commercial interests, i.e., by economic factors. It is clear that, through the system of free evaluation of proof, a very considerable domain which was once subject to formal juristic thought is being increasingly withdrawn therefrom. But we are here more concerned with the corresponding trends in the sphere of substantive law. One such trend lies in the intrinsic necessities of legal thought. Its growing logical sublimation has meant everywhere the substitution for a dependence on externally tangible formal characteristics of an increasingly logical interpretation of meaning in relation to the legal norms themselves as well as in relation to legal transactions. In the doctrine of the continental "common law" this interpretation claimed that it would give effect to the "real" intentions of the parties; in precisely this manner it introduced an individualizing and relatively substantive factor into legal formalism. This kind of interpretation seeks to construct the relations of the parties to one another from the point of view of the "inner" kernel of their behavior, from the point of view of their mental "attitudes" (such as good faith or malice). Thus it relates legal consequences to informal elements of the situation. . . . . Much of the system of commodity exchange, in primitive as well as in technically differentiated patterns of trade, is possible only on the basis of farreaching personal confidence and trust in the loyalty of others. Moreover, as commodity exchange increases in importance, the need in legal practice to guarantee or secure such trustworthy conduct becomes proportionally greater. But in the very nature of the case, we cannot, of course, define with formal certainty the legal tests according to which the new relations of trust and confidence are to be governed. Hence, through such ethical rationalization the courts have been helpful to powerful interests. Also, outside of the sphere of commodity exchange, the rationalization of the law has substituted attitude-evaluation as the significant element for assessment of events according to external criteria. In criminal law, legal rationalization has replaced the purely mechanistic remedy of vengeance by rational "ends of punishment" of an either ethical or utilitarian character, and has thereby introduced increasingly nonformal elements into legal practice. In the sphere of private law the concern for a party's mental attitude has quite generally entailed evaluation by the judge. "Good faith and fair dealing" or the "good" usage of trade or, in other words, ethical categories have become the test of what the parties are entitled to mean by their "intention." Yet, the reference to the "good" usage of trade implies in substance the recognition of such attitudes which are held by the average party concerned with the case, i.e., a general and purely business criterion of an essentially factual nature, such as the average expectation of the parties in a given transaction. It is this standard which the law has consequently to accept.

Now we have already seen that the expectations of parties will often be disappointed by the results of a strictly professional legal logic. Such disappointments are inevitable indeed where the facts of life are juridically "construed" in order to make them fit the abstract propositions of law and in accordance with the maxim that nothing can exist in the realm of law unless it can be "conceived" by the jurist in conformity with those "principles" which are revealed to him by juristic science. The expectations of the parties are oriented towards the economic and utilitarian meaning of a legal proposition. However, from the point of view of legal logic, this meaning is an "irrational" one. For example, the layman will never understand why it should be impossible under the traditional definition of larceny to commit a larceny of electric power. It is by no means the peculiar foolishness of modern jurisprudence which leads to such conflicts. To a large extent such conflicts rather are the inevitable consequence of the incompatibility that exists between the intrinsic necessities of logically consistent formal legal thinking and the fact that the legally relevant agreements and activities of private parties are aimed at economic results and oriented towards economically determined expectations. It is for this reason that we find the ever-recurrent protests against the professional legal method of thought as such, which are finding support even in the lawyers' own reflections on their work. But a "lawyers' law" has never been and never will be brought into conformity with lay expectation unless it totally renounce that formal character which is immanent in it. This is just as true of the English law which we glorify so much today, as it has been of the ancient Roman jurists or of the methods of modern continental legal thought. . . .

New demands for a "social law" to be based upon such emotionally colored ethical postulates as justice or human dignity, and thus directed against the very dominance of a mere business morality have arisen in modern times with the emergence of the modern class problem. They are advocated not only by labor and other interested groups but also by legal ideologists. By these demands legal formalism itself has been challenged. Such a concept as economic duress, or the attempt to treat as immoral, and thus as invalid, a contract because of a gross disproportion between promise and consideration, are derived from norms which, from the legal standpoint, are entirely amorphous and which are neither juristic nor conventional nor traditional in character but ethical and which claim as their legitimation substantive justice rather than formal legality.

Internal professional ideologies of the lawyers themselves have been operative in legal theory and practice along with those influences which have been engendered by both the social demands of democracy and the welfare ideology of monarchical bureaucracy. The status of being confined to the interpretation of statutes and contracts, like a slot machine into which one just drops the facts (plus the fee) in order to have it spew out the decision (plus opinion), appears to the modern lawyer as beneath his dignity; and the more universal the codified formal statute law has become, the more unattractive has this notion come to be. The present demand is for "judicial creativeness," at least where the statute is silent. The school of "free law" has undertaken to prove that such silence is the inevitable fate of every statute in view of the irrationality of the facts of life; that in countless instances the application of the statutes as "interpreted" is a delusion, and that the decision is, and ought to be, made in the light of concrete evaluations rather than in accordance with formal norms. . . .

[T]here have also arisen attempts to reestablish an objective standard of values. The more the impression grows that legal orders as such are no more than "technical tools," the more violently will such degradation be rejected by the lawyers. For to place on the same level such merely "technical rules" as a customs tariff and legal norms concerning marriage, parental power, or the incidents of ownership, offends the sentiment of the legal practitioners, and there emerges the nostalgic notion of a transpositive law above that merely technical positive law which is acknowledged to be subject to change. . . .

There are now advanced . . . certain efforts to deduce objective standards from the "nature" of the law itself. The latter effort has taken two forms. In the aprioristic, neo-Kantian doctrines, the "right law," as the normative system of a "society of free men," is to be both a legislative standard for rational legislation and a source for judicial decisions where the law refers the judge to apparently nonformal criteria. In the empiricist, Comtean, way those "expectations" which private parties are justified to have in view of the average conception existing with regard to the obligations of others, are to serve as the ultimate standard, which is to be superior even to the statute and which is to replace such concepts as equity, etc., which are felt to be too vague. . . .

The . . . trends have also been inspired by the desire of the modern lawyers, through the pressure groups in which they are

so effectively organized, to heighten their feeling of self-impor-
tance and to increase their sense of power. This is undoubtedly
one of the reasons why in Germany such continuous reference is
made to the "distinguished" position of the English judge who
is said not to be bound to any rational law. Yet, the differences
in the attribution of honorific status on the continent and in England are rather rooted in circumstances which are connected with
differences in the general structure of authority.

Contemporary Anglo-American Law. The differences between
continental and common law methods of legal thought have
been produced mostly by factors which are respectively connected with the internal structure and the modes of existence of
the legal profession as well as by factors related to differences in
political development. The economic elements, however, have
been determinative only in connection with these elements. What
we are concerned with here is the fact that, once everything is
said and done about these differences in historical developments,
modern capitalism prospers equally and manifests essentially identical economic traits under legal systems containing rules and
institutions which considerably differ from each other at least
from the juridical point of view. . . .

Indeed, we may say that the legal systems under which modern
capitalism has been prospering differ profoundly from each other
even in their ultimate principles of formal structure.

Even today, and in spite of all influences by the ever more
rigorous demands for academic training, English legal thought is
essentially an empirical art. Precedent still fully retains its old
significance, except that it is regarded as unfair to invoke a case
from too remote a past, which means older than about a century.
One can also still observe the charismatic character of lawfinding,
especially, although not exclusively, in the new countries, and
quite particularly the United States. In practice, varying significance is given to a decided case not only, as happens everywhere, in accordance with the hierarchal position of the court by
which it was decided but also in accordance with the very personal authority of an individual judge. This is true for the entire
common-law sphere, as illustrated, for instance, by the prestige
of Lord Mansfield. But in the American view, the judgment is
the very personal creation of the concrete individual judge, to
whom one is accustomed to refer by name, in contrast to the
impersonal "District Court" of Continental-European officialese.
The English judge, too, lays claim to such a position. All these
circumstances are tied up with the fact that the degree of legal
rationality is essentially lower than, and of a type different from,

that of continental Europe. Up to the recent past, and at any rate up to the time of Austin, there was practically no English legal science which would have merited the name of "learning" in the continental sense. This fact alone would have sufficed to render any such codification as was desired by Bentham practically impossible. But it is also this feature which has been responsible for the "practical" adaptability of English law and its "practical" character from the standpoint of the public.

The legal thinking of the layman is, on the one hand, literalistic. He tends to be a definition-monger when he believes he is arguing "legally." Closely connected with this trait is the tendency to draw conclusions from individual case to individual case; the abstractionism of the "professional" lawyer is far from the layman's mind. In both respects, however, the art of empirical jurisprudence is cognate to him, although he may not like it. No country, indeed, has produced more bitter complaints and satires about the legal profession than England. The formularies of the conveyancers, too, may be quite unintelligible to the layman, as again is the case in England. Yet, he can understand the basic character of the English way of legal thinking, he can identify himself with it and, above all, he can make his peace with it by retaining once and for all a solicitor as his legal father confessor for all contingencies of life, as is indeed done by practically every English businessman. He simply neither demands nor expects of the law anything which could be frustrated by "logical" legal construction.

Safety valves are also provided against legal formalism. As a matter of fact, in the sphere of private law, both common law and equity are "formalistic" to a considerable extent in their practical treatment. It would hardly be otherwise under a system of stare decisis and the traditionalist spirit of the legal profession. But the institution of the civil jury imposes on rationality limits which are not merely accepted as inevitable but are actually prized because of the binding force of precedent and the fear that a precedent might thus create "bad law" in a sphere which one wishes to keep open for a concrete balancing of interests. We must forego the analysis of the way in which this division of the two spheres of stare decisis and concrete balancing of interests is actually functioning in practice. It does in any case represent a softening of rationality in the administration of justice. Alongside all this we find the still quite patriarchal, summary and highly irrational jurisdiction of the justices of the peace. They deal with the petty causes of everyday life and . . . they represent a kind of Khadi* justice which is quite unknown in Germany. All in all, the Common Law thus presents a picture of an administration of justice which in the most fundamental formal features of both substantive law and procedure differs from the structure of continental law as much as is possible within a secular system of justice, that is, a system that is free from theocratic and patrimonial powers. Quite definitely, English law-finding is not, like that of the Continent, "application" of "legal propositions" logically derived from statutory texts.

These differences have had some tangible consequences both economically and socially; but these consequences have all been isolated single phenomena rather than differences touching upon the total structure of the economic system. For the development of capitalism two features have been relevant and both have helped to support the capitalistic system. Legal training has primarily been in the hands of the lawyers from among whom also the judges are recruited, i.e., in the hands of a group which is active in the service of propertied, and particularly capitalistic, private interests and which has to gain its livelihood from them. Furthermore and in close connection with this, the concentration of the administration of justice at the central courts in London and its extreme costliness have amounted almost to a denial of access to the courts for those with inadequate means. At any rate, the essential similarity of the capitalistic development on the Continent and in England has not been able to eliminate the sharp contrasts between the two types of legal systems. Nor is there any visible tendency towards a transformation of the English legal system in the direction of the continental under the impetus of the capitalist economy. On the contrary, wherever the two kinds of administration of justice and of legal training have had the opportunity to compete with one another, as for instance in Canada, the Common Law way has come out on top and has overcome the continental alternative rather quickly. We may thus conclude that capitalism has not been a decisive factor in the promotion of that form of rationalization of the law which has been peculiar to the continental West ever since the rise of Romanist studies in the medieval universities.

Lay Justice and Corporative Tendencies in the Modern Legal Profession. Modern social development, aside from the already mentioned political and internal professional motives, has given rise to certain other factors by which formal legal rationalism

---

* Khadi: the "Moslem judge who sits in the market place and, at least seemingly, renders his decisions without any reference to rules or norms but in what appears to be a completely free evaluation of the particular merits of every single case." Rheinstein, Preface at xlviii. [Eds. note]

is being weakened. Irrational Khadi justice is exercised today in criminal cases clearly and extensively in the "popular" justice of the jury. It appeals to the sentiments of the layman, who feels annoyed whenever he meets with formalism in a concrete case, and it satisfies the emotional demands of those underprivileged classes which clamor for substantive justice.

Against this "popular justice" element of the jury system, attacks have been directed from two quarters. The jury has been attacked because of the strong interest orientation of the jurors as against the technical matter-of-factness of the specialist. Just as in ancient Rome the jurors' list was the object of class conflict, so today the selection of jurors is attacked, especially by the working class, as favoring class justice, upon the ground that the jurors, even though they may be "plebeians," are picked predominantly from among those who can afford the loss of time. Although such a test of selection can hardly be avoided entirely, it also depends, in part at least, on political considerations. Where, on the other hand, the jurors' bench is occupied by working-class people, it is attacked by the propertied class. Moreover, not only "classes" as such are the interested parties. In Germany, for instance, male jurors can practically never be moved to find a fellow male guilty of rape, especially where they are not absolutely convinced of the girl's chaste character. But in this connection we must consider that in Germany female virtue is not held in great respect anyway.

From the standpoint of professional legal training lay justice has been criticized on the ground that the laymen's verdict is delivered as an irrational oracle without any statement of reasons and without the possibility of any substantive criticism. Thus one has come to demand that the lay judges be subjected to the control of the legal experts. . . . The professional judges, in turn, are threatened, in the sphere of criminal law, by the overshadowing power of the professional psychiatrist, onto whom more and more responsibility is passed, especially in the most serious cases, and on whom rationalism is thus imposing a task which can by no means be solved by means of pure science.

Obviously all of these conflicts are caused by the course of technical and economic development only indirectly, namely in so far as it has favored intellectualism. Primarily they are rather consequences of the insoluble conflict between the formal and the substantive principles of justice, which may clash with one another even where their respective protagonists belong to one and the same social class. Moreover, it is by no means certain that those classes which are underprivileged today, especially the working class, may safely expect from an informal administration

of justice those results which are claimed for it by the ideology
of the jurists. A bureaucratized judiciary, which is being plan-
fully recruited in the higher ranks from among the personnel
of the career service of the prosecutor's office and which is completely dependent on the politically ruling powers for advancement, cannot be set alongside the Swiss or English judiciary, and
even less the (federal) judges in the United States. If one takes
away from such judges their belief in the sacredness of the purely
objective legal formalism and directs them simply to balance
interests, the result will be very different from those legal systems
to which we have just referred. . . .

Prophets are the only ones who have taken a really consciously
"creative" attitude toward existing law; only through them has
new law been consciously created. For the rest, as must be stressed
again and again, even those jurists who, from the objective point
of view, have been the most creative ones, have always and not
only in modern times, regarded themselves to be but the mouth-
piece of norms already existing, though, perhaps, only latently,
and to be their interpreters or appliers rather than their creators.
This subjective belief is held by even the most eminent jurists.
It is due to the disillusionment of the intellectuals that today
this belief is being confronted with objectively different facts and
that one is trying to elevate this state of facts to the status of
a norm for subjective judicial behavior. As the bureaucratization
of formal legislation progresses, the traditional position of the
English judge is also likely to be transformed permanently and
profoundly. On the other hand, it may be doubted whether, in
a code country, the bestowal of the "creator's" crown upon bureaucratic judges will really turn them into law prophets. In any
case, the juristic precision of judicial opinions will be seriously
impaired if sociological, economic, or ethical argument were to
take the place of legal concepts.

All in all the movement is one of those characteristic onslaughts
against the dominance of "specialization" and rationalism, which
latter has in the last analysis been its very parent. Thus the development of the formal qualities of the law appears to have
produced peculiar antinomies. Rigorously formalistic and dependent on what is tangibly perceivable as far as it is required
for security to do business, the law has at the same time become
informal for the sake of business loyalty, in so far as required
by the logical interpretation of the intention of the parties or
by the "good usage" of business intercourse, which is understood
to be tending toward some "ethical minimum."

The law is drawn into antiformal directions, moreover, by all
those powers which demand that it be more than a mere means

of pacifying conflicts of interests. These forces include the demand for substantive justice by certain social class interests and ideologies; they also include the tendencies inherent in certain forms of political authority of either authoritarian or democratic character concerning the ends of law which are respectively appropriate to them; and also the demand of the "laity" for a system of justice which would be intelligible to them; finally, as we have seen, anti-formal tendencies are being promoted by the ideologically rooted power aspirations of the legal profession itself.

Whatever form law and legal practice may come to assume under the impact of these various influences, it will be inevitable that, as a result of technical and economic developments, the legal ignorance of the layman will increase. The use of jurors and similar lay judges will not suffice to stop the continuous growth of the technical element in the law and hence of its character as a specialists' domain. Inevitably the notion must expand that the law is a rational technical apparatus, which is continually transformable in the light of expediential considerations and devoid of all sacredness of content. This fate may be obscured by the tendency of acquiescence in the existing law, which is growing in many ways for several reasons, but it cannot really be stayed. All of the modern sociological and philosophical analyses, many of which are of a high scholarly value, can only contribute to strengthen this impression, regardless of the content of their theories concerning the nature of law and the judicial process.
. . .

The decisive reason for the success of bureaucratic organization has always been its purely technical superiority over every other form. A fully developed bureaucratic administration stands in the same relationship to nonbureaucratic forms as machinery to nonmechanical modes of production. Precision, speed, consistency, availability of records, continuity, possibility of secrecy, unity, rigorous coordination, and minimization of friction and of expense for materials and personnel are achieved in a strictly bureaucratized, especially in a monocratically organized, administration conducted by trained officials to an extent incomparably greater than in any collegial form of administration. . . .

The utmost possible speed, precision, definiteness, and continuity in the execution of official business are demanded of the administration particularly in the modern capitalistic economy. The great modern capitalist enterprises are themselves normally unrivaled models of thoroughgoing bureaucratic organization. Their handling of business rests entirely on increasing precision, continuity, and especially speed of operation. This in its turn is conditioned by the nature of the modern means of communication, in which we include the news services. The extraordinary acceleration of the transmission of public announcements and of economic or political events exercises a steady and definite pressure in the direction of the maximum acceleration of the reaction of the administration to the given situation; this maximum can normally be reached only by thoroughgoing bureaucratic organization. . . .

Above all, bureaucratization offers the optimal possibility for the realization of the principle of division of labor in administration according to purely technical considerations, allocating individual tasks to functionaries who are trained as specialists and who continuously add to their experience by constant practice. "Professional" execution in this case means primarily execution "without regard to person" in accordance with calculable rules. The consistent carrying through of bureaucratic authority produces a leveling of differences in social "honor" or status, and, consequently, unless the principle of freedom in the market is simultaneously restricted, the universal sway of economic "class position." The fact that this result of bureaucratic authority has not always appeared concurrently with bureaucratization is based on the diversity of the possible principles by which political communities have fulfilled their tasks. But for modern bureaucracy, the element of "calculability of its rules" has really been of decisive significance. The nature of modern civilization, especially its technical-economic substructure, requires this "calculability" of consequences. . . . In the place of the old-type ruler who is moved by sympathy, favor, grace, and gratitude, modern culture requires for its sustaining external apparatus the emotionally detached, and hence rigorously "professional," expert; and the more complicated and the more specialized it is, the more it needs him. All these elements are provided by the bureaucratic structure. Bureaucracy provides the administration of justice with a foundation for the realization of a conceptually systematized rational body of law on the basis of "laws," as it was achieved for the first time to a high degree of technical perfection in the late Roman Empire. In the Middle Ages the reception of this law proceeded hand in hand with the bureaucratization of the administration of justice. Adjudication by rationally trained specialists had to take the place of the older type of adjudication on the basis of tradition or irrational presuppositions.

Rational adjudication on the basis of rigorously formal legal concepts is to be contrasted with a type of adjudication which is guided primarily by sacred traditions without finding therein a clear basis for the decision of concrete cases. It thus decides cases either as charismatic justice, i.e., by the concrete "revelations" of

an oracle, a prophet's doom, or an ordeal; or as khadi justice
non-formalistically and in accordance with concrete ethical or
other practical value-judgments; or as empirical justice, formal-
istically, but not by subsumption of the case under rational concepts but by the use of "analogies" and the reference to and
interpretation of "precedents." The last two cases are particularly interesting for us here. In khadi justice, there are no "rational" bases of "judgment" at all, and in the pure form of
empirical justice we do not find such rational bases, at least in
that sense in which we are using the term. The concrete value-
judgment aspect of khadi justice can be intensified until it leads
to a prophetic break with all tradition, while empirical justice
can be sublimated and rationalized into a veritable technique.
Since the non-bureaucratic forms of authority exhibit a peculiar
juxtaposition of a sphere of rigorous subordination to tradition
on the one hand and a sphere of free discretion and grace of the
ruler on the other, combinations and marginal manifestations of
both principles are frequent. In contemporary England, for instance, we still find a broad substratum of the legal system which
is in substance khadi justice to an extent which cannot be easily
visualized on the Continent. Our own jury system, in which the
reasons of the verdict are not pronounced, frequently operates in
practice in the same way. One should thus be careful not to
assume that "democratic" principles of adjudication are identical
with rational, i.e., formalistic, adjudication. The very opposite
is the truth, as we have shown in another place. Even American
and British justice in the great national courts still is to a large
extent empirical adjudication, based on precedent. The reason
for the failure of all attempts to codify English law in a rational
way as well as for the rejection of Roman law lay in the successful resistance of the great, centrally organized lawyers' guilds, a
monopolistic stratum of honoratiores, who have produced from
their ranks the judges of the great courts. They kept legal education as a highly developed empirical technique in their own hands
and combated the menace to their social and material position
which threatened to arise from the ecclesiastical courts and, for
a time, also from the universities in their attempts to rationalize
the legal system. The struggle of the common law lawyers against
Roman and ecclesiastical law and against the power position of
the church was to a large extent economically caused by their
interest in fees, as was demonstrated by the royal intervention in
this conflict. But their power position, which successfully with-
stood his conflict, was a result of political centralization. In Germany, there was lacking, for predominantly political reasons, any
socially powerful estate of honoratiores who, like the English

lawyers, could have been the bearers of a national legal tradition, could have developed the national law as a veritable art with an orderly doctrine, and could have resisted the invasion of the technically superior training of the jurists educated in Roman law. It was not the greater suitability of substantive Roman law to the needs of emerging capitalism which decided the victory here. As a matter of fact, the specific legal institutions of modern capitalism were unknown to Roman law and are of medieval origin. No, the victory of the Roman law was due to its rational form and the technical necessity of placing procedure in the hands of rationally trained specialists, i.e., the Roman law trained university graduates. The increasingly complicated nature of the cases arising out of the more and more rationalized economy was no longer satisfied with the old crude techniques of trial by ordeal or oath but required a rational technique of fact-finding such as the one in which these university men were trained. The factor of a changing economic structure operated, it is true, everywhere including England, where rational procedures of proof were introduced by the royal authority especially in the interest of the merchants. The main cause for the difference which nonetheless exists between the development of substantive law in England and Germany is not, as is already apparent, to be found here but rather in the autonomous tendencies of the two types of organization of authority. In England there was a centralized system of courts and, simultaneously, rule by honoratiores; in Germany there was no political centralization but yet there was bureaucracy. The first country of modern times to reach a high level of capitalistic development, i.e., England, thus preserved a less rational and less bureaucratic legal system. That capitalism could nevertheless make its way so well in England was largely because the court system and trial procedure amounted until well in the modern age to a denial of justice to the economically weaker groups. This fact and the cost in time and money of transfers of landed property, which was also influenced by the economic interests of the lawyers, influenced the structure of agrarian England in the direction of the accumulation and immobilization of landed property. . . .

The demands for "legal equality" and of guaranties against arbitrariness require formal rational objectivity in administration in contrast to personal free choice on the basis of grace, as characterized the older type of patrimonial authority. The democratic ethos, where it pervades the masses in connection with a concrete question, based as it is on the postulate of substantive justice in concrete cases for concrete individuals, inevitably comes into conflict with the formalism and the rule-bound, detached objectivity of bureaucratic administration. For this reason it must emotionally reject what is rationally demanded. The propertyless classes in particular are not served, in the way in which bourgeois are, by formal "legal equality" and "calculable" adjudication and administration. The propertyless demand that law and administration serve the equalization of economic and social opportunities vis-à-vis the propertied classes, and judges or administrators cannot perform this function unless they assume the substantively ethical and hence nonformalistic character of the Khadi. The rational course of justice and administration is interfered with not only by every form of "popular justice," which is little concerned with rational norms and reasons, but also by every type of intensive influencing of the course of administration by "public opinion," that is, in a mass democracy, that communal activity which is born of irrational "feelings" and which is normally instigated or guided by party leaders or the press. As a matter of fact, these interferences can be as disturbing as, or, under circumstances, even more disturbing than, those of the star chamber practices of an "absolute" monarch.

NOTES AND QUESTIONS

1. Max Weber was born in 1864 in Germany, and he died there in 1920. A number of studies of his thought have appeared in English, including Reinhard Bendix's *Max Weber: An Intellectual Portrait* (Doubleday 1960). On Weber's sociology of law, the introduction to *Max Weber on Law in Economy and Society*, by Professor Max Rheinstein, is well worth reading. Weber's typology has been an important influence on other sociologists who have attempted to classify the legal systems of whole societies. For example, Georges Gurvitch, in his *Sociology of Law* 203-26 (Alliance Book Corp. 1947), expands Weber's types of legal systems to seven, classified in terms of the type of society to which they pertain, from "Polysegmentary societies" (*i.e.*, tribal) "having a Magical-religious Base," through "Entirely secularized and logicized Systems of Law of Societies unified by the pre-eminence of the Territorial State and the autonomy of individual Wills." The latter is the sixth type, which is decaying into the seventh type, the "transitional" system of contemporary society.

2. A typology is created for some purpose. One could classify legal systems by whether or not their courtrooms, if there were any courtrooms, were air conditioned, but for most purposes such a classification would be meaningless. To what, if anything, are Weber's formal-substantive, rational-irrational variables relevant?

Is there any sense in which "rationality" (in Weber's definition) must be preferred to "irrationality"? Is it better? more
efficient? Weber clearly believed that bureaucracy was an inevitable and improved mode of organizing economic and social
life as compared to pre-modern modes of organization. What is
the relationship between bureaucracy and rationality in the legal
system? Is the legal system becoming more or less bureaucratic?
Are the pressures which Weber sees militating against "rationality" in law equally militating against "bureaucracy" in administration and business organization?

3. You will recall Weber's typology: Laws can be classed as
formally irrational, substantively irrational, formally rational, and
substantively rational. The Weber typology is not as simple to
use as it may appear at first. How would you classify the following examples of lawmaking and lawfinding, in Weber's terms:

(a) the passage of medicare by Congress;

(b) two boys, quarreling over a brightly-colored pebble
which they both claim to have seen first, toss a coin
and award the pebble to the one who wins the toss;

(c) the medieval legal institution of trial by battle;

(d) the decision by the United States Supreme Court, in
1954, that school segregation was a denial of equal protection of the laws under the 14th amendment to the
United States Constitution;

(e) in the early years of the Chinese Revolution, "tribunals"
were empowered to roam the countryside and administer revolutionary justice; landlords and other "class
enemies" were driven together, denounced by members
of the community and punished by the tribunals; there
was no right of appeal;

(f) a judge is empowered to award the custody of the children of divorced parents to one or the other parent, as the child's "best interests" demand; the judge
hears argument in chambers, reads the report of a social
worker and makes decisions, sometimes (but not always)
filing a written opinion; there is no jury;

(g) same as (f), but a sociologist has discovered that the
judge in county A always awards custody to the mother,
unless she is an alcoholic;

(h) a statute of an American state forbids the hunting of
deer without a license; in order to procure a license,
an applicant must demonstrate to the Department of

Conservation that he is twenty-one years old or more and pay a $10 fee; an applicant fills out a form, pays $10 to a clerk at the office of the Department and shows his driver's license, which indicates that he is forty-three years of age; the clerk issues a license;

(i) a statute forbids a divorced person from remarrying within one year from the date of the initial decree; Mr. and Mrs. Jones obtain a divorce decree on June 1st; later, they reconcile and on July 1st go through a ceremony of marriage; on the question of the validity of their remarriage, a court later holds that their remarriage is within the literal meaning of the statute, and hence is invalid, citing a number of cases.

4. What does Weber mean by a "gapless" system of legal propositions? Which of the following, if any, would constitute such a system:

(a) the federal Constitution, with respect to constitutional law;

(b) the Restatement of Contracts;

(c) the collected statutes of a state;

(d) a policeman's manual, with respect to his duties, rights and obligations;

(e) the common law and statutes of England.

5. What, in Weber's view, is the relationship between capitalism and a "rational" legal system? How does his view differ from that of, say, orthodox Marxist philosophers of law, or from that of "Spartacist"? *See* Readings 65 & 67, at 577, 587, *supra*.

6. At 920-21, Weber is quoted as saying that the general development of law can be looked upon "from a theoretical point of view," as passing through certain stages. Weber denies, however, that any such evolution is necessary or inevitable; indeed, only the West has gone through these stages. If these are not evolutionary stages, what is their relationship to each other? What causes a legal system to change so significantly that one could say that it had passed from one stage to another?

108. Justice and Judgment Among the Tiv

PAUL BOHANNAN*

The Death of Gesa

Gesa's . . . compound was several miles from mine, but I visited it occasionally. I went there one afternoon in March 1950.
. . .

Orya, the compound head, . . . asked me to come along to Gesa's reception hut and have a look at him.

Gesa was lying on a mat, breathing with difficulty. His senior wife told me, when I asked, that he hadn't eaten or drunk or been awake for over two days. He could still hear conversation, however, and when I, wondering if he had some sort of paralysis, asked his wife if he could still move his legs, he did so. I turned to him, and told him to move his fingers if he could hear me. He did so. Outside again, the compound head told me that about two or three months ago Gesa had been working together with his age-set in a communal task of road-building. Not feeling well, he had come home. He had got steadily worse and in the last three days his feet and his belly swelled up.

Orya described the symptoms in the words always used in describing the action of *swem*—'your feet and your belly and your head swell, and you die'. I went back to look more closely at Gesa. He was a man in good physical condition, in spite of his illness, and there was no sign that any part of his body had swelled.

On my walk home, I was accompanied part of the way by the oldest man of Gesa's lineage, whose compound lay in my general direction. Once we were on the path, he turned to me and said simply, 'He will die.' I asked him what the trouble was. He said he didn't know. . . .

I thought that the old man was probably right—that Gesa would die. The next morning at dawn I started in that general direction soon after waking. On the way I encountered two

---

* Professor of Social Anthropology, Northwestern University. From Justice and Judgment Among the Tiv, pp. 199-203, by Paul Bohannan. Published by the Oxford University Press for the International African Institute. Reprinted by permission.

youths bathing in a stream. One of them, whom I knew slightly, asked if I was going to the funeral. I asked who had died. He replied that it was Gesa; he had heard this from a woman who had come to the stream for water some time after having seen people from Gesa's compound. . . .

A full sister of Gesa had died some three or four months earlier. The divination apparatus indicated that she had been killed by *tsav*, but nobody had asked the apparatus whose *tsav* had been responsible. At the funeral, her body was examined and it was found that she herself did not have *tsav* on her heart; therefore she did not die from her own evil, but was killed by someone else—either the elders *qua mbatsav* or by an evil man of *tsav*. Loud and bitter accusations had taken place among her close male kinsmen though only a small moot had been convened. At the end of this moot, *swem* had been dressed and broken, so that whosoever might have caused this death would be caught by *swem*.

Within a month, Gesa had fallen ill. By the time his death was imminent, most of the people nearby were describing his suffering in terms of the symptoms of *swem* [although I could not see them]. Therefore, the exchange among the agnates* and the age-set amounted to: 'Did Gesa die by means of his own *tsav* and the force of *swem* that was, of course, stronger, or was he bewitched and killed as a sacrifice by his agnates or by one of them acting individually and *ipso facto* evilly?' There is only one sure way to determine this fact; the divination apparatus—except the sasswood ordeal—is fallible. That one sure way was to hold a post-mortem examination of Gesa's heart. If it were found to have *tsav* growing on it, then Gesa would be buried and it would be said that his own evil had killed him. If his heart was found to be sound and healthy, without *tsav*—if, as Tiv would put it, his chest was found to be empty, the age-set would know that he had been killed by his agnates: probably the same persons who had killed his sister and were trying to kill his second sister's daughter.

There were loud arguments, shouts, and accusations. The agnates constantly contradicted themselves, for it was necessary for them both to protest their own innocence and to uphold the innocence of their 'child'. The age-set, on the other hand, said repeatedly, 'We must know. Our duty is to protect and revenge our age-mate if he be innocent. But we must know if he is innocent before we dare to raise our hands for him. You are his agnates, but you are also our agnates.'

---

* Agnates are those related through male descent. [Eds. note]

Had Gesa been found innocent, the age-set might—in the days before the effective government of the British Administration—have attacked, punished, and perhaps even killed those members of Gesa's lineage who were deemed to have caused his death. This institution, known as *hoyo*, is no longer practised. Today the age-set, if it were to do anything in such a situation, must either resort to magical means or hire someone else to do so.

By about half-past twelve the grave had been dug by the same men who had washed the corpse. The body was, after a series of moves requiring some twenty minutes, transported to its side. All sorts of delaying tactics were employed. The age-set was reluctant to perform the post-mortem operation; they would have been saved from doing so by a tacit admission from the elders that Gesa's death was 'natural'—that is, that they had needed his body for sacrificial purposes. But the elders, each knowing that such was not the case and that no decision had ever been reached about Gesa, would not make the admission.

The age-set and the elders faced one another grimly over the grave. Finally Kwaghwam said to the elders and Orya, 'Shall we look and leave?' The eldest replied, 'This is Orya's child. You must ask him. It is your matter and Orya's—but I should say, don't do it.' Orya said nothing. Kwaghwam decided to force the issue. 'We, his age-set, must know why he died. We will look.' One of the elders brought up the case of Gbannor, who, I discovered later, had been examined, and the examination didn't help him, his age-set, or his agnates; his chest had been empty, and Gesa's chest, this elder had implied, would also be empty.

Another elder, feeling himself supported, said, 'We know that our child is right. We would bury him and break *swem*. But his age-set will not believe.'

Kwaghwam said, 'His age-set must know.' He thereupon dispatched some of his age-mates to find a suitable knife. 'Bring Gesa's own knife,' he told one of them.

Orya said sadly, 'Who will do it?'

Kwaghwam said, 'His agnates should do it, but they fear. His innocence must be proved by his age-mates, for his agnates have nothing but fear.'

A few of the elders and age-mates stood and watched; most of them withdrew. Kwaghwam appointed one of his age-mates to perform the operation. The operator unwrapped the corpse from its cloths and mats. It lay on its back in the sun on the pile of dirt beside its grave. Standing above the body, straddling it, the operator made a neat initial incision horizontally on the chest about two inches below the top of the sternum. Each corner, then, he turned down along the lower ribs so as to make the

arc of an oval. The incision was deepened until he struck the
bone of the ribs. He then drove the knife between two ribs,
tapped its sides with an axe-handle, neatly cutting through each
rib, one at a time, and finally through the top portion of the
sternum. The knife was sharp and worked quickly. There was
no sound except his tapping. When he had finished cutting, he
took a hook (made from a forked branch which had been cut
by another age-mate) and pried upwards the flap of flesh and
bone. It rose with the slight sound of tearing perichondrium.
It opened like a trap door and was laid down on the corpse's
belly. Another layer of perichondrium was visible. The operator cut through it; the organs were exposed. He placed his
knife and hook carefully below the trap-door of flesh and bone
and reached in, slowly, with his right hand. Again, there were
a few sounds of tearing ligament and pericardium. He lifted the
heart out of the opening, turned it slowly and said, 'You see?'
   They all looked. A few said 'Mmmmmm.'
   Kwaghwam turned to me and said, 'Jim, do you see the *tsav*?'
I asked him to point it out precisely. He and the operator
used their explanation to me as an excuse to describe it aloud
so that all could hear, including those who would not come to
look. *Tsav* is a growth on the heart. It looked to me as if
blood had been forced into sacks in the pericardium. There were
two such sacks on Gesa's heart. The larger, dull blue in colour,
was about three inches long and half as wide. The smaller, about
half that size, was bright red. I do not know what they were.
If they were sacks of blood, one must have been arterial blood,
the other venous.
   'Do you see?' Kwaghwam repeated.
   'Yes, I see,' I answered. 'And that is *tsav*?'
   'You have seen *tsav*,' the operator said. 'You yourself have *tsav*
to look on *tsav*.'
   'But *tsav* need not be evil,' Kwaghwam added a moment later.
'But this *tsav* is evil. It is large and it is of two colours.'
   The operator replaced the heart in Gesa's chest, closed the trap
door and wrapped the chest about with a strip of cloth torn from
that about Gesa's loins. The body was again wrapped in the mat,
lowered into the grave, and moved with some difficulty on to the
shelf that had been prepared for it. The white cloth was spread
over it, and everybody present helped to cover the grave.
   The operator took the knife he had used for the operation and,
with the aid of a small stone, drove it point first up to its hilt
into a tree. Such a knife must never be used again—if brought
back into the compound, it might accidentally be used to cut
food, in which case anyone who ate such food would have eaten

the human flesh that had contaminated the knife. The wooden hook was buried with the corpse.

The tension was over. The moot could be finished quickly: Gesa had brought about his own death. Someone tried to joke about the elders and their knowledge that the situation would be as it was (i.e. one witch knows another); someone else tried to laugh. Then Orya began a dirge. He walked heavily back into the compound, singing as he came, those peculiarly Tiv dirges which start high and come down a minor scale for two octaves or more and end in formalized sobs. He sat down slowly and silently. The other agnates and the age-set also resumed their positions. The women, who had all gone down to the stream, did not return for another half-hour.

One of the elders said, 'It was the age-set. It was they who wanted him opened.'

Kwaghwam replied, 'I don't like it. But was it a lie (*yie*) which we did?'

One of the junior elders, a man very little older than the age-set, said that the whole thing was a matter of *swem*. '*Swem* killed him,' he noted through the other platitudes.

Slowly, over about fifteen minutes, they all admitted that this was indeed the case: *swem* had killed Gesa. Meanwhile, the women began to come back, a few at a time, into the compound.

There was nothing more to say. Someone in the age-set said, 'We have looked. We know. Let us go.' (*Se nenge mfe. Mough sha.*)

Then Kwaghwam rose and went before the elders. 'We must have his people,' he said.

This statement raised a turmoil again. Finally, however, Orya formally took each of Gesa's widows by the wrist and handed them to Kwaghwam, who grasped their wrists, thus signifying that he, for the age-set, was offering them protection. Gesa had a third wife, who had been absent for three months. The age-set asked several questions about her. Orya said he knew nothing about her, but would ask and be responsible for her well-being.

Kwaghwam said, 'What about Gesa's other people?' He referred to Gesa's younger full brother. The agnates shouted in anger, 'We did not kill Gesa. *Swem* killed Gesa. Why should Gesa's age-set seek to protect his brother, as if it had been we who killed Gesa?'

Kwaghwam was firm. Finally the agnates concurred, and the younger brother was handed to Kwaghwam, who grasped his wrist also, thus putting him under the protection of the age-set.

Kwaghwam then asked, 'What about the sick daughter of Gesa's sister?'

This time the agnates were more firm. 'She is here,' one elder said. 'She is safe with her mother's agnates. No one can harm her here, for we have refused to let them.' This point took almost ten minutes to settle. But the agnates were adamant—this child was not one of 'Gesa's people'. Had the elders let her go, it might some day be interpreted as an admission that they were bewitching her. If she remained 'in the palm' of her mother's agnates, then the assumption would be that it was Gesa who had bewitched her. The age-set eventually conceded the point.

The oldest man of the lineage then dressed a new *swem* in a large potsherd. He stood in the clear space, surrounded by all the participants, and held it high above his head. 'If we have not discussed this *jir* properly,' he said in a loud voice, 'and if we are wrong, then *swem* will catch anyone who has done evil deeds (*ishor i bo*) in this matter.' He dashed *swem* to the ground; the ashes in it raised a small cloud of dust which was carried away in the breeze.

The funeral—or moot, for it was both and could be called either *ku* or *jir*—was ended. It was a little after 4 o'clock in the afternoon. The whole procedure had taken about eight hours.

The first thing to note about this moot, as with the others, is that it was ended with a ritual: the dressing and smashing of *swem*. All the moots we have considered—and this applies, I believe, to all moots that are successfully concluded—ended with ceremonies of repairing fetishes, ceremonies of 'blowing out the curse', or ceremonies involving *swem*.

The second point of importance is that the moot settled a multitude of quarrels and fears among the people of the community: the volition for several past deaths was now 'known', and the atmosphere was cleared of suspicion. All the dependants of Gesa had been assured that they and their interests were being mystically protected by his age-set, for his wrongdoing did not relieve them of their responsibilities to his dependants: he was still their age-mate; his wives were still their *mtene*, and his sons were still their sons. The first steps toward re-establishing social relationships on a new footing, in the absence of the dead man, had been achieved. They grieved for Gesa and about Gesa, but now they 'knew'.

NOTES AND QUESTIONS

1. Which category of Weber's typology does the funeral-moot described by Bohannan fall into? Would you give the same answer if you believed that there is really such a thing as *tsav*? Is a coroner's inquest rational or irrational as a means of determining whether a person has met death from foul play?

[Reading 109]

2. Compare the following description of an ordeal from Jan Vansina, "A Traditional Legal System: The Kuba," in *African Law: Adaptation and Development* (Kuper & Kuper eds. 1965).*

Vansina has been describing the legal institutions of the Kuba, a group of tribes who live in the Republic of the Congo. The Kuba have a regular court system, and also a system of "moots," which are less formal and which attempt to settle disputes by conciliating the various parties to them.

The legal institutions described so far cannot cope with accusations of witchcraft, which are made very frequently. Yet no moot, no court, will accept them. The proper technique is to ask for a poison ordeal. The accused drinks poison; if he dies he is guilty, and if he survives he is innocent. Normally the head of the clan of the victim— often the clan of the suspected witch as well—makes a public accusation and asks the suspect to drink poison. A village headman may do the same with regard to suspects in his village, but he may not accuse dependents (slaves, serf women, spouses married into the village) without the permission of their masters; if they drank poison, they would take it in their villages of origin. If the suspect does not belong to the clan of the victim, the head of the victim's clan asks the head of the suspect's clan to submit his man to the ordeal. The request is almost never refused, but, if the man is innocent, compensation must be given by the victim's clan, either by payment of 200-400 cowries or, as is often done, by having one of their men take the poison. This is the closest the Kuba ever come to a feud, and they recognize that such cases may create permanent hatred between some clans.

After the accusation is formally voiced, the accused person agrees to take the poison. If he should refuse, the poison would be slipped into his food or drink anyway. Many suspects themselves cheerfully ask to drink the poison so as to clear their names. The ordeal itself is a complete ritual performed by a specialist. It is supposed to be directed supernaturally by the Creator God and the nature spirits. . . .

The Kuba recognize that in a way the poison ordeal is a legal instrument; in the myth that supports the institution, the ordeal is invented by a man named Justice. After his

---

* Professor of History, University of Wisconsin. Copyright © 1965 University of California Press. Reprinted from pp. 113-14, by permission.

death, long ago, the courts used to administer the preliminary ordeal leading to the poison ordeal, if no witnesses
were available and an oath had been taken. But later the
ordeal developed in its present form and became restricted
to accusations of witchcraft. The courts withdrew completely from this field. It is tempting, but untenable, to
hold that the courts are not concerned with witchcraft because the alleged crime is supernatural and cannot be established by natural means. The use of black magic is forbidden, and action is taken in court when accusations of
this nature arise. That no material evidence can be offered
in cases of witchcraft should not necessarily stop the courts,
for, when there are no witnesses and there is no evidence,
the defendant takes an oath which the court accepts as
evidence.

In fact, alongside the moots and the courts, the poison
ordeal may be considered the third major institution of the
Kuba legal system. It might be argued that the poison ordeal
is not administered by the courts partly because of the large
number of cases that arise, which would have justified the
creation of a special court to deal with the problem. But the
nature of the ordeal is such that the whole community in
which the drama of witchcraft has unfolded itself plays a part
in the drama, in a way not unlike the participation of the
whole village in a moot. This community encompasses all
persons who are interested in the case, and none of those
who are not. The latter circumstance suggests that cases of
witchcraft are not seen as affecting the whole large political
community, and can be dealt with by an institution like the
moot at the village level. That the ordeal has to be impartial, and not a condemnation, is clear from the type of
crime—it cannot be traced—and from the type of judging
body—no person could condemn a fellow villager or clans-
man and not disrupt the fabric of social relations in the
village. The condemnation is not given by the villagers; it
comes from above, and nobody but the dying witch can be
blamed for it. [pp. 113-14]

Would Vansina's explanation account for the Tiv funeral-moot
as well? Would it account for the institution of a jury system
in Western countries? for the decision, taken in the days just
before World War II, to select young men for the draft by having a Selective Service official, blindfolded, pull numbers from a
fishbowl? for the reliance on psychiatric testimony in a murder
trial in a state of the United States which has capital punishment?

3. Max Gluckman,* in 1955 (2d enlarged ed. 1967), published an important anthropological study, *The Judicial Process Among the Barotse of Northern Rhodesia.* Gluckman stressed many similarities between the law of the Barotse and those of Western systems. Unlike many students of primitive law, he emphasized the rationality rather than the irrationality of legal process among the people he studied. He found that Barotse courts were conciliatory and compromise-minded. This he ascribed to the fact that most relationships among the peoples he studied were "multiplex, enduring through the lives of individuals and even generations. Each . . . is part of an intricate network of similar relationships." Disputes, then, do not arise "in ephemeral relations involving single interests, but in relationships which embrace many interests." Hence there is no tendency in a dispute to limit it to a single "issue," and to restrict the inflow of evidence.

Compare the practices described by Macaulay in Reading 13, at 145, *supra.* The Barotse have built into their formal legal system considerations relevant to supporting continuing relationships among members of the society. American businessmen are just as interested in continuing relationships but these considerations find expression in negotiations that take place before resort is made to the formal legal system. The formal legal system in the United States tends to ignore the impact of its judgments on continuing relationships. Which legal system is more primitive? which better meets the needs of its society? *See also* Aubert, Reading 18, at 175, *supra.* In our society, many "multiplex relationships" exist—within the family, for example. To what extent does the legal system fail to take these relationships into account?

In Weber's terms, what kind of legal system do the Barotse have? Once we have classified it, how does that help us think about the Barotse's legal system or legal systems in general?

_____

* Professor of Social Anthropology, University of Manchester, England. Published by the Manchester University Press for the Rhodes-Livingstone Institute. Reprinted by permission.

110. The Differing Realms of the Law

PAUL BOHANNAN*

THE ETHNOLOGY OF LAW (L. Nader ed. 1965)

To summarize the position so far [see Reading 5, at 47, supra], it is the essence of "law" to present a double institutionalization of norms. A secondary criterion was added: a unicentric political unit (no matter how pluralistic) is the device most commonly utilized to carry out the secondary, or legal, institutionalization (a "sovereign"). Such a theory—although it may be charged with being simplistic—is, it would seem, consonant with the state type of organization. However, the theory of double institutionalization seems inadequate thus far to explain three related situations: the situations of (1) law in a stateless society, (2) law in a colonial society, and (3) international law.

So far we have two assumptions. First, we have assumed a power or a state, whether it be seen as an Austinian sovereign, or as the greater entity that assumes the court whose actions are to be predicted with greater or lesser accuracy. Second, we have assumed that there is also only one legal culture in such a situation—no matter, for the moment, how many contradictions are to be found in it. A legal culture, for the present purposes, is that which is subscribed to (whether they know anything about it or

	Unicentric Power	Bicentric (or Multicentric) Power
One culture	Municipal systems of "law"	Law in stateless societies
Two (or more) cultures	Colonial law	International law

The Legal Realm.

not, and whether they act within it or "agree" with it or not) by the people of a society. The secondary institutionalization forms a more or less consistent cultural unit.

* Professor of Social Anthropology, Northwestern University. Reproduced by permission of the American Anthropological Association from the American Anthropologist: Vol. 67, No. 6, Part 2, pp. 33, 37-41 (1965).

With these ideas in mind, it is possible to question both assumptions and hence to build a four-square diagram in order to
extend our views for examining the realm of the legal (see figure). Municipal systems, of the sort studied by most jurists, deal
with a single legal culture within a unicentric power system. Sub-
cultures in such a society may create vast problems of law's being
out of phase with the customs and mores of parts of the society,
but it is a problem of phase.

Colonial law

Colonial law is marked by a unicentric power system, with
greater or lesser problems of conjoining the colonial government
with the local government, and more and less overt theories (such
as the British "indirect rule") of accomplishing the conjunction.
All are marked, however, by two (or more) legal cultures. Sometimes this situation is recognized, as it was in preindependence
Kenya with its two hierarchies of courts, one for "European" law
and the other for African law joined only at the top in the
Supreme Court. The mark of a colonial situation might be said
to be a systematic misunderstanding between the two cultures
within the single power system, with constant revolutionary proclivities resulting from what is, at best, a "working misunderstanding."

In colonial law, the problem of disengaging a problem case
from the milieu in which it arises is often complicated by the
existence of directly opposed ideas about the motives and goals
to be achieved in resorting to court action. Once disengaged, the
culture of the court officials may be completely different from
that of the principals and witnesses in the cases, so that the outcome at best may seem arbitrary. Once "settled" in this more
or less arbitrary way, the re-engagement in the institutions of
society may be very imperfect, because of lack of consensus about
what was decided or lack of agreement about the binding qualities and the justice of it.

We are only now far enough removed from colonies—now that
they are obsolete—to begin a thorough examination of the effect
that colonial powers had, via such a system, on the legal systems
of the countries in which they were found.

Law in stateless societies

The mark of the stateless society is the absence of a unicentric
power system. All situations of dispute that occur between people
not within the same domestic unit *ipso facto* occur between two

more or less equal power units. The prime example of a bicentric system is, of course, the lineage [ancestry] system based on the principle of segmental opposition, but there is no reason that this type of solution need be limited to such situations. There is, however, only a single culture: the principals and witnesses in a case may be at vast odds about who did what and to whom, and hence where justice lies. But they understand one another's activities and plots—perhaps they understand them only too well.

In such a situation, all trouble cases are settled by some form of compromise, more or less in accordance with a set of overt "rules." Instead of "decisions" there are "compromises." In a unicentric system, it is possible to have judicial decision and a recognized mechanism of enforcement which presents problems merely of efficiency, not of substance. In a bicentric situation, nobody can be in a position to make decisions—it is organized so that there cannot be. The "judges" must make compromises, and their compromises must be enforced from two power centers, which often—to a citizen of a "state"—looks like no enforcement at all. Instead of implementing decisions, the parties are made to accept the principles and provisions of a compromise.

It is my feeling—but I cannot claim it is any more than that— that the compromise, bicentric solution of problems leads to very much less precise restatements of norms as law than does the decision-based unicentric solution. Bodies of rules in stateless societies seem to be less precise, scarcely made into anything resembling a *corpus juris* although, of course, the anthropologist or the intellectually inclined informant can create a system—even a system of precedents—from the regularities that result from compromise between units in terms of their common cultural recognition of their common institutions.

In some societies the compromiser may be quite firmly insti-tutionalized. Among the Nuer (Evans-Pritchard 1940), for ex-ample, the leopard-skin chief is a firmly institutionalized com-promiser who may or may not be resorted to in any specific instance. If he is, his task is to create a compromise to which both parties will concur, saving the face of all by his religious position and "sanctions."

Most specifically, perhaps, the court—a body of men repre-sentative of the political power—cannot have any part in a bicentric system, unless there is some mode of organizing mul-tiple judges. The more common methods of procedures are moots, contests, oracles, and self-help. In short, the bicentric, unicultural system may not have a very great potential for or-ganized, neat systems of "law."

International law

[T]here has been a long dispute in jurisprudence about whether international law is *really* "law." . . .

The difficulty arises among scholars who derive their model too narrowly from that law which is associated with a unicentric power system. It is undoubtedly true that the most "developed" legal systems occur within organizations such as states that have a single power system—indeed, the growth of states has been co-incident with the growth of such legal systems. For all that such a power system may be pluralistic, it nevertheless is not legally divisible into warring and treating factions. "Law" is seen as one of the supreme activities of such an institution. The elements of coercion and prediction that have been emphasized in the definitions of law have lent credence to the point. These qualities have carried over and indeed obscured discussions of international law.

The situation in international law is, however, made more complex in that two or more unicentric power systems are bound together by means other than a more inclusive unicentric power system. In each of them, custom is "legalized." In international law, then, the process of "reinstitutionalization" must take place yet again—but with the qualitative difference that this time it must be done within the limitations of a multicentric power system. The difficulties in this secondary reinstitutionalization of international law are compounded because there are likely to be cultural differences in the two or more primary legal systems.

The "law" must, in short, be reinstitutionalized not out of a single related set of institutions, but rather out of two separate sets of interrelated institutions, including the interrelationship of the two unicentric power systems. Many cultures can exist within a unicentric system—the United States provides a vivid example; moreover, what might in other aspects be neatly regarded as a single culture may be representative of two or more states. However, it is usually reasonable to assume that the two separate but interrelated sets of institutions on which international law must draw in the process of legalization, exhibit somewhat different cultures. Therefore legalization must take place in terms of two cultures that are often vastly foreign to one another.

Obviously, the legal institutions of a bicentric and bicultural system exhibit different types of organization, different goals— different customs all round—from those of unicentric systems. More specifically, they must have different ways of disengaging the trouble situation from its matrix. Probably those ways must be more subtle precisely because the power distribution stems from two centers, and a preliminary legalization has likely been made in each. We do not as yet have adequate legal institutions for bicentric systems, nor do we have agreed ways for legalizing international law that are sufficiently subtle and consonant with multiple cultural evaluations. . . . The problem will not be solved merely by the creation of a single "sovereign," as was supposed only a few years ago.

It is a characteristic of unicentric legal systems that they are empowered to reach and enforce decisions. It is, just so, characteristic of bicentric systems that they must reach legal compromises that are sufficiently compatible with both cultures as to be acceptable and ultimately enforceable from the two power centers. Western judges have lost and are just regaining some of their rights to compromise within the framework of the adversary procedure. Other societies such as some of those in Africa, are only beginning to adopt a "decision" procedure in place of or in addition to a compromise procedure.

In short, it would appear that in international law—or at least in the old-fashioned view of it—there is a *treble* institutionalization: once at the level of custom, once at the level of the legal institutions of states, and again at the level of the bicentric, bicultural "international" accord. . . .

111. Justice in Moscow

GEORGE FEIFER*

I began an unhurried, unguided tour of the People's Courts, bottom rung in the Soviet judicial hierarchy. To the great mass of Russian people, the Law means the People's Courts, for almost all civil and criminal cases are heard here first. Here, where the printed words on the page—the articles of the code, the rules of socialist behavior—are translated into terms of human conduct, where the living law is germinated.

There are seventeen People's Courts in Moscow, one to each city district: Kalininskii, Leninskii, Oktyabrskii, Kirovskii, Dzerzhinskii, Moskvoretskii, Krasnopresnenskii, Pervomaiskii. . . . The courthouses are scattered about town in buildings of every sort. Most of them, however, are worn and dry, mournful and bare. They reminded me of the ancient, soulless city hall in the town where I grew up: no comfort anywhere to mitigate the civic gloom.

Each court has eight to twelve judges—"People's Judges"—and a "chairman" in charge. The judges have a courtroom more or less permanently assigned to them and, adjacent, a tiny, sparsely furnished office which serves as chambers, lunchroom, deliberating room and, for some intimate personal cases, courtroom. Somewhere in the building is a larger office for the court as a whole, dealing in the inevitable exasperations of petty bureaucracy. Somewhere sits a duty lawyer on watch, offering on-the-spot consultations for a trifling fee.

Here, in these plainest of settings, the coating of mystery, enigma and mumbo jumbo surrounding the law dissolves, leaving the commonplace.

The corridors of all the People's Courts offer similar joyless scenes. A crowd, made up of quiet couples waiting their turns, bunches outside the room in which suits for divorce are being heard. Police lead defendants, heads bowed and hands clasped always behind their backs, to and from their trials. Inquisitive time-wasters open doors, peek in, search for a good case. Witnesses pass around cigarettes and the morning's *Pravda*. Rela-

---

tives—mostly older, black-clothed, wrinkled relatives—wait out the writing of verdicts. Lawyers between cases prepare their next speech, or answer queries of prospective clients. A queue forms haphazardly to see the judge, who is giving consultations about alimony, the necessary papers, the procedure for appeal, the insults of a neighbor or a foreman.

Opening a door along one hallway, I would come upon a typical scene. The first impression of a court in session was of drabness and routine; had I been seeking sensation, I would have left soon. I stayed a long time, however, even after my understanding of trial procedure was clear, for here was exposure to Soviet working-class life that a foreigner can get nowhere else. Here was detailed scrutiny of life in a country where such material is not much publicized.

Behind a door picked at random, the case on trial was likely to be minor, one I had seen many times before. For there is no summary procedure in Soviet criminal law, and the simplest cases are tried under the same general rules of procedure as the most serious and complex. The People's Judge—who is more often than not a woman—would be questioning the defendant or a witness in tones that reached the back of the room as a drone. The lay assessors would simply be in attendance, like bodyguards for the judge. The court secretary, often a fresh young girl just out of school, would be jotting down essential facts at a desk alongside the judge's bench. A small, dark group of spectators smelling of pomade, strong tobacco and uncleaned wool—mostly the family and friends of the parties involved—would be listening glumly, whispering their comments and sometimes shouting them to the bench. The door would creak as stray spectators or extra policemen would wander in or out.

Probably there would be no procurator, for he, the Moscow equivalent of an American district attorney, is overworked and cannot afford to assign his men and women to minor trials. (Or, as a procurator explained to me, he does not want to—for the law requires that when a procurator prosecutes, the accused *must* be represented by counsel, and "dragging a lawyer in makes unnecessary difficulty for everyone; it is better to keep him out, to keep a simple case simple.") More often there would be a defense counsel, for defendants *may* be represented whether or not the procurator attends, and Muscovites seem to value representation, even when the facts are obvious.

Sometimes the accused would be in the dock, watched by a surprising number of policemen. His head is shaved (in accordance with Russian prison rules), and in all respects he is a marked man, silly- or sad-looking. Among certain middle-aged

Russian men a shaved head is still a mark of fashion, but for prisoners it is humiliating, a badge of guilt which keeps the head hung low. Sometimes, if he has not been taken into custody but has appeared at the trial still a free man, the defendant may sit in the first row of public benches and testify from his place.

In the first weeks, I was surprised by the informality, the lack of legal phraseology, of practiced, self-conscious precision, of esoteric procedural niceties and devotion to form. Much has changed since the early years of Soviet rule, when judges drew upon their "revolutionary consciousness" as the new law. But something of that amateur spirit has remained. A Soviet trial is informal by any standards; there is nothing a layman cannot understand. The rules of the game (or compulsions of the ritual) are not treasured like intricate, ancient plumage. What the people in court have to say is more important than how they must say it. In the trials that I observed, when an interested observer had some relevant information to give, he gave it, even if it would have been inadmissible as evidence in a foreign court and even if he was not, at the moment, in the witness stand. . . .

People's Court, Dzerzhinskii District. The courthouse is [on] the second and third floors of a narrow old office building on Srentenka, a busy central shopping street. Its façade is nine-teenth-century Russian classical, the pasty-yellow plaster surface of most of downtown Moscow. The interior is dark and in need of paint. Just inside the entrance is a red banner with an inscription lettered in white: "THE TINIEST ILLEGALITY, THE TINIEST VIOLATION OF THE SOVIET LEGAL ORDER IS A CHINK WHICH IS IMMEDIATELY USED BY THE ENEMIES OF THE TOILERS.—V. I. LENIN." A tinted portrait of Lenin hangs in every room.

Open a door along one of the corridors . . . I am selecting from ten days' normal fare.

Article 144: Theft[1]

The accused is a muscular young man, born in Moscow but, like so many, reeking of peasant ancestry. He has admitted stealing a *papakha* (a tall fur hat popular in winter), which had been lying on the seat next to his, late one evening in the metro. Next to it, dozing, had been a hatless man, obviously the owner. This man, the complainant, works for the K.G.B. [secret police].

"What do you do there, if it is not a secret?" the judge asks. "Do not tell us anything you shouldn't."

---

[1] The articles are those of the Criminal Code of the Russian Soviet Feder-ated Socialist Republic-Russia.

"I am a driver. I don't know *anything* secret."

The accused has been convicted of crimes twice before, for hooliganism and for theft of a watch.

"Now this is the third time, Solovyev. What's it all about? What are you doing with your life? Do you want to be a common criminal? That's where you're headed, you know."

No answer.

"What is your explanation, if you please?"

No answer.

"I don't understand. You know there is nothing romantic about this—you know jail. Do you like it there?"

An answer is formed but not spoken.

"Now look, you are a trained worker, you were taught a trade valuable to Soviet society, you have a decent income; your mother and father are both on pension. *How do you explain this thing?* Were things difficult for you? I would like to understand what made you steal again. I cannot. *Why?*"

"I did it, I told you that, I admit I took it. I already told you everything." The youth half whines, half defies.

"I'm trying to find out *why*."

"I . . . didn't know it was his hat."

"Why didn't you ask? Why just take it?"

"I don't know. I didn't know who to ask. I thought . . ."

"In February, a man walking around with a bare head, and on the seat next to him an unattached hat. Nonsense! Do you think anyone is going to believe that?"

"It's not so strange. There are lots of people without hats. *I* don't always wear one."

"Maybe you'll think this over a minute and tell the court what really happened. Don't think I'm talking you into anything. But if you have made mistakes in life you yourself must be the first to recognize them; then things will go better for you."

Solovyev winces. "I didn't intend to steal it."

"But it's still theft. When you take someone else's things without asking, that is theft. Do you understand that?"

"I understand . . . but I wasn't trying to steal."

"What *were* you trying to do? For heaven's sake, isn't it the normal thing to ask before you walk off with a hat that belongs to someone else? What did you have in mind?"

"I don't know. I really don't know what I had in mind. I just did it."

"Come on, tell us now. What were your motives? We want to hear what you were thinking in that metro."

"I wasn't thinking anything. I just picked up the *papakha* when I came to my station and . . ."

"You *stole* the *papakha*. Look, Solovyev, I want to hear one thing from you. When you take a hat from a seat without asking, do you understand that that is a *crime*, that you are stealing?"

"Yes, I do understand."

A second lesson remains to be taught. It turns out that the young man, a lathe operator, had not been working for some ten weeks before the incident. He had quit his job, drifted around, gone to movies, met his buddies in the park, done odd jobs, drunk in the afternoons and evenings, and lived principally on doles from his parents. Hearing this confirmed by the offender, the judge berates him.

"How could you permit yourself to go for weeks without work? Why did you quit? Why didn't you get a new job? Where is your honor as a Soviet citizen? How could you, a healthy young man with strong hands and an honest profession, refuse to work, disregard your civic duty for the sake of loafing? Aren't you ashamed of yourself? Do you understand how wastefully and decadently you spent your time? Do you understand that there is a direct correlation between not working—the idle hours, the drinking, the loss of self-respect—and the crime? What right have you to expect the support of society without your support of it?"

Solovyev seems indifferent. He replies in words of one syllable.

"And how do you regard your actions now? What can you say about the way you behaved?"

"Not very good."

"That's all? 'Not very good'?"

"Terrible."

In appointing punishment, the court takes into consideration the defendant's disrespect for his obligations as a citizen as evidenced by his unwillingness to work. The sentence is one year in a labor colony, normal regime.

Article 211: Reckless Driving by a Professional Driver

The defendant, thirty-two, clean-cut, Driver Third Class, bounced the factory's *pik-ap* ("pickup truck") over a curb one icy February evening, slightly injuring two schoolgirls who had been playing in the snow. He had been rushing home from work "terribly upset" by a telephone call informing him that his brother, a tuberculosis victim, had been taken to the hospital after a relapse. He had dashed to the store for some things for his brother, forgetting his license in another jacket, had gulped a few swallows of vodka for his nerves, and then had skidded on the ice in the truck.

His own lawyer, counsel for the defense, grills him determinedly. Had he behaved well? No, very badly. Not *badly*, the lawyer says, but *criminally*; does he understand that he committed a serious crime, not only in hitting the girls, but in sitting behind the wheel with vodka in him? Does he know that every Soviet life is sacred? Will he do it again, will he drink and drive? Will he promise he will never, never do it again? Does he understand that that kind of irresponsibility cannot be tolerated in Soviet society?

The driver, voice unsteady and hands stiff at his sides, is too upset to play a part; he manages only a look of sincere shame and a simple apology: "I behaved very badly." While the court is out, his relatives pounce on him for his weak performance and for not emphasizing that he helps support his mother and invalid brother. "I couldn't say more; I am guilty, I hurt those poor girls. The court must decide what to do with me."

It decides mercifully: corrective labor and loss of driving rights for a year, but no imprisonment.

Article 154, Paragraph III: Petty Speculation

At the famous outdoor market-fair in Luzhniki, alongside Lenin Stadium, a young man, the picture of innocence, had sold his place near the head of a queue for Polish raincoats to a Georgian—the latter had been 465th in line—for three rubles. When he had successfully made his sale, the accused realized another ruble profit by selling to his victim two pairs of men's socks for six rubles instead of the five he had just paid. He had a history of such speculation: a camera bought and sold, jazz records, a rug; and once he peddled a trip to Leningrad that his brigade had been awarded for outstanding production.

The Georgian glowers menacingly, seemingly galled for having been taken in. His excuse is that he had wasted the entire previous afternoon standing vainly in line for a sweater; the supply had given out before his turn came up. The judge gives him a lecture, and to the speculator a look of disgust and a year's corrective labor.

Article 96: Petty Theft of State Property

Dozens of packs of Dukat cigarettes, totaling twenty rubles in value, had been filched from a tobacco factory in several installments. The accused is twenty-eight; like many Russian workers, he looks ten years older. He had been caught stealing before, had been warned, and had been reprimanded by the factory's Comradely Court. Now he can offer the judge no excuse other than vodka. He agrees that his wages had been sufficient for a comfortable life and that nothing had forced him to steal.

When the court retires, the man's wife turns on him. "Oh God, Andrei, why did you pretend we are not lacking for anything? You *know* that we hardly manage each month, with the children and everything. You were never able to speak up for yourself, you! Why didn't you say that your father and brother are sick and that you have helped them all these years? Oh, God. Or that our girl is weak and constantly needs milk? Besides, you earn sixty rubles, not seventy. The children ask already, 'What are we going to do without papa?' We will go hungry, that's what we'll do. Oh, God, Andrei."

The children are with them in the courtroom, two well-formed blond cherubs, too young to understand. They have a grand time, playing peek-a-boo behind their parents' motionless forms, giggling quietly, forming their newly learned words, and crawling up on the bench from time to time to embrace *mamachka* and *papachka*.

Then mother and father embrace, before he is led away to begin a two-year term in a labor colony.

Article 145, Paragraph II: Robbery

"I was on my way home at midnight," recounts the victim, a plump woman in her thirties, "when he grabbed me, took my watch, and searched my bag. I told him I had nothing besides the watch. When he unbuttoned my coat, I screamed—hard. Lord knows what he had in mind. I'm a married woman."

The attacker, an unskilled laborer, does not know himself what he had in mind. He was drunk. Now he admits his guilt "fully and completely," is eager to explain how it happened, and keeps repeating, "That's correct, that's correct," to all the charges. "Yes, it was a stupid, criminal action."

He looks up plaintively. "Comrade Judges, what can I say?"

"That is your affair."

"I have nothing to say."

This was his third robbery in three years. The court, "considering that the earlier sentences had no educative effect," orders deprivation of freedom for four years.

Article 211: Reckless Driving by a Professional Driver

A woman was slightly injured by a truck and spent three days in a hospital. The driver had been drinking.

The judge informs her that she is entitled to make a claim against the driver.

"Do you mean money? Oh, no, I don't want any money."

"Are you sure?" the Judge asks. "Nothing?"

"Well, perhaps enough to replace my stockings and skirt which were ruined. But money has nothing to do with it; my claim is only that such an untrustworthy man should not be allowed to drive in our socialist society."

Article 206: Hooliganism

The code defines hooliganism as "intentional actions grossly violating social order and expressing obvious disrespect to society."* Rowdyism, in other words; being drunk and disorderly and disturbing the peace.

Predictably, it is the most frequent single charge; twenty-eight cases fall under this article during the ten-day period—more than one third of the total calendar. The defendants are mostly men, mostly seedy, mostly repeaters—and mostly drunk. After drinking followed scenes, slaps, street fighting, or swearing—foul language in public is also hooliganism.

"Hooliganism" is an indispensable word in Moscow. A mother tells her young son to stop "hooliganizing"; a procurator says it can be grounds for capital punishment.

The criminal code provides a wide range of punishments: social censure, fine up to fifty rubles, corrective labor up to a year, detention up to five years (when the defendant has been convicted before of hooliganism or has resisted the police or has behaved really outrageously). The twenty-eight cases here fell in between: from six months' corrective labor to two years' detention in a labor colony.

Articles 91, 144, 145 and 146: Armed Robbery with Intent to Seize State Property; Theft; Robbery; and Armed Robbery

Ten thin seventeen-year-old boys, their faces already hardened by vodka and factory work, sit on two benches in the dock, watched by nine policemen in boots, belts, and pistols, five facing the boys, a foot away.

The youths formed a neighborhood gang, which grew spontaneously, and spontaneously went wild, beating up and robbing people (with a 1903 German pistol that did not work), to keep themselves in vodka, or just for the fun of it. There were nine

---

* From Hooligan, the name of an Irish family in southeast London, famous in the late 19th Century for ruffianism and street fighting. [Eds. note]

incidents in a three-week period. The victims were boys they disliked, random boys, a taxi driver, a policeman, salesgirls, and watchmen.

The judge is old enough to be their mother and acts as if she is. With tender concern, she asks each boy to have respect for the court, and then: "*Why*? What made you do it? What were your thoughts? Tell the court how you feel about it now. It is your future we are concerned with. Do you realize what you have done with your young life?"

Two boys got ten years; the others, eight, six, and five. . . .

Article 206: Hooliganism

The accused is not present; he is not permitted to leave the mental hospital where he is confined. He is charged with systematically creating disturbances in his apartment house, swearing vilely, distributing foul letters, frightening children, shutting off the electricity, chasing women with knives—for no apparent reason. His neighbors confirm it, each standing about two minutes in the witness stand. Various remedies have been tried in vain.

The procurator says that psychiatrists have found him mentally unbalanced, and he urges that the accused be absolved from criminal responsibility. The defense counsel agrees, referring to war wounds and a medical history. The court is out eight minutes: it finds the accused guilty, but applies "enforced medical treatment" in the hospital, instead of criminal punishment. For how long? I ask. Until the doctors say he is well.

This is the shortest case, thirty-five minutes in all. Obviously, procurator and judge had settled everything beforehand on the strength of the psychiatric report. . . .

Articles 147 and 198: Swindling and Violation of Passport Regulations

The defendant, a skinny, dark, itinerant Azerbaijanian born in Baku, grins uncontrollably. (Is it the pleasure of confession, or the embarrassment of being caught, that forces that grin on so many defendants' faces? It is the grin of young boys found at mischief and not entirely ashamed. Defendants realize, of course, that they ought to look contrite; but the confessional grin operates on its own.)

He has admitted guilt on both charges. The swindling was attempted in a local *rinok* (an open market where collective farmers are permitted to sell produce from their private plots). With a fellow Azerbaijanian he worked a variation of an old confidence game, known in both the East and West as the "pocketbook drop," on a dashing Uzbek soldier on leave in Moscow. Promising to split the contents of a wallet they supposedly found, the two accomplices enticed the victim to part with his own fortune of sixty-three rubles. (The mustached soldier, a Lermontov character, carried his money in a clip under his tunic, next to his golden skin.) A plainclothes policeman became suspicious when he saw the transfer of money. The soldier had to be restrained when he realized he had been duped.

The second charge is illegal residence in Moscow: the accused has no *propiska* (a residence permit, issued by the police). This permission, which is stamped in the citizen's (internal) passport, is required in the major Soviet cities—Moscow, Leningrad, Kiev—and in the coastal strip along the Black Sea and in other popular areas. A Soviet citizen cannot simply take up residence in these areas as he could, for instance, in Irkutsk. For a newcomer, permission to stay usually depends upon his having a job which would entitle him to a *propiska*; but for most jobs—to complete the vicious cycle—possession of the *propiska* is a prerequisite. The purpose is to deter migration to already overcrowded cities. Thus, the Azerbaijanian, having no steady job, has no legal right to live in Moscow; he has been warned four times during the past two years about his being there.

The judge is a ponderous man who plays with his words and his fingers. "Young man, you have got to get a job, you have got to find yourself an honest place in our socialist society. And you cannot do it in Moscow. Do you understand that you are living at the expense of society? Young man, you are a piece of fungus. You have done nothing with your life but practice the bourgeois creed of getting something for nothing. Why didn't you go back to your homeland and work, like a Soviet man?"

Grinning, the skinny defendant asks for mercy. He knows that he must be punished, of course; he understands that he did wrong—but could the court please make it as light as possible. You see, he has a sick mother in Baku, he has asthma, and he has a burning desire to reform. . . .

But the sentence is four years in a labor colony, strict regime. The Azerbaijanian is stunned; the grin becomes a mouth agape, then a grimace of hatred.

"Defendant, is the sentence of this court clear to you?"

"Yes, your great humanity is very clear. Thank you"—and under his breath, but loud enough for the fat judge to hear— "you bastard."

Four youths stole three rolls of tar paper from their factory: three years each. A drunk sneaked a mirror from a grammar school on Election Day: two years. A sober man took the windshield wipers and mirror from a parked car: one year. An obviously imbecilic old lush insisted on annoying strangers at a metro station: one year. A waitress had been pouring each glass of wine a few drops short and taking home a bottle a fortnight for herself: two years. A man rolled a drunk for his greasy jacket and scruffy shoes: one year. The punishments are astonishingly severe.

Much is written in Soviet legal literature about the need to re-educate and reform, rather than simply to punish, criminals. Lenin's pronouncement that it is the inevitability of punishment, rather than its severity, that is crucial to the elimination of crime, is everywhere quoted. And the penal policy seems to conform to this enlightened spirit. In labor colonies, at least under normal regime, the lot of prisoners is said to approach the level of ordinary backwoods life. Men live in barracks, work at jobs that are not humiliating, receive wages, and are visited overnight by their wives. It is a far cry from the rot of jail, which in Russia is reserved only for the most dangerous criminals.

Yet, in the courtroom, the doctrine of rehabilitation seems to evaporate. Judges are simply impatient with the wrongdoer and quick to hand him a stiff sentence. "We are building Communism," they seem to say (and often they do say it), "and if you are not willing to help after we have given you every opportunity to do so, then you are not worth our effort and we are not willing to help you."

In these ordinary trials the cardinal concern is much broader than the facts and the juridical significance of a single crime, or even a single criminal. A greater task faces the court—no less a task than the remaking of a society. Remaking society means work, toil, labor, in its most direct sense, on farm and in factory. The task of the court is to put every man behind his machine.

But these defendants, like defendants everywhere, are mostly society's outcasts, those who do the least to improve it. Rarely are they the capable, respectable, steady citizens who keep the wheels turning. Usually the wrongdoer has an indifferent history of employment at an unskilled trade. "No established place of work" is mentioned often in indictments and sentences. And much is made of this; for these undesirables, the law is harsh.

The trials run aground on universal human frailties: a judge misses the crucial point in a defendant's testimony because she is fuming at her secretary for opening the window. A witness remembers, after he sits down, that he has forgotten to mention

the most important fact. A court is so annoyed with a lawyer's
nasal interruptions that it deafens itself to his client's appeal.
And trials run aground, too, on the limitations of the trial form
itself; no code, indictment or summation is exact enough to re-
capture the subtleties of even the simplest case. A trial is an
attempt to reproduce episodes and circumstances from life. But
where to stop and where to start? How deep to probe? What to
simplify and what to leave out? A woman defendant wants to
talk about her family troubles, her husband's drinking; a mother
thinks she can explain why her son went wrong; a witness struggles to remember who insulted whom first, who bought the
vodka, why blows were reached. . . . But the court has neither
time nor means for exactitude of that kind. It is a cardinal principle of Soviet legal theory that the sentence in every criminal
case should reflect *materialnaya istina*—"material," or "objective," or "absolute truth." But it is a regular condition of Soviet
trial practice that judges are satisfied with much less in dealing
with the oral testimony. Even to the untrained ear many facts
go undisclosed, and seemingly essential questions go unasked.

NOTES AND QUESTIONS

1. Where do the People's Courts fit in Weber's typology?
What kind of justice do they dispense? Again, how does such a
classification help us to understand Soviet justice, if at all?

2. Does the picture of the administration of justice in Feifer's
account conform to the remarks on socialist law in Golunskii &
Strogovich, Reading 65, at 577, *supra*? If not, in what ways do
they differ, and can these differences be reconciled?

3. American judges have been known to lecture defendants
and apply community standards in sentencing those involved in
the types of offenses described by Feifer. For example, one county
judge, who sits in a large midwestern city, is famous locally for
these qualities. He has called defendants "hoodlum," "punk"
and "bum." In response to criticism he responded, "I am talking to some people who don't understand any other kind of language." He has dismissed charges against men playing a Serbian
card game where no player can lose more than $1 per hour. The
judge commented that he had "played poker at police socials"
and that "we would have to raid every home . . . in [the city]
on Saturday night if we wanted to break up every card game."
In every case he asks whether or not the defendant or his family
is receiving welfare payments. If the defendant is not supporting
his family, and if there is an issue of whether or not to grant

probation, the judge gives the defendant a choice of finding a job or going to jail. When young defendants appear before him for sentencing, he considers community standards of dress and grooming. He placed one young man on probation if the young man would get his hair "cut so short that I can't grab a single hair." When Civil Rights groups organized a boycott against the city's schools for what they charged was *de facto* segregation, the judge stated his views while sentencing a Negro prostitute. He commented that he ought to place women such as the defendant on probation to the leaders of the school boycott. "If the time and money spent on the boycott had been spent on learning family living and parenthood or trying to get parents to motivate their children to go to school and take advantage of job opportunities, more good would have been done. You are not going to get civil rights by civil wrongs."

The judge is very popular with most of the white community and regularly wins reelection by a wide margin. He is not popular among the black community.

4. Many of the readings in the early section of these materials described the administration of justice as essentially a bargaining process. To what extent does justice in the People's Courts conform to the picture of justice as a bargaining process, and to what extent does it differ?

5. Among the factors which may have gone into molding the kind of administration of justice found in the People's Courts are (a) the professional training and predilections of the judges; (b) the "taught tradition" of the law; (c) Russian history, culture and experience; (d) the resources, including time, available to the court; (e) the kind of case and the kind of litigant coming before the court; (f) government policies, decrees and ideologies. Can one guess which of these is most influential? Is there any way to find out?

112. Delinquency and Drift

DAVID MATZA*

The Impression of Inconsistency and Individualized Justice

Individualized justice is *the* basic precept in the philosophy of the juvenile court. More generally, it is recommended to all officials who deal with juveniles. We should, it is suggested by enlightened professionals, gear our official dispositions to suit the individual needs of the accused rather than respond in automatic fashion to the offense that he has allegedly committed. The relating of disposition to individual needs instead of to the offense is a central aspect of the modern *treatment* viewpoint. . . . The usual claim that equality is violated by individualized justice is at least in theory wrong, or beside the point.

The principle of equality is a misnomer. All principles, to the extent that they are formulated, stress equality in that they commend a *framework of relevance* by which all cases are to be judged. The principle of equality can be reduced to the dictum of treating like cases in like manner. This, as [H.L.A.] Hart suggests, is an empty formula unless we are told the criteria by which to determine the like cases. The principle of equality refers to a specific set of substantive criteria that are awarded central relevance and, historically, to a set of considerations that were specifically and momentously precluded. Its meaning, especially in criminal proceedings, has been to give a central and unrivaled position in the framework of relevance to considerations of *offense* and conditions closely related to offense like prior record, and to more or less preclude considerations of status and circumstance. This has been the overall substantive meaning of the principle of equality and the only grounds on which it may be distinguished from other principles, which logically are equally equal. Thus, strictly speaking, the principle of equality should be called the *principle of offense*.

The principle of individualized justice is a distinct departure from that of offense, but not in the sense of liquidating the norm of equality. Principles cannot depart from the norm of

---

* Professor of Sociology, University of California, Berkeley. Copyright © 1964 John Wiley & Sons, Inc. Reprinted from pp. 111-26, 128, by permission.

equality. Their function is to suggest a framework of relevance by which we may infer the meaning of the recommendation that we treat like cases alike. Internal equality of treatment within a category is the very meaning of a principle. A principle informs us of the particular mode of equality we will apply to juveniles even though juveniles as a category may be treated differently than adults. Such different treatment may be justified on the grounds that juvenile and adult matters are not like cases. The separate jurisdiction of juvenile and adult matters, the differences in the statutory expectations, and the differences in procedure may be tenable or untenable. But in either case that issue should not be confused with the internal equality of treatment suggested by a principle.

If the principle of individualized justice does not differ from that of offense with respect to equality, how does it differ? It differs in two fundamental ways. First, it is much more inclusive: it contains many more items in its framework of relevance. Second, the kinds of criteria it includes are more diffuse than those commended in the principle of offense.

The principle of individualized justice is more inclusive than the principle of offense. It contains many more criteria in its framework of relevance. Its greater inclusiveness is assured by the fact that the older principle, that of offense, is included in the newer one, that of individualized justice. Spokesmen for individualized justice do not suggest that offense is irrelevant; rather, that it is one of many considerations that are to be used in arriving at a sound disposition. Offense, like many other forms of behavior, is to be taken as an indication or "symptom" of the juvenile's personal and social disorder. The principle of individualized justice suggests that disposition is to be guided by a *full understanding* of the client's personal and social character and by his "individual needs." This view is well captured by the slogan which suggests that nowadays the treatment fits the individual whereas in olden times the punishment fit the crime. Needless to say, the transition from olden to modern times is taken as one manifestation of a major historical transformation commonly called the enlightenment. I want to suggest that the character of this transformation is completely missed and distorted if we take it as part of the wider process of enlightenment. We come closer to assessing its real character by insisting that its impact has been the very opposite of enlightenment. The consequence of the principle of individualized justice has been mystification. . . .

The inclusion of personal and social character as relevant criteria in judgment has been consequential. Its consequence has been that hardly anyone, and least of all the recipients of judgment who have some special interest in these matters, is at all sure what combinations of the widely inclusive relevant criteria yield what sorts of specific disposition. Indeed, no one has even attempted such a task. The task is manifestly an immense if not an impossible one.

A combination of impoverished economic position, a marginal scholastic record, a particular kind of disrupted family situation, a current infraction of burglary, and two past citations for auto theft yields a disposition. What disposition? If we ask court agents, they will honestly and appropriately answer that it depends. On what does it depend? It depends on other factors. On what other factors? Well, perhaps on a diagnosis of the child's personality, but that too depends. On what does that depend? Ultimately, it depends on the needs of the child. And, on what do these needs depend? And eventually we come to the final and only possible answer. It depends on the professional training, experience, and judgment of the court agents. Any system with an extremely wide frame of relevance in which the items included in the frame are neither specifically enumerated nor weighted must come to rely heavily on professional judgment. . . .

What of the clarity of the many criteria that are included in a principle of individualized justice? Surely, the principle of offense is itself no pinnacle of clarity. . . .

However, . . . compared to most systems the law works arduously and sometimes even successfully toward clarity and specificity of definitions of offense. Little that is included in the frame of relevance sponsored by those guided by a principle of individualized justice approaches even the most vaguely formulated criminal statute. Indeed, many spokesmen for individualized justice would not want it so. If the categories of offense vary by jurisdiction, and if the same terms often pertain to different referents, what can be said of the categories implicit in the more inclusive framework stressing personal and social background? Many of the categories implicit in those frameworks at best approach the clarity of the most diffuse legal categories, say, incorrigibility.

Some categories used by court agents have rather specific referents, for instance, age, occupation of father, and perhaps school performance. Others, which occupy an important place in the frame of relevance, are hardly as specific as the legal term incorrigibility. The "home situation," which is regularly described in the probation worker's report, is an example. What is a home situation? With what degree of assurance may we utter the designations adequate, inadequate, or poor? And what forms of evidence are used to associate or dissociate persons with each of these categories? Finally, there are the categories of personality and the multitude of assessments that appear in each of them. My aim here is not to criticize the social and psychological categories that are used and sometimes abused by court agents. In some instances, they happen to be the best we can do and in many kinds of research they do well enough. The point is that compared to offense categories they are necessarily more diffuse. They are more diffuse not so much because lawyers are more practiced in the arts of clarity than those who create social and personal categories, though they surely are, but because the degree of complexity in the respective tasks fundamentally differs. It is, at this juncture and perhaps eternally, more difficult to locate and specifically define relevant personal and social categories than offense categories. Consequently, the criteria implicit in a principle of individualized justice are not only more numerous than those implicit in a principle of offense; they are more diffusely defined, too. Thus, court agents are dependent on wisdom in a double sense. They must use wisdom in deciding which portion of the wide frame of relevance they will assign greatest weight and thus invoke in any particular case. Moreover, they must use their judgment in applying whichever portion of the frame of relevance they choose since each portion in itself tends to be diffusely defined. . . . Great variation in the practice and sentiment of the dispensing units is and always has been a central characteristic of this kind of justice. The claim that there is great variation from one juvenile court to another within the same jurisdiction, or even the same building, has traditionally been taken as a warning against generalization concerning the court. I suggest contrarily that the great variation from court to court is one of the most important and revealing generalizations one can make about the type of justice regularly dispensed in juvenile courts.

The juvenile court is not the first court marked by great variation among the dispensing units. That sort of variation is a general feature of *kadi* justice—the brand of justice most closely approximated by the juvenile court, to the extent that it is guided by the canons of individualized justice. Kadi is a variety of justice that is unified by the great variation of practice and sentiment appearing within its realm. The particular form taken depends mainly on the special attributes of judgment and wisdom possessed by the kadi. . . . The kadi does not really render his decisions without any reference to rules or norms. What the kadi in all likelihood does should by now be obvious. He operates with an extremely wide frame of relevance in which, in principle, everything matters. In each particular case he implicitly chooses that section of the frame of relevance he wishes to invoke. He is under no sustained obligation to choose the same section of the frame of relevance in every case. That is the kadi's distinctive prerogative which he may or may not exercise. . . .

The kadi *seems* to render decisions without reference to rules or norms and is engaged in what *appears to be* a completely free evaluation of the particular merits of each case. . . . Of immediate relevance is the sense in which the kadi seems *to the recipients of justice* to render decisions without reference to rules or norms. *It appears to them* that he is engaged in a completely free evaluation of the case.

Before turning to the way in which kadi justice appears to its recipients, let us explore its meaning a little further. Max Weber distinguishes among rational, empirical, kadi, and charismatic justice. He says:

> The rational interpretation of law on the basis of strictly formal conceptions stands opposite the kind of adjudication that is primarily bound to sacred traditions. The single case that cannot be unambiguously decided by tradition is either settled by concrete "revelation" (oracle, prophetic dicta, or ordeal—that is by charismatic justice) or—and only these cases interest us here—*by informal judgments rendered in terms of concrete ethical or other practical evaluations.* This is *"kadi justice,"* as R. Schmidt fittingly called it. Or formal judgments are rendered, though not by subsumption under rational concepts, but by drawing on "analogies" and by depending upon and interpreting concrete "precedents." This is "empirical justice."

Thus, kadi stands between empirical and charismatic justice. All three, kadi, empirical, and charismatic justice, depart from rational justice which is based on "strictly formal conceptions." But the three differ with respect to the kinds of tradition that guide judgments: empirical justice is guided by the interpretation of concrete *legal precedents;* kadi justice, by concrete *ethical and practical valuations;* charismatic justice, by concrete *revelation.*

Thus far, I have suggested the similarity between the contemporary juvenile court and kadi justice. But if the juvenile court is an instance of kadi justice, it is a very special instance. Weber correctly considers ideal kadi justice a nonbureaucratic form of domination. . . . Contemporary juvenile justice is a peculiar form of kadi justice in which the reliance on judgment and wisdom persists but is fundamentally modified and distorted by the strange, one might almost say unseemly, setting in which it appears. The juvenile court exercises kadi justice in a bureaucratic context. This is a feature of the juvenile court to which I shall return in the discussion of the ways in which the *competence* of some of its agents is challenged by its juvenile clientele. Now I want simply to note the peculiarity inherent in the transfer of an independent kadi from his original and natural setting, the market place, to a career position in the wider bureaucratic establishment entrusted with the administration of justice. The current setting of kadi is, to say the least, a very different kind of market place.

What is so peculiar about kadi justice being dispensed within a bureaucratic context? Kadi justice, both in general and in its current rendition stressing the principle of individualized treatment, tends in the main to widen discretion, whereas bureaucratization tends in the main to limit discretion.

Legal bureaucracies, like any other, must concern themselves with routines, work flow, public relations, maintenance of reasonable internal harmony, record keeping, and a variety of other forms of business. What does this tell us about the way in which the setting will influence the principle of justice being espoused? It informs us, I believe, that the kadi will undergo persistent and often self-imposed stress, especially since he happens to be the manager of the court as well as its kadi, to bend his decisions in a manner that will serve institutional needs. The wide discretion given him by the principle of individualized judgment is limited in a way that will be consistent with the bureaucratic norms of efficiency, good public relations, and the maintenance of harmony and *esprit de corps* among his underlings. Thus, the kadi's initially free-wheeling choice is restricted by his structural situation.

However, it would be inaccurate as well as unfair to leave the discussion at that. The kadi in the juvenile court is susceptible to another set of pressures because of the peculiar sort of bureaucracy in which he finds himself, and specifically because of the strange sentiments espoused by many of his underlings. In some measure, and the measure is closely related to the extent to which the court is guided by the principle of individualized justice, the judge precariously rules over what to him must surely seem a *social-work* bureaucracy. If internal harmony is to be maintained, if work is to flow, if the embarrassment of frequent reversal of the probation worker's recommendation is to be avoided, and all of these are in some measure necessary, then the kadi must succumb to another set of pressures. These too serve to limit his discretion. In what direction do the social-work pressures push him? There are two ways of answering that question. One would

be to indulge in and describe the mystifications that pervade social-work theory. This would be of little help since they merely
duplicate and are in fact the basis of the kadi's aimless guide to
action—the principle of individualized justice. The second way
of answering the question is more open to controversy, but I
believe it to be true in the main. The pressure exerted on the
judge by his social-work underlings is, to state it simply, for
mercy.

Now, a statement as bald as that, especially when it seems to
confirm the public criticism of the social-work view, surely seems
calculated to provoke disagreement from the practitioners in that
profession. Many spokesmen for social work would argue that I
have misunderstood their basic point of view, taken it out of context and thus distorted it. That claim would be partly true. I
have taken the quality of mercy out of the context in which it
appears in social-work pronouncements, and in that sense distorted their complex and sometimes mysterious message. My only
defense is that I believe that the kadi oversimplifies the message
of his social-work underlings in a manner similar to that expressed here. It seems to him that what his underlings ask for
most of the time is mercy for the offender. He may understand,
appreciate, and even concur with the elaborate social-work theory
that underlies the plea for one sort of mercy or another. However, that is of little consequence. By this time, the kadi is seeking a guide to action, and the flimsiest sort of justification may
suffice.

The kadi is subject to one final pressure. Since he manages the
court, it is he who is ultimately responsible to the public. He
will have to explain to those specialists in indignation—newspapermen—why the 17-year-old murderer of an innocent matron
was allowed to roam the streets, on probation, when just last year
he was booked for mugging. This is no easy question to answer.
Somehow, an invoking of the principle of individualized justice
and a justification of mercy on the basis of accredited social-work
theory hardly seems appropriate on these occasions. Thus, the
kadi anticipates the situation. He worries about it. He talks
about it to almost anyone who cares to listen. It is the awesome
hazard of his calling. Consequently, he becomes subjected to a
pressure exactly contradicting that emanating from his underlings. It is his sense that the public demands *severity*. And, in a
sense, he is quite right. The public, whenever it speaks to the
kadi, does seem to be demanding severity.

In summary, the contemporary kadi's situation is one in which
the principle of individualized justice gives him incredibly wide
discretion and incredibly little guide for action. But his tradi-

tional freedom is restricted by the peculiar bureaucratic setting in which it appears. His judgment and wisdom may reign but only precariously since he is simultaneously the manager of the court and must thus concern himself with public relations, internal harmony, efficient work flow, and the rest. How does the kadi handle and respond to the pressures in which he is caught? The answer to that question returns us to what must seem to the reader a round-about way of arriving at the basis of the delinquent's sense of injustice. But there is no other way. The *delinquent's* sense of injustice is partially rooted in the *kadi's* response to his own delicate situation.

The kadi's responses to the crosspressures obviously vary but not as much as one might imagine. If we pay attention to what he actually does and not to the rhetoric by which he justifies his dispositions, some interesting and by no means unprecedented things seem to happen. A first order of business is to merely get through the day's work. The flow of juvenile cases is something to behold. Falling behind is consequential since there are other points on the juvenile assembly line, detention halls, for instance, that will suffer pile-ups. Cases must be handled routinely and efficiently or else there will be complaints to the management from other parts of the system. Much of the real work and real decision making is done behind the scenes where the recipient of justice cannot observe it. It is completely obscured from him. His court hearing is typically perfunctory, though occasionally a case is rather thoroughly explored.

Within the limits set by the demands of time, efficiency, and work flow, the kadi's wisdom and judgment may operate. He must decide which portion of the wide frame of relevance to invoke in each case, and in every case he is subjected to the remaining crosspressures; one calling for severity, the other for mercy; one emanating from far-off and occasional critics, the other from nearby and ever-present underlings with whom he must work; one irrelevant to the day-to-day administration of an efficient court, the other crucially relevant; but one representing what he takes to be public opinion, the other what he takes to be professional opinion; and one holding the sanction of public scandal, the other of professional criticism. Indeed, the kadi must be bestowed with judgment and wisdom. His frame of relevance for the disposition of cases is truly one in which many things matter.

His typical solution, and in a sense it is the only solution open to ordinary mortals, is compromise. However, his compromise is of the sort that suggests the surrender of authority rather than a wily manipulation of sovereignty. He renders unto each camp what seems to be their due, and, if his social-work underlings display the normal sensitivity of those who ply that trade, they will protect their kadi from embarrassment by not asking him for what is not properly theirs. . . . The mystery, of course, is how a court that publicly announces adherence to an aimless guide to action—the principle of individualized justice—makes decisions and quickly disposes of cases. . . . I believe the answer to be quite simple. The court's solution contains two elements. One, the main part of the solution, is to more or less reinstore—*sub rosa*—the *principle of offense.* Those delinquents who sense this flagrant violation of the court's publicly espoused philosophy take the amazing hullaballoo regarding individualized justice and treatment to be pious cant, abortive mystification, and patent "snow job." Are they right in their assessment? Not completely, because the concern with individual characteristics and with treatment is not completely surrendered by the court. These concerns remain but they are transformed, *as they must be* in any ongoing system of bureaucratic domination, into workable doctrines that may routinely function as enlightening guides to action rather than mystifying obstacles. The workable bureaucratic equivalents of the stress on extraordinary individual characteristics—equity—and the philosophy of treatment are the doctrines of *parental sponsorship* and *residential availability.* . . . This means that whether a juvenile goes to some manner of prison or is put on some manner of probation—the alternative sentences from which the kadi mainly chooses—depends first, on a traditional rule-of-thumb assessment of the total risk of danger and thus scandal evident in the juvenile's current offense and prior record of offenses; this initial reckoning is then importantly qualified by an assessment of the potentialities of "out-patient supervision" and the guarantee against scandal inherent in the willingness and ability of parents or surrogates to sponsor the child. If the reckoning of danger and thus potential scandal is extremely high, then no amount of parental or surrogate sponsorship will result in mere probation. The offender will be rendered unto those who support and man the prison. If the reckoning of danger is moderate then the decision will turn on an assessment of the presence, the amount, the quality, and the dependability of parental sponsorship. The cumulative reckoning of offense and prior record being equal, those with adequate sponsorship will be rendered unto probation, and those inadequately sponsored to prison. If the reckoning of danger is very low, then only those with virtually no visible or foreseeable parental sponsorship whatever will go to prison. . . .

The second doctrinal qualification on the principle of offense pertains to the availability of residential treatment or, to revert to the older usage, prison space. . . . Justice must possess cutting points in order to achieve decision. Thus, when the original principles guiding a legal institution are so aimless as to forget cutting points, those who man the institution will themselves elaborate them over the course of experience. The cutting point is supplied by the publicly obscure doctrine of residential availability. . . . The doctrine of residential availability is wittingly or unwittingly invoked only when *no obvious decision* ensues from the main reckoning based on the principle of offense and the primary doctrine of parental sponsorship. . . . In some cases, probably a small minority, the decision is far from obvious. In those few cases, the choice between probation or prison is exceedingly difficult. In those cases, the judge is likely to invoke the doctrine of residential availability. What else is there? The judge and his helpers have already teased whatever guidance they could from the principle of offense and the doctrine of parental sponsorship. The judge like his academic counterpart must make a decision. . . .

The emergent reliance on the reinstituted principle of offense, qualified not by equity and treatment but by their routinized equivalents, parental sponsorship and residential availability, is founded on the connected facts that they can provide the kadi with substantive guides to action, allow him to maintain peace in the internal court establishment, and deflect or at least minimize the chances of public scandal introduced by the external presence of specialists in indignation. This amalgam emerged and persists because it was a workable accommodation to the originally aimless principles of individualized justice and treatment. In considerable measure this accommodating amalgam has satisfied everyone who partakes of the system—everyone, that is, who matters.

NOTES AND QUESTIONS

1. Compare the picture of the juvenile court in Matza with the description of the commitment process in Scheff, Reading 78, at 654, *supra*.

2. Matza is obviously indebted to Weber for a number of his concepts and terms. Is he also criticizing Weber? Despite some hedging, Weber seems to imply that there is a definite movement *away* from "kadi justice" and irrationality in modern law. Matza examines a pocket of kadi justice *within* a largely rational system of law (rational in Weber's sense). Does the survival of

this pocket of kadi justice tend to cast any doubt on at least the *evolutionary* aspects of Weber's argument?

In connection with this last question, the reader will recall (a) that the juvenile court was created in this country around 1900, partly to avoid the use of criminal law in the treatment of juveniles; criminal law processes are highly individuated, but do not, as Matza points out, permit as wide a scope of discretion (or Weberian kadi justice) as do the juvenile courts; (b) quite recently, the Supreme Court of the United States in *In re* Gault, 387 U.S. 1 (1967), held that juveniles have at least *some* rights to be represented by attorneys; and widespread criticism of the operation of juvenile courts has led to a movement to *cut down* the discretion of the "kadi."

Is Matza taking the Weber categories out of a historical-cultural context, and making kadi justice a matter of structure, expedience and power distribution *within* a legal system?

3. Note the careful distinction made by Matza between the *actual* behavior of the judge and the great freedom accorded him by governing law. To what levels of analysis, the formal or the informal, do Weber's categories apply? Is kadi justice simply a matter of unreviewability of decisions (or, in other words, discretion)?

4. Note the discussion at 966, of "individualized justice" in criminal law, where disposition is to be guided by a "full understanding of the client's personal and social character." This leads, Matza argues, to mystification and resentment on the part of the client. Would Feifer agree? Does the description—and the critique—fit the work of the People's Courts in Moscow?

5. Matza states at 967, that any system with "an extremely wide frame of relevance in which the items included in the frame are neither specifically enumerated nor weighted must come to rely heavily on professional judgment." Can this statement be reconciled with the studies of Barotse, Kuba and Tiv law?

6. In general, how culturally specific are Matza's findings and arguments about the juvenile court? Would they hold for any culture without a "deviant subculture" such as is often posited for the juvenile delinquent?

C. EVOLUTIONARY THEORIES OF LAW

113. Legal Evolution and Societal Complexity

RICHARD D. SCHWARTZ AND
JAMES C. MILLER*

70 AMERICAN JOURNAL OF SOCIOLOGY
159-69 (1964)

The study of legal evolution has traditionally commended itself to scholars in a variety of fields. . . .

There are theoretical and practical reasons for this interest. Legal evolution provides an opportunity to investigate the relations between law and other major aspects and institutions of society. Thus [Sir Henry] Maine explained the rise of contract in terms of the declining role of kinship as an exclusive basis of social organization. [Emile] Durkheim saw restitutive sanctions replacing repressive ones as a result of the growth of the division of labor and the corresponding shift from mechanical to organic solidarity. [Albert V.] Dicey traced the growth of statutory law-making in terms of the increasing articulateness and power of public opinion. [Max] Weber viewed the development of formal legal rationality as an expression of, and precondition for, the growth of modern capitalism.

For the most part, these writers were interested in the development of legal norms and not in the evolution of legal organization. The latter subject warrants attention for several reasons. As the mechanism through which substantive law is formulated, invoked, and administered, legal organization is of primary importance for understanding the process by which legal norms are evolved and implemented. Moreover, legal organization seems to develop with a degree of regularity that in itself invites attention and explanation. The present study suggests that elements of legal organization emerge in a sequence, such that each consti-

---

* Richard Schwartz, Professor of Sociology and Law, Northwestern University; James Miller, Department of Psychology, Yale University.

tutes a necessary condition for the next. A second type of regularity appears in the relationship between changes in legal organization and other aspects of social organization, notably the division of labor.

By exploring such regularities intensively, it may be possible to learn more about the dynamics of institutional differentiation. Legal organization is a particularly promising subject from this point of view. It tends toward a unified, easily identifiable structure in any given society. Its form and procedures are likely to be explicitly stated. Its central function, legitimation, promotes crossculturally recurrent instances of conflict with, and adaptation to, other institutional systems such as religion, polity, economy, and family. Before these relationships can be adequately explored, however, certain gross regularities of development should be noted and it is with these that the present paper is primarily concerned.

This article reports preliminary findings from cross-cultural research that show a rather startling consistency in the pattern of legal evolution. In a sample of fifty-one societies, compensatory damages and mediation of disputes were found in every society having specialized legal counsel. In addition, a large majority (85 per cent) of societies that develop specialized police also employ damages and mediation. These findings suggest a variety of explanations. It may be necessary, for instance, for a society to accept the principles of mediation and compensation before formalized agencies of adjudication and control can be evolved. Alternatively or concurrently, non-legal changes may explain the results. A formalized means of exchange, some degree of specialization, and writing appear almost universally to follow certain of these legal developments and to precede others. If such sequences are inevitable, they suggest theoretically interesting causative relationships and provide a possible basis for assigning priorities in stimulating the evolution of complex legal institutions in the contemporary world.

METHOD

This research employed a method used by Freeman and Winch in their analysis of societal complexity.[13] Studying a sample of forty-eight societies, they noted a Guttman-scale relationship among six items associated with the folk-urban continuum. The following items were found to fall in a single dimension rang-

---

[13] Linton C. Freeman and Robert F. Winch, "Societal Complexity: An Empirical Test of a Typology of Societies," *American Journal of Sociology*, LXII (March, 1957), 461-66.

ing, the authors suggest, from simple to complex: a symbolic medium of exchange; punishment of crimes through government action; religious, educational, and government specialization; and writing.

To permit the location of legal characteristics on the Freeman-Winch scale, substantially the same sample was used in this study. Three societies were dropped because of uncertainty as to date and source of description or because of inadequate material on legal characteristics. Six societies were added, three to cover the legally developed societies more adequately and three to permit the inclusion of certain well-described control systems.

Several characteristics of a fully developed legal system were isolated for purposes of study. These included counsel, mediation, and police. These three characteristics, which will constitute the focus of the present paper,[19] are defined as follows:

> *counsel:* regular use of specialized non-kin advocates in the settlement of disputes
> *mediation:* regular use of non-kin third party intervention in dispute settlement
> *police:* specialized armed force used partially or wholly for norm enforcement.

These three items, all referring to specialized roles relevant to dispute resolution, were found to fall in a near-perfect Guttman scale. Before the central findings are described and discussed, several methodological limitations should be noted.

First, despite efforts by Murdock and others, no wholly satisfactory method has been devised for obtaining a representative sample of the world's societies. Since the universe of separate societies has not been adequately defined, much less enumerated, the representativeness of the sample cannot be ascertained. Nevertheless, an effort has been made to include societies drawn from the major culture areas and from diverse stages of technological development.

Second, societies have been selected in terms of the availability of adequate ethnographic reports. As a result, a bias may have entered the sample through the selection of societies that were particularly accessible—and hospitable—to anthropological observers. Such societies may differ in their patterns of development from societies that have been less well studied.

---

[19] The original study also included damages, imprisonment, and execution. These were dropped from the present analysis, even though this unfortunately limited the scale to three items, to permit focus on statuses rather than sanction. Data on damages will be introduced, however, where relevant to the discussion of restitution.

Third, despite the selection of relatively well-studied societies, the quality of reports varies widely. Like the preceding limitations, this problem is common to all cross-cultural comparisons. The difficulty is mitigated, however, by the fact that the results of this study are positive. The effect of poor reporting should generally be to randomize the apparent occurrence of the variables studied. Where systematic patterns of relationship emerge, as they do in the present research, it would seem to indicate considerable accuracy in the original reports.

Fourth, this study deals with characteristics whose presence or absence can be determined with relative accuracy. In so doing, it may neglect elements of fundamental importance to the basic inquiry. Thus no effort is made to observe the presence of such important phenomena as respect for law, the use of generalized norms, and the pervasiveness of deviance-induced disturbance. Although all of these should be included in a comprehensive theory of legal evolution, they are omitted here in the interest of observational reliability.[22]

Fifth, the Guttman scale is here pressed into service beyond that for which it was developed. Originally conceived as a technique for the isolation of uni-dimensional attitudes, it has also been used as a means of studying the interrelationship of behavior patterns. It should be particularly valuable, however, in testing hypotheses concerning developmental sequences, whether in individuals or in societies. Thus, if we hypothesize that A must

---

[22] Determination of the presence of a characteristic was made after a detailed search by Miller of the materials on each society in the Human Relations Area Files. His search began with a thorough reading for all societies of the material filed under category 18, "total culture." (All categories used are described in detail in George P. Murdock *et al., Outline of Cultural Materials* [4th rev. ed.; New Haven, Conn.: Human Relations Area Files, 1961].) This was followed by a search of the annotated bibliography (category 111) to locate any works specifically dealing with legal or dispute settling processes. When found, works of this kind were examined in detail. In addition, materials filed under the following categories were read: community structure (621), headmen (622), councils (623), police (625), informal in-group justice (627), intercommunity relations (628), territorial hierarchy (631), legal norms (671), liability (672), offenses and sanctions (68), litigation (691), judicial authority (692), legal and judicial personnel (693), initiation of judicial proceedings (694), trial procedure (695), execution of justice (696), prisons and jails (697), and special courts (698). If this search did not reveal the presence of the practice or status under investigation, it was assumed absent. . . .

A reliability check on Miller's judgments was provided by Robert C. Scholl, to whom the writers are indebted. Working independently and without knowledge of the hypotheses, Scholl examined a randomly selected third of the total sample. His judgments agreed with those of Miller 88 per cent, disagreed 4 per cent, and he was unable to reach conclusions on 8 per cent of the items. If the inconclusive judgments are excluded, the reliability reaches the remarkable level of 96 per cent.

TABLE 1

SCALE OF LEGAL CHARACTERISTICS

Society	Counsel	Police	Media-tion	Errors	Legal Scale Type	Freeman-Winch Scale Type
Cambodians	x	x	x		3	*
Czechs	x	x	x		3	6
Elizabethan English	x	x	x		3	6
Imperial Romans	x	x	x		3	6
Indonesians	x	x	x		3	*
Syrians	x	x	x		3	*
Ukranians	x	x	x		3	6
Ashanti		x	x		2	5
Cheyenne		x	x		2	*
Creek		x	x		2	5
Cuna		x	x		2	4
Crow		x		1	2	0
Hopi		x	x		2	5
Iranians		x	x		2	6
Koreans		x	x		2	6
Lapps		x	x		2	6
Maori		x	x		2	4
Riffians		x	x		2	6
Thonga		x		1	2	2
Vietnamese		x	x		2	6
Andamanese			x		1	0
Azande			x		1	0
Balinese			x		1	4
Cayapa			x		1	2
Chagga			x		1	4
Formosan aborigines			x		1	0
Hottentot			x		1	0
Ifugao			x		1	0
Lakher			x		1	2
Lepcha			x		1	3
Menomini			x		1	0
Mbundu			x		1	3
Navaho			x		1	5
Ossett			x		1	1
Siwans			x		1	1
Trobrianders			x		1	*
Tupinamba			x		1	0
Venda			x		1	5
Woleaians			x		1	0
Yakut			x		1	1
Aranda					0	0
Buka					0	0
Chukchee					0	*
Comanche					0	0
Copper Eskimo					0	0
Jivaro					0	0
Kababish					0	1
Kazak					0	0
Siriono					0	0
Yaruro					0	1
Yurok					0	1

* Not included in Freeman-Winch sample.

Coefficient of reproductibility $= 1 - 2/153 = .987$; coefficient of scalability $= 1 - 2/153\text{-}120 = .94$; Kendall's tau $= +.68$.

precede B, supporting data should show three scale types: neither A nor B, A but not B, and A and B. Instances of B occurring without A represent errors which lower the reproducibility of the scale and, by the same token, throw doubt in measurable degree on the developmental hypothesis. Although the occurrence of developmental sequences ultimately requires verification by the observation of historic changes in given units, substantiating evidence can be derived from the comparative study of units at varying stages of development. The Guttman scale seems an appropriate quantitative instrument for this purpose.

FINDINGS

In the fifty-one societies studied, as indicated in Table 1, four scale types emerged. Eleven societies showed none of the three characteristics; eighteen had only mediation; eleven had only mediation and police; and seven had mediation, police, and specialized counsel. Two societies departed from these patterns: the Crow and the Thonga had police, but showed no evidence of mediation. While these deviant cases merit detailed study, they reduce the reproducibility of the scale by less than 2 per cent, leaving the coefficient at the extraordinarily high level of better than .98. Each characteristic of legal organization may now be

TABLE 2

DAMAGES IN RELATION TO LEGAL FUNCTIONARIES

	No Mediation	Mediation Only	Mediation and Police	Mediation, Police, and Counsel	Total
Damages.........	7	17	10	7	41
No damages......	6*	3	1	0	10
Total..........	13	20	11	7	51

* Includes Thonga, who have neither mediation nor damages, but have police.

discussed in terms of the sociolegal conditions in which it is found.

MEDIATION

Societies that lack mediation, constituting less than a third of the entire sample, appear to be the simplest societies. None of them has writing or any substantial degree of specialization. Only three of the thirteen (Yurok, Kababish, and Thonga) use money, whereas almost three-fourths of the societies with mediation have a symbolic means of exchange. We can only speculate at present on the reasons why mediation is absent in these societies. Data on size, using Naroll's definition of the social unit, indicate that the maximum community size of societies without mediation is substantially smaller than that of societies with mediation.[28] Because of their small size, mediationless societies may have fewer disputes and thus have less opportunity to evolve regularized patterns of dispute settlement. Moreover, smaller societies may be better able to develop mores and informal controls which tend to prevent the occurrence of disputes. Also, the usually desperate struggle for existence of such societies may strengthen the common goal of survival and thus produce a lessening of intragroup hostility.

The lack of money and substantial property may also help to explain the absence of mediation in these societies. There is much evidence to support the hypothesis that property provides something to quarrel about. In addition, it seems to provide something to mediate with as well. Where private property is extremely limited, one would be less likely to find a concept of damages, that is, property payments in lieu of other sanctions. The development of a concept of damages should greatly increase the range of alternative settlements. This in turn might be expected to create a place for the mediator as a person charged with locating a settlement point satisfactory to the parties and the society.

This hypothesis derives support from the data in Table 2. The concept of damages occur in all but four of the thirty-eight societies that have mediation and thus appears to be virtually a precondition for mediation. It should be noted, however, that damages are also found in several (seven of thirteen) of the societies that lack mediation. The relationship that emerges is one of damages as a necessary but not sufficient condition for mediation. At present it is impossible to ascertain whether the absence of mediation in societies having the damage concept results from a simple time lag or whether some other factor, not considered in this study, distinguishes these societies from those that have developed mediation.

---

[28] Data were obtained for thirty-nine of the fifty-one societies in the sample on the size of their largest settlement. Societies with mediation have a median largest settlement size of 1,000, while those without mediation have a median of 346. Even eliminating the societies with developed cities, the median largest settlement size remains above 500 for societies with mediation,

POLICE

Twenty societies in the sample had police—that is, a specialized armed force available for norm enforcement. As noted, all of these but the Crow and Thonga had the concept of damages and some kind of mediation as well. Nevertheless, the occurrence of twenty societies with mediation but without police makes it clear that mediation is not inevitably accompanied by the systematic enforcement of decisions. The separability of these two characteristics is graphically illustrated in ethnographic reports. A striking instance is found among the Albanian tribesmen whose elaborately developed code for settling disputes, Lek's Kanun, was used for centuries as a basis for mediation. But in the absence of mutual agreements by the disputants, feuds often began immediately after adjudication and continued unhampered by any constituted police.[29]

From the data it is possible to determine some of the characteristics of societies that develop police. Eighteen of the twenty in our sample are economically advanced enough to use money. They also have a substantial degree of specialization, with full-time priests and teachers found in all but three (Cheyenne, Thonga, and Crow), and full-time governmental officials, not mere relatives of the chief, present in all but four (Cuna, Maori, Thonga, and Crow).

Superficially at least, these findings seem directly contradictory to [Emile] Durkheim's major thesis in *The Division of Labor in Society*. He hypothesized that penal law—the effort of the organized society to punish offenses against itself—occurs in societies with the simplest division of labor. As indicated, however, our data show that police are found only in association with a substantial degree of division of labor. Even the practice of governmental punishment for wrongs against the society (as noted by Freeman and Winch) does not appear in simpler societies. By contrast, restitutive sanctions—damages and mediation—which Durkheim believed to be associated with an increasing division of labor, are found in many societies that lack even rudimentary specialization. Thus Durkheim's hypothesis seems the reverse of the empirical situation in the range of societies studied here.[30]

---

[29] Margaret Hasluck, *The Unwritten Law in Albania* (Cambridge: Cambridge University Press, 1954).

[30] A basic difficulty in testing Durkheim's thesis arises from his manner of formulating it. His principal interest, as we understand it, was to show the relationship between division of labor and type of sanction (using type of solidarity as the intervening variable). However, in distinguishing systems of law, he added the criterion of organization. The difficulty is that he was very broad in his criterion of organization required for penal law, but quite

COUNSEL

Seven societies in the sample employ specialized advocates in the settlement of disputes. As noted, all of these societies also use mediation. There are, however, another thirty-one societies that have mediation but do not employ specialized counsel. It is a striking feature of the data that damages and mediation are characteristic of the simplest (as well as the most complex) societies, while legal counsel are found only in the most complex. The societies with counsel also have, without exception, not only damages, mediation, and police but, in addition, all of the complexity characteristics identified by Freeman and Winch.

It is not surprising that mediation is not universally associated with counsel. In many mediation systems the parties are expected to speak for themselves. The mediator tends to perform a variety of functions, questioning disputants as well as deciding on the facts and interpreting the law. Such a system is found even in complex societies, such as Imperial China. There the prefect acted as counsel, judge, and jury, using a whip to wring the truth from the parties who were assumed a priori to be lying. To serve as counsel in that setting would have been painful as well as superfluous. Even where specialized counsel emerge, their role tends to be ambiguous. In ancient Greece, for instance, counsel acted principally as advisors on strategy. Upon appearance in court they sought to conceal the fact that they were specialists in legal matters, presenting themselves merely as friends of the parties or even on occasion assuming the identity of the parties themselves.

---

narrow in describing the kind of organization needed for non-penal law. For the former, the "assembly of the whole people" sufficed . . . ; for the latter on the other hand, he suggested the following criteria: "restitutive law creates organs which are more and more specialized: consular tribunals, councils of arbitration, administrative tribunals of every sort. Even in its most general part, that which pertains to civil law, it is exercised only through particular functionaries: magistrates, lawyers, etc., who have become apt in this role because of very special training." . . . In thus suggesting that restitutive law exists only with highly complex organizational forms, Durkheim virtually insured that his thesis would be proven—that restitutive law would be found only in complex societies.

Such a "proof," however, would miss the major point of his argument. In testing the main hypothesis it would seem preferable, therefore, to specify a common and minimal organizational criterion, such as public support. Then the key question might be phrased: Is there a tendency toward restitutive rather than repressive sanctions which develops as an increasing function of the division of labor? Although our present data are not conclusive, the finding of damages and mediation in societies with minimal division of labor implies a negative answer. This suggests that the restitutive principle is not contingent on social heterogeneity or that heterogeneity is not contingent on the division of labor.

At all events, lawyers are here found only in quite urbanized societies, all of which are based upon fully developed agricultural economies. The data suggest at least two possible explanations. First, all of the sample societies with counsel have a substantial division of labor, including priests, teachers, police, and government officials. This implies an economic base strong enough to support a variety of secondary and tertiary occupations as well as an understanding of the advantages of specialization. Eleven societies in the sample, however, have all of these specialized statuses but lack specialized counsel. What distinguishes the societies that develop counsel? Literacy would seem to be an important factor. Only five of the twelve literate societies in the sample do not have counsel. Writing, of course, makes possible the formulation of a legal code with its advantages of forewarning the violator and promoting uniformity in judicial administration. The need to interpret a legal code provides a niche for specialized counsel, especially where a substantial segment of the population is illiterate.

Conclusions

These data, taken as a whole, lend support to the belief that an evolutionary sequence occurs in the development of legal institutions. Alternative interpretations are, to be sure, not precluded. The scale analysis might fail to discern short-lived occurrences of items. For instance, counsel might regularly develop as a variation in simple societies even before police, only to drop out rapidly enough so that the sample picks up no such instances. Even though this is a possibility in principle, no cases of this kind have come to the authors' attention.

Another and more realistic possibility is that the sequence noted in this sample does not occur in societies in a state of rapid transition. Developing societies undergoing intensive cultural contact might provide an economic and social basis for specialized lawyers, even in the absence of police or dispute mediation. Until such societies are included in the sample, these findings must be limited to relatively isolated, slowly changing societies.

The study also raises but does not answer questions concerning the evolution of an international legal order. It would be foolhardy to generalize from the primitive world directly to the international scene and to assume that the same sequences must occur here as there. There is no certainty that subtribal units can be analogized to nations, because the latter tend to be so much more powerful, independent, and relatively deficient in common culture and interests. In other ways, the individual nations are farther along the path of legal development than subtribal units because all of them have their own domestic systems of mediation, police, and counsel. This state of affairs might well provide a basis for short-circuiting an evolutionary tendency operative in primitive societies. Then too, the emergent world order appears to lack the incentive of common interest against a hostile environment that gave primitive societies a motive for legal control. Even though the survival value of a legal system may be fully as great for today's world as for primitive societies, the existence of multiple units in the latter case permitted selection for survival of those societies that had developed the adaptive characteristic. The same principle cannot be expected to operate where the existence of "one world" permits no opportunity for variation and consequent selection.

Nonetheless, it is worth speculating that some of the same forces may operate in both situations. We have seen that damages and mediation almost always precede police in the primitive world. This sequence could result from the need to build certain cultural foundations in the community before a central regime of control, as reflected in a police force, can develop. Hypothetically, this cultural foundation might include a determination to avoid disputes, an appreciation of the value of third-party intervention, and the development of a set of norms both for preventive purposes and as a basis for allocating blame and punishment when disputes arise. Compensation by damages and the use of mediators might well contribute to the development of such a cultural foundation, as well as reflecting its growth. If so, their occurrence prior to specialized police would be understandable. This raises the question as to whether the same kind of cultural foundation is not a necessary condition for the establishment of an effective world police force and whether, in the interest of that objective, it might not be appropriate to stress the principles of compensatory damages and mediation as preconditions for the growth of a world rule of law.

NOTES AND QUESTIONS

1. In a footnote omitted from the main reading, Schwartz and Miller remark:

To test whether the legal sequence has a "dynamic of its own," it would seem necessary to examine the growth of legal systems independent of folk-urban changes, as in subsystems or in societies where the process of urbanization has already occurred. The data covered here do not permit such a test.

By "subsystems" they may mean such things as the development of the "legal system" of a university as the institution grows in size.

a. Do you think it is true that "subsystems" go through the same set of stages that whole legal systems do? Think of as many "subsystems" as you can—the "legal" system of a major organization such as General Motors, or of a church in process of expansion, or of the Army, or of the university.

b. What implications would you draw from your conclusions, either way? What would these implications tell you about the factors which induce a legal system to move from one phase to another phase of the cycle?

2. In mature legal systems in industrial countries, legal development in some areas appears to be cyclical. A matter is handled by the adversary-adjudication system, with rules, procedures and lawyers. Then there is dissatisfaction with the results reached and the costs of the process. A new system is introduced without lawyers, with loose procedure, and with wide discretion given to experts or representatives of the community to apply the most general kinds of standards. Then as a result of dissatisfaction with the results reached by this system and its costs, reforms are instituted to "judicialize" the process, and so on. The developments in the area of juvenile justice illustrate such a process.

Does the Schwartz and Miller data preclude a cyclical theory of this sort? If not, how general do you think such a process is? How would you go about investigating whether it is prevalent or not?

3. Are Schwartz and Miller's findings relevant primarily in the evolution of some legal *institutions* or of the whole legal system? Is their scheme of any utility in explaining evolution past the development of literacy and a moderately urbanized society? How valid is their projection of their scheme onto international law?

4. Among other evolutionary and semi-evolutionary theories of law, one must mention (in addition to Emile Durkheim, discussed by Schwartz and Miller) Sir Henry Maine, who, in his book *Ancient Law,* first published in 1861, argued that in "progressive" societies the legal system moved "from status to contract." By status he meant a situation in which legal relationships depended upon one's status, largely a matter of birth and inherited place in the social structure, excluding all relationships which

were the immediate or remote result of agreement. Contract meant a situation in which free, voluntary agreements formed the basis on which law rested. In status-societies, the legal unit tends to be the family; in contract-societies, the individual.

114. The Modernization of Law

MARC GALANTER*

In the past two centuries, the whole legal landscape of the world has altered dramatically. Throughout the world, there has been a proliferation of governmental responsibility and a growth of new areas of law; social life is regulated increasingly through law, rather than through market pressure, custom and informal controls, fiat, or force. During this period, the industrializing nations of the West have developed and consolidated unified national legal systems of a kind not known before. And in the poorer parts of the earth, the nineteenth and early twentieth centuries have seen an influx of foreign law unprecedented in scope (even by the acceptance of Roman law in medieval Europe). The incorporation of large blocs of civil and common law in the nineteenth century has been followed, since World War II and the end of Western dominance, by the reception of new constitutional models and by a postindependence wave of reform and rationalization.

In both older and newer nations, the development, expansion, and consolidation of these national legal systems seem to involve certain common directions of change. Laws are applied over wider spatial, ethnic, and class areas; personal law is replaced by territorial law, special law by general law, customary law by statute law. Corporate rights and responsibilities are replaced by individual ones. Religious sanctions and inspiration are replaced by secular motives and techniques; moral intuition is replaced by technical expertise. Law making and law applying move from authorities with local accountability and diffuse responsibility to specialized professionals representing central national power.

In speaking of modern law, one may mean many things. The term "modern" is used here to refer to a cluster of features that characterize, to a greater or lesser extent, the legal systems of the industrial societies of the last century. Many of these features are to be found elsewhere; some of them are absent to some

* Professor, College, University of Chicago. Chapter 11 of Modernization, pp. 153-65, edited by Myron Weiner. Copyright © 1966 by Basic Books, Inc., Publishers, New York.

degree in one or another advanced industrial society. However, I am putting forth, not a description, but a model. Modern legal systems differ in many important respects. This model attempts to isolate their common salient features.

Let us begin by considering the kinds of legal rules.

First, modern law consists of rules that are uniform and unvarying in their application. The incidence of these rules is territorial rather than "personal"; that is, the same rules are applicable to members of all religions, tribes, classes, castes, and localities and to both sexes. The differences among persons that are recognized by the law are not differences in intrinsic kind or quality, such as differences between nobles and serfs or between Brahmans and lower castes, but differences in function, condition, and achievement in mundane pursuits.

Second, modern law is transactional. Rights and obligations are apportioned as they result from transactions (contractual, tortious, criminal, and so on) between parties rather than aggregated in unchanging clusters that attach to persons because of determinants outside the particular transactions. That is, legal rights and duties are not determined by factors such as age, class, religion, sex, which are unrelated to the particular transaction or encounter. Such status clusters of rights and obligations as do exist are based on mundane function or condition (for example, employer, a business enterprise, wife) rather than on differences in inherent worth or sacramental honor.

Third, modern legal norms are universalistic. Particular instances of regulating are devised to exemplify a valid standard of general applicability, rather than to express that which is unique and intuited. Thus the application of law is reproducible and predictable. [Khadi] justice is replaced by Kant's Categorical Imperative.

Now let us consider the kind of institutional arrangements and techniques for administering these rules.

Fourth, the system is hierarchical. There is a regular network of courts of first instance to apply this law and a regular structure of layers of appeal and review to ensure that local action conforms to national standards. This enables the system to be uniform and predictable. This kind of hierarchy, with active supervision of subordinates, is to be distinguished from hierarchic systems in which there is a delegation of functions to subordinates who enjoy complete discretion within their jurisdictions. Independent legal fiefdoms are transformed into provinces.

Fifth, the system is organized bureaucratically. In order to achieve uniformity, the system must operate impersonally, following prescribed procedures in each case and deciding each case in accordance with written rules. In order to permit review, written records in prescribed form must be kept in each case.

Sixth, the system is rational. Its procedures are ascertainable from written sources by techniques that can be learned and transmitted without special nonrational gifts. Rules are valued for their instrumental utility in producing consciously chosen ends, rather than for their formal qualities. Theological and formalistic techniques, for example, in the field of evidence are replaced by functional ones.

Seventh, the system is run by professionals. It is staffed by persons chosen in accordance with testable mundane qualifications for this work. They are full-time professionals, not persons who engage in it sporadically or avocationally. Their qualifications come from mastery of the techniques of the legal system itself, not from possession of special gifts or talents or from eminence in some other area of life. The lord of the manor and religious dignitaries are replaced by trained professional jurists, by police, examiners, and other enforcement specialists.

Eighth, as the system becomes more technical and complex, there appear specialized professional intermediaries between the courts and the persons who must deal with them. Lawyers replace mere general agents.

Ninth, the system is amendable. There is no sacred fixity to the system. It contains regular and avowed methods for explicitly revising rules and procedures to meet changing needs or to express changing preferences. Thus it is possible to have deliberate and measured innovation for the achievement of specific objectives. Legislation replaces the slow reworking of customary law.

Finally, let us consider the relation of law to political authority. Tenth, the system is political. Law is so connected to the state that the state enjoys a monopoly over disputes within its cognizance. Other tribunals for settling disputes, such as ecclesiastical courts and trade associations, operate only by the state's sufferance or in its interstices and are liable to supervision by it.

Eleventh, the task of finding law and applying it to concrete cases is differentiated in personnel and technique from other governmental functions. Legislative, judicial, and executive are separate and distinct.

By modernization I mean the development of the features mentioned above or sustained movement toward these features. Such a movement may be discerned in Europe as far back as the reception of Roman law, beginning in the eleventh century. But the development of national legal systems of this kind gathered momentum in Europe at the very end of the eighteenth century and spread over most of Europe in the early part of the nineteenth century. The foundations of such systems were laid in many other parts of the world in the nineteenth century. Thus, the "modern" legal experience in most of the world began only a short time after the European. Although in many non-European nations modernization has been intimately connected with the importation of European law, developments in Europe and elsewhere should be seen as phases in a world-wide transformation to legal systems of this "modern" type. This sort of modernization continues today in both new and old states.

It must be emphasized that this process of modernization is still going on in the West. There is no shortage of examples in the contemporary United States: the abolition of racial classifications in the law, the persistent trend to bring state law into line with federal standards in racial matters and in criminal procedure; the movement to make state laws in commercial fields uniform; the movements toward professional judges at the lower levels of the legal system. In the newer nations, the process goes on even more rapidly, more visibly, and often more painfully. But the point is that all legal systems are comprised of these "modern" features in uneven mixtures with traditional ones, just as modern and traditional features are interwoven throughout almost every society.

Our model of modern law emphasizes its unity, uniformity, and universality. Our model pictures a machinery for the relentless imposition of prevailing central rules and procedures over all that is local and parochial and deviant. But no actual legal system is really so unified, regular, and universalistic. Let us look, then, at the sources of diversity, variety, irregularity, and particularism in legal systems.

Every legal system that embraces a diverse population faces the problem of accommodating local norms and giving expression to local concerns while securing uniformity. Again, any legal system that extends over a wide area must be multilevel. It must have at centers of political power some superior agencies that are acknowledged to be authoritative and are engaged in formulating and elaborating important social norms. But it must also have a multitude of lesser and local agencies to apply this law to everyday occurrences in many places. Finally, any legal system must take account of the fact that at any given time there is inevitably a discrepancy between the highest normative standards that are embodied in the law and the going usages of officials, lay people, and legal professionals themselves.

Thus we come to the basic sources of diversity and discrepancy between the law in books and the law in action—the multiplicity of legal agencies themselves, the necessity of accommodating local interests and concerns, the necessity of accommodating values and interests that are not explicitly acknowledged by the legal system. These basic sources of diversity and deviance may be handled very differently by different legal systems. What we have characterized here as modern law can be thought of as one fairly distinct style of balancing unity and diversity, the center and the periphery, the legitimate and the disapproved.

So far, we have talked lawyers' law—the law on the books. But we know that there is no exact correspondence between the law on the books and the law in action. To understand how this modern system works and how it is really different from earlier legal systems, we must ask what happens when we put it in context— where this official lawyers' law is juxtaposed with local legal tradition, deviant practices, and divergent popular attitudes.

The lawyers' law is not the whole of the law. By lawyers' law I refer to those elements of the legal system that are national, formal, impersonal, written, refined, and elaborate, articulated and applied by specialists arranged in a hierarchic network of communications and involving reference to universal norms and independently verifiable facts. On the other hand, the going practice of any legal agency or locality involves local standards and understandings, informal relations, and personal judgments. There are some legal systems that are so simple that no such lawyers' law is differentiated as a distinct and recognizable entity from going practice; for example, the self-contained traditional communities studied by students of primitive law. On the other hand, there are legal systems in which this official lawyers' law has in the main absorbed and effaced the local law traditions. In both of these situations, "official" law is well integrated with popular attitudes about legality; lawyers' law is indistinguishable from local law. Most theories of law, strangely to me, are based on the assumption of a high degree of unity of this kind. Law is said to be the command of the sovereign or the expression of the jural postulates of the society.

But these highly unified legal situations are extreme or ideal types. Plainly there is an intermediate type in which there is an unresolved tension between the national and local, the formal and the informal, the official and the popular. The clearest instance of this is when a colonizing power superimposes uniform law over a territory formerly governed by a diversity of legal traditions. But it is important to recognize that this kind of legal colonization may come from within as well as from without, as it did in Japan in the nineteenth century and Turkey in the twentieth century and as it proceeds today in the reforms instituted in many new nations or in the United States. We may call this intermediate type the dualistic legal situation.

In a relatively homogeneous society, one may visualize law as the expression of shared social norms. But in a heterogeneous society (differentiated horizontally by culture or region or vertically by caste or class), the law expresses primarily the aspirations, not of "the society," but of the groups and strata that promulgate, formulate, and apply the law. The official law embodies norms and procedures that are congenial to the governing classes and may be more or less remote from the attitudes and concerns of many of the people ruled by it. As an astute Nigerian lawyer recently observed, "The law and the constitution of a people are an expression of the social consciousness of their leaders."[1]

A gap between official law, on the one hand, and popular or local law on the other, is not a rare phenomenon. It is probably typical of most large political entities or those with intensive social differentiation. This dualistic legal situation is present with special intensity in the newer states, but it obtains in most modern societies to a greater or lesser degree.

This multilayered legal situation is not new; it long antedates modern systems of law. What is distinctive is how modern law deals with this situation and the processes of change that it sets in motion. There is a striking contrast between modern and premodern law in the way in which the higher and most authoritative elements in the legal system address themselves to the local and discordant elements.

Take the example of India, where there has been and continues to be legal pluralism on the most massive scale. In the Hindu law system, before the coming of the British, law was for the most part a local matter. Besides the courts of kings, there were innumerable tribunals, formal and informal, applying myriad bodies of customary law to their respective castes, localities, and guilds. There was classical Hindu law or *dharmaśāstra*, a widespread and prestigious system of law. But in spite of the plenary power of the kings' courts, official or higher law did not operate to override and displace local law. *Dharmaśāstra* itself incorporated the widest tolerance for local law. The king was instructed to recognize the binding authority of these lesser bodies of law. The fact that *dharmaśāstra* was the only body of law that was written, studied, and systematically cultivated combined with the prestige of its Brahman expositors, the patronage of royal authority, and the striving of many groups for social advancement

---

[1] H. O. Davies, "The Legal and Constitutional Problems of Independence," in Peter Judd, ed., *African Independence* New York: Dell, 1962, p. 328.

to spread this "higher" law to more groups on more topics of law. But this was by absorption and acceptance, not by imposition. At the same time that custom was gradually aligned in some respects with śāstric standards, the textual law itself was continuously reinterpreted to accommodate a variety of going usages.

Thus, in the Hindu system, the existence of royal courts and a refined and respected system of written law did not serve to unify the system in the way that national law did in the West. In Europe and America, local law was absorbed into and gradually displaced by law promulgated by state authorities. But Hindu law did not visualize the respective authoritativeness of its governmental, śāstric, and local components in a way that supplied either the techniques or the ideology for the ruthless suppression of local law. The relation of the highest and most authoritative parts of the legal system to the lower end of the system was not that of superior to subordinate in a bureaucratic hierarchy. It was perhaps closer to the relations that obtain between Paris designers and American department-store fashions, or between prestigious universities and smaller colleges, than to anything in modern legal experience. Instead of systematic imposition, there is a general diffusion by example and persuasion, by the filtering down (and up) of ideas and techniques, by some conscious imitation and imitation of imitations.

Hindu law, then, is the prime example of the ancient maxim that "special law prevails over general law." Let us take another premodern example: that of Muslim law. Here, too, we find a body of authoritative and universal legal norms worked out in an elaborate and refined legal literature. But here, too, we find that the local, the particular, the deviant, the customary, are accommodated, not, as in the Hindu system, by simply absorbing them and conferring legitimacy on them, but rather by an elaborate series of technical devices to make the law comport with going practice and by a delimitation of spheres by which troublesome matters were left to custom or to royal prerogative.

In modern law, the relatively stable and slowly changing balance between higher and local components in a legal system is shattered beyond repair. In earlier systems, there was a mutual influence and interchange between higher general law and special local law. The higher law might deflect the local and might be deflected by it. They might coexist without much friction. Now, as we shall see, there is an end to the possibility of coexistence and there is an acceleration of the rate of influence in one direction and an inhibition of influence in the other.

In a modern system, there is a strong and persistent tendency toward the replacement of local and popular law by official law-

yers' law. The most powerful agency of dissemination is a hierarchical system of courts. The nationwide rules and standards
propounded at the upper reaches of the hierarchy are applied by
local courts. The decrees of these courts can be enforced by compulsory process, independently of local opinion. Even where official courts attempt to apply indigenous law, the latter is transformed in the process. Hindu or Moslem law, applied in courts
with different rules of procedure and by judges with different
training, preconceptions, and traditions, takes on a new character.
And this even more so with unwritten customary law. From an
orally transmitted body of precepts and precedents, subject to
variable interpretation and quasi-legislative innovation at the discretion of village notables, it becomes a body of fixed written
laws to be applied by a professional court. Variable sanctions
imposed with an eye to the total situation of the parties are
replaced by the compulsory and drastic execution of the decree
of the official court.

This process of modernization is accompanied by characteristic
discomforts. In nineteenth- and twentieth-century India, we hear
complaints that are strikingly reminiscent of those in medieval
Germany at the time of the reception of Roman law, applied by
professional judges—judges unfamiliar with local customs, delay,
expense, unnecessarily complicated procedure.

In this process, the official law does not remain static. If official law is borrowed, it is refined more or less to distill out some
of the localisms of its original historic embodiment, as the common law, in being transplanted to India, was stripped of technicalities and historical anomalies and rendered symmetrical and
orderly. Again, the lawyers' law must be elaborated to assimilate
new kinds of persons and transactions, as the English law of
crimes had to deal with new kinds of offenses and new kinds of
property in India and Africa. The dissemination of lawyers' law
is not wholly a one-way process. But official law is limited and
contained by the very conditions of its success. The law on the
books does not represent the attitudes and concerns of the local
people. The demise of traditional law does not automatically
bring the demise of traditional society. People learn to manipulate it for their purposes, to make it express their concerns and
serve their ambitions. They devise new patterns of avoidance and
evasion of the rules promulgated at the upper reaches of the
system. The law in operation is always a compromise between
lawyers' law and parochial notions of legality.

Every legal system purports to cover everything under the
mantle of elevated general standards. But it always has pockets
in which to accommodate local and parochial interests and atti-

tudes. In premodern systems, the smaller groups enjoyed autonomy in their own law work, and the government tended to absorb
and apply local standards. Under a modern system, these methods
are no longer available.

A modern system breaks the tie of law with local and group
opinion; this can be liberating for the dissenter and the deviant.
The individual is freed from the prescriptive usage of the local
group; the group itself must now be responsive to norms of a
much wider collectivity. Local attitudes and concerns can no
longer find direct embodiment in law. They become law only
when mediated through ideas of remote lawmakers and the techniques of professional judges. The legal world is transformed
from congeries of more or less independent chapels into a few
hierarchic churches.

In this new dispensation, parochial interests and concerns find
expression in new ways. Federalism, limitations on government,
rules of contract, and voluntary association all provide enclaves;
influence through representation at the law-making centers makes
official law responsive. Devices like juries, and locally elected
judges and prosecutors, permit differences under the veneer of
uniformity. Selective nonenforcement, planned inefficiency, *sub
rosa* compromise, tolerated evasion, and, finally, corruption—all
these permit the local, the particularistic, the deviant, to assert
themselves while maintaining the fiction that the law is uniform
and unvarying.

In spite of its discomforts, there seems to be a certain irre-
versibility in this process of forming a modern legal system.
Schemes to revive the "simplicity" of local customary law by
reconstituting village courts cannot put together the broken vessel
of traditional law. Legal revivalist movements such as those in
Ireland, Pakistan, and Israel, whatever their limited success in
changing substantive norms, seem similarly doomed to have little
effect on the basic character of the legal system.

It is instructive to compare the fate of colonial law with that
of colonial languages. While the languages of the colonizing
powers sometimes recede from their former pre-eminence as a
medium of public business and public life, the tide of modern
law that colonization brought in its train continues to advance.
For modern law includes techniques for eroding away and sup-
pressing local law by official law; it accomplishes its own imposition, even inadvertently. And this imposition seems to be enduring in a way that language is not. An official language does not
become a household language; each generation must undergo
anew the process of estrangement. But the official language does
not necessarily gain at the expense of household languages. On

the contrary, we find in India, for example, an enrichment and development of indigenous languages during British rule. However, official law of the modern type does not promote the enrichment and development of indigenous legal systems. It tolerates no rivals; it dissolves away that which cannot be transformed into modern law and absorbs the remainder.

But it should be emphasized that the process of modernization does not continue relentlessly until it produces a legal system that corresponds to our model in every detail—that is, completely unified, uniform, hierarchic, and so on. As society becomes modernized in all spheres, new kinds of diversity and complexity are generated. Intense concentrations of population, mobility, occupational specialization, mass media of communication—all create counter pressures that demand differentiation, responsiveness, and flexibility in the law. So the very factors that encourage modernization of law and are encouraged by it finally impede and undermine it.

Modern societies develop new devices to blunt and deflect the drive toward modernization of law—new techniques of local autonomy through federalism, voluntary associations, and contractual undertakings; new methods of making law flexible and responsive, such as we find in juvenile courts, administrative agencies, and arbitration. Modern law as we have depicted it in our model is not a destination, but rather a focus or vector toward which societies move. But the very forces that support this movement and are released by it deflect it from its apparent destination. . . .

NOTES AND QUESTIONS

1. Carefully note Galanter's eleven characteristics of a modern legal system. Are they to be considered functional prerequisites of modernization of the society, or merely concomitants? It can be shown, for example, that there is a strong correlation between literacy and a high standard of living, between urbanism and a high gross national product, and between the wearing of Western style clothing and high standards of living and gross national product. Yet no one would argue that the wearing of Western style clothing is a precondition for standard of living and gross national product, although one might so argue as to urbanization and literacy.

2. What is Galanter's conception of "modernity"? Does it make sense to you? In Galanter's terms, which is the more modern society, the Union of South Africa or Mexico? the Soviet Union or the United States?

3. What does "universalistic" mean? In what sense is the law of the United States more or less universalistic than that of the Kuba? Is the comparison meaningful?

4. An evolutionary theory may be one which (a) posits a development which is necessary and inevitable—all societies must go through stages *A, B,* and *C* in that order; or (b) posits a contingent development—*if* society is to reach stage *C* at all, it must go through *A* and *B,* and in that order; but societies need not reach stage *C* since they may rest at *B.* Classify the various evolutionary theories in this section in terms of this distinction.

5. The term "evolution" is often used in reference to the biological theories of Darwin and later biologists. It is largely an unconscious process. But man has in some ways reached a position where he can affect his own evolution. He can certainly make changes that alter or speed up the evolutionary process in plants and animals, by selective breeding. Is there an analogous fact in legal systems too, which evolutionary theorists neglect— the extent to which, in modern times, and with modern instruments of development, societies can control themselves and engineer needed change through law?

D. LAW AND CULTURE

115. Legal Culture and Social Development

LAWRENCE M. FRIEDMAN*

In the modern world, the boundaries between legal systems are largely territorial. Legal power follows political lines, and is divided into jurisdictions. Every independent country has its own body of laws. Many have more than one—for example, federations. Many countries are or have been legally plural without being federal. In most African countries, the law of the colonial masters applied most completely to those parts of society which had adopted Western ways and which took part in some kind of market economy. In the interior, native ethnic groups settled disputes through the use of so-called customary law, which differed from the law applied at the center, even when judges sent out from the center applied it. In the old Ottoman Empire, each ethnic group enjoyed its own family law and its own system of courts.

Every body of laws, together with its supporting institutions, whether national or part of a federal or pluralistic system, can be called, somewhat loosely, a legal system. One can speak of the federal law of the United States, and also of the legal systems of Colorado, Florida, and Maine. National legal systems in turn can be grouped and classified into larger units, or families of law, also loosely called "legal systems." One speaks, for example, of the common law legal system, in England, the United States and most of the English-speaking world, and the civil law systems of France, Germany, Italy, and Spain.

* Professor of Law, Stanford University. This is a revised version of a paper originally delivered as part of a panel discussion sponsored by the Association of American Law Schools at its meeting in December 1968 in New Orleans, Louisiana, U.S.A. The author wishes to thank Robert Alford, Daniel Lev, Marc Galanter, Carl Spaeth, and David Trubek, whose comments on earlier drafts were enormously helpful to him. This paper contains no citations to authorities. The reader will nonetheless recognize an indebtedness to a whole line of political and social scientists whose influence is felt at many places.

Classification of legal systems into families assumes that national legal systems are more than the sum of their parts; that they have a definite character and style. Within the family of law, all members share certain basic legal traits. These traits or characteristics are consistent with each other, persist over time, and permeate the legal institutions of the society in such a way as to give a legal system a definite flavor or character. The classifiers, like taxonomists in biology and linguistics, single out certain basic or core features as diagnostic. The core features are then used to assign a body of law to this or that system. The diagnostic features tend to be highly "legal." That is, they pertain to those parts of law which are most exclusively controlled by lawyers, or which, for some reason of history or social position of the profession, loom large in lawyers' minds and are stressed in their training. If one asks a traditional legal scholar how the common law system of an American state differs from the law of Italy or France, he might mention the doctrine of precedent, point out that American law is not wholly codified, refer to the civil jury, and perhaps mention a few concepts, such as consideration in the law of contracts—all these as opposed to the civil law system.

But no one would single out these traits because they were known to be important to the way the law actually operates in contemporary times. The traits, the typology, the classification scheme are based on historical evolution. To be sure, evolutionary theories have yielded useful classifications in linguistics and biology. This has been the model for the classification of systems of law. But what is the utility of the evolutionary scheme as the basis for classification and evaluation of legal systems? Of course, it is true that in one interesting sense, American law "descends" from English law; and the law of Louisiana from the civil law of France and Spain. But does the language of evolution, and the typology that results, explain anything, except the formal sources of those traits selected as "basic"? Moreover, the traits were selected as basic precisely because they were valuable to the classification scheme. Does classification of legal systems by the historical evolutionary method tell us anything about *other* characteristics of a nation or society? Is there a causal connection between membership in one of these families and some level of social or economic development? Many scholars have speculated on this general subject; it was, in a way, one of Max Weber's central themes. It is fair to say that nothing has been proven. The jury is a common law institution, for example. Through jury service, ordinary people make law, or at least take part in decisions. Does this kind of participation in law mean that the jury is vital to the growth of democratic government? It would be rash indeed to answer "yes" too boldly. That would mean that systems without a jury would be less likely to evolve democratic institutions, or to keep them, than systems with a jury. Not enough is known about the effect of this kind of participation on the political system. Perhaps there is some functional equivalent to the jury in systems that do not exactly have a jury. Perhaps the actual impact of a jury is far less democratic than it seems. Some countries with juries seem less participatory than some countries without juries. Similar doubts can be expressed about *any* of the diagnostic features of the traditional classification—and about the features as a whole. One simply cannot say that the common law system, as it evolved in England, was a decisive factor in the rise of the English form of government. Even less could one say that it had anything to do with the flowering of the industrial revolution. Could we even say that it *contributed* to economic or political change? And what does it do today? What would it do in Burma or Iran?

Notice that our skepticism was limited to the common law "system." We neither asserted nor denied that English *law* had an influence on political or economic development in England. We drew a sharp line between what is conventionally called the common law system, and English law (or the English legal system), which is something broader and quite different. All we are saying, for now, is that the conventional concept of the *legal system*, based on historical evolution, is not a helpful tool of research and theory, if the purpose of classifying bodies of law and generalizing about them is to understand the relationship between law and society. This is so for at least two reasons. First, the conventional concept does not do an adequate job of describing how legal systems work. The traits it singles out have not been tested empirically for their impact on the economy, the political system, or on society in general. Second, the conventional concept does not presuppose or yield any coherent theory of the relationship of law and society. It may even be inimical to development of such a theory.

Very often, when people speak of "the legal system" of their community, they are not thinking of that static bundle of traits traditionally used to classify legal systems. They are speaking rather of concrete activities going on about them. They are thinking of lawyers and judges at work, legislators passing laws, administrative agencies making rules and settling disputes. One way to look at the legal system is to consider it as a process—what legal institutions do, and how they do it. This is one meaning of the word "system" in modern social science—an actual operating unit in society, which takes in raw materials, processes them, and produces an output. The comparison between the legal system and a machine is vulgar but useful. It directs our attention to actual moving parts. In these terms, study of the legal system would include study, first of all, of the demands made upon legal institutions calling for action of one sort or another; second, the responses made by legal institutions; third, the impact of these responses on the persons making the demands; and fourth, the effect on society as a whole.

The concept of "demand," as used here, is very broad. Any request for action or redress of grievance, any use of legal or administrative process, would be considered a demand. Litigation is a demand made upon a court. When one or more persons bring a law-suit, they are asking for a response from the court as well as from the defendant. The defendant, too, can be looked upon as making a demand upon the court; he demands justice or vindication. Even if the court dismisses the case or refuses jurisdiction, it has made a response. And whatever response it makes has an impact on the litigants, and very often on others. The legal system as a whole consists of the universe of demands upon legal institutions—not only courts, of course—together with the responses and the effects of the responses. The current social meaning of a legal system can be discovered only if one has some idea what these institutions, demands, and responses are, and some notion of their quality and quantity.

A working legal system can be analyzed further into three kinds of components. Some are *structural*. By structural, we mean the institutions themselves, the forms they take, and the processes that they perform. Structure includes the number and type of courts; presence or absence of a constitution; presence or absence of federalism or pluralism; division of powers between judges, legislatures, governors, kings, juries, and administrative officers; modes of procedure in various institutions; and the like.

Other elements in the system are *cultural*. These are the values and attitudes which bind the system together and which determine the place of the legal system in the culture of the society as a whole. What kind of training and habits do the lawyers and judges have? What do people think of law? Do groups or individuals willingly go to court? For what purposes do people turn to lawyers, for what purposes do they make use of other officials and intermediaries? Is there respect for law, government, tradition? What is the relationship between class structure and the use or non-use of legal institutions? What informal social controls exist in addition to or in place of formal ones? Who prefers which kind of controls, and why? These aspects of law—the legal culture—influence all of the legal system. But they are particularly important as the source of the demands made upon the system. It is the legal culture, that is, the network of values and attitudes relating to law, which determines when and why and where people turn to the law, or to government, or turn away.

Still other components are *substantive*. This is the output side of the legal system. These are the "laws" themselves—the rules, doctrines, statutes and decrees, to the extent they are actually used by the rulers and the ruled, and, in addition, all other rules which govern, whatever their formal status.

The three elements together—structural, cultural, and substantive—make up a totality which, for want of a better term, we can call the legal system. The living law of a society, its *legal system* in this revised sense, is the law as actual process. It is the way in which structural, cultural, and substantive elements interact with each other, under the influence too, of external, *situational* factors, pressing in from the larger society.

In this revised definition, the key concept, perhaps, is that of the legal culture. People are quite accustomed to comparing legal structures and substantive law. They fall into error when they fail to distinguish between mere paper systems and reality; between dead rules and institutions and living ones. Hence they may be enormously misguided in their view of a country's legal system, even from the structural or the substantive viewpoint. But even this mistake is a mistake with respect to the legal culture. This is so because legal culture is the term we apply to those values and attitudes in society which determine what structures are used and why; which rules work and which do not, and why.

Legal cultures obviously differ in ways that cut across the conventional similarities and differences of legal systems as classified by historical evolution; so, therefore, do legal systems differ. Louisiana, for example, is said to belong to the civil law family. By convention, this makes it a close relative of the legal system of France; and a stranger to the system of its sister states. Yet the *cultural* elements of Louisiana's legal life undoubtedly are closer to those of Arkansas or Texas than to France. The number of lawyers and judges, the jobs they do, their place in Louisiana society, what the public thinks of law and lawyers, the kinds of disputes that go to court and stay out of court—these are probably very similar in Louisiana's neighboring states, and quite different in France. Actually, culture is only the most striking case. The textbooks sharply distinguish the substance of Louisiana law from the substantive law of Mississippi, stressing historical and diagnostic traits. Yet the laws of the two states are not that different, if we look instead at the working law of social and economic life: tax law, economic regulation, the law of race relations, occupational licensing, or labor codes. Federal law, of course, is identical in the two states, and it is of great importance. French tax and regulatory law, on the other hand, are quite remote from Louisiana. Even the *structural* elements of law in Louisiana are closer to those of its neighboring states than one might expect from traditional theory. The states are parts of a federal system; all are subject to the constitution. They have shared a century and a half of a common history; they are all part of a single large free-trade area, the United States. Population streams freely across borders; and so the public image of law tends to be much the same in Louisiana and its neighboring states. Finally, Louisiana lawyers speak English; in their training they are exposed to the influence of common law institutions. Hence the legal systems, as a whole, are very similar in the neighboring states.

Contrariwise, two members of what was historically one legal family may move along separate paths as their societies diverge. American law obviously owes a great deal to English law. But British and American law have grown significantly apart over the last three centuries. A great deal of the actual working law in a mature, industrial society is comparatively new law, and it is comparatively specific to the country. In the United States, this includes a vast sea of regulatory law, tax law, labor law, insurance and corporation law, welfare and planning law, and an enormous body of administrative rules and codes. Regulatory and planning law are vital parts of the legal system. They provide a good share of the daily business of lawyers and government officials. They are obviously of first importance in economic and social development. Comparative legal studies traditionally paid little attention to these modern aspects of law. But these parts of law, because they are living, and important, are part of the legal culture, and are deeply rooted in the culture of the society as a whole. They cannot be ignored if one is interested in principles that may explain the relationship of law and the process of social growth.

A comparison of British and American law, for example, would no doubt yield important differences in legal culture, which affect the way in which the rules of law have been elaborated, and the way in which institutions work. The rules, of course, are different; and so are the institutions. But these are probably only the outer form of underlying differences in style, in the effect of public opinion, in short, in culture. What these are, exactly, is a subject for research. The possibilities are intriguing. In Eng-

land, the statutes that govern land use are broadly worded. They
vest enormous power in local authorities; judicial review of land-
use decisions is rare and ineffective. By way of contrast, the
United States is the homeland of *zoning*—a rigid, specific mode
of land-use control. Cities enact a land-use map which determines, for considerable periods of time, the fate of particular
parcels of land. On the other hand, landowners can get "variances"; and zoning decisions may be reviewed in court, and are,
with some frequency.

There are other differences between the two countries which
seem to run parallel to the differences in land-use control. There
seems to be an American attitude toward law and toward power,
which fears centralization and likes to split authority into frag-
ments which counterbalance each other. This cultural attitude,
perhaps, explains the rejection here of the English style of planning law. American law, at least in this area, seems to prefer
to control agencies collaterally, so to speak; English law seems
to prefer control through hierarchy, with a regular chain of command. It does not necessarily follow, however, that the *outcomes*
of land-use control in the two countries are necessarily different.
That depends in turn on the substance of the law (though in
the living-law, not the formal-law sense). And any "gap" between
theory and practice will turn out to be influenced by the legal
culture, that is, by the values and attitudes of the rulers and the
ruled.

Distinguishing between the two definitions of legal system—
one historical and evolutionary, one based on a process model
and stressing the legal culture—may bring some clarity into discussion of general theoretical questions of the relationship between law and society. There are a number of extreme positions
that stand in contrast to each other. One position is that the
law is insulated from the general social system. It is not culturally specific, but is rather adaptable to any level of social
development. The legal system has habits, and embodies values;
but these habits and values, reduced to essentials, are timeless;
different legal systems are different ways of looking at the world
that are in eternal dialogue. Law, then, is analogous to language,
which is another rather insulated social phenomenon. The Japanese speak Japanese now, in the midst of their economic miracle,
just as they spoke Japanese in the middle ages. French is spoken
in France, a rich, sophisticated, urban country; it is spoken, too,
in rural backward Haiti. French, like all languages, can invent
or adopt new words; it can assimilate changes in technology or
art or thought, without a significant time lag, or serious social
disruption. Japanese adapts itself to the modern world without

fundamental structural change. Legal systems can be looked at in the same way. Edward I and Elizabeth II both reigned over a country that was English-speaking and professed the common law. For a thousand years, the common law maintained some sort of continuity, while absorbing and responding to the most fundamental kinds of social change. Law, in this view, is a tough, persistent, relatively self-contained social subsystem. It can accommodate itself to social change, of course, but its basic structure is firm and tenacious.

Another extreme position asserts that a system or body of law is tied to specific levels or kinds of culture. Law is not self-contained; it is culturally very specific. If a community wants to put through some program of drastic political and economic change, it must make drastic changes in its laws. If it wants to modernize, and especially if it wants to modernize fast, the legal system has to be radically altered, or even replaced. Some scholars, for example, might argue that the new African nations must stamp out all traces of customary law, not merely in the name of national unity, but also because customary law is incompatible with modern agriculture, business, and trade, and with the modern state. They do not look on customary law as containing any values worth preserving or as providing any basis for adaptation to modern needs. In most of Africa and much of Asia, colonial powers introduced some parts of the law of the mother country; and this law had some effect, at least on the upper class in the colonial capital. The new nations, however, have been scarcely less avid in seeking legal models outside of their own experience. Mostly these have been Western models, sometimes Socialist models. In either case, the new nations have acted on the assumption that only these models are conducive to the kind of economic growth they want.

There are many other ways of looking at legal systems and their relationship to the larger society, and many hybrid views. Most of them rest on observations that are undeniably true in part. The various theories simply assume different conceptions of the legal system. It is certainly true that legal systems, in the historical and evolutionary sense, are tough and persistent; and can be adapted to societies of quite different types and levels of culture. France and Haiti share a "legal system" as well as a language. It is also clear that any radical social change implies a radical change in the law. When a community moves from tribal organization to nationhood and a money economy, the legal organization of the community will have to be changed to implement and support the new political, social, and economic realities. If the legal tradition does not support these programs, new law—sometimes in massive doses—must be manufactured or brought in from outside.

These general points suggest that discussion of the relationship between the legal system and social development does well to begin by asking what is meant by the legal system. As far as we know, any one of the great historical evolutionary families is *capable* of supporting any level of economy or culture. But this point is not very helpful, because all that it means is that over a long enough period of time legal institutions can accommodate themselves to a variety of social arrangements. It also requires us to define "legal institutions" very narrowly, using, as tools of definition, criteria which do not relate to the question at hand. On the other hand, legal systems are not collections of brittle little sticks to be picked up and discarded at the command of the rulers. Some parts of the living law are deeply imbedded in national culture; and to replace major parts of it either means to uproot something quite fundamental, at considerable costs in disruption; or face the possibility that the new law will not be effective. What the study of legal culture promises is the discovery of the conditions under which legal change occurs, either spontaneous change or imposed change; and, in the case of imposed change, the conditions which make it fail or succeed.

This is an age, by common consent, of rapid and continuous social change. On the legal side, it is an age which is interested, as few periods have been before, in law reform and in social reform through law. This means that those who are concerned, either as legal scholars or social scientists, with the working of the legal system, will probably have to pay increasing attention to that aspect of the legal system which we have called legal culture. We wish to suggest, first, that the idea of social engineering through law is itself an important aspect of the legal culture; second, that this means turning scholarly attention to the question of the conditions under which law is "effective." Here, again, we meet with the legal culture as a critical variable.

On the first point: it hardly needs to be demonstrated that modern societies, as opposed to those societies which we call primitive or traditional, are change-oriented. This means not only that they are changing, but that they also *want* to change. The public as a whole, or some significant elite, has the attitude that change is necessary and desirable, and that the state, the government, the authorities, have the duty to put programs into effect that will move society in the proper direction. In this respect, all modern societies are alike. Whatever vast differences separate the laissez-faire governments of the nineteenth century from the government of Maoist China, to take two extreme examples, this cultural attitude is held in common. Modern societies share a belief in the directive power of government and law. They have different definitions of law. They have different philosophies of law. But they all believe in the duty of the authorities to put in operation effective programs that allow or push society toward the goals they seek. No modern society believes absolutely in the fixity and permanence of law. They may believe in some absolutes, whether the bill of rights, the ban on birth control, or the inviolability of Marx; but they all assume that there is a sphere of human life in which governments can act and must act on behalf of the common good. Demands for change are addressed to governments. It is the rulers who must respond. They, not the gods, must bring on the magic.

The question of effectiveness is more difficult. In one sense legal institutions are effective if society is stable, that is, if the demand side and the supply side of the legal system are in some sort of equilibrium. They are effective at least in the sense that they keep society going without a major breakdown. In some societies, it is easy to see this equilibrium. This is true of static or traditional societies. Members of the community make demands on public authorities, of course; grievances are addressed to chiefs, or bureaucrats; trouble cases go to court. But these demands are routinely handled. They put no unbearable stress on legal institutions, or on the general structure of society. The *capacity* of the authorities—their ability to meet routine demands—is sufficient to keep society in a steady state. Equilibrium is not only a characteristic of primitive or traditional peoples. Ordinary legal process, even in complex societies, is in equilibrium. The traffic court judge comes to court and does his job, day in and day out. Demands flow in, decisions flow out, fines flow in, flagrant violators go to jail, drivers with good stories get off free. The system is stable, and, in its own terms, effective. Probably the whole court system in Western countries is stable and effective in this sense.

But courts are only part of the picture. Today all complex societies are change-oriented. Demands are made on all legal institutions; and the demands are demands for progress, improvement, reallocation, reform. This factor on the demand side—a push toward change—does not necessarily mean that modern governments live in a perpetual state of political or legal crisis. Stable governments are not changeless governments, in the modern world, but governments which are lucky enough or sound enough to find ways to satisfy the most pressing demands made upon them. Their legal systems are equilibrium systems, in the sense that they are stable. But they differ from the simpler equi-

librium of traditional society, in that they accept, process, and produce change, just as a functioning market system accepts, processes
and produces outputs that reflect all sorts of changes in consumer
demand. The restlessness of twentieth century life, then, does
not *necessarily* mean a state of crisis. But often enough crisis does
come. Some intrusive force, some novelty occurs, and the number or type of demands is thrown out of balance. There may
be, for example, demands from some economic class for a higher
national income, or for better distribution of the country's
wealth; and such demands, whether they stem only from a West-
ernized elite, or from the mass of the people, desirous of better
food, more bicycles, or a greater say in their lives, very often
cannot be met without radically changing society. Nor are radical
demands by any means confined to the less developed nations.

On the supply side, then, the critical question is whether the
legal system is responsive enough or effective enough, measured
by some ideal, or end product, or goal. There is no such thing
as effectiveness in the abstract. Effectiveness may be judged from
the inside of the system—does the system *survive* without overthrow, does it satisfy its own customers? Or effectiveness may be
judged by some outside ideal or product, whether an abstract
product (justice), or some concrete goal, like a lower crime rate
or a higher amount of wealth. Once effectiveness is concretely defined, however, it is possible to compare legal systems in terms
of such a concept.

At the present time, legal research is in no position to identify
legal factors that make for successful economic development, for
political stability, or indeed for any reasonable measure of the
effectiveness of law. For one thing, no country, not even the
United States, has an accurate bank of quantitative information
about its legal system. For non-Western countries there is even
less information. Not even such simple things as the number of
lawyers is known for many countries. But an accurate description, or "map" of the legal system, is vitally important for generating comparative social theory, and for learning the conditions
under which legal systems work and fail. What is most notably
missing, even for the Western countries, is information on what
we have called the legal culture. What are the attitudes of different populations toward various parts of the legal system? Are
courts used or avoided? Who goes to court and why? What legal
roles—lawyers, judges, policemen—exist in society? Who occupies these roles and what functions do they perform? What is the
conversion process of the legal system, that is, how are demands
handled, and by whom; how are decisions made? Which officials
have discretion, which do not? What questions are matters of rule,

and what questions are matters of discretion? Are various parts of the system bureaucratic or flexible? What are the effects of the outputs on the population and how can these effects be measured? What is the source of the legitimacy of various parts of the system? Who is supposed to make law, who is supposed to carry it out? How much corruption and maladministration is there and why?

In the best of all possible worlds, one would approach the unresolved questions of law and society armed with answers to these and to countless other questions. Obviously, no one is going to gather all this data; the costs would be enormous, the obstacles insurmountable. But selective research on the legal culture, to answer some specific preliminary questions, seems to be a logical and necessary first step. This is because the legal culture is first of all a major unknown; and second, because legal culture is the key to the effectiveness of law.

Both points are obvious. Opinion research that touches on law is rare. And legal culture is far more than "public opinion" in the crude sense of the polls. For one thing, "the public" is a myth; to understand the law, one must carefully define *a* relevant public; and its identity will differ as issues differ.

It is clear, however, that the effectiveness of any law, actual or proposed, depends on the response of some public that is sought to be moved, or whose interests seem to be at issue. But response by a public is determined by cultural factors. The relevant values and attitudes are not easy to get at. If one proposes that some nation adopt for itself an income tax law more or less on the American plan, can one know in advance whether the law will actually work? How much money will it raise, and at what economic and social cost? The dollars and cents that would be raised by a perfectly enforced law can be computed by economists. But one still needs to know the cost from evasion and disobedience, costs that may flow from lack of public support. Italy and the United States are both modern industrial nations; it is notoriously hard to collect income tax in Italy, but not in the United States. Yet it would be no simple matter to discover the precise social conditions that lead to obedience or compliance with particular forms of law (or to respect for law in general) in two countries such as Italy and the United States.

To take another example, litigiousness varies from culture to culture; the social meaning of litigation is different in different countries and sometimes in adjoining villages. What a public agency means to its community should be taken into account when decisions are made to assign particular social tasks to that agency. There is no inherent social role that must be played by any particular institution or agency. Courts, for example, have been used in many ways in different societies. They have served as instruments to carry into effect decisions and policies of the executive, a use that comes out in political trials and purges, or in a court such as Star Chamber in Tudor England. They may act as agencies of conciliation and dispute-settlement, as in many traditional societies, and to some extent in American family courts. They may act as oracles of law and makers of law, as is true of Anglo-American appellate courts, and in the courts of some theocratic systems. These functions act as both cause and effect of the cultural meanings that surround the idea of judges and courts. And this cluster of cultural meanings in turn determines whether the court can be useful in taking on some slightly different role.

Much of the discussion so far has dealt with engineered social change, a polite way of speaking about change imposed from above. There is, in this approach, a certain danger of treating culture purely as an obstacle. The word culture reminds us of the term "tradition"; and tradition, in modern discourse, is a word often used with a slight sneer. A traditional society is a society which is primitive, torpid, obsolete. It would be unfortunate to think of culture in such a pejorative sense. If one assumes that enacted laws, ideally and magically, ought to work exactly as planned, then culture is indeed an obstacle, since it is the culture which determines the amount of deviance from the norm. But the assumption is of course absurd. One might just as easily assume that no law printed on paper ever came to life without some cultural input; in which case, it is the culture which is the sole source of effectiveness of law.

Modern regulatory law stands in a particularly complex relationship to culture. Most of the research on the effectiveness of law (hence on legal culture) has shied away from this area. Many social scientists have warned of the limits of legal effectiveness; formal changes in law are doomed to failure if they ignore the restraints imposed by custom and culture. But this point of view can be carried much too far. Taken literally, it would mean that important changes in law would be impossible, unless they were preceded by cultural change; and law reform would mean little more than the codification of custom. There are aspects of law which do codify custom; and probably no law is effective that does not make some use of the culture of its society. Still, regulatory law in general is far more than the codification of custom. In a modern state, tax law and the law regulating industry are not really customary law. Law may be able only weakly and slowly to change people's minds on questions that affect their basic drives and values. But it does not follow that the law cannot achieve a particular result, *within* a certain culture, by making use of the tools which work best for that culture.

Attitudes toward law within a community can act as an obstacle to social change or they can serve as a tremendous source of strength—a value which can be tapped at low cost or no cost to the government. If people habitually obey the law, for example, high compliance with new regulation can be achieved at very low cost. Imagine trying to assign a value to this aspect of legal culture. Americans, for example, seem willing to pay taxes when they are asked to; they evade, but within acceptable limits. This attitude, and this behavior, have made it possible to raise enormous sums of money through the income tax. And if somewhat more money is needed, it can be raised through adjusting the tax rates upward, with relatively small additional loss through evasion or rebellion. On the other hand, attempts to use law to eliminate adultery in the United States create entirely different problems of enforcement. No one obeys adultery laws simply because they are laws. Large segments of the population disapprove of the laws; others feel that these laws are not worth enforcing. Adultery laws, then, have an uphill battle for enforcement; state intervention in private sexual behavior is culturally disapproved. It would require a great input, in real enforcement resources, to raise the rate of effectiveness even a little. At the same time, enforcement would cause costly disruptions in social life and create great public dissatisfaction. The culture, in this case, is truly an obstacle. Yet, in some societies, "adultery," as defined in the United States, is not even considered immoral, and attempts to ban it by law would be even more futile. In still other societies, adultery is deemed far more serious an offense than in the United States, and violators of the norm are punished swiftly and without social disruption. Even for the United States, where adultery laws are unenforceable, the actual incidence of adultery is limited by the strength of cultural and religious taboos.

Legal research might wish, then, to explore the cultural factors that influence the cost and effectiveness of law. The cost and effectiveness of attempts to bring about economic development through law would be of particular interest. Some countries have achieved high levels of national income—the United States, Western Europe, Japan, the Soviet Union. Are there elements in their legal culture, which, in partnership with specific economic and social policies, were conducive to economic growth? If there are, can they be transferred or applied to other countries? Or are there functional substitutes that can be tapped in these other countries?

Research on the legal culture might be helpful in increasing our understanding of the cultural specificity or nonspecificity of particular kinds of law, or of whole bodies or codes of law. The twentieth century is an age of cross-cultural influence, of wholesale diffusion of laws and borrowing of legal institutions and codes. Conquerors have often imposed their legal systems on the people they conquered; but only recently, perhaps, have societies borrowed codes, legal systems, and whole bodies of law, in order to upgrade themselves in some way. Japan and Turkey are among the countries that have borrowed Western codes, lock, stock, and barrel. We know that the engineering of social change does not require the replacement of a whole legal system (in the historical-evolutionary sense), or even a whole code. An indigenous system is not inherently incapable of adjusting to the needs and interests of the society. Changing systems is sometimes the only way to ensure the success of a conquest. It might be functional, for example, to stamp out tribal law, if this is the sole way to destroy the power of the chiefs. It might have been right for Ataturk to adopt the Swiss code, to break the *political* power of the Moslem elites. But this is a special sense of the effect of borrowing of laws, and it is one that is not closely related to the content of those laws. It is another question, whether these borrowings are effective in the substantive sense. Under what cultural conditions does borrowing result in real changes in behavior, and under what conditions does it not?

We may apply the term *penetration* to the degree to which a rule, code, or law takes hold in its population. Penetration refers, then, to the number of actors and spheres of action that a particular rule, legal institution, code, or system of law actually reaches. How far are rules paper rules? Who really governs in the country? How far does the power of the central government extend? What is the living law of the provinces, or the streets, or the corporation, in comparison to the law on the books?

Over the last two centuries there has been a growing tendency for the legal system of the capital, or the central political organs of a country, or its ruling class, to extend its reign deeper down into the population and further out into the land. No community or group is truly lawless. But if law is defined to mean the formal law of the capital or the rulers, then there are lawless groups and territories in every country. In Africa, the colonialist's law governed, if at all, chiefly in the capital; native or customary law shared power in most of the colony. But there were, and are, equally real dualities in Western countries. The common law was not the law of the English manor; American book law does not really describe the living law of the urban ghettoes; the Uniform Commercial Code or a treatise on corporation law do not really illuminate the norms of business behavior. All modern nation-states have been endeavoring, sometimes quite ruthlessly, to increase the degree of penetration of their central legal system, at least geographically, usually in other senses too. In the United States, federal rule has been crowding the states, and the tax collectors and the regulators have brought more and more men and affairs into their orbit. In some parts of Africa, the new nations have been trying to stamp out their plural legal systems. All countries have been struggling to exert their authority on outlying areas and on more and more of their population. Perhaps some aspects of the rage for increased legal unity, legal penetration, and centralization are less rational than these governments imagine. Active government is an unavoidable necessity in the modern world; a higher degree of legal penetration is therefore equally unavoidable. But not *all* forms of the imperialism of the center can stand the test of reason. Pluralism, like federalism, is not merely a structural matter. It rests on cultural differences. That is easy enough to see in plural legal systems; but it is even true of a country like the United States, where decentralization has flourished, though not because of any tribal differences between Maine and California. There are, however, aspects of American legal culture that stand in the way of a strong central government, peculiar American attitudes toward government, power, and law. In the light of a country's legal culture, what are the gains and costs of increasing legal penetration? This is a question that badly needs research. The concept must, of course, be further refined. It must be broken down into its components for purposes of measurement and study.

Penetration is a concept of command; it refers to the degree that government is successfully imposed. But government is a two-way street. *Participation* is a twin concept of penetration. It refers to the role of members of the general public, or some special public, in making and carrying out law. Juries and elections are forms of participation. Intriguing questions can be asked about participation, similar to questions about penetration. Is a legal system more stable, the more it is participatory? Can a system with more participation more effectively meet demands; or are the costs in lost efficiency too great? Can one define participation in the legal system and measure it?

It is not likely, in the near future, that anyone will prove or disprove propositions made up of concepts so general and abstract, and which cut across most national boundaries, periods, and problems. But these concepts, and others, may provide the vocabulary for more modest proposals in specific fields. If it could be shown, for example, what elements of legal culture are supportive of a collectivized form of land tenure and which of cooperative or individual ownership of land, this would be a major advance in theory, and one of great practical effect. The traditional approaches to foreign law by American lawyers would not be likely to come up with the right kind of hypothesis. Concepts of culture and process may possibly bring better results.

NOTES AND QUESTIONS

1. In a note on the effectiveness of legal systems (Reading 41, at 398, *supra*), Talcott Parsons was quoted as saying that the specific development of English law was decisive in producing the industrial revolution. Max Weber contended, however, that "modern capitalism prospers equally and manifests essentially identical economic traits under legal systems containing rules and institutions which considerably differ from each other. . . . ." Does Professor Friedman side with one or the other, or does he take a distinct third position?

2. Macaulay, Reading 13, at 145, *supra*, quoted American businessmen as saying, "One doesn't run to lawyers if he wants to stay in business because one must behave decently. . . . One businessman said that customers had better not rely on legal rights or threaten to bring a breach of contract action against him since he 'would not be treated like a criminal' and would fight back with every means available." In a similar vein, Professor Pyong-Choon Hahm, in *The Korean Political Tradition and Law* 190 (Seoul, Korea 1967), remarks that:

> For a Korean, it is not decent or "nice" to insist on one's legal right. When a person hauls another person into court, he is in fact declaring war on him. . . . He has lined himself up on the side of the bureaucrats to use the power of the state to oppress his fellow man. Thus, a Korean cannot think of law as anything other than oppressive. . . . This reluctance to maintain one's legal right is particularly pronounced in the area of property.

To what extent, if at all, do these parallel opinions indicate that attitudes toward litigation are irrelevant to the development of a modern industrial economy?

See also J. Toshio Sawada,* *Subsequent Conduct and Super-vening Events* 225, 226 (U. of Tokyo Press 1968), where the author comments, "The notion of 'legal right' does not flourish in an interdependent, communal society, where the supreme social dictate is spontaneous mutual help. In a society where the concept of 'right' is absent and 'neglect of logic' is notable, codified private laws cannot take deep roots. Contracts are viewed not as a set of legal claims, but as an evidence of certain social or personal relations. Litigation, or even mediation by a third person, is repugnant. Whenever adjustment of interests becomes necessary, the Japanese prefer settlement in private. . . . The lawyers' task would seem to be limited to drafting comprehensive contracts, which serve to suggest reasonable standards when the parties' pre-modern machinery fails to resolve differences."

---

* Professor, Sophia University, Tokyo, Japan. Reprinted by permission of University of Tokyo Press.

Index

M